ENCYCLOPEDIA OF CULTS AND NEW RELIGIONS

John Ankerberg
John Weldon

HARVEST HOUSE PUBLISHERS
Eugene, Oregon 97402

Cover by Left Coast Design, Portland Oregon

Note to the Reader: In a few cases reference citations are absent or inadequate due to lost, damaged, or stolen materials or circumstances beyond the authors' control.

ENCYCLOPEDIA OF CULTS AND NEW RELIGIONS

Copyright © 1999 by John Ankerberg and John Weldon
Published by Harvest House Publishers
Eugene, Oregon 97402

ISBN 1-7369-0074-8

Printed in the United States of America.

For the members of these groups.

Mai ke kanaka i aloha
i ka 'āina 'iu lani no
ka manawa a pau no ka
hanohano o ke Akua i
ho'ohana ia 'āina.

John Weldon would like to acknowledge the following individuals for their help in the production of this volume: Pastor Mike MacIntosh for grateful research funding assistance, Charles Strohmer for his fine editing of the condensed manuscript, Dr. Clifford Wilson for his many graciously offered hours editing an earlier draft of the full manuscript; Ruth and Esther Wilson for initial copy editing and for checking most of the citations; Rhonda and Madison Leigh Spence for an excellent job inputting the manuscript, and the staff at Harvest House Publishers for an excellent job overall. I would also like to thank Jim and Leeha Chadwell, Phil and Georgia Calhoun, Fred and Jani Russell, and Rich and Pam Boyer for their financial assistance.

CONTENTS

CONTENTS

How to Use This Book

Seven helpful features will assist the reader in using this encyclopedia more effectively.

FIRST, every chapter begins with three short sections carrying quick facts about a group: 1) a primary Table of Contents (for secondary Table of Contents see tip four), 2) Info at a Glance (briefly stated key information about the group), and 3) a Doctrinal Summary.

SECOND, every chapter is divided into time-saving sections so that you do not need to read an entire chapter unless you wish to. For example, if you just need information about what a group believes about God, or Jesus or salvation, or whether it encourages the occult, or if you want critiques or tips for talking with members, just turn to those particular sections. Thus, familiarizing yourself with the Table of Contents may save time. We have tried to make each section more or less self-contained, but of necessity there is some overlap between the sections. In this encyclopedia we could not, of course, cover all that could be said. A good companion to our *Encyclopedia of New Age Beliefs* and this encyclopedia is Charles Strohmer's book *The Gospel and the New Spirituality: Communicating the Truth in a World of Spiritual Seekers* (Thomas Nelson, 1996). This book develops an in-depth, easy-to-use biblical model for talking to nonChristian spiritual seekers. Its principles are well worth picking up and putting into practice when talking with members of cults and new religions.

Further, even though a group's doctrines about God and salvation are the only ones nec-essary to examine, despite a group's claims, that the group is Christian, we have included a relatively large number of doctrinal topics because one never knows what information may prove useful in talking with members. What a group specifically teaches about Christianity, man or the afterlife, for instance, may prove useful in developing a particular approach or apologetic for a certain person. Many followers have little or no idea concerning the real teachings of their religion. When exposed to such teachings, especially if the member is from a Christian background, it may give reason for pause and open doors otherwise closed.

THIRD, while we have frequently included brief scriptural responses within each chapter, a more thorough general treatment of most major doctrinal sections is provided in the Doctrinal Appendix at the end of this encyclopedia. This offers a strong biblical corrective to what a given religion believes about a given doctrine. Thus, it is important to peruse the contents of the Doctrinal Appendix, which may also be useful for Bible studies and other areas outside cult research. In addition, some chapters end with a Scripture contrast section that may prove useful in discussions.

FOURTH, we have provided Info at a Glance sections which, when relevant, contain references to volume one of this series—*Encyclopedia of New Age Beliefs* (Harvest House, 1996). It contains 27 chapters that are frequently relevant to the topics in this encyclopedia. In effect, volume one as a companion to volume two will be useful to further critique the practices and teachings of many of these groups. Volume one also contains chapters on other religions not covered in this book, including Eastern Gurus, Scientology, and Silva Mind Control.

FIFTH, whenever possible, we have cited the first editions of the standard works that a group considers authoritative. Because these are often seen as divine revelation or divinely authoritative, if the citations given today are different than what we cite, and if there is no error on our part, this means that the group has changed their divine revelation, with all that implies. If a group has revised their texts—for whatever reasons; social, cultural, political, ethical—they are guilty of rejecting their own divine revelation and members are then faced with the dilemma of determining who to believe, if anyone. Sometimes, these changes have been so significant that we are almost dealing with a 'different' religion, as in Mormonism and Jehovah's Witnesses. We emphasize that no religion can logically claim to accept the divine authority of its founder and simultaneously change, suppress or deny his teachings. If the founder was wrong in the first place, it is difficult to see how members can logically place faith in their religion at all. Further, if the religion is wrong because it incorrectly accepts a false claim to divine inspiration, then it has no credibility either. This 'lose-lose' situation is a more frequent occurrence than supposed.

SIXTH, as theologian Harold O. J. Brown points out in his fine work, *Heresies,* the cults have a positive side. They offer valuable lessons to the Church, something heresy has always accomplished historically. The most important message these religions have for Christianity is to triple underscore the necessity for the dissemination of doctrinal, apologetic and hermeneutical knowledge at the local church level. (See our Introduction for some additional reasons why this is so vital.) For example, the sufficiency of Scripture alone and the extent of the Canon, and the necessity of salvation by grace alone through faith alone in Christ alone, are perhaps the most crucial, and yet among the most neglected doctrines. If the Church is to prosper in the twenty-first century, then doctrine, apologetics and hermeneutics

must be more widely taught to the average church member.

As always, the best offense against spiritual counterfeits is knowledge of the truth, how to defend the truth and, most importantly, how to apply the truth. Those searching for the truth need look no further than Jesus Himself, who declared, "I am the way and the truth and the life. No one comes to the Father except through me" (John 14:6). On trial before Pilate, Jesus answered, "You are right in saying I am a king. In fact, for this reason I was born, and for this I came into the world, to testify to the truth. Everyone on the side of the truth listens to me" (John 18:37). To testify to the truth is the purpose of the Church, and also our purpose at the John Ankerberg Show. Readers should take advantage of our material, as well as that from related organizations, to secure the information they need. The information in these chapters may be used at the local church level in sermons, conferences or Bible studies to illustrate the importance of doctrine, apologetic knowledge, hermeneutics and related themes for the health of the Church. (Again, we would also suggest purchasing Volume One in this series, *Encyclopedia of New Age Beliefs,* for similar reasons, as well as the third volume, *Encyclopedia of Christian Apologetics,* when it is published.)

The groups in this encyclopedia often illustrate larger cultic themes and their implications for our society. For example, collating the "moral concerns" sections alone would prove to be an enlightening study on the ethical implications of the cults and new religions. Thus most chapters offer a "larger lesson" than the mere detailing of their theological beliefs, important as that is. These lessons may be used profitably in teaching at all levels. For example:

—Buddhism shows how a study of comparative religion (Christianity and Buddhism in this case) can illustrate the great error in claims to alleged compatibility between religious faiths.

—Jehovah's Witnesses, The Way International and New Thought depict the inaccuracies of cultic translations of the Bible and how misuse of biblical languages can be used in support of cult theology.

—The Masonic Lodge powerfully displays the consequences of the Christian church compromising with the truth of Scripture.

—Mormonism and Jehovah's Witnesses illustrate the tremendous consequence of deceptive semantics, deliberate changes in doctrine, alteration of history and suppression of data. Jehovah's Witnesses also illustrate how the cost of false religion can induce physical or mental illness or even death to oneself or one's children.

—Oneness Pentecostalism, Jehovah's Witnesses and classical Armstrongism show the folly of rationalism when applied to Scripture. (The *new* Worldwide Church of God is a powerful testimony to God's grace and mercy.)

— Religious Science, Unity School of Christianity, New Thought and Buddhism reveal the all too common problems of human potential approaches to human well-being and spiritual enlightenment.

—Self-Realization Fellowship illustrates the Hindu, not Christian, derivation of New Thought religions such as Religious Science and Unity School of Christianity. In turn, these New Thought religions demonstrate the folly of assuming the latent divinity of the human mind, a common New Age theme.

—The Unification Church illustrates the folly and consequence of trusting in spiritism, indicating the true nature of the spirits and showing how the origin and worldview of the Unification Church can lead people into a terrible bondage to the spirits.

—Unitarian Universalism reveals the consequences of liberal theology in society.

—Zen illustrates the personal and social cost of irrationalism.

Religion can be good or bad. If this encyclopedia illustrates anything, it is the consequence of bad religion. The lowest common denominator revolving around most of these groups, intentional or not, is a kaleidoscope of deception which, unfortunately, the unsuspecting public (and most in the Christian church) have little cognizance of. Indeed, had we wished to do it, a far darker picture could have been painted.

SEVENTH, you can find information on almost any subject by using our listed resources. The scope of any one-volume work is limited, and thus the religions and cults in this encyclopedia are only the tip of the iceberg. Worldwide, there are thousands of new religions today with a membership of one-hundred-fifty million. Given their relatively minor influence only a generation ago, this would seem to indicate an almost unparalleled explosion. Offering a significant critique of them all would take a lifetime, or more. Therefore, to help the reader become even more informed, we offer the following list of resources.

HOW TO FIND INFORMATION ON ANY RELIGIOUS GROUP, PHILOSOPHY OR SUBJECT

As far as new religions and cults are concerned, the following key resources are invaluable. When possible, synopses were supplied by the organization itself to illustrate its purpose, resources and uniqueness. Space limited our selection, but Internet links can be made from these sites to many other organizations we would have recommended.

The John Ankerberg Show—The John Ankerberg Show is an award-winning weekly TV program on a variety of subjects relevant to the Christian faith. General categories include apologetics, prophecy, world religions, cults and new religions, the New Age movement, social issues, cultural critique and Christian growth. Dr. John Ankerberg is the program moderator for the show, which often includes debate style format on various topics. The John Ankerberg Show is televised nationally on the Inspiration Channel and on dozens of local markets in cities nationwide. Its research division, the Ankerberg Theological Research Institute (ATRI), has produced over 60 books, including the best-selling "Facts On" series, which discuss several dozen contemporary topics in a brief question and answer format.

Over 100 videos, cassettes or transcripts of the TV programs are available; these are discounted for those who become part of the 30/30 club and receive materials on a regular basis. The Ankerberg website also offers a variety of materials and articles online as well as a real media broadcast of the weekly John Ankerberg Show. A subscription service to a larger database of 15 categories with articles by scores of evangelistic scholars is also available. See www.harborlighthouse.com or visit www.anker berg.com for details. To order materials only call toll free 1-800-805-3030. For a catalog or additional information, write or call The John Ankerberg show, PO Box 8977, Chattanooga, TN 37414; 423–892–7722.

Watchman Fellowship—Watchman Fellowship is one of the oldest and largest evangelical Christian discernment ministries in America established in 1979, with offices in seven states. Specializing in counter-cult apologetics, they maintain a forty thousand volume research library (including files and periodicals) on cults and new religions. They focus primarily on Mormonism, Jehovah's Witnesses and the New Age Movement, but they have files and information on hundreds of other groups and organizations. Their website, www.watchman.org, contains hundreds of articles from past issues of their magazine and a helpful word-searchable database, The Index of Cults and Religions, which contains over 1,100 cults, new religious movements, New Age groups, occult organizations and world religions, with related terms, doctrines and cross-references. They publish a bimonthly magazine, The Watchman Expositor. Write or visit their website for subscription information or to order a free resource catalog. Watchman Fellowship, Inc., PO Box 13340, Arlington, TX 76094; 817–277–0023. Their regional offices are: Georgia Office: 706–576– 4321, email: wfidh@aol.com; Alabama Office: 205–871–2858, email: wfial@aol.com; Pennsylvania Office: 724–327–2948, email: wfp a@nb.net; Illinois Office: 773–381–5086, email: tdmwfi@aol.com; Tennessee Office: 931–358–3012, email: taftj@ juno.com; Mississippi Office: 601–924–3879, email: malinmin @meta3.net.

Spiritual Counterfeits Project—Since 1973, the Spiritual Counterfeits Project, or SCP, Inc., has been a frontline ministry confronting the occult, the cults and the New Age movement, explaining why these are influencing our society. SCP gained national prominence after condemning the use of Trancendal Meditation (TM) as a relaxation centering exercise in public schools. The case went to Federal Court in the mid-70s, and SCP won the case. SCP's evidence on TM, much of it secret and previously unseen, exposed TM for what it was, a version of Hinduism. Today SCP is a Christian think tank comprised of people from top universities who have spent years on various spiritual paths before becoming Christians. SCP has six thousand groups on file, which the New York City Library assesses as the most complete collection of such materials in the United States. *Time, Newsweek,* ABC and other major media quote SCP about a wide range of movements and issues. The award winning *SCP Journal* (three times a First Place EPA winner) is unsurpassed in the field of analyzing and discerning the inside workings of new spiritual trends. SCP is headed by best selling author Tal Brooke, a graduate of the University of Virginia and Princeton, who speaks regularly at Cambridge and Oxford Universities. Historian Dr. Gregory S. Camp, author of *Selling Fear,* described him as "one of Christian America's intellectual and spiritual treasures." SCP offers information and counseling without charge by telephone through its ACCESS line (510–540–5767). Its journals and published materials are available for a minimum donation of $25.00 per year ($35 outside USA) at: SCP, Inc., Box 4308, Berkeley, CA, 94704. Phone a visa order to 510–540–0300. SCP can be accessed on the web, where its materials can be ordered: http://www.scp-inc.org.

Alpha and Omega Ministries—This site associated with Dr. James White offers an online debate center, chat room and good quality materials on apologetics, Mormonism, Jehovah's Witnesses, Roman Catholicism and biblical doctrine. Its website states: "Alpha and Omega Ministries is dedicated to providing the most up-to-date, faithful defense of the historic Protestant position on the sufficiency of Scripture and salvation. We are a Reformed ministry, fully believing in what are commonly called the 'doctrines of grace.' We firmly believe in the Trinity, the deity of Christ, the person of the Holy Spirit, and salvation by grace through faith alone. We hold to the 'solas' of the Reformation: sola scriptura, sola gratia, sola fide, soli Deo gloria." Contact: www.aomin.org; email @ xapis@ aomin. org, or write to PO Box 37106, Phoenix, AZ, 85069.

The Christian Research Institute—The Christian Research Institute was founded by the late Dr. Walter Martin, a respected authority on cults, apologetics and comparative religion. The Christian Research Institute is currently headed by Hank Hanegraaff of the Bible Answer Man broadcast and publishes a quality periodical, the *Christian Research Journal.* Extensive archives of the journal at their website offer a large variety of materials on apologetics, doctrine, cults and new religions, witnessing tips, book reviews and more. Contact: www.equip.org, or CRI International, P.O. Box 7000, Rancho Santa, CA 92688; 949–858–6100.

Personal Freedom Outreach—Personal Freedom Outreach is able to supply a variety of printed and audio-visual resources to help the Christian respond to many of the threats that face American culture today. Visit the "PFO Ministry Resources" section of its website for a listing of the available materials (http://www. pfo.org/index.htm). This website carries a complete index to over 700 articles, editorials, news update items and book reviews, which have appeared in the PFO quarterly newsletter publication since its inception in 1981. This index is located in "The Quarterly Journal" category of this website. Also, PFO can be contacted at any one of its office locations in Bricktown, NJ; Niles, OH; Peoria, AZ or Kunkletown, PA. For prompt delivery of witnessing tracts, books or other resource materials, send your order to PFO's St. Louis address: PO Box 26062, St. Louis, MO, 63136; 314–921–9800.

The 1996 Directory of Cult Research Organizations—Updated irregularly, the 1996 edition contains a worldwide listing of over 750 agencies or individuals involved in cult research (arranged by state or country according to an Evangelical, Roman Catholic, Behaviorist or Sociological approach). Index and appendicies. Contact American Religions Center, PO Box 168, Trenton, MI, 48183; 313–692–7772, or Cornerstone Apologetics Research Team, 312–561–2450 x2084, or 312–878–6030.

The Institute for The Study of American Religions—This is headed by Dr. J. Gordon Melton, author of the standard work, *The Encyclopedia of American Religions,* listing some 2500 groups. This institute is also associated with the International Religions Directory Project. Contact: http://www.americanreligion.org/ or the Institute for the Study of American Religions, PO Box 90709, Santa Barbara, CA, 93190; 805–967–7721.

The Internet—The Internet has become a primary information source and will soon be indispensable for researchers, if it isn't already. The previous groups all have websites; one could start with these, noting and exploring links to related sites. Before long one will be able to find information on almost anything. (If you can't find what you are looking for on these sites, try key search engines such as go.com, snap.com, webcrawler and google.com inputting a specific inquiry.)

Apologetics Index, headed by Anton Hein in Holland, offers an invaluable and extensive listing of articles on apologetics, cults and new religions, doctrine, links and a discussion format. Color-coded and indexed. See: http://www. apologeticsindex.org/.

Apologia **Report**—Publishes the international e-mail weekly, *Apologia Report,* for career apologists, educators, pastors and missionaries ($15 per year) *Apologia Report* surveys new resources in Christian apologetics and the arena of competing worldviews. Its specific focus includes "cults and alternative religions, as well as spiritual trends and movements in modern culture and theology." Editor Rich Poll, formerly in charge of research material at Christian Research Institute, used a similar publication to train new research staff at CRI from 1985-1995. Paul Carden and Ron Rhodes are contributing editors. To aid *Apologia Report* readers in finding and sharing resources in the field of Christian apologetics, Apologia hosts the free AR-talk discussion group on the Internet (open to the public). A sister listserv group, AR-vent, is available to AR-talk members for the discussion of issues in apologetics. As a part of the Mission America coalition, Apologia is constructing a select list of the best Christian responses to alternative religions at www.apologia. org/ resources, for over 200 national Christian ministries and 65+ denominations representing over 180,000 churches. Apologia, 24040 Alpin Dr./Box 552, Crestline, CA, 92325; ph/fx: 909–338–4873; email: apologia@xc.org; www.apologia. org.

Office hours: 11:00 A.M.–1:00 P.M. PST, M-F; VISA, Discover, Mastercard accepted.

www.trancenet.org provides current up-to-date news and information on a variety of cults and new religions.

Stand to Reason provides a link to over 50 worthwhile apologetic sites at: http://www.str.org/index.htm.

Among invaluable general resources: The Internet Christian Library @ http://www.iclnet. org and The Worldwide Christian Web @ http:// www.superb.com/ www/pages/wwcw.

Your local library and its interlibrary loan service—For those without a computer, the librarian is always one's best friend when information is required. Many major branches offer limited, free over the phone research, as well as photocopy and fax service. For a small fee, the inter-library loan service can track down almost any book ever printed.

Library of Congress—have loads of fun at http://lcweb.loc.gov/harvest/query-lc.html.

Christadelphians were included because their claims influence biblical Christianity and because almost no literature can be found offering even a modest-sized biblical critique.

A few groups, such as The Way International, presented something of a dilemma. While their membership is down more than 50 percent, such groups could always rebound to previous or even greater levels of influence.

It should be noted that when many people leave a particular group, for whatever reasons, this does not necessarily mean official membership figures are a true reflection of the actual number of believers. In the case of The Way International, many splinter groups were formed which have kept the numbers of believers much higher than The Way International "membership" figures would suggest. Traditional Armstrong theology has now been rejected by the new Worldwide Church of God, but nearly three dozen splinter groups continue to teach Herbert W. Armstrong's doctrines.

Million member groups such as Iglisio ni Christi, which denies the trinity, and Black Muslims, who deny Christ, and Seventh-day Adventism, which often teaches salvation by works, were deleted for lack of space, most members were outside the U.S., or because the doctrinal deviation, while important, was not as serious as in other groups.

CATEGORIZATION OF SUBJECTS

Generally, we included those groups having the largest membership, most significant impact on Christianity or greatest social influence.

DOCTRINAL APPENDIX

Located at the end of this encyclopedia, the Doctrinal Appendix provides brief information on these major biblical themes:

- The Christian Faith—Why It's True
- The Bible—The Most Unique Book in the World
- God/The Trinity
- Jesus Christ: Lord and Savior
- The Deity of Jesus Christ
- The Deity of Christ and Early Church Testimony
- Religions, Cults and the Deity of Jesus Christ
- The Personality and Deity of the Holy Spirit
- Salvation: The Glory of the Gospel
- Forgiveness of Sin Through God's Grace and the Atonement of Christ
- The Doctrine of Justification
- Death and the Afterlife: Eternity Decided in Time
- The Occult: The Modern Spiritual Counterfeit
- Scriptures Relating to Cults and New Religions

Then Jesus cried out, "When a man believes in me, he does not believe in me only, but in the one who sent me. When he looks at me, he sees the one who sent me. I have come into the world as a light, so that no one who believes in me should stay in darkness. As for the person who hears my words but does not keep them, I do not judge him. For I did not come to judge the world, but to save it. There is a judge for the one who rejects me and does not accept my words; that very word which I spoke will condemn him at the last day. For I did not speak of my own accord, but the Father who sent me commanded me what to say and how to say it. I know that his command leads to eternal life. So whatever I say is just what the Father has told me to say" (John 12: 44-50).

INTRODUCTION

A WORLDWIDE PROBLEM

"The 21st Century will be spiritual or it will be nothing."

— Andre Malraux (1901–1976), noted French Minister of Information and Cultural Affairs

"All warfare is deception."

—Chinese General, 500 B.C.

Some researchers estimate that new religions and cults originating in the last two hundred years have increased their membership figures in this century by 2,000 percent to 3,000 percent.[1] According to J. Gordon Melton and others, Europe has 3–4 times as many new religious groups per capita as the U.S.[2]

The American Family Federation (AFF) is a 20-year old nonprofit research center and educational organization founded to study cults, educate the public and professionals, examine the psychological dangers and assist those who have been adversely affected by involvement with cults. It has an experienced staff plus a network of over 150 volunteer professionals in diverse fields including education, psychology, religion, journalism and law enforcement. AFF publishes a peer reviewed, multi-disciplinary, award winning scholarly journal, *Cultic Studies Journal* (www.csj.org). The AFF reported on its website in mid-1999:

Cults are a worldwide problem. European concerns about cults led to the European Parliament's passing a Resolution on Cults in 1984, and to three international conferences on cults, and to a report by the Council of Europe. The French government has twice studied the cult problem and issued book-length reports on the problem in France. Similar reports have been issued in Germany. Even in Latin America, cults have generated considerable concern. *Cultic Studies Journal* has published two articles on the cult problem in Latin America.

There have been at least five international conferences about cults in the last 10 years. In 1993 the International Humanist and Ethical Union (IHEU) expressed "grave concern about the growth of destructive cults and sects throughout the world." AFF estimates [there are] between 3,000 to 5,000 active groups.

The extent of concern over cults in Europe is illustrated by the number of political measures and recommendations that attempt to protect the public. For example, consider the *Common Declaration of the European Conference 23–24 April 1999 by the European Federation of Centers of Research and Information on Sectarianism* (FECRIS). Here, members of the European Association are "united in fighting the effects of adverse sectarian [the term is similar to 'cultic' in America] practices and to assist the victims of such practices." While being seriously committed to freedom of thought and worship, they also "recognize that it is the duty of public authorities to make available free information to enable individuals to protect themselves against the adverse practices of sectarianism; to protect individuals against any form of mental manipulation and psychological conditioning in whatever context." Thus, these associations "support resolution 134 of 15 April 1999 of the European Parliament's Committee of Civil Liberties and Internal Affairs. This resolution invites Member States to 'take measures, in compliance with the principles of legality, with a view to fighting abuses caused to people by certain sects which should be denied the statutes of cult or religious organization endowing them with certain tax advantages and legal protection.'" FECRIS thereby affirms the following:

1. To deny the existence of national, regional, or transnational sectarian organizations, whether hidden or not under mask of philosophical or religious belief, cannot but abuse public opinion and refrain the authorities from taking action against the same.

2. We must not confuse "spiritual seeking", be it related or not to a well-established philosophical or religious movement, with sectarian groups whose practices impede the aspiration of individuals.

3. The philosophical or religious claims of a group does not entitle it to violate human rights, the law or to disturb or unsettle social balance.

FECRIS has therefore made the following requests.

1. "The official recognition of the European Federation of Associations for the defense against the totalitarian practices of sectarianism, in order that it should be consulted by the European Parliament, the Council of Europe, the Organization for Cooperation and Security in Europe (OSCE), and the United Nations and their organizations and commissions. FECRIS should, furthermore be in continual liaison with the administrative authorities empowered to apply fiscal and custom procedures for states and for the European Union, and with other international organizations having the same aims."

2. "The creation within the national parliaments, the European Parliament, and the Parliamentary Assembly of the Council of Europe, of permanent study groups charged with the observation of the sectarian phenomenon and, in the event, to vote legislative measures and executive measures."

3. "Alongside this, the setting up of a permanent European organization charged with gathering information on sectarianism and in collaboration with national authorities to take preventive measures and provide public information."

Europe is clearly concerned about the cults politically, and it may only be a matter of time before similar concerns and measures are politically expressed and adopted in the U.S. Where all this will lead and how it will affect established and traditional religion is anyone's guess. With estimates as high as 5,000 cults worldwide, and estimates of as many as 150 million people worldwide belonging to cults, few can afford to ignore this issue. In a sense, cults are the latest "world religion." Yet when cults and alternative religions hit the scene in the 60s and 70s, most religious and social commentators believed that they were a passing phenomenon soon to die out. Obviously, the scholars and commentators who thought this way were wrong. As Associated Press religion writer George W. Cornell wrote on November 26, 1988, "New religions that have proliferated in America in the last two decades aren't fading away as they had been widely expected to do, but instead are growing and multiplying." One reason is that virtually anyone can be recruited into a cult—even those who think that they are most resistant. A major factor is not the individual's resistance, for that can vary, but the individual's personal circumstances and the cult recruiter's skill. Another chief factor—one that is, unfortunately, rarely considered by prospective converts—is the power of the devil, who, spiritually speaking, reaps significant rewards from cult membership.

THE NEED FOR MEANING

Why are hundreds, even thousands, of cults and new, or alternative, religions "here to stay," so to speak? Obviously they are filling a need in people for stability and meaning in life. They are filling a spiritual vacuum created by the inability of materialism, hedonism and existentialism to supply lasting purpose to one's existence. When life is no longer satisfying, people naturally look for ultimate answers and a greater meaning to their existence.

Also, as our culture increasingly implodes on the weight of its own sin, the meaning people once found in "worldly" pursuits is no longer as satisfying. This shows why polls consistently reveal that, in a broad sense, people look more and more to religion today. Of course, this is what people have done historically—the history of humanity is the history of religion. Not surprisingly, then, recent issues of magazines like *Time* and *Newsweek* have run cover stories on the topics of God, Jesus, angels, life after death and related issues. Bill Moyers' PBS series, "Genesis: A living Conversation" and Joseph Campbell's PBS "Myth" series all reflect the truth of Augustine's observation that there is a God-shaped vacuum in everyone's heart and that people will be unsatisfied until it is filled. This unremitting need for meaning shows why there are thousands of large and small new religions and cults in the world today. Indeed, even science itself, long considered the "enemy" of religion, has often become "religious" in its search for answers to the meaning of life, such as evolutionary theory claiming it has revealed the secret to creation, or speculations in quantum physics to find the "final theory" of life. Parapsychology, thanatology (clinical death) research, exobiology (the search for extraterrestrial life) and many other basically religious quests lie within science and are evident today. (See our book *Darwin's Leap of Faith* [Harvest House, 1997).

People will even invent religions to satisfy their needs, as, e.g., can be seen in the chapter on Religious Science. Ernest Holmes admitted he simply invented Religious Science by selecting beliefs and practices he liked from other religions. (The truth is that almost all religion is invented, either by people or spirits. As we will see, the intrusion of spirits in the new religions is almost ubiquitous.) In seeming mimicry, a July-August 1998 article in the *Utne Reader,* "God with a Million Faces," observed many people were now engaging in "designer religion." It addressed the pros and cons of this—inventing your own religion by selecting bits and pieces you like from a variety of sources. Referring to this "cafeteria religion," the article stated that "the land now abounds with these private belief systems, each tailored to fit the believer's individual needs."

Clearly, the religion many people are looking to today is not biblical Christianity, but various counterfeits. When J. K. van Baalen referred to the cults as the "unpaid bills of the church," in many ways he hit the mark. A church with a robust faith grounded in theology and apologetics and an emphasis on cultural critique and evangelism would have seriously blunted the rise of the cults. But that bridge is now burned. Pollsters Barna and others have found that Americans are "basically ignorant" of even simple Bible teachings, and the connection here to the rise of the cults is more than incidental. Most people cannot even recite the Ten Commandments, let alone define "justification," but perhaps most Christians can't either.

Part of the ebb of Christian influence in America can be traced to the cults and new religions. They have helped transform America religiously from a nation of basically just two religions (Christianity and Judaism, plus a few cults) a mere generation ago, to a nation of hundreds, if not thousands, of religions today. (Perhaps U.S. coins should now read "In gods we trust"!) This transformation from monotheism to polytheism, from religious concord to religious pluralism and paganism, has marked a major turning point in American, and thus in Western civilization itself. America is no longer a Judeo-Christian nation. It once was (clearly in principle if not state sanction), but is no more, and we say this with heartache because, unfortunately, the bill will be paid by everyone. We are reminded of Jeremiah 19:4 in ancient Israel, "For they have forsaken me and made this a place of foreign gods."

Wherever we look we see the influence of the new religions. The Internet has become a vast spiritual marketplace for the cults and new religions, with hundreds of millions of onlookers. Hundreds of cults have their own websites. There are some 200 million–300 million pages related to religion on the Internet. Internet compilers have called the religion presence on the Web "staggering," referring to the number of sites as "expanding exponentially."

During the past few decades, thousands of books have been published on cults, new religions and related themes. Indeed, there are several multiple volume series costing hundreds or thousands of dollars each. Some 500 groups are discussed in *The Encyclopedic Handbook of Cults in America*, Vol. 7 of the series published by Religious Information Systems; 1100 entries are found in Roger Rosen (ed.), *The Illustrated Encyclopedia of Active New Religions, Sects, and Cults;* 2100 groups (including Christian denominations and sects) are briefly covered in J. Gordon Melton's *The Encyclopedia of American Religions* (Gale research). Then there is the dozen plus volume, *Bibliographies on Sects and Cults in America Series* (Garland).

Unfortunately, as this Volume documents, the cults and new religions are not the good news that they are made out to be by their promoters and advertisers. This can be argued forcefully from a secular perspective and definitively from a Christian perspective. Religious pluralism is a good thing only if the cults and new religions are a good thing. The problem is that they are not. The difficulty is that a counterfeit initially looks so good and feels so good that one rarely suspects something is wrong. Only when the counterfeit is examined and compared with the real thing does the counterfeit become apparent. By then it's often too late.

RELIGIONS AND TRUTH

So people are searching for the truth today because, in the end, the truth is the only thing that finally matters. Apart from truth, people are bewildered. And apart from truth, goodness itself is unlikely to be found because deception and evil are never far apart. Put simply, truth matters more than most other things. Plato declared, "Truth is the beginning of every good thing, both in Heaven and on earth, and he who would be blessed and happy should be from the first a partaker of the truth." When people join a new religion or a cult, they are promised the truth and assume that it will give them the truth. They believe that they have found the truth because this is what the cult has told them. Unfortunately, in the world in which we live, this is not possible. When religions multiply out of control, truth inevitably suffers. Because all religions can't possibly be true, confusion reigns when all religions claim to be true. Having no standard for judgement, most people who are relativists don't know what to believe and, depending on their disposition, they conclude that either somehow, mystically, all religions are true, or that no religion is true.

When it comes to the subject of religion and truth, the choices are powerfully restricted. Thousands of contrary religions cannot all be true. Put another way, every religion might be false, but when thousands of religions contradict one another, only one might be true. If there is one true God, it makes sense there is one true religion. (See Doctrinal Appendix, "Christianity.") As one TV character said, facing a difficult personal situation, "The truth isn't easy, but it's real—it opens your eyes."

In our relativistic, pluralistic, "tolerant" and "open minded" culture, saying something like "Christianity alone is fully true" is considered politically incorrect—worse, a religious blasphemy. Still, the truth always wins out in the end. It's really just a matter of letting historical and other evidence logically lead where it will, being sure not to let our own personal agendas interfere with the process. But that's the difficult part for people who wish the world different from how God has made it. In a world ruled by relativism, it is often easier to find the truth we like rather than to accept the truth that is.

If the historical evidence strongly favors the conclusion that Christianity alone is fully true, is it not better to be open-minded and tolerant with the evidence and let it escort us where it leads? Why deride Christians for speaking the truth about Christianity? As the Apostle Paul wondered, "Have I now become your enemy by telling you the truth?"(Galatians 4:16). If historical and other evidence proves Christianity true, it is the fault of none but the evidence. As we commented in *Ready with an Answer* (Harvest House, 1997, p. 11), "There is little need to examine 500 different religions in A to Z fashion (even if that were possible), when there is one religion that stands out from all the others in almost every respect. Christianity is the only religion that is simultaneously most likely to be true, and, given its claims, the easiest to disprove if false."[3]

Being politically correct or religiously intolerant certainly has its problems. One wonders, what is the point of defending relativism when it means that, if truth does exist, one could never find it? What is the point of being "open-minded" if our personal preferences or philosophical premises require that we be closed-minded to everything we happen not to like? What happens to truth then? And what is the point of being tolerant of everything when many things we tolerate now, including the cults and new religions, are clearly harming us, our children and our society?

THE PRICE OF TOLERANCE

We pay for what we tolerate, whether it be crime, drug use, murderers or not disciplining our kids. The worse the thing tolerated, the higher the price imposed. Merely the financial cost to society from tolerance of sexual promiscuity alone is trillions of dollars—in prostitution, abortion, pornography, rape, incarceration, abuse of children, AIDS and dozens of other sexually transmitted diseases, not to mention homosexuality, gender confusion, divorce, suicide, psychological consequences to children and much more. Our modern media, driven by its own brand of lusts, still doesn't get it, and they continue to promote sexual license, violence and amorality in our culture.

Tolerance is not always a virtue. In a *Newsweek* column supporting the death penalty ("Intolerable Tolerance," May 11, 1998), George F. Will pointed out: "Tolerance that reflects the absence of strong beliefs is a symptom of a distinctively contemporary form of decadence—the comfortable disbelief in the propriety or importance of never making emphatic judgments about behavior." Will cites as one sobering example: "Society increasingly flinches from judgments commensurate with the worst crimes. That is one reason, in the estimate of John DiIulio, a Princeton political scientist and criminologist, there are walking around in American society about 500,000 murderers who have not been caught or who have served time and been released."

"Live and let live" in the spheres of morality, decency and the golden rule can only give us what we deserve. A tolerance of evils that can be hindered or prevented by our social will, prevented to everyone's benefit, is itself evil. That is the very reason God sent the prophets to Israel—because the nation was tolerating things that would destroy it—and did destroy it. And it will destroy our nation also. Hardly anyone argues we should be tolerant of everything, for this would include things like pedophilia and human sacrifice. If tolerance must have limits, then we should learn what it is wise to be intolerant of and how the judgement is to be made. This has nothing to do with the curtailment of necessary individual freedoms. But it has everything to do with limiting individual freedoms to larger moral considerations, as well as the necessity of morality being based in absolutes. Freedom based in morality is the only true freedom.

When weird and bad things were once in the closet, the majority in society never considered getting involved in them because of social convention that accepted general Christian principles regardless of religious persuasion. Those who wished to were still free to pursue their own frequently depraved (now often "enlightened") interests, but most people never even heard of the depravities. Today they are broadcast to our children from the print media, and they are increasingly on movies, TV, and the Internet. (Indeed, pornography and pedophilia are supposedly the top draws on the Internet.)

THE VIRTUE OF INTOLERANCE

Like so many other things today, cults themselves have become tolerated, even praised by many. The reasons for our "intolerance" of cults and new religions—why we are critical of them—are more soundly based than our critics would be willing to concede. Facts are facts. Some will be mentioned in this Introduction and many more in the individual chapters. We would hope that those who would condemn others for their "intolerance" would try to understand that it is not intolerant to have exclusive views in religious matters and therefore to reject other views. It is only logical, especially if the other views can be demonstrated to be false, harmful and destructive.

During the twentieth century, tens of millions of lives were damaged or ruined by the cults. One wonders, do the "tolerant" care? Anyone who wishes can be tolerant of the kinds of things described in this encyclopedia. That is their right, even if it is coming back to haunt the rest of society. But that does not mean that others have no right to be critical of the beliefs and practices of those whom they think are detrimental to individuals and to society, especially if good evidence exist in support of such claims. Politically correct folks aside, it is still a free country. You can think on your own and disagree with anyone. Thank heaven not everyone is convinced the cults are above criticism.[4]

EVALUATING CULTS: THE STANDARD

Without intending to sound presumptuous, and this may surprise some people, it is a fact that only biblical Christianity offers serious evidence for its claim to be a divine revelation. Whether people like this is not the issue. Again, facts are facts even when people don't like them. The premise of this Encyclopedia is therefore that only biblical Christianity is fully true. By this we do not mean that Christianity is without problems, or that some truth cannot be found in other religions. But if anyone wants the one true religion, they have to come to grips with the evidence for biblical Christianity. (See "Christianity" in Doctrinal Appendix.) This is why it is important to start with Christianity and why Christianity is our standard of measurement to evaluate religious truth claims, especially claims to be Christian or claims to be in harmony with the Bible and Christianity—something all the groups covered in this Encyclopedia and hundreds of others assert without blinking.

Only Christianity has a logical, absolute basis for judging religious truth claims. Some of the evidence for this conclusion was presented in our book *Ready with an Answer* and its companion volume *Knowing the Truth About Salvation* (Harvest House 1997). For example: the fact that Christianity (as opposed to all other religions) would never have been born were its claims false; the fact that Christianity (as opposed to all other religions) was founded by the only Person in history to prove that He was God-incarnate; the fact that Christianity (as opposed to all other religions) can offer a high quality and quantity of fulfilled prophecy in its Scripture; and, also unique to Christianity, the scientific prevision of its Scripture. Further, Christianity (as opposed to all other religions) has a central proof—the resurrection of Christ from the dead, which will withstand legal cross-examination as a fact of history. Christianity (as opposed to all other religions) also has textual and archaeological confirmation of its Scripture, and the fact that no other religion anywhere offers credible evidence for the truth of its worldview and major religious claims. This makes Christianity quite unlike the cults, which offer subjective experience, which proves nothing.

The great German reformer Martin Luther was correct when he wrote that, in the end, there were only two religions in the world, the religion of works and the religion of grace. No one has yet satisfactorily explained how, apart from divine revelation, we find only one religion of grace among thousands professing works.

USE OF THE TERM "CULT"

We had little desire to spend seven years compiling and writing this Encyclopedia merely for fun or profit. We wrote it for others to try to help them. We wrote it for people on the outside who are unknowingly misled by the claims of these groups who are thinking of joining. We wrote it for people on the inside who are members of these groups, to help them do some reality testing. We also wrote it for Christians who may unsuspectingly join these groups, or be introduced to them and confused by their claims to be compatible with Christianity.

Historically, the term cult has been used as a religious term, not a psychological or sociological one. To examine cults and new religions culturally, anthropologically, sociologically, behaviorally, phenomenologically and politically leaves undecided the most important question of all: are these cults and religions true? It goes without saying that only a religion established as true can answer that question. Put another way, what does not agree with the truth can not be true by definition. As the Bible comments, "No lie comes from the truth." (1 John 2:21). Thus our analysis in this Encyclopedia centers on doctrinal and apologetic issues.

If, as Socrates said, the unexamined life is not worth living, certainly this must be true for the unexamined belief or religion. Yet the whole point of religion is to find the truth. While on trial, Jesus said to Pilate, "You are right in saying I am a king. In fact, for this reason I was born, and for this I came into the world, to testify to the truth. Everyone on the side of truth listens to me" (John 18:37). Those who want the truth need to listen to Jesus' words. It may take courage to accept the truth when it is unpopular or costly, but it clearly has its rewards. One would hope that people who are searching for the truth would be willing to re-examine incorrect ideas if the evidence clearly indicated this.

We may offend some people by using the term "cult," and the issue is by no means an easy one to resolve. We use it largely because it is too late to start over. Actually, we gave thought to not using the term entirely. But as we considered it more, given its widespread cultural acceptance, we retained the term because, overall, no designation seems quite as accurate or apropos; although from a Christian perspective, "spiritual counterfeits" or "heretical groups" is just as fitting and in some ways preferable.

The use of terms such as "alternate faiths" or "new religious movements" tends to imply that all religions have equal validity, which does not convey what needs to be conveyed about the groups in this Encyclopedia. Used properly, the term "cult" also has particular value for secularists who are unconcerned about theological matters yet very concerned about the ethical, psychological and social consequences of cults; although, as we will see, there are dangers for the church here. And for Christians, "cult" implies that which is "destructive to people's spiritual welfare," which is what the authors believe. So, for the sake of people's welfare, we believe that exclusively using a term like "alternate faiths" would have been inaccurate and unfair, and a term like "heretical" irrelevant to many people. While "spiritual counterfeits" is good, it does not convey the contemporary force of the term "cult."

These groups cannot, in all frankness, be seen as something neutral, biblical, divine or benign. Consciously or not, intentional or not, their agenda is often anti-moral, anti-social and anti-Christian, and they pursue their agenda. Thus, our purpose is: a) to show people what these groups really believe, in spite of claims to the contrary, b) to show that their teachings are not biblical, in spite of claims to the contrary and c) to assist people in understanding what may be expected of them spiritually and otherwise before they join a cult. People have a right to know what may be demanded by these groups. Even outwardly very respectable groups, such as Mormonism, can have a dark side to them. (See our book *Behind the Mask of Mormonism*, Harvest House, 1996.)

Properly defined and understood, the term "cult" is not necessarily pejorative, just descriptive. And with varying degrees of applicability, the groups herein deserve the title, even if they disagree. If, after a reading of the evidence, the shoe actually fits but no one wants to wear it, that is not the problem of a descriptive term. It is not just the truth that has bedeviled the term cult, it is the cults themselves—what they do and believe.

The term "cult" comes from the French *culte* and Latin *cultus*, "cultivation," "reverence," from *colere*, "to cultivate worship." According to Shipley's *Dictionary of Word Origins*, the word can be traced back to "agriculture" and indirectly to "acorn": the term "agriculture" is Latin, *agri cultura*, "tilling the field, from *colere, cult,* to *cultivate* (*cultivating* the favor of the gods is to attend them, to worship them). . . ." The definition of the term is problematic because it has been used in so many different ways and can be approached from so many different vantage points. *Webster's Third New International Dictionary* (unabridged) supplies the following definitions of the term "cult" or "cultic":

1) religious practice: worship; 2) a system of belief and ritual connected with worship of a deity or a spirit, or a group of deities or spirits; 3) the rites, ceremonies and practices of a religion as the *cultus* of Roman Catholicism, involving ceremonial veneration paid to God, Virgin Mary or the saints; 4) a religion regarded as unorthodox or spurious; 5) a system for curing disease based on dogma or principles set forth to the exclusion of scientific evidence; and 6) excessive devotion to a person, idea or thing.

All but definition 5 are applicable to the topics in this Encyclopedia, although number 5 is applicable to groups like Christian Science.

For our purposes, and from a Christian perspective, a cult may be briefly defined as "a separate religious group generally claiming compatibility with Christianity but whose doctrines contradict those of historic Christianity and whose practices and ethical standards violate those of biblical Christianity." A more expanded definition would include: "any religious organization (not a standard world religion): 1) promoting the indoctrination ('to teach to accept the system of thought uncritically') of unbiblical theology in key doctrinal areas; 2) demanding submission to a unbiblical authoritarian structure, or an individual leader; and 3) promoting excessive spiritual or psychological regulation or dependence."

In one of his lectures, Dr. Gordon Lewis of Denver Seminary provided a helpful definition of a related term, allegedly biblical group: "a religious group claiming to be based on Christ and the Bible, but whose characteristic teachings contradict the essentials of Christian teachings, whose standard of life contradicts the essentials of Christian ethics and whose standard of leadership contradicts the standards of Christian ministerial standards."

A sect may be defined as: "a smaller religious body separated from a larger established denomination, usually over doctrinal matters." A group like Seventh-day Adventism is often cited as an example because, while it has similarities with cults, it is more commonly considered a sect of Protestant Christianity, for it holds to many biblical teachings that cults generally reject. On the other hand, others classify it as a cult because the issue is not always so clear-cut. To the extent Seventh-day Adventism rejects salvation by grace through faith alone and teaches salvation by works, it must at least be classified as heretical.[5]

A cult should also be distinguished from what we may term an aberrational Christian group that is more or less doctrinally sound but contains some or many of the behavioral or other aberrations found in cults: authoritarianism, isolationism, financial exploitation, elitism, legalism, spiritual and psychological intimidation. A cult teaches heretical doctrine that is generally not found in aberrational Christian sects, while aberrational Christian sects have truly regenerated individuals generally not found in cults, although this is changing. However, even aberrational Christian groups may have elements of serious doctrinal error, such as the "positive confession" or "word-faith" movement and the modalistic (Unitarian) Oneness Pentecostal movement, although the latter may more properly be classified as a cult (see that chapter). Nevertheless, an aberrational Christian sect is one whose doctoral teachings are generally in accord with historic Christianity but whose standards of life or leadership are not. In aberrational Christian sects, certain unbiblical beliefs may be held in order to justify the sects' lifestyles. Such teachings are an aftereffect of aberrational practices, hence these groups may deny: 1) the universal priesthood of the believer; 2) full forgiveness of sin; 3) independent Bible study; 4) universal accountability (clearly, leaders should be accountable to someone); 5) the truth that ministers are servants.[6]

CHARACTERISTICS OF CULTS

Thousands of families have been battered by destructive cults. Some parents have had to spend 20 years or more searching for their children, who have been taught to reject their parents as agents of the devil, rather than to honor them as the Bible teaches. Books such as Margaret Singer's *Cults in Our Midst* (1996) show the threat that cults pose to members, families and society generally and how the cults can radically and harmfully alter members' perception. Singer has interviewed thousands of former cult members, so what she says is difficult to ignore. Other studies with thousands of ex-cult members have further proven cult dangers. As Dr. Paul Martin points out, there are "countless tales of woe related by thousands of former cult members."[7]

The consequence of cults related to overall health is an often neglected problem:

Compared to other social or medical problems, the havoc created by destructive cultism . . . is the most under-studied, neglected and ignored mental and social problem in the world. (The most conservative estimates based on a number of surveys are that 185,000 Americans alone join a destructive cult each year. Of those 185,000 at least 25% will suffer enduring irreversible harm that will affect their ability to function adequately in the emotional, social, family, and occupational domains.) The rate of numbers of people joining destructive cults in other countries equals or exceeds the rates observed in the United States.[8]

According to the *Journal of the American Medical Association*, June 10, 1998, some irrational folk beliefs, beliefs often found in the cults, may even be responsible for some forms of cancer.

The characteristics of the cults illustrates the applicability of the term. Here are a dozen characteristics of cults and new religions that we have documented in both Volume One (*The Encyclopedia of New Age Beliefs*) and in this current Encyclopedia on the cults and new religions. The list is not exhaustive. Not all groups have all the characteristics and not all groups have every characteristic in equal measure, but if we were to make "the perfect cult," criminal cults excluded, it would include the following.

1) Despite the claim to be a friend of Christianity, the new religions are rejecting or hostile to Christianity. Despite the claims to compatibility with Christianity, we find, variously,

humanism, nihilism, escapism, syncretism, eclecticism, spiritism and other occultism, polytheism, liberal theology, monism, mental science, Hinduism, mysticism, paganism, gnosticism, rationalism and pantheism. Despite the claim to be Christian or to be compatible with Christianity, there is a misrepresentation of Christianity, such as the distortion of the Christian gospel and Christian theology, and, further, an insulation against the gospel with pervasive unbiblical theology generally. For example, the two most vital biblical doctrines are universally rejected. First, there is a denial of the Holy Trinity itself and each member of the Holy Trinity: God, Jesus Christ and the Holy Spirit. Second, despite a claim to teach salvation by grace, salvation by effort and character is universal and pervasive, often logically connected to a devaluation or rejection of the atonement. And in many groups, there is a hostility to Christianity once you get past the outer friendly face. (This brings to mind the saying, "If you live in a glass house don't throw stones.")

2) Despite the claim to allow for individual expression and to respect members as individuals, we discover a destructive authoritarianism and sanction-oriented mentality: members must obey explicitly or be punished or ex-communicated.

3) Despite a claim to interpret the Bible properly, the Bible is systematically misinterpreted, either through additional revelation that distorts proper biblical interpretation or through alien (mystical, symbolic, subjective) methods of interpretation. Despite a claim to respect and honor the Bible, especially independent Bible study, a philosophical indoctrination in biblical interpretation unique to the cult and its worldview remains hostile to accepted biblical interpretation. Claiming the "latest scholarship," cultists by and large also employ the literature of liberal rationalistic theologians and higher critical methodologies (source, form and redaction criticism) to document their rejection of the established conservative view and interpretation of the Bible. Not surprisingly, even scholars who study the cults have been corrupted. Extremely wealthy organizations, such as the Unification Church, have no qualms about using their funds to influence scholarly opinion in their behalf. For their part, some scholars seem

to have no qualms about accepting funding from these groups even if it means whitewashing the truth.[9]

4) Despite a claim to care for members, members are often subject to psychological, physical and spiritual harm through cult dynamics that reject biblical, ethical and pastoral standards. Related to this, there is often distortion of the biblical view of human sexuality or the degradation or perversion of sexuality.

5) Despite a claim to allow independent thinking, there is a restriction of independent thought, a rejection of reason and logic, and often unquestioning obedience to the leader or organization.

6) Despite public claims for openness and tolerance to other religions, exclusivism and intolerance are taught privately.

7) Despite a claim for independent verification and objective evidence in support of a group's beliefs and practices, the evidence is almost exclusively based in undocumented claims or the subjective realm—mystical experience or powerful occult experience. In contrast to Christianity, the cults and new religions require blind faith, not reasoned faith.

8) Despite the claim to offer true spirituality and a genuine experience of God or ultimate reality, and despite the claim not to be occult, what is offered is often occult practices and beliefs. These may be redefined in neutral, divine, scientific or psychological categories, but what is present is occult activity in a group's history and current practice. Almost every chapter in this Encyclopedia has a section on the occult. What the Berkeley-based Spiritual Counterfeits Project noted over 20 years ago in its *Newsletter* of Jan./Feb., 1979 remains true today: "Our research has revealed that the lowest common denominator is often that of direct spirit influence." In similar confirmation, religion professor Dr. Robert S. Ellwood, of the University of Southern California, wrote in his text covering some 40 new religions, *Religious and Spiritual Groups in Modern America* (1973, p. 12), that one of the most potent and destructive forms of spiritism, shamanism, "has striking parallels to all the groups under consideration in this study. The cult phenomena could almost be called a

modern resurgence of shamanism." As we pointed out in Volume One, the widespread acceptance of shamanism and spiritism will cost a society dearly in terms of moral, social and even economic consequences. (See also our *The Coming Darkness;* Harvest House, 1992.) If, according to George Barna, 20% of the adult American population is already following the New Age movement in some fashion, and if we add membership in the cults* and *all* forms of the occult, it might not be an exaggeration to say perhaps as much as 50 % of American adults have been influenced, directly or indirectly, by the spirits (demons) who associate themselves with the cults and the occult. If so, the implications should not be lost on anyone.

9) Despite the claim for accurately representing one's history and to give a true portrait of a group's leader(s), there is a distortion—reinvention and cover-up—of a group's history and leader for purely advantageous interests. The reason is usually because a group's history and leader(s) are a moral and spiritual embarrassment, denying the claim to divine revelation and guidance.

10) Despite the claim to trust others, cults may be paranoid or persecution conscious, and they may be oppositional or alienated from the culture, having beliefs, values and practices opposed to those in the dominant culture.

11) Despite the claim for honesty there is use of intimidation or deception on both members and outsiders. There is often fraud or deception concerning a group's true teachings, the life of the founder, the group's history, fund-raising, front groups and financial cost. An American Bar Association report title says it all: *Cults in American Society: A Legal Analysis of Undue Influence, Fraud and Misrepresentation.*

12) Despite the claim for openness, there is secrecy.

---

*E.g., there are at least 1 million–6 million each (in the U.S. alone) of Mormons, Transcendental Meditators, Jehovah's Witnesses, Buddhists, Muslims, Masons, Hindus, est/the Forum graduates, Christian Scientists, Edgar Cayce believers, Oneness Pentecostals, New Thought followers, Silva Mind Control graduates and others.

Another problem with the term "cult" is that, in many quarters today, the plea is made that the term be restricted to bizarre or negative fringe groups where a more pejorative term is justified. The idea is that new religions generally do not deserve the term cult. For example, in *How Wide the Divide: A Mormon and an Evangelical in Conversation* (Inter-Varsity 1997, p.193), we read that Mormonism does not deserve the term: "it should be reserved for the kind of small, bizarre fringe groups sociologists more technically label as cultic (such as those lead to their deaths by Jim Jones or David Koresh). As applied to contemporary Latter-day Saints, the term is technically incorrect."

Granted, few would object to applying the term cult to groups like Jim Jones' People's Temple, Aum Shinryko (still alive and well), UFO cult Heaven's Gate, satanic cults or David Koreshs' Branch Davidians, which have resulted in the deaths of many people. Even today, in spite of many groups like this, some argue—even in the church—that the cults are unimportant. But they have and can have more influence than we suspect. For example, a 1999 History channel program on Hitler and the occult revealed the significant impact that Theosophy had on the madness of the Third Reich. On March 20, 1999, the fourth anniversary of the Aum Shinrikyo sarin nerve gas attack in Japan, which killed 12 and injured over 5300 others, some 2500 victims continue to suffer the after-affects of the gassing. But the question of what truly deserves the name "cult" in a depreciative or even evil sense is somewhat more complex than this. For example, we see a dictionary definition of cult as: "a religion regarded as unorthodox or spurious." From the perspective of orthodox Christianity, Mormonism clearly fits this definition, and from the perspective of historical facts, it is clearly a spurious religion with no small amount of evil historically. And given its teachings and practices historically and today, it can hardly be considered a benign religion. (See our book *Behind the Mask of Mormonism*).

The decision to use or not use the term cult takes us to the issue of how we should view the new religions from the vantage point of not just orthodox Christianity but also common social convention. Despite the cultural breakdown in America, there are still often agreed upon standards of right and wrong, decency, the importance of trust and so on. It would seem that neutral terminology is not deserved when the new religions are almost universally deceptive, frequently reject common moral concerns and often harm people in different ways. Thus, what if the term "cult" in a generally negative sense really *is* appropriate? Of course, for the overly tolerant we arrive back at the issue of "sensitivity" and not wishing to offend people by referring to their religion as a cult. Apparently, we are not to offend anyone even if it costs people their peace of mind, family, finances, overall health, sanity or soul.

Put another way, from a Christian perspective, is it not wrong to lead others astray spiritually or take advantage of people's ignorance of the Bible by distorting its doctrines? If there is a hell, is it not wrong to assist people in their journey there in the name of God, religion, truth and "Christianity"? Did not Jesus warn that stumbling blocks must come, but woe to the one through whom the stumbling block comes (Matthew 18:7)? Nor is ignorance without some culpability. Aldous Huxley adopted a platform of nihilism in defense of his radical moral, sexual and political views. He noted frankly, "Most ignorance is vincible ignorance. We don't know because we don't want to know. It is our will that decides how and upon which subjects we shall use our intelligence."[10]

When people are manipulated in different ways for ulterior motives, as cults are shown to do in this Encyclopedia, is not this to be condemned? Those cult leaders or gurus who have encouraged their followers to oppose moral convention, denied their followers blood transfusions and medical access, encouraged prostitution for making converts, sometimes raped women, beaten their disciples, molested children, practiced black magic and witchcraft, engaged in drug smuggling and other criminal activity, including murder—do they not deserve the condemnation of us all? And such things have occasionally happened even in what many people regard as the "respectable" cults.

If physical poisons like arsenic, strychnine and cyanide kill quickly, spiritual poisons like cults kill slowly, for they induce the deadly elements piecemeal. That makes them no less dangerous, just less visible. Thus, is not the greatest threat of the cults their obstruction of salvation? As Dr. Harold O. J. Brown observed in his fine work, *Heresies* (1984, p.3):

> The early Christians felt a measure of tolerance for the pagans, even though they were persecuted by them, for the pagans were ignorant. "This ignorance," Paul told the Athenians, "God winked at" (Acts 17:30). But Paul did not wink at him who brought "any other Gospel" within the context of the Christian community. "Let him be accursed," he said in Galatians 1:8. Honorable enemies are regarded with less hostility than the traitor from within one's own camp. The Christian life is often presented as spiritual warfare; if the pagans are the enemies, the heretics are the traitors.

So is it "bad faith" or "intolerance" to criticize a cult or new religion if its beliefs and behavior deserve exposing? Indeed, the hatred that some of the "tolerant" have expressed toward Christianity is hardly a shining example of compassion. In *The Psychology of Self-esteem* (Bantam, 1969) Nathaniel Brandon, a disciple of Ayn Rand, refers to Christian belief in sin and self-sacrifice as, incredibly, "as monstrous an injustice, as profound a perversion of morality as the human mind can conceive."[11] Others have actually argued that Christians who accept certain Christian doctrines, like belief in biblical creation, should be put in mental institutions and prevented from having children! How's that for tolerance?

The *Macmillan Dictionary for Students* defines "tolerance" as the "ability or willingness to accept or respect the behavior, customs, opinions, or beliefs of others." Barring illegalities, or perversions, Christians are certainly willing to accept the beliefs and practices of others and·to respect their right to hold them; after all, this is a God-given right. How is this being intolerant, as critics charge? Worse, to criticize Christians and call them intolerant for holding to a demonstrated truth is sheer nonsense. Indeed, Christians are frequently more tolerant of others' beliefs than their own critics are, who carelessly categorize Christians as representing the essence of intolerance. "The fundamentalism of tolerance is just as dogmatic as any other fundamentalism, only it is deceptive in its *profession* of tolerance. . . . Actually, it is only tolerant of other expressions of the same world view. . . . It may actually prove to be less tolerant, since it does not seem to recognize the right of others to reject its relativistic view."[12] Today, then, "tolerance" has often become a code word for intolerance toward exclusivistic beliefs. (See the chapter on Unitarian Universalism.)

Of course not all cults are equally culpable when it comes to unsavory teachings and practices, but enough are. What we have discussed in this Encyclopedia stands as a testimony to what we say about the continuing relevance of the term cult. And it must be remembered that what is recorded is merely the tip of the iceberg.

In sum, when people really understand what the cults are like, it becomes difficult to trust them in mundane matters, let alone in the salvation of one's soul. It is like the TV ad that runs during income tax season: "For help with your tax preperation, call . . ." If inaccuracies in little things do not inspire confidence, how much less do the inaccuracies in big things? The problem with the cults is that people don't know the inaccuracies, and this we have tried to remedy, to help people know.

LEGAL PROBLEMS

There are many documented things that we could not even mention or discuss in this work, simply because time and funds were unavailable to defend against frivolous lawsuits—lawsuits designed strictly to intimidate researchers and keep them quiet. (Thankfully, at least some of this material has been placed on the Web by cult-watchers with financial backing.) For example, *Time* magazine's 1991 cover story on Scientology, labeling it a "thriving cult of greed and power," cost the magazine $7 million before a federal District Court Judge dismissed the case five years later. (Scientology has filed hundreds of lawsuits against its critics.) Intimidating lawsuits can and have destroyed individuals and entire ministries because the purpose of the law is less and less justice than expediency—winning at any price by any means for your own personal cause. Here is only one consequence of a culture's unwillingness to stand for truth, common sense and morality: corruption of the legal system to such an extent the truth dies and falsehood and vice prosper. Most people still believe that America is the land of the free, but things are changing. America has become a nation that as often as not protects the freedom to do evil as much as the freedom to do good, because we no longer know the difference. Not infrequently, the evils that cults do are protected by one set of laws while traditional religious freedoms are harmed by another set of laws. For example, some cults are free to continue bizarre practices that can harm people under a liberal interpretation of the "freedom of religion" statute. According to *The Honolulu Advertiser,* March 22, 1999, in the last 7 years, Medicare has paid out over $50 million to Christian Science facilities that treat the sick with mental affirmations which imply denial of the reality of sickness. Thousands have died early deaths. Yet a time-honored religion like Christianity is widely discriminated against or even persecuted by a conservative (and false) interpretation of the "establishment of religion" clause.[15]

Those with the power to interpret and apply the law increasingly seem to be using the law to endorse their agenda of tolerance for almost everything—tolerance being denied to that expression of religion they personally do not like. The law is manipulated by convention or preference when it has no moral basis to secure its judgements. The more we travel down this road, the more everyone's freedoms will be eroded.

CHRISTIANS AS CULTISTS?

When Christians merely share their faith, this is now seen in some quarters as "religious intolerance," "hate crimes" or "cultural violence." Further, if intolerance toward Christianity continues to increase, what is happening globally in some nonChristian nations may start happening in so-called Christian nations. There are many cases in the courts overseas where Christians are treated as if they were cultists. But consider this: Evangelical Christian Mark Harding was the first individual to be convicted and almost sent to prison for "hate crimes" in criticizing another religion (Islam) during his personal evangelism in Canada. Apparently, his prison time was commuted to a sentence (on appeal) of 240 hours attendance at a mosque, where he is court-ordered to attend *indoctrination classes* in Islam. He is not permitted to defend his faith or even contradict what the Muslim clerics will be teaching him. Muslims, of course, would *never* put up with this. And neither should Christians.

In a culture grounded in relativism and tolerance of everything but absolutes, American churches could be prohibited the right of excommunication for serious moral sin or heresy, and face prosecuting for refusing gay or women's ordination or even for teaching moral absolutes. Moral absolutes are in fact "violence" against the cultural norm of relativism. Our society "will not tolerate criticism of anything except what we wish criticized." Tolerance is now perverted from its true definition to mean *intolerance* for whatever a particular group doesn't like. In the "old" Soviet Union, people could be jailed merely for expressing belief in God. If America becomes a true secular state, then totalitarian, will the outcome be different here?

Let's look at one of the lesser known but potentially more powerful arguments for abandoning the term cult. In the *Evangelical Dictionary of Theology,* I. Hexham points out that the first modern use of the term cult was in 1912 in Ernst Troeltsch's text, *The Social Teaching of the Christian Churches.* Here the word was used in a more positive sense as it referred to a form of religion attempting to enliven a dead orthodoxy. Luther, many of the Puritans and perhaps Charismatics today would thus be examples of cultic religion. Eventually the term came to be viewed more negatively in association with polemics against heretical groups, as in J. K. van Baalen's 1938 work, *The Chaos of Cults* and in

Walter Martin's *The Kingdom of the Cults* (1960). Hexham points out that along with concern over theological heresy, a concern developed with the psychological dynamics of cults which suggested that members were brainwashed. This idea was turned against the church with books like William Sargent's 1957 text, *The Battle for the Mind,* a text that cites evangelical conversion as an example of brainwashing. Jim Siegelman and Flo Conway's 1979 text *Snapping,* argues that Christian conversion—being born again—is an experience similar to the process by which people join cults. Hexham writes:

> Such books as these and stories in the media about brainwashing have led to considerable pressure on governments in various American states, Canada, Britain, and Germany for anti-conversion laws. These laws are supposedly aimed at groups like the Moonies. But because of their lack of definition. . . . they are in practice aimed at any form of change of lifestyle brought about by a religious conversion.

> Today the real problem of cults is the propaganda value of the word "cult" in a secular society. . . . These groups are presented [by cult watchers] as a major threat to society. As a result secularists are able to urge the acceptance of laws which replace religious freedom by a grudgingly granted religious tolerance. Rather than persist with the use of a word which has now become a propaganda weapon, the academic practice of calling such groups "new religious movements" should be followed. An alternative to this neutral terminology available for Christians who oppose such groups on theological grounds would be to revive the usage of "heretic" or simply call such groups "spiritual counterfeits." Such a procedure would move the debate away from psychological theories that can be used by secularists against Christianity to the arena of theological discussion and religious argument.[14]

Consider the following June 15, 1997 Internet comment quoting, again, evangelical Christian Irving Hexham:

> Evangelical criticisms of cults play a role in the formation of government policy toward religious freedom in Europe. The irony here is that North American criticisms of cults have been cited in

German courts to limit religious activity. These restrictions make no distinction between groups like Satanism, Hare Krishnas, the Unification Church and evangelical groups like Campus Crusade. It is also important to realize that under the guise of the "danger" of "fundamentalism" counter cult legislation is being used to hinder conservative Christians in various German State churches. Further. . . . German established church "cult experts" are playing an important role in encouraging the Russian Duma and other newly liberated East European countries to outlaw evangelical activity.

There are no easy answers here. Regardless, the term cult is so entrenched in culture that we are unlikely to be able to avoid it.

DEFENDING RESPONSIBLE RELIGIOUS FREEDOM

What should be done? On the one hand, responsible religious freedom must be defended, vigorously, including the responsible religious freedoms of cults and new religions. Simultaneously, the legitimate distinctions between cults and biblical Christianity must be demonstrated, distinctions such as the generally positive influence for society from Christianity and the generally negative impact for society from the cults. (On the former, see D. James Kennedy, *What If Jesus Had Never Been Born?* It would also need to be stressed that aberrational Christianity is not biblical Christianity.) The approach that we have taken in this Encyclopedia is to illustrate as best we can, given legal threats, that the cults do pose a significant threat to society.

On the other hand, Christian leaders should call for and institute a national discussion over how we protect legitimate religious freedoms and simultaneously protect ourselves from "freedom of religion." In fact there may be no solution here, but we need to try. (compare *Cultic Studies Journal,* Vol. 9 No. 2 (1992), "The Council Of Europe's Report on Sects and New Religious Movements"; the "Europe and Cults" section posted at www.apologeticsindex.org, especially "Illegal Activities of Sects" (and responses); and the 13 April, 1999 "Report of the

Committee on Legal Affairs and Human Rights" of the Council of Europe Parliamentary Assembly, Document 8373).

In America, the problems raised by the dominance of relativism and secularism vis a vis first amendment religious issues is forbidding at best. A generation ago we had very few cults and no problem with intolerance or persecution of Christians because the cultural consensus was Christian. This seems to have been the divine plan. In establishing a nation solidly based in clear Christian beliefs and principles (see the crucial John Ankerberg show interview with David Barton, "The Founding Fathers"), God may have ordained a built-in penalty that could not be avoided should we forsake our Christian foundations and responsibilities. In other words, the First Amendment only works as long as the nation accepts Christian principles. If it does not, then it gets what it gets—all kinds of religious evils protected by the very amendment by which God intended to bless the nation.

Of course, what Hexham mentions above illustrates the problem precisely: state authorities unable to distinguish good religion from bad religion because as relativists they have no logical basis for doing so. But that is hardly the fault of Christianity. In the end, the persecution of the state brought upon Christians that may occur will result from the state's unwillingness to take religious truth claims seriously, and from the church's unwillingness to take theology and apologetics seriously, for these are the most authoritative means to distinguish good and bad religion.

Nevertheless, those who wish that Christians would go away, or who may wish to persecute them legally, need to consider the practical consequences, if not the spiritual consequences (see 2 Thessalonians 1:4–10). Mature Christian faith is not only a stabilizing force in society morally and spiritually, it is a powerful antidote to the cults, the occult, pseudo-science, irrationalism and the moral and philosophical chaos that have ruined countless lives in our generation. People who are law-abiding, who live and encourage common sense morality, who love their neighbors as themselves, who encourage fairness and justice and who help the poor and needy are far more of a social godsend than secularists may realize.

THE CULTS' INFLUENCES ON CHRISTIANITY

Wherever cult dynamics operate, they harm people. This is especially true in the church. Dr. Paul R. Martin is a cult expert and the author of *How to Cult-Proof Your Kid*. He is also Executive Director of the Wellspring Retreat and Resource Center, an organization helping individuals and families deal with their cult experiences. "My own research (with several hundred ex-cultists and about 50 on an intensive basis totaling about 2000 hours) indicates that the severity of problems suffered by those in the extremist evangelical sects may be equal to or greater than that experienced by members of the better known cults such as is ISKCON, the Church of Scientology, the Moonies, the Divine Light Mission and The Way."[15] Further research indicates that "a sizable proportion of those involved in cults or extremist groups come from some type of evangelical church base. Of the cultists I have personally worked with, approximately 25% came from evangelical or fundamental churches and over 40% had backgrounds in the large, more liberal Protestant denominations."[16] Dr. Martin estimates that there are several hundred thousand *evangelical* Christians that have been harmed by the cults.[17]

For anyone who has come out of a cult, he writes, "I cannot underscore enough the importance of getting these ex-members to think, and to think critically."[18] This also is one purpose of this Encyclopedia, that Christians will hopefully encourage other Christians who were once cult members to read the material we have put together.

CULTIC BEHAVIOR AND SERIOUS ERRORS ON CHURCH FRINGES

Sadly, an increasing problem exists in the church today that is related to the phenomenon of the cults. It exists because of a lack of biblical knowledge, apologetics and spiritual discernment. There are groups who use "Christian" as a screen to mask their actions. For example, the "Concerned Christians," who were arrested in Jerusalem in 1999 had decidedly unbiblical plans for inducing violence, perhaps mass suicide, to allegedly "hasten the return of Jesus Christ." Certain "Christian militia" and racist groups may also be stepping over true Christianity by planning violent outbreaks. Despite their unbiblical actions, in the eyes of the world these groups appear Christian, just like the more traditional cults. With Christian names and claims, how is the world to tell a real Christian from a false one? Apart from biblical knowledge and biblical actions, they can't. Unfortunately, genuine Christians sometimes do join these groups, just as they ignorantly join other more traditional cults. Many years ago John Weldon remembers reading the book *Unholy Devotion,* which spoke to this issue. It argued persuasively that a major reason Christians join cults is because they don't know any better—based, in part, on their experience in aberrational evangelical churches. In other words, when they joined the cult, they could not tell much difference between their own evangelical church and the cult they were now in. Certainly, if they had been taught proper doctrine (especially the doctrine of full salvation by grace), apologetics, biblical morality and how to interpret the Bible properly, they may never have joined a cult in the first place.

But the problem is not only in the church; it appears in the home as well. We do not seem to be training our kids properly in biblical truths. On January 11, 1997, Josh McDowell stated in a lecture, "I would estimate 98.9% of all evangelical fundamental kids are living legalism. . . . 95% of parents don't know how to communicate their values to their children." Today, the situation is of sufficient concern that many books have been written describing otherwise evangelical churches abuse of members through spiritual intimidation, financial manipulation, authoritarianism, legalism and other means.[19]

Consider a few other facts that may help explain the influence of cults among Christians: national opinion polls reveal that 35 percent of America's evangelical seminarians deny that faith in Christ is absolutely necessary for salvation; 35 percent of the entire adult evangelical population agrees that "God will save all good people when they die, regardless of whether they've trusted in Christ"; 30 to 51 percent of

Protestant pastors do not believe in the physical resurrection of Jesus Christ; 53 percent of those claiming to be Bible-believing conservative Christians "said there is no such thing as absolute truth"; 43 percent of born again Christians agree that "it does not matter what religious faith you follow because all faiths teach similar lessons about life"; 30 percent of born again Christians do not believe that "Jesus came back to physical life after He was crucified." Up to 70 percent of adults generally believe that "it does not matter what God, force or higher power you pray to because it will respond regardless."[20]

Have our own churches and homes, by default, become ripe fields for cult evangelism? Hopefully not to a significant degree. But only God knows the whole story.

NOTES

1. Robert M. Bowman Jr. estimated a factor of 18 with 108 million worldwide in November 1987, "What's New in the New Religions," *Moody Monthly,* November 1987, p. 69.

2. (Florida) *Sun-Sentinel,* June 8, 1991.

3. Incidentally, God has very good reasons for leaving the evidence convincing but not literally compelling. For God to shout would generate worse problems. See, e.g., J. P. Moreland, ed., *The Creation Hypothesis,* pp. 117-18 and the essay, "Why Isn't the Evidence Clearer?" in John Warwick Montgomery, ed., *Evidence for Faith: Deciding the God Question.*

4. Consider some recent titles: Miriam Williams, *Heaven's Harlots: My 15 Years as a Sacred Prostitute in the Children of God;* Anton Shupe, *The Darker Side of Virtue: Corruption, Scandal and the Mormon Empire;* Brian Lane, *Killer Cults: Murderous Messiahs & Their Fanatical Followers* (Lane is author of *The Encyclopedia of Serial Killers* and related texts); James J. Boyle, *Killer Cults;* James Randall Noblitt, Pamela Sue Perskin, *Cult & Ritual Abuse: Its History, Anthropology & Recent Discovery;* Marc Breault, Martin King, *Inside the Cult: A Member's Chilling, Exclusive Account of Madness and Depravity in David Koresh's Compound;* Michael Barkun, *Religion and the Racist Right: The Origins of the Christian Identity Movement;* William Henry, *The Keepers of Heaven's Gate: The Millennial Madness, the Religion Behind the Rancho Sante Fe Suicides;* Lawrence J. Gesy, Carol Giambalvo, *Today's Destructive Cults & Religious Movements;* Larry Kaehner, *Cults That Kill;* Michael D. Langone, Linda O. Blood, *Satanism and Occult Related Violence;* George Feuerstein, *Holy Madness: The Shock Tactics and Radical Teachings of Crazy-Wise Adepts, Holy Fools and Rascal Gurus.*

5. For the controversy, see Walter R. Martin, *Seventh-day Adventism;* Anthony Hoekema, *The Four Major Cults;* Geoffrey Paxton, *The Shaking of Adventism;* Dale Ratzlaff, *Cultic Doctrine of the Seventh-Day Adventists;* Robert Brinsmead, *1844 Re-examined;* Kenneth R. Samples, "An Updated Assessment of Seventh-day Adventism," *Christian Research Journal,* Summer, 1988; Walter Rea, *The White Lie;* Mark Martin, *Seventh-day Adventism and the Writings of Ellen G. White;* and Jeremiah Films, "Seventh-day Adventism."

6. Members of such groups might be termed schismatic sheep, and verses like 2 Timothy 2:23–26; Titus 1:9, 3:1, 2, 10, 11; and Romans 16:17 apply.

7. Paul R. Martin, "The Psychological Consequences of Cultic Involvement," *Christian Research Journal,* Winter/Spring 1989, Internet Copy.

8. Paul R. Martin, "Cults and Health," *Well Spring Messenger,* Winter 1996, p. 3.

9. We have noticed several recent examples on the Internet, e.g., the following book review from *Apologia Report* discusses J. Gordon Melton's association with the channeled entity, "Ramtha": "Finding Enlightenment: Ramtha's School of Ancient Wisdom" by J. Gordon Melton (Beyond Words Publishing, 1998)—reviewer Siobhan Houston observes: "Melton's high praise for the RSE [Ramtha School of Enlightenment] does not sit well with critics of Ramtha. . . . Melton devotes a chapter to defending [channeler J.Z.] Knight and the RSE against various accusations, but I couldn't help feeling this was not a full and unbiased disclosure of the various disputes surrounding the group." Case in point: Houston cites evidence that Melton has received funds from the RSE and/or its affiliates on more than one occasion. "The close connection between Melton and the RSE raises a problematic issue that confronts the scholars of new religious movements (NRMs). People from both inside and outside the academy charge that certain researchers have close ties to and accept financial support from the groups they purport to study in an objec-

tive manner. Common sense and professional ethics suggest that scholars of NRMs should be especially vigilant to maintain a professional distance between themselves and the subjects of their research." (*Gnosis,* Wtr. '99, p. 60.)

10. Aldous Huxley, *Ends and Means* (London: Chatto & Windus, 1946), pp. 270–73.

11. Cited in Paul R. Martin, "The Psychological Consequences of Cultic Involvement," *Christian Research Journal,* Winter/Spring 1989, Internet copy.

12. Elliott Miller, "The 1993 Parliament of the Worlds Religions Part Two: The Fundamentalism of Tolerance," *Christian Research Journal,* Winter 1994.

13. The incidents would fill a book this size and can be documented by contacting organizations such as the Rutherford Institute, the Christian Legal Society or the American Institute for Law and Justice.

14. I. Hexham, "Cults" in Walter A. Elwell, ed., *Evangelical Dictionary of Theology* (Baker, 1984), p. 289.

15. Martin, "The Psychological Consequences of Cultic Involvement."

16. Ibid.

17. Ibid.

18. Ibid.

19. Dr. Ronald Enroth, *Churches that Abuse,* and *Recovering from Churches that Abuse;* David Johnson and Jeff Van Vonderen, *The Subtle Power of Spiritual Abuse;* Ken Blue, *Healing Spiritual Abuse;* Agnes C. and John W. Lawless, *The Drift into Deception: The Eight Characteristics of Abusive Christianity;* Harold Bussell, *By Hook or Crook: How Cults Lure Christians;* Ron and Vicki Burk, *Damaged Disciples;* and Tim Brauns, et. al., eds., *Twisted Scriptures: A Path to Freedom From Abusive Churches.* These are only a few titles. John McArthur's *Reckless Faith: When the Church Loses Its Will to Discern,* although a book on discernment, is also important.

20. Documentation on file at the Ankerberg Theological Research Institute; cf., *Chattanooga New Free Press,* September 7, 1991.

This is the message we have
heard from him and declare to you:
God is light; in him there is no darkness at all.
—1 John 1:5

Jesus said, "My kingdom is not of this world. . . ."
"You are a king, then!" said Pilate.
Jesus answered, "You are right in saying I am a king.
In fact, for this reason I was born,
and for this I came into the world, to testify to the truth.
Everyone on the side of truth listens to me."
—John 18:36,37

Armstrongism

Note: In the late 1980s, in an almost unprecedented move historically, the Worldwide Church of God (WCG) began radically changing its doctrines from heresy to orthodoxy. From 1988 to 1997, the transformation occurred gradually to the point that in 1997 the church was accepted as a member of the National Association of Evangelicals. Thus, the WCG Website now declares, "Today the church and *The Plain Truth* [magazine] are in full agreement with the statement of faith of the National Association of Evangelicals."

The cost was great. The television ministry was lost, as was over 50 percent of church membership. *The Plain Truth* had its circulation decline from 8 million to less than 150,000, and the Pasadena employees fell from around 1,000 to 180.[1] But history and eternity will prove the rewards worth the sacrifice. As the WCG church website declares, "Organizationally this doctrinal change had catastrophic results. But spiritually, it was the best thing that ever happened to the WCG."

Of course, we welcome the fact that the Pasadena WCG has changed its course. Nevertheless, we have included H. Armstrong's teachings because the information is still relevant for numerous offshoots of the WCG that refused the changes, left the WCG, and began their own churches in order to preserve Armstrong doctrines. The Global Church of God, The Associated Church of God, Philadelphia Church of God, United Church of God and others, still hold to Armstrong doctrines.

While the WCG has made truly dramatic doctrinal changes, it still has a way to go.[2] It is understandable that some things which need changing remain unchanged given where the church has come from as a full blown cult and the cost of its transformation. In some areas it has moved slowly, apparently in its desire to reach as many members for Christ as possible. But there will come a point when certain issues can no longer be avoided, such as the full truth about its own history and Herbert W. Armstrong's status as a heretic. Armstrong was never a "minister of the gospel" and the old WCG was never a Christian church, although statements by the new WCG in 1996–1998 have allegedly said that the old WCG was Christian. In addition, the truth of the doctrine of eternal punishment needs to be recognized. Clearly, the old church denied this, and at this point the new church doesn't seem to have made much progress.

For all we know, these issues are in the process of being addressed, and the Evangelical Church should do all in its power to continue to encourage and assist the new WCG toward a complete and robust evangelical faith, and be grateful to God for the historic changes already accomplished. Our prayers for the leadership of the church are especially important.

DOCTRINAL SUMMARY

God: Currently, two Persons, the Father and Jesus; now reproducing themselves into billions of Persons.

Jesus: Jehovah of the Old Testament; triparte.

Holy Spirit: God's mind and power, God's life and love, but not the third Person of the Godhead.

Trinity: A satanic, pagan doctrine.

Salvation: By works.

Man: Becomes a God at the resurrection.

Fall: Instituted by God to help people eventually attain perfection.

Bible: Accepted as authoritative when interpreted by Herbert W. Armstrong.

Death: Soul sleep; annihilation for the wicked.

Hell and Heaven: Hell is a pagan teaching; no heaven, as taught in Christianity, exists.

NOTES

1. Internet copy: *A Brief History of the Worldwide Church of God—Transformed by Christ: The New Worldwide Church of God.*
2. See the articles in, e.g., *The Quarterly Journal,* July-September 1998.

ASTARA

INFO AT A GLANCE

Name: Astara.

Purpose: To awaken a person's inner potential through psychic development and to promote spiritistic contact with the Masters.

Founder: Earlyne and Robert Chaney.

Source of authority: Psychic messages published as numerous books and lessons.

Revealed teachings: Yes.

Claim: To be a New Age religion of mystical Christianity, supportive of every religion and free of dogmatism.

Examples of occult potential: Yoga, psychic development, spiritism.

Examples of key literature: Books by Earlyne and Robert Chaney: *Remembering: The Autobiography of a Mystic; The Great Work of the Penetralia; Mysticism: The Journey Within.*

Attitude toward Christianity: Rejecting.

Quote:

"Astara differs completely from the orthodox and traditional. A church of free souls, Astara encourages each Astarian to seek God in his own way, recognizing authority in no one man or leader, but only in Truth. As a church, Astara follows the leadership of the great Master Jesus the Christ, but pays reverent homage to saints of all religions. . . . Presenting no creeds, dogmas, nor precepts which bind the mind in any way. Holding to no exoteric dogma, Astara embraces the esoteric or inner teachings of all religions."

(Earlyne Chaney, *The Great Work of the Penetralia I,* pp. 58–59)

"You [are] an emissary of the Infinite, the Cosmic Being we call God or Brahma or Allah or any of a thousand different names!" (Robert Chaney, *Awaken Your Higher Potential,* p. 19)

"The three Masters of Astara [Rama, Kuthumi and Zoser—Astara's principal spirit guides] follow the leadership of Jesus most reverently. . . . It is the Master Jesus who is Astara's leader and light, and it is his inner Teachings which the Astarian disciples follow as devout Astarian mystic Christians." (Earlyne Chaney, *The Great Work of the Penetralia I,* p. 23)

Note: In places, the philosophy of Astara is influenced by the surat shabd yoga of the Radhasoami sect.

DOCTRINAL SUMMARY

God: Universal cosmic energy.

Jesus: The Master of Astara, a man who attained a high degree of cosmic consciousness.

The Christ: Higher consciousness.

The Holy Spirit: The *Nahd,* or divine sound current.

The Trinity: Divine essence, creation, *Nahd.*

Salvation: Achieving higher consciousness through psychic methods.

Man: Inwardly divine.

Sin: Ignorance of one's divinity and true reality.

Satan: A figurative term for sickness, karmic law, negativity.

The Second Coming: The coming of higher consciousness for mankind.

The Fall: Into matter.

The Bible: One of many relevant scriptures when interpreted mystically.

Death: Ultimately beneficial, a path to final liberation through reincarnation.

Heaven and Hell: Temporary places or states of consciousness.

BAHA'I

INFO AT A GLANCE

Purpose: To unite the entire world in one common faith.

Founders: "The Bab" (Syyid, or Mirza, Ali Muhammed); Baha'u'llah. (In Baha'ism, the words "Syyid" and "Mizra" are designations of spiritual authority.)

Source of authority: The writings of Baha'u'llah.

Revealed teachings: Yes.

Claim: To be the fulfillment of all world religions and prophecies.

Occult dynamics: Mystical practices influenced by Shiite Islam.

Examples of key literature: *The Al-Kitab Al-Aqdas (The Most Holy Book), The Kitab-I-Iqan (The Book of Certitude), Gleanings From the Writings of Baha'u'llah; Baha'i World Faith.*

Attitude toward Christianity: Rejecting.

Quotes:

"The Cause of Baha'u'llah is the same as the Cause of Christ. It is the same Temple and the same Foundation."[1]

—'Abdu'l-Baha the infallible interpreter of Baha'u'llah,

"Verily if he declares the right to be left, or the south to be north, it is true and there is no doubt therein."[2]

—Baha'u'llah on himself

"There are some people who, even if all the proofs in the world would be adduced before them, still will not judge justly."[3]

—'Abdu'l-Baha

"He (Baha'u'llah) sets forth a new principle for this day in the announcement that religion must be the cause of unity, harmony and agreement among mankind." "All these [religious] divisions we see on all sides, all these disputes and opposition, are caused because men cling to ritual and outward observances, and forget the simple, underlying truth. It is the outward practices of religion that are so different, and it is they that cause disputes and enmity—while the [doctrinal] reality is always the same, and one. The Reality is the Truth, and truth has no division."[4]

—Baha'i World Faith website

Note: For a similar approach to religious syncretism, see The Masonic Lodge chapter.

DOCTRINAL SUMMARY

God: Unknowable, except through His or Its historic Manifestations. (See citation at note 83.)

Jesus: A Prophet; a Manifestation of God (one of nine or more); never God-incarnate.

Holy Spirit: The "impersonal" active force of God.

Trinity: An irrational concept reinterpreted in light of Baha'i teachings, especially by Baha'u'llah.

Salvation: By belief in the Manifestations of God and good works.

Man: A son of God.

Satan: A Christian myth.

Second coming: Baha'u'llah represents the Second Coming of Christ.

Bible: One of many divine scriptures.

Death: Generally, death brings an improved state of existence.

Heaven and Hell: Conditions, not places.

INTRODUCTION AND HISTORY

"The claim which Baha'u'llah has advanced is no ordinary claim, and He does not ask anyone to accept it without serious investigation. Indeed, one of His most important Teachings is on the subject of independent investigation of the truth."[5]

—Gloria Faizi, *The Baha'i Faith—*
An Introduction

Within the world of modern religions, the Baha'i faith is known by its claims for religious tolerance. Baha'is with pride declare, "We accept all the manifestations of God." In fact, Baha'is make such substantial claims here that we feel it best to start with a short treatment of this idea to set the stage for our subsequent discussion.

Throughout the chapters in this encyclopedia we have witnessed a number of common themes. One is that religions which earnestly allege to be religiously open-minded are in actuality often the opposite. In the end, what they believe is that *they* have the only way to God, or at least the best way. Despite their claims for tolerance, it is frequently an empty gesture; upon examination, an obvious lack of tolerance often exists.

The Baha'i faith stands at the pinnacle, perhaps, in claims for religious harmony and tolerance. Yet, as we shall see, these claims are essentially without foundation, since each religion it claims to accept is not permitted to speak for itself but is re-interpreted to conform, more or less, to the teachings of the Baha'i faith. In essence, other religions are reinvented to teach the Baha'i philosophy. Whether it be Hinduism, Buddhism, Judaism, Christianity or Islam, when sifted through Baha'i apologists, such religions are recreated in the image of Baha'i. No amount of intellectual gymnastics can change this basic fact: the Baha'i faith is not as tolerant as it would have us believe. Fundamentally, it recognizes what all religions have accepted: only absolute truths have value. It is thus underhanded in claiming one thing (the acceptance of the basic teachings of all religions) while teaching another (religious exclusivism).

The Baha'i faith does not claim to be a new religion, but instead a *renewal* of religion. It claims to be a renewal of the true teaching of all religions, which time has corrupted. Baha'is stress "we are *not* a new religion" because they wish to harmonize all religion under Baha'i teachings, and thus they cannot be understood as being just one more "competing" religion. This is why Baha'i literature argues that all *other* religions are "obsolete," that they have "bankrupt and broken" beliefs which are mere "imitations" of God's true religion, and that Baha'i's alone have the true way.[6] The truth according to Baha'i is that its religion is unique and represents the essence of Divine Truth that God has molded throughout history in various religions, but which has become distorted. Nevertheless, in spite of this claim that they are not a new religion, even Shoghi Effendi, the one-time "Guardian" and absolute ruler[7] of the Baha'i faith, once approved of an Islamic court verdict declaring that "The Baha'i Faith is a new religion, entirely independent, with beliefs, principles and laws of its own, which differ from, and are utterly in conflict with, the beliefs, principles, and laws of Islam."[8]

Before continuing, three other facts of Baha'ism bear stressing. First, while the articles in the leading Baha'i periodical *World Order* do not necessarily reflect "official" Baha'i views, they are a valid source of Baha'i teachings on many subjects. (*World Order* encourages non-Baha'is to write articles as an expression of religious unity. To our knowledge no conservative Christian articles examining Baha'i claims critically have ever been accepted.)

Second, since Baha'is at least *proclaim* belief in an independent search for truth, there is a sense in which the Baha'is are similar to the Unitarian-Universalists and modern New Age religions, where ultimate authority resides in the individual. Hence, not everything quoted herein will necessarily be accepted by every Baha'i. On the other hand, there are also limits to individual opinion. Baha'is have their own scriptures, which are believed to be divinely inspired, and these carry authority above any individual's personal views. From the beginning, members have been required to submit to a higher authority, whether it be the divine Manifestations (the Bab, Baha'u'llah), the infallible interpreters of them (such as 'Abdu'l-Baha), the Guardian of the Faith (Shoghi Effendi) or, today,

the "Universal House of Justice," which is the nine-member authoritative ruling body. "Baha'u'llah says that all Baha'is must obey the Universal House of Justice because anything they decide is the Will of God."[9] The fact is, then, that the Baha'i claim to "independent investigation of the truth" is true only insofar as members first obey a higher authority and accept its rule over their lives. As we will see, this claim to independent investigation of truth turns out to be artificial.

Our third point is that many Baha'i writers think that Protestant critiques of Baha'i incorporate a "one-sided bias" in that they employ secondary literature, with a "preference given to unreliable sources" on Baha'i. These supposedly cause "gross misrepresentation of Baha'i," "false interpretations of the Bible" and "many misunderstandings." Such claims are made despite Baha'i's *own* historic misrepresentations of other religions and their own lack of primary source documentation.[10] Regardless, the claim is not true, at least of the evangelical critiques of Baha'i which we cite in this chapter.

For our own, we have answered this criticism beforehand by quoting from accepted authoritative Baha'i sources that contain primary documents: *Baha'i World Faith—Selected Writings of Baha'u'llah and 'Abdu'l-Baha; Gleanings from the Writings of Baha'u'llah; The Al Kitab al-Aqdas* (the Most Holy Book) by Baha'u'llah; *The Revelation of Baha'u'llah* by Adib Taherzadeh; *The Kitab-I-Ian* (the Book of Certitude); *Christ's Promise Fulfilled* by 'Abdu'l-Baha; *The Seven Valleys and the Four Valleys* by Baha'u'llah; *The Hidden Words of Baha'u'llah* (transl.) by Shoghi Effendi; and Esslemont's *Baha'u'llah and the New Era* (a text with over sixty printings and recognized as accurate by the Baha'i Publishing Trust). We have also used secondary sources by modern Baha'is. Generally, these reflect historic Baha'i teachings, at least as far as our doctrinal concerns extend—for example, George Townshend's *The Heart of the Gospel* and *Christ and Baha'u'llah.*

The Baha'is represent a fairly solid international movement. Despite severe persecution in Iran and elsewhere, often by Muslims who see them as the worst of heretics, they remain stable and evangelistic. In the United States, Baha'is claim that membership doubled from 25,000 to 50,000 in less than two years (1970 to 1971). By 1975, there were over 1,000 local spiritual assemblies ("churches") in the United States, and Baha'is resided in over 5,300 cities and towns. There were also three permanent schools and the Baha'i Publishing Trust distributed over three hundred book titles.[11]

By 1976 their writings had been translated into 546 languages, and they claimed 2,000,000 plus adherents around the globe in some 18,000 "churches" in over 72,000 localities (330 countries and territories, including 119 National Spiritual assemblies).[12] In 1999, according to their website, they claimed membership in 200 countries and territories with Baha'i literature being translated into over 700 different languages. U.S. membership is now estimated at 40,000–75,000. (Baha'is do not supply precise figures.) The religion also has official parliamentary (although non-voting) recognition within the United Nations.

The four principal individuals of Baha'i history are:

1. Mirza Ali Muhammad ("the Bab," 1819–1850, author of *The Bayan*).

2. Mirza Husayn Ali ("Baha'u'llah," 1817–1892, author of the *Al-Kitab-Al-Aqdas* (The Most Holy Book), and the *Kitab-I-Iqan* (The Book of Certitude).

3. 'Abdu'l-Baha (1844–1921, son of Baha'u'llah).

4. Shoghi Effendi, grandson of 'Abdu'l-Baha and Guardian of the Faith, who died in 1957.

The history of the Baha'is begins in 1844. This was the year that Mizra Ali Muhammad, otherwise known as "the Bab," proclaimed to the world that he was the greatest Manifestation of God to date and the fulfillment of prophecies in all world Scriptures. Baha'is believe that of the nine or more historic manifestations of God (for example, Krishna, Buddha, Jesus—the exact number has changed historically), the Bab was the greatest revealer of truth up to his time.

However, the Bab also told of another Manifestation, even greater, who would follow him. The Baha'is interpret this (erroneously in all likelihood) as Mirza Husayn Ali, otherwise

known as Baha'u'llah. Baha'u'llah (meaning "the Glory of God") is as close as one can come to a Baha'i equivalent of Jesus Christ. Baha'is today view the Bab as his forerunner and give Baha'u'llah preeminence. Hence the teachings and writings of the Bab are of less import, as they are superseded by those of Baha'u'llah, who brought greater revelation to light.

Critique of Baha'i History

No discussion of Baha'i history is complete without noting Dr. William Miller's detailed research in *The Baha'i Faith: Its History and Teachings* (1974, 464 pages). This critical text is more than a headache to faithful Baha'is. In essence, Miller documents why he believes that the Bab did, in fact, teach that the *next* Manifestation of God would not appear for another 1511 to 2001 years, well into the fourth millennium A.D.[13] If true, Baha'u'llah was an impostor and the foundation of the Baha'i World Faith crumbles because Baha'i religion is based squarely on the divine authority of Baha'u'llah.

"Was Baha'u'llah actually the next Manifestation?" is a question that is crucial for Baha'is. If not, the Bab is still the true (current) Manifestation and the one he prophesied about has not yet appeared. If the Bab is still the true Manifestation, then Baha'is have abandoned the true prophet and largely discarded his writings for a false prophet, Baha'u'llah. Put simply, the Baha'is have chosen to trust Baha'u'llah's own claim that he was indeed the prophesied one.[14]

Although Baha'i writer Douglas Martin[15] has raised a few minor technical issues in response to Miller's work, a discussion of which goes beyond the purpose of this present volume, we believe that Miller is correct in his analysis: Baha'u'llah was not the next Manifestation. Significantly, not all of the Bab's followers accepted Baha'u'llah as the next true Prophet.[16]

It should also be pointed out the Martin analysis does not have all its facts straight. For example, another problem for Baha'is is their inaccurate translation of their own *Al-Kitab-Al-Aqdas*, or "Most Holy Book," written by Baha'-u'llah. Thus, Martin calls the Elder-Miller translation of *The Most Holy Book* (found in an Appendix to Miller's *The Baha'i Faith*) "often misleadingly inaccurate."[17] This is in spite of the fact that Elder is an Arabic scholar, and that the translation was checked by scholars familiar with both Arabic and Baha'ism. It was published by the eminent Royal Asiatic Society in London, hardly known to publish inaccurate translations. Thus, the accuracy of the Elder-Miller translation places Baha'i authorities in a dilemma. Why did they reject this translation and forbid their members to read it, unless they disapproved of its contents? But if it is translated accurately, how could its contents be rejected by them, since it is Baha'i's "Most Holy Book" and considered divine scripture?

Altering Their History

According to Miller, the Baha'is have had to alter their own history to escape embarrassment caused by their own scriptures and prophets. While this is not uncommon in the history of religion, to suppress and then seriously tamper with one's own "Most Holy Book" and the commands of one's own divine prophets is hypocrisy and, one would think, egregious folly. One may check these facts by reading Dr. Miller's text (the unabridged version) where he has documented the additions, deliberate changes and omissions in the official Baha'i translation.[18] In a brief personal letter to us, despite the recent death of his wife, he very graciously responded to Martin's charges: "I stand by what I wrote in *The Baha'i Faith*. . . . I believe my documentation is an adequate reply for anyone who is able and willing to read the references in the Arabic texts. It makes no matter who supplies the material; if it is true, one should accept it. . . ."[19] It seems that Baha'is, like Mormons, Jehovah's Witnesses, Christian Scientists and other sects with suppressed and altered histories, or biased translations of "divine" books, should exercise some "independent investigation" here. (See respective chapters for documentation.) Baha'is might do well to remember the statement of Baha'i writer Gloria Faizi, cited at the beginning of this chapter.

The value of Dr. Miller's text is that no well documented, extensive objective-critical history of the Baha'i movement had been available previously. Nearly all Baha'i histories were written

by Baha'is. Dr. Miller provided the impetus for examining Baha'ism in a different, if less favorable, light. Based on his research alone, Baha'i claims to the divine origin and guidance of the movement are dramatically called into question. Indeed, they no longer ought to be believed by those who pride themselves on rationality and impartial inquiry, as Baha'is do. Douglas Martin correctly noted, in a critical review of Miller's book, that the picture painted by Dr. Miller is that the Baha'i faith "is a product of a century-long conspiracy conceived by persons of the basest character and motive. Its present-day followers . . . are entirely deceived as to their Faith's real nature," although he admits Dr. Miller is much more gracious in tone than the above assessment.[20]

Nevertheless, since Dr. Miller's analysis is heavily documented (over 800 footnotes of largely primary sources), it is up to Baha'i historians to refute its arguments objectively and not merely present a self serving use of the facts to support *modern* Baha'i interpretations, beliefs and practices. If, as Dr. Miller claims, Baha'i leaders are guilty of altering or suppressing the commands of their own divine prophets, and of severely altering and pasteurizing their history, the Baha'i laity is in deep trouble if such prophets were indeed "Manifestations" of God. Baha'is at this point cannot appeal to the "infallible" pronouncements of their leaders because the Baha'i claim of an *infallible* leader or governing body (Shoghi Effendi, the House of Justice, etc.) has been disproven by false prophecies, changes in earlier divine pronouncements and simple errors.[20a] For example, Charles Mason Remey, once President of the International Baha'i Council and a committed seventy-year Baha'i, was expelled by the governing body (the Universal House of Justice or UHJ) after he charged them (correctly) with abandoning fidelity to the laws of God—to the earlier divine pronouncements of Shoghi Effendi and the then held doctrine of the perpetuity of the Guardian's role.

During Shoghi Effendi's lifetime, Baha'is agreed that there would always be "in perpetuity" a "Guardian of the Cause" (cf., *World Order*, April, 1937). However, when Shoghi Effendi died without appointing the new Guardian successor, a nine-member "House of Justice" was set up, supposedly having the infallibility that Baha'u'llah said belonged only to the Manifestations. Dr. Miller responds, "The indispensability of the Guardianship has been forgotten by most of the Baha'is, and their literature has been rewritten to suit the new situation. It is as though the Cardinals of the Roman Catholic Church should suddenly decide that the Church no longer needs a Pope, and all the Catholics should silently acquiesce."[21] In essence, the UHJ usurped the allegedly divinely instituted role of the Guardian and then covered their tracks by altering Baha'i history and scripture.

Remey himself wrote in 1968, "One of the greatest sins that a believer can commit is to change the Holy Baha'i Texts. I am now finding how confused [even] the most sincere believers are becoming by these alterations and changes and additions to the Holy Teachings."[22]

Altered histories, teachings and doctrinal confusion explain why there are several different Baha'i sects today. Thus, despite the Baha'i claim to be without schism, the "unorthodox" Baha'i sects include: "The Free Baha'is," who denounce Shoghi Effendi as the "orthodox" successor to 'Abdu'l-Baha and "The Orthodox Baha'i Faith," which also originated with disputes over leadership, in this case after Shoghi Effendi's death. Organized by excommunicated member Mason Remey, it denies that the UHJ was the true successor of Shoghi Effendi. Another of their sects is "Baha'is Under the Provision of the Covenant" (BUPC), headed by chiropractor Leland Jensen.

Apparently, once those in power discovered that the proclaimed infallible "Guardian" of the faith (Shoghi Effendi) was quite fallible and had made serious errors, there was little desire for a repeat performance; that is, that a future "infallible" Guardian would again prove embarrassing. Hence a supposedly more "democratic" form of government, The Universal House of Justice, was selected to be the governing body of the Baha'i faith.

Like most Mormons, most Baha'is have little or no idea of the serious distortions that have transpired in their history, because they uncritically accept the pronouncements of the governing body. But the UHJ was not breaking new Baha'i ground with its chicanery. Just as the nine historic Baha'i Manifestations have contradicted one another on basic points, even the four cornerstone Baha'i prophets have contradicted one another and altered one another's teachings through infallible (mis)interpretation or outright subversion. For example, Miller points out that Baha'u'llah's son, 'Abdu'l-Baha (who, incidentally, left little of the Bab's teachings intact) violated his father's legal will by appointing his grandson, Shoghi Effendi, as successor rather than Baha'u'llah's brother, who had been stipulated in Baha'u'llah's will. This leaves the Baha'is in the embarrassing position of accepting that a *non*-Manifestation of God can overrule the legally declared wishes of a Manifestation of God. The Baha'i website agrees that "'Abdu'l-Baha was *not* a Manifestation of God" and yet declares his decisions are considered binding. "Although He is not considered to be a Manifestation of God like the Bab and Baha'u'llah, Abdu'l-Baha's decisions are believed to have been divinely guided and His writings (along with the Bab's and Baha'u'llah's) are considered a part of the Baha'i sacred scripture."

If such extensive corruption of the Baha'i faith has occurred, it is at least consistent with their belief that *all* religions become corrupted in time. As 'Abdu'l-Baha argued, "In the passage of time religions become entirely changed and altered."[23] "The essential realities . . . have now well nigh vanished."[24] If so, one wonders how Baha'is can logically argue that all other religions need to have their "original truths" restored to pristine Baha'i purity when it is their own religion that remains so corrupted? How can Baha'is pride themselves on the uniqueness and incorruptibility of their religion?

Other questions can be raised here as well. Baha'u'llah himself said that the biblical and Koranic texts had *not* been corrupted textually but hermeneutically:

That the meaning of the Word of God hath been perverted, not that the actual words have been effaced. To the truth of this testify they that are sound of mind. . . . We have also heard a number of the foolish of the earth assert that the genuine text of the heavenly Gospel doth not exist amongst the Christians. . . . How grievously they have erred! . . . How could God . . . cause His holy Book, His most great testimony amongst His creatures, to disappear also? What would be left to that People? . . . What law could be their stay and guide?[25]

In light of this, the claim of some modern Baha'is, who appeal to a *textual* corruption of the Gospels in order to support their denials of biblical teaching, would seem to number them among "the foolish of the earth."

TEACHINGS AND PRACTICE

In this section we will discuss two principal tenets of Baha'i, "one worldism" and the Baha'i concept of the "Manifestation." Because of the nature of the Manifestation as disclosure of "God," some overlap will be found between this section and our discussion of the Baha'i concept of God that follows later.

One Worldism

The fundamental principles of Baha'i revolve around an emphasis on world unity. Thus Baha'is emphasize belief in the oneness of God, the oneness of religion (in a sense, a world religion evolving "into" oneness through progressive revelation) and the oneness of mankind. They also stress the harmony of science and religion and universal compulsory education—presumably this would incorporate Baha'i teachings. They advocate the equality of the sexes, a universal auxiliary language, religion as a source of unity, international peace maintained by a one-world government, "the elimination of all forms of prejudice," the abolition of extremes of wealth and poverty and so on.[26] In general, they advocate things that allegedly help to promote the growth of mankind into a united, peaceful and prosperous planetary body.

A key element for instituting this one-worldism is their syncretistic theology of accommodation, the idea of "religion as a source of unity." It is also their Achilles heel, which abandons them to an indefensible position.

As we have seen, Baha'is insist that they are a progressive, uniting factor among all religions, and that they are not a new religion. Nevertheless, their writings prove that the Baha'i faith is a new religion, one in active competition with all others and hence not a uniting factor. This rejection of other faiths is maintained even while Baha'i offers the other faiths the hand of unity and friendship. When this is seen for what it is, this spiritual pretense is distasteful to the neutral observer or committed member of another faith. Baha'is only tells a member of another religion exactly what he or she may wish to hear: "Baha'i does not deny your beliefs, it teaches that you can be a devout Christian and also a Baha'i." Thus new prospects are promised, "The Baha'i Faith invites us to broaden our religious horizons, not to become an apostate."[27]

Unfortunately, this is precisely what happens. After one commits oneself to the Baha'i faith, one learns that "true religion" is found only in the teachings of Baha'u'llah; it is one's own religion that has been seriously corrupted. Given the lofty ideals espoused by Baha'is (religious harmony, racial brotherhood, world peace), which naturally attract many people, usually one does not discover this religious "subversion" until it is too late. After all, if world religions do not teach "One Truth," the only way Baha'is can make it seem so is by deceptive methods, intentional or not. Not unexpectedly, as an article in *World Order* observes, "Baha'is have always evinced a profound reticence with regard to theology."[28]

"Properly" understood then, all religions teach the same truth, despite variation due to local customs, cultures and the depth of religious evolution of man at that point. The world's religions will eventually accept the truth and unite under Baha'i teachings into one grand ecumenical brotherhood. The Baha'i community itself is held to represents a miniature version of this coming, divinely-ordained utopia.

The Manifestations and the Nature of God

To understand the origin of the Baha'i concept of the Manifestation, we need to understand the Islamic and mystical origins of the Baha'i faith. Although Baha'is claim that they are not a

Muslim sect, their leader, the Bab (Syyid Ali Muhammad), was in fact a heretical Shi'ite Muslim and Iranian mystic who based his teachings on gnostic and neo-Platonic ideas, which had found their way into Islam (for example, through the mystical Sufis).[29] He was also the leader of the stronger section of a split in the spiritistic Shaykhis Shi'ite sect. This stronger group became known as the "Babis," after the name "Bab," which Syyid Ali Muhammad took for himself.

Because it is true in traditional Islam that Muhammad is the last and greatest prophet, the Bab's heralding of himself as a greater manifestation of truth classified him as a Shi'ite Muslim apostate. This explains why Baha'is have been persecuted and murdered by Muslims, especially Shi'ite Muslims, from the beginning. The Bab taught that he was a greater revealer of truth than Muhammad, and that an even greater prophet than him would some day appear. Orthodox Sunni or Shi'ite Muslims will not tolerate such teaching.

Reflecting Islamic influence, however, the Baha'i faith believes that God is fundamentally and eternally unknowable. He "reveals" himself in historic Manifestations, which are not incarnations since the Baha'i faith, again reflecting Islamic influence, rejects the possibility of an incarnation of God. These prophets, or Manifestations of God, have revealed truth to mankind in progressively larger and larger increments and taught that no Manifestation is a final revelation of God.

This revelation is accomplished either in harmony with the evolutionary level of mankind or as it becomes necessary. And because the Manifestations all represent revelation from the same God, allegedly they do not contradict one another. As their website declares, citing Baha'u'llah:

Every true Prophet hath regarded His message as fundamentally the same as the Revelation of every other prophet gone before him.

Baha'is view religion as a progressive, evolutionary process which needs to be updated as humanity evolves mentally, socially, and spiritually. Every so often a new Prophet is sent to humanity to update religion to the current needs of mankind. These Prophets bring essentially the same spiritual message to mankind; in a form that meets the need of the people of their time. Baha'is believe that Baha'u'llah has brought an updated message for mankind today.[30]

Even though the most recent Baha'i prophet in many ways replaces the previous one, one prophet is supposedly not superior to another. Thus Muhammad and Baha'u'llah are not superior to Jesus, even though their revelation of truth is allegedly much greater. Unfortunately, the Baha'is have differed historically as to the exact number of their prophets, apparently uncertain as to who the exact Manifestations of God are. The Bab and Baha'u'llah (having been influenced by Shi'ite teachings) spoke of six previous Manifestations of God: Adam, Noah, Abraham, Moses, Jesus and Muhammad. Because of their Koranic background, the Manifestations were entirely semitic. 'Abdu'l-Baha, however, was more ecumenical, adding Manifestations of a more oriental flavor: Zoroaster and the Buddha.[31] Modern Baha'is, deleting Adam and Noah, believe in nine to 12 Manifestations: an unknown Prophet, Krishna, Abraham, Hud (an ancient Arabian prophet; the eleventh surah of the Koran is named after him), Salih, Moses, Zoroaster, Buddha, Christ, Muhammad, the Bab and Baha'u'llah.[32]

The Baha'is have never declared the exact number of prophets (nine is often used), nor precisely how a Prophet is to be known.[33] The most recent prophet, Baha'u'llah, is the most complete Manifestation to date. But as we have seen, there is genuine reason to doubt his authenticity based on the teachings of the Bab. Nevertheless, even though Baha'u'llah is *not* the final prophet, his words are absolutely binding as the words of God, despite their replacement some day through the revelations of a prophet with more spiritually evolved teachings. In addition, the interpretation of Baha'u'llah's writings by 'Abdu'l-Baha and Shoghi Effendi are held to be infallible.

What is the nature of the Baha'i prophet or Manifestation? He is seen as divine in that he reflects the divine nature, but he is not God, only a revealer and servant of God. He reflects or even contains the divine attributes, but he is ultimately only a divinely enlightened human. In other words, the prophet is a combination of the human and in some sense the divine, but ultimately only a very special man.

Baha'u'llah's mysticism led to declarations about the prophet that did not always clarify matters. On the one hand, he asserted they are *not* incarnations of God: "Know thou of a certainty that the Unseen can in no wise incarnate His Essence and reveal it unto men."[34] But then he spoke more forcefully in terms of their divine nature. Apparently referring to himself: "Unto this subtle, this mysterious and ethereal Being [Baha'u'llah] He [God] hath assigned a twofold nature; the physical, pertaining to the world of matter, and the spiritual, *which is born of the substance of God Himself.* . . . 'Manifold and mysterious is My relationship with God. *I am He, Himself, and He is I, Myself,* except that I am that I am and He is that He is.'"[35]

Baha'u'llah alleges that the Bab declared of him, "There is none other God but Him."[36] Baha'u'llah also says unashamedly, "When I contemplate, O My God, the relationship that bindeth me to Thee . . . I am moved to proclaim to all created things, '*verily I am God!*'; and when I consider my own self, lo, I find it coarser than clay."[37] Nevertheless, the rationalistic influence in modern Baha'i theology, as well as its Islamic roots, dictate that the prophet cannot be deity, and this is the official teaching.

And there are other difficulties. Baha'u'llah attempted to distinguish between the prophets' *station* (rank) and *mission.* As to their station, the prophets are all equal in an absolute sense. "No distinction do We make between any of His Messengers"; they "are regarded as one soul and the same person."[38] They all have the same value, even though the most recent Manifestation supersedes the others in importance by means of progressive or superior revelation. As to the prophets' mission, however, "the words and utterances . . . appear to diverge and differ . . . [still] all their utterances are, in reality, but the expressions of one Truth."[39] Even though their teachings *appear* as contradictory, they really aren't because all the prophets "are re-garded as one soul and the same person" giving revelation from the one and same God. Supposedly then, in the end, Krishna, a polytheist, and Jesus, a monotheist, are One, despite their vast theological differences, not to mention natures. Buddha and Muhammad are One, despite Buddha's practical atheism and Muhammad's zealous theism.

The problem with a mystic is that one does not always know when to take him literally, but we assume literalness was not the intent when Baha'u'llah stated: "Were any of the all-embracing Manifestations of God to declare: 'I am God,' He, verily, speaketh the truth, and no doubt attacheth thereto."[40] Certainly the biblical Abraham or Moses (or Buddha or the Muslim Muhammad) would react with horror to such an expression literally meant. Regardless, this statement still cannot be reconciled with the teachings of Abraham, Muhammad, Buddha, Moses or Jesus, for it is also implying that all the Manifestations were God-sent and God-empowered to teach Baha'i truths, "truths" which these other religions deny. In effect, the Baha'i Achilles heel is that nothing they can ever do will justify their approach to comparative religion, at least not if we examine religious scriptures frankly and let words mean what they say. Unfortunately, verbal clarity of expression is not the goal of a mystic who wishes to unify all religions into his own personal truth.

Baha'is may respond to these problems by declaring that the prophets' progressive revelation is only relative and that therefore no prophet has ever denied an absolute truth of another prophet. But if all revelation is relative, no absolute truth exists and Baha'i claims to absolute truth are spurious:

> The problem with this concept of revelation is that it is self-defeating. The statement, 'revelation is relative,' which is allegedly a revelation spoken by Baha'u'llah, must be either relative or absolute. If the statement is relative, it is not absolutely binding, and it is possible that absolute revelation does exist. If the statement, 'revelation is relative,' is absolute, then the statement, 'revelation is relative,' cannot be true. Thus, the Baha'i doctrine of relative revelation is self-defeating and untrue.[41]

Further, we know with certainty what the basic doctrines of the major world religions are. The Baha'i faith is wrong to declare that the real differences among religions are in outer form and ritual and not in fundamental doctrine. In fact, almost all religions, more or less, are similar in outer form and ritual but distinct in doctrine. No orthodox Christian, Muslim or Jew, for example, would accept Krishna or Buddha as prophets of God. No orthodox Buddhist or Muslim could ever accept Jesus as the atoning Savior and Son of God. Only if Baha'i can presuppose religious unity by *discarding* the teachings of the prophets can it find a way to "harmonize" fundamentally contrary faiths. Unfortunately for Baha'i, the horse was dead at the gate. Prophets who collectively contradict one another on essential doctrinal teachings have nothing to say to anyone. And at that point it is then impossible to determine *any* religious truth from them. All that can remain from the Baha'i approach to religion is skepticism and agnosticism. As Francis Beckwith points out in his study *Baha'i:*

> Though Shoghi Effendi has said that the manifestations disagree on "non-essential aspects of their doctrine," it would stretch credibility to the limit to suppose that the nature of God is one of these non-essential aspects. God cannot be impersonal, personal, transcendent, polytheistic, pantheistic, monotheistic, able to beget, not able to beget, relevant, and irrelevant all at the same time. If it is true that God is all those things, then we are driven to agnosticism. Such an illogical God can never be known based on the contradictory information given to us by His alleged manifestations. Irreconcilable data gives us no knowledge of God whatsoever.[42]
>
> In order to be fair to any world religious leader, one should accept what the leader says at face value, instead of twisting it in order to fit a predetermined belief. In other words, if the leader says, "I am a sinner," or "I have failed God," this must be accepted. It should not be distorted in order to fit a particular prejudice of the reader (such in the case of "'Abdu'l-Baha"—"the manifestations never sin."). The burden of proof is on the Baha'i leaders to justify their interpretation. Since they have not done so, we must accept what has been written at face value. This

is the only honest and fair way to read any given text.

> It could be said, without fear of contradiction, that the religious leaders who the Baha'i faith believes to be manifestations, are "authorities" with wax noses—noses which can be twisted in any way the Baha'i apologist sees fit, in order to keep his religious beliefs "consistent."[43]

Thus, in the following quotation, note that the basic message that Baha'u'llah communicates is of *not* listening to the meaning of the prophet's words themselves. His teaching is that, regardless of how contradictory the prophets' words are, all of them must be seen as valid regardless! Baha'u'llah declares of the Manifestations what any first year comparative religion major would know is false: "If thou wilt observe with discriminating eyes, thou wilt behold them all abiding in the same tabernacle, soaring in the same heaven, seated upon the same throne, uttering the same speech, and proclaiming the same Faith. . . . Whoso maketh the slightest possible difference between their persons, their words, their messages, their acts and manners, hath indeed disbelieved in God, hath repudiated His signs, and betrayed the Cause of His Messengers."[44]

The truth is that the Baha'i prophets have not simply amended or expanded the *minor* teachings of the prophets before them; they have *rejected* the major teachings. For example, how could the Buddha "establish the Oneness of God" when he didn't even believe in God?[45] Buddhism actually nullified Hinduism (there is no absolute deity); Islam "nullified" Christianity ("God has no Son"); Baha'i nullified Islam (Muhammad is not the final prophet). How then can the prophets be prophets of the *same* God? Further, why do Baha'is maintain that *their* faith is the one being misrepresented? Where have Muslims, Christians, Buddhists and Jews misrepresented Baha'i? Is not the reverse true, and is it not their own personal religious biases and intolerance that cause them to claim misrepresentation?

Essentially, then, it is hardly unexpected to discover Baha'is stressing their basic ideals to potential converts, such as world peace and brotherhood, rather than an actual study of different religions to prove their alleged unity.

Yet in order to maintain their superior status, Baha'is emphasize that they are neither eclectic nor syncretistic. Incredibly, Sabet declares that such an idea is "historically incorrect and unfounded in substance. . . . Baha'u'llah's teaching is not syncretic."[46] But isn't the dictionary definition of syncretism, "the attempt or tendency to combine or reconcile differing beliefs, as in philosophy or religion"? Baha'is must adopt a circular argument, assuming the truth of what is argued. Supposedly, Baha'i is not syncretistic because it presupposes the truth that all religions are One. So how can it be syncretistic: Baha'i is only teaching the original truth of all religion. Unenlightened people and their false doctrines and interpretations of their scriptures have clouded the primordial unity.[47] Not surprisingly, in "Baha'i Houses of Worship the Holy Scriptures must not be interpreted by the word of man,"[48] and no sermons are ever given on the Holy Books. As a result, Baha'is remain safe in their world of religious "unity."

Undoubtedly, having an infallible interpreter or spokesman that proclaims "all religions are one" by fiat solves many difficulties, but it also denies the individual his fundamental right to examine "God's Word" to make up his or her own mind as to what it teaches. If we truly accept the idea of an independent investigation of the truth, then we may expect that, with reverent and objective study, we will not fall prey to *another's* false interpretation. As there can be no more vital a topic than the Word of God, no one should have the right to deny another person the opportunity of determining what God does or does not say. God places no premium on credulity (Proverbs 14:15) or ignorance (Hosea 4:1, 6; 2 Timothy 2:15). Giving infallible authority to one person or governing body may "solve" problems for those in power, but the problems it creates for the laity are far more serious.

Thus, if we take a critical look at the teachings of the Bab, Baha'u'llah, 'Abdu'l-Baha and modern Baha'i writers, we find not only antiChristian, anti-Islamic, anti-Buddhist and anti-Hindu teachings but also serious internal problems for the Baha'i member. There are numerous false biblical interpretations, and many denials of earlier proclaimed infallible truths. Such basic errors are inconsistent with the divine nature. For God to be unknowable is one thing; for Him to change His mind every time He manifests, for Him to pronounce error and misinterpret His own Scripture, is another thing entirely. What kind of God is this?

Just as many people would rather be in the company of an honest sinner than a hypocritical saint, so they would rather have an honest disunity in religion that is respectful of other people's religious beliefs than a contrived unity that is disrespectful to other people's religious beliefs and undermines them by stealth, all the while claiming friendship. The Baha'i approach to Christianity illustrates this problem clearly.

THEOLOGY

Christianity

While Baha'is tell potential converts that they are not antiChristian, their prophets and modern writers are denouncing Christianity in four major areas:

1. the authority of the Bible

2. the Trinity

3. Christology (from the Virgin Birth to Christ's unique Deity and mediatorial atonement)

4. salvation by grace through faith alone

Certainly, Baha'is may *sound* Christian. Consider the following Baha'i statement: "Baha'is believe in Jesus Christ. Baha'is believe that Christ was the son of God, born of the Virgin Mary. Christ came to bring salvation to mankind. . . . A person cannot be a Baha'i unless he believes in Christ."[49] But do Baha'is really believe this?

The Baha'i message for Christians is that *Baha'u'llah* is the promised Messiah of the Bible and other holy scriptures, and that Baha'u'llah's teachings supersede all others. Baha'u'llah was none other than Jesus Christ returned, and it is to him, not Jesus, that Christians and others must look. Why then are orthodox Christians still looking for Jesus' return? Because Christ's erring disciples falsely interpreted Jesus' teachings. This explains why such teachings do not seem to conform to Baha'u'llah's revelations.

Consider several examples. William Sears declares that because he *was* a Christian (but one who did not know Christ was the Messiah![50]), he was compelled to accept Baha'u'llah as Christ returned. For this, he was told, was the true teaching of Christ that the disciples had distorted. "I had to accept Baha'u'llah or deny Christ. . . . To deny Moses and Christ would be to deny Baha'u'llah. . . . I could not refuse to accept Baha'u'llah or I would be denying Christ Himself. . . ."[51] Although his book *Thief in the Night* is allegedly a reputable Baha'i apologetic for their view that Baha'u'llah is Christ returned, anyone with a modicum of doctrinal and biblical knowledge may easily uncover the historical, biblical and religious errors that run throughout his book.[52]

A related effort is by George Townshend. His book *The Heart of the Gospel* tells us, "Within the Baha'i Faith the spirit of the early Christian Church has risen again. . . . Christ is adored as the very Word of God sharing God's glory from all eternity. . . . Christ's message is renewed, elucidated, expanded, carried forward."[53]

In his book *Baha'u'llah and the New Era,* J. E. Esslemont states that Baha'u'llah "comes to make Christians better Christians."[54] He quotes 'Abdu'l-Baha: "The principles of Christianity and the commandments of Baha'u'llah are identical and their paths are the same."[55] Horace Holley avers, "Baha'u'llah's message does not *repeat* the message of Christ—it *completes* that message."[56]

Baha'is, then, are uncompromising in asserting that they are genuine Christians. Naturally, it is the "true Christians [who] will accept Jesus in his returned form [as] Baha'u'llah. The Baha'i Faith thus becomes . . . a truer form . . . of Christianity"; "The Baha'i Faith is Christianity today; the Baha'i Faith is Islam today."[57] Richardson even claims that "Christians by the thousands have deserted the banner of Jesus for that of Baha'u'llah."[58] Unfortunately, because of Baha'i distortions about Jesus, many people from mainline Christian churches have become Baha'is.

To win over Christians, the Baha'i faith destroys Christian faith and replaces it with Baha'i doctrines. Nominal Christians who are now Baha'is and Baha'is themselves need to ask some serious questions concerning this approach. How can Baha'is be Christian and followers of Jesus Christ when their teachings are anti-Christian and opposed to Christ? How do they objectively know that the Jesus they believe in is the real Jesus? What if historical proof exists that their Jesus is the corrupted Jesus? (See our book *Ready with an Answer,* chapters 4–6, 8, 14–16 and Unitarian Universalism, appendix.) If the path of Baha'i and Christianity is the same, why did orthodox Christians reject the subsequent Baha'i Manifestation of God after Jesus, Muhammad? Why did they reject the Bab? And why did they reject the most complete Manifestation of God to date, Baha'u'llah?

Also, how can Baha'is logically claim to honor Christianity when their own teachings demand that they reject it as an evil religion? All true Christians worship Jesus as God, but this is something that Baha'is declare is an idolatrous blasphemy. What about the "ancient dogma" and "error of exclusivism" in Christianity that hinders the Baha'i march toward world unity? Is not the Christian belief in miracles a "primitive rejection" of the "victory of science" proclaimed by Baha'is?[59] And do Baha'is not believe that the apostle Paul, whom Christians accept as divinely inspired, is a perverter and destroyer of Jesus' teachings? (For a disproof of this claim, see additional Baha'i errors below.) One could go on and on, but knowledgeable Baha'is know their adversary. Christians do not persecute Baha'is as Muslims do, but to the Baha'i cause, Christian doctrine is almost as dangerous.

Despite the claim to accept the Christian faith, the following sentiments represent a more accurate portrayal of the Baha'i view of Christianity. First, according to Baha'ism Christians have an antiquated religion, deformed teachings, do not understand the words of Jesus and are spiritually destitute:

Mason Remey: The Baha'i Faith is not a renewal of Christianity. It is an entirely New Religion that is going to supersede Christianity.[60]

Udo Schaefer (Chairman National Spiritual Assembly of Baha'is of Germany): Measured by the standard of Baha'u'llah's revelation, the Pauline doctrine of Justification, the doctrine of Original Sin, the doctrine of the Holy Trinity . . . the whole Church plan of salvation . . . these are a deformation of Jesus's teaching.[61]

Baha'u'llah: As the adherents of Jesus have never understood the hidden meaning of these words . . . they therefore refused to acknowledge, even until now, the truth of those Manifestations of Holiness that have since the days of Jesus been made manifest. They have thus deprived themselves of the outpourings of God's holy grace, and of the wonders of His divine utterance. Such is their low estate in this, the Day of Resurrection![62]

'Abdu'l-Baha: The clergy have neither understood the meaning of the Gospels nor comprehended the symbols.[63]

Baha'is tell Christian clergy that they do not understand their own Scriptures. Baha'is believe Christians are false prophets and apostates. George Townshend tells us that "unenlightened" Christians have actually committed the crime of *rejecting* Christ (Baha'u'llah), who brought "a new, different, and more advanced Revelation."[64]

Second, Sabet, in another effervescent display of Baha'i religious tolerance, describes those who believe Baha'u'llah to be a false prophet as:

The real false prophets—narrow-minded and intolerant clergy and theologians who have perverted Christ's real teachings.[65]

Today, Christians make the same mistake the Jews made 2,000 years ago. They are so concerned with their own ideas of what Christ is that they cannot see the spirit of Christ in Baha'u'llah.[66]

Christ was a perfect Man. . . . Baha'u'llah . . . is the Christ for this day. . . . If you turn away from Baha'u'llah, you turn away from Christ.[67]

But Jesus Himself warned us about "false Christs" and He gave very specific signs of his personal return (Matthew 24); none, repeat none, of which were fulfilled by Baha'u'llah. The only "ideas" Christians have about Jesus Christ are those He spoke Himself, which were accurately recorded by His disciples. Those disciples have never been shown to have been untrustworthy or dishonest. So, is it true that the "spirit of Christ" is also in Baha'u'llah? (See chart below.)

Third, Baha'i claims to being Christian and religiously tolerant tend to suffer even more when one views their overall attitude towards Christianity seen throughout their literature. By implication or statement Christian leaders "verily, are of the fallen," and "by one stroke of His exalted Pen" Baha'u'llah stripped them of their power and abolished their church.[68] They have rejected Christ and God and failed. "Ye, and all ye possess, shall pass away," including Christians' "corrupt desires," which they love to rove in [69] They are "inwardly wolves" and "inwardly foul."[70] Christians have blurred vision causing ignorance of the facts.[71] Christian leaders writing against Baha'is are considered "foolish divines."[72] Orthodox Christians engage in "folly" and "are seized by the frenzy of their vain fancies."[73] Those who believe Christ was the final revelation utter "vain and absurd sayings" and are said to be afflicted with a "spiritual disease."[74] Christians are likened to blasphemers who have made an idol out of Jesus.[75]

Christianity "is now obsolete. It was valid only for a particular tribe, a particular period in history."[76] Biblical miracles are "mythology,"

CHRIST	BAHA'U'LLAH
Orthodox Jew	Muslim mystic
Trusted in a holy, knowable personal Father	Praised an unknowable, unreachable Deity
Exclusivist	Syncretist
Atoning Savior	Allegedly exemplary way shower

and "superstitions." Baha'is have no attraction to these, nor to a "morbid devotion to the letter of the Scriptures."[77] Christians who refuse to repent of their spiritual errors, according to Baha'is, have been warned. As Townshend asserts, Baha'u'llah "directed numerous and repeated exhortations and warnings to the entire Christian world. These without exception were ignored by Christendom when they were made, and they have now been set aside and disregarded for some eighty years."[78] For example, Baha'u'llah spoke of his God, who "hath solemnly warned them that have repudiated the verses of God, and hath disowned them that have denied His holy words. Consider how far the people have strayed . . . and how grievous hath been the faithlessness and arrogance of the spiritually destitute."[79]

Here is how the *Macmillian Dictionary for Students* defines "tolerance": "ability or willingness to accept or respect the behavior, customs, opinions or beliefs of others." Baha'is may claim tolerance for other religions, but the truth lies elsewhere. What they do for Christianity they do for all faiths. The chart below summarizes just a few of the contrasts between Baha'i doctrine and Christianity.

God

The Baha'i faith teaches an absolute monotheism, stressing the unity of God. In particular ways, however, God's nature is unspecified and, as a result, described in very general terms and is an unknowable essence. For the Baha'i, "God is greater than all words," and, conveniently, doctrinal approaches to God are sternly rejected.[80] This is one reason Baha'is disdain systematic theology.

There are, of course, "benefits" to a hidden deity. If the one true God is unknowable and

BAHA'I VS. CHRISTIANITY	
BAHA'I	CHRISTIANITY
GOD	GOD
God is unknowable except through conflicting manifestations. God cannot incarnate Himself.	God is knowable personally through Jesus Christ (John 17:3), and through a self-revelation which is not contradictory (the Bible). God did incarnate Himself in the person of Jesus (Philippians 2).
JESUS CHRIST	JESUS CHRIST
One of many manifestations of the divine; Jesus Christ returned as Baha'u'llah.	The unique incarnation of God (Philippians 2:1-9; John 1:1, 14, 6:46); the Second Person of the Holy Trinity; Jesus Christ will return as Himself in the glorified Person of Jesus of Nazareth (Matthew 24).
NATURE OF REVELATION	NATURE OF REVELATION
Written revelation is incomplete and continuing; religious truth is ultimately relative.	Written revelation is complete and has ended; religious truth is absolute.
In their true essence and teaching all religions are true or reflect facets of the truth.	The revelation of the one true God alone is true; what conflicts with truth is error (John 17:17; 1 John 2:21).
METHOD OF BIBLICAL INTERPRETATION	METHOD OF BIBLICAL INTERPRETATION
Biased: employs Baha'i assumptions; non-literal (for example, cf. Beckwith *Baha'i* 1985, pp. 23–25 and chapter 4).	Objective: employs universally accepted principles; literal.

undefined (except in general terms necessary to any rational concept of Deity—eternal, infinite, righteous, omnipotent and so on), then other religions' concepts of the Deity have little to contrast it with. While other religions may know their God as "B," they cannot immediately deny the Baha'i God as "non-B" if the Baha'i God is spoken of only in general terms acceptable to most faiths.

Baha'u'llah describes God as "the innermost Spirit of Spirits and eternal Essence of Essences"; "the Most Exalted, the Inaccessible"; "the invisible and unknowable Essence"; "the All-Pervading, the Incorruptible" and a plethora of other descriptive terms that still leave one wondering what God is really like.[81] However, reflecting Islam, Baha'u'llah did describe God as "Supreme Singleness," an apparent reference denying the Christian doctrine of the Trinity.[82]

In Baha'i, God does not incarnate Himself. Also, God is incapable of being known personally; at best, only the Manifestations reveal something of God's nature. God then, is an unknowable essence who is believed to manifest (to a degree) through the prophets. Even the Manifestations, of course, can be "known" only through historical records (not personally).

As we consider the Baha'i theology we discover the Baha'i relationship to God is quite unlike the kind of relationship the Christian has with God and Christ, where there is on-going direct personal knowledge and intimacy (John 17:3). Christians talk to God through Christ daily in the manner of normal conversation, and through the presence of His Holy Spirit and by His Word, He replies. Christians do not talk to the prophets—for example, Moses and Abraham. Thus, without such personal communication, it seems doubtful that the Baha'i would talk to or pray to their God (or His prophets) in the same way (if at all) that a Christian would to Jesus. They could praise their God, as Baha'u'llah did, and seem to talk to him, but the conversation would be one-sided, apart from mystical experiences that might be interpreted as a "reply." Communication with or response from an impersonal and unknowable Deity would, it seems, be rather like interaction with a new type of unknown energy, such as some mag-

netic force. How would one evaluate a response or even know it was one? "Personality is in the Manifestation of the Divinity, not in the essence of the Divinity."[83]

Thus, if God cannot be known personally in the Christian sense, it is hard to conceive of having a personal relationship to Him, or even with the Manifestations, which allegedly reveal Him, for they are, after all, dead and gone. All that is left are historical records, a "relationship" with the God described therein (the difference between, say, reading about Jesus and knowing Him), and perhaps, again, mystical experiences.

Clearly, historic knowledge of the Baha'i prophets is not the same as being known by God (Galatians 4:9); as being loved by him (John 14:21, 23; 16:27); as being adopted into his family (Galatians 4:5–9; Ephesians 1:5); and as being united to Him intimately (1 Corinthians 12:27). After all, does the Baha'i God work within the Baha'i convert personally and come to dwell within him and sanctify him in the way the triune God of the Scriptures does (1 Corinthians 6:19; Philippians 2:13)?

Thus, an immense gulf exists between the relationship of the believer to his God in Baha'i and to that relationship found in Christianity. The Christian God is vastly more related to His people than the Baha'i God is: the image of God in man, the incarnation, the atonement and all aspects of Christian salvation (such as union with Christ) are intensely personal and underlie the deep bond that exists between the Christian God and the redeemed believer.

This human need for personal relationship and divine communion was one reason why the "far-off" God of Islam gave birth to the mystical Sufi movement. The wholly transcendent Allah could not provide the immanence of truly personal interaction, whereas mystical experience could. No doubt it explains Baha'i mysticism as well. Thus, this is the manner in which a Baha'i could have a "personal" relationship to God—through mystical experience. But isn't it true that such experience can give only the illusion of that relationship, since it is one which is primarily psychological or occult? Further, from the Christian perspective no God ever responds because no such God exists to respond.

Nevertheless, mysticism is not the manner in which Jesus Christ bridges the gap between people and God. In His person at the Cross, Jesus paid the penalty of divine justice against sin (Romans 3:23–26; 2 Corinthians 5:17–21). He reconciled people to Himself so that through faith people can be on intimate terms with God. Then, through the indwelling of the Holy Spirit and through the Bible, the Word of God, people can study and learn of God and His will and grow in personal relationship to Him (2 Peter 3:18). Regardless of what one thinks about mysticism, a personal relationship with God through Jesus Christ would seem far preferable to faith in an unknowable, hidden deity.

Not surprisingly, the Baha'i God is, in many respects, similar to the Allah of the Koran—majestic, utterly separate from people, unreachable, "the Compassionate, the All Merciful" and so on. (In his *The Kitab-I-Iqan*, Baha'u'llah quotes the Koran about 145 times, the Bible only ten.) Baha'u'llah described God as follows:

> God, the unknowable Essence, the divine Being, is immensely exalted beyond every human attribute, such as corporeal existence, ascent and descent, egress and regress. . . . He is and hath ever been veiled in ancient eternity of His Essence, and will remain in His Reality everlastingly hidden from the sight of men. . . . No tie of direct intercourse can possibly bind Him to His creatures. He standeth exalted beyond and above all separation and union, all proximity and remoteness.[84]

Such a statement, for one, reveals the Baha'i (and Islamic) antipathy towards the Christian concept of the incarnation (Philippians 2:1–10). In such theology, the very idea that God would "degrade" Himself so as to become one of His creatures (let alone die in their stead) is unthinkable; indeed it is demeaning and blasphemous to the grandeur and transcendent majesty of God.

Again, as one reads Baha'i descriptions, it becomes clear that people can never really know this God personally. So one wonders how one really trusts a God one does not know, and never can know? References to His "closeness" are rare and, although present,[85] seem to be ir-

relevant in a personal sense. The "attaining unto the Presence" of God is only possible in "the Day of Resurrection" and refers to attaining God's "Beauty" through the prophet.[86] God Himself is still not known directly or personally: "From time immemorial He hath been veiled in the ineffable sanctity of His exalted Self, and will everlastingly continue to be wrapt in the impenetrable mystery of His Unknowable Essence."[87] "No one hath any access to the Invisible Essence. The way is barred and the road impassable."[88] The contrast to Christianity is marked. Jesus taught, "Now this is eternal life: that they may know you, the only true God, and Jesus Christ, whom you have sent" (John 17:3).

An article in *World Order*, "The God of Baha'u'llah," also discusses the unknowableness of God. The author discusses with accuracy and some satisfaction the contrast between the Christian and Baha'i viewpoints: "The God of the Baha'is seems more distant, more unapproachable than the Father evoked in the Gospels. It is no longer a question of man 'made in the image of God.' The Godhead is an alien and inconceivable Being nearer to the God of Spinoza than to the God of Genesis."[89] The Baha'i author goes on to point out that in spite of our inability to know this alien God, we can nevertheless, "open ourselves" to Him. Thus, "God remains in His heights, but His Spirit, the Holy Spirit (which is in no way here the "third person" of an impossible "trinity" but, more logically, the spirit of God and of the love given by God), throws a bridge across the chasm and annuls the separation."[90]

Presumably God is able to remain alien while we simultaneously come to experience Him in some sense through the prophets or "the Holy Spirit." This may be accomplished "mystically." But this is not an intimate knowledge involving personal fellowship, communion and union with God as in Christianity. In essence, the divine love of the Baha'i God is one of limited self-disclosure and perhaps of mystical experience but worlds apart from the love of God seen at the Cross (John 3:16), which is personal redemption.

At best Baha'i knowledge of God is intellectual at one level and mystical at another. Thus, as 'Abdu'l-Baha stated, knowing about the Manifestations is knowing about God. "If man attains to the knowledge of the Manifestations of God, he will attain to the knowledge of God."[91] Baha'is also stress the importance of mystical knowledge of God. In his essay "The Knowledge of God: An Essay on Baha'i Epistemology," Jack McLean refers to the mystical approach to "knowing" (cf. section on "Occult"). He refers to "Baha'u'llah's notion of purifying the consciousness from all previous presuppositions of knowledge in order to gain true knowledge," and he states that "Baha'u'llah is clearly saying that one must empty himself of worldly knowledge in order to discover the knowledge of God"[92] (cf. Romans 1:18–21). Baha'u'llah declared that the seeker after knowledge of God, "Must before all else, cleanse and purify his heart, which is the seat of the revelation of the inner mysteries of God, from the obscuring dust of all acquired knowledge, and the allusions of the embodiments of satanic fancy. He must purge his breast . . . from all shadowy and ephemeral attachments."[93]

Divine mystical knowledge of God is to be sought in place of worldly, normal knowledge: "The most grievous of all veils is the veil of knowledge. Upon its ashes, we have reared the tabernacle of divine knowledge."[94] Hence it is not surprising that "the Bab, therefore, forbade the reading of all non-Babi books, and commanded that they be burned. . . . Believers must read only the *Bayan*, and books written by eminent Babi scholars under the shadow of the *Bayan*. No one is permitted to own more than nineteen books, the first of which is to be the *Bayan*."*[95] This sentiment, obviously, was quite contrary to the "free inquiry" and "scientific approach" of modern Baha'i leaders.

The Trinity

The Baha'i religion declares that the Trinity is an irrational concept. Given his presuppositions, Baha'u'llah could hardly compromise here. There could be no Incarnation, in spite of Jesus' claims (six times in John 6:33–58 alone) and

other biblical declarations (Philippians 2:1–9). God could never "descend" into the world; at best his "Manifestations" could only dimly reveal Him. The following statement by 'Abdu'l-Baha rejects both the Trinity and the Incarnation: "The Divine Reality . . . admits of no division; for division and multiplicity are properties of creatures. . . . The Divine Reality is sanctified from singleness,[*] then how much more from plurality. The descent [of God] into conditions and degrees [the material world] would be equivalent to imperfection and contrary to perfection, and is, therefore, absolutely impossible. . . . For God to descend into the conditions of existence would be the greatest of imperfections."[95a]

Jesus Christ

"The Christology of the Church and the teachings of Baha'u'llah about Christ's mission are on essential questions irreconcilable."[96]

—Sabet, *The Heavens Are Cleft Asunder*

In our study of some 40 Baha'i books and periodicals, we discovered enough denials of the Gospel teachings and the person and work of Jesus Christ to fill what remains of this chapter. Yet Udo Schaefer claims, "One thing, however, must be stressed. The attitude of the Baha'i towards Christianity is clear: he acknowledges its divine origin and believes in the Word of God as testified by the Gospels."[97] It is odd, then, that the Baha'i believer entirely leaves out the Gospels in his "independent investigation of truth." For if the Gospels are uncorrupted, and this is historic fact, then Jesus taught that He and His words were *eternally* authoritative and that He alone, the Person of Jesus, was the only way to God (Matthew 24:35; John 14:6). "If anyone is ashamed of me and my words, the Son of Man will be ashamed of him when he comes in his glory and in the glory of the Father and of the holy angels" (Luke 9:26).

It is a sign of the times—and quite disquieting, if not surprising—to see how people can sincerely claim to be true followers of Christ and yet accept such comprehensive denials of the

---

*Followers of Bab were Babis. Baha'u'llah rescinded this command.

*Apparently due to God's ineffable nature, though they speak of "God" in such terminology.

person and work of Christ as found in Baha'i. Baha'i theology denies the Incarnation, the virgin birth, the unique deity, the saving death, the miracles, the resurrection and the ascension of Jesus Christ. The chart below provides several examples.

Despite this comprehensive denial of Jesus Christ, we are told that "a person cannot be a Baha'i unless he believes in Jesus Christ"! Obviously, then, Baha'is believe in "another Jesus" (2 Corinthians 11:4 NAS), and not the biblical Jesus.

The Baha'i view of Christ is radically different from the biblical view. Jesus is called "the Spirit of God" and is equated with the Holy Spirit; that is, the Spirit of the Baha'i God, who allegedly inspired the biblical prophets.[104] Baha'u'llah is a far superior revelation of God than that found in Jesus. Baha'u'llah declared: "O Jews! If ye be intent on crucifying once again Jesus, the Spirit of God, put Me to death, for He hath once more, in My person, been made manifest unto you. . . . Followers of the Gospel! If ye cherish the desire to slay Muhammad, the Apostle of God, seize Me and put an end to My life, for I am He, and My Self is His Self."[105]

Baha'u'llah was "a fuller and more glorious Revelation" of God than Jesus Christ despite Scripture telling us that Jesus Christ is the radiance of His [God's] glory [cf. Colossians 1:15, 2:2–3] and the exact representation [Gk. *charakter*] of His nature, and upholds all things by the word of His power (Hebrews 1:3). Anyone who reads the Gospels will see at once that a fuller revelation of God than in Jesus is not possible.

In keeping with their exalted view of Baha'u'llah, 'Abdu'l-Baha, Baha'u'llah himself, and modern Baha'is apply biblical texts that refer to the second coming of Christ to the coming of Baha'u'llah (for example, Isaiah. 9:2–7; 11:1–2; 40:1–5). In *Thief in the Night*, William Sears spends almost 300 pages attempting to prove that Old Testament prophecies refer to Baha'u'llah and not to Christ. Sears attempts to make Baha'u'llah more or less *literally* fulfill biblical prophecy, but then he declares in midstream

BAHA'I VS. THE GOSPELS	
BAHA'I TEACHES	THE GOSPELS TEACH
"True Christians worship God in Jesus,* not [God in] the person of Jesus."[98]	"Thomas said to him [Jesus], 'My Lord and my God!'" (John 20:28).
"To worship Baha'u'llah . . . is as vain, as idolatrous as to worship Jesus."[99]	Jesus accepted worship of His *person* throughout the Gospels, e.g., "Then those who were in the boat worshiped him, saying, 'Truly you are the Son of God'" (Matthew 14:33).
Jesus does not once say, "I am God's only Son."[100]	"[Jesus is speaking of Himself] For God so loved the world that he gave his one and only Son. . . . whoever does not believe stands condemned already because he has not believed in the name of God's one and only Son" (John 3:16,18).
"God could not be a man."[101]	"He who has seen me has seen the Father" (John 14:9; cf., Philippians 2:6-8).
"Not that . . . Jesus was God the Creator."[102]	"Through him all things were made; without him nothing was made that has been made" (John 1:3; cf., Isaiah 44:24; Colossians 1:16; Hebrews 1:1-3,10).
"Jesus was not the only-begotten Son of God come down from Heaven, crucified and resurrected, nor the unique Saviour."[103]	See John 6:38-40; Acts 4:12; 1 Corinthians 3:11; 15:3-4.

*As they should worship God in Buddha, Krishna, Baha'u'llah, etc.

that Christians misunderstand the Bible today because they take it literally and not symbolically![106]

For example, Isaiah 53 is applied to the Persian Baha'u'llah[107] despite the fact that the prophecy refers to the Hebrew Messiah (and also to the Jewish nation's rejection of the Messiah). How can Isaiah 40–55 possibly predict Baha'u'llah when so much of it (for example, chapter 53) was already fulfilled at the time of Christ, 1900 years before Baha'u'llah even existed? And why does Sears leave out Isaiah 53:6 and 12, which refer to the Messiah dying for our sins? Did Baha'u'llah claim to do this, or are those verses omitted because Jesus did?*

Because Baha'is seek to deal with biblical data concerning the Messiah, they should abide by the biblical data in its entirety. What does the Bible say about the Messiah? The Messiah was Jewish, and of course will be Jewish when He returns in His second Advent (see Isaiah 11:1–2 NAS, out of "the stem of Jesse," King David's father). Baha'u'llah was not Jewish, a descendent of King David, but Iranian. Very specific and dramatic signs are to accompany the Messiah's return (see, for example, Matthew 24), *none* of which were present for Baha'u'llah's arrival. The Messiah would not have human birth at His return (2 Thessalonians 1:7–10), but Baha'u'llah did. The Messiah would return directly from heaven to Jerusalem (Acts 1; Zechariah 14), but Baha'u'llah did not. The Messiah would set up an *immediate* worldwide Kingdom (Zechariah 14), which Baha'u'llah apparently forgot.

It may not be appreciated by Christians enamored with Baha'i just how thoroughly Baha'u'llah erases Jesus Christ. The Jesus Christ of the Gospels is simply no longer relevant. Thus "when Baha'u'llah instituted the great Feast of Ridvan" on April 21, 1863, as a declaration of his own "power and sovereignty," he called it "the Day of God." Townshend comments, "Now it was that Jesus Christ [Baha'u'llah] ascended His throne in the power of God the Father. Now it

was that He took upon Himself the scepter of the fullness of God's might and thus set Himself as Supreme Overlord of all that is in heaven and on earth."[108]

Baha'u'llah had no misgivings at all with usurping Christ's glory for himself. He tells us, "I am the One Whom the tongue of Isaiah hath extolled.... Jesus, the spirit of God ... hath once more, in My person, been made manifest unto you."[109] According to Dr. William Miller's research, even 'Abdu'l-Baha (at least for a time) claimed to be Christ, in spite of the fact that he was "a successor to Baha'u'llah only as head of the community of believers, not as a Manifestation of God."[110] However, he eventually repudiated the claims, as they apparently caused him some embarrassment: "I am Abdu'l Baha and no more"; "I am not Christ, I am not Eternal God."[111]

Other Baha'is deny that Jesus is the Christ. Referring to John 8:58, where Jesus declares His eternalness, Townshend states, "Believers know that He [Jesus] spoke not of the individual Jesus but of the Eternal Christ. The Christ ... which spoke through Jesus ... had not confined its energies, its appearances, its utterances to the Hebrews alone."[112] In other words, "the Christ" is kind of a universal divine Spirit that speaks through all religions. But the Bible clearly states, "Who is the liar? It is the man who denies that Jesus is the Christ" (1 John 2:22).

Baha'is also deny Christ's physical resurrection and ascension. 'Abdu'l-Baha argued that, "The resurrections of the Divine Manifestations are not of the body ... likewise, His [Jesus'] ascension to heaven is a spiritual and not material ascension."[113] In essence, despite claims to the contrary, Baha'is believe Baha'u'llah was better than Jesus—much better.[114]

But a Baha'i view of Christ is not what we get from reading the Bible. The importance of Jesus and His words cannot be underestimated. Those who claim to believe in Him should listen carefully to what he says:

Heaven and earth will pass away, but my words will never pass away. (Matthew 24:35)

God is spirit, and his worshipers must worship in spirit and truth. (John 4:24)

---

*Sears also confuses the Holy Spirit with Christ (p. 172), and Christ with Satan (p. 174). He engages in selective use of data (pp. 150, 118), and he denies clear biblical teachings (on p. 122 he claims the Messiah would come from Assyria). The book has many such errors.

For not even the Father judges any one, but He has given all judgment to the Son, in order that all may honor the Son, even as they honor the Father. He who does not honor the Son does not honor the Father who sent Him. (John 5:22–23 NAS)

Whoever denies the Son does not have the Father; the one who confesses the Son has the Father also. (1 John 2:23 NAS)

Jesus answered and said to him, "If anyone loves Me, he will keep My word; and My Father will love him, and We will come to him, and make Our abode with him. He who does not love Me does not keep My words; and the word which you hear is not Mine, but the Father's who sent Me." (John 14:23–24 NAS)

Perhaps Baha'is should also listen carefully to Baha'u'llah when he speaks of Jesus that "whatsoever hath proceeded after his blameless, his truth-speaking, trustworthy mouth, can never be altered. . . ."[115]

Nevertheless, Jesus had absolute faith in a literal reading of the Old Testament (Matthew 19:4–5; John 5:47; 17:17), which Baha'i denies, and He emphatically denied people's ability to self-perfect or save themselves, (John 6:29, 47, 63), which Baha'i affirms.

According to the Bible, Jesus Christ is not some special creature whom God chose to dimly manifest His unknown being. He is God Himself: "for in Christ all the fullness of Deity dwells in bodily form" (Colossians 2:9). He is above all rule and authority:

Which He brought about in Christ, when He raised Him from the dead, and seated Him at His right hand in the heavenly places, far above all rule and authority and power and dominion, and every name that is named, not only in this age, but also in the one to come. (Ephesians 1:20–21 NAS)

"THOU HAST PUT ALL THINGS IN SUBJECTION UNDER HIS FEET." For in subjecting all things to him, He left nothing that is not subject to him. (Hebrews 2:8 NAS)

One day every person will bow and worship Him:

Therefore also God highly exalted Him, and bestowed on Him the name which is above every name, that at the name of Jesus every knee should bow, of those who are in heaven, and on earth, and under the earth, and that every tongue should confess that Jesus Christ is Lord, to the glory of God the Father. (Philippians 2:9–11 NAS)

Indeed, no greater wisdom can be found anywhere than in Jesus, "in whom are hidden all the treasures of wisdom and knowledge" (Colossians 2:3). His relevance and reign was not for a temporal age, but forever:

to be put into effect when the times will have reached their fulfillment—to bring all things in heaven and on earth together under one head, even Christ. (Ephesians 1:10)

according to his eternal purpose which he accomplished in Christ Jesus our Lord. (Ephesians 3:11)

because Jesus lives forever, he has a permanent priesthood. Therefore he is able to save completely those who come to God through him, because he always lives to intercede for them. (Hebrews 7:24–25)

The seventh angel sounded his trumpet, and there were loud voices in heaven, which said, "The kingdom of the world has become the kingdom of our Lord and of His Christ, and he will reign forever and ever." (Revelation 11:15)

For conservative, staunchly monotheistic Jews to say such things of a mere "man" is either utter blasphemy or absolute truth. Jesus' Jewish disciples conceded the latter for the following reasons:

1. Christ claimed to be God and performed attesting miracles, the quantity and quality of which have never been duplicated throughout history (John 5:18; 10:30–33; 19:7).

2. He resurrected Himself from the dead to prove His claims (John 2:19; cf. Matthew 27–28; Mark 16; Luke 24; Acts 2:24; Romans 4:24).

3. The Jews could turn to their divinely inspired Old Testament and see that the Messiah *was* to be God (Isaiah 9:6; Micah 5:2; cf. Matthew 22:43–46) not a Baha'i-type manifestation, and that Jesus had fulfilled Old Testament messianic prophecy in detail (as

we documented in *The Case for Jesus the Messiah*).

This is why the Jewish authors of the New Testament told the world that Jesus Christ is the radiance of His [God's] glory [cf. Colossians 1:15,24] and the exact representation [Gk. *charakter*] of His nature and that He upholds all things by the word of His power (Hebrews 1:3). The Greek word *charakter* denies the Baha'i assertion that the "essence" of God cannot become incarnate. It means literally the "exact reproduction" and is a stronger word than "image," as in 2 Corinthians 4:4 and Colossians 1:15. As noted biblical scholar F. F. Bruce says in his Hebrews commentary (1:3), "The substance of God [Gk. *hypostasis*] is really in Christ, Who is its impress, its exact representation [*charakter*] and embodiment. What God essentially is is made manifest in Christ."[116]

Salvation by Works

Baha'u'llah reputedly "ascended in 'Akka in 1892, His Revelation completed, His Mission fulfilled."[117] Baha'is rejoice that their greatest Manifestation had fulfilled his mission. But like the followers of Sun Myung Moon, they will teach Christians that Jesus Christ did *not* fulfill His mission, because His mission was never as Christians interpreted it. God intended Jesus only to be one of many Manifestations, but not a divine Savior. When Christians teach about Christ's death atoning for the world's sin (1 John 2:2), this is something Jesus never intended to do, never could do and never did do.

Thus, as far as the Baha'i concept of salvation is concerned, Baha'is have no solution to the problem of sin. Baha'i forgiveness of sin and salvation rests upon personal merit and law-keeping. From a biblical perspective, there is little or no understanding of the human impossibility of keeping God's law or the holy wrath of God against sin. Udo Schaefer, in his rejection of "Paul's" doctrine of justification by faith alone, never deals with the key issues of how one logically achieves a right standing before God and forgiveness of sins when one is a sinner who cannot keep the Law. Note, for example, the following statement by Schaefer glorifying the merits of the Law as a means of salvation. Faith is said to be powerless because Baha'i "is a religion of the Law": "Belief alone has no power to bring salvation. That demands responsive action, for the greater the effort, the more faithfully will man 'reflect the glory of the names and attributes of God'. . . . The Baha'i Faith is a religion of the Law. . . . For 'the essence of faith is fewness of words and abundance of deeds.' From the Law man discovers what he owes God. And only in striving to fulfil the Law does he come into the right relationship with God."[118]

Schaefer digs the grave deeper by declaring that the Law must be kept inwardly as well as outwardly, and that it is thus logically impossible for an individual to know that he or she is saved:

But the Law is not satisfied by being literally fulfilled, by a mere external legality; it demands to be carried out from inner devotion: "Walk in My statutes for love of Me." . . . No believer can be sure of God's acceptance of his works and aware of his state in God's eyes: "He [the true believer] should forgive the sinful, and never despise his low estate, for none knoweth what his own end shall be." . . . In view of the fact that every man falls short of the demands of the Law and thereby falls into sin, what happens about the "Justification" before God? The answer is that justification does not take place—no one is just except God—because, as explained, the purpose of the Law is not to justify the individual before God, but to make him holy in carrying it out. God's forgiveness goes to the man who strives with all his might and with all his heart to obey the demands of the Law. . . . In the *Qur'an*, too, we are assured: "If you avoid the great sins, which are forbidden to you, We will cover your smaller sins and lead you in honour into Paradise."[119]

Clearly, however, the Bible rejects the Baha'i view of salvation through law-keeping:

I tell you the truth, he who believes has everlasting life. (John 6:47)

For we maintain that a man is justified by faith apart from observing the law. (Romans 3:28)

Know that a man is not justified by observing the law, but by faith in Jesus Christ. So we, too, have put our faith in Christ Jesus that we may be justified by faith in Christ and not by observing the law, because by observing the law no one will be justified. (Galatians 2:16)

All who rely on observing the law are under a curse, for it is written: "Cursed is everyone who does not continue to do everything written in the Book of the Law." (Galatians 3:10)

he saved us, not because of righteous things we had done, but because of his mercy. He saved us through the washing of rebirth and renewal by the Holy Spirit. (Titus 3:5)

The Atonement

Baha'i stresses salvation by works because it has no other means of salvation. It denies the mediatorial atonement of Christ (1 John 2:2), seeing such "sacrifice" as a "service characteristic" of the prophets, and even of the prophet's disciples. Note Baha'u'llah's teaching:

That which thou hast heard concerning Abraham, the Friend of the All-Merciful, is the truth, and no doubt is there about it. The Voice of God commanded Him to offer up Ishmael [sic; this is the Muslim teaching] as a sacrifice. . . . The purpose of God, moreover, was to sacrifice him as a ransom for the sins and iniquities of all the peoples of the earth. This same honor, Jesus, the Son of Mary, besought the one true God, exalted be His name and glory, to confer upon Him. For the same reason was Husayn offered up as a sacrifice by Muhammad, the Apostle of God.[120]

That this "ransom" is not literal is evident from the emphasis upon works-salvation as well as from the Baha'i denial of Christian teaching generally. Thus Sabet informs us: "For the Baha'is it would make no difference to the station of Christ . . . if He had not been crucified but had [died] . . . by stoning or a normal death. . . . The Baha'is cannot conceive of a Deity who prescribes for man an unconditional love of neighbour and enemy, but who is Himself unable to forgive unless He has had 'satisfaction' . . . through the blood of His son."[121]

In a similar vein, Udo Schaefer's approach is typical of the Baha'i approach to biblical theology generally. Using the biased "insights" of higher critical methods and liberal theologians, he tells us that we cannot really say anything certain about Jesus,[122] and this obviously includes anything about the atonement. Sabet tells

us just what we might expect: that such higher critical theology "is bringing results irreconcilable with the Church's teaching positions but remarkably in accord with the teachings of the Baha'i Faith."[123] (In *The Facts on False Views of Jesus,* we refuted higher critical methods, showing their historical and theological deficiency.) Nevertheless, in a teaching reminiscent of the Holy Order of Mans and Unity, Baha'u'llah did teach that Christ's death somehow "infused" the creation with spiritual energy: "a fresh capacity was infused into all created things."[124] But no more.

Finally, Baha'is either misunderstand or ignore the biblical concept of spiritual rebirth (regeneration), reinterpreting it to "confirm" Baha'i doctrine. Thus Baha'u'llah says being "born again" is belief in the Manifestations,[125] and a Baha'i book for children, *God and His Messengers,* under the section "The Message of Jesus," declares: "So that's what being born again means. It means your spirit comes to know God because of His Messengers. . . . That's why it's so important to try hard in this world. Because if you try hard here, and are loving and good, you will be born again and go to heaven one day, where you will be closer to God, and will even *see* His beautiful Messengers."[126]

Again, Baha'is may claim "tolerance" and "non-finality" even for their own religion, but in fact they are intolerant and absolutist. If people want the truth, at least for the next thousand years or so, they must listen to Baha'u'llah. As Baha'u'llah gushed over the greatness of his own person: "Empty thyself of all learning, that thou mayest partake of My knowledge. . . . Blind thine eyes, that is, to all save My beauty; stop thine ears to all save My word; empty thyself of all learning save the knowledge of Me. . . . Seek none other than Me. . . . quaff the stream of mystic holiness from My sugar-shedding lips."[127]

Man, Sin, the Fall

In Baha'i, all men are "sons of the Supreme Being," capable of perfecting themselves.[128] 'Abdu'l-Baha said that "all the souls are created according to the nature of God and all are in the state of purity at the times of their births."[129] Thus for Baha'is there is no original sin. Sabet claims, "Original sin in its present sense and content did not become dogma until the sixteenth century."[130] Udo Schaefer maintains that the biblical Fall is merely an allegory and the idea of original sin a "corruption" by the Apostle Paul. Sabet does at least acknowledge the reason for the Baha'i rejection of scriptural teaching when he admits that Baha'is "could never accept the logic of the doctrine of original sin, which would make all men sinners, including saints and prophets."[131] But this is exactly the teaching of Jesus and the Bible (Matthew 7:20-23; Romans 3; 5:12-19). Which biblical prophet—or prophet of any religion—was without sin?

Reminiscent of gnosticism, the Baha'i teaching declares that man has a pure and perfect spiritual nature, but that the physical nature "is the source of all imperfection."[132] Biblically, however, man's physical being is fallen, but it is not the source of "all imperfection." The source of all imperfection is man's inner being, as Christ taught (Mark 7:20-23). Man's whole nature is corrupted—mind, emotions, will and so on. Thus people sin, because their innermost nature is sinful, and therefore all are sinners.

Baha'is believe that all of man's imperfections can eventually "be transformed into human perfections."[133] If man is born perfect and only "learns" sin, he can "unlearn" it and regain original perfection. This explains why Baha'i teaches that people need no Savior. Udo Schaefer tells us, "Jesus too knows nothing of the total corruption of man."[134] If true, this would mean Jesus died on the Cross for nothing.

The Afterlife

The Baha'i believes in a personal immortality based on good works, with rewards for the faithful. Beyond that, little appears to be said. Nevertheless, what is said is once again difficult to reconcile with the Baha'i acceptance of all religions and its religious tolerance. For instance, Baha'i strongly reject reincarnation, which is accepted by hundreds of millions of Hindus and Buddhists, and they also reject the Christian concept of heaven and hell. Heaven and hell are more conditions of positive and negative actions, not places.[135] "For the Baha'is, hell signifies remoteness from God, and heaven, nearness to Him."[136] "Hell," perhaps, would constitute a very slow progression toward God; "heaven"

would involve a rapid progression towards God. While hell as a place sometimes seems to be referred to by Baha'u'llah,[137] it is often denied by Baha'is, probably because Baha'u'llah characteristically spoke of it symbolically, as he did of heaven.[138] "Heaven and Hell: These are not places. Heaven is knowing about God and doing what He wants. Hell is not knowing about God or not doing what He wants. A person who is happy and is obeying God is in heaven. A person is in hell when he dislikes others or himself, or is always unhappy."[139]

Baha'is also offer a "second chance" for salvation after death. Prayer for the dead is recommended and specific prayers are offered. The living can pray for the dead, and when the living die they can continue to pray for those dead who are less advanced spiritually, so that "they can make progress." The dead can also progress by means of their own prayers, especially if a Manifestation prays for them.[140]

Whether people should look forward to death, or fear it, is uncertain. Thus, some teachings indicate that death will be "better" for almost all and worse for some.[141] But generally speaking, everyone will progress at some point after death. Also, a kind of mediumistic view of development after death is taught. However, the Christian doctrine of bodily resurrection tends to be rejected.[142]

The Occult

There is a psychic dynamic to the Baha'i faith, both in terms of its occult history and also, potentially, in the mysticism of some Baha'i practices. It is often argued that mysticism and the occult are distinct categories, and, while this is true in certain particulars, our own research leads us to argue that mysticism has a stronger connection to the occult than many practitioners are willing to concede. Nevertheless, while some public pronouncements of Baha'i may deny an interest in the psychic and mystical realms, we are not thereby convinced of its absence.

Shi'ite Muslim religion, from which Baha'i developed, has been influenced historically by spiritism. To explain this, some background history is necessary. Shi'ites acknowledge twelve *Imams*, or familial successors to Muhammad, appointed by God through the previous Imam. Shi'ites believe there is a special hidden *Imam*, and they look for him as earnestly as Jews did for the Messiah.[143] This twelfth Inman reportedly disappeared as a child in 873 A.D., and it is believed he is still alive. For seventy years after the disappearance of the last Imam, four "Babs" (gates) communicated with him psychically, directing his will to the people. After the fourth Bab died, there was no Babi-successor and the Shi'ites were cast off from direct contact with "The Lord of the Age." Today they still pray for his return, as they have for over 1,000 years. One day he will reappear to usher in a theocratic utopia. (Speculation here, incidentally, was one reason for the popularity of the Ayatollah Khomani in Iran.)

How does this relate to Baha'i? Of the various heretical Shi'ite sects known as *ghulat* (they usually believe in reincarnation), the Bab's Shaykhi sect held to a belief that "there must always exist among men on earth some person who is in direct supernatural communication with the Hidden *Imam*."[144] Again, the Baha'i faith stems from this group.

The Shaykhi sect split over the issue of a successor to Syyid Kazim, the second psychic intermediary who died in 1843. Two men claimed successorship. One was Syyid Ali Muhammad who took the title *Bab*. His became the stronger faction, and his followers became known as Babis, forerunners of the Baha'is.[145]

As a Muslim, the Bab would have believed, as Muhammad taught, that God had sent mankind various great prophets, like Moses and Jesus. According to orthodox Islam (Sunni or shi'ite), however, Muhammad was the final and greatest prophet. But as a mystic, and probably as a result of spiritistic influence,[146] the Bab came to believe that *he*, not Muhammad, was the greatest Manifestation of God to date, and with this conviction the Baha'i faith was born.

Some of the Bab's occult activities are noted by Miller. The Bab supported mystical meditation and repetitious prayer was used to enter altered states of consciousness. And, "The Bab placed great importance on talismans. . . . All believers were commanded to wear certain amulets and charms and seals designed by the Bab himself. Charms were to be tied about the necks of infants. It seemed to Gobineau that the Bab wished to revive the ancient paganism of Chaldea. . . . For in his opinion the Babi system was full of animistic practices, and even polytheistic features were not wanting."[147]

The Bab's successor was also a mystic: "The mysticism of Baha'u'llah is in conformity with that of the "perennial philosophy" dear to Aldous Huxley, that of Meister Eckhart, Saint John of the cross, Jakob Boehme, that also which is expressed in the Bhagavad-Gita and the writings of the great Sufis."[148] Chouleur observes, "It would be regrettable . . . if the essentially mystical origin of the Baha'i Faith were lost from view."[149] But the public relations efforts of Baha'i tend to play down the mystical side of that faith.

Baha'u'llah, supposedly somewhat less mystical than his predecessor, was no stranger to occult revelations. The *Kitab-I-Iqan* itself was "revealed" to him in 1862 in two days and nights.[150] In fact, given the extent of literary output by the Bab, Baha'u'llah and 'Abdu'l-Baha, it would not be surprising to learn that much or most of their writings were supernaturally revealed. (Certainly, the precedent had been laid long ago with Muhammad and the "angel Gabriel," who Muslims believe revealed the Koran.) In 1852 "The 'Most Great Spirit' appeared to Him [Baha'u'llah] in a dream and on every side was heard these words: 'Verily, we shall render Thee victorious by Thyself and by Thy pen.'"[151] Such mystical occult writings of Baha'u'llah include *The Seven Valleys and the Four Valleys, The Hidden Words of Baha'u'llah* and *Tablet of the Holy Mariner*.[152]

'Abdu'l-Baha continued the tradition. In *The Wisdom of Abdul-Baha*, he said: "Through the faculty of meditation man attains to eternal life; through it he receives the breath of the Holy Spirit—the bestowal of the Spirit is given in reflection and meditation. This faculty of meditation frees man from the animal nature, discerns the reality of things, puts man in touch with God. . . . Let us keep this faculty rightly directed—turning it to the heavenly Sun [spiritual reality] and not to earthly objects—so that we may discover . . . the mysteries of the Spirit."[153]

In almost any mystical system, exploring the "mysteries of Spirit" is a potential door to the world of the occult. The possibility of mystical experiences among modern Baha'is is clearly present. Several illustrations follow. McLean refers to an experience of "intuitive knowledge" during the Baha'i Nineteen Day Feast, which can apparently be a mystical attempt to unite with the revelations of Baha'u'llah.[154] This is a way of "knowing" beyond the rational. One empties himself of all rational knowledge and opens himself to mystical knowledge of the "Holy Spirit." Baha'u'llah said, "Know verily that Knowledge is of two kinds: Divine and Satanic. The one welleth out from the fountain of divine inspiration. . . . The other is but a confirmation of the truth: 'Knowledge is the most grievous veil between man and his Creator.'"[155] Baha'u'llah did not mean one should give up all learning (compulsory education was one of his teachings), however God could never be found through what he believed was "satanic knowledge." McLean also discusses this mystical-psychic approach to knowing God:

> Baha'u'llah and 'Abdu'l-Baha taught that where the knowledge of God is concerned (this also applies to other forms of knowledge), emotion is a valid and indeed indispensable aspect of the epistemological process. . . . For a Baha'i the method of securing knowledge is not a detached and objective exercise of reason alone. It involves his participation at the deepest levels of his being. The exercise of the passions must also involve the use of volition. If he finds difficulty in attaining these states, he must intently desire their realization. . . . As for the nature of the mystical experience itself, the Baha'i Faith recognizes its intrinsic value. . . . While nothing in the Faith prevents individuals from sharing such experiences with others, under no circumstances do they take on an authoritative character to be imposed upon the body of the believers. Baha'u'llah's Revelation and the authorized interpretations of 'Abdu'l-Baha and Shoghi Effendi remain the definitive statement for the believers. Any mystical experience the individual may have, moreover, ought to be set within a theological and metaphysical framework that is the means of verifying its validity.[156]

Baha'u'llah's *Seven Valleys* describes seven often interrelated "stages" that the soul must pass through before it reaches its final goal. Three of these include:

1. A transcending of duality into a monistic-pantheistic awareness: "He pierceth the veils of plurality. . . . He looketh on all things with the eye of oneness." "There was God and there was naught beside Him." The spiritual wayfarer leaves behind him the stages of "'oneness of Being and Manifestation' and reacheth a oneness that is sanctified above these two stations."[157]

2. The transformation of normal perception into mystical perception: "inwardly they are throned in the heights of mystic meaning; they eat of the endless bounties of inner significances."[158]

3. The death of the limited ego and mind for "annihilation" in God: "then shalt thou gaze on the Beloved, and forget all else. . . . Now hast thou abandoned the drop of life and come to the sea of the Life-Bestower"; "strive with all thy soul that thou may disappear and be lost, like unto a drop, in the ocean of God's love" ('Abdu'l-Baha).[159]

Clearly, Baha'u'llah was familiar with mystical-occult experiences, and just as clearly we can see this approach in many of his followers.

CRITIQUE

In this section we will briefly examine: (1) the Baha'i approach to other religions; (2) the absence of the personal requirements Baha'i demands for the Manifestations; (3) anachronistic Baha'i scriptures; (4) the Miller analysis of the Baha'i faith; (5) moral concerns; (6) some Baha'i errors; and (7) failed prophecy and Baha'i misuse of Christian prophecy.

The Baha'i Approach to Other Religions

Udo Schaefer tells us that his rejection of historic Christianity was not based on science (presumably meaning facts) but on his own faith in the truth of Baha'u'llah's claim that all religions are one. Assuming the truth of this, religions must then contain "no essential contradictions," "for God does not contradict Himself."[160] The truth is that every religion in the world conflicts with every other religion.

In his article, "Baha'i-Christian Dialogue" in the *Christian Research Journal*, Dr. Francis J. Beckwith makes a good point here, which will

BAHA'I VS. OTHER RELIGIONS	
THE TEACHINGS OF BAHA'I WORLD FAITH	THE TEACHINGS OF OTHER RELIGIONS
Opposes reincarnation.	Hindus, Buddhists, others teach reincarnation.
Man is not one essence with God. There is no final mystical merger with God.[162]	Hinduism believes man is God inwardly and finally merges with God mystically.
Numerous religious duties in the *Aqdas* oppose Muslim/Koranic beliefs.[163]	Islam rejects such religious duties. Muslims view Baha'is as heretics, hence Baha'is admittedly keep very low profiles in Islamic nations. As Chouleur notes, "Baha'is have to make themselves invisible in most Muslim states."[164]
Monotheistic, unitarian.	Buddhism is atheistic (*Hinayana*) or polytheistic (*Mahayana*).[165] Christianity is monotheistic and trinitarian.
Accepts Baha'u'llah as a prophet of God.	Judaism, Hinduism, Buddhism, Islam and Christianity reject him as a prophet of God.
Continuing prophets.	Islam teaches Muhammad was the seal of the prophets and the final prophet.
Islam, etc., perverted divine revelation. "The people of the Qur'an have perverted [misinterpreted] the text of God's holy Book."[166] (The same argument is used for other religions)	Orthodox Muslims disagree, as do orthodox members of all non-Baha'i faiths.
Christ has returned as Baha'u'llah.[167]	Christians believe Christ has yet to return.

introduce our discussion of the Baha'i approach to comparative religion:

> The fact that the various alleged manifestations of God represented God in contradictory ways implies either that manifestations of God can contradict one another or that God's own nature is contradictory. If manifestations are allowed to contradict one another, then there is no way to separate false manifestations from true ones or to discover if any of them really speak for the true and living God. . . . If, on the other hand, God's own nature is said to be contradictory, that is, that God is both one God and many gods, that God is both able and not able to have a son, personal and impersonal, etc., then the Baha'i concept of God is reduced to meaninglessness.[161]

Consider just several discrepancies between the teachings of the Baha'i World Faith and the teachings of other religions (see chart).

The problem for Baha'i World Faith is clear. How can Baha'is retain credibility for their claim to accept and honor other religions? The only way Baha'is can "successfully" defend their syncretism is through a subjective, mystical approach to other scriptures, or through emphasis on a monistic religious experience to the exclusion of scriptural study, or by attempting to unite all religions merely upon surface or common characteristics (generally vague ideas on love, worship, God and so on).

To illustrate further, there are irresolvable theological problems in attempting this kind of religious syncretism. For example, how can the concepts of God in the "Religious Founders' Concepts of God" chart *ever* be reconciled?

Even when we compare Baha'i with just *one* other religion, Christianity, the problems are still insurmountable.

Finally, putting comparative religion aside for the most part, even Baha'i claims relative to itself are problematic.

The Absence of the Personal Requirements
Baha'i Demands for the Manifestations

We even discover irreconcilable difficulties when we examine the alleged attributes of the

RELIGIOUS FOUNDERS' CONCEPTS OF GOD	
LEADER	GOD
Krishna	polytheistic; pantheistic; Hinduism ultimately adopts a monistic/impersonal ultimate reality.
Moses	monotheistic, personal.
Zoroaster	dualistic; two supreme beings (one good and one evil).
Confucius	polytheistic; but gods are secondary in importance to ultimate reality.
Buddha	a supreme God is irrelevant; the gods are also; modern Buddhism is, variously, polytheistic or humanistic.
Jesus	monotheistic, personal, trinitarian. God has a Son who reveals God perfectly.
Muhammad	monotheistic, personal, unitarian. God has no Son.
The Bab/Baha'u'llah	ineffable, unknowable.

Manifestations and the denial of the attributes in history by those very Manifestations. For example, the Baha'i faith claims that all the Manifestations fit the following requirements, most of which are given in George Townshend's *Promise of All Ages* (1974). These requirements are that the Manifestations will:

1. Be sinless
2. Be uneducated, with no status
3. Fulfill prophecy and foretell their successor
4. Maintain a very high ethical standard
5. Bring harmony among men
6. Have a self-validating truth based on their character

However, even a cursory examination of the Manifestations, whether they number six, eight, nine, ten or fourteen (as they have been numbered throughout Baha'i history) fail to fulfill the above criteria. For example:

1. Only Jesus was sinless; all other Manifestations admitted to their sin (for example, Adam, Moses, Mohammed, Abraham, Buddha, Confucious, etc.).

2. Neither Moses nor Confucius were uneducated or without status.

3. Neither Krishna, Muhammad nor Buddha maintained a particularly high ethical standard in conduct or philosophy. Moses committed murder and Abraham sometimes lacked faith and committed adultery with Hagar.

4. Jesus foretold no successor; indeed considered sequentially in history none of the Manifestations ever prophesied their specific historic successor. Nor, as claimed, have any of them accepted the teachings of their alleged predecessor, Baha'u'llah included.

5. None brought true harmony among men, even among their own followers. Jesus specifically prophesied He would bring great division (Matthew 10:34-37).

6. As a whole, the Manifestations self-validating truth can hardly be based on their character and teachings, when apart from Jesus, they are morally flawed or contradictory.

The simple fact is that the historic manifestations do *not* qualify as divine manifestations, even according to *Baha'i* precepts.

BAHA'I VS. CHRISTIANITY		
TOPIC	BAHA'I	CHRISTIANITY
Manifestations:	Nine or more non-divine Manifestations of God to date, who accomplish God's will progressively in larger and larger increments.	One (divine) Manifestation who accomplished God's will and purpose "once for all" (Hebrews 9).
God:	God is unknowable: monotheistic/unitarian.	God is knowable/monotheistic/trinitarian.
Salvation:	Salvation is by works and belief in the Manifestations. No repentance from sin or new birth is needed.	Salvation is by grace through faith in Christ alone; repentance from sin and regeneration are vital.
Revelation:	Progressive revelation—each Manifestation reveals God more perfectly. The "Word of God" is syncretistic.	Perfect (inerrant) and final revelation; Christ alone perfectly revealed God; the Word of God is found in the Bible alone, normally interpreted.
The person and work of Jesus Christ:	Denies biblical Christology (Christ is not the *monogenes* of God; Christ is not God). Spiritualizes or ignores the atonement. No physical resurrection and second coming. Christ is One with other manifestations.	Christ is the *monogenes* (John 3:16, 18) of God and God incarnate. Christ's atonement was the propitiation for the world's sin. Christ Himself resurrected physically, and He will return again. He is unique.
Miracles:	Rejects the miraculous.	Accepts the miraculous.
Morality:	Relative.	Absolute.

BAHA'I CLAIMS VS. BAHA'I REALITY	
CLAIM	REALITY
Not a new religion.	A new religion.
Independent investigation of truth.	Authoritarian.
Tolerant of other religions.	Intolerant.
Stresses reason.	Irrational in its syncretism.
Believes in Christ.	Denies Christ.

Anachronistic Baha'i Scripture

The scriptures of the Baha'i faith present serious problems for the faithful who believe in science, reason and progressive revelation. Indeed, in light of the "divine" requirements expressed in the Baha'i Bible, the *Most Holy Book* (The *Al-Kitab-al Aqdas*), written by Baha'u'llah, one can but wonder whether Baha'u'llah would look with favor or scorn upon most Baha'is today, for they do *not* abide by its divinely authoritative teachings. The *Aqdas* is, as Miller notes, a divine revelation more relevant to the middle ages than to the twenty-first century. For the greater part it comprises a restatement of the Bab's *Bayan*, which Baha'u'llah, strangely, forbade others to read.[168] It embodies few of the major principles for which Baha'is are known today.

Anyone who reads the *Aqdas* will recognize how antiquated it is. Yet this is the Baha'i Bible, the most important text of all. In his will, 'Abdu'l-Baha declared that to it "everyone must turn," and this was also a reflection of his father's sentiment.[169] Indeed, so important is this alleged divine revelation that it is the text upon which the "theocratic" millennium will be based, wherein Baha'is will rule the world. Its provisions "must remain inviolate for no less than a thousand years, and whose system will embrace the entire planet."[170] In other words, this book will remain binding well into the 29th century.

One can appreciate the dilemma here. Is a "medieval" "scripture" truly authoritative for the next eight or nine centuries, or was Baha'u'llah simply wrong? If the latter, he cannot be a prophet. But if it is authoritative, why do not even Baha'is practice its precepts, as "commanded by God"? For example, "*worship* for the dead" (emphasis added); intricate inheritance laws (to children 9/42 or 540/2520; to teachers 3/42 or 180/2520 and so on),[171] regulations for daily worship, regulations for fasting, punishments for criminals (the branding of third-offense thieves; payment of $21 for committing adultery; the burning of arsonists; use of capital punishment; required marriage (to one or two wives; Baha'u'llah had three).[172] Do Baha'is wash their hands every day, then their face, then sit facing God and say ninety-five times, "God is most Splendid"?

Yet these are all laws by which Baha'is are to be living. But do Baha'is believe these laws? Do they live by them? If not, why not? Are they *not* God's commandments? Can Baha'u'llah be believed in anything if not in all things?

Baha'is respond by claiming that the time "has not yet come" for the laws of the *Aqdas* to be put into effect. But a reading of the *Aqdas* indicates that Baha'u'llah *expected* his people to *abide by the Aqdas* for at least *a thousand years.* "Perform the stipulations and ordinances of

God. Then keep them as you keep your eyes."[173] One wonders why Baha'u'llah, the most superior Manifestation of God to date, would write a book containing so many laws and regulations if not to have his people obey them? Of course, if the Baha'i community began following the commands of the *Aqdas*, it would have to abandon its modern "progressive" reputation. Thus, the fact that Baha'is do not obey the commands of God's Manifestations would seem to indicate they do not believe that such writings are truly authoritative. Our conclusion must be either that the *Aqdas* is outdated or that it is not a divine revelation. It would seem difficult for Baha'is to expect others to accept their Bible as divine if the community of believers does not treat it as such.

The Miller Analysis

The Miller text should, if at all possible, be read in its unabridged entirety, as it comprises a devastating and, to our way of thinking, fatal evaluation for the Baha'i community.* Miller's unabridged edition is one of the few places where one can find an unbiased translation of the *Aqdas*. With our space limitations here, however, we can at best scratch the surface of this text. To begin, Dr. Miller ends his analysis with a relevant criticism of the Baha'i World Faith and its claim to represent a valid religion for the world and its future:

> With its lack of clarity in its doctrine of God; with its legalism which characterizes its Most Holy Book; with its prescription in this Book of practices long since outdated; with the inadequacy of its treatment of sin and of its provision for the cure of evil in man; with the vagueness of its teaching about life after death; with the gross failure of its founders to exemplify among their own families the love they so strongly advocated—with these and other defects which are manifest in its history, can the Baha'i World Faith be an adequate religion for the world for today, and for the millennium to come? Only

---

*The original William Carey Library edition (1974) is currently out of print, although large libraries should carry a copy or an interlibrary loan may be employed.

one answer is possible, and that is decidedly negative.[174]

Miller discusses many interesting points, some of which we reproduce in abbreviated fashion and others which were pointed out in the section "Critique of Baha'i History."

1. The Bab expected to be the true Manifestation for at least 1511 years. Again, this is one reason why not all Babi's accepted Baha'u'llah as the next manifestation.[175] The Bab had said that the next prophet would abrogate his laws (as each one is free to do), but if, in retrospect, the Bab was wrong about the next prophet and Baha'u'llah was the legitimate successor, how could he himself be a legitimate prophet?

2. Why has the Bab's *Bayan* been kept from the laity? Is it due to the fact that much of it is "of almost inconceivable incomprehensibility"? Or is it because its laws that were *not* abrogated by Baha'u'llah must then still be in effect and ruling Baha'is find them difficult to believe, let alone implement?[176]

3. Shoghi Effendi (not a prophet but supposedly an infallible interpreter of Baha'u'llah) clearly contradicts the teaching of Baha'u'llah.[177] Also, Baha'u'llah declared that only the prophet had infallibility,[178] so how then did 'Abdu'l-Baha, Shoghi Effendi and others claim it for themselves?[179]

4. Baha'is, of course, reject Millers' work. "Anyone who questions the accuracy of the authorized version of Baba-Baha'i history is denounced as an enemy of the Cause of God."[180] Given this fact, isn't the Baha'i principle of "independent investigation of truth" then hypocritical? If Baha'is are forbidden to read any translation of the *Aqdas* by non-Baha'i scholars, if the House of Justice has sole authority to interpret Baha'i scripture, how can the Baha'i member possibly live by his own principles?

5. Miller supplies numerous examples of the moral failure and authoritarianism of Baha'i founders. For example, a quarrel between Baha'u'llah and his brother led to the murder of several people on both sides, and Shoghi Effendi excommunicated his parents and many relatives for disagreeing with his policies.[181] Baha'u'llah's authoritarianism was evident:[182] "If

He declares water to be wine, or heaven to be earth, or light to be fire, it is true and there is no doubt therein; and no one has the right to oppose Him, or to say 'why' or 'wherefore'. . . . Verily no account shall be demanded of Him for what He shall do. . . ."[183]

6. Miller documents numerous errors by "infallible" Baha'i leaders. Baha'u'llah and 'Abdu'l-Baha both engaged in exaggeration, inaccuracies and deception.[184] For example, we are told that the name of Moses had not been heard in Iran before the time of Christ. We are told that Baha'u'llah achieved (past tense) the uniting of all religious faiths in the Orient into a brotherhood of love. We are told that he spent forty years in prison, when he didn't.[185]

In light of the sobering facts that Miller brings to light, only a fraction of which has been presented here, one would think that it would be incumbent for every Baha'i to re-evaluate the validity of Baha'i religion. What genuine evidence exists for the truth of the Baha'i faith? Does its founders' lives reflect a godliness such as that found in the life of Jesus Christ or the Apostle Paul? True, many of the Baha'i ideals are commendable, but are they divinely inspired? Is their ideal of religious unity based on divine revelation or on religious deception?

We cannot stress enough that Baha'is should become independently acquainted with the other side of their history through Dr. Miller's analysis. If their own research confirms his conclusions, they should, at the least, act in accordance with their individual conscience.

Morality

Parts of Baha'u'llah's mystical philosophy and experience are troubling because they tend to blur moral categories. In part, they may explain his own purported moral evils, as discussed in Miller.[186] Remember, Baha'u'llah is the greatest Manifestation of God to date. If so, what are we to make of teachings like the following? If, as Sabet declares, Baha'i teaches that "good and evil are not fixed in their value once for all, but are themselves subject to development," why cannot the evil of today be the good of tomorrow?[187] If one prophet speaking *the Word of God* nullifies or contradicts the moral teachings of another, do we still live in a moral universe? If even "love becometh an obstruction and a barrier," where are we headed?[188]

When Baha'u'llah declared that "the works and acts of each and every one" of the prophets "are all ordained by God, and are a reflection of His Will and Purpose,"[189] it would seem that the Baha'i faith must thereby endorse as the divine will much or all of the personal evils and immoral teachings of Krishna, the sins of Moses, the practical atheism of Buddha and the religious violence of Muhammad, not to mention the sins of the Bab and Baha'u'llah himself. Is this in harmony with a progressive and enlightened outlook on religion?

Some Additional Baha'i Errors

1. Discarding historical evidence, Baha'is teach that the Apostle Paul was unconcerned with the historic Jesus, perverted His teachings and was a superstitious ascetic. In order to make such statements, one would have to assume Baha'is have not even read the Apostle Paul, since such charges are demonstrably false. In 1 Corinthians 15:3-8 we see that what the Apostle Paul considered as having "first importance" was precisely the historic Jesus. Far from perverting Jesus' teaching, Paul held to it strictly, as J. Gresham Machen's *The Origin of Paul's Religion* proves in detail. Consider a few examples from our own reading of Jesus and Paul. We present a number of basic Christian doctrines showing the theological harmony of Jesus Christ and the Apostle Paul. Baha'is and other liberal critics allege these were never Jesus' original teachings but "invented" by the Apostle Paul. Since the following are agreed to by almost everyone to be Paul's teachings, we only need to document that they are also Jesus' teachings:

Jesus Christ as the only Son of God and the Savior. Luke 10:16; John 3:16, 18; 5:34-40; 6:27-40; 8:12; 11:25-27; 12:47.

The Trinity. Matthew 28:19; John 5:18; 10:33-38; 14:9, 16-18; 16:13-15.

Salvation by grace. Luke 18:9-14; John 5:24; 6:29,47.

Jesus Christ is the only way. John 3:14-18; 8:24; 10:1, 7-9, 28; 14:6; 17:3.

Heaven and Hell. Matthew 25:46; Luke 16:19-31; John 14:2-3; 17:24.

Belief in a personal triune God. Matthew 28:19; John 17.

Death of Jesus Christ for the world's sins (the atonement). Matthew 20:28; 26:28; John 10:11, 17.

The Church as the institution of believers. Matthew 16:15-19.

Creation of Adam and Eve and the Fall. Matthew 19:4; Luke 10:18; John 8:44.

Resurrection of Jesus Christ. Matthew 16:21; 26:32; John 2:19.

Satan and demons are real. Mark 9:25-29; Luke 4:1-13, 33-35.

Sin is real. John 3:19-20; 5:14; 8:7-11, 34.

Importance of salvation by faith. Luke 7:9; 18:42; John 5:24; 6:47.

Death is an enemy. John 11:32-44.

Jesus is the Christ, the Jewish Messiah. Matthew 16:15-17; Mark 14:61-64; Luke 18:31; 20:41-44; 22:67-71; John 4:25-26; 5:38-47; 7:26-29; 8:42-47; 10:24-26.

The kingdom of God. Matthew 13:44-53; 18:1-4; Luke 9:62; 19:11; John 18:36.

The resurrection of people. Luke 20:35-38.

Jesus Christ's second coming. Matthew 24:27-31; 25:31.

Necessity of repentance. Matthew 18:3-4; Mark 6:7; 12; Luke 17:1-4.

Literal interpretation of the Bible. John 8:30-32; 18:19-21.

Immorality condemned. Matthew 19:5-9.

Importance of prayer. Matthew 21:13, 22; Luke 5:16; 6:12.

The Old Testament as the Word of God. Matthew 4:4; Mark 7:6-10,13; John 17:17.

The fear of God. Luke 12:4-5.

Inspiration of the New Testament. John 14:16-17; 14:26; 16:13-15.

Communion and baptism. Matthew 3:16; 21:25; 28:19; Luke 22:15-20; John 6:53-56.

Jesus' acceptance of worship. Matthew 8:2; 9:18; 14:33; John 9:38.

How could the Apostle Peter, who knew Jesus so well, accept Paul if he were a falsifier of Jesus' teachings (Acts 26:22; 2 Peter 3:15–16)? The testimony of both Paul and Jesus is that He, Jesus Christ, is wholly unique. Jesus has universal and eternal relevance; that is, not merely relevance for His own place and time (Matthew 24:30, 35; 28:18; John 5:20–29; Philippians 2:9-11). As far as being a "superstitious ascetic," Paul's own life and teachings deny this repeatedly (Colossians 2:8, 23).

Regardless, Baha'is fail to mention that Jesus' own disciple Peter declared Paul's writings the Word of God (2 Peter 3:15–16). If Baha'u'llah *himself* confirmed Peter's station and said God caused "wisdom . . . to flow out of his mouth," and if Shoghi Effendi further declared that "the primacy of Peter, the prince of the apostles, is upheld and defended," how do they proceed to deny the divine authority of Paul whom Peter upheld?[190]

2. The "infallible" Baha'u'llah quite erroneously declared of Muhammad that he claimed to be Jesus. No orthodox Muslim believes this, nor is it taught in the Koran. Baha'u'llah says, again falsely, "Neither the person of Jesus nor His writings hath differed from that of Muhammed and of His holy Book."[191] In *The Facts on Islam,* we have shown how wrong such a declaration is.

3. Baha'is have written various books to convert Christians to the Baha'i faith. The errors in these books are extremely numerous and often unconscionable.[192] As one example, observe Townshend's interpretation of Deuteronomy 33:2, where Moses is blessing the Sons of Israel just before he dies. The parentheses are Townshend's: "The Lord came from Sinai (meaning Himself [Moses]), and rose up from Seir (meaning Jesus Christ); he shined forth from Mount Paran (meaning Muhammad) and he came with ten thousands of saints (meaning Baha'u'llah)." These are supposedly "the undoubted facts of history."[193] Interpretations as this are not only

preposterous but also extremely embarrassing to Baha'i claims to represent enlightened religion.

4. "In the synoptic Gospels, there is nowhere to be found any allusion to a miraculous birth."[194] But the virgin birth of Jesus is mentioned in two synoptic Gospels (Matthew 1:23; Luke 1:27; cf. Isaiah 7:14).

5. Jesus never spoke of Himself as the only Son of God. But in John 3:16 and 18 Jesus very clearly speaks of Himself as the only (*monogenes*) Son of God.[195]

6. Christianity was influenced by the mystery religions.[196] This historical error was never tenable and we refuted it in chapter 7 of our *Ready with an Answer.* (Ronald Nash's *Christianity and the Hellenistic World* also provides a detailed analysis.)

7. The Trinity "cannot be found in Paul's writings," and Paul never thought of Jesus as "in any sense identical or equal to God."[197] In fact, Paul's writings contain some of the most definitive statements for belief in the Trinity and he not infrequently declared the full deity of Jesus Christ (for example, Titus 2:13). (See Doctrinal Appendix at end of this book.)

Failed Prophecy and Misinterpretation of Christian Prophecy

The Baha'is religious presuppositions force them to misinterpret the Bible virtually wherever they discuss it. This is particularly true with Baha'i prophetic scriptures. In his text *Baha'i* (chapter 4, 1975) Dr. Francis Beckwith critically analyzes Baha'i misinterpretations of Daniel 8:13–17; Isaiah 11:1–10; Isaiah 35:1–2; Isaiah 1:1, 6, 7 and other passages. He also documents a particularly damaging false prophecy—and its cover-up—that universal peace would be established in 1957. This was a prophecy of 'Abdu'l-Baha cited by J. E. Esslemont in 1923 but removed (after his death) in the 1970 edition of Esslemont's text, *Baha'u'llah and the New Era.* Beckwith then concludes:

The chief representatives of Baha'i scholarship show an absolute ignorance of properly interpreting any given Biblical text. They ignore context, language, intent, and historical setting. They seek only to twist biblical passages so as to fit their presupposed doctrines which, in their opinion, justify these presupposed doctrines. This seems to be the continuing fallacy lurking behind almost every Baha'i apologetic use of the Bible: Baha'i apologists (defenders) reason in a circle.

Concerning ethical character, upon which the Baha'is put a premium, the censorship of J. E. Esslemont's book, after his death, is indeed a black mark upon all Baha'ism. Changing an eyewitness testimony (of 'Abdu'l-Baha's false prophecy) after the death of the eyewitness is blatantly unethical.[198]

Nevertheless, the Baha'i syncretism demands that virtually any prophetic scripture can be misinterpreted, and dozens of additional cases can be referenced.[199] Such misinterpretation is found throughout their literature. We shall, however, discuss only one example of their misuse of prophetic scripture in Daniel chapters 8–9.

Dr. John Walvoord offers a clear and detailed analysis of the book of Daniel in *The Prophecy of Daniel*. This may be compared to the Baha'i booklet "Prophecy Fulfilled" by E. H. Cheney, who expounds 'Abdu'l-Baha's views on Daniel.

'Abdu'l Baha attempts to find Daniel's prophecy fulfilled in the Baha'i religion, using Daniel chapters 8 and 9. In Daniel 8:14, the 2,300 "evenings and mornings" are wrongly interpreted by Baha'i's as 2,300 years. The Hebrew term referred to "evening and morning" sacrifices (see 9:21; Exodus 29:38–42), which would be 1150 days or about three years, not *2,300* years. The prophecy in Daniel 8 deals directly with Antiochus IV Epiphanes, the eighth ruler of the Syrian dynasty during the time of the Maccabees. The "2,300 evenings and mornings" were fulfilled within a few years, some 2,000 years *before* Baha'is even existed. As the NIV text note (Zondervan Study Bible) for Daniel 8:14 reads, "The 2,300 evenings and mornings probably refer to the number of sacrifices consecutively offered on 1,150 days, the interval between the desecration of the Lord's altar and its reconsecration by Judas Maccabeus on Kislev 25, 165 B.C. The pagan altar set up by Antiochus on Kislev 25, 168, was apparently installed almost 2 months after the Lord's altar was removed, accounting for the difference between 1,095 days

(an exact three years) and the 1,150 specified here."

'Abdu'l-Baha uses Daniel 9:24–26 and applies it contextually to Daniel chapter 8, ignoring the fact that it deals with the first coming of the Messiah, which occurred 2,000 years ago. (Only in verse 27 is the second coming referred to.) In other words, 'Abdu'l-Baha ties together entirely unrelated prophecies, each fulfilled some two millennia ago, as relating to the nineteenth century A.D. Baha'i origins. In that way he can use the decree of Artaxerxes (Daniel 9:25; Ezra 7; 457 B.C.), add 2,300 years (Daniel 8) and come up with the year 1844, the time of the Bab's Pronouncement that he was God's Messenger. He can also claim that Baha'u'llah is the "prince" foretold by Daniel. The difficulty is that there are two princes foretold at Daniel 9:24–27, and neither refer to Baha'u'llah. One is the Messiah, who is "cut off" (Jesus, who died on the Cross), and the other prince who destroys the sanctuary, the anti-Christ. Contextually, Jesus Christ is the only person who could fit the prophecy here. (Cf. Dr. A. J. McClain, *Daniel's Prophecy of the 70 Weeks* and Sir Robert Anderson, *The Coming Prince*.)

It is, of course, easy to misinterpret prophecy without careful study. The Seventh day Adventists made the same error as the Baha'is (interpreting the 2,300 mornings and evenings for years), and thus they expected Christ's return in 1844. Incidentally, the same Baha'i booklet interprets Nahum 2:3–4 as a prophecy about automobiles of our own era, even though the book of Nahum is a prophecy against Assyria, to whom Jonah had earlier preached. The language in 2:3–4 is a mildly poetic description of chariots of the time.

TALKING WITH MEMBERS

Clearly, Baha'is have an interpretation of Christianity that is inconsistent with the facts of history, biblical theology and comparative religion. They may feel justified in their views because they have the support of "higher critical" scholarship, not realizing that the biased premises, methods and conclusions of such scholarship *also* does not have the support of the facts of history and theology. Several books demonstrate why this is true, such as our *The Facts on False View of Jesus: Knowing the Truth about the Jesus Seminar;* Dr. Gleason Archer's *A Survey of Old Testament Introduction;* Josh McDowell's *More Evidence That Demands a Verdict* and Gundry and Johnson's *Tensions in Contemporary Theology* (Revised Edition).

So one good approach for discussion with a Baha'i concerning Christianity is to show the person why the New Testament is reliable historically and textually. (See Unitarian Universalism appendix. Other good sources are F. F. Bruce's *The New Testament Documents: Are They Reliable?;* John Warwick Montgomery's *History and Christianity;* Norman Geisler's *Inerrancy* and Rene Pache, *The Inspiration and Authority of Scripture*). It should also be shown why the Apostle Paul could not have perverted Jesus' teachings and did not borrow his ideas from the pagan mystery religions. (See J. Gresham Machen's *The Origin of Paul's Religion* and John Whenham's *Christ and the Bible.*)

Baha'is who truly believe in an "*independent investigation of the truth*" should, by the data, concede the bankruptcy of higher criticism and the truth of biblical reliability. As we have seen, if the Bible is accepted as historically reliable, it is easy to prove that it does not agree with Baha'i teachings and that the Apostle Paul did not invent the Jesus of the Gospels. Of course, all this presupposes that we interpret the Bible literally; that is, normally. In that Baha'is have never once justified their non-literal approach to the Bible, the standard method of interpreting it must be conceded. At this point, a decision can be pressed based on the following question: if the Christian interpretation of the Bible is accurate, how can the Baha'i faith constitute a divine revelation when it has rejected something so important and witnessed against one of God's revelations? If Baha'is follow this reasoning logically, they must conclude Baha'i is not a divine revelation. And if only Jesus has ever risen from the dead, one would have to assume His religion was the true one.

True Christianity and the Baha'i faith cannot, then, be part of One Truth; at least one teaching must be wrong. The Baha'i has a choice between a man who claimed to be a prophet of God without offering any evidence, Baha'u'llah, or a person who claimed to be God incarnate and provided evidence of this by resurrecting physically from the dead. Further, can a Baha'i in good conscience really compare men like the Bab and Baha'u'llah (especially in light of Miller's findings) to the Jesus Christ of the New Testament? Are they proud of either their syncretistic endeavors or the biased writings of their apologists? Since Baha'is claim consistently to respect history and reason, isn't it the Baha'i religion itself that is an embarrassment?

Baha'is often have a strong emotional investment in the Baha'i ideals—world peace, brotherhood, racial equality and so on, which is all very good. The problem is they do not want to see these ideals "lost" by an "independent investigation of the truth" that would undermine the very organization promoting them. In effect, if emotion holds sway over reason, they will be unwilling to undertake an unbiased personal look at both sides of the question concerning a normal reading of the New Testament documents and the relationship between Baha'i and original Christianity. At this point one must assist members to understand that truth found late is better than truth not found at all. If an independent investigation of the truth leads them to reject Baha'i, then the ideal still stands even if the religion espousing it does not. This exchange is not something bad if it leads to genuine truth. It might be appropriate to assist their independent investigation—not with a Bible study only but with a weekly study about the Bible or hermeneutics. They could study one Bible topic or chapter for a week (or month) along with discussion of one chapter a week in, for instance, F. F. Bruce's *The New Testament Documents,* or McDowell's *More than a Carpenter* or a simple text on Bible interpretation. A discussion of additional supporting evidence could be included, as in the less exhaustive chapters in McDowell's *Evidence That Demands a Verdict* or our *Ready with an Answer.* As their trust in the "integrity" of the Baha'i position weakens, it can perhaps be replaced with a growing trust in Jesus' words.

Baha'is, like all people, are aware of their limitations. So even Baha'u'llah can be quoted, but used in a Christian context: "It is the way-wardness of the heart that removeth it far from God, and condemneth it to remoteness from Him."[200] The Baha'i God declares, "The best beloved of all things in My sight is Justice."[201] "Waywardness of heart" and its solution could lead to a discussion of sin and its remedy. "Justice" could lead to a discussion of Baha'i syncretism, or to a discussion of whether divine justice is avoidable. Do Baha'is honestly believe that they can perfect themselves, or that a holy God can forgive them without judgment of their sins? Do they understand the severity of God's justice and the immensity of human sin before Him, that God is so holy that it required the tortured death of His Son? Further, does the Baha'i member believe in his heart he or she can attain to any of the following?

1. knowledge of God

2. love of God

3. faith

4. philanthropic deeds

5. self-sacrifice

6. severance from the world

7. living in the utmost state of sanctity and holiness

But this is what they must attain: "Unless he acquires these forces and attains to these requirements he will surely be deprived of the life that is eternal."[202] But how can Baha'is attain knowledge and love of God when their God is inherently self-contradictory?

How much simpler, yet more profound, is the Gospel, in which eternal life comes by simple faith in Jesus Christ, who said: "For God so loved the world that he gave his one and only Son, that whoever believes in him shall not perish but have eternal life" (John 3:16). That Gospel also has power to transform a life for righteous living, as it has done for two millennia.

On the other hand, if Baha'is *reject* an "*independent* investigation of the truth" how can they claim to be good Baha'is? If they understand the dictionary definition of "independent" and fol-low accepted principles of independent investigation (such as objective assessment of the evidence), they will be required to reject Baha'i religion.

Here is another point of possible dialogue. Baha'is believe that Christians have *rejected* God. They decry the fact that the prophets, especially Baha'u'llah, have not been accepted by Christians. Baha'u'llah stressed, "Whoso turneth away from them, hath turned away from God, and whoso disbelieveth in them, hath disbelieved in God."[203] Let us accept the argument for a moment. Christians deny Baha'u'llah. But Baha'is also teach, "If we deny *one* of the Manifestations of God we deny *all*."[204] Now, the truth is that Baha'is *deny* Christ. If we are fair, we must be willing to accept that. Therefore, *they* deny Baha'u'llah. Only illogical reasoning or a biased refusal to accept the integrity of the Gospels can change this conclusion.

Jesus claimed that His words were relevant for *all* time (Matthew 24:35), and He said, "No man comes to the Father but by Me" (John 14:6). If His words *are* relevant today, then neither fol-lowers of Baha'u'llah, nor one who is a Christian, can *accept* Baha'u'llah without *denying* Jesus. And to deny one prophet is to deny all, which must also be to deny Baha'u'llah. Baha'is own doctrine thus forces them to deny Baha'u'llah. Since they will not see this on their own, it could be pointed out to them.

Their only solution to this dilemma is to deny Christ's words as being His own. However, then they are no longer engaging in "independent investigation of truth," as they have *no* historical or factual basis on which to discount the Gospels.

It is not that we oppose the right of the Baha'is to believe in and propagate a new religion to which we disagree. It is their disregard for the proven teachings of other religions that is difficult to accept in light of their support for ideals such as tolerance and "independent investigation of the truth." Let them truly engage in this, and see if they can remain Baha'is.

If Baha'is were truly pro-Islam, would Muslims kill them as heretics? It is a horrendous sin to kill a brother in the faith according to the Koran, although it is right to kill heretics. Likewise, if Baha'is were truly pro-Christian, would

Christians everywhere reject their claims concerning Christianity?

One might also ask a Baha'i believer to place himself or herself in the position of a Christian, that they may more easily see the problem their approach presents. For example, on their own terms Baha'is accept the Gospels as teaching Baha'i truths, but they reject the Pauline Epistles as distortions of Jesus' teachings, even though from day one Paul's writings were believed to have been divinely inspired, as Peter testified (2 Peter 3:15–16). In other words, they are merely refuting their contrived gross distortion of Christianity. Would Baha'is be content if Christians accepted only their *Aqdas, The Most Holy Book,* and distorted it to teach Christian doctrine and then rejected the rest of their holy scriptures as spurious? Would this be fair? If we were to approach the Baha'i faith in the same way Baha'is approach Christianity, would it not be easy for Christians to simply disregard other Baha'i scriptures as "perversions" of the original *Aqdas* and then misrepresent the Baha'i religion as teaching Christianity through citing only the *Aqdas*?

If Baha'is would *not* permit such an approach by a Christian, how then can Baha'is accept it for themselves? Indeed, isn't it also true that if we were to accept only the *Aqdas* and interpret it properly (literally), that a far more critical and grimmer picture of Baha'i could then be painted?[205] Would Baha'is be pleased if Christians accepted their *Aqdas* literally and ignored their other scripture, forcing Baha'ism into the mold of an antiquated religion? So, if Christians have respected the Baha'i faith by declaring its doctrines correctly, why can't Baha'is grant Christians the same courtesy?

Because Baha'i is a religion that denies the truth and ignores an independent investigation of the truth, we would, first, simply urge Baha'i's to listen once more to their own prophets: "*Truthfulness* is the foundation of all human virtues. Without *truthfulness,* progress and success, in all the worlds of God, are impossible for any soul. . . . You must live and act with the utmost *truthfulness* . . . let *truthfulness* and courtesy be your adorning. Be fair to yourselves and to others that the evidences of Justice may be revealed through your deeds among our faithful servants."[206]

In light of this emphasis on the vital importance of truth, we have two questions. First, why do 'Abdu'l-Baha and the Baha'i prophets subvert the truth by misquoting the Bible by changing its words[207] or by deletion? For example, 'Abdu'l-Baha leaves out the third clause of John 1:1, and quotes the verse only as declaring "In the beginning was the Word and the Word was with God." Why is "and the Word was God" deleted?[208] If he was infallible, as he claimed, why did he misquote the Bible by carelessness?[209] Or was it deliberately misquoted? Was 'Abdu'l-Baha truthful, and if not, what are the implications? As Gloria Faizi correctly warned: "It would be foolish, of course, to accept anyone as God's Mouthpiece on earth without being absolutely sure of his station."[210]

The second question relative to the importance of truth is this: are not all spiritual truths eternal? Baha'is divide each prophet's revelation into two parts: the essential and eternal, and the non-essential and temporal.[211] All religions teach key doctrines that they claim as essential and eternal. But Baha'i ignores these claims of the other religions and argues that the central doctrines of other religions are really just peripheral. On what logical, historical or other basis does Baha'i "reinvent" the vital teachings of other religions as "nonessential and temporal"? Would Baha'is ever permit such a distortion to be implemented upon their own revelation, so that all their essential and eternal truths become non-essential and temporal throwaways? If they did, could they remain Baha'is?

Perhaps the Baha'is have some house-cleaning to attend to? If the Baha'i faith is to continue to claim that it treats other scriptures and religions fairly, it should undertake that house-cleaning as a matter of some urgency. Further, in light of our analysis in this chapter, Baha'is should clearly reconsider 'Abdu'l-Baha's assessment that "religion must be in harmony with science and reason. If it does not conform to science and reconcile with reason it is superstition."[212] In his *Portals to Freedom,* Howard Ives, a Unitarian minister-convert to Baha'i, also quoted Abdu'l-Baha as stating, "If religion is opposed to reason and science, faith is impossible" and, "It were better to have no religion than a religion which did not conform to reason." He also prided himself on the fact the "the first principle under which the consistent Baha'i thinker acts is *the independent investigation of truth.*"[213]

The simple fact is that the Baha'i approach to religion is opposed to reason. If anything has been demonstrated by this chapter, that has. By its own principles, then, the Baha'i World Faith stands condemned as superstition and it would be better for Baha'is to have no religion.

Finally, we would urge Baha'is to listen to the words of Jesus, as their own prophet Baha'u'llah told them to. "If you reflect upon the essential teachings of Jesus you will realize that they are the light of the world. Nobody can question their truth. They are the very source of life and the cause of happiness to the human race."[214] Here are some of the essential teachings of Jesus, and as Baha'u'llah said, "Nobody can question their truth":

"You are a king, then!" said Pilate. Jesus answered, "You are right in saying I am a king. In fact, for this reason I was born, and for this I came into the world, to testify to the truth. Everyone on the side of truth listens to me." (John 18:37)

Jesus answered, "I am the way and the truth and the life. No one comes to the Father except through me." (John 14:6)

As the Apostle John declared:

No who one denies the Son has the Father; whoever acknowledges the Son has the Father also. (1 John 2:23)

We accept man's testimony, but God's testimony is greater because it is the testimony of God, which he has given about his Son. Anyone who believes in the Son of God has this testimony in his heart. Anyone who does not believe God has made him out to be a liar, because he has not believed the testimony God has given about his Son. And this is the testimony: God has given us eternal life, and this life is in his Son. He who has the Son has life; he who does not have the Son of God does not have life. (1 John 5:9–13)

We know that we have come to know him if we obey his commands. (1 John 2:3)

In that day you shall know that I am in My Father, and you in Me, and I in you. He who has My commandments and keeps them, he it is who loves Me; and he who loves Me shall be loved by My Father, and I will love him, and will disclose Myself to him. (John 14:20–21 NAS)

If Baha'is truly wish to know God and be known by God, they need to listen more carefully to the words of Jesus and *truly* perform "an independent investigation of the truth." As their own prophet said, "God has bestowed upon man the gift of mind in order that he may weigh every fact or truth presented to him and adjudge it to be reasonable."[215]

Scripture Contrasts

The process of His creation that had no beginning, and can have no end. [216]	Thus the heavens and the earth were completed, in all their vast array. (Genesis 2:1; cf. 2:2–3, 1:1)
This universe has no beginning.[217]	In the beginning God created the heavens and the earth. (Genesis 1:1)
The Greatest name, Baha'u'llah.[218]	Therefore also God highly exalted Him, and bestowed on Him the name which is above every name, that at the name of Jesus every knee should bow, of those who are in heaven, and on earth, and under the earth, and that every tongue should confess that Jesus Christ is Lord, to the glory of God the Father. (Philippians 2:9–11 NAS)
	(continues)

41

Scripture Contrasts, cont.

The Church gave pride of place not to his [Jesus'] faith but to a faith in him which he had not preached.[219]	For if you believed Moses, you would believe Me; for he wrote of Me. . . . this is the work of God, that you believe in Him whom He has sent. (John 5:46; 6:29; see context NAS)
So we can say that there must be a Mediator between God and man, and this is none other than the Holy Spirit.[220]	For there is one God, and one mediator also between God and men, the man Christ Jesus, who gave Himself as a ransom for all, the testimony borne at the proper time. (1 Timothy 2:5–6 NAS)
All of you were created from water and you will return to the earth.[221]	The LORD God formed the man from the dust of the ground and breathed into his nostrils the breath of life, and the man became a living being. (Genesis 2:7)

NOTES

1. 'Abdu'l-Baha, *Baha'i World Faith* (Wilmette, IL: Baha'i Publishing Trust, 1976), p. 400.
2. Baha'u'llah, ed. H. Holley, *The Baha'i Scriptures* (New York: Brentane's, 1923), p. 243, cited in Miller, *The Baha'i Faith*, p. 140.
3. 'Abdu'l-Baha, *Some Answered Questions* (Baha'i Publishing Trust, 1930), p. 44, cited in Francis Beckwith, *Baha'i* (Bethany, 1985), p. 28.
4. Baha'i World Faith website at: http://oneworld.wa.com/ bahai/srb-faq.html.
5. Gloria Faizi, *The Baha'i Faith An Introduction* (Wilmette, IL: Baha'i Publishing Trust, 1978), p. 35.
6. *World Order*, Fall 1977, p. 11; "Baha'i Teachings for a World Faith," Baha'i Publishing Trust, 1943, pp. 5-7, 20.
7. Cf. William McLwee Miller, *The Baha'i Faith: Its History and Teachings* (South Pasadena, CA: William Carey Library, 1974), chapters 12–13.
8. Huschmand Sabet, *The Heavens Are Cleft Asunder* (Oxford, England: George Ronald Publishing, 1975), p. 51; verdict of May 10, 1925, by the Islamic Court of Appeal of Beba, Egypt, quoted in *God Passes By*, p. 365.
9. Peter Simple, Kolstoe, *Baha'i Teachings, Light for All Regions* (Wilmette, IL: Baha'i Publishing Trust, 1970), pp. 17-18.
10. Udo Schaefer, *The Light Shineth in Darkness* (Oxford, England: George Ronald, 1973) p. 1; J. E. Esslemont, *Baha'u'lla'h and the New Era* (Wilmette, IL: Baha'i Publishing Trust, 1970), p. 9.
11. The National Spiritual Assembly of the Baha'is of the United States, 1975, p. 8; various introductory literature and pamphlets.
12. Sabet, p. 143.
13. Miller, *The Baha'i Faith: Its History and Teachings*, p. 54.
14. See Douglas Martin, *World Order*, Spring 1976, p. 46. Much depends here on the words of Shoghi Effendi and the clarity with which the Bab expressed his teachings about the next Manifestation. Obviously, if his statements were unclear or contradictory, *anyone* could claim to be the next Prophet and, if luck were with him, succeed. Clear or unclear, the Baha'is have problems.
15. Ibid.
16. Adib Taherzadeh, *The Revelation of Baha'u'llah Adrianople 1863-68* (Oxford: George Ronald), pp. 120, 146, ch. 7; *Abington Dictionary of Living Religions*, p. 87.
17. Martin, p. 61.
18. Miller, *The Baha'i Faith: Its History and Teaching*, pp. 323, 327, 343-346.
19. Letter dated February 10, 1981.
20. *World Order*, Spring 1976, pp. 43-44.
20a. Miller, *The Baha'i Faith*, chs. 12-14, for example, pp. 310-322. On Baha'i authoritarianism, see the *Journal for Scientific Study of Religion*, June 1998.
21. Miller, "What Is the Baha'i World Faith?" (pamphlet), p. 13.
22. Miller, *The Baha'i Faith*, p. 321.
23. Abdu'l-Baha, *Christ's Promise Fulfilled* (Wilmette, IL: Baha'i Publishing Trust, 1978), p. 72.
24. *Baha'i World Faith*, p. 225; Abdu'l-Baha, *Christ's Promise Fulfilled*, pp. 66-67.
25. Baha'u'llah, *The Kitab-I-Iqan The Book of Certitude* (Wilmette, IL: Baha'i Publishing Trust, 1974), pp. 87, 89, see also p. 86.
26. Baha'i World Faith website.
27. *World Order*, Fall, 1977, p. 11.
28. Ibid., Fall 1978, p. 10.
29. Miller, *The Baha'i Faith*, pp. 52-59, 11.
30. Baha'i World Faith website.
31. Miller, *The Baha'i Faith*, p. 227, citing *Baha'i Scriptures* (1923), p. 330, cf. Miller, p. 53 (book).
32. Baha'i introductory literature; *World Order*, Fall 1978, p. 14.
33. *World Order*, Fall 1978, p. 14. The alleged characteristics of a Manifestation are no guide at this point. See the section in this chapter: "The Absence of the Personal Requirements Baha'i Demands for the Manifestations."
34. *Baha'i World Faith*, p. 20.

35. Shoghi Effendi, *Gleanings from the Writings of Baha'u'llah* (Wilmette, IL: Baha'i Publishing Trust, 1976), pp. 66-67, emphasis added.
36. Taherzadeh, p. 146, citing Epistle to the Son of the Wolf (p. 141).
37. Ibid., p. 80 citing Shoghi Effendi, *World Order of Baha'u'llah*, p. 113, emphasis added.
38. *Gleanings from the Writings of Baha'u'llah*, pp. 50-51.
39. Ibid., p. 53.
40. *Baha'i World Faith*, p. 24.
41. Francis Beckwith, *Baha'i* (Bethany, 1985), pp. 20-21.
42. Ibid., p. 18.
43. Ibid., pp. 18-19.
44. *Baha'i World Faith*, pp. 20-28.
45. Abdu'l-Baha, *Christ's Promise Fulfilled*, p. 71.
46. For example, cf. Sabet, *The Heavens Are Cleft Asunder*, pp. 48-49.
47. Ibid., pp. 49-50.
48. Ibid., p. 49.
49. Ibid., pp. 9, 11.
50. William Sears, *Thief in the Night* (Oxford, England: George Ronald, 1973), pp. 252-255.
51. Ibid., pp. 253-255.
52. For example, pp. 117-119, 148-150, 172-175, 203-207.
53. George Townshend, *The Heart of the Gospel* (London, England, George Ronald, 1960), pp. 156-157.
54. Esslemont, p. 256.
55. Ibid., p. 257.
56. *World Order*, Spring 1978, p. 5.
57. Ibid., Spring 1976, p. 36.
58. Ibid., p. 35.
59. Abdu'l-Baha, *Christ's Promise Fulfilled*, p. 30.
60. Miller, *The Baha'i Faith*, p. 321; cf. p. 62 for a statement by the Bab.
61. Schaefer, p. 87.
62. *The Kitab-I-Iqan*, p. 80.
63. Abdu'l-Baha, *Christ's Promise Fulfilled*, p. 33.
64. Townshend, *The Heart of the Gospel*, p. 147; cf. pp. 149, 117, 77, 75.
65. Sabet, pp. 123-124.
66. *Baha'i Teachings*, p. 6.
67. Ibid., pp. 7, 11.
68. Taherzadeh, pp. 271-272.
69. Ibid., p. 312.
70. Ibid., p. 350.
71. Schaefer, p. 61.
72. Baha'u'llah, *The Kitab-I-Iqan*, p. 27.
73. Ibid., p. 135.
74. Ibid., p. 213, cf. p. 27.
75. *World Order*, Fall 1978, p. 15.
76. Ibid., Fall 1977, p. 11.
77. Ibid., p. 15.
78. Abdu'l-Baha, *Christ's Promise Fulfilled*, p. 75.
79. *The Kitab-I-Iqan*, p. 215.
80. *World Order*, Fall 1978, p. 11.
81. *The Kitab-I-Iqan*, pp. 177, 179, 180; *Baha'i World Faith*, p. 39; *Gleanings from the Writings of Baha'u'llah*, p. 62.
82. Ibid.
83. Miller, *The Baha'i Faith*, p. 226, citing *Baha'i Scriptures* (1923), p. 481.

84. *The Kitab-I-Iqan*, p. 98.
85. *Gleanings from the Writings of Baha'u'llah*, p. 186.
86. *The Kitab-I-Iqan*, pp. 140-145; 169-170.
87. *Gleanings from the Writings of Baha'u'llah*, p. 63.
88. Miller, *The Baha'i Faith*, p. 226, citing *Baha'i Scriptures* (1923), p. 459.
89. *World Order*, Fall 1978, p. 12.
90. Ibid., p. 13.
91. *Baha'i World Faith*, p. 323.
92. *World Order*, Spring 1978, pp. 48-49.
93. *The Kitab-I-Iqan*, pp. 192-193.
94. Ibid., p. 188.
95. Miller, *The Baha'i Faith*, p. 64.
95a. *World Order*, Winter 1966, p. 27.
96. Sabet, p. 110.
97. Schaefer, pp. 4-5.
98. *World Order*, Fall 1978, p. 16.
99. Ibid.
100. Ibid., p. 14.
101. Ibid., p. 12.
102. Ibid., Summer 1978, p. 39.
103. Ibid.
104. *Gleanings from the Writings of Baha'u'llah*, p. 57; *Baha'i World Faith*, p. 49.
105. *Gleanings from the Writings of Baha'u'llah*, p. 101.
106. Sears, pp. 203-208.
107. Ibid., pp. 156-159.
108. George Townshend, *Christ and Baha'u'llah* (Oxford, England: George Ronald, 1977), p. 77.
109. *World Order*, Winter 1966, p. 27.
110. Ibid., Fall 1978, p. 17; Miller, *The Baha'i Faith*, pp. 224-227.
111. Miller, *The Baha'i Faith*, p. 225.
112. Townshend, *The Heart of the Gospel*, p. 80.
113. Abdu'l-Baha, *Christ's Promise Fulfilled*, pp. 31-32; Schaefer, p. 78; Esslemont, p. 222.
114. Townshend, *Christ and Baha'u'llah*, pp. 115, 65, 77; *World Order*, Fall 1978, p. 16.
115. *Baha'i World Faith*, pp. 60-61, cf. pp. 15, 49, 51, 62, 71, 20.
116. F. F. Bruce, *The Epistle to the Hebrews*, New International Commentary (Grand Rapids, MI: Eerdmans, 1973), p. 6.
117. *Baha'i World Faith*, p. v.
118. Schaefer, pp. 93-100.
119. Ibid.
120. *Gleanings from the Writings of Baha'u'llah*, pp. 75-76.
121. Sabet, p. 117.
122. Schaefer, pp. 77-79.
123. Sabet, p. 110.
124. *Gleanings from the Writings of Baha'u'llah*, p. 85.
125. *The Kitab-I-Iqan*, p. 118.
126. David Hofman, *God and His Messengers* (Oxford, England: George Ronald, 1973), p. 21.
127. Shoghi Effendi (trans.) *The Hidden Words of Baha'u'llah* (Wilmette, IL: Bah'i Publishing Trust, 1975), pp. 25, 33.
128. *World Order*, Fall 1978, p. 18; Summer 1978, p. 37.
129. *Baha'i World Faith*, p. 388.
130. Sabet, p. 112.
131. Ibid., p. 117.
132. Schaefer, p. 93.

133. Ibid.
134. Ibid., p. 90.
135. Sabet, p. 128.
136. Ibid., p. 117.
137. *Gleanings from the Writings of Baha'u'llah*, p. 158.
138. *The Kitab-I-Iqan*, pp. 44, 62-71; Mabel Hyde Pain, *The Divine Art of Living* (Wilmette, IL: Baha'i Publishing Trust, 1974), p. 124.
139. Simple, p. 21.
140. Pain, pp. 126-128.
141. Ibid., pp. 122-128.
142. Ibid., p. 126; *World Order*, Fall 1977, p. 17.
143. Taken from Miller, *The Baha'i Faith*, pp. 6-8.
144. Ibid., p. 9.
145. Ibid., pp. 9-10.
146. Miller, *The Baha'i Faith*, p. 9.
147. Ibid., p. 59.
148. *World Order*, Fall 1978, pp. 17-18.
149. Ibid., p. 18.
150. Book cover.
151. Baha'u'llah, *The Seven Valleys and the Four Valleys* (Wilmette, IL: Baha'i Publishing Trust, 1971), p. iv.
152. *World Order*, Fall 1978, p. 17.
153. Pain, p. 39.
154. *World Order*, Spring 1978, pp. 44-45.
155. *The Kitab-I-Iqan*, p. 69.
156. *World Order*, Spring 1978, pp. 49-50.
157. *The Seven Valleys and the Four Valleys*, pp. 17-18, 31, 39.
158. Ibid., p. 30.
159. Ibid., p. 38; cf. 39-41; Pain, p. 74.
160. Schaefer, p. 86.
161. *Christian Research Journal*, Winter/Spring, 1989, p. 2, internet copy.
162. *World Order*, Spring 1978, p. 51.
163. Miller, *Aqdas*, pp. 24-25, 42, 66, etc.
164. See "A Look at Islam," *World Order*, Spring 1978; cf. Fall 1977, p. 13.
165. See "Buddhism and the Baha'i Faith," *World Order*, Winter 1971–1972.
166. Baha'u'llah, *The Kitab-I-Iqan*, p. 87.
167. Cf. "Baha'u'llah to the Christians," *World Order*, Winter 1966.
168. Miller, *The Baha'i Faith*, pp. 142-144.
169. Ibid., p. 142, citing *Baha'i Scriptures*, pp. 261, 554.
170. Miller, *The Baha'i Faith*, p. 142, citing *God Passes By*, p. 213.
171. Miller, *The Baha'i Faith*, Appendix; *Aqdas*, p. 29.
172. Ibid., pp. 40-41.
173. Ibid., p. 63.
174. Miller, *The Baha'i Faith*, pp. 357-358.
175. Ibid., pp. 54-55; *Aqdas*, 71-72n.
176. Miller, pp. 49, 159-160.
177. Ibid., p. 345.
178. *Aqdas*, p. 37.
179. Miller, p. 342.
180. Ibid., p. 354.
181. Ibid., pp. 357, 423.
182. Ibid., p. 140, citing *Baha'i Scriptures* (1923), pp. 241, 243.
183. Miller, p. 140.
184. Ibid., pp. 165-166, 225-231, 353.
185. Ibid., citing *Baha'i Scriptures*, pp. 286, 289, 361, 309, 316, 317, 393, 394, 335-336, 351; *A Traveler's Narrative*, pp. 156-160.
186. *The Seven Valleys and the Four Valleys*, pp. 52, 57.
187. Sabet, p. 116.
188. *The Seven Valleys and the Four Valleys*, p. 57.
189. *Baha'i World Faith*, p. 27.
190. *World Order*, Summer 1979, p. 7; Summer 1978, p. 3; Schaefer, pp. 80-87.
191. *Gleanings from the Writings of Baha'u'llah*, pp. 21-22.
192. Sabet, chapter 8 and Schaefer, pp. 55-113 are the more "scholarly"; Townshend is replete with error. *Christ and Baha'u'llah*, pp. 11-100 (see pp. 32, 69); *The Heart of the Gospel*, pp. 11-153.
193. *Christ and Baha'u'llah*, pp. 13, 32.
194. *World Order*, Fall 1978, p. 14.
195. *Christ and Baha'u'llah*, p. 25.
196. *World Order*, p. 10; 1978, p. 38.
197. Ibid., Winter 1978–1979, pp. 7-8.
198. Beckwith, p. 39.
199. *The Kitab-I-Iqan*, pp. 66, 119; cf. pp. 82, 84-87, 199; Schaefer, pp. 72-90; Townshend, *Christ and Baha'u'llah*, pp. 16, 24, 27-29, 31-32, 58, 69, 110; *World Order*, Winter 1966, pp. 30-31; Sabet, chapters 13-14, pp. 106, 109, 134. That Sabet would quote Sears in support is indicative of the book's quality; Pain, p. 49; Abdu'l-Baha, *Christ's Promise Fulfilled*, pp. 13, 30, 58, 61; *Baha'i World Faith*, p. 38.
200. *Gleanings from the Writings of Baha'u'llah*, p. 186.
201. Ibid., p. viii.
202. Pain, p. 19.
203. *Baha'i World Faith*, p. 21.
204. Pain, p. 114, citing *Some Answered Questions*, p. 269.
205. See Sabet, p. 120.
206. Pain, pp. 78-79.
207. *Christ's Promise Fulfilled*, p. 30.
208. Ibid., p. 58.
209. Ibid., pp. 61, 17.
210. Faizi, p. 37.
211. Esslemont, p. 125.
212. *Baha'i World Faith*, p. 247.
213. Ives, *Portals to Freedom*, pp. 171-172.
214. *Baha'i World Faith*, p. 250.
215. Ives, *Portals to Freedom*, p. 172.
216. *Gleanings from the Writings of Baha'u'llah*, p. 61.
217. Abdu'l-Baha, *Christ's Promise Fulfilled*, p. 67.
218. Ibid., p. 54.
219. Sabet, p. 114.
220. Pain, p. 43.
221. Miller, *Aqdas*, p. 63.

Buddhism and Nichiren Shoshu Buddhism

Info at a Glance

Name: Buddhism (B); Nichiren Shoshu Buddhism or Nichiren Shoshu of America (NS).

Purpose: (B) To eradicate suffering and attain enlightenment; (NS) to receive material benefits and find happiness.

Founder: (B) Gautama Siddhartha (ca. 563–483 B.C.); (NS) Nichiren Daishonin (1222–1282 A.D.)

Source of authority: (B) The Pali canon and other Buddhist Scripture, personal experience; (NS) The Lotus Sutra and Nichiren Daishonin's writings (Gosho), personal experience.

Claim: (B) Through the Buddha's teachings, one can attain true enlightenment and find contentment; (NS) to represent the only true Buddhism.

Revealed teachings: (B) No (early Buddhism), Yes (later Buddhism); (NS) Yes

Theology: (B) Nontheistic or atheistic (early Buddhism), polytheistic (later Buddhism); (NS) polytheistic.

Occult dynamics: (B & NS) Altered states of consciousness, ritual, psychic powers, spiritism.

Key literature: (B) The Pali Canon, various other scriptures; (NS) The Lotus Sutra, the writings of Nichiren Daishonin, Daisku Ikeda and principal periodicals: *The Seikyo Times, The World Tribune,* NSA Quarterly (defunct).

Attitude toward Christianity: Rejecting.

Quote:

Rely upon yourself: do not depend upon anyone else. Make my teachings your light. Rely upon them: do not depend upon any other teaching.[1]

—The Buddha

This whole world of delusion is nothing but a shadow caused by the mind.... there is no world ... outside the mind ... To Buddha every definitive thing is illusion.... things have no reality in themselves but are like heat haze.[2]

—The Buddha

Note: In America today, there are an estimated 1,000 plus Buddhist centers and millions of practicing Buddhists. "Later," or Mahayana Buddhism, is predominate in the West, and this includes Zen, Tibetan/Tantric and Nichiren schools of Buddhism. In this chapter we will first examine Buddhism in general from a Christian perspective and then proceed to discuss the most influential Buddhist sect in the United States, Nichiren Shoshu of America (NSA or NS). Our discussion of Zen Buddhism is in the chapter entitled "Zen." A brief treatment of Tibetan Buddhism can be found in Part Two of this chapter. Also included is the testimony of a former Tibetan Buddhist and why she became a Christian.

Because we cover three different Buddhist sects, we felt a general treatment of Buddhism was warranted, although as a world faith, Buddhism is not properly included in a text on cults and new religions. This was especially necessary to indicate how far removed from "true" Buddhism NSA is. Thus, the NSA emphasis on materialism and the promotion of and seeking ones desires by worship of the Gohonzon would have been strongly repudiated by the Buddha.

DOCTRINAL SUMMARY

God: Ultimate reality is a condition of "existence" called nirvana; no supreme God exists. In NS, the equivalent is an impersonal life essence "incarnated" in the Lotus Sutra and Ghonzon.

Jesus: A wise sage (perhaps enlightened), whose teachings were distorted by Christian myths.

Salvation: Through occult meditation and ritual to attain enlightenment or true understanding of and control over "reality."

Man: In his true essence and enlightenment, one with the Buddha.

Sin: Ignorance.

Satan: An impersonal force within Nature, the personification of "evil."

Bible: Generally, a scripture containing true and false teachings.

Death: Reincarnation into nirvana.

Heaven and Hell: Temporary states of mind or places.

PART ONE:
BUDDHISM, AN OVERVIEW

A recent cover story of *Time* magazine was titled "America's Fascination with Buddhism." It noted that Buddhism was now growing "ever stronger roots" in America and the West, pointing out that American entertainment had also "become fascinated with Buddhism." Celebrity Buddhists or those somewhat interested include: Steven Seagal, who was declared the reincarnation of a fifteenth-century lama by the head of the Nyingma lineage of Tibetan Buddhism; Richard Gere, the most famous disciple of the Dalai Lama; director Martin Scorsese of *The Last Temptation of Christ* fame; rocker Tina Turner, who follows Nichiren Shoshu Buddhism; Adam Yauch, the punk rock singer of the Beastie Boys; movie producer Oliver Stone; Phil Jackson, the Chicago Bulls coach who refers to himself as a "Zen-Christian" and is author of *Sacred Hoops;* and grunger Courtney Love. (The same issue of *Time* observed that Jewish, Protestant and Catholic Buddhists believe that "Buddhist practice can be maintained without leaving one's faith of birth," however insofar as Buddhist practice supports or inculcates a Buddhist worldview,* we will see that such a view is incorrect.)

Buddhism's increasing popularity can be seen on the Internet bookstore "amazon.com," which lists more than 1,200 titles on Buddhism. *Living Buddha, Living Christ* alone has sold more than 150,000 hardcover copies. A supposedly non-religious Buddhist meditation is now taught to hundreds and probably thousands of business executives in such companies as Monsanto, where the potentially dangerous Vipassana meditation is said to be offered. Since 1988 the number of *English* language Buddhist teaching centers in America has increased from 429 to more than 1,200—almost threefold.

---

*See John Ankerberg and John Weldon, *Encyclopedia of New Age Beliefs,* chapter on Meditation.

INTRODUCTION:
BUDDHISM IN AMERICA

We have included Buddhism in an encyclopedia on cults and new religions because there are so many new Buddhist religions in America. Estimates of practicing Buddhists in America range from 1 million–6 million. It is safe to say that millions of Americans fall into three categories: practicing Buddhists, syncretists who combine Buddhism with Christianity or those who have been seriously influenced by Buddhism in their worldview through various human potential seminars, such as est. Hawaii and California have significant Buddhist influence and large Buddhist populations. The Asian population and tourism are so large in Hawaii that a Buddhist "bible" can be found next to every Gideon Bible in hotel rooms (*The Teaching of Buddha*, donated by the Buddhist Promoting Foundation of Tokyo). The American Buddhist Directory, published by The American Buddhist Movement in New York and other sources list more than 1,000 Buddhist groups and organizations currently active in the United States (each major school is represented: Theravadin, Mahayana and Tibetan/Tantric). Men like D. T. Suzuki, the late Chogyam Trungpa, Daisku Ikeda and the Dalai Lama are having considerable impact through their writings and translations or as founders and leaders of American Buddhist religions.

The 1960s–1990s also saw an increase both in academic studies of Buddhism and in the number of courses in Buddhism at American colleges and universities. A number of Buddhist schools were founded (e.g., the fully accredited Naropa Institute in Denver, Colorado; the Institute of Buddhist Studies in Berkeley, California and the College of Oriental Studies in Los Angeles). Publications promoting Buddhism are on the rise. One of the most influential of Buddhist publications is the quarterly *Tricycle*. Buddhist psychotherapy is prominent within the pages of *The Journal of Transpersonal Psychology,* the most scholarly periodical of the so-called fourth force psychology (behind psychoanalysis, behaviorism and humanistic psychology). Publishers have devoted themselves to expanding

Buddhist literature and influence in the United States (e.g., Shambala of Boston). And, again, Buddhism also has many indirect influences, as in Werner Erhard's est and The Forum.*

If all this explains why there are now so many Buddhists in the U.S., how did America come to smile so much on the Buddha? After the landmark meeting in Chicago of the "World Parliament of Religions" in 1893, Buddhist teachers and missionaries began to arrive—namely, D. T. Suzuki, Nyogen Senzaki and others—and established Buddhist subcultures in America. The new faith was soon popularized by American devotees such as Christmas Humphreys and Alan Watts, and by "beat writers" Alan Ginsberg, Jack Kerouac and Gary Snyder. (Like many others, Alan Watts had maintained that Buddhism enabled him to "get out from under the monstrously oppressive God the Father.") Waves of Indochinese war refugees continued to bring Buddhist peoples to America. Between 1970 and 1980, when the U.S. population increased by 11 percent, the Asian population increased by more than 140 percent. There are now (year 2000) more than 10 million Asians living in America, making them the third largest minority, behind blacks and Hispanics. These facts alone underscore the need for the Christian church to undertake an active encounter with Buddhism. Hundreds of thousands of mainline Christians have already converted to Buddhism or some form of its hybridization.

BUDDHISM IN THE WORLD

Buddhism encompasses both the teachings ascribed to Gautama Siddhartha (the Buddha) (563–483? B.C.) and the subsequent if question-able development of his thoughts by Buddhists in later centuries. (Such an assessment assumes that we know the true teachings of the Buddha. A number of scholars argue that the late nature of the manuscripts and other factors make it virtually impossible to know what the Buddha actually taught.) Almost innumerable forms of Buddhism exist. Some 200 sects can be found in Japan alone, many of them opposing one another in doctrine or practice. Our analysis must be recognized as being general, for there is no doctrinally precise Buddhism in the same sense that there is a doctrinally precise Christianity.*

Still, nearly all Buddhism accepts certain key teachings: a) the four noble truths; b) the eightfold path; c) the impermanence or *ultimate* nonexistence of all *dharmas* (things, events); and d) the need for enlightenment (liberation through awareness) in one form or another. We will discuss these later. Other common beliefs in Buddhism include:

1. *The Three Jewels* (also known as "the Three Refuges"): Buddha, Dharma and Sangha. These refer to 1) following the Buddha, the enlightened one; 2) accepting the Buddha's Dharma or teaching; and 3) living in harmony with the Sangha, the Buddhist community. In other words, one finds refuge in the Buddha, his teachings and the Buddhist community.

2. *The Five Precepts:* these involve rules of ethical practice, such as abstaining from harming all living things (ahimsa), false speech and sexual misconduct.

---

*Werner Erhard acknowledges his indebtedness to many religious systems. But he states, "I don't think that any one of them in particular was more important than any other with the possible exception of Zen being the most influential."[3] In the official biography of Erhard by philosopher William Warren Bartley III, *Werner Erhard: The Transformation of a Man: The Founding of Est,* Erhard is quoted as saying, ". . . of all the disciplines I studied, practiced and learned, Zen was the essential one. . . . It is entirely appropriate for persons interested in est to also be interested in Zen."[4] (For a thorough analysis of est/The Forum, see our *Encyclopedia of New Age Beliefs* (Harvest House, 1996).

*For example, biblical Christianity everywhere has the same beliefs concerning the nature of God (infinite, personal and triune), the Person and work of Jesus Christ (incarnate, atoning Savior), the means of salvation (by grace through faith alone), and so on. Buddhism, on the other hand, has within itself quite different views as to the nature of ultimate reality, the nature of the Buddha and the means of salvation. Considered historically, of course, there are endless sects and cults of Christianity, from gnosticism, modalism and Arianism in the early centuries to their counterparts today, such as Christian Science, "Jesus Only" and Jehovah's Witnesses. But none are truly Christian. By contrast, almost all Buddhists sects, even those Buddha himself would probably or certainly not accept, are considered Buddhist by Buddhists today.

3. *The Ten Precepts:* these include the five precepts and the aspiration to abstain from certain activities, such as accepting gold or silver, taking untimely meals, dancing and singing, forms of personal adornment and taking high seats or seats of honor.

The hundreds of millions of Buddhists worldwide can be divided into two broad schools, Theravada and Mahayana.* While the Mahayanist is by far the largest, the Theravada is generally held to be the original, "true" Buddhism. (According to majority opinion, Mahayanism developed centuries later.) The Theravada school is the only survivor of some 18 sects that arose in the first four centuries after Buddha's death. The sects were collectively termed *Hinayana,* or "lesser vehicle," by the *Mahayanists* (meaning "greater vehicle"). According to some, the term *Hinayana* was used because in the Hinayanist perspective enlightenment "salvation" (due to the rigors of the path) was possible for only a select few, whereas the later Mahayanists made enlightenment the possibility for all. According to others, the terms are used as follows: Hinayana Buddhists are those who seek to reach enlightenment merely for their own personal welfare, whereas Mahayana Buddhists seek to help others attain enlightenment as well, even though this involves the obligation to reincarnate time and time again until all "sentient beings" have attained enlightenment.

Geographically, Theravada is "Southern Buddhism" (the national religion of Siam, Ceylon, Laos, Cambodia and Burma); Mahayana is "Northern Buddhism" (China, Korea, Japan, Tibet and Nepal). In the U.S., two typical Mahayanist schools are Zen and Nichiren Buddhism. Although Buddhism may be broadly classified into these two schools, the Theravada and Mahayanist, many Buddhist scholars refer to three schools, adding the controversial Tibetan, or Tantric, Buddhism as a separate school.

The first Buddhist scriptures were written down by Theravadin monks about 400 years after the Buddha lived. These scriptures were written on palm leaves and became known as the Tipitaka or Pali Canon. The former term means "three baskets" and refers to the threefold division of the scriptures termed Vinaya Pitaka, Sutta Pitaka and Abhidhamma Pitaka. The first division, the Vinaya Pitaka, involves discipline for Buddhist monks concerning the 227 rules by which they are to live. The second division, the Sutta Pitaka, comprises the teachings of the Buddha on the four noble truths and the eightfold path as well as popular Buddhist literature such as the Dhammapada and the Jataka Tales (the Dhammapada is an anthology of the Buddha's sayings and the Jataka Tales are stories of Buddha's [alleged] previous lives). The Abhidhamma Pitaka involves philosophical teachings that underscore how Buddhists understand the meaning and purpose of life.

As Buddhism spread outward in different geographical directions, a number of different doctrines and scriptures developed. The Theravada school believes that scriptural authenticity is determined by the texts that were allegedly derived from the Buddha's teachings. The Mahayana school added additional scriptures that it claimed were just as authoritative, even though these scriptures had little to do with the Buddha's teaching as handed down by the Theravadin school. These scriptures seemed to have originated by mystical revelations and "vary in form and introduce both mythological and philosophical features not found in the *Theravada.*"[5] Some general differences between the Theravadin and Mahayana schools can be seen on the chart on page 84.

THE BUDDHA AND HIS TEACHING

According to Buddhist history, Siddhartha Gautama was raised in a wealthy family and sheltered and protected from life's unpleasantness and tragedies. One day, however, he saw the world as it really was. In observing a decrepit old

---

*Buddhist terms are frequently spelled differently. This is because the Buddhist scriptures are divided into those of the Theravadins, which use the Pali language, and those of the Mahayanists, which use the Sanskrit language. Thus, Nirvana in Sanskrit is Nibbana in Pali. The Buddha is Siddhartha Gautama in Sanskrit but Siddhatta Gotama in Pali and so on.

THERAVADA	MAHAYANA
Buddha is a human teacher	Buddha is an enlightened, supermundane eternal being and/or "god"
Complete self-effort for enlightenment	Self-effort is necessary, however additional help from Buddha, Bodhisattvas (Buddhist "saviors") and Buddhist gods is accepted
Gods are rejected	Gods are accepted
Prayer equals meditation	Prayer may also be petitionary
Anti-supernatural	The supernatural is accepted
Attains the state of Buddhahood (Nirvana apart from the world; one can only help oneself)	Attains the state of Bodhisattva (Nirvana in the world; e.g., a Bodhisattva postpones Nirvana to help others find it)
Atheism or agnosticism	Atheism, agnosticism or polytheism
Nirvana replaces Samsara (existence)	Nirvana is Samsara (existence)

man, a corpse, a diseased man and a beggar, he realized the fundamental human condition was one of suffering. For the Buddha, the essential problem of humanity was not really one of sin, selfishness or rebellion against God, as Christianity teaches. It was suffering and misery. But how could suffering be alleviated? This occupied the Buddha's thoughts and he eventually received "enlightenment" on the matter and formulated the foundation of Buddhism: the four noble truths and the eightfold path.[6]

The Four Noble Truths and the Eightfold Path

From a Christian perspective, Siddhartha attempted to find a solution to the *symptoms* of our problem instead of the basic, or underlying, problem itself. In Christianity, suffering and misery are caused largely by our sin and rebellion against God. Rejecting God and the dynamics of our relationship to God, Buddha dealt with symptoms (e.g., suffering) instead of causes (e.g., sin). In turn, this basic misdiagnosis of the human problem conditions everything subsequent in Buddhism.

In brief, the four noble truths are: (1) all life involves suffering; (2) suffering is caused by desire (e.g., "selfish" craving defined, in part, as the desire to exist as an independent self); (3) desire can be overcome; and (4) the means to overcome desire is the eightfold path. The eightfold path comprises the proper, or correct, exercise of eight conditions or actions aimed at eliminating desire and hence suffering. These include: (1) right vision (knowledge or views); (2) right conception (aspirations); (3) right speech; (4) right behavior (conduct); (5) right livelihood; (6) right effort; (7) right concentration or mindfulness; and (8) right one-pointed contemplation (or meditation).

One must remember to interpret these eight requirements from a *Buddhist* rather than from a Western or Christian perspective. Thus, with distinctly Buddhist implications, they become implicitly or explicitly nonChristian. Further, given Buddhist premises, the Christian worldview is easily considered a spiritual detriment or evil.[7] For example, right understanding is the correct understanding and acceptance of the four noble truths and the Buddhist perception of the world and self. Right concentration, or mindfulness, is the sense of awareness of one's own actions as achieved by meditation (often leading to occult trance states or the development of psychic powers). Right morality "does not consist in passive obedience to a code imposed by a God . . ." but is determined by tradition (ultimately determined by the Buddha, i.e., the first Buddhist traditions).[8] In fact, according to Buddha, belief in the Christian God and morality would have been considered by him to be delusive, harmful beliefs. He thus argued, "It is no wonder that people holding these conceptions lose hope and neglect efforts to act wisely and avoid evil."[9]

The Law of Dependent Origination

The dilemma of suffering is exemplified by the Buddhist "law of dependent origination," which asserts that existence itself perpetuates suffering in a vicious cycle. Thus, existence itself (the ever impermanent flux of phenomena, both mental and physical) causes corresponding effects. These effects result in more impermanent phenomena, and these in turn cause ignorance of the permanent state (nirvana). Such ignorance of reality brings more harmful desires, which result in more suffering, which brings karmic rebirth. All this perpetuates a bondage to individual existence from which there is no escape. In *The Teaching of Buddha* we read the following statements by Buddha:

> Because of ignorance and greed, people imagine discriminations where, in reality, there are no discriminations. Inherently, there is no discrimination of right and wrong in human behavior; but people, because of ignorance, imagine such distinctions and judge them as right or wrong. . . . As a result, they become attached to a delusive existence. . . . In reality, therefore, it is their own mind that causes the delusions of grief, lamentation, pain and agony. This whole world of delusion is nothing but a shadow caused by the mind. . . . It is from ignorance and greed that the world of delusion is born, and all the vast complexity of coordinating causes and conditions exists within the mind and nowhere else. Both life and death arise from the mind and exist within the mind. . . . An unenlightened life rises from a mind that is bewildered by its own world of delusion. If we learn that there is no world of delusion outside the mind, the bewildered mind becomes clear; and because we cease to create impure surroundings, we attain Enlightenment. . . . Since everything in this world is brought about by causes and conditions, there can be no fundamental distinctions among things. The apparent distinctions exist because of people's absurd and discriminating thoughts. . . . In action there is no discrimination between right in wrong, but people make a distinction for their own convenience. Buddha keeps away from these discriminations and looks upon the world as upon a passing cloud. To Buddha every definitive thing is delusion. . . .[10]

So how does the Buddhist escape from the endless round of desire, karma and more desire?

In order to understand the Buddhist solution, we must further understand how Buddhism views reality.

In Buddhism, existence is believed to be made up of extremely temporary and ever changing phenomena or aggregates. These are termed dharmas or skandhas. *Dharmas* are experiential moments that are the building blocks of existence. (In another definition, Dharma means Buddhist Law, i.e., Buddha's teachings).[11] *Skandhas* refer to the five aggregates making up the person: (1) the body; (2) feelings; (3) perceptions; (4) volition, impulses and emotions; and (5) consciousness.[12] Buddhism maintains that existence by its very nature is so fleeting that none of its components can in any sense be held to be permanent. Such phenomena (broken down to their constituent parts) exist for so short a time (e.g., nano-seconds) that they cannot be said to resemble permanence. However, reality must be something permanent if it is to be real. That which is impermanent cannot be real. Hence, one must transcend all impermanence and arrive at nirvana, the only permanent and real state.[13]

Naturally, if existence is impermanent and "unreal," the logical solution is to eradicate *our* personal existence and achieve permanence: that alone which is real. As noted, this is the Buddhist goal: to attain the state of nirvana. The Buddha, who sometimes had little love for common sense, argued that since existence is unreal to treat it as real is absurd. Further, to treat it as real is a grave error preventing enlightenment. And so he scolded the ignorant masses for believing that the world is real. "It is a mistake to regard this world as either a temporal world or as a real one. But ignorant people of this world assume that this is a real world and proceed to act upon that absurd assumption. But as this world is only an illusion, their acts, being based on error, only lead them into harm and suffering. A wise man, recognizing the world is but an illusion, does not act as if it were real, so he escapes the suffering."[14]

Again, the Buddhist view of phenomenal existence (things, people, the universe) is that it is in such a state of constant flux and impermanence that, ultimately, it has no reality in any meaningful, personal or eternal sense. It is not, for example, that the ego (personal existence) does not exist; it "exists" as the sum of its various constituents, which are in constant flux, and as such it can be perceived and distinguished as a separate entity. Still, our existence has no reality in the sense of being something permanent. This is because the Buddhist concept of impermanence does not believe anything phenomenal can be permanent long enough to be real. Existence is the delusory creation of our minds. Thus, even the perception of the individual self is a delusion. "Separate individual existence is really an illusion, for the self has neither beginning nor ending, is eternally changing, and possesses only a phenomenal existence."[15] "Existence consists of dharmas, things or objects, but what can be said of these objects? They are all impermanent and changing, and nothing can be said of them at one moment which is not false the next. They are as unreal as the atman [self] itself."[16]

One Buddhist scripture complains that the "foolish common people do not understand that what is seen is merely (the product of) their own mind. Being convinced that there exists outside a variety of objects . . . they produce false imaginings."[17] Reminiscent of advita Vedanta, other scriptures liken conventional reality to a magical illusion, a mirage and a dream.[18] Buddhism tells us that since reality as we perceive it does not exist, we should strive to arrive at this awareness and come to that state which alone is permanent, the state of nirvana. Ostensibly, this state lies somewhere "in-between" personal existence (which it isn't) and complete annihilation (which it also, allegedly, isn't). The person who recognizes this Buddhist truth is held to be in an enlightened state of being, for one now understands what is real and what is not real.

Essentially, Buddhism is a religion with one principal goal: to eliminate individual suffering by attaining the permanent state—nirvana. In attaining this goal, one does not look to God for help but, paradoxically, only to the impermanent: to man himself. From the delusory mind, the illusory world appears, but "from this same mind, the world of enlightenment appears."[19] (One wonders how a mind so deluded and dis-ordered—that it creates a world of illusion—could ever discover enlightenment from that delusion?) In spite of its denial of any permanent reality to man, Buddhism is essentially, if paradoxically, a humanistic faith that in the end destroys what it virtually worships: man as man. As Hendrik Kraemer, former professor of the History of Religions at the University of Leiden, Netherlands, asserts: "Buddhism teaches with a kind of prophetic rigour that what really matters is man and his deliverance, and nothing else. . . . Behind the screen of sublime philosophies and mystical and ethical 'ways' to deliverance, or in the garb of fantastic textures of magic and occultism, man remains the measure of all things."[20]

In Buddhism, man has no savior but himself; hence people need only look inward for deliverance. "Since Buddhism does not have a God, it cannot have somebody who is regarded as God's prophet or messiah."[21] Buddhism, then, is: (1) atheistic, practically speaking; (2) agnostic, in that most Buddhists don't really care if a *supreme* God exists (irrespective of the polytheism of later Buddhism); and (3) antitheistic, in that belief in a supreme Creator God, as in Christianity, is something evil because it prohibits personal liberation.

We now turn to a discussion of Buddhist and Christian philosophy, where these ideas and their implications are seen more fully.

BUDDHISM VS. CHRISTIANITY

In this section, we will briefly evaluate Buddhist attempts to reach Christians by maintaining that there are few or no essential differences between the two faiths. Then we will show how the basic philosophy of Buddhism makes such attempts futile. Such attempts may indeed be fruitful for Buddhist proselytisation, but they are fundamentally dishonest.

The *Christian Research Journal* for Summer 1996 contained the following account: "A few months ago my mother sent me a monthly newsletter that the San Jose Buddhist church distributes among its members. My mother thought the major article in the newsletter would prove what she had been saying for nearly 30 years—that the differences between Buddhism and Christianity are insignificant compared to what they have in common, and therefore any further discussion between us about these differences would be a waste of time."[22] That newsletter article by Buddhist Rev. Ronald Y. Nakasone claimed that Jesus and Buddha taught basically the same things and that Jesus was "close to Buddhahood." Like many other Buddhists, Nakasone based his rejection of the Christ of the New Testament on the highly questionable findings of liberal theologians, in particular, Burton L. Mack of the so-called Jesus Seminar. Those who disagreed with his assessment of Jesus were said to be intolerant and narrow-minded. On p. 47, the same issue critiqued the best-selling book, *Living Buddha, Living Christ,* by Thich Nhat Hahn. Hahn believes that Christians who teach that Jesus is the only Way are potential murderers who foster "religious intolerance and discrimination."

Yet one can only ask, aren't Buddhists who argue this way being intolerant of Christianity? Aren't they discriminating against Christianity when they distort it and make it teach things it does not? This is clearly evident in Hahn's attempt to reinterpret "true" Christianity as Buddhism. He claims, "I do not think there is that much difference between Christians and Buddhists," and "when you are a truly happy Christian, you are also a Buddhist. And vice versa." Thus, in order to support Buddhist doctrine, Christian distinctives are ignored and Christian doctrine is reinterpreted as Buddhist belief. How is that fair—or ethical? For example, even though the Buddhist concept of nirvana and the biblical concept of the kingdom of God are contradictory, and worlds apart philosophically and theologically, Hahn sees them as equivalent: "Buddhists and Christians know that nirvana or the kingdom of God is within our hearts." Again, is this being fair to Christianity? Is it being tolerant of Christian beliefs? Hahn also says, "We are of the same reality as Jesus . . . Jesus is not only our Lord, but he is also our Father, our Teacher, our Brother, and our Self." Again, he is egregiously making Christianity teach Buddhist beliefs. Yet Hahn claims that it "would be cruel" to have Buddhists "abandon their own spiritual roots and embrace your [Christian] faith." But this is exactly what he asks Christians to do with their own spiritual roots, to abandon Christianity and embrace Buddhism. Again, is this being tolerant of Christianity?

Buddhist-Christian dialogue will be equitable only when Buddhists treat Christianity and Christians fairly. This means they must stop assuming that their own presuppositions about life and religion are absolute truth while Christian beliefs are as changeable as the seasons, based on nothing more than Buddhists' personal preference. In books of this nature we often find such double standards. Quite in error, Christianity is held out as irrational and intolerant while Buddhism is declared to be supremely rational and open-minded. But what we actually find is that Buddhists are genuinely intolerant of Christianity and that their own doctrines are irrational. For example, the same *CRI Journal* review quotes Hahn as declaring, "For a Buddhist to be attached to any doctrine, even a Buddhist one, is to betray the Buddha," because Buddhists believe it is impossible for a doctrine to adequately convey reality. Further, "nothing can be talked about, perceived, or described by representation." Yet Hahn and other Buddhists are clearly attached to Buddhist doctrine; after all, they spend so much time writing books in defense of it and trying to live it. And of course if nothing can be described by representation, the very words that Buddhist writers use to describe Buddhism are meaningless.

Thus, in an era pregnant with tolerance for everything, some Christians have embraced Buddhism and numerous attempts have been made to unify Buddhism and Christianity by ecumenically minded members of both faiths. Friendly Buddhist and Christian encounters are the vogue on some university campuses. Through no fault of its own however, "Christianity" is frequently the loser in such encounters. Thus, mainline Christians who have no real comprehension of biblical Christianity but are fascinated by the alluring or mystical nature of Buddhist metaphysics may leave their "faith" and become Buddhists. Or, they may maintain an odd mixture of both religions, one that is ultimately unfaithful to both. As we have indicated,

Buddhists who "accept" Christianity merely do so to transform it into Buddhism. Professor of Buddhism and Japanese Studies at Tokyo and Harvard Universities respectively, Masaharu Anesaki, illustrates this by his assimilation of Jesus with the Buddha. "In short we Buddhists are ready to accept Christianity; nay, more, our faith in Buddha is faith in Christ. *We see Christ because we see Buddha*. . . . We can hope not in vain for the *second advent* of Christ [that is] the appearance of the [prophesied] future *Buddha Metteya*."[23]

Nevertheless, rather than seeking a unity among these religions, the truth is much closer to the gut feeling of Zen Buddhist D. T. Suzuki, who states, as he undoubtedly reflects upon the Buddhist concept of suffering, "Whenever I see a crucified figure of Christ, I cannot help thinking of the gap that lies deep between Christianity and Buddhism."[24] Or, as a Buddhist monk once told us, "Buddhism and Christianity are forever irreconcilable—one is based on enlightenment, the other on delusion."

Contrasts Between Buddhism and Christianity

The truth is that similarities between Buddhism and Christianity are only on the surface. For example, many have claimed a similarity between Jesus Christ's saving role in Christianity and the Bodhisattva's savior role in later Buddhism. But these roles are entirely contradictory. In Christianity, "Christ died for our sins" (1 Corinthians 15:3). This means He saves us from the penalty of our sins by taking God's judgment of sin in His own Person. Jesus paid the penalty of sin (death) for sinners by dying in their place. Thus, He offers a free gift of salvation to anyone who believes and accepts what He has done on their behalf (John 3:16). The central ideas involved in Christ's saving role—God's holiness, propitiatory atonement, forgiveness of sin, salvation as a free gift of God's grace through faith in Christ and so on—are all foreign to Buddhism. The Bodhisattva's role of savior is entirely different than that of Jesus Christ's. The Bodhisattva has no concern with sin in an ultimate sense, only with the end of suffering. He has no concept of God's wrath against sin or the need for a propitiatory atone-

ment. He has no belief in an infinite personal God who created men and women in His image. He has no belief in a loving God who freely forgives sinners. His only sacrifice is his postponement of entering nirvana so that he can help others find Buddhist enlightenment. That is, having achieved self-perfection, the Bodhisattva could have freely entered nirvana at death. Instead, he chose another incarnation in order to help others attain self-perfection and nirvana more quickly.

Anyone who argues that there is an essential similarity between the Buddhist and Christian concepts of a savior is quite mistaken. In fact, at their core Buddhism and Christianity are irreconcilable. Indeed, virtually every major Christian doctrine is denied in Buddhism and vice versa. Merging the two traditions only results in a disservice to both.

Many Buddhists, however, have long recognized the differences between the two faiths. The knowledgeable Buddhist is aware that the doctrines and teachings of biblical Christianity hold to and proclaim openly those things which Buddhists reject (as mere ignorance and spiritual hindrances); further, Christianity openly opposes those things which Buddhism endorses as essential for genuine enlightenment.

For example, Christianity is interwoven with the monotheistic grandeur of an infinite, personal, triune God (Matthew 28:19; John 17:3; Isaiah 43:10-11, 44:6); Buddhism is agnostic and, practically speaking, atheistic (or in later form, polytheistic). Christianity involves the absolute necessity for belief in Jesus Christ as personal Savior from sin (John 14:6; Acts 4:12; 1 Timothy 2:5-6); Buddhism has no Savior from sin, and even in the Mahayana tradition, as we have seen, the savior concepts are quite dissimilar. Christianity stresses salvation by grace through faith alone (John 3:16; Ephesians 2:8-9); Buddhism stresses enlightenment by works through meditative practices that seek the alleviation of "ignorance" and desire. Christianity promises forgiveness of *all* sin now (Ephesians 1:7; Colossians 2:13) and the eventual elimination of sin and suffering for all eternity (Revelation 21:3-4); Buddhism, since it holds that there is no God, promises not the forgiveness and eradication of sin but the elimination of suffering (eventually) and the ultimate eradication of the individual. Christianity rejects pagan mysticism and all occultism (e.g., Deuteronomy 18:9–12); Buddhism accepts or actively endorses them.

Wherever we look philosophically, we see the irreconcilable contrasts between these two faiths. Christianity stresses salvation from sin, not from life itself (1 John 2:2). Christianity exalts personal existence as innately good, since man was created in God's image, and thus Christianity promises eternal life and fellowship with a personal God (Genesis 1:26, 31; Revelation 21:3–4). Christianity has a distinctly defined teaching about the afterlife (heaven or hell, e.g., Matthew 25:46; Revelation 20:10–15). It promises eternal immortality for man as man, but perfected in every way (Revelation 21:3–4).

On the other hand, Buddhism teaches reincarnation and has only a mercurial nirvana, wherein man no longer remains man or, where, in Mahayana, there exists temporary heavens or hells and the final "deification" of man through a merging with the ultimate pantheistic-cosmic Buddha nature. But Christianity denies that reincarnation is a valid belief, a denial based on the fact of Christ's propitiatory atonement for sin. In other words, if Christ died to forgive *all* sin, there is no reason for a person to pay the penalty for their own sin ("karma") over many lifetimes (Colossians 2:13; Hebrews 9:27–28; 10:10, 14).

Consider further contrasts. In Christianity life itself is good and given honor and meaning; in Buddhism one finds it difficult to affirm that life is ultimately worth living, for life and suffering are always inseparable. In Christianity, Jesus Christ came that people "might have life and have it more abundantly" (John 10:10); in Buddhism, Buddha came that people might rid themselves of personal existence. In Christianity, the world is the loving creation of God; in Buddhism it is only the temporary illusion of a deluded mind. In Christianity, God will either glorify or punish the spirit of man (John 5:28–29); in Buddhism no spirit exists to be glorified or punished. In Christianity, absolute morality is a central theme (Ephesians 1:4); in Buddhism absolute morality is nonexistent.

Christianity is essentially theistic, stressing God's self-revelation and gracious initiative on behalf of man's helpless moral and spiritual condition. Buddhism is essentially humanistic, stressing man's self-achievement. Thus, in Buddhism man alone is the author of salvation; Christianity sees this as an absolute impossibility because innately man has no power to save himself (Ephesians 2:8–9; Titus 3:5).

We could go on. Suffice it to say that the form of romantic humanism that inspires liberal religionists to see fundamental similarities in the two faiths is no more than wishful thinking. It is not utterly surprising, however, that Western religious humanists would promote Buddhism, for in both systems man is the measure of all things (a god of sorts), even if in the latter the end result is a form of personal self-annihilation. But to that extent both are humanistic, they encompass the antithesis of Christianity, whose goal is to glorify God and not man (Jeremiah 17:5; Jude 24–25).

Glorifying God is unimportant and irrelevant to Buddhists. But biblically, to the extent that God is ignored or opposed, people must correspondingly suffer. Here we see the ultimate irony of Buddhism: in ignoring God, Buddhists believe they can escape suffering, but this will only perpetuate it forever. This is the real tragedy of Buddhism, especially of so-called Christian Buddhism. The very means to escape suffering (true faith in the biblical Christ) is rejected in favor of a self-salvation, which can result only in eternal suffering (Matthew 25:46; Revelation 20:10–15).

The following discussion further illustrates how Buddhism seeks to eliminate that which Christianity sees as foundational: (1) the glorification of God and Christ, (2) a real permanent existence and (3) personal individual salvation.

1. Buddhism rejects the God of Christian worship. In this three-volume *Hinduism and Buddhism*, Sir Charles Eliot acknowledges: "On the whole it is correct to say that Buddhism (except perhaps in very exceptional sects) has always taken and still takes a point of view which has little in common with European theism. The world is not thought of as the handiwork of a divine personality, nor the moral law as his will."[25] Several Buddhists have told us, "The Christian God is irrelevant." A former Buddhist told us, "One of my favorite Tibetan Lamas told me: 'We simply don't have a clue what these Jews and Christians mean when they talk about their God.'" Buddhism is fundamentally atheistic, and therefore the words of the psalmist come to mind, "The fool has said in his heart, 'There is no God.'"

2. Buddhism rejects God's creation. While Theravada believes that reality is temporarily "real," it is nevertheless insubstantial, impermanent and in a continual state of flux. It is not, as God's creation is now, real, nor as it will be, eternal but perfect. Thus, Theravada denies that the universe will have an eternal existence, because only nirvana is permanent. For Theravada *nirvana* is set in *contrast* to *samsara,* which is the world of impermanent existence as we know it.

The Mahayanists, on the other hand, believe that in addition to its constant flux, the universe is "empty"; that is, when broken down to its smallest components the universe is "nothing" in and of itself and ultimately "non-existent." We see this Mahayanist perspective in *Buddhism: Its Doctrines and Methods* by Tibetan Buddhist Alexandra David-Neel:

> The elements called illusion, desire, karma, and birth, which constitute the individual life, have no real existence in the absolute meaning of this word; they have none even in the restricted sense as regards the conditions of life in samsara. The rope which was taken for a snake is not in itself a snake, nor is it ever a snake, either in the darkness or in the light. What is it, then, that is called phenomenal reality (samsara)? Obsessed by the unreal demons of their "ego" and their "mind," stupid people—those who are of the world—imagine that they can perceive separate entities, whereas in reality these do not exist. . . .[26]

3. Buddhism rejects Christian salvation as ignorance. In the Christian sense, Buddhists have no concept of a personal creator and no concept of a savior. In Buddhism, the concept of Christian salvation is not only irrelevant, it is even spiritually dangerous. Why? Because it seeks to save and perpetuate an illusion, the personal self. According to Buddhism, any desire to affirm and perpetuate what Christianity calls "the image of God" in us would logically be considered evil. "Desire in itself is not evil. It is desire to affirm the lower self [the image of God in us], to live in it, cling to it, identify oneself with it, instead of with the Universal self, that is evil."[27] But this is the essence of what it means to be human according to Christianity. In a clinging to temporal existence, to the personal desires that Christianity finds good (e.g., the desire to glorify God and to live the Christian life), in hoping for personal immortality, and in much more that is Christian, all these, according to Buddhism, are ignorant approaches to life preventing enlightenment, true salvation.

By definition then, Christianity insulates against and prevents Buddhist enlightenment. But the reverse is also true. Buddhism insulates against and prevents biblical salvation. Where God, Christ and the atonement are denied, there can be no salvation. How then can Buddhism look with favor upon Christianity? How can the serene and compassionate Buddha sit and smile unperturbed at the bloody cross? In Buddhism: "Ignorance, then, is not only lack of knowledge, but wrong knowledge; it is that which hides things and prevents one from seeing them as they are in reality."[28] "There is no mention of a Supreme Divinity, nor any promise of superhuman aid for suffering humanity."[29]

In *Conversations: Christian and Buddhist,* Father Dom Aelred Graham (author of *Zen Catholicism*) talked with various Buddhists; in the following, Buddhist instructor Fujimoto Roshi. Roshi is speaking: "Father Graham asked whether it is possible for a Christian to attain Enlightenment. I would say that it is. However, as long as Christians are attached to *the* Christianity [i.e., exclusivistic, doctrinal Christianity], as they have been, it is *not* possible."[30]

Clearly, Buddhism and Christianity are antagonistic to one another and only when this is accepted will Christians feel the necessity to uncompromisingly share the truth of Jesus Christ with Buddhists. And perhaps then Buddhists will recognize that an urgent choice must be made:

> Jesus said to him, "I am the way, and the truth, and the life; no one comes to the Father, but through Me." (John 14:6 NAS)

> Salvation is found in no one else, for there is no other name under heaven given to men by which we must be saved. (Acts 4:12)

> And this is eternal life, that they may know Thee, the only true God, and Jesus Christ whom Thou hast sent. (John 17:3 NAS)

> The one who believes in the Son of God has the witness in himself; the one who does not believe God has made Him a liar, because he has not believed in the witness that God has borne concerning His Son. And the witness is this, that God has given us eternal life, and this life is in His Son. He who has the Son has the life; he who does not have the Son of God does not have the life. (1 John 5:10–12 NAS)

BUDDHISM AND JESUS CHRIST

As a whole, Buddhism has little directly to say about Jesus Christ. It does acknowledge what most men do: that He was a great person. For the most part, however, His Gospel teachings are largely ignored and a more convenient Jesus is accepted: one who, along with the Buddha, smiles serenely. On the other hand, there is a sense in which Buddhism explicitly rejects Jesus Christ. After all, if no "person" exists, then no "personal savior" exists either. So what is there to save? The central message of Christianity (John 3:16) is thus dismissed as remnants of beclouded consciousness.

This explicit rejection of the biblical Jesus is to be expected, for He rejects what Buddhism accepts. The biblical Jesus stresses repentance before God (Matthew 4:17). He believes in a loving, infinite, personal Creator who makes moral demands upon and judges His creatures (Luke 12:5). He denies the possibility of self-perfection and refers to Himself alone as the Savior of the world (Matthew 20:28; 26:28; John 6:29, 47; 14:6). He is God's unique and only Son (John 3:16, 18), and the creator God is His personal Father (John 14:5–6). Spiritual enlightenment and salvation come only by Him (John 14:6) because He is "the true light" of the world (John 1:9; 8:12; 12:46). It is impossible that these could come through Buddha and his philosophy, or through Bodhisattvas and their sacrifice of remaining in the world, or through any other self-achieving method (cf. Matthew 19:24–26). Jesus Christ utterly rejects polytheism and paganism (e.g., Matthew 6:7; 22:37; Luke 4:8). His worldview is thoroughly based on moral absolutes, and it is by His moral standards that all creatures, heavenly and earthly, will be judged and required to give an account (Luke 10:19–20; John 5:22–29; Colossians 1:16–18; 1 Corinthians 6:3). Jesus accepted the permanency (Matthew 25:46) and utility of suffering in this life (Hebrews 2:10; 5:8–9); indeed, it is by Jesus' suffering alone that the world is redeemed and through which (in part) God sanctifies His people (Philippians 3:10; 1 Peter 2:21, 24; 3:18; 4:1).

Although ecumenically minded people would find it difficult to accept, the Jesus Christ of history is not merely un-Buddhist but anti-Buddhist. If we could bring Jesus and Buddha together for a discussion, neither Jesus nor Gautama would find the other's worldview acceptable. According to Christ, Buddha would certainly not have been spiritually enlightened—far from it. His rejection of a creator God would classify him as a pagan unbeliever, however adept he was at philosophical speculation. Jesus would view Gautama as in need of salvation as much as everyone else. Conversely, Buddha would have no need for Christ as Savior, for Buddha taught total, unswerving self-reliance. As we quoted earlier, "Rely upon yourself: do not depend on anyone else." Compare this with Jeremiah 17:5: "Cursed is the man who trusts in mankind and makes flesh his strength and whose heart turns away from the Lord." Thus, in discussing Buddhism's appeal to modern people, Stephen Neill correctly observes that this appeal is based squarely upon prideful self-sufficiency:

> For the modern man one of the most attractive things in this scheme is that in it he is entirely cast back upon himself. "Therefore, O Ananda, take the self as a lamp; take the self as a refuge.

Betake yourselves to no external refuges. Hold fast as a refuge to the truth. Look not for refuge to anyone besides yourself. Work out your own salvation with diligence." [In] the Maha-Parinibbana-Sutta, one of the most famous of Buddhist classics. . . . The Buddha attained to enlightenment by his own intense concentration; he called in no help from any god or savior. So it must be with the disciple. God has been abolished, at least as far as any possibility of a practical relationship to him is concerned. There is no hope for a man outside of himself—or rather in his inner apprehension of the meaning of the Buddha, the Law and the Order. "Man for himself." That is the modern mood. The last thing that a modern man desires is to be told that he needs to be saved, or that he requires the help of a savior. . . . So naturally Buddhism has attractive power. . . .[31]

Whereas Theravada views the Buddha as an enlightened man (more enlightened, no doubt, than the biblical Christ, but still a man), Mahayana places Buddha on the level of a divine being who rivals Christ in his deity, although still falling far short of the biblical concept.

The Mahayana text *Matrceta Satapancasatkastotra I*, 2–4 states of Buddha: "To go to him for refuge, to praise and to honor him, to abide in his religion, that is fit for those with sense. The only Protector, he is without faults or their residues; The all-knowing, he has all the virtues, and that without fail. For even the spiteful cannot find with any justice any fault in the Lord—in his thought, words or deeds."[32] The Lotus Sutra (Saddharmapundarika) says of him: "He thus becomes the Saviour of the world with its Gods" (XXIV, 17).[33]

And in the area of miraculous we find another disagreement with Christian faith: "It may be fairly said that Buddhism is not a miraculous religion in the sense that none of its central doctrines depend on miracles."[34] By contrast how many Christological themes or doctrines depend upon the miraculous? To name just several: messianic prophecy (Psalm 22; Isaiah 9:6); the incarnation (Philippians 2); the virgin birth (Matthew 1:25); Christ's miracles as proof of his Messiahship (Matthew 8:15–17); the miracles associated with the crucifixion (Matthew 27:50–53); the resurrection (Luke 24:36–39); the

ascension (Acts 1:9–10); and the second coming (Matthew 24).

Clearly, Buddha and Jesus are not just a little bit short of being friends! The suffering and exaltation of Jesus Christ is hardly equivalent to the serene peacefulness of the Buddha entering nirvana. Jesus came to save the world, not himself (John 12:27). Indeed, Jesus said, "Whoever wants to save his life will lose it" (Matthew 16:25). He obeyed and glorified the very God whom Buddha so contentedly and forcefully rejected (John 17:4).

TALKING WITH BUDDHISTS

The weaknesses of Buddhism are so vast and the strengths of Christianity so powerful that anyone with a grasp of the details of Buddhist and Christian philosophy should at least be able to give their Buddhist friends something to think about. Clive Erricker, a lecturer and prolific writer in the field of religious studies, with a special interest in Buddhism, writes accurately of the Buddha when he discusses what the Buddha did *not* claim. In stark contrast to Jesus, "[Buddha] did not even claim that his teachings were a unique and original source of wisdom. . . . [Citing John Bowker in *Worlds of Faith*, 1983] Buddha always said, 'Don't take what I'm saying [on my own authority], just try to analyze as far as possible and see whether what I'm saying makes sense or not. If it doesn't make sense, discard it. If it does make sense, then pick it up.'"[35]

Now we will employ the Buddha's own admonition to see if what he taught "makes sense." If it does not, let's simply follow his admonition and discard it. To begin, consider the following statement by noted theologian J. I. Packer:

God's world is never friendly to those who forget its Maker. The Buddhists, who link their atheism with a thorough pessimism about life, are to that extent correct. Without God, man loses his bearings in this world. He cannot find them again until he has found the One whose world it is. It is natural that non-believers feel their existence is pointless and miserable. . . . God made life, and God alone can tell us its meaning. If we are to make sense of life in this world, then, we must know about God. And if we want to know about God, we must turn to the Bible.[36]

Buddhism of course rejects both God and the Bible and thus finds itself in the dilemma mentioned by Packer.[37] Arguments against Buddhism (historical, logical, theological) will not necessarily persuade the convinced Buddhist of this, though they may be effective with a recent Western convert to Buddhism. They do, nevertheless, help the Christian to emphasize the differences between Buddhism and Christianity and to strengthen the Christian's own conviction as to the truth of the faith.

One of the most fundamental problems in Buddhism is that no one is certain what "true Buddhism" is. For one thing, the manuscript evidence is far too late and unreliable. Buddha's words were never recorded, which makes it impossible to ascertain if what we have are the genuine words of Buddha or merely those of his disciples centuries later. Second, the manuscripts we do possess are so contradictory that one despairs of ever finding truth. Charles Prebish is Professor of Religious Studies at Pennsylvania State University and editor of *Buddhism: A Modern Perspective.* In his essay he points out that Buddha told his disciples they could "abolish all the lesser and minor precepts."[38] Unfortunately, he never identified what these precepts were, leading to great confusion among his disciples and the sects. Buddhism has thousands of works that claim the authority of the Buddha, and yet they contain endlessly contrary teachings. Where, then, does the Buddhist turn to find truth?

Then there are the many internal contradictions of Buddhist philosophy itself. Buddhist scholar Edward Conze notes in *Buddhist Thought in India* that the Mahayanists "prefer lucid paradoxes which always remain mindful of logic and deliberately defy it. For they do not mind contradicting themselves."[39] Buddhism teaches reincarnation but denies the soul, so what can possibly reincarnate? Spiritually "enlightened" Bodhisattvas vow to work for the enlightenment of all beings, fully knowing such beings never existed to begin with. So how can one grant wisdom to those who have compassion on non-entities? Why should enlightened beings toy with illusions? Why help save a thing which, according to Buddhist philosophy, must save itself solely by its own efforts? But it doesn't really matter, for nothing is saved and no soul exists to be enlightened. Then what of the Buddha and his mission? Does it have any relevance? And what of Buddhism? What's the point to all its efforts? The truth is, given Buddhist assumptions, it makes no difference at all whether Buddha, Bodhisattvas or Buddhism ever existed. They can bring no fundamental change to the world and they are as much an illusion as everything else.

There are many other internal contradictions. By definition, sense perceptions do not exist in nirvana. What then exists to perceive nirvana? And even in samsara, without a soul what permanently exists to perceive suffering? And how can samsara possibly be nirvana? Or, how can Buddhism logically uphold morality when its own philosophy requires it to conclude that even the most noble and virtuous actions can be evil because all unenlightened actions produce suffering and self-defeating karma by definition. Conversely, by definition, the enlightened supposedly can do no evil. But is this what we see among the ranks of the enlightened? To the contrary! They are as subject to evil as the rest of us, often even more so, if the reports of former disciples are to be believed.*

The Problem of Social Apathy

One of the greatest problems of Buddhism is its logically derived social apathy. Professor of Religion Robert E. Hume was correct when he wrote in *The World's Living Religions* that, in one sense, "the main trend in Buddhist ethics is negative, repressive, quietistic, non-social."[40] Christmas Humphreys, an influential Western Buddhist, admits this but seems to argue that

---

*In our *Encyclopedia of New Age Beliefs* we showed how Eastern philosophy logically increases evil by denying that evil has any reality and maintaining that the disciple must go beyond good and evil to find enlightenment (see the chapters on Altered States of Consciousness, Eastern Gurus, Enlightenment, Meditation, Yoga).

the alleged self-satisfaction offered by Buddhism is reason enough to become a Buddhist. "It may be asked, what contribution Buddhism is making to world problems, national problems, social problems, appearing among every group of men. The answer is as clear as it is perhaps unique. Comparatively speaking, none. And the reason is clear. One man at peace within lives happily."[41]

But a man content and at peace with himself who does nothing for anyone is perhaps the worst man of all. Personal contentment is hardly sufficient reason to remain indifferent to the world's problems. Jesus Christ provides all the personal contentment one can ask for, but He also commanded His disciples to be salt and light in the world. Jesus impells men and women into society to help others, the poor, the needy, the discouraged, the lost. The Christian loves his neighbor, and indeed all people, because the God who is there loves them and because they are made in his image (James 3:9–10). Because God cares, they care. Because He acts, they act. But if people are illusions, and if Nirvana has no concern with them, why should the Buddhist? In fact, a number of Buddhists have recognized the superiority of Christianity at this point. Monk Shojun Bano confesses that "Buddhism is far behind Christianity. . . . Buddhism should learn more from Christianity," and noted popularizer of Buddhism in the West, D. T. Suzuki, agrees that "Buddhism has a great deal to learn from Christianity."[42] The eminent Christian historian Kenneth S. Latourette was certainly correct when he wrote the following in *Introducing Buddhism:*

> Christianity has been the source of far more movements and measures to fight chronic evils and improve the lot of mankind than has Buddhism. . . . Christianity has been the motivating impetus behind anti-slavery campaigns, public health drives, relief activities in behalf of sufferers of war, and the establishment of the nursing profession. It has been responsible for the building of institutions to care for the mentally ill, hospitals, schools and universities, and for the reduction of more languages to writing than can be ascribed to all other forces put together. . . . More than any other religion, it has made life this side of the grave richer.[43]

This is not to say that individual Buddhists never do social good. It is to say their philosophy cannot logically establish social concerns, so if that is achieved, they are acting inconsistent with their philosophy. In light of this, and by Buddha's own admonition, Buddhists should forsake Buddhism.

Heaven or The Void?

No one who enjoys life and understands what Christianity offers can logically think Buddhism offers more. Christianity promises abundant life not just now but forever. It offers a personal immortality in a perfected state of existence where all suffering and sin are forever vanquished and the redeemed exist forever with a loving God who has promised they will inherit all that is His. By contrast, Buddhism promises only an arduous, lengthy road toward personal non-existence in a nebulous nirvana. Consider the contrast provided by Clive Erricker in comparing the Buddhist nirvana and the Christian heaven:

> There is a continuing selfhood in heaven which Nirvana denies; there is a tendency to understand heaven as a future state, following on from earthly life, that Nirvana is not; there is a belief that heaven is, at least to some degree, understandable in earthly terms, whereas, Nirvana is not even the opposite of Samsaric existence. Samsaric existence entails the cessation of everything. The problem we then have is that Nirvana sounds dreadfully negative, as though everything precious to us is denied and destroyed.[44]

Erricker's statements are true. Since the goal of Buddhism is to destroy the individual person, who is merely an illusion, everything precious to the individual is also "denied and destroyed." But notice the Buddhist response to this unlovely state of affairs: "The Buddhist response to this is that speculation of this kind is simply unhelpful."[45] In other words, Buddhist teaching does deny and destroy all that is meaningful to human existence, but Buddhism has no answers as to the implications. It merely retreats into its particular worldview declaring that critical evaluation is "unhelpful." Former Buddhist J. I. Yamamoto observes: "My hunger and my thirst cannot be satisfied in Buddhism because I know that the Buddha neither created me nor offers for me to live forever with him. . . . Beyond the Buddha is the void, and the void does not answer the needs of my humanity."[46] As one Buddhist convert to Christianity remarked, "I did not want nirvana. I wanted eternal life."

Sin and Redemption or Karmic Justice?

But there is a deeper issue in Buddhism that must be addressed: the real problem of humanity and the implications of Eastern notions of karmic "justice" and morality. At this point, the Buddhist needs to understand that the problem of humanity is much deeper than ignorance or suffering. The problem is sin, rebellion against God. Thus the Buddhist needs to understand the absolute necessity of forgiveness through Christ and the loving sacrifice He made at the Cross. But the Buddhist has a real problem here because love is a foreign concept to Buddhist ultimate reality (nirvana) and to its gods. Buddhist "love" is impersonal; it exists without relationships. But if a God of love really exists, why would one exchange this God for a reality that is impersonal and whose deities are frequently and arbitrarily wrathful or evil?[47] In essence, Buddhists need to understand that their basic analysis of the human condition is flawed. Far from accomplishing its goal—the ending of suffering—Buddhism has no real solution to suffering.

To begin with, Buddha's analysis of the human condition was incomplete. His surface perception was valid, that suffering was universal. But his perception was not adequate. *Why* was the man old? *Why* was the man sick? *Why* was the beggar suffering? *Why* had the man died? When Buddha sought an answer to the "whys," he concluded (falsely) that personal existence itself was the cause of all suffering and therefore that the goal must be to annihilate personal existence. Yet in offering so radical a solution as the destruction of individual existence, Buddha went too far. People don't want to be annihilated, they want to live forever, hopefully in a much better place—exactly what Christianity offers.

Another error of the Buddha was to assume that suffering is wholly evil. Thus Buddha re-jects the knowledge that suffering can be something good (Romans 5:3–4; 8:34–39; James 1:2; 5:20; 1 Peter 2:20; 3:14, 17; 4:1, 17; 5:10). Nevertheless, people who suffer will often admit that suffering has made them better persons in ways that only it could. Even Jesus as a man "learned obedience from the things which He suffered" (Hebrews 5:8 NAS). The suffering of Jesus on the Cross, of course, became the salvation of the world (1 John 2:2).

Further biblically, there is a great deal that is predicated upon that which Buddhism rejects, the satisfaction of desires and the hope for personal immortality. It is good and right to desire the glory of God, personal salvation and sanctification, love for others and eternal life. Consider just a few scriptures which tells us that God is there, that He is personal, that He is gracious and that He desires for us to enjoy life. That God is good to everyone is indeed the scriptural testimony:

> God does not desire "anyone to perish" (2 Peter 3:9); He wants people to "love life and see good days" (1 Peter 3:10).

> God "has shown kindness by giving you rain . . . and crops . . . plenty of food and [He] fills your hearts with joy" (Acts 14:17).

> I know that there is nothing better for men than to be happy and to do good while they live. That everyone may eat and drink, and find satisfaction in all his toil—this is the gift of God (Ecclesiastes 3:12–13).

> The earth is full of the goodness of the LORD (Psalm 33 KJV).

> The LORD is gracious and compassionate, slow to anger and rich in love. The LORD is good to all; he has compassion on all he has made. . . . The LORD is faithful to all his promises and loving toward all he has made. The LORD upholds all those who fall and lifts up all who are bowed down. . . . You open your hand and satisfy the desires of every living thing (Psalm 145:8–16).

Of course, although God is good and loving, this is not necessarily true of men and it is certainly not true of the devil and demons. These are the source of most evil and suffering in the world.

Whenever there are problems or tragedies in life and God does not seem to be kind and good, we should not suspect that God lacks goodness (see John Wenham, *The Goodness of God*; C. S. Lewis, *The Problem of Pain*). In fact, the Bible tells us people intuitively know God is good despite the evil in the world (Romans 1:18-21; 2:14-16; 3:4-6). If God were *truly* evil, there would be no hope and the conditions of life and our sense of things would be quite different. This is why we never ask, "Why is there so much good in the world?" It's always, "Why is there so much evil in the world?" We know that evil is the aberration in a universe whose Ruler is good and righteous.

Buddha, however, promised, "If you follow these teachings, you will always be happy."[48] One wonders how many of the 400,000,000–600,000,000 Buddhists in the world are happy? At best, their lot in life is rather like the rest of the world. It is difficult to assume that their pessimistic philosophy and the outworking of Buddhist ideas in their cultures would offer blessings of true and lasting happiness. If Buddhism does not cease suffering even in this life, how can there be any guarantee that it will do so in the next life, or even in so-called nirvana?

Ironically, due to karmic belief, which says that suffering is inevitable due to misdeeds in a past life, Buddhism may not only ignore the suffering of others but also perpetuate it. Although, given a Buddhist perspective, karma does uphold a form of morality, in another sense karma merely becomes the dispenser of pain. That is, it justifies the acts of the sin nature as inevitable. Ultimately, there are no victims, for the acts of evil merely represent people fulfilling their karma. Thus it can easily be a "justice" which ordains that the murderer in this life be murdered in the next. It therefore can perpetuate crime and evil on the pretense of satisfying justice. In part, then, Buddhism itself perpetuates the very suffering it seeks to alleviate.

The problem, then, is that the two greatest *desires* of the Buddhist—cessation of personal existence and cessation of suffering—are the two things that can never be attained: As long as one remains a Buddhist one can do nothing to prevent the former and can only ensure the latter.

The one thing that will end their suffering (faith in Jesus' atonement) is rejected on philosophical grounds. Buddhists need to know that *personal* immortality *is* a possibility without the necessity of concomitant suffering. In fact, God has promised this as a free gift to those who believe in His Son (John 6:47).

That the gift is free means it cannot be earned. Buddhists hope to gain merit in this life by pilgrimages to Buddhist temples, assisting monks, giving alms to the needy, preaching Buddhism and so on. This, among many other things, is good karma (deeds, actions) by which Buddhists strive to attain nirvana. But it is precisely this kind of works-salvation that is condemned biblically:

> For we maintain that a man is justified by faith apart from works of the Law. (Romans 3:28)

> ... to the one who does not work [for salvation], but believes in Him who justifies the ungodly, his faith is reckoned as righteousness, just as David also speaks of the blessing upon the man to whom God reckons righteousness apart from works. (Romans 4:5, 6 NAS)

> But even if we or an angel from heaven should preach a gospel other than the one we preached to you, let him be eternally condemned! (Galatians 1:8)

> Nevertheless knowing that a man is not justified by the works of the Law but through faith in Christ Jesus, even we have believed in Christ Jesus, that we may be justified by faith in Christ, and not by the works of the Law; since by the works of the Law shall no flesh be justified. (Galatians 2:16 NAS)

Finally, above all else Buddhism is an experientially based religion founded in subjectivism. Its "confirmation" lies solely in the realm of inner experience not divine revelation:

> Buddhism is not primarily a religion of faith or obedience to a superior being. It stresses the importance of personal experience of the goal. While in the earlier stages of the religious life the Buddhist must of necessity take the teachings of Buddhism on faith, it is agreed that finally these teachings must be validated through the experience of enlightenment and nirvana.[49]

Buddhism . . . does not make a strong distinction between objective and subjective reality. . . .[50]

How can any Buddhist have the assurance of final success based upon a highly speculative philosophy sustained only by mystical experience? Should even the occasional subjective experience (in meditation) of something the philosophy calls "nirvana" be taken as evidence that its religious doctrines are true? And if in the end no one ultimately exists to experience nirvana, what's the point?

Perhaps we should cite the Buddha once again: "Do not believe [me] merely because I am your master. But when you yourselves have seen that a thing is evil and leads to harm and suffering then you should reject it." But the Buddha also said, "And when you see that a thing is good and blameless, and leads to blessing and welfare, then you should do such a thing."[51] Buddhists, then, who agree that Christ was good and blameless, should consider His life and words far more soberly than they do. And Buddhists who agree that Christianity has far outstripped Buddhism in positive social works, and accomplished great good for mankind, should also look more closely at its message. Buddhists may indeed be content to live within the confines of the Buddhist worldview. But look what they are missing—eternal life in heaven! Unfortunately, continued indifference to Jesus will cost them dearly. As Christians, we have the privilege of sharing the truth about Jesus with our Buddhist friends, in the hope that they too may inherit eternal life. What could be more wonderful for a Buddhist?

TESTIMONY OF A FORMER TIBETAN BUDDHIST

We now complement our conclusions by sharing the testimony of Katja Zink formerly a leading disciple of Buddhist teacher Jamgon Kontrul Rinpoche. In 1995 Katja converted from Buddhism to the Christian faith and gave the following account of that to John Weldon. The reasons for her conversion should be of interest not only to Buddhists but also to Christians.

"Always looking for a deeper meaning in our existence on this planet earth, I became interested in various philosophies in my early pu-

berty and later was drawn increasingly towards Eastern spiritual disciplines. My Christian background in Germany seemed shallow and in fact was spiritually uninspiring. Christians often seemed narrow-minded, judgmental and self-righteous. The hypocrisy bothered me the most. As far as the Christian faith was concerned, Europe seemed spiritually dead, either because the churches which claimed to be Christian had no heartfelt connection to the living Jesus of the Gospels or because they tried to confine him into some rigid old-fashioned frames and rituals, diminishing his uniqueness and majesty more than exalting it.

"Christianity appeared to be a nice comfort zone for simple-minded people who thought that there really was a personal and loving creator God. But this assumption already bothered me. How could there be such a God? How could He create this broken world with all its pain, poverty, injustice and despair? And how could he just watch this chaos going on? How could this God be a truly loving God, a God who cares? Besides that the crucifixion did not make any sense at all to me: The idea of God brutally crucifying his own son, so we would be redeemed of our sins, seemed to be the ultimate karmic escape fantasy, an easy cop-out deal on a pretty cruel basis.

"Buddhism made a lot more sense. Karma and the cycle of samsara including the assumption of numerous reincarnations explained the evil in this world and the possibility of liberation in a far more reasonable way. As far as I could see, Buddhism offered the only truthful path towards real enlightenment. So I became deeply involved with Tibetan Buddhism through a friend of mine in Germany. I liked its vastness of symbolism and variety of meditation practices and learned that this world is a samsaric network of conglomerated karmically trapped minds whose inherent, diamond-like, radiant Buddha-nature can only be revealed through a strict discipline of meditation and ethically pure motivated actions, offering us at least a chance to free ourselves from this useless merry-go-round of reincarnation.

"For almost seven years I became entirely devoted to the Buddhist tradition of the Karmapa, the Karma Kagyu Lineage (similar to the Gelgpa-Lineage of the Dalai Lama). My teacher was the third Jamgon Kontrul Rinpoche, one of the four 'heartsons' of the Karmapa. The concrete path of different meditation tools and the close connection to a teacher who had mastered the transformation from samsara to nirvana was very appealing to me. Besides that I was blessed with a truly beautiful being accepting me as a disciple. I also saw the benefits of a consistent practice of contemplation and meditation in my own mind: more stability, clarity, inner peace and a sparkling sensation of joy. The purifying effect of the so-called Ngandra, the four preliminary practices with hundred thousand repetitions each, impressed me. I was convinced to finally have found the right spiritual path towards the perfect union of ultimate wisdom and compassion.

"But unforeseen changes were already lurking. Through an unusual set of circumstances, I ended up moving to the island of Maui in Hawaii. My next-door neighbor was an interesting man with a fascinating background. About three years ago I asked him why he became a Christian since I knew that he also denied the existence of God for many years. (I didn't know at the time that he had been praying to God that I would ask him that question.) In response, he told me that no other spiritual teacher ever had the impact that Jesus Christ did, neither did anybody ever claim to be what he claimed to be, namely the unique son of God. I just laughed, because somebody who claimed to be the unique son of a God who did not even give evidence for his own existence seemed more a lunatic than anything else to me.

"However, as a Buddhist I was soon to be faced with my own spiritual perplexities. The sudden and entirely unexpected death of my young, spiritual teacher, Jamgon Kongtrul Rinpoche, in a car accident in Sikkim, northern India, was devastating. It also irritated me deeply, because when I saw him the last time three months before his death, he gave me no warning of his death or any upcoming threat that he had to face. Instead he reassured me several times that he would come to Europe in the coming fall, where I was supposed to meet him

again. But I was taught that an enlightened being had perfect insight into the future and makes careful preparations for his death as well as gives careful last instructions to all his disciples. So what went wrong? And why?

"The whole lineage entered into a time of intense mourning. Then something wonderful happened. But instead of uplifting hope, despair and confusion were heightened when the recent incarnation of the Karmapa was finally found in eastern Tibet after years of intense searching and brought back to his original monastery in central Tibet near Lhasa. The reason for confusion instead of hope was due to the fact that another one of Karmapa's 'heartsons,' Sharmar Rinpoche, refused to accept the boy as the true incarnation and proposed a different candidate. That started a roller-coaster of power-struggles in the lineage, ending in a severe political split. (Although the Dalai Lama and the Chinese government, for the first time in the history of Tibet, agreed in the acknowledgement of the Tibetan boy as the only legitimate, official reincarnation.)

"In addition, several personal experiences during a four month retreat created more questions and doubts concerning Buddhism. For example, it brought out all the contradictions I stumbled over in Buddhism to the forefront when one of my Buddhist friends quoted a highly respected Lama: 'Vajrayana [the Tibetan Buddhist path] is like a jump between the two World Trade Centers. If you make it to the other building—amazing! Otherwise it's a long fall down.'

"Buddhists do not at all soften the outlook on reincarnation. The human realm is—according to their teachings—the only realm out of six in which you can reach spiritual enlightenment. Nevertheless, 'the human birth is as rare and precious as a star in the daytime sky' as every sincere Tibetan teacher will tell you. The chance of a rebirth in one of the other realms, particularly the lower realms is far, far greater. Another illustration gives an even more vivid impression of this: imagine the whole earth was covered by water. Somewhere in this vast ocean stirred up by heavy winds, is one lone turtle swimming beneath the waves. Somewhere else in this vast ocean is a ring floating on the surface, moved by the ocean's currents. The ring fits right around the neck of the turtle. The turtle comes up for air only once every hundred years. The chance of a human rebirth, Tibetans say, is equivalent to the chance of the turtle finding the ring around its neck when lifting its head out of the water! Yet this is only an illustration of the chance of human rebirth *not* the chance of enlightenment which is far rarer.

"In essence, during this retreat I was forced to consider the severe difficulty of the Buddhist path. I also saw firsthand the helplessness and despair created in my spiritual leaders by the split in the lineage and the lack of 'enlightened' solutions. My doubts about Buddhism being a path of ultimate truth started to grow. The answers the Lamas gave me in response to my questions were not enough nourishment for my inquisitive mind and all my meditation practices just could not erase them either. Besides that, I felt trapped in a hopeless attempt 'to reach the other building,' facing 'the long fall down,' realizing that if my own spiritual leaders as 'enlightened beings' in their twelfth or fourteenth consciously chosen reincarnation were not able to find all the answers and clues, I as an ordinary being certainly had even much less of a chance.

"Looking at myself with greater honesty, I saw plenty of weaknesses in my own heart and mind. As much as Buddhists rejected the existence of a Creator God, memories of my earlier Christian teachings started to come alive again. If I indeed wanted to find ultimate truth; as I did, I had to consider there may be a permanent factor behind all the obvious impermanence of this world and thus consider the possibility of God's existence.

"I started to cry out to Him, to plead and wrestle with Him through numerous prayers. I was almost shockingly surprised when I found them heard and answered, because if this holy God did exist indeed, I knew my shortcomings before Him would be a problem.

"Slowly, I began to realize why the Christian message was called the gospel. If such a God existed, it was good news indeed to be able to have your sins forgiven. I cannot even begin to describe the level of my shame before God when—

after months of research—I finally realized the Jesus Christ surrendered to that terrifying death on the cross as an atonement for my and ALL of our sins. Simultaneously, my heart was overwhelmed with the deepest joy by the experience of his incredible mercy and forgiveness, and I was even more delighted by the historical evidence of the resurrection of Jesus Christ which gives all of us solid hope for eternal life.

"I am now fully convinced that Jesus' death on the cross is the single most transforming spiritual event in the history of mankind. More than anybody else, C. S. Lewis helped me to understand this, looking at it from kind of a Buddhist perspective by evaluating the karmic merit of the Jewish people. He explains in *Mere Christianity* that the constant failure in perfect obedience by God's chosen people brought the 'karmic scales' so hopelessly out of balance that only the spiritual weight of sacrificing himself through a human incarnation and a truly sacrificial death could create balance again and serve as a fundamental hope and inspiration for the redemption of our sins and failures. By the measurement of God's law, the future of mankind was hopelessly lost in sin, but by the gift of His grace—and only by that—we all receive a chance to be saved from final fatal judgement. So God actually did crucify His own Son to spare us the divine judgement due to our sin. But by faith in Jesus we could be forgiven and the resurrection of Christ proved it. Suddenly the words from the Gospel of John (Chapter 3, verse 16) became transparent and alive to me in all their truthful, joyous glory: 'For God so loved the world that he gave his one and only Son, that whoever believes in Him shall not perish but have eternal life.' In return, all God expects from us is to accept this and acknowledge Jesus' sacrifice with gratitude while living up to Jesus' level of obedience and surrender the best we can.

"My Buddhist friends were puzzled, amused, amazed, partly confused and mostly convinced that I had become deceived in a spiritual mind trap. Buddhists generally do not understand Christianity, as I can well remember. That response was hard to face and still is difficult. Nevertheless, the gift of inner joy that comes with the Christian faith is worth all the price this world extracts. The assurance of eternal life I have through faith in Jesus is indisputably more precious than anything I have ever found in Buddhism, because Jesus Christ is "the true light that gives light to every man" (John 1:9).

"For thirty-three years of my life I lived without God. Whatever may happen in the future, I never want to be without Him again. As Jesus once told his disciples, 'I am the resurrection and the life: he who believes in me shall live even if he dies. And everyone who lives and believes in me shall never die' (John 11:25-26), and 'I have told you this so that my joy may be in you and that your joy may be complete' (John 15:11), because, as Lewis once wrote, 'joy is the serious business of heaven.'"

PART TWO:
NICHIREN SHOSHU BUDDHISM

For Info at a Glance and Doctrinal Summary of Nichiren Shoshu, see these two sections at the beginning of this chapter. Additional Info at a Glance material follows here.

Claims: Nichiren Shoshu (NS) claims to represent true Buddhism and to offer the world a scientifically enlightened form of religious practice. It teaches that by chanting before and worshipping the Gohonzon, a sacred mandala, believers can bring their lives into harmony with ultimate reality, producing wealth, health and success—sort of a Buddhist form of "name it and claim it," or word-faith teachings. However, NS constitutes a late form of Buddhism whose emphasis upon materialism would have been repudiated by the Buddha. Furthermore, its claim to be compatible with Christianity is contradicted by its Buddhist philosophy and basic approach to life.

Quote: "The demon of worldly desires is always seeking chances to deceive the mind"[52] (The Buddha).

Note: NS is among the most influential of the new religions that have come on the scene in recent decades. Overall, the movement claims 17 million members in more than 117 countries.[53] As a mystical faith with a materialistic emphasis (one that constantly stresses its "scientific" nature), it is uniquely suited for success in America.

INTRODUCTION AND HISTORY: IN SEARCH OF "TRUE" BUDDHISM

The founder of Nichiren Shoshu, Nichiren Daishonin, was one of the most controversial and important figures in Japanese Buddhism. Daishonin lived during a period of Japanese history that was embroiled in political and religious turmoil. With many of the Buddhist sects in conflicting disarray, he longed for the reality of one true and united Buddhism, and he devoted tireless efforts to this end.

From the age of 12, Daishonin researched various schools of Buddhism, including the Tendai, Zen and Shingon sects. Although he consumed years studying at the esoteric monastery of the Tendai school on Mt. Hiei, and at 16 became a monk there, it was only through intensive and prolonged meditation at the Shingon Monastery at Mt. Koya that he became convinced of the "truth" that has become the heart of Nichiren Buddhism. Through this revelation, Daishonin determined that the essence of the Buddha's true teachings were crystallized in the writing we know today as the *Lotus Sutra,* or *Saddharma-Pundarika* (the Sutra of the Lotus of the True Law). Daishonin believed that the mystical essence of this sutra was embodied in the invocation "Nam-myoho-renge-kyo," the ceremonial chant used by Nichiren Shoshu Buddhists. The chant is believed to be a repository of magical power so that the disciple can instill the (alleged) material and spiritual benefits of the sutra into his life, even without reading it.

Daishonin was persuaded not only that his life's mission was to clarify true Buddhism but also that he was the sole repository of Buddhist truth, and that only his interpretation of the Lotus Sutra was correct. He argued that "the Pure Land Sect (*Nembutsu*) is the Everlasting Hell; *Zen* devotees are demons; *Shingon* devotees are ruining the nation; the *Vanaya* sect are traitors to the country."[54] To anyone who opposed him, he warned, "Those who despise and slander me will have their head broken into seven pieces."[55] He even threatened destruction of the Japanese state unless it united under true Buddhism (his teachings). Nichiren Daishonin thus aroused no small amount of opposition by his robust intolerance of all other Buddhism. During his life, he was expelled from his own monastery, exiled twice, sentenced to death once and repeatedly suffered from persecution (his death sentence was commuted).

In spite of his heartfelt desire to unify Japan and all Buddhism, his intolerance and inability to accept compromise had merely saddled Japan with one more competing sect. As Brandon's *Dictionary of Comparative Religion* observes, "Nichiren's teaching, which was meant to unify Buddhism, gave rise to [the] most intolerant of Japanese Buddhist sects."[56] Noted Buddhist scholar Dr. Edward Conze declares that Nichiren "suffered from self-assertiveness and bad temper, and he manifested a degree of personal and tribal egotism which disqualifies him as a Buddhist teacher."[57]

Not unexpectedly, Nichiren and his most prominent disciples discovered that they could not agree on what constituted true Buddhism, and this led to initial charges of heresy among their ranks and eventual historic fragmentation. Although Nichiren Shoshu is the largest of the more than 40 Nichiren sects today, each sect maintains that it is the "true" guardian of Nichiren Daishonin's teachings.

NICHIREN SHOSHU TODAY

In 1930 a lay movement was founded to promote Nichiren Shoshu: Soka Gakkai International (SGI). From 1960–90, the leader of SGI was the prolific and energetic Daisaku Ikeda. One evidence of his dynamism is that under his leadership NS expanded into more than 100 nations, and his picture was placed prominently near NS altars around the world. Apparently, this success caused a major rift in the movement. A devastating split between the lay organization and the priesthood emerged in the late 1980s–early 90s, with serious charges being leveled back and forth.[58] In unbuddhist-like fash-

ion, it appears that the Japanese priesthood became jealous and even resentful of the phenomenal prosperity of the lay movement. In December 1990, the priesthood stripped Ikeda of his sokoto title: head of all Nichiren lay believers. They took this action in spite of the fact that for years Ikeda had been heralded by the Soka Gakkai as "the living Buddha for today" and even as the reincarnation of Nichiren Daishonin. The image of Nichiren Shoshu has thus suffered much from quarreling, threats, negative publicity, power plays and even several recent financial scandals. An early editorial in SGI's *World Tribune* confessed: "When priests denounce President Ikeda and confuse members in order to gain followers, this . . . is wrong. . . . the priesthood's recent actions are disrupting unity and hindering the propagation of [Nichiren's] teachings."[59] By stripping Ikeda of his authority and consolidating power to themselves under the local Danto movement (followers of NS who identify with the priesthood rather than the lay organization), the Nichiren Shoshu priesthood has effectively asserted supreme jurisdiction, but it has also caused a rift that has the potential to fragment the movement even further.

Today in Japan, the Soka Gakkai has the third largest political party, the Komeito. It advocates a one-world government based upon Buddhist politics and universal pacifism.[60] Soka Gakkai International continues to devote strenuous efforts to its ultimate aim of Kosen-rufu: the conversion of the entire world to its teachings.

PRACTICE AND TEACHING: IN SEARCH OF "BENEFITS"

Nichiren Shoshu Buddhism teaches that an omnipresent and ultimately impersonal "essential life" flows throughout the totality of the universe, both the animate and the inanimate. This life, however, assumes different forms. For example, in people, the life essence has manifested itself as consciousness, emotions and mental capacities. In trees, rocks, air, water and so forth the life essence is present, but latent or dormant.

One conclusion we may draw from this teaching is that in terms of their true nature, man and the universe are ultimately one: their inner nature is identical, despite any differences in outward form. However, NS claims that until we practice the teachings of Nichiren Shoshu this unity is neither realized nor appropriated, and "spiritual" benefits cannot be acquired until this occurs. By chanting "Nam-myoho-renge-kyo" (the magical invocation believed to summarize and internalize the essence of the Lotus Sutra), one's individual nature is brought into harmony with the "essential life" of the universe. Eventually, the highest expression of essential life, the Buddha nature, which is dormant in the inner self, is brought to the surface. The individual nature thus becomes united to the Buddha nature, the result (allegedly) being new spiritual power, self-renewal, greater wisdom, more vitality and, not the least, material wealth.

In order to achieve this state of Buddhahood, each morning and night the NS member kneels, chants Nam-myoho-renge-kyo and recites sections from the Lotus Sutra. This ritual is performed before the Gohonzon, a small altar comprised of a Buddhist mandala. This mandala is a sacred piece of paper. It contains the sacred chant, written vertically in the center, and the name of Nichiren, around which are written the names of various Buddhist gods which are mentioned in the Lotus Sutra, including a demon god. (In NS, Buddhist gods and demons are not, officially, personal spirits, but positive and negative life functions.)

The daily ritual worship is termed gongyo and consists of three aspects. The first (as noted) involves kneeling before the Gohonzon and reciting passages from the Lotus Sutra. This constitutes a mystical, not an intellectual, endeavor. The second aspect of gongyo is chanting the daimoku "Nam-myoho-renge-kyo" while rubbing a string of Juzu (prayer beads). Daimoku is also done throughout the day and is the most important form of gongyo. The third aspect involves five prayers: prayers of gratitude to (1) various deities, (2) the Gohonzon and (3) Nichiren; (4) a prayer to fulfill one's wishes; and (5) a prayer to the dead. The Sutra passages are recited five times in the morning and three times in the evening. Chanting is performed until one "feels satisfied." This may last many hours, producing a hypnotic or trance-like effect. One individual claimed to have chanted 12 *million* daimoku which, purportedly, led her into spirit contact. She claimed that "she directly met Nichiren Daishonin and received his guidance."[61]

The emphasis on materialism and the element of personal power are the most obvious attractions of Nichiren Shoshu. Chanting is believed to bring "benefits" (answered "prayer") in the form of acquiring possessions, money, health and control over both one's own circumstances and those of others. By chanting, one can allegedly acquire anything one desires: "Through faith in the Gohonzon he can fulfill any wish and control his environment...."[62]

The philosophy underlying this idea is probably of little concern to most followers, who are satisfied simply to be "receiving benefits." Nevertheless, it is integral to NS theology. According to President Daisaku Ikeda, "There is a single, underlying rhythm which controls the constant shifting of nature and the play of her interlocking harmonies—a fundamental law which also moves and supports human life. Nichiren Daishonin's Buddhism defines it as Nam-myoho-renge-kyo...."[63]

"Nam" means the consecration of one's entire being into believing in the Gohonzon and all it represents. "Myoho" is the supreme law of the universe, its natural working principle: "Buddhism interprets nature itself as the great life. There is no such god outside the great universe. The great universe itself is mysterious (Myo), and yet has a strict law (ho) in itself. Therefore, it should be termed Myoho, i.e., the Mystic Law."[64] "Renge" refers to the lotus flower and represents karma, interpreted as the "simultaneous nature of cause and effect." Chanting is the highest possible cause, resulting in the natural effect of answered prayer or benefits. "Kyo" is the "sound or vibration within the universe." The sound and rhythm of the chant places one into harmony with the stream of life.[65]

By chanting, one (allegedly) brings one's self into harmony with the laws of the universe and the fundamental flow of life. As we become united with the universe "behavior will become synonymous with Mystic Law which leads to eternal happiness."[66] The objects of our desires are now capable of flowing naturally to us; hence, regular practice allows us to achieve our desires and thereby produces happiness. According to President Ikeda, Nam-myoho-renge-kyo "is the origin of everything."[67] "Nam-myoho-renge-kyo is the essence of all life and the rhythm of the universe itself. Life can never be apart from Nam-myoho-renge-kyo, and yet, because we have forgotten this, we have come out of rhythm with life itself. When we chant, we enter back into that basic rhythm and once again have the potential for indestructible happiness. ... [because] our life force will permeate the universe and the Buddha nature will emerge within ourselves, *enabling us to fulfill our wishes*."[68]

THEOLOGY:
IN SEARCH OF SALVATION

According to Daishonin, the cause of all unhappiness is evil religion, which is more or less all religious interpretations apart from his own. "Shakubuku" (to break and subdue) is one NS term descriptive of his attitude toward other religions. Shakubuku is the forceful method of conversion, whereas "shoju" is the more moderate approach. According to Harry Thomsen, author of *The New Religions of Japan*, "Nichiren maintained that to kill heretics is not murder, and that it is the duty of the government to extirpate heresy with the sword."[69]

Shakubuku is considered an act of great love and mercy because it breaks the evil religion of the person being converted.[70] The second president, Josei Toda, stated on May 3, 1951, "*Kosen-rufu* [mass conversion] of today can be attained only when all of you take on evil religions and convert everyone in the country and let him accept a *Gohonzon*."[71] Professor Noah S. Brannen, author of *Soka Gakkai: Japan's Militant Buddhists*, states that Shakubuku "designates intolerant propaganda and pressure to produce a forced conversion. . . . [It] often employs a technique of intimidation carried out in a very systematic manner."[72] Although the practice has allegedly been modified, Brannen and others list earlier incidents of threats of injury against a prospective convert and family members, actual beatings, cases of arson, and so on.[73]

Nichiren Shoshu vs. Christianity

Perhaps it is not surprising, then, that despite attempts at accommodation hostility toward Christianity has remained a feature of the writings of Nichiren Shoshu and President Ikeda. Regrettably, Christianity is often misrepresented and then attacked as an inferior and irrational belief. Thus, in the authoritative NS literature the major doctrines of Christianity are described as: "unscientific nonsense"; "stupid superstition"; "ridiculous"; "fantasy"; "irrational"; "morbid"; "shallow"[74] and so forth. NS believes "[the Christian] God is dead . . .", and "it is apparent that Christian life has, in fact, repeated every kind of atrocity."[75] The Genesis doctrine of creation is "foolish and childish."[76] Heaven is seen as "an enticement toward some illusionary paradise."[77] Under a belief in absolute monotheism, "the people are powerless beings."[78]

In essence, being a Christian brings only "bad karma."[79] Relying upon Jesus Christ for salvation will "ultimately lead to confusion."[80] Christian teachings are "destructive of people's happiness."[81] And, referring to the Christian concepts of God and salvation, we are told that there is no need to seek salvation outside ourselves in the Christian God, nor is there any reason to believe in Him, nor is there any need for the concept of God's grace.[82] Professor N. S. Brannen observes, "Christianity is the universal non-Buddhist religion singled out for attack."[83]

God

Nichiren Shoshu replaces God with an impersonal omnipresent essence that eternally fluctuates in cycles of manifestation and dormancy. Practically speaking, Nichiren Shoshu is an atheistic system, for any concept of a personal God is irrelevant and, to their way of thinking, spiritually harmful. Nichiren Shoshu teaches that "Life has no beginning; therefore it was not created by God."[84] "God is not the Creator. . . . Our life is not given to us by our parents, and is not either given by God."[85] Perhaps the clearest expression of their humanistic theology is given in *The Complete Works of Daisku Ikeda*, volume 1. There it simply, if succinctly, states: "God is nothing but man"[86] (cf. Psalm 9:15, 20; 10:3–4; Jeremiah 17:5).

While it is true that NS rejects the Christian concept of God, it is also clear that the mystical life essence ("the very source of the universe") is divinized and that the Gohonzon is the visible expression of it. Thus, while the biblical God is ridiculed as a myth, the Gohonzon is deified and worshipped.

Even though common sense tells us that the Gohonzon is merely a piece of paper (Nichiren Shoshu stresses that it is a religion of common sense), throughout Nichiren Shoshu writings we find that it is constantly worshipped, personalized, held to be eternal, omnipotent, omniscient and the ultimate source of everything. It alone saves, supports, protects, purifies and physically heals the believer. It alone answers prayer, forgives sin, punishes evil and gives great wisdom.[87] It alone brings happiness and good fortune.[88] It alone is the Savior of the world and anxiously awaits the world's worship. To slander or disbelieve in the Gohonzon is to fall into the lowest hell. "Nothing can surpass the *Gohonzon* . . . All of us are children of the Gohonzon . . . The Gohonzon witnesses everything . . . The Gohonzon's blessings are as vast as the universe . . . The Gohonzon's mercy is equal to all."[89]

Jesus Christ and Salvation

Statements about Jesus Christ are usually general and given within a Buddhist context. For example, "Because of his love, Jesus of Nazareth is comparable to a Bodhisattva"; that is, one full of compassion who sacrifices himself to help others attain "enlightenment" (Buddhahood).[90] Nichiren Shoshu rejects the biblical portrait of Christ's person and mission, His unique deity (John 1:1; 3:16, 18; 10:30, 33) and His atoning death (Matthew 26:28; Ephesians 1:7). For example, "Jesus died on the Cross. This fact shows that he was defeated by opposition, whatever interpretation posterity may have given to this fact. . . ."[91] While the Bible teaches that "there is one God and one mediator between God and men, the man Christ Jesus" (1 Timothy 2:5), who is "the Savior of all men" (1 Timothy 4:10), Nichiren Shoshu teaches it Nichiren is "the true Savior of mankind,"[92] only he is to be worshipped, through the Gohonzon, because he reflects the true Buddha.[93]

According to Nichiren Shoshu, "Nichiren Daishonin's Buddhism alone can save all of the people."[94] But what is salvation here? In its essence, salvation is humanistic. Salvation is equivalent to lasting personal happiness or satisfaction ("Buddhahood"); it does not involve deliverance from sin and from spiritual death as Christianity maintains (Ephesians 2:1–4). In a nutshell, one is "saved" from suffering, ignorance and unhappiness, and this results from appropriating the Buddha nature within, which is achieved through one's practice of the spiritual mechanics of Nichiren Shoshu. "The true intention of the Daishonin is to save the whole world through the attainment of each individual's happiness in life."[95]

The biblical concept of atonement (John 3:16; 1 John 2:22) is rejected on multiple grounds. First, the Christian God is held to be a myth, and so Christianity's teaching on the atoning death of Jesus Christ—God's Son—is held to be a myth. There is no Christian God who exists, so He could not have a Son to give. "Faith in the saving power of Christ is fundamental to every Christian teaching. . . . Buddhism paints a vastly different picture."[96] Second, the miraculous is rejected. The idea of a divine incarnation or of a God who intervenes in history is seen as "irrational, unscientific nonsense."[97] Yet salvation in Christianity is miraculous from start to finish, as can be seen in Christ's miraculous birth, ministry, death, resurrection, ascension, intercession and Second Coming. Third, the concept of substitutionary death for our sins violates the heart of a major Buddhist doctrine, the law of karma—the relationship between cause and effect and the necessity to "pay for" one's own misdeeds. Fourth, Christ's atonement is innately repugnant to Buddhists since it implies that ultimate reality is somehow fundamentally linked to suffering, the very thing Buddhists work so diligently to eradicate. In the Buddhist universe, suffering is an illusion to be dispensed with, forever vanquished by absorption into the ultimate reality of a blissful, if impersonal, nirvana. It is not something that can be related to ultimate reality ("God") in any way.

Nichiren Shoshu clearly offers a system of salvation by merit and personal effort. God is an entirely irrelevant consideration. By chanting, one removes karma, becomes happy and, finally, attains Buddhahood ("eternal happiness," but not in a personal, individual sense). Thus President Ikeda emphasizes, "We must seek the source of the meaning in life within man himself, instead of finding it in another transcendental being, God."[98]

But Jesus Himself taught: "This is eternal life, that they may know Thee, the only true God, and Jesus Christ whom Thou has sent" (John 17:3 NAS). "I am the light of the world; he who follows Me shall not walk in the darkness, but shall have the light of life (John 8:12 NAS).

CRITIQUE: THREE PROBLEMS FOR NICHIREN SHOSHU

In the areas of spirituality, religious claims and morality, NS Buddhism falls short of what a seeker might legitimately expect of true religion. We will first summarize these three problems and then examine the most critical problem for NS claims in depth. First, despite its claims to offer true spirituality, NS offers just another occult-based system of religion. Nichiren Shoshu priests and some laypersons have claimed occult or shamanistic powers, and part of daily worship involves ritual prayers to the dead. The Gohonzon itself is seen as a repository of magical powers available to anyone who recites the incantation and therefore "has the power to bless or curse" its worshipper, depending upon the treatment given it.[99]

Second, NS's claims to be true Buddhism are false. As Yale historian Kenneth Scott Latourette concludes, "[Nichiren] was mistaken in his conviction that the Lotus Sutra contained the primitive Buddhism. As a matter of fact, it was a late production, an expression of a form of Buddhism that would scarcely have been recognized by Gautama, or if recognized would have been repudiated."[100] Nor can NS offer the world the true interpretation of the Lotus Sutra, for the important NS doctrines are absent from the Lotus Sutra, and its mythological content is incapable of uniform interpretation. (This most fundamental NS claim is demonstrably false, as we will soon discuss in depth.)

Third, John Weldon has talked with NS members who have attempted to utilize chanting to bring about evil: to obtain drugs, commit crimes or magically control other people's decisions. They told him that "chanting works as well for these things as for any others." How can the NS member justify this? But even when they chant for "good" things it can be morally indefensible, such as when the emphasis is materialism. NS maintains that those who chant properly "will surely become rich."[101] "Let's make money and build health and enjoy life to our heart's content before we die!"[102] Many more examples of materialism could be cited if space permitted. In NS it becomes all too easy to replace moral integrity with personal self-indulgence. In contrast, Jesus warned, "Beware, and be on your guard against every form of greed; for not even when one has an abundance does his life consist of his possessions" (Luke 12:15 NAS). He also said, "For what will a man be profited, if he gains the whole world, and forfeits his soul? Or what will a man give in exchange for his soul" (Matthew 16:26)? Even if NS believers don't want to believe Jesus, they might want to believe former disciples who have admitted that NS benefits are few and far between. The *Ex-NSA Journal* reports: "Ex-members . . . will tell you that the really *important* things never did materialize [and that] they never *really* became happy."[103]

THE LOTUS SUTRA, NICHIREN SHOSHU OF AMERICA CREDIBILITY AND MYSTICAL HERMENEUTICS

Introduction

In Nichiren Shoshu, virtually everything rests upon the claim that it has the true interpretation of the Lotus Sutra, their principal Scripture. If this cannot be objectively substantiated, Nichiren Shoshu is invalidated as to its basic claims. Nichiren Shoshu then becomes culpable, even by Buddhist standards, for teaching its members a false religion, and it must then be considered fraudulent on this basis alone, other grounds notwithstanding.

The date of this Buddhist Sutra must be our first concern, for if it was not written ca. 900 B.C., (four centuries before the Buddha!) NS has a serious problem, for that is when NS maintains it was written. There is no consensus on when the Lotus Sutra, one of the most revered of Mahayana texts, was written, but it could not have been written 900 B.C. This may be why Ikeda writes that "just how the Lotus Sutra came into being is a question involving a number of historical riddles. . . ."[104] Scholars are, however, generally certain that it is a later Buddhist document and probably composed over a period of several centuries. M. A. Ehman states, "Some passages of the sutra may antedate the Christian era, but the entire text could not have been completed much before A.D. 200."[105] Again, Latourette argued that the Lotus Sutra "was a late production, an expression of a form of Buddhism that would scarcely have been recognized by Gautama, or if recognized would have been repudiated."[106]

According to a standard modern Sanskrit translation by Kern, the Lotus Sutra was in existence before 250 A.D., and he believes the earlier portions (Chapters 1–20; 27) date "some centuries earlier."[107] Its first known commentary was penned around 550–600 A.D.[108] Hence, it would seem nearly impossible to stretch its origin to 500 B.C. (the generally accepted date of Buddha), let alone to 900 B.C. How could a clearly Buddhist document be written 400 years before the Buddha was born? Yet this 900 B.C. date must be true in order for NS claims to be valid. Why?

Nichiren declared that he was the fulfillment of a prophecy in the Lotus Sutra predicting a coming Buddha who would return 2,000 years after Gautama's death. Two thousand years after Gautama's death is ca. 1517 A.D. , 300 years after Nichiren was born in 1222. So, the only way the prophecy can be fulfilled in Nichiren is for Buddha and the Lotus Sutra to have existed ca. 900 B.C. Nichiren, then, was in error not only in believing that the Lotus Sutra was written by Buddha but also in thinking that he was the fulfillment of its alleged prophecy.[109] Brannen states, "The sutra is obviously a treatise written to defend the worship of Gautama as the primordial Buddha which had developed in Mahayana Buddhism and to justify the origin of the Mahayana school."[110]

Further, besides difficulty with the text's time of composition and degree of corruption there is a serious problem with its content. Since the Lotus Sutra is obviously contradictory in itself, NS divides it into two parts: the "theoretical teaching" (the first half) and the "essential teaching" (the last half). Kirimura acknowledged when comparing the seventh and sixteenth chapters that "clearly the teaching of these two chapters of the Sutra are contradictory."[111] And, as we will document in the next section, some important NS doctrines are absent from the Lotus Sutra. This forces NS into a subjective, mystical hermeneutic in order to justify expounding the text "accurately." That the text itself is incapable of objective or uniform interpretation calls into question both Daishonin's interpretation of the Lotus Sutra and modern Nichiren Shoshu's interpretation of Daishonin.[112] Consider the following statement in the forward to Josei Toda's commentary on Chapters 2 and 16 of the Lotus Sutra, titled *Lectures on the Sutra* (1984 rev. ed.). In essence, the writer asserts that the study of the Lotus Sutra is not made in order to comprehend the text itself but to understand that the true essence of the Buddha's teachings can become meaningful only through chanting to the Gohonzon. "The study of the Lotus Sutra in Nichiren Shoshu is not undertaken as an intellectual exercise merely with the goal of comprehending ancient writings and teachings. Rather, it pursues the essence of the Buddhist teachings—an essence which comes alive through the practice of Nichiren Daishonin's Buddhism, i.e., the recitation of gongyo to the Gohonzon."[113]

That NS should rest its claims for religious truth upon a mystical approach to a corrupted and contradictory text is not surprising, but neither is it conducive to the frequent assertions of NS regarding its scientific objectivity and its claim to have uncovered "Buddhist truth." Kern points out that even the Buddhist scribes seemed not to care for their Scripture: "In general, it may be said that all the known copies of the Saddharma-pundarika [the Lotus Sutra] are written with a want of care, little in harmony with the holy character of the book."[114]

This is one reason why NS relies heavily on its mystical approach toward chanting, for the essence and benefits ("knowledge") of the Lotus Sutra are said to be absorbed through the invocation, not through study of the text. Obviously, then, problems relative to a corrupted text become less relevant. Nevertheless, on the basis of objective textual data that does exist, one cannot honestly maintain that the historic Buddha penned the Lotus Sutra, nor can one argue that the Sutra is capable of uniform interpretation. Further, as we will see, neither Nichiren Shoshu nor Nichiren Daishonin could have interpreted it accurately. The simple fact is that there is no "true" or "accurate" interpretation.

The Mythological Nature of the Lotus Sutra and Its Mystical Interpretation

Being a pagan, mythological text, the Lotus Sutra is full of vast numbers of gods, demons, bodhisattvas, giantesses, goblins, garudas (bird gods), great serpents and other mythological creatures. We find worship endorsed for "thirty hundred thousands myriads of kotis (kotis = tens of millions) of Buddhas" (an infinite number). Further, the eternal Buddha states that after his "complete extinction" he will send "gods and goblins in great number" to the proclaimers of the Lotus Sutra.[115]

Two examples of the mythical content will help us understand the difficulty the Lotus Sutra offers for any religion based on it. (These are taken from its chapters 7 and 20, respectively.) This will also illustrate its lack of practical application to the believer,* and the necessity to absorb its teachings mystically through chanting.

> ... the great Brahma-angels in the fifty hundred thousand myriads of kotis of spheres mounted all together their own divine aerial cars, took with them divine bags, as large as mount Sumeru [the largest mountain of all, located in the center of the earth], with celestial flowers. . . .

---

*The problem is recognized though not dealt with; cf. *Seiko Times*, Nov. 1978, p. 22, and July 1975, p. 40; *Lectures on the Sutra*, p. 22.

until they arrived at the western quarter. . . . [and saw the Lord Buddha] seated on the royal throne at the foot of the tree of enlightenment, surrounded and attended by gods, Nagaas [serpent deities], goblins, Gandharvas [half man–half bird creatures], demons, Garudas, Kinnaras, great serpents, men and beings not human. . . .[116]

Thereupon the Lord Sakyamuni [Gautama-Buddha] . . . and the wholly extinct Lord Prabhutaratna . . . commenced smiling to one another, and from their opened mouths stretched out their tongues, so that with their tongues they reached the Brahma-world [nearly an infinite distance away], and from those two tongues issued many hundred thousand myriads of kotis of rays.

From each of those rays issued many hundred thousand disciples, with gold coloured bodies and possessed of the thirty-two characteristic signs of a great man, and seated on thrones consisting of the interior of lotuses. Those Bodhisattvas spread in all directions in hundred thousands of worlds, and while on every side stationed in the sky preached the law. Just as the Lord Sakyamuni . . . produced a miracle of magic by his tongue, so, too . . . [did the others].[117]

Naturally, the only way a religion claiming strict allegiance to science can deal with the extensive myth and supernaturalism of the Sutra is to demythologize the text. No matter how fantastic a given scene, it can always be said to describe some particular "aspect" of human life. Exactly which aspect is anybody's guess; however, NS trusts in Nichiren's views and in the official interpretation of him. Nevertheless, even an appeal to (1) figurative language or (2) Buddha's cryptic teaching methods offers little solution to knowing what the original authors meant or how to apply their teaching today. This is why we find numerous contradictory interpretations and numerous competing Nichiren sects.[118] It then becomes clear that NS does not have *the* correct interpretation of the Lotus Sutra, simply because there is none. Ikeda quotes the Buddha himself as saying in Chapter 10, stanza 15, of the Sutra: "The Sutras which I have expounded number in the countless millions, those I have expounded in the past, those I expound now, and those I shall expound in the future. But among all those, this Lotus Sutra is the most difficult to believe and the most difficult to understand."*[119]

Objective understanding is therefore impossible. The Lotus Sutra can mean anything to anyone and is therefore useless as an authoritative standard for doctrine or practice. In a "Reply to Myoho-ama," Nichiren declared that those "who can explain the meaning of the Lotus Sutra and clearly answer questions concerning it" are as rare as "those who are able to kick the entire galaxy away like a ball."[120] Indeed, perhaps this is why he said in the same letter that if you chant the daimoku and do nothing else you are reading the Sutra correctly! "If you ceaselessly chant Daimoku, you will be continually reading the Lotus Sutra."[121] Ikeda states, "Nam-myoho-renge-kyo *is the Lotus Sutra and everything it means.*"[122] In other words, simply by chanting one "properly" interprets the Sutra. But how can this approach be a satisfying one for those who are allegedly a scientific, rationally minded people? Should potential converts accept that a mystical practice will allow them to "read" a text correctly? And if the Sutra cannot be properly interpreted, what happens to the religion based on it? Nichiren Daishonin put all his trust in *his* interpretation of the Lotus Sutra, but his followers have offered *their own* (conflicting) interpretations. Who can know that Nichiren Daishonin's interpretation of the Sutra is correct? Further, in light of the many conflicting Nichiren sects, how can the NS disciple know if the NS interpretation of Nichiren's writings is the true one?

Who Has the Correct Interpretation?

There are even clear differences between NS and the Lotus Sutra. For example, NS defines the ultimate law as Nam-myoho-renge-kyo, and it propounds the crucial doctrine of "ichinen sanzen" (the theory of 3,000 worlds in each moment) and other teachings that it admits are neither mentioned nor defined in the Lotus Sutra.[123] NS also maintains an antisupernatural approach, which is totally repudiated by the Lotus Sutra itself. Thus, even though Nichiren and NS claim they are the guardians of the true interpretation of the Lotus Sutra, that Sutra itself rejects some of their key beliefs. To get around this, NS literature claims that such doctrines are present but hidden from profane eyes. The doctrines exist in the "*unwritten* truth *behind* the letter."[124] Even so, given a written document, how is an *unwritten* truth acceptable as orthodox doctrine? By occult meditation, which is where its mysticism becomes evident.

The doctrines of the Sutra "are not always written in language plain enough for all to comprehend," hence only through "long hours of contemplation" was even Tendai able "to identify the principles hidden within the Sutra."[125] Nichiren himself first learned how to interpret it "correctly" by deep meditation. The preface to *The Major Writings of Nichiren Daishonin* Vol. II declares that "in it [the Lotus Sutra] the timeless principles of Buddhism are clarified *from the standpoint of the Daishonin's enlightenment. . . .*"[126] Josei Toda, the second president, was to no one's surprise hopelessly confused about Buddhism and the Lotus Sutra. Who was the Buddha? What does the Lotus Sutra mean? He repeatedly asked himself these questions during his time in prison. Eventually, only after hundreds of thousands of daimoku (chants) and "long, deep meditation," did he realize who the Buddha was.[127] He also received the answer to his question about the Lotus Sutra mystically:

> Later on, another crucial question struck him. What is the truth of the Lotus Sutra? And he devoted his entire being to pondering on this until he had chanted on a million and eight hundred thousand *daimoku.* In mid-November 1944, while chanting daimoku, he found himself in the air worshipping the Dai-Gohonzon together with innumerable others. Returning to reality, he found himself again in the cold prison. Overjoyed, he began to read the Lotus Sutra which had been too difficult for him to understand until that time. However, now he could comprehend it as easily and accurately as if he had picked up a notebook he himself had written long ago.[128]

---

*Kern's translation reads, ". . . is apt to meet with no acceptance with everybody, to find no belief with everybody" (p. 219).

Although Toda and Ikeda (his pupil) both claimed to be able to interpret the Sutra "easily and accurately," interpretations originating from altered states of consciousness are hardly reliable. A number of examples from *Lectures on the Sutra* and *Fundamentals of Buddhism* illustrate this.[129] When Sakyamuni states in the Sutra that "once Taho practiced the bodhisattva austerities," this is interpreted by NS to mean "that at one time he practiced this Law—Nam-myoho-renge-kyo—to attain enlightenment."[130] In another part of the Sutra, Bodhisattvas spring from the earth. The "earth" is interpreted as "Nam-myoho-renge-kyo," or the "essential life" but also as the philosophy and cultures of the various continents.[131]

Another passage in the Sutra reads, "This efficacious medicine I now leave here for you to take. Do not fear that you will not be cured." According to NS the "proper" interpretation is that "the medicine" is the Gohonzon, that "I now leave here" is the kaidan or place of worship and that "for you to take" means chanting daimoku.[132] But none of these key NS doctrines are found in the Lotus Sutra and NS admits as much. "The Three Great Secret Laws [Gohonzon, daimoku, kaidan] . . . are called secret because neither Sakyamuni nor his successors in India and China ever revealed them. Nichiren Daishonin was the first."[133] Again, on what basis does NS lay claim to finding "true" Buddhism in the Lotus Sutra?

"The Ceremony in the Air" is another key event recorded in the text. This discusses a vital assembly convened by the gods to spread the teachings of the Lotus Sutra. How does NS interpret it? In Chapter 11 of the Lotus Sutra, the Treasure Tower appears (half the size of the world), rising from the interior of the earth ascending into the sky. Taho Buddha announces from the tower that all of Sakyamuni's (Gautama's) teachings are true. Sakyamuni then summons all the Buddhas in the universe, seats himself alongside Taho, and through his occult powers transports the entire assembly into the air. There, in "The Ceremony in the Air," he preaches about spreading the teachings of the Lotus Sutra. NS interprets this as supporting its doctrines. Thus, when Sakyamuni and Taho

Buddha were in the Treasure Tower together this is seen as a lesson on the three characteristics, or phases, of the Buddha. The former (Sakyamuni) represented the subject (the wisdom to know reality), the latter (Taho Buddha) the object (reality itself). The third characteristic is their unity. "That they sat beside each other signifies the unity of subject and object,"[134] one being the Buddha nature inherent in our lives, the other the wisdom to realize it. All the other Buddhas present represent "merciful functions arising from the combination of the two," and "the gathering of all these Buddhas . . . signifies that the life of the Eternal Buddha of Nam-myoho-renge-kyo [Nichiren] is endowed with the three phases."[135]

Of course the list for other possible interpretations is endless. Elsewhere we find that it is the Treasure Tower which is variously interpreted as Nam-myoho-renge-kyo, or as the Gohonzon, or as one's own life, or as Buddhahood and so on. But, "The Ceremony in the Air" is given the same interpretations and is also said to "signify the principle of *Kyochi myogo*, 'the oneness of subjective enlightenment and objective verification.'"[136] In the following quotation, note that the "true" meaning of the Sutra is found only through the unconscious mind. "As Bodhisattvas of the Earth, however, we have all attended the eternal ceremony [in the air] in which the Lotus Sutra was taught, and that experience is indelibly recorded in the deepest realms of our unconsciousness. It is therefore in the depths of our lives, *in the realm of the unconscious mind, where we grasp the meaning of the Lotus Sutra.*"[137]

In *A Reply to Lord Nanjo*, Nichiren told Nanjo, "Try to come see me at the earliest possible occasion. I am awaiting you here." NS argues, "This statement should be interpreted today to mean that the Dai-Gohonzon is anxiously awaiting all the people of the earth to come and worship."[138] NS claims to be a rational religion, but is it?

We have labored to arrive at this point in order to introduce a key apologetic of NS. According to George Williams, director of NS, NS proves that it is *the* true religion by three tests. Writing in *NSA Seminars: An Introduction to*

True Buddhism, he argues that the true religion must have: 1) literal proof—a reliable, written scripture; 2) theoretical proof—the true interpretation of that scripture; evidence that no changes have been made in original doctrines and that the scripture harmonizes with science and logic and 3) actual proof—the experience of chanting and receiving benefits.[139]

Our earlier discussions show that the available evidence disproves the first two tests. The Lotus Sutra is not a literal proof, not accurately transmitted. And NS has not always interpreted it in harmony with Nichiren, and there have been substantial doctrinal changes made. Here we will show that NS theory is anything but logical or scientific. Williams himself even declares that "the Buddhist teachings state, 'if their use neither document nor have logic, one should not believe.' Who can disagree with this rational attitude?"[140] A good point. As Ikeda is quoted in *The Soka Gakkai* (1962, pp. 131-32), "True religion must not be unscientific on even the smallest point. . . . Unless a religion is infallible from the scientific, philosophical and moral standpoints, it cannot be called true or absolute."

In the first chapter of the Lotus Sutra, Buddha is sitting on the Vulture Peak surrounded by 1,200 monks with occult powers, 6,000 nuns, 80,000 Bodhisattvas, 80,000 gods (including the sun, moon and wind gods), millions of Gandharvas and an infinite number of demons and other beings.[141] The Buddha enters a trance state, celestial flowers gently fall and cover the assembly and "the Buddha field" shakes in six different ways. A ray issues from the circle of hair between the eyebrows of Buddha extending over 1,800,000 Buddha fields. This causes all beings everywhere to become visible and hear the message preached by the Buddha.

Commenting on this chapter (and the entire Lotus Sutra), the *Seikyo Times* does not declare the events to be myth. To the contrary, "just imagine hundreds of thousands of people gathered on top of a rocky mountain peak! The Eagle [vulture] Peak still exists in India, but it seems far too small to accommodate such a vast host . . . yet the Buddha had the attention of everyone present and his words appear to have reached them all. . . . The appearance of this [treasure] tower, which was about half the size of the earth itself, must have absolutely astounded the people gathered there."[142]

This analysis comes from the same group that adamantly preaches that "true religion" must harmonize with science and logic:

If the literature is not rational, logical and scientific, it cannot be a basic teaching for modern people who have acquired the scientific way of thinking and living. . . . The history of Buddhism can be cited as an example proving that Buddhism is scientific. No evidence can be found of struggle between it and science throughout its long history, as often occurred in the history of Christianity. Superstitious and unscientific doctrines contradict scientific logic and cause strife. . . . How about Christianity? . . . Who can believe such unscientific nonsense?![143]

The commentary in *Seikyo Times* asks a crucial question of this event:

Is it reality or illusion? Whoever reads the Lotus Sutra will face this question, since the story goes so far from what we think of as common sense. Assemblies of hundreds of thousands of people, the appearance of the 500-yujun-high Treasure Tower, the emergence of as many Bodhisattvas of the Earth as the sands of the Ganges—these all are staggering to the imagination. However, they are *not mere illusions or grandiose tales.*[*] Some scholars criticize the Lotus Sutra as being a product of the unique imagination of the Indian people. It is easy to reach this conclusion, but to discover what the ancient Indians desired to tell with this sutra is not easy at all. Criticism such as that mentioned above only shows the arrogant reliance some contemporaries have on the current limits of science and rational thought. Yet modern thought is not automatically more correct. Our first requirement is to view this sutra with an open mind. With a seeking attitude, the living story of the Lotus Sutra becomes meaningful.[144]

In the previous quote we see: (1) an admission that the Sutra goes beyond the bounds of common sense; (2) openness to the possibility of

---

*Yet the *Seikyo Times* of Jan. 1979, states: ". . . these cannot be considered historical facts" (p. 58).

a literal interpretation; (3) the admission that the Sutra's intent and purpose is obscure; (4) a possible denial of rationality and modern science when it opposes the Sutra and (5) the necessity of an "open mind" and a "seeking attitude" for the Sutra to have any real meaning.

The article also admits that many readers "may still find it difficult to grasp its actual relationship to our daily lives."[145] Yet Ikeda states that "if one cannot apply the teachings of the text in one's daily life . . . then one's understanding of the Sutra is valueless."[146] Unfortunately, some disciples took the Lotus Sutra's "relationship" to daily life quite literally and injuriously. In Chapter 23, the Sutra contains examples of Bodhisattvas igniting themselves and burning for thousands of years, illuminating the galaxy. Murata comments: "In ancient China, some devotees took these allegories literally and burned their fingers or arms and even incarcerated themselves in drastic affirmation of their faith, and to early followers of the Lotus Sutra in Japan, such acts of devotion were thought more important than the intellectual comprehension of the sutra."[147]

NS disciples have the same problem with the founder of their religion that they have with their Scripture. In reading *The Gosho Reference*, Vol. 1, the NS translation and commentary on 34 of Nichiren's letters (more than half incompletely translated), we find that according to the normal reading of the text there is often an ambiguous interpretation and that Nichiren had the same difficulties in interpreting the Sutra as everyone else.*[148] Also, Nichiren at times views himself as no more than a common mortal, and in what he called "his most important teachings" ("The True Nature of Life") even he expressed doubts about his own Buddhist mission.[149] Nevertheless, Nichiren claimed that only the Lotus Sutra was valid and that only his interpretation was true. But NS declares that only their interpretation of Nichiren is correct, even though they distort him.

For example, it is clear that Nichiren's worldview was thirteenth century magical and polytheistic, not twentieth century rational and

scientific. In "Reply to *Kyo'o-dono*," he declares that he is praying to Nitten and Gatten (the sun and moon gods), "each and every moment of the day."[150] Therefore, to interpret his writings solely in light of twentieth century science (the gods being "natural functions of the universe") is to distort his writings, offering ideas that Nichiren could never have intended. We could cite many examples, such as in "A Reply to Lord Ueno" and "The Proof of the Lotus Sutra," where he clearly believes in spirits as personal entities. He says of King Asoka, "He even kept spirits in his service."[151] Demons, too, are clearly personal spirits.[152] But in the NS commentary following these sections, the demons are spoken of as impersonal concepts. Elsewhere Nichiren sees heaven as a place and gods as spirits, but Ikeda maintains that heaven is "nature" and the gods' "life itself."[153] Another commentator admits that some Sutras state, ". . . hell is found under the ground"; yet he goes on to state, "This may be interpreted to mean that it is such an extremely oppressed condition of life that one feels as if he were sinking into the depths of the earth."[154] Modern NS leaders offer no solution to such dilemmas.

For many years, NS disciples have continued to trust these spiritual guides, even though the guides do not trust Nichiren. In an embarrassing statement, Nichiren declared that his followers were to believe in the Lotus Sutra "exactly as it teaches," and accept that "the entire Lotus Sutra is true."[155] So how is it that even President Ikeda admitted the Lotus Sutra contains "fables"? Why did he declare of The Ceremony in the Air that "it is difficult to believe . . . it is too unrealistic to be true"? Why did he admit that the Lotus Sutra contained "the element of the fantastic and irrational"?[156] Does he have the same faith in the Lotus Sutra as Nichiren, and if not, what of those he leads?

Although Nichiren did interpret at least part of the Lotus Sutra symbolically (The Treasure Tower represented the true Buddhist and was the daimoku), in "Reply to Lord Nanjo" he stated, "If there should be any falsity in the Sutra whatsoever, what is there [left] in which one can believe?"[157] This is the point. Daishonin maintained that "there can be not the least falsity in

---

*There are some 300 explanatory notes for 34 short letters.

the Lotus Sutra. . . ."[158] But did even Nichiren believe that the body of a Bodhisattva "continued blazing for twelve thousand years without ceasing to burn," lighting up the whole galaxy?[159] Apparently so. For moderns, the accepted method for sidestepping such difficulties is either to ignore the text or to claim that only the truly enlightened will understand. Ikeda argued, ". . . unless one to some extent is able to enter the realm of the enlightenment of a Buddha, he can hardly hope to grasp its truths."[160] Thus, understanding the Sutra "from a literary point of view" is fruitless; unless one chants daimoku, all the study in the world of the Sutra is valueless for comprehending it.[161] Ikeda says, "It is useless to ask whether any such miraculous phenomenon actually took place at the time when Sakyamuni was preaching the Lotus Sutra, nor would there be any point to such a question. The important message . . . is that Buddha world is present within the life force of every single person. . . ."[162]

But why is *his* interpretation valid? How can we say the Buddha's preaching or teaching was real, when the miracle in which the preaching occurred, The Ceremony in the Air, was not? Chris Roman, an associate editor of *Seikyo Times*, admits that if we apply the same method of interpretation to the Bible (that they apply to the Sutra), "It becomes apparent that [the Christian] God is inherent in nature itself, a force eternal, working to maintain harmony between all its various existences and reacting on the basis of a fundamental law of cause and effect."[163] Again, this is exactly the point. Once we remove the Bible from its history, culture and context, it becomes a useless document. In the same manner, NS has removed the Lotus Sutra from its cultural environment and twisted it to conform to the modern "scientific" worldview of NS, and it has become a useless document. Roman also denies any validity to a magical ceremony that actually took place in the sky at some historical point in time. However, when a person chants *daimoku*, "He is attesting to the truth of The Ceremony in the Air within his own life," that 3,000 conditions exist in his life at every moment. Thus, ". . . only when we understand the proper way of reading the Lotus Sutra

can we come to grasp its profound view of life. . . . In other words the Lotus Sutra contains a detailed analysis of what life is."[164]

Nam-myoho-renge-kyo Is Not in the Lotus Sutra

But how does any believer know this? How can the NS believer chant daily when the chant does not even exist in one's Scripture? For NS perhaps the most crucial "doctrine" is Nam-myoho-renge-kyo. It is as central to NS as Christ is to Christianity. But we do not find this term or its meaning mentioned anywhere in the Lotus Sutra. What if Jesus Christ were not mentioned anywhere in the New Testament? Would there be a Christianity? "In what part of the Lotus Sutra did Sakyamuni clarify this law? Even if we peruse the Sutra over and over again, we are unable to know what the law is."[165] "For some untold reasons, Sakyamuni did not define the law as Nam Myoho Renge Kyo, but gave somewhat abstract explanations in what was later called the Lotus Sutra."[166] Clearly, the "law" was not there *until* Nichiren supplied the new interpretation, because the law was hidden "beneath the Letter."[167] Nichiren, who entered the scene at least a thousand years after the Lotus Sutra was written, was the first to "clarify the entity of life" as Nam-myoho-renge-kyo, despite the fact that the Lotus Sutra is believed to be the Buddha's "highest" teachings and therefore should have been "clarified" when he first composed it. In the January 1979 *Seikyo Times,* Yasuji Kirimura admits, "There is one essential point which we might think should have been revealed, but which was in actuality omitted"; and he laments, "There can be no such vital omission, however. Simply, the Sutra does not state it explicitly."[168] One might think that such a fact would cause one to doubt Nichiren's wisdom in selecting the Lotus Sutra as the "true" teaching of Buddhism, if not NS altogether. However, rather than admit that Nichiren was in error, one discovers that the truth is really there after all, but it is "between the lines" and "beneath the letter." After all, since Nichiren is the true Eternal Buddha, only he could show us what it *really* means. "Incidentally, to think that Nichiren Daishonin delved into the Lotus Sutra and therein found the ultimate law is a mistake [because it is not there]. Actually, no one except the Daishonin could clarify what The Ceremony in the Air expresses. From his enlightenment to the ultimate law, *the Daishonin shed new light upon the Lotus sutra. . . .* The true purpose of this great Sutra was revealed and fulfilled for the first and last time by Nichiren Daishonin."[169]

Further, as noted, the central doctrine of ichinen sanzen is also absent from the Lotus Sutra. Brannen points out, "The teaching of the ichinen sanzen is not made explicit in the basic doctrine of the Lotus Sutra. It was Tendai Daishi [a predecessor to Nichiren] who discovered the truth, but Nichiren alone was able to . . . interpret the unwritten truth behind the letter."[170] The *Seikyo Times* of January 1979 states: "The doctrine of ichinen sanzen is found only in one place, *hidden in the depths* of the Juryo chapter [16] of the Lotus Sutra."[171] But *Lectures on the Sutra* states ichinen sunzen is missing: "The Juryo chapter does not necessarily reveal the 'eternity of life' however."[172]

What we have, then, is a religion made of whole cloth. NS doctrine is "kept in secret in the depths" of the chapters and found "between the lines."[173] NS doctrine, according to Nichiren, is "hidden truth . . . which lies beneath the letter."[174]

Just as the Buddha did not really compose the Lotus Sutra, the Lotus Sutra does not really contain the doctrines of Nichiren Shoshu. Of course even these issues are academic, for if, as NS teaches, the Buddha "guided the masses by various fables" for 42 years, on what basis can we be certain his last few years of alleged teaching in the Lotus Sutra was any different?[175] Is not "his" Sutra little more than "various fables"?

Conclusion

Since precious little of objective reality is left us here, perhaps it is not surprising that Nichiren finally concluded that the Lotus Sutra itself was unimportant!

"This teaching (Nam-myoho-renge-kyo) was not propagated in the Former and Middle days of the Law because it incapacitated other sutras. Now, in the Latter Day of The Law, neither the Lotus Sutra or the other sutras are useful [valid].* Only Nam-myoho-renge-kyo is beneficial."[176] This quote is found in "A Reply to Lord Ueno."[177] In it Nichiren refers to both Sakyamuni and the Lotus Sutra. Note Ikeda's interpretation (Ikeda himself was guided by the High Priest of NS, Nittatsu Hosoi): "Whenever the Daishonin refers to the Lotus Sutra as the teaching to spread in the Latter Day, he means the essence of the sutra [not found in it], Nam-myoho-renge-kyo. Thus devotion to Sakyamuni and the Lotus Sutra means 'devotion to Nichiren Daishonin and Nam-myoho-renge-kyo.'"[178]

Nichiren Daishonin claimed to find the true teachings of the Buddha in the Lotus Sutra. Besides being wrong on this most crucial point, he even misinterpreted the Lotus Sutra and made it declare doctrines absent from the text itself, as have his followers. In that the entire NS religion is based upon Daishonin's erroneous claims and interpretation, the credibility of NS is eroded. The Lotus Sutra, Nichiren's interpretation of it and the NS interpretation of both the Sutra and Nichiren present insurmountable difficulties for NSA.

All that remains is a four-word chant.

COMPARATIVE CHARTS

In the following six charts, we compare and contrast Buddhism, including its most influential American sect, Nichiren Shoshu Buddhism, with the beliefs of Christianity. These charts will further illustrate the problems involved when people claim that Buddhism and Christianity are compatible or complementary.

---

*Ikeda translates "useful" as "valid" in *The True Object of Worship*, Part 1, p. 5.

Chart One: Buddhism vs. Christianity	
BUDDHISM	CHRISTIANITY
Seeks release from suffering	Seeks knowledge of God and His glory
"Unreal" (impermanent) world	Real world
Nihilistic, pessimistic outlook	Hopeful, optimistic outlook
No God or Savior exists	One God and Savior exists
Apologetic centered in subjective experience	Apologetic centered in objective history
Trusts self	Trusts God
Morality self-derived	Morality based on the infinitely holy character of God
Devalues man (e.g., man is a bundle of flux; the body is evil, the mind is deceptive)	Dignifies man (e.g., man is made in God's own image; the believer's body is the temple of the Holy Spirit; the believer's mind can glorify God)
Activity and individual life are "evil" and hamper salvation	Activity and individual life can be good and glorify God
Atheistic/polytheistic	Theistic
Impersonal ultimate reality	Personal ultimate reality
Often anti-social	Responsible social action
Enlightened by works	Salvation by grace
Mysticism and the occult are spiritual activities	Mysticism and the occult are rejected as evil and as opposed to God
The afterlife constitutes an impersonal, uncertain nirvana	The afterlife is clearly delineated and involves personal immortality
Spiritual truth is discovered by disciplined effort	Spiritual truth is revealed by God

Chart Two: Buddha vs. Jesus	
BUDDHA	JESUS
Buddha is dead	Jesus is alive
In many ways the Buddha is a mystery (no contemporary biographies exist); "apart from flegends we know very little about the the the circumstances of his life"[179]	Jesus was a historic person of whom four reliable, early "biographies" were penned; "It is a historic fact that Jesus Christ lived and taught taught what the New Testament says He taught"[180]
Teachings uncertain	Teachings certain
Buddha was only a man: "Notwithstanding his own objectivity toward himself, there was constant pressure during his lifetime to turn him into a god. He rebuffed all these categorically, insisting that he was human in every respect. He made no attempt to conceal his temptations and weaknesses, how difficult it had been to attain enlightenment, how narrow the margin by which he had won through, how fallible he still remained."[181]	Jesus is incarnate God: "I am the light of the world"; "I am the way, the truth and the Life"; "He who believes in Me will never die"; "He who has seen Me has seen the Father." "I and the Father are One." "You believe in God, Believe also in Me." "All that the Father has is Mine." "All power andauthority in heaven and earth have been given to Me" — Jesus *(continues)*

Chart Two: Buddha vs. Jesus, cont.	
BUDDHA	**JESUS**
Non-theistic worldview	Theistic worldview
A way-shower; Buddha as a person is unnecessary for achieving enlightenment	The Savior; salvation is impossible apart from the Person of Jesus
Encouraged men to follow a philosophy	Encouraged people to follow Him
Never appealed to faith	Stressed the importance of faith in God and Himself
Rejected God	Called God His own Father
Undogmatic	Dogmatic
Offered a way	Taught that He was the only way between the temporal and the eternal

Chart Three: Buddhist Enlightenment vs. Christian Salvation	
BUDDHIST ENLIGHTENMENT	**CHRISTIAN SALVATION**
Man's nature remains fundamentally unchanged; the individual Buddhist accomplishes "enlightenment," but this is only a new *perspective* on life- undergirded by carefully cultivated altered states of consciousness (the experience of "nirvana" in meditation)	Man's nature is changed forever. This is accomplished wholly by God through an inner change of one's nature (regeneration) a new legal standing before God (justification) and, logically, a corresponding "outer" transformation (sanctification)
Eradicates "ignorance" of the truths of Buddhism and ostensibly, in the end, suffering	Eradicates sin
History is irrelevant; salvation is experientially based and possible through mysticism; inner experience supplants historical concerns; the person of Buddha irrelevant to process of enlightenment	Historically based; salvation is objectively based and impossible apart from the person of Jesus Christ of Nazareth
The believer is saved from life; sin is not forgiven	The believer is saved from divine judgment; all his sins are forgiven
Humanistic: man instituted	Theological: God instituted
Escapist (salvation *from* the world)	Realist (salvation *of* the world, i.e., of all believers)
One cannot be reconciled to an impersonal nirvana; one can only "realize" it or "achieve" it; technically, one cannot even experience it	Reconciliation to God
Eternal existence allegedly constitutes an ineffable existence somewhere in between (not comprising either) total annihilation or personal immortality	Eternal life constitutes personal immortality and fellowship with a loving God
Derives from a finite source of change utilizing the power of self-perfection	Derives from an infinite source of change utilizing the power of divine grace
Ultimate Reality is the *experience* of emptiness or ineffable impersonal "existence"	Ultimate Reality *is* the infinite personal triune God
Faith is denied or placed in Buddhist gods plus works	Based on faith in Christ alone apart from works

Chart Four: Buddhist Teaching vs. Christian Scripture	
BUDDHISM	**CHRISTIANITY**
Those who, relying upon themselves only, shall is the one who trusts in not look for assistance to any one besides themselves, it is they who shall reach the topmost height[182]	The LORD says: "Cursed man, who depends on flesh for his strength, and whose heart turns away from the LORD" (Jeremiah 17:5)
By this ye shall know that a man is *not* my disciple—that he tries to work a miracle[183]	But many of the multitude believed in Him; and they were saying, "When the Christ shall come, He will not perform more signs than those which this man has, will He?" (John 7:31 NAS)
"One thing I teach," said Buddha: "suffering and the end of suffering. . . . It is just ill and the ceasing of ill that I proclaim"[184]	But to the degree that you share the sufferings of Christ, keep on rejoicing; so that also at the revelation of His glory, you may rejoice with exultation. . . . Therefore, let those also who suffer according to the will of God entrust their souls to a faithful Creator in doing what is right (1 Peter 4:13, 19 NAS)
The self we think to be true and important is pure illusion, and a lie that is the cause of a large proportion of human suffering[185]	So God created man in his own image, in the image of God he created him; male and female he created them. . . . The LORD God formed the man from the dust of the ground and breathed into his nostrils the breath of life, and the man became a living being (Genesis 1:27; 2:7)
Perhaps the greatest difference between Buddhism and Christianity is that Buddhism very explicitly does not require an act of faith[186]	And without faith it is impossible to please Him, for he who comes to God must believe that He is, and that He is a rewarder of those who seek Him. (Hebrews 11:6 NAS)
There is no permanent self in Buddhism. In fact, nothing is permanent[187]	(See John 6:47.) Your kingdom is an everlasting kingdom, and your dominion endures through all generations. (Psalm 145:13) But Thou, O LORD, dost abide forever (Psalm 102:12 NAS)
Do not believe in that which you have yourselves imagined, thinking that a god has inspired it[188]	All scripture is inspired by God and profitable for teaching, for reproof, for correction, for training in righteousness; that the man of God may be adequate, equipped for every good work (2 Timothy 3:16–17 NAS)
According to Buddhism the universe evolved, but it did not evolve out of nothingness; it evolved out of the dispersed matter of a previous universe, and when this universe is dissolved, its dispersed matter—or, its residual energy which is continually renewing itself—will in time give rise to another universe in the same way. The process is therefore cyclical and continuous. The universe is composed of millions of millions of world-systems like our solar system, each with its various planes of existence[189]	In the beginning God created the heavens and the earth. (Genesis 1:1) By faith we understand that the worlds were prepared by the word of God, so that what is seen was not made out of things which are visible (Hebrews 11:3 NAS)

Chart Five: Nichiren Shoshu Buddhism vs. Christianity	
NICHIREN SHOSHU	CHRISTIANITY
Eternal cyclic-universe ("illusion")	Finished creation (real)
Man is "eternal," the manifestation of an impersonal God (man in the image of the universe and/or "life essence")	Man is the creation of a personal God (man in the image of God)
Monistic (all life is one essence)	Monotheistic (God is triune; man, animal and matter are all created by God but generically distinct)
Ultimate reality is an impersonal life essence (amoral)	Ultimate reality is a loving, personal, just deity (absolutely moral)
Salvation by personal effort (self-perfection)	Salvation by grace through faith (involving the imputed righteousness of Christ)
The Buddha nature resides universally in everyone	God dwells only in the regenerate
Universal salvation (reincarnation)	Particular redemption (eternal heaven or hell)
Key historical apologetic spurious and subjective evidential and objective (e.g., the mystical interpretation of the Lotus Sutra)	Key historic apologetic (e.g., fulfilled prophecy, the resurrection of Christ)
Anti-supernatural	Supernatural

Chart Six: Nichiren Shoshu Buddhism vs. Christian Scripture	
NICHIREN SHOSHU	CHRISTIAN SCRIPTURE
In Buddhist thinking, each of us alone is responsible for our destiny, individual and joint. We are not in God's hands; we are in our own[190]	You did not honor the God who holds in his hand your life and all your ways (Daniel 5:23)
The Gohonzon [altar] is the only True Object of Worship in the World[191]	You shall worship the Lord your God and serve Him only(Luke 4:8 NAS)
Anyone with the Gohonzon is already a perfect and beautiful human being[192]	If we say we have no sin, we are deceiving ourselves, and the truth is not in us (1 John 1:8 NAS)
Christianity must not be our guiding philosophy of life[193]	I am the way, and the truth, and the life; no one comes to the Father, but through Me. (John 14:6 NAS) Everyone on the side of truth listens to me (John 18:37)
Let us resolve to chant a million more *Daimoku*. Two million—that would be fine of course[194]	And when you are praying, do not use meaningless repetition, as the Gentiles do, for they suppose they will be heard for their many words. Therefore do not be like them (Matthew 6:7; see Isaiah 29:13)
You can see how much more demanding and full of conditions Christianity is, when you compare this with Buddhism, where you have only one condition: to believe. It shows the difficulty of practice and the inferiority of the teachings of Christianity[195]	These things I have written to you who believe in the name of the Son of God, in order that you might *know* that you have eternal life (1 John 5:14 NAS) He who believes has eternal life (John 6:47)

(continues)

Chart Six: Nichiren Shoshu Buddhism vs. Christian Scripture, cont.	
NICHIREN SHOSHU	CHRISTIAN SCRIPTURE
If we simply worship the Gohonzon . . . we will surely become rich[196]	Beware, and be on your guard against every form of greed; for not even when one has an abundance does his life consist of his possessions. (Luke 12:15 NAS) For what does it profit a man to gain the whole world, and forfeit his own soul? For what shall a man give in exchange for his soul? (Mark 8:36–37 NAS)
The truth itself is no standard of judgment because truth doesn't invariably lead to human happiness[197]	We know that God's judgment . . . is based on truth. (Romans 2:2) No lie is of the truth (1 John 2:21 NAS)
If you give up now, all your efforts will be meaningless[198]	For God is not so unjust to forget your work and the love which you have shown toward His name, in having ministered and in still ministering to the saints (Hebrews 6:10)
The Buddhists would find no objection in the cult of many gods because the idea of a jealous God is quite alien to them[199]	You shall have no other gods before Me. . . . You shall not make for yourself an idol. . . . You shall not worship them or serve them; for I the LORD your God, am a jealous God, visiting the iniquity of the fathers on the children, on the third and fourth generation of those who hate Me (Exodus 20:3–5 NAS)
If you seek enlightenment outside of yourself, any kind of practice or good acts will be completely meaningless[200]	Stop trusting in man, who has but a breath in his nostrils. Of what account is he? (Isaiah 2:22)
A person who says "I keep faith" . . . when he is poor, I don't consider him my pupil[201]	Turning His gaze on His disciples, He began to say, "Blessed are you who are poor, for yours is the Kingdom of God" (Luke 6:20 NAS)
In contrast, the Lotus Sutra holds that worldly affairs are the entity of Buddhism[202]	Do not be conformed to this world. (Romans 12:2 NAS) Set your mind on the things above, not on the things that are on the earth (Colossians 3:2 NAS)
Nothing in the universe is immune to the dynamics of the cycle of jo-ju-e-ku (constant change and flux—birth, growth, maturity, waining stage, return to the void)[203]	Jesus Christ is the same yesterday and today and forever (Hebrews 13:8)
Everything undergoes constant change and this is the real aspect of the universe[204]	For I, the LORD; do not change (Malachi 3:6 NAS)
There is in Buddhism no myth of creation nor any idea of an original beginning . . . the universe is itself an eternal existence without beginning or end[205]	In the beginning God created the heavens and the earth (Genesis 1:1)
Life has no beginning, therefore it was not created by God[206]	It is I who made the earth and created mankind upon it (Isaiah 45:12 NAS)

(continues)

Chart Six: Nichiren Shoshu Buddhism vs. Christian Scripture, cont.	
NICHIREN SHOSHU	CHRISTIAN SCRIPTURE
With our total devotion to the Gohonzon, we should promote Kosenrufu [prosleytization] since . . . this, and only this will assure us of eternal happiness[207]	And we know that the Son of God has come, and has given us understanding, in order that we might know Him who is true, and we are in Him who is true, in His Son Jesus Christ. This is the true God and eternal life. Little children, guard yourself from idols (1 John 5:20–21 NAS)
In Buddhahood, one "experiences eternal life in its true sense"[208]	This is eternal life, that they may know Thee, the only true God, and Jesus Christ whom Thou hast sent (John 17:3 NAS)
There is no other way to be enlightened except by receiving Nam-myoho-renge-kyo [Buddhist mystical chant][209]	But as many as received Him [Jesus], to them He gave the right to become children of God, even to those who believe in His name (John 1:12 NAS)
It is only Daishonin's Buddhism that can save modern man[210]	And there is salvation in no one else; for there is no other name under heaven that has been given among men, by which we must be saved (Acts 4:12 NAS)
There is no danger of damnation.[211]	Do not marvel at this; for an hour is coming, in which all who are in the tombs shall hear His voice, and shall come forth . . . those who committed the evil deeds to a resurrection of judgment. (John 5:28 NAS) He that believeth not shall be damned (Mark 16:16 KJV)

NOTES

1. *The Teaching of the Buddha*, p.18.
2. Ibid., pp. 86, 100, 104, 108.
3. Werner Erhard Interview, *New Age Journal*, No. 7, p. 20.
4. William Warren Bartley, III, *Werner Erhard the Transformation of a Man: The Founding of Est* (New York: Clarkson N. Potter, 1978), p. 121, italics in original.
5. Clive Erricker, *Buddhism* (Chicago, IL: NTC Publishing, 1995), p. 65, cf. 61-65.
6. For a description of these in more detail see Richard A. Gard (ed.), *Buddhism* (New York: George Braziller, Inc., 1961), pp. 106-167.
7. F.L. Woodward, trans., *Some Sayings of the Buddha* (New York: Oxford University Press, 1973), pp. 124-125.
8. Alexandria David-Neel, *Buddhism: Its Doctrines and Its Methods* (New York: St. Martin's Press, 1977), p. 25; Charles Prebish, "Doctrines of Early Buddhists," in *Buddhism: A Modern Perspective* (ed.), Charles S. Prebish (University Park & London: Pennsylvania University Press, 1975), p. 30.
9. *The Teaching of Buddha*, p. 88.
10. Ibid., pp. 84-104.
11. See e.g., T. O. Ling, *A Dictionary of Buddhism: A Guide to Thought and Tradition* (New York: Charles Schribners' Sons, 1972), pp. 96-97.
12. Ibid., pp. 156-158.
13. Nyanatiloka, *Buddhist Dictionary* (Colombo, Ceylon: Frewin and Company, Ltd., 1972), pp. 105-107.
14. *The Teaching of Buddha*, p. 112.
15. J.N.D. Anderson (ed.), *The World's Religions* (Grand Rapids, MI: Eerdman's Publishing Co., 1968), p. 124. See the Dhyayitamushti sutra quoted in *The History of Buddhist Thought*, Edward J. Thomas (London: Reutledge and Kegan Paul Ltd., 1975), p. 223.
16. Edward J. Thomas, *The History of Buddhist Thought*, p. 218. He cites Sutta-Nipata 1119; Majjhima 121, 122; Samy. iv, 54; the two Prajnaparmita-hrdaya-sutras, etc.
17. Edward Conze, et al. (eds.), *Buddhist Texts Through the Ages* (New York: Philosophical Libary, Inc., 1954), p. 212, citing Lankavatara Sutra, pp. 90-96.
18. Ibid., pp. 215-216 citing Asanga Mahayanasamgraha II, 27, including Vasubandhu's comments.
19. *The Teaching of Buddha*, p. 86.
20. Hendrik Kraemer, *The Christian Message in a Non-Christian World* (Grand Rapids, MI: Kregel Publ., 1977), pp. 174-175, 177.
21. Walt Anderson, *Open Secrets, A Western Guide to Tibetan Buddhism* (New York: Viking Press, 1979), p. 23.
22. *Christian Research Journal*, Summer 1996, p. 8.
23. Masaharu Anesaki, "How Christianity Appeals to a Japanese Buddhist," in David W. McKain (ed.), *Christianity: Some Non-Christian Appraisals*, (Westport, CT: Greenwood Press, 1976), pp. 102-103, italics in original.

24. D. T. Suzuki, "Mysticism: Christian and Buddhist," in McKain (ed.), p. 111.
25. Sir Charles Eliot, *Hinduism and Buddhism*, Vol. I. (New York: Barnes and Noble, Inc., 1971), p. xcv.
26. David-Neel, p. 247.
27. Stephen Neill, *Christian Faith and Other Faiths* (2nd ed.) (Great Britain: Oxford University Press, 1970), p. 117.
28. Ibid., p. 51.
29. Ibid., p. 28.
30. Dom Aelred Graham, *Conversations: Christian and Buddhist* (New York: Harcourt, Brace, Jovanovich, 1968), p. 104, second emphasis added.
31. Neill, *Christian Faith*, pp. 118-119.
32. Conze (ed.), *Buddhist Texts Through the Ages*, pp. 194.
33. Ibid.
34. Eliot, p. 325.
35. Erricker, pp. 2-3.
36. J. I. Packer, *Hot Tub Religion*, p. 22.
37. *The Teaching of Buddha*, p. 96.
38. Charles Prebish, *Buddhism: A Modern Perspective*, essay, p. 21.
39. Edward Conze, *Buddhist Thought in India*, p. 262.
40. Robert E. Hume, *The World's Living Religions*, p. 73.
41. In F. L. Woodward, Trans., *Some Sayings of the Buddha* (New York: Oxford University Press 1973), p. X. X. I. I.
42. Dom Aelred Graham, *Conversations: Christian and Buddhist*, p. 172; T. N. Callaway, *Zen-Way, Jesus-Way*, pp. 147-48.
43. Kenneth S. Latourette, *Introducing Buddhism* (1956), p. 59.
44. Erricker, p. 51.
45. Ibid.
46. J. Isamu Yamamoto, *Beyond Buddhism* (Dowers Grover, Il: Intervarsity Press, 1982), p. 118, 123.
47. E.g., C. Burrows, "The Fierce and Erotic Gods of Buddhism," *Natural History*, April 1972, p. 26ff.
48. *The Teaching of Buddha*, p. 20.
49. Francis H. Cook, "Nirvana" in Prebish (ed.), p. 133.
50. Walt Anderson, p. 36.
51. Kalama Sutta, in D.T. Niles, *Buddhism and the Claims of Christ*, p. 20.
52. *The Teaching of Buddha*, p. 24.
53. William M. Alnor, "Name It and Claim It Style of Buddhism Called America's Fastest Growing Religion," *Christian Research Institute Journal*, Winter/Spring 1989, p. 26.
54. R. H. Robinson, "Buddhism in China and Japan," in *The Concise Encyclopedia of Living Faiths*, ed. R. C. Zaehner (Boston: Beacon, 1959), p. 346; cf. Harry Thomsen, *The New Religions of Japan* (Rutland, Vermont: Charles E. Tuttle, 1963), p. 101.
55. "The Buddha's Perception into the Three Existences of Life," *Seikyo Times*, Dec. 1978, p. 7.
56. Charles Brandon, ed., *Dictionary of Comparative Religion* (New York: Charles Schribner's Sons, 1970), p. 470.
57. Edward Conze, *Buddhism, Its Essence and Development* (New York: Harper & Row, 1959), p. 206.
58. See William M. Alnor, "Infighting, Division, and Scandal Afflicting Nichiren Shoshu Buddhists," *Christian Research Journal*, Winter 1992, pp. 5-6.
59. Editorial, *World Tribune*, 1 April 1991, p .2.
60. Kiyoaki Murata, *Japan's New Buddhism* (New York: Walker, 1969), pp. 169-170; Daisaku Ikeda, *Lectures on Buddhism* Vol. V (Tokyo: Seikyo Press, 1970), p. 44.
61. "Twelve Million Daimoku," *World Tribune*, 31 August 1970, p. 7.
62. Ibid., 1 July 1970, p. 7.
63. Daisaku Ikeda, "Be Envoys of Peace for a Troubled Age," *NSA Quarterly*, Winter 1976, p. 42.
64. Daisaku Ikeda, *Complete Works*, Vol. 1 (Tokyo: The Seikyo Press, 1968), pp. 478-479.
65. *NSA Quarterly*, Spring 1973, pp. 59-60.
66. Daisaku Ikeda, *Lectures on Buddhism*, Vol. IV (Tokyo: The Seikyo Press, 1969), p. 119.
67. Daisaku Ikeda, "Life's Ultimate Fulfillment," *NSA Quarterly*, Fall 1975, p. 68.
68. *NSA Quarterly*, Spring 1973, pp. 59-60.
69. Thomsen, p. 101.
70. Murata, p. 103, citing Soka Gakkai Kyogakubu (Study Dept., Soka Gakkai) *Shakubuku Kyoten* (Tokyo, 1967), p. 244.
71. Murata, p. 104.
72. Noah Brannen, *Soka Gakkai: Japan's Militant Buddhists* (Richmond, VA: John Knox, 1968), pp. 100-101; cf., pp. 103-106 and Thomsen, pp. 104-115.
73. Ibid.; cf. Murata, p. 102.
74. *The Sokagakkai*, rev. ed. (Tokyo: The Seikyo Press, 1962), pp. 78, 82, 143, 148; Daisaku Ikeda, *Science and Religion* (Tokyo: The Sokagakkai 1965), p. 47; Daisaku Ikeda, "Salvation of Mankind in Our Times," *The East*, Jan. 1973, p. 25; *Seikyo Times*, Nov. 1972, p. 45; Ikeda, *Complete Works I*, p. 442; *NSA Quarterly*, Fall 1973, passim.
75. *Seikyo Times*, Nov. 1972, p. 45; Ikeda, *Complete Works I*, 442; *NSA Quarterly*, Fall 1973, pp. 18-127.
76. Ikeda, *Complete Works I*, p. 462.
77. Editorial, "Three Guiding Principles," *Seikyo Times*, Jan. 1979, p. 4.
78. Daisaku Ikeda, *Heritage of the Ultimate Law of Life*, Part II (Santa Monica, CA: World Tribune Press, 1977), p. 12.
79. "To Secure Human Happiness," *Seikyo Times*, Oct. 1982, p. 52.
80. "The Reality of Evil," *Seikyo Times*, Nov. 1982, p. 58.
81. "Heaven and Hell versus Life in the Ten Worlds," *Seikyo Times*, June 1982, p. 56.
82. "The Innate Power of Life," *Seikyo Times*, Dec. 1982, pp. 43-44.
83. Brannen, pp. 98-99.
84. Ikeda, *Complete Works I*, p. 395.
85. Y. Kohira, *Shakubuku Kyoten*, p. 344 (1954 ed.), from Thomsen, p. 103.
86. Ikeda, *Complete Works I*, p. 8.
87. E.g., *The Soka Gakkai*, pp. 48, 50, 60, 126, 144; Ikeda, *Lectures on Buddhism V*, pp. 6, 10, 15, 19, 59, 70-71, 73, 112, 115, 144, 161; *Seikyo Times*, March 1973, pp. 23-24, 49-54; *NSA Quarterly*, Spring 1973, p. 87; and Winter 1976, p. 8; Ikeda, *Heritage of the Ultimate Law of Life*, Part 2, p. 78.
88. Takashi Harashima, "Faith and Study," *Seikyo Times*, Nov. 1978, p. 6; Ikeda, *Complete Works I*, pp. 550-551.

89. Ikeda, *Lectures on Buddhism V,* 19, 144; *Seikyo Times,* March 1973, pp. 23-24, 49-54.
90. Ysuji Kirimura, *Fundamentals of Buddhism* (Tokyo: Nichiren Shoshu International Center, 1978), p. 161; cf. p. 45.
91. Thomsen, p. 103.
92. *The Soka Gakkai,* 47-48; Ikeda, *Lectures on Buddhism IV,* p. 307.
93. "Ho'on Sho," *NSA Quarterly,* Fall 1975, p. 130.
94. "Practice of the Buddha's Teaching," *Seikyo Times,* Sept. 1975, p. 46.
95. *The Soka Gakkai,* p. 15.
96. "The Roots of Suffering," *Seikyo Times,* July 1982, p. 51.
97. This quote is derived from personal conversations with many members.
98. See "Buddhism and Traditional Western Concepts Series," *Seikyo Times,* June 1982, p. 55 and October 1982, pp. 52-53.
99. Brannen, p. 34.
100. Kenneth Scott Latourette, *Introduction to Buddhism* (New York: Friendship Press, 1956), p. 38; cf. Mark A. Ehman, "The Saddharmapundarika Sutra" in Charles S. Prebish ed., *Buddhism: A Modern Perspective* (Pennsylvania State University Press, 1975), p. 102; cf. Murata, p. 24.
101. *The Soka Gakkai,* p. 141.
102. In Murata, pp. 107-108.
103. *Ex-NSA Journal,* Vol. 4, no. 5, p. 1.
104. Daisaku Ikeda, "Guidance Summary," *Seikyo Times,* Nov. 1978, p. 21.
105. A. Ehman, "The Saddharmapundarika—Sutra" in Prebish ed., p. 102; cf. Murata, p. 24.
106. Kenneth Scott Latourette, *Introducing Buddhism* (New York: Friendship Press, 1956), p. 38.
107. H. Kern (trans.), *Saddharma-Pundarika or the Lotus of the True Law* (New York: Dover Press, 1963), p. 22.
108. Ibid., p. xxii.
109. Nichiren Daishonin, "Letter to Myomitsu Shonin," in Williams, p. 70. Nichiren claims he was born 2,220 years after Sakyamuni's death.
110. Brannen, p. 66.
111. Kirimura, p. 104.
112. Brannen, pp. 66-70; Thomsen, pp. 87-88.
113. Nichiren Shoshu International Center Editorial Department, *Lectures on the Sutra,* rev. ed. 1984, pp. XIV-XV.
114. Kern, p. xxxix.
115. Ibid., pp. 145, 225.
116. Ibid., pp. 161-162.
117. Ibid., pp. 364-365.
118. Thomsen, p. 82; Brannen; *Seikyo Times,* Jan. 1979, p. 14.
119. Daisaku Ikeda, "Guidance Summary," *Seikyo Times,* Nov. 1978, p. 22.
120. Nichiren Daishonin, "Reply to Myoho-ama" in *The Gosho Reference,* Williams, p. 96.
121. Ibid., pp. 97-99.
122. Ikeda, *Buddhism The Living Philosophy,* p. 56, emphasis added.
123. "The Opening of the eyes," *Seikyo Times,* Jan. 1979, p. 14; Yasuji Kirimura, "Nichiren Daishonin's Life," *Seikyo Times,* Jan. 1979, p. 51; cf. Brannen, p. 70.

124. Brannen, p. 70; cf. "Contradictions" and below, emphasis added.
125. *Lectures on the Sutra,* p. 17; cf. p. 171.
126. The Gosho Translation Committee, *The Major Writings of Nichiren Daishonin,* Vol. II (Tokyo: Nichiren Shoshu International Center, 1982), p. vii., emphasis added.
127. Kirimura, p. 169.
128. Ibid., pp. 169-170.
129. *Lectures on the Sutra,* pp. 167-168; Kirimura, pp. 93, 96, 97, 106, 107, 119.
130. *Lectures on the Sutra,* pp. 167-168.
131. Kirimura, pp. 96-97.
132. Ibid., pp. 119-120.
133. Ibid., p. 119.
134. Ibid., p. 106.
135. Ibid., pp. 106-107.
136. Ibid., pp. 92-93.
137. *Lectures on the Sutra,* p. 23, emphasis added.
138. "Tozan—Pilgrimage to Mankind's Home," *Seikyo Times,* Oct. 1971, p. 55.
139. *NSA Seminars: An Introduction to True Buddhism* (World Tribune Press, 1974), pp. 51-54.
140. Ibid.
141. Kern, chapter 1; cf. "Mankind's Eternal Heritage," *Seikyo Times,* July 1975, pp. 38-40 and "The Proof of the Lotus Sutra," *Seikyo Times,* Nov. 1978, p. 11.
142. "Mankind's Eternal Heritage," *Seikyo Times,* July 1975, pp. 38-39.
143. Seikyo Press, *The Soka Gakkai,* pp. 78-79.
144. "Mankind's Eternal Heritage," *Seikyo Times,* July 1975, p. 40.
145. Ibid.
146. Daisaku Ikeda, "Guidance Summary," *Seikyo Times,* Nov. 1978, p. 22.
147. Murata, p. 28.
148. E.g., Williams, *The Gosho Reference,* pp. 55, 66, 69, 78-81, 90-100, 105, 123, 146, 212, etc.
149. Ibid., pp. 70, 89-91.
150. Nichiren Daishonin, "Reply to Kyo'o-don" in Williams, p. 52 cf. 54-55.
151. Nichiren Daishonin, "Reply to Lord Ueno," in Williams, p. 121.
152. Nichiren Daishonin, "The Proof of the Lotus Sutra," *Seikyo Times,* Sept. 1975, pp. 55-57; *NSA Quarterly,* Summer 1974, pp. 46-48; *Seikyo Times,* Nov. 1978, p. 11; *Soka Gakkai,* pp. 94.
153. Daisaku Ikeda, "Religion Is Man's Fundamental Force to Humanize Culture," *Seikyo Times,* Jan. 1972, p. 21.
154. "Theory of Ten Worlds," *Seikyo Times,* Apr. 1971, p. 58.
155. "The Proof of the Lotus Sutra, *Seikyo Times,* Nov. 1978, p. 11; "Gosho for Practice," *Seikyo Times,* Jan. 1975, p. 58.
156. Chris Roman, "Buddhism and the Western-Philosophical Tradition" (4), *Seikyo Times,* Nov. 1978, pp. 43, cf. p. 22; Ikeda, *Heritage of the Ultimate Law of Life II,* p. 16.
157. Nichiren Daishonin, "Reply to Lord Nanjo," in *The Gosho Reference,* Williams, p. 119.
158. Ibid.
159. Kern, ch. 22.
160. Daisaku Ikeda, "Guidance Summary," *Seikyo Times,* Nov. 1978, p. 22.

161. Ibid.
162. Daisaku Ikeda, "The Spirit of the Mahayana Buddhists," *Seikyo Times*, Dec. 1978, p. 22.
163. Chris Roman, *Seikyo Times*, Nov. 1978, p. 43.
164. Ibid., p. 44.
165. "The Lotus Sutra's Intention," *Seikyo Times*, Dec. 1978, p. 47; cf. Nov. 1978, p. 6.
166. "Part 1: What Is Buddhism?" *Seikyo Times*, April 1971, p. 60.
167. Brannen, p. 70; "The Opening of the Eyes," *Seikyo Times*, Jan. 1979, p. 14, cf. p. 51.
168. "Nichiren Daishonin's Life," *Seikyo Times*, January 1979, p. 51.
169. "The Lotus Sutra's Intention," Dec. 1978, p. 48, emphasis added; cf. July 1975, p. 49, Apr. 1971, p. 60.
170. Brannen, p. 70.
171. "The Opening of the Eyes," *Seikyo Times*, January 1979, p. 14.
172. *Lectures on the Sutra*, p. 28, emphasis added.
173. Takashi Harashima, "Faith and Study," *Seikyo Times*, Nov. 1978, p. 6.
174. Brannon, p. 70 (see also p. 173), citing Nichiren's *Hon'inmyosho*, from Nakamura, *Bukkyo Tehodoke* (Hosoi Seido: Tokyo, 1959), p. 159; cf. *The Gosko Reference*, Vol. 1, forward; Brannon, p. 146.
175. Seikyo Press, *The Soka Gakkai*, p. 74.
176. "Applying Faith in Society," *Seikyo Times*, Nov. 1978, p. 39; see Ikeda, *The True Object of Worship Part I*, p. 5, from "Reply to Lord Uno."
177. *The Gosho Reference* does not contain this statement; see also "Questions and Answers on the Practice of Faith," *NSA Quarterly*, Fall 1975, p. 77.
178. Ikeda, *The True Object of Worship Part I* (Santa Monica: World Tribune Press, 1977), p. 5.
179. David-Neel, p. 15.
180. Norman Geisler, *A Popular Survey of the Old Testament* (Chicaco, IL: Moody Press, 1978), p. 11.
181. Smith, *The Religions of Man*, p. 99.
182. Smith, p. 107, quoting E. A. Burt (ed.), *The Teachings of the Compassionate Buddha* (New York: Mentor, 1955), p. 50.
183. Smith, p. 108.
184. Woodward (tr.), p. XXI.
185. Ibid., p. 109.
186. Walt Anderson, p. 26.
187. Ibid., p. 32.
188. David-Neel, p. 123.
189. Neill, p. 121, citing Maha Thera U Tittila in *The Path of the Buddha* (ed.), K.W. Morgan (1956), pp. 77-78.
190. *Seikyo Times*, October 1982, p. 55.
191. Seikyo Press, *The Soka Gakkai*, rev. ed. (Tokyo: Seikyo Press, 1962), p.144.
192. George Williams, *The Gosho Reference*, Vol. 1 (Los Angeles: The World Tribune Press, 1976), p. 137.
193. *The Soka Gakkai*, p.79.
194. Daisaku Ikeda, *Lectures on Buddhism*, Vol. V (Tokyo: The Seikyo Press, 1970), p. 117.
195. Y. Kohira, *Shakubuku Kyoten* (1954 ed.; rev. Tokyo, 1967), pp. 340-343, from Thomsen, p. 102.
196. *The Soka Gakkai*, p. 141.
197. *Seikyo Times*, Dec. 1978, p. 45.
198. *NSA Quarterly*, Fall 1975, p. 72.
199. Edward Conze, *Buddhism: Its Essence and Development* (New York: Harper Torch Books, 1959), p. 42.
200. Nichiren, "On Attaining Enlightenment," *The Gosho Reference*, p. 13.
201. Josei Toda in Kiyoaki Murata, *Japan's New Buddhism: An Objective Account of Soka Czakkai* (New York: Walker/Weatherhill, 1969), p. 108.
202. Nichiren Daishonin, *On the Gift of Rice* in Williams, *The Gosho Reference*, p. 130.
203. Yasuji Kirimura, *Fundamentals of Buddhism* (Tokyo: Nichiren Shoshu International Center, 1977), p. 110.
204. Daisaku Ikeda, *Complete Works of Daisaku Ikeda*, Vol. I (Tokyo: Seikyo Press, 1968), p. 541.
205. *Fundamentals of Buddhism*, p. 65.
206. Ikeda, *Complete Works I*, p. 395n.
207. *Seikyo Times*, April 1971, p. 61.
208. Daisaku Ikeda, *Buddhism: The Living Philosophy* (Tokyo: The East Publications, 1974), p. 38.
209. *World Tribune*, Sept. 10, 1966, p. 2.
210. *The Soka Gakkai*, Preface, p. 3.
211. *Seikyo Times*, November 1982, p. 59.

Edgar Cayce and the Association for Research and Enlightenment

Info at a Glance

Name: The Association for Research and Enlightenment (ARE) was founded in 1931 "to preserve, research and disseminate the psychic work of Edgar Cayce."

Founder: Edgar Cayce (1877–1945).

Source of authority: The trance readings of Edgar Cayce's alleged unconscious mind. These are often claimed to have originated from "the akashic records," purportedly a storehouse of universal knowledge which many occultists cite as a source of inspiration.

Claim: The revelations of Edgar Cayce represent one of the most significant psychic phenomena of our time.

Occult dynamics: Spiritistic revelations and various occult practices, e.g., astrology.

Key literature: *The Circulating Files* (only ARE members can obtain the nearly 400 topically arranged transcripts of the Cayce Trance readings); the *ARE Journal* and *Newsletter; New Millennium Journal; Venture Inward* magazines; *A Search for God* (2 Vols.); *The Edgar Cayce Library* (topically organized volumes of the Cayce readings—e.g., Vol. 6 is *The Early Christian Epoch*); and the multi-volume *Individual Reference File*. These last two are continually expanding.

Attitude toward Christianity: Rejecting.

Quote:

Q. "How should we present the [Edgar Cayce] work to one in orthodox faith?"

A. ... "If they are satisfied in their own mire, or their own vomit, then do not disturb." (254–87).

Note: In this chapter, hyphenated numbers after quotations (as above) refer to original Edgar Cayce Reading numbers.

References to *Encyclopedia of New Age Beliefs:* Altered States of Consciousness, Angels, Astrology, Channeling, Dream Work, Hypnosis, Meditation, New Age Inner Work/ Intuition, New Age Medicine, Shamanism, Yoga.

Doctrinal Summary

God: A pantheistic, impersonal force.

Jesus: A man who attained Christ consciousness.

(The) Christ: A state of higher (occult) consciousness.

Trinity: Reinterpreted as e.g., Time, Space and Patience.

Man: Part of God.

Fall: The fall occurred in heaven, not on the earth, and man fell "into matter," not sin. Matter and spirit are "opposed" to one another. When pre-existing spirits fell into matter they lost their spiritual understanding and awareness of their divinity.

Sin: Error (e.g., not recognizing or appropriating one's deity). "Sin" is more a defect in awareness than violation of a moral standard.

Salvation: Salvation is through knowledge, not faith, and involves the attainment of higher consciousness and realization of one's divinity.

Satan: A symbol of "evil."

Second coming: The subjective experience within each person of the internal coming of "the Christ."

Bible: One of many holy books, interpreted symbolically.

Death: A spiritual advancement.

Heaven and Hell: Inward states of consciousness or good or bad experiences in life.

IMPACT ON SOCIETY

Be able to look EVERYMAN in the face and tell him to go to hell—but LIVE as He did, the lowly Nazarene![1]

—From an Edgar Cayce reading

Few other modern spiritists have been more prolific or had more written about them than Edgar Cayce. He has been lauded by psychic researchers and liberal theologians alike as "A healer of thousands" and "a wonderful prophet of God." Others acclaim him as the "Muhammad Ali" of psychics. Occultists too have lauded his virtues and influence. Bestselling author and spiritist Ruth Montgomery recalls: "The man who is rightly credited with having done more than any other to awaken popular Western interest in reincarnation is Edgar Cayce, the late seer of Virginia Beach."[2] The late famous astrologer and psychic Jeane Dixon declared: "Edgar Cayce was a great, great person, a great medium."[3]

Others however have expressed a far different opinion. The late German theologian and authority on occultism Dr. Kurt Koch was convinced that "Cayce was not a prophet in the true sense of the word, but rather a sorcerer. . . . In fact, he was the means of oppressing many. Cayce was only a spiritist and a mediumistic trance healer. He has thereby rendered the American nation a bad service."[4]

The life of Edgar Cayce represents one of the most grimly fascinating and tragic examples of the individual and social consequences of failing to exercise spiritual discernment. With millions of people today emulating Cayce in various ways, the implications are sobering indeed.

The Readings

In four decades (1901–1944) Edgar Cayce entered an unconscious hypnotic state some 16,000 times, of which 14,249 were recorded in writing. At each "reading" Cayce would be asked questions about any number of matters, usually how to diagnose and cure some person's illness. In trance, he would provide answers and comments, which were hand-recorded by a stenographer. At the end of each session, Cayce would awaken but remember nothing of what he had said while in trance. Oddly, having only a sixth grade education, Cayce sometimes supplied almost perfect diagnoses in proper medical terms, confounding the medical authorities of his day. It made no difference if the person were visibly present or on the other side of the world.

Some idea of the magnitude of the Cayce phenomenon is found by the tremendous variety and content of the readings. Copies of the earliest readings were lost (1901–1908), hence the oldest copy on file is dated 1909. The readings from 1909–1944 comprise more than 13 million words, and cover topics that include:

NUMBER	READING
8976	Physical (diagnosis of physical and mental problems)
2500	Life and past life (vocational, psychological, human relations problems— information and advice helpful to "the

soul" in its development throughout its "various lives" since "the creation")

794	Business
677	Dream interpretation
401	Mental-spiritual
223	Land readings (locating oil wells, investments, etc.)
130	Spiritual laws for Edgar Cayce study groups
116	Work readings (developing the Association for Research and Enlightenment)
76	Buried treasure
65	Group study of prayer and meditation for healing
35	Aura charts

The Association for Research and Enlightenment (ARE)

The Association for Research and Enlightenment (ARE) was set up to study and disseminate Cayce's trance information. While in trance, Cayce had urged the formation of the Association to "preserve, study and present the Edgar Cayce readings." Not surprisingly, the early ARE was heavily dependent upon psychic advice for guidance. In the early days "hardly a move was taken by the ARE without the help of psychic forces to organize and carry on its work."[5] Recently, it has become one of the largest coordinated bodies promoting occultism in America today and its influence has moved into the international arena. Nationwide, hundreds of major conferences have been sponsored. These usually concentrate in the areas of popular parapsychology (representing a wide variety of psychic and occult topics such as psychic development, reincarnation and astrology) and holistic health (a movement often integrating the occult and medicine). Indeed, Edgar Cayce is popularly known as the "father of holistic medicine."

The ARE publishes two periodicals *The New Millennium* journal and *Venture Inward* magazine, and it sponsors hundreds of Cayce study groups nationwide. It has also published over 100 books on the occult, most based on Edgar Cayce's work or philosophy; these include *Astral Forecast; Past-Life Profile; Numerology Profile; The Complete Cayce Reading's on CD-Rom; The Christmas Story; Dreams—Your Magic Mirror; Edgar Cayce on the Akashic Records* and *Money Freedom*. Almost 50 ARE television programs are aired each month on the so-called Wisdom channel. Topics include "Awakening Your Seven Spiritual Centers," "Be Your Own Psychic," "Reincarnation," "Meditation Made Easy" and "Making the Edgar Cayce Remedies at Home."

NOTES

1. Edgar Cayce, reading #2869-1 from *Circulating File: Jesus the Pattern and You* (Virginia Beach, VA: A.R.E. Press, 1971), p. 67.
2. Ruth Montgomery, *Here and Hereafter*, p. 84.
3. Jeane Dixon, as quoted in interview in M.M. Delfano, *The Living Prophets* (1972), p. 125.
4. Kurt Koch, *Occult Bondage and Deliverance* (1970), p. 24.
5. Mary Ellen Carter (Hugh Lynn Cayce, ed.), *Edgar Cayce on Prophecy* (New York: Paperback Library, 1972), p. 17.

CHRISTADELPHIANS

INFO AT A GLANCE

Name: The Christadelphians.

Purpose: To disseminate the true interpretation of the Bible.

Founder: John Thomas (1805–1871).

Source of authority: The Bible.

Revealed teachings: No.

Claim: To comprise the only true church; only those who accept Christadelphian doctrine and its interpretation of the Bible will be saved.

Example of Key literature: John Thomas, *Elpis Israel;* Robert Roberts, *Christendom Astray; A Declaration of the Truth Revealed in the Bible.*

Attitude toward Christianity: Rejecting.

Quote:

"Jesus Christ, the Son of God, is not the 'second person' of an eternal Trinity."[1]

DOCTRINAL SUMMARY

God: One Person only (Unitarian)

Jesus: A created being in need of redemption.

Holy Spirit: The impersonal power of God.

Trinity: A pagan teaching.

Salvation: By faith in Christ and works of righteousness.

Man: A physical being without an immortal soul.

Sin: Transgression of God's law.

Satan: Synonym for sin; any adversary.

Second coming: Jesus will return to reign on earth.

Fall: Sexual in nature.

Bible: The Word of God, the final authority for faith and practice.

Death: Unconsciousness or annihilation.

Hell and Heaven: Myths.

INTRODUCTION AND HISTORY

The founder of the Christadelphians ("brethren of Christ") was John Thomas, a physician turned Bible teacher, born in London on April 12, 1805. In 1832, during a brush with death in a shipwreck, he resolved to look into the truth about the afterlife and vowed to dedicate his life to religion if he was spared. His first experience with "Christianity" was with the often unbiblical Campbellite movement (today known as the "Church of Christ," "Christian Church" or the "Disciples of Christ").* In 1833 Dr. Thomas had met Alexander Campbell and was influenced by his teachings.[2] Eventually he left the Campbellites and continued studies on his own. In 1847, he claimed that he had arrived at "the truth of the gospel."[3] His best known works are *Elpis Israel* ("Israel's Hope," 1849) and *Eureka* (1862), a 2,000 page study of the book of Revelation. Both are published and used by Christadelphians today. *The Christadelphian* is the principal periodical of the church. It was originally titled *The Ambassador of the Coming Age* and begun by Robert Roberts, one of Thomas' earliest converts. Roberts became the leader of the Christadelphians after Thomas died in 1871.

Like Joseph Smith in Mormonism, John Thomas seems to have derived many of his ideas from the theological climate of the day. Although he believed that he was reviving "original Christianity," some of his teachings paralleled the early Unitarians, while other teachings were drawn from diverse sources. In *The Protesters,* Christadelphian writer Alan Eyre expresses his surprise upon learning of Dr. Thomas' many borrowings: "The writer, once naively and unquestioningly accepting a popular view that Dr. John Thomas 'discovered,' as if from a void, the totality of Bible truth as believed by Christadelphians, was amazed to discover

___

*In his *Campbellism: Its History and Heresies,* Bob L. Ross cites a number of unbiblical teachings providing original sources (all page references are from the fourth edition, 1976, published by Pilgrim Publications, Pasadena, TX, 77501). A few examples include: (1) an exclusivistic attitude resulting in the condemnation of all other denominations. Campbell (called "the Master Spirit") allegedly believed he was infallible in understanding the Scriptures, automatically making everyone who disagreed with him wrong (pp. 8, 30–35, 171); (2) restorationism: the true gospel was lost in the dark ages and not restored to its original state until 1827 by Campbell (pp. 78, 132); (3) works-salvation through e.g., the teaching of baptismal regeneration. Baptism in water provides forgiveness of sins and is equivalent to regeneration or being 'born again' (pp. 78–81, 157); (4) the natural man does not require the assistance of the Holy Spirit to believe (p. 153); (5) the Holy Spirit is not sovereign (p. 156); (6) God is not omniscient (p. 173).

source after source which showed that this was at least a serious misrepresentation."[4]

The Christadelphians meet in "Ecclesias" or local congregations. The first were established by Thomas in 1838 in Illinois and Virginia. The church was officially incorporated in 1864, being registered at the county court house in Oregon, Illinois. Today the church is scattered around the world and is principally found in the United States, Europe and Africa.

THEOLOGY

Christianity

Many modern religious cults claim not only that they are Christian but also that they represent the restoration of original Christianity. Along with Mormons, Jehovah's Witnesses and Christian Scientists, this is also true for the Christadelphians. For example, Christadelphian author Alan Haywood quotes skeptical philosopher Bertrand Russell, author of *Why I Am Not a Christian,* in alleged support of Christadelphian apostolic Christian claims: "The best representatives of the primitive [Christian] tradition in our time are the Christadelphians."[5] Other Christadelphians declare, "In short we are people of the Bible."[6] "First-century Christianity was thoroughly Bible based, and so we try to make our faith like that, too."[7] "The Bible is our only authority, and we teach that it should be read prayerfully and with care at every opportunity."[8]

The truth is that Christadelphians oppose historic orthodoxy and view biblical Christianity as a pagan religion. This is why it is declared to be "paganized theology,"[9] and even "meaningless."[10] Christadelphians are told that the true church of Jesus "and modern Christianity are as different as night and day."[11] "The creeds of Christendom are based on *false* doctrines, compounded of a little Bible teaching, but mostly composed of fables, based upon pagan mythology."[12]

In addition, Christadelphians see little difference between Protestants and Catholics, almost as if the Reformation had never occurred. In essence, Christadelphianism condemns Protestantism because it has many of the same doctrines of Rome:

The principal doctrines of the churches of Christendom are these same Romish doctrines. They are as follows: 1. The Trinity, 2. The pre-existence of Christ, 3. Christ the Creator, 4. The immortality of the soul, 5. Eternal torments, 6. Heaven-going, 7. A supernatural, fallen-angel Devil and Satan, 8. A substitutionary Christ. . . . The popular churches of Christendom teach some, if not all of these Romish doctrines. Therefore they come under the same condemnation as Rome.[13]

Of course, biblical teaching alone determines what is true and what is false doctrinally. Protestant Christianity can hardly be in error if the above doctrines are established as biblical teaching. Clearly, as we documented in *Protestants and Catholics* (Harvest House, 1995), Catholic doctrine is unbiblical at many important points, especially the doctrine of salvation. Nevertheless, for Christadelphians, because Protestantism accepts *some* of the same doctrines as Catholics, it is declared to be just as "iniquitous" and "false" as Catholicism.[14] But obviously, we could apply the same reasoning to Christadelphian beliefs. As we will see, Christadelphian teaching bears certain important doctrinal resemblances to traditional Armstrongism and the Jehovah's Witnesses: rejection of the Trinity as Satanic; Christ's atonement for past sins only; the necessity of good works for salvation; the impersonality of the Holy Spirit; a denial of eternal punishment and so on. Would Christadelphians consider it fair of Christians to conclude that Christadelphians were in error solely because of some similarity in doctrine to other religions?

Further, when Christadelphianism rejects Protestantism on the basis of similarity to Catholicism, it uses a double-standard. Catholicism also believes in works-salvation, the authority of the Bible and other Christadelphian teachings. But Christadelphians will never classify their own church as "pagan" and "iniquitous" on this basis. So why argue it in such a manner with Protestantism?

Nevertheless, when Christadelphians maintain that "traditional church teachings do not reflect the truth of the Bible in a number of key areas,"[15] this is precisely what they have never

established. Nor can they, since basic biblical doctrine is accepted as established by almost everyone but cultists. Still, as in Mormonism, the Christadelphian church claims that after 1,800 years of apostasy it alone has restored the true gospel. To emphasize this point to the faithful, again as with Mormonism, it attacks the Christian church uncharitably and undeservedly. John Thomas asserted that biblical preachers were the epitome of evil:

> What base views must such men have of the God whose ministers they pretend to be! Their "consolations" are unmitigated blasphemy, and false from first to last. . . . It is the preachers that make men infidels by the preposterous absurdities they preach in the much-abused name of Christianity. . . . Their ministrations have no vitality in them, and leave their flocks in their own predicament, "dead in trespasses and in sins." Therefore "come out from among them, and be ye separate, and touch not the unclean, and I will receive you, and will be a Father to you, and ye shall be my sons and daughters, saith the Lord Almighty."[16]

Citing Galatians 1:8, the *Christadelphian Messenger* declares that the Gospel Christians teach will only curse those who preach it or accept it. "The conglomerate mixture of Christianity, paganism and assorted doctrines of men preached by the popular churches of Christendom is not the Gospel of salvation which Christ and the apostles preached, and it contains not enough salvation to save one human soul. It is error, and will accurse all who preach it, and all who accept it."[17] Christadelphians even argue that Christians are so deceived that they will, at the Second Coming, reject Jesus Himself as the Antichrist:

> No one desires to be in the position where he or she might reject Jesus when he comes because of an incorrect understanding of the prophetic events related to his second coming. Yet the framework has already been laid throughout Christianity for most Christians to do exactly that. . . . This false teaching is preparing millions of Christians throughout the earth to reject Jesus at his return because they will be convinced, by the things he will do, that he is "the Antichrist" and will oppose him.[18]

And Christians will die with a lie on their souls. "Neither Protestants nor Papists 'believe in God.' They have a system of faith which bears no affinity to the religion of God; and hence they hope for things which He has not promised; and consequently the most pious of them die with a lie."[19] Not surprisingly, John Thomas believed that Christian churches do not teach the Gospel:

> Let the reader search the scriptures from beginning to end, and he will nowhere find such systems of faith and worship as those comprehended in the Papal and Protestant systems. The gospel of the Kingdom of God in the name of Jesus is not preached among them. . . . They are dead, twice dead, plucked up by the roots, and therefore the time is come to cut them off as a rotten branch from the good olive tree. . . . By remaining in them, a man partakes of their evil deeds, and subjects himself to their evil influences.[20]

For Thomas, the Christian churches represented a "thousand-headed monster" that was "devoted to mammon" and the commandments of men, wallowing in "its ignorance of the Scriptures."[21]

God and the Trinity

Christadelphians believe that God is one Person only and thus maintain that belief in the "Trinity is unscriptural."[22] (See Doctrinal Appendix.)

When Christadelphians evaluate the biblical doctrine of God, they are perhaps at their most superficial. As in Jehovah's Witnesses and Oneness Pentecostalism, the doctrine of God is misrepresented and the arguments given are illogical and irrelevant. For example:

> Most churches of Christendom teach that He is a triune God; others, such as the Christadelphians, teach that He is one, the Father. . . . This [trinity] doctrine is not drawn from the Bible (where the term Trinity never appears) but from what is known as the Athanasian Creed. . . . In short, to believe in what most churches teach concerning the Godhead is to believe an impossibility, a contradiction . . . [and] "God is not the author of confusion." . . . The Bible nowhere teaches that God is a triune Being or that the Lord Jesus

Christ is co-equal and co-eternal with the Father, but *the very opposite*. Actually, the word "Trinity" is not found in the Bible. . . . They cannot explain why one God should also be three Gods and vice versa; how God should have substance but no form; or how the Son of God is at the same time his own Father. The doctrine is one of confusion, because it is drawn not from the Bible, but from pagan mythology.[23]

First, the Trinity was never derived from pagan mythology, as we documented elsewhere.[24] Second, it is irrelevant whether the term "Trinity" appears in the Bible. The Trinity is merely the term used to describe biblical teachings about the "tri-unity" of God, just as the term "monotheism" (which is also absent from the Bible) is used to describe the biblical teaching of one God. No Christadelphian would argue that monotheism is unscriptural merely because the term is absent from the Bible. So why single out the word "Trinity" this way?

Third, the doctrine is not impossible, confusing or contradictory. It is not entirely comprehensible, true, but this cannot be proof that it is wrong. (See the Doctrinal Appendix and Oneness Pentecostalism for documentation.) Many things in life are incapable of being fully comprehended, but this does not mean that they are "impossible" or "irrational." Are the Christadelphians saying that in order for them to believe in the Trinity they must first fully and logically understand how God can be everywhere present, infinite and eternal? Do they deny the reality of particle physics because they don't fully grasp it or because it is paradoxical? So it is with the doctrine of the Trinity. If it is a biblical teaching, we should accept it. A Christadelphian publication admits: "Nor can we hope for a full comprehension of all that is implied in the statement that in Jesus Christ there 'dwelleth all the fullness of the Godhead bodily.'"[25] If they admit that, why reject the Trinity simply because it cannot be fully comprehended?

Fourth, Christians have never believed in "three Gods," only one God who exists externally in three Persons. Nor have Christians confused the Persons in the Godhead, so that the Person of the Son is the Person of the Father. Such teachings were universally condemned by the early church (see Oneness Pentecostalism). Christians have always taught there is only one God.

Fifth, the doctrine of the Trinity is clearly taught in the Bible. The Christian creeds merely stated in systematic doctrinal form what the Bible already taught and what the Church accepted from its beginning. To argue that the doctrines of Christianity were invented by church councils to distort the Bible is nonsense.

The Father creates but the Son creates also (John 1:3). The Son atones, and the Father is in the Son reconciling the world to Himself (2 Corinthians 5:19). The Spirit sanctifies believers, and so does the Father and the Son (1 Thessalonians 5:23). The Holy Spirit indwells believers and so does Jesus and the Father (John 14:23). The Father raised Jesus from the dead (Acts 3:26), and so did Jesus (John 2:19-21), the Holy Spirit (Romans 8:11) and God (Acts 17:31). Only the doctrine of the Trinity can explain many scriptures like these.

If anyone has invented doctrines to distort the Bible, it is the Christadelphians. Christadelphians also publish E. J. Newman's *The Doctrine of the Trinity*. Newman accurately points out that "Athanasius contended successfully against Arius for the view that Christ was of the same nature as God and not merely of like nature."[26] However, he goes on to declare that John's gospel does not teach that "it is God Himself who comes into the world to redeem it.[27] But John 1:1, 14 declares that "the Word was God" and that "the Word was made flesh" (v. 14) in Jesus. John 3:16-17 declares that Jesus (who John has already declared God) came into the world to save it "through him."

Newman further contends that in the Gospel of John, Christ does "not proclaim himself as God."[28] But Jesus clearly asserted His deity in both statement and action. He claimed equality with God (John 5:18), and this was the very meaning of His claim to be the Son of God (John 19:7). He exercised the prerogatives of deity throughout the Gospel (John 5:17, 21-24; 10:28-30, 33; 14:7-9; 15:23).

Jesus Christ

Christadelphians believe that Jesus is more than a man but less than God. He is "the mani-

festation of God" in a unique way, which no other man duplicates.[29] He is not God incarnate but a very special man. Unfortunately, Christadelphianism denies almost everything biblical about Jesus Christ.

Christadelphian doctrine states that Christ is not eternal but was a created being, and as such, God "gave him immortality."[30] Thus He was not incarnated.[31] "Jesus Christ did not exist as a person from eternity as one of the triune Godhead. . . . He did not actually come into being until He was begotten of the Holy Spirit and born in Bethlehem."[32] He was a man only. "Though he was only a mortal man in those days, he still had the strength of character to right some of the most appalling wrongs of his time."[33]

Second, in one of its more blasphemous doctrines, Christadelphians teach that Jesus had a sinful nature and needed salvation from sin:

> Though He was begotten of Holy Spirit power, though He was the Son of God, and a manifestation of the Father in human flesh, yet He inherited from His mother Mary, the same sinful nature of those He came to redeem. . . . If Jesus had not been of sin-nature, sin could not have been condemned in Him. . . . There is no reason to recoil at the thought of Jesus' possessing sinful nature. It is, on the other hand, a glorious thought that He was really like us in nature. . . . Jesus was included in all that He did for us. He had our death-stricken nature and needed salvation the same as we. . . . The terms upon which He accepts the sinner are belief in His word and obedience to His commands. . . . It is by righteous works that he is perfected in divine character and made a fit subject for the eternal inheritance.[34]

> Christ was the first to attain eternal life.[35]

> Sin could not have been condemned in the body of Jesus, if it had not existed there. His body was as unclean as the bodies of those for whom he died; for he was born of a woman, and "not one" can bring a clean body out of a defiled body; for "that," says Jesus himself, "which is born of the flesh is flesh." . . . Sinful flesh being the hereditary nature of the Lord Jesus, he was a fit and proper sacrifice for sin.[36, 37]

The Bible declares exactly the opposite, that Jesus was sinless. He "committed no sin"

(1 Peter 2:22); "in him is no sin" (1 John 3:5); He "had no sin" (2 Corinthians 5:21); He was "tempted in every way . . . yet was without sin (Hebrews 4:15).

The Holy Spirit

As Jehovah's Witnesses believe, Christadelphians maintain that the Holy Spirit is simply the impersonal power of God, a "concentrated spirit power which took complete possession of the apostles" to miraculously empower their ministry. Thus, "The Spirit of God is another name for the Power of God."[38] In Christadelphianism, God empowered Jesus with the Holy Spirit at His baptism, making Him capable of performing miracles, but today this special manifestation of power is no longer available. In *Christendom Astray* Robert Roberts declares, "There is no manifestation of the Spirit in these days. The power of continuing the manifestation [of miracles] doubtless died with the apostles."[39] Further, the biblical doctrine of the Holy Spirit is denied:

> The term Holy Spirit does not refer to a person, as some erroneously suppose, neither does it refer to a different spirit from that spirit of God referred to generally in the scriptures, but it refers to the one and same spirit power, separated and set apart for special purposes, for the performance of special miraculous works. . . . The notion that the Holy Spirit is a person, one of a trinity of Gods, involves the whole subject in utter confusion.[40] (For the biblical teaching on the Holy Spirit, see the Doctrinal Appendix.)

Salvation, Works, Atonement

Christadelphians believe that people are saved by faith in Jesus as Savior plus good works qualifying them for eternal life. However, as is true in Mormonism and most other cults, while they may claim to teach "salvation by grace," the claim is buried beneath a landslide of demands for works righteousness. We may note the following seven points.

First, salvation is a process. "Salvation . . . commences with a belief of the gospel, but is by no means completed thereby; it takes a life-time for its scope and untiring diligence for its accomplishment . . . [It] is a work of slow development, and can only be achieved by the industrious ap-plication of the individual to the means which God has given for the purpose."[41]

Second, eternal life is given at the resurrection, not the point of one's faith in Christ. In a teaching similar to traditional Armstrongism, Christadelphians allege that we are first "conceived." This is the process of salvation begun by faith and baptism. Then we experience growth "in the womb" by obedience. After death, at the resurrection—assuming we have maintained righteousness in life—we are then spiritually "born." In other words, at the resurrection we become spirit beings. Then, and only then, are we saved. The following statements reflect the Christadelphian misunderstanding of biblical salvation, especially the nature and interrelationship between regeneration, justification, sanctification and glorification:

> The Bible calls this continuing process "salvation." Because it begins at baptism Peter says "baptism now saves you" (1 Peter 3:21 NAS), while Jesus promises that "whoever believes and is baptized will be saved" (Mark 16:16). But the process of salvation cannot be completed until Christ comes again, when he will give everlasting life to those who have grown fit for it. Hence the New Testament also speaks of salvation as something we must wait for.[42]

> The New Birth, like the old one of the flesh, is not an abstract principle, but a process. It begins with the begettal and ends with the having been born. . . . Having been begotten by the Father by the word of truth, and born of water, the first stage of the process is completed. He is *constitutionally* "in Christ." When a child is born, the next thing is to train him up in the way he should go. . . . This is also the arrangement of God in relation to those who are born out of water into His family on earth. . . . That by so doing he may be accounted worthy of being "born of spirit," that he may become "spirit," or a spiritual body; and so enter the kingdom of God, crowned with "glory, honor, incorruptibility, and life." . . . He is then an incorruptible and living man, "equal to the angels"; and like them capable of reflecting the glory of Him that made him. This is the end of the process. He is like Jesus himself.[43]

To the contrary, the Bible is clear that eternal life is given at the point of faith in Christ and is therefore not a lifelong process such as sanctification (John 5:24; 6:47; 1 John 5:13). Thus, at the point of faith a person has *already* been regenerated (born again) and justified (declared righteous). (See Doctrinal Appendix.)

Third, belief in the covenants is necessary to salvation. In Christadelphianism, belief in Jesus alone is not sufficient for salvation. One must believe in the covenants also, and that one will inherit the land of Canaan and eventually the world. One must also possess knowledge of what the Bible teaches if one would be saved.[44] "Salvation in the kingdom is not promised to those who only believe that Jesus is the Son of God, and died and rose again for sin. It is equally necessary to believe in the promises of the covenants; not more so, but equally so."[45] "By '*the great salvation*' is meant deliverance from the grave by a resurrection to life, and a share in the kingdom of God. This, as we have seen, is predicated on faith in the promises made to the Fathers, an Abrahamic disposition [the same mental attitude and knowledge], baptism into the name of the Holy Ones, and faith made perfect by works."[46]

Fourth, people are saved unto equality with Christ. "They can attain unto the 'glory of God,' 'divine nature,' the 'name of God,' and complete 'oneness with Him.' The Lord Jesus attained unto all this, and thus had the name of God bestowed upon himself, a name that he promises all true believers, who are described as being 'heirs of God' with him (Romans 8:17). . . . In short, the Bible sets out the hope that what Jesus Christ is now—glorious, divine, immortal—the redeemed can become."[47]

Fifth, the biblical doctrine of justification by faith alone is erroneous:

> Christendom, which has gone astray from the doctrines, has also forsaken the commandments of Christ, if ever it made them a rule of life. . . . Popular theology has reduced them to a practical nullity. It has totally obscured the principle of obedience as the basis of our acceptance with God in Christ, by its doctrine of 'justification by faith alone'. . . . While faith turns a sinner into a saint; obedience only will secure a saint's acceptance at the judgment seat of Christ; . . . a disobedient saint will be rejected more decidedly than even an unjustified sinner.[48]

> *It is not at the instant a man believes that he is justified.*[49]

> I have termed it a twofold justification by way of illustration; but it is, in fact, only one. The two stand related as cause and effect; faith being the motive principle it is a justification which *begins* with the remission of sins that are past, and is *perfected* in obedience unto death. The idea may be simplified thus. No exaltation without probation.[50]

For the biblical teaching, see Doctrinal Appendix on justification.

Sixth, good works are essential to salvation. This idea reflects John Thomas' belief that people are "justified by works unto eternal life."[51] Faith only secures forgiveness of past sins. "Faith justifies from all past sins, and ensures peace with God; but works are requisite to retain His favor and secure acceptance at the last."[52] In the end, good works and obedience are what forgives future sin and establishes acceptance with God. "God forgives sins and bestows rewards only on the basis of belief in His word and obedience of His commands."[53] "'Be ye holy, for I am holy' is the fundamental principle of man's relationship with God and the recognition of this must shape his life."[54] "The plan of salvation will be fulfilled in those (and only those) who hear, believe and obey the commandments of God."[55]

John Thomas further declared that a "law of works" was required for salvation. "Hence, '*the obedience of faith*' is made the condition of righteousness; and this obedience implies the existence of a '*law of faith*,' as attested by that of Moses, which is '*the law of works.*'"[56] "Salvation is the gift of God but he will only bestow it upon those who have works meet for repentance. It is impossible to do too much for the Lord."[57]

Thus, for salvation one must strive diligently to live as Jesus did, because only a few are good enough to earn their salvation:

> Let him continue in the daily practice of ALL THINGS commanded by Christ, and in the daily cultivation of that exalted character which was exemplified in Christ himself. . . . If he put himself into this position, and faithfully occupy it to the end, he will certainly be approved when the Lord comes.[58]

The terms upon which He accepts the sinner are belief in His word and obedience to His commands.... It is by righteous works that he is perfected in divine character and made a fit subject for the eternal inheritance.[59]

This precious life and immortality brought to light by Jesus Christ is not to be indiscriminately bestowed. All men will not attain to it; only a few will be counted worthy. The precious gift is freely offered to all; but it is conditional. It is not to be given to the faithless and the impure. Perfection of character must precede perfection of nature. Moral fitness is the indispensable pre-requisite, and God is the judge and the prescriber of the peculiar moral fitness necessary in the case.[60]

Seventh, baptism is also essential for salvation. So essential that even a true believer in Jesus will die in his sins apart from it. "Baptism is an act of obedience required of all who believe the Gospel.... It is, therefore, necessary to salvation."[61] "There is no other way than this, and even a believer of the truth will die in his sins unless he submit to it."[62]

In light of the foregoing, it is hardly surprising that we find Christadelphians stating that they "do things for God every day. Constantly and consistently we pray, we do our Bible readings, we are faithful in our attendance at every kind of meeting.... We are always willing to serve.... We do a hundred and one little things and we do them every day, not for the praise of man but for the Lord. We keep pounding, and we pound every day."[63] The Christadelphianism list of things that one must do for salvation is reminiscent of what one finds in Mormonism. Although we have quoted over a dozen different sources in this section, one still does not understand the full impact of just how fully "salvation by grace" is denied until one reads statements like the following:

Is faith by itself enough to secure for us the benefit of the work of Christ? Answer: No: there must be obedience, or "works" also....

[What are] a few of the things we are to do. Answer: 1) We are to love God and Christ; 2) to do to men as we would that they should do to us; 3) to love one another; 4) to sympathize with men in their joys and sorrows; 5) to love even our enemies, blessing those who curse us, doing good to those who hate us, and praying for those who badly use us; 6) we are to be ready to do every good work, to give to those who ask, to relieve the afflicted; 7) to be faithful even to bad masters; 8) to pray always and in everything give thanks; 9) to speak the truth always; 10) to be blameless and harmless; 11) to be humble, brave, joyful, courteous and manly; 12) to follow after whatsoever things are true, honest, pure, just, lovely and of good report.

Can you enumerate some of the things we are not to do? Answer: 1) We are not to be masterful and lordly; 2) we care not to return evil for evil; 3) we are not to avenge ourselves, but rather give place to wrath, and suffer ourselves to be defrauded; 4) we are not to do our alms before men, or let our left hand know what our right hand doeth; 5) we are not to labor to be rich or to love the world; 6) we are not to return cursing for cursing, or railing for railing, but contrariwise, blessing; 7) we are not to grudge, judge, complain, or condemn; 8) we are not to give way to anger, wrath, bitterness, or evil speaking; 9) we are not to conform to the world or to be ambitious after higher things; 10) we are not to be slack in paying our debts; 11) we are not to backbite or speak of other men's sins until we have spoken to themselves first; 12) we are not to be guilty of adultery; fornication, uncleanness, drunkenness, covetousness, wrath, strife, sedition, hatred, emulation, boasting, vainglory, envy, jesting or foolish talking.

Will the Gospel save us if we are disobedient to those commandments? Answer: No; our belief of the Gospel and baptism will only be to our condemnation if we live in disobedience to the commandments of Christ. Only those who do his commandments will at last be among the blessed.

Is there forgiveness for those who, having submitted to the Gospel, may fail in rendering a perfect obedience to the commandments of Christ? Answer: Yes if there were not, no flesh could be saved. But forgiveness is conditional on our confession and forsaking our sins; and also on our being forgiving to others; and forgiveness is only granted at the intercession of Christ. If we are unforgiving, or if he refuses to intercede, there is no hope for us.[64]

Christadelphians may also occasionally assert that they "cannot hope to achieve perfection" in this life,[65] but in light of the above requirements one would hardly suspect it. Here is the Achilles heel of systems of works righteousness. Besides being impossible before God, we are never told how much obedience is necessary or at what point a believer is perhaps forever lost. The Bible refers to the absolute hopelessness of all forms of works-salvation, and it declares that the completed nature of the atonement makes them unnecessary (Galatians 2:15–4:31; Ephesians 2:8–9; Romans 9:30–10:4; Hebrews 10:14). Scripture declares that today we may know, with absolute certainty, that our sins are forgiven, future sins included, and that we actually, now, possess eternal life (John 5:24; 6:47; Ephesians 1:7; Colossians 2:13; Hebrews 10:14; 1 John 5:13). Eternal life, once acquired as a present possession, can never be lost, since it is eternal by definition. "Truly, truly, I say to you, he who hears My word, and believes Him who sent Me, has eternal life, and does not come into judgment, but has passed out of death into life" (John 5:24 NAS).

Further, Christadelphians stress that Jesus Christ was only a representative, not the atoning Savior of the world. "A very circumscribed and superficial view of the gospel is that which finds it stated in the words 'Christ died for our sins according to the scriptures.'"[66] The Apostle Paul, however, said just the opposite when he emphasized, "Now I make known to you, brethren, *the gospel* which I preached to you . . . by which also you are saved . . . unless you believed in vain [i.e., falsely]. For I delivered to you *as of first importance* what I also received, that Christ died for our sins according to the Scriptures" (1 Corinthians 15:1–3 NAS, emphasis added).

In Christadelphianism, the reason Christ had to die was not because God's wrath was outraged at sin, but only because God required the death of the sinful nature. Thus when Christ died, the death of His sinful nature somehow secured forgiveness of our past sins. Further, Christians who believe in the atonement by that belief cut themselves off from salvation:

We wish to emphasize the fact that Jesus Christ came as a representative, and not a substitute for man. It is common to represent Christ as one of a trinity of Gods who came down to earth, entered a mortal body and substituted Himself for sinful man, enduring the suffering and death due to sinful man, thus saving them from the wrath of God and eternal torment in a lake of fire. Then there is the teaching that Christ was the subject of "immaculate conception," therefore being sinless in nature. Again, there are numerous "clean flesh" theories which seek to show that Christ's nature was different from the rest of humanity. All such theorists succeed in one thing: They forever cut themselves off *from any hope of salvation.* For such a redeemer could not fulfill the requirements of the redemptive plan. The divine scheme of redemption *required the death of the nature that had sinned.*[67]

The Death of Christ was not to appease the wrath of offended Deity, but to express the love of the Father in a necessary sacrifice for sin that the law of sin and death which came into force by the first Adam might be nullified in the second in a full discharge of its claims through a temporary surrender to its power; after which immortality by resurrection might be acquired, in harmony with the law of obedience. Thus sin is taken away, and righteousness established.[68]

Clearly, the death of Christ means something entirely different to the Christadelphian than what it means for the Christian. On the following page we note some of the contrasts.

CRITIQUE AND DIALOGUE

Our Doctrinal Appendix adequately documents Christian belief biblically, which refutes that of the Christadelphians. Also many of the arguments disproving the teachings of the traditional Worldwide Church of God (see Armstrongism appendix) and Jehovah's Witnesses will be applicable to Christadelphian beliefs.

When talking with a member, one of the most fruitful areas of discussion will be a thorough presentation of salvation, including our inability to keep the Law of God, especially in light of God's requirements for moral perfection (Galatians 3:10–13). The Scriptures cited in the Doctrinal Appendix will be helpful here. Once Christadelphians understand the extent of their sinfulness before God, that even their *righteousness* is "filthy rages" (Isaiah 64:6), and once they further ponder the infinite nature of God's holiness, they have no alternative but to cast themselves upon the mercy of God and to trust in the biblical Christ alone for salvation. Only the true Jesus can save because only He could pay the divine penalty for sin. Stressing the completed nature of the atonement should also be a priority (Hebrews 9:26–8; 10:10–18). Discussion of relatively minor teachings (such as their belief in nonparticipatory democracy—no voting, politics, or military service) is better avoided, regardless of personal feelings on the subject.

A second major issue to stress is "who is Jesus Christ"? If the Christadelphians are wrong about Jesus, it matters little what else they may be right on, because a denial of Jesus Christ will prevent salvation and lead to damnation. The Bible is clear on this. "He who has the Son has life; he who does not have the Son of God does not have life" (1 John 5:12). "No one who denies the Son has the Father . . ." (1 John 2:23). Jesus Himself warned, "If you do not believe I am the one I claim to be, you will indeed die in your sins" (John 8:24). "No one comes to the Father except through me" (John 14:6). "He who rejects me rejects him who sent me" (Luke 10:16) "There is a judge for the one who rejects me and does not accept my words; that very word which I spoke will condemn him at the last day" (John 12:48).

Christadelphians argue that Jesus was only a man and not God, and they cite many scriptures to prove that Jesus was a man. Of course, it is easy to select scriptures that will prove Christ was a man. No Christian denies this. Thus, as a man He was weary, thirsty, wept, prayed, submitted to the Father and died. After the resurrection He said, "I am returning to my Father and your Father, to my God and your God" (John 20:17), a perfectly reasonable statement coming from one who was a man (1 Timothy 2:5). But it is irrational to argue that, because the Bible calls Jesus a man, the Scriptures that speak of His deity cannot be true. To maintain that the second Person of the Trinity could never incarnate is logically indefensible if Scripture declares that He did incarnate (Philippians 2). Simply listing Scriptures stressing Christ's manhood prove nothing. The issue is, "Was he also God?"

Some of the common Christadephian (and cultic) arguments used to deny Christ's Deity are:

—God cannot be tempted; therefore Christ is not God.[69]

—God cannot be born; therefore Christ is not God.[70]

—Jesus could not be a true conqueror or exalted were He God, since God is sovereign and omnipotent (Acts 5:30–31).[71]

—It is a logical impossibility for Jesus to be both God and God's son.[72]

Jesus is described in the Bible "as being in need of redemption (Hebrews 5:7–9; 9:12; 13:20),"[73] hence he could not have been God.

—He is referred to as "the MAN Christ Jesus" (1 Timothy 2:5; Acts 2:22).[74]

—He calls the redeemed "brethren"; he could not speak this way if He were God.[75]

—He admitted limitations on His knowledge (Mark 13:32; Revelation 1:1).

THE DEATH OF CHRIST	
CHRISTADELPHIAN	CHRISTIAN
Forgives past sins (incomplete)	Forgives all sins, past, present, future (complete)
Representation and sacrificial	Propitiatory and atoning
Provides the *possibility* of earning salvation by works and obedience (conditional)	*Secures* salvation by faith alone (unconditional)
To secure the death of the sinful nature	To secure full forgiveness of all sins
Died also for his own salvation	Died for others' salvation

—He could not be forsaken if He were God (Mark 15:34).[76]

—He could not be subject to the Father if He were God (1 Corinthians 15:28).[77]

—Christ disowned co-equality with the Father; and co-eternity is impossible for a Son.[78]

We will discuss some of these points. However, it goes without saying that nearly all of these statements *are* possible if Jesus was both God *and* man. Philippians 2:6-8 clearly tells us that Jesus Christ preexisted as God (cf. Greek), but that He willingly became a man (took on a sinless human nature) and submitted Himself to the Father's will by dying on the Cross. Jesus laid aside the prerogatives of deity, so He could truly represent humanity, but He could never relinquish His own divine nature. Thus, in the incarnation He was the true God-Man.

As for the idea that Jesus needed redemption from sin, this is a terrible blasphemy. The Bible repeatedly tells us Jesus was without sin (John 8:46; 2 Corinthians 5:21; 1 Peter 1:19; 1 John 3:5). Speaking of logical impossibilities, if Christ needed redemption from sin, how could He redeem others from sin? How can a mere man pay the cost of infinite justice for the sins of billions of people? "No man can redeem the life of another or give to God a ransom for him—the ransom for a life is costly . . ." (Psalm 49:7-8).

Concerning Jesus' subjection to the Father, this hardly requires His inequality with God, no more than a wife submitting to her husband means she is inferior. Christians are to submit to one another, but this does not mean they are unequal. United States citizens are not inferior in nature to their President simply because they are subject to him.

Clearly, a few Scriptures do refer to Christ's limitation in knowledge. But again, He relinquished the use of His divine powers. Every day there are people who, for various reasons, give up a capacity to do something that they are capable of doing. Lack of use does not require the absence of ability. Further, Christ did not disown equality with the Father; He pronounced it (John 10:30-33). And co-eternity is not impossible for a son if the second Person of the Godhead became God's Son through the incarnation and virgin birth.

Christadelphians will, of course, admit that Jesus is called "God," but, like Jehovah's Witnesses, they assert that it is only because such a "title" may apply to people if they are given positions of divine authority. Although such designations are rare in the Bible, Christadelphians argue they are "frequently applied throughout Scripture for those who manifest the authority of God."[79] The Apostle Thomas' declaration (John 20:28), Jesus' own declaration (John 10:30), Moses (Exodus 7:1, and Zechariah 12:8) are given as examples. These verses are misunderstood by Christadelphians. Whenever Scripture expresses the divine authority of a person this way it is only a figurative expression to refer to them as "gods." In Psalm 82, the phrase "You are gods" is an example. In Exodus 7:1 Moses was to be "a god" to the Egyptians, which he was. With the powers God gave him, it was as if one of their mythical gods had come to life. But no Christadelphian believes that Moses was actually God. However, Scripture demands that we come to such a conclusion about Jesus. Declarations of Jesus' deity are frequent in the New Testament (John 1:1, 3; 5:18; Acts 20:28; Colossians 2:9; Titus 2:13; Hebrews 1:3, 8-10; 2 Peter 1:1). Contextually, Zechariah 12:8 means that the house of David will be divine-like in its invincibility. (But also verse 10 shows that Jesus is God, for when was the Father ever pierced? The Hebrew *dagar* means "to pierce through" as with a lance. Note also the significant change in pronouns.)

Regarding John 10:30, grammar and context dictate that the term "one" means "one" in essence with God. Christadelphians argue that in John 10:30 ("I and the Father are one"), the Jews simply misunderstood Christ's words of unity, or "oneness of purpose," as a claim to deity. This view is difficult to accept in light of Jesus' immediately preceding statement that He retains the same power of the Father to keep His sheep. He then says, "the Father is greater than all," and declares "I and the Father are one." The meaning is obvious. The Jews did not misunderstand Him. Their response to try and stone Him to death shows how clearly they did understand Him. In falsely claiming to be God (as they saw it), He was guilty of a capital offense. If the Jews misunderstood Him, Jesus (not to mention the Apostle John who recorded the incident), never bothered to correct their error. Certainly the Apostle John would have indicated their misunderstanding if this was actually the case. As a devout Jew, would the Apostle have left his readers with the blasphemously false impression that Jesus was God? And did the Jews also "misunderstand" Jesus in John 5:18, where His claim to deity was based on His own declaration that God was His very own Father? If the phrase "making Himself equal with God" does not mean Christ believed He was God, what does it mean?

Finally, Thomas' statement in John 20:28 would surely have been rejected by Jesus if *Jesus* knew He were only a devout Jew. As a godly Jew Jesus would never have tolerated others confusing Him with God. Further, the word Thomas uses in 20:29 is *theos*, the common word for God.

Christadelphians further argue that, because Jesus received glory from God, He could not be God, whose glory is immanent and cannot be received. However, we are dealing with different kinds of glory here: divine glory and human glory. The glory Jesus received as a man and passed on (John 17:22) is the glory of servanthood. Here, Jesus' glory was glory of service given Him by the Father in His incarnation (for example of bearing the Cross; John 5:36, 44; 17:4–5). But the glory He had with the Father "before the world began" is eternal (John 17:5).

When Christadelphians stress that "the simple appellation of 'Son' as applied to Christ is sufficient to prove that His existence is derived not eternal,"[80] they misunderstand the biblical meaning of the term. ("Did you ever hear of a son who did not have a beginning" is one argument. Of course, the same can be said for the term "Father.") Men can be children ("sons") of God by adoption (1 John 3:1–2). Jesus, however, was the Son of God by nature (Luke 3:22; Romans 1:1–4). To be "the Son of God" in this sense was to be deity, just as Scripture declares (John 5:18; 19:7).

Christadelphians interpret John 1:1 in the following manner: "It is assumed (and it is pure assumption) that 'Word' here used refers to Jesus Christ as a person. We shall see that such is not the meaning, but that it has reference to the manifestation of the eternal Deity in Jesus, who first actually came into being when He was born in Bethlehem."[81]

Supposedly, Jesus had two sides—"one Deity and the other Man. . . . The Deity dwelling in him was the Father."[82] In other words, His so-called "deity" was not innate, but simply because the Father indwelt Him. In response, according to John 1:1–3, the Word is clearly declared to be God. The Word is God: Jesus is the Word; therefore Jesus is God—this is John's argument. John 1:14–17 further declares that the Word became flesh and that the Word was the person whom John the Baptist bore witness of, saying "He existed before me." Jesus is clearly the Word. If He is not, what was John trying to communicate in verses 14–17? And how could John the Baptist say of Jesus, "He existed before me," if Jesus did not even exist until His conception? Jesus was conceived six months after John the Baptist (Luke 1:24–31, 35–36). Jesus existed before John because He pre-existed in eternity.

In conclusion, the Christadelphian view of Jesus Christ is both deficient and demeaning. Christians should help Christadelphians ponder Jesus' words more soberly: "If you do not believe that I am the one I claim to be, you will indeed die in your sins" (John 8:24). The following declaration is one all Christadelphians would subscribe to: "We believe there is *one God*, who is the *Creator* and *sustainer of all things, Lord of heaven and earth*, the *Alpha and Omega*, the *Lord God Almighty*." There is indeed "one God" and Jesus is part of that one Triune Deity (Colossians 2:9; Titus 2:13; 2 Peter 1:1). There is only one God, "Who is the Creator" (*Jesus*: John 1:3; Colossians 1:16; Hebrews 1:2, 10), "sustainer of all things" (*Jesus*: Colossians 1:17; Hebrews 1:3), "Lord of heaven" (*Jesus*: Revelation 19:16) "and earth" (*Jesus*: Revelation 1:5), "The Alpha and Omega" (*Jesus*: Revelation 22:13 with 1:17; 2:8; 21:6), and "the Lord God Almighty" (*Jesus*: Revelation 1:8 with Revelation 22:20; 21:22–23; 22:3, 5 with Revelation 4:8–10; 5:8 and 7:11–12, 17).

Christadelphians may deny that Jesus is God. This they are free to do. But they cannot logically deny this on biblical grounds, much less claim that they are "true Christians" for doing so.

NOTES

1. A. Hayward, *Great News for the World*, p. 41.
2. John Thomas, *Elpis Israel*, p. xiii.
3. Ibid., p. xiv.
4. Alan Eyre, *The Protesters*, p. 7.
5. A. Hayward, *Great News for the World*, p. 82, cf. p. 87.
6. A. Norris, *The Things We Stand For*, p. 6.
7. A. Hayward, *Great News for the World*, p. 83.
8. "Answering Your Questions About the Christadelphians," pamphlet, p. 2.
9. R. Roberts, *Christendom Astray*, p. 55.
10. H. A. Twelves, *The Only Day of Salvation*, p. 8.
11. *Christadelphian Messenger*, No. 50, "The Church of the Living God," p. 4.
12. Ibid., No. 47, "Christendom's Creeds Not Christianity," p. 2.
13. Ibid., No. 47, p. 4.
14. Ibid., pp. 3-4.
15. "God Cares What We Believe," p. 6.
16. John Thomas, *Elpis Israel*, pp. 319-320.
17. *Christadelphian Messenger*, No. 11, "A Refuge from the Judgment Storm," p. 3.
18. *The Great Delusion*, p. 6, cf. pp. 5-10, 30-31.
19. John Thomas, *Elpis Israel*, p. 278.
20. Ibid., pp. 7-8.
21. Ibid., p. 140.
22. *The Christadelphian Instructor*, p. 9.
23. *Who Do You Worship?* pp. 51-52. (Birmington, England: pamphlet, Christadelphains).
24. John Ankerberg, *Knowing the Truth About the Trinity* (Eugene, OR: Harvest House, 1997); cf. John Weldon, *Ready with an Answer* (Eugene, OR: Harvest House, 1997), pp. 119-29.
25. *God Whom We Worship*, p. 6.
26. *The Doctrine of the Trinity*, p. 7.
27. Ibid., p. 13.
28. Ibid., p. 14.
29. *The Christadelphian Instructor*, p. 18; *Who Do You Worship?* p. 56.
30. "Answering Your Questions About the Christadelphians," p. 2.
31. *The Christadelphian Messenger*, No. 56, "The Divine Plan of Redemption," pp. 3-4.
32. Ibid., No. 46, "The Word Made Flesh," p. 3.
33. A. Hayward, *Great News for the World*, p. 41.
34. Ibid., p. 69.
35. *A Declaration of the Truth Revealed in the Bible*, p. 26.
36. Thomas, *Elpis Israel*, p. 128.
37. R. Roberts, *Christendom Astray*, p. 89.
38. A. Hayward, *Great News for the World*, p. 89; cf. *Who Do You Worship?* p. 51.
39. Roberts, *Christendom Astray*, p. 42.
40. *Christadelphian Messenger*, No. 40, "The Holy Spirit," pp. 1 -2; cf. *The Christadelphian Instructor*, p. 10.
41. *The Bible Companion*, p. 1.
42. *Great News for the World*, p. 53.
43. John Thomas, *Elpis Israel*, pp. 135-136, cf. p. 128.
44. *Christadelphian Messenger*, No. 4, "The One Hope of Everlasting Salvation"; No. 47 "Christendom Creeds not Christianity," p. 1; No. 11 "A Refuge from the Judgment Storm," p. 4.
45. Thomas, *Elpis Israel*, p. 315.
46. Ibid., p. 318.
47. *Who Do You Worship?* pp. 62-63.
48. R. Roberts, *Christendom Astray*, p. 241.
49. Thomas, *Elpis Israel*, p. 259.
50. Ibid., p. 261.
51. Ibid., p. 259.
52. *Christadelphian Instructor*, p. 17.
53. *Christadelphian Messenger*, No. 26, "It Does Make a Difference What WE Believe," p. 3.
54. *God Whom We Worship*, p. 22.
55. *What Is Death?* p. 15.
56. Thomas, *Elpis Israel*, p. 133.
57. *Minute Meditations*, pp. 25, 34.
58. R. Roberts, *Christendom Astray*, p. 240.
59. *Christadelphian Messenger*, No. 56, p. 4.
60. R. Roberts, *Christendom Astray*, pp. 53-54.
61. *A Declaration of the Truth Revealed in the Bible*, p. 51.
62. Thomas, *Elpis Israel*, p. 260.
63. *Minute Meditations*, p. 85.
64. *Christadelphian Instructor*, p. 225.
65. J. Marshall, *Portrait of the Saint*, p. 76.
66. Thomas, *Elpis Israel*, p. 315.
67. *Christadelphian Messenger*, No. 56, p. 3.
68. *A Declaration of the Truth Revealed in the Bible*, p. 28.
69. A. Norris, *The Things We Stand For*, p. 11.
70. Ibid.
71. Ibid.
72. A. Hayward, *Great News for the World*, p. 41.
73. *Who Do You Worship?* p. 59.
74. Ibid., p. 58.
75. Ibid.
76. Ibid.
77. Ibid.
78. *The Christadelphian Instructor*, pp. 18-19.
79. *Who Do You Worship?* pp. 60-61.
80. R. Roberts, *Christendom Astray*, p. 93.
81. *The Christadelphian Messenger*, No. 46, p. 1.
82. *A Declaration of the Truth Revealed in the Bible*, p. 26.

CHRISTIAN SCIENCE

INFO AT A GLANCE

Name: Christian Science

Purpose: The realization of God and Good as the means to health and prosperity.

Founder: Mary Baker Eddy (1821–1910).

Source of authority: The writings of Eddy as interpreted by Christian Science.

Revealed teachings: Yes. Christian Science is the outcome of Eddy's involvement in mediumism and Quimbyism. (Phineas Parker Quimby promoted an early form of mental/psychic healing that strongly influenced Eddy.)

Examples of occult potential: Mrs. Eddy was a spiritistic medium for about 25 years. There is an openness to certain psychic abilities in *Science and Health,* although misinterpreted in divine terms. Telepathy is possible in treatments, and Christian Science healing may be considered a form of psychic healing.

Examples of key literature: *Science and Health with Key to the Scriptures; Miscellaneous Writings; Seven Messages to the Mother Church; Church Manual;* and other texts by Mary Baker Eddy.

Attitude toward Christianity: Rejecting.

Quotes:

"If there had never existed such a person as the Galilean Prophet, it would make no difference to me." (Mary Baker Eddy, *First Church of Christ Scientist and Miscellany,* pp. 318–319.)

"We have no more proof of human discord, sin, sickness, disease, or death,—than we have that the earth's surface is flat, and her motions imaginary." (Mary Baker Eddy, *Miscellaneous Writings,* p. 65.)

"False theology would tell you that it is sin we need to be saved from." (Edward Kimball, *Lectures and Articles on Christian Science,* p. 209.)

"Does erudite theology regard the crucifixion of Jesus chiefly as providing a ready pardon for all sinners who ask for it and are willing to be forgiven? . . . Then we must differ from them. . . . The efficacy of the crucifixion lay in the practical affection and goodness it demonstrated for mankind. . . . The material blood of Jesus was no more efficacious to cleanse from sin when it was shed upon 'the accursed tree,' than when it was flowing in his veins as he went daily about his Father's business." (*Science and Health,* pp. 24–25.)

Note: Eddy's writings can be confusing or contradictory. Also, early editions of *Science and Health* are in places significantly different from the modern edition.

DOCTRINAL SUMMARY

God: Impersonal-personal; "spiritually pantheistic" (someone who believes God is everything and that matter is an illusion; Unipersonal.

Jesus: A highly enlightened Christian Scientist.

The Christ: The divine manifestation of God/Christian Science.

The Holy Spirit: Christian Science.

The Trinity: Interpreted as "Life, Truth and Love," and other triplets.

Salvation: By awareness, divine realization.

Man: Part of God.

Sin: Ignorance; the false beliefs of "mortal mind."

Satan: A Christian myth.

The Second Coming: Christian Science.

The Fall: A Christian myth.

The Bible: An inferior revelation properly interpreted only by *Science and Health with Key to the Scriptures.*

Death: Non-existent.

Heaven and Hell: Mental states, not places.

CHURCH UNIVERSAL AND TRIUMPHANT

INFO AT A GLANCE

Name: The Church Universal and Triumphant

Purpose: To help "dethrone the Synthetic [false] Image of Man and replace it with man's Real Image as Deity." By obedience to the teachings of the Ascended Masters and occult practices such as yoga, visualization, occult chanting (e.g., decreeing things to happen) and energy manipulation, the planet can be cleansed of its karma and a New Era entered into. The Church claims to offer the best path to spiritual enlightenment and the true interpretation of the Bible. Current leader Elizabeth Clare Prophet is nearly deified and is held to be the only mouthpiece for God on earth.

Founder: Mark Prophet.

Source of authority: The teachings of the Ascended Masters and Elizabeth Clare Prophet.

Revealed teachings: Yes.

Occult dynamics: Spiritism, necromancy, kundalini yoga, a form of ritual "magic" in which "decreeing" is practiced up to five hours per day.

Examples of key literature: *Climb the Highest Mountain*; *Pearls of Wisdom* (weekly tract); *Heart to Heart* (formerly *Royal Teton Ranch News*).

Attitude toward Christianity: Rejecting.

Quotes:

"Be of good cheer. The Ascended Masters have overcome the world" (citing John 16:33 in El Morya, *The Chela and the Path*, p. 70).

"The Ascended Masters are not only sane and well organized, but they are also godly and profound to the nth degree." (*Climb the Highest Mountain*, p. 209.)

Note: As in many other cults and new religions, the Church Universal and Triumphant (CUT) Ascended Masters go out of their way to reach those in the Christian church. Their revelations contain hundreds of Scripture references, they claim their church is truly Christian and that they honor and believe in Jesus Christ. Further, they claim that they do not deny true biblical doctrine and they maintain their church is not an occult group practicing spiritism.

The theme of the "Ascended Masters" is not unique to the Church Universal; a number of other occult organizations lay claim to contact with the same allegedly advanced spirit entities. The church itself claims to be founded by the same "Ascended Masters" that, in their eyes began H. P. Bavatsky's Theosophical Society, Mary Baker Eddy's Christian Science movement and Guy and Edna Ballard's "Mighty I AM" religion.[1] Nevertheless, while Christian Science does have some similar teachings, it is Theosophy and the "Mighty I Am" cult that bear the closest similarities in belief and practice to the Church Universal and Triumphant.

Other occult groups who believe they are receiving revelations from this conglomeration of spirit hierarchies (the Ascended Masters) include The Holy Order of Mans (which recently claimed to have revised its theology along biblical lines) and The White Lodge in Del Mar, California (publishing the multi-volume spirit-written "Books of Azrael"). It should be noted, however, that the White Lodge appears to be a part of The Church Universal and Triumphant, as indicated by CUT records.[2]

Nickolay Roerich (1874–1947), the famous painter, set designer and archaeologist was one of many people heavily influenced by the Theosophical "Masters," and he made archaeological expeditions to the Far East as a result of their influence in his life. His book of spiritistic revelations, *Leaves of Morya's Garden* ("Morya" or "El Morya" being an Ascended Master), reportedly helped lay the foundation for Mark Prophet's Summit Lighthouse organization in 1958, the precursor to the Church Universal and Triumphant. Mark Prophet claimed that his personal contact with "El Morya" was instrumental in founding the Church Universal.

Another link to the Ascended Masters is Baird T. Spalding's popular five-volume *Life and Teachings of the Masters of the Far East.* This is an account of Spalding and friends' alleged amazing occult experiences with "the Masters" while on a purported research trip in the Far East in 1894. No one on the trip remains alive, and none of the story was ever documented, but thousands today accept the books as true accounts. DeVorss and Co., the books metaphysical publishing house admits that despite several publisher investigations to document the story, no evidence could be found in substantiation (publisher's note to the 1964 edition).

Characteristic with the teachings of "Ascended Masters" everywhere, the theology of *Life and Teachings* is typically unbiblical. The teachings of Ascended Master "Jesus" are pantheistic, monistic, gnostic and occult, not biblical. "Jesus" denies and opposes His earlier biblical teachings about Himself, God, salvation and hell. Volume two, chapter five has "Jesus" making such declarations as, "Hell or the devil has no abiding place except in man's mortal [erroneous] thought. . . . If God rules all and is All, where could either

be placed in God's perfect plan?" "God is Impersonal Principle." "When I said 'I am the Christ, the only begotten of God', I did not declare this for myself alone." "The Christ means more than the man Jesus. . . ."[3]

References to *Encyclopedia of New Age Beliefs:* Altered States of Consciousness, Channeling, Enlightenment, Meditation, New Age Inner Work, Visualization, Yoga.

DOCTRINAL SUMMARY

God: An impersonal energy that can be manipulated by man.

Jesus: Currently an Ascended Master, highly evolved spirit guide.

The Christ: Higher consciousness.

The Holy Spirit: Cosmic energy sustaining the cosmos.

The Trinity: A symbol for man's inward divinity.

Salvation: Realization of one's inner divine nature through occult practice and development. All people will eventually find enlightenment or salvation.

Man: In his true nature, one essence with God.

Sin: Ignorance as to one's divine nature.

Satan: A lieutenant of Lucifer.

The Second Coming: Receiving the Christ consciousness.

The Fall: A descent into "material consciousness" that masks awareness of one's divinity.

The Bible: The Bible is seen as an historically unreliable text whose teachings were further perverted by Christian misinterpretation. The Ascended Master's teachings correct biblical errors and generally replace the Bible as the "true word of God."

Death: Transition to a new incarnation on earth or a higher spiritual plane. Reincarnation culminates in an eventual reabsorption to the Divine essence.

Heaven and Hell: States of consciousness.

NOTES

1. El Morya, dictated to Elizabeth Clare Prophet, *The Chela and the Path* (Los Angeles: Summit University Press, 1977), pp. 121-22.

2. The author has a xerox coy of a canceled check associating the Lodge with the Church; a decree from the Keepers of the Flame handbook said that at 10 P.M. every night decrees of protection are said for "The White Lodge in Del Mar."

3. *Life and Teachings,* Vol. 2, pp. 50-55.

DA FREE JOHN

INFO AT A GLANCE

Name: The Free Communion Church (originally The Dawn Horse Communion).

Purpose: To disseminate the teaching of the Way of Divine Ignorance or Radical Understanding.

Founder: Da (Bubba) Free John (Franklin Jones).

Source of authority: Ultimately Da Free John, although "enlightened" disciples now conduct many activities.

Revealed teachings: Yes.

Claim: To be the pinnacle of spiritual teachings in the West, and to represent in clarified form the essence of the genuine Truth of the spiritual traditions of man.

Examples of occult potential: Psychic powers, yoga, spirit possession.

Key literature: The Enlightenment of the Whole Body, and numerous other books by Da Free John.

Attitude toward Christianity: Rejecting.

Quotes:

"No one is the beloved of God, absolutely no one." (Bubba Free John, The Way That I Teach, p. 183)

"I am the Essential Truth. . . . I am God. Without a doubt. . . . This is the core of My Revelation. I am God. I am your own Truth." (Bubba Free John, Vision Mound, Vol. 2, no. 7, pp. 14, 53)

"Motherhood . . . is an illusion. Giving birth is no more divine than taking a crap. . . . Motherhood is garbage. It is all garbage . . . the whole drama of existence . . . is garbage." (Bubba Free John, Garbage and the Goddess, pp. 119-20)

"True Wisdom is the capacity for perfect madness." (Da Free John, "A New Tradition," 1980, p. 1).

DOCTRINAL SUMMARY

God: Divine Energy.

Jesus: A higher being.

The Christ: The divine part of man; divine consciousness.

The Holy Spirit: Energy; "the white light vibration" (Enlightenment, p. 446).

Salvation: By surrender to spiritual power.

Man: One with God inwardly.

Sin: Ignorance.

The Fall: Into the illusion of matter.

The Bible: Mystically interpreted.

Death: A benevolent transition through reincarnation to higher levels.

Heaven and Hell: Positive or negative states of consciousness.

ROY E. DAVIS—
CENTER FOR
SPIRITUAL AWARENESS/
CHRISTIAN SPIRITUAL
ALLIANCE

INFO AT A GLANCE

Name: Roy Eugene Davis and the Center for Spiritual Awareness/Christian Spiritual Alliance (CSA).

Purpose: To serve as a catalyst for ushering in the "New Age."

Founder: Roy Eugene Davis.

Source of authority: The writings of Paramahansa Yogananda, Roy Davis, Masaharu Taniguichi and various New Thought writers.

Revealed teachings: Yes.

Claim: To be a vanguard movement for the New Age of enlightenment.

Examples of occult potential: Meditation; psychic development.

Key literature: Various books by Roy Eugene Davis: *This Is Reality; Time Space and Circumstance; Creative Imagination; With God We Can; Darshan: The Vision of Light.*

Attitude toward Christianity: Rejecting.

Quotes:

"To those who need Jesus as a god, the virgin birth concept helps them maintain their illusions" (Roy Eugene Davis, *The Hidden Teachings of Jesus Revealed*, p. 51).

"We are all incarnations of God"; "We are what God is" (Davis, *Truth Journal*, December-January 1977–1978, p. 5; *With God We Can*, p. 213).

DOCTRINAL SUMMARY

God: Brahman; impersonal energy.

Jesus: A man who attained realization of oneness with Spirit.

The Christ: A state of mystical consciousness.

The Holy Spirit: Creative vibration/Lord Shiva.

The Trinity: Being, Consciousness, Bliss; Brahma, Vishu, Shiva.

Salvation: By occult meditation and higher consciousness.

Man: Inwardly divine.

Sin: Error; lower consciousness.

Satan: Illusion or *maya*.

The Second Coming: Awakening in higher consciousness.

The Fall: Into matter.

The Bible: A usable source of information when interpreted mystically.

Death: Transition to the next life or level of spiritual advancement.

Heaven and Hell: Higher or lower states of mind.

The Divine Life Society/Integral Yoga Institute

Name: The Divine Life Society/Integral Yoga Institute.

Purpose: The dissemination of Sivananda's and Satchidananda's Vedantic teachings and yoga practice.

Founder: Swami Sivananda and Swami Satchidananda.

Source of authority: The founders' writings and standard Hindu scriptures (Bhagavad Gita, Upanishads).

Revealed teachings: Besides the Hindu scriptures, Sivananda's alleged post-mortem communications are accepted as genuine.

Examples of occult potential: Development of psychic powers, kundalini arousal, spiritism.

Attitude toward Christianity: Rejecting.

Quotes:

"I am a true Christian, a true Musalman [Muslim], a true Hindu, a true Buddhist, a true Sikh, and a True Parsi." (Swami Sivananda, *Divine Nectar,* p. 81.)

"The Lord has many names, many forms and many attributes. Call Him by any name, any form or any attribute. He will hear you." (Sivananda, *Divine Nectar,* p. 251.)

"Guru is God in human form." (Sivananda, *Divine Nectar,* pp. 185, 226.)

Note: Chinmayananda was a disciple of Sivananda and his work (Chinmaya Mission) and teachings are very similar to the Divine Life Society.

DOCTRINAL SUMMARY

God: The Vedantic Brahman; impersonal, ineffable; *Satchidananda* (impersonal Being, consciousness, bliss).

Jesus: A great prophet; one of many great souls; a spirit in the astral world.

Salvation: By knowledge and spiritual practice (yoga, meditation). Man is never separate from God, but must seek to become conscious of his divinity.

Man: Inwardly divine.

Sin: Ignorance of one's true divine nature.

Satan: Figurative for false perception.

The Fall: In consciousness, not history.

The Bible: Sivananda's words are the true word of God, and his interpretation of the Bible is considered divine revelation.

Death: A normal transition, or spiritual advance.

Heaven and Hell: States of consciousness or temporary places.

DIVINE LIGHT MISSION/ ELAN VITAL

INFO AT A GLANCE

Name: Guru Maharaj Ji and the Divine Light Mission (DLM)/Elan Vital.

Purpose: To dispense DLM's brand of special "knowledge" as subjective experiences of "God."

Founder: Shri Hans Ji Maharaj Ji.

Source of authority: Hindu scriptures; Maharaj Ji.

Revealed teachings: Yes.

Claim: To be the only path to "divine light."

Examples of occult potential: Psychic meditation.

Key literature: *Divine Times* (formerly *And It Is Divine*), *Elan Vital.*

Attitude toward Christianity: Rejecting.

Quotes:

Without Guru Maharaj Ji nobody is going to find the path.... Without the Perfect Master you cannot find God. (*Divine Times,* May/June 1979, p. 17.)

Christ was not crucified for forgiving sins of human beings. How is sin forgiven? Sin is forgiven by meditation. Because where is the sin? Sin is in the mind and meditation wipes away the mind, hence the sin.... How are sins forgiven? That our minds become stilled. The mind loses the tendency of evil propensity, and then it will become sinless. All sins are gone. *So by giving knowledge, Jesus Christ made people sinless*

... not by being crucified on the cross.... Without receiving that practical Knowledge, one who thinks that the sins will be forgiven.... It is impossible. (Word for word transcript of conversation between Guru Rajeswar and Jack Cheetham of *Magnum* magazine at the San Francisco DLM ashram, the last week of September 1973, emphasis added.)

DOCTRINAL SUMMARY

God: Primordial impersonal energy; Brahman.

Jesus: A man who realized his divinity through receiving DLM's Knowledge.

The Christ: Divine consciousness.

The Holy Spirit: Maharaj Ji; Shiva; impersonal divine essence.

Salvation: Through initiation, meditation and personal spiritual development.

Man: Inwardly divine.

Sin: Ignorance, mistakes.

Satan: Ego, ignorance.

The Second Coming: Fulfilled in the person of Maharaj Ji.

The Bible: Relevant when interpreted mystically.

Death: Transition to the next life or spiritual level.

Heaven and Hell: Positive or negative states of consciousness.

ECKANKAR

Name: Eckankar.

Purpose: To help people directly experience God (the "Sugmad") as sound and light in nonphysical states; to achieve spiritual liberation in this life by returning the soul to its true home in the god worlds.

Founders: Paul Twitchell, Darwin Gross and Harold Klemp are the most recent in a purported six million year line of "Living ECK Masters."

Source of authority: The writings of Twitchell, Gross and Klemp.

Revealed teachings: Yes.

Claim: Eckankar is the most ancient religion known to man. It is the only path providing true salvation by unfolding unique spiritual experiences that no other teaching replicates.

Examples of occult potential: Altered states of consciousness, occult visualization, spiritism, similarity to occult magic.

Examples of key literature: Paul Twitchell's *The Tiger's Fang; The Far Country; In My Soul I am Free* (with Brad Steiger); *Dialogues with the Masters; Eckankar; Letters to Gail; The Spiritual Notebook; The Shariyat-Ki-Sugmad;* Periodicals: *The Eck Mata Journal; Eck World News;* Darwin Gross, *Your Right to Know;* Harold Klemp, *The Spiritual Exercises of ECK; A Modern Prophet Answers Your Key Questions About Life; A Cosmic Sea of Words: The Eckankar Lexicon;* and *The Mahanta Transcripts,* some two dozen books derived from Klemp's speech excerpts (*How the Inner Master Works; The Dram Master;* and others).

Attitude toward Christianity: Rejecting.

Quotes:

I am the Deity! . . . I am the trinity, the holy trinity. I am God the Father, I am God the Son, Jesus Christ . . . the King of Glory. . . . I bring salvation to all souls . . ." (Paul Twitchell—The First Living Eck Master, *The Tiger's Fang,* pp. 110–111.)

"The Living ECK Master . . . never lays down laws and proclaims his way to God as the better way, although it is. He knows that *all religions* are pseudo and in the minority, but he never states this in any of his works. . . . All religions are [only] for the benefit of the leader with exception of the Path of ECKANKAR. . . . The chela must learn to separate truth from false teachings." (Darwin Gross—The Second Living Eck Master, *Your Right to Know,* p. 107, emphasis added.)

"Every man, woman and child is God! No one can dispute this basic fact of cosmic wisdom." (Paul Twitchell, *ECK World News,* March 1979, p. 15.)

"The Mahanta, the Living ECK Master, is so frank about everything in life that no one believes him" (Paul Twitchell, *The Shariyat-Ki-Sugmad,* Vol. 2, p. 30).

Note: Eckankar believes it is the oldest religion on earth and was begun by a former inhabitant of the planet Venus whose name was "Gakko" and who came to earth six million years ago. (C. F. David Lane, "Eckankar in

Turmoil, Part 1," *Understanding Cults and Spiritual Movements-Research Series, Vol. 2, No. 1* (Del Mar, CA: Del Mar Press), pp. 1–6, 17–19) Although Eckankar claims to be unique, Paul Twitchell actually acquired much of the teachings of Eckankar from a Hindu school. This group of teachings, called "Surat Shabd Yoga," was systematized in India by Sawan Singh (died 1948) in his Radhasoami Beas sect. It was continued to Kirpal Singh (died 1974) in his Ruhani Satsang sect (into which Twitchell was initiated in 1955), and it was popularized in America by Dr. Julian Johnson in his book *The Path of the Masters* (1939). (Cf. *SCP Journal*, "Eckankar: A Hard Look at a New Religion," Vol 1. No. 2, pp. 7–22.)

A popular humanistic new-age group, the Movement of Spiritual Inner Awareness (MSIA, pronounced Messiah), sponsor of the "Insight Training Seminars," was started by graduate John-Roger Hinkins in 1968. Through out of body episodes ("soul transcendence") and psychic awareness, the student is led to the sound and light within, basic Radhasoami theology.

DOCTRINAL SUMMARY

God: (The *Sugmad*). Impersonal, amoral, pantheistic spirit.

Jesus: Biblically, a son of Kal (the "devil"); otherwise a chela (Eckankar disciple) of 2,000 years ago.

The Holy Spirit: The divine sound current.

The Trinity: Biblically Satanic; otherwise variously integrated into Eckankar philosophy.

Salvation: By great personal effort and soul travel.

Man: Inwardly divine.

Sin: "Mistakes" in consciousness, or spiritual ignorance.

Satan: A Christian myth; otherwise Kal Niranjan, an evil God controlling the illusive worlds and deceiving man.

The Second Coming: A Christian Myth.

The Fall: Biblically a myth; otherwise there was a fall of spirit-souls into illusionary materialistic worlds (for example, earth).

The Bible: A corrupted work of unenlightened men.

Death: Spiritual advancement or regression depending on one's spiritual condition at death.

Heaven and Hell: Christian myths; otherwise temporary places or states of consciousness.

THE FAMILY/
CHILDREN OF GOD

INFO AT A GLANCE

Name: The Family (earlier The Love Family); The Children of God.

Purpose: To spread the teachings of the late David Berg throughout the world emphasizing an apocalyptic end to the world.

Founder: David Berg, aka "Moses David," "Mo," "Father David," "King David."

Source of authority: Spiritistic revelations given to David Berg.

Revealed teachings: Yes.

Examples of occult potential: Spiritism, contacting the dead.

Key literature: "The Mo Letters," which are the individual writings of David Berg on a wide variety of topics (Bible, religion, politics, government, family, sex and so on).

Attitude toward Christianity: Rejecting. Christians are viewed as enemies; the Church is a "God-damned whore" that God has abandoned and to which He has sent "strong delusion."

Quotes:

"*GOOD* SPIRITISM IS SUCH A NEGLECTED FIELD, WE DO NOT EVEN HAVE WORDS FOR IT. . . . THE CHURCH HAS BEEN SO WEAK SPIRITUALLY that it could not cast good spells or do good magic or have good witches or wizards, so that there are not even words for them! . . . WHERE ARE *GOD'S* WITCHES? Where are His wizards? Where are *His* magicians? Where are those of *us* who can cast spells over others? WELL, THEY'RE *HERE*—ITS *YOU!*" (David Berg, *The Mo Letters*, Vol. 4, p. 4274, "God's Witches," June 6, 1976, DO No. 573: 139, 141, 146, 147.)

Note: The "author" of many volumes of "Mo Letters" is stated to be "God." Not surprisingly, many members accept whatever Berg said as God's word. While all letters are inspired by God ("it's *all* given by inspiration"), it is also claimed that not all his letters are inspired to the same degree as the Bible. Thus, Berg declares that his business-administrative correspondence and other teaching aspects of his letters were "*not* on the level of the Bible," but that the other letters are. "God" declares through Berg: "Should ye not print for them the Mo Letters? . . . Give them My letters. . . . I will feed them My words" (Introduction to Vol. 1 of *The Mo Letters*, p. 3; "More Precious Pearls," Sept. 1976, DO [Disciples Only] No. 540: 4).

DOCTRINAL SUMMARY

God: Vaguely defined; immoral.

Jesus: Divine, not necessarily God.

The Christ: Feminine aspect of deity; at times seemingly impersonal.

The Trinity: Variously affirmed or denied.

Salvation: By faith and works but apparently universalistic.

Man: The creation of God in spirit, soul and body.

Sin: Sometimes viewed biblically, but in practice certain sins are often redefined as performing God's will, such as fornication or adultery as a "spiritual" means to gather converts.

Satan: Biblically defined, although he will finally inherit salvation.

The Bible: A divine revelation properly interpreted by David Berg's revelations.

Heaven and Hell: Hell is apparently not an eternal place, but purgatorial and redemptive, not retributive.

FOUNDATION OF HUMAN UNDERSTANDING

INFO AT A GLANCE

Name: The Foundation of Human Understanding.

Purpose: To help man contact his inner Self to solve his problems.

Founder: Roy Masters.

Source of authority: Roy Masters; the inner Self.

Revealed teachings: Yes.

Claim: "Roy Masters has nothing less to offer you than the secret of life itself." (Roy Masters, *How Your Mind Can Keep You Well*, back cover.)

Examples of occult potential: Psychic meditation.

Key literature: The books of Roy Masters.

Attitude toward Christianity: Rejecting.

Quote:

"Don't ever let it be said that I am against Christianity . . ." (Roy Masters, *The Satan Principle*, p. 76).

DOCTRINAL SUMMARY

God: Ineffable.

Jesus: A man.

The Holy Spirit: A synonym for God.

Salvation: Inner awareness by meditation.

Man: Inwardly divine.

Sin: Emotional disability.

Satan: Personal "devils"; a synonym for evil.

The Fall: From light into darkness.

The Bible: Spiritually inadequate; at best a pointer to Reality.

Heaven and Hell: Positive or negative states of consciousness.

GURDJIEFF FOUNDATIONS

Name: The Gurdjieff Foundations.

Purpose: The attainment of higher consciousness.

Founder: George Gurdjieff.

Source of authority: Gurdjieff.

Revealed teachings: Yes.

Examples of occult potential: Psychic powers; spiritism.

Key literature: *All and Everything; Beelzebub's Tales to His Grandson* and other literature by Gurdjieff and Peter D. Ouspensky.

Attitude toward Christianity: Rejecting.

Quotes:

"I hate your Jesus" (Gurdjieff, C. S. Nott, *Teachings of Gurdjieff*, p. 103). "He never spoke well of the Christian Churches" (J. G. Bennett, *Gurdjieff: Making a New World*, p. 141).

"Everyone idiot. I am idiot. Even God is idiot" (Gurdjieff, *Further Teachings of Gurdjieff*, p. 70).

Note: J. G. Bennett, a 30 year Gurdjieff disciple, was instrumental in helping propagate the occult Subud teachings in the U.S. Although he is said to have changed his mind, he once believed Subud to be the "logical" culmination of Gurdjieff's teachings. Werner Erhard, the founder of est/the Forum, was also influenced by Gurdjieff/Subud.

DOCTRINAL SUMMARY

God: Ineffable, although conceived in quasi-Christian terms.

Jesus: A Master.

Salvation: Enlightenment is achieved through specific techniques, sometimes involving strenuous human efforts toward the attainment of systematic "self-observation" leading to the comprehending of "objective" reality or true consciousness.

Man: Inwardly divine (potentially), although currently asleep.

The Bible: Interpreted mystically.

Death: Some individuals experience reincarnation, others are "annihilated."

THE HOLY ORDER
OF MANS (HOOM)

INFO AT A GLANCE

Name: The Holy Order of Mans (HOOM).

Purpose: To help unify all religions and bring in the "New Age."

Founder: Paul Blighton.

Source of authority: The books of Paul Blighton.

Revealed teachings: Yes.

Claim: HOOM is the one principal organization that "the Christ" is using to set up the New Age.

Examples of occult potential: Development of psychic powers, Eastern meditation, spiritism.

Key literature: *Book of the Master Jesus* (3 vols.); *The Golden Force; The Golden Nugget; History of the White Brotherhood; Keystone of Tarot; Sonflowers Discipleship Journal.*

Attitude toward Christianity: While claiming to be a Roman Catholic order, its attitude to Christianity is one of rejection.

Quote:

"The term 'Christ' as used in the New Testament represents that holy power which Christed or anointed the blessed Jesus at his time of Baptisms, by virtue of which he became the most perfect of men and the highest Initiate of Earth's humanity." (Paul Blighton, *Book of the Master Jesus,* Vol. I, p. 46.)

"We cannot limit ourselves to any denomination, or sect, or religion, and still maintain the universal consciousness which is called Christ. It is impossible to speak of universal Consciousness without the inclusion of Buddha, Moses, Mohammed, Krishna, Zoroaster, or any other of the avatars and teachers of men." (*Sonflowers,* Jan. 1978, p. 22.)

Note: In the last few years HOOM claims that it has rejected its earlier teachings for biblical faith, making the content here possibly outdated. HOOM information on the Internet would indicate that if such a change has occurred, its major replacement is "Christ the Savior Brotherhood," a sect of Eastern Orthodoxy which, however much improved, is still not biblical faith. Apparently, at least five distinct groups today replace the HOOM: Christ the Savior Brotherhood; The Gnostic Order of Christ; Science of Man; American Temple; and The Foundation of Christ Church. (See www.angelfire.com/hi/HOOM/index2.html)

DOCTRINAL SUMMARY

God: Pantheistic (an omnipresent impersonal force), psychic energy.

Jesus: An extremely advanced mystic who attained perfection and "Christ" awareness.

The Christ: Universal consciousness; divine nature.

The Holy Spirit: Part of the force of God.

Salvation: By psychic exercises; knowledge; social good works.

Man: Inwardly divine.

Sin: Error.

Satan: Myth.

The Second Coming: The worldwide increase of interest in psychicism.

The Fall: Symbolic.

The Bible: A guidebook containing truth and error.

Death: Transition to a higher plane.

Hell and Heaven: Positive or negative states of consciousness.

HUMAN POTENTIAL SEMINARS—
est/THE FORUM, LIFESPRING, ACTUALIZATIONS, MOMENTUS

INFO AT A GLANCE

Description: Human Potential seminars are often 50-60 hour intensive programs designed to unleash "human potential" and achieve enlightenment. A number of significant New Age seminars are offshoots of the philosophy of Werner Erhard or Jose Silva (Silva Mind Control).

Founder(s): Werner Erhard (est/The Forum); John Hanley (Lifespring); Stewart Emery (Actualizations); Daniel Tocchini (Momentus). Related seminars include founders John-Roger (Insight Seminars); Dennis Becker (Impact Seminars); Bob White and Duncan Callister (Life Dynamics); William Patrick (the now defunct Mind Dynamics).

How do they claim to work?: Forum leaders allege their methods have the ability to radically empower individuals through unleashing the untapped powers of the mind. Because each individual's mind determines or shapes reality, once people experience their true (divine) potential, they are allegedly able to influence all areas of their lives for the better.

Examples of occult potential: Altered states of consciousness, psychic development, spiritism.

Major problem: The generally monistic or solipsistic worldview assumes a false view of man, a false view of the world and a false view of how people are to live in the world.

Biblical and Christian evaluation: In general, both the antiChristian teachings (monism, humanism, occult philosophy) and practices (visualization, meditation, self-hypnosis, psychic development) mean that participation in these seminars is proscribed.

Potential dangers: Self-deception over one's abilities; possible occult influences; conversion to Eastern-occult worldviews.

Quote:

> "I believe that the 'belief' in God is the greatest barrier to God in the universe—the single greatest barrier. I would prefer someone who is ignorant to someone who believes in God. Because the belief in God is a total barrier, almost a total barrier to the experience of God." (Werner Erhard, "All I Can Do Is Lie," *East-West Journal*, September 1974 (rpt), p. 2.)

> "How do I know I'm not the reincarnation of Jesus Christ? You wouldn't believe the feelings I have inside me." (Cited in Jesse Kornbluth, "The Fuhrer Over Est," *New Times Magazine*, March 19, 1976, p. 42.)

Note: Est was "retired" in 1985, however, the beliefs of Werner Erhard and est live on in the Forum, Lifespring, Actualizations and in other ways and places in society.

The change from est to The Landmark Forum had more to do with public relations and marketability than with any fundamental change in philosophy. The duplicity in how est was packaged and the many legal, financial and ethical allegations against Werner Erhard were causing a significant problem for public perception of est, not to mention its profitability. Soon after the revealing "60 Minutes" expose of est on March 3,

1991, Erhard left the country. Two years later Erhard's problems were chronicled in the scathing unofficial biography by Steven Pressman, *Outrageous Betrayal: The Dark Journey of Werner Erhard from est to Exile* (St. Martin's, 1993).

In essence, est was repackaged by Werner, his brother Harry Rosenberg and other leaders to resolve its public relation problems. The public liability of Erhard was dealt with while the same basic philosophy remained. In a similar vein, a more tolerant and sophisticated Lifespring today has resulted in major increases of its attendees, not to mention revenues. And now we even have a "Christianized" Lifespring called Momentus.

Erhard is "gone," but his philosophy remains and it would not be surprising to discover, despite denials, that, wherever he is, he still pulls the strings. Landmark alumnus Walter Plywaski, a Colorado electronics engineer, commented in *Time* magazine March 16, 1998, "Erhard is like the Cheshire cat. He has gone away, but the smile is there, hanging over everything."

There are many places where the similarities between Scientology, est/The Forum and Lifespring are clear. To fully understand est, one must also understand Scientology. In fact, Scientology has allegedly accused Erhard of stealing the essence of his program from L. Ron Hubbard, the founder of Scientology. To fully understand The Forum (or Lifespring) it is essential to understand est. To fully understand Momentus, one must understand both est and Lifespring.

Through human potential seminars, millions of people today have paid hundreds of millions of dollars to try and find everything from solutions to their personal problems to meaning in life. But despite the promises made by promoters and the relatively brief expense of time—one or two weekends—the problem is that the "enlightenment" these seminars deliver is unhealthy and potentially dangerous.

In terms of their worldview and ethical impact, despite the "profound psychological insights" and "dramatic personal transformation," from a Christian perspective they remain deceptive and inconsequential. Indeed, little or no research is done by these groups to validate objective claims, or to establish unambiguous criteria for evaluation, or to define successful training or to record the failures and harm done some participants and the implications thereof.

Since so many human potential seminars are modified clones of one another, it is relatively easy to diagram a basic evolution:

Scientology, Zen and other disciplines

↓

est ⟶ the Forum

↓

Lifespring, etc. Actualizations

↓

Momentus

MOMENTUS AND MASHIYACH MINISTRIES

In our *Encyclopedia of New Age Beliefs* we very briefly touched upon Momentus Seminars. We were unable to find sufficient information to do other than issue a general warning. In the last two years however, more information has come to light so that we may clearly declare it off limits for Christians. The problem is not the good motives of founder and former Lifespring trainer Daniel Tocchini, or whatever Christian elements or instruction are in the training. The problem is the nature of the training as a whole. From Internet reports and those who have taken the training we may discern the following:

1. Momentus appears to be a toned down "Lifespring for Christians" in an outwardly Christian format and with a somewhat Christian philosophy. Given the fact that Momentus founder Daniel Tocchini was a Lifespring trainer for almost ten years after he became a Christian in the early 1980s the influence of Lifespring could be expected.

2. Manipulative methods are used that exceed the bounds of Christian ethical instruction. "The basic Momentus training involves four

intense, 13-hour days of group personal teachings and exercises designed, as one graduate put it, 'To tear down who you are and then rebuild you from the bottom up.'"[1]

3. Sin is primarily defined as being a victim. As it was in est, there are no true (adult) victims; you are responsible for what happens in your life.

4. As far as changing one's behavior, Momentus training is as important as sanctification by the Holy Spirit.

5. The Momentus vision of Christian discipleship is one in which Christ and the Cross are not central in the training.

6. The philosophy is more humanistic than biblical, more therapy than theology, and it includes elements of Gestalt, Transactional Analysis and abuse recovery methodology. Truth is apparently judged by emotions more than by Scripture.

7. The same kinds of negative reports by graduates found in est/The Forum and Lifespring appear to be present in Momentus.

On its website, the Messiah Lutheran Church in Highland, California, concluded, "By first-hand accounts and Momentus literature, this organization appears not to be Christian but rather est and Lifespring-type training with a Christian veneer." It also noted (we have heard similar accounts) that Momentus has caused division in churches and even church splits. In addition, the following similarities are noted to est/The Forum and Lifespring:

• There is a controlled, regimented environment.

• Lifespring processes are used, such as the Red/Black game and Lifeboat.

• High pressure tactics break down participants.

• It can be powerfully life changing.

• Existing paradigms are broken down to create a new reality; "reality is defined by present experience" not objective truth.

• Experimental and anti-intellectual emphasis; the focus is on "being rather than doing."

• A mandatory two-page "hold harmless" release and a psychologist release for those in therapy: "Each prospective trainee is asked to sign a 'hold-harmless' contract acknowledging . . . that emotional and/or psychological damage may occur but is not the legal responsibility of Mashiyach Ministries and that the trainee will never reveal the contents of the training to any non-graduate. . . . This contract is virtually identical to the contracts used in Lifespring, The Forum, and other human potential movement groups."[2]

• Graduate testimonials are nearly identical to est/The Forum and Lifespring.

• The Momentus experience can be difficult, even harrowing. *Killing the Victim*, a standard Momentus text, explains: "In the training, there is no attempt to relieve the pressure that comes from the confrontation between what you say you believe and inconsistent behavior. Participants are encouraged to use the discomfort and tension they may experience as energy to compel them to change their lives."[3]

[The Messiah Lutheran Church] website also reviewed the first Momentus book, which summarizes the philosophy underlying Momentus, *Killing the Victim Before the Victim Kills You* by Tocchini and two associates, Derek M. Watson and Larry Pinci. Significantly, the book positively acknowledges Lifespring founder John Hanley. Excerpts of the review follow:

There is a blurring or twisting of concepts of subjectivity throughout the book. At heart, what they seem to promote is a "mind over matter" philosophy, where if I can just change my attitude, I can change reality. . . . I think it is probably closer to the truth to say that they have taken the program from EST and added a veneer of Christianity. The flaws in their theology indicate that they don't have a truly Christian model of personal transformation. All the psychological and spiritual dangers of EST are probably present in Momentus.

Their attitude toward the church in general is suspicious and critical. They seem to have encountered a lot of suspicion from local churches whose members have gotten involved in Momentus. . . . They attack churches for being either "gnostic" (their code word for charismatic, experience centered) or "textualists" (a code word for doctrinally centered).... At least four of the many people listed in their acknowledgments are former leaders in The Way International....[4]

A former Way member and Momentus trainer recalls:

I was Team Captain in the April and July trainings. My husband and I became sponsors for the September training; we sponsored two more trainings (and lost about five to six thousand dollars doing so) before severing ties with Mashiyach. Perhaps half the area sponsors were ex-Wayers, as was founder Daniel Tocchini. He wasn't deeply involved.... At one point I heard one of the trainers say that there are no victims (except for children who were sexually abused). I did my best to adapt this stance for my experience and myself but it did not work.... As team captain and then sponsor of the Momentus Training, Mashiyach held my husband and I responsible for everything that went wrong with any training. For example, a few people who took the training had to be either heavily medicated or hospitalized after the training due to the emotional intensity of the training. As sponsors we were blamed (although they avoided using that word) for not coaching the team on whom to enroll in the training. No responsibility was taken by the trainer for what occurred during the training that would cause such a response....

John [ex-Way leader John Lynn] recruited participants directly from his mailing list of former The Way International (TWI) members. I believe John had an interest in leading former TWI members to feel that they were responsible for whatever abuse they endured while associated with TWI so that he could absolve himself of his responsibility.... The Momentus Training was a convenient tool for ex-TWI leaders to absolve themselves of any responsibility for the pain and abuse they had a hand in causing.... Daniel is not trying to brainwash people and he does not believe brainwashing is possible. However, after reading about brainwashing, I think some of the exercises in the training could be considered brainwashing techniques....

So many Way people are drawn to this in my opinion because they are so accustomed to doing what a Way leader tells them that they just do what John (or whoever) tells them to do. John has a big mailing list of ex-Way people. I have seen him pull it out and just make call after call to sign people up for the training. That is NOT how people are supposed to be enrolled by MMI's usual standards.[5]

All this is probably why the "News Watch" section of the *Christian Research Journal* reported:

Mashiyach Ministries has received considerable criticism from secular and Christian religious movement researchers, both for its roots in the New Age human potential group Lifespring, and for its assumptions and practices that critics say are contrary to social and mental health and to sound biblical principles of discipleship and personal growth.... the persistence and consistency of negative reports from dissatisfied graduates do indicate that a fundamental problem surfaces wherever the trainings are held.... Critics also point to the "fruit" of Mashiyach Ministries, which includes a significant number of emotionally troubled graduates; failure to produce tangible, notable changes in many graduates' lives; and a number of churches that have undergone destructive internal battles and divisions between the Momentus advocates and church members who have not attended any trainings.... Santa Rosa Christian Church eventually suffered a church split over the issue.[6]

Est/The Forum reserves the very last portion of its training for recruitment to additional seminars like Momentus. When participants are in a state of emotional exaltation over their "incredible transformational insights," they are at that moment signed up for more seminars (save $100 off the $700 Advanced Program, etc.). In a similar fashion:

... By conducting the "free-will" offering at the end of the training, Mashiyach Ministries realizes its maximum benefit from grateful new graduates before they have a chance to think twice about their experiences. As one recent graduate told the JOURNAL concerning his donation, "If I was willing to invest $150 in something I hadn't even experienced and knew relatively little about, how much more do you think I was willing to give when I thought I had just experienced the greatest life-transforming event of my Christian walk?" . . . There is also a strong motivation to press Momentus graduates to attend the variety of additional advanced programs, each with its own price tag.[7]

Finally, the abusive language of est/The Forum is also present in Momentus:

Dick Williams of Grace Fellowship in Santa Rosa, California, notes that "The foundational presuppositions behind the training are essentially the same as Lifespring." Williams also brings up the use of swearing during the trainings. . . . One of the more persistent complaints received by the Christian Research Institute from churches is that parishioners who have completed the Momentus trainings develop speech habits of swearing that are highly offensive to other Christians. As one pastor told the JOURNAL, "Liberty in Christ is one thing. This isn't liberty, it's an offense to Christ." David Serio, a Christian who left part way through a Momentus training, comments, "The very act of regressing people back to their past and encouraging the free, uninhibited expression of anger, including the use of profanity, if need be, is totally and completely unbiblical. This is not biblical Christianity, it is humanistic psychology.[8]

Although Tocchini briefly suspended trainings in 1993 with the stated goal of making Momentus training biblically compatible, this information indicates that this has not yet occurred, and it may not even be possible. "The organization has yet to silence successfully the concerns raised by critics. Nor has it successfully convinced critics that its behavior and teaching are essentially and qualitatively different from the human potential movement and are instead throw away Christian."[9] That is to say, Momentus' connection to Christianity is tenuous at best.

NOTES

1. "New Watch," "'Lifespring' for Christians? Momentus and Mashiyach Ministries Attract Followers and Controversy," *Christian Research Journal*, January–March 1998, p. 43.
2. Ibid.
3. In ibid.
4. "Summary of Problems in Momentus Training," from Messiah Lutheran Church website, http://e2.empirenet.com/~messiah7/tw_momentus sumary.htm.
5. Ibid.
6. "News Watch," *Christian Research Journal*, pp. 6-7.
7. Ibid., p. 7.
8. Ibid.
9. Ibid.

JEHOVAH'S WITNESSES

INFO AT A GLANCE

Name: Jehovah's Witnesses and the New World Society. The Watchtower Bible and Tract Society. International Bible Students.

Purpose: To declare the name and coming Kingdom of Jehovah God.

Founder: Charles Taze Russell (1852–1916).

Source of authority: The Watchtower Society (splinter groups often still hold Charles Russell as the authority and reject subsequent changes in doctrine).

Revealed teachings: Yes.

Claim: To represent the only organization on earth through which Jehovah God operates and disseminates His will; to supply the true interpretation of the Bible.

Theology: Historically eclectic; parallels with Arianism and Socinianism.

Occult dynamics: A reliance upon "angelic" revelation, guidance, biblical interpretation and translation of the Bible.

Key literature: Scores of books published by the Watchtower Society. Key periodicals are "The Watchtower Announcing Jehovah's Kindom" ("The Watchtower"; formerly "Zion's Watchtower and Herald of Christ's Presence"), and "Awake" (formerly "The Golden Age"; "Consolation").

Attitude towards Christianity: Rejecting.

Quotes:

"Haters of God and His people . . . are to be hated. . . . We must hate in the truest sense, which is to regard with extreme and active aversion, to consider as loathsome, odious, filthy, to detest. Surely any haters of God are not fit to live on his beautiful earth. The earth will be rid of the wicked and we shall not need to lift a finger to cause physical harm to come to them, for God will attend to that, but we must have a proper perspective of these enemies. . . . We pray with intensity . . . and plead that his anger be made manifest. . . . O Jehovah God of hosts . . . be not merciful to any wicked transgressors. . . . Consume them in wrath, consume them so that they shall be no more."

—*The Watchtower,* October 1, 1952, pp. 596-604 (in Martin, *Jehovah of the Watchtower,* p. 109).

"It is entirely unsafe for the people to rely upon the words and doctrines of imperfect men."

— Judge Rutherford, second Watchtower president, Gerstner, p. 34, citing Stoup *The Jehovah's Witnesses* (1945), p. 125.

The Watchtower . . . "is the first paper ever to make announcement of the invisible presence of our Lord and to submit clear, Scriptural proof to show that since 1874 he has been present." (*Reprints of the Original Watchtower and Herald of Christ's Presence,* Vol. 1, Prefatory Note, July 1, 1979.)

Note: *New World Translation* (the Watchtower Society Bible) verses in past or present editions may be cited.

There are some 24+ sects of the Jehovah's Witnesses (Gruss, *We Left Jehovah's Witnesses,* p. 6). About one-third of these are analyzed in Gruss, *Apostles of Denial,* Appendix A. These sects retain the heretical teachings of Charles Russell in spite of sounding Christian. They include:

a) The 50,000–100,000 member Layman's Home Missionary Movement of Chester Springs, PA, which although Russellite in theology has been endorsed by some Christian organizations. (See *Apostles of Denial,* pp. 269-272);

b) The 20,000–40,000 member Dawn Bible Students Association of East Rutherford, NJ. These are also heretical, denying, for example, the biblical nature of Christ and salvation (see *The Dawn: A Herald of Christ's Presence,* Nov. 1979, pp. 29-31, 38-43; April 1979, pp. 41-48; May 1979, pp. 43-45);

c) The Associated Bible Students and the Pastoral Bible Institute (also Berean Bible Institute);

d) Back to the Bible Way;

e) The Christian Believers;

f) The New Creation Bible Student's Association and others.

The authors wish to note their indebtedness to Professor Edmond Gruss for much of the original materials no longer published by the Watchtower Society. It is apparently standing Watchtower Society policy to remove books or revise them when sufficient publicity comes to light documenting their errors. (See Gruss, *Apostles of Denial,* p. 261.) Good literature and further study can be found at Free Minds, Inc. at http://www.freemmds.org, which has links to over 75 other Christian and secular sites that critique Jehovah's Witnesses. Further documentation for virtually everything in the chapter is available on the Web, especially at the above site and its links. For example, this site links to R & W (Researching the Watchtower), which links to the "Top 100 sites about Jehovah's Witnesses." All in all, there are hundreds of Jehovah's Witnesses related links.

DOCTRINAL SUMMARY

God: Unipersonal; His proper name is Jehovah.

Jesus: A created angel who has existed in three stages or phases (the archangel Michael, Jesus of Nazareth, an exalted Michael).

The Christ: The anointed one; Jesus became "the Christ" at his baptism, at which point He was also spiritually reborn.

Holy Spirit: The impersonal active force of Jehovah.

Trinity: A pagan superstition devised by Satan to blaspheme Jehovah.

Salvation: By faith and works. (Man is capable of achieving salvation without spiritual rebirth.)

Man: A material (not spiritual) creation of Jehovah.

Sin: Soteriologically, a weak view of sin is held.

Satan: Generally orthodox teaching, except for the fact of Satan's annihilation and Watchtower Society confusion over good and evil angels.

Second Coming: Occurred invisibly in 1874 (date later changed to 1914).

Bible: Authoritative only when interpreted by the Watchtower Society.

Death: Death brings annihilation—temporary for those "resurrected" (recreated) to life, eternal for the wicked.

Heaven and Hell: Heaven is a place reserved for only the 144,000 "elect"; the idea of an eternal hell is a "doctrine of demons."

INTRODUCTION AND HISTORY

An aggressive brand of proselytizing has made the Jehovah's Witnesses one of the most successful religious cults in this century. A few statistics enable one to appreciate its growth from a small group of Bible students in 1870. According to the late Dr. Walter Martin, a recognized authority on the cult: "During the years 1942–52, the membership of Jehovah's Witnesses doubled in North America, multiplied fifteen times in South America, twelve times in the Atlantic islands, five times in Asia, seven times in Europe and Africa, and six times in the islands of the Pacific. By 1973 these figures had almost doubled. Such is the evolution of Pastor Russell's 'Zion.'"[1]

Twenty years later the figures had doubled again. As of 1999 there were approximately 5 million to 6 million "publishers," or active members, plus 5 million to 7 million additional interested persons, or inactive members, who attended the yearly April "memorial" service—the Witnesses version of the Lord's supper. This means that in terms of influence, the number of active members only tells half the story. In many respects, the Watchtower Society (WS), begun by C. T. Russell, is today just as influential as the LDS church begun by Joseph Smith.

Since 1928 the Watchtower printing plant has sent out *billions* of pieces of literature.[2] In 1975, the Watchtower yearbook (p. 32) listed for 1974 a print run of 51,663,097 bound books, 18,239,169 booklets and almost a half billion *Watchtower* and *Awake* magazines. The ten billionth piece of literature was reached sometime in 1988 or 1989; the twenty billionth about the time this encyclopedia was published. Today the WS sponsors some 5 million Bible studies each month, and followers spend almost 2 billion hours witnessing.[3] There are over 75,000 congregations in some 230 countries.

The two key periodicals, *The Watchtower* and *Awake,* have a combined yearly circulation of over 600,000,000 in some 150 languages.[4] Watchtower literature as a whole is published in some 230 languages. The circulations of the two Watchtower magazines rival *TV Guide* and *Reader's Digest* and outsells *Time, Newsweek* and *US News and World Report* combined. Also, possibly one-hundred million copies of the Watchtower Society's *New World Translation* (NWT) of the Bible are now in some 30 languages, in whole or part. Perhaps no other single religious organization uses the printed page so extensively, dwarfing by comparison the majority of other religious bodies, even, it is claimed, the U.S. Catholic Church.[5]

Of course, there are other ways to look at such figures that are less flattering to the Witnesses. In light of such vast publication figures, one is surprised at the relatively small numbers of converts. Edmond Gruss, Professor of Apologetics at the Masters College in Los Angeles, California and an expert on Jehovah's Witnesses, calculates that to bring one convert to baptism (the final step in becoming a Witness) involves 10 active Witnesses and some 1,800 hours of service.[6] Freeminds.org on the Web ("How Big is the Watchtower") estimates that it takes about 15 years for the average "publisher" (active member) to make one convert. It is also true that since its inception in the 1880s, there has been a steady exodus of members from the movement.[7] From 1949 to 1973 at least 400,000 baptized Witnesses apparently left the Witnesses and are no longer active members, half the number occurring between 1969 and 1973.[8] From 1970–1979, over 750,000 left the organization or were disfellowshipped, according to former Governing Board Member and Witness leader, Raymand Franz, nephew of the fourth WS president, Frederick W. Franz.[9] Matters have apparently not improved in the subsequent two decades, in large part due to the authoritarianism, legalism, stress and even medical hazards resulting from Watchtower doctrines.

In examining the history of WS we should note the influence of several different religions upon WS doctrine, especially Seventh-day Adventism.

Charles Taze Russell had a church upbringing but eventually became dissatisfied with certain teachings. After a period of agnosticism, he began exploring other religions to see if he could find something more to his liking. Seventh Day Adventism and Christadelphianism exerted a marked influence upon him, and they clearly became a source of his theology, in spite of official silence or denials. In a recent edition of *The Chaos of the Cults,* Dr. Van Baalen declared: "The origin of the Russell-Rutherford-Knorr theology, especially of its eschatology, lies in Seventh-day Adventism. This was asserted in *The Chaos of the Cults* in 1929, hotly disclaimed by LeRoy E. Froom, and has since then been reaffirmed by Lehman Strauss, F. E. Mayer, and E. G. Gruss."[10] In *The Theology of the Major Sects,* Dr. Gerstner concurs:

It is quite clear that the Jehovah's Witnesses are an offshoot of the Seventh-day Adventists.... As Ferguson observes, "Evidently his [Russell's] youth was dominated by morbid pictures of a sizzling hell, for as a boy he used to go around the city of Pittsburgh every Saturday evening and write signs with chalk on the fences, warning people to attend Church on the following Sabbath that they might escape the ghastly torments of everlasting fire." From this fiery orthodoxy, Russell, when he found himself unable to answer certain questions of a skeptic, passed over into a frigid unbelief. It was then that he met the Seventh-day Adventists, and his faith in Christianity, especially the Second Advent, was restored.[11]

While Russell was heavily influenced by Adventism, he also modified it. In 1877 he published a book with N. H. Barbour (leader of an Adventist sect), *Three Worlds or Plan of Redemption.* (Both Russell and Barbour denied the physical resurrection and return of Christ.) Together they published a magazine, *The Herald of the Morning.* When Russell split with Barbour he began a new magazine, *Zion's Watchtower and Herald of Christ's Presence,* which is today *The Watchtower Announcing Jehovah's Kingdom.*

Adventist doctrines in harmony with Jehovah's Witnesses include: 1) the rejection of a biblical hell, 2) the rejection of an immortal soul, 3) in part, the Adventists have a works emphasis in salvation, 4) like the Witnesses, they believe themselves to be the only true remnant church.*

If one examines the doctrines of the Christadelphians, it seems evident they also exerted an influence upon Russell. For example, they express hostility towards the Church, and they

---

*Insofar as Adventism rejects salvation by grace through faith alone and other key doctrines, it cannot be classified as biblical Christianity. Insofar as it accepts biblical teaching on the nature of God and other key doctrines, it cannot properly be classified as a cult. Unfortunately, in recent years traditionalists have squashed biblical reform movements within Adventism, leaving its future health subject to doubt.

deny the Trinity, Jesus' deity, hell and an immortal soul. They teach a partial atonement, an "end times" restored church and the necessity of works-salvation (see Christadelphian chapter).[12] Professor Gruss, a former member of the Witnesses and author of one of the best texts on the Witnesses, *Apostles of Denial*, points out: "It is difficult to understand why the Jehovah's Witnesses do not claim or even mention in their history the Christadelphian movement. . . . It is certain that this group is a definite source of Russellite theology. Except for minor differences, there is almost a word-for-word agreement between the Christadelphian and the Russellite theology in several areas."[13]

At the least, this suggests that the origin of the Jehovah's Witnesses is not as original or as unique as claimed. Their teachings also bear similarities to some earlier heresies, notably Arianism (it denied Christ's deity) and Socinianism (it denied the Trinity on the basis of reason and held the Holy Spirit to be an influence or energy coming from God). In fact, Professor Gruss discusses the extent of heresy represented by the WS:

> William J. Schnell, a member of the Jehovah's Witnesses for more than thirty years, views the background of Russellite theology as a background of heresies, the Watchtower Society having "succeeded in weaving the threads of all former heresies and cults in the make-up for a New World Society." That this statement is true, and is even an understatement, can be seen in a careful study of the history of Christian doctrine; an understatement, in that Russell and his successors not only accepted old heresies but created new heresy which had never appeared before. Russell, directly or indirectly, picked up such errors as Universalism (later modified), Unitarianism, second probationism, restorationism, and a peculiar method of Biblical interpretation—a mixture of Swedenborgian or Pietist and Socinian methods.[14]

Five Eras

In that the president of the Watchtower Society tends to leave his own particular imprint upon the Society, we may note five particular "eras" to date:

1)	Charles T. Russell	(1872–1916)
2)	Joseph F. Rutherford	(1917–1942)
3)	Nathan H. Knorr	(1942–1977)
4)	Frederick W. Franz	(1977–1992)
5)	Milton G. Herschel	(1992–)

1) Russell stressed the reconciliation of God and man through the atonement of Christ and the coming restoration of all things in the millennial kingdom, the latter being a continuous Watchtower Society theme of today. Russell's magnum opus—a seven volume set of writings called *Studies in the Scriptures*—became a new "Bible" for the faithful Russellites of his era; although today, despite its claim to divine revelation, it is largely neglected. Nevertheless, its theology was typically nonChristian. For example, Russell's *The Atonement Between God and Man* (Vol. 5) contains most of his theology including denials of: 1) Christ's deity—study III (cf. pp. 83–95); 2) the personality of the Holy Spirit, study VIII (cf. pp. 165–172); 3) hell and the immortality of the soul, study XII-XIII (cf. pp. 301–333); 4) the atonement, study XV, XVI (cf. pp. 422–429); and others.[15]

2) In the second era (Rutherford as Witness president) many of Russell's distinctive teachings were largely ignored (the basic theology remained the same), and the Jehovah of the Old Testament replaced the Christ of the New Testament, an emphasis that remains today. Rutherford initiated the new name, "Jehovah's Witnesses" and placed more importance on the vindication of God's name than on Russell's teaching on the atonement. He also increased the level of attack upon Christendom. Rutherford began an open verbal war against the visible segment of the devil's earthly kingdom, the military-political-religious world system. This has also continued to this day, although in milder form.

Under Rutherford's direction the Society became an authoritarian organization within whose ranks dissent was not tolerated, also something that has remained to this day. Rutherford expanded the use of an allegorical interpretation of the Old Testament, which has also continued. He further stressed the idea of "progressive revelation," which allowed him to shed "new light" on Russell's earlier teachings. Actually, his idea of progressive revelation was a denial of the Christian concept. Rather than giving new information on dimly revealed doctrines (in the Bible, the doctrine of the Trinity and the doctrine of eternal punishment, while present in the Old Testament, are more fully revealed in the New Testament), Rutherford changed Russell's divinely revealed truths into errors and taught new concepts and biblical interpretations that forcefully denied earlier ones.[16] (cf. Critique section). Thus, during Rutherford's "era of changes," thousands of faithful Russellites, perceiving a betrayal of Russell, left the organization and started some of the two dozen sects of the Jehovah's Witnesses that we find today.

3) The period under Nathan H. Knorr (1942-1977) greatly expanded the organization's numbers (105,000 when he began; 2.2 million when he left). New stress was placed on training in the Jehovah's Witnesses interpretation of the Bible. This accounts for Witnesses' success today with uninformed Christians, and in more or less liberal mainline denominations and the spiritually searching segments of the general public. Also, their own doctrinally biased translation of the Bible, the *New World Translation,* was produced in 1950, and became an invaluable asset in Watchtower doctrinal apologetics and witnessing. (See Critique section.)

Under Knorr, literature produced by the WS became anonymous, although it was accepted that it originated from the Watchtower Society leadership. Changes continued to be made, justified by "progressive revelation"; for example, the term "religion," once universally condemned as entirely satanic, was now acceptable. Also during this period, more alterations in biblical interpretation are evident.[17] There was also something of a desire to be seen as respectable in a scholarly sense, and a new stress was laid upon recording the group's history.

4, 5) Subsequent presidents Franz and Herschel have continued the same tradition of leaving their unique marks upon the WS beliefs and practices.

What is clear from this is that WS claims for an immutable revelation of doctrine are without foundation.*

Characteristics

In this section we consider some characteristics of the Watchtower Society (WS) which are relevant to later discussions. For example, understanding their concept of a dual classification of the believer is vital to comprehending their doctrines in general, especially as they relate to salvation. Similarly, their claim to divine guidance and inspiration allows us to understand their placing WS literature on equal footing with the Bible. Understanding the rationalistic emphasis of the WS helps one comprehend their rejection of "unreasonable" doctrines such as the Trinity, hell, and the deity of Christ. Their authoritarianism makes it easier to understand members' absolute submission to Watchtower programs and practices such as refusing blood transfusions and nonobservance of holidays (Christmas, Easter, etc.). Indeed, the average member is quite fearful of Watchtower Society disapproval, since to be cut off from the WS is to be cut off from God and salvation. We shall examine these and other characteristics in turn.

Two Classes of Believers

One cannot fully understand Watchtower Society (WS) literature unless one understands that there are two distinct classes of believers within the Witnesses. Without realizing who a given section of literature is referring to, one may become confused; for example, by assuming that terms like "anointed class" refer to all Jehovah's Witnesses when in fact they do not.

---

*Anyone interested in a reliable history of Jehovah's Witnesses should not consult their own histories, for as in Mormonism and other cults, they are largely unreliable.[18] Gruss suggests Herbert H. Stroup's *The Jehovah's Witnesses* (a published Ph.D. thesis, 1945); Edgar R. Pike's *Jehovah's Witnesses* (1954); William H. Cumberland's *A History of Jehovah's Witnesses* (unpublished Ph.D. thesis, The State University of Iowa, 1958); J. William Whalen's *Armageddon Around the Corner* (1962); and Timothy White's *A People for His Name: A History of the Jehovah's Witnesses and an Evaluation* (1968).[19] Gruss' own text *Apostles of Denial,* presents an excellent survey of Witness history.[20]

The first class, the "anointed class," are the 144,000 specific Jehovah's Witnesses (God's elect), and only they are "born again." This class is explained by the Witness theory that since 33 A.D. Jehovah has been choosing 144,000 individuals as a special class of people to rule with Him in heaven. (No one in Old Testament times can be part of this class, since before Christ no one could be "born again.") The 144,000 have different responsibilities, a different way of salvation and a different destiny than the "second" class of individuals, which are the "other sheep," the vast majority of Jehovah's Witnesses. So the Witnesses have two distinct classes of believers: the elect 144,000 and all other Jehovah's Witnesses.

The elect are also referred to as the "faithful and discreet slave" of Matthew 24:45. Although they number 144,000, their most crucial segment is the small group of leaders of the Watchtower headquarters at Bethel who write and publish the literature of the Society. While they will one day rule in heaven with their elder brother Jesus, they now rule the "other sheep" here on earth, seeing themselves in a servant role. Concerning Jesus' parable in Matthew 24:45-51 it is said: "Jesus' illustration began fulfillment at his departure in the year 33 C.E., and this composite 'slave' has been existing since then, namely, 'the Israel of God,' the spirit-begotten, anointed congregation of Christ, the membership of which will finally reach 144,000."[21]

It appears that virtually all of the 144,000 have already been selected, so that among the millions of Witnesses the average person today has virtually no expectation of being the elect. A few may express the "hope" of election, and this seems to be determined by personal conviction. Thus the vast majority of Witnesses have no desire to be "born again," and they do not expect, or intend, to go to heaven. They expect to live on a "paradise earth" forever, assuming they pass the many future divine tests required of them.

Exclusivism

Since their beginning, Jehovah's Witnesses, like the Mormons and hundreds of other cults, have claimed to be the only organization on earth through which God directs His will and purposes. Most importantly, only through the Watchtower Society (WS) and its publications can one find the true meaning of the Bible. The WS is "God's sole collective channel for the flow of Biblical truth to men on earth."[22] WS exclusivism is perceived in two ways: negatively, as separation from the entire world system—political, military and religious (the latter being exclusively the "Great Whore Babylon"*); and positively, as being the sole instrument of God's use:

> What about those whom Jehovah today calls "my people"? These are commanded to "get out" of modern Babylon the Great before she is destroyed in the coming "great tribulation" foretold by Jesus Christ.... Jehovah's dedicated people have gotten out of her since the postwar year of 1919 C.E.**[23]

> We belong to NO *earthly organization*.... We adhere only to that *heavenly organization*.... All the saints now living, or that have lived during this age, belonged to OUR CHURCH ORGANIZATION: such are all ONE Church, and there is NO OTHER recognized by the Lord. Hence any earthly organization which in the least interferes with this union of saints is contrary to the teachings of Scripture and opposed to the Lord's will.[24] (Emphasis in original.)

Along with numerous other unbiblical religions (such as traditional Armstrongism, Christian Science and Mormonism), the WS claims to be a restored remnant of true believers that has been absent on earth for almost 1900 years. "The falling away of Christian leaders from true Christianity to form a 'man of lawlessness' class or system began shortly after the twelve apostles died.... The composite lawless man came out into the open and followed his self-exalting, lawless course of conduct. He set himself up as an apostate clergy."[25]

---

*The beast of Revelation 13 is the political-military system; the whore Babylon rides on the back of the beast. Many years ago, the whore Babylon was viewed as the political, military and religious system; today it is exclusively all false (non WS) religions.

**The significance of this date is related to the start of the Rutherford era and reflects the year he began his reorganization of the "theocratic kingdom."

Claim to Divine Inspiration

The WS leadership claims to receive divine guidance and new revelation, including from angels. However, the great number of changes in doctrines, Bible interpretations, "ethical" guidelines and failures in prophecy have forced them to admit human fallibility in the reception of this divine guidance. This allows them to receive the obedience due divine revelation while providing an "explanation" for their many errors. For all practical purpose, WS membership believes that the Watchtower Society is fully inspired, and members are generally unaware of the extensive nature of the problem. (See Critique section.) One former 20-year member noted that members commonly believe "the idea that the *Watchtower* and *Awake* magazines are inspired publications. . . . One JW stated to a Christian, 'Your Bible was finished 2,000 years ago, but our Bible has 32 pages added to it every week.' "[26] In other words, the divine authority of the Watchtower was equated with the divine authority of the Bible. In the minds of JW's this is a given.

Watchtower literature provides many examples of claims to divine guidance. Volume seven of Russell's *Studies in the Scriptures* (published posthumously) declares that Russell "said that he could never have written his books himself. It all came from God through the enlightenment of the Holy Spirit."[27] Judge Rutherford said, "[My] speeches do not contain my message, but do contain the expression of Jehovah's purpose which he commands must now be told to the people."[28] "It is entirely unsafe for the people to rely upon the words and doctrines of imperfect men."[29] Anthony Hoekema quotes their history, *Jehovah's Witnesses in the Divine Purpose*, 1959, p. 46 (quoting a 1909 Watchtower article, p. 371):

> In 1909 certain leaders of study classes were asking that Watch Tower publications should no longer be referred to in their meetings, but only the Bible. Russell himself replied to this suggestion in a Watch Tower article: "This (the suggestion just made) sounded loyal to God's Word; but it was not so. It was merely the effort of those teachers to come between the people of God and the *Divinely provided light upon God's Word.*"[30]

Throughout WS literature, claims are made that their writings are "Christ's message," "God's message" and "God's truth," and the implications are clear. The Watchtower for July 1, 1973, p. 402, stated that for their group "*alone* God's sacred Word the Bible, is not a sealed book" (emphasis added). One may thus trust in the Watchtower Society as one trusts in God. Our section "Prophetic Failures" documents this attitude more clearly. Note the comments of former members:

> In retrospect, I can understand how easily we were attracted by this organization that claimed to be the *only* organization on earth guided by God's "holy spirit," and the only organization capable of understanding the meaning of the Holy Scriptures (*The Watchtower*, July 1, 1973, p. 402). . . . When questions arose, other Watchtower publications were cited as references because it was claimed that the Watchtower Bible and Tract Society was God's "sole collective channel for the flow of Biblical truth to men on earth" in these last days (*The Watchtower*, July 15, 1960, p. 439). We were taught that we must adhere absolutely to the decisions and scriptural understandings of the Society because God had given it this authority over his people (*The Watchtower*, May 1, 1972, p. 272). . . . To gain . . . eternal life, I was told, certain things were necessary: 1) I should study the Bible diligently, and only through Watchtower publications. . . .[31]

Authoritarian

Since the WS believes itself divinely guided and inspired, dissent is not permitted. Charles S. Braden, author of *These Also Believe*, observes, "Criticism of the decisions or policies of the headquarters group are likely to be labeled as 'Satan-inspired.' "[32] Gerstner, author of *The Theology of the Major Sects*, asserts:

> The organization of the Witnesses is utterly authoritarian. Differences of opinion are simply not tolerated. Defectors from the party line are liquidated from the membership. . . . So then, their nominal acceptance of the principle of an authoritative Scripture is vitiated by the practical acceptance of an infallible interpreter. The right of private judgment is, for all practical purposes, done away with, as the Witness bows to the hierarchy, or rather, the one at the head of the hierarchy.[33]

As anyone knows who has talked in depth with a Witness, dissent, criticism or independent questioning and reading of "unauthorized" literature is not permitted. One may ask the questions, but one may not question the answers. To do so is to invite disfellowship, which, practically speaking, constitutes the rejection of and by Jehovah God. This carries a potential sentence of eternal annihilation at the judgment, and thus is not something to be taken lightly. Again, to reject the Watchtower Society is to reject God. A former 10 year Witness, Bill Cetnar, observes, "Whatever word comes from the Watchtower is equal to Scripture."[54] In effect, the WS has made biblical literacy dependent upon Jehovah's Witnesses membership.[35] God's "theocratic headquarters" must be accepted in "its every aspect."[36] In fact, responsible members will be careful to "not be so foolish" as to place "their own human reasoning" above the divinely guided pronouncements of the Watchtower Society.[37]

Emphasis on Reason

Jehovah's Witnesses claim undying allegiance to the Bible. But it is clear that this is allegiance to the Bible as interpreted by the Watchtower Society. For WS leadership, whatever is "unreasonable" to them is summarily rejected. Paradoxically, members must not use their "human reasoning" to question Watchtower Society teachings, but they must use it to question non-WS teachings. Russell's *Studies in the Scriptures* declares:

We have endeavored to build upon that foundation [of reason] the teachings of Scripture, in such a manner that, so far as possible, pure human judgment may try its squares and angles by the most exacting rules of justice which it can command.[38]

Let us examine the character of the writings claimed as inspired, to see whether their teachings correspond with the character we have reasonably imputed to God.[39]

Professor Gruss observed: "The natural outgrowth of such an approach is the rejection of all that is beyond reason's comprehension. In place of sound principles of interpretation based upon the Bible, Russell substituted a preconceived theology based on reason."[40] As a result, the Trinity is "unreasonable." Since "trying to reason out the Trinity teaching leads to confusion of mind," it cannot possibly be true.[41] The deity of Christ is also "unreasonable," as is eternal punishment, and so both are rejected.[42] (Paradoxically, members who have tried to reconcile, or "reason out," confusing and conflicting Watchtower Society policies, doctrines and biblical interpretation rarely seem to apply the same methodology to their own beliefs.)

Organizational Structure

The organizational structure of the Society begins at the top with Jehovah God. He communicates His will and biblical interpretation to the Watchtower upper echelon (the president and his close associates), who then pass it on to others, where it finally reaches the printing presses and is sent out as Watchtower literature. Former member William Cetnar observes:

President Knorr made a very significant and revealing statement in 1952 after some of the brothers in editorial had argued over a doctrinal matter. He stated, "Brothers, you can argue all you want about it, but when it gets off the sixth floor *it is the truth.*" What he was saying was that once it was in print (the presses were on the sixth floor), it is the truth and we had to stand unitedly behind it. Franz in court admitted the same; however, he did not speak the truth when he said [under oath] there were no differences of opinion. . . . Often I have been asked, "What gives the Witnesses such fervent zeal . . . ?" The answer is that Jehovah's Witnesses believe that the Society has the authority to speak for God.[43]

The literature of the Society is sold by loyal members who meet several times a week in Kingdom Halls, the Watchtower Society's churches. Active members are known as "publishers" because they secure their literature from the WS and offer it to prospective converts. Active members are to witness as much as possible, carefully recording the number of homes visited (an average of 10 or more a week)[44] and the number of hours spent in various activities (back calls, Bible studies and so on). They are assigned certain "territories" and attempt to make at least two calls a year at each house.[45] Two Witnesses usually work together as a team, one often being a beginner.

As in Mormonism, a systematic program exists for winning new members. In the WS, if it is carried through to the sixth step, conversion is usually successful. These steps are:

1. Place Watchtower Society literature into the hands of the household.

2. Call again to encourage the person to read and study the literature, using current events to spark interest. *Awake!* magazine especially is used for this purpose.

3. Start a weekly home Bible study on the literature received. (These are not true Bible studies but studies of Watchtower Society literature offering its distorted interpretation of the Bible).

4. Invite the potential convert to an area study group where the person can be engaged in a carefully controlled dialogue with Witnesses.

5. Invite the prospect to attend a "Watchtower Study" at a Kingdom Hall.

6. Start the person on a similar program of reaching his neighbors, under Watchtower Society care and guidance.

7. Have a person in regular attendance at Watchtower Society meetings dedicate himself to God's service through water baptism, which officially makes the person a "minister" of Jehovah and a representative of the Watchtower Society.[46]

The Watchtower Society takes pride in noting the harmony and efficiency of its organization, but this is mere outward appearance. Dr. Montague, a 20-year member and current Christian psychiatrist with inside information on the problems of Jehovah's Witnesses (author of *Jehovah's Witnesses and Mental Illness*), provides some enlightening comments, which we will soon cite. Some religions attempt to justify their unethical behavior in proselytizing or other activities on the basis that it makes converts or offers other benefits. The followers of Sun Myung Moon have "heavenly deception," Hare Krishnas use "transcendental trickery," and the older Children of God (now "The Family") "plunder the Whore Babylon." The Watchtower Society has "theocratic tact" to sanction its own behavior.

The problem with suppressing ethics is that it returns to haunt us. In the case of the WS, one generally does not discover the extent of Society problems until one has been a member for several years and has been appointed an elder. Dr. Montague informs us that within the organization at all levels, there exists a great deal of cover-up, authoritarianism, legalism, selfishness, lack of love, power struggles, personality conflicts and complaints, and he asserts that such things "are common."[47] This has been confirmed in much greater detail by former Watchtower leader Raymond Franz in his enlightening and powerful exposés *Crisis of Conscience* and *Searching for Christian Freedom*. Nevertheless, Dr. Montague observes that the Society goes to great pains to cover up its unwashed laundry:

> When we look beyond the attractive veneer, we find an endless number of a wide variety of problems rampant both within the typical congregation and the whole Watchtower organization. The J.W.'s are anxious to present a favorable picture of themselves to others because this helps "sell" their organization. And selling the Watchtower Society is an important goal of every J.W. Conversion, in the Witness sense, is actually conversion to accepting the idea that the Watchtower Society is God's channel.... The key goal of the Witnesses is to help the J.W. to become loyal to the organization, and once loyalty is achieved, passive consent in all other areas usually follows.... Thus the J.W.'s take pains to cover these [problems] up, especially from neophytes....[48]

Montague observes that once a member becomes an elder he discovers even more serious concerns, involving mental problems and serious doubts as to the reliability of the WS:

> The new elder discovers J.W.'s have a large number of problems, including emotional and mental health problems, as well as spiritual problems. There is much unhappiness, restlessness, doubts, and misgivings about the Wt. Society and the Wt. teachings. Further, the fact that a number of Witnesses have been abused by either the Society or its representatives comes to

light. As one elder stated after six months in this role, "I never dreamed that Witnesses had so many problems—I have seen problems almost without end. I never realized a group of people could have so many problems including, and by far not the least common, doubts about the validity of the Wt. teachings."[49]

Montague also notes the ethical dilemma raised by Watchtower operations:

The fact that these problems are hidden from the typical J.W., and especially newer J.W.'s by concealment, prevarication, and open lying raises ethical problems which could cause one to question the validity of the rest of the teachings of the Wt. Society. . . . Witnesses in high positions generally recognize that this is deceitful, but feel that the ends justify the means. . . . If the person can achieve according to Witness doctrine, everlasting life, deceiving him in the early stages of conversion, J.W.'s feel, is justified. The Society has openly justified this under the rubric of "theocratic tact" or where it is felt proper to protect "the Wt. organization."[50]

Thus, despite the Watchtower website claim that "the most outstanding mark of true Christians is that they have real love among themselves,"[51] the truth is much closer to the sentiments expressed by Dr. Montague: "J.W.'s tend to look out for their own interests, and especially their own ego needs, and are only outwardly concerned about others. Probably the most common complaint among the congregations today is that there is 'a lack of love.' This 'lack of love' is commonly bemoaned among Witnesses everywhere."[52]

As is generally true in the world of the cults, far from being the model of organizational efficiency, inner harmony and Christian love presented to the world, the reality is quite different.[53] Granting divine authority to the WS is the fundamental reason for these problems. As in Mormonism, the leadership is biblically untrustworthy and self-serving if not corrupt because, as is so often true, absolute power corrupts absolutely. Despite abundant claims to "follow Christian principles" and to "obey Jesus," the words ring hollow given WS history. The kinds of things one can find on the Web

about the Witness leadership is proof enough. Practically speaking, in the lives of most devoted members, the Watchtower organization is more important than Christ is.[54] The WS is God's sole channel on earth to accomplish His will, but no matter how important the WS argues that He is, Christ is only a created angel.

THEOLOGY

Christianity

Jehovah's Witnesses claim to be Christian and this is usually how non-Witnesses view them. For the Watchtower Society (WS), this is all to the good, as a large part of their membership is derived from Christendom in general: Catholics; nominal Protestants; new or immature believers. Professor Edmond Gruss points out some consequences:

The work of the Witnesses among nominal Christians and new converts has caused the Church of Christ much trouble. With a missionary background, William Kneedler, in his booklet, *Christian Answers to Jehovah's Witnesses*, rightly states that their "work is parasitic on established Christian work and very confusing to new Christians and to those not well-grounded in the reasons for their beliefs." The shame is that most Christians and pastors are not sufficiently aware of the Witnesses' history, their doctrines and their methods to deal intelligently with them.[55]

For the Witnesses, both Catholicism and Protestantism (liberal and conservative) are lumped together under the derogatory terms "Christendom" or "Religionists." As in Mormonism, since the beginning, the Witnesses have instituted a broad-based vitriolic attack against Christianity as satanic, pagan, evil and under the judgment of God. For example, the fervent denunciations against false prophets in the Old Testament are routinely applied to Christian pastors.[56] Numerous researchers have noted this fact of Witness hostility to the Christian Church. Charles S. Braden, in *These Also Believe*, states, "Toward the churches the Witnesses are quite hostile."[57] Anthony Hoekema, in *The Four Major Cults*, observes, "The attitude of the Jehovah's Witnesses toward the Christian Church in general is so utterly bigoted as to be almost unbelievable."[58] The late Dr. Walter Martin noted, "Reviewing the mass of indictments and undocumented charges against Christendom and the clergy, the Christian cannot help but be shocked at the accusations hurled helter-skelter by the Witnesses."[59]

The WS sees Christendom as militantly engaged in a life or death battle against God's true people. Satan's conspiratorial efforts are especially directed against Jehovah's "Theocratic Kingdom." His minions are organized into two divisions: a visible segment (the political-religious empire of the world) and an invisible segment (the spirit world of demons). It is hardly surprising that some Jehovah's Witnesses may border on paranoia: Both what they see and what they do not see are seeking their spiritual ruin. Although the attacks against Christianity have been somewhat toned down recently, they have never really let up since the days of Russell and Rutherford. Christianity has been portrayed in the following ways.

1. Satanic.

The Anglo-American empire system, which chiefly is "Christendom," Satan makes his chief spokesman on earth, and therefore in the Scriptures this system is called the "false prophet"; and by this beastly organization Satan speaks to and deceives the people. . . . That conspiracy is formed, and the overt acts are committed against God's anointed within the realms of "Christendom," and this is further proof that "Christendom" is Satan's instrument.[60]

Christendoms' religion is demonism.[61]

2. Immoral.

In his 1937 book *Enemies*, Judge Rutherford stated, "All liars and murderers are religionists."[62] "In these religious organizations are included thieves, robbers, liars, whoremongers, murderers, manstealers or kidnappers, frauds, cheats . . . using a great mountain of lies behind which the racketeers hide themselves."[63] The September 1, 1979, *Watchtower* declared: "Today the immoral condition of Christendom is notorious, 'horrible,' on a scale grander than in

Sodom and Gomorrah. Deservedly Christendom will suffer the fate of those ancient immoral cities. As the most reprehensible ones among the people of Christendom, the clergy and religious leaders will drink the potion of death."[64]

3. A wicked persecutor.

Christendom's clergy, like Zedekiah and his band of false prophets . . . have tried to suppress the preaching done by the anointed remnant.[65]

She has been . . . treacherous. . . . Heartlessly she has despoiled such Christians because they keep the commandments of Jehovah God. . . . Christendom has been foremost in this program of dealing treacherously and despoiling.[66]

4. The chief component of "Babylon the Great."

Jehovah's Christian witnesses are the ones that have identified who Babylon the Great is. . . . Her blasphemies exceed those of "pagandom". . . . Her bloodguilt exceeds that of all the non-Christian religious realm! Not out of line with this, Christendom will be given first attention in the execution of divine judgment upon Babylon the Great, according to what appears from the inspired Scriptures.[67]

5. Hateful to God and His people.

Down will come the Devil's agency of religious persecution, Christendom, as utterly rejected by Jehovah God and Jesus Christ. . . . Up will come Jehovah's persecuted witnesses in an overwhelming display of his choice and approval of them before all heaven and earth.[68]

By His destruction of Christendom the Sovereign Lord Jehovah must absolve himself from all responsibility for her shameful course throughout the centuries of her existence.[69]

6. Inferior to Jehovah's Witnesses.

In sharp contrast to Christendom and Judaism, Jehovah's Christian witnesses, who are residing in the spiritual paradise of his favor and protection, are the ones that have taken Jehovah as their King. . . . They are therefore the ones that are safeguarded from the spiritual sicknesses and maladies and plagues that afflict Christendom and Judaism.[70]

7. The way of death.

"Christendom's course is 'the way of death.' Let us go no farther in it. Time still allows for a person's escape from being executed with her."[71]

8. Worthy of death.

Today Christendom's clergy-prophets outspokenly back up the international conspiracy against Jehovah's kingdom by his Christ. Jehovah's Witnesses are not authorized to pronounce the death sentence upon any of them. But they can take up the inspired utterance of Jehovah and apply it against the clerical false prophets. . . . So, here now let us read of Jeremiah's prophetic actions. . . . "Look! I am sending you away from off the surface of the ground. This year you yourself must die, for you have spoken outright revolt against Jehovah."

—Jeremiah 28:15, 16[72]

Jehovah today has not minced words in stating his judicial decision against Christendom. He has commissioned his Jeremiah class [Jehovah's Witnesses] to declare a correspondingly straightforward message of calamity to the modern counterpart of ancient Jerusalem and Judah. Unsparingly, unwaveringly, the Jeremiah class must adhere to all that He commands them in His Word.[73]

9. The anti-Christ.

Ever since the first century the identity of what the apostle Paul called "the son of perdition" or "son of destruction" had puzzled Christians. But in Jehovah's due time this "mystery of iniquity" or "mystery of lawlessness" was scheduled to be unraveled . . . as an apostate clergy.[74]

The Watchtower Society even alleges that Christianity is "responsible for the physical and spiritual miseries of the poor," that their "pretended interest in the poor is sheer hypocrisy" and that Christianity is also "responsible" for World Wars I and II.[75] Not surprisingly, Christian missionaries often find that the Witnesses have gone ahead of them in many countries. Over the years we have received several letters indicating this, such as the following from a missionary team in Mazatlan, Mexico: "In exploring new areas [Tehuacan and elsewhere] we

were astounded at the amount of work the Jehovah's Witnesses have done here. Almost every village we have visited has some Jehovah's Witnesses and there are areas where entire towns have converted to this cult. Jehovah's Witnesses make conversions doubly difficult."[76]

The Bible and Watchtower Hermeneutics

Jehovah's Witnesses believe that the Bible is the inspired Word of God. However, they believe only the Watchtower Society can properly interpret it for them, because only the WS receives divine illumination as to its true meaning. In other words, the Bible is a closed book to all non-Jehovah's Witnesses, who, bereft of God's official interpretation of His word, are incapable of understanding its true teachings. Indeed, apart from WS leadership, it would be a closed book even to ordinary Jehovah's Witnesses. Thus the Bible must be illuminated through its "official interpreter," the WS. WS interpretation could also be said to be a Bible above the Bible, since the Bible we have is, for all practical purposes, useless without it. In the early days the interpreter was Russell, and then Rutherford; today it is the Watchtower Society as represented by their published literature. In Russell's era, it was stated that his *Studies in the Scriptures* were necessary to comprehend the Bible accurately. In fact, *Studies* were more important than the Bible, for without them the Bible was only a closed book leading to spiritual darkness:

We might not improperly name the volumes "The Bible in an Arranged Form." That is to say, they are not mere comments on the Bible, but they are practically the Bible itself. Furthermore, not only do we find that people cannot see the divine plan in studying the Bible by itself, but we see, also, that if anyone lays the "Scripture Studies" aside . . . and ignores them and goes to the Bible alone, though he has understood his Bible for ten years, our experience shows that within two years he goes into darkness. On the other hand, if he had merely read the "Scripture Studies" with their references and had not read a page of the Bible as such, he would be in the light at the end of two years, because he would have the light of the Scriptures.[77]

Since Russell's time, WS publications have occupied the same prominence in the Society as Russell's *Studies in the Scriptures*. No matter how much one studies the Bible, one will end up in spiritual darkness apart from WS publications. One former member complained, "Real Bible study has been gagged and suppressed by the organization."[78]

Thus, although Jehovah's Witnesses adamantly claim to believe in the Bible as the inspired Word of God, their assumptions and false hermeneutical methods force a preconceived theology into its pages.[79] It is not surprising that any number of researchers have noted that the Watchtower Society has an entirely unjustifiable methodology at this point. Anthony Hoekema categorized four errors of their interpretive methods:

1. Absurd literalism and spiritualizing (for example, Leviticus 17:14 being used to deny blood transfusions);

2. Absurd typology (for example, Noah's wife as a type of the "144,000" elect);

3. "Knight-jump exegesis,"* jumping from one part of the Bible to another in complete disregard of the context in order to "prove" their teachings (examples can be seen later);

4. A "rear view method" of prophetic interpretation, or arbitrarily selecting certain events, "aligning" them with a particular Biblical passage, and then claiming "prophetic fulfillment."[80]

As one example of this fourth method, consider their interpretation that the 1918 jailing of Watchtower Society leaders was a fulfillment of Zechariah 13:7, which refers to Jesus Christ and not to Judge Rutherford. This was what was being asserted in 1973.[81] However, in 1933 the same event was being proclaimed as a fulfillment of Daniel 8:9–12, which has nothing to do with the internal events of the Watchtower Society in 1918.[82] Hoekema concludes: "Their very method of interpreting the Scriptures makes it impossible for them really to listen to God's

Word. Given the methods previously described, one can draw from the Bible virtually any doctrine his imagination can concoct."[83]

Professor Gruss points out nine errors of Watchtower hermeneutics, all of which will be illustrated as we proceed:

1. A rationalistic premise that discards "unreasonable" teachings;

2. A concept of "progressive revelation" that changes error to truth and truth to error;

3. An allegorical method whereby the Bible "becomes like putty" in the interpreter's hand;

4. Unwarranted speculation, especially in the area of prophetic chronology;

5. An arbitrary division of biblical contents where certain Scriptures refer only to: a) the "144,000," or b) the "Great Multitude" (the rest of the Witnesses);

6. Ignoring the context; for example, Jeremiah 10:3–4 to teach against Christmas trees and Galatians 4:8–11 to teach against observing holidays;

7. Repeated violation of rules of grammar;

8. Violating word meanings (for example *kolasin* in Matthew 25:46 is translated as "cutting off," not its real meaning of punishment; *theotes* in Colossians 2:9 is translated as "divine quality" rather than "fullness of deity");

9. Ignoring the tenor of Scripture.[84]

Gruss concludes correctly that WS hermeneutics powerfully refute their claims to accept biblical authority. The infallible interpreter is for all practical purposes more inspired than the Bible. Thus, as C. T. Russell pointed out, one does not even need to read the Bible, only the literature of its official interpreter. Gruss concluded: "With the methods employed by the Society in interpreting the Scriptures, it really would not matter if the Witnesses held the doctrine of inspiration or not, for the Word of God is twisted so that the infallible (at the time of the doctrinal pronouncement at least) interpreter is more inspired than the Bible. . . . The Bible has been subordinated to the subjective outlook of the interpreter."[85]

---

*An allusion to chess where the knight is able to jump in an "L" shape fashion, circumventing pieces "in the way."

God and the Trinity

The Jehovah's Witnesses deviate from the biblical view of God in two important areas. First, God is only one person, not three persons or triune. Second, God is limited to a specific locale and is not omnipresent. Thus the Jehovah's Witnesses' God is "not part of [the] Triune Godhead, with other coequal members."[86] "The true God is not omnipresent, for he is spoken of as having a location (1 Kings 8:49; John 16:28; Hebrews 9:24). His throne is in heaven (Isaiah 66:1)."[87] "[God is] not omnipresent, but can project spirit anywhere to accomplish His purpose."[88]

As we will see in our discussion of WS salvation, it is also true in Watchtower theology that as far as God is concerned "the stress appears clearly to lie upon the side of his power and his inexorable justice rather than upon the side of his love and forgiveness."[89] Nevertheless, the WS abhorrence of a "pagan Trinity" makes the Christian God abhorrent to Witnesses. C. T. Russell blasphemously taught that the Christian God was, in fact, the devil: "The clergy's God is plainly not Jehovah but the ancient deity, hoary with the iniquity of the ages—Baal, the Devil Himself."[90]

There are five principal reasons why the Trinity is rejected by the Watchtower Society: 1) claimed associations with paganism; 2) the lack of the word "Trinity" in the Bible; 3) supposedly defames Jehovah's name; 4) claimed polytheism and 5) alleged irrational nature. The following briefly documents these five reasons.

1. The Trinity was not part of the early church but a development from paganism.

This doctrine was unknown to the Hebrew prophets and Christian apostles. . . . The early Christians who were taught directly by Jesus Christ did not believe that God is a "Trinity." The trinity is referred to as "that idea of pagan imagination."[91] (See our Doctrinal Appendix, and the book *The Way* and our *Knowing the Truth About the Trinity.*)

2. The Trinity is not found in the Bible.

Their word "Trinity" does not occur in the Holy Bible.[92] [Neither does "monotheism," "Jehovah," "theocratic" or "New World Society."]

3. The Trinity is satanic because it maligns Jehovah's name.

The doctrine of the Trinity is a false doctrine and is promulgated by Satan for the purpose of defaming Jehovah's name.[93]

The plain truth is that this is another of Satan's attempts to keep God-fearing persons from learning the truth of Jehovah and his Son, Christ Jesus.[94] [The doctrine cannot be satanic or malign God's name if it is biblical teaching. See our Doctrinal Appendix.]

4. The Trinity is a doctrine of polytheism, teaching three gods.

If there are three Almighty Ones, how could there be one most mighty?[95]

However, according to Trinity teachers, when "the Word became flesh," Mary became the mother of God. But since they say God is a Trinity, then the Jewish virgin Mary became the mother of merely a third of God, not "the mother of God."[96]

[It is] a bit difficult to love and worship a complicated, freakish-looking, three-headed God.[97]

These are all incorrect descriptions or caricatures of the historic doctrine of the Trinity, which teaches belief in one God. We expound on this in *Knowing the Truth About the Trinity.*

5. The doctrine of the Trinity is irrational.[98] Many things are beyond our full comprehension, such as particle physics; this does not make them irrational.

The extent of WS distortion surrounding the doctrine of the Trinity, even in its more recent scholarly literature, such as Greg Stafford's *Jehovah's Witnesses Defended,* is difficult to imagine for those who have not read it. After analyzing the anti-Trinitarian argumentation in *Let God Be True* (a brief statement of Watchtower beliefs in outline form), Gruss makes the comment: "After starting with no evidence, misrepresenting orthodoxy, using Scripture out of context, not understanding the meaning of a word, misrepresenting the source of the Trinity doctrine, bringing in irrelevant material and changing the events of church history, the

Witnesses make this 'authoritative' statement: 'The obvious conclusion is, therefore, that Satan is the originator of the trinity doctrine.' "[99]

Jesus Christ

The Watchtower "Jesus" existed in three different stages or phases, even, in a sense, as three different persons: 1) the Archangel Michael (also "the Word"); 2) the man Jesus of Nazareth; 3) a new superior, recreated Michael.

Clearly, there is believed to be a correspondence between the three. For example, the first person, Michael the Archangel, became Jesus; this "second" Jesus became a new Michael and so on, so that when Jesus came into existence, Michael was no longer, and when Jesus of Nazareth "resurrected" (was recreated) and became a new Michael, Jesus was no longer. To further confuse matters, it also appears from WS writings that the human Jesus was *not* the same person as the pre-human or the post-human Jesus. The Witnesses are ambiguous at this point, seeming to both affirm and deny connections between the three entities. In light of WS concern with "rational" doctrine, not to mention their consternation with the doctrine of the Trinity, we could conclude, since trying to reason out WS Christology leads to confusion of mind, that it can't possibly be true. Nevertheless, here are the Society's three phases of Jesus.

Jesus as Michael the Archangel (also "the Word").

> Scriptural evidence indicates that the name Michael applied to God's Son before he left heaven to become Jesus Christ and also after his return. Michael is the only one said to be the "archangel," meaning "chief angel" or "principal angel."[100]

Michael was the first "spirit-son" of God. He was a direct creation of God (thereby becoming His Son) and finds his uniqueness in that fact. God eventually created other spirit-sons (angels) through this Michael. In heaven Michael was the head of the angels, or the archangel. "However, by virtue of his being the sole direct creation of his Father, the firstborn Son was unique, different from all others of God's sons,

all of whom were created or begotten by Jehovah through that firstborn Son."[101]

Jesus as a unique man. The Watchtower Society denies the Christian doctrine of the incarnation.[102] When Jesus was conceived, "Michael" no longer existed: the life force of the person that was Michael was transferred to a female ovum:

> Since actual conception took place, it appears that Jehovah God caused an ovum or egg cell in Mary's womb to become fertile, accomplishing this by the transferral of the life of his firstborn Son from the spirit realm to earth (Galatians 4:4). Only in this way could the child eventually born have retained identity as the same person who had resided in heaven as the Word. . . . From the results revealed in the Bible, it would appear that the perfect male life force (causing the conception) canceled out any imperfection existent in Mary's ovum. . . . Since it was God's holy spirit that made the birth possible, Jesus owed his human life to his heavenly Father, not to any man.[103]

As noted, the Society claims that Jesus "retained identity as the *same* person who had resided in heaven." Thus, when Jesus was born, Michael per se ceased to exist for "He laid aside completely his spirit existence."[104] "Almighty God divested the Son of his heavenly godlike existence and transferred his life from heaven to Mary's womb."[105] However, not all commentators would agree that Watchtower theology permits a continuity of identity between the pre-incarnate Michael, the incarnate Jesus and the new post-incarnate Michael. In part this is due to conflicting data in Watchtower theology itself and in part to "Michael's" own transformation from a special but mortal angel to a literal human being to a new improved, spiritually recreated and more powerful immortal angel.

Dr. James Bjornstad observes:

> This doctrine reveals a disjointed view of Christ, even though Jehovah's Witnesses seem to portray continuity between the various states of existence. According to the Jehovah's Witnesses, the one who laid down his life at Calvary for our sins was not the one who existed in heaven and

had been the Father's agent in creation. Furthermore, he was not the one who was raised from the dead and who now rules in heaven over his kingdom.[106]

Hoekema asks:

Is there real continuity between the Son of God in his prehuman and his human state? Was the child born of Mary really the same individual who existed previously in heaven as the Archangel Michael? To this question it is difficult to give an unambiguous answer. On the one hand, Jehovah's Witnesses frequently speak of "Christ's prehuman existence," [they] say that the angel Michael was actually Jesus Christ in his prehuman spirit form, and assert that it was God's only-begotten Son who became a man. Other passages from their writings, however, imply that there was no real continuity between Michael and the man Jesus Christ.[107]

Nevertheless, when Michael became Jesus upon the earth, this is when he earned his immortality. "Christ Jesus was first to receive immortality as a reward for his faithful course on earth. . . ."[108] "Finishing his earthly course free from flaw in any sense of the word, Jesus was acknowledged by God as justified. He was thus the only man who, through test, stood firmly and positively just, or righteous before God on his own merit. . . . Jesus Christ, after his faithful course until death was 'made alive in the spirit,' given immortality and incorruption."[109]

The WS also teaches Jesus became "the Christ" at his baptism. "As regards Jesus, according to the angel's announcement at his birth in Bethlehem he was to become a 'Savior, who is Christ the Lord.' When did he become Christ or 'Anointed One'? After the prophet John the son of priest Zechariah baptized Jesus in the Jordan River. . . . Not at birth, but at thirty years of age Jesus became Christ or 'Anointed One.'"[110] This contradicts Luke 2:11, which declares that Jesus was born the Christ. Nevertheless, the Society at this point believes that Jesus was "born-again," becoming the first born of all begotten sons of God.

Jesus as a new improved Michael. According to Jehovah's Witnesses, when Jesus of Nazareth

died, He ceased to exist. C.T. Russell stated, "The *man* Jesus is dead, forever dead."[111] The body of Jesus, whether, as they claim, it was dissolved into gases or preserved as a future memorial, was not what was raised from the dead.[112] A new creation—the "better" Michael—was the one who appeared to the disciples by temporarily materializing a human body for them to see, much as the angels had in Genesis Chapter 19.

In light of this we may deduce several conclusions concerning the Jesus of the Watchtower Society.

1. Jesus never incarnated.

As Nelson and Smith conclude: "The 1921 edition of *The Harp of God* declares, 'The incarnation is scripturally erroneous. Indeed, if he (Christ) had been an incarnate being, he could never have redeemed mankind' (p. 101). Witnesses teach a total *kenosis*, that is, Christ had been a spiritual being, but on coming to this world he ceased being such and became nothing more than a perfect man."[113]

2. Jesus of Nazareth is dead.

Today only the new Michael exists. Dr. Bjornstad observes: "When Jesus died, he was annihilated. As a human being he was simply blotted out of existence. He just ceased to exist."[114]

3. Jesus was not bodily resurrected.

If Jesus ceased to exist, He could not have been resurrected. According to the WS, there was only an improved spiritual *recreation* of the old Michael.[115] Thus, the new Jesus (Michael) bears no marks of the crucifixion and thus could *not* have been the same person as Jesus on earth.[116] (But again, Jehovah's Witnesses speak of him as being the same person: "Regarding a future 'coming,' *Jesus himself* made it plain that at *his* second coming he would not be in the flesh, visible to humans. *He* was resurrected as a spirit.")[117] At this point, Bjornstad comments that Watchtower theology actually requires the permanent extinction of Jesus:

If it was not the material part of Jesus that was raised, perhaps it was his immaterial nature—his soul and/or his spirit. According to the Jehovah's Witnesses, the soul and the body are the same thing. So, if his body did not rise, his soul did not rise from the dead. Furthermore, the Jehovah's Witnesses believe that the spirit is nothing more than breath. In dying Jesus gave up this spirit or breathed his last breath, and thus his spirit could not be raised from the dead. If it was not the body of Jesus nor his soul nor his spirit that was raised from the dead, what then was resurrected according to Jehovah's Witnesses? In actuality it was nothing. It was not Jesus who rose from the dead.[118]

This is why Jehovah had to recreate Michael as a new immortal spirit, for nothing was left of Jesus of Nazareth:

Though Jehovah's Witnesses affirm belief in the resurrection of Jesus Christ, they do not really believe in his resurrection. Jehovah's Witnesses believe in re-creation. They believe that Jehovah remembers your life pattern and then creates you again, or re-creates you after death as He remembers you. In Jesus' case, Jehovah remembered the pre-human existence of Jesus as an angel, and thus re-created the angel Michael, the archangel, only this time immortal and of a divine order.[119]

In the process of recreation, Jehovah did not look to the material human stage of "Jesus" existence, but to His previous existence as an "angel."

4. The second coming of "Jesus" has already occurred invisibly.

Jehovah's Witnesses initially taught that Christ returned in 1874; however, the date was later changed to 1914 (see Prophecy section). Since He was "resurrected" (recreated) as a spirit creature, His return could not possibly be in a physical body, but it had to be in a spiritual body. Thus His coming was "invisible."

Since the 1914 return of Jesus, He is now more important than He was prior to 1914. Why? Because for 1900 years, practically speaking, He was not a King. He obtained His kingdom in 1914 and as a result entered into an exalted status. Therefore, He was infused with a new "royal capacity such as he had not possessed when he was down here on earth in the first century.... [He was now] a personage who had greater rank, authority and power than the one [before].... This made service to him much more important now. It was a higher honor now to be in his service."[120]

In conclusion, the WS doctrine of Jesus Christ logically denies his deity, immutability, sovereignty, eternity, birth as the Messiah, bodily resurrection, kingdom prior to 1914, physical return and even His very existence! Yet in their door-to-door witnessing Jehovah's Witnesses have told hundreds of millions of people, "We believe in the biblical Jesus Christ as our Lord and Savior!"

The Holy Spirit

Jehovah's Witnesses teach that the Holy Spirit is not a distinct person of the Godhead but Jehovah's "impersonal active force." Their teachings on this subject are given in their text *Holy Spirit—The Force Behind the Coming New Order* and elsewhere. We summarize some principal ideas here.

The Holy Spirit is a force or energy that accomplishes God's will.

From God there goes forth an invisible active force by means of which he gets his will done. It is not a mere influence.... It is a force that is operative, and it issues forth from God who is holy.... He sends it forth to accomplish what is holy. So it is correctly called "holy spirit."[121]

It is not Jehovah's "power".... "Power" is basically the ability or capacity to act or do things and it can be latent, dormant, inactively resident in someone or something. "Force," on the other hand, more specifically describes energy projected and exerted on persons or things, and may be defined as "an influence which produces or tends to produce motion, or change of motion."[122]

The Holy Spirit is impersonal, not personal.

It was not until the fourth century C.E. that the teaching that the holy spirit was a person and part of the "Godhead" became official church dogma. Earlier Christians, sometimes called church "fathers," did not so teach.... The Scriptures themselves unite to show that God's holy spirit is not a person but is God's active force by which he accomplishes his purpose and executes his will.[123]

... this spirit is not a person at all.[124]

Salvation

Nothing is more important in life than having a correct understanding of salvation. As Jesus Himself taught at the start of His longest recorded prayer: "Now this is eternal life: that they may know you, the only true God, and Jesus Christ, whom you have sent" (John 17:3). Eternal life comes through a personal relationship with the one true God and His only Son, Jesus Christ (John 3:16; 5:24; 6:47).

Jehovah's Witnesses claim that they offer people the true way of salvation. The issue under consideration is whether such claims are valid and how one can know if they are or are not. Christians have always believed that a proper understanding of God and His will for mankind can be determined by *anyone* through an objective interpretation of God's Word, the Bible. The Jehovah's Witnesses however, believe that they *alone* constitute God's channel for disseminating divine truth. This truth is determined solely by the governing body, the Watchtower Society, through its own interpretation of the Bible, and then it is dispersed to the rest of the world by loyal believers, through door to door witnessing, Bible studies, literature distribution and so on.

In summary form, the Jehovah's Witnesses believe that concerning salvation only a special "elect" class of people, 144,000 individuals, will actually go to heaven to be with Jehovah God and their elder brother, Jesus. The rest of redeemed humanity will inherit a paradise on earth as a result of their good works in this life and during the millennium.

In principle, salvation in the Jehovah's Witness religion is based upon the death of Christ that atoned for Adam's sin. But somehow the Witnesses apply that view of Christ's death to all individuals, not just Adam, although in their doctrine whether or not this actually occurs is determined on the basis of personal merit. (We say "somehow atones" because even though Witnesses believe Jesus was only a man, they have never explained how the death of one man can atone for the sins of billions of people; we will return to this problem later.)

There are three disparate classes of individuals who are "resurrected" (recreated) and potential heirs of salvation: 1) the 144,000 elect of God; 2) the Jehovah's Witnesses "earthly class," all other Jehovah's Witnesses; 3) the rest of mankind. We will discuss these in more detail in a moment. Here it is important to note that there are three different salvation teachings for each of these groups of people. (A fourth class of individuals, the unsaved, obviously, receive no form of salvation at all. Since Jehovah's Witnesses reject the doctrine of eternal punishment, they teach these individuals are, or will be, forever annihilated.)

Salvation for the individual Jehovah's Witness begins with his entrance into the Watchtower organization and subsequent obedience to that organization. In other words, only those who are Jehovah's Witnesses in good standing with the Watchtower Society can be saved in this life. In speaking of the requirements of salvation we are told, "A third requirement is that we be associated with God's channel, his organization. ... To receive everlasting life in the [coming] earthly paradise, we must identify that organization and serve God as part of it."[125]

The first two classes of people mentioned (the 144,000 and all other Jehovah's Witnesses) are, by definition, members of the Watchtower Society. The third class, the remainder of humanity (at least most of them), have the opportunity to earn salvation after death in their resurrection to paradise earth. We will now discuss these three groups in a bit more detail before proceeding with our general analysis of the Watchtower doctrine of salvation.

The minority 144,000. These are called "anointed" and are allegedly chosen sovereignly by God. They are said to be saved on the basis of *faith* in Jesus' ransom sacrifice. However, they must earn and maintain their own salvation, and it is on this basis that they are "elected." God provides these individuals with at least five benefits that He does not give to the two other classes of "saved" people:

1. They are now *presently* "justified" by God as long as they maintain their justified status.

2. They are now consecrated and anointed as priests.

3. They are specially sanctified for Jehovah's purposes.

4. If they remain faithful, at death they will be regenerated or born again just like Jesus.

5. They will then rule in heaven with God and Jesus.

At the "resurrection," the 144,000 will be changed into spirit creatures, just as they believe Jesus was at His "resurrection." This constitutes being "born again." Thus, just like the Watchtower Jesus, they will live in heaven as spirits but not on earth as physical persons. They are thus said to be given *immortality* as spirits in heaven, in contrast to a physical *eternal life* on earth.

The majority earthly class. This includes the vast majority of Jehovah's Witnesses—well over 99.99 percent. They are called the "other sheep" or the "great crowd." These must earn salvation while on earth, but they must do so without the five benefits provided above for the 144,000. From a Christian perspective, the difficulty here is obvious. Jehovah's Witnesses reserve the new birth only for the 144,000 and this only at death. The *average* Jehovah's Witness, however, has no desire or need for spiritual rebirth or being "born-again" in this life because he or she thinks that the "new birth" has relevance only for the 144,000. The average Witness sincerely believes he or she *cannot* be born-again. Biblically, of course, the new birth is equivalent to salvation, and to be without the new birth is to be without salvation, as Jesus made clear in John 3:3-5. In effect, to its discredit, the Watchtower Society has denied biblical salvation to the average member, who believes he or she must earn their salvation without being "born-again." They are then taught that *if* they are successful in earning their salvation they will be given positions of leadership in the millennial age. However, they are also warned that if they do not pass *additional* millennial tests, they will forfeit their eternal life and be annihilated.

Biblically, of course, no one can do anything to earn salvation. All men and women prior to salvation "are dead [to God spiritually] in [their] transgressions and sins" (Ephesians 2:1), and so they "do not accept the things that come from the Spirit of God" (1 Corinthians 2:14). The Scripture describes them as "hostile to God"; "alienated from God"; "God's enemies"; "unable to please God"; and thus as "objects of wrath" (Romans 5:10; 8:7-8; Ephesians 2:1-3; Colossians 1:21; please read Ephesians 2:1-10). These descriptions may be considered particularly relevant for those in religions that are especially hostile to God's revelation in the Bible. (And unfortunately, this includes most religions. In one manner or another, the Bible constantly warns against false religion [Matthew 7:15; Colossians 2:8-23; 2 Timothy 3:5].)

Those who follow any given religion apart from the one true religion revealed by the one true God, despite their sincerity, obviously cannot please God if they deny Him and oppose His way of salvation. Clearly, if there is one true God, a logical conclusion is that there is one true salvation. Therefore, those who do not know the one true God (John 17:3), and those outside the one true way of salvation (John 3:16; 14:6; Acts 4:12), however devout they may be, and whatever their God, cannot be worshipping and serving the one true God.

Unfortunately, Witnesses who sincerely believe they are living for God and pleasing Him do not have salvation. Because of WS teaching, they have no desire to be born again. Thus, all their efforts are, as far as God is concerned, profitless for salvation. In effect, Jehovah's Witnesses teach that *unsaved* men and women can please God entirely in their own power apart from regeneration. Nothing could be more untrue (Ephesians 2:1-10). Thus, when the Witnesses speak of the effects of Adam's sin on the human race, it hardly matters:

These other sheep however, *cannot be born again.* Yet they are said to be able to exercise true faith, to be faithful to Jehovah, to belong to "obedient mankind," and to dedicate themselves to do God's will. The Witnesses, therefore, teach that a person can believe and be faithful to Jehovah without having been born again!

I conclude that, though Jehovah's Witnesses appear to teach an inherited disability on account of Adam's sin, their theology belies this assertion. For a "disability" which enables unregenerate man to have true faith, to dedicate his life to God, and to remain faithful to Jehovah is no disability at all![126]

The rest of mankind. These are resurrected to life on earth in the exact moral condition in which they died (good or evil), and they must then seek to attain their own perfection during the millennium. *If* they attain perfection *and* also pass the final millennial test by avoiding the judgment of God in Revelation 20:7-9, they will obtain eternal life on earth, which, being earthly, is distinguished from the immortality of the spiritually recreated 144,000.

Salvation by Works

As we will emphasize throughout this section, Jehovah's Witnesses stress works-salvation, something the Bible condemns in the clearest terms (Galatians 2-3; Ephesians 2:8-9). This emphasis on salvation by works is frankly admitted in Watchtower publications.

In *Man's Salvation Out of World Distress at Hand!* a chapter is titled "Requirements for Entering Spiritual Paradise." Here it is asserted: "Ways and thoughts approved by the God of righteousness are a requirement for gaining entrance to the spiritual paradise of His worshipers and servants."[127] "For persons who listen to and obey God's commandments it can mean an eternal future."[128] The "doctrinal" text *Make Sure of All Things* contains the following subheadings, quoted verbatim here:

For one to be declared righteous, he must exercise faith in the shed blood of Christ and conduct himself in harmony with that faith.[129]

Following the Test at the End of Christ's Thousand-Year Reign, Obedient Ones Will Have Their Names Written in the Book of Life as Justified.[130]

Knowledge of God's Word [WS doctrines] Necessary to Gain Salvation.[131]

Not "Once Saved, Always Saved"; Endurance Required.[132] [Earlier editions of the last quote (1953) stated, "Salvation a goal to be attained— Not 'Once Saved Always Saved'."]

In *Aid to Bible Understanding* (The Watchtower's biblical and theological dictionary) we find the following: "There is no substitute for obedience, no gaining of God's favor without it."[133] *The Watchtower* magazine also contains numerous examples indicating that *faith alone* is insufficient for salvation:

It is evident from this that besides faith and baptism, "public declaration" to the effect that Jesus Christ is Lord and that God raised him up from the dead is a requirement for salvation.... Clearly, for all who wish to gain an approved standing with God, Christian baptism is a requirement.[134]

So taking a comprehensive view of our sacrifices, we must admit that at meetings, when sharing the "good news" with others, and in attitude, word and action, yes, in all areas of life, we should be prepared to give our very best. We should not be halfhearted about such vital matters. What is at stake is Jehovah's approval and our being granted life.[135]

Persons desiring divine approval and eternal life must understand God's Word, declare it to others and live according to the Bible.[136]

After following through on what Jehovah God requires, the baptized disciple comes into possession of a good conscience. As long as he maintains that good conscience he is in a saved condition. Divine condemnatory judgment will not be expressed against him.[137]

The emphasis on works-salvation is true even for the 144,000, who are said to be elected by Jehovah and saved by grace. Dr. Anthony Hoekema, author of *The Four Major Cults*, points out that even after their faith, repentance, baptism and willingness to sacrifice all their rights on earth for the *hope* of heavenly life, even though they are allegedly "justified" (that is, have the *hope* of final justification after death), they are still not immortal and must yet earn their immortality. Only if they maintain their integrity until death will they have the opportunity for immortality, to be among the 144,000. Thus their "election" by God is on the basis of personal merit:

Jehovah's Witnesses teach that the selection of the 144,000 is a sovereign act on God's part. This selection, however, is made on the basis of their having met the requirements for membership in this class. One is chosen to belong to this group, therefore, on the basis of his worthiness. We must remember, too, that the first steps in the process that leads to salvation for this class are faith, repentance and dedication to Christ—steps that these individuals themselves must take. It is only after they have taken these steps that God justifies, regenerates, and sanctifies them. It should further be noted that much emphasis is laid on continued faithfulness to God.[138]

Hoekema refutes the Witnesses' claim that they believe in salvation by grace:

Hence, though Jehovah's Witnesses' claim that salvation is of grace, and that all credit for salvation belongs to Jehovah, we conclude that in Watchtower theology it is not really God's sovereign grace that saves even the 144,000, but rather man who saves himself by grasping the ransom, by showing himself worthy of being selected as a member of the anointed class, and by carrying out his dedication to Jehovah faithfully until death.[139]

And yet, as Hoekema also observes, the remaining vast majority of Witnesses are expected to believe that they can also earn their own salvation without any of the declared advantages of the 144,000:

According to Watchtower teaching, most of those who are to be saved will attain this salvation without being regenerated, justified (in the Christian sense), anointed to office, and sanctified (in the Christian sense). This means that, without having their sinful natures renewed, this "great crowd" will be able to have faith in Christ, to dedicate their lives wholly to him, and to remain faithful to the end![140]

Biblical response. Biblically speaking then, we are asked to accept that Jehovah's Witnesses and the rest of humanity will be able to save themselves. If anything in this life is to be considered impossible, it must be this. The very reason Christ died for us was because we were helpless to save ourselves. "You see, at just the right time, *when we were still powerless*, Christ died for the ungodly" (Romans 5:6). Indeed, to argue we can save ourselves is to repudiate the atonement, "for if righteousness could be gained

through the law, Christ died for nothing" (Galatians 2:21). The Bible is clear on this. First, no person can be saved apart from the divine miracle of regeneration that enlivens the spirit and changes ones disposition toward the things of God (John 3:3-5; 1 Corinthians 2:14-15; 2 Corinthians 5:16-17). This the Jehovah's Witnesses forbid to everyone but the 144,000, and even these are believed to receive spiritual rebirth only *after* death.

Second, no one can be saved apart from final justification in this life, which occurs at the point of salvation and legally declares one eternally righteous before God (Romans 3:21-31; Philippians 3:3-9). In WS doctrine, this is prohibited for the "other sheep" and for the rest of mankind. Third, no one can find acceptance with God apart from having their sins forgiven—fully and totally—something the Witnesses claim the "ransom" of Christ, by itself, did not effect (cf. Revelation 21:27). Fourth, no person can live for God and please Him apart from the empowerment of the Holy Spirit, whom Witnesses believe does not exist. Clearly, the Watchtower doctrine of salvation is anything but biblical.

The Bible denies Jehovah's Witnesses doctrines when it teaches (emphasis added):

1) That salvation is by grace through faith, *not* through works. "For it is by grace you have been saved, through faith—and this *not from yourselves,* it is the gift of God—not *by works,* so that no one can boast" (Ephesians 2:8-9).

2) That *complete* forgiveness of *all* sins occurred at Calvary. "In him [Jesus] we *have* redemption through his blood, the forgiveness of sins . . ." and, "He forgave us *all* our sins . . ." (Ephesians 1:7; Colossians 2:13).

3) That full and entire justification occurs in *this* life at the *moment* of faith. "Therefore, since we *have been justified* through faith, we *have peace* with God through our Lord Jesus Christ. . . . Since we have *now been justified* by his blood, *how much more* shall we be saved from God's wrath through him" (Romans 5:1, 9).

4) That eternal life is a *present* possession of all true believers. "I tell you the truth, he who believes *has everlasting life*" (John 6:47).

The truth is that Christ atoned for *all* our sins on the Cross, not just the sins of Adam or potentially the sins of most. This is why salvation is entirely by grace and why God does not expect us to earn our salvation by good works, or to achieve the potential forgiveness of our sins by obedience. Christ earned full salvation for us so that we only need receive it as a gift.

The Bible clearly teaches that salvation is a free gift. By definition, a free gift cannot be paid for. The *Oxford American Dictionary* defines gift as "a thing given or received without payment." No man takes a gift of flowers home to his wife and says, "Hi, honey, these are yours after you wash the car." In the same way, no one pays for salvation with his or her works when it has been freely given as a gift. Biblically, "the *gift* of God is eternal life" (Romans 6:23); and we are "justified *freely* by his grace" (Romans 3:17), because we have "the *gift* of righteousness" (Romans 5:17). The Witness concept of salvation, then, disavows the biblical teaching on salvation by grace through faith alone (Romans 3:28):

> William J. Schnell points out that during his years with the movement the other sheep were told that if they stayed close to the Watchtower organization, listened attentively to its indoctrination, went out regularly to distribute literature, and rigidly reported the time spent in doing so, they might be saved at Armageddon! All the emphasis, he insists, was on works, particularly on witnessing, as the way to arrive at a reasonable certainty of future salvation, rather than on faith in Jesus Christ as Saviour.[141]

The irrelevance of salvation. Here is the crux of the problem: Witnesses do not teach that salvation comes by faith in Jesus but, in essence, by faith in what the Watchtower Society tells them to believe and do. William Schnell also points out another major consequence of the Witness view of salvation. It nullifies the relevance of most New Testament texts related to salvation for the vast majority of Jehovah's Witnesses. Why? Because only the 144,000 are declared to be regenerated, chosen, justified, saints, part of the body of Christ, sanctified, heaven-bound and so on. Therefore, all the biblical passages that speak of these and related things do not apply,

according to WS doctrine, to the average Jehovah's Witness. It's not just that they cannot be born-again, it's that most of the biblical doctrines related to regeneration are denied them as well.

Thus, according to WS teaching, what the Bible teaches about salvation is really applicable to only a handful of people. In effect, as far as salvation is concerned, the Bible is simply irrelevant for 99.999999 percent of humanity:

> By their sharp division of believers into two classes, the Watchtower Society actually makes a large part of the Bible, particularly of the New Testament, meaningless for the majority of its adherents. For all Scriptural passages dealing with regeneration, sanctification, anointing, and consecration; all passages which speak of being sealed by the Spirit, filled with the Spirit, or testified to by the Spirit; all passages which describe the body of Christ, the bride of Christ, the new creation, the holy nation, and the elect (the list is far from exhaustive) are intended, so the Witnesses say, only for the anointed class and mean nothing for the other sheep.[142]

Schnell correctly points out the end result: a teaching as fully destructive to the Bible's message of salvation as that of the biases of higher critical approaches to Scripture, such as the form and redaction criticism of the "Jesus Seminar" (critiqued in the chapter on Unitarian Universalism, and more extensively in our book *The Facts on the False Views of Jesus*). "Surely this is a kind of divisive [WS] criticism of the Bible that is just as damaging to its authority and comfort as are the irreverent scissors of the higher critic!"[143]

In 1980 it was reported that a number of high-ranking Jehovah's Witnesses at Bethel headquarters were disfellowshipped or voluntarily left the Watchtower Society. It seems that their personal Bible studies had caused them to believe—quite correctly—that everyone, not just the 144,000, needed to be born-again. Among this new crop of outcasts were Raymond Franz, nephew of former president F.W. Franz, and Edward Dunlap, former 12 year head of the Watchtower Society Gilead School of the Bible, its missionary training arm.[144] But, as is so often the case with authoritarian religions, the Watchtower Society would not tolerate dissent; appropriate action was taken to silence the "heresy." In response, Raymond Franz has written *Crisis of Conscience* and *Searching for Christian Freedom,* detailed and scathing exposés of Witness life and policies. These should be considered must reading for all Jehovah's Witnesses and those interested in the Watchtower Society.

The denial of grace, works and maintaining one's righteousness under threat of annihilation. We have seen that Jehovah's Witnesses hold that unregenerate men and women can exercise faith, live for God and even perfect themselves without spiritual rebirth or regeneration. This teaching, of course, denies the biblical doctrine of grace, for if we can do all these, we certainly need little or no "grace." Clearly, Jehovah's Witnesses speak of "grace," but not in a biblical sense. The Jehovah God of the Watchtower is said to be a God of "grace" because without Jesus' death for our sins, no one would have the opportunity to merit salvation. It should be evident, then, that the word "grace" for the Watchtower Society simply means the *chance* to earn one's own redemption.

The problem with a salvation dependent on personal worthiness is that it must be maintained by great effort and can so easily be lost if one fails to meet the proper standards. If the 144,000 do not continue in service, good works and obedience to the Watchtower Society, which is believed to equal obedience to Jehovah, they will lose their "justification" and become worthy of eternal death. In the following citation, observe how being "justified" (biblically, being *declared* righteous apart from works, Titus 3:5-7) is dependent on continued works and faithfulness. Obviously, then, the 144,000 are not declared righteous by God in a biblical sense; they are only given the opportunity to prove themselves righteous by maintaining a favored status before God. Their "present justification" may be lost at any time:

> The followers of Jesus Christ . . . are first declared righteous by God on the basis of their faith in Jesus Christ (Romans 3:24, 28). . . . They are therefore "counted" or "credited" as being

completely righteous persons, all their sins being forgiven. . . . To win [the battle with present sin], however, they must constantly exercise faith in Christ's ransom sacrifice and follow him, thus *maintaining their righteousness* in God's eyes. . . . If, on the other hand, they take up the *practice* of sin, falling away from the faith, they lose their favored standing before God as righteous persons. . . . Such ones face destruction [eternal annihilation].[145]

This claim to being *credited* as righteous and having *all* ones sins forgiven is either not true or not believed by the Watchtower. If it were considered true, there would never be any legal or just basis for Jehovah to annihilate people. Just as the WS claim to believe in God's grace is disproven by its emphasis on works, so its claim to believe in justification and full forgiveness of sins (at least for the 144,000) is disproven by their emphasis on the requirement to maintain salvation. Thus, the elect 144,000 are chosen on the basis of their own worthiness, and then they must maintain worthiness until death to be insured a spiritual "resurrection," finally giving them immortality. The other Witnesses, as we shall see, must also do good works and remain faithful in this life, and then both they and the rest of resurrected mankind must later attain sinless perfection if they also are to finally inherit "eternal life" on earth.

Salvation in the battle of Armageddon and beyond to the millennium: When too much is too little. The Witness concept of salvation is also related to the ever approaching "battle of Armageddon," the last great World War prior to the millennial age of God's theocratic kingdom. Only Jehovah's Witnesses are survivors of this Great Tribulation, and they will be joined on earth by the resurrected faithful saints (the 144,000) and later by the resurrected unbelievers. These recreated Witnesses will become the righteous example for the rest of resurrected mankind (the unbelievers, whether good or evil), who now have the opportunity to earn their salvation during the millennium. Here we have an irony of sorts: evil people in this life fare better than unfaithful Witnesses, even if the Witnesses had been faithful most of their lives.

Jehovah's Witnesses can be faithful for most of their lives and still lose their salvation, which relegates them to the "unfaithful" category. All "unfaithful" Jehovah's Witnesses throughout history were forever annihilated when they died. But even evil non-Witnesses now get to be resurrected and are offered a second chance for immortality on earth. Obviously, it is more preferable to be an evil person in this life than an "unfaithful" Jehovah's Witness.

But even faithful Jehovah's Witnesses are not off the hook. The Watchtower teaches that the Jehovah's Witnesses who will survive Armageddon had previously attained righteousness on earth, although not yet perfection. Hence their righteousness only provides them a privileged *position* in the millennial age. Over the next 1,000 years they must still earn their eternal life. The rest of earthly mankind must do the same. Thus, while Jesus and the 144,000 rule from heaven, everyone on earth must now attempt to perfect themselves. For the Jehovah's Witnesses who survive Armageddon: "Jesus Christ . . . can do priestly service for them throughout the thousand years of his reign till at last they reach human perfection, if they are willing."[146] For the remainder of mankind: "The 'great crowd' of survivors of the war of [Armageddon] . . . will then be on their way to gaining absolute righteousness and perfection in the flesh . . . actual human perfection in the flesh. . . . They will be able to stand before the God of holiness on the basis of their own righteousness."[147]

But that's not all. Even after attaining perfection, no one is yet truly justified or a possessor of eternal life. All must yet pass the final test spoken of in Revelation 20:7-9, the test that countless numbers are destined to fail:

Up in heaven in association with the High Priest Jesus Christ, great will be the privilege of his 144,000 immortal joint heirs. . . . Having been imperfect, sin-laden humans themselves on earth, they too will be able to sympathize with men on earth in their efforts to get rid of the "law of sin and death" in their members and to attain to human perfection, innocence, sinlessness. . . . All mankind will then be, like the perfect man Adam in the Garden of Eden. . . . [Nevertheless] before adopting them as his free

sons through Jesus Christ, Jehovah God will subject all these perfected human creatures to a thorough test for all time. . . . The ones to be tested then will be, not the holy angels of heaven but only perfected mankind on earth. . . . So an indefinite number of perfected, human free moral agents will let themselves be misled. . . . These willful rebels will be summarily executed.[148]

In Witness terms, according to Revelation 20:7-9, the number of the perfected class who will rebel against God are like the "sand on the seashore." One wonders how these "perfect," "innocent," and "sinless" people (according to the Witnesses) could ever rebel against God in the manner spoken of? The answer, biblically, is because these people of the millennium are not perfect but still sinners. But the Watchtower teaches that these individuals have sinless perfection and yet still rebel. This does not offer individual Witnesses much hope for their eternal future.

Thus, all the heroic efforts a Jehovah's Witness engages in during this life only secure him a better *political* position in the New World. His many good works offer him precious little in relation to his *spiritual* position before God. Along with everyone else, including the wicked, Witnesses with a lifetime of good works and righteousness must now work even harder not only for one normal lifetime but also for their life during the entire length of the millennium. They must strive toward literal perfection and somehow attain it, and then they must pass the final test before they can be counted among those with eternal life.

Only the "second death"—extinction—remains for those who fail the final test. This eternal judgment is applied even though people have attained perfection; they somehow rebel against God at the last moment. However, even from a Witness perspective, it hardly seems just. Although original sin bringing death was supposedly canceled by the atonement, these "perfect" men and women can still die (be annihilated) by their own rebellion. "After that, if any lifted up to a perfect human image and likeness of God die, it will not be a death traceable to Adam but be a death due to the perfect sinner's[!]

151

own willfulness and rebellion. . . . So at the end of Christ's millennial reign he turns over the perfected human race to stand trial before God, for only God is the one who can justify creatures to everlasting life—Romans 8:33."[149]

Here, people spend hundreds and hundreds of years striving and straining to attain sinless perfection during the millennium. Finally, they achieve it. And then find themselves annihilated for one transgression! What was the point to all that effort if it could so easily be lost? (If countless people are lost at this point, one presumes that the transgression itself, whatever it is, can hardly be that difficult to fall into.)

Here we find illustrated another Achilles heel of Watchtower salvation. It is so fragile that it can be lost at any point, no matter how heroic the efforts on behalf of salvation up to that point. Of course, if human nature tells us anything, it is that a salvation dependent on us must, in the end, always fail. No one can ever perfect themselves or be good enough to merit God's acceptance and salvation. Unfortunately, Jehovah's Witnesses have little understanding of either the depth of human sin, which reveals our predicament, or the depth of the grace of God, which solves it.

The Watchtower doctrine of salvation is an impossible burden. Perhaps this may explain why different studies indicate that mental illness among Witnesses is 4 to 16 times higher than that of the general population—people break down under the strain.[150] Has anyone in human history ever been able to perfect himself or herself? This is a reason why Christ lovingly died—to make possible as a free gift what we could never earn on our own merits because of the depth of our sinfulness (Romans 3:10–18). The glory of God's free grace is that the salvation once received is forever; it can never be lost (John 5:24; Romans 8:28–38; 1 John 5:13). We documented this biblically in *Knowing the Truth About Eternal Security* (Harvest House, 1998). The reason salvation by works is terminally insecure is because it is dependent on what man cannot do. The reason salvation by grace is eternally secure is because it is dependent upon what God can do—and has done.

Unfortunately, in the logic of WS doctrine, no Jehovah's Witnesses anywhere can have any assurance of their salvation. Former Jehovah's Witnesses themselves have pointed out the uncertain and tenuous nature of their status before God. "I never had any assurance of my salvation; it was something to be obtained by right conduct and good works as a theocratic slave. In spite of all my efforts I did not have a personal relationship with the Lord Jesus Christ. If a Witness does not maintain a faithful course of integrity, he loses his chance of gaining everlasting life. . . . This teaching applied even to the 'heavenly class' of 144,000."[151] "The Witnesses' plan of salvation is based primarily on one's personal good works. Each Witness is working his way to everlasting life and cannot know that he is saved."[152]

What a contrast with the Gospel. "He who has the Son has life; he who does not have the Son of God does not have life. I write these things to you who believe in the name of the Son of God *so that you may know that you have eternal life*" (1 John 5:12–13). Jesus Himself emphasized, "I tell you the truth, whoever hears my word and believes him who sent me *has eternal life and will not be condemned; he has crossed over from death to life*" (John 5:24).

To summarize, we may observe four categories of people in WS doctrine, each of which must earn their own salvation:

1. The 144,000 (the elect historically).

The "resurrection of life" includes the "first resurrection," which is the resurrection to instantaneous perfection of life, spirit life, in which Jesus himself participated and in which only the 144,000 joint heirs participate with him.[153]

The way to heavenly life involves more than just faith in Christ's ransom sacrifice and works of faith in obedience to God's instructions.[154]

2. The "other sheep" (other faithful Jehovah's Witnesses historically).

Others who "did good things" in God's sight and who will share in the "resurrection of life" will be those of the "great crowd" of sheeplike persons who may die before Armageddon; also the faithful witnesses of Jehovah who died before Pentecost A.D. 33. . . . Their resurrection will be early after Armageddon, because many of these will be made theocratic princes in all parts of the earth.[155]

3. The unjust who attain perfection.

This includes only "resurrected" unbelievers (non-Jehovah's Witnesses). (When the millennium begins there are only two categories of people: the 144,000, who rule from heaven, and the faithful Witnesses, who survived Armageddon. The "resurrected" unbelievers will join them later in the millennium.) In the following, note again that WS teaching involves the opportunity for salvation after death. Speaking of the "resurrected" unrighteous we are told that Jesus Christ will provide:

> A period of judgment in the new world in hope of their reforming and practicing good things and deserving to be lifted up to human perfection. . . . As Jehovah's High Priest, the Shepherd King will be able to apply the merit of his atoning sacrifice . . . in behalf of their sins. In that way their sins may be forgiven and canceled and they may be cured of their imperfections and brought to the image and likeness of God by the end of Christ's thousand-year reign.[156]

4. The rebellious who fail.

This includes: a) certain categories of people who are forever annihilated at death (they are never resurrected in the first place); b) the resurrected just or unjust who fail to attain perfection in the millennium (Jehovah's Witnesses and non-Jehovah's Witnesses); c) all those deceived in the final test, whether the faithful Jehovah's Witnesses ("other sheep") or non-Jehovah's Witnesses:

> If any resurrected ones then under judgment prove unreformable or turn rebellious after a sufficient period of trial, they may be executed, destroyed in the second death, without further delay.[157]

Not only these people but also everyone who is alive anywhere on earth will have to face this last test, even the princes of the "new earth" and the sheeplike people who lived through Armageddon. Everyone on earth will be judged according to how he meets this test.[158]

In *Life Everlasting* we read, "Jehovah God will justify, declare righteous, on the basis of their own merit all perfected humans who have withstood that final, decisive test of mankind."[159]

Watchtower Denials. Like Mormons, Jehovah's Witnesses may stress that they do not teach salvation on the basis of works of righteousness. They do this by maintaining an arbitrary distinction between Mosaic works, which cannot save, and New Testament works, which can save. The goal is to attempt to reconcile their doctrine of works-salvation with biblical statements denying works-salvation. Whenever the Bible denies works-salvation, the WS argues it must be referring to trying to earn one's salvation by outdated Mosaic works, not required Gospel works. In effect, there are dead works of "the Law" and saving works of "the Gospel." In denying salvation by works of the Law[160] while asserting salvation by works of the Gospel,[161] Witnesses may claim to deny works-salvation while in fact supporting it. Thus we find both a denial and affirmation of self-righteousness.[162]

The difficulty with the Watchtower argument is that, morally speaking, Mosaic law and Gospel law are not that easily separated. Further, the requirements of the Gospel law are considerably more stringent than the law of Moses, as passages like the Sermon on the Mount (Matthew 5–7) make clear.

The Atonement of Christ

In speaking with individual Jehovah's Witnesses, it may initially seem as if they believe in Christ's atoning death on the Cross. Certainly they claim this. But the Witnesses oppose the biblical doctrine of the atonement, as numerous Christian scholars and researchers have recognized. The late Dr. Walter Martin called their view of the atonement "completely unscriptural."[163] Professor Edmond Gruss, a former Jehovah's Witness and author of the definitive *Apostles of Denial*, declares, "The Witnesses' view of the atonement is very different from that held by orthodoxy and in essence is a rejection of that Biblical doctrine."[164] In his book *Four Major Cults*, Anthony Hoekema agrees.[165]

Gruss points out that during their early history the Witnesses actually had three entirely different views of the "ransom" of Christ. "The teaching of the Society on the ransom of Christ has been confused from the beginning, with C. T. Russell presenting three differing positions on this doctrine in the publications of the Watchtower Society. The teaching on the subject since Russell's death has also been unsteady as to the extent and application of the ransom."[166]

How does the Witness view of the atonement differ from the biblical view? The key difference can be seen in their *limitation* of the atonement. Christ's death made *potential* forgiveness available for others by faith and works. Just as Adam's disobedience brought death, so Christ's obedience brought life—resurrection (recreation)—with the potential to earn eternal life. But Christ's death alone did not atone for everyone's sins; in the end, good works and good character do this. Thus the Christian concept of a completed atonement of infinite value is rejected.

For some people, according to WS teaching, Christ's death has no value at all because there are some sins that are simply unforgivable. Apparently, certain murderers and the willfully rebellious receive no benefit. For example, Adam is stated to be exempt from the benefits of the atonement because he was a "willful sinner."[167] "Under the law the deliberate murderer could not be ransomed. Adam, by his willful course, brought death on all mankind, hence was a murderer" (Romans 5:12). "Thus the sacrificed life of Jesus is not acceptable to God as a ransom for the sinner Adam."[168]

What the Watchtower fails to recognize is that *all* people everywhere are "willful sinners." That is the essence of being a sinner, as the Bible plainly declares (Romans 1:18–2:5; 3:9–20; Ephesians 2:1–3; Colossians 1:21). In addition, the Bible teaches that murderers can be forgiven, and there are fine biblical examples, such as Moses (Exodus 2:12); King David (2 Samuel 11:14–15; 12:9); possibly the Apostle Paul (Acts 8:1; 9:1; 22:4–5; 26:10). Even to those who murdered Him, Jesus responded, "Father, forgive them . . ." (Luke 23:34). But according to the Watchtower, there are millions of other people for whom the atonement has had no value, and they have already been annihilated forever:

> Some people have already been judged. They have shown that they do not deserve life. These

people will not be resurrected from the dead in the new world. Adam and Eve were judged unworthy of life. They were put to death by Jehovah. The people who died in the flood of Noah's day received this same kind of unfavorable judgment. God brought the flood that "destroyed them all" (Luke 17:27). The people of the city of Sodom died by a rain of fire from heaven after receiving an unfavorable judgment. At other times other groups also have received an unfavorable judgment. They proved that they were not worthy of life, and they will not be resurrected.[169]

Even though the atonement, according to WS doctrine, involved the death of one man for one man, Jehovah's Witnesses believe it could somehow be applied to more than one man. The Witnesses refer to a "corresponding ransom" theory in presenting this idea. As is true in The Way International, another Arian cult, the Witnesses argue Jesus had to be *only* a man in order to be our Savior:

> If Jesus, when he was baptized at thirty years of age, had been a so-called God-man . . . he would have been superhuman and would have had more value than a ransom for all mankind. The perfect justice of God would not unjustly accept more value than that of the thing to be ransomed. . . . It was the perfect man Adam that had sinned and so had lost for his offspring human perfection and its privileges. Jesus must likewise be humanly perfect, to correspond with the sinless Adam in Eden. In that way he could offer a ransom that *exactly* corresponded in value with what the sinner Adam lost for his descendants. This requirement of divine justice did not allow for Jesus to be more than a perfect man. That is why, in writing 1 Timothy 2:5, 6, the apostle Paul uses a special word in Greek, *antilutron*, to describe what Jesus offered in sacrifice to God.[170]

> The human life that Jesus Christ laid down in sacrifice must be exactly equal to that life which Adam forfeited for all his offspring: it must be a perfect human life, no more, no less. It must be a "corresponding ransom."[171]

What the Witnesses miss here is that one *man* alone could never atone for the sins of *billions* of sinners. Only if Jesus were both God and man could His atonement forgive all human sin.

Nevertheless, somehow, Jehovah's Witnesses apply the death of one man to all "capable" of receiving it through good works (some murderers and certain others being excluded):

At the time of Adam's sin and his being sentenced to death, his offspring or race were all unborn in his loins and so all died with him. (Compare Hebrews 7:4–10; Romans 7:9.) Jesus as a perfect man, "the last Adam" (1 Corinthians 15:45), had a race or offspring unborn in his loins, and when he died innocently as a perfect human sacrifice this potential human race died with him. Thus, Jesus was indeed a "corresponding ransom," not for the redemption of the one sinner, Adam, but for the redemption of all mankind descended from Adam. He repurchased them so that they could become his family, doing this by presenting the full value of his ransom sacrifice to the God of absolute justice in heaven.[172]

Hoekema correctly questions this reasoning:

For, as has been pointed out, there is no real continuity between Christ as he appeared in the flesh and [as] the previously existing Archangel Michael. For the Witnesses, therefore, God did not really send his only-begotten Son (even if one understands this term as designating the created Logos) into the world to ransom man from his sins. Rather, He caused a sinless man to be miraculously conceived by Mary; this man was not even a "spirit-begotten son of God" at birth, but only a human son. He was different from other men only in two respects: (1) he had been born of a virgin, and (2) he lived a perfect life. . . . At this point the question cannot be suppressed: Why should the sacrificed life of Jesus Christ have so much value that it can serve to ransom millions of people from annihilation? It was a perfect human life which was sacrificed, to be sure; we must not minimize this point. But it was the perfect human life of someone who was *only a man*. Could the life of a mere man, offered in sacrifice, serve to purchase a multitude which no man can number?[173]

The Scripture is clear on this: the death of one *man* is insufficient to ransom another: "No *man* can redeem the life of another or give to God a ransom for him—the ransom for a life is costly, no payment is ever enough. . . ." (Psalm 49:7–8, emphasis added). Only God can redeem

a life, which is precisely why Christ had to be God and precisely why Christ died.

The "corresponding ransom" theory of the Watchtower is not at all equivalent to the substitutionary and propitiatory atonement of Jesus Christ. The WS view pays only for the sins of one man and is of limited value and somehow applied to others, while the biblical view pays for the sins of all the redeemed and is of infinite value. As Gruss points out, the Greek word *antilutron* does not carry the meaning of "exact correspondence," which the Witnesses have attributed to it:

The "corresponding ransom" doctrine should be rejected on the following grounds: First, the Greek word *antilutron* occurs only once in the Bible (1 Timothy 2:6) and the meaning need not be much different than *lutron* ("ransom"). After an examination of the words in the *lutron* group in the New Testament, Morris concludes that in meaning *antilutron* "does not seem to differ greatly from the simple *lutron*, but the preposition emphasizes the thought of substitution; it is a 'substitute-ransom' that is signified. Such a term well suits the context, for we read of Christ 'who gave himself on behalf of all' (1 Timothy 2:6). The thought clearly resembles that of Mark 10:45, i.e. that Jesus had died in the stead of those who deserved death. If the thought of substitution is there, we find it here to an even greater degree in view of the addition of the preposition which emphasizes substitution."

It should be obvious to the reader that what the Watchtower writers convey with the words "corresponding ransom" and what is conveyed by the words "substitute ransom" as explained by Morris and the rest of the Scriptures are not remotely the same.[174]

As in Mormonism, Watchtower writings speak highly of "the atonement." But as to its importance, the WS relegates it to a secondary status behind human good works. It is not faith in Christ that applies the merits of Christ, but the good works and perseverance of the individual and his faith in the Watchtower Society. Without these, the merits of Christ are worthless. Apparently for the Watchtower Society, what the Bible describes as "filthy rags" (our works of righteousness [Isaiah 64:6]) has more value for salvation than the sacrificial and sanctified death of Jesus Christ Himself! "The Witnesses' doctrine of the ransom largely ignores the Biblical teaching on the subject, by claiming to accept the 'ransom sacrifice' which was provided in the death of Christ not as a finished work, but only as a foundation from which man works to provide his own salvation."[175] A former Witness of 16 years points out that, despite their claims to believe in the atonement, the witnesses deny this through their demand for works:

As I laid aside *The Watchtower* and other study guides of the Jehovah's Witnesses and read the New Testament with an open mind, I became aware of two things. First, salvation comes by faith in Jesus Christ and not by works (Ephesians 2:8–10). . . . I found out that they said one thing but believed another. They will often speak highly of Jesus' sacrifice and yet deny its efficacy by saying that to be saved one must do all the things the organization directs.[176]

There is an additional sense in which the death of Christ is secondary. Jehovah's Witnesses teach that the primary goal of Jesus was to vindicate the name of Jehovah in response to a challenge of Satan's; it was only Jesus' secondary purpose to die for Adam's sin. In other words Jesus' principal goal was *not* to die for our sins.[177] Dr. James Bjornstad comments:

His primary purpose was to vindicate (provide a defense for Jehovah's name) and establish Jehovah's kingdom. . . . After Adam disobeyed God, Satan challenged God to put a creature on earth who could experience all the temptations Satan could give and still remain faithful to God until death. . . . The burden fell upon His first created being, His son, Michael the archangel. God's son came to earth as Jesus and met all the temptations of Satan, according to the Jehovah's Witnesses. Moreover, he remained true to God until death. In so doing he was able to establish God's kingdom. Thus Jesus was Jehovah's chief witness. Jehovah's Witnesses claim Jesus also had a secondary purpose in being here. He came to sacrifice his human body as a ransom to God for Adam's sin.[178]

Further, Jehovah's Witnesses not only deny a *completed* atonement by declaring its practical application dependent on works, but also deny it by declaring its future application occurs only at the end of the millennium. It is at "the end of Christ's thousand-year reign as King when he finishes applying the merit of his human sacrifice."[179] Dr. Martin correctly observes: "Jehovah's Witnesses argue that the atonement is not wholly of God, despite 2 Corinthians 5:21, but rather half of God and half of man. Jesus, according to their argument, removed the effects of Adam's sin by His sacrifice on Calvary, but the work will not be fully completed until the survivors of Armageddon return to God through free will and become subject to the theocratic rule of Jehovah."[180]

In conclusion, the Jehovah's Witnesses view of salvation and the atonement of Christ must be considered deficient and powerless to save. It does not accept God's teaching about salvation, and therefore cannot have God's blessing.

Man

Jehovah's Witnesses believe that man is a creation of Jehovah but deny that man is created in God's image with an immortal soul. In Watchtower theology the body is the soul. Man consists of a mortal body (the soul) and the mortal life energy that activates it (the spirit or breath, or "life force"). For Jehovah's Witnesses, the devil is the author of the idea of an eternal soul, as he is the author of all Christian doctrine.[181]

1. The soul is material and mortal, not immaterial and immortal.

The Scriptures show that both *psy-khe* and *ne'phesh*, as used with reference to earthly creatures, refer to that which is material, tangible, visible and mortal. . . . The Scriptures clearly show that *ne'phesh* and *psy-khe* are used to designate the animal creation lower than man. The same terms apply to man. . . . So, too, the "spirit" . . . or life force of man is not distinct from the life force in animals. . . . *Psy-khe* does not refer to something immortal or indestructible.[182]

2. The spirit is not the soul.

The "spirit" (Hebrew, *ru'ahh*: Greek *pneu'ma*) should not be confused with the "soul" (Hebrew, *ne'phesh;* Greek, *psy-khe'*), for they refer to different things. . . . As has been shown, the soul *(ne'phesh; psy-khe')* is the creature itself.

The spirit *(ru'ahh; pneu'ma)* generally refers to the life force of the living creature or soul, though the original language terms may also have other meanings.[183]

The Afterlife

If man has no immortal spirit, he cannot be subject to eternal punishment. Again, for the WS, the soul is the body and the spirit is just the breath, so when the body dies, the person is extinguished. (This explains why Jehovah's Witnesses actually believe in recreation, not resurrection.) As a result, Jehovah's Witnesses deny the biblical teaching of death as separation from God; they prefer a materialistic interpretation of total annihilation or extinction. The doctrine of hell is believed to be a Satanic teaching. Annihilation is God's only judgment or "punishment" on sin.

1. There is no hell.

"The teaching about a fiery hell . . . can rightly be designated as a 'teaching of demons.' . . . Has not this doctrine. . . grossly misrepresented God? . . . Those teaching the hellfire doctrine are therefore saying blasphemous things against God. . . . That being the case, would you want to continue supporting any religious system that teaches a fiery hell?"[184]

2. Death is extinction.

"Biblical evidence thus makes it plain that those whom God judges as undeserving of life will experience, not eternal torment in a literal fire, but 'everlasting destruction.' They will not be preserved alive anywhere. The fire of Gehenna is therefore not a symbol of the totality and thoroughness of that destruction."[185]

3. Heaven is only for the elect (144,000).

As we have seen, the vast majority of Jehovah's Witnesses and recreated mankind inherit an earthly paradise; only the 144,000 go to heaven. The subheadings in *Make Sure of All Things* declare: "Only a limited number from among mankind to be in heaven with the Lamb Jesus Christ. . . . 144,000 are spiritual Israelites, include both Jews and Gentiles. . . . Chosen by God for heavenly life. . . . Other faithful servants of God to be rewarded with life on earth, not in heaven."[186]

In the end, there are three basic possibilities for the future state after death:

1. Recreation as a spirit in heaven (immortality as one of the 144,000 elect).

2. Recreation to a probationary general future physical life on earth for a thousand years.

3. Depending upon the outcome of this life and its testings there will result either eternal life upon earth or extinction forever.

THE OCCULT

"This is not what some may regard as spiritism by any means. . . ."

—Judge Rutherford describing his angelic inspiration (*Light*, Book 1, 1930, p. 64.)

Jehovah's Witnesses claim to oppose occult involvement. However, when it comes to accepting spiritistic inspiration, they have simply redefined this as inspiration from "angels" or "holy spirit." The WS has been involved in occult activity historically. The Bible Way Productions, Inc. (a Watchtower sect headed by Roy D. Goodrich of Ft. Lauderdale, FL), publishes a 36 page pamphlet (1969 ed.), No. 272, "Demonism and the Watchtower," which gives some evidence that during significant portions of the Rutherford era the Society apparently engaged in work with spiritistically associated radionic devices such as the Abrams' "black-box." (Abrams, like practitioners of occult radionics and psychometry generally, was involved with spiritism). Although the "devices" are held to be the source of psychic power (for example, healing energy), it is invariably the spirit behind the device which is the real source of power, as we documented elsewhere.[187] In light of this involvement the author raises a significant question: "Since the 'Diagnostic Machine of Dr. Albert Abrams' at Jonesboro, Ark., and the 'Radioclast,' its present counterpart so long housed and used at the Bethel home, are both ideal for receiving 'yes' and 'no' answers from the occult realm, have we any assurance that these have not been so used in the formulation of Watch Tower doctrines, policies and commandments?"[188]

As we will see, they were so used. Also, Russell's and the Society's endorsement of numerological-prophetic power to the Great Pyramid of Egypt seems to have had occult associations.[189] Thus it can be documented that the Watchtower Society in its early years was involved in the occult,[190] even though the Society's official position toward occult activity is supposedly in agreement with the prohibition found in Deuteronomy 18:9-12. That this is not the case can be seen from recent research into the Watchtower and the occult. For example, one website, "Index of Watchtower Society and the Occult" (http://home.sol.nol.~jansh/wteng/a-2.html), includes sections on astrology, spiritism, demonism, divination, necromancy, Egyptian religion, numerology, radionics and pyramidology. The first six or seven issues of Ken Raines' *JW Research Journal* also have the Watchtower Society and the occult as a principal theme. At Raines' website, http://www.premier1.net1~raines, one can find many articles like the following: *The Spirit World Guided Rutherford*; *Was Rutherford a Spirit Medium?* and *Talking with the Dead: JW's and Necromancy.*

Today the Watchtower Society appears to be unsuspectingly involved in the occult in principally one manner: it seems to accept demonic guidance and revelations that come to it in the guise of angelic contacts. For example, "Judge" Rutherford practiced what a channeler or medium would, when wanting to contact the spirit world. But Rutherford defined his practice differently, as godly contact with angels. This, too, is what countless channelers today would say. But no godly angel is going to supply revelations that deny God and Christ as the Bible teaches them.

Since the Watchtower's translation, doctrines and practices have failed to meet biblical, moral[191] and scholarly standards, how could the supernatural assistance have orginated in God? Would godly angels lend help to an organization that denies the true nature of God, deliberately distorts His word and rejects His Son? The Bible says that fallen angels—demons—would do this. The Bible further declares that demons masquerade as "angels of light" while doing this (2 Corinthians 11:14).

The Watchtower Society claims that angels guided its translators in translating the *New World Translation* of the Bible, but former service department member in the Jehovah's Witnesses headquarters at Brooklyn, New York, Bill Cetnar, found that many Watchtower beliefs were professed by Johannes Greber, a spirit-possessed medium the Society was quoting.[192]

Let's look at some examples of Watchtower's claims to supernatural guidance. Judge Rutherford openly stated that angels helped write *The Watchtower* magazine when he said that "the Lord through His angel sees to it that the information is given to His people in due time...."[193] Former worldwide president of Jehovah's Witnesses F. W. Franz also spoke of angels guiding the Watchtower: "We believe that the angels of God are used in directing Jehovah's Witnesses."[194]

Among other things *The Watchtower* claims that angels: 1) enlighten and comfort; 2) bring refreshing truths; and 3) transmit information to "God's anointed people."[195] In another clear statement, *The Watchtower* magazine admits, "Jehovah's Witnesses today make their declaration of the good news of the kingdom under angelic direction and support."[196]

In *The Watchtower*, Dec. 1, 1981 (p. 27) and Jul. 15, 1960 (p. 439), the leaders of the Jehovah's Witnesses claim to be God's "channel of communication," actively "channeling" (the early use of this common New Age term is theirs) since the days of Rutherford. In the issue of Apr. 1, 1972 (p. 200), they claim that all spiritual direction is supplied by invisible angels. In the issues of Nov. 15, 1933 (p. 344), Nov. 1, 1935 (p. 331) and Dec. 15, 1987 (p. 7), they claim that the name "Jehovah's Witnesses" and their key doctrine of "Christ's" invisible return in 1914 were channeled by invisible angels. Today the Society's leaders claim that both "holy spirit" and "angels" communicate information to them (*The Watchtower*, Mar. 1, 1972, p. 155; Aug. 1, 1987, p. 19).[197] "Angels may share in directing us, or we may receive guidance by holy spirit" (*The Watchtower*, Jul.15, 1992, p. 21).

Under the second president of the Jehovah's Witnesses, Judge Rutherford, the Witnesses received most of their basic doctrines of today.

Rutherford believed that God's "holy spirit" had ceased to function as his teacher and had been replaced by angels who taught him in his mind (*The Watchtower,* Sept. 1, 1930, p. 263; Feb. 1, 1935, p. 41; Rutherford, *Riches* (1936), p. 316).

Direct "angelic" guidance was the source behind the *New World Translation.* According to the Scottish *Daily Express,* F. W. Franz testified:

1) That he and N. H. Knorr headed the secret Translation Committee of seven.

2) That he and Knorr, not the Committee, had the last word.

3) That he, Franz, was the head of the Society's Publicity Department.

4) That translations and interpretations emanated from God in this way:

    a) They are INVISIBLY COMMUNICATED to the Publicity Department.

    b) This is accomplished by "ANGELS OF DIFFERENT RANKS WHO CONTROL WITNESSES."[198]

This statement, cited by Professor Gruss, was checked by him for accuracy, and is also quoted by Goodrick as accurate.[199] Alleged "angels who control witnesses" sounds suspiciously like demonism.

Much additional information on the occult in Watchtower history can be found at the previous websites and in Vols. 1–3 of Ken Raines' *JW Research* (PO Box 5534, Everett, WA 98206, 1994–95). Raines points out that Rutherford claimed that Jehovah God was the actual editor of *The Watchtower* magazine, and that "angels transmitted the divine interpretation of Scripture into his mind." Further, "Most of the unique doctrines and chronology that JWs believe today came from angels via Rutherford's angelic channeling."[200] Rutherford also endorsed a book called *Angels and Women,* which was received through automatic writing, admittedly "by one of the fallen angels who desired to come back into divine favor."[201] Allegedly, Rutherford endorsed this book because he truly believed that some demons were honest and could still be saved from annihilation. So we see numerous WS claims that *The Watchtower* was inspired by angels or holy spirit. "*The Watchtower* is not the instrument of any man or set of men. . . . No man's opinion is expressed in *The Watchtower.*"[202]

In essence, most WS doctrines of today were received from "angels." The only question is what kind of angels. These frank admissions from the Watchtower—documenting that it receives information and guidance from angels—coupled with the fact of all its false prophecies, biased Bible translation and unbiblical teachings, lead us to believe that it is receiving its information from demons, not from godly angels. In light of the anti-biblical doctrines of the Watchtower Society, in view of its denial of the Holy Trinity as satanic, its demeaning of Christ and His atonement—not to mention its unrelenting hostility to the church and its unorthodox interpretations and translation of the Bible—if the Watchtower Society leadership truly was "possessed by angels," it seems evident that they were not of the kind that ministered to Jesus.

It would appear, then, that the WS has been extensively involved in the occult, albeit under another name, throughout its history. Since it continues to claim to receive supernatural revelation as to biblical interpretation, prophecy and teaching, from angels and holy spirit, the Jehovah's Witnesses should be classed as an occult religion despite its denials of occult involvement.

CRITIQUE

In this section we will concentrate on documenting one basic point: the inherent untrustworthiness of the Watchtower Society. Although we do touch on other areas, we emphasize this one because of its importance. If a Jehovah's Witness finds that he cannot trust that the Watchtower Society is the sole channel of God on earth, it will be difficult for him to remain a Witness. As we saw earlier many do have doubts. Either the Watchtower Society *is* God's sole channel, and as such should be, at least generally, morally upright and trustworthy, or it *is not* God's channel. If it is an organization propagating the conflicting beliefs and theories of men, or perhaps so-called "angels," who are not receiving direction and guidance from God, it is better avoided. As we quoted Judge Rutherford earlier, "It is entirely unsafe for the people to rely upon the words and doctrines of imperfect men."

The following information will adequately answer the question, "Is the WS God's true channel for giving truth to the world or is it a fallible organization beset with sufficient corruption to forever dispel its claims to divine guidance?" We think the latter, and many openminded former Witnesses will agree. As an Internet blurb on Randall Waters, *Thus Saith the Governing Body of Jehovah's Witnesses,* noted, the WS "has made more changes in doctrine, more coverups and has promoted more outright deceptions than most religions put together." The question must be asked: if truth is what we should expect from men directly guided by God for over 100 years, how is it we get the opposite in the WS? We have selected four principal "tests":

1) Does the WS uphold honesty and integrity in translating the Bible, God's Word?

2) Is the WS trustworthy and accurate in its prophetic statements?

3) Has the WS changed its own divine revelations?

4) Is the WS fair in quoting other sources and authors in support of its views?

Bible Translation

Our first test will be to examine the Watchtower translation, *The New World Translation of the Holy Scriptures* (NWT). As we will note, both their English Bible and their Interlinear claim great fidelity to the original languages and entire accuracy in translation. If the Witnesses have not translated God's revelation with care and accuracy, but have incorporated their own doctrinal bias in complete disregard of the Greek text, then it is unlikely that the Watchtower Bible and Tract Society (WBTS) is God's sole channel for communicating His will to mankind today. (The numerous false translations also prove that divine angels were not involved.) Indeed, the combined weight of the

following four indisputable facts proves that the Watchtower Society has no regard at all for the Word of God. These four facts are: 1) pervasive unbiblical theology; 2) clear bias in translation; 3) numerous false prophecies historically; 4) changes and contradictions in their own revealed doctrines.[203]

The Emphatic Diaglott

Before we begin our analysis of the NWT, we should note that for about 70 years it was preceded in use by the *Emphatic Diaglott,* published in 1864 by Benjamin Wilson and based on the 1806 recension of J. J. Griesbach. In utilizing this translation, the Witnesses never informed their members that the translation was flawed and that Wilson was a Christadelphian, who, holding similar doctrines with Jehovah's Witnesses, naturally sought a translation in harmony with Christadelphian bias. For example, the *Diaglott* (like the *NWT*) translates Matthew 25:46 "agelasting cutting-off" and John 1:1 "the Word was a god," both in harmony with Christadelphian (and Watchtower) denials of eternal punishment and Christ's deity respectively.[204] Professor Edmond Gruss, of the Master's College in Southern California, author of a standard work on Jehovah's Witnesses, *Apostles of Denial,* and a former member of the group, observes how the *Diaglott* fit the needs of the newly formed Russellite (Jehovah's Witnesses) religion:

> Wilson was self-educated; his work shows that he certainly was not a scholar. Neither did he have the respect of those who were scholars. Obviously, his purpose was not to translate, but to justify his theological views.... It may be concluded, then, that the *Emphatic Diaglott* was adopted because of its Christadelphian bias which agreed almost perfectly with the new Russellite group that was forming. The Russellites accepted the renderings of Wilson, for they did not have the linguistic ability either to evaluate or to determine their correctness, nor did they wish to question that which so perfectly supported their theories....[205]

In spite of his bias and errors in translation, Wilson claimed "scrupulous fidelity" to the original languages. "Scrupulous fidelity has been maintained throughout this version in giving the true rendering of the original text into English; no regard whatever being paid to the prevailing doctrines or prejudices of sects, or the peculiar tenets of theologians. To the Divine authority of the original Scriptures alone has there been the most humble and unbiased submission."[206]

As we will see, the Jehovah's Witnesses make similar claims to scholarly objectivity in Bible translations and yet fail miserably to live up to them.

The New World Translation (NWT) of the Holy Scriptures

Another mark of true religion is that its members have a *deep respect for the Bible.* They accept it as the Word of God and believe what it says.[207]

After using the *Diaglott* for many years, eventually the Watchtower Society produced its own translation, *The New World Translation of the Holy Scriptures.* Testimony under oath by then vice-president F. W. Franz revealed that translations and interpretations came from God in such a way that they were invisibly communicated to the Publicity Department via "angels of various ranks who control witnesses."[208] One mediumistic translation that claims to originate in the spirit world has translations similar to those of the NWT. The 1937 New Testament translation by spiritistic medium Johannes Greber has similar translations for John 1:1, Hebrews 1:8 and other verses and is quoted by the WBTS in several of its books.[209] Spirit possession would indeed explain the theological bias and antiChristian nature of the WS translation.

Robert M. Bowman, Jr. points out that readers should not assume that the NWT only has a relatively small number of errors in its translation relative to key doctrines, and that, for the most part, the NWT is an acceptable translation. The truth is that there are hundreds and thousands of distortions of the Bible in the NWT. "The JWs *systematically* distort the Bible to make it fit their preconceived beliefs. . . . The NWT itself reflects this systematic distortion in a vast number of texts relating to practically every area of biblical doctrine."[210] Indeed, even a small listing of WS mistranslations, in addition to those listed below, include: Genesis 1:2; Exo-

dus 3:14; Numbers 1:52; Ecclesiastes 12:7; Isaiah 43:10; Matthew 2:11; Mark 1:4; Luke 23:43; John 6:56; 14:17; Acts 2:42; 10:36; Romans 2:29; 8:1; 8:23; 8:28; 8:29; 8:32; 9:5; 13:1; 1 Corinthians 6:19; 10:4; 12:11; 14:12-16; 15:2; Philippians 1:23; 2:9; Colossians 1:19; 2:6-12; 1 Timothy 4:1; Hebrews 12:9; 12:23; 1 John 5:20. (Many of these scriptural mistranslations will not seem significant unless one understands Watchtower theology. Securing a book such as Bowman's *Jehovah's Witnesses Answered Verse by Verse* will be a good reference for those readers wishing to pursue the matter.)

Nevertheless, the Watchtower Society has made many statements concerning NWT translation accuracy. Of course, if Witnesses really believed the translators were possessed by "angels," it would be easy to assume the translation was accurate even when the translators themselves did not know the original languages. Regardless, we find the WBTS claiming absolute fidelity to the Greek and Hebrew text. Their *Kingdom Interlinear Translation of the Greek Scriptures* declares: "Its literal interlinear English translation is specially designed to open up to the student of the Sacred Scriptures what the original Koine Greek basically or literally says, without any sectarian religious coloration."[211] And of the NWT, the Society asserts:

The translators who have a fear and love of the divine Author of the Holy Scriptures feel especially a responsibility toward Him to transmit his thoughts and declarations as accurately as possible. They also feel a responsibility toward the searching readers of the modern translation who depend upon the inspired Word of the Most High God for their everlasting salvation. It was with such a sense of solemn responsibility that the committee of dedicated men have produced the New World Translation of the Holy Scriptures, over the course of many years.[212]

In its text *All Scripture Is Inspired of God and Beneficial,* the Society makes similar claims. Note for example the assertion to grammatical accuracy:

The New World Translation . . . conveys accurately the action or state expressed in the Hebrew and Greek verbs. . . . .The conveying of the state of the Hebrew verb accurately into English is most important, otherwise the meaning may be distorted. . . . Similar care has been exercised in the translating of the Greek verbs. . . . The New World Translation . . . is accurate and reliable . . . a faithful translation of God's Word.[213]

We will later document comments on the NWT by those familiar with the original languages who have made a study of the Jehovah's Witnesses a scholarly pursuit, or are Greek scholars themselves. Then we will document the accuracy of NWT claims by citing specific examples of mistranslation from the NWT.

Scholars' Comments on the
New World Translation

Dr. Robert Countess' published doctoral dissertation, *The Jehovah's Witness New Testament: A Critical Analysis of the New World Translation of the Christian Greek Scriptures* (Phillipsburg, NJ: Presbyterian and Reformed Publications, 1982), offers a most thorough and devastating critique of the NWT. His overall conclusion is that the NWT:

. . . has been sharply unsuccessful in keeping doctrinal considerations from influencing the actual translation . . . [The] New World Translation of the Christian Greek Scriptures must be viewed as a radically biased piece of work. At some points it is actually dishonest. At others it is neither modern or scholarly. And interwoven throughout its fabric is inconsistent application of its own principles enunciated in the Foreword and Appendix.[214]

Professor Edmond Gruss, author of a standard historical and theological work, *Apostles of Denial*, writes:

A sound interpretation of any passage requires a careful grammatical exegesis. Watchtower publications repeatedly present doctrines and interpretations of the Scriptures which completely misunderstand or ignore grammar. Before the Society entered into the field of translation, there were many verses which gave them trouble because of their direct contradiction of the Witnesses' doctrines. With the appearance of the New World Translation the difficult passages in many cases were weakened or eliminated by a translation that violated or ignored the rules of grammar.[215]

Dr. Anthony Hoekema, author of *The Four Major Cults*, points out: ". . . the Jehovah's Witnesses actually impose their own theological system upon Scripture and force it to comply with their beliefs. . . . [Their] New World Translation of the Bible is by no means an objective rendering of the sacred text into modern English, but is a biased translation in which many of their peculiar teachings of the Watchtower Society are smuggled into the text of the Bible itself."[216]

The late Dr. Walter Martin, author of *Jehovah of the Watchtower,* observed that of the anonymous seven-member translation committee at least five had no training in Greek:

These books possess a veneer of scholarship unrivaled for its daring and boldness in a field that all informed scholars know Jehovah's Witnesses are almost totally unprepared to venture into. As a matter of fact, the authors have been able to uncover partially a carefully guarded Watchtower secret: the names of five of the members of the New World Translation committee. Not one of these five people has any training in Greek . . . [or Hebrew].[217]

Dr. Bruce Metzger, professor of New Testament Language and Literature at Princeton Theological Seminary and author of *The Text of the New Testament,* states: ". . . the Jehovah's Witnesses have incorporated in their translation of the New Testament several quite erroneous renderings of the Greek."[218]

Dr. Julius Mantey was one of the leading Greek scholars in the world and co-author of *The Dana-Mantey Greek Grammar* and *A Hellenistic Greek Reader.* He stated:

I have never read any New Testament so badly translated as *The Kingdom Interlinear Translation of the Greek Scriptures.* In fact, it is not their translation at all. Rather, it is a distortion of the New Testament. The translators used what J. B. Rotherham had translated in 1893, in modern speech, and changed the readings in scores of passages to state what Jehovah's Witnesses believe and teach. That is distortion, not translation.[219]

In light of the previous testimony, it must be concluded that the NWT cannot be trusted to accurately convey God's Word because of its biases in translation and lack of scholarship in many areas. Nor can Jehovah's Witnesses appeal to an alleged "trinitarian bias" on the part of the previous scholars, for the issue is not personal theology but accuracy in translation. Even non-Christian scholars of New Testament Greek would agree that the NWT is not accurate; after all, rules of languages, grammar and translation are true regardless of personal theological belief.

Examples of Mistranslation

Watchtower literature states:

> Jehovah is against such clergy prophets whom he did not send forth from his intimate group and who "steal" words from his Bible in order to make a wrong application of them. . . . he will rid himself of this "burden" by abandoning Christendom to calamity. . . . To such self-opinionated religionists, the Jeremiah class [Jehovah's Witnesses] say: "You have changed the words of the living God. . . ."[220]

> God does not deal with persons who ignore his Word and go according to their own independent ideas.[221]

But who is it that really "steals" or "ignores" God's words in order to bolster their own independent ideas?

In the following section we have utilized the Watchtower Society's *New World Translation* (NWT) and *Kingdom Interlinear Translation of the Greek Scriptures* (KIT). The latter gives the Greek text, a word for word English translation below the Greek text and a column containing the NWT to the right. In the following examples we have provided the NWT and the *New American Standard* (NAS) translation so the reader may make a quick comparison prior to the discussions. The NWT mistranslation is in small capital letters.

1. Matthew 25:46. ["Punishment," *kolasin,* is translated *"cutting off"* in order to escape the text's teaching of eternal punishment and to support their theology of annihilation of the wicked or conditional immortality.]

> "And these will depart into everlasting CUTTING-OFF but the righteous ones into everlasting life." NWT

> "And these will go away into eternal punishment, but the righteous into eternal life." NAS

How do standard Greek lexicons define *kolasin*? J. H. Moulton and G. Milligan in *The Vocabulary of the Greek New Testament* (Grand Rapids, MI: Eerdmans, 1980, p. 352) give an illustration of *kolasin* as "punishment and much torment." H. K. Moulton in *The Analytical Greek Lexicon Revised* (Grand Rapids, MI: Zondervan, 1978, p. 235) defines it as "chastisement, punishment." *New Thayer's Greek English Lexicon* (Wilmington, DE: Associated Publishers and Authors, 1974, 1977, p. 353) defines it as "correction, punishment, penalty." The *Arndt and Gingrich Greek-English Lexicon* (Chicago: University of Chicago, 1967, p. 441) states "1. punishment . . . 2. of divine retribution . . . go away into eternal punishment. . . ." Gerhard Kittle (ed.), in the standard work *Theological Dictionary of New Testament* (Grand Rapids, MI: Eerdmans, 1978, Vol. 3, p. 816), defines it as "punishment."

Over hundreds of years, words may evolve in meaning; hence *kolasin* at one time could have been translated "cutting-off," meaning the removal of that which is evil. It could also have the meaning of punishment for the purposes of correction.[222] But this was not its intended meaning in biblical times, as is evident from Greek scholars Mantey and Trench (Greek words are transliterated by the authors):

> In Jehovah's Witnesses' *New World Translation* and *Kingdom Interlinear Translation* (Matthew 25:46), the Greek word [*kolasin*], which is regularly defined as "punishment" in Greek lexicons, is translated "cutting-off," in spite of the fact that there isn't a shred of lexical evidence anywhere for such a translation. We have found this word in first-century Greek writings in 107 different contexts and in every one of them, it has the meaning of "punishment," and never "cutting-off." But since their premise is that there can be no eternal punishment, they have translated the Scripture to make it somewhat compatible with their theology. . . . *Kolasin* is also mistranslated "restraint" in 1 John 4:18.[223]

> The [*kolasis aionios*] of Matthew xxv.46, as it is plain, is not merely corrective, and therefore temporary, discipline; . . . for in proof that [*kolasis*] with [*kolazesthai*] had acquired in Hellenistic Greek this severer sense, and was used

simply as "punishment" or "torment," with no necessary underthought of the bettering through it of him who endured it, we have only to refer to such passages as the following: Josephus, Antt.xv. 2.2; Phil, De Agric. 9; Mart. Polycarp. 2; 2 Macc iv 38; Wisd. xix.4; and indeed the words of St. Peter himself (2 Ephesians II.9).[224]

2. John 8:58. ["I AM" is translated "I have been" in order to circumvent Christ's deity].

"Jesus said to them: "Most truly I say to you, before Abraham came into existence, I HAVE BEEN." NWT

"Jesus said to them, 'Truly, truly, I say to you, before Abraham was born, I AM.'" NAS

The proper translation of the Greek *ego eimi* is "I Am" not "I have been." This is a WS attempt to deny Christ's statement of deity (cf. context) and to replace it with something compatible to the Witnesses' concept of Christ's limited preexistence. Dr. Mantey observes: "The translation of it as 'I have been' by Jehovah's Witnesses is wrong. The footnote stating that it is in 'the perfect indefinite tense' is also wrong. No Greek grammar, to my knowledge, has such a statement. In fact, there is no form *eimi* in the perfect tense in the Greek New Testament."[225]

It is also noteworthy that Michael Van Buskirk, author of *The Scholastic Dishonesty of the Watchtower,* has two official Watchtower Society letters showing that the Society has assumed four different grammatical positions in regard to *ego eimi*: a) "present indicative first person singular" (the correct designation); b) "a historical present"; c) the "perfect indefinite tense," but only "in a general sense"; d) "perfect tense indicative."[226] But again, there is no "perfect indefinite tense" as they claim (see 1950, 1953 eds. of the NWT). Dr. Mantey also states that there is no "perfect indicative in this verse in Greek."[227] The correct answer is "present indicative, first person singular," which translates as "I Am," not as "I have been." If the Watchtower Society had admitted (at least once) that the grammatical construction was a "present indicative, first person singular," why did they never translate it as such? In fact, one can look

at their KIT (p. 467) and directly beneath the Greek *ego eimi* we find "I Am"; but the translation column to the right reads "I have been."

3. Hebrews 9:27. [This verse has the insertion of "for all time" to justify WS belief in conditional immortality.]

"And as it is reserved for men to die once FOR ALL TIME [eternally] but after this a judgment." NWT

"And inasmuch as it is appointed for men to die once, and after this comes judgment." NAS

Looking at the KIT (p. 988) we find the addition of the words "for all time" is without any justification. There is no Greek correspondence. Mantey states: "Hebrews 9:27, which without any grounds for it in the Greek, is mistranslated in the J. W. Translation. . . . Note that the phrase 'for all time' was inserted in the former versions without any basis in the original for it. No honest scholar would attempt to so pervert the Word of God!"[228]

4. Luke 23:43. [This verse inserts a comma after "today," to support their belief in soul sleep.]

"And he said to him: 'Truly I tell you today, You will [i.e., later] be with me in Paradise.'" NWT

"And He said to him, 'Truly I say to you, today you shall be with Me in Paradise.'" NAS

KIT (p. 408) admits that "in the original Greek no comma is found." The noted commentator Lenski explains why the NWT is incorrect here:

It should no longer be necessary to explain that "today" cannot be construed with "I say to thee." To be sure, Jesus is saying this today—when else would he be saying it? The adverb "today" is a necessary part of Jesus' promise to the malefactor. In fact, it has the emphasis. It would usually take three or four days until a man would die on the cross, so lingering was death by crucifixion. But Jesus assures this malefactor that his sufferings will cease "today." This is plain prophecy and at the same time blessed news to this sufferer. But Jesus says vastly more: "Today in company with me shalt thou be in Paradise!" This is an absolution. By this word Jesus acquits this criminal of sin and guilt.[229]

5. Matthew 27:50; Luke 23:46. [The term "spirit" is translated as "breath" and/or "spirit" in order to support conditional immortality.]

"Again Jesus cried out with a loud voice, and yielded up (his) BREATH." NWT

"And Jesus cried out again with a loud voice, and yielded up His spirit." NAS

"And Jesus called with a loud voice and said 'Father into your hands I entrust my spirit.' When he had said this he expired." NWT (This case "spirit" is translated correctly.)

"And Jesus, crying out with a loud voice, said, 'Father, into thy hands I commit My spirit.' And having said this, He breathed His last." NAS

In Matthew 27:50 *pneuma* (spirit) is mistranslated "breath" to support WS belief that no immortal spirit exists to be "yielded up." Yet Luke 23:46, the parallel account of this same event, which includes the actual cry of Jesus, shows that the translation "breath" is an impossible rendering, as it would have Jesus crying out, "Father into your hands I entrust my *breath*." The question is this. If in the NWT *pneuma* is translated "spirit" in Luke, why is it translated "breath" in the parallel passage in Matthew unless it is an obvious attempt to deny that Jesus' spirit continued after His physical death? Clearly, the Witnesses have distorted Matthew 27:50 although nothing could really be done by them with the passage in Luke.[230] KIT directly beneath the Greek translates *"pneuma"* as "spirit" in both places (pp. 168, 409). Why then not in both translations?

6. Acts 20:28. [The phrase "with his own blood" is translated as "the blood of his own (Son)," to circumvent Christ's deity.]

"Pay attention to yourselves and to all the flock, among which the holy spirit has appointed you overseers, to shepherd the congregation of God, which he purchased with THE BLOOD OF HIS OWN (SON)." NWT

"Be on guard for yourselves and for all the flock, among which the Holy Spirit has made you overseers, to shepherd the church of God which He purchased with His own blood." NAS

The KIT appendix justifying this translation (pp. 1160–61) refers to some manuscripts that use "Lord" (supposedly Jesus) instead of God and mentions "troublesome Greek words." It can offer this translation only by unnaturally translating the Greek, and it concludes, "The entire expression could therefore be translated 'with the blood of his own.' "[231]

Nigel Turner, an authority who wrote the volume on Greek syntax in Moulton's three volume *Grammar of New Testament Greek*, explains why the Witnesses are wrong at this point:

The dying proto-martyr, St. Stephen, addressed Jesus as if he were God. A pious Hellenistic Jew would not pray at one less than God. It may not be so generally appreciated that St. Paul slipped naturally and casually into the affirmation that he who shed his blood upon the cross was God. The reference is to Acts 20:28, where St. Paul at Miletus spoke to the Christian elders about "the church of God which he bought for himself by his own blood." The blood of God! Some aberrant manuscripts have the inoffensive reading, "the church of the Lord"—implying the Lord Jesus. But they must be rejected on the ground that the more startling or difficult reading is the one likely to be correct; scribes would not invent a conception of such unexpected originality as "the blood of God." We are left with the original and plain statement of St. Paul that Jesus is God, and it worries those scholars who think that it represents a Christology grammatical expedient whereby "his own" is understood as a noun ("his own One"), rather than a possessive adjective. In consequence, standing as it does in the genitive case, one may place before it the word "of": i.e., "of his Own." The expedient lowers the Christology drastically and reduces St. Paul's affirmation to something like this: "the church of God which he bought for himself by the blood of his Own"—as in the margin of the NEB. It is a theological expedient, foisting imaginary distinctions into a spontaneous affirmation, and is not the natural way to take the Greek. It is unlikely to have been the meaning envisaged either by St. Paul or the writer of the narrative. The easy thing would be for them to add the word "Son," if that was intended.[232]

Even the KIT appendix admits:

Grammatically, this passage could be translated, as in the King James Version and Douay Version, "with his own blood." In such case the verse would be saying that God purchased his congregation with his own blood. That has been a difficult thought with many . . . the ordinary translation would mean to say "God's blood."[233]

Nevertheless, the more accurate and natural translation is rejected since it cannot be true according to Watchtower theology, which denies the deity of Jesus Christ.

7. Hebrews 1:8. ["Thy throne O God" is translated "God is your throne" in order to circumvent Christ's deity.]

"But with the reference to the Son: 'GOD IS YOUR THRONE forever, and (the) scepter of your kingdom is the scepter of uprightness.'" NWT

"But of the Son He says, 'Thy throne, O God, is forever and ever, and the righteous scepter is the scepter of His kingdom.'" NAS

Nigel Turner comments: "Happily in Hebrews 1:8 the NEB (New English Bible) no longer hesitates to accept in its text the statement that Jesus is God. 'Thy throne, O God, is for ever and ever.' It consigns to the margin the grotesque interpretation which obscures the godhead of Jesus ('God is thy throne for ever and ever')."[234]

Thomas Hewitt states:

Some commentators have taken "O God" to be nominative, either subject or predicate. If subject, the translation would be "God is thy throne for ever and ever." If predicate "Thy throne is God," or "The foundation of thy throne is God." Such translations sound very strange and have no parallel elsewhere. The AV, RV and RSV rightly support the vocative and translate "Thy throne, O God". . . . The Son, on the contrary, is addressed by the Father not as a messenger but as God, who occupies an eternal throne, and as Sovereign, who rules His Kingdom with righteousness.[235]

Former Ryland's Professor of Biblical Criticism and Exegesis at the University of Manchester, F. F. Bruce, declares that here the "Messiah can be addressed not merely as God's Son (verse 5) but actually as God. . . ."[236] As anyone can see, verse 10 corroborates that the intent of verse 8 is to declare Jesus as God (note the conjunction "and").

8. Colossians 1:15–20. [These verses insert the word "other" in parenthesis in order to deny the eternal existence of Christ.]

"He is the image of the invisible God, the firstborn of all creation; because by means of him all (OTHER) things were created in the heavens and upon the earth, the things visible and the things invisible, no matter whether they are thrones or lordships or governments or authorities. All (OTHER) things have been created through him and for him. Also, he is before all (OTHER) things and by means of him all (OTHER) things were made to exist, and he is the head of the body, the congregation. He is the beginning, the first-born from the dead, that he might become the one who is first-born from the dead, that he might become the one who is first in all things; because (God) saw good for all fullness to dwell in him, and through him to reconcile again to himself all (OTHER) things by making peace through the blood (he shed) on the torture stake, no matter whether they are the things upon the earth or the things in heaven." NWT

"And He is the image of the invisible God, the first-born of all creation. For in Him all things were created, both in the heavens and on earth, visible and invisible, whether thrones or dominions or rulers or authorities—all things have been created through Him and for Him. And He is before all things, and in Him all things hold together. He is also head of the body, the church; and He is the beginning, the first-born from the dead; so that He Himself might come to have first place in everything. For it was the Father's good pleasure for all the fullness to dwell in Him, and through Him to reconcile all things to Himself, having made peace through the blood of His cross; through Him, I say, whether things on earth or things in heaven." NAS

In the NWT, the term "other" is inserted to imply that the meaning of the passage is that

Christ Himself is not *the* Creator. We grant that a translator may insert a word in italics or brackets if it is necessary to express the thought of the original accurately. But even a cursory reading of the context here will show that Christ *is* the Creator. KIT is again embarrassing itself (p. 896), for it proves that the word "other" is not in the Greek. Yet this did not prevent earlier editions of the NWT from using "other" *without* brackets, implying that it was part of the Greek (see the 1950,1953 eds.). Even the 1965 edition of *Make Sure of All things Hold Fast to What is Fine* quotes Colossians 1:15–18 as if "other" were part of the original Greek. No parenthetical brackets are present: "because by means of him all OTHER things were created.... All OTHER things have been created through him and for him."[237] In addition, modern versions of the NWT insert the word "other" in Philippians 2:9, again changing the meaning ("the name above every OTHER name"), and again without brackets or italics, implying that it is in the original when in fact it is not, as their own interlinear once again demonstrates.

Jehovah's Witnesses' objectivity cannot become more questionable than through examples of this type, where the Society adds to the divine text what is simply not present in order to deny what is clearly taught. Nevertheless, the Witnesses have somehow overlooked John 1:3 (which the NWT translates correctly) and which clearly declares the doctrine of Christ's deity, which they spuriously removed from Colossians: that if Christ is the Creator of *all* things, He Himself must be uncreated. The NWT translates John 1:3 as: "All things came into existence through him, and apart from him not even one thing came into existence."

While on the subject of Christ as Creator, Jehovah's Witnesses refer to the word *prototokos* ("first-born" in Colossians 1:15) as alleged evidence of Christ being "created." However, the word means priority and sovereignty over creation, as the context reveals. Bruce Metzger observes:

Here he is spoken of as "the first begotten of all creation," which is something quite different from saying that he was made or created. If Paul had wished to express the latter idea, he had

available a Greek word to do so, the word *protoktistos,* meaning "first created." Actually, however, Paul uses the *prototokes,* meaning "first begotten," which signifies something quite different, as the following explanation by a modern lay theologian makes clear:

"One of the creeds says that Christ is the Son of God 'begotten, not created' and it adds 'begotten by his Father before all worlds.' Will you please get it quite clear that this has nothing to do with the fact that when Christ was born on earth as a man, that man was the son of a virgin? We are not now thinking about the Virgin Birth. We're thinking about something that happened before Nature was created at all, before time began. 'Before all worlds' Christ is begotten, not created. What does it mean?

"We don't use the words *begetting* or *begotten* much in modern English, but everyone still knows what they mean. To beget is to become the father of: to create is to make. And the difference is just this. When you beget, you beget something of the same kind as yourself. A man begets human babies, a beaver begets little beavers, and a bird begets eggs which turn into little birds. But when you make, you make something of a different kind from yourself. A bird makes a nest, a beaver builds a dam, a man makes a wireless set.... Now that's the first thing to get clear.

"What God begets is God; just as what man begets is man. What God creates is not God; just as what man makes is not man."

To return now to Colossians 1:15 where Paul speaks of Christ as "the first begotten of all creation," it is important to observe that the adjective "first" refers both to rank as well as time. In other words, the Apostle alludes here not only to Christ's *priority* to all creation, but also to his *sovereignty* over all creation.[238]

One can mention other Scriptures. In Psalms 89:27, "firstborn" clearly means preeminence. In Jeremiah 31:9, Ephraim is the "firstborn" although Manasseh was literally born first; hence "firstborn" must refer to rank or preeminence.

9. Colossians 2:9. [In this verse "deity" is translated as "divine quality" in order to circumvent Christ's deity.]

"... because it is in him that all the fullness of the DIVINE QUALITY dwells bodily." NWT

167

"For in Him all the fullness of Deity dwells in bodily form." NAS

The great grammarian, A. T. Robertson, author of *A Grammar of the Greek New Testament,* declares:

In this sentence . . . Paul states the heart of his message about the Person of Christ. There dwells (at home) in Christ not one or more aspects of the Godhead (the very essence of God, from *theos, deitas*) and not to be confused with *theiotes* in Romans 1:20 (from *theios,* the quality of God, *divinitas*), here only in N. T. as *theiotes* only in Romans 1:20. The distinction is observed in Lucian and Plutarch. *Theiotes* occurs in the papyri and inscriptions. Paul here asserts that "all the pleroma (fullness) of the Godhead," not just certain aspects, dwells in Christ and in bodily form . . . dwells now in Christ in his glorified humanity. . . . He asserts plainly the deity and the humanity of Jesus Christ in corporeal form.[239]

Metzger asserts:

Nothing could be clearer or more emphatic than this declaration. It means that everything without exception which goes to make the godhead, or divine quality, dwells or resides in Jesus Christ bodily, that is, is invested with a body in Jesus Christ. It is to be noticed also that Paul uses the present tense of the verb, "dwells." He does not say that the fullness of the divine quality "has dwelt" in Jesus Christ, but that it "dwells" there.[240]

Gruss concurs:

The word *theotes* is here translated "divine quality" which is not a literal or correct rendering. Grimm-Thayer gave as the meaning of his word, "*deity* i.e., the state of being God, Godhead: Colossians ii. 9." The word for "divinity" or "divine character" is found in Romans 1:20 and is *theiotes* which is rendered by Grimm-Thayer as divinity, divine nature." Cremer gives "the Godhead" as the meaning of *theotes* and then says that the two words are to be distinguished: "*theotes*—that which God is, *theiotes*—that which is of God." In the discussion of these two words Trench writes concerning Colossians 2:9:

". . . St. Paul is declaring that in the Son there dwells all the fullness of absolute Godhead: they were no mere rays of divine glory which gilded Him lighting up his person for a season and with a splendour not his own; but He was, and is, absolute and perfect God. . . ."[241]

10. Titus 2:13, 2 Peter 1:1. (Cf. Ephesians 5:5, 2 Thessalonians 1:12). [In these verses "our great God and Savior" is translated as "the great God and the Savior" in order to deny Christ's deity.]

". . . while we wait for the happy hope and glorious manifestation of the great God AND OF (THE) Savior of us, Christ Jesus." NWT (Titus 2:13)

". . . looking for the blessed hope and the appearing of the glory of our great God and Savior, Christ Jesus." NAS (Titus 2:13)

The Greek of Titus 2:13 and 2 Peter 1:1 is very similar, with *megalou,* "great," being absent in 2 Peter.

The NWT changes the proper translation to separate Jesus Christ from the term God, thereby denying His deity. In the NWT, the verse is translated as if two persons are being spoken of, God and Jesus, rather than one person only, Jesus Christ. This violates a rule of Greek grammar called the Granville Sharp rule. In simplified form it states that when two singular personal nouns (a personal noun is distinguished from a proper noun in this rule) of the same case ending (God and Savior, genitive case) are connected by "and" (*kai*) and only the first noun has the modifying article "the" (*tou*) (the second noun does not), it always means that both nouns uniformly refer to the same person. When defined properly, the rule has no exceptions in the New Testament.[242] John Weldon remembers being challenged publicly, at this point, by a Greek expert concerning his "error" regarding the universality of Granville Sharp, which illustrates that even otherwise well-informed people can be in error concerning this rule (see Appendix 2).

Thus "God" and "Savior" must both refer to one person, to Jesus, in Titus 2:13 and 2 Peter 1:1. In fact, in ancient times the same phraseology ("god and savior") was used of a ruling king.

These two verses, then, must be translated as "our great God and Savior Jesus Christ."[243]

The KIT explanation for the WS translation (p. 1163) is typically biased, sounding scholarly but misquoting Moulton's *Grammar,* as we will later document. In *A Manual Grammar of the Greek New Testament,* Dana and Mantey state: "The following rule by Granville Sharp of a century back still proves to be true: . . . 2 Peter 1:1 . . . means that Jesus is our God and Savior. After the same manner Titus 2:13 . . . asserts that Jesus is the great God and Savior."[244] (The reason why the King James Version, the American Standard Version and a few additional earlier versions incorrectly translate such passages is, in part, according to Robertson, due to the influence of the grammatical work of George B. Winer.[245] (See Appendix 2.)

11. John 1:1. ["God" is translated as "a god" in order to deny Christ's deity.]

"In (the) beginning the Word was, and the Word was with God, and the Word was a god." NWT

"In the beginning was the Word, and the Word was with God, and the Word was God." NAS

The transliterated Greek of this verse looks like this:

En arche en ho logos kai ho logos
In beginning was the Word and the Word
en pros ton theon kai theos en ho logos
was toward the God and God was the Word

In essence, the Watchtower Society, violating another rule of Greek grammar, Colwell's rule, claims that it can translate *theos* as "a god" because there is no definite article before this usage of *theos* (God) in the last clause of John 1:1. Note that the first use (*pros ton theon*) has the article (ton, "the"). The second use simply states *kai theos,* "and God," (not "and the God"). Because it does not say "and *the* God" Jehovah's Witnesses argue that they are free to interpret this second usage of "God" as, figuratively, meaning a lesser deity, "a god," a designation signifying Christ's exalted status, even though He is still only a creature.

The WS concern here is to escape the clear and forceful meaning of this passage, in which Christ is called *theos,* God. But had the apostle John used the article, he would have declared "*the* God was the Word." Had he done so, he would have confused the persons of the Trinity and supported modalism (in the early church this was known as the heresy of Sabellianism, see the chapter Oneness Pentecostalism). In other words, to say that "*the* God was the Word (Jesus)" would have declared that all of God, the whole trinity, was Jesus. This would have supported modern modalistic belief that there is only one Person in the Godhead (Jesus, i.e., "Jesus only") and that the terms Father, Son and Spirit in Scripture only refer to modes or offices of the one God, who exists as one person.

The Apostle John had to make a finer distinction and, on the one hand, clearly declare that the person of Jesus was deity but, on the other hand, not make it seem as if all three persons in the Godhead were to be considered the same as the person of Jesus. To make this fine distinction he had to use the exact wording he used.

We should note that KIT (pp. 1158-59) utilizes both Mantey's and Robertson's *Grammar* in defense of their John 1:1 translation. However, Dr. Mantey publicly rebuked them:

Since my name is used and our [Daney & Mantey] *Manual Grammar of the Greek New Testament* is quoted on page 744 to seek to justify their translation, I am making this statement . . . of all the scholars in the world, as far as we know none have translated this verse as Jehovah's Witnesses have done. If the Greek article occurred with both Word and God in John 1:1, the implication would be that they are one and the same person, absolutely identical. But John affirmed that "the Word was with (the) God" (the definite article preceding each noun), and in so writing, he indicated his belief that they are distinct and separate personalities. Then John next stated that the Word was God, i.e., of the same family or essence that characterizes the Creator. Or, in other words, that both are of the same nature, and that nature is the highest in existence, namely divine. . . . The apostle John in the context of the introduction to his Gospel, is pulling all the stops out of language to portray not only the deity of Christ, but also his equality with the Father. He states that the Word was in the beginning, that He was with God, that He was God and that all creation came into existence through him and that not even one thing exists that was not created by Christ. What else could be said that John did not say?[246]

For more of Dr. Mantey's letter see Appendix 2. As for Dr. Robertson, the WS misstates his position by selectively quoting him. As they observe, Robertson does say that "the absence of the article here is on purpose." But Jehovah's Witnesses do not explain *why* Robertson says this. He does so to indicate that to include the article "would have been Sabellianism."[247] In his *Word Pictures*, Robertson provides a succinct analysis:

> By exact and careful language John denied Sabellianism by not saying *ho theos enho logos.* (The God was the Word). That would mean that all of God was expressed in *ho logos* (the Word) and the terms would be interchangeable, each having the article. The subject is made plain by the article (*ho logos*) and the predicate without it (*theos*) just as in John 4:24 *pneuma ho theos* can only mean "God is spirit," not "spirit is God." So in I John 4:16 *ho theos agape estin* can only mean "God is love," not "love is God" as a so-called Christian scientist would confusedly say. For the article with the predicate see Robertson, Grammar, pp. 767f. So in John 1:14 *ho Logos sarx egeneto,* "the Word became flesh," not "the flesh became Word."[248]

The Watchtower Society appendix defending their rendering "a god" (KIT, pp. 1158–60) appears scholarly but is not. For example, they misquote Dana and Mantey's *Grammar.* In a letter dated July 11, 1974 to the WS, Mantey demanded a public apology for their repeated misquotings (in millions of printings), and he requested their discontinuance of the use of his grammar. (See Appendix 2 in this section.)

A related argument the WS uses here is given as follows: "At Acts 28:6 we have a case paralleling that of John 1:1 with exactly the same predicate construction, namely, with an anarthrous [no definite article] OEOS [*theos*]" (KIT, p. 1160). This at first seems to be true, for there is no definite article in Acts 28:6. What the Witnesses fail

to mention is that in John 1:1 the predicate nominative (*theos*) precedes the verb, but in Acts it follows the verb and thus is not applicable. Colwell's rule, which is at issue here, states that a definite predicate nominative has the article when it follows the verb and lacks the article when it precedes it:

> . . . such a rendering is a frightful mistranslation. It overlooks entirely an established rule of Greek grammar which necessitates the rendering, ". . . and the Word was God." Some years ago Dr. Ernest Cadman Colwell of the University of Chicago pointed out in a study of the Greek definite article that, "A definite predicate nominative has the article when it follows the verb; it does not have the article when it precedes the verb. . . . In a lengthy Appendix in the Jehovah's Witnesses' translation, which was added to support the mistranslation of John 1:1, there are quoted thirty-five other passages in John where the predicate noun has the definite article in Greek. These are intended to prove that the absence of the article in John 1:1 requires that OEOS must be translated "a god." None of the thirty-five instances is parallel, however, for in every case the predicate noun stands after the verb, and so, according to Colwell's rule, properly has the article. So far, therefore, from being evidence against the usual translation of John 1:1, these instances add confirmation to the full enunciation of the rule of the Greek definite article. Furthermore, the additional references quoted in the New World Translation from the Greek of the Septuagint translation of the Old Testament, in order to give further support to the erroneous rendering in the opening verse of John, are exactly in conformity with Colwell's rule, and therefore are added proof of the accuracy of the rule. The other passages adduced in the Appendix are, for one reason or another, not applicable to the question at issue. (Particularly inappropriate is the reference to Acts 28:6, for no one has ever maintained that the pagan natives of Malta regarded Paul as anything other than "a god.")[249]

Van Buskirk points out that the Witnesses have attempted to deny Colwell's Rule by quoting Phillip B. Harner's article in *Journal of Biblical Literature*, "Qualitative Anarthrous Predicate Nouns: Mark 15:39 and John 1:1" (Vol. 92, 1973,

p. 87). However, a full *year* earlier Dr. Mantey sent a letter to the Watchtower Society demanding they stop misquoting him. He pointed out that not only had they misquoted Colwell's rule but also that it is impossible to quote Harner in denial of Colwell since Harner himself supports the rule and denies the possibility of an "a god" translation. Van Buskirk observes: "One's mind staggers at the depths to which someone will sink to prove his point. In the Watchtower's case both Colwell and Harner show that in John 1:1 'a god' is not a permissible translation. Yet without blinking an eye they will quote, out of context, the man who refutes them. Harner's article in no way concludes what the Watchtower makes it conclude in their letter."[250] (Van Buskirk goes on to discuss exactly what Harner concluded and how his research is complementary to Colwell's; it simply brings out new information.)

Nevertheless, even if we were to assume the truth of what the Watchtower Society claims in their KIT appendix, they have violated their own John 1:1 "rule" 94 percent of the time. Robert H. Countess, writing in *The Jehovah's Witnesses' New Testament*, documents this in detail.[251] In John 1 alone they violate their principle at least five times. Checking their interlinear (pp. 417–19) we see the following: John 1:6 *para theou*—no definite article; John 1:12 *tekna theou*—no definite article; John 1:13 *ek theou*—no definite article; John 1:18 *Theon*—no definite article; John 1:23 *odon Kuriou*—no definite article.

If, according to WS standards, the absence of the article demands the rendering "a god," why do they not so render it here? In fact, where is it in 94 percent of the instances of such construction in the NWT? Clearly, translating John 1:1 as saying "a god" is not only a violation of Greek grammar but also unjustified even in light of the vast majority of their own translation. Obviously, then, in the preceding passages and in John 1:1, the translation should be "God," not "a god." (As an aside, the NWT at John 1:23 translates the Greek *kurios* [Lord] as "Jehovah," since it is a clear reference to Jehovah God from Isaiah. Yet, according to their John 1:1 rendering, with no definite article, it should be "a Jehovah." If "a god" must be different from God, "a Jehovah" must then be different from Jehovah. At this point we would have three "Gods": "Jehovah," "a god" and "a Jehovah.")

12. Philippians 1:23. [The word "depart" is translated as "releasing" to support a belief in soul sleep.]

> "I am under pressure from these two things; but what I do desire is the RELEASING and the being with Christ. . . ." NWT

> "But I am hard pressed from both directions, having the desire to depart and be with Christ, for that is very much better." NAS

Dr. Walter Martin comments: "The rendering, 'but what I do desire is the releasing,' particularly the last word, is a gross imposition upon the principles of Greek exegesis because the untutored Russellites have rendered the first aorist active infinitive of the verb *analuoo* (*analusai*) as a substantive (the releasing), which in this context is unscholarly and atrocious Greek. In order to translate it 'the releasing' the form would have to be the participle construction (*analusas*)."[252] (Martin also shows that in 2 Timothy 4:6 the Witnesses accept the similar form of the same word as meaning "death," but they cannot do so in Philippians 1:23 for reasons of theological bias.)

13. Matthew 24:3. [The word "coming" is translated as "presence" to justify the "invisible presence" of Jesus since 1914.]

> ". . . . Tell us, when will these things be, and what will be the sign of your PRESENCE and of the conclusion of the system of these things?" NWT

> ". . . . Tell us, when will these things be, and what will be the sign of Your coming, and of the end of the age?" NAS

The Greek word *parousia*, according to its context, should be translated "coming." (It can be translated "presence," but context must determine which is correct.) As Martin points out:

> Jehovah's Witnesses claim scholarship for this blanket translation of *parousia*, yet not one great scholar in the history of Greek exegesis

and translation has ever held this view. Since 1871, when Pastor Russell produced this concept, upon examination, it has been denounced by every competent scholar. The reason this Russellite rendering is so dangerous is that it attempts to prove that *parousia*, in regard to Christ's second advent, really means that His return or "presence" was to be invisible and unknown to all but "the faithful" (Russellites, of course). . . . To conclude that presence necessarily implies invisibility is also another flaw in the Watchtower's argument, for in numerous places where they render parousia "presence," the persons spoken of were hardly invisible. (See 1 Corinthians 16:17; 2 Corinthians 7:6; and 10:10.)[253]

In the *New Thayer's Greek-English Lexicon* we find these comments under the word *parousia*: "In the N.T., esp. of the advent, i.e., the future, visible, return from heaven of Jesus, the Messiah, to raise the dead, hold the last judgment, and set up formally and gloriously the kingdom of God: Matthew 24:3."[254]

14. Over 200 verses: the translation of YHWH as "Jehovah." We can see biased translations even in the Witnesses' own term "Jehovah," which is so important to them as allegedly signifying the "true" name of God. The NWT adds "Jehovah" to the New Testament text over 200 times, in spite of the fact that "Jehovah" is not found anywhere in the Bible, New or Old Testament. WS claims that the New Testament originals were "tampered with," and that the tetragrammaton (YHWH) was surreptitiously removed, substituting *kurios* (Lord) and *theos* (God).

The truth is that YHWH never occurs in any New Testament Greek manuscript, and it occurs in only one Septuagint copy.[255] There is simply no evidence of tampering.[256] YHWH itself can be translated different ways, since the insertion of vowels is arbitrary. YHWH could have been Jehovah, or JiHiViH or JaHiVeH and so on. In other words, the translation of *kurios* and *theos* as JEHOVAH in the NWT (some 237 times) is a completely unjustified translation. We simply do not know the "true" name of God. Metzger observes: "The introduction of the word 'Jehovah' into the New Testament text, in spite of much in-

genuity in an argument filled with a considerable amount of irrelevant material (pp. 10–25), is a plain piece of special pleading."[257]

There is another reason for the WS use of "Jehovah" in place of "Lord"; it thereby denies the deity of Christ where the term "Lord" (applied to Jesus) connotes the meaning of Jehovah in the Old Testament. Often, when the New Testament refers to Christ as "Lord," it is associating Him with Jehovah in the Old Testament. The Watchtower Society has had to be inconsistent in its translation, translating *kurios* variously as "Jehovah" or "Lord" to suit their own theology. For example, if we look at KIT (p. 723) for Romans 10:11, *kurios* is translated "Lord," but in verse 13 the same word, which here clearly refers to Jesus, is now translated "Jehovah" rather than "Lord" or "Jesus." In both places the term "Lord" refers to Jesus and connotes His deity, but the NWT hides this by the translation of "Lord" in verse 11 and "Jehovah" in verse 13, implying that the entire section refers to Jehovah, but not to Jesus. Likewise, Philippians 2:10–11 clearly refers to Jesus and is based on Isaiah 45:22–25, referring to Jehovah (see Romans 14:9–11). If *kurios* were translated "Jehovah" in Philippians 2 it would mean that Jesus is identified with Jehovah, and the Watchtower Society could not permit such a translation. Hence, *kurios* is here translated "Lord," not Jehovah. Thus, it is only where *kurios* can be translated Jesus and simultaneously *not* imply His deity, that it is so translated.

15. Additional examples. We may note that Professor Gruss observes a number of other errors in WS translation.[258] In Matthew 24:6,14; 1 Peter 4:7; 2 Corinthians 11:15; Revelation 19:20 and elsewhere words are added that are not in the Greek. And despite the WS claim not to engage in paraphrasing, the NWT repeatedly paraphrases when Scripture refers to believers being "in Christ." *All* believers everywhere can be in Christ only if Jesus is God. But in the NWT the term "in" (Greek *en*), in "in Christ," is often mistranslated, such as as "in union with" (Christ) or something similar. The Witnesses then interpret this to mean a union of purpose rather than a spiritual union. Gruss comments:

"With the same Greek word being translated properly in every case except when it refers to the believer's personal relationship with Christ, it must be concluded that the translator's paraphrasing is nothing less than interpretation. One loses confidence in a translation which professes to be literal when it is replete with biased paraphrases."[259]

In Philippians 3:11 the Greek *exanastasis* (resurrection) is erroneously translated "earlier resurrection." And, in John 13:18; 17:12; 19:24,36, the exact same Greek words are translated four different ways. Robert H. Countess refers to additional mistranslations.[260]

In light of such examples our only conclusion is that the Watchtower Bible and Tract Society (WBTS) can hardly be concerned with accurately translating the New Testament.

So far we have referred to the New Testament portion of the *New World Translation*. What of the Old Testament? Although space does not permit illustrations, according to reviewers it is not much improved. British scholar H. H. Rowley asserts, "From beginning to end this volume is a shining example of how the Bible should not be translated. . . .", and he calls it "an insult to the Word of God."[261] Gruss points out that the WS translation of the Old Testament has the same basic purpose as that of the New, to justify preconceived Watchtower theology.[262]

We should emphasize again that our analysis of the *New World Translation* here is not a result of "biased trinitarian theology," as Witnesses are fond of claiming. If the scholars quoted above are biased, it is toward a respect for rules of grammar and divine revelation. A Christian should feel free to challenge a Witness by appealing to nonChristian authorities at this point. Any university Greek professor could be consulted for his view of the *New World Translation* at John 1:1, Matthew 25:46 and so on.

Since the Watchtower Society has failed the test of accurately translating the Bible, it cannot claim adherence to or a respect for divine revelation. Can it then possibly be a channel through which God has chosen to operate on earth?

Having established that the Watchtower society has produced an unconscionably biased translation of God's Word, we proceed to our second test: the prophetic record of the Watchtower Society.*

The Watchtower Society and Prophetic Speculation

Is it for God that you speak falsehood? (Job 13:7 NAS)

Must you go on "speaking for God" when he never once has said the things that you are putting in his mouth? (Job 13:7 TLB)

Will you speak wickedly on God's behalf? Will you speak deceitfully for him? Will you show him partiality? Will you argue the case for God? Would it turn out well if he examined you? Could you deceive him as you might deceive men? (Job 13:7-9 NIV)

By establishing the Watchtower Society's definition and view of prophecy, we will be able to establish whether the WS meets its own standards for prophetic fulfillment. *The Watchtower* of March 1, 1975 declares, "The Bible itself establishes the rules for testing a prophecy at Deuteronomy 18:20-22 and 13:1-8."[263] In Deuteronomy 18, the Bible states that prophets who presume, falsely, to speak in God's name that which He never commanded them to speak shall be put to death (18:20), and also that: If what a prophet proclaims in the name of the LORD does not take place or come true, that is a message the LORD has not spoken. That prophet has spoken presumptuously. Do not be afraid of him" (18:22). In Deuteronomy 13 we are warned that if a prophet does a miracle but tells people to follow false gods, he must be put to death, because he is a false prophet in spite of displaying a miracle. Although the historical contexts differ in the following verses, the principle remains. God Himself declares the prophet is "recognized as one truly sent by the LORD *only* if his prediction comes true" (Jeremiah 28:9, emphasis added), because "Whatever I say will be fulfilled,

---

*The authors express their gratitude to Professor Edmond Gruss of the Masters College for copies of early Watchtower Literature and for much of the data in this section. Many of the early books he cites can be difficult or impossible to locate.

declares the Sovereign LORD" (Ezekiel 12:28). The biblical standard is clear.

Note further that the Watchtower Society's *Aid to Bible Understanding* states that prophecy includes "a declaration of something to come," that "the source of all true prophecy is Jehovah God," and that "correct understanding of prophecy would still be made available by God . . . particularly in the foretold 'time of the end'"[264] (a reference to the Watchtower Society). A "prophet" is defined as "one through whom the divine will and purpose are made known," which reflect the claims of the Watchtower Society for itself.[265] Also, we are told that "the three essentials for establishing the credentials of the true prophet" are: 1) speaking in Jehovah's name; 2) that "the things foretold would come to pass"; 3) promoting true worship by being in harmony with God's already revealed word.[266] The true prophet "expressed God's mind on matters. . . . Every prediction related to God's will, purpose, standards or judgment."[267]

In light of these claims, the WS has little room in which to maneuver, for it claims to speak in the name of Jehovah, to be His prophet predicting future events, to predict those events accurately and to be in harmony with His Word. In the September 1, 1979, *Watchtower,* the Society declares that "for nearly 60 years now [since Rutherford's post-1918 era] the Jeremiah class have faithfully spoken forth Jehovah's Word."[268] Clearly, then, "the things foretold (would) come to pass." But have they? Not even once!

The Jehovah's Witnesses are confronted with an intractable problem here. Yet many fail to recognize the quandary. John Weldon remembers a three-hour discussion he and a friend had with two Jehovah's Witnesses, one of whom had the reputation of being one of their best apologists. The apologist was shown numerous false prophecies in *The Watchtower* magazine. It hardly seemed to bother him. He admitted, "There have been some errors in prophetic interpretation." While he was willing to accept "a few" genuine errors, he entirely ignored the implications. We have two points in response to this.

First, divine guidance is divine guidance. The Watchtower Society claims to be God's prophet and His *only* channel on earth for disseminating divine truth. This includes the "true interpreta-

tion" of the Bible and disclosing true and relevant prophetic information on a regular basis. Thus, based on the Society's own acceptance of biblical standards and its own claim for accuracy, one should expect an inerrant record. If the Watchtower is divinely guided in the manner it claims to be, inerrancy is the proof of their claims. Even "a few errors" nullify WS claims to genuine divine guidance. And if the Society leadership admits that it is incapable of accurately receiving or interpreting such guidance, this in effect nullifies the very claim, for guidance must be accurate if it is to have any value. Imagine the Pentagon informing Congress that a 25 billion-dollar missile tracking system is 100 percent accurate, but then informing Congress that they can give no assurance that military officers will be able to interpret the tracking accurately.

Second, we are not dealing here with "a few" or "some" errors of biblical prophecy. We are dealing with hundreds of prophetic errors. These have proliferated from the start of WS, and they continue to this day. This is why the issue of false prophecy ought to be so relevant to the average Witness, because it represents a *continual pervasive pattern* in Watchtower history, not just an exception "here and there" which blemishes an otherwise perfect record. In other words, as with their Bible translation, the Watchtower prophetic record is one of repeated failure, not even marginal success. It is this fact that the average witness must come to grips with.

Further, WS leadership knows the dismal record of failure. Former leader Raymond Franz wrote in *Crisis of Conscience:*

During the first twenty years or so of my active association with Jehovah's Witnesses, I had at most a hazy idea about any failures in past predictions and simply did not attach any great importance to them. . . . It was not until the late 1970s that I learned just how far the matter went. I learned it then, not from so-called "opposition literature," but from Watchtower publications themselves and from active and respected Witnesses, including members of the Governing Body of Jehovah's Witnesses.[269]

How can such a fact possibly be reconciled with *any* claim to divine guidance? Further, if

God had been guiding the Watchtower Society, and if they had been receiving this guidance accurately, then they have a much more serious problem than if they claimed no guidance, for God would obviously be neither omnipotent nor omniscient.

The key issue is this. If the Watchtower cannot be trusted in prophecy, if they have misperceived the "holy spirit's" guidance here, how can anyone be assured they have not misperceived "its" guidance elsewhere, as in doctrine? If they are fallible at one point, they are potentially fallible at any point. Given their penchant for biased translation and exegesis, deliberate cover-up of earlier errors and other dubious matters, one can argue that the WS should not be trusted in any area.

Claims to Divine Guidance

If we thoroughly document the pervasive nature of WS claims to divine guidance, the extent of prophetic failure will be highlighted beyond doubt. These claims are established by: 1) claims to prophethood; 2) claims to guidance from "Holy Spirit" or angels; 3) other direct claims.

1. Claims to prophethood. The Jehovah's Witnesses are collectively held to be a "prophet" of God and to receive divine guidance from Jehovah through the Watchtower Society and its publications. The WS, then, is the true prophet who distributes Jehovah's prophecies to the faithful for dissemination to others. Here are some examples from WS literature:

> *The Nations Shall Know that I Am Jehovah* (1971): [Jehovah's Witnesses] serve as the mouthpiece . . . of Jehovah [and . . .] speak as a prophet in the name of Jehovah. . . . (pp. 58–59)

> *The Watchtower,* November 1, 1956: Who controls the organization, who directs it? . . . the living God Jehovah. (p. 666)

> *The Watchtower,* April 1, 1972: These questions can be answered in the affirmative. Who is this prophet? . . . This "prophet" was not one man, but was a body of men and women. It was the small group of footstep followers of Jesus Christ, known at that time as International Bible Students. Today they are known as Jehovah's Christian witnesses. . . . Of course, it is easy to say that this group acts as a "prophet" of God. It

is another thing to prove it. The only way that this can be done is to review the record. What does it show? (p. 197)

> Jehovah is interested not only in the vindication of his own name but also in vindicating his "prophet." (p. 200)

The book *Holy Spirit* declares that the Witnesses have been "prophesying from house to house" and "prophesying to all the nations."[270]

2. Claims to guidance by Holy Spirit or angels. This has already been established. The WS receives guidance from Jehovah and Jesus through "angels." In *The Watchtower* April 1, 1972 we read: "This would indicate that Jehovah's witnesses today make their declaration of the good news of the Kingdom under angelic direction and support (Revelation 14:6, 7; Matthew 25:31, 32). "And since no word or work of Jehovah can fail, for he is God Almighty, the nations will see the fulfillment of what these witnesses say as directed from heaven" (p. 200). *The Watchtower* of July 1, 1973 states: "Jehovah's organization alone, in all the earth, is directed by God's holy spirit or active force. . . . To it alone God's Sacred Word, the Bible, is not a sealed book" (p. 402).

3. Other direct claims to divine guidance. Judge Rutherford implied that his books and the Watchtower publications were "the word of God" (*The Watchtower,* April 1, 1932). Other WS publications from that era state:

> *The Watchtower,* December 1, 1933: No man is given credit for the wonderful truths which the Lord has revealed to his people through the Watch Tower publications. (p. 263)

> *The 1934, 1935 and 1936* Yearbooks respectively: All credit and honor are due to the Lord for what appears in the Watchtower. (p. 69)

> It is announced with confidence that the Lord uses the columns of the Watchtower to transmit to his consecrated people things that he reveals to them and provides for them to know. It is the privilege of the Watchtower to publish explanation of the prophecies. . . . There is no attempt on the part of the Watchtower to interpret prophecy, for the reason that no human creature can interpret prophecy. (p. 52)

No human creature is entitled to any credit for what appears in the Watchtower. (p. 63)

The Watchtower February 1, 1938, Vol. LIX, No. 3: All this information came not from or by man, but by the Lord God. (p. 35)

The Watchtower January 1, 1942: Those who are convinced that the Watchtower is publishing the opinion or expression of a man should not waste time looking at it at all. (p. 5)

The Watchtower of April 15, 1943: *The Watchtower* is a magazine without equal in the earth. . . . The getting of correct information and instruction, just such as is required for the times. . . was never more vital than now. . . . This is not giving any credit to the magazine's publishers, but is due to the great Author of the Bible with its truths and prophecies, and who now interprets its prophecies. (p. 129)

Judge Rutherford authored every Jehovah's Witness book from 1926 to 1942 and supervised virtually everything that went into *The Watchtower* magazine. The claims here are clear: Rutherford received divine inspiration-revelation and it is impossible to understand any biblical passage unless one was reading one of Rutherford's books that explained it, which is precisely the claim of the Watchtower Society today with its literature.

The 1950 edition of the *New World Translation of the Christian Greek Scriptures* carried an advertisement on page 793 for *The Watchtower Magazine,* where it was declared to be "a dependable Bible study aid," and that "since 1879 . . . the Watchtower has consistently proved itself dependable." With all these claims, and many more, can anyone logically doubt that if they are true then the WS must have a virtually perfect prophetic record.*

The following cases represent only a sampling; the actual number of false prophecies is far greater. Unless otherwise noted, all statements are taken from *The Watchtower.* We should remember that the average Jehovah's

Witness does not look forward to the Second Coming of Christ, since according to the WS this has already occurred, but they look forward to the Battle of Armageddon, which will end with the new millennium. Hence most prophecies deal with the coming battle of Armageddon.

Prophetic Failures

The Failure of the 1914 prediction. Jehovah's Witnesses repeatedly prophesied 1914 as the year to mark the end of the battle of Armageddon and the beginning of the millennial reign. As early as 1877, warnings were being given of the imminent end of the world:

1877—THE END OF THIS WORLD . . . is nearer than most men suppose.[272]

1889—In subsequent chapters we present proofs that the setting up of the Kingdom of God is already begun. . . . And that the "battle of the great day of God Almighty" (Revelations 16:14), which will end in a.d. 1914 with the complete overthrow of earth's present rulership, is already commenced.[273] [The 1915 edition of this book changed "A.D. 1914" to "A.D. 1915."]

July 15, 1894—We see no reason for changing the futures—nor could we change them if we would. *They are, we believe, God's dates, not ours.* But bear in mind that the end of 1914 is not the date for the *beginning,* but for the *end* of the time of trouble. We see no reason for changing from our opinion expressed in the view presented in the WATCH TOWER of January 15, '92. We advise that it be read again. [First emphasis added.][274]

1904—The stress of the great time of trouble will be on us soon, somewhere between 1910 and 1912—culminating with the end of the "Times of the Gentiles," October, 1914.[275]

May 1, 1914—There is absolutely no ground for Bible students to question that the consummation of this Gospel age is now even at the door. . . . The great crisis . . . that will consume the ecclesiastical heavens and the social earth, is very near.[276]

The year 1914 ended without a single prediction of Russell's coming true.[277] Before we comment further, let us also note that Russell did not predict a *spiritual* fulfillment in 1914, as modern

---

*When Russell or Rutherford expressed such sentiments as "we have never claimed inspiration or prophetic vision,"[271] they were self-deceived, engaging in rationalization or lying, because as we just saw, this is exactly what they expressed in different terminology.

Jehovah's Witnesses claim; that is, he did not predict that Jesus would set up his Kingdom in *heaven.* Russell predicted a physical kingdom on earth. But modern Jehovah's Witnesses have denied that the original prediction was earthly. Speaking of Jehovah's Witnesses in 1880, modern Witnesses claim that the earlier Witnesses predicted a heavenly kingdom: "In the 'Watchtower' magazine of March, 1880, they said: 'The Times of the Gentiles extend to 1914, and the heavenly kingdom will not have full sway till then.' Of all people, only the witnesses pointed to 1914 as the year for God's kingdom to be fully set up in heaven."[278] But let us go back to the March, 1880, *Zion's Watch Tower* (the original name of *The Watchtower* magazine), where we find the original prophecy, which is only quoted in part above. *Zion's Watch Tower* for March 1880 carries the full quote. In the Reprint Index, this very article is included under the title "*earthly* kingdom" (p. 6569). The original material clearly referred to an earthly, not a heavenly, rule:

> The "Times of the Gentiles" extend to 1914, and the heavenly kingdom will not have full sway till then, but as a "Stone" the kingdom of God is set up "*in the days* of these (ten gentile) kings," and by consumating [sic] them it becomes a universal kingdom—a "great mountain and fills the whole Earth."[279]

For Russell, "the heavenly kingdom" "fills the whole *Earth.*" Further, Russell's third volume of *Studies in the Scriptures* (1891) declared that there would exist "the full establishment of the Kingdom of God *in the earth* at A.D. 1914."[280] In another book published in 1899 he stated that he would "prove that *before that date* [1914; emphasis his] God's Kingdom, organized in power, will be *in the earth,*" and that before the end of 1914: a) the last member of the church of Christ would be glorified; b) Jerusalem and Israel would be restored to divine favor; c) there would be "a worldwide reign of anarchy"; d) the Kingdom of the world would be destroyed.[281] By the end of 1914, none of these predictions came true.

Like false prophets generally, Russell was undaunted. The April 1, 1915 issue of *Zion's Watch Tower*[282] referred to the faithful taking

"the Bible view of the Great Armageddon, of which we are now having the prelude," and "the battle of Armageddon to which this war [World War I] is leading." In the September 1, 1916 issue he continued to hope: "We see no reason for doubting, therefore, that the Times of the Gentiles ended in October, 1914; and that a few more years will witness their utter collapse and the full establishment of God's kingdom in the hands of Messiah."[283] This prophecy (the "few more years") also failed. Gruss further points out that the WS is incorrect in claiming that Russell at least predicted World War I.[284] To the contrary, Russell only confirmed his own status as a false prophet. Listen to Russell's own words eight years prior in *The Watchtower* of October 1, 1907:[285]

> But let us suppose a case far from our expectations.... Suppose that A.D. 1915 should pass with the world's affairs all serene and with evidence that the "very elect" had not been "changed" and without the restoration of natural Israel to favor under the New Covenant (Romans 11:12, 15). What then? Would not that prove a keen disappointment? Indeed it would! It would work irreparable wreck to the parallel dispensations and Israel's trouble, and to the Jubilee calculations, and to the prophecy of the 2300 days of Daniel, and to the epoch called "Gentile Times," and to the 1,260, 1,290 and 1,335 days.... None of these would be available longer.... What a blow that would be.[286]

As we will note, the Watchtower Society's eventual response was to either change the dates or to admit human error, but not to admit false prophecy.

When the 1914 events did not occur, they were rescheduled for 1918–1925. When they did not occur in 1918–1925, the WS again changed or deleted the dates in its literature.[287] In the 1917 edition of *The Finished Mystery* (claimed to be the posthumous work of Russell and Volume 7 of his *Studies in the Scriptures*),[288] Armageddon was to begin in "the Spring of 1918" (p. 62). There was to be "worldwide all-embracing anarchy" in the "fall of 1920" (p. 542; the 1926 ed. reads "in the end of the time of trouble"). Likewise the 1917 edition asserts that Revelation 11:13 would be fulfilled "early in 1918" (the "earthquake") and in "the fall of 1920" (the fire, p. 178). The 1926 edition is again altered.[289]

After Russell's death, Rutherford continued and expanded this tradition of making false prophecies and covering up their failures. He believed that 1925 would mark the year of Christ's Kingdom. He was wrong.[290] *The Watchtower* of September 1, 1922 (page 262) stated, "The date 1925 is even more distinctly indicated by the Scriptures because it is fixed by the law of God to Israel. . . . [One can see how] even before 1925 the great crisis would be reached and probably passed." *The Watchtower* of April 1, 1923 (page 106) stated, "Our thought is that 1925 is definitely settled by the Scriptures." But what happened when 1925 arrived? *The Watchtower* of January 1, 1925 was less certain: "The year 1925 is here. With great expectation Christians have looked forward to this year. Many have confidently expected that all members of the body of Christ will be changed to heavenly glory during the year. This may be accomplished. It may not be."[291]

What happened near the end of 1925? In the September, 1925 *Watchtower,* we find the importance of 1925 being denied: "It is to be expected that Satan will try to inject into the minds of the consecrated the thought that 1925 should see an end of the work, and that therefore it would be needless for them to do more."[292] After all the divinely inspired WS promises for 1925, all of a sudden Satan, not God, becomes the one prophesying. Rutherford noted in 1931:

> There was a measure of disappointment on the part of Jehovah's faithful ones on earth concerning the years 1914, 1918 and 1925, which disappointment lasted for a time. Later the faithful learned that these dates were definitely fixed in the Scriptures [concerning other matters]; and they also learned to quit fixing dates for the future and predicting what would come to pass on certain dates, but to rely (and they do rely) upon the Word of God as to the events that must come to pass.[293]

Jehovah's Witnesses apparently stopped date-setting, at least for about 40 years, but they continued to hold out the promise of the immanency of Armageddon and the subsequent Kingdom. Again, the Witness looks forward to the Battle of Armageddon in the same manner that the Christian looks forward to the Second Coming of Christ, because both usher in the New World. From 1930 to 1939 there were numerous predictions:

> 1930—The great climax is at hand.[294]

> 1931—God's Kingdom has begun to operate. His day of vengeance is here and Armageddon is at hand.[295]

> 1933—The overwhelming testimony of the prophecy and of the supporting facts shows that the cleansing of the sanctuary has been accomplished and this indicates that Armageddon draws nigh.[296]

In a "Testimony to the Rulers of the World," Rutherford stated:

> That Satan's lease of power is done, that the old world has ended, and that the time is at hand when Christ Jesus . . . will oust Satan the [wicked] one and begin His righteous government which will establish God's will on earth. . . . Evil forces are gathering the whole world unto the great battle of the Lord God Almighty; that there is now impending a time of trouble such as the world has never known.[297]

> 1939—The battle of the great day of God Almighty is very near.[298]

We have in our files 44 predictions, from May, 1940 to April 15, 1943, of the immanence of Armageddon, variously phrased. We list only the briefest data here. All but two are quotations from *The Watchtower.* Some are qualified by "all the facts now indicate," "strongly indicates," "suggests" and such like, but the overall message is undeniable:

> May 1940—Armageddon is very near (May 1940, *Informant,* p. 1).

> September 1940—The Kingdom is here, the King is enthroned. Armageddon is just ahead. . . . The great climax has been reached (September 1940, *The Messenger,* p. 6).

> January 1, 1941—Armageddon is very near (p. 11).

> May 15, 1941—The time is short now till the universal war of Armageddon (p. 159).

August 1, 1941—Armageddon, which is near (p. 235).

September 15, 1941—The FINAL END IS VERY NEAR (p. 276; cf. p. 287).

October 15, 1941—The battle of Armageddon is quite near (p. 319).

November 1, 1941—Armageddon is very near (p. 325).

January 15, 1942—The time is at hand for Jesus Christ to take possession of all things (p. 28).

February 1, 1942—The time is short (p. 45; cf. p. 39).

March 1, 1942—The "end of the world" at Armageddon, now near (p. 74; cf. p. 69).

May 1, 1942—Now, with Armageddon immediately before us (p. 139).

May 15, 1942—All such are the sure signs of the FINAL END (p. 157).

June 15, 1942—The glorious day of the triumph of Jehovah's THEOCRACY . . . is at hand (p. 188).

July 15, 1942—Armageddon, which final battle is very near (p. 224).

August 15, 1942—The impending battle of Armageddon (p. 243; cf. p. 253).

April 15, 1943—The impending cataclysm of Armageddon (p. 126).

May 1, 1943—The final end of all things . . . is at hand (p. 139).

August 15, 1943—The battle of Armageddon cannot be sidetracked; all nations are remorsely marching nearer and nearer to it (p. 252).

September 1, 1944—Armageddon is near at hand (p. 264).

Even after World War II had ended, in 1946 we read, "The disaster of Armageddon . . . is at the door."[299] And the period of 1950 to 1980 is full of "announcements" similar to what we have just quoted. Numerous books and *The Watchtower* have continued what Gruss labels "the illusion of urgency." Several from the 1950s are typical:

1950—The March is on! Where? To the field of Armageddon for the "war of the great day of God the Almighty."[300]

1953—Armageddon is so near at hand it will strike the generation now living.[301] The year 1954 was thought by many Witnesses to be "the Year."[302]

1955—It is becoming clear that the war of Armageddon is near its breaking-out point.[303]

1958—When will Armageddon be fought? Jehovah the great Timekeeper has scheduled Armageddon to come at the close of the "time of the end." That time is near. How near? . . . No man knows that date, but we do know it will be very soon. How do we know it is soon? Because the time left for the Devil, now that Christ has hurled the Devil down to the earth, is called "a short period of time" (Revelation 12:12). The time left for the Devil's world is now very short.[304]

The long march of the world powers is nearing its end. World-shattering events are just before us. Jehovah's history written in advance makes certain of this to us [sic].[305]

The October 8, 1968, *Awake* (page 23), stated that "certain persons" had previously *falsely* predicted the end of the world, and that what they lacked was God's guidance! It even said that "they were guilty of false prophesying." But now, supposedly, this false prophesying is over:

True, there have been those in times past who predicted an "end to the world," even announcing a specific date. Some have gathered groups of people with them and fled to the hills or withdrawn into their houses waiting for the end. Yet, nothing happened. The "end" did not come. *They were guilty of false prophesying.* Why? What was missing? Missing was the full measure of evidence required in fulfillment of Bible prophecy. *Missing from such people were God's truths and the evidence that he was guiding and using them.* But what about today? Today we have the evidence required, all of it. And it is overwhelming! [Emphasis added.]

Here the Watchtower Society admits to false prophecy, explaining it as a lack of God's guidance. But they next claim that the situation is far different now, because they have "all the evidence" that God is guiding them, and "it is overwhelming." The stage had been set for the 1975 prophecy of Armageddon. In 1973 we read, "The day when the unparalleled 'great tribulation' breaks upon . . . Christendom, is very near. . . . There is no reason for us to be uncertain with regard to the period of time in which we are living."[306]

Prior to 1975, Jehovah's Witnesses were once again led to believe in date-setting for the year 1975, in spite of the fact that in 1963 they were told that "it does no good to use Bible chronology for speculating on dates that are still future."[307] Edmond Gruss' devastating exposé, *Jehovah's Witnesses and Prophetic Speculation*, published in 1972, stated: "In the mind of the average Witness there is little or no doubt that the [1975] date is correct. This conclusion was drawn by the writer from his conversations with individual Jehovah's Witnesses. The same impression was reported by Ruth Brandon in her article, 'Jehovah 1975: For the Witness', there's no question of "if." Armageddon *will* happen in 1975, if not earlier.'"[308]

Why did the WS return to date setting? Because they had no choice. Their own (again false) chronology demanded it. The Witnesses had taught that Armageddon must precede the 1,000 year reign of Christ, and their chronology taught that there was a literal 6,000 years of human history prior to this. Thus, when they declared that the 6,000 years was to end in 1975, Armageddon had to occur before or in 1975. In the following quote (made in 1966) they stated that the year of the Jubilee would parallel the seventh millennium and begin in 1975:

> God's own written Word indicates it is the appointed time for it [the Jubilee year, i.e., the millennium]. . . . According to this trustworthy Bible chronology six thousand years from man's creation will end in 1975, and the seventh period of a thousand years of human history will begin in the fall of 1975 C.E. . . . How appropriate it would be for Jehovah God to make of this coming seventh period of a thousand years a sabbath period of rest and release, a great Jubilee sabbath. . . . It would not be by mere chance of accident but would be according to the loving purpose of Jehovah God for the reign of Jesus Christ, the "Lord of the sabbath," to run parallel with the seventh millennium of man's existence. . . . The blessed time for its introduction is fast approaching. . . . The long-awaited time for this is at hand![309]

Thus there can be no doubt that for Jehovah's Witnesses 1975 was to be "the Year." In 1975, as if there were no possibility of failure, the Society states: "The fulfillment . . . is immediately ahead of us."[310] "Unequaled world distress lies just ahead of us."[311] And that there is "Lifesaving work . . . [which] yet remains to be done before the current world distress reaches it culmination in the 'great tribulation.'"[312] The October 1, 1975 issue (p. 94) referred to "the approaching great tribulation." Despite the additional failure, *The Watchtower* continued its emphasis on Armageddon. The September 22, 1976 issue (p. 31), declared "a global disaster, unparalleled in human history, is very near."

The mid-late 1970s had article titles such as the following, which were emphasized on the front cover of *The Watchtower:*

March 15, 1976—Reconciliation Through God's Mercy Before Har-Magedon.

December 15, 1976—Hold on—the Promise Nears Fulfillment.

March 1, 1978—Our Incoming World Government—God's Kingdom.

June 15, 1979—A Day of Reckoning at Hand.

November 1, 1979—Christian Neutrality as God's War Approaches.

October 15, 1979—Take Courage the Millennium is at Hand.

The 1980s and 1990s have shown no WS repentance in this area; in fact, they have continued these deceptive practices and false prophecies.

We have now listed a reasonable number of statements showing that the Watchtower Society, since its beginnings, has been claiming an immanent end to the world. The issue is simple. If the Watchtower Society has been indisputably *wrong* in every era it has been prophesying, how can it possibly be trusted by modern Jehovah's Witnesses in their own era? How can their prophetic statements be true, accurate and genuinely reflect God's guidance of the Watchtower when they are proved false by the calendar? Calendars have no bias against the WS! Would any employer in his right mind hire a criminal for the tenth time after nine repeated jailings for offenses against the employer? How can that Society possibly claim to be the "faithful, reliable, trustworthy" servant of God?[313] Read these 1975 Watchtower Society statements carefully:

A new and better world is at hand. . . . There is no room for doubt about this. . . . [Jehovah's Witnesses] unswerving attention to such inspired prophecy has held them true to the right course till now. And now the new day is dawning and the daystar has risen, and their eyes are blessed with seeing the modern-day fulfillment of Bible prophecy.[314]

Over the endorsement of God's own name the grand things to come—soon—stand fully guaranteed in prophecies of his indestructible Word.[315]

The same book even claims of Armageddon that "Jehovah has his own *fixed* date for its arrival."[316] How can "Jehovah God" possibly have been guiding the Watchtower Society for over 100 years when He has His "own fixed date for its arrival"? Clearly, either God has changed His mind from generation to generation, or fallible or corrupt men who have *never* received divine guidance have been directing the Watchtower for the last century.

With all due respect, what can one say of Witnesses who know all this and yet continue to believe in the Watchtower Society as God's true prophet? As Proverbs notes, "Wisdom is too high for a fool . . ." (Proverbs 24:7). Yet Witnesses are the very ones who assert, "Christians holding to true prophecy do not follow . . . false teachers."[317] Naturally. Then why do Witnesses follow the Watchtower Society?

What makes things worse is that individual Witnesses are pressured to deny the existence of false prophecy because to admit to their existence might lead to the consequences of disfellowship, which makes one worthy of death and eternal annihilation. As Gruss documents, citing court records, a facade of unity is far more important to the Society than any concern with truth.[318] The following brief excerpt is taken from the Pursuer's Proof of a trial held in the Scottish Court of Sessions, November 1954. Microfilm copies are available from The Scottish Records Office, H.M. General Register House,

Edinburgh, Scotland. Ask for *The Pursuer's Proof* of Douglas Walsh vs. The Right Honorable James Latham Clyde, M.P., P.C., as representing the Minister of Labour and National Service. The pages in question are numbers 340–343. Haydon C. Covington (who is interviewed here by James Latham Clyde) was the Watchtower's legal counsel and its former Vice-President:

Q. Back to the point now. A false prophecy was promulgated?

A. I agree to that.

Q. It had to be accepted by Jehovah's Witnesses?

A. That is correct. . . .

Q. Unity at all costs?

A. Unity at all costs, because we believe and are sure that Jehovah God is using our organization, the governing body of our organization to direct it, even though mistakes are made from time to time.

Q. And unity based upon an enforced acceptance of false prophecy?

A. That is conceded to be true.

Q. And the person who expressed his view, as you say, that it was wrong, and was disfellowshipped, would be in breach of the Covenant, if he was baptized?

A. That is correct.

Q. And as you said yesterday expressly, would be worthy of death?

A. I think—

Q. Would you say yes or no?

A. I will answer yes, unhesitatingly.[319]

Does the Watchtower Admit to False Prophecy?

Despite its continuous claims to divine guidance, the WS now admits some failures; it could do little else given all the advance publication for 1874, 1914, 1925 and 1975. As we saw, even Rutherford, in his book *Vindication*, confessed, "There was a measurement of disappointment on the part of Jehovah's faithful ones on earth concerning the years 1914, 1918 and 1925 . . ."[320]

Any member who knows that the WS has publicly confessed to false prophecies should immediately recognize that the Society is not guided by God and leave. Nowhere in the Bible do we find God claiming that a prophet might misinterpret Him or that His prophecies may not accurately be received. Nowhere in the Bible do we find a prophet of God having to explain why his prophecies failed. In the following material, we will document that the WS has admitted its errors.

1) In *Man's Salvation* (1975) the WS admits that Russell was wrong in his 1874 prediction of Christ's second coming.[321] (According to *Studies in the Scriptures*,[322] Russell claimed "Our Lord, the appointed King, is now present, since October 1874, A.D.")

2) The WS admitted that it was wrong in the 1914 prediction. The Grieshabers quote the Watchtower publication *Light* (Book One), undated (page 194), as confessing that they were wrong for 40 years in their 1914 prophecy:

> The Watch Tower, and its companion publications of the Society, for forty years emphasized the fact that 1914 would witness the establishment of God's kingdom and the complete glorification of the church. . . . All of the Lord's people looked forward to 1914 with joyful expectation. When that time came and passed there was much disappointment, chagrin and mourning, and the Lord's people were greatly in reproach. They were ridiculed by the clergy and their allies in particular, and pointed to with scorn, because they had said so much about 1914, and what would come to pass, and their 'prophecies' had not been fulfilled.[323]

> True, the Bible students were not "taken home" to heaven in October 1914. But the 2,520-year-long Gentile Times then ended.[324]

3) The WS admitted that it was wrong in 1925. As the start of the new millennium, 1925 was to mark the resurrection of the prophets of old for ruling in the millennial age. "Therefore we may confidently expect that 1925 will mark the return of Abraham, Isaac, Jacob and the faithful prophets of old."[325] Yet the 1975 Witness *Yearbook* confesses that it was, in effect, wrong in the 1925 prophecy, also rationalizing its failure:

> Jehovah certainly blessed his people back in the 1920's and provided the things they needed to advance the interests of the Kingdom. He also

proved himself to be a God of progressive revelation. The Bible Students, in turn, found it necessary to adjust their thinking to some extent. . . . God's people had to adjust their thinking about 1925, for instance . . . 1925 was a sad year for many brothers. Some of them were stumbled; their hopes were dashed. They had hoped to see some of the "ancient worthies" [men of old like Abraham] resurrected. Instead of its being considered a "probability," they read into it that it was a "certainty" and some prepared for their own loved ones with expectancy of their resurrection.[326]

Does the earlier quote, stating "we may confidently expect" 1925 to be "the year" sound like a "probability"? Clearly, the date was fixed.

The *1980 Yearbook* (pp. 30–31) declares of 1925: "The brothers also appreciated the candor of this same talk, which acknowledged the Society's responsibility for some of the disappointment a number felt regarding 1925." Gruss, in *Apostles of Denial* (p. 26), and others have given further data concerning the certainty of the 1925 date. The WS also admitted to false prophecy in the October 8, 1968, *Awake* magazine. And they admitted that they were wrong in 1975. In what must be one of the great understatements of the twentieth century, the Society's *1975 Yearbook* explains: "If for any reason the Lord has permitted us to miscalculate the prophecies, the signs of the times assure us that the miscalculations cannot be very great. . . . Jehovah certainly had not forsaken his people or allowed them to be misled."[327] Unbelievably, the same text asserts that "Jehovah's servants" for over 100 years "enjoyed spiritual enlightenment and divine direction" (p. 245).

Did they? Has the Watchtower Society passed the second "test," of having their prophecies "come to pass"? Since biblical standards are the admitted WS standard for judging prophetic accuracy, we can but cite it once more. The prophet is "recognized as one truly sent by the Lord *only* if his prediction comes true" (Jeremiah 28:9).

Changes in Divine Revelation

Another test concerns the immutability of divine revelation. An immutable God who faithfully guides the Watchtower Society would, by definition, not repeatedly change His mind on numerous important issues.

Granted, the Jehovah's Witnesses teaching on progressive revelation does allow for new information to be brought to light. The Bible itself is an example of progressive revelation. For example, there is fuller information in the New Testament on matters only hinted at, or summarily mentioned, in the Old Testament. However, biblically, progressive revelation never contradicts, denies or changes earlier revelation. Yet this is exactly what we find in the Watchtower and it raises the question: how can a God who repeatedly changes His word be trusted? Further, if the Watchtower has changed its mind before, how do we know that what members have complete faith in today will not be changed by the WS tomorrow? Indeed, a number of former Witnesses have cited this quandary as one reason for their leaving the organization. Gruss recounts an incident and then comments on it:

A short time later the Society changed the meaning of a Bible passage for the second time (Romans 13:1, 2). This was the final straw!... It was then that I started searching through the back issues of The Watchtower. I found many more discrepancies, contradictions, and changes of interpretation.[328]

Considering the changes in doctrinal matters and the errors in prophetic speculation over the years, it is difficult, if not impossible to believe that this organization is the sole recipient of, or is guided at all by God's Holy Spirit.[329]

How big is the problem? Gruss asserts that "*thousands* of reinterpretations of Scripture and many new doctrinal points have evolved since Russell's death," and he provides a number of examples in his book.[330] Van Baalen observes that W. J. Schnell reports, "As a progressive light worshipper and Jehovah's Witness in good standing, I had observed the *Watchtower* magazine change our doctrines between 1917 and 1928, no less than 148 times."[331] An example can be seen at Luke 16:19–31, where Jesus discusses the reality of hell. This has been interpreted by the Society in at least five different ways. These are not minor changes but major reinterpretations.[332] These changes took place in:

1908 during the Russell-White debate

1928 in Rutherford's *Reconciliation* (pp. 175, 176)

1942 in *The New World* (pp. 360–361)

1946 in *Let God Be True* (1st ed., p. 79)

1952 in *Let God Be True* (revised, p. 98)

The WS claims that God has always guided WS leadership to give its people the true interpretation of the Bible "in due time." How does God change His mind so easily on thousands of occasions? If the dismal record of the WS is our guide, how is it possible to know what the true interpretation of *any* biblical passage is?

Another example is their history text, *Jehovah's Witnesses in the Divine Purpose* (1959), which "rewrites the history and the facts in many places, and authority for almost every statement is from Watchtower sources. Many views held in the early years of the movement are either reinterpreted or not mentioned.... This history is full of inaccuracies...."[333] Gruss provides 17 examples of rewriting the facts, distortions, biased reporting and unjustified changes in the Watchtower Society's own history and doctrines.[334] All this was done under "God's guidance and direction"! Gruss concludes: "The speculations which have been presented are only a small example of what can be found in a limited area. It should be remembered that this speculation was presented with definiteness, as reasonable and as Scriptural."[335]

The faithful and wise servant. A crucial example worth noting of change in WS doctrine involves the "faithful and wise servant" in Matthew 24:45. The average Jehovah's Witness today believes that the "faithful and wise servant" refers to a servant class of people, the "144,000 elect," particularly the ones living at Watchtower headquarters in Bethel, who dispense the true food of God (properly interpreting His Word and will) to over 10 million Jehovah's Witnesses. Truth comes from God only by means of "the faithful and wise servant," now believed to be this class of people.[336] Yet the Watchtower Society claims that C. T. Russell never claimed to be "that servant." "From this it is clearly seen that the editor and publisher of

Zion's Watch Tower disavowed any claim to being individually, in his person, that 'faithful and wise servant.' He never did claim to be such."[337]

True, as a young man, Russell claimed that he was not that servant, but under "divine guidance" he later changed his mind and taught he was that servant. Now, if God's truth is said to come *only* from this servant, if it were Russell, then God's channel was permanently terminated with his death, since Russell never changed his mind about his status or appointed a successor. Further, since the WS has altered or denied so many of Russell's earlier "divinely guided" teachings, the Society must be guilty of altering God's personal revelation of His will for His people.

When Judge Rutherford entered the picture, he had his own ideas besides those of Russell. He changed Russell's teaching to apply the "faithful and wise servant" to a group of people, to those whom he headed, presumably to justify his own divine authority and guidance. This new teaching ("that servant" being a class of people rather than a person, Russell) caused a serious rift in the membership: numerous splinter groups arose who claimed allegiance (and still do) to Russell alone as God's channel of truth. Today, the Layman's Home Missionary Movement strongly opposes the Watchtower Society where it has altered Russell's teachings; it believes Russell to be "the servant" of Matthew 24. This movement was begun by Paul Johnson, who, believing himself to be Russell's successor, wrote the 17 volume *Epiphany Studies in the Scriptures*. In Volume 4, *Merariism:*

> Johnson . . . gives numerous additional examples of changes in doctrine and interpretation. He lists 140 contradictions where Rutherford violates Russell's teaching on pages 373–376, and then comments: "If we would point out the details coming under point (62) above—'Misrepresenting thousands of verses properly interpreted by "that Servant" [Russell]'—our list would swell into thousands of details; for almost never does he allude to or quote a passage in an article on his pet views but he corrupts its sense" (p. 377).[338]

The Dawn Bible Students Association is a similar group that originated as Rutherford

began to alter Russell's teachings. (Jehovah's Witnesses splinter groups generally have the same basic doctrine, since all are essentially Russellite. The division is over the changes instituted by Rutherford.)[339]

If Russell was "that servant," such a role ended with his death, and the Watchtower Society pronouncements from the beginning that contradict him are merely those of deceived men without divine guidance. If Russell was not "that servant," he was in grave error concerning his own divine mission and unlikely to be trustworthy on other matters. Either way, the WS loses. Rival sects, of course, argue that the data strongly affirm that divine revelation ended with Russell. "If Pastor Russell were 'that servant,' then his death would stop all subsequent revelations and the Society's publications would only be a rehash of what Russell taught. So with the establishing of 'the faithful and wise servant' as a class, the Society has left the door open to create or abolish doctrine and policy at will, and without question!"[340]

What did Russell himself teach? The rival sects are correct here. Russell, as early as 1896, wrote that "that servant" was an individual and that he was "that servant."[341] *The Watchtower* of December 1, 1916 (pp. 356–357; reprints, p. 5998) agreed: "Thousands of the readers of Pastor Russell's writings believe that he filled the office of 'that faithful and wise servant,' and that his great work was giving to the household of faith meat in due season [proper Bible interpretation]. His modesty and humility precluded him from openly claiming this title, but he admitted as much in private conversation."[342]

Even Rutherford admitted in *The Watchtower* (March 1, 1917, p. 67): "The Watchtower unhesitatingly proclaims Brother Russell as 'that faithful and wise servant.'" *The Watchtower* (December 15, 1916; Reprints, p. 6024) stated of Russell (for example, his *Studies in the Scriptures*), "To disregard the message would mean to disregard the Lord." *The Watchtower* (December 15, 1918, p. 396) also stated the belief in Russell as "that servant": "This we most certainly hold, both as a fact and as a necessity of faith." Duane Magnani's study, *Who Is the Faithful and Wise Servant?* from which this material was taken, concludes: "Russell never believed another person held this special position of 'That Servant.' Neither did he rebuke his followers for referring to him as this Servant. The record plainly shows that Charles Taze Russell BELIEVED AND TAUGHT that he alone was the Faithful and Wise Servant. . . . [Yet] the present day Society rejects his claims of spiritual authority."[343]

So one reason the modern Watchtower Society rejects many of Russell's teachings is because his claims, having divine sanction, *deny their own authority.* Yet without Russell's authority, they would not even exist. The WS alteration has been so complete that ordinary Jehovah's Witnesses today will deny that they are Russellites.[344] Not surprisingly, the Watchtower Society does not sell Russell's *Studies in the Scriptures,* and it has not for many years; they can be purchased only from Russellite sects.

But there could be another reason for the WS to de-emphasize Russell. As a false prophet who lied under oath and was unqualified as a Bible teacher, he was one more embarrassment. All this and more is public record concerning Russell.[345] This may explain why Rutherford apparently attempted a "theocratic coup," wherein Russell and the problems associated with him could be eliminated and Rutherford himself could start fresh as "God's new channel." Thus, Rutherford changed a number of things. He instituted the name "Jehovah's Witnesses"—a reflection of his shifting the emphasis from Russell's theology on Christ's atonement to the vindication of Jehovah's name. Rutherford may have felt that Russell had not sufficiently vindicated Jehovah's name. Rutherford also claimed that only with him was divine light now being shed upon certain books. His characteristic approach is typified when in 1931 he said of Ezekiel: "During the centuries that prophecy has been a mystery sealed to all who have sought to unlock it. God's due time has come for the prophecy to be understood."[346] Likewise he said that Daniel could not be understood until post-1918, when it was "revealed" that the League of Nations was the abomination of desolation.[347] Russell, however, had already written some 200 pages on Ezekiel in *The Finished Mystery* (1917). This was now discarded, because it did not fit the new teachings of the Watchtower Society; that is,

Rutherford's interpretations. Of course, Rutherford could not dispense with Russell entirely, for he was still the founder and head.

According to Gruss, Rutherford, in his 1929 book, *Prophecy,* began a dual-era interpretation of Watchtower history based on the Elijah-Elisha partnership in the Old Testament. Russell was Elijah, Rutherford was Elisha. The "Elijah era" was that time wherein God was restoring basic truths to his people (through Russell). This ended in 1918, only two years after Russell's death. The "Elisha era" began in 1919, the year Rutherford was released from prison,* and began reorganization of the society. Rutherford, like Elisha, had a "double portion" of the Spirit. He would continue and complete the work "Elijah" had begun, and so he moved quickly to purge his opposition and consolidate his power.[348] During this era some 40,000 of the faithful left the movement.[349] This became the source of the splinter Russellite groups already mentioned.

Russell's prophecies had largely failed, since his prophetic revelation dealt with the 1874 to 1914 era, and his claims did not come to pass. Rutherford "saved the day" by reinterpreting the Scriptures to apply them to his post-1918 era, although in the end he failed just as miserably as Russell. Nevertheless, the idea that new revelation was being given, bringing "new light" upon the Scriptures, was sufficient to satisfy many and to solidify the movement. Under Rutherford's leadership the Society greatly expanded. Major changes were made in Russell's teachings, in effect denying all possibility to Russell's divine inspiration. Thus Russell is largely ignored today by the very organization he founded.

Although there are thousands of changes in divine revelation only a few illustrations are needed here.** The purpose of this brief section is to document that the average Jehovah's Witness has no basis for trusting the WS claim to properly interpret the Bible under divine guidance.[350]

---

*He and other Watchtower Society staff were jailed in accordance with the Antiespionage Act due to their pacifist, anti-Government philosophy.

**These are excerpted for convenient reference, and used with permission, from Gruss' *We Left Jehovah's Witnesses—A Non-Prophet Organization,* pp. 156–59.

1. Abaddon, Apollyon—from Satan to Jesus Christ. This concerns Revelation 9:11 and the identification of the angel of the bottomless pit:

Original doctrine: "The prince of the power of the air." Ephesians 2:2. . . . That is, Destroyer. But in plain English his name is Satan, the Devil.[351]

Changed doctrine: "In Hebrew his name is Abaddon, meaning 'Destruction'; and in the Greek it is Apollyon, meaning 'Destroyer.' All this plainly identifies the 'angel' as picturing Jesus Christ, the Son of Jehovah God."[352]

2. Adam—from resurrection to no resurrection.

Original doctrine: "Just when Adam will be awakened, only the Lord knows. It may be early or it may be late during the period of restoration."[353]

Changed doctrine: "There is no promise found in the Scriptures that Adam's redemption and resurrection and salvation will take place at any time. Adam had a fair trial for life and completely failed."[354] In recent writings, Adam and Eve were viewed as among those who are incorrigible sinners who "proved that they were not worthy of life, and they will not be resurrected."[355]

3. Sodom and Gomorrah—resurrection promised, resurrection denied, resurrection reinstated.

Original doctrine: "Thus our Lord teaches that the Sodomites did not have a full opportunity; and he guarantees them such opportunity."[356]

Changed doctrine: "He was pinpointing the utter impossibility of ransom for unbelievers or those willfully wicked, because Sodom and Gomorrah were irrevocably condemned and destroyed, beyond any possible recovery."[357]

Return to former position: "As in the case of Tyre and Sidon, Jesus showed that Sodom, bad as it was, had not got to the state of being unable to repent. . . . So the spiritual recovery of the dead people of Sodom is not hopeless."[358]

4. Worship of Jesus Christ—from acceptance to rejection.

Original doctrine: "*Question.* . . . Was he *really* worshiped or is the translation faulty? *Answer.* Yes, we believe our Lord while on earth was really worshiped, and properly so. . . . It was proper for our Lord to receive worship."[359] "He was the object of unreproved worship even when a babe, by the wise men who came to see the new-born king. . . . He never reproved any for acts of worship offered to Himself. . . . Had Christ not been *more* than man the same reason would have prevented Him from receiving worship."[360] "The purposes of this Society are: . . . public Christian worship of Almighty God and Jesus Christ; to arrange for and hold local and world-wide assemblies for such worship."[361]

Changed doctrine: "No distinct worship is to be rendered to Jesus Christ now glorified in heaven. Our worship is to go to Jehovah God."[362] "For example, the magi from the east and King Herod said they wanted to 'do obeisance to' (*proskyneo*) the babe that had been born King of the Jews. 'Do obeisance' is preferable here because neither the magi nor King Herod meant to worship the babe as God."[363]

5. Resurrection from the dead—from all to some.

Original doctrine: "All are to be awakened from the Adamic death, as though from a sleep, by virtue of the ransom given."[364] "Under this new covenant the whole human race shall have the opportunity to come back to God through Jesus Christ the mediator."[365]

Changed doctrine: "It has been held by many that the Scriptures guarantee that 'all must come back from the dead' at Christ's return and during his thousand-year rule."[366] "That conclusion does not appear to have support in reason or in the Scriptures."[367]

6. Israel—literal Israel to spiritual Israel.

Original doctrine: "That the re-establishment of Israel in the land of Palestine is one of the events to be expected in this Day of the Lord, we are fully assured by the above expression of the Prophet [commenting on Amos 9:11, 14, 15]. Notice, particularly, that the prophecy cannot be interpreted in any symbolic sense."[368] "The promise, time and again repeated, that the Lord would regather them and bless them in the land and *keep them there* and bless them forever is conclusive proof that, the promise must be fulfilled. . . . Behold, that time is now at hand![369] (See also Rutherford's *Life*.)

Changed doctrine: "Nothing in the modern return of Jews to Palestine and the setting up of the Israeli republic corresponds with the Bible prophecies concerning the restoration of Jehovah's name-people to his favor and organization. . . . The remnant of spiritual Israelites, as Jehovah's Witnesses, have proclaimed world-wide the establishment of God's kingdom in 1914."[370]

7. The "superior authorities" of Romans 13—from earthly rulers, to Jehovah and Jesus, to earthly rulers.

Original doctrine: Until 1929 it was taught that the "higher powers" or "superior authorities" (*New World Translation*) were the earthly rulers to whom the Christian paid taxes, etc.[371]

Changed doctrine: From 1929 to 1962 the "superior authorities" were explained as "the Most High God Jehovah and his exalted Son Jesus Christ."[372]

Return to former position: "In spite of the end of the Gentile Times in 1914, God permitted the political authorities of this world to continue as the 'higher powers' or the 'powers that be,' which are 'ordained of God.' "[373]

8. The great crowd ("other sheep," the non-144,000 Jehovah's Witnesses) as a spiritual class—yes, no.

Original doctrine: "*Does the Great Company receive life direct from God on the spirit plane?* Answer—Yes, they receive life direct in that they have been begotten of the Holy Spirit, and when they are begotten they are just the same way as the little flock, because we are called in the one hope of our calling. They do not make their calling and election sure, but not being worthy of second death, they therefore receive life on the spirit plane."[374] "Ever and anon someone advances the conclusion that the 'great multitude' will not be a spiritual class. The prophecy of Ezekiel shows that such conclusion is erroneous. The fact that their position is seven steps higher than the outside shows that they must be made spirit creatures. . . . They must be spirit creatures in order to be in the outer court of the divine structure, described by Ezekiel."[375]

Changed doctrine: "Thus the great multitude is definitely identified, not as a spirit-begotten class whose hopes are for a place in heaven, but a class trusting in the Lord, and who hope for everlasting life on earth."[376]

Do the previous examples support the claim that the Watchtower Bible and Tract Society "from the time of its organization until now" has been God's "sole collective channel for the flow of Biblical truth to men on earth"? Do the examples support the claim that all Witness interpretations emanate from God? Or do they prove that the interpretations merely originate from the minds of confused men? Indeed, at this point, one can only agree with the Watchtower Society: "Jehovah never makes any mistakes. Where the student relies upon man, he is certain to be led into difficulties."[377] "Men not only contradict God, they contradict one another. How can they be reliable guides—unless their words are based on God's words? But how can you know whether they are or not? By going directly to God's Word as your source of authority. Search for yourself and let God be true!"[378] Not surprisingly, many former Jehovah's Witnesses will testify to leaving the Watchtower Society because of "going directly to God's Word" as their source of authority and spiritual enlightenment. More than one Witness has broken ranks with the WS after taking to heart signs at rallies protesting the WS that say "Read the Bible, not the Watchtower."

In conclusion, the Watchtower Society has not passed this test, concerning the veracity of divine revelation, because it has changed its own divine revelations in countless places.

Misuse of Quoted Sources

It is obvious that the true God, who is himself "the God of truth" and who hates lies, will not look with favor on persons who cling to organizations that teach falsehood. (Psalms 31:5; Proverbs 6:16–19; Revelations 21:8). And, really, would you want to be even associated with a religion that had not been honest with you? (*Is This Life All There Is?*; 1974, p. 46.)

A fourth and final test concerns fairness in quoting other sources and authors. Watchtower defenses of their beliefs often appeal to Greek grammars or lexicons, Bible dictionaries and encyclopedias and other authoritative sources, and they seem quite convincing to someone who reads them and assumes the integrity of the Watchtower. However, as with Mormonism, a cardinal rule when studying Watchtower literature is always to read the quoted sources in their original context, because the original will often be misquoted. Many researchers have noted this tendency. In his detailed study, Gruss discovered: "This writer has found that in many cases the Watchtower publications have either misrepresented or misunderstood the sources they have utilized."[379] In *The Scholastic Dishonesty of The Watchtower,* Van Buskirk agreed: "In reviewing the above subjects one finds that the Watchtower Bible and Tract Society thinks nothing of misquoting and misrepresenting historians.... Several Greek scholars are quoted completely out of context.... There is no hesitancy to twist and to lie outright about the earlier doctrines held by their own founders."[380] In addition, the Watchtower Society also employs the writings of liberal theologians and agnostics—virtually anyone they can squeeze doctrinal support from.[381]

Gruss and Van Buskirk have checked a number of Watchtower quotations, to which we add our own here. Only a sampling can be listed.

1. McClintock and Strong's *Cyclopaedia of Biblical Theological and Ecclesiastical Literature* (1871). The article under "Trinity" is cited in support of WS belief that the Trinity is a pagan concept. In WS books *Let God Be True* (1946, 1952) and *Make Sure of All Things* (1953), this source is used to document such an allegation. Gruss remarks: "This writer would strongly urge the reader to read the 'Trinity' article which completely refutes the position set forth in both *Let God Be True* and *Make Sure of All Things.* Possibly the compilers of *Make Sure of All Things* actually wished to refer the reader to the article 'Trinity, Heathen Notions of,' which follows the 'Trinity' article. If this is true the compilers again have their position refuted."[382]

2. The same Watchtower Society sources also cite Alexander Hislop's *The Two Babylons* as proof of a pagan trinity. However, Hislop is not

dealing with the orthodox teaching at all, but with its corruption by the Catholic Church and paganism: "The purpose of the author of *The Two Babylons* is not to show the origin of the doctrine from the ancient pagans, but to show the corruption of the Trinity by the Catholic Church, as Mary is inserted into the Trinity. Hislop shows that paganism *corrupted* the Trinity and did not originate it. ... Hislop completely exposes the Witnesses' appeal to his book."[383]

3. Edwin R. Thiele's *The Mysterious Numbers of the Hebrew Kings.* Professor Gruss wrote a letter to Dr. Thiele, a recognized authority on biblical chronology, and included the Watchtower Society quotation of his book in their February 1, 1969 *Watchtower* (p. 90). The subject concerned Ptolemy's Canon and Babylonian chronology. The Witnesses cannot accept the full accuracy of the Canon since it refutes their assertion that Jerusalem fell in 607 B.C., a date vital to their own chronology (Jerusalem actually fell to Babylon in 586–587 B.C.). Watchtower Society chronology declares that the "times of the Gentiles" began in 607 B.C. This had to be true in order for them to establish their 1914 chronology concerning the end of the "Times of the Gentiles" and the "Second Coming."[384] Gruss received the following reply concerning the Witnesses' use of Thiele's text in support of their claims:

In regard to your request for my comment on the use of my quotation in the WATCHTOWER concerning Ptolemy's Canon, I will say that it is misleading and unscrupulous. It is misleading in that it would give an entirely different impression concerning this important canon of Ptolemy than I hold. It is unscrupulous, because a procedure of this type is not honest. If the writer of this article had been honest—or informed—he would have known that I use Ptolemy's Canon in an entirely different way than he would have it used. ... What would I say about the article in general? I would say that such a writer and reader has no business writing about such a subject. He does not know the facts, or if he does, he does not use them in an honest manner. It reminds me of the way an unscrupulous lawyer would deal with facts in order to support a case he knows not to be sound. Let us be charitable with the man and say that in his reading he does not read as an informed scholar should. In other words, let us accuse him rather of ignorance than dishonesty.[385]

4. Robertson's *A Grammar of the Greek New Testament*. In the WS Interlinear appendix (p. 1159) they misquote Robertson's grammar three times to "support" their translation "a god" of John 1:1.[386]

5. Westcott and Hort. The January 15, 1975, *Watchtower* (p. 63), quotes the Westcott and Hort Greek text referring to the predicate "God" of John 1:1 as stating that "it describes the nature of the Word and does not identify His Person." The *Watchtower* quoted Westcott and Hort as *denying* the deity of Christ. In actual fact, Westcott and Hort were saying that the absence of the article before *theos* was necessary in order not to be declaring the modalistic heresy that Jesus was the person of the Father. Thus, they clearly assert that Christ is deity, only that He is not the person of the Father. Reading Westcott and Hort under John 1:1 we find:

> The predicate [God]   is necessarily without the article . . . inasmuch as it describes the nature of the word and does not identify His person. It would be pure Sabellianism to say "the Word was ὁ ΘΕΟΣ" (the God). No idea of inferiority of nature is suggested by this form of expression, which simply affirms the true deity of the Word. . . . The Word is declared to be "God" and included in the unity of the Godhead. . . . The Son can be regarded . . . in relation to God as God.[387]

6. William Barclay's *Many Witnesses, One Lord*. The May 15, 1977, *Watchtower* (p. 320), cites this text from the 1963 edition.[388] Baker Books reprinted this volume in 1973. The quoted material is on the same pages in the 1973 edition. The Watchtower Society quotes Barclay, again dishonestly, as denying Christ's deity, which he does not do. Like Westcott and Hort, Barclay is pointing out that the definite article is absent in John 1:1 so that "the Word" is not identified with the entirety of God; that is, by Himself Jesus does not constitute all of God in the sense that He is the Trinity. *The Watchtower* quotes only that part of Barclay's discussion

which seems to deny Christ's deity; it leaves out what Barclay says next: "The only modern translator who fairly and squarely faced this problem is Kenneth Wuest, who [says]: 'The Word was as to his essence essential deity.' But it is here that the NEB has brilliantly solved the problem with the absolutely accurate rendering: 'What God was the Word was.'"[389]

The WS article continues quoting Barclay: "John is not here identifying the Word with God. To put it very simply, he does not say that Jesus was God." This ends the Watchtower Society quote. In his entire discussion (not just the part cited by the WS), Barclay argues that while the Apostle John does declare that Jesus is God, he (John) does not declare that Jesus is all that God is; that is, that the person of Jesus comprises the entire Trinity. Thus, Barclay clearly asserts Christ's deity: "What he [John] does say is that no human description of Jesus can be adequate, and that Jesus, however you are going to define it, must be described in terms of God."[390]

7. In the May 15, 1979, *Watchtower* (p. 31), the Society quotes Volume Two of the *New International Dictionary of New Testament Theology* to *support* WS denial of the deity of Christ. The Witnesses fail to mention that the author of the dictionary article expressly denies the validity of the Watchtower translation of John 1:1 *by name*, going on to assert that "hence, the RSV translation [of John 1:1] would be the correct one."[391] After noting earlier that "theos is the most frequent designation of God in the NT" (p. 73), the author concludes his article, which the Jehovah's Witnesses quote from, with: "E. Stauffer is doubtless correct when he writes: 'the Christology of the NT is carried to its logical conclusion with the thorough-going designation of Christ as *theos*.'"[392]

8. Dana and Mantey's *Manual Grammar of the Greek New Testament*. Mick Van Buskirk provides a number of examples of the Watchtower Society misquoting and misrepresenting Greek grammars.[393] For example, the WS quotes *A Manual Grammar of the Greek New Testament* in support of their John 1:1 translation the "word was a god" (see the *Kingdom Interlinear Translation of the Greek Scriptures*, 1969, Appendix, p. 1158). Van Buskirk first sent a letter to Dr.

Mantey asking for his comments. In Mantey's letter of reply, February 25, 1974, he noted, "I was quoted out of context," and he stated that he was not even talking about what they claimed he asserted.[394] Van Buskirk next sent Dr. Mantey's reply to the Watchtower Headquarters in Brooklyn. In their three page letter, the Watchtower clearly maintained the correctness of their usage of Mantey's grammar. Van Buskirk then sent their reply to Dr. Mantey, who then sent them a letter (dated July 11, 1974) in which he noted a number of their mistranslations and demanded that they stop misquoting him. (See Appendix 2 for this letter.) In a letter to Van Buskirk, Mantey asserted: "After studying their mistranslation in hundreds of N.T. verses, it has dawned upon me that when Scripture disagreed with their peculiar teachings they deliberately mistranslated it or so altered the reading that there would be some apparent support for their unbiblical views."[395]

9. The Watchtower Society has misquoted *The Encyclopedia Britannica, The New Catholic Encyclopedia, The Encyclopedia Americana* and other encyclopedias.[396]

The Watchtower Society has now miserably failed four tests of its claim to be God's sole channel for accurately disseminating the true interpretation of God's word and will. It has failed accuracy of biblical translation by deliberately mistranslating the Bible in thousands of places. It has failed accuracy in prophecy by declaring countless of false prophecies as God's truth. It has failed in consistency as to divine revelation. It has failed accuracy in history, doctrine, interpretation and documentation by misrepresenting or lying about thousands of things. Why then should the WS be taken seriously by anyone?

Moral Concerns

According to other researchers and former members, Watchtower Society leaders have apparently been involved in shady financial activities, racism, vulgar language at Bethel, fraudulent schemes, cruelty, false advertising, lies, perjury and bribery, much of this being documented by court records.[397] Dr. Walter Martin refers to "proof of their founder's inherent dishonesty and lack of morals."[398] Evidently

the lives of both Russell and Rutherford[399] were not shining examples of Christian character and the legacy has, variously, continued to the present. More recently the books by Raymond Franz, *Crisis of Conscience* (400 pages) and *In Search of Christian Freedom* (700 pages), have further substantiated some of these charges.

The WS position on blood transfusions, wherein thousands have needlessly lost their lives,[400] is clearly a moral issue and one we will comment on. Of course, so is WS deception in Bible translation, prophecy and other areas, which has brought grief or ruin to thousands. What of the many Witnesses, believing the end of the world was immanent, sold homes, quit jobs and made financial decisions that reduced them to poverty? According to former members, it appears that irresponsibility, "callousness and indifference [are] often shown by the Watchtower Society hierarchy" in situations like this or when WS interests are at stake.[401] There is also the unconscionable fact that the WS has not taken responsibility for any of this.

Blood Transfusion

No one knows how many Witnesses have voluntarily taken their own lives or sacrificed the lives of their children due to the Watchtower Society's ban on blood transfusions, but the number is in the thousands. David A. Reed's *Blood on the Altar* (Prometheus, 1996) offers details, pointing out that thousands of Witnesses have literally bled to death in obedience to the Watchtower. Reed offers medical statistics and case histories that include names, dates, attending physicians and hospitals.

As in Christian Science (for different reasons), a Witness will actually allow himself or his own child to die rather than permit a medical solution if it involves a blood transfusion. The reasoning is as follows. Because transfusions are a violation of God's "law," and can result in *eternal* death, its better to die physically and at least have the hope of recreation. As one faithful witness declared, "I would rather see my boy dead and in the grave than see him violate Jehovah God's commandment against blood." In this case, as so often happens, she received her wish and saw her son placed in the grave.[402]

In defending this doctrine, the Watchtower Society utilizes Genesis 9:4, Leviticus 17:14 and other biblical passages as proof texts. The above Scriptures prohibit the eating of blood, which has nothing to do with transfusion for medical purposes. In addition, they refer to animal blood in sacred Old Testament sacrifices, not human blood. The reason for the prohibition is given in Leviticus 17:11: the blood of animals partaking in sacrifice was sacred, and since "the life of a creature is in the blood" it must be respected, not eaten. Genesis 9:4 also refers to the eating of animal blood, a not infrequent pagan practice done in the assumption that one is transferring the animal's life-force into oneself for power. In Acts 15:20, 29, abstaining "from blood" also refers to animal blood and has nothing to do with transfusions or eternal death. Not one biblical verse prohibits blood transfusions.

Blood transfusion involves the saving of life. Even orthodox Jews who hold to strict Old Testament laws, and who certainly know how to translate the Old Testament more accurately that the WS, accept the practice of blood transfusion. The Watchtower Society ban is simply a result of the unfortunate irresponsibility of biblically ignorant people. Even if eating blood meant transfusion, in his *Jehovah's Witnesses and Blood Transfusion* Dr. Havor Montague shows that under Jewish law such transfusion would have been permitted in order to save a life, since to save a life is more important than to not eat blood.[403] His analysis refutes a number of other Watchtower Society positions on this issue.

Probably at the cost of many lives and much misery, the Watchtower Society also once denied immunizations as being "against the law of God," but years later changed its mind. For many years the Society also denied organ transplants, which it now accepts. If Internet reports are correct, in recent years the WS has apparently, incrementally, begun to lift its ban on blood transfusions, largely with the teaching that certain unique blood products may be used in some cases. While full recision may eventually happen with blood transfusions, so many lives have already been lost defending the practice that it would be difficult for the Society to admit its error. We can expect, then, that before needed change arrives, thousands more lives may be callously and needlessly discarded:

> Extensive research will reveal that the arguments presented here cannot be answered by the Watchtower with its invalid positions. Extensive communication with prominent members of the Society has not produced any satisfactory answers to the question against the blood issue put forth here.... Neither the Society nor its publications can justify the deaths of faithful Witnesses on the basis that the Society tries to present as Biblical evidence.[404]

> What is the significance of this vaccination position held by the Society until 1952? Thousands of Witness parents and children were placed in the position of keeping "God's law" (the erroneous Watchtower dictum) and lying to school authorities. Men were needlessly in solitary confinement because of the error of the Society. Why did the official position of the Society not change until 1952? Will a discovery of erroneous teaching also be found in the Society's ban on blood transfusions? The problem on this point is that thousands will have already sacrificed their lives on the altar of Watchtower error.[405]

We think that Jehovah's Witnesses who have lost their loved ones to WS doctrine and then realized their error should begin considering class action lawsuits to stop the practice.

The Jehovah's Witnesses and Mental Illness

It is often claimed by Jehovah's Witnesses that they are the "happiest and most content" people on earth, that their families are more successful than others and that "they have the least need for psychiatrists."[406] Unfortunately this is not true. Witnesses often have emotional problems. Disfellowshipped Witnesses (there are many) are regarded as "dead" by active members and even at times by their own families. It goes without saying that this can produce severe emotional stress.[407] We reproduce, in part (with permission), "Jehovah's Witness and Mental Illness," an article written by Christian psychiatrist Dr. John Stedman (pen name), who has had an interest in the field of Jehovah's Witnesses' mental health for a number of years. He begins by noting the common knowledge of

Jehovah's Witnesses mental health problems and the sect's denial of them:

> Psychiatrists and others who have worked with Jehovah's Witnesses have been aware for a number of years that both the mental illness rate and the suicide rate is very high among the Witnesses. . . . Indeed the rate is so high that some hospitals are literally 'stuffed with JW's'— one mental hospital is nick-named 'The Watchtower House' because the number of JW's is so high.

> This is common knowledge and the reasons are generally well-known among mental health personnel, but when the typical JW is confronted with this information he often violently refuses to acknowledge its validity.[408]

There is extreme Witness reluctance to submit their faith to the confines of a psychiatric setting. Since a Witness is by definition a happy, well-adjusted person, the Witness who has problems assumes that the fault is his, not the Society's. The true number of troubled Witnesses is unknown because those who seek help often shift the blame. "As discussed, the reporting probably represents much lower rates than actually is the case."[409] Stedman continues:

> Most Witnesses who are forced to seek psychiatric services are extremely reluctant to admit they are a Witness. A large number of JW's whom the writer has worked with put down "Protestant" or even "none" instead of their true affiliation. JW's are typically extremely ashamed of the fact that they are mentally ill and often will not be open and honest with the therapist because of the fear that his illness may bring reproach upon the Wt. Society.[410]

Subsequent research has confirmed the severity of the situation. As Dr. Jerry Bergman wrote in "Paradise Postponed . . . And Postponed: Why Jehovah's Witnesses Have a High Mental Illness":

> Several academic studies have explored the problem of mental illness among the Witnesses. . . . Licensed therapist Havor Montague monitored the admissions to state and private mental hospitals and local mental health clinics in Ohio

from 1972 to 1976. From this study of 102 cases, he estimated, "the mental illness rate of JWs is approximately 10 to 16 times higher than the rate for the general, non-Witness population. . . . About 10% of the publishers (full members) in the average congregation are in serious need of professional help . . . [although they are often] able to hide this fact quite well, especially from outsiders". . . . Another study was completed in 1985 by Robert Potter as part of a Ph.D. thesis on religion and mental health. He concluded that there exists "a strong positive correlation between Witness membership and clinical schizophrenia". . . . In addition, a 1985 German study by Elmer Koppl came to similar conclusions, as did a study by Norwegian psychologist, Kjell Totland. Using Oakland County, Michigan court records from 1965 to 1973, this writer found that not only is the mental illness rate above average, but the suicide and crime rates are also high, especially aggressive crimes against persons. (See also the *British Journal of Psychiatry*, June 1975; the *American Journal of Psychiatry*, March 1949; *Social Compass* Vol. 24 [1977]; and Kjell Totland, "The Mental Health of Jehovah's Witnesses," *Journal of the Norwegian Psychological Association* 1999 [in press].)

Bergman attributes the high mental illness rate to a variety of factors, including the extreme emphasis upon door-to-door witnessing, which can require, in addition to one's normal job, 20 hours to 30 hours per week. He also cites WS prohibitions against normal social relations and most school activities for children who, not infrequently, grow up lonely and troubled because the WS has not issued proper guidelines to help them live their lives. He concludes that the average Witness serves the Watchtower, not God, because serving the Watchtower is serving God. "Discouraged from many normal means of self-fulfillment, Witnesses slavishly devote their time and energy to serving an organization that does not care about them as individuals. . . . Many feel they are trapped in a way of life in which virtually every alternative is undesirable." When WS service does not satisfy or solve one's problems, this, Bergman writes, causes guilt leading "Witnesses to feel that they are evil and will not survive Armageddon. The depression and hopelessness have led to a disproportionate number of suicides and homicides among Witnesses."[411]

TALKING WITH MEMBERS

If we want to worship God acceptably, we must know the truth. This is an important issue. Our eternal happiness depends on it. Therefore, everyone should ask himself: "Is my way of worship acceptable to God? Am I genuinely interested in learning the truth of God's Word? Or am I afraid of what a careful investigation might reveal?" (Watchtower Society website, "Do You Know the Truth?" April 1, 1999)

Anyone talking with Jehovah's Witnesses will sooner or later discover that they avoid examining works critical of the WS. This is because the leadership at Bethel headquarters has told members that they are to avoid critical materials as they would pornography (*The Watchtower*, March 15, 1986, p. 12). The reason is clear: their eternal life is at stake if they become deceived by the devil's false teachings.

By insulating Witnesses from all critical materials, the WS intends to ensure that members hear only what Society leaders wish them to hear. The quote beginning this section may be cited to members, especially the last sentence. The WS cannot logically expect its membership to engage in "careful investigation" and simultaneously prohibit it by requiring members to investigate only WS materials. Clearly, only people who have something to fear demand intolerance toward responsible opposition literature. As a result, time spent thinking on how best to drive this point home may prove rewarding.

While the vast majority of active Witnesses probably will not read critical literature, some for different reasons will, and if so, this chapter or additional literature may be suggested.*

Until recently, the Jehovah's Witnesses have largely avoided engaging in scholarly apologetic dialogue. The 1998 publication of Greg Stafford's *Jehovah's Witnesses Defended: An Answer to Scholars and Critics* may signal a turning point. Despite the book's weaknesses, by increasing the level of scholarly discussion it is probably the best Witness apologetic to date. Stafford does not make his case because he is still attempting to defend the indefensible: biblical unitarianism and its denial of the Trinity. There are arguments here new to most Witnesses and so a reading of this book may be necessary for those engaged in regular contact and discussion. Dr. James White points out, in his review published in the *Christian Research Journal*, Vol. 21, #2 (1999, p. 49), that a basic flaw is Stafford's assumption that the terms "God," "Jehovah," and "Father" refer to the same person (unitarianism); thus if Jesus is not the person of the Father, He cannot be God. But to prove that the Son is not the Father only proves that the person of the Son is not the person of the Father, not that the Son is not God. The doctrine of the Trinity holds that one divine essence—the one Being of God—is shared by the person of the Father, Son and Holy Spirit: three persons or centers of consciousness in the one divine essence. Therefore, proving Jesus is not the Father is only proving biblical teaching. What Stafford needed to do is prove that Jesus is not deity, and in this he has clearly failed.

Our approach in this section will be to continue to familiarize readers with a sampling of WS argumentation. Jehovah's Witnesses are one of the few groups trained in argumentation, which is why we will cite specific illustrations.

---

*Some texts we recommend are: Randall Walters, *Refuting Jehovah's Witnesses, Letters to the Editor-Book One* (1983–1989), *Book Two* (1989–1995), *Thus Saith the Governing Body of Jehovah's Witnesses* (cf. his *The Governing Body's Famous Sayings of the 80's*); M. James Patton, *Apocalypse Delayed* (1997 rev.); Raymond Franz, *Crisis of Conscience, In Search of Christian Freedom;* Lynn Lundquist, *The Tetragrammaton and the Christian Greek Scriptures;* Carl Olof Johnson, *Gentile Times Reconsidered;* David A. Reed, ed., *Answering the Jehovah's Witnesses Verse by Verse, Index of Watchtower Errors, Behind the Watchtower Curtain;* Edmund Gruss, Leonard Chretien, *Jehovah's Witnesses: Their Monuments to False Prophecy;* Wilbur Lingle, *How to Use the 1995 Watchtower Publication: "Knowledge that Leads to Everlasting Life" To Witness Effectively to Jehovah's Witnesses;* Ken Raines, *Jehovah: Ancient Astronaut from the Pleiades?;* Heather and Gary Botling, *The Orwellian World of Jehovah's Witnesses* (University of Toronto Press, 1984); Havor Montague, "The Pessimistic Sect's Influence on the Mental Health of Its Members: The Case of Jehovah's Witnesses," *Social Compass,* Vol 24, 1977.

Before we begin we introduce a point mentioned by Dr. Robert Morey:

> Over a period of many years we have had contact with Jehovah's Witnesses who have steadfastly remained in the Watchtower despite their being refuted on many occasions. Fighting with them verse by verse never seemed to get anywhere because the Watchtower headquarters would always come up with an "answer." We must remember that the Watchtower has had 100 years to come up with answers to orthodox arguments. But these Witnesses, once their confidence and trust in the organization was shaken, were brought to salvation.[412]

This is one reason we have spent so much time documenting the Watchtower Society's fatal unreliability—mistranslations, errors in prophecy, contradictions in doctrines and interpretation and so on. It is logically impossible to remain a Jehovah's Witness once faith in the Watchtower Society as "God's channel" has been undermined. Members can at least be encouraged to investigate this subject on their own using Watchtower magazine reprints, first editions of WS literature and so on. Of course, if they will not read a critical text to at least find the alleged errors, so they can then check them personally, they will have to read much more widely to find them on their own.

As noted, Witnesses have "answers" for WS problems, which appear to satisfy most members.[413] In the area of prophecy they may admit to a "few" errors, and the Witness who does not take the time to see how extensive these "few" errors are will remain loyal. "Progressive revelation" may explain doctrinal "refinements" if one never takes the time to see that the "refinements" are flat out denials of earlier doctrine! For "true believers," the solution to problems is not, unfortunately, the facts, but the will to believe. By whatever means, members may defend their beliefs with reasons that appear satisfying to them, but the issue is the illegitimacy of the WS counterarguments in face of such damaging evidence. The fact that virtually all Greek scholars recognize the Society's *New World Translation* as biased, in error and unscholarly is no less damaging than its perfect failure rate in prophecy. The issue is not can they come up with ever new reasons for explaining their failures, but whether the level of failure is already sufficient to disprove WS claims to any impartial party.

Isaiah 9:6 is a case in point. It clearly refers to the Messiah (whom the WS acknowledges is Jesus Christ) as "Mighty God" (NWT). The Hebrew is *el gibbor*, "el" being a common name for Jehovah God. One might think this were enough. But for Jehovah's Witnesses, the Messiah simply cannot be God because of their theological presuppositions as to the unitarian nature of God. Therefore they reply, "It is true Jesus is *a* Mighty god, but not *Al*mighty God Jehovah. Only if Isaiah said Jesus were the *Al*mighty God would it be saying Jesus is God." But if a descriptive prefix "Al" denotes a qualitative difference in nature between Jesus and Jehovah, then it must also be true that Jehovah must be inferior to Jesus on the same reasoning: Jehovah is merely "the Shepherd" in Psalm 23:1. But Jesus is the great Shepherd in Hebrews 13:20 and the Chief Shepherd in 1 Peter 5:4.

Obviously, the context must determine the use of words, and in Isaiah 9:6 the term "mighty God" is asserting Jesus' deity. Both the original language and the context demand this conclusion. Rather than accept this, the Witnesses will find a reason for evading it: "At Isaiah 9:6 Jesus Christ is prophetically called 'El Gib·bohr, 'Mighty God' (not 'El Shad·day which applies to Jehovah at Genesis 17:1). 'El is used of idol gods at Psalm 81:9."[414] The reasoning is that since El Shaddai is used only of Jehovah and never of Jesus (which is true), Jesus cannot be God. But this does not logically follow. The fact that "El Shaddai" is not used of Jesus is irrelevant if Jesus is clearly declared God in Isaiah 9:6 and elsewhere. They also mention that the definite article is not used, but it is also missing in Isaiah 10:21, which is clearly a reference to Jehovah. Further, "el" may be used of the one true God or false gods, but in Isaiah 9:6 it can only refer to the true God: ". . . the Hebrew word 'el' in Isaiah usually denotes Jehovah, the only true God; when it does not do so (in 44:10, 15, 17; 45:20; 46:6), it is used to describe an idol made by men's hands. Surely Isaiah did not intend to say that the coming Messiah would be an idol god! It ought also be noted that the expression 'el gibboor' is in Old Testament literature a traditional designation of Jehovah—see Deuteronomy 10:17; Jeremiah 32:18; and Nehemiah 9:32."[415] The larger context is also relevant; for example, in Isaiah 10:21 Jehovah is described as "mighty God," the exact phrase used to describe Jesus in Isaiah 9:6.

The Witnesses response? They will drop the issue and find another argument. For example, they may point out this verse also calls Jesus "eternal Father." If orthodoxy does not believe Jesus is the person of the Father, then why believe He is literally the Mighty God? The point missed is that Jesus is also a father to us if He is God, who is our Father (Psalm 103:13), and as such it is proper to describe Him as a father. (Nowhere does Isaiah 9:6 teach that the Person of the Son is the Person of the Father.) The same argument is true for the designation "eternal." Only if He is God is it proper to refer to Him as eternal. But is it proper to describe him as "Mighty God" if he is not God? Clearly, it is not.

If the Watchtower Society has admitted that it makes errors and is not infallible, how much more important is it that a member think for himself and be willing to examine critically what he has been taught? To cite an analogy, one day at the brake shop we notice a man with the same model car we have. We also notice that the mechanic is putting in the wrong brake system, a mistake which could have fatal consequences. We tell this to the car owner, but he assures us the mechanic is qualified because he has read the owner's manual carefully. We tell him, "We have read it carefully ourselves and it is the wrong brake system; your life and others will be in peril if you drive your car." Unless the owner will actually read the manual for himself and carefully study it to see who is correct, he could be making a fatal error. Claims and counter-claims can be made all day long. The individual must study these issues for himself. Even if the mechanic has some apparent explanation for his interpretation of the manual, other qualified mechanics need to be consulted.

Note some examples of what happens when a Jehovah's Witness studies the Bible on his own:

After I looked through the publications and found other similar problems, I set them aside and began studying the Bible without literature aids of any kind. I read chapter by chapter, looking up cross references wherever necessary. The Holy Spirit revealed many things to me, and I was amazed to find that orthodox Christianity was really true. I discovered that the Bible taught such doctrines as: the Trinity, the deity of Christ, the personality of the Holy Spirit, the immortality of the soul, and the visible return of Christ—*all* the doctrines the Watchtower Society had brainwashed us into rejecting![416]

Of course after doing a bit of background reading I began to see the utter temporal relativism of W.T. truth. Conflicting doctrines were held at various times, all with the infallible authority of Jehovah behind them....

I spent the most of my life in an organization of HATE, until now I feel like a bird out of a cage. Keep a bird in a cage for twenty-five years, then turn it out, it is slow learning to fly again.... I have been taught the Watchtower language so long I feel very weak in learning the language of love.[417]

There are other ways to approach a Jehovah's Witness. One may read the *New World Translation* and find areas that clearly teach biblical truths, which the Witness may then be challenged to believe. (Not every "error" has been corrected or addressed in WS literature.) Obviously, one will need a *New World Translation* to use these scriptures. (If their translation has changed from what we cite, seek the reason and ask them to justify the change. Were they wrong in the previous translation? Then what about the present translation?) Here are numerous passages from the NWT that can be used.

Salvation by faith alone. Titus 3:5; Ephesians 2:8-9; 2 Timothy 1:9; Romans 3:28, 4:5, 5:9, 6:23; John 6:29, 5:24; 1 John 3:14.

Christ as God, (for example, Redeemer, Creator). John 1:3; John 5:18,23 with 19:7; Zechariah 11:13; John 1:2; Matthew 3:3; Micah 5:2 with Psalms 102:12 and Isaiah 40:28.

How Many Lord of Lords? Deuteronomy 10:17; Revelation 19:16. There is only one. Witnesses will say Jesus is Lord of Lords on earth but not in heaven. Yet in Revelation 19:11,14, where is Jesus when John called him Lord of Lords but in heaven?

Who was with the Israelites? In Deuteronomy 32:12 it is Jehovah. In Deuteronomy 32:15 Jehovah is the Rock. In Isaiah 44:8, there is no other Rock. In 1 Corinthians 10:1–4, the Rock was Christ. Their interlinear shows that their translation is unjustified in translating "the rock-mass meant the Christ" (cf., Romans 9:33). *Petra* means rock (rock-mass is an attempt to avoid the similarity to Deuteronomy 32). Their own Greek is translated as "was," not "meant." The Rock was Christ (that is, based on the previous Scriptures, Christ is deity).

Who is the Eternal Light? In Isaiah 60:19–20 it is Jehovah. In Revelation 21:23 it is Jesus, cf. Revelation 22:5.

Who sits in the center of Jehovah's Throne? In Revelation 7:10–12 it is Jehovah. In Revelation 7:17, it is Jesus. *Meson* means center or middle of, the NWT "midst" is less clear but to the point.

Who sheds the light in the new Jerusalem? In Revelation 22:5 it is Jehovah. In Revelation 21:23 it is Jesus. (Other examples of Christ's deity can be found in the *New World Translation.* Any systematic theology or topical Bible can be used to check which verses in the *New World Translation* teach this.)

Eternal punishment. Daniel 12:2 and Revelation 20:10. That Revelation 20:10 is not symbolic, as maintained by the NWT, is seen by the Greek word translated "tormented." It is the same word in Matthew 8:6, 19 and Revelation 14:11, which means literal torment. The Greek word "for ever and ever" is the same word used in Hebrews 1:8, which the Witnesses interpret as referring to Jehovah and must therefore mean eternal. Also, see the *Kingdom Interlinear* at Jude 7. And in Hebrews 10:28–29 the one who tramples under foot the blood of Jesus receives a *worse* judgment than death. How can there be a "much more severe punishment" than death, which is only annihilation to Witnesses? To re-ceive a worse punishment than death, the spirit must remain alive.

The deity of the Holy Spirit. Acts 5:3, 4; Hebrews 10:15; Hebrews 3:7; Isaiah 6:8–9 with Acts 28:25–26; Isaiah 40:28 with 1 Corinthians 2:10–11; Isaiah 63:10 with Psalm 78:17.

Assurance of salvation. 1 John 5:13; John 6:39, 47; Romans 8:1.

Everyone needs spiritual rebirth. 1 John 5:1 and related passages.

The personality of the Holy Spirit. John 14:26; 16:13; Acts 16:6, 7; 10:19; 1 Corinthians 2:10; 12:11; John 14:16, 26; 15:26; 16:7; Romans 8:26–27; Acts 13:4; Matthew 28:19; Ephesians 4:30; Matthew 12:31; Acts 5:3; 7:51; Hebrews 10:29.

Immediate judgment at death (no second chance). John 5:28–29; 13:18.

A related approach, in this case to the doctrine of the Trinity, was given in our *The Facts on Jehovah's Witnesses,* (pp. 12–13), which we will reproduce. "The doctrine of the Trinity can be seen from five simple statements supported by the Bible. (The following scriptures taken from the Jehovah's Witnesses' *New World Translation,* 1970 ed., are abbreviated "NWT.")[418]

There is only one true God. "For there is one God, and one mediator between God and men. . . ." (1 Timothy 2:5 NWT; cf. Deuteronomy 4:35; 6:4; Isaiah 43:10)

The Father is God. "There is actually to us one God the Father. . . ." (1 Corinthians 8:6 NWT; cf. John 17:1–3; 2 Corinthians 1:3; Philippians 2:11; Colossians 1:3; 1 Peter 1:2)

Jesus Christ, the Son, is God. ". . . but he [Jesus] was also calling God his own Father, making himself equal to God" (John 5:18 NWT). "In answer Thomas said to him [Jesus]: 'My Lord and my God!'" (John 20:28 NWT; cf. Isaiah 9:6; John 1:1; Romans 9:5; Titus 2:13; 2 Peter 1:1; see note 418)

The Holy Spirit is a Person, is eternal and is therefore God. The Holy Spirit is a Person: "However, when that one arrives, the spirit of the truth, *he* will guide you into all the truth, for *he* will not speak of *his* own impulse, but what things *he* hears *he* will speak, and *he* will declare to you the things coming" (John 14:13, NWT, emphasis added). The Holy Spirit is *eternal*: "How much more will the blood of the Christ, who through an everlasting spirit offered himself without blemish to God . . . (Hebrews 9:14, NWT). The Holy Spirit is *therefore God*: "But Peter said: 'Ananias, why has Satan emboldened you to play false to the holy spirit. . . . You have played false, not to men, but to God.'" (Acts 5:3,4 NWT)

The Father, Son and Holy Spirit are distinct Persons. ". . . Baptizing them in the name of the Father and of the Son and of the holy spirit"; "The undeserved kindness of the Lord Jesus Christ and the love of God and the sharing in the holy spirit be with all of you." (Matthew 28:19; 2 Corinthians 13:14 NWT).

It is clear from these verses, read either from the NWT or a modern version like the NIV, that the Bible teaches the one true God exists eternally as Father, Son and Holy Spirit.

Another approach is to discuss individual Scriptures with members, knowing their response beforehand and having thought through a reply. Samples are provided here.

John 20:28 (NWT). Thomas' response to Jesus as "My God" is not clear enough for Witnesses. The standard response is that Thomas did not mean "my only *true* God," or else Jesus would have reproved him. Thomas really meant that Jesus was the Son of God, or that he was only using this as a figure of speech intended as respect towards Christ. But in John 5:18 and John 10:30, the Apostle John makes no qualifying note stating Jesus attempted to correct other people's "misperception" of Him as God. This would be a serious error in an inerrant Bible. Also, Thomas did not say "My Son of God," but rather "My God." The Greek is *ho theos mou*, "the God of me"; that is, my God. What else can "My God" mean but "my only true God"? Thomas

was no polytheist. Jesus recognized only one true God, and He did not rebuke Thomas for calling Him God.

John 10:30–33. Jehovah's Witnesses will say that by "I and the Father are one" Jesus meant, "I and the Father are one in purpose and unity," even though this is not what the verse says. The neuter (*hen*) implies one in essence. Clearly the Jews understood the claim, for they would not seek to stone him (a capital offense) for merely claiming to be one in purpose with God. They would, however, stone Jesus for blaspheming, for falsely claiming to be God. The NWT mistranslates John 10:33 as "a god." As their interlinear indicates, *poieis seauton theos* is without the article, hence underneath the Greek text, the English reads "making yourself God." (The distinction between capital and non-capital letters was not made in the Greek.)

Jesus did not try to convince the Jews that they had misunderstood Him here. He simply reasserted His deity. In John 10:34–38, He reasoned that if even Scripture calls men "gods" figuratively, how can the very One whom the Father sanctified and sent into the world (by virgin birth, that is, as the prophesied divine Messiah) be blaspheming when he claims to be God's Son and does the miracles that prove His claims? Even the NWT claims at John 19:7 that to be God's Son meant claiming to be God. In other words, Jesus is saying, "If it is possible for anyone to claim equality with God, it is possible for Me. I came from the Father, I do His works and We are one." Jesus then says, "If I am not doing the works of my Father (doing God's works, doing the works only God can do) do not believe me"; that is, do not believe that "I and the Father are one" in essence. "But if I am doing the works, at least believe them, that you may know that I and the Father are one" (that He is God).

John 14:28. Jesus said that the Father was greater than He was. This verse teaches the Father was greater than Jesus in His human incarnation and servant role. Jesus had by His own volition humbled and limited Himself (Philippians 2:6–7). The Father was greater in that Jesus submitted to Him, but mere submission does not demand inferiority as to nature, whether in the Godhead or among men and women in Christian marriage or between a king and his subjects. The Greek *meizon* implies a quantitative aspect. If John meant "inferior" he should have used *kreitton*, which means qualitatively better, as is used in Hebrews 1:4.

Revelation 3:14. Dr. Bruce Metzger comments:

> The New World Translation . . . is also in error at Revelations 3:14, where it makes the exalted Christ refer to himself as "the beginning of the creation by God." The Greek text of this verse . . . is far from saying that Christ was created by God, for the genitive case . . . means "of God" and not "by God," which would require the preposition. . . . Actually the word *arche*, translated "beginning," carries with it the Pauline idea expressed in Colossians 1:15-18, and signifies that Christ is the origin, or primary source, of God's creation (compare also John 1:3, "Apart from him not even one thing came into existence").[419]

Hebrews 1:8-10. We have noted that Hebrews 1:8 in the NWT is a biased translation. We have not noted that Hebrews 1:10 refers to Jesus, as clearly evidenced by the conjunction "and" (NWT). But Hebrews 1:10 is a quote of Psalm 102:25, referring to Jehovah creating the world. Here this Scripture is applied to Jesus. We might also observe the Greek word *charakter* in Hebrews 1:3 ("exact representation of his very being," NWT). The Greek word was taken from a word used to describe an impression produced by a seal or a die stamp in wax or metal. Moulton and Milligan defined it as "an exact reproduction."[420] If Jesus is the "exact reproduction" of Jehovah is He a creature? The answer is that He and His Father are indeed One.

Nehemiah 9:6. Here all the angels of heaven worship Jehovah alone. In Luke 4:8 worship is to be given to God only. In Hebrews 1:6 Jesus receives angelic worship. How can Jesus receive the worship of the angels if He is only a created angel Himself?

John 17:22. Jesus received glory from God. The Witnesses reply, "Can God receive glory from God"? But there are different types of glory. For example, Jesus' essential glory is the glory of His deity, which cannot be communicated. His moral glory is the glory of His character, and his acquired glory is the glory received through His incarnation, death and resurrection. Clearly, the glory Jesus received from God was the glory of his incarnation and His death, the commission to save believers (John 5:36, 44; 17:4-5), not the glory of His innate deity, which He could never receive and which He had with the Father before the world was (John 17:5).

John 20:17. Jesus said, "I ascend to My God." The Witnesses reply, "If he were God how could he refer to 'His God'?" As a true man, Jesus could properly speak of God as "My God," just as through the virgin birth He could speak of God as "My Father."

Other verses could be listed, but these are sufficient to indicate that the quality of the Watchtower Society's apologetic is insufficient to warrant trust.

Finally, in any discussion with the Witnesses, it should be remembered that they have little or no assurance of salvation. Someone who has this assurance and can communicate it biblically will present an attractive alternative. M. J. Schnell remarks: "Assurance of salvation is prized amidst Jehovah's Witnesses. You work hard for it. But as you perform one task, other tasks loom ahead and you are never sure. For thirty years I sought assurance in this manner. I had not found it."[421] Members of Jehovah's Witnesses thus need to know the blessed hope that: "I write these things to you who believe in the name of the Son of God so that you may *know* that you have eternal life" (1 John 5:13, emphasis added).

Even the Watchtower Society agrees that "sincere seekers for the truth want to know what is right. They realize that they would only be fooling themselves if they rejected portions of God's Word while claiming to base their beliefs on other parts."[422]

In our book *Facts on Jehovah's Witnesses*, we spoke personally to Jehovah's Witnesses in the following manner, and we repeat our concerns here: "What can you do if you are a Jehovah's Witness who desires to live for God and Christ and yet are unsure about what you have been taught?"

First, if you are a Jehovah's Witness, don't be discouraged. Don't give up on God because someone lied to you. Perhaps you accepted the Watchtower's claims without first testing them carefully. Possibly your own doubts and discouragement will become the means by which God leads you into the truth and into a personal relationship with Him.

Second, realize that you aren't alone. Millions of others were disfellowshipped or left the Watchtower organization.[423] It's not the end of the world.

Third, take the initiative: get at the truth for yourself. The Watchtower has told you before that "sincere seekers for the truth want to know what is right."[424] If you study the Bible on your own, in humility before God, God says that He Himself will show you the truth:

> But if any of you lacks wisdom, let him ask of God, who gives to all men generously and without reproach, and it will be given to Him. . . . Draw near to God and He will draw near to you. (James 1:5; 4:8 NAS)

> Ask Him, and He'll help you. Believe and obey His Word, don't alter it, and you will know the truth and as Jesus promised "the truth will make you free. (John 8:31,32)

Fourth, accept God's loving and free gift of salvation in Christ Jesus. There are no works to earn it! It's a gift. God never intended for you to spend your life in a hopeless, never-ending attempt to earn your own salvation by measuring up to His standard of perfection. He has already told us that it is impossible for any person to do so. Because of your fallen nature, you'll never be able to do it (Romans 8:3). "But because of His great love for us, God, who is rich in mercy, made us alive with Christ even when we were dead in transgressions—it is by grace you have been saved" (Ephesians 2:4-5). The really good news that God gives to all of us is:

> Therefore, there is now no condemnation for those who are in Christ Jesus. (Romans 8:1)

> You see, at just the right time, when we were still powerless, Christ died for the ungodly. (Romans 5:6)

> But the gift of God is eternal life in Christ Jesus our Lord. (Romans 6:23)

> However, to the man who does not work [for salvation] but trusts God who justifies the wicked, his faith is credited as righteousness. (Romans 4:5)

> So we, too, have put our faith in Christ Jesus that we may be justified by faith in Christ and not by observing the law, because by observing the law no one will be justified. . . . I do not set aside the grace of God, for if righteousness could be gained through the law, Christ died for nothing! (Galatians 2:16, 21)

Fifth, God wants you to confess your sins and accept the forgiveness He provided through Christ's shed blood. Read Isaiah 55:1-3 and see how eagerly God longs for you to come to Him to rest. Do you long for eternal life and the assurance of it? God's Word says you can know that you have it:

> The one who believes in the Son of God has the witness in himself; the one who does not believe God has made Him a liar, because he has not believed in the witness that God has borne concerning His Son. And the witness is this, that God has *given us* eternal life, and this life is in His Son. *He who has the Son has the life;* he who does not have the Son of God *does not* have the life. These things I have written to you who believe in the name of the Son of God, in order that *you may know that you have eternal life* (1 John 5:10-13, emphasis added).

You can receive the gift of salvation and know that you have eternal life, right now, by praying sincerely:

> Dear God, I'm confused. But I long to know You and serve You as You really are. Please reveal Yourself to me. I confess that I'm a sinner and incapable of earning merit in Your eyes. I believe Jesus' words, "You must be born again." I now receive Jesus Christ as my personal Lord and Savior. I receive Him as my God. I commit myself to Him and to Your Word. Please help me to understand it correctly. Amen.

APPENDIX 1:
THE ACCURACY OF THE GRANVILLE SHARP RULE

Is the Granville Sharp Rule so accurate that it is without demonstrable exception in the entire

New Testament? The Granville Sharp rule of Greek grammar is important for proving the deity of Christ and refuting Sabellianism, since it absolutely requires that distinct persons be spoken of in places like Matthew 28:19. Here we concentrate on its application to the deity of Christ in Titus 2:13 and 2 Peter 1:1. A transliteration of the last part of the Greek for Titus 2:13 reads as follows:

(The)	TOU	MEGALOU	*THEOU*	KAI
	(of our)	great	God	and
SOTEROS	HEMON	CHRISTOU	IESOU.	
savior	of us	Christ	Jesus	

The Jehovah's Witnesses' *New World Translation* changes the proper translation here to separate the term "Christ Jesus" from the term "God," thereby attempting to deny His deity in their rendering "the great God and of the Savior of us, Christ Jesus." The NWT verse is translated as if two persons are being spoken of, God and Jesus, rather than one person only, Jesus Christ. This violates Sharp's rule. In simplified form it states that when two singular personal nouns of the same case ending (God and Savior, genitive case) are connected by "and" (*kai*) and only the first noun has the modifying article "the" (*tou*) (the second noun does not), it always means both nouns uniformly refer to the same person. (The rule applies to personal nouns, singular not plural. A personal noun is distinguished from a proper noun in this rule.) Thus "God" and "Savior" must *both* refer to one person, to "Jesus," in Titus 2:13 and 2 Peter 1:1. In fact in ancient times, the same phraseology ("god and savior") was used of a ruling king, so it is obvious that only one person was meant.

In an exhaustive study of the Granville Sharp rule, including its critics, C. Kuehne, in the *Journal of Theology—Church of the Lutheran Confession* (September 1973 to Dec. 1974, Vols. 13, nos. 3, 4; Vol. 14, nos. 1–4), found the Sharp rule to be without demonstrable exception in the entire New Testament.[425] Other authorities agree. Noted Greek scholar Bruce Metzger observes:

> In support of this translation there may be quoted such eminent grammarians of the Greek

New Testament as P. W. Schmiedel, J. H. Moulton, A. T. Robertson, and Blass-Debrunner. All of these scholars concur in the judgment that only one person is referred to in Titus 2:13 and that therefore it must be rendered, "Our great God and Savior Jesus Christ.... All that has been written in the preceding section, including the judgment of the grammatical authorities cited there, applies with equal appropriateness to the correct rendering of II Peter 1:1. Accordingly, in this verse also there is an express declaration of the deity of Jesus Christ," ... of our God and Savior Jesus Christ.[426]

Dana and Mantey, in *A Manual Grammar of the Greek New Testament,* state: "The following rule by Granville Sharp of a century back still proves to be true: ... 2 Peter 1:1 ... means that Jesus is our God and Savior. After the same manner Titus 2:13 ... asserts that Jesus is the great God and Savior."[427] One may also note the Greek scholar A. T. Robertson in his *Word Pictures,* Vol. 6, p. 147 ("One Person not two"), and Wener-Schmiedel's *Grammatik* 8th ed., Leipeig, Germany, p. 158 ("Grammar demands that one person be met").

In *The King James Only Controversy,* Dr. James White points out that, "Most attacks upon Granville Sharp's Rule happened to be based upon less-than-full or accurate definitions of it. A review of the current literature shows that most modern grammars do not give full definitions when presenting Granville Sharp's work."[428] He cites Kenneth West, Curtis Vaughan and Vitrus Gideon as examples. In their grammar Dana and Mantey "give probably the most accurate definition," but even here the definition is not a fully accurate rendering of what Granville Sharp actually stated. "It has been due to these less-than-accurate definitions that Sharp's Rule has become the target of much criticism."[429] White cites A. T. Robertson's *The Minister and His Greek New Testament,* pages 61–68 under the title "The Greek Article and the Deity of Christ," as having one of the best discussions on the subject. Robertson provided an accurate rendering of Sharp's Rule and much relevant discussion. White also tracked down an 1807 edition of Sharp's work entitled "Remarks on the Uses of the Definitive Article in the Greek Text of the New Testament: Containing Many New

Proofs of the Divinity of Christ, from Passages which are Wrongly Translated in the Common English Version [the KJV]" (Philadelphia: B.B. Hopkins & Co., 1807). Sharp's Rule, according to Sharp, is given as follows in this work:

> When the copulative *kai* connects two nouns of the same case [viz. nouns (either substantive or adjective, or participles) of personal description, respecting office, dignity, affinity, or connexion, and attributes, properties, or qualities, good or ill] if the article *ho,* or any of its cases, precedes the first of the set nouns or participles, and is not repeated before the second noun or participle, the latter *always* relates to the same person that is expressed or described by the first noun or participle: i.e., it denotes a farther [further] description of the first named person.[430]

White points out that the issue here is that Sharp's rule is valid only for singulars not plurals and is not intended to be applied to proper names. In other words, the rule applies to persons, not things. This means that Sharp's Rule is significantly more limited in scope than many modern definitions indicate:

> Does this more accurate and definite definition make a big difference? Indeed it does! There are seventy-nine occurrences of "Granville Sharp" constructions in the writings of Paul, using Vaughan and Gideon's definition. Hence, here we have constructions that mix singulars and plurals, descriptions of places and things, and constructions that reflect both nouns as having the article. A quick glance over the list reveals a maximum of fifteen exceptions, and a minimum of five. Even this ratio would be considered very good for a general rule of grammar. However, Sharp claimed that the rule *always* held true. Obviously, if the modern versions of his rule are accurate, Sharp was not.[431]

White also points out the fact that when the rule *is* properly defined, it is without exception in the entire New Testament:

> But when the constructions in the New Testament that truly follow Granville Sharp's Rule are examined, a very unusual thing happens: *it is found to be entirely without exception!* As Robertson quotes from Sharp's work, "But, though Sharp's principle was attacked, he held to it and affirms (p. 115) that though he had ex-

amined several thousand examples of this type, . . . he had never found an exception."[432]

The reason why the King James Version, the American Standard Version and a few additional earlier versions incorrectly translate such passages as Titus 2:13, 2 Peter 1:1 and others is, according to Robertson, due to the influence of the grammatical work of George B. Winer. For over 100 years his work was considered the best and scholars were not inclined to disagree with him:

> However, Winer himself, being an anti-trinitarian, admitted that it was not grammatical grounds that led him to reject the correct rendering of Titus 2:13, but theological ones. In the Winer-Moulton Grammar (as cited by Robertson) page 162, Winer said, "Considerations derived from Paul's system of doctrine lead me to believe that *soteros* is not a second predicate, co-ordinate with *theou,* Christ being first called *megas theos,* and then *sotar.*" However, Robertson put it well when he said, "Sharp stands vindicated after all the dust has settled. We must let these passages mean what they want to mean regardless of our theories about the theology of the writers."[433]

APPENDIX 2:
LETTER OF DR. JULIUS
R. MANTEY TO THE
WATCHTOWER SOCIETY

"I haven't read any translation that is as diabolical and as damnable as the JW so-called translation. . . . They (the Society) hate Jesus Christ."

—Dr. Julius Mantey; "Distortions of the New Testament," Tape "T-2," available from Witness, Inc., Clayton, CA

July 11, 1974
Watchtower Bible & Tract Society
117 Adams St.
Brooklyn
New York 11201

Dear Sirs:

I have a copy of your letter addressed to *Caris* in Santa Ana, California, and I am writing to express my disagreement with statements made in that letter, as well as in quotations you have made from the Dana-Mantey Greek Grammar.

(1) Your statement: "their work allows for the rendering found in the *Kingdom Interlinear Translation of the Greek Scriptures* at John 1:1." There is no statement in our grammar that was ever meant to imply that "a god" was a permissible translation in John 1:1.

A. We had no "rule" to argue in support of the trinity.

B. Neither did we state that we did have such intention. We were simply delineating the facts inherent in Biblical language.

C. Your quotation from p. 148 (3) was in a paragraph under the heading: "*With the Subject in a Copulative sentence.*" Two examples occur there to illustrate that "the article points out the subject in these examples." But we made no statement in this paragraph about the predicate except that, "as it stands the other persons of the trinity may be implied in *theos.*" And isn't that the opposite of what your translation "a god" infers? You quoted me out of context. On pages 139 and 149 (VI) in our grammar we stated: "without the article *theos* signifies divine essence . . . *theos en ho logos* emphasizes Christ's participation in the essence of the divine nature." Our interpretation is in agreement with that in NEB and the TEV: "What God was, the Word was"; and with that of Barclay: "The nature of the Word was the same as the nature of God", which you quoted in your letter to *Caris.*

(2) Since Colwell's and Harner's articles in JBL [*Journal of Biblical Literature*], especially that of Harner, it is neither scholarly nor reasonable to translate John 1:1 "The Word was a god." Word-order has made obsolete and incorrect such a rendering.

(3) Your quotation of Colwell's rule is inadequate because it quotes only a part of his findings. You did not quote this strong assertion: "A predicate nominative which precedes the verb cannot be translated as an indefinite or a 'qualitative' noun solely because of the absence of the article."

(4) Prof. Harner, vol. 92:1 (1973) in *JBL,* has gone beyond Colwell's research and has discovered that anarthrous predicate nouns preceding the verb function primarily to express the na-

ture or character of the subject. He found this true in 53 passages in the Gospel of John and 8 in the Gospel of Mark. Both scholars wrote that when indefiniteness was intended the gospel writers regularly placed the predicate noun after the verb, and both Colwell and Harner have stated that *theos* in John 1:1 is not indefinite and should not be translated "a god." Watchtower writers appear to be the only ones advocating such a translation now. The evidence appears to be 99% against them.

(5) Your statement in your letter that the sacred text itself should guide one and "not just someone's rule book." We agree with you. But our study proves that Jehovah's Witnesses do the opposite of that whenever the "sacred text" differs with their heretical beliefs. For example the translation of *kolasis* as "*cutting off*" when punishment is the only meaning cited in the lexicons for it. The mistranslation of *ego eimi* as "I have been" in John 8:58. The addition of "for all time" in Hebrews 9:27 when nothing in the Greek New Testament supports it. The attempt to belittle Christ by mistranslating *arche tes ktiseos* "beginning of the creation" when he is magnified as "the creator of all things" (John 1:2) and as "equal with God" (Philippians 2:6) before he humbled himself and lived in a human body here on earth. Your quotation of "The Father is greater than I am" (John 14:28) to prove that Jesus was not equal to God overlooks the fact stated in Philippians 2:6–8, when Jesus said that he was still in his voluntary state of humiliation. That state ended when he ascended to heaven. Why the attempt to deliberately deceive people by mispunctuation by placing a comma after "today" in Luke 23:43 when in the Greek, Latin, German and all English translations except yours, *even in the Greek in your KIT,* the comma occurs after *lego* (I say)?—"Today you will be with me in Paradise." 2 Corinthians 5:8, "to be out of the body and at home with the Lord". These passages teach that the redeemed go immediately to heaven [after] death, which does not agree with your teachings that death ends all life until the resurrection. Cf. Psalms 23:6 and Hebrews 1:10.

The above are only a few examples of Watchtower mistranslations and perversions of God's Word.

In view of the preceding facts, especially because you have been quoting me out of context, I herewith request you not to quote the *Manual Grammar of the Greek New Testament* again, which you have been doing for 24 years. Also that you not quote it or me in any of your publications from this time on.

Also that you publicly and immediately apologize in the Watchtower magazine, since my words had no relevance to the absence of the article before *theos* in John 1:1. And please write to *Caris* and state that you misused and misquoted my "rule."

On the page before the *Preface* in the grammar are these words: "All rights reserved—no part of this book may be reproduced in any form without permission in writing from the publisher."

If you have such permission, please send me a photocopy of it.

If you do not heed these requests you will suffer the consequences.

Regretfully yours,
Julius R. Mantey

NOTES

Note: All Jehovah's Witnesses texts are published by the Watchtower Bible and Tract Society (WBTS, 25 Columbia Heights, Brooklyn, NY 11021).

1. Walter Martin and Norman Klann, *Jehovah of the Watchtower* (Chicago: Moody Press, 1974), p. 15.
2. Based on *Yearbook* reports.
3. *1997 Report of Jehovah's Witnesses Worldwide* (1998) at www.watchtower.org; website changed online topics in early 1999.
4. See the 1999 *Yearbook* and the WS website.
5. W. M. Nelson, R. K. Smith, "Jehovah's Witnesses Part II: Their Mission" in Hesselgrave (ed.), *Dynamic Religious Movements*, p. 192.
6. Edmond C. Gruss, *We Left Jehovah's Witnesses a Non-Profit Organization*, p. 6.
7. Ibid., pp. 6-11.
8. Ibid., p. 11.
9. Raymond Franz, *Crisis of Conscience* (Atlanta: Commentary, 1983), p. 31.
10. Van Baalen, J.K., *Chaos of the Cults*, p. 257.
11. Gerstner, *The Theology of the Major Sects*, p. 29.
12. See "The Christadelphians" in the *Ankerberg Theological Research Institute Magazine*, March/April 1999.
13. Edmund Gruss, *Apostles of Denial: An Examination and Exposé of the History, Doctrines and Claims of the Jehovah's Witnesses* (Grand Rapids, MI: Baker Book House, 1976), pp. 15-16.

14. Ibid., p. 14.
15. Charles T. Russell, *Studies in the Scriptures* (East Rutherford, NJ: Dawn Bible Students' Association, 6 Vols.; Vol. 5, *The Atonement Between God and Man*, n.d., reprint of 1886 ed.).
16. Gruss, *Apostles of Denial*, ch. 5.
17. Ibid., p. 76.
18. Ibid., pp. 19-33.
19. Ibid., p. 37.
20. Ibid., chs. 2-7.
21. Watch Tower Bible & Tract Society, *God's Kingdom of a Thousand Years Has Approached* (Brooklyn: WTB & TS, 1973), p. 342.
22. *The Watchtower*, July 15, 1960, p. 439, cited in Michael Van Buskirk, *The Scholastic Dishonesty of the Watchtower* (Santa Ana, CA: CARIS, 1976), p. 26.
23. *The Watchtower*, May 15, 1980, pp. 17-18.
24. *The Watchtower*, March 1, 1979, p. 16.
25. *The Watchtower*, September 1, 1979, p. 21.
26. H. Montague, "Watchtower Congregations: Communion or Conflict," p. 7 published by CARIS, Costa Mesa, CA.
27. C. J. Woodsworth, G. H. Fisher (comp. and ed.), *The Finished Mystery* (Brooklyn: International Bible Students Assoc., 1918), p. 387.
28. Gerstner, *Theology*, p. 34, citing Stroup, *The Jehovah's Witnesses* (1945) citing Rutherford, *Why Serve Jehovah*, p. 62.
29. Gerstner, p. 34, citing Stroup, p. 125.
30. Anthony Hoekema, *The Four Major Cults* (Eerdmans, 1970), p. 245, emphasis Russell's.
31. Gruss, *We Left Jehovah's Witnesses*, p. 41.
32. Charles S. Braden, *These Also Believe*, p. 365.
33. Gerstner, *Theology*, pp. 34-35.
34. William Cotnar, "Why I Was Kicked out of the Watchtower," *Eternity*, October 1980, p. 41.
35. *The Watchtower*, November 1, 1901, p. 660.
36. *The Watchtower*, October 1, 1967, p. 591.
37. *The Watchtower*, February 1, 1952, p. 80. The previous three references are cited by Van Buskirk in *The Scholastic Dishonesty of the Watchtower*, pp. 24-26 in fuller quotations.
38. Russell, *Studies in the Scriptures*, Vol. 1 (1907), pp. 10-11, cited in Gruss, *Apostles of Denial*, p. 220.
39. Russell, *Studies in the Scriptures*, Vol. 1, p. 41, cited in Gruss, *Apostles of Denial*, p. 221.
40. Gruss, *Apostles of Denial*, p. 221.
41. *"The Word"—Who Is He According to John?* (1962), p. 7.
42. Watch Tower Bible & Tract Society, *The Truth that leads to Eternal Life* (Brooklyn: WTB & TS, 1968), pp. 22, 42; 1975 Yearbook, p. 36.
43. Gruss, *We Left Jehovah's Witnesses*, pp. 77-78.
44. Nelson and Smith, "Jehovah's Witnesses Part II," in Hesselgrave (ed.), *Dynamic Religious Movements*, p. 193.
45. Ibid.
46. Ibid., pp. 194-197.
47. H. Montague, "Watchtower Congregations: Communion or Conflict?" pp. 1-7, CARIS tract.
48. Ibid.
49. Ibid.
50. Ibid.

51. Website, "How can you find the true religion?" Lesson 13.
52. Montague, "Watchtower Congregations," pp. 1-7, CARIS tract.
53. On, e.g., Mormonism see our book *Behind the Mask of Mormonism*, especially pp. 68-71.
54. Gruss, *We Left Jehovah's Witnesses*, pp. 19, 22.
55. Gruss, *Apostles of Denial*, pp. 4-5; *The Watchtower*, April 15, 1978, p. 15.
56. For example see *Paradise Restored*, p. 307; *The Nations Shall Know That I Am Jehovah—How?* pp. 6, 10.
57. Braden, *These Also Believe*, p. 380.
58. Hoekema, *Four Major Cults*, p. 285.
59. Martin, *Jehovah of the Watchtower*, p. 114.
60. J. F. Rutherford, Commentator *Preparation* (Brooklyn: Watch Tower Bible and Tract Society, 1933), pp. 19-20.
61. J. F. Rutherford, *Religion* (WBTS, 1940), p. 104, cited in Gruss, *Apostles of Denial*, p. 63.
62. J. F. Rutherford, *Enemies*, p. 118, cited in Gruss, *Apostles of Denial*, p. 63.
63. Ibid., p. 306, cited in Gruss, *Apostles of Denial*, p. 64.
64. *The Watchtower*, September 1, 1979, p. 28.
65. *The Watchtower*, November 1, 1976, p. 665.
66. *The Watchtower*, July 1, 1980, p. 12.
67. Watch Tower Bible & Tract Society, *Man's Salvation Out of World Distress at Hand* (Brooklyn: WTB & TS, 1975), pp. 335, 216.
68. *The Watchtower*, March 1, 1979, p. 18.
69. *Man's Salvation*, pp. 338-339, 226-227; *The Watchtower*, March 1, 1980, p. 21.
70. *Man's Salvation*, p. 215.
71. *The Watchtower*, September 1, 1979, p. 21.
72. *The Watchtower*, November 1, 1979, p. 26; *The Watchtower*, May 15, 1980, p. 27; *The Watchtower*, August 15, 1979, p. 27.
73. *The Watchtower*, September 1, 1979, p. 22.
74. Ibid., September 1, 1979, pp. 20-21.
75. *The Watchtower*, December 1951, pp. 731-732, cited in Martin, *Jehovah of the Watchtower*, p. 106; *The Watchtower*, September 1, 1979, p. 29.
76. Letter of August 1987.
77. *The Watchtower*, September 15, 1910, p. 298, cited in *Reprints of the Original Watchtower and Herald of Christ's Presence*, p. 4685.
78. Gruss, *We Left Jehovah's Witnesses*, p. 7.
79. For example, cf. Rutherford, *Preparation*, pp. 343-344.
80. Hoekema, *Four Major Cults*, pp. 249-255.
81. *God's Kingdom*, p. 352.
82. Rutherford, *Preparation*, pp. 342-344.
83. Hoekema, *Four Major Cults*, p. 255.
84. Gruss, *Apostles of Denial*, ch. 11.
85. Ibid., pp. 238-239.
86. Watch Tower Bible & Tract Society, *Make Sure of All Things Hold Fast to What Is Fine* (Brooklyn: WTB & TS, 1965), p. 267.
87. Watch Tower Bible & Tract Society, *Aid to Bible Understanding* (Brooklyn, NY: WTB & TS, 1971), p. 665.
88. *Make Sure*, p. 267.
89. W. M. Nelson, R. K. Smith, "Jehovah's Witnesses, Part II, Their Mission," in David Hesselgrave, *Dynamic Religious Movements*, p. 188.
90. Quoted in Nelson and Smith, ibid., in Hesselgrave, p. 181; *Studies in the Scriptures*, Vol. 7 (*The Finished Mystery*), p. 410.
91. *The Truth that Leads to Eternal Life*, p. 22; Watch Tower Bible & Tract Society, *Then Is Finished the Mystery of God* (Brooklyn: WTB & TS, 1969), p. 10.
92. Watch Tower Bible & Tract Society, *Things in Which It Is Impossible for God to Lie* (Brooklyn: WTB & TS, 1965), p. 256.
93. Rutherford, *Uncovered* (1937), pp. 48-49 cited in Braden, *These Also Believe*, p. 371.
94. *Let God Be True*, 2nd ed., p. 111, cited in Van Baalen, *The Chaos of the Cults*, p. 268.
95. *Things in Which It Is Impossible for God to Lie*, p. 259.
96. *"The Word"—Who Is He According to John?* p. 12.
97. *Let God be True* (1946, rev. 1952), p. 102, cited in Gruss, *Apostles of Denial*, p. 110.
98. Personal conversations with Jehovah's Witnesses. Incomprehensibility is not the same as irrationality.
99. Gruss, *Apostles of Denial*, pp. 101, 109-110.
100. *Aid to Bible Understanding*, p. 1152.
101. Ibid., p. 918.
102. Ibid., p. 920.
103. Ibid.
104. *The Truth Shall Make You Free* (1943), p. 246, cited in James Bjornstad, *Counterfeits at your Door* (Glendale, CA: Regal, 1979), p. 67.
105. *Things in Which It Is Impossible for God to Lie*, p. 231.
106. Bjornstad, *Counterfeits at Your Door*, p. 68.
107. Hoekema, *Four Major Cults*, p. 272.
108. *Let God Be True* (1946, Rev. 1952), p. 74, cited in Hoekema, *Four Major Cults*, p. 295.
109. *Aid to Bible Understanding*, p. 437.
110. *Things in Which It Is Impossible for God to Lie*, p. 211.
111. Russell, *Studies in the Scriptures*, Vol. 5 (1906), p. 454.
112. *The Truth Shall Make You Free* (1943), p. 264, cited in Bjornstad, *Counterfeits*, p. 93.
113. Nelson and Smith, "Jehovah's Witnesses," in Hesselgrave, *Dynamic*, pp. 178-179.
114. Bjornstad, *Counterfeits at Your Door*, p. 67.
115. Ibid., p. 68; see *Let Your Name be Sanctified* (1961), p. 272.
116. *Man's Salvation Out of World Distress*, pp. 42-43.
117. *The Watchtower*, January 15, 1980, p. 31, emphasis added.
118. Bjornstad, *Counterfeits at Your Door*, pp. 92-94; see *Make Sure of All Things*, p. 255.
119. Ibid.
120. *God's Kingdom of a Thousand Years*, p. 354; cf. *Man's Salvation Out of World Distress*, p. 42.
121. *Holy Spirit, The Force Behind the Coming New Order* (Brooklyn: WTB & TS, 1976), p. 11.
122. *Aid to Bible Understanding*, pp. 1543-1544; *The Watchtower*, November 1, 1976, p. 656.
123. *Aid to Bible Understanding*, pp. 1542-1543.
124. *Things in Which It Is Impossible for God to Lie*, p. 269.
125. *The Watchtower*, February 15, 1983, p. 12.
126. Anthony A. Hoekema, *Four Major Cults*, p. 269.
127. *Man's Salvation Out of World Distress at Hand!* (1975), p. 112.

128. *Making Your Family Life Happy* (1978), pp. 182-183.
129. *Make Sure of All Things, Hold Fast to What Is Fine* (1965), p. 296.
130. Ibid., p. 297.
131. Ibid., p. 439.
132. Ibid.
133. *Aid to Bible Understanding* (1971), p. 1240.
134. *The Watchtower*, May 1, 1979, p. 15.
135. Ibid., p. 20.
136. *The Watchtower*, June 15, 1977, p. 373.
137. *The Watchtower*, May 1, 1980, p. 13.
138. Hoekema, *Four Major Cults*, pp. 282-283.
139. Ibid.
140. Ibid., pp. 284-285.
141. Ibid., p. 285.
142. Ibid.
143. Ibid.
144. *Christianity Today*, December 12, 1980, pp. 68-71.
145. *Aid to Bible Understanding* (1971), p. 437, emphasis added.
146. *Life Everlasting in Freedom of the Sons of God* (1969), pp. 397-399.
147. Ibid., pp. 391 393, cf. pp. 396, 397.
148. Ibid., pp. 397-399.
149. *You May Survive Armageddon into God's New World* (1955), pp. 357-360.
150. See Jerry Bergman, "Paradise Postponed . . . And Postponed: Why Jehovah's Witnesses Have a High Mental Illness Level" *Christian Research Journal*, Summer 1996.
151. Edmond Gruss, *We Left Jehovah's Witnesses*, p. 132.
152. Ibid.
153. *You May Survive Armageddon*, pp. 354-355
154. *Aid to Bible Understanding*, p. 735.
155. *You May Survive Armageddon*, p. 355.
156. Ibid., p. 356.
157. Ibid., pp. 356-357.
158. *From Paradise Lost to Paradise Regained* (1958), p. 238.
159. *Life Everlasting*, p. 400.
160. *Things in Which It Is Impossible for God to Lie* (1965), p. 396.
161. *Aid to Bible Understanding*, p. 1671.
162. *Things in Which it Is Impossible for God to Lie*, p. 401; pp. 401-404; *From Paradise Lost to Paradise Regained*, p. 152; see also pp. 242, 244, 246 247, 249.
163. Walter Martin and Norman Klann, *Jehovah of the Watchtower* (Chicago: Moody Press, 1974), p. 71.
164. Edmond Gruss, *Apostles of Denial*, p. 90.
165. Hoekema, *Four Major Cults*, pp. 276-279.
166. Gruss, *Apostles of Denial*, pp. 142-143.
167. *Aid to Bible Understanding*, p. 33; cf. *Let God be True* (1946), p. 119, cited in Hoekema, *Four Major Cults*, p. 277.
168. *Aid to Bible Understanding*, p. 1373.
169. *From Paradise Lost*, p. 236.
170. *Things in Which It Is Impossible for God to Lie*, p. 232.
171. *You May Survive*, pp. 38-39.
172. *Aid to Bible Understanding*, p. 1373.
173. Hoekema, *Four Major Cults*, pp. 278-279.
174. Gruss, *Apostles of Denial*, p. 144.
175. Ibid., p. 145.
176. Gruss, *We Left Jehovah's Witnesses*, pp. 37-38.
177. Bjornstad, *Counterfeits*, p. 85, cites *New Heavens and a New Earth* (1953), pp. 147-148; *What Has Religion Done for Mankind* (1951), pp. 240-245.
178. Bjornstad, *Counterfeits*, p. 85.
179. *You May Survive*, p. 357.
180. Martin, *Jehovah of the Watchtower*, pp. 71-72.
181. *Let God Be True* (1946, rev. 1952), p. 74.
182. *Aid to Bible Understanding*, pp. 1532-1534.
183. Ibid., p. 1535.
184. *Is This Life All There Is?* pp. 96-97, 119.
185. Ibid., pp. 115-116, 120.
186. *Make Sure of All Things*, pp. 226-227.
187. See John Weldon, *Psychic Healing* (1982), chapter on psychometry and radionics; see also *Encyclopedia of New Age Beliefs*, chapter on divination.
188. *Demonism and the Watchtower* (1969), p. 14. (Gruss believes that much of what Goodrich claims in this area is accurate—see Gruss, *Apostles of Denial*, p. 33n.)
189. See Gruss, *Jehovah's Witnesses and Prophetic Speculation*, Appendix A, p. 113.
190. See Note 192, under Roy Goodrich.
191. For primary documentation consult Martin, *Jehovah of the Watchtower*, pp. 19-23; Gruss, *Apostles of Denial*, pp. 27, 45, 294-295; Gruss, *Jehovah's Witnesses and Prophetic Speculation*, chapter 6; Hoekema, *Four Major Cults*, p. 243; Van Baalen, *Chaos*, p. 259; Gruss, *We Left Jehovah's Witnesses*, op. cit., pp. 7, 65-66, 70, 74-75, 80-81, 83, 111, 118-119, 129; Montague, "Watchtower Congregations"; Hesselgrave, *Dynamic*, p. 183. For problems on the high incidents of mental illness among Jehovah's Witnesses, see Dr. Jerry Bergman, *The Mental Health of Jehovah's Witnesses* (Clayton, CA: Witness, Inc., 1987).
192. William and Joan Cetnar, *Questions for Jehovah's Witnesses* (Kunkleton, PA, 1983), p. 53 (cf. pp. 48-55). The Johannes Greber translation is cited in, e.g., *Make Sure of All Things*, p. 489. Greber was a spirit medium who claimed his translation originated in the spirit world. It translates John 1:1; Hebrews 1:8 and other passages the way the *NWT* does. Roy Goodrich, head of the Jehovah's Witness splinter sect Back to the Bible Way, discusses the Society's involvement with psychometry and radionics in his "Demonism and the Watchtower." These are spiritistic forms of medical diagnosis. See John Weldon and Zola Levitt, *Psychic Healing* (Chicago: Moody Press, 1982), pp. 53-65. The last known address of Back to the Bible Way was 517 N.E. Second St., Ft. Lauderdale, FL 33301.
193. Rutherford, *Riches* (WBTS, 1936), p. 316, and *Vindication* (WBTS, 1932), vol. 3, p. 250.
194. William and Joan Cetnar, *Questions*, p. 55.
195. Rutherford, *Preparation*, pp. 35-38, 67.
196. *The Watchtower*, April 1, 1972, p. 200; cf. Sept. 1, 1932, p. 263. For further information and documentation as to the Society's claim to direction and guidance from the spirit world see Witness, Inc.'s tape "Angels of the New Light" and the text *The Heavenly Weatherman* (p. 3).
197. Much of this information was supplied by Duane Magnani of Witness, Inc., P.O. Box 597, Clayton, CA 94517. For further information and documentation as to the

Societies claim to direction and guidance from the spirit world see Witness, Inc.'s tape "Angels of the New Light" and the text *The Heavenly Weatherman* (p. 3). A free catalogue of materials may be requested.

198. Gruss, *Apostles of Denial*, p. 32.

199. Ibid., 15-16.

200. Ken Raines, "Rutherford and Biblical Interpretation: Angelic Channeling, Part 1, *JW Research*, Vol. 1, no. 1, Winter, 1994, p. 2.

201. *Angels and Women*, 1924, p. 5.

202. "Taught of God," *The Watchtower*, November 1, 1931.

203. See our book *The Facts on the Jehovah's Witnesses* (Eugene, OR: Harvest House); also Gruss discusses each of these, see his *The Jehovah's Witness and Prophetic Speculation* (Nutley, NJ: Presbyterian and Reformed, 1972).

204. Benjamin Wilson, *The Emphatic Diaglott New Testament* (Interlinear Edition, Brooklyn: Watchtower Bible and Tract Society, 1942), pp. 106, 372.

205. Gruss, *Apostles*, pp. 194-96.

206. Wilson, *Emphatic Diaglott*, "Preface," p. 3.

207. Website, "How Can You Find the True Religion?" Lesson 13, point 4, emphasis in original.

208. Gruss, pp. 32-33, 219. See also *The Watchtower*, September 1, 1932, p. 263; *Light*, Vol. 1, 1930, pp. 106, 120, 218; Vol. 2, 1930, pp. 12, 20; *Vindication*, Vol. 3, 1932, p. 250, *Preparation*, 1933, pp. 36, 67.

209. For documentation see Cetnar and Cetnar, *Questions*, pp. 48-55.

210. See Robert M. Bowman, Jr., 4-part series on Jehovah's Witnesses and the Bible, see especially parts 1 & 2, *Christian Research Journal*, Fall 1989, taken from internet copy part 2, p. 1.

211. *The Kingdom Interlinear Translation of the Greek Scriptures* (Brooklyn: WBTS, 1969), p. 5.

212. *The New World Translation of the Holy Scriptures* (Brooklyn: WBTS, 1961), p. 5.

213. *All Scripture Is Inspired by God and Beneficial* (Brooklyn: WBTS, 1963), pp. 226-30.

214. Robert Countess, *The Jehovah's Witnesses New Testament* (Phillipsburg, NJ: Presbyterian and Reformed, 1983), pp. 91, 93.

215. Gruss, pp. 236-37.

216. Anthony Hoekema, *Four Major Cults*, pp. 238-39.

217. Martin, pp. 129, 175-78, cf. Gruss, p. 198.

218. Bruce Metzger, "The Jehovah's Witnesses and Jesus Christ," report of April 1953, *Theology Today* (Princeton, NJ: Theological Book Agency, 1953), p. 74.

219. Julius Mantey, *Depth Exploration in the New Testament* (New York: Vantage Press, 1980), pp. 136-37.

220. "The Royal Shepherd of Bible Prophecy," *The Watchtower*, Vol. 100, no. 17, Sept. 1, 1979 (Brooklyn: WBTS), p. 30.

221. *The Watchtower*, March 15, 1972, p. 189.

222. Colin Brown, *The New International Dictionary of New Testament Theology* (Grand Rapids, MI: Zondervan, 1973), Vol. 3, "Punishment"; R. C. Trench, *Synonyms of the New Testament* (Grand Rapids, MI: Eerdmans, 1978), pp. 24-25.

223. Mantey, *Depth*, p. 142.

224. Trench, *Synonyms*, pp. 25-26.

225. Mantey, *Depth*, p. 137.

226. Michael Van Buskirk, *The Scholastic Dishonesty of the Watchtower* (Santa Ana, CA: Christian Apologetics and Research Information Service, 1976).

227. Ibid.

228. Mantey, *Depth*, pp. 142-43.

229. R. C. H. Lenski, *The Interpretations of St. Luke's Gospel* (Minneapolis: Augsburg Publishers House, 1961), pp. 1145-46.

230. Martin, *Jehovah of the Watchtower*, p. 135.

231. *The Kingdom Interlinear Translation of the Greek Scriptures*, p. 1160.

232. Nigel Turner, *Grammatical Insights into the New Testament* (Edinburgh: T. and T. Clarke, 1965), pp. 14-15.

233. *The Kingdom Interlinear Translation*, p. 1160.

234. Turner, *Grammatical*, p. 15.

235. Thomas Hewitt, in the Tyndale's New Testament Commentary Series, *The Epistle to the Hebrews* (Grand Rapids, MI: Eerdmans, 1973), pp. 56-57.

236. F. F. Bruce, *The Epistle to the Hebrews* in *The New International Commentary of the New Testament* (Grand Rapids, MI: Eerdmans, 1973), p. 20.

237. *Make Sure of All Things, Hold Fast to That Which Is Fine*, p. 364.

238. Metzger, "Jehovah's Witnesses and Jesus Christ," p. 77; also Kenneth Wuest, *Word Studies in the Greek New Testament*, Vol. 2, "Hebrews" (Grand Rapids, MI: Eerdmans, 1971), p. 46.

239. A. T. Robertson, *Word Pictures in the New Testament*, Vol. 4 (Nashville: Broadman, 1930), p. 491.

240. Metzger, "Jehovah's Witnesses and Jesus Christ," pp. 77-78.

241. Gruss, *Apostles*, pp. 204-205.

242. From a condensation of Kuehne's article published in the CARIS newsletter May 1978, Vol. 2, no. 2, stated to be accurate by Kuehne in Vol. 2, no. 3, "letters".

243. Metzger, "Jehovah's Witnesses and Jesus Christ," p. 79.

244. Dana and Mantey, *A Manual Grammar of the Greek New Testament* (Toronto, Canada: MacMillian, 1957), p. 147.

245. James White, *The King James Only Controversy* (Minneapolis: Bethany 1995) p. 270.

246. Mantey, *Depth*, pp. 138-39.

247. A. T. Robertson, *A Grammar of the Greek New Testament* (Nashville: Broadman Press, 1934), pp. 767-68.

248. A. T. Robertson, *Word Pictures*, Vol. 5, pp. 4-5.

249. Metzger, "Jehovah's Witnesses and Jesus Christ," pp 75-76.

250. Van Buskirk, *Scholastic Dishonesty*, p. 16.

251. Countess, Chapter 4, pp. 54-55; Appendix Table 5.

252. Martin, *Jehovah of the Watchtower*, p. 136.

253. Ibid., p. 141.

254. J. H. Thayer, *New Thayer's Greek-English Lexicon* (Wilmington, DE: Associated Publishers and Authors, 1977), p. 490.

255. Countess, *Jehovah's Witnesses New Testament*, p. 23; Gruss, *Apostles*, pp. 198-99.

256. Gruss, *Apostles*, pp. 198-200; Martin, *Jehovah of the Watchtower*, pp. 129-31.

257. Bruce Metzger, *The Bible Translator*, July 1964, p. 152, cited in Gruss, *Apostles*, p. 200.

258. Gruss, *Apostles*, pp. 200-205.

259. Ibid., p. 201.
260. Countess, *Jehovah's Witnesses New Testament*, ch. 6.
261. Rowley, "How Not to Translate the Bible," *The Expository Times*, Nov. 1953, pp. 41-42, cf. Jan. 1956, p. 107; cited by Gruss, *Apostles of Denial*, pp. 212-13.
262. Gruss, *Apostles*, p. 213.
263. *The Watchtower*, March 1, 1975, p. 151.
264. *Aid to Bible Understanding*, pp. 1344, 1346.
265. Ibid., p. 1347.
266. Ibid., p. 1348.
267. Ibid.
268. *The Watchtower*, September 1, 1979, p. 29.
269. Franz, *Crisis of Conscience* (1993), p. 138.
270. *Holy Spirit, The Force Behind the Coming New Order*, pp. 148, 150.
271. *The Watchtower*, May 1, 1914, reprints Vol. 12, p. 5450.
272. N.H. Barbour and C.T. Russell, *Three Worlds and the Harvest of this World* (1877), p. 17, cited in Gruss, *Jehovah's Witnesses and Prophetic Speculation*, p. 82.
273. C.T. Russell, *The Time Is at Hand* (1889), p. 101, cited in Gruss, *Jehovah's Witnesses and Prophetic Speculation*, p. 83.
274. *The Watchtower* reprints, vol. 4, p. 1677.
275. C.T. Russell, *The New Creation* (1904), p. 579, cited in Gruss, *Jehovah's Witnesses' and Prophetic Speculation*, p. 84.
276. *The Watchtower* reprints vol. 6, p. 5450, cited in Gruss, *Jehovah's Witnesses and Prophetic Speculation*, p. 84.
277. Gruss, *Jehovah's Witnesses and Prophetic Speculation*, pp. 23-26.
278. *From Paradise Lost to Paradise Regained* (1958), p. 170.
279. C.T. Russell, *Thy Kingdom Come* (1891), p. 126, cited in Gruss, *Jehovah's Witnesses and Prophetic Speculation*, p. 21.
280. See Charles T. Russell, *Studies in the Scriptures*, Vol. 3, (1891), p. 284; cf., Gruss, *Apostles of Denial*, pp. 232-34.
281. C.T. Russell, *The Time Is at Hand* (1889), pp. 76-78 cited in Gruss, *Jehovah's Witnesses and Prophetic Speculation*, p. 23.
282. *The Watchtower* reprints, Vol. 12, p. 5659.
283. Ibid., p. 5950.
284. Gruss, *Jehovah's Witnesses and Prophetic Speculation*, pp. 24-25.
285. *The Watchtower* reprints, Vol. 9, p. 4067.
286. *The Watchtower* reprints, Vol. 9, (1907), p. 4067.
287. Gruss, *Jehovah's Witnesses and Prophetic Speculation*, pp. 85-86.
288. C.J. Woodsworth and G.H. Fisher (eds.), *The Finished Mystery* (1917).
289. Gruss, *Jehovah's Witnesses and Prophetic Speculation*, pp. 85-86.
290. See Rutherford's *Millions Now Living Will Never Die* (1920), pp. 97, 105, 140, and Gruss, *Jehovah's Witnesses and Prophetic Speculation*, p. 87.
291. *The Watchtower*, January 1, 1925, p. 3.
292. *The Watchtower*, September, 1925, p. 262.
293. Rutherford, *Vindication* (1931), pp. 338-339, cited in Gruss, *Jehovah's Witnesses and Prophetic Speculation*, p. 89.
294. J.F. Rutherford, *Light*, Vol. 2, p. 327 (1930), cited in Gruss, *Jehovah's Witnesses and Prophetic Speculation*, p. 89.
295. J.F. Rutherford, *Vindication*, Vol. 1 (1931), p. 147.
296. J.F. Rutherford, *Preparation* (1933), p. 341.
297. Ibid., pp. 348-349.
298. Rutherford, *Vindication*, p. 310, cited in Gruss, *Jehovah's Witnesses and Prophetic Speculation*, p. 89.
299. *Let God Be True* (1946), p. 194, cited in Gruss, *Jehovah's Witnesses and Prophetic Speculation*, p. 92.
300. *This Means Everlasting Life* (1950), p. 311, cited in Gruss, *Jehovah's Witnesses and Prophetic Speculation*, p. 93.
301. *You May Survive Armageddon*, p. 11; cf. p. 362.
302. Gruss, *Jehovah's Witnesses and Prophetic Speculation*, p. 93.
303. *You May Survive Armageddon*, p. 331.
304. *From Paradise Lost*, p. 205.
305. *Your Will Be Done on Earth*, p. 105.
306. *God's Kingdom of a Thousand Years Has Approached*, p. 363; cf. pp. 24, 14, 18-21, 28, 332, 336-363.
307. *All Scripture Is Inspired by God and Beneficial* (1963), p. 286, cited in Gruss, *Jehovah's Witnesses and Prophetic Speculation*, p. 93.
308. Gruss, *Jehovah's Witnesses and Prophetic Speculation*, p. 59.
309. *Life Everlasting*, pp. 27, 29-30. As if to cover itself, *The Watchtower* of August 15, 1968, p. 494, warned against looking to 1975.
310. *Man's Salvation Out of World Distress at Hand*, p. 312.
311. Ibid., p. 369.
312. Ibid., p. 371.
313. *God's Kingdom*, p. 361.
314. *Man's Salvation Out of World Distress at Hand*, pp. 283-284.
315. Ibid., p. 366.
316. Ibid., p. 309, emphasis added.
317. Ibid., p. 308.
318. Gruss, *Jehovah's Witnesses and Prophetic Speculation*, pp. 99-101.
319. Ibid., p. 100.
320. *1975 Yearbook*, pp. 74-75.
321. *Man's Salvation*, p. 287.
322. Russell, *Studies in Scriptures*, Vol. 4, p. 621.
323. Eric and Jean Grueshaber, *Exposé of Jehovah's Witnesses* (1978), p. 14.
324. *1975 Yearbook*, p. 76.
325. Rutherford, *Millions Now Living Will Never Die*, pp. 89-90, cited in Gruss, *Apostles of Denial*, p. 26.
326. *1975 Yearbook*, pp. 145-146.
327. Ibid., pp. 74-75.
328. Gruss, *We Left Jehovah's Witnesses*, p. 20.
329. Ibid., p. 44.
330. Gruss, *Apostles of Denial*, p. 104n; cf. pp. 56-66, 76.
331. Van Baalen, *Chaos of the Cults*, p. 258.
332. Ibid., pp. 228-229.
333. Gruss, *Apostles of Denial*, pp. 19, 33.
334. Ibid., pp. 19-37.
335. Gruss, *Apostles of Denial*, p. 234n.
336. *The Watchtower*, January 15, 1969, p. 51.
337. *God's Kingdom*, p. 346.
338. Cited in Gruss, *Apostles of Denial*, p. 62n.
339. Cf. Gruss, *Apostles of Denial*, Appendix A., for example see the April, 1979 issue of *Dawn: A Herald of Christ's Presence*, pp. 41-48.

340. Van Buskirk, *Scholastic Dishonesty*, p. 24.
341. *Zion's Watchtower*, March 1, 1896, p. 47; cf. *Studies in the Scriptures*, Vol. 4, pp. 613- 614; *Zion's Watchtower*, April 15, 1904, p. 125; *The Watchtower*, March 1, 1923, p. 68, cited in Van Buskirk, *Scholastic Dishonesty*, pp. 27-42.
342. Van Buskirk, *Scholastic Dishonesty*, p. 32.
343. Duane Magnani, *Who Is the Faithful and Wise Servant?* pp. 31-32.
344. Martin, *Jehovah of the Watchtower*, pp. 41-42.
345. Ibid., pp. 21-24, 36, 41-42.
346. Rutherford, *Vindication*, 1931, cited in Gruss, *Apostles of Denial*, p. 57.
347. Rutherford, *Preparation*, p. 343.
348. Gruss, *Apostles of Denial*, pp. 57, 59.
349. Ibid., p. 57.
350. *The Watchtower*, July 15, 1960, p. 439.
351. *Studies in the Scriptures*, vol. 7, p. 159.
352. *Then Is Finished the Mystery of God*, p. 232.
353. Rutherford, *Reconciliation*, pp. 323-324.
354. Rutherford, *Salvation*, p. 43.
355. *From Paradise Lost to Paradise Regained*, p. 236.
356. C.T. Russell, *Studies in the Scriptures*, Vol. 1, p. 110.
357. *The Watchtower*, February 1, 1954, p. 85.
358. *The Watchtower*, March 1, 1965, p. 139.
359. *The Watchtower* reprints, July 15, 1898, p. 2337.
360. *The Watchtower* reprints October 1880, p. 144.
361. Charter of the Watchtower Society of Pennsylvania, Article II.
362. *The Watchtower*, January 1, 1954, p. 31.
363. *The Watchtower*, May 15, 1954, p. 317.
364. Russell, *Studies in the Scriptures*, Vol. 5, p. 478.
365. J.F. Rutherford, *The Harp of God*, pp. 328 or 334 depending on edition.
366. Russell, *Studies in the Scriptures*, Vol. 5, pp. 478-486.
367. Rutherford, *Salvation*, p. 224.
368. Russell, *Studies in the Scriptures*, Vol. 3, p. 244.
369. Rutherford, *Comfort for the Jews*, p. 55.
370. *Let God be True*, 2nd ed., pp. 217-218.
371. Russell, *Studies in the Scriptures*, Vol. 1, p. 266.
372. *This Means Everlasting Life*, p. 197.
373. *Babylon The Great Has Fallen! God's Kingdom Rules!* p. 548.
374. *What Pastor Russell Said*, p. 297.
375. Rutherford, *Vindication*, Vol. 3, p. 204.
376. Rutherford, *Riches*, pp. 324-325.
377. Rutherford, *Prophecy*, pp. 67-68.
378. *Awake!* March 22, 1963, p. 32.
379. Gruss, *Apostles of Denial*, p. 255.
380. Van Buskirk, *Scholastic Dishonesty*, p. 47.
381. Gruss, *Apostles of Denial*, p. 193.
382. Ibid., p. 107.
383. Ibid., pp. 107-108.
384. Gruss, *Jehovah's Witnesses and Prophetic Speculation*, ch. 3.
385. Ibid., p. 37.
386. Van Buskirk, *Scholastic Dishonesty*, p. 15.
387. The xeroxed reproduction of the Westcott and Hort Text (p. v) is from note 432.
388. William Barclay, *Many Witnesses, One Lord* (1963), pp. 23-24.
389. Ibid., p. 23.

390. Ibid., p. 24.
391. Colin Brown (ed.), *The New International Dictionary of New Testament Theology* (1977), pp. 81, 82.
392. Ibid., p. 82.
393. As far as we can determine this practice has not been discontinued.
394. Van Buskirk, *Scholastic Dishonesty*, p. 7.
395. Ibid., pp. 12-13.
396. See, e.g., the *New World Translation* 1953 appendix, pp. 770-71 and the original *Britannica* article edition 11, vol. 7, p. 506; *The New Catholic Encyclopedia*, 1967, vol. 14, p. 306 with *The Truth that Leads to Eternal Life*, 1968, p. 22; *The Quarterly Journal*, July-Sept. 1990, p. 10.
397. For primary documentation consult Martin, *Jehovah of the Watchtower*; Gruss, *Apostles of Denial*, pp. 27, 45, 294-295; Gruss, *Jehovah's Witnesses and Prophetic Speculation*, ch. 6; Hoekema, *Four Major Cults*, p. 243; Van Baalen, *Chaos*, p. 259; Gruss, *We Left Jehovah's Witnesses*, pp. 7, 65-66, 70, 74- 75, 80-81, 83, 111, 118-119, 129; H. Montague, *Watchtower Congregations—Communion or Conflict: An Inside Look at the Kingdom Hall* published by CARIS, and Hesselgrave, *Dynamic Religious Movements*, p. 183.
398. Martin, *Jehovah of the Watchtower*, p. 21.
399. Gruss, *We Left Jehovah's Witnesses*, p. 7.
400. Ibid., p. 66.
401. H. Montague, *Watchtower Congregations—Communion or Conflict: An Inside Look at the Kingdom Hall* published by CARIS.
402. Gruss, *We Left Jehovah's Witnesses*, pp. 118-119.
403. Montague, *Jehovah's Witnesses and Blood Transfusions*.
404. Ibid., p. 19.
405. Gruss, *We Left Jehovah's Witnesses*, p. 66.
406. *Awake!* March 8, 1960, p. 27.
407. *Christianity Today*, December 12, 1980, p. 69.
408. John Stedman, "Jehovah's Witnesses and Mental Illness," *CARIS Newsletter*, February–March, 1977; Vol. 1, no. 2.
409. Ibid.
410. Ibid.
411. Jerry Bergman, "Paradise Postponed . . . And Postponed: Why Jehovah's Witnesses Have a High Mental Illness Level," *Christian Research Journal*, Summer 1976, pp. 36, 37, 41. See especially Lois Randel, "The Apocalypticism of the Jehovah's Witnesses," *Free Inquiry*, Winter 1984, pp. 18-24 as well as *The British Journal of Psychiatry*, June 1975; *Social Compass*, March 1976; *The American Journal of Psychiatry*, March 1949; Robert Potter, "A Social Psychological Study of Fundamentalist Christianity" (Ph.D. Dissertation, Sussex University, England, 1985); and Kjell Totland, "The Mental Health of Jehovah's Witnesses," *Journal of the Norwegian Psychological Association*, 1996.
412. Morey, *How to Answer a Jehovah's Witness*, pp. 14-15.
413. See, e.g., *The Watchtower*, June, 1906, from Gerstner, *The Theology of the Major Sects*, p. 34.
414. *Aid to Understanding the Bible*, p. 500.
415. Hoekema, *Four Major Cults*, p. 332.
416. Gruss, *We Left Jehovah's Witnesses*, p. 21.
417. Gruss, *Apostles of Denial*, pp. 261-263.
418. The verses listed with each of these five points should be read in a good, modern translation like the New

International Version or the New American Standard Bible, since some were mistranslated in the King James Version and in the *New World Translation.*

419. Metzger, *The Bible Translator,* pp. 79-80.
420. Moulton and Milligan, *The Vocabulary of the Greek Testament* (1980), p. 683. See F. F. Bruce, *The Epistle to the Hebrews; The New International Commentary on the New Testament* (1973), pp. 5-6.
421. Schnell, *Jehovah's Witnesses' Errors Exposed,* pp. 13; cf. p. 100.
422. *Is This Life All There Is?* p. 99.
423. Franz, *Crisis of Conscience,* p. 31.
424. *Is This Life All There Is?* p. 99.
425. From a condensation published in the CARIS newsletter May 1978 Vol. 2, no. 2, stated to be accurate by the author (Vol. 2, no. 3 "letter").

426. Bruce M. Metzger, "The Jehovah's Witnesses and Jesus Christ: A Biblical and Theological Appraisal," rpt. of *Theology Today* article April 1953 (Princeton, NJ: Theological Book Agency), p. 79.
427. Dana and Mantey, *A Manual Grammar of the Greek New Testament* (Toronto, Canada: MacMillian) 1957, p. 147.
428. James White, *The King James Only Controversy* (Minneapolis: Bethany, 1995), p. 268.
429. Ibid., p. 269.
430. Ibid., p. 3, emphasis added.
431. Ibid., p. 270.
432. Ibid., citing Robertson, *The Minister and His Greek New Testament,* p. 62.
433. White, *King James Only Controversy,* p. 270; Greek words transliterated by the authors.

KRISHNAMURTI FOUNDATION

INFO AT A GLANCE

Name: Krishnamurti Foundation of America.

Purpose: To disseminate Krishnamurti's teachings and set people free from their enslavements. "My only concern is to set men absolutely unconditionally free." (Lutyens' biography, p. 297.)

Founder: Jiddhu Krishnamurti.

Source of authority: Self.

Examples of occult potential: "Awareness" meditation.

Key literature: *The Awakening of Intelligence; Commentaries on Living* (multivolume); *Freedom from the Known.*

Attitude toward Christianity: Rejecting.

Quotes:

"The worship of authority, whether in big or little things, is evil, the more so in religious matters. There is no intermediary between you and reality; and if there is one, he is a perverter, a mischief-maker, it does not matter who he is, whether the highest savior or your latest guru or teachers." (D. Rajaqupal, ed., *Commentaries on Living, First Series from the Notebooks of J. Krishnamurti,* p. 66.)

"One has to be a light unto oneself; following the light of another only leads one into darkness." (D. Rajaqupal, ed., *Commentaries on Living, Third Series from the Notebooks of J. Krishnamurti,* p. 207.)

DOCTRINAL SUMMARY

God: Ineffable.

Jesus: A crutch; mythic.

Salvation: By "exact awareness" as defined by Krishnamurti.

Death: Concept vague.

THE LOCAL CHURCH

INFO AT A GLANCE

Name: The Local Church; Living Stream Ministry.

Purpose: To build God a body.

Founder: Witness Lee (The Local Church claim Watchman Nee as their founder).

Source of authority: Witness Lee; individual revelations; Watchman Nee.

Revealed teachings: Yes.

Claim: To be the only true church that God is satisfied with.

Examples of occult potential: Whatever might exist would probably originate in the mystical approach and claims of new revelation. Lee, however, was not very supportive of supernatural experiences.

Key literature: The books of Witness Lee and Watchman Nee.

Attitude toward Christianity: Rejecting. (When Lee refers to "Christians" or even "religion," he is generally referring to true believers.)

Quotes:

"If you keep religion [Christianity], you will lose Christ." (Witness Lee, *Christ vs. Religion*, p. 157.)

"Our own distinctive understanding of God's economy rests upon the simple premise that God operates in time upon His elect to make them the same as He is in life, nature, and expression. . . . His elect become God by their union and communion with Him and by their continual dependence on Him and on what He

is in Himself." (Kerry S. Robichaux, "The Divine Trinity in the Divine Economy," *Affirmation & Critique*, April 1999, p. 37.)

"If people ask if I come from China, I would tell them, 'No, I come from the third heaven!'" (Witness Lee, *How to Meet*, p. 31.)

Brothers, while you are gardening, you have to say something for Christ. You can speak to the birds: "Little bird, I want to tell you that Christ is my life. My life is better than yours. I am so proud of Him." Tell the creatures something about Christ. I am not joking. You will learn how to function. Then, when you come to the meeting, it will be easy for you to say something . . . . And again I say, we have many opportunities every day to practice. We may not have a human audience, but we can always speak to the beings in the air. When we speak to human beings, there may not be so much need of exercising the spirit, but when we speak to the beings in the air, the mind does not work. To exercise the mind to speak to the angels is useless; we must exercise our spirit to speak to them. (Witness Lee, *How to Meet*, pp. 112–113.)

DOCTRINAL SUMMARY

God: Contrary views, such as Modalism (God is one Person with three modes) or historic trinitarianism.

Jesus: God as a man; the Trinity; after the resurrection He became the Holy Spirit or the "Lord Spirit."

Holy Spirit: Jesus Christ as Spirit; "The Lord Spirit," the Trinity.

211

Trinity: Orthodox and unorthodox views; "The Lord Spirit." The Trinity was "assumed" so God could mingle Himself with man. (See *Affirmation & Critique*, the Living Stream Ministry Quarterly, 1996–1997, all issues for a detailed treatment of their unorthodox views [www.lsm.org].)

Salvation: Orthodox and unorthodox views. The infusing of God's uncreated life; complex ideas on sanctification.

Man: Redeemed man is part of God.

Sin: Orthodox and unorthodox views. Variously personified as Satan, or used in the biblical meaning. Lee's views on morality may tend to depreciate the biblical emphasis.

Satan: Variously; a personification of sin, God's enemy.

The Fall: A nullifying of the spirit's ability to contact God through Satan's invading of the flesh. In a sense even created man was "fallen" man since he still required redemption.

The Second Coming: Christ will return visibly but as the "Lord Spirit," not necessarily as the biblical Jesus Christ.

Bible: Often viewed as "the dead letter" (in contrast to "new revelations") and interpreted figuratively or allegorically.

Heaven and Hell: Redeemed man exists as God's body; Satan and unredeemed man would seem to be annihilated in the lake of fire.

LUCIS TRUST

Name: The Arcane School, Full Moon Meditation Group, Lucis Trust.

Purpose: To help institute the "reappearance" of the Christ; to help foster love and brotherhood in the world through occult power.

Founder: Alice A. Bailey.

Source of authority: The spiritistic writings of A. A. Bailey received from an alleged "ascended master" (spirit) who called himself "the Tibetan."

Revealed teachings: Yes.

Examples of occult potential: Spiritism, contacting the dead, psychic development.

Key literature: Alice Bailey, *From Bethlehem to Calvary; The Reappearance of the Christ;* and other books.

Attitude toward Christianity: Rejecting.

Quote:

"Jehovah [is] the tribal God of the Jews. Jehovah is not God." (Alice Bailey, *Esoteric Healing,* p. 393.)

"Always down the centuries . . . a divine Son of God has come forth and under many different names. Then the Christ came and apparently left us, with His work unfinished and His vision for mankind not yet consummated. For two thousand years it has seemed as if all His work had been blocked, frustrated and of no avail." (Alice Bailey, *From Bethlehem to Calvary,* p. 191.)

Note: The writings of Alice Bailey have resulted in a number of "New Age" groups. Those based to one degree or another on her writing (all make use of them) include the Arcane School, Meditation Group of the New Age, Full Moon Meditation Groups, School of Esoteric Studies, Arcana Workshops, Aquarian Educational Group and the School of Light and Realization (SOLAR). Robert Assagioli, founder of the Psychosynthesis movement, was the Arcane School representative of Italy for many years (Alice Bailey, *The Unfinished Autobiography,* p. 224).

DOCTRINAL SUMMARY

God: Energy; indefinable; still evolving.

Jesus: An advanced occult initiate; indwelt by the Christ.

The Christ: An advanced cosmic Being.

The Holy Spirit: The part of divinity active in matter.

Salvation: Through occult development and good works.

Man: Part of God.

Sin: Ignorance.

The Bible: Interpreted mystically or esoterically.

Heaven and Hell: Positive or negative states of consciousness and experiences.

THE MASONIC LODGE

INFO AT A GLANCE

Name: The Masonic Lodge (Masonry, Freemasonry, or sometimes "Speculative" or "Symbolic" Masonry)

Purpose: The uniting of men in fellowship under the principal themes of the Fatherhood of God, the brotherhood of man, and the immortality of the soul. For many Masons Masonry is a religious quest for spiritual enlightenment; however, ultimately, in the higher degrees the purpose is to conform the world to Masonic beliefs.

Founder: No single individual. Masonry gradually evolved into its present form, known as "speculative" Masonry. This distinguishes it from the "operative" or "working" Masonry of the medieval stone masons. Operative

Masonry slowly assimilated the mysticism and occultism of numerous religions and philosophies of the Middle Ages to become what is known as modern speculative Masonry. Most scholars trace modern Masonry to the time when four lodges merged in London in 1717 to form the first Grand Lodge.

Theology: Polytheistic, syncretistic.

Practice: Secret ritual, individual spiritual quest.

Historic antecedents: Ancient pagan mystery religion, medieval trade unions and occult practices.

Spheres of influence: Church, education, business, politics, charitable agency.

Ethics: Subjective, relative, amoral.

Levels of initiation: Social, religious, mystical.

Worldview: Humanistic, eclectic, mystical.

Source of authority: Masonic ritual, "landmarks" (principles or doctrines), Grand Lodges and prominent Masonic authorities and writers.

Revealed teachings: Technically, yes, even though Masonry has deistic tendencies. The ritual of the Scottish Rite teaches, "Masonry is of divine origin."[1] The Iowa Quarterly Bulletin teaches, "Masonry is a divinely appointed institution. . . ."[2] The charge to the candidate for the second degree (Fellowcraft) tells him, "Masonry [is] of a divine and moral nature. . . ."[3]

Attitude to other religions: Condescending.

Key literature: Masonic Monitors (texts of ritual) and writings of prominent Masons such as Mackey, Coil and Pike.

Occult dynamics: Masonry has a number of similarities to ancient pagan mystery religion. In addition, for many, Masonry provides an introduction to mysticism, paganism and the occult, which may culminate with involvement in occult philosophy and practices.

False claims: Masonry is not a religion or a substitute for religion. The following is either implied or stated in Masonic literature:

Masonry is not occultic.
Masonry does not offer a system of salvation.
To be merely a fraternal brotherhood.
To constitute the one true religion.
To support the church.
To be tolerant of all religions; further, to unite all religions.
To honor the Bible and all Scriptures.
To not interfere with one's religion or politics.

Quote:

"Hear us with indulgence, O infinite Deity. . . . Help us to perform all our Masonic duties, to ourselves, to other men, and to Thee. Let the great flood of Masonic light flow in a perpetual current over the whole world and make Masonry the creed of all mankind."[4]

—J. Blanchard,
Scottish Rite Masonry Illustrated

Note: Besides this chapter in this book, the authors have published four additional texts on Masonry. Unfortunately, the response of the Lodge to these texts in reviews and personal conversation shows that Masons prefer not to deal forthrightly with the issues we have raised. Until the Lodge does so we will stand by our conviction that Masonry is an anti-Christian religion and that Christians, in good conscience, can neither logically join nor remain in the Lodge. Because the material in these other texts is relevant to our discussion here, we will comment briefly on it.

In *The Facts on the Masonic Lodge* we extensively cited the foundation of Masonry, the ritual of the Blue Lodge. We proved from the authoritative ritual that Masonry is a religion. We also showed that at every point Masonry opposes Christian faith. The purpose of that short text was to document from the ritual that Masonry is engaging in deception when it claims that it (1) is not a religion and (2) does not conflict with Christian faith but complements and encourages it.

In our larger book, *Christianity and the Secret Teachings of the Masonic Lodge,* we wrote specifically to the Christian Mason, again documenting Masonic doctrines from the ritual of the Blue Lodge, but also extending the discussion into the higher degrees of the York and Scottish rites. This book also proves (in more detail than *The Facts on the Masonic Lodge*) that it is logically impossible for one who professes Christian faith to become or remain a Mason.

In *Bowing at Strange Altars* (Ankerberg Theological Research Institute, 1993), we critiqued the Southern Baptist Convention's report on its acceptance of Masonry. In a point by point discussion, we showed why it was wrong for Southern Baptists to conclude that Christians could join the Lodge. Because the Lodge is so influential in the Baptist Church—an estimated 500,000 to 1,300,000 Southern Baptist men are Masons—we have appended from *Bowing at Strange Altars* both our "Word to Masons" and the table of contents as an Appendix at the end of this chapter. This volume may be ordered from The John Ankerberg Show (1-800-805-3030).

These three books assume a somewhat different approach to Masonry than that found in this chapter. While these earlier books were written for Christian Masons, this chapter is written also for the nonChristian Mason. Further, in our earlier books we stressed the ritual of Masonry because Masons, whatever their specific additional beliefs, are not permitted to disagree with the ritual. To disagree with the ritual is to deny Masonry and this carries severe penalties. These rituals are kept secret: "Much of this Ritual is esoteric [hidden], and, not being permitted to be committed to writing is communicated only by oral instruction."[5] To discuss and document the rituals, these had to be uncovered from authoritative sources. This was accomplished, but it required sufficient space that key topics relating to Masonry were omitted. In this chapter, therefore, we cover important additional topics that could not be discussed in the aforementioned texts. Space does not permit us to again document every Masonic doctrine by appeal to the ritual, although this has been done in some places here. Those requiring proof that the teachings found in this chapter are reflected in the ritual of the Lodge should consult these texts. Specifically, those needing clear information about Christian Masons should con-

sult *Christianity and the Secret Teachings of the Masonic Lodge* (Ankerberg Theological Research Institute [ATRI], 1989).

Following sections are updated and much condensed from an earlier and significantly different draft of *The Secret Teachings of the Masonic Lodge*.* The material is offered here in a different format and contains new information. The reader is encouraged to consult *Secret Teachings* for further documentation on the subjects discussed as well as other topics.

DOCTRINAL SUMMARY

God: Unitarian, deistic, pantheistic; The Grand Architect of the Universe (GAOTU); variously defined and incorporated with pagan elements.

Jesus Christ: A supremely good man who understood divine [Masonic] truth.

Salvation: By personal character: good works and individual merit.

Sin: Character flaws, ignorance of spiritual [Masonic] reality, i.e., a flaw in human nature which men are able to correct through Masonic enlightenment.

Man: Flawed but not sinful in a biblical sense; potentially divine, however all non-Masons exist in spiritual darkness.

The Bible: A *symbol* of the divine will, not to be taken literally.

Afterlife: Universalisitc.

INTRODUCTION AND HISTORY

"As a fraternity, we are always ready to be judged—severely and critically."[6]

—Francis G. Paul, 33rd Degree, Sovereign Grand Commander

The Nature and Definition of Masonry

Masonry (also known as Freemasonry or "the Lodge") is a powerful, centuries-old fraternal

---

* © 1990, Moody Bible Institute of Chicago, Moody Press. Used by permission.

order that began early in the eighteenth century. According to most Masonic authorities, modern Masonry (also called "speculative" Masonry) can be traced to the founding of the first Grand Lodge in London in 1717 A.D.[7] The Lodge is also a secret society. To maintain its secrets, Masonry uses symbolism, secret oaths and secret rituals to instruct new members called "initiates." Each new member swears during these secret ceremonies to remain loyal to the Lodge and its teachings. The teachings instruct each new candidate how to serve the Lodge and the rewards he can expect. In addition, Masonry views its mission as being to help conform the beliefs of all men into harmony, a harmony based primarily on Masonic teachings.[8]

Two of these teachings form the foundation of all Masonry. The first is a belief in the universal Fatherhood of God and brotherhood of man. By this, Masons teach that all men, whether Muslims, Jews, Hindus, Mormons, Buddhists, Christians or whatever, regardless of their personal religious views, are the spiritual sons of God. Masonry's second foundational belief is that the reform of personal character and the practice of good works will secure God's favor. In other words, the Masonic Lodge clearly teaches that the good character and good works of a Mason will earn him a place in heaven, which is called the "Celestial Lodge Above."

Let us examine the definition and descriptions of Masonry as given by Masonic authorities themselves. In Albert G. Mackey's *Revised Encyclopedia of Freemasonry* he states, "All [Masons] unite in declaring it to be a system of morality, by the practice of which its members may advance their spiritual interest, and mount by the theological ladder from the Lodge on earth to the Lodge in heaven."[9] Other respected Masonic authorities define Masonry in the following words:

1. "Masonry is the realization of God by the practice of Brotherhood."[10]

2. "It is a science which is engaged in the search after Divine Truth, and which employs symbolism as its method of instruction."[11]

3. "[Masonry is] that religious and mystical society whose aim is moral perfection on the basis of general equality and fraternity."[12]

4. "Freemasonry, in its broadest and most comprehensive sense, is a system of morality and social ethics, a primitive religion, and a philosophy of life, . . . incorporating a broad humanitarianism, . . . it is a religion without a creed, being of no sect but finding truth in all. . . . [It] seeks truth but does not define truth. . . ."[13]

On the one hand, defining Masonry presents us with a dilemma. There is no single universal definition of Masonry accepted by all Masons because the practice means different and sometimes contrary things to individual Masons. Masonry, for some of its members, has largely become a social club, while for others Masonry dominates their life and work as a religion they trust in for their salvation. This point is well stated by leading Masonic authority Henry Wilson Coil in his *A Comprehensive View of Freemasonry*. Here, he discusses the contradictory nature of Masonry:

Nobody knows what Freemasonry is, or, if that statement be deemed too strong, at least no one has been able to demonstrate that he knows the answer to the question. What one [Mason, or Masonic authority] asserts another of apparently equal ability doubts or denies. . . . Nor is this divergence of opinion due to ignorance or lack of investigation, for conflicts arise principally among the most zealous and erudite of Masonic students. The Fraternity has no central authority to declare its creed and no censor of books to check aberrations. Anyone, either within or without the Society, may speak or write about it what he wills, and many have taken advantage of that liberty.[14]

Coil also discusses the basic problem represented by Freemasonry:

Freemasonry has spread so widely, has expanded into so many degrees [up to 1,100 degrees[15]], and has undergone so many changes, to say nothing of having been subjected to so many diverse interpretations, that the question: What is Freemasonry? must first be answered by another question: When, where, and what phase of it? Though much of Masonic doctrine has remained remarkably well fixed and stable, its laws have changed, its degrees have changed, its ceremonies have changed, its religion has changed, and doubtless the concepts of it by its members have changed.[16]

Historically, Masonry has changed, and even today Masonry worldwide is not uniform. This characteristic of Masonry presents us with an important issue that any critical work needs to resolve at the outset: Does Masonry's lack of a central authority and its acceptance of contrary opinions mean one cannot authoritatively determine Masonic beliefs? Many Masons have argued that because Masonry has no "official voice" Masonic writers generally are only voicing "opinions that have no authority." But this is irrelevant when it comes to ascertaining a general wordview and commonly accepted beliefs. The real issue is whether the statements made by Masonic authors and authorities are in harmony with what Masonry represents historically in terms of its overall worldview. Few Masons will dispute that Masonry *itself* is the authority. In his *The Newly Made Mason*, H. L. Haywood refers to the obligations placed upon the new Mason:

> I hereby solemnly and sincerely promise and swear that as a beginning Craftsman in the Masonry of the mind and as a Newly-Made Mason I will not permit myself to be led into making hasty conclusions. I promise and swear that I will not listen to those who are not competent to teach me. There will be nothing binding on me except the truth. If there be those who say one thing and if there be others who say the opposite thing, I will consider that it is *Freemasonry itself* which finally is to decide between them.[17]

Obviously, if Masonry itself is the authority, then those Masons who are agreed to have most accurately represented Masonry must be considered authorities on what the Lodge believes and teaches. This chapter is therefore an analysis of Masonry itself as stated by Masonic authorities recommended to us by at least half of the Grand Lodges in the United States. We agree that what is presented may not necessarily coincide with the individual beliefs of any given Mason. Some Masons have no interest in the history and doctrines of Masonry. But for others, Masonry is a religious worldview that dominates their life and their work. Before we proceed, we should note there are at least three distinct levels of religious awareness or "consciousness" which exist in Masonry:

1. The nominally religious Mason. This Mason has been through the Masonic rites, stressing the importance of Masonic religion, but he has turned Masonry into a social club and secular brotherhood. For him, Masonry is a means to social standing and advancement, such as by assisting his business or employment opportunities through contacts with other Masons. He is content to view Masonry like this; the entire subject of religion is largely irrelevant to him. Many Masons, possibly even a slight majority, fall into this category. But many other Masons see a trend within Masonry toward the next two categories.

2. The humanistically religious Mason. This Mason accepts, lives and promotes the religious nature of Masonry, largely at its face value. He accepts the literal, or "outer," meaning of Masonry. He is committed to Masonic truth as he sees it and seeks to live according to Masonic ideals: the Fatherhood of God, the brotherhood of man, the immortality of the soul and Masonry as the hope of the future. This Mason could view the first-category Mason as an apostate who has denied and dishonored the sacred truths of Masonry. For the humanistically religious Mason, the *claims* of Masonry about the inherent harmony of religions are key. Thus, he believes that Masonry seeks true religious brotherhood where men of all faiths may unite in worship to the one true God. He does not consider the matter further and never tries to understand the deeper nature of Masonry. The Mason who lives at this level of Masonry has still not understood Masonry as it really is. In order to truly understand Masonry, we must examine the third level of Masonry.

3. The mystically religious Mason. This Mason looks at Masonry at an esoteric level. He finds in Masonry, correctly so, a thorough-going system of mysticism offering occult enlightenment for those who seek it. He sees almost everything in Masonry as part of the tradition of the ancient mystery schools, gnostic religions whose "outer forms" (category "2" above) preserve the genuine secrets of "true" Masonry from the profane (the unenlightened, whether Mason or non-Mason). This Mason views Masons in the second category as somewhat ignorant and naive, as unenlightened to the real nature of Masonry. For the mystically religious Mason, Masonry is the one true religion whose mystical core constitutes the inner truths of all religions.

Here is the reason many Masons confess that other Masons live in spiritual ignorance. All of the following statements are by Masons or former Masons. Allen E. Roberts: "There is much that is still unknown to even the ardent Masonic student."[18] Masonic authority Rollin C. Blackmer: "It is a lamentable fact that the great mass of our membership are . . . densely ignorant of everything connected with Masonry. . . ."[19] An official Masonic text: "The majority of Masons are sadly lacking in the knowledge of the height, breadth and depth of Masonic teachings as contained in the meanings of the many symbols of Masonry. . . ."[20] Edmond Ronayne: "[T]hose who know the least about Freemasonry are the Masons themselves."[21] Reverend William M. Russell: "[N]early every Mason thinks he knows all about Masonry, and also what Speculative [modern] Masonry is. As a matter of fact however, he does not."[22]

George H. Steinmetz summarizes the condition of at least half of Masonry when he writes, "Most of the truly great Masonic writers have deplored the lack of esoteric Masonic knowledge among the Craft in general. . . . The average Mason is lamentably ignorant of the real meaning of Masonic Symbology and knows as little of its esoteric teaching."[23]

What all of this means is that an individual Mason may be (1) unaware of the teachings of the higher degrees of Masonry or (2) unaware of the true inner meaning of Masonry.

Determining the Authoritative Sources in Masonry

If anyone is going to investigate the teachings of the Masonic Lodge, who or what authority should they listen to? Mr. Bill Mankin, a thirty-second degree Mason, admitted to the following on The John Ankerberg Show, "The authorita-

tive source for Masonry is the ritual. The ritual—what happens in the Lodge, what goes on."[24] But, as Coil says, there is "the misconception that originally there was somewhere one authorized ritual. The Masonic rituals were not created: they grew and there never was only one Masonic ritual; there have always been many."[25] The question then becomes, "Who determines what the ritual will consist of in each Masonic Lodge?" The answer is that the Grand Lodge of each state has the power to regulate the ritual practiced in that Lodge. For example, Coil writes that it is "well understood that Grand Lodges are the highest Masonic authorities in both law and doctrine."[26]

But, if one examines Masonry historically, the Grand Lodges of each state have disagreed on many of the landmarks (principles of Masonry) and precisely what should be included in the ritual.[27] However, when one examines Masonry *today* and compares the different manuals containing the ritual for each state, it is apparent that *today* the ritual and the interpretations given are very close or almost identical. In *Bowing at Strange Altars* (ATRI, 1993; pp. 74–75), we compared Lodge rituals in Alabama, Illinois, Georgia, North Carolina, Texas, Virginia, Oregon and other places and found them very similar. Therefore the ritual in the Masonic Manuals can be considered the authoritative teachings of the Lodge. Former Worshipful Master Jack Harris reveals: "In [all] other states . . . the principle and the doctrines are exactly the same. The wording only varies slightly."[28]

In addition, there is a vast amount of Masonic literature available to researchers. This includes at least 100,000 volumes, among which are a minimum of 600 analytical works giving a broad treatment of the subject of Masonry.[29] There are also numerous exposés of Masonry by former members who have revealed virtually all the secrets of the Craft. In this sense, Masonry is a "secret society" only to those who have not read such literature.

But which authors and books do Masons themselves recommend to outsiders as authoritative? A letter was sent to each of the 50 Grand Lodges in America in order to answer this question. Remember, according to Coil it is "well understood that Grand Lodges are the highest

Masonic authorities in both law and doctrine." The letter was addressed to the Grand Master of each of the Grand Lodges, asking him to respond to the question: "As an official Masonic leader, which books and authors do you recommend as being authoritative on the subject of Freemasonry?"[30] When a reply from a Grand Lodge was received, we added it to the replies from the other Grand Lodges. Twenty-five, or half, of the Grand Lodges responded, a sufficiently high percentage to be considered representative. These authors and books were most often recommended by these Grand Lodges:

44% recommended Henry Wilson Coil, *Coil's Masonic Encyclopedia*
36% Joseph Fort Newton, *The Builders*
32% Albert G. Mackey, *Mackey's Revised Encyclopedia of Freemasonry*
24% Carl H. Claudy, *Introduction to Freemasonry*
24% H. L. Haywood, *The Newly Made Mason*
20% Alphonse Cerza, *A Masonic Reader's Guide*
20% Robert F. Gould, *History of Freemasonry*
20% Allen E. Roberts, *The Craft and Its Symbols*
16% Albert Pike, *Morals and Dogma*

Because Coil, Newton and Mackey were recommended most often, we have cited them frequently. Other authors recommended included: W. R. Denslow, R. V. Denslow, Charles C. Hunt, Bernard Jones, Roscoe Pound, James Anderson, Henry Clausen, D. Darrah, Manly Hall, W. Hutchinson, M. M. Johnson, Karl C. F. Krause, W. Preston, G. Steinmetz, J. H. Van Gorden, T. S. Webb and Louis Williams.[31] We secured these responses and have them on file so that Masons can see that we have based our arguments on material that half of their Grand Lodges consider authoritative and reliable. These authors and books represent the most authoritative interpreters of Freemasonry.

The Blue Lodge, the Scottish Rite, the York Rite
The Blue Lodge is the parent, or mother, Lodge of Freemasonry. The Blue Lodge confers the first three Masonic degrees: (1) the Entered Apprentice, where a man is initiated into the beginning mysteries of the fraternity of Free-

masonry; (2) the degree of Fellow Craft and (3) the Master Mason degree. Before they may proceed to the higher degrees, all men must go through the first three degrees of the Blue Lodge.* After passing the three Blue Lodge degrees, the candidate may choose not to proceed further. Many and perhaps most Masons stop with the first three degrees. If the candidate chooses to proceed higher, it must be along one or both of two other branches in Masonry. One branch is the Scottish Rite, which advances by numerical degrees, beginning with the fourth and ending with the thirty-second, the thirty-third degree being either active or honorary. The other major branch is the York Rite, which goes through designations called the "Chapter," "Council" and "Commandery" degrees, ending with the degree of Knights Templar.

Anyone who passes the first three degrees and becomes a Master Mason may visit Blue Lodges other than his own. If a Mason is suspended or expelled from his Blue Lodge, it automatically severs his connection from all other Masonic bodies.

In the next column is a diagram of all the degrees.[32] Usually only the Scottish Rite cites its degrees by number; the York Rite designates its degrees by name. For example, the fourth degree of the York Rite is termed "Mark Master."

Blue Lodge
1. Entered Apprentice
2. Fellow Craft
3. Master Mason

York Rite	Scottish Rite
Chapter (capitular degrees)	*Lodge of Perfection*
Mark Master	4. Secret Master
	5. Perfect Master
	6. Intimate Secretary
Past Master	7. Provost & Judge
(Virtual)	8. Intendant of the Building
	9. Elu of the Nine
	10. Elu of the Fifteen

---

*It is possible to stop at only the first or second degree, but the candidate can progress to the higher degrees only after completing the Blue Lodge.

Most Excellent Master	11. Elu of the Twelve
	12. Master Architect
	13. Royal Arch of Solomon
Royal Arch Mason	14. Perfect Elu
	Chapter Rose Croix
	15. Knight of the East or Sword
Council (cryptic degrees)	16. Prince of Jerusalem
Royal Master	17. Knight of the East & West
	18. Knight Rose Croix
	Council of Kadosh
	19. Grand Pontiff
Select Master	20. Master of the Symbolic Lodge
	21. Noachite or Prussian Knight
	22. Knight of the Royal Axe
Super Excellent Master	23. Chief of the Tabernacle
Commandery	24. Prince of the Tabernacle
(chivalric degrees)	25. Knight of the Brazen Serpent
Order of the Red Cross	26. Prince of Mercy
	27. Knight Commander of the Temple
	28. Knight of the Sun
Order of the Knights of Malta	29. Knight of St. Andrew
	30. Knight Kadosh
	Consistory
	31. Inspector Inquisitor
Order of Knights Templar	32. Master of the Royal Secret
Commandery	33. (Active or Honorary)

Besides the degrees, there are many affiliated, appendant organizations or side degrees of Masonry. These are orders with specific memberships (youth, women, relatives, collegians) or goals, such as the Shriners (the Ancient Arabic Order of Nobles of the Mystic Shrine).

Although the Blue Lodge is Masonry, and it appears to be the Masonry of most Masons, it is clearly not all that Masonry constitutes. Some Masons would view Blue Lodge Masonry—at least as it is usually interpreted—as an initial, or beginning, form of Masonry. These Masons would maintain that the real substance of Ma-

sonry—its lifeblood—lies in the higher degrees and in the initiate's search for their true meaning. Some Masons would consider Blue Lodge Masonry as only the cover of the book, not the book itself. These Masons would say that to truly understand Masonry one must open the book and understand what lies between the covers. As Sovereign Grand Commander Henry C. Clausen admits, "It must be apparent that the Blue Lodge . . . degrees cannot explain the whole of Masonry. They are the foundation. . . . An initiate may imagine he understands the ethics, symbols and enigmas, whereas a true explanation of these is reserved for the more adept."[33]

The Influence of Masonry in Culture

Until recently, Masonry existed in 164 countries.[34] According to the *Encyclopedia Britannica*, its membership of 6 million qualified Masonry as "the largest worldwide secret society."[35] At least 15,300 Lodges once operated in the U.S. and more than 33,700 around the world.[36] Today these figures are down somewhat. As of 1998 there were 13,200 U.S. Lodges and a worldwide membership of fewer than 5,000,000. England has more than 7,000 Lodges; Canada, 1,600; Cuba, India and West Germany each have more than 300. Recent efforts are underway to increase Masonic membership and influence worldwide.

The large numbers of Masons is one reason why Masonry has exerted a considerable influence in society and in the Church for at least 200 years:

One member of the Craft pointed out that there are at least 160 organizations (which he did not identify) that require their members to also be initiates into the Masonic Fraternity. In 1948, *The New Age* boasted that some ten million adults were linked directly, or were indirectly associated with the nation's three million Master Masons. The Scottish Rite publication estimated that "between one in five and one in 10 of the adult thinking population come directly within the circle of Masonic influences."[37]

Even in 1912, scholar Martin Wagner could observe in his critical treatment on Masonry: "Masonry, with its numerous offsprings is a powerful factor in our civilization. It is influencing our civic, our social, our family, our moral and our religious life far more than is generally realized."[38] Critic Paul A. Fisher, with a background in military intelligence and politics, observes that Masons have dominated the U.S. Supreme Court since 1941–1971. From 1941–1946 the ratio was 5 to 4; from 1949–1956 it was 8 to 1; from 1969–1971 it was again 5 to 4.[39] He concludes that such influence may have contributed to the high court's "determination to move the nation away from an emphasis on Judeo-Christian values in public life," helping further to secularize society and sustain "an epoch of revolutionary liberalism" with far reaching consequences.[40] If there is any substance at all to Fisher's claims, then addressing the religious views, content and goals of Freemasonry is hardly an idle task but personally relevant for all of us (see "Theology" section following). In the 13th degree of the Scottish Rite the oath reads: "I furthermore promise and swear to use every means in my power . . . to contribute with all my might to the . . . propagation of liberal ideas wheresoever I may be."[41]

According to Masonic and Congressional records, as many as 14 U.S. presidents have been Masons (George Washington, James Monroe, Andrew Jackson, James Polk, James Buchanan, Andrew Johnson, James Garfield, William McKinley, Teddy Roosevelt, William Howard Taft, Warren Harding, Franklin Delano Roosevelt, Harry Truman and Gerald Ford,[42] plus 14 vice presidents.[43]

The influence of Masonry in U.S. government was revealed by the Senate Congressional record of September 9, 1987.[44] In the proceedings some members of the Senate Judiciary Committee had questioned the propriety of appointing Judge David Sentelle as a U.S. Circuit Judge for the District of Columbia. The objection was raised on the grounds that he was a Mason. In response to this a number of Senators who were Masons vigorously protested. They felt it was unthinkable to question an appointee merely because he was a member of the Lodge. They considered it: "extraordinary," "totally unwarranted," "most absurd," "galling and preposterous" and so on. They were "astounded" and "aghast."

During the debate, Masonic Senators Thurmond and Simpson and Senate Majority Leader Robert Byrd (33rd degree), all of whom admitted pride of membership, revealed that Masons comprised:

—Forty-one members of the Federal Judiciary

—Half the membership of the Senate Judiciary Committee

—Eighteen Senators, including Lloyd Bentsen, Sam Nun, Bob Dole (33rd degree), Jesse Helms, John Glenn and Mark Hatfield

—Seventy-six members of the House of Representatives, including Speaker of the House Jim Wright, Claude Pepper, William Ford, Dan Glickman, Trent Lott and others. At least two Senators are 33rd degree Masons, Bob Dole and Robert Byrd.

Objections were raised against questioning Masonry because "Masonry in this country is the bedrock" and because being a Mason "simply means people who believe in God and love their fellow man." If that's all Masonry is, it's unlikely any objection would have been raised.

According to Masonic records, many other famous and influential persons have become Masons. These include Norman Vincent Peale,* Senator Howard H. Baker, [45] Congressman Jack Kemp,[46] Irving Berlin, actor Ernest Borgnine, William Jennings Bryan, scientist Luther Burbank, comedian Bob Burns, Christopher "Kit" Carson, Sir Winston Churchill, Samuel Clemons (Mark Twain), Tyrus (Ty) Cobb, William "Buffalo Bill" Cody, motion picture producer Cecil B. DeMille, Thomas E. Dewey, Major General James R. Doolittle, "Sherlock Holmes" author Sir Arthur Conan Doyle, Edward VIII (Duke of Windsor), Douglas Fairbanks, Sr., comedian W. C. Fields, Henry Ford, Benjamin Franklin, Arthur Godfrey, Johann Wolfgang von Goethe, Barry M. Goldwater, astronaut Virgil E. Grissom, Oliver Hardy (of "Laurel and Hardy"), influential Hindu guru Swami Vivekananda, Fahruddin Ali Ahmed (the President of India),

---

*Peale was once featured on the cover of *The New Age*, a Masonic magazine, as a 33rd degree Mason. He wrote the article, "What Freemasonry Means to Me."

composer Franz Joseph Hayden, FBI director J. Edgar Hoover, magician Harry Houdini, John Paul Jones, King Kamehameha V (king of Hawaii), Rudyard Kipling, Colonel Charles A. Lindberg, General Douglas MacArthur, Chief Justice of the Supreme Court John Marshall, Presbyterian clergyman and chaplain of the U.S. Senate Peter Marshall, motion picture producer Lewis B. Mayer, Charles H. Mayo (founder of the Mayo Clinic), Wolfgang Amadaus Mozart, Admiral Robert E. Peary, James C. Penney (founder of J. C. Penney Company), General John J. Pershing, Paul Revere, all seven of the Ringling Brothers, cowboy hero Roy Rogers, Will Rogers, Sir Walter Scott, comedian Richard Bernard "Red" Skelton, French writer and philosopher Francois Voltaire, General Jonathan M. Wainwright, Lou Wallace (author of *Ben Hur*), Chief Justice of the Supreme Court Earl Warren, Booker T. Washington and many others.[47]

The Lodge also exerts considerable influence through affiliated or appendant organizations, which usually espouse similar beliefs. Masonry is generally considered to be the "mother organization" of these groups, whose rituals, secrets or goals may have similar characteristics to those of Freemasonry.[48] In 1912 Wagner observed: "The whole secret society system with its countless lodges and their organizations, is an outgrowth of Masonry. All the secret societies, even the so-called minor orders, have assimilated and incorporated more or less of the fundamental principles of Masonry. A comparison of their various rituals with the rituals of Masonry demonstrates this fact."[49]

Some of these organizations are officially Masonic and others are not, but all of them have been influenced by Masonry. For example, the so-called animal lodges reflect Masonic influence but are not, strictly, Masonic organizations. Among these are the Fraternal Order of Eagles (FOE), the Benevolent and Protective Order of Elks (BPOE) and the Loyal Order of Moose (LOOM). Others include the Independent Order of Odd Fellows, the Woodsmen of the World, the Knights of Pythias, Tall Cedars in Lebanon, the Mystic Order of Veil Prophets of the Enchanted Realm (Grotto), Acacia Fraternity and the Knights of the Red Cross of Constantine.[50]

There are Masonically affiliated female organizations such as Daughters of the Nile, the Order of the Eastern Star, the Order of Amaranth, the White Shrine of Jerusalem and the Daughters of Mokanna. In *Secret Teachings* (pp. 26–30) we showed how the teachings of the Order of the Eastern Star parallel those of Masonry. Recently, full length books critiquing the Order and showing its connection to Masonry have appeared, including *Hidden Secrets of the Eastern Star* and *The Masonic Connection.*

There are also numerous affiliated youth organizations such as the Order of DeMolay, Order of Job's Daughters, Order of the Builders and Order of the Rainbow. (Occasionally, the Kiwanis, Rotary, Lion's Club, American Legion and Veterans of Foreign Wars are incorrectly associated with Masonry or its affiliated organizations. Unlike Masonry, these are not religious groups having religious goals[51] and should not be confused with Masonry.)

Finally, the Lodge has exerted its influence in the history of Mormonism and in liberal religion such as Unitarian Universalism.[52]

The Influence of Masonry in the Church

As we documented in *Secret Teachings*, Masonry is influential enough within the Church that most major conservative Christian denominational bodies have issued official declarations condemning Masonry as a non-Christian or an antiChristian religion. Most of these reports acknowledge that the principal reason many Christians have joined Freemasonry is out of simple ignorance; they do not know the contradictions between Masonry and Christianity.[53] This indicates that the Church must do a better job educating her members about the Craft. Former Mason Jack Harris observes that "many ministers, elders, deacons, trustees and Sunday school teachers" are Masons.[54]

Wherever we look in the Christian world we find the influence of Masonry. Masonic author Cerza divulges that many officers of the Salvation Army are Masons.[55] Investigator Stephen Knight supplies evidence "the Vatican itself is infiltrated by Freemasons."[56] In Europe, the Presbyterian Church of Wales is "strongly influenced" by Masonry.[57] Knight observes that "thousands of practicing Christians in Britain today worship the Freemasonic God believing it to be precisely the same as the Christian God. . . ."[58] He further states: "Despite overwhelming evidence of Masonry's incompatibility with Christianity, . . . the Church of England has been a stronghold of Freemasonry for more than 200 years. Traditionally, joining the Brotherhood and advancing within it has always been the key to preferment in the church."[59] In fact, Masonic power is so strong that "the church . . . dares not offend or provoke thousands of influential and often financially substantial laymen by inquiring into the religious implications of Freemasonry."[60] Although Knight is neither a Christian nor a Freemason, he does note that "Freemasonry is extremely anxious to have—or appear to have—good relations with all Christian churches. . . ."[61]

Freemasonry is anxious to maintain good relations with the Church for one principle reason. The Church continues to provide a large number of converts to Freemasonry. And there is a particular oath offered specifically for Christian ministers who are joining the Lodge. This oath pledges them the idea that true Christianity must safeguard the interests of Masonry: "You, brother, are a preacher of [Christian] religion, . . . You cannot, therefore, but be fond of the [Masonic] Order, and zealous for the interests of Freemasonry. . . . Whoever is warmed with the spirit of Christianity, must esteem, must love Freemasonry."[62]

Why has Masonry infiltrated the Church? One reason is that Masonry asserts everywhere that it is *not* a religion or a substitute for religion. It claims to be merely a fraternal brotherhood seeking to better the world. It asserts that it is fully compatible with all religions and that there is absolutely nothing in Masonry that is in opposed to Christian belief. In addition, Masonry speaks openly of the importance of belief in God and claims that each member is free to interpret God in any manner. Further, many Masons openly proclaim that Freemasonry "exists to assist or to support the church."[63]

But as we will see in the following, Masonry is also a nonChristian religion. Also, it is a substitute for the Christian faith (and for all other faiths), and it believes it is superior to every other religion.

The Appeal of Masonry

Masonry is attractive to people for many reasons. For instance, it claims to be divinely instituted and therefore appeals to man's search for God.[64] Some are curious and are allured by its secrecy. They enjoy belonging to a society in which only they have access to its inner mysteries. And because Masonry enjoys a measure of respect in society, some people are attracted by its lofty ideals and humanitarian works. Others are drawn to Masonry because they like the idea of a worldwide brotherhood encompassing idealistic goals by which to better the world. Some, too, are charmed simply by its social fellowship.

Others are fascinated by the symbolism and the pagan mysteries of Masonry. They enjoy its similarities to many older religions. Such persons "love ritual and are held enthralled by the wonder and mystery of the Masonic work and rituals."[65] Consider the following statement in Roberts' book, *The Craft and Its Symbols,* describing how a Mason feels in the ritual of the first degree of Masonry, the Entered Apprentice: "You could not have helped but to be thrilled and full of pride when you reached the Northeast Corner of the Lodge. There you stood, a just and upright Mason! Every brother present exulted with you. You were about to complete the first step of the most meaningful journey of your life."[66]

Some people are allured by the power of Masonry. For example, the Worshipful Master (W.M.) exercises absolute control over his Lodge. Others see in Masonry the ability to seek occult power, "a secret order which can have great power if properly developed. . . ."[67]

All in all, Masonry is attractive because it offers brotherhood, social prestige, mystery, lofty ideals, the lure of secrecy, the hope of religious quest and spiritual power. But as we will see, Masonry has hidden motives for its lofty ideals, its humanitarianism and all else that makes it attractive to outsiders.

The Origins of Masonry

The origins of Masonry (at least its historical antecedents) are shrouded in antiquity. As Coil observes in his *Freemasonry Through Six Centuries,* "The origin of Freemasonry, its early development and character, are unknown, and are likely to remain so."[68] Most scholars believe it is difficult to trace the origins of Masonry (as it is known today) to before the early 1700s. We do know that in 1717, four Lodges combined to form the first Grand Lodge in London, England. Today, all Masonic Grand Lodges in the world trace their origin to this first Grand Lodge. The first U.S. Lodge began in 1729, and the first Canadian Lodge started in 1745.[69]

However, an older type of Masonry, the "operative," or "working" Masons (essentially itinerant craftsmen) can be traced back to the Middle Ages. These persons formed primitive trade unions (Lodges) for protection and professional credibility. These Lodges were the foundation for modern Masonry, which is termed "speculative Masonry" to contrast it from the older "operative Masonry." Some of the rituals, the symbolisms and many of the teachings of Masonry, however, can be traced to ancient paganism, and in particular to the ancient mystery religions of Egypt, Rome, Greece and other cultures.

In the transitional phase from operative to speculative, or modern, Masonry, membership was not restricted to stone masons. The doors swung open to anyone seeking membership. Interest in the Lodge mushroomed and a wide diversity of membership resulted. Among the members of the Lodges were clergymen, politicians, scientists, astrologers and other occultists, and these individuals became involved in formulating the ritual, doctrine, degrees of advancement and other important aspects of Masonry. "In fact, men in all ranks of life became actively engaged in manufacturing degrees and arranging rites to advance their particular interests, theories, dogmas, or ambitious pretensions."[70] This is why more than 1,100 degrees were eventually produced.[71]

In particular, modern Masonry owes a great deal to several medieval occult practices and religions, from which many of its teachings were derived. Haywood states in *The Great Teachings of Masonry:* "All our historians, at least nearly all of them, agree that Freemasonry owes very much to certain occult societies or groups that flourished—often in secret—during the late middle ages, and even into the after-Reformation times. Chief among these were the Rosicrucians and the Knights Templar."[72] Another form

of influential medieval occultism, Kabbalism, also exerted great influence upon Masonry, as virtually all Masonic historians admit.[73]

Scholar Dr. Shildes Johnson, who holds three earned doctorates, lists such groups as the Rosicrucians and two other occult orders, the Golden Dawn and the Illuminati, as having influenced Masonry. He also observes, "Today, the chief religious influence of Masonry may be observed in the Unitarian-Universalist Church, in the Church of Jesus Christ of Latter-Day Saints (Mormons), and in witchcraft."[74]

In summary, there are three basic influences responsible for the teachings of Masonry:

1. *Ancient paganism:* the ancient pagan mystery religions practiced in Egypt, Asia Minor and later in Greece. These appear to have formed the religious basis of much Masonic teaching, symbolism and ritual, although no direct link can be established.

2. *Medieval stonemasonry:* the "operative" or "working" Masonry of the Middle Ages (500–1500)—the itinerant craftsmen known as stone Masons. Many symbols of modern Masonry were derived from their tools of the trade.

3. *Modern Masonry:* "speculative" or "symbolic" Freemasonry. A gradual change took place in operative Masonry through the infusion of medieval occultism and other elements and transformations, resulting in the development of modern Masonry.

Thus, modern Masonry combines elements of both of its earlier counterparts. For example, the working tools of the stone Masons, such as the square and the compass, have been changed into symbols expressing moral and spiritual lessons, and the teachings and rites of the ancient mystery religions, also found variously in medieval occultism, can also be found in Masonry, although they have sometimes undergone considerable modification.

Why Masonry Is a Secret Society

Masonry stresses the importance of secrecy for at least two principal reasons. The first is that the element of secrecy itself is something that can attract men and make them feel important. They have access to vital secrets and truths that other men do not share. The second reason is that secrecy offers the Craft a stabilizing influence. Men who swear extremely solemn oaths of secrecy conclude not only the information received is important but also that it must be protected at all costs. For example, the *Guide to the Royal Arch Chapter* observes, "Mystery has charms as well as power. 'The entire fabric of the universe is founded on secrecy; and the great Life-force which vivifies, moves, and beautifies the whole, is the profoundest of all mysteries.... The first obligation of a Mason—his supreme duty—his chief virtue—is that of silence and secrecy.'"[75]

But there are other reasons for Masonry's secrecy, reasons both religious and sometimes political. By maintaining secrecy, Masonry can hide its religious nature from the outside world and secure converts who would not otherwise join. In addition, some believe there are secret political goals of the Lodge. Paul A. Fisher observes:

Masonry has 25 "landmarks," or canons which are "unrepealable," and can "never be changed." Landmark no. 23 concerns "secrecy of the Institution." It admonishes initiates that to change or abrogate such a requirement of confidentiality "would be social suicide, and death of the Order would follow its legalized exposure." Continuing, the same Landmark notes that Freemasonry has lived unchanged for centuries as a secret association, but as an open society, "it would not last for many years."

One wonders why the organization must be so secret. Why would openness bring "death of the Order"? Why would it "not last for many years" if its secret activities were unmasked? Certainly, the landmark suggests the Craft is something more than a fraternal and charitable organization. Why hide good works?

The answer is: Freemasonry in America and elsewhere is far more than a fraternal organization. It never hides its charitable endeavors. But its secret work is something else entirely. And that secret work frequently has involved subversion of the existing political order in any given State.[76]

THE GOALS OF MASONRY

Masonry Is More Than a Fraternal Fellowship

For some Masons, Masonry is merely a fraternal fellowship. For many, Masonry is a vital worldwide organization, which they hope will help bring peace and universal brotherhood to all mankind. This is because Masonry sees itself as a "world Fraternity": "There is no such thing as 'Lodge Masonry.' The Masonic Fraternity is a single, indivisible fellowship which is neither divided nor affected by local or by national boundaries.... It has one set of Landmarks, one set of Degrees, one teaching for the whole world.... The one World Fraternity is everywhere one and the same thing...."[77]

The goals of Masonry are to unite the world under the umbrella of a doctrine teaching the Fatherhood of God, the brotherhood of man and the immortality of the soul. Masons foresee the day when all religious division and sectarianism (i.e., what Masonry views as specific or exclusivistic and therefore "divisive" religious beliefs) will be wiped away and a new era of universal peace, brotherhood and religious faith will emerge.

In the most widely read and influential book in Masonry, *The Builders,* author Joseph Newton explains what Masonry "is trying to do in the world." He cites the following as the objectives of Masonry:

To bring about a universal league of mankind.[78]

Masonry seeks to free men from a limiting conception of religion, and thus to remove one of the chief causes of sectarianism.[79]

Its mission is to form mankind into a great redemptive brotherhood....[80]

Why does Masonry seek to change the world? Because it teaches that all non-Masons are living in spiritual darkness. The Masonry ritual for the first degree teaches the candidate that he "has long been in darkness, and now seeks to be brought to light...."[81] The Lodge teaches that true Masons are enlightened and live in the Truth. Masonry claims that "each member is a living stone in this Holy House"—the Masonic temple.[82] It refers to itself as a "Holy Empire" whose mission is "to dispel darkness."[83] Thus it is the mission and "duty of its initiates to diffuse among men its ideals, without which error, superstition and spiritual subjugation must be *eternal*."[84] The result of this premise is that if true world brotherhood is ever to be achieved, it demands for its success a worldwide religion of Masonry. Thus, informed Masons partake in "the glorious privilege which belongs to Masonry as the precious jewel of its prerogative, to be *the chiefest of human agencies* used by God to bring forward the rosy dawn of this magnificent future."[85]

If Masonry is to one day rule the world, then all non-Masonic beliefs must either be abandoned or absorbed into Masonry. "Sectarian" religions with exclusive teachings, such as the Christian faith (John 14:6; Acts 4:12), simply cannot be permitted if Masonry is to succeed. Masonry then, claims that it is the light of the world and that only "its ideals" can save the world from its errors and superstition. All of this is why Masonry is far more than simply a worldwide fraternal brotherhood. Masonry desires to change the world, and one way to do this is by influencing the Church.

IMPORTANCE OF SYMBOLS AND RITUAL

The symbols and ritual in Masonry are important because they are used as a principal method of teaching Masonic ideals. In *The Facts on the Masonic Lodge* and *Christianity and the Secret Teachings of the Masonic Lodge* we have documented the teachings of Masonry by citing their ritual and symbols. Here we will simply document that this is a principal teaching method of Freemasonry and cite some illustrations. In Masonic authority Allen E. Roberts' text, *The Craft and Its Symbols: Opening the Door to Masonic Symbolism,* the author observes that "symbolism is the lifeblood of the Craft. . . . It is the principal vehicle by which the ritual teaches Masonic philosophy and moral lessons."[86] Albert Mackey asserts, "Freemasonry is . . . a system of doctrines which [are] taught . . . by allegories and symbols."[87] This is why use of symbols is interwoven throughout Masonic Ritual.

In addition, the rituals themselves are tied to ancient legends and myths that are replete with symbolic content. Like an onion, the symbols in Masonry may have layers of meaning. At one level of initiation a symbol may mean one thing, and at a higher level of initiation it may mean something else.[88] In the beginning, most Masonic symbols have certain more or less universally accepted meanings. But in the end, each symbol can mean virtually anything a Mason wants it to mean. Following are a few illustrations of Masonic symbols used during ritualistic initiations:[89]

—The square and compass (sometimes with a capital "G" in the middle). The square symbolizes morality; the compass symbolizes spirituality; and the "G" symbolizes God or geometry.

—The cable tow with which the Mason is tied up during the ritual symbolizes the tie of Masonic brotherhood.

—The candidate's removal of his shoes symbolizes humility.

—The apron that the candidate wears symbolizes innocence, purity and honor.

—The three burning tapers symbolize the sun, moon and Worshipful Master.

The sword pointing to a naked heart symbolizes justice and the knowledge that God will reward men according to their deeds. (The candidate walks in a circle [circumnambulation] to symbolize the spiritual [e.g., mystical and occult] links to the past that represent man's dependence upon man.)

—The sprig of acacia symbolizes faith in the promises of God in the "Volume of the Sacred Law" (e.g., the Bible, Koran, Upanishads, and others).

That the Masonic Rituals are composed of myths and legends, even of pagan myths and legends, is not as important as what they mean to the candidate in his search for "light" and "truth."[90] Here the subjectivism of the Craft is plain, for there is no "final word" on the Masonic symbols because "there is no limitation to what a person can find in this or any other symbol."[91] Thus, the "symbols [of Masonry] have a variety of meanings for everyone."[92] The lessons and secrets of Freemasonry can be seen differently by each person who brings a unique perspective to them.[93] The problem here is that if no one has the final say, then no Mason can ever know if he has arrived.

THE WORLDVIEW AND CHARACTERISTICS OF MASONRY

A worldview is a set of assumptions about life through which people interpret themselves, their universe and their place in the universe. Because Masonry is a religion, it offers a comprehensive view of man and man's place in the world. This was why former Master Mason W. L. Wilmshurst states, "Masonry, then, is a system of religious philosophy in that it provides us with a doctrine of the universe and of our place in it. It indicates whence we are come and whither we may return."[94] Freemason Allen E. Roberts confesses, "Freemasonry is many things, but most of all: FREEMASONRY IS A WAY OF LIFE."[95]

If we understand the worldview of Masonry, then we will understand how Masonry influences the life of an individual Mason. In this section we will briefly examine six principal characteristics of Masonry which help to form its worldview.

1. Masonry is both static and fluid. In key doctrines Masonry exhibits general stability. *Duncan's Masonic Ritual and Monitor* (New York: David McKay, n.d., p. 148) states, ". . . the essential points of Masonry are identical the world over." But Masonry is also fluid, historically. It changes with the times. For instance, in the Middle Ages Masonry was often compatible with Christianity; today it is not.

2. Masonry is liberal religion. It is a humanistic religion stressing the inherent divinity and universal brotherhood of mankind. Liberal religion has long stressed the Fatherhood of God, brotherhood of man and salvation by works and character, and it characteristically teaches unitarianism and universalism. This is why Masonry reaches out to liberal ministers. "The Relation of the Liberal Churches to the Fraternal Orders" is a pamphlet published by the American Unitarian Association and written by E. A. Coil, a Unitarian minister and Mason. In that article he pleads for a closer cooperation between Masonry and liberal religion because of their similar beliefs about God, man and salvation by character. "Modern Freemasonry owes much to the thought of the eighteenth century, and this concept of God reflects the prevalent Deism, in which God is the Supreme Being, the Creator who has set the world in motion, laid down His moral laws for men to obey, but does not continue to act personally in the world in mercy or in judgment."[96] Further, ". . . the study of man leads to knowledge of God, by revealing to man the ultimate divinity at the base of human nature."[97] And, "We must return to a faith in man himself. . . ."[98]

3. Masonry is a hierarchical system. It offers different levels of practice, interpretation and belief. "There is much that is still unknown to even the ardent Masonic student."[99] "Most of the truly great Masonic writers have deplored the lack of esoteric Masonic knowledge among the Craft in general. . . . The average Mason is lamentably ignorant of the real meaning of Masonic Symbology and knows as little of its esoteric teaching."[100]

4. Masonry is a syncretistic faith. It claims that it alone is the true religion behind all (limiting lesser) religions and dogmas:

> The true disciple of ancient Masonry has given up forever the worship of personalities. . . . As a Mason his religion must be universal: Christ, Buddha or Mohammed, the names mean little, for he recognizes only the light and not the bearer. He worships at every shrine, bows before every altar, whether in temple, mosque or cathedral, realizing with his *truer understanding* the oneness of all spiritual truth. . . . No true Mason can be narrow, for his Lodge is the divine expression of all broadness. There is no place for little minds in a great work.[101]

> Masonry is not *a* religion but Religion—not a church but a worship, in which men of all religions may unite. . . . It is not the rival of any religion, but the friend of all, laying emphasis upon those truths which underlie all religions and are the basis and consecration of each.[102]

5. Masonry is a "New Age" mysticism. It offers an individual Mason the potential for higher consciousness and occult development. (See "The Occult" section in this chapter.)

In other words, a Mason may in his ignorance worship the God or gods of his specific religion whether it be Christianity or Hinduism. But these are really false Gods and idols.

6. Masonry is the one true religion. As the Mason becomes instructed in the truths of Masonry and is re-educated along the lines of Masonic religion, he will realize the one true religion lies far beyond the limiting doctrines of the religions that others follow. This is why many Masons see the work of Masonry as that of "rebuilding the temple of fallen humanity," and it is why they see Masonry as "a *world mission* in aid of all men everywhere in the world, and that this mission is spiritual."[103] The goal of Masonry certainly is worldwide in scope. If Masons are "awakening" to this fact, the Church had better take note.

THEOLOGY: THE RELIGIOUS NATURE AND THEOLOGY OF MASONRY

Is Masonry a Religion?

Despite some of the foregoing quotes from Masonic literature, many Masons go out of their way to claim that Masonry is not a religion nor a substitute for religion. The claim that "Masonry is not a religion"[104] is found throughout Masonic literature. For example, Masonic authority Silas H. Shepherd claims: "There is nothing *better understood* among Masons than that it is not a religion; it is not a religious institution in the sense that it is an instrument for the propagation of religious doctrines."[105] Nevertheless, Masonry is a religion. When Masons say that Masonry is not a religion, they are either misinformed or perhaps even lying.

What is religion? By any accepted dictionary definition of religion, Masonry qualifies as a religion. In *The Facts on the Masonic Lodge* and *Christianity and the Secret Teachings of the Masonic Lodge* we have gone into great detail to prove beyond any doubt that Masonry is a religion. In *The Encyclopedia of Philosophy* (1972;

Vol. 7, pp. 141–42), Professor of Philosophy at the University of Michigan William Alston cites the following characteristics of religion:

- A belief in supernatural beings (God or gods)
- A distinction between sacred and profane objects
- Ritual acts focused on these sacred objects
- A moral code with supernatural sanction
- Religious feelings which are aroused by sacred objects or ritual and connected to the idea of a divine being or beings
- Prayer
- A particular worldview which encompasses the individual's place within the world
- The organization of one's life based on such a worldview
- A social group that is bound together by the above traits

After reading or perusing more than 100 books by Masons or about Masonry, we believe that it is absolutely undeniable that Masonry contains all the above characteristics. This is why many Masonic authorities who have written on this issue have concluded that Masonry is a religion or religious. In Coil's *A Comprehensive View of Freemasonry* we find: "Religion is espoused by the Masonic ritual and required of the candidate."[106] In fact, Coil's entire discussion of some 15,000 words proves Masonry is a religion. This is why he states, "Freemasonry is undoubtedly religion...."[107] Other Masonic authorities also state that Masonry is a religion:

...the religion of Masonry is cosmopolitan, universal....[108] —Albert G. Mackey

Many Freemasons makes this flight [to heaven] with no other guarantee of a safe landing than their belief in the religion of Freemasonry.[109] — Henry Wilson Coil

Masonry ... is the universal, eternal, immutable religion....[110] —Albert Pike

Everything in Masonry has reference to God, implies God, speaks of God, points and leads to God. Not a degree, not a symbol, not an obligation, not a lecture, not a charge but finds its meaning and derives its beauty from God the Great Architect, in whose temple all Masons are workmen.[111] —Joseph Fort Newton

Another standard Masonic authority, *Mackey's Revised Encyclopedia of Freemasonry*, agrees: "Freemasonry may rightfully claim to be called a religious institution. . . . The tendency of all true Freemasonry is toward religion. . . . Look at its ancient landmarks [doctrines], its sublime ceremonies, it profound symbols and allegories—all inculcating religious doctrine, commanding religious observance, and teaching religious truth, and who can deny that it is eminently a religious Institution?"[112]*

Experts in comparative religion have also declared Masonry to be a religion. Shildes Johnson, who holds three doctorates in religion or fields relating to religion, concludes: "A comparison of the moral, allegorical, and symbolic teachings of Freemasonry with these definitions of a religion reveals that the lodge is a theistic, non-Christian, man-centered and universal religion."[114] Yet Masons constantly claim Masonry is not a religion. Even the report of the Southern Baptist Home Mission Board, March 17, 1993, concluded: "Freemasonry is not a religion."

If Freemasonry is a religion, as even many Masonic scholars confess, why then do virtually all Masons say Masonry is not a religion? Do they deny the truth to gain converts to Masonry, who otherwise might not join? Is lying about the nature of Masonry necessary to furthering the goals of the venerable Lodge? And does Masonry in fact teach that it is a religion superior to all other faiths? It is to this question that we now turn.

---

*In his encyclopedia of Masonry, Mackey quotes Webster's four principal definitions of religion and then comments, "Now, it is plain that in either of the first three senses in which we take the word religion . . . Freemasonry may rightfully claim to be called a religious institution."[113] But Masonry also fits Webster's fourth definition, of religion. Mackey did not apply the fourth definition, which would imply that Masonry assumes a rightful place among the religions of the world. His objection is that this would make Masonry a competing religion with other religions. This would, of course, nullify Masonry's attempts to have "universal" appeal to all religions and so he cannot accept this definition.

Masonry teaches it is superior to all other faiths. Masonry is allegedly the genuine friend of all the world's religions. As Joseph Fort Newton asserts, "Masonry is . . . a worship, in which men of all religions may unite. . . . It is not the rival of any religion, but the friend of all, laying emphasis upon those truths which underlie all religions and are the basis and consecration of each."[115] Nevertheless, Masonry does teach that it is a religion superior to all other faiths.

The following statements by Masonic authorities prove that Masonry teaches that it is a religion superior to all others. Albert Mackey held the highest positions Masonry has to offer. For many years he was a 33rd degree Mason and Secretary General of the Supreme Council of the Thirty-Third Degree Scottish Rite. In his book, *The Manual of the Lodge,* Mackey describes the candidate who seeks to enter the Masonic Lodge. No matter what religious belief he brings to Masonry, such belief did not bring him into the light but kept him in darkness. Whether Christian, Jew, Hindu, Muslim or Buddhist, all candidates live in equal darkness outside of Masonry. "There he stands without [outside] our portals, on the threshold of his new Masonic life, in darkness, helplessness and ignorance. Having been wandering amid the errors and covered over with the pollutions of the outer and profane world, he comes inquiringly to our door, seeking the new birth, and asking a withdrawal of the veil which conceals divine truth from his uninitiated sight."[116]

Again, if all non-Masons are in spiritual darkness, and if Masonry is spiritual light and teaches that its ideals will one day rule the world, then Masonry must, of logical necessity, view itself as the one true religion. In referring to the Masonic believer, 33rd degree Mason and occultist Manly P. Hall says that because he is "freed of limitation of creed and sect, he stands as a master of all faiths. . . ."[117]

Time and again in Masonic literature, the teachings of Masonry become the substitute faith for the outmoded dogmas and particular tenets of any other religious belief. All doctrinal beliefs of non-Masonic religions are considered subsidiary and secondary beliefs, teachings relatively unimportant compared with the absolute truths of Masonry.[118] This is why Wagner, an authority on Masonry, can observe: "While it tacitly admits the existence of other gods in allowing its disciples to hold their private views, it does so on the theory that these god-ideas are perversions and corruptions of its own theistic conceptions and which it aims to correct. . . . It reduces all monotheistic deities to one and the same thing as its Great Architect, and all the great religions as identical with itself."[119]

Former Freemason Edmond Ronayne admits: "Freemasonry claims to be the only true religion now in the world," and he quotes from McClenachan in his *Book of the Ancient and Accepted Scottish Rite,* page 575, that "Masonry at last shall conquer, and its altar be the world."[120] Haywood declares, "[Masonry] is a world law destined to change the earth into conformity with itself. . . ."[121] Masonic authors have believed and taught:

There is under all creeds one universal religion.

This one true religion . . . is the very soul of Masonry.

The true disciple of ancient Masonry has given up forever the worship of personalities. . . . As a Mason his religion must be universal: Christ Buddha or Mohammed, the names mean little, for he recognizes only the Light and not the bearer [the person].

It is true that Masonry is not a religion, but it is Religion. . . . Religions are many; Religion is one. . . . It brings together men of all creeds in behalf of those truths which are greater than all sects, deeper than all doctrines.

Scarcely a Masonic discourse is pronounced, or a Masonic lesson read, by the highest officer or the humblest lecturer, *that does not earnestly teach this one true religion which is the very soul of Masonry,* its basis and apex, its light and power. Upon that faith it rests; and in that faith it lives and labors; and by that faith it will conquer at last.[122]

From Masonic literature, it becomes quite clear that Masonry is a religion, however emphatically it may also attempt to deny this. The more one reads in Masonry, the most obvious and undeniable is the fact that it believes itself to be the One True Religion.[123]

Christianity

The great thrust of Masonry does not establish the Kingdom of Christ; it is in fact hostile to Christ.[124]

Masonry claims it is compatible with Christian faith. But, as we will show, Masons themselves admit that Masonry is not Christian. In fact, as we will show, Masonry is antiChristian.

In Albert Mackey's *The Symbolism of Freemasonry,* it is acknowledged that the "Christianization of Freemasonry (the interpretation of its symbols from a Christian point of view)"[125] is wrong. "This is an error into which [some] have fallen. It is impossible to derive Freemasonry from Christianity. . . . [Freemasonry's] religion was derived from the ancient priesthood."[126] Joseph Fort Newton, perhaps the most popular Masonic writer of all time, acknowledges that, "The pilgrims and the Puritans were not of our Craft, and if we may judge from their real interests we may be sure that they did not care anything about it."[127] He also observes that Masonry did "finally emancipate itself from any sectarian and dogmatic interpretation of Christianity. . . ."[128]

In his *The Great Teachings of Masonry,* Haywood argues that Christians who think that Masonry is Christian are simply wrong: "Many brethren, misled by the predominantly Scriptural cast of the Work, and misunderstanding a few scattered references here and there, assume that in some sense Freemasonry is specifically a Christian institution. . . . These brethren should be made to understand the facts in the case. . . . The ritual [of Masonry] is not built on the text of the Bible, for the great major incidents in the ritual—and this applies to all the grades—are not found in the Book at all."[129] He acknowledges that the main reason, historically, why Christians joined Masonry was because of the "serious and religious nature of the ritual" as well as the citations from the Bible.[130] In other words, Christians joined Masonry because it appeared devout and biblical, even though this was not its intent or its true nature.

On this subject almost everyone agrees— Masonic, secular and Christian authorities alike—Masonry is not Christian.[131] The standard work on Masonic history freely admits that in the Constitutions of 1723, "Christianity was discarded."[132]

It seems, therefore, that only Christian Masons believe that Masonry is Christian. Other fellow Masons do not believe this, nor do former Masons who are now Christians, nor do secular researchers on the subject. Even Stephen Knight, who defines himself "as a neutral investigator holding no brief for Christianity"[133] admits, "One does not have to be a theologian—nor even a Freemason or a Christian—to recognize that Christians and Freemasons would have to worship the same God for the two to be compatible. . . . [But] Masonry and Christianity are mutually exclusive. . . . [There is] overwhelming evidence of Masonry's incompatibility with Christianity. . . ."[134]

One of the clearest statements documenting the true goal of Masonry comes from the 28th and 30th degrees. Masonry had earlier promised the candidate that it would not hinder him from following his own religious beliefs. But Masonry shows that this was only a ruse in order to get a person started in Masonry, for the goal was that the Lodge would eventually change a person's original beliefs. And notice that in the following block quote, one's original religious beliefs are called "superstition." This ritual teaches that all men are lost, in spiritual darkness, and not *true* Masons until they accept this. This statement also reveals that the true goal of the Masonic Lodge is to have its initiates finally drop and repudiate their previous religious beliefs—their "superstitions and prejudices"—and to accept the final and only truth of Masonry. Thus, the 28th degree teaches that "the first degree represents man, when he had sunken from his original lofty estate. . . . He is emphatically profane, enveloped in darkness, poor and destitute of spiritual knowledge, and emblematically naked. The material darkness which is produced by the bandage over his eyes, is an emblem of the darkness of his soul."[135] In the 30th degree it is revealed to the initiate that his earlier religious beliefs are "superstition" and that the claim of religious compatibility was only a ruse to get him started in Masonry:

In all the preceding degrees you must have observed that *the object of Scotch Masonry is to*

overthrow all kinds of superstition, and that by admitting in her bosom on the terms of the strictest equality, the members of all religions, of all creeds and of all countries, without any distinction whatever, she has, and indeed can have, but *one single object* and that is *to restore to the Grand Architect of the Universe; to the common father of the human race those who are lost in the maze of impostures, invented for the sole purpose of enslaving them.* The Knights Kadosh recognize no particular religion, and for that reason we demand of you nothing more than to worship God. And whatever may be the religious forms *imposed upon you by superstition* at a period of your life when you were incapable of discerning truth from falsehood, we do not even require you to relinquish them. *Time and study alone can enlighten you. But remember that you will never be a true mason unless you repudiate forever all superstitions and prejudices.*[136]

From this it can be seen that Masonry teaches that of all the faiths in the world it alone is the true faith and that ultimately all other religions are false superstition. With such a belief, Masonry can hardly claim that it seeks to unite all religions into a common brotherhood. The only way Masonry unites all men is if they abandon their former beliefs. As Joseph Fort Newton states, "Masonry seeks to free men from a limiting conception of religion, and thus to remove one of the chief causes of sectarianism." Newton hopes that as Masonry expands around the world, all religious creeds and dogmas will "cease to be," and that what remains will be "the one eternal religion—the Fatherhood of God, the brotherhood of man, the moral law, the golden rule, and the hope of a life everlasting."[137]

Do these sentiments of Masonic authorities sound "tolerant" toward the Christian faith—or any faith?

The Bible

Masonry claims to honor, reverence and respect the Bible as a great light for mankind. One standard Masonic authority states:

Upon the Altar of every Masonic lodge, . . . lies the Holy Bible. . . . our Volume of Sacred Law [VSL] and a Great Light in Masonry. The Bible opens when the lodge opens; and closes when the lodge closes. . . . The book of the Will of God rules the lodge in its labors, as the sun rules the day. . . . No Mason needs to be told what a great place the Bible has in the Masonry of our day. . . . Almost every name found in our ceremonies is a biblical name. . . . The spirit of the Bible, its faith, its attitude toward life, pervades Masonry. . . . Upon the Bible every Mason takes solemn vows of loyalty. . . . [It is] the book which tells us the purest truth about God. . . . While we honor every Book of Faith . . . with us the Bible is supreme. . . . Its truth is inwrought in the fiber of our being. . . .[138]

Masonry rejects the authority of the Bible and denies what the Bible teaches about itself. For Masonry, the Bible, like the Scriptures of all religions (the Upanishads, Koran, and so on) is merely a *symbol*[139] and not the literal Word of God to us. Albert Pike (see Appendix 2 at the end of this chapter) emphasized that, "The Hebrew books [the Bible] were written in Symbols unintelligible to the Profane [the non-Mason]."[140] So only Masons can "properly interpret the Bible." And when the Bible is "properly" interpreted, it teaches Masonic doctrine. This is why Martin L. Wagner observes: "Charles Sotheran speaks of the Bible as a pseudo-revelation. . . . Many Masonic writers ridicule the Christian doctrine that the Bible is a supernatural revelation from God. They say it is a book written for the vulgar, by the ancient priests, and that they concealed under its exoteric [outer or normal] language, the secret doctrine, which is the true Freemasonry."[141]

Chase's *Digest of Masonic Law* (pp. 207-8) states the Masonic view of the Bible clearly:

To require that a candidate profess a belief in the divine authority of the Bible is a serious innovation [violation] in the very body of Masonry. The Jews, the Chinese, the Turks, each reject either the Old or the New Testament, or both, and yet we see no good reason why they should not be made Masons. In fact, Blue Lodge Masonry has nothing whatever to do with the Bible. It is not founded on the Bible. If it were, it would not be Masonry.[142]

All Masonic authorities: "Establish three things: 1) that the Bible is only a symbol, 2) that a Mason is not required to believe its teachings and 3) that some other book may be substituted for it."[143]

Though the Bible is one of the three great "lights" of Masonry it is a "light" only in the sense that it is a mere symbol of divine truth or of the will of God *as individually interpreted by a Mason.*[144] For example: "When our rituals and Monitors tell us the Bible is one of the Great Lights of Masonry and that as such it is the rule and guide to our faith, it can only be speaking symbolically as it certainly is when speaking of the other two Great Lights, the square and the compass."[145] But the square and compass are universal symbols throughout Masonry. The Bible is not granted such status. That is why the Masonic *Volume of Sacred Law* (the religious Scripture appropriate to a given culture) and not the Bible is the true "great light." The Bible is only a limited symbol. It is only a localized "light" for Christian lands.

One of the reasons the Bible is used in Masonry is the same reason the Scriptures of other religions are used in other countries. The Lodge tricks men into swearing to uphold Masonry on the basis of that which they consider most holy, their own Scriptures. Thus, a Christian swears on the Bible to uphold Masonry without understanding that Masonry denies or distorts every major doctrine the Bible teaches. A leading Masonic authority, Rollin C. Blackmer, M.D., observes that the Bible "is almost never read in the lodge. In thirty years of almost constant attendance at lodge in many jurisdictions, the writer has never heard the Bible read in the lodge, though portions of Scriptures are occasionally quoted in the ritualistic work."[146]

As noted, Masons believe that it is a mistake to interpret the Bible literally. In harmony with a cultic and mystical approach to the Bible, they believe it is to be interpreted allegorically, symbolically or mystically.[147] For example in *Decoding the Bible Code,* Dr. Weldon showed how destructive Kabbalistic Bible interpretation is to the Scriptures. But Masons seem unaware of this, for Wagner states: "Freemasons take it for granted and as proved that the mystical interpretation of the scriptures according to Kabbalistic principles and methods is the correct one. The eminent Masons all contend that there is a veil upon the scriptures, which when removed, leaves them clearly in accord with Masonic teachings and in essential harmony with other sacred books."[148] The fact that there are now several Masonic editions of the Bible—all seeking to lend scriptural authority to Masonry[149]—merely adds insult to injury.

All of this makes a mockery of the Masonic claim to reverence and respect the Bible: "... there is a very large element of the Craft the world over who do not believe the teachings of the New Testament. ... Unless we are perpetrating a grim mockery, we do not employ the Bible as a profession that we as a society accept all its teachings and doctrines."[150]

What does the Bible teach about itself? It teaches it is the revealed Word of God, not just a symbol, or "a piece of [lodge] furniture."[151] (See Doctrinal Appendix.)

God

Those who become Masons must declare belief in a "supreme being." Most Christian Masons assume that this supreme being is the God of the Bible. However, it is easy to prove that Masonry does not believe in and worship the same God as the biblical Deity.

What does Masonry believe about God? It teaches the general concept of God as the Creator, Sustainer and Creative Principle (Architect) of the universe. This is why Masons refer to God as the Great Architect of the Universe (G.A.O.T.U.). Without doubt, this is the God of Masonry:

> It is faith in this deity [G.A.O.T.U.] that, as a prerequisite for membership, is demanded at the door of the lodge of every candidate for Masonic honors. It is this deity in whose name the covenant is made, and who is invoked for help to keep it inviolate. It is to him that the prayers in the lodge are addressed, ... whose praises are sung in Masonic odes and whose divinity is extolled. It is to him that Masonic alters are built, priests consecrated, sacrifices made, temples erected and solemnly dedicated. This Great Architect of the Universe is the "one God" in Freemasonry and besides him there is no other in that institution. Freemasonry as such knows no deity save the Great Architect of the Universe.[152]

But Masons have different and conflicting views about this God. Initially, Masons are simply required to have a belief in God (atheists are not permitted membership), but beyond this, no questions are asked. Any God will do: Allah, Krishna, Buddha, whoever. It may be the God of whichever religion the person brings to Masonry, or it may be any particular belief about God the Mason chooses to adopt in the future.

Some Masons believe (falsely, as we have noted) that the true God of Masonry is the God of their particular religion. Other Masons believe that God is a composite of every God that people worship; that is God has revealed Himself differently to different people but nevertheless encompasses all such revelations. In other words, similar for instance to the teachings of the Baha'i faith, the one true unknowable and indescribable God has made Himself known through a series of historical manifestations that have resulted in the major world religions.

Masonry offers so many different views of God because it refuses to define God clearly. Masonry admits that God is infinite, eternal, unitarian, boundless, universal and undenominational—a vast, cosmic Divine Spirit. But it goes no further. Thus in its ranks is found a morass of conflicting and competing concepts of God.

Logically, at one level, Masonry must encourage all members of different religions to pray to their own respective gods, for this is the means by which Masonry can appeal to members of different religions. But then Masons cannot all be praying to the *same* God because gods are different in nature and in what they expect of people and in what people expect of them. This means that the concept of the "Fatherhood of God and the brotherhood of man"—a Masonic ideal—is a myth. It is *not* a myth only if there is some *larger* God beyond the contradictory lesser gods that men worship. And this is why Freemasonry has a supreme God, G.A.O.T.U., supposedly the one true God all men are really praying to and which is beyond all the inferior, primitive concepts of individual religions.

There is a serious problem for Christian Masons in all this. When the Masonic Lodge allows its members obedience and allegiance to their different gods, the result, from a Christian perspective at least, can only be spiritual deception and idolatry. For Masonry argues that all Masons must worship their own gods, whatever those gods may be. For example, the Baptist Study cites *The Freemasons' Diary* as setting *"this priority for a Mason* concerning his *faith* and *religious practice:* a Freemason is encouraged to do his duty first to his God (*by whatever name he is known*) *through his faith and religious practice....* "[153]

But if there is only one true God, as Jesus Christ taught (John 17:3), then the Masonic approach is engaging in spiritual deception and promoting a belief in a multitude of *false* gods (idolatry). So how can Christian Masons logically join and swear allegiance to this? If Christian Masons really believe that there is only one true God, aren't they encouraging the acceptance of false gods with all that this implies? Isn't this idolatry? If it is idolatry, do Christian Masons really believe Masonry is as concerned about the Truth as it claims? After all, Jesus emphasized, "Now this is eternal life: that they may know you, *the only true God,* and Jesus Christ, whom you have sent" (John 17:3). For Christian Masons to encourage all Masons to worship and do their duty to their various gods constitutes the very kind of idolatry that God severely judged Israel for.

In teaching Christian Masons to accept all these false concepts of God, how is Masonry helping the Christian? The same question holds true for nonChristian Masons: how is Masonry helping anyone by leading them to worship false gods?

The Baptist Study says the following about God: "Every Mason is required to profess a belief in God, but each Mason is allowed to define his understanding of God as he wants. There is no doubt that Masons take belief in God seriously."[154] But how can "Masons take belief in God seriously" under such a principle? If there is only one true God and Masonry promotes the worship of a variety of false gods, how does it possibly take "belief in God seriously"? The *Scottish Rite Journal* itself confesses that Masonry strengthens one's "sense of responsibility to God and dependence on God is taught in our Ritual."[155] Again, which God?

Masonry teaches that the one true God is indescribable and unknowable. Consider the following comments by Coil:

> Men have to decide whether they want a God like the ancient Hebrew *Jahweh,* a partisan, tribal God, with whom they can talk and argue and from whom they can hide if necessary, or a boundless, eternal, universal, undenominational, and international, Divine Spirit, so vastly removed from the speck called *man,* that He cannot be known, named, or approached. So soon as man begins to laud his God and endow him with the most perfect human attributes such as justice, mercy, beneficence, etc., the Divine essence is depreciated and despoiled.... The Masonic test [for admission] is a *Supreme Being,* and any qualification added is an innovation and distortion.[156]

In a similar vein, Albert Pike taught in *Morals and Dogma,* "Every religion and every conception of God is idolatrous, insofar as it is imperfect, and as it substitutes a feeble and temporary idea in the shrine of that Undiscoverable Being [of Masonry]" (1906, p. 516). But Masonry offers the conception and qulification of God at its higher levels as pantheistic. Further, the Masonic God is clearly a deistic God. This, too, is a particular conception in that it rules out many other aspects of the Deity. The Masonic God is also a unitarian God; the concept of a triune nature in God is clearly rejected. And, as noted below, there are pagan conceptions of the Masonic God, which are implied through Masonic Ritual and belief. For example, Masonry accepts a particular form of pantheism called panentheism. "In its doctrines concerning the divine imminence Freemasonry is decidedly pantheistic, partaking of the various shades of that view of the divine. God (the Great Architect) is the great 'soul' of the universe, and the universe is the garment in which he is clothed."[157] "The Masonic view of the revelation of God, in the lower degrees, is deistic, but in the higher degrees it becomes pantheistic. The writings of Garrison, Buck, Pike, and other imminent Masons show this unmistakably. It is this peculiar pantheistic conception of deity which has passed from India through the secret doctrines of the Kabbalah into modern speculative

Freemasonry. . . . In Masonry, a god distinct from the life of nature has no existence."[158]

Masonry contains pagan conceptions of deity. An occult view of God in Masonry is just as appropriate as a Christian one,[159] and one writer in *The New Age* (April 1945, p. 159) asserted, "When we talk to God we are talking to ourselves, for God and Man are one and the same through the ties of love. . . ."[160]

Although the ultimate deity of Masonry is allegedly unapproachable and unknowable, parts of Masonry clearly reflect a pagan concept of the deity. In the Royal Arch Degree of the York Rite the secret name of the Masonic deity is revealed to be "Jabulon." Masons below that degree, therefore, such as those who have only taken the first three degrees of the Blue Lodge, do not understand that the Great Architect of the Universe (G.A.O.T.U.) is also this deity Jabulon.[161]

Jabulon is an embarrassment to many Masons. For example, speaking of one Masonic researcher, Steven Knight in his exposé *The Brotherhood* reveals: "'I have spoken to no less than 57 long-standing Royal Arch Freemasons' who he says were happy to discuss all aspects of Masonry with him. 'However, all but four lost their self-assurance and composure when I said, "What about Jah-bul-on?" All of the Masons attempted to move the conversation to another topic. If I insisted on returning to Jah-bul-on, almost invariably the interview would be unceremoniously terminated."[162] According to Knight, even Albert Pike had a problem with the word. Pike allegedly stated, "No man or body of men can make me accept as a sacred word, as a symbol of the infinite and eternal Godhead, a mongrel word, in part composed of the name of an accursed and beastly heathen god, whose name has been for more than 2,000 years an appellation of the devil."[163] On that we can agree with Albert Pike!

Who or what is Jabulon? Masonic authorities give different specific meanings to the term, but they are in agreement that the syllables of the term invoke pagan deities.[164] Most probably, the word is a composite of the Hebrew God Jehovah (Ja), the Canaanite god Baal (Bul) and the Egyptian god Osiris (On, a corruption of "Os"?). In this ritual Masonry connects the one true and

righteous God of the Bible with evil and pagan deities of the ancients. In other words, every Royal Arch Mason is told that the true name for the God he has been praying to throughout the different degrees of Masonry is Jehovah joined with the Canaanite Baal and Egyptian On (or possibly Osiris). Wagner observes: "In this compound name an attempt is made to show by a coordination of divine names . . . the unity, identity and harmony of the Hebrew, Assyrian and Egyptian god-ideas, and the harmony of the Royal Arch religion with these ancient religions. This Masonic 'unity of God' is peculiar. It is the doctrine that the different names of gods, Brahma, Jehovah, Baal, Bel, Om, On, etc., all denote the generate principle, in that all religions are essentially the same in their ideas of the divine."[165]

Coil's Masonic Encyclopedia declares, "Jah, Bel, and On appear in the American ritual of the Royal Arch degree on the supposition that Jah was the Syriac name of god, Bel (Baal), the Chaldean, and On, the Egyptian."[166] Here Coil himself admits that Bel refers to the Babylonian god "Baal." We will show how serious this is by illustrating the nature of the second deity in the composite term Jabulon, Bul or Baal. Baal was a Canaanite nature deity.[167] We have selected this deity because it is the god that is emphasized in Masonry in another manner as well:

There is no dispute between Freemasons and their fiercest critics that both the word Jehovah and the composite word, Jahbulon, appear on the [Masonic] altar, on top of which is inscribed a circle, containing a triangle. Around the circle is inscribed the name JEHOVAH and on the three sides of the triangle the letters JAH BUL ON. . . . To all of this must be added the third and final feature of the top of the pedestal: the Hebrew characters set at the angles of the triangle: Alif, Beth, and Lamed, each of which is said to have reference to the deity or to some divine attribute. [Quoting a Masonic source]: "Take each combination [of the letters] with the whole, and it will read this: Ab Bal, [meaning] Father, Lord; Al Bal, Word, Lord; Lab Bal, Spirit, Lord." The obvious result of such juggling of the Hebrew characters is to emphasize the formation of Bal, the name of a Semitic deity bitterly opposed by Elijah and the later Hebrew prophets; to associate this name in any way with that of Jehovah would have deeply shocked them.[168]

This quote identifies each Person of the holy trinity—Father, Son, Spirit—with Baal. This would have shocked the Jews because Baal was associated with incredibly evil practices, including the murder of children in sacrifice to the god. It would have shocked them in the same way it shocks us to read of modern cases of human sacrifice. Baal practice was sufficiently Satanic that both Jesus and the New Testament used the name of Baal in an extended manner for Satan himself. Beelzeboul is the New Testament form of the Old Testament Baalzebub.[169] In fact, one wonders whether "Jabulon" may be a satanic parody on the Trinity, much in the same way that the religion of Satanism attempts to parody the rituals and beliefs of Christianity. (For a more comprehensive look at the evil practices involved in Baal worship, see Judges 2:10-19; 1 Kings 18:16-40; Jeremiah 7:9; 11:13; 19:4-6).

Pike and other Masonic authorities have stated that "we utter no word that can be deemed irreverent by anyone of any faith" in Masonic Ritual or belief.[170] But how can Masonry claim this? Does a man feel offended when someone calls his mother a whore? How much more when someone calls his God a devil? God warns, "You shall not take the name of the Lord your God in vain, for the Lord will not leave him unpunished who takes His name in vain" (Exodus 20:3, 7). Does the Christian Mason assume God is pleased when he swears a solemn oath implying that God is associated with a devil? Does he believe that something evil can have no effect on his spiritual life? Is God mocked (Galatians 6:7)?

But the Christian Mason will reply, "Masonry is not idolatry." But Masonry is idolatry. The first commandment reads, "Thou shalt have no other gods before me." The biblical God will have no other gods before Him because at best they are lifeless idols, at worst demonic counterfeits. Wagner observes:

The Christian cannot, he dare not recognize other deities, or assent to their worship. This God is of necessity jealous of his honor, and he cannot give his glory to another.... Biblical

monotheism is an absolute monotheism, a solity of God and demands a worship of him and him only and in his name only. It demands that there be neither belief in the existence, neither the recognition, nor the worship of other gods. It denies that God can be known from speculation, but only by the revelation of Himself, in His Word.[171]

Wagner also states that the attempt to make Jehovah and the God of Masonry into the same God involves a subtle trick. Even while the Christian Mason professes adherence to the first commandment, he violates it openly:

... these attempts are simply cunning devices for misleading and deceiving both the Mason and the profane. They are examples of clever sophistry, of skillful syncretism, of cunningly devised fables and delusive fictions, which have a semblance of truth and fact, but which in reality are only veils and disguises for its refined idolatry. They are skillful professions of adherence to the first commandment while in fact they are palpable violations of it.[172]

There is absolutely no doubt that Masonry offers another god besides the one true God. Hence Masonry is both blasphemous and idolatrous. This is why a Committee of the General Synod of the Church of England concluded: "JAHBULON (whether it is a name or description), which appears in all the rituals, must be considered blasphemous: in Christian theology the name of God (Yahweh/Jehovah) must not be taken in vain, nor can it be replaced by an amalgam of the names of pagan deities."[173] In light of all this, how can the Christian Mason justify remaining a Mason?

Jesus Christ

"Holiness to the Lord"

—Motto on the official seal of the Grand Lodge of New York

Masonry claims that it does not offend a Christian's belief about Jesus Christ. For example: "We do not say to Christians that Christ was a mere man, whose life's story is only a revival of similar older [pagan] stories. To do any of these things would be irreverent. We utter no such words."[174] But Masonry does teach that Jesus Christ was merely a man. Concerning the denial of Christ's deity we may note the observations of Masonic leader Jim Shaw. Shaw was a 33rd degree Mason, a Past Worshipful Master of the Blue Lodge, Past Master of all Scottish Rite bodies, and a Knight Commander of the Court of Honor. He acknowledges that official Masonic doctrine maintains that "Jesus was just a man. He was one of the 'exemplars,' one of the great men of the past, but not divine and certainly not the only means of redemption of lost mankind."[175] The Masonic Maundy Thursday Ritual of the chapter of Rose Croix states officially, "We meet this day to commemorate the death [of Jesus], not as inspired or divine, for this is not for us to decide."[176] One Mason told us, "Jesus and Krishna are the same!"[177]

In his spiritual darkness or ignorance, the Christian Mason may choose to believe that Jesus was God and Savior of the world, but this is not Masonic truth. Those who consider themselves enlightened Masons hope that their unenlightened Christian brethren will realize that *all* specific dogmas about Christ are in error. As Clausen emphasizes, Masons hope to "strip from all religions their orthodox tenets, legends, allegories and dogmas."[178] This is why the Masonic scholar Albert Pike asserts that Jesus was "a great teacher of morality"—but no more.[179]

So Masonry teaches that Jesus was only a man. Why does Masonry say that, and thereby offend the beliefs of Christians? It does this because it does not wish to offend the religious sensibilities of nonChristian Masons, those members of other faiths who deny that Jesus is the only Incarnation of God and Savior of the world. The unique nature and mission of Christ is denied by Hindus, Buddhists, Muslims and Jews. In order to not offend these people, it offends Christians.

Masonry excludes all particular biblical teachings about Christ, such as His Incarnation, redemptive mission, death and resurrection. In fact, there is no biblical truth about Jesus Christ affirmed anywhere in Masonry. Mason Edmond Ronayne confesses: "Freemasonry 'carefully excludes' the Lord Jesus Christ from the Lodge and chapter, repudiates his mediatorship, re-

jects his atonement, denies and disowns his gospel, frowns upon his religion and his church, ignores the Holy Spirit, and sets up for itself a spiritual empire, a religious theocracy, at the head of which it places the G.A.O.T.U.—the god of nature—and from which the one only living and true God is expelled by resolution. . . ."[180]

Although there are many possible beliefs that Masons hold about Jesus, one of the more prevalent beliefs can be traced to Masonry's ties to the ancient mystery religions. Many Masons believe that the biblical teaching of Christ as God and Savior is merely a corruption of "similar," more "pure" stories in some of the earlier pagan religions.[181] (For a refutation, see our *Ready with an Answer* [Harvest House, 1997].) These Masons teach that the New Testament is a corrupted version of such stories and that Christianity as normally interpreted by the Church is false. In fact, many of these Masons are offended that Christianity teaches that only Jesus is God. They prefer a more mystical Christ, a Christ who recognizes that all men are divine.[182] For example, Dr. R. Swineburne Clymer, M.D., recognized as a high Mason, teaches in *The Mysticism of Masonry* (1900, p. 47): "In deifying Jesus, the whole humanity is bereft of Christos as an eternal potency within every human soul, a latent (embryonic) Christ in every man. In thus deifying one man, they have orphaned the whole of humanity [of its divinity]."[183]

But none of the Masonic teachings about Christ agree with what Jesus taught about Himself and with what the Church has maintained for 2,000 years. If Masonry does not even respect the teachings of Jesus, how can it claim to be a tolerant religion? (See chapter 4 of *Bowing at Strange Altars* and chapter 10 of *Secret Teachings* for more information on Masonry and Jesus Christ. See the Doctrinal Appendix in this book for the biblical view of Jesus Christ.)

Salvation

There are five important teachings related to the Masonic idea of salvation. Although Masonry incorporates different levels of Masonic "enlightenment," not all Masons are aware of the teachings of the higher degrees. For example,

Masons who have only completed the first three degrees of the Blue Lodge may not be aware of the teachings of the higher degrees or how Masonry can open the door to occult concepts of salvation. What Masonic rituals clearly imply, and what Masonic doctrines clearly state, is that Masonry itself enlightens a man to his proper place in the universe. It offers him the true way to live and supplies him with the manner in which he can be in a right relationship with God. In fact, it is everywhere implied that the non-Mason (the profane) exists in a state of spiritual ignorance. Here we will examine five teachings of Masonry concerning salvation: 1) *"Universalism"*—the teaching that all men are going to live forever in the afterlife with God (not necessarily heaven); 2) *"Salvation by works"*—good works earn salvation in the afterlife; 3) *"Reformation as regeneration"*—Masonic reformation of character as the new birth; 4) *A form of "gnosticism"*—the teaching that a Mason is saved from his own ignorance of Masonic truths; 5) *"Occult Enlightenment"*—a Mason may travel the higher Masonic path of enlightened consciousness and occultism.

1. Universalism: in the end, all men will be saved.

The Masonic doctrine of the universal "Fatherhood of God" assures them that nothing can possibly separate them from their Father in the afterlife. Masonry does not believe that man is born sinful or that he needs deliverance from his sin and God's wrath against it. In reference to a belief in original sin, Masonry rejects the concept: "Nor does Masonry teach that human nature is a depraved thing, like the ruin of a once proud building. Many think that man was once a perfect being but that through some unimaginable moral catastrophe he became corrupt unto the last moral fiber of his being, so that, without some kind of supernatural or miraculous help from outside him, he can never [be saved]."[184] As one official Baptist report on Masonry concluded: "Freemasonry teaches much about moral righteousness but almost nothing about sin and repentance. There appears to be no need for the forgiveness of sins and reconciliation to God through the shed blood of Jesus Christ. Masons are encouraged to become involved in charitable causes, and in the minds of many these good works may be their idea of earning salvation."[185]

If all men are already going to heaven regardless of their personal morality or religious beliefs, then they need nothing from God concerning a basic change in their condition before entrance. All they need is to discover God within themselves. "We are taught that if we would find God, look for his revelation within our own souls. We are a part of him and he of us."[186] In teaching that all men are already saved, Masonry dismantles the heart of the Christian Gospel. If men do not need to be saved from their sins, why did Christ die on the Cross? Why did He teach that faith in Him was necessary to deliver a man from God's wrath against sin? (See Matthew 20:28; John 3:16; 5:24; 6:47; 1 John 2:2.)

2. Salvation by Works.

Masonry claims that it does not teach salvation by works. For example, in 1985 the Board of General Purposes of the United Grand Lodge of England published a tract titled "Freemasonry and Religion,"[187] asserting that Masonry "does not claim to lead to salvation by works, by secret knowledge, or by any other means."[188] But this is false. Lynn Perkins writes in *The Meaning of Masonry* (CSA Press, p. 95), "Every man is in essence his own savior and redeemer; for if he does not save himself, he will not be saved."

Masonic rituals teach things very clearly. Freemasonry is the best way to live and die and the best way to be in a correct relationship to God. Sovereign Grand Commander Clausen emphasizes that *each* of the 32 degrees of the Scottish Rite "teach by ceremony and instruction" that the "noblest purposes and duties of man" are to struggle for his own salvation, to overcome and win, "to reach the spiritual and divine within himself" because "man is . . . an eternal soul advancing ever nearer and nearer to perfection."[189] Pike taught that "step by step men must advance toward Perfection; and each Masonic Degree is meant to be one of those steps."[190] In other words, all of Masonry is actively committed to teaching works-salvation, which by implication opposes the Gospel of

Jesus Christ. Masonry teaches that a man must be "worthy of life after death,"[191] which can only be achieved by "service and obedience" to Masonry[192] and by a life regulated by "morality, faith and justice."[193]

This pride-based teaching of self-salvation helps Masonry feel superior to Christianity. Former 33rd degree Worshipful Master Jim Shaw recalls: "Never in all my years of dedicated service to Masonry did anyone in the lodge witness to me about the love and saving grace of Jesus. The lodge attended a church once each year as a group. Each time the pastor (who was himself a Mason) would introduce us to the congregation and then exalt the craft, telling them about all our wonderful works. We usually left the church thinking of how wonderful we were and feeling sorry for all those in the church who were not Masons, participating in all our good deeds."[194]

Consider the symbolism of the lambskin (the white linen apron) that is presented to a Mason during the first (Entered Apprentice) degree of the ritual: "Because the lamb, in all ages, has been deemed an emblem of innocence; he, therefore, who wears the lambskin as a badge of a Mason is thereby continually reminded of that purity of life and conduct which is essentially necessary to his gaining admission into that celestial Lodge above, where the Supreme Architect of the universe presides."[195] In the second (Fellow Craft) degree, the ritual imparts the following instruction: "The apron of a Mason is intended to remind him of purity of mind and morals.... Thus you will wear your apron while laboring among us as a speculative Fellow Craft, to distinguish you from the Entered Apprentices, ever remembering that you are to wear it as an emblem of that purity of heart and conscience that is necessary to obtain for you the approval of the Grand Architect of the Universe."[196] Virtually every degree in Masonry teaches or implies salvation by works.

In spite of all this evidence, Masons officially deny teaching salvation by works. In a debate on "The John Ankerberg Show," Mason William Mankin, a professing Christian, looked straight into the eyes of the audience and said:

[Masonry] is not a religion. *It offers no system of salvation.* . . . Our symbols are related to the development of character, of the relationship of man to man. They are working tools to be used in the building of life. These working tools have been used from time immemorial to build buildings, and all we are saying is that if you as an individual adopt the principles represented [in Masonry], . . . that you will be a better person. *Not that you're going to go to heaven.*[197]

But former Worshipful Master Mason Jack Harris flatly contradicts this:

In all the rituals that I taught for eleven years, Masonry did teach how to get to *heaven.* They taught it with the apron that I wore, by my purity [of] life and conduct. They taught it in the Hiram Abiff legend in the third degree [symbolizing] the immortality of the soul. Through all their writings they say they are teaching the immortality of the soul to the Mason. But the Word of God tells me that the only way to have immortal life is through the Person of Jesus Christ. Never at any Masonic ritual did they point out that Jesus is the way of salvation.[198]

But how can Masons speak of earning entrance to heaven on the basis of good works if heaven is the inalienable right of all men? Entrance to heaven cannot logically be gained by good works if it is automatic by virtue of being human.*

In his *Lexicon of Freemasonry,* Mackey defined "acacian" as "a term signifying a Mason who by living in strict obedience to obligations and precepts of the fraternity is free from sin."[199] Presumably, good works forgive sin only

---

*Technically, Masonry's doctrine of universalism assumes men will get to heaven with or without good works. Logically then, Masonry should teach that although all men will go to heaven, only Masons will be specially rewarded for their being Masons and doing Masonic works. But many of its statements imply that heaven, or the afterlife, is a reward for good works. Thus, Masonry must either deny its universalism, which it cannot do, or deny the value and uniqueness of Masonry as a way to heaven, which it also cannot do. Masonry must continue to imply that a Mason earns his way to heaven—a false conclusion in any system of universalism. Masonry is thus placed in the uncomfortable position of either teaching a lie to its members (Masonry gets them to heaven) or of confessing that Masonry does not get one to heaven (because all men are predestined to heaven regardless).

in the sense that good works are pleasing to God, who overlooks sin because of a Mason's good works. In other words, to be redeemed from sin is to become a moral person. By his initiation and resolve to enter the Masonic life, the master Mason "has discovered the knowledge of God and His salvation, and been redeemed from the death of sin and the sepulcher of pollution and unrighteousness."[200]

3. Reformation as regeneration: Masonry and the new birth.

A Christian Mason may respond, "Doesn't Masonry believe in the new birth and doesn't the symbolism of the third degree clearly deal with Christian rebirth?" A Christian who interprets the nonChristian rituals and symbols of Masonry through Christian eyes is seeing in them what he chooses to see, rather than what is there. Masonry does speak of a "new birth." Carl Claudy maintains, "The candidate for the Entered Apprentice Degree must be born again, before he really *entered;* and when his preparation is so regarded, the rite becomes solemn, convincing, sacred...."[201] But this is principally a moral reformation or enlightenment to the alleged spiritual truths of Masonry and has nothing to do with biblical regeneration. Thus, the new life or new birth of the Mason may in one sense be considered "spiritual," but it is not supernatural. The Masonic candidate is "reborn spiritually" in the sense that he now comes to *realize* that eternal life or immortality is his divine right as a child of God, something he did not understand before coming to Masonry.[202] The following statements by Masonic authorities reveal the true nature of the Masonic rebirth:

> Your preparation to become an entered apprentice has taught you that you are to be reborn. This rebirth is spiritual and mental. Through Freemasonry's universal forms and ceremonies you are united with millions of [Masonic] men.[203]

But as profound as it is hoped to be, it is emphasized that this rebirth is *not* supernatural:

> It is true that the lesson in the Third Degree is the lesson of regeneration: the candidate comes as one whose old self must die in order that a new self may be born; but this new life into which the candidate is born is *not in any sense supernatural.*[204]

This means that the "rebirth" according to Masonry has nothing to do with biblical rebirth. Rather, it is mere human reformation as found in cultic and occult religion. Thus cultists and occultists by the thousands, from Mormons to witches, speak of similar changed lives like those found among Masons. In fact, the Masonic candidate is "reborn" in a fashion similar to an initiate in the ancient mystery schools:

> In the Ancient Mysteries the doctrine of regeneration was taught by symbols: not the theological dogma of regeneration peculiar to the Christian church, but the philosophical dogma, as a change from death to life—a new birth to [the realization of] immortal existence.... This is the doctrine in the Masonic mysteries, and more especially in the symbolism of the Third Degree. We must not say the Freemason is regenerated when he is initiated—but that he has been indoctrinated into the philosophy of the regeneration, or the new birth of all things—of light out of darkness, of life out of death, of eternal life out of temporal death.[205]

Christian regeneration, however, radically changes a person's disposition, spirit and destiny. (See Doctrinal Appendix.) Masonic regeneration only gives the Mason new ideas. It tells the Mason to believe something he did not believe before: that because he is allegedly God's child, he will inherit immortality as a result.

4. Gnosticism: a Mason is saved only from his ignorance of Masonic truths.

If a Mason is "saved" from anything it is only from his ignorance of the eternal truths of Masonry. Whether he is a Christian or not, as a Masonic initiate he comes to Masonry in spiritual darkness and is delivered from spiritual darkness by the truths of Masonry. *The Standard Masonic Monitor* teaches, "Hence the great, the primary object of the first degree is to symbolize the birth of the intellectual light in the mind; and the Entered Apprentice is the type of unregenerate man, groping in moral and mental darkness, and seeking for the light [of Masonry] which is to guide his steps and point him to the path which leads to duty and to Him [God] who gives to duty its reward."[206]

Thus, in harmony with ancient gnosticism, the occult and many Eastern religions and cults, Masonry teaches that man's principal problem is ignorance: he simply does not know that he already maintains a perfect relationship with God and in his true nature partakes of divinity. What he needs is knowledge: enlightenment as to his true condition, in this case, Masonically interpreted. He does not require repentance from sin, faith in Jesus Christ and salvation in a biblical sense.

5. Occult enlightenment: the Mason may travel the higher Masonic path of enlightened consciousness and occultism. "Salvation" can mean different things to different Masons. The Christian Mason will interpret "salvation" far differently from a Mason who may be a nominal Christian, or a Hindu, Buddhist, Muslim or occultist. In general, salvation can mean whatever an individual Mason wishes it to mean. In his text *Freemasonry: Its Aims and Ideals,* p. 187, Ward states, "Freemasonry has taught each man can, by himself, work out his conception of God and thereby achieve salvation."[207] *The Short Talk Bulletin,* a publication of the Masonic Service Association of the United States (Vol. 43, no. 5, May 1964, p. 3), asserts, "The fraternity is, to me, man's organized attempt in an orderly way to proceed in a direction of life that is orientated toward what *he feels is* creation's design for him in this universe. It is the reach of man for God."[208]

But there is another sense in which Masonry teaches that salvation is a lengthy process, that it may continue for eons. In its inquiry into Freemasonry, the Baptist Union of Scotland concluded, "There is another strand in Freemasonry which implies salvation through enlightenment, after the manner of the ancient mystery religions."[209] Masonic scholar Albert Pike taught that the essence of Freemasonry was that of a struggle with the material and sensual world that would begin an eternal process of the soul's advancement toward perfection.[210] Thus, a belief in reincarnation may be accepted.

Along this path, *consciousness* and *realization* are key. The Mason who seeks enlightenment does not just blindly accept the idea that he is inwardly divine (as many other Masons may); he seeks to experientially realize it through occult technique. Thus, a man must "refine" his consciousness to realize (not just intellectually accept) his inner divinity. Developing altered states of consciousness or attending other occult pursuits are not only accepted but encouraged as the means to such refinement of consciousness. Here, Masonry is not only connected to its occult counterparts, such as Rosicrucianism, Theosophy and the Ancient Mysteries, it also opens the door in the life of an individual Mason to a greater personal pursuit of the occult. One leading Mason argues: ". . . the soul of man has ceased to be God-conscious and has degenerated into the limited terrestrial consciousness of the ordinary human being. . . . Yet there remains a way of regaining [higher] consciousness of that higher world and life. It is by bringing into function a now dormant and submerged faculty resident at the depth and center of his [a man's] being."[211]

These citations demonstrate that Ma-sonry is both nonChristian and antiChristian in its view of salvation. How then can a Christian Mason support the cause of Masonry?

THE OCCULT

"It is one of your great duties as a Most Excellent Master to dispense light to the uninformed Mason."[212]

—Charge to the Most Excellent Master upon his initiation

Most Masons scoff at the idea that Masonry is occult. They claim that Masonry has nothing to do with the occult. Coil asserts, "Freemasonry is no more occult than the Golden Rule; no more mysterious than Morality."[213] Of course, many people would say something similar about astrology, the Ouija board and other occult activities. Coil's statement is true only at one level of Masonry and then at best a half truth.

Most Masons who participate in the rituals do not understand their occult significance. If they pursue Masonry no further than this, it may be true for them that Masonry is not something occult. If so, this is only because these Masons are unaware of the occult meaning of the Masonic symbols or ritual and have chosen not to pursue the issue further. The fact that most Masons choose not to pursue the hidden meaning of Masonry is why Steinmetz laments, "Most of the truly great Masonic writers have deplored the lack of esoteric Masonic knowledge among the craft in general. Mackey speaks of the Parrot Mason, describing him as: 'One who commits to memory questions and answers of the catechetical lectures, and the formulas of the ritual, but pays no attention to the history and philosophy of the institution; [he is] called a Parrot Mason because he repeats what he has learned without any conception of its true meaning.' "[214]

For those with eyes to see, Masonry is full of the occult. One researcher concludes, "Behind all Masonic symbolism there is an undisclosed occult interpretation of which most Freemasons are ignorant."[215] One spiritist confesses of the Scottish Rite, "From the Nineteenth to the Twenty-eighth [degree] the work is most deeply occult. . . ."[216] One official inquiry into Masonry concluded, "The whole complex of ideas inherent in Masonry bears close similarities to occultism. . . ."[217]

In this section we will document four different ways in which Masonry may encourage the pursuit of the occult.

New Age and Parapsychological Premise
Masonry accepts the premise of the New Age and modern parapsychology: "unlimited" power within man. The modern New Age movement teaches that man is invariably divine, a god in the making. Its adherents see in the modern discipline of parapsychology (the scientific study of the occult) the confirmation of the idea that man has latent psychic powers. All people need to do is to learn to unleash these "divine" powers. A number of prominent Masons share similar beliefs. Sovereign Grand Commander Henry C. Clausen refers to achieving "a true New Age" and asserts that potentially, "We have within us an infinite, unlimited source of power. . . . Perhaps the stars in transition have a message for us, as the world plunges through space into the Age of Aquarius. . . . Our

altar is in the East. . . . We know that the new division we are entering will bring new energies. These may have tremendous effects upon us, our civilization and our earth. . . ."[218] Consider also Clausen's commentary on the 28th degree of the Scottish Rite: "This is a Kabalistic and Hermetic Degree of the greatest antiquity, dealing with the primal matter of all things. . . . There are seven stations representing planets that anciently explained the passage of souls between heaven and earth. . . . What we see in this life are reflections of things that exist in the invisible spiritual world. . . . Faith is taught as the miraculous lever that can move humanity . . . [and] senses an underlying divinity in all things."[219] In his discussion of the 32nd degree he reveals the secret nature of Masonry, which promises occult knowledge and power by revealing the true laws of nature:

As we progress toward the end of this Degree and seek seriously the Royal Secret which is concealed like the occult science of the ancients, we remember, 'Faith begins where reason sinks exhausted.' Magic, after all, is but the absolute science of nature and its laws. . . . You will seek the Holy Doctrine—the Blazing Star of Truth, the Royal Secret—of creation. So do we slowly climb toward the final goal, the state of perfection . . . ? Some modern scientists concede that in the search for enlightenment, recourse must be made to the mystic. . . . William James . . . harmonized religion and mysticism, concluding that 'personal religious experience has its roots and center in mystical states of consciousness.' . . . Telepathy and esoteric psychology can work within us and release energy, insight and imagination. . . . The Holy Doctrine—the Royal Secret—heretofore has been concealed. . . . But the veil now has been lifted for you. . . . The Scottish Rite symbology and teachings and studies have made the creative law of the universe susceptible of discovery. . . . Nature's secrets are those of the supernatural [occult] sciences. . . . Man has an immortal soul, imprisoned for a time within a mortal body, which is capable of improvement and of spiritual development. It is released when death occurs, thus mingling the divine with the human. . . . So, if you will seek and discover, you can travel beyond the material, you can grasp the supersensual, you can touch the Divine. You will be carried toward total truth and to that rare and ultimate mystic understanding of self and the universe. You then will know why we are here, what we are doing, and where we are going.[220]

These teachings are in a number of important respects indistinguishable from the teachings of the New Age movement and human potential parapsychology.

Relation to Occult Practices
Masonry is an introduction to the occult because in symbolism and philosophy it is similar to many occult practices. That Masonry is related to other occult arts is acknowledged by Masonic authorities.

A. *Kabalism.* Kabalism* is a complex, symbolical occult art that began among the Jewish people in the first century A.D., flowered in the Middle Ages and is experiencing a revival today, in part a consequence of widespread interest in an alleged Kabalistic-based "Bible Code" hidden in the Torah. (See John Weldon's *Decoding the Bible Code,* Harvest House, 1998.) Albert Pike confesses that "the Kabalah is the key of the occult sciences. . . ."[221] He also sees Kabalism in Masonry at every turn, which is why he encourages the Mason to familiarize himself with Kabalistic doctrine.[222] He claims, "All the Masonic associations owe to it [Kabalism] their Secrets and their Symbols."[223] And, "Masonry is a search after Light. That search leads us directly back, as you see, to the Kabalah. . . . [there] the Initiate will find the source of many [Masonic] doctrines; and may in time come to understand the Hermetic philosophers, the Alchemists . . . and [spiritist] Emanuel Swedenborg."[224] The *Liturgy of the Ancient and Accepted Scottish Rite* describes the 13th degree as follows: "There are profounder meanings concealed in the symbols of this degree, connected with the philosophical system of the Hebrew Kabalists which you will learn hereafter, if you should be so fortunate as to advance. They are unfolded in the higher degrees."[225]

*Also spelled Kabbalism, Cabalism, Qabbalism.

Any study of Kabalism will quickly reveal that Kabalism was and is used today for all types of occult practice—black and white magic, conjuring spirits, divination, developing psychic powers, etc.[226] Is it truly wise, let alone Christian, to partake in rites and be a member of a religion that is based upon Kabalistic philosophy or that encourages the study of such philosophy?

B. *Rosicrucianism.* The connection between Rosicrucianism and Freemasonry is also clear. Even a review of W. B. Crow's book *Witchcraft, Magic and Occultism* in the March 1975 issue of *Masonic Square* admitted the connection between English Masons and Rosicrucianism.[227] Although many authorities could be given recognizing this connection, space only permits our citing one here, Manly Hall:

Many of those connected with development of Freemasonry were suspected of being Rosicrucians. . . . Frank C. Higgins, a modern Masonic symbolist, writes: "Dr. Ashmole, a member of this fraternity [Rosicrucianism], is revered by Masons as one of the founders of the first Grand Lodge in London." . . . Elias Ashmole is but one of many intellectual links connecting Rosicrucianism with the genesis of Freemasonry. The *Encyclopaedia Britannica* notes that Elias Ashmole was initiated into the Freemasonic order in 1646. . . . Speculators have gone so far as to state that, in their opinion, modern Freemasonry has completely absorbed Rosicrucianism and succeeded it as the world's greatest secret society. Other minds of equal learning declare that the Rosicrucian brotherhood still exist, preserving its individuality as a result of having withdrawn from the Masonic Order. . . . One thing is certain: with the rise of Freemasonry, the Rosicrucian Order in Europe practically disappeared, and notwithstanding existing statements to the contrary, it is certain that the Eighteenth degree (commonly known as the Rose-Croix) perpetuates many of the symbols of the Rosicrucian Fire Alchemist.[228]

C. *Hermetic Philosophy.* Hermetic philosophy (also known as "alchemy") is a pillar of ancient and modern occultism. The Greek god *Hermes* (the Roman *Mercury* and Egyptian *Thoth*) was held to be the originator of many occult arts. According to Mackey, "In all the old manuscript records which contain the legend of the Craft, mention is made of *Hermes* as one of the founders of Freemasonry."[229] Coil, who seems somewhat embarrassed by the Masonic connection to the occult, objects to any association in the following terms:

There has been a tendency for two centuries among imaginative and sensational writers to corrupt Freemasonry by coating it with all sorts of mystical and occult veneers, of which Alchemy is but one. So successful have they been that many within and many without the Society assume that there is some affiliation of Freemasonry with theosophy, astrology, spiritualism, occultism, magism, or even fortune telling and sleight of hand. There has never been any association between Freemasonry and the mystical arts, especially alchemy, though, doubtless, the formulators of the numerous *hauts grades* and other higher degrees around the middle of the Eighteenth Century resorted to many such sources for interesting and impressive material, which was as valuable in promotion as it was supernatural. Accordingly, the twenty-eighth degree of the Scottish Rite, called *knight of the sun* is partly Hermetic, just as the twenty-first or *Prussian* knight furnishes an example of sorcery.[230]

But Albert Mackey simply confesses, "There is a very great similarity between their doctrines and those of the Freemasons; so much so that the two associations have sometimes been confused."[231]

In conclusion, these connections of Masonry to various occult arts is one reason why many Masons are also occultists and why many occultists have chosen to pursue the path of esoteric Masonry.

Mysticism
Masonry is an introduction to the occult because Masonry is a system of mysticism which accepts the development of altered states of consciousness. Dozens of books have been published on the mystical side of Masonry, such as Arthur Ward's *Masonic Symbolism and the Mystic Way* and J. D. Buck's *Mystic Masonry.* Many of these Masonic writers have inspired other Masons to look to Eastern or Western

mysticism and the occult as a means of spiritual development.[232] For these authors the real meaning of Masonry is hidden in the mystical quest. This is why Carl H. Claudy refers to Masonic authority and scholar Albert Pike as the "greatest of Masons as he was greatest of mystics"[233]—because he did as much as anyone to promote the mystical side of Masonry. (See Appendix 2.) Masonic authorities H. L. Haywood and A. E. Waite both agree that, "There is a class of religious practices (or experiences) called mysticism; *Freemasonry is a religious mysticism;* whatever may be the place belonging to religious mysticism in the world *is the place belonging to Freemasonry.*"[234]

Anyone who studies mysticism will realize that a large part of that "place belonging to religious mysticism" deals with altered states of consciousness.[235] This is why mystical Masons stress the importance of developing altered states.[236] For example, 32nd degree Mason Foster Bailey refers to "the necessity . . . for complete self mastery and expansion of consciousness before the achieving of the degree of Master [Mason]."[237]

Masonic authority Wilmshurst[238] and other mystic Masons allege that each degree of the Blue Lodge is able to open one's consciousness to progressively higher levels of being. For instance, the second degree of Masonry, Fellowcraft, involves "the use of the psychic and higher intellectual nature," and the third degree, Master Mason, may involve "an opening up of consciousness to the very center and depths of one's being," that is, to the divinity within.[239] In noting the connection between the initiations of the ancient pagans and modern Masonry, Wilmshurst observes that both had a common goal: "Initiation, therefore, meant a process whereby natural man became transformed into spiritual or ultra-natural man, and to effect this it was necessary to *change his consciousness,* to gear it to a new and higher principle, and so, as it were, make of him a new man in the sense of attaining a new method of life and a new outlook upon the universe.[240]

Why is the cultivation of occult and mystical altered states of consciousness of concern? It is of great concern because a psychic altered consciousness is a characteristic door to establishing contact with the spirit (demon) world. (We documented this in detail in our *Encyclopedia of New Age Beliefs*.) Cambridge educated John Ferguson goes so far as to assert that a state of voluntary spirit possession is "the core of mystical experience."[241]

Occult Masonry
Masonry is an introduction to the occult because many Masons are working for an awakening of occult Masonry. Because the occult is now socially out of the closet, many Masons are recognizing that the time is "ripe" to return Masonry to its occult heritage. The curator and librarian of the Grand Lodge of Free and Accepted Masons of New York points out, "In this new Aquarian age, when many individuals and groups are working in various ways for the eventual restoration of the [ancient] mysteries, an increasing number of aspirants are beginning to recognize that Freemasonry may well be the vehicle for this achievement."[242] Hall argues that there is more than sufficient precedent within the domains of Masonic scholarship for the modern Mason to return to the ancient meanings of the Craft.[243] Wilmshurst sees that "a higher Masonic consciousness is awakening in the Craft. Members of the Order are gradually, and here and there, becoming alive to the fact that much more than meets the eye and ear lies beneath the surface of Masonic doctrine and symbols."[244] Should Masonry as a whole ever return to its ancient roots, it could become a significant power for the expansion of the occult in the Western World.

These four considerations reveal that Masonry has both the means and the motivation to encourage its members to pursue the world of the occult. Masonry therefore encourages Masons to pursue its esoteric side and to pursue altered states of consciousness and the development of "higher" (psychic) powers. Thus Masonry is related to other occult practices, and many Masons are actively working for the revival of occult Masonry.

All of this is why we find many examples where the search for "Masonic light" leads to the dead end of the occult. Indeed, it is also the reason that we find the spirit world promotes Masonry, as was documented in our chapter on Masonry and spiritism in *Secret Teachings*. For example, Djwhal Khul was one of the principal spirit guides of occultist Alice Bailey. Of Masonry this spirit teaches, "The Masonic movement . . . is the home of the Mysteries and the seat of initiation. . . . It is a far more occult organization than can be realized, and is intended to be the training school for the coming advanced occultists."[245]

Keep in mind that a spirit is speaking these words through a possessed medium. This entity also revealed that the spirit Hierarchy directs specific persons within each field to perform the will of the spirits: "In all these bodies there are to be found esoteric groups. . . . These inner groups consist of occult students and of those who are in direct or occasional touch with the Masters [spirits] and of those whose souls are in sufficient control so that the will of the Hierarchy [the governing spirit hierarchy] may be communicated and gradually filtered down to the channel of the physical brain."[246] In other words, this spirit claims that such individuals are under the guidance and control of the spirit world.

Masonic Lynn F. Perkins wrote *Masonry in the New Age*, in which he thoroughly integrated Masonry with occult and New Age philosophy. Yet he too claims his ideas were inspired by the spirits.[247] Another illustration of the spirits' interests in Masonry is the writings of Harold Walden Percival, a mystic and spiritist. While he was functioning as a channel for the spirits, they generated through him an influential occult text called *Thinking and Destiny*. What was later published separately as *Masonry and Its Symbols in the Light of "Thinking and Destiny"* was originally part of the manuscript of *Thinking and Destiny*. In other words, the material on Masonry was the result of the spirits' inspiration through Percival. According to Percival it was later published separately with the approval of Masons. The goal of this text is to awaken Masons to "true Masonry" and to show how the spirits, or "intelligences in the earth's sphere," work through Masonry behind the scenes.[248] The spirits reveal:

the Brotherhood of Freemasons is the largest of the bodies in the world which are outposts to prepare possible candidates for an inward [mystical] life. . . . Intelligences in the earth's sphere [spirits] are behind Masonry, though the lodges are not aware of this in the present age. The spirit [philosophy] that runs through the system of the Masonic teachings connects these Intelligences with every Mason, from the greatest to the least, who practices them.[249]

So again we see that the spirits claim their involvement with Masonry. Manly P. Hall also notes the interest of the spirit world in Masonry. He teaches that this spirit world ("celestial intelligences") operates invisibly and imperceptibly behind the man who becomes a Mason and recognizes its true meaning.[250]

Foster Bailey was a 32nd degree Mason and husband of Alice Bailey, a prominent late-nineteenth-century occultist and founder of Lucius Trust. Foster Bailey believed that Masonry "was created by the Most High as an instrument in His hands by which to raise humanity." "Masonry is not man-made; it is God-made. . . . Masonry has survived the ages because in truth and fact we have been guided by inspiration and by intuition, by [spirits of the] Grand Lodge on High, whose members are not dead Masons, but a living Society of Illumined Minds, the Knowers of God's Plan."[251] In other words, Bailey is teaching that Masonry has been guided by the spirits of the dead who are in tune with God and able to use the Society to fulfill God's will. (Mediums by the thousands teach the same belief concerning their own philosophy and practices, yet all such activity is condemned by God in Deuteronomy 18:9-12.) Bailey calls such spirits "the Builders of the occult tradition," the "Illuminati," and other names. Step by step these spirits guide the Masonic candidate:

They prepare the candidate for those great revelations and expansions of consciousness. . . . Step by step They guide the candidate until he has gained the right to stand in the East before the Presence. . . . Stage by stage They assist at the unfolding of the consciousness of the candidate until the time comes when he can "enter into light" and, in his turn become a light-bearer, one of the Illuminati who can assist the Lodge on High in bringing humanity to light.[252]

CRITIQUE

My estimation of Freemasonry has been well stated by Chief Justice John Marshall: "The institution of Masonry ought to be abandoned as one capable of much evil, and incapable of producing any good which might not be effected by safe and open means."

—Everett C. DeVelde, Jr.

Most Masons assume that any criticism of Masonry is invalid or irrelevant. Cerza states, "Those who have opposed the craft have done so because of selfish motives or from lack of information."[253] Earl B. Delzell, Secretary of the Grand Lodge of Iowa, stated in his address to the Conference of Grand Secretaries meeting in Washington: "We have our foes. They are persistent. They attempt to tell us what's wrong with Masonry. They speak from ignorance. We Masons must be informed."[254] Cerza further declares of Christian responses to Masonry, "All that can be said of these Christians is that they have studied the words of Christ and closed their hearts to the spirit of toleration that pervades the gentle teachings of the Master."[255] Masons have personally charged us with all sorts of devilry—poor scholarship, persecution of Masons, bigotry and such like, to which we responded in *Bowing at Strange Altars*.

The thrust of Cerza's book, *Let There Be Light: A Study in Anti-Masonry,* is that every criticism of Masonry is invalid. But Masonry would not have been subjected to the degree of criticism that it has been if there were nothing of concern in Masonry. The real question is not whether Masonry can meet people's needs, or if it has a good reputation in society, or if it is powerful and influential, or if clergymen and members of Congress support it, or if it has charitable works. The issue is, "Is it true?"

We need to remember that many Masons are unfamiliar not only with much of the foregoing material but also with the material that follows, and they would even be shocked with parts of it. Others have simply not thought through the logical implications of their oaths or their religious worldview. It is our sincere hope and intent that the following two basic criticisms, of its religious brotherhood and its oaths, will help the Mason to reexamine his religious commitment.

Religious Brotherhood

The most fundamental Masonic goal of all, religious brotherhood, is doomed from the start. This is because the "true teachings" of every religion are *not* the same as Masonic doctrine. The deities of Buddhism, Hinduism, Islam, Judaism, Christianity, animism and other religions are not simply the same, contrary to Masonic teaching.

Jehovah (the God of Christianity) is infinite, personal, triune, loving and holy. Allah (the deity of the Muslims) is unitarian (not triune); he is merciful, but he is not necessarily loving or holy. Brahman (a major deity of the Hindus) is impersonal and monistic (neither unitarian nor triune). Most all Hindus are *polytheistic* (believing in thousands of finite gods, both good and evil). Buddhism is either polytheistic, believing in Buddha and in hundreds of other good and evil gods, or completely *non-theistic,* claiming there is no God. As such, it replaces an absolute God with a confusing "state of being" called Nirvana. Mormonism is different still in that it is *henotheistic,* accepting worship of one central deity (Elohim) for this world, yet also accepting endless similar gods for other worlds.

Masonry is completely wrong in teaching that all religions ultimately have the same God or concept of God.[256] The world religions all have widely divergent concepts of God: He is either (1) personal or impersonal, (2) holy amoral or evil, (3) unitarian or trinitarian or monistic, (4) infinite or finite, (5) loving or not loving, (6) existent or nonexistent, to name just several. These are not superficial distinctions. In fact, in some cases they are exact opposites (personal or impersonal, for instance). When Masonry claims that all men worship the same Masonic god within the Lodge, in actuality Masonry has a concept of God that disagrees with all the other religions' concepts. It has its own distinct concept of God.

The different religions also have different concepts of the nature of man, the nature of salvation and what one can expect after death. For Masonry to claim otherwise is absurd. Two examples are Masonry's pronouncement that Mithra (an evil and finite god) is omnipotent and beneficent and that the "Tao" (an impersonal concept) is really a "loving creator."[257] Think also of the hundreds of millions of secularists in the world who do not believe in any religion. How will Masonry unite them?

Masonry's claim to be able to form a religious brotherhood in Masonry is an impossibility. Masonry has only further splintered mankind by adding one more competing religious sect to those that currently exist.

Masonry's distinctive religious beliefs are usually attractive only to those who are nominal members of their particular religious faith.[258] Knowledgeable believers of every religion will immediately recognize that Masonry denies their deity and particular beliefs. For the Lodge to claim that Buddha was an early Mason will not endear knowledgeable Buddhists to Masonry.[259] Buddha rejected and repudiated belief in a supreme being, a belief that is a requirement in Masonry. Whatever Buddha believed, it was clearly not Masonic.

Evidence that Masonry will never be able to unite the different religions in brotherhood can also be found in the history of the Lodge itself. Masonry has not even united its own brotherhood into harmony, let alone the vastly competing religions of the world. The disputes among Masons are well documented. In 1858, Albert Pike wrote an article titled "The Evil Consequences of Schisms and Disputes for Power in Masonry, and of Jealousies and Dissensions Between Masonic Rites." In that article, Pike referred to the problems and errors of Masonry that tended to justify Masonry's critics. He felt that this was accomplished "more than all, in the angry disputes which rend the bosom of the Order, accompanied with bitter words, harsh epithets and loud denunciations, that give the lie to the combatants' claim of brotherhood. . . ."[260] A century later little has changed. An article in *Masonic Square* entitled, "Freemasonry International" December 1976, carefully noted:

Each Grand Lodge makes its own judgment in the light of its own approach to what Freemasonry means. . . . So, of course, many opinions differ on what is considered basic Masonry. . . . All this goes to demonstrate that one must be very careful before applying the practices of one Grand Lodge in the lodges of another, for they may be based on quite different esoteric [hidden] thinking to an extent where one can be a complete contradiction of the meaning behind another. This can apply even within one jurisdiction.[261]

Another Mason states that Masonry must change its "evil activities":

Certain undesirable aspects of the Masonic work and organization must inevitably disappear. The appetite of the curiosity seekers, the private political machinations of certain Masonic groups, and the purely social and commercial incentives which govern much of the Masonic politics in many lands must end. . . . Old and evil activities will come to an end. . . . Selfishness, ambition, separativeness, wrong motives and political propaganda must fade out all together. They have no place in Masonry. They run counter to the plans of the Divine Design.[262]

One big problem with Masonry is that it denies the sinful nature of man and subscribes to a naive idealism that romanticizes and fantasizes a world brotherhood. Masons in today's Lodge seem unable to agree even on major issues, such as who God is and whether He is relevant:

. . . we see scarcely any two of our ablest Masonic scholars agreeing on it [the nature of God].

British, Irish, Colonial, American, and other Grand Lodges have broken off communication and the right of inter-visitations with lodges and members of Latin Freemasonry who do not insist upon subscription to a belief in the existence of a Supreme Being and the doctrine of immortality.[263]

Masons cannot even agree on minor issues. In one of the most damning indictments ever written about Masonry's claim to brotherhood, Masonic scholar Oliver D. Street confessed:

We read in our Monitors and in the effusions of Masonic orators of the "Universality of Ma-

sonry," and how that Masonry "unites men of every country, sect and opinion." . . . Our bosoms heave with pride that we belong to so beneficial and so universal a brotherhood. It is a beautiful fiction which it is a pity to destroy, but the lamentable fact is there is not a word of truth in it. . . . There is not and never has been and, if many of our most estimable brethren can have their way, *there never will be universal Masonry*. . . . The Masonries which exist among many others are repudiated and denied by one another and by the Masonry of the English-speaking countries in particular. . . .

The most trivial and absurd difference in either doctrine or practice is seized upon by some Grand Lodge, which imagines it is the conservator of pure and unadulterated Freemasonry, to erect impassible barriers between the Masonic bodies of the world. *Among the most rancorous disputes that the world has ever witnessed are those that have raged among Masons* during the last 200 years over questions of minor or no importance. . . . The intolerance on the part of many Masons and Masonic bodies towards others claiming to be Masonic are so extreme that they frown even on any suggestion of getting acquainted or of even conferring together. . . . Self sufficient in our own conceit, we will not admit that we can learn anything of value from the Masons of other countries and in our smug complacence we say that they are "impossible" as Masons. It is precisely the same mental attitude of Greek toward Barbarian, ancient Hebrew toward Gentile, Pharisee toward Samaritan which we so unsparingly condemn in others, but which we, like them, cannot see in ourselves. . . . This ignorant and narrow provincialism will *forever prevent the Masons of the world getting together*. . . .

Yet, 200 years after that liberal and fraternal declaration [of brotherhood], and in spite of it, we see "good men and true, men of honor and honesty," those who "obey the moral law" still being kept at a distance from each other by "their particular opinions," by their "denominations or persuasions" concerning God and religion. Shall this keeping them at a distance be made perpetual? If so, one of the great objects of our Institution will be defeated.[264]

If Masons cannot achieve brotherhood *inside* the Lodge, how will they ever achieve it among the rest of the world that disagrees with them?

Morality and Oaths

A second concern lies in the moral sphere. Masonic ritual and doctrine stress the importance of leading a moral lifestyle. Many Masons attempt to live such a lifestyle, although it is often through the eyes of nominal Christian faith or conventional social morality. But there is another side to Masonic teaching that merits examination. Masonry does teach a system of morality, but it may make this morality subservient to the interests of Masonry. In addition, as is true for its religion, Masonic morality has a hidden or esoteric side that is unknown to most Masons. In his critique of Freemasonry, Wagner discusses this in some detail.[265]

The common definition of Masonry asserts: "Freemasonry is a system of morality veiled in allegory and illustrated by symbols." This is why Wagner maintains that the outer morality of Masonry is only part of the story. He argues convincingly that the only way one may truly understand Masonic ethics is to view them in light of the Masonic standard of morals—the law of nature—and not to judge, estimate or interpret Masonic morals through a Christian worldview or conventional social morality.[266] He explains: "The symbolic illustrations [of morality in Masonry] are double veils; they conceal rather than reveal the true ethical ideas. Masonry employs to some extent the terms of Christian ethics under which to hide its peculiar moral ideas. In its ethical expressions the words do not mean what they say. It is esoteric [secret, hidden] in its ethics as well as in its religion."[267]

The following three concerns are cited as genuine or potential issues of conflict in the area of Masonic ethics and moral behavior. They are explained by the fact that the foundation of Masonic morality is not God's Word but Masonic religion.[268]

1. The Oaths of Masonry. Following are some Masonic oaths that every Mason must swear by. They are taken from Masonic Monitors, other Masonic literature and confirmed as accurate by former Masons. Masonry claims they are symbolic only, but this is not really true. Regardless, their force and soberness are intended to convey the solemn nature of the oaths by which the

Mason is binding himself. It is generally accepted that these oaths are sworn for the entire Mason's life, indeed, "for all time."[269]

Before we read these oaths, let us examine what Masonic literature itself teaches about them. The presentation volume for Masonry in Virginia states that "the penalties incurred for willful violation of your Masonic obligation will not be of a physical nature"; they are retained "to impress upon the mind of each brother how serious a violation will be regarded by the members of the fraternity."[270] Carl H. Claudy, Litt.D., was a Master Mason, a former Grand Master of Masons in the District of Columbia and a member of all the coordinate rites of Masonry. He was a noted Masonic writer and was awarded many Lodge honors and distinctions.[271] He confesses that those who framed the penalties "intended to inspire terror" and that if a Mason ever broke the oaths, he should fear: "the loss of my self-respect. [Including] the self-abasement any true man feels who has broken a solemn pledge. The wrath of a God blasphemed. The horror of a sin in which there is none greater. ... These, then, are what the penalties really mean; these are the real consequences to me, if I violate my solemn obligations, these are what will be done to me if I fail in living up, so far as I am able, to the covenants I made with my brethren."[272]

It appears that the intent to inspire terror is effective for some, and probably many, Masons. In 1912, Wagner could observe the following from personal experience: "That Masons believe that these penalties will be mercilessly inflicted upon them, should they betray its secrets, we know to be true in many cases. The convictions of those who have exposed the ritualism of the order, that they took their lives into their hands in doing so, is proof. The numerous confessions made to the writer, on the part of both Masons and ex-Masons, is further proof."[273]

It even appears that on rare occasions Masons of the past have taken the oaths of revenge quite literally. Wagner observed of the infamous Morgan case: "That William Morgan was murdered in obedience to a Masonic decree, is in the opinion of all non-Masons who have carefully and impartially examined the evidence, proven beyond a doubt, and that his murderers were protected from summary justice, by the institution, is equally proven."[274] He also claims that a Judge Whitney of the Belvidere Lodge in Illinois "escaped assassination at the hands of Master Masons."[275]

Here are several of the many oaths in Masonry.

1. The oath for the Entered Apprentice obligations declares:

I, _____, of my own free will and accord, in the presence of almighty God, and this worshipful Lodge, erected to him ... most solemnly and sincerely promise and swear, that I will always hail, ever conceal, and never reveal, any of the arts, parts or points of the hidden mysteries of ancient Freemasonry. ... All this I most solemnly, sincerely promise and swear, with a firm and steadfast resolution to perform the same, without any mental reservation or secret evasion of mine whatever, binding myself under no less penalty than that of having my throat cut across, my tongue torn out from its roots, and my body buried in the rough sands of the sea ... should I ever knowingly violate this my Entered Apprentice obligation. So help me God. ...[276]

2. The oath for the Master Mason degree includes:

I furthermore promise and swear, that I will stand to and abide by all laws, rules, and regulations of the Master Masons' Degree, and of the Lodge of which I may hereafter become a member, as far as the same shall come to my knowledge; and that I will ever maintain and support the constitution, laws, and edicts of the Grand Lodge under which the same shall be holden. Further, that I will acknowledge and obey all due signs and summonses sent to me from a Master Masons' Lodge, or given me by a brother of that Degree. ... Further, that I will keep a worthy brother Master Mason's secrets inviolable, when communicated to and received by me as such, murder and treason excepted ... binding myself, under no less penalty than that of having my body severed in two, my bowels taken from thence and burned to ashes, the ashes scattered before the four winds of heaven, that no more remembrance might be had of so vile and wicked a wretch as I would be, should

I ever, knowingly, violate this my Master Mason's obligation. So help me God. ...[277]

3. From the initiation of the tenth degree of the Scottish Rite:

I do promise and swear upon the Holy Bible ... to keep exactly in my heart all the secrets that shall be revealed to me. And in failure of this my obligation, I consent to have my body opened perpendicularly, and to be exposed for eight hours in the open air, that the venomous flies may eat of my entrails, my head to be cut off and put on the highest pinnacle of the world, and I will always be ready to inflict the same punishment on those who shall disclose this degree and break this obligation. So may God help and maintain me. Amen.[278]

The sign of this oath is to "place the point of the poniard under the chin, and draw it downward to the waist, as if in the act of ripping open the abdomen."[279]

4. From the seventeenth degree of the Scottish Rite:

I _____ do promise and solemnly swear and declare in the awful presence of the Only One Most Holy Puissant Almighty and Most Merciful Grand Architect of Heaven and Earth ... that I will never reveal to any person whomsoever below me ... the secrets of this degree which is now about to be communicated to me, under the penalty of not only being dishonored, but to consider my life as the immediate forfeiture, and that to be taken from me with all the torture and pains to be inflicted in manner as I have consented to in the preceding degrees.[280]

During this ritual the All Puissant teaches: "The skull is the image of a brother who is excluded from a Lodge or Council. The cloth stained with blood, that we should not hesitate to spill ours for the good of Masonry."[281]

5. From the eighteenth degree of the Scottish Rite:

I _____ do solemnly and sincerely promise and swear under the penalty of all my former obligations which I have taken in the preceding degrees, never to reveal directly or indirectly, the secrets or mysteries of [this degree] . . . under the penalty of being forever deprived of the true word, to be perpetually in darkness, my blood continually running from my body, to suffer without intermission the cruel remorse of soul; that the bitterest gall, mixed with vinegar, be my constant drink; the sharpest thorns for my pillow and that the death of the cross may complete my punishment should I ever infringe or violate in any manner or form the laws and rules which have been, are now, or may be hereafter made known or prescribed to me.

And I do furthermore swear, promise and engage on my sacred word of honor, to observe and obey all the decrees which may be transmitted to me by the Grand Inspectors General in Supreme Council of the thirty-third degree. . . . So help me God and keep me steadfast in this my solemn obligation. Amen. (Candidate kisses the Bible.)[282]

For this oath, the candidate kneels on the step to the altar with his right hand on the Bible.

6. From the thirtieth degree of the Scottish Rite:

I _____ of my own free will and accord, do hereby solemnly and sincerely promise and swear to keep faithful the secrets of the sublime degree of Knights Kadosh and strictly to obey the statutes of the order. . . . All of which I promise to do, under the penalty of death. So help me God.[283]

The Grand Provost of Justice holds the point of his sword to the heart of the candidate who is taking this oath.

This degree also has the following oath:

When your rashness prompted you to enter this awful Sanctuary, you were no doubt informed of the danger which threatened you, and of the trials which still await you. Swear therefore, upon your word of honor, never to reveal what you have seen or heard hitherto. . . . Forget not that the slightest indiscretion will cost you your life. Are you still willing to proceed?[284]

The fact is that no Mason is told during the ritual that the penalties are merely symbolic. In his mind, Masonic obligations appear to deal with vows of life and death. If mere critics of

Masonry have received threats of death or retribution, as we have, how can the Mason think his more severe violation removes him from all risk?

A further question remains about *who* inflicts the penalties. Candidates must swear by God, not by Masonry, to having these penalties inflicted on them. Thus God is the One (not Masonry) who is to take responsibility for inflicting punishment on the violators. Consider the following statement by leading Masonic authority Albert Mackey in his *Encyclopedia.* The Mason who disobeys his oaths is worthy of death and that it is up to God, not men, to inflict the penalty:

We may say of what are called Masonic *penalties,* that they refer in no case to any kind of human punishment; that is to say, to any kind of punishment which is to be inflicted by human hand or instrumentality. . . . The obsecration of a Freemason simply means that if he violates his vows or betrays his trust *he is worthy of such penalty,* and that if such penalty were inflicted on him *it would be just and proper.* . . . The ritualistic penalties of Freemasonry, supposing such to be, are in the hands not of men, *but of God,* and *are to be inflicted by God,* and not by men.[285]

Does anyone think that threats like these will not strike fear into a Masonic initiate? And is this not a form of cultic intimidation—using threats of divine retribution to force compliance to a false religion? (See Appendix 4.)

But will God never use men as the sword of His justice? Can solemn penalties sworn to God be only symbolic? Is God only a symbol? And isn't it true that most Masons take the oaths literally and many fear literal consequences for breaking them? In fact, isn't this how the entire system of Masonry perpetuates itself, the means by which it maintains the Mason's loyalty and obedience? Isn't this why so many Christian Masons have refused to deny Masonry, because they are fearful of the consequences of breaking their oaths?

Masons themselves have admitted that the Lodge would probably dissolve were it not for the secrecy of the organization and the fear of the penalties inflicted by the oaths. Is this any way to promote and advance a religion, especially one based on brotherhood?

2. The first duty of the Mason is to Masonry.

When Masonic secrets or vital interests are at stake, the rights of Masonry are apparently above duty to country, family, church and possibly even law.[286] The *Mentor's Manual of Masonry* admits, "The obligation is the heart of the degree, for when it is assumed by the candidate, he has solemnly bound himself to Freemasonry and assumed certain duties which are his for the rest of his life."[287] In his covenant with Masonry, the candidate solemnly promises that he "will forever conceal and never reveal" the secrets of Masonry.[288] According to Past Master Edmond Ronayne, page 196 of "Webb's Monitor" reads: "The first duty of the reader of this synopsis is to obey the edicts of his Grand Lodge. Right or wrong, his very existence as a Mason hangs upon obedience to the powers immediately set above him. The one unpardonable crime in a Mason is . . . disobedience."[289]

The ritual of the 17th degree of the Scottish Rite divulges: "A Mason should not hesitate to spill his blood for the support of Masonry."[290] In discussing the symbolic meaning of certain items this ritual explains: "The bow, arrows and crown signify that the orders of this respectable Council should be executed with as much quickness as the arrow flies from the bow, and be received with as much submission as if it came from a crowned head or a chief of a nation. The sword [signifies] that the Council is always armed to punish the guilty. . . . The skull is the image of a brother who is excluded from a lodge or Council. The cloth stained with blood, that we should not hesitate to spill ours for the good of Masonry."[291]

In addition, Masons are sworn to protect fellow Masons, right or wrong. The Georgia Monitor teaches, "Secrecy is an essential element of Freemasonry, and every Mason is bound by irrevocable ties to keep inviolate its private ceremonies, signs, words, the business of the lodge, and (excepting treason and murder) never to divulge any secret that may be confided by a brother if accepted as such."[292]

The problem here is obvious. Suppose a Mason is a witness in a criminal case involving another Mason in, say, embezzlement. What if the witness receives a sign from the brother Mason charged with the crime? He is sworn to retain the secrets of his brother Mason. Does this not place both Masons above the law? The standard Masonic Monitor states, "I furthermore promise and swear, that I will assist a companion Royal Arch Mason when I see him engaged in any difficulty, and will espouse his cause so far as to extricate him from the same, *whether he be right or wrong.*"[293] This oath gave as two exceptions "murder and treason." But here no exceptions are given. Apparently the Mason is free to decide the issue for himself.

Former Mason Ronayne believed that by its absolute stress on secrecy, keeping oaths and believing in Masonry as the highest good, that in effect Masonry taught the following:

> Whenever you see any of our signs made by a brother Mason, and especially the *Grand Hailing sign of distress,* you must always be sure to *obey* them, even at the risk of your life. If you're on a jury, and the defendant is a Mason, and makes the Grand Hailing sign, you must obey it; you must disagree with your brother jurors, if necessary, but you must be very sure not to bring the Mason guilty, for that would bring disgrace upon our order. It may be perjury, to be sure, to do this, but then you're fulfilling your obligation, and you know if you "live up to your obligations you'll be free from sin." . . . you must conceal all the crimes of your brother Mason, except murder and treason, and these only at your own option, and should you be summoned as a witness against a brother Mason be always sure to shield him. Prevaricate, don't tell the whole truth in this case, keep his secrets. . . .[294]

This is why many persons express concern about the potential for conflict between the duties the Mason owes first to Masonry and second to other institutions, national, military or political. Cerza admits, "Occasionally individual Masons in European countries have used their Lodge connections to promote their political ambitions."[295] (See Appendix 4, point 5 for one example.) Dr. R. A. Torrey, a founder of what later became Biola College and Talbot Theological

Seminary in La Mirada, California, and superintendent of the Moody Bible Institute, had personal experience on this issue. In his tract "My Reasons for Not Joining the Masonic Fraternity" he states: "To my own personal knowledge, Masonry has been used to protect criminals and other evil doers from the just consequences of their wrong doing."[296] Perhaps this is why U.S. President Grant observed, "All secret, oath-bound, political parties are dangerous to any nation."[297] President John Quincy Adams was more severe. After an impartial investigation of Freemasonry he concluded in his "Address to the People of Massachusetts":

> I saw a code of Masonic legislation adapted to prostrate every principle of equal justice and to corrupt every sentiment of virtuous feeling in the soul of him who bound his allegiance to it. I saw the practice of common honesty, the kindness of Christian benevolence, even the abstinence of atrocious crimes, limited exclusively by lawless oaths and barbarous penalties, to the social relations between the Brotherhood and the Craft. I saw slander organize into a secret, widespread and affiliated agency ... saw self-invoked imprecations of throats cut from ear to ear, of hearts and vitals torn out and cast off and hung on spires. I saw wine drank from a human skull with solemn invocation of all the sins of its owner upon the head of him who drank it.[298]

The response of Masonry to all of this is simply to remain silent. The Mason is charged in the first degree: "Neither are you to suffer your zeal for the institution to lead you into argument with those who through ignorance may ridicule it."[299] Cerza urges, "Let us not dispute, or argue, or engage in discussion on this subject of Anti-Masonry.... Let us continue to maintain a discreet silence."[300]

Cerza and all Masons would probably deny the charges. They would claim Masonry is harmless and innocent. But this would make the testimonies those of liars. And what motive would they have? The problem with a secret society is precisely in its secrecy. And if the secret society has no absolute standard of morality, what then? Given sinful human nature, should we be optimistic? And if these are true reflec-

tions of Masonic morality, can the Mason justify them before his God?

3. Masonry may be racist or otherwise prejudiced. The *Encyclopaedia Britannica* observes: "In practice, some lodges have been charged with prejudice against Jews, Catholics, and non-whites. U.S. lodges rejected the legitimacy of Negro Masonic Lodges, the Prince Hall lodges...."[301] Another researcher concludes, "It appears that most lodges, especially the Masonic Lodge, discriminate racially (even as they freely admit 'unanimous consent' is necessary for any candidate to be 'entered' into the craft)."[302] This is further documented by Fisher.[303] Masons are also apparently told to exclude the unintelligent and the handicapped from their lodges: "You agree to be cautious to admit none but good men into your lodge, to receive no one who does not do his duty as a Blue [Lodge] Mason, and who is not of good character, intelligent and respectable."[304] Carl Claudy writes,"A candidate for initiation must be a man, free born, unmutilated and of mature age.... These landmarks can never be changed."[305]

TALKING WITH MEMBERS

In talking with a Mason, one should determine what category of Mason one is dealing with: Christian, social, mystical and so on, and approach the individual on that basis. For example, a Christian Mason needs to see how antiChristian Masonry is. He needs to see that he is denying the Lord and his faith by supporting an organization that opposes God, Christ, the Bible, evangelism and so on. The social Mason needs to decide if he wishes to continue being a Mason in light of the information revealed in this chapter and in our other books on this subject. In essence, are the social benefits of Masonry worth the cost of belonging to an organization that is deceptive, antiChristian and potentially occult? The mystical Mason needs to be aware of the dangers and consequences of mysticism, paganism and the occult, generally which we documented in detail in *The Coming Darkness*.

Whatever category of Mason one encounters, in light of their own conscience they all must face the issue of Masonic deception of the general public, its own initiates, Christians and others, as we have documented here and, further, in chapter two of *Secret Teachings*. How can Masons continue to be part of an organization that lies and deceives?

Most Masons will be reluctant to discuss these issues. They will wrongly assume that they are betraying their oaths to Masonry. But they should understand that breaking an evil oath, particularly one taken in ignorance, is far preferable to permitting that oath to continue to bind one in evil. As we emphasized elsewhere,[306] if a Mason has sworn allegiance to the Lodge, he should break his oaths.

What can one do who has already taken the oath "for all time"? Is that person bound to keep his oath? The Bible says no:

If a person swears, speaking thoughtlessly with his lips to do evil or to do good, whatever it is that a man may pronounce by an oath, and it is hidden from him—when he realizes it, then he shall be guilty in any of these matters. And it shall be, when he is guilty in any of these matters, that he shall confess that he has sinned in that thing; and he shall bring his trespass offering to the Lord for his sin which he has sinned . . . so the priest shall make atonement on his behalf for his sin which he has sinned, and it shall be forgiven him (Leviticus 5:4–6, 10 NJKV).

In the Old Testament, a person was to go the the priest, confess his sin and offer a sacrifice of atonement. Today, a Christian is to come to his eternal high priest, the Lord Jesus Christ, who died on the cross to cleanse mankind from sin. The believer is to confess he is guilty of swearing wrongly, repent of his oath, ask God for forgiveness and acknowledge he will obey God. The Bible promises us, "If we confess our sins, he is faithful and just and will forgive us our sins and purify us from all unrighteousness" (1 John 1:9). Why is this important?

By taking the Masonic oaths, the Mason is swearing to uphold Masonry and its teachings. Swearing to uphold the Masonic oaths is sinful, unscriptural and should not be a part of the Christian's life for the following reasons.

1) They make a Christian man swear by God to doctrines which God has pronounced false and sinful. For example, Masonry teaches a universalist doctrine of "the Fatherhood of God" (John 8:42).

2) The Christian man is made to swear his acceptance of the lie that salvation, the reward of Heaven, can be gained by man's good works (Ephesians 2:8–9).

3) The Christian man swears to accept and promote the Masonic lie that Jesus is just one of many equally revered prophets in the world. He does this when agreeing that all religions can lead a man to God (Acts 4:12; Philippians 2:9–11; Colossians 1:16–18).

4) The Christian man swears he will remain silent in the Lodge and not talk of Christ when God commands every Christian to be a witness (Matthew 28:19).

5) The Christian swears that he is approaching the Lodge while he is in spiritual ignorance and moral darkness, when the Bible says Christians are children of light and are indwelt by the Light of the world (John 8:12; Ephesians 5:8).

6) By taking the Masonic oath, the Christian is guilty of taking the name of the Lord in vain, because he has sworn unlawfully to things God has forbidden him to swear to. God says He will not leave such a person unpunished (Exodus 20:7).

7) The Christian falsely swears that the God of the Bible is equally present in all religions (1 Timothy 2:5–6).

8) The Christian falsely swears to the teaching that true worship can be offered in the Lodge to God without the mediatorship of Jesus (Hebrews 9:14).

9) By swearing the Masonic oath, Christians are perpetuating a false gospel to

other Lodge members who look only to the gospel of Masonry to get them to Heaven (Galatians 1:6–8).

10) The Christian's spirit, mind and body are the temple of the Holy Spirit, "bought with a price" (1 Corinthians 6:19–20). By taking the Masonic obligations he could be agreeing to allow the pollution of his mind and spirit by pagan religion or even occult practices.

It is the Christian's duty to break and renounce any evil oath that binds him. Every Christian Lodge member should renounce his Masonic oath and confess it as a sin and be forgiven, and so stop adding his influence to the sins of the Lodge which, with their false religion, result in the damnation of so many souls.[307]

Christian Masons must confess to God that they have ignorantly taken a vow against Him and His teaching and ask His forgiveness. Then they should notify their Lodge in writing that they have decided to leave the Lodge, explaining that Masonic teaching and vows are not biblical and, as Christians, they can no longer participate according to 2 Corinthians 6:14–18 and Ephesians 5:8–17. (See Appendix 3.)

Will a Mason face the truth (John 14:6)? Did not Claudy himself teach that "a Master Mason who is afraid to face the truth is not a good Master Mason!"?[308] Do not the Masonic oaths obligate the Mason to truth itself: "There will be nothing binding on me except the truth"?[309]

APPENDIX 1:
A WORD TO MASONS

The Masonic Lodge has millions of men in it worldwide who look to Masonry for the brotherhood and fellowship that it has brought into their lives. They believe they are part of an organization that attempts to engage in worthwhile causes, such as children's hospitals, and they feel strongly about the Masonic tenets of the Fatherhood of God, the brotherhood of man and the immortality of the soul.

We acknowledge the good which Masonry has done in the world through its philanthropic endeavors. Some wonder how we can still be critical of Masonry. Many Masons do not seem to understand the issues we address in our television programs and books on Masonry. Because we have raised these issues, we have often been labeled "anti-Mason." But we would ask that Masons attempt to understand our criticism from the following perspective.

There is a big difference between someone who criticizes people's views because he doesn't like them and is trying to hurt them, versus someone who criticizes people's views because he is trying to save them from error. We have entered this debate because we honor and respect individual Masons as fellow human beings made in the image of God. Although Masons might not believe it, we really do care for them as people for whom Christ died. Because Jesus commanded us as Christians to go into all the world and preach the Gospel, and because the apostles instructed Christians to earnestly contend for the faith (Jude 3), we have written books comparing biblical teaching with Masonic ritual. But we have also compared biblical teachings with the literature of such organizations as the Watchtower Society (Jehovah's Witnesses), the Church of Jesus Christ of Latter-day Saints (Mormonism) and others. Just as we did with the truth claims of these other groups, it is the nature of the claims made by the Masonic Lodge that we have taken issue with, not individual Masons.

When an organization such as Masonry makes certain claims that are contrary to biblical teaching, we believe it is our obligation to point this out, both for the sake of Masons and for those who might yet become Masons. The issue of Masonry and its relationship to Christian faith have been controversial for at least 200 years. This means at least two things: (1) different sides have taken different positions on the same issue and attempted to defend their positions to the best of their ability; (2) confusion has occurred more often for the layperson, who has to wade through arguments on both sides before resolving the issue responsibly.

For those who consider us "anti-Mason," we would hope that they would remember that to argue with a philosophy is not to reject the value or importance of the person who holds that philosophy. The Apostle Peter commanded all Christians: "But in your hearts set apart Christ as Lord. Always be prepared to give an answer to everyone who asks you to give the reason for the hope that you have. But do this with gentleness and respect . . ." (1 Peter 3:15).

APPENDIX 2:
WHERE THE SOUTHERN
BAPTISTS WENT WRONG

A committee in the largest Protestant denomination in America, the Southern Baptists, concluded in its 1993 Study on Freemasonry that it cannot frankly state that it is wrong for a Christian to join the Masonic Lodge. In spite of the biblical prohibitions the Study documented, it recommended that Lodge membership be left to the Christian's own conscience. In doing so, the Southern Baptists may be the only conservative Christian denomination in America not to warn their constituents that membership in the Masonic Lodge is not biblically appropriate.

Many other churches and denominations will face the issue of whether its members should participate in the Masonic Lodge. We believe they will have to deal with many of the same circumstances and issues that the Interfaith Witness Department of the Home Mission Board (HMB) of the Southern Baptist Convention (SBC) has had to face. We will attempt to briefly document what took place and show why they issued a contradictory and self-defending Study. Also, what happened in the Southern Baptist Convention's examination of the subject of Masonry will reveal the absolute importance for churches and other denominations examining Freemasonry to select committees carefully, composing them of men who accept the authority of Scripture and will not be influenced by political pressures.

In the case of the Southern Baptists, at their 1992 convention they passed a resolution to appoint a committee to study Freemasonry and its compatibility with Christianity. The Home Mission Board charged the Interfaith Witness Department with preparing this study and admonished them to give "special attention . . . to the compatibility of Freemasonry with Christianity and Southern Baptist doctrine."[310] In the end, the Interfaith Witness Department compiled a 107-page analysis that was eventually condensed to a 75-page study and submitted to the HMB entitled, *A Study of Freemasonry* (1993). They urged the HMB to advance the position that membership in Freemasonry "be left with the judgment of the individual."[311] The HMB then developed and approved their own 6-page summary conclusion ("A Report on Freemasonry," March 17, 1993), which ended with the following recommendation to be presented and voted upon by the delegates at the 1993 convention:

> In light of the fact that many tenets and teachings of Freemasonry are not compatible with Christianity and Southern Baptist doctrine, while others are compatible with Christianity and Southern Baptist doctrine, we therefore recommend, that consistent with our denomination's deep convictions regarding the priesthood of the believer and the autonomy of the local church, membership in a Masonic Order be a matter of personal conscience. Therefore, we exhort Southern Baptists to prayerfully and carefully evaluate Freemasonry in light of the Lordship of Christ, the teachings of the Scripture, and the findings of this report, as led by the Holy Spirit of God.[312]

As we have shown in *Bowing at Strange Altars* (chapters 2–10), both the Interfaith Witness Department (IWD) Study and the HMB Report ignore biblical instruction and overlook Masonic ritual in order to defend their final conclusion.

Our advice to Southern Baptists is to either amend this resolution or vote it down. We will document that the IWD Study and HMB Report conceded point after point concerning Masonic ritual in light of the Christian faith, even though in their six-page Summary Report on Masonry, the HMB listed many reasons why it is wrong for a Christian to be a member of the Masonic Lodge. For example, it cited several examples from the Blue Lodge degrees concerning the taking of bloody oaths by the Masonic initiate. It warned, "Even though these oaths, obligations and rituals may or may not be taken seriously by the initiate, it is *inappropriate* for a Christian to 'sincerely promise and swear,' with the hand on the Holy Bible, any such promises or oaths, or to *participate* in any such pagan rituals."[313] The Report also stated, "Many tenets and teachings of Freemasonry are not compatible with Christianity and Southern Baptist doctrine . . .", and it cited several examples.[314] In fact, the Report offered solid reasons why Masonry and Christianity are incompatible and why Christians shouldn't participate in the Lodge. But then, shockingly and illogically, it offered the contradictory advice that "membership in a Masonic Order be a matter of personal conscience." If the committee's own evidence leads to the conclusion that Masonry is incompatible with Christian teaching, how can the committee conclude that the matter should be left up to the individual conscience of a Christian?

The real question is: "Why did the IWD Study and the HMB Report conclude what they did?" In spite of all the evidence they presented *against* Masonry, what led the committee to conclude that any Christian could possibly join the Lodge in good conscience? Consider the comments of Dr. Larry Holly, M.D., president of Mission and Ministry to Men, Inc. He was instrumental in having the SBC confront the issue of Masonry by organizing a committee to study the issue and make its recommendation. He is also the author of *The Southern Baptist Convention and Freemasonry* (1993). Dr. Holly felt that despite its weaknesses the Board of Trustees' condemnations of Masonry in the Summary Report were sufficiently strong for any Christian who read it to conclude that membership in the Lodge was wrong. However, in his response to the larger 75-page Study that was finally published, plus the 107-page Study on which it was based, Holly takes a much stronger stance. In a supplement to his initial press release, March 22, 1993, he stated:

> Since then, I have seen and read the 107-page report written by Dr. Gary Leazer. That report is a virtual whitewash of the Masonic Lodge, totally in keeping with Dr. Leazer's January, 1993 letter in which he indicated his affinity for the Masonic brotherhood. In my opinion, the report represents extremely poor scholarship, is an embarrassment to the Southern Baptist Convention, and if it is the best that Southern Baptists

can do, demonstrates how poorly we are represented in the Inter-faith Witness Department.

> The 107-page staff report *contradicts* the trustees' 7-page recommendation, both in content, spirit and conclusion. The report will reassure Masons, while a recommendation should warn Masons. With the publication of the 107-page report Southern Baptists have tragically become the first Christian denomination to exonerate the Masonic Lodge, and they did it with half truths, poor research and prejudicial conclusions. It has also been done with a staff report which did not have trustee input, oversight or approval.

> The only way in which the 7-page recommendation could have been written and approved by the trustees was to totally ignore the implications and conclusions of the 107-page report. The question should be asked by every Southern Baptist: "Why does the Home Mission Board persist in publishing and distributing a report which has been superseded, and implicitly rejected, by official sanction of the trustees of the Home Mission Board?"[315]

In another letter, March 25, 1993, he stated:

> What is impossible to accept is the fact that some state Baptist papers are ignoring your recommendation and are only reporting the conclusions of Dr. Leazer and Dr. Lewis as presented in the 107-page staff study. What is impossible to accept is that after the Houston SBC, your recommendation will not be circulated by the HMB, but the 107-page study which contradicts your recommendation will continue to be sold by the HMB. The contradiction between your recommendation and the staff study has the HMB giving an "uncertain sound." . . . The problem for the HMB, and thus for Southern Baptists, is that the trustees have drawn one conclusion and the staff is drawing another.[316]

In another letter Dr. Holly comments: "Make no mistake about it, God will not prosper Southern Baptists if we compromise on this critical issue."[317]

Now, how could the Study of the Interfaith Witness Department end up contradicting the six-page Report of the Trustees of the Home Mission Board? The evidence seems to indicate that this took place as a result of three things:

(1) deceptive practices, (2) a Masonic agenda and (3) biased scholarship.

DECEPTIVE PRACTICES

Dr. Gary Leazer was a staff member with the Home Mission Board. He was assigned to be Director of the IWD Committee and given the responsibility of preparing a study on Masonry. He was later removed from his position as Director of the Interfaith Witness Department because he allowed Masons to read and critique his committee's study and then accepted their suggestions for changes. At the same time, he deliberately did not allow Christians opposed to Masonry, such as Dr. Holly, to read the Study.

Evidence of this is found in a letter Dr. Leazer wrote to Mason Don L. Talbert in Chattanooga. He wrote, "I appreciate all of the help that Masons have been to me. Jim Tresner, Editor of *The Oklahoma Mason,* and Dr. Abner McCall, former President of Baylor University, have each read the Report and offered suggestions which I used."[318] (Dr. Abner McCall is one of the Masonic authors in the February 1993 *Scottish Rite Journal* who argued that Christianity and Freemasonry are compatible. See *Bowing at Strange Altars,* chapters 10, 11.)

Dr. Leazer's allegiance and friendship to Masonry is apparent since he was asked to read and proof the February issue of the *Scottish Rite Journal.* In fact, that issue was devoted to arguing that membership in the Masonic Lodge is compatible with Christian faith. The journal even confessed that the Center for Masonic Information was sending the magazine to 30,000 Blue Lodges in America and to 5,000 Southern Baptist leaders, many of whom are delegates who might attend the Southern Baptist Convention.

In Dr. Leazer's letter he stated that "John Boettjer [the journal editor] asked me to read the proof of the February issue of *The Scottish Rite Journal,* which I did in December. It will be on Freemasonry and religion and will be sent to either three or four thousand non-Mason Southern Baptists." He further confessed, "James L. Holly is quite upset with me as I will not meet with him again to let him approve the report before it is submitted. He, of course, will explode when he sees it. I am reaffirming our depart-

ment's 1986 position that Freemasonry is NOT a religion and recommending that the SBC take a stand neither for nor against Freemasonry."[319]

Here we have an apparently Masonic-biased employee of an agency who supposedly agreed to do an objective evaluation of the doctrinal relationship between Freemasonry and Christianity. He supplied the conclusions of his study to the people who had caused the doctrinal controversy to begin, the Masons. And he apparently showed them his conclusions not simply to inform the Masons of his committee's findings, but to see if the Masons wanted to change the committee's findings, and he admitted that he accepted their recommended changes. This would be like an evangelical Christian Seminary offering its report on the Jehovah's Witnesses to the Watchtower Society for inspection and then incorporating their recommendations into its conclusions. What do you think the Masons wanted changed in the Interfaith Witness Department Study? What do you think Masons wanted changed in the Home Mission Board's recommendation to the SBC's delegates?

A MASONIC AGENDA

Worse than this, there seemed to be an agenda, even a conspiracy, to encourage the acceptance of Masonry within the Southern Baptist denomination. For example, Christian Masons were actively encouraged to attend the Southern Baptist Convention by Masonic leaders and authors (e.g., in Masonry publications) as well as by other Christian Masons. They did this in order to make certain that no negative vote was made against Masonry. In *Bowing at Strange Altars,* chapter 10, we document that the Masonic Lodge confesses it attempted to infiltrate the Southern Baptist Convention in order to influence its vote. In Gary Leazer's letter he stated: "It is essential that as many Southern Baptist Masons get to the SBC as possible."[320] Here, an employee of an agency at the Southern Baptist Convention conspires with the Masons to manipulate the convention in favor of Masonry. His words and actions certainly disqualify him as a fair and impartial party. Is anyone surprised he later joined the Lodge?

BIASED SCHOLARSHIP

We believe the evidence is clear that the HMB report concluded as it did because of its philosophical bias in favor of Masonry. In *Bowing at Strange Altars,* chapters 2–10, we documented this biased reporting.

So what can we learn from this unfortunate situation? The Bible clearly teaches that the leaders of the Church are to "keep watch over . . . all the flock of which the Holy Spirit has made you overseers. . . . Even from your own number men will arise and distort the truth in order to draw disciples after them. So be on your guard!" (Acts 20:28–31).

This issue is of enough importance that when we became aware of what was happening in the Southern Baptist Convention, we wanted to make this information known to the public. So at The John Ankerberg Show we extended invitations to all the relevant principals involved to appear on our television program to present their particular views. We did this so that before the convention vote was taken, people would be able to decide for themselves.

First, we asked Gary Leazer to come. We also asked Dr. Larry Lewis, the HMB president, to come and explain how the HMB issued a seemingly contradictory resolution and why he was cited in *The Atlanta Constitution* as saying that the issue of Freemasonry was so *un*important it probably should never have been raised in the first place. We also invited Dr. John Boettjer, editor for the *Scottish Rite Journal* to defend the issues he raised in his magazine concerning the compatibility of the Masonic Lodge with Christian faith. We also wanted him to address any additional plans the Masonic Lodge might have to attempt to influence Christianity in America. We next issued an invitation to Dr. Herbert H. Reynolds, president of Baylor University and one of the authors of an article in the February *Scottish Rite Journal,* which presented his thoughts that Christians could be a part of the Lodge. We also extended an invitation to Mason Dr. John J. Robinson, author of *A Pilgrim's Path* and *Born in Blood.* Dr. Weldon had earlier debated Dr. Robinson on radio and found the exchange worth repeating. Dr. Robinson has traveled more than 150,000 miles and spoken to millions of people in the last three years defending Masonry on more than 100 radio and TV appearances. All of these men declined our invitation. (Letters on file.) Clearly, Masons and members of the HMB did not want to debate the issues in an open forum publicly. After studying what they have said, we believe we understand why.

Sadly, the conclusions of the Home Mission Board were used to advance the cause of Masonry even before the vote at the convention was taken. A number of secular media sources cited the conclusions of the HMB to the effect that Masonry and Christianity are compatible. The way they viewed it, the HMB Report signified that the largest Christian denomination in America had concluded that Masonry is not of sufficient concern to advise against it. It has not been difficult for the Masonic Lodge and those sympathetic to it to use this recommendation to promote the Lodge's agenda.

Bowing at Strange Altars: The Masonic Lodge and the Christian Conscience

TABLE OF CONTENTS

APPENDIX 3:
MASONRY AND ALBERT PIKE

Members of the Masonic Lodge, especially Christian Masons, will frequently argue that the occultist Albert Pike had little if any noticeable influence upon Masonry. As we will see, this is incorrect and illustrates one of the many concerns with the IWD study. In other words, why would a Christian organization acknowledge that Masonry was strongly influenced by a noted occultist and then proceed to declare that it was permissible for Christians to join such an organization?

The Interfaith Witness Department Study agreed to the great influence of Albert Pike on Masonry. It pointed out that Pike's pagan text, *Morals and Dogma*, was traditionally given to the candidate upon receipt of the 14th degree of the Scottish Rite. It also cited Walter Lee Brown, who observes that Pike "intended it [*Morals and Dogma*] to be a supplement to that great 'connected system of moral, religious, and philosophical instruction' that he had developed in his revision of the Scottish ritual."[321]

Pike has always been honored by leading Masons. Not long ago, Sovereign Grand Commander of the Scottish Rite, C. Fred Kleinknecht, said of Pike, "Albert Pike remains today an inspiration for Masons everywhere. His great book, *Morals and Dogma*, endures as the *most complete exposition* of Scottish Rite philosophy. He will always be remembered and revered as the *Master Builder of Scottish Rite*."[322] Writing in *The Scottish Rite Journal*, February 1993, p. 95, Dr. S. Brent Morris, 33rd degree, refers to *Morals and Dogmas* as "this great work of our Order."[323] Incredibly, he cites the arcane text *The Bible in Albert Pike's Morals and Dogma* (1992), published by the Lodge, as proof of Pike's "rich biblical context." Perhaps instead of calling Christian books on Masonry "the trash they are," Dr. Morris might look a bit closer to home.[324]

The Bible in Albert Pike's Morals and Dogma was one of many recent attempts of the Lodge to answer accusations and to make the Lodge seem compatible with Christian faith. Yet this text itself, quoting Pike, has the following false statement concerning the Bible:

> The Deity of the Old Testament is everywhere represented as the direct author of Evil, commissioning evil and lying spirits to men, hardening the heart of Pharaoh, and visiting the iniquity of the individual sinner on the whole people. The rude conception of sternness predominating over mercy in the Deity, can alone account for the human sacrifice, purposed, if not executed, by Abraham and Jepthah.[325]

The fact that Masons have officially supplied Pike's *Morals and Dogma* to Masons, until 1974, and have now replaced it with Hutchens' *A Bridge to Light,* which promotes Pike, indicates that Masons want their members to learn Pike *and* the greater pagan truths symbolized in the Masonic degrees. *A Bridge to Light* was written by Rex R. Hutchens and is now given to all 14th degree Scottish Rite candidates. As noted earlier, Hutchens was disturbed that *Morals and Dogma* was read by so few Masons, so he wrote *A Bridge to Light* to be "a bridge between the ceremonies of the degrees and their lectures in *Morals and Dogma.*"[326]

The Baptist Study on Masonry admitted that the influence of Albert Pike's pagan philosophy on Scottish Rite Masonry continues. Yet in its section on Pike, the Study downplays the issues involved in Masonry's acceptance and endorsement of Pike. Even so, it states that ". . . Hindu-occult philosophy is found in *Morals and Dogma.* That Pike revered the Aryans of early India is beyond doubt."[327] The Study continues by citing Christian apologist Dr. Robert Morey, who points out in *The Origins and Teachings of Freemasonry,* p. 41, that Pike's *Morals and Dogma* includes the teachings that (1) man is divine, (2) truth is relative and cultural, (3) only God or Mind ultimately exists, (4) evil does not exist, (5) the belief in reincarnation and astrology, and (6) the idea that various magical or occult arts are acceptable.[328] The Baptist Study then quotes the Sovereign Grand Commander of the Southern Jurisdiction of Scottish Rite Freemasonry Kleinknecht, who says, "*Morals and Dogma* represents the opinions of Albert Pike. It does not represent dogmatic teachings for Freemasonry or for the Scottish Rite. . . ."[329]

We think that the Baptist Study should have quoted what else Kleinknecht said about Albert Pike and *Morals and Dogma,* which we just cited. Kleinknecht even wrote the preface to *The Bible in Albert Pike's Morals and Dogma,* which attempts to document that Pike's book is compatible with the Bible. One wonders why Kleinknecht would, on the one hand, revere Pike as the Master Builder of the Scottish Rite and say that his *Morals and Dogma* is the greatest exposition of the Scottish Rite, but then on the other hand imply that the book is merely the opinions of Albert Pike?

If Masonry had no paganism in it, why would the Lodge officially endorse such a pagan text at all? Or, why would they endorse this text if any and all parts of it can be rejected by Masons? Certainly they don't believe that all Masons will reject all of Pike, do they? If not, then they are encouraging Masons, including Christian Masons, to study and absorb the paganism and occultism of Pike. A former 32nd degree Mason told us, "Upon graduating the 32nd degree, we were told *Morals and Dogma* was *the* source book for Freemasonry and its meaning."

APPENDIX 4:
HOW TO RECEIVE A
DEMIT FROM THE LODGE

The rules and orders of the Lodge specify that if your letter meets the following requirement, it must be read before the members of the Lodge. If done in this fashion, your letter will become a testimony to others in the Lodge concerning the truth of Jesus Christ.

In your letter, tell them the reason that you are leaving the Lodge is because it conflicts with the teaching of the Bible and especially the teachings of Christ. Give a few Bible verses to prove where it conflicts (e.g., you might bring up John 8:12, which asserts the Christian is not in darkness when following Jesus, not Masonry). You could refer to the nature (deity) and mission of Christ (redeeming Savior) or to the nature of salvation—by grace through faith—not works (Ephesians 2:8-9). If the letter is addressed in the following manner, according to Masonic law, it must be read before the Lodge:

Both the letterhead and envelope must be addressed to the *Members of the Lodge.* Never address your letter to the Lodge Master or merely to, say, "Lodge 202," because this refers to the officers, who will simply process your request without reading it to the Lodge membership. Again: (1) Your letter must be addressed (on the outside of the envelope) "To the members of the Lodge number _____," then give the address. (2) The letter itself must begin with "To the members of Lodge number _____" and not to any particular person, but only to Lodge members.

To help you officially sever your ties from the Lodge, we recommend the following sample letter as given by former Mason Dale Byers:

Sample Letter for Receiving a Demit

To the members of Lodge number _____:

This letter is a formal request for my demit from the Masonic Lodge. Please remove my name from your membership rolls and mail to me a copy of my demit.

Thank you for allowing me an opportunity to express my reasons for withdrawing from the Lodge. Do understand that my withdrawal has no personal bearing upon individual members or any personal conflicts with members. Those in the Lodge who are my friends know that I still treasure their personal friendships.

However, I am a Christian and must forsake the Lodge because its teachings are contrary to the true teachings of the Bible. Freemasonry rejects the Lord Jesus Christ Who is the Lord and Master of my life. I cannot with a clear conscience be a Mason because Jesus Christ is not allowed to be named or worshiped in the Lodge as it might offend another Mason. Masonry's respected authors, Albert Mackey and Albert Pike, openly claim that Masonry is a religion. They are right! It is a religion without Christ.

Many of us have heard that the Lodge is based on the Bible. However, in Freemasonry the Bible is rejected and God's Word is misused and misquoted. The Lodge's religion is universalism and the Bible is nothing more than a symbol.

Masonry promises to its members the blessings of Heaven and acceptance before God. [But] The Masonic plan of salvation is totally contrary to what the Bible teaches. Men cannot be saved apart from Jesus Christ as Savior.

In closing, may I express my love for you as individuals and if you desire, I will gladly share how I became a Christian and help you to understand how you, too, may become a follower of Jesus Christ.

Your friend in Christ, [330]

APPENDIX 5:
IS MASONRY A CULT?

In order to answer the question of whether Masonry is a cult, one must first determine which type or level of Masonry is being discussed and what definition of a cult is being considered. Not all Masonry is the same; a purely social Mason would be far less influenced by any cultic elements in Masonry than a religiously committed Mason.

Theologically, Masonry may be classified as a cult from the perspective of biblical revelation. If we define a cult as a religious group which claims compatibility with Christian faith but deviates seriously from orthodox Christianity in doctrine and practice, Masonry qualifies. In addition, there are certain historic associations, levels of initiation and levels of interpretation of Masonry that reveal a more broad-based cultic nature.

Consider the more outlandish characteristics of a cult such as: (1) a more or less complete withdrawal from all non-cultic social and family contact; (2) the physical or spiritual mistreating or abuse of cult members; (3) the inhibition of independent thinking and deliberate cultivation of dependency upon an authoritarian leader; (4) indoctrination reinforced through intimidation such as threats of reprisal by physical violence or severe spiritual consequence.

Masonry contains elements of some of these characteristics. It keeps Masonic secrets from family members, its oaths can be spiritually abusive, manipulative and intimidating, and they imply retribution for their violation. The ritual may in certain ways function to suppress independent thinking and dependency on Masonry. Masons must obey Lodge authority and Masonry itself.

Here are eight characteristics of cults that are to varying degrees shared with Masonry. Full documentation may be found in our four books on Masonry.

1. Masonry has parallels to ancient pagan cultic themes and beliefs. This has been documented in chapters 17–19 of *Secret Teachings* (ST), dealing with the occult generally (chapter 17), spiritism specifically (chapter 18) and the Ancient Mystery Religions (chapter 19). Many other researchers have noted the correlations. Martin L. Wagner spent years of diligent study of Masonry.[331] He was the pastor of Saint John's

English Evangelical Lutheran Church in Dayton, Ohio, and he concluded that the peculiar views of Masonry harmonize it "with the religions of the ancient cults."[332] "The Masonic ritual has many elements which have come down from antiquity, and connect the modern institution with the cults of the ancients not so much in form as in doctrine."[333] In speaking of the unity of Freemasonry with such pagan cults, he emphasizes that this is not to be seen in the externals of the Craft, "not in exact identity of ceremony and symbol, but in the religious ideas, in the object of its adoration, in its conception and definition of the deity."[334]

2. The deception of the profane (the unworthy), whether Mason or non-Mason. In *Secret Teachings,* chapter 20, "Masonry and Deception," we have examined and documented this.

3. Spiritual intimidation or secrecy reinforced by penalty. In our discussion on the oaths of Masonry (*Secret Teachings,* chapter 14), we said that the retributions were claimed as merely symbolic but that this was not true and, regardless, they were punitive and intimidating. To violate Masonic secrets is to offend the Deity seriously[335] and to risk severe divine penalty, not to mention censure and rejection by the Lodge. The penalties may be physical, psychological or spiritual. To divulge Masonic secrets is to be branded a traitor by fellow Masons, to lose important alliances and friendships, and to suffer whatever consequences arise from Masonic censorship. Among families of Masons, in business relations and in social bonds these consequences can be significant.

The oaths and their penalties are intended to instill fear in the initiate, and they are effective. One only needs to talk to a Mason to realize that he fears the consequences of violating Masonic secrets. We cited the bloodthirsty nature of these oaths, and we will document that Masonry shares a characteristic common to cultism: spiritual intimidation and fear.

Manly Hall, a 33rd degree Mason, concedes: "Every Mason knows that a broken vow brings with it a terrible penalty. . . . When a Mason swears that he will devote his life to [Masonry, and then violates his oath] . . . he is breaking a

vow which imposes not hours but *ages of misery.*"[336] Elsewhere Hall even declares that spirits will bring retribution to the Mason who violates his vows:

> The average Mason, as well as the modern student of Masonic ideals, little realizes the cosmic obligation he takes upon himself when he begins his search for those sacred truths of Nature as they are concealed in the ancient and modern rituals. He *must not lightly regard his vows,* and if he would not bring upon himself *years and ages of suffering* he must cease to consider Freemasonry solely as a social order only a few centuries old. He must realize that the ancient mystic teachings as perpetuated in the modern rites are sacred, and that powers unseen and unrecognized [the spirit world[337]] mold the destiny of those who consciously and of their own free will take upon themselves the obligations of the Fraternity.[338]

The "presentation volume" of the Grand Lodge of Ancient Free and Accepted Masons of Virginia observes: "The ancient oral penalties already mentioned are retained in our ritual to impress upon the mind of each brother how serious a violation will be regarded by the members of the Fraternity. . . . Every means possible is used to impress the new Mason with the solemnity and the necessity for faithful performance of them."[339] Masonic authority Carl H. Claudy states that the Mason who violates his oaths must consider bringing upon himself the divine wrath for such blasphemy:

> . . . there are penalties in all three [Blue Lodge] obligations and a discussion of one will do for all. . . . The penalty should be read symbolically, each man for himself. "I have taken an obligation. In it is a penalty by which those who framed it *intended to inspire terror;* to be binding upon those who then took it *through fear.* I fear . . . what? The contempt of my fellows. The loss of my self respect. The self abasement any true man feels who has broken a solemn pledge. The wrath of a God blasphemed. The horror of a sin than which there is *none greater;* breaking faith pledged in honor. These, then, are what the penalties really mean; these are the *real consequences* to me, if I violate my solemn obligation; these are what will be done to me if I fail in living up, so far as I am able, to

the covenants I made with my brethren. And may all of this be done unto me, *in full measure* should I fail my brethren."[340]

Some have responded by saying that Christianity also utilizes fear and threats. But any fear Christianity inspires is merely a proper and respectful fear of God; it is not a fear generated to retain secrets of doubtful value or outright falsehoods. In addition, Christianity inspires fear of God's holiness for a legitimate reason: hell is real. So to do otherwise would be cruel and ludicrous.

4. The justification, whether intended or otherwise, of unethical practices. This cultic characteristic can be seen in our discussion on Masonry and morality (*Secret Teachings,* chapter 4). Cult groups often claim that they uphold morality, but in fact the situation is usually quite different. This is also the case in Masonry.

5. An element of authoritarianism. Masonry is not authoritarian in the same sense that many cults are; however there is an element of authoritarianism. For example, L. James Rongstad observes that in the Lodge, "Rule is autocratic. The Worshipful Master of a local lodge, for example, has supreme and total control."[341] In his *Introduction to Freemasonry,* Volume 2, Carl H. Claudy observes,

The incumbent of the Oriental Chair [Worshipful Master] has powers peculiar to his station which are far greater than those of the president of a society or the chairman of a meeting of any kind.... It is the Master's right to control lodge business and work. It is in a very real sense *his* lodge. He decides all points of order and no appeal from his decision may be taken to the lodge.... The Master has the right to say who may enter and who may leave the lodge room. ... Only the Master may order a committee to examine a visiting brother.... If he keeps within the laws, resolutions, and edicts of his Grand Lodge [and the Landmarks] ... the power of the Worshipful Master is that of an absolute monarch.[342]

The Masonic scandal in the Italian government in 1981 illustrates how such power may be abused. By 1975, more than 100 Masons were members of the Italian Parliament.[343] The controversy centered around *Propaganda Due* ("P2"), a secret grouping of Masons that constituted an "illegal" Masonic Lodge (it was never officially constituted and never held regular meetings of all members[344]). According to investigator Stephen Knight, P2 was formed in 1966 at the request of the then Grand Master of the Grand Orient of Italy, Giordano Gamberini. His goal was apparently to establish a group of eminent persons who could be useful to the cause of Freemasonry.[345] Gamberini chose Licio Gelli to form this group of respected individuals. But Gelli was a fascist and a supporter of Mussalini.[346] In effect, Gelli became the "Venerable Master" (the Italian equivalent of Master Mason) of an unofficial Lodge. According to Knight:

Many men joined P2 because they believed the Venerable Master's patronage was indispensable to the furtherance of their careers. By this self-perpetuating process, Gelli's purported power became real. Others joined the lodge because Gelli used ruthless blackmail. The "Masonic dues" Gelli extracted from the brethren of Lodge P2 were not primarily financial. What the Venerable Master demanded—and got—were secrets. official secrets which he could use to consolidate and extend his power, and personal secrets he could use to blackmail others into joining his lodge. This most sensitive information from all areas of government was passed to him by his members, *who seem to have obeyed him with unquestioning devotion.*[347]

A secret society can be only as moral and patriotic as those who rule it. If those who have absolute power rule for personal ends, expect miscarriages of justice. Almost a thousand of Italy's most powerful men were secret members of P2, and a prosecutor's report observed: "Lodge Propaganda Due [P2] is a secret sect that has combined business and politics with the intention of destroying the country's constitutional order."[348] Eventually, the "power of Gelli was found to have undermined not only the national security of Italy, but to have struck at the roots of Western strength in Southern Europe and the Middle East. NATO was forced to support the attitude of the corrupt Freemasons in Italy's armed forces."[349] "Gelli had his Freemasons in every decision-making center in Italian politics, and was able to exert significant influence over those decisions."[350]

Knight also reveals that "P2 was the very embodiment of the fear that had haunted Italy's undersecretary of state in 1913 when he had called for a law that 'declared the unsuitability of members of the Masonic Lodge to hold certain offices (such as those in the judiciary, in the army, in the education department, etc.), the high moral and social value of which is compromised by any hidden and therefore uncontrollable tie, and by any motive of suspicion, and lack of trust on the part of the public.' "[351]

A parliamentary committee which investigated the scandal charged that the Lodge was engaged in a conspiracy to set up an authoritarian government in Italy—in effect, attempting to overturn the Italian Republic.[352] Knight concluded, "There can be no doubt that many others have suffered because of Freemasonry entering into areas of life where, according to all its publicly proclaimed principles, it should never intrude. The abuse of Freemasonry causes alarming miscarriages of justice."[353] He even cites Scotland Yard, which was "heavily Masonic," as an example.[354]

6. The attempt at suppression of critical literature. Many cult groups today like Mormonism, Christian Science and Scientology have something to hide. It may be an unsavory past, current abuse of members, leaders' immorality or destructive secret teachings. These groups often attempt to undermine, discredit or suppress works that are critical or too revealing. Stephen Knight observes, "There is evidence of very considerable efforts being made by Masons—including pressures on publishers, distributors and libraries—to suppress works critical of the brotherhood. . . . This even extends to the brotherhood's own publications."[355]

According to Knight, Walton Hannah, author of the critical work on Masonry, *Darkness Visible,* was offered a thousand British pounds by "a mysterious gentleman" not to publish his book.[356] Knight's own text, *The Brotherhood,* also encountered publishing problems. His first

publisher was fearful of Masonic attempts to inhibit its publication.[357] This publisher, NEL, was taken over by Hodder and Stoughton. The chairman and managing director were Philip and Michael Attenborough. But their father, John Attenborough, was a devoted Freemason and Christian. The book was killed because the publishers "realized they would cause their father very great pain by publishing *The Brotherhood.*"[358] The book was eventually published in 1983 in England by Grenada Publishing. It went through numerous printings, causing a furor.[359] Knight claims that Freemasons were officially warned about owning, discussing or even reading the book.[360] The "official" attitude of Masonry toward critical works is to simply ignore them and maintain silence.[361] But it appears that some Masons, officially or otherwise, have proceeded to take matters into their own hands.

7. The distortion of Scripture. Cults often cite Scripture, sometimes extensively, but the manner in which Scripture is interpreted involves a deliberate distortion to make them conform to the beliefs of a particular group. Many illustrations are found in our book *Secret Teachings* and in James Sire's *Scripture Twisting.* Masonry engages in similar quoting and misuse of the Scriptures. As one official Presbyterian inquiry noted:

> It is significant, however, that in Masonic ritual in use in so called Christian lands, as Great Britain and the United States, quotations from Holy Scripture abound. It cannot be doubted that this fact has blinded the eyes of many to the real character of the Masonic order. . . . Time and again in Masonic ritual portions of the Word of God are erroneously—and, it must be said, even blasphemously—applied. . . . Masonry does most serious violence to the inscripturated Word of God and does the gravest despite to Jesus Christ, the personal Word.[362]

8. Theologically, the denial of Christian truth and blaspheming God. In our theological analysis and elsewhere (*Secret Teachings,* chapters 5–16) we have seen that Masonry: (1) denies the deity of Christ, (2) rejects the nature of God,

(3) denies salvation by grace and teaches salvation by works, (4) distorts the Scriptures;[363] (reinterprets the Bible to teach the "truths" of Masonry), (5) replaces allegiance to God with allegiance to Masonry, (6) contains contradictory theology, and 7) blasphemes God.

All these are characteristic of allegedly "biblical" cults. What these characteristics represent are (1) a rejection of God's interests and (2) a corruption of the Church. The late Dr. Walter Martin, an acknowledged authority on comparative religion and cultism, observed:

> I think there is a motivation in Masonry as there is in the entire cultic structure that we study in *The Kingdom of the Cults.* "Human nature is perfectible by an intensive process of purification and initiation." That is the Masonic initiation. Good works is the pathway to salvation in all pagan religions and the pathway to justification. ... What we are dealing with in Masonry is a non-Christian cult with a lot of very nice people in it who are very sincere and very dedicated but very mistaken. In the words of Scripture, "There is a way that seems right unto a man but the end thereof are the ways of death."[364]

If the supreme allegiance of the Mason must be to Masonry, then it cannot be to God, particularly if the teachings and goals of the two are at variance. Masonry does not add membership to the Christian Church; rather, it lures members away and corrupts their faith. In a sense, it is parasitic, nurturing itself by draining the life from another living organism.

All of this indicates that Masonry, in various ways and at various levels, contains many of the characteristics of a cult and is therefore properly classified as a cult, or at least cultic.

NOTES

1. J. Blanchard, *Scottish Rite Masonry Illustrated: The Complete Ritual of the Ancient and Accepted Scottish Rite*, Vol. I (Chicago, IL: Charles T. Powner, Co., 1979), p. 455.
2. *Iowa Quarterly Bulletin*, April 1917, p. 54.
3. Grand Lodge of Texas, A. F. and A. M., *Monitor of the Lodge: Monitorial Instructions in the Three Degrees of Symbolic Masonry* (Grand Lodge of Texas, 1982), p. 63.
4. Blanchard, *Scottish Rite Masonry Illustrated*, Vol. II, p. 320.
5. Albert Mackey, *Mackey's Revised Encyclopedia of Freemasonry*, Vol. 2 (revised and enlarged by Robert I. Clegg) (Richmond, VA, Macoy Publishing and Masonic Supply, 1966), p. 859.
6. Editorial by Francis G. Paul, The Sovereign Grand Commander, "The Test Never Changes," *The Northern Light: A Window for Freemasonry*, May 1988, p. 1.
7. Henry Wilson Coil, *Freemasonry Through Six Centuries*, Vol. I (Richmond, VA, Macoy Publishing and Masonic Supply, 1967), pp. 131, 152; Transcript, "Christianity and the Masonic Lodge: Are They Compatible?" (guests: William Mankin, Dr. Walter Martin), (Chattanooga, TN, The John Ankerberg Evangelistic Association, 1985), p. 3; Shildes Johnson, *Is Masonry a Religion?* (Oakland, NJ., Institute for Contemporary Christianity, 1978), p. 12.
8. H. L. Haywood, *The Great Teachings of Masonry* (Richmond, VA, Macoy Publishing and Masonic Supply, 1971), p. 90; Foster Bailey, *The Spirit of Masonry* (Hampstead, London, Lucius Press, Ltd., 1972), p. 125; Legenda 32 (Part 1). (This is a Masonic source apparently used for instruction, Circa 1920-1930. No publisher, author or date is given), p. 33; Mackey, *Mackey's Revised Encyclopedia of Freemasonry*, Vol. I, p. 269; Joseph Fort Newton, *The Builders: A Story and Study of Freemasonry* (Richmond, VA, Macoy Publishing and Masonic Supply, 1951), pp. 233, 243, 275.
9. Mackey, *Mackey's Revised Encyclopedia of Freemasonry*, Vol. I, p. 269.
10. Joseph Fort Newton, *The Religion of Masonry: An Interpretation* (Richmond, VA: Macoy Publishing and Masonic Supply Co., Inc., 1969), p. 116.
11. Mackey, *Mackey's Revised Encyclopedia of Freemasonry*, Vol. I, p. 269.
12. Ibid.
13. Henry Wilson Coil, *A Comprehensive View of Freemasonry* (Richmond, VA: Macoy Publishing and Masonic Supply Co., 1973), p. 234.
14. Ibid., pp. 214-215.
15. Henry Wilson Coil, *Coil's Masonic Encyclopedia* (New York: Macoy Publishing and Masonic Supply, 1961), p. 600; "Freemasonry," *Encyclopedia Britannica Micropedia*, Vol. 4, p. 302.
16. Coil, *A Comprehensive View of Freemasonry*, p. 216.
17. H. L. Haywood, *The Newly-Made Mason: What He and Every Mason Should Know About Masonry* (Richmond, VA: Macoy Publishing and Masonic Supply, 1973), pp. v-vi, emphasis added.
18. Allen E. Roberts, *The Craft and Its Symbols: Opening the Door to Masonic Symbolism* (Richmond, VA: Macoy Publishing and Masonic Supply, 1974), p. 6.
19. Rollin C. Blackmer, *The Lodge and the Craft* (Richmond, VA: Macoy Publishing and Masonic Supply, 1976), p. 1.
20. Educational and Historical Commission of the Grand Lodge of Georgia, *Leaves from Georgia Masonry* (Educational and Historical Commission of the Grand Lodge of Georgia, 1947), p. 65.
21. Edmond Ronayne, *The Master's Carpet; or Masonry and Baal-Worship—Identical*, nd., np. (distributed by

Missionary Service and Supply, Route 2, Columbiana, OH 44408), p. 242.

22. William H. Russell, *Masonic Facts for Masons* (Chicago, IL: Charles T. Powner Co., 1968), p. 7.

23. George H. Steinmetz, *Freemasonry—Its Hidden Meaning* (Chicago, IL: Charles T. Powner Co., 1976), pp. 2, 5.

24. Transcript, "Christianity and the Masonic Lodge: Are They Compatible?" p. 3, cf. p. 5.

25. Coil, *Coil's Masonic Encyclopedia,* p. 569.

26. Ibid., p. 369.

27. Various authors, *Little Masonic Library,* Vol. I (Richmond, VA: Macoy Publishing and Masonic Supply, 1977), pp. 2-3.

28. Transcript, "The Masonic Lodge: What Goes on Behind Closed Doors?" (guests: Jack Harris, William Mankin, Dr. Walter Martin, Paul Pantzer) (Chattanooga, TN: The John Ankerberg Evangelistic Association, 1986), p. 29.

29. Alphonse Cerza, *A Masonic Reader's Guide* (Thomas C. Warden, ed.), Transactions of the Missouri Lodge of Research, Vol. 34 (1978-1979), 1980, p. ix; Coil, *Coil's Masonic Encyclopedia,* p. 376; "Freemasonry" in Richard Cavendish (ed.), *Man, Myth and Magic: An Illustrated Encyclopedia of the Supernatural* (New York: Marshall Cavendish Corporation, 1970), p. 1035.

30. The John Ankerberg Evangelistic Association, "Freemasonry on Its Own Terms," *News & Views* (Chattanooga, TN: The John Ankerberg Evangelistic Association) May, 1986, p. 1.

31. Ibid., p. 1.

32. Haywood, *The Newly Made Mason;* cf. Henry Pirtle, *Kentucky Monitor: Complete Monitorial Ceremonies of the Blue Lodge* (Louisville, KY: Standard Printing Co., 1921).

33. Henry C. Clausen, *Clausen's Commentaries on Morals and Dogma* (The Supreme Council, 33rd Degree, Ancient and Accepted Scottish Rite of Freemasonry, Southern Jurisdiction of the USA, 1976), p. 148.

34. Kent Henderson, *Masonic World Guide* (Richmond, VA: Macoy Publishing and Masonic Supply Co., 1984).

35. "Freemasonry," *Encyclopaedia Britannica Micropedia,* Vol. 4, p. 302.

36. H. V. B. Voorhis, *Facts for Freemasons: A Storehouse of Masonic Knowledge in Question and Answer Form,* rev. (Richmond, VA: Macoy Publishing and Masonic Supply, 1979), p. 190.

37. Paul A. Fisher, *Behind the Lodge Door: Church, State & Freemasonry* (Washington, D.C.: Shield Press, 1987), p. 248.

38. Martin L. Wagner, *Freemasonry: An Interpretation,* nd., np. (distributed by Missionary Service and Supply, Route 2, Columbiana, OH, 44408), p. 23.

39. Paul A. Fisher, *Behind the Lodge Door: Church, State & Freemasonry* (Washington, D.C.: Shield Press, 1987), pp. 244, 260-68.

40. Ibid., pp. 1-17.

41. Blanchard, *Scottish Rite Masonry Illustrated,* Vol. II, p. 284.

42. Voorhis, *Facts for Freemasons,* p. 191.

43. Ibid.; cf. 56-117.

44. *Congressional Record,* Senate, September 9, 1987, pp. S11868-70.

45. Voorhis, *Facts for Freemasons,* p. 125.

46. Fisher, *Behind the Lodge Door,* p. 246.

47. Voorhis, *Facts for Freemasons,* pp. 128-170; cf. 56.

48. Committee on Secret Societies of the Ninth General Assembly of the Orthodox Presbyterian Church (meeting at Rochester, NY, June 2-5, 1942), *Christ or the Lodge?* (Philadelphia, PA: Great Commission Publications, nd.), p. 2; Rongstad, *How to Respond to the Lodge,* p. 10.

49. Wagner, *Freemasonry,* p. 23.

50. J. W. Acker, *Stange Altars: A Scriptural Appraisal of the Lodge* (St. Louis, MO: Concordia, 1959), pp. 18-22, 48-58; L. James Rongstad, *How to Respond to the Lodge* (St. Louis: Concordia, 1977.), p. 13; Committee on Secret Societies, *Christ or the Lodge?* p. 2; Haywood, *The Newly Made Mason.*

51. Acker, *Stange Altars,* pp. 71-83.

52. Gerald and Sandra Tanner, *Mormonism: Shadow or Reality?* (1972), pp. 484-492; Fisher, *Behind the Lodge Door,* p. 1-15, 187; Rongstad, *How to Respond to the Lodge,* p. 10.

53. Rongstad, *How to Respond to the Lodge,* p. 28.

54. Jack Harris, *Freemasonry: The Invisible Cult in Our Midst* (Chattanooga, TN: Global, 1983), p. x.

55. Alphonse Cerza, *Let There Be Light: A Study in Anti Masonry* (Silver Spring, MD: The Masonic Service Association, 1983), p. 28.

56. Stephen Knight, *The Brotherhood: The Explosive Exposé of the Secret World of the Freemasons* (London: Grenada Publishing, Ltd./Panther Books, 1983), p. 246.

57. Ibid., p. 263.

58. Ibid., p. 233.

59. Ibid., p. 240.

60. Ibid., p. 242.

61. Ibid., p. 244.

62. Malcom C. Duncan, *Masonic Ritual and Monitor* (New York: David Mckay Co., n.d.), p. 57.

63. Haywood, *The Newly Made Mason,* p. 211.

64. Grand Lodge of Texas, A. F. and A. M., *Monitor of the Lodge,* p. 63.

65. Bailey, *The Spirit of Masonry,* p. 12.

66. Roberts, *The Craft and Its Symbols,* p. 36.

67. Bailey, *The Spirit of Masonry,* p. 12.

68. Coil, *Freemasonry Through Six Centuries,* Vol. I, p. 5.

69. Johnson, *Is Masonry a Religion?* p. 12.

70. Ronayne, *The Master's Carpet,* p. 210.

71. Coil, *Coil's Masonic Encyclopedia,* p. 600.

72. Haywood, *The Great Teachings of Masonry,* p. 94.

73. Ibid., p. 95.

74. Johnson, *Is Masonry a Religion?* pp. 12-13.

75. John Sheville and James Gould, *Guide to the Royal Arch Chapter: A Complete Monitor with Full Instructions in the Degrees of Mark Master, Past Master, Most Excellent Master and Royal Arch Together With the Order of High Priesthood* (Richmond, VA: Macoy Publishing and Masonic Supply Co., 1981), p. 145.

76. Fisher, *Behind the Lodge Door,* p. 206.

77. Haywood, *The Newly Made Mason,* pp. 215-216.

78. Newton, *The Builders,* p. 233.

79. Ibid., p. 243.

80. Ibid., p. 275.

81. Duncan, *Masonic Ritual and Monitor*, p. 29; cf. transcript, "The Masonic Lodge: What Goes on Behind Closed Doors?" p. 4.

82. The Ancient and Accepted Scottish Rite of Freemasonry, Southern Jurisdiction USA, *Ceremonies of Installation and Dedication* (1954, rev.), p. 119.

83. Ibid., p. 123.

84. Ibid., p.123, emphasis added.

85. Ibid., p. 29.

86. Roberts, *The Craft and Its Symbols*, p. ix.

87. Albert G. Mackey, *The Symbolism of Freemasonry: Illustrating and Explaining Its Science and Philosophy, Its Legends, Myths, and Symbols* (Chicago, IL: Charles T. Powner Co., 1975), p. 10.

88. Roberts, *The Craft and Its Symbols*, p. 24.

89. Ibid., pp. 23, 13-14, 16, 31, 32, 76, 20, 80, respectively.

90. Mackey, *The Symbolism of Freemasonry*, pp. 3-5.

91. Roberts, *The Craft and Its Symbols*, p. 10.

92. Ibid., p. 82.

93. Ibid., p. 84.

94. W. L. Wilmshurst, *The Meaning of Masonry* (New York: Bell Publishing Co., 1980), p. 74.

95. Allen E. Roberts, *Key to Freemasonry's Growth* (Richmond, VA: Macoy Publishing and Masonic Supply, 1969), p. 18.

96. The Baptist Union of Scotland (endorsed by the Baptist Union of Great Britain and Ireland), *Baptists and Freemasonry* (Baptist Church House, 1987), pp. 4-5.

97. Wilmshurst, *The Meaning of Masonry*, p. 121.

98. Clausen, *Clausen's Commentaries on Morals and Dogma*, p. xviii.

99. Roberts, *The Craft and Its Symbols*, p. 6.

100. Steinmetz, *Freemasonry—Its Hidden Meaning*, pp. 2, 5.

101. Manley P. Hall, *The Lost Keys of Freemasonry or the Secret of Hiram Abiff* (Richmond, VA: Macoy Publishing and Masonic Supply Co., Inc., 1976), pp. 64-65, emphasis added.

102. Newton, *The Religion of Masonry*, pp. 11-12.

103. Bailey, *The Spirit of Masonry*, p. 125.

104. *Ceremonies of Installation and Dedication*, p. 24.

105. *Little Masonic Library*, Vol. I, p. 138, emphasis added.

106. Coil, *A Comprehensive View of Freemasonry*, p. 186.

107. Coil, *Coil's Masonic Encyclopedia*, p. 158.

108. Albert G. Mackey, *An Encyclopedia of Freemasonry and Its Kindred Sciences* (Chicago: Masonic History Company, 1921), Vol. 1, p. 301.

109. Henry Wilson Coil, *Coil's Masonic Encyclopedia* (NY: Macoy, 1961), p. 512.

110. Albert Pike, *Morals and Dogma of the Ancient and Accepted Scottish Rite of Freemasonry* (Charleston, SC: Supreme Council of the 33rd Degree for the Southern Jurisdiction of the United States, 1927), p. 219.

111. Joseph Fort Newton, *The Religion of Masonry: An Interpretation* (Richmond: Macoy, 1969), pp. 58-89.

112. Mackey, *Mackey's Revised Encyclopedia of Freemasonry*, Vol. II, p. 847.

113. Ibid., p. 848.

114. Shildes Johnson, *Is Masonry a Religion?* (Oakland, NJ: Institute of Contemporary Christianity, 1978), p. 21.

115. Newton, *The Religion of Masonry*, pp. 11-12.

116. Albert Mackey, *The Manual of the Lodge* (New York: Clark Maynard, 1870), p. 20, cf. Transcript, "The Masonic Lodge: What Goes On Behind Closed Doors?" p. 5.

117. Hall, *The Lost Keys of Freemasonry*, p. 13.

118. Knight, *The Brotherhood*, p. 234; *Little Masonic Library*, Vol. V, pp. 43-44.

119. Wagner, *Freemasonry*, pp. 289, 336, cf., p. 330.

120. Ronayne, *The Master's Carpet*, pp. 111-112.

121. H. L. Haywood, *The Great Teachings of Masonry* (Richmond, Macoy, 1971), p. 90.

122. Ibid., p. 99; Newton, *The Builders*, p. 258; Hall, *The Lost Keys of Freemasonry*, pp. 64-65; Newton, *The Builders*, pp. 243, 258, emphasis added.

123. Coil, *Coil's Masonic Encyclopedia*, p. 512; Roberts, *Key to Freemasonry's Growth*, p. 18; *Little Masonic Library*, Vol. V, p. 35; Newton, *The Builders*, pp. 62-63, 275.

124. Everette C. DeVelde, Jr., "A Reformed View of Freemasonry" in James B. Jordan, ed., *Christianity and Civilization*, Vol. 1: The Failure of the American Baptist Culture (Tyler, TX: Geneva Divinity School Press, 1982), p. 281.

125. Mackey, *The Symbolism of Freemasonry*, p. 326.

126. Ibid., p. 327.

127. *Little Masonic Library*, Vol. II, p. 143.

128. Ibid., p. 92.

129. Haywood, *The Great Teachings of Masonry*, pp. 97-98.

130. Ibid., pp. 96-98.

131. Rongstad, *How to Respond to the Lodge*, p. 24; Committee on Secret Societies, *Christ or the Lodge?* pp. 22-23; Wagner, *Freemasonry*, pp. 24, 282; Acker, *Stange Altars*, pp. 58-61; Harris, *Freemasonry*, p. 143; "Freemasonry," *Encyclopedia Britannica Micropedia*, Vol. 4, p. 502; E. M Storms, *Should a Christian Be a Mason?* (Route 1, Lytle Road, Fletcher, NC, New Puritan Library, 1980), pp. 4, 78-79; John R. Rice, *Lodges Examined by the Bible* (Murfreesboro, TN: Sword of the Lord Publishers, 1943), p. 47; H. J. Rogers, *The Word of God vs. Masonry* (Van Alstyne, TX: B & R Publishers, nd.), pp. 1-2; Alva J. Mc Clain, *Freemasonry and Christianity* (Winona Lake, IN: BMH Books, 1977), p. 32; The Working Group established by the Standing Committee of the General Synod of the Church of England, *Freemasonry and Christianity: Are They Compatible?* (London: Church House Publishing, 1987); The Baptist Union of Scotland, *Baptists and Freemasonry,* Report of the Faith and Order Committee of the British Methodist Church, *Freemasonry and Methodism*, 1985 (presented to the General Assembly of the British Methodist Church and adopted by them Wednesday, July 3, 1985).

132. Coil, *Freemasonry Through Six Centuries*, Vol. I, p. 174.

133. Knight, *The Brotherhood*, p. 230.

134. Ibid., pp. 230, 231, 234, 240.

135. Blanchard, *Scottish Rite Masonry Illustrated;* Rongstad, *How to Respond to the Lodge*, pp. 221-22.

136. Blanchard, *Scottish Rite Masonry Illustrated*, Vol. II, pp. 263-264, emphasis added.

137. Newton, *The Builders*, pp. 243, 246, 247.

138. *Little Masonic Library*, Vol. IV, pp. 215-218.

139. Mackey, *Mackey's Revised Encyclopedia of Freemasonry*, Vol. I, p. 133.

140. Albert Pike, *Morals and Dogma of the Ancient and Accepted Scottish Rite of Freemasonry* (Charleston, SC: The Supreme Council of the 33rd Degree for the Southern Jurisdiction of the United States, 1906), pp. 744-45.

141. Wagner, *Freemasonry*, p. 285.

142. Acker, *Strange Altars*, p. 29.

143. *Little Masonic Library*, Vol. I, p. 132.

144. Ibid., pp. 128-32; Coil, *Coil's Masonic Encyclopedia*, p. 520.

145. *Little Masonic Library*, Vol. I, pp. 129-30.

146. Blackmer, *The Lodge and the Craft*, p. 22.

147. Pike, *Morals and Dogma* (1906), pp. 224, 715, 741, 744, 818; Jim Shaw and Tom McKenney, *The Deadly Deception: Freemasonry Exposed by One of Its Top Leaders* (Lafayette, LA: Huntington House, 1988), pp. 128-129; Legenda 32 (Part 1), p. 15; The Baptist Union of Scotland, *Baptists and Freemasonry*, p. 5.

148. Wagner, *Freemasonry*, pp. 335-336, cf. pp. 341-42; cf. Harold Waldwin Percival, *Masonry and Its Symbols in the Light of "Thinking and Destiny"* (Forest Hills, NY: The Word Foundation, Inc., 1979), pp. 45; John Dove (comp.), *Virginia Textbook* (containing *"The Book of Constitutions," Illustrations of the Work, Forms and Ceremonies of the Grand Lodge of Virginia*, Vol. II (Grand Lodge of Virginia, nd.), p. 52; Acker, *Strange Altars*, p. 43.

149. "The Bible and Freemasonry" in *Holy Bible—Masonic Edition* (Terminal House, Shepperton, London: A. Lewis (Masonic Publishers Ltd., 1975); Holy Bible (Temple Illustrated edition), (Nashville, TN: A. J. Holman Co., 1968).

150. *Little Masonic Library*, Vol. I, p. 129.

151. Mackey, *Mackey's Revised Encyclopedia of Freemasonry*, Vol. I, p. 133.

152. Wagner, *Freemasonry*, pp. 292-293.

153. "A Study of Freemasonry" (Atlanta, GA: Home Mission Board of the Southern Baptist Convention, 1993), available from Home Mission Board, SBC, 1350 Spring Street, N.W., Atlanta, GA, 30367-5601 (1-800-634-2462), p. 26, emphasis added (hereinafter referred to as *Study*.)

154. Ibid., p. 38.

155. Rev. Thomas Sherrard Roy, 33rd Degree, "An Answer to Anti-Masonic Religious Propaganda," *The Scottish Rite Journal*, February 1993, p. 71.

156. Coil, *Coil's Masonic Encyclopedia*, pp. 516-517.

157. Wagner, *Freemasonry*, p. 286.

158. Ibid., pp. 309-310.

159. Bailey, *The Spirit of Masonry*, p. 112.

160. Fisher, *Behind the Lodge Door*, p. 54.

161. Knight, *The Brotherhood*, p. 243; Acker, *Strange Altars*, p. 32.

162. Knight, *The Brotherhood*, p. 237.

163. Ibid., pp. 236-237.

164. F. De P. Castells, *The Genuine Secrets in Freemasonry Prior to A.D. 1717* (London, England: A. Lewis, 1971), p. 221.

165. Wagner, *Freemasonry*, pp. 338-399.

166. Coil, *Coil's Masonic Encyclopedia*, p. 516.

167. A. E. Cundall, "Baal" in Merril C. Tenney (ed.), *The Zondervan Pictorial Encyclopedia of the Bible*, Vol. 1 (Grand Rapids, MI: Zondervan, 1975); "Baal" in *Encyclopedia*

Britannica—Micropedia, Vol. 1 (Chicago, IL: University of Chicago, 1978); "Baal" in *The New Schaff-Herzog Encyclopedia of Religious Knowledge*, Vol. 1 (Grand Rapids, MI: Baker, 1977), pp. 390-393; Lewis Bayles Payton, "Baal, Beel, Bel" in James Hastings (ed.), *Encyclopedia of Religion and Ethics*, Vol. 2 (New York: Charles Schribner's Sons, n.d.); George A. Barton, "Baalzebub and Beelzaboul" in No. 114, subsequent article.

168. General Synod of the Church of England, *Freemasonry and Christianity: Are They Compatible?* pp. 27, 29.

169. Barton, "Baalzebub and Beelzaboul" in No. 114, p. 298; cf. Luke 11:15-19; Matthew 10:25-27.

170. Pike, *Morals and Dogma* (1906), p. 524; cf. Clausen, *Clausen's Commentaries on Morals and Dogma*, p. 159.

171. Wagner, *Freemasonry*, pp. 319, 343.

172. Ibid., p. 299.

173. *Freemasonry and Christianity: Are They Compatible?* p. 30.

174. Clausen, *Clausen's Commentaries on Morals and Dogma*, p. 159.

175. Shaw and McKenney, *The Deadly Deception*, pp. 126-127.

176. Ibid., p. 127, cf. Henry C. Clausen, *Practice and Procedure for the Scottish Rite* (Washington, DC: The Supreme Council, 33rd Degree, Ancient and Accepted Scottish Rite of Freemasonry Mother Jurisdiction of the World, 1981), pp. 75-77.

177. Cf. *The Kentucky Monitor*, 1946, p. xv.

178. Clausen, *Clausen's Commentaries on Morals and Dogma*, p. 157.

179. Pike, *Morals and Dogma* (1906), p. 525.

180. Ronayne, *The Master's Carpet*, p. 87.

181. Shaw and McKenney, *The Deadly Deception*, p. 127; Pike, *Morals and Dogma* (1906), p. 524; Harris, *Freemasonry*, pp. 102-103.

182. Cf. Corinne Heline, *Mystic Masonry and the Bible* (La Cañada, CA: New Age Press, 1975), pp. 19, 33, 47, 90-91.

183. Harris, *Freemasonry*, p. 102.

184. Haywood, *The Great Teachings of Masonry*, p. 138.

185. The Baptist Union of Scotland, *Baptists and Freemasonry*, pp. 5-6.

186. Grand Lodge of Georgia, *Leaves from Georgia Masonry*, p. 67.

187. General Synod of the Church of England, *Freemasonry and Christianity: Are They Compatible?* p. 20.

188. Ibid., p. 34.

189. Clausen, *Clausen's Commentaries on Morals and Dogma*, p. 156.

190. Pike, *Morals and Dogma* (1906), p. 136.

191. Grand Lodge of Georgia, *Leaves from Georgia Masonry*, p. 140; cf. Southern Jurisdiction of the United States of America, *Funeral Ceremony and Offices of a Lodge of Sorrow of the Ancient and Accepted Scottish Rite of Freemasonry* (Charleston, SC, 1946, rpt.), p. 76.

192. *Ceremonies of Installation and Dedication*, p. 85.

193. Dove (compiler), *Virginia Textbook*, Vol. II, p. 38.

194. Shaw and McKenney, *The Deadly Deception*, p. 125.

195. Duncan, *Masonic Ritual and Monitor*, p. 50.

196. Raymond Lee Allen, et. al., *Tennessee Craftsmen or Masonic Textbook*, 14th ed. (Nashville: Tennessee Board of Custodians Members, 1963), p. 41.

197. John Ankerberg, William Mankin, and Walter Martin, *Christianity and the Masonic Lodge; Are They Compatible?* "The John Ankerberg Show," transcript (Chattanooga, TN: Ankerberg Theological Research Institute, 1985), p. 2.

198. Ankerberg, et al., *The Masonic Lodge*, p. 35, emphasis added.

199. Shaw and McKenney, *The Deadly Deception*, p. 132; cf. W. J. Morris, *Pocket Lexicon of Freemasonry* (Chicago, IL: Ezra A. Cook Publications, nd.), p. 5.

200. Mackey, *The Symbolism of Freemasonry*, p. 44.

201. Carl H. Claudy, *Foreign Countries: A Gateway to the Interpretation and Development of Certain Symbols of Freemasonry* (Richmond, VA: Macoy Publishing and Masonic Supply, 1971), p. 18.

202. Arthur Edward Waite, *A New Encyclopedia of Freemasonry*, Vol. I (New York: Weather Vane Books, 1970 [combined edition), pp. 395-396.

203. Roberts, *The Craft and Its Symbols*, p. 17.

204. Haywood, *The Great Teachings of Masonry*, p. 139, emphasis added.

205. Mackey, *Mackey's Revised Encyclopedia of Freemasonry*, Vol. II, p. 844.

206. George Simmons and Robert Macoy, *Standard Masonic Monitor of the Degrees of Entered Apprentice, Fellow Craft and Master Mason* (Richmond, VA: Macoy Publishing and Masonic Supply, 1984), p. 46.

207. Rongstad, cited in *How to Respond to the Lodge*, p. 17.

208. Ibid., emphasis added.

209. The Baptist Union of Scotland, *Baptists and Freemasonry*, p. 6.

210. Pike, *Morals and Dogma* (1906), pp. 854-55, cf. Clausen, *Clausen's Commentaries on Morals and Dogma*, p. 156.

211. Wilmshurst, *The Meaning of Masonry*, pp. 130-131.

212. The General Grand Chapter of Royal Arch Masons International, Committee on Revision of the Ritual, William F. Kuhn, et al., *The Manual of Ritual for Royal Arch Masons* (45th ed., 1983), p. 81.

213. Coil, *A Comprehensive View of Freemasonry*, p. 184.

214. Steinmetz, *Freemasonry—Its Hidden Meaning*, p. 2.

215. Storms, *Should a Christian Be a Mason?* p. 43.

216. Heline, *Mystic Masonry and the Bible*, p. 91.

217. The Baptist Union of Scotland, *Baptists and Freemasonry*, p. 7.

218. Clausen, *Clausen's Commentaries on Morals and Dogma*, pp. 157-158.

219. Ibid., pp. 172, 174.

220. Ibid., pp. 203, 204, 210-212.

221. Pike, *Morals and Dogma* (1906), p. 626.

222. Ibid., p. 745.

223. Ibid., p. 744.

224. Ibid., p. 741.

225. The Supreme Council, *Liturgy of the Ancient and Accepted Scottish Rite of Freemasonry*, p. 166.

226. John Weldon, *Decoding the Bible Code*, chapter 8, "Understanding the Kabalah."

227. *Masonic Square for 1975 and 1976* (bound volume), (Vol. 1—March 1975–December 1975), p. 29.

228. Manly Hall, *An Encyclopedic Outline of Masonic Hermetic Qabbalistic and Rosicrucian Symbolical Philosophy* (Los Angeles: Philosophical Research Society, 1977), p. 139.

229. Mackey, *Mackey's Revised Encyclopedia of Freemasonry*, Vol. I, p. 449.

230. Coil, *Coil's Masonic Encyclopedia*, p. 25.

231. Mackey, *The Symbolism of Freemasonry*, p. 338.

232. Ibid., p. 333; Hall, *The Lost Keys of Freemasonry*, p. 100; Isabel Cooper-Oakley, *Masonry and Medieval Mysticism: Traces of a Hidden Tradition* (Wheaton, IL: Theosophical Publishing House, 1977), p. 34; Claudy, *Foreign Countries*, p. ix; Wilmshurst, *The Meaning of Masonry*, p. 177, etc.

233. Claudy, *Foreign Countries*, p. ix.

234. Haywood, *The Newly Made Mason*, p. 211.

235. Frits Staal, *Exploring Mysticism* (Berkeley University of California Press, 1975); Benjamin B. Wolman, Montague Ullman (eds.), *Handbook of States of Consciousness* (New York: Van Nostrand Reinhold, 1986).

236. Clausen, *Clausen's Commentaries on Morals and Dogma*, p. 210.

237. Bailey, *The Spirit of Masonry*, p. 127.

238. Transcript, "Christianity and the Masonic Lodge: Are They Compatible?" p. 29.

239. Wilmshurst, *The Meaning of Masonry*, p. 1112, cf. pp. 74-75, 174-185.

240. Ibid., p. 185.

241. John Ferguson, *An Illustrated Encyclopedia of Mysticism and the Mystery Religions* (New York: Seabury Press, 1977), p.148; cf. Staal, *Exploring Mysticism* and Wolman and Ullman (eds.), pp. 286-90.

242. Wilmshurst, *The Meaning of Masonry*, p. 4.

243. Hall, *The Lost Keys of Freemasonry*, p. 102.

244. Wilmshurst, *The Meaning of Masonry*, p. 54.

245. Djwhal Khul, "The Restoration of the Mysteries," *The Beacon* (May 1963), in Corinne Heline, *Mystic Masonry and the Bible* (La Cañada, CA: New Age, 1975), pp. xiv-xvi; cf. p. xvi.

246. Ibid., p. xv.

247. Lynn F. Perkins, *Masonry in the New Age* (Lakemont, GA: CSA, 1971), pp. 18-19.

248. Percival rejected the more typical occult descriptions as to how *Thinking and Destiny* was produced (Harold Walden Percival, *Masonry and Its Symbols in the Light of "Thinking and Destiny"* [Forest Hills, NY: The Word Foundation, Inc., 1979], pp. xi-xlii), possibly the result of his allegedly "devout Christian" upbringing (Percival, *Masonry and Its Symbols*, p. xiv). But that it was not a product of his own mind but was rather the result of spiritistic inspiration should be clear to anyone who is familiar with the various forms that spiritistic inspiration takes and who reads Percival's own description of the process of his inspiration (Percival, *Masonry and Its Symbols*, pp. xv-xvi, xi, 47, 53-58).

249. Percival, *Masonry and Its Symbols*, pp. 1, 2.

250. Hall, *The Lost Keys of Freemasonry*, pp. 11-13.

251. Foster Bailey, *The Spirit of Masonry* (Hampstead, London: Lucius, 1972), p. 119.

252. Ibid., p. 21.

253. Cerza, *Let There Be Light*, p. 55.

254. Ibid., p. 2.

255. Ibid., p. 43.
256. Wagner, *Freemasonry*, pp. 288-302.
257. Henry C. Clausen, *Beyond the Ordinary: Toward a Better, Wiser and Happier World* (Washington, DC: The Supreme Council, 33rd Degree, Ancient and Accepted Scottish Rite of Freemasonry, 1983), p. 253.
258. *Little Masonic Library*, Vol. V, pp. 102-103.
259. Pike, *Morals and Dogma* (1906), p. 277.
260. *Little Masonic Library*, Vol. V, p. 14.
261. *Masonic Square for 1975 and 1976*, Vol. 2—March 1976–December 1976, pp. 122-123.
262. Bailey, *The Spirit of Masonry*, pp. 24-25.
263. *Little Masonic Library*, Vol. I, p. 118; cf. Coil, *A Comprehensive View of Freemasonry*, p. 192; *Little Masonic Library*, Vol. IV, p. 258.
264. *Little Masonic Library*, Vol. I, pp. 115-117, emphasis added; *Little Masonic Library*, Vol. I, p. 134.
265. Wagner, *Freemasonry*, pp. 487-563.
266. Ibid., p. 489.
267. Ibid., p. 490.
268. Ibid., pp. 487-563.
269. Cerza, *Let There Be Light*, p. 53.
270. Dove (comp.), *Virginia Textbook*, Vol. II, p. 21.
271. Carl H. Claudy, *The Master's Book* (Washington, DC: The Temple Publishers, 1985), pp. V-VII.
272. Claudy, *Foreign Countries*, p. 90.
273. Wagner, *Freemasonry*, p. 550.
274. Ibid., p. 551.
275. Ibid., p. 552.
276. Duncan, *Masonic Ritual and Monitor*, pp. 34-35.
277. Ibid., pp. 95, 96.
278. Blanchard, *Scottish Rite Masonry Illustrated*, Vol. I, p. 196.
279. Ibid., p. 197.
280. Ibid., p. 448.
281. Ibid., Vol. II, p. 457.
282. Ibid., Vol. I, p. 473.
283. Ibid., Vol. II, pp. 269-270, emphasis added.
284. Ibid., p. 275, emphasis added.
285. Mackey, *Mackey's Revised Encyclopedia of Freemasonry*, Vol. II, p. 760, first emphasis Mackey's.
286. Rice, *Lodges Examined by the Bible*, pp. 13-14, 25-27, cf. Fisher, *Behind the Lodge Door*.
287. Dove (comp.), *Virginia Textbook*, Vol. II, p. 21.
288. Wagner, *Freemasonry*, p. 513.
289. Ronayne, *The Master's Carpet*, p. 72.
290. Blanchard, *Scottish Rite Masonry Illustrated*, Vol. I, p. 454.
291. Ibid., p. 457.
292. William W. Daniel, et al., *Masonic Manual of the Grand Lodge of Georgia, Free and Accepted Masons* (Grand Lodge of Georgia, 9th ed., 1973), p. 190.
293. Duncan, *Masonic Ritual and Monitor*, p. 230.
294. Ronayne, *The Master's Carpet*, pp. 105-106.
295. Cerza, *Let There Be Light*, p. 55.
296. Rice, *Lodges Examined by the Bible*, p. 27.
297. Ibid., p. 27.
298. Wagner, *Freemasonry*, p. 555.
299. Ibid., p. 514.
300. Cerza, *Let There Be Light*, p. 55.
301. "Freemasonry," *Encyclopaedia Britannica Micropedia*, Vol. 4, p. 302.
302. Rongstad, *How to Respond to the Lodge*, p. 14.
303. Fisher, *Behind the Lodge Door*, pp. 50-52.
304. *Ceremonies of Installation and Dedication*, p. 12.
305. Carl H. Claudy, *Introduction to Freemasonry*, Vol. III (Washington, DC: The Temple Publishers, 1984), p. 161.
306. John Ankerberg, John Weldon, *The Facts on the Masonic Lodge* (Eugene OR: Harvest House, 1989); John Ankerberg, John Weldon, *Christianity and the Secret Teachings of the Masonic Lodge: What Goes on Behind Closed Doors?* (Chattanooga, TN: JAEA, 1989).
307. "Freemasonry on Its Own Terms," *News & Views*, pp. 6-8; cf. John 3:18, 36; 8:24, Knight, *The Brotherhood*, p. 48.
308. Claudy, *Foreign Countries*, p. 87.
309. Haywood, *The Newly Made Mason*, p. VI.
310. "*A Report on Freemasonry*," published by the Home Mission Board, SBC, 1350 Spring Street, N.W., Atlanta, GA, 30367-5601 (1-800-634-2462), p. 1, hereinafter referred to as *Summary Report*.
311. *Study*, p. 75.
312. *Summary Report*, p. 6.
313. Ibid., emphasis added.
314. Ibid., p. 5.
315. Press Release 22 March 1993, emphasis added. Copy on file.
316. Letter of 25 March 1993. Copy on file.
317. Letter received 20 March 1993. Copy on file.
318. Transcript of phone conversation with Dr. Holly, 23 March 1993, pp. 2-3.
319. Letter of Gary Leazer to Don L. Talbert of Chattanooga, 17 January 1993. Copy on file.
320. Ibid.
321. *Study*, p. 57.
322. See Fred Kleinknecht, *The House of the Temple of Supreme Council* (Washington, DC: The Supreme Council 33rd Degree, 1988), p. 23, emphasis added.
323. S. Brent Morris, "The Sound and the Fury," *Scottish Rite Journal*, February 1993, p. 95.
324. Ibid., p. 88.
325. Southern Jurisdiction of Scottish Rite Freemasonry, Washington, DC: Supreme Council 33rd Degree, *The Bible in Albert Pike's Morals and Dogma*, p. 165, citing Albert Pike, *Morals and Dogma*, p. 687 from Holly, p. 42.
326. *Study*, p. 57, citing Hutchens, *A Bridge to Light*, p. 4.
327. *Study*, p. 58.
328. Ibid.
329. Ibid., p. 59.
330. Dale A. Byers, *I Left the Lodge* (Schaumburg, IL: Regular Baptist Press, 1988), pp. 125-126.
331. Wagner, *Freemasonry*, p. 140.
332. Ibid., p. 283.
333. Ibid., p. 138.
334. Ibid., pp. 252-253.
335. Carl Claudy, *Foreign Countries: A Gateway to the Interpretation and Development of Certain Symbols of Freemasonry*, p. 90.
336. Hall, *The Lost Keys of Freemasonry*, p. 68, emphasis added.
337. Cf. ibid., pp. 11-13, 17-18, 25, 57, 60, 62.
338. Hall, *The Lost Keys of Freemasonry*, p. 11, emphasis added.

339. Dove (comp.), *Virginia Textbook*, Vol. II, p. 21.
340. Claudy, *Foreign Countries*, p. 90, emphasis added.
341. Rongstad, *How to Respond to the Lodge*, p. 14.
342. Claudy, *Introduction to Freemasonry*, Vol. II, pp. 89-92.
343. Stephen R. Sywulka, "The Pope Uses Masonic Scandal to Stiffen Traditional Stance," *Christianity Today*, June 26, 1981, p. 38.
344. Knight, *The Brotherhood*, p. 270.
345. Ibid.
346. Ibid., pp. 270-271.
347. Ibid., p. 271, emphasis added.
348. Ibid., p. 273.
349. Ibid., p. 273, cf. p. 277.
350. Ibid., p. 275.
351. Ibid., pp. 273-274.
352. Sywulka, "The Pope Uses Masonic Scandal to Stiffen Traditional Stance," p. 38; Knight, *The Brotherhood*, p. 274.
353. Knight, *The Brotherhood*, p. 4.
354. Ibid., p. 85; cf. pp. 269-77, 298-307.
355. Ibid., pp. 244-245.
356. Ibid., p. 245.
357. Ibid., p. 10.
358. Ibid., p. 11.
359. Ibid., p. 12.
360. Ibid.
361. Cerza, *Let There Be Light*, pp. 29, 55.
362. Committee on Secret Societies, *Christ or the Lodge?* pp. 12-13.
363. Ibid., pp. 12-13; Harris, *Freemasonry*, p. 97.
364. Transcript, "Christianity and the Masonic Lodge: Are They Compatible?" pp. 33-34.

Mormonism

Info at a Glance

Name: The Church of Jesus Christ of Latter-day Saints (Mormon).

Purpose: To evangelize the world with the message of Jesus Christ as interpreted by Joseph Smith and the Mormon church; to baptize the dead for their salvation; for individual members to strive to attain godhood on the basis of personal righteousness and merit.

Founder: Joseph Smith (1805–1844).

Source of authority: Supernatural revelations received by Joseph Smith, Brigham Young and other prophets and presidents.

Revealed teachings: Yes.

Claim: To be the only true church of Jesus Christ on earth.

Occult dynamics: Historically and at present necromantic and spiritistic revelations and other contacts; development of psychic powers interpreted as gifts of the Holy Spirit.

Key literature: Scripture: The Bible, the *Book of Mormon, Doctrine and Covenants, The Pearl of Great Price;* while the revelations of Mormon prophets and presidents are also considered scripture, these are only occasionally added to the canon.

Other authoritative literature: *Journal of Discourses* (26 volumes of writings by leading early Mormon presidents and prophets and other authorities); *Joseph Smith's History of the Church* (7 volumes); Bruce McConkie's *Mormon Doctrine* and *Doctrinal New Testament Commentary* (3 vols.); Joseph Fielding Smith's *Doctrines of Salvation* (3 vols.); *Answers to Gospel Questions* (4 vols.); *Teachings of the Prophet Joseph Smith;* and *Gospel Doctrine;* James Talmage's *Articles of Faith* and *Jesus the Christ;* LeGrand Richards' *A Marvelous Work and a Wonder; Ensign* (periodical) conference addresses; and others.

Attitude toward Christianity: Rejecting.

Quote:

> Convince us of our errors of doctrine, if we have any, by reason, by logical arguments, or by the Word of God, and we will be ever grateful for the information, and you will ever have the pleasing reflection that you have been the instruments in the hands of God of redeeming your fellow beings from the darkness which you may see enveloping their minds. Come, then, let us reason together, and try to discover the true light upon all subjects, connected with our temporal or eternal happiness.[1]

—Apostle Orson Pratt

Note: It should be stressed that any claims by Mormon leaders and writers concerning official Mormon history, early doctrine, apologetics and so on are generally not to be trusted. The Mormon church has engaged in a protracted whitewashing of its early history and doctrines. As a result, most Mormons are unaware that previous divinely inspired teachings may contradict official Mormon doctrine today.

Christians should also be aware that the LDS church has programs specifically designed to reach Christians and convert them to Mormonism. Indeed, there are many Mormons who promote their religion strategically through several popular programs and courses. Two prominent examples are the multimillion dollar bestseller by Stephen Covey, *The Seven Habits for Highly Effective People* (millions have attended courses based on this book) and the Power-Glide Language Courses created by BYU professor Dr. Robert Blair. (On Power-Glide see Richard Stout's articles by Iouda 3 Press, e-mail.IOUDA3@aol.com.)

These individuals are committed Mormons whose venues have had a large impact in Christian circles: "[Covey's] book *The Divine Center* (1982) is about centering one's life in the god of Mormonism and reads like an LDS primer. In fact, it seems to be the basis for *SH [Seven Habits]* as many of the ideas Covey wrote in it in 1982 are included and built upon in the *SH*, published in 1989. . . . Covey's organization, the Franklin Covey Company, claims to have over 19,000 licensed, client facilitators teaching its curriculum to over 750,000 participants annually. Yearly book sales are over 1.5 million with over 15 million individuals using their planner products. Included among these participants and book purchasers are Christians, including business leaders, pastors and denominational leaders."* Bill Gordon with the Southern Baptist Convention's Home Mission Board points out: "Many church and religious organizations are using this program to train ministers and leaders. One of the reasons they find this program attractive is because it gives a prominent place to spirituality in personal growth. However, most of those who take this training are unaware of the specific religious beliefs that are behind many of Covey's principles. Covey has stated these religious beliefs in an earlier book entitled *The Divine Center*. This book contains many of the same principles that are found in *7 Habits*. Many of the anecdotes and illustrations in the two books are also similar. An analysis of *The Divine Center* reveals that Covey's religious beliefs are Mormon. Covey explains in this book that he has discovered how to communicate Mormon truths to non-Mormons by simply changing his vocabulary. He writes, "I have found in speaking to

---

*Bob Waldrep, "The Shifting Paradigms of Stephen Covey," at: www.apologeticsindex.org.

various non-LDS groups in different cultures that we can teach and testify of many gospel [LDS] principles if we are careful in selecting words which carry our meaning but come from their experience and frame of mind" [*Divine Center,* p. 240].*

References to *Enclyopedia of New Age Beliefs:* Altered States of Consciousness, Angel Contact, Astrology, Channeling, Crystal Work, Divination Practices, Dowsing.

DOCTRINAL SUMMARY

God: An exalted physical man; "Elohim" of the Old Testament; a deity "created" (technically, "fashioned") by the sexual union of his divine mother and father. As an infinite number of gods and earths exist, God the Father of Jesus Christ is creator and ruler of this earth only. He is (in early Mormonism) Adam who fell in the Garden of Eden, which was then located, according to Mormonism, in what is now Independence, Missouri.

Jesus: "Jehovah" of the Old Testament (Moroni 10:34 n.); the first begotten spirit child of Elohim ("God the Father"), who "created" (or fashioned) him by physical sexual union with Mary, one of his wives.

Trinity: Mormonism rejects the Christian Trinity for a belief in henotheism, the worship of one principal God (Elohim) among many. Mormonism is also tri-theistic, stressing three primary earth gods, the Father, Son and Holy Ghost, and it is polytheistic, accepting endless additional gods of other worlds.

Holy Ghost: A man with a spiritual body of matter.

Salvation: True salvation in Mormonism is achieved by personal merit and effort with the goal of attaining "exaltation," or godhood, in the highest part of the celestial kingdom. There one may participate in "eternal increase"; that is, as a god one may beget (or fashion) innumerable spirit children just as Elohim has. All other salvation is considered

---

*Bill Gordon, "A Closer Look at Stephen Covey" at www.apologeticsindex.org.

"damnation," which to Mormons does include participation in various degrees of glory. Mormonism is almost universalistic, teaching that all will be saved except a very few "sons of perdition." Some Mormons teach that even these will be saved.

Death: Mormonism teaches that salvation is possible after physical death. Most people apparently go to a "waiting" area and are eventually assigned one of three principal kingdoms where opportunities exist for advancement, possibly to a higher kingdom, at least according to some authorities.

Heaven and Hell: There are three principal kingdoms of heaven. The celestial heaven is the highest, and below it are the terrestrial and telestial heavens. These constitute various "degrees of glory" and privilege. Personal entrance is based upon individual merit in this life, which is itself based upon individual merit in preexistence. In its most important sense, heaven consists only of three departments in the highest, or celestial, kingdom. Further, true salvation (exaltation or godhood) is found only by those worthy to be granted access to the highest part of the celestial kingdom. Hell is not eternal, but a temporal purgatory. The vast majority who go there will, in their punishment, pay the penalty for their sins, be raised after the millennium and inherit a "degree of glory." The only category of persons who apparently inherit literal eternal hell are "the sons of perdition," principally composed of a few apostate Mormons (Mormons who deny their faith) and possibly some adulterers or murderers.

Man: An eternal refashioned spirit intelligence having the innate capacity to evolve into godhood. Men on earth were first created as spirit offspring of Elohim and his wife through physical sexual intercourse. Thus, men are created or fashioned as preexistent spirits and subsequently inhabit the products of human sexual intercourse (a physical body) in order to attempt to gain exaltation or godhood.

Sin: Mormonism holds a less than biblically orthodox view of sin in that its scriptural content is downplayed in some way. First, the Mormon concept of works-salvation teaches that good works cancel the penalty of sin. Second, its teachings give the Fall a positive role in fostering spiritual growth and maturity.

Satan and demons: Satan is one of the innumerable preexistent spirits created by Elohim and his wife; hence the spirit brother of all men and women, including Christ Himself. Because of his primeval rebellion, he was not permitted to inherit a body as the rest of his brothers and sisters. In essence, Satan and demons once represented potential men and women but are now consigned to live as spirits forever.

The Second Coming of Christ: Mormons speak of the Second Coming of the earth god Jesus, but they have also referred to the Second Coming of the god Joseph Smith (*Journal of Discourses*, 7:289; 5:19).

The Fall: Ultimately beneficial; predestined by Elohim for the spiritual progress and ultimate welfare of all mankind.

The Bible: The Word of God as long as it is translated correctly. Wherever it disagrees with Mormon theology, it is considered incorrect due to textual corruption or false translation or interpretation.

Note: This chapter was reorganized, condensed and updated from the authors' 500-page *Behind the Mask of Mormonism* (Harvest House, 1996). Readers seeking additional information or documentation on Mormonism are encouraged to consult this book. The chapter here has been kept brief so that a series of appendices could be included. We encourage reading this material, which critiques Mormon apologetics, revisionism and its attempts to influence evangelicalism.

INFLUENCE AND BEGINNINGS

The need for this chapter arises from particular claims made by the Mormon church that cause widespread confusion concerning the nature of Mormonism. For instance, Mormonism claims to represent true Christianity and to believe in the biblical God. It teaches that it trusts in the true Jesus Christ and that He alone is the atoning savior who died for the sins of the world. Mormonism emphasizes that it depends on salvation by grace and that it places full confidence in the Bible as the authoritative Word of God, including its teaching concerning heaven and hell. But none of these claims are true, as we will document. We hope to clear up this confusion on two fronts: 1) by showing that even though Mormon literature frequently uses biblical and Christian terms, they are given entirely different meanings; 2) by giving Mormons themselves, who are often uninformed about it, a sampling of their religion's true history and teachings.

This may be hard to swallow because in the minds of many people Mormonism has a good clean reputation and is often thought to be a respectable Christian religion. This is partly because in recent years the Church of Jesus Christ of Latter-day Saints (Mormon) has initiated a powerful campaign to influence millions of people with its message, including evangelical churches. Sophisticated magazine, newspaper and television ads have reached tens of millions of people with the claims of Mormonism. Multiple full-page newspaper inserts proclaim, "We believe the New Testament Scriptures are true and that they testify that Jesus is indeed the Promised Messiah and Savior of the world." Headlines blare, "Mormons believe Jesus Christ is Lord and Savior" and "Mormons testify Jesus is the Christ."

These advertisements have also been placed in *Reader's Digest* (March 1990) and *TV Guide* (December 9, 1990), and they include an 800 number that respondents could call to receive a free copy of the Bible and the *Book of Mormon*, which is boldly advertised as "another testament of Jesus Christ." (Almost 100,000,000 million copies of the *Book of Mormon* have been published since 1830, according to the LDS website.)

The success of these ads is evident. In 1989 almost 260,000 requests for a free *Book of Mormon* were received, and 86,000 of those responding wanted missionaries to make a personal visit. In addition, 40 percent of the respondents said they "believed the book was the Word of God" and that "they had a special feeling about it."[2] By the late 1990s, these television campaigns sometimes ran twice during an hour program.

Direct advertising is not the only way the Mormon church seeks converts. Its methods of proselytizing are as varied as its corporate holdings. For example, the church takes advantage of the fact that every year millions of people visit Hawaii:

> Mormons own a substantial portion of Hawaii [including] the major financial institutions of this area. When you go to the [Mormon sponsored] Polynesian Culture Center they offer you a tour to [visit] their Temple. . . . Soon after you return from your visit . . . you will receive a knock from a Mormon missionary asking how you enjoyed your visit and whether you would like to know more about the Church. The Mormons have many other ways of recruiting members: through door-to-door missionaries, visitor centers, the thousands of church sponsored Boy Scout troops and educational institutions, and . . . the Marriott Hotel chain which places Mormon literature in every room.[3]

The power of Mormonism also stems from the fact that it is perhaps the largest, most influential and missionary minded of the various unconventional religions of the United States. The church maintains some 65,000–70,000 missionaries (LDS website), who engage in proselytizing activities around the world, and its current membership of ten million is expected to double in the next ten years. Some have estimated that in less than two generations Mormon membership will reach nearly a quarter billion. Moreover, the church maintains financial assets valued at billions of dollars, a testimony to the power of faithful tithing by members. In 1991, *Time* magazine reported, "In business terms, the Church is an $8 billion-a-year conglomerate that employs about 10,000 people."[4] This makes it one of the wealthiest churches per capita in the entire world. Not unexpectedly, many of the lay leaders within the Mormon church are businessmen who help the church oversee a vast and growing worldwide financial empire. For example, the church owns real estate management and trust holding firms which alone have assets of two billion dollars. In addition, it owns

or has owned five insurance companies, a newspaper, two television stations, a chain of bookstores, a shopping mall, eleven radio stations, hundreds of thousands of acres of farmland, one of the nation's largest private television networks and most of Salt Lake City's tallest skyscrapers.[5] (Compare the extensive report in *The Arizona Republic*, June 30, 1991.)

The church is also a large stockholder in Utah Power and Light Company, with assets of over one billion dollars. The Mormon empire runs several colleges, such as Brigham Young University (with 60 language departments and an enrollment of over 30,000), plus other schools, factories and businesses. According to the late Dr. Walter Martin, the church owns Bonneville International Corporation, Zion's Securities Corporation and Deseret Ranches of Florida, some 315,000 acres near Disney World, which are worth at least a billion dollars.[6] According to "The God Makers," a critical film on Mormonism:

> The Mormon Church is the second largest financial institution west of the Mississippi River. The Mormon Church wields economic power more effectively than any other organized religion in the world. They own the $2.6 million Beneficial Life Insurance Company, The Deseret Management and Trust Corp., hospitals, schools, apartment buildings, farms. They are a major stockholder in the *LA Times*. They own TV and radio stations (and) the ZCMI Department Store chain. They have vast land holdings with ownerships in all 50 American states, throughout Canada and Europe and on every continent. Two thirds of their properties are tax exempt.[7]

Mormons tend to view financial prosperity as a sign of God's blessing (cf. Alma 1:29; 4 Nephi 1:23). Their corporate wealth confirms their belief that Mormonism is wealthy because it is pleasing to God, and tithing is a principle means of church income. According to Mormon doctrine, tithing is a law of God commanded upon the people. *Doctrine and Covenants* (*D&C*) 119:3, 4 calls it a "standing law . . . forever." A devoted former church member estimates that many Mormons "will be paying 20%–25% of their gross income to the Church."[8] Wealthy Mormon celebrities and business executives also tend to tithe generously. For example, the Osmond and Marriott families are two large contributors to the Mormon empire.[9]

In state[10] and national[11] politics, Mormons have retained more than their share of influence. Richard Beal, one of the most powerful men in the Reagan administration, was a Mormon.[12] Mormons have headed the following posts and departments: Assistant Attorney General, head of the National Security Council, Secretary of Agriculture, Treasurer of the United States, the United States Department of Commerce, the Department of Interior, the Federal Communications Commission, the Department of Housing and Urban Development, the Federal Research Board, the Securities and Exchange Commission and various state government posts.[13] Mormons also head or have headed Walt Disney Productions, Save-On Drugs, Max Factor, Standard Oil and many other conglomerates.[14]

The Mormon church is also the single largest sponsor of Boy Scout units in the United States (seventeen thousand), and Mormon officials have admitted this is an effective manner in which to share the faith.[15] For example, former Secretary of Agriculture in the Eisenhower administration and the former Mormon prophet and president, Ezra Taft Benson, commented·

Scouting is Church work. It is part of the (Mormon) Church program.[16]

I have been deeply impressed with the record that has been made by the Church. . . . In no other field do we have a better reputation than in the field of Scouting. . . . We have . . . a higher proportion of Scout troops sponsored by the Church than any other church or civic organization in the world. . . . [And] we have the highest enrollment of boys in Scouting of any church on the earth.[17]

Religious emphasis is a part of Scouting. . . . Scouting helps prepare boys for [Mormon] Church responsibility. . . . We want these boys to become better men and boys and honor their [Mormon] priesthood and to be faithful members of the [Mormon] Church and kingdom of God.[18]

Thus the positive image of Mormonism is undergirded by many factors: their scouting leadership, their financial reputation, their moral emphasis and their Christian appearance. All this is why even many Christians think that the Mormon church is a Christian organization and that individual Mormons are Christians.

In fact, the Mormon church's successful portrayal of itself as Christian explains why there are apparently more converts to Mormonism from Christian churches than there are official defections from Mormonism. According to the *Mormon Church Almanac,* seventy-five percent of newly baptized Mormons each year are converts from Protestant churches. As one Mormon magazine noted: "Far more persons convert to the Mormon Church from other churches or from a status of no religious affiliation than leave."[19] The report cited a 1990 study published by Mormons Howard M. Bahr and David Hunt relying on NORC General Social Survey data from 1972–1988 and the University of Wisconsin National Survey of Families and Households, 1987–1988. This study also indicated that the conversion rates from various Christian denominations to Mormonism were proportionately similar. However, Jewish, Catholic, Baptist and Christian Reformed churches had somewhat lower conversion rates than several evangelical and fundamentalist denominations and some mainline denominations (Presbyterian, Episcopal, Christian and United Churches of Christ, among others). Studies also indicated that among leading world religions, Mormonism has the fourth highest retention rate: Islam (92 percent), Jewish (88 percent), Catholic (83.5 percent), Mormon (82 percent).[20] But such studies do not give us the whole picture.

Even though global membership of the Mormon church has climbed more than sevenfold since 1947, making it the fifth or sixth largest religious denomination in America, not all is well with Mormonism. For example, according to the *Los Angeles Times,* several analysts familiar with the Mormon church have stated that at least forty percent of Mormons are inactive and that many of these are disillusioned.[21] But if even thirty percent of Mormons are inactive or disillusioned, the Mormon empire could face some serious future problems.

Joseph Smith

How did Mormonism begin? The official version is recorded in the Mormon scripture *The Pearl of Great Price* (1851). By this account, the seeds of Mormonism were sown in Joseph Smith, Mormonism's founder, during a powerful divine visitation. This encounter is known as the "first vision." Allegedly, God the Father and Jesus Christ appeared to Smith as part of their plan to begin the Mormon religion and reestablish "true Christianity." This "first vision" episode is crucial to the claims of the Mormon religion.

Joseph Smith claimed that in his fifteenth year (1820), while living in Manchester, New York, a religious revival of significant proportions took place and "great multitudes united themselves to the different religious parties."[22] However, Smith alleges that the doctrinal strife among these religious parties was so great as to confuse a person entirely: with such conflicting claims, how could anyone determine which religion was correct—Presbyterians, Methodists, Baptists or any other denomination? Furthermore, according to Smith, the teachers of the various denominations allegedly "understood the same passage of Scripture so differently as to destroy all confidence in settling the question [of which group to join] by an appeal to the Bible." Because of his confusion, Smith determined to seek God's counsel as to which of the various denominations was true, so that he might know which church he should join. As he explains it, James 1:5, which refers to asking God for wisdom, had a crucial impact at this juncture. In Smith's own words:

> Never did any passage of Scripture come with more power to the heart of man than this did at this time to mine. It seemed to enter with great force into every feeling of my heart. I reflected on it again and again, knowing that if any person needed wisdom from God, I did; for how to act I did not know and unless I could get more wisdom than I then had, I would never know.[23]

He concluded that either he must "remain in darkness and confusion" or "do as James directs, that is, ask of God."[24] In his attempt to seek God, the teenage Joseph Smith retired to a secluded place in the woods in order to pray. He notes that it was on the morning of a "beautiful, clear day, early in the spring of 1820."[25] After finding an appropriate spot, Smith reports that he "kneeled down and began to offer up the desires of my heart to God." But what Smith encountered terrified him:

> I had scarcely done so, when immediately I was seized upon by some power which entirely overcame me, and had such an astonishing influence over me as to bind my tongue so that I could not speak. Thick darkness gathered around me, and it seemed to me for a time as if I were doomed to sudden destruction.[26]

Smith then describes how, fearing immediate death, he called upon God for deliverance:

> But, exerting all my powers to call upon God to deliver me out of the power of this enemy which had seized upon me, and at the very moment which I was ready to sink into despair and abandon myself to destruction—not to an imaginary ruin, but to the power of some actual being from the unseen world, who had such marvelous power as I had never before felt in any being—just at this moment of great alarm, I saw a pillar of light exactly over my head, above the brightness of the sun, which descended gradually until it fell upon me.[27]

Having felt the panic of imminent destruction, Smith was amazed to find himself delivered:

> It no sooner appeared when I found myself delivered from the enemy which held me bound. When the light rested upon me I saw two personages, whose brightness and glory defy all description, standing above me in the air. One of them spake unto me, calling me by name, and said—pointing to the other—"THIS IS MY BELOVED SON, HEAR HIM."[28]

At this point, the claims of Joseph Smith are clear. Having called on God for help, he has been immediately delivered by nothing less than the astonishing appearance of God the Father and His Son Jesus Christ. At this juncture, Smith collected his senses and recalled his mission:

> My object in going to inquire of the Lord was to know which of all the sects was right, that I

might know which to join. No sooner, therefore, did I get possession of myself, so as to be able to speak, than I asked the personages who stood above me in the light, which of all the sects was right—and which I should join.[29]

Smith was answered immediately. In fact, to answer the question of "How did Mormonism begin?" we only need read the reply that the two supernatural personages supplied to Joseph Smith's question. According to Joseph Smith, God the Father and God the Son said:

I must join none of them, for they were all wrong, and the Personage who addressed me [God the Father] said that all their creeds were an abomination in his sight: that those professors [of Christian religion] were all corrupt; that "they draw near to me with their lips, but their hearts are far from me, they teach for doctrines the commandments of men, having a form of godliness, but they deny the power thereof."

He [God the Father] again forbade me to join with any of them; and many other things did he say unto me, which I can not write at this time. When I came to myself again [fully regained his senses], I found myself lying on my back, looking up into heaven. When the light had departed, I had no strength; but soon recovering it in some degree, I went home.[30]

Joseph Smith had found his answer. He was convinced that God had appeared to him to inform him that Christianity was a false religion. He recalls, "My mind [was] satisfied so far as the sectarian [Christian] world was concerned . . . [It] was not my duty to join with any of them, but to continue as I was until further directed."[31] Smith became persuaded that, out of all the men in the world, he had been uniquely called of God. Although he admits that he "frequently fell into many foolish errors," he waited patiently until the next revelation.[32]

Three years later, on September 21, 1823, Smith experienced the first of several major necromantic encounters (contacts with the dead). A spirit appeared to Smith to tell him the location of certain "gold plates." These gold plates contained the purported historical records of the Jewish "Nephite" peoples concerning their early migration to the Americas. In his *History of*

the Church, Smith records the visit by this spirit, who identified itself as "Moroni" (the son of a "Nephite" historian named Mormon, the alleged author of the "gold plates" from which the Book of Mormon was "translated"):

While I was thus in the act of calling upon God, I discovered a light appearing in my room, which continued to increase until the room was lighter than at noonday, when immediately a [spirit] personage appeared at my bed side, standing in the air. . . . He called me by name, and said unto me that he was a messenger sent from the presence of God to me and that his name was Moroni; that God had a work for me to do. . . . He said there was a book deposited, written upon gold plates, giving an account of the former inhabitants of this [American] continent, and the sources from whence they sprang. He also said that the fullness of the everlasting Gospel was contained in it, as delivered by the Savior [Jesus] to the ancient inhabitants [of America]; also that there were two stones in silver bows—and these stones, fastened to a breastplate, constituted what is called the Urim and Thummim—deposited with the plates; and the possession and use of these stones were what constituted [the category of] "seers" in ancient or former times; and that God had prepared them for the purpose of translating the book.[33]

In addition, the spirit quoted numerous passages of prophetic scripture, either implying or stating that some of them were about to be fulfilled. The spirit then departed, although it soon reappeared twice to state the same message.[34] These and other necromantic contacts were probably the result of Joseph Smith's use of magic ritual to invoke the spirit world (see "The Occult" section). The specific nature of the encounters frequently fit the pattern for magical occult contacts.

Further supernatural encounters continued to influence the young Joseph Smith profoundly. The next day, the seventeen-year-old lad was crossing a field when suddenly his strength entirely failed him: "I fell helpless on the ground, and for a time was unconscious of anything."[35] The first thing Smith remembered was hearing the same spirit calling his name. Regaining his senses, he was commanded to go and locate the "gold plates" buried in a certain hill named

Cumorah. After that, according to the spirit, he was to return yearly to that same spot for further instructions and teaching, and in the fourth year (in 1827) the translation of the "gold plates" would be permitted. By 1829 the translation was completed, and in 1830 the *Book of Mormon* was published. Named after its author, the Nephite historian Mormon, it became one of the three scriptures unique to the Mormon faith.

BOOK OF MORMON: DIVINE REVELATION?

Even though Mormon prophets and leaders have always stressed the divine authority of the *Book of Mormon,* and therefore that it could withstand any and all critical scrutiny, many theologians and scholars over the years have shown the falsity of the claim. Here we will briefly highlight just several of the many facts that disqualify the *Book of Mormon* for any serious consideration of revelation from God. A full discussion can be found in our book *Behind the Mask of Mormonism* (Harvest House, 1996).

Psychic Method of Writing

Even though the Mormon church claims that Joseph Smith translated the alleged gold plates (containing the alleged historical records of the "Nephites" and "Lamanites") by the power of God using divine implements called the Urim and Thummim,* the *Book of Mormon* was actually produced through psychic methods and has nothing to do with ancient history. It is merely a product of nineteenth-century occultism.

---

*In the *Book of Mormon* Introduction—testimony of Joseph Smith—the Urim and Thummim are described as two stones in silver bows fastened to a breastplate. We do not know exactly what the Old Testament Urim and Thummim were. Nevertheless: 1) they were restricted in usage to the high priest; 2) the God of the Bible only rarely "spoke" through them to reveal his will; and 3) apparently they were two separate objects, not a single stone, which is what Smith used. Thus, in each category Mormon claims are refuted. Whatever Smith used, it was not the biblical Urim and Thummim (Exodus 28:30; Numbers 27:21). Joseph Smith was not an Old Testament high priest who used these implements to reveal God's will. He used an occult seer stone to divine the "translation" of a "text" that denies God's Word (cf. Mosiah 28 preface and verse 13).

Historical documents prove that when Smith translated the *Book of Mormon* he was only engaging in his usual practice of crystal gazing. The testimonies of David Whitmer (one of the three key "witnesses" to the *Book of Mormon),* Emma Smith (one of Joseph Smith's wives and scribes) and William Smith (Joseph's brother) make this clear.

In 1877, Whitmer confessed that the alleged "Egyptian" characters on the gold plates (Nephi 1:2) and their English interpretation appeared to Joseph Smith while using his seer stone with his face buried inside a hat:

> I will now give you a description of the manner in which the *Book of Mormon* was translated. Joseph Smith would put the seer stone into a hat, and put his face in the hat, drawing it closely around his face to exclude the light; and in the darkness the spiritual light would shine. A piece of something resembling parchment would appear, and on that appeared the writing. One character at a time would appear, and under it was the interpretation in English. Brother Joseph would read off the English to Oliver Crowdery, who was his principal scribe, and when it was written down and repeated to Brother Joseph to see if it was correct, then it would disappear, and another character with the interpretation would appear. Thus the *Book of Mormon* was translated. . . .[36]

Emma Smith revealed the same occult method. "In writing for your father, I frequently wrote day after day. . . . He sitting with his face buried in his hat, with the stone in it, and dictating hour after hour with nothing between us."[37] Clearly, the *Book of Mormon* was produced through a form of crystal gazing. Testimonies such as these (and others)[38] have brought even some Mormons who reject the idea to at least concede its possibility. The tenth president and prophet, Joseph Fielding Smith, confessed in his *Doctrines of Salvation* (Vol. 3, p. 225) that "it may have been so."

Human Sources

The Mormon church believes that the *Book of Mormon* is an account of ancient writings first inscribed on gold plates at least fifteen hundred years ago that chronicled the history of the so-called "Nephite" and "Lamanite" peoples, who spanned a period from 600 B.C.–A.D. 421. The *Book of Mormon* therefore claims to be a translation of ancient historical records that date long before Joseph Smith lived, and Mormons maintain that apart from divine revelation it would have been impossible for Joseph Smith to have done this translation. Thus they consider this a great proof of its heavenly derivation. Mormons, however, rarely consider the other possibilities that explain the origin of the *Book of Mormon* far better; for example, that it could have been a combination of Smith's natural talent and spiritistic revelation from crystal gazing. Concerning the former, there are several possible human sources for the *Book of Mormon*.

Fawn Brodie, who was excommunicated from the Mormon church for her scholarly critical study on Joseph Smith, *No Man Knows My History: The Life of Joseph Smith,*[39] cites persuasive evidence for the likelihood of a nineteenth-century origin of the *Book of Mormon*. For example, how likely is it that Jewish writers between 600 B.C.–A.D. 421 would discuss the social and religious issues common to nineteenth-century Christian America?

Any theory of the origin of the *Book of Mormon* that spotlights the prophet [alone] and blacks out the stage on which he performed is certain to be a distortion.

[For example, in] the speeches of the Nephi prophets one may find [discussions of] the religious conflicts that were splitting the churches in the 1820's. Alexander Campbell, founder of the Disciples of Christ, wrote in the first able review of the *Book of Mormon:* "This prophet Smith, through his stone spectacles, wrote on the plates of Nephi, in his *Book of Mormon,* every error and almost every truth discussed in New York for the last ten years. He decided all the great [religious] controversies . . . [and even the questions of] Freemasonry, Republican government and the rights of man. But he is better skilled in the controversies in New York than in the geography or history of Judea. He makes John baptize in the village of Bethabara and says Jesus was born in Jerusalem."

The theology of the *Book of Mormon,* like its anthropology, was only a potpourri. . . . Always an eclectic, Joseph never exhausted any theory he had appropriated. He seized a fragment here

and another there and of the odd assortment built his history.[40]

In his study *A Parallel, The Basis of the Book of Mormon,* Hal Hougey observes a number of striking similarities between the *Book of Mormon* and Ethan Smith's 1823 text *View of the Hebrews,* a book that was available to Joseph Smith.[41] Parallels between the *Book of Mormon* and *View of the Hebrews* were sufficient enough to prompt no less an authority than Mormon historian B. H. Roberts to study the issue. He concluded that it was possible for Smith alone to have written the *Book of Mormon.*[42]

The language of the King James Bible is also enlightening. According to Dr. Anthony Hoekema, some 27,000 words taken from the King James Bible appear in the *Book of Mormon.* Anyone who compares the following list, which carries just several examples, will see that Smith copied material from the King James Bible:

> 1 Nephi chapters 20,21—Isaiah chapters 48, 49
> 2 Nephi chapters 7,8—Isaiah chapters 50, 51
> 2 Nephi chapters 12,24—Isaiah chapters 2–14
> Mosiah chapter 14—Isaiah chapter 53
> 3 Nephi chapters 12,14—Matthew chapters 5–7
> 3 Nephi chapter 22—Isaiah chapter 54
> 3 Nephi chapters 24,25—Malachi chapters 3,4
> Moroni chapter 10—1 Corinthians 12:1–11.[43]

Jerald and Sandra Tanner, who have done massive amounts of research on Mormonism, have also supplied evidence for other sources for the creation of the *Book of Mormon,* including: Josiah Priest's *The Wonders of Nature and Providence Displayed* (Albany, NY: 1825); *The Wayne Sentinel; The Apocrypha,* a dream of Joseph Smith's father and *The Westminster Confession and Catechism.* All this indicates that the *Book of Mormon* could not have been a translation of ancient records. What then is the real source of the *Book of Mormon?* The most appropriate answer is that it combines human sources from other books and spiritistic revelation through Smith's use of the seer stone.

Archaeology and the Book

If the *Book of Mormon* were truly an historical record of ancient peoples inhabiting a vast civilization, it is probable that at least some archaeological data would confirm the civilization, just as it has confirmed, in varying degrees, biblical and other ancient histories. The *Book of Mormon* claims to represent the history of three different groups of people, all of whom allegedly migrated from the Near East to Central and South America. Two of the groups supposedly traveled as far north as Mexico and North America (the *Book of Mormon*, Ether and 1 Nephi).* The Nephites and Lamanites are said to have been Semitic, with the most important group being led by Lehi of Jerusalem. His descendants became the Nephites. The main history of the *Book of Mormon* concerns the Nephites.

But not a shred of archaeological evidence exists to support that any of this is history, despite many vigorous archaeological excavations financed by the Mormon church. This has forced any number of non-Mormon researchers to conclude that the *Book of Mormon* is primarily myth and historical invention. Dr. Walter Martin refers to "the hundreds of areas where this book defies reason or common sense."[45] Both the prestigious National Geographic Society and the Bureau of American Ethnology of the Smithsonian Institute have issued official statements denying Mormon claims, and the Tanners' book *Archaeology and the Book of Mormon*, and other works, show that archaeological confirmation claimed by the Mormon church is untrustworthy.[46] Dr. Gordon Fraser, observing that Mormons still accept their book as history, asserts that it in no way corresponds to the known facts of the ancient Americas.[47]

Nevertheless, Mormon apologists and lay writers alike claim that archaeology proves that the *Book of Mormon* is true. In fact, this is a standard argument frequently used by Mormon missionaries around the world in their attempts to convert people. As Hal Hougey observes in *Ar-*

*Although the traditional view is that the *Book of Mormon* story covers North and South America, some modern Brigham Young University academicians, apparently attempting to coordinate *Book of Mormon* claims and geography with existing data back pedal and accept a more limited geography.[44] (They believe, for example, that the Cumorah in New York was really in Southern Mexico.)

chaeology and the Book of Mormon, most Mormons think that archaeology is on their side. "The numerous books and articles by Latter-day Saints over the years have shown that Mormons believe that the fruits of archaeological research may properly be applied to verify the *Book of Mormon*. Dr. Ross T. Christensen, a Mormon anthropologist, agrees: "If the book's history is fallacious, its doctrine cannot be genuine. . . . I am fully confident that the nature of the Book is such that a definitive archaeological test can be applied to it."[48] But definitive archaeological tests have already been applied, and they have discredited the *Book of Mormon* as history. Mormon authority Gordon Fraser correctly observes the *Book of Mormon's* fictitious nature:

Mormon archaeologists have been trying for years to establish some evidence that will confirm the presence of the [Mormon] church in America. There is still not a scintilla of evidence, either in the religious philosophy of the ancient writings or in the presence of artifacts, that could lead to such a belief.

The whole array of anachronisms [historical errors] in the book stamps it as written by someone who knew nothing about ancient America and presumed that no one ever would know. It is total fiction, done by one who assumed that cultures in ancient America would probably be about the same as those of our own north eastern states in the 19th Century. While certain Mormon apologists are pledged to the task of defending the credibility of the *Book of Mormon*, because the church demands it, some professors at Brigham Young University are demanding caution concerning claims that the ruins of old temples and other artifacts found in Mexico and Central America are positive evidence of the claims of the *Book of Mormon*.

The problem has become a sticky one for Mormon scholars who would like to be investigators in depth but are forbidden by their church authorities.[49]

Lack of Manuscript Evidence

Another problem with Mormon claims about ancient Nephite history is the lack of ancient manuscript evidence. Because of their perceived importance, the religious scriptures of most ancient peoples have been preserved, despite the sometimes incredible odds against it. Occasionally, the preservation is almost perfect, and the Bible of the Jews and the New Testament of the Christians are unique in this regard.[50] Even with the Koran of the Muslims and with Hindu and Buddhist scriptures some evidence exists to determine a religious document's genuineness. For example, sufficient extant manuscript evidence may exist to prove that a document is as old as its proponents claim it to be.

This is not true for the *Book of Mormon*. While the manuscript evidence for the Bible is rich and abundant, for the Mormon scriptures it is nonexistent.[51] There is no textual evidence for either an ancient *Book of Mormon* or for any of Smith's other alleged ancient records. Is there a single ancient manuscript? Is there even a portion of one, or even one fragment of a page? No. There is none of this. Can the "gold plates" from which Smith allegedly translated the *Book of Mormon* be produced? Were these ancient records ever cited by another writer? No. There is none of this either:

As far as historical and manuscript evidence is concerned, Joseph Smith's scriptures have absolutely no foundation. The "records of the Nephites," for instance, were never cited by any ancient writer, nor are there any known manuscripts or even fragments of manuscripts in existence older than the ones dictated by Joseph Smith in the late 1820's. Joseph Smith's "Book of Moses" is likewise without documentary support. The only handwritten manuscripts for the "Book of Moses" are those dictated by Joseph Smith in the early 1830's. The "Book of Abraham" purports to be a translation of an ancient Egyptian papyrus. However, the original papyrus is in reality the Egyptian "Book of Breathings" and has nothing to do with Abraham or his religion. Therefore, we have no evidence for the "Book of Abraham" prior to the handwritten manuscripts dictated by Joseph Smith in the 1830's. It would appear, then, that there is no documentary evidence for any of Joseph Smith's works that date back prior to the late 1820's.[52]

Lack of Mormon Doctrines

A further point, briefly made here, but which should be of particular interest to many Mor-

mons, is that Mormon teachings are not principally derived from the *Book of Mormon*. Mormon doctrine is derived primarily from another Mormon scripture, *Doctrine and Covenants*. Thus, ". . . doctrinally the *Book of Mormon* is a dead book for most Mormons. . . . The *Book of Mormon* teachings have little bearing upon current Mormon doctrine."[53]

The dilemma that this poses for the Mormon church is a serious one because *D&C* emphasizes that the *Book of Mormon* contains basic, or fundamental, Mormon teachings. For example, according to *D&C*, the *Book of Mormon* contains "the truth and the Word of God" (*D&C*, 19:26); "the fullness of the gospel of Jesus Christ" (that is, Mormon teachings, *D&C*, 20:9); and "the *fullness* of the *everlasting* gospel" (*D&C*, 135:3). *Doctrine and Covenants* also has Jesus claiming that the *Book of Mormon* has "the principles of my gospel" (*D&C*, 42:12) and "*all things written* concerning the foundation of my church, my gospel, and my rock" (*D&C*, 18:4, cf. 17:1–6; emphasis added; see also *Book of Mormon*, Introduction).

According to *Doctrine and Covenants*, then, the *Book of Mormon* must contain at the very least most of the central doctrines of Mormon faith. But the *Book of Mormon* contains few major Mormon teachings. It does not teach any of the following central Mormon principles, which form the foundation of the Mormon church and its "gospel": polytheism; God as the product of an eternal progression; eternal marriage; polygamy; human deification; the Trinity as three separate Gods; baptism for the dead; maintaining genealogical records; universalism; God has a physical body and was once a man; God organized, not created, the world; mother gods (heavenly mothers); temple marriage as a requirement for exaltation; the concept of eternal intelligences; three degrees of heavenly glory (telestial, terrestrial, celestial); salvation after death in the spirit world; a New Testament era of Mormon organizational offices and functions such as the Melchizedek and Aaronic priesthoods; stake president and first presidency.[54]

All this is why some Mormon writers have noted the theological irrelevance of the *Book of Mormon* to Mormonism. For example, John H.

Evans observed "how little the whole body of belief of the Latter-day Saints really depends on the revelation of the Nephite record [the *Book of Mormon*]."[55]

Given the vast amounts of scholarly research that is similar to and affirms our brief survey of the *Book of Mormon,* all the evidence points to the unavoidable conclusion that the *Book of Mormon* is really a piece of nineteenth-century fiction. Whatever else it is, it cannot be a divine revelation. Writing in "The Centennial of Mormonism" in *American Mercury,* Bernard De Voto described it as "a yeasty fermentation, formless, aimless and inconceivably absurd."[56] All this is why Mormon leaders tell potential converts to ignore criticism of the *Book of Mormon* and rely entirely upon subjective (completely personal) "confirmation." Nevertheless, the church's appeal to subjectivity does nothing to convince a rational person why he or she should believe in the *Book of Mormon.* To believe without any evidence is troublesome enough; to believe in spite of the evidence is folly.

TEACHINGS AND PROPHECIES

Contradictions in Mormon Doctrine

We receive continuing guidance from inspired leaders chosen by the Lord. Through these leaders, the Lord speaks to us and ensures that the true gospel of Jesus Christ is taught.

—*Membership in the Kingdom,*
Discussion 6, 8

Mormons claim that they have additional scripture as well as "Latter-day prophets" to help them correctly understand "doctrines that have confused apostate Christianity for centuries."[57] The late president and prophet of the Mormon church, Ezra Taft Benson, emphasized that "the [Mormon] gospel encompasses all truth; it is consistent, without conflict, eternal."[58] Mormon scholar Hugh Nibley states: "Of all churches in the world only this one has not found it necessary to readjust any part of doctrine in the last hundred years."[59] Mormons repeatedly claim that their scriptures are not contradictory.[60] Why then, when early and modern Mormon teachings are compared, does one discover clear doctrinal contradictions on many key issues? Rather than affirm existing doctrines, the "inspired leaders" are involved in quite a different task. They have had "to go back and rework, rewrite, cover-up, change, delete and add [material throughout] all of their books—their histories, their Scriptures. They [also] suppress their diaries because these things show the confusion and the man-made nature of their theology and religion."[61]

Because Mormon theology is replete with contradictions, the church has attempted to suppress information that it has found embarrassing. This includes the Reorganized Church.[62] Church leaders have apparently felt that this approach was justified for at least two reasons. One is that the real Joseph Smith is not a person that the church desires to present to the world, hence suppression of true biographical data is necessary. The other is that modern Mormonism rejects many of its earlier prophets' divinely revealed teachings, and its earlier prophets would reject many of the teachings now approved by church leadership.

In the charts on the following pages we provide just a fraction of the many verbatim contradictions found within Mormon doctrines.

The modern Mormon has no logical solution to the problems that such changes in doctrine represent, and the response of church leadership has been to suppress information surrounding the contradictions.

Contradictions to the Bible's Teachings

A more serious problem is the clear contradiction of Mormon doctrine to that of the Bible. Hundreds of contrasts could be given. The "Contradictions Between Mormon Doctrine and Biblical Truth" chart lists several.

Prophetic Record

The only way of ascertaining a true prophet is to compare his prophecies with the ancient Word of God, and see if they agree, and if they do and come to pass, then certainly he is a true prophet. . . . When, therefore any man, *no matter who,* or how high his standing may be, utters, or publishes, anything that afterwards proves to be untrue, *he is a false prophet.*[63]

—Joseph Smith

Verbatim Contradictions in Mormon Doctrine

THE DOCTRINE OF POLYGAMY	
Plural marriage is not essential to salvation or exaltation (McConkie, *Mormon Doctrine*, 578).	For behold, I reveal unto you a new and everlasting covenant; and if ye abide not [in] that covenant, then are ye damned; for no one can reject this covenant and be permitted to enter into my glory (*D&C*, 132:4).
Now Zeezrom said: Is there more than one God? And he answered, No (*Book of Mormon*, Alma 11:28, 29).	There are three Gods—the Father, the Son, and the Holy Ghost (McConkie, *Mormon Doctrine*, 317).
ADAM IN THE GARDEN	
The *Book of Mormon*, the Bible, *Doctrine and Covenants*, and *The Pearl of Great Price* all declare that Adam's body was created from the dust of the ground, that is, from the dust of this ground, this earth (Joseph Fielding Smith, *Doctrines of Salvation*, 1:90).	Adam was made from the dust of an earth, but not from the dust of this earth (Brigham Young, *Journal of Discourses*, 3:319).
When our father Adam came into the Garden of Eden, he came into it with a celestial body (Brigham Young, *Journal of Discourses*, 1:50).	We hear a lot of people talk about Adam passing through mortality and the resurrection on another earth and then coming here to live and die again. Well, that is a contradiction of the word of the Lord, for a resurrected being does not die. . . . Adam had not passed through a resurrection when he was in the Garden of Eden (Joseph Fielding Smith, *Doctrines of Salvation*, 1:91).
THE OMNISCIENCE AND OMNIPOTENCE OF GOD	
Each of these personal Gods has equal knowledge with all the rest. . . . None of these Gods are progressing in knowledge: neither can they progress in the acquirement of any truth. . . . Some have gone so far as to say that all the Gods were progressing in truth, and would continue to progress to all eternity . . . but let us examine, for a moment, the absurdity of such a conjecture (Pratt, *The Seer*, Aug. 1853, 117).	We might ask, when shall we cease to learn? I will give you my opinion about it; never never . . . both in time and eternity (Brigham Young, *Journal of Discourses*, 3:203). God is not progressing in knowledge (McConkie, *Mormon Doctrine*, 1966, 239).
Do not . . . say that he cannot learn anymore . . . (Brigham Young, *Deseret Weekly News*, 22:309).	[God has] knowledge of all things . . . (Joseph Smith, *Lectures on Faith*, 44, cited in McConkie, *Mormon Doctrine*, 545).
[The teaching that] God is progressing or increasing in any of these attributes, [knowledge, faith, power, justice, judgment, mercy, truth is] false heresy (McConkie, *Mormon Doctrine*, 263).	God . . . is not advancing in knowledge. . . . He is increasing in power (Joseph Fielding Smith, as cited in Joseph W. Musser, *Michael Our Father and Our God*, 27, emphasis added).

(continues)

Verbatim Contradictions, cont.

THE FALL OF MAN	
That old serpent that did beguile our first parents, which was the cause of their fall; which was the cause of all mankind becoming carnal, sensual, devilish, knowing evil from good, subjecting themselves to the devil. Thus all mankind were lost (*Book of Mormon*, Mosiah 16:3, 4).	In the true gospel of Jesus Christ there is no original sin (John Widstoe, *Evidences and Reconciliation*, 195, in Cowan, 75).
For the natural man is an enemy to God, and has been from the fall of Adam, and will be, forever and ever, unless he yields to the enticings of the Holy Spirit (Mosiah 3:19).	
[God] showed unto all men that they were lost, because of the transgression of their parents (*Book of Mormon*, 2 Nephi 2:21).	

TREATMENT OF ENEMIES	
As I remarked, we were then very pious, and we prayed the Lord to kill the mob (Apostle George A. Smith, *Journal of Discourses*, 5:107). (C.f. the discussion of blood atonement, etc., in *Behind the Mask of Mormonism*, chapter 2, 28.)	But behold I say unto you, love your enemies, bless them that curse you, do good to them that hate you and pray for them who despitefully use you and persecute you; that ye may be the children of your Father who is in heaven (*Book of Mormon*, 3 Nephi 12:44, 45).

THE INDWELLING OF GOD	
The Lord hath said . . . in the hearts of the righteous doth he dwell (*Book of Mormon*, Alma 34:36).	The idea that the Father and the Son dwell in a man's heart is an old sectarian notion, and is false (*D&C*, 130:3).

SALVATION BY GRACE	
Remember, after ye are reconciled to God, that it is only in and through the grace of God that ye are saved (*Book of Mormon*, 2 Nephi 10:24).	Fulfilling the commandments bringeth remission of sins (*Book of Mormon*, Moroni 8:25). Except ye shall keep my commandments. . . . Ye shall in no case enter into the kingdom of heaven (*Book of Mormon*, 3 Nephi 12:20).

GOD'S IMMUTABILITY	
Mormon prophets have continuously taught the sublime truth that God the Eternal Father was once a mortal man (M.R. Hunter, *Gospel Through the Ages*, 104).	Behold I say unto you, he that denieth these things knoweth not the gospel of Christ; yea, he has not read the Scriptures; if so, he does not understand them. For do we not read that God is the same yesterday, today, and forever, and in him there is no variableness neither shadow or changing? And now if ye have imagined up unto yourselves a god who doth vary, and in whom there is shadow of changing, then have ye imagined up unto yourselves a god who is not a God of miracles (*Book of Mormon*, Mormon 9:8–10).

THE CREATION OF MAN	
God . . . created man, as we create our children; for there is no other process of creation in heaven, on the earth, in the earth, or under the earth, or in all the eternities that is, that were, or that ever will be (Brigham Young, *Journal of Discourses,* 11:122).	By the power of his word man came upon the face of the earth which earth was created by the power of his word. Wherefore, if God being able to speak and the world was, and to speak and man was created, O then, why is he not able to command the earth or the workmanship of his hands upon the face of it, according to his will and pleasure? (*Book of Mormon,* Jac. 4:9).

THE FALL PRODUCING CHILDREN	
If Adam had not transgressed he would not have fallen. . . . And they would have had no children (*Book of Mormon,* 2 Nephi 2:22, 23). Were it not for our transgressions we never should have had seed (*The Pearl of Great Price,* Moses 5:11).	And I, God, created man in mine own image. . . . Male and female created I them. And I, God, blessed them, and said unto them: Be fruitful and multiply (*The Pearl of Great Price,* Moses 2:27, 28).

CHILD BAPTISM	
And their children shall be baptized for the remission of their sins when eight years old (*D&C,* 68:27).	Listen to the words of Christ . . . your Lord and God. . . . I know that it is solemn mockery before God, that ye should baptize little children. . . . Yea, teach parents that they must repent and be baptized (*Book of Mormon,* Moroni 8:8–10).

Contradictions Between Mormon Doctrine and Biblical Truth

THE GATES OF HELL PREVAILED	
The gates of hell have prevailed and will continue to prevail over the Catholic Mother of Harlots, and over *all* her Protestant Daughters (*Pamphlets* by Orson Pratt, 112, cited by Jerald and Sandra Tanner, *Changing World,* 27). The kingdoms of this world made war against the kingdom of God . . . and they prevailed against it. . . . [It has been] overcome and nothing is left (Orson Pratt, *Journal of Discourses,* 13:125).	I will build my church, and the gates of Hades will not overcome it (Matthew 16:18).

JUSTIFICATION BY POLYGAMY	
Abraham received concubines, and they bore him children; and it was accounted unto him for righteousness (*D&C,* 132:37).	For what does the Scripture say? "Abraham believed God, and it was credited to him as righteousness" (Romans 4:3).

(continues)

Contradictions Between Mormon Dictrine and Biblical Truth, cont.

JUSTIFICATION BY WORKS	
Man is justified by works (McConkie, *Doctrinal New Testament Commentary*, 3:260).	For we maintain that a man is justified by faith apart from observing the law (Romans 3:28). By the works of the Law no flesh will be justified in His sight (Romans 3:20 NAS).
HATRED OF ENEMIES	
In Missouri we were taught to "pray for our enemies, that *God would damn them, and give us power to kill them*" (Letter, B. F. Johnson, 1903, cited in Jerald and Sandra Tanner, *Changing World*, p. 485, see *Journal of Discourses* 5:32, 95, 107, 133; 7:122 for similar examples).	You have heard that it was said, "YOU SHALL LOVE YOUR NEIGHBOR, and hate your enemy." But I say to you, love your enemies, and pray for those who persecute you (Matthew 5:43–44 NAS). Do not repay anyone evil for evil. Be careful to do what is right in the eyes of everybody (Romans 12:17).
MAN AS INHERENTLY GOOD	
It is, however, universally received by professors of religion as a Scriptural doctrine that man is naturally opposed to God. This is not so. Paul says in his Epistle to the Corinthians, "But the natural man receiveth not the things of God." But I say it is the unnatural "man that receiveth not the things of God." . . . *The natural man is of God* (Brigham Young, *Journal of Discourses*, 9:305).	But a natural man does not accept the things of the Spirit of God; for they are foolishness to him, and he cannot understand them, because they are spiritually appraised (1 Corinthians 2:14 NAS). This I say therefore, and affirm together with the Lord, that you walk no longer just as the Gentiles also walk, in the futility of their mind, being darkened in their understanding, excluded from the life of God, because of the ignorance that is in them, because of the hardness of their heart (Ephesians 4:17–18 NAS).
It is not natural for men to be evil (John Taylor, 3rd President, *Journal of Discourses*, 10:50).	As it is written: "There is no one righteous, not even one; there is no one who understands, no one who seeks God. All have turned away, they have together become worthless; there is no one who does good, not even one" (Romans 3:10–12).
NO ORIGINAL SIN	
In the true gospel of Jesus Christ there is no original sin (John Widtsoe, *Evidences and Reconciliations*, 195, in Cowan, 75).	One trespass was condemnation for all men (Romans 5:18).
REJECTION OF CHRIST'S DEITY	
Jesus *became* a God . . . through consistent effort (M. R. Hunter, *Gospel Through the Ages*, Salt Lake City: *Deseret*, 1945, 51, in McElveen, 154).	The Word was God (John 1:1). Jesus Christ is the same yesterday and today and forever (Hebrews 13:8). His goings forth are from long ago, from the days of eternity (Micah 5:2 NAS).

THE INDWELLING OF GOD	
The idea that the Father and the Son dwell in a man's heart is an old sectarian notion, and is false (*D&C*, 130:3).	Jesus answered and said to him, "If anyone loves Me, he will keep My word; and My Father will love him, and We will come to him, and make Our abode with him" (John 14:23 NAS).
ADAM AS GOD	
Adam is our Father and Our God (Brigham Young, *Journal of Discourses*, 1:50).	Then to Adam He said, ". . . you are dust, and to dust you shall return" (Genesis 3:17, 19).
SOURCE OF SALVATION	
There is no salvation outside the Church of Jesus Christ of Latter-day Saints (McConkie, *Mormon Doctrine*, 670).	Yet to all who received him, to those who believed in his name, he gave the right to become children of God (John 1:12). Whoever believes in the Son has eternal life, but whoever rejects the Son will not see life, for God's wrath remains on him (John 3:36).
THE HOLY SPIRIT AND BAPTISM	
Cornelius . . . could not receive the gift of the Holy Ghost until after he was baptized (Joseph Smith, *Teachings*, 199).	Cornelius received "the gift of the Holy Spirit" before he was baptized (Acts 10:43–48).
THE CREATION	
There really was no beginning because God and matter are eternal (Wallace, *Can Mormonism Be Proven Experimentally?* 163).	In the beginning God created the heavens and the earth (Genesis 1:1).

Another vital area relative to Mormon claims to divine revelation is its prophetic record. The many fake prophecies found throughout its history, beginning with Joseph Smith, also disprove that Mormonism is divine revelation. While we have not examined every Mormon prophecy, the many we did study proved untrue. We include several here, which are typical of what one finds throughout Mormon history.

Joseph Smith's Canadian prophecy. David Whitmer (one of the three principal witnesses to the writing of the *Book of Mormon*) tells a highly relevant story that reveals Joseph Smith to be a false prophet. Here are Whitmer's own words:

When the Book of Mormon was in the hands of the printer, more money was needed to finish the printing of it. . . . Brother Hyrum said it had been suggested to him that some of the brethren might go to Toronto, Canada and sell the copyright of the Book of Mormon for considerable money: and he persuaded Joseph to inquire of the Lord about it. Joseph concluded to do so. He had not yet given up the [seer] stone. Joseph looked into the hat in which he placed the stone, and *received a revelation* that some of the brethren should go to Toronto, Canada, *and that they would sell the copyright* of the Book of Mormon. Hyrum Page and Oliver Crowdery went to Toronto on this mission, but *they failed entirely to sell the copyright*, returning without any money. Joseph was at my father's house when they returned. I was there also, and am *an eyewitness* to these facts. Jacob Whitmer and John Whitmer were also present when Hyrum Page and Oliver Crowdery returned from Canada.

Well, we were all in great trouble; and we asked Joseph how it was that he had received a revelation from the Lord for some brethren to go to Toronto and sell the copyright and the brethren had utterly failed in their undertaking. Joseph did not know how it was, so he inquired of the Lord about it, and behold the following revelation came through the stone:

> Some revelations are of God: some revelations are of man: and some revelations are of the devil.

So we see that the revelation to go to Toronto and sell the copyright was not of God [even though Smith claimed it was], but was of the devil or of the heart of man.... This was a lesson for our benefit *and we should have profited by it in [the] future more than we did.*

Whitmer concludes his discussion with a warning to every living Mormon:

> Remember this matter brethren; it is very important.... Now is it wisdom to put your trust in Joseph Smith, and believe all his revelations in the *Doctrine and Covenants* to be of God?... I will say here, that I could tell you *other false revelations* that came through Brother Joseph as mouthpiece (not through the stone), but this will suffice. Many of Brother Joseph's revelations were never printed. The revelation to go to Canada was written down on paper, but was never printed.[64]

The "City and Temple" prophecy. In a revelation given to Joseph Smith on September 22–23, 1832, "The word of the Lord" declared that both a city and a temple are to be built "in the western boundaries of the state of Missouri" (that is, in Independence, Missouri):

> A revelation of Jesus Christ unto his servant Joseph Smith, Jun[ior].... *Yea, the word of the Lord* concerning his church ... for the gathering of his saints to stand upon Mount Zion, which shall be the city of New Jerusalem. Which *city shall be built*, beginning at the temple lot ... *in the western boundaries of the state of Missouri,* and dedicated by the hand of Joseph Smith.... Verily *this is the word of the Lord,* that the city

New Jerusalem shall be built by the gathering of saints, beginning at this place, even the place of the temple, which temple shall be reared *in this generation. For verily this generation shall not all pass away* until an house shall be built unto the Lord, and a cloud shall rest upon it, which cloud shall be even the glory of the Lord, which shall fill the house.... Therefore, as I said concerning the sons of Moses—for the sons of Moses and also *the sons of Aaron shall offer an acceptable offering and sacrifice in the house of the Lord,* which house shall be built under the Lord in this generation, upon the consecrated spot as *I have appointed* (*D&C,* 84:1–5, 31, emphasis added).

This prophecy clearly teaches that a temple and a city will be built in western Missouri in the generation of the people *then living* and that it will be dedicated by the hand of Joseph Smith himself. This temple will stand (in western Missouri) "upon Mount Zion" and the city will be named "the city of New Jerusalem." It was to be the place Christ returned to at His Second Coming.[65]

In *Doctrine and Covenants,* 97:19 (August, 1833) and 101:17–21 (December, 1833), "God" declares that He is absolutely certain as to His intent and the location of this temple: "Zion cannot fall, nor be moved out of her place, for God is there, and the hand of the Lord is there," and "there is none other place appointed than that which I have appointed; neither shall there be any other place." Interestingly, on July 20, 1833, when Smith was giving this particular prophecy in Kirtland, Ohio, unaware of events occurring in Missouri, the Mormon community had already agreed to leave Missouri because of "persecution." In other words, even as Smith was giving the prophecy "in the name of the Lord," "Zion" was already being "moved out of her place."[66]

In spite of the numerous ways that Mormon leaders have tried to justify the "City and Temple" prophecy since it was made, 170 years have passed and neither the temple nor the city has been built. Thus there is no way to escape the conclusion that this is a false prophecy. But since Mormonism assumes that Joseph

Smith was a true prophet, it cannot be a false prophecy. So a process of rationalization sets in. For example, Joseph Fielding Smith dealt with the "generation problem" by claiming that the term "generation" meant an *indefinite* period of time, and that due to "persecution" God had "absolved the saints and postponed the day."[67] Now everyone could relax. There never was a false prophecy.

The "Second Coming" prophecy. Along with Jehovah's Witnesses and Seventh-day Adventists, Joseph Smith predicted that the Second Coming of Christ would occur in the latter part of the nineteenth century. In his *History of the Church,* Smith taught that the Second Coming would occur between 1890 and 1891. In 1835 he declared that Christ's return would occur fifty-six years later, and in 1843 that it would occur in forty-eight years. Smith claimed that the generation then living would not die "till Christ comes."[68] For example, under the date of April 6, 1843, in his *original* History (taken from Smith's diary, March 10, 1843 to July 14, 1843), one can read: "I prophecy [sic] *in the name of the Lord God*—& let it be written; that the Son of Man will not come in the heavens until I am 85 years old, 48 years hence or about 1890."[69] Smith, however, was dead within a year, and Christ still has not returned.

Some of the twelve Mormon apostles were told that they also would remain until Christ returned. For example, the Tanners note that Lyman E. Johnson was told that he would "see the Savior come and stand upon the earth with power and great glory"; and William Smith was told that he would "be preserved and remain on the earth, until Christ shall come."[70] Because of such a strong belief in the imminence of the Second Coming, Apostle Parley P. Pratt wrote in 1838: "I will state *as a prophesy* [sic], that there will not be an unbelieving Gentile upon this continent 50 years hence; and if they are not greatly scourged, and in a great measure overthrown, within five or ten years from this date, *then the Book of Mormon will have proved itself false.*"[71] Not unexpectedly, the prophecy has been deleted from the modern versions of the *Writings of Parley P. Pratt.*

There have been many other false prophecies throughout the history of the Mormon church, far too numerous to cite here.* These include prophecies given to Mormon individuals that were never fulfilled, such as that Brigham Young would become president of the United States, and a Smith prophecy about the complete overthrow of the U.S. government.

With so many false prophecies by Smith and other Mormons, one is tempted to assume that they were either carried away by false visions of their own mind or through spiritistic duplicity. Certainly a truthful God could not be the author of wrong predictions. In spite of all these false prophecies, Mormons do not show much concern about the issue. Apparently, this is because they have never come to grips with the biblical teaching on what God requires of a true prophet (Deuteronomy 13; 18; Jeremiah 28:9; Ezekiel 12:28) and what a false prophet really is:

> It is somewhat ironic that most Mormons are basically unimpressed by the evidence against their "prophets" concerning the many false prophecies that have issued forth from them. This behavior is so unusual because of the reverence Mormons give their Presidents as "prophets of God." Their attitude of indifference is primarily based upon ignorance and conditioning. The average Mormon is unaware of the biblical tests for a true prophet and is therefore ignorant of how to properly determine if a man is a true prophet or a false prophet. However, the greatest difficulty Mormons have is overcoming their "conditioning." They have been programmed to believe that the greatest test of a prophet is their own personal "testimony" that he is a prophet.[72]

But it must also be said that many Mormons are not even aware of the false prophecies. For

---

*Ralson lists the following examples: *D&C*, 42:39; 62:6; 69:8; 84:114, 115; 88:87; 97:19; 101:11, 17; 103:6, 7; 111:2, 4–10; 112:15, 19; 115:14, 17; 117:12. Walter Martin refers to several false prophecies in *D&C*, 97:22–24 (with *D&C* commentary, appropriate section) and also in *Teachings of Joseph Smith* (pp. 17, 18). Jerald and Sandra Tanner refer to false prophecies in *Journal of Discourses* 3:228, 253, 262; 4:40; 5:10, 93, 94, 164, 173–174, 274, 275 and in other sources. The resource text, *Where Does It Say That?* by former Mormon Bob Witte, contains others.

example, if one examines the *D&C* student manual, an extensive five-hundred-page commentary on *D&C*, one finds that the false prophecies are either ignored or carefully reinterpreted.

THEOLOGY

Jesus emphasized the importance of the one true God. He said, "And this is eternal life, that they may know Thee, the only true God, and Jesus Christ whom Thou hast sent" (John 17:3 NASB). Thus accurate knowledge of who that God is is vital. In this section we will examine aspects of the Mormon view of God and contrast them with the biblical Christian view to show that the Mormon view is not compatible with orthodox Christianity. (See also the Doctrinal Section at the end of this book.)

The Mormon church emphasizes the importance of a correct understanding of God. In *Doctrines of the Gospel,* published by the Mormon church, it reads: "Central to our faith as Latter-day Saints is a correct understanding of God the Father."[73] This is the student manual used at Brigham Young University for Religion course 231 and 232. The problem is that the Mormon church claims that only they understand God truly; all others are wrong. Joseph Smith testifies, "There are but a few beings in the world who understand rightly the character of God."[74] Likewise the leading Mormon theologian James Talmage claims, "[The] sectarian [Christian] view of the Godhead [contains] . . . numerous theories and dogmas of men, many of which are utterly incomprehensible in their inconsistency and mysticism."[75]

This riddle between what they claim and what is actually true can be solved by understanding that when Mormons claim that they believe in the *biblical* God what they mean is that the Bible teaches the *Mormon* concept of God. Further, because of its alleged apostasy, Christianity lost the true teaching of God and therefore the historic Christian doctrine of God is not truly biblical. This leaves Mormons free to concede that their concept of deity is contrary to traditional Christian faith. And this they do. William O. Nelson, Director of the Melchizedek Priesthood Department, agrees, "Some who write anti-Mormon pamphlets insist that the Latter-day Saint concept of Deity is contrary to what is recognized as traditional Christian doctrine. In this they are quite correct."[76] So the real issue is to ascertain the true biblical teaching on the nature of God. See the next chart, "The Nature of God," which notes major differences between the Mormon and biblical Christian views of God.

Many Gods or One?

Christianity is monotheistic. Mormonism is polytheistic. Of course, Mormons are very uncomfortable with the charge of polytheism. No less a church authority than Bruce McConkie categorically insists that "the saints [Mormons] are not polytheists."[77] Stephen Robinson, chairman of the Department of Ancient Scripture at Brigham Young University and author of *Are Mormons Christians?* (which he emphatically affirms), argues that "the Latter-day Saints [doctrine does not] . . . constitute genuine polytheism." He takes pains to argue that "the Latter-day Saints [should] be considered worshipers of the one true God."[78]

But if Mormons are really polytheists, why do they think they are monotheists? Principally, it is through the uncritical acceptance of the statements of church authorities, and secondarily it is by a process of seemingly deliberate self-deception caused by the improper use of words. When Mormons deny the charge of polytheism, they illustrate a characteristic feature of Mormon apologetics: equivocation, which involves the ambiguous use of words in order to conceal something. The truth is that Mormons are polytheists by any standard definition of the term. The *Oxford American Dictionary* defines polytheism as "belief in or worship of more than one god."[79] And this, as we will see, is true.

Technically, Mormon theology is "henotheistic," a form of polytheism that stresses worship of a central deity. In Mormonism, the central deity is Elohim, whom Mormons call "God the Father." But henotheism also accepts other deities. In Mormonism the other deities accepted include Jesus, the Holy Ghost and endless other gods who were once men and who have now evolved into godhood.

Polytheism can be seen in the words of Joseph Smith. "In the beginning, the head of the

The Nature of God

MORMON CONCEPT OF DEITY	BIBLICAL CHRISTIAN CONCEPT OF DEITY
Material (a physical body of flesh and bones)	Immaterial (spirit)
Mortal, finite	Immortal, infinite
Changeable, evolving	Immutable
Physically localized	Omnipresent
Polygamous or incestuous	Jesus was monogamous (celibate)
Polytheistic	Monotheistic
Tri-theistic (three earth gods)	Trinitarian
Exalted saved man	Eternal deity
Eternally progressing in certain attributes (early Mormonism)	Eternally immutable in all characteristics
Feminine counterpart (heavenly mother)	No feminine counterpart
Adam, once considered God (early Mormonism)	Adam, a creation of God
Jesus, begotten by Elohim's physical intercourse with Mary	Jesus, begotten supernaturally by the Holy Spirit (virgin birth)
Polygamist Jesus (some early Mormons)	Celibate Jesus

Gods called a council of the Gods; and they came together and concocted a plan to create the world and people in it."[80] Consider also the following excerpts from Smith's new revelation of the Creation account in the Mormon scripture known as *The Pearl of Great Price:*

At the beginning . . . the Gods organized and formed the heavens and the earth. . . . And the Gods called the light Day. . . . And the Gods also said: let there be an expanse in the midst of the waters. . . . And the Gods ordered the expanse, so that it divided the waters. . . . And the Gods called the expanse Heaven. . . . And the Gods pronounced the dry land Earth. . . . And the Gods said: let us prepare the earth to bring forth grass. . . . And the Gods organized the lights in the expanse of the heaven. . . . And the Gods organized the two great lights, the greater light to rule the day, and the lesser light to rule the night. . . . And the Gods set them in the expanse of the heavens. . . . And the Gods organized the earth to bring forth the beasts after their kind. . . . And the Gods took counsel among themselves and said: let us go down and form man in our image. . . . So the Gods went down to organize man in their own image. . . . And the Gods

said: we will bless them. . . . And the Gods said: Behold, we will give them every herb bearing seed. . . . And the Gods formed man from the dust of the ground. . . . And the Gods planted a garden, eastward in Eden. . . . And the Gods took the man and put him in the Garden of Eden. . . . And the Gods said: let us make an help meet for the man.[81]

Mormon polytheism encompasses two aspects. First there is a predominant "local" polytheism as far as the earth is concerned. That is, the earth has three distinct gods who "rule it." This ties in with the Mormon concept that the biblical Trinity is tri-theistic (three Gods), not monotheistic. In *Mormon Doctrine*, McConkie declares, "There are three Gods—the Father, the Son and the Holy Ghost."[82] The principal deity is the Father, a physical god named "Elohim," said to be the primary and most "advanced" god. Mormonism teaches, "The Father is the supreme member of the Godhead."[83] The Son is the physical God "Jehovah" of the Old Testament: "Jesus Christ is Jehovah, the God of the Old Testament."[84] The Holy Ghost is a former man who has become a god, although unlike the Father and the Son he does not have a concrete physical body but is a man with a spiritual body of matter. These three beings, all former men, are the three gods that Mormons are to concern themselves with. But because Mormonism claims that extra-solar gods are not the church's particular concern, their tri-theism is somehow held to be monotheistic by them. In any case, Mormons assure everyone that they believe in only one true God.

The second aspect of Mormon polytheism moves beyond the earth. If there are an infinite number of earths, each with its god or gods, then there are an infinite number of gods. Whether or not Mormons on earth are "concerned" with them, they do believe in them. McConkie declares:

> To us, speaking in the proper finite sense, these three [the principal Gods of earth] are the only Gods we worship. But in addition there is an infinite number of holy personages, drawn from worlds without number, who have passed on to exaltation [Godhood] and are thus gods.... This doctrine of plurality of Gods is so comprehensive and glorious that it reaches out and embraces every exalted personage [God]. Those who attain exaltation are gods.[85]

Brigham Young declared: "How many Gods there are I do not know, but there never was a time when there were not Gods."[86]

The Bible clearly rejects polytheism in the most straightforward terms. God Himself declares in Isaiah: "Before me no God was formed, nor will there be one after me" (43:10). "I am the first and I am the last; apart from Me there is no God . . . Is there any God besides me? . . . I know not one" (44:6, 8). "I am the LORD, and there is no other; apart from me there is no God. . . . There is no God apart from me" (45:5, 21). From Genesis to Revelation, the Bible teaches monotheism.

A Tri-Theistic Trinity

Mormonism claims that it believes in the Trinity. Dr. Stephen E. Robinson is chairman of the Department of Ancient Scripture at Brigham Young University and director of "Pearl of Great Price" research for the Religious Studies Center. He claims that Mormonism believes in the biblical God: "The Latter-day Saints accept unequiv-

ocally *all the biblical teachings* on the nature of God."[87] He also claims that Mormons believe in the biblical doctrine of the Trinity: "Latter-day Saints believe in the *biblical* Father, Son, and Holy Ghost."[88] Even more explicitly, "If by 'the doctrine of the Trinity' one means *the New Testament teaching* that there is a Father, a Son, and Holy Ghost, all three of whom are fully divine, then Latter-day Saints *believe in the doctrine of the Trinity*. It's as simple as that. The Latter-day Saints' first *Article of Faith*, written by Joseph Smith in 1842, states, 'We believe in the God, the Eternal Father, and in His Son, Jesus Christ, and in the Holy Ghost.'"[89]

To the contrary, Mormons do not believe in the biblical Trinity; they believe in *tri-theism*, three gods for this particular earth. Joseph Smith himself was a tri-theist:

> Many men say there is one God; the Father, the Son and the Holy Ghost are only one God. I say that is a strange God anyhow–three in one, and one in three! It is curious organization. . . . All are to be crammed into one God according to sectarianism [Christian faith]. It would make the biggest God in all the world. He would be a wonderfully big God—he would be a giant or a monster.[90]

> I will preach on the plurality of Gods. I have selected this text [Genesis 1:1] for that express purpose. I wish to declare that I have always and in all congregations when I have preached on the subject of the Deity, it has been on the plurality of Gods.[91]

Nevertheless, as we documented in *Knowing the Truth About the Trinity* (Harvest House, 1997), this contradicts two thousand years of Christian tradition, in which the Christian church has found the doctrine of the Trinity (one God in three Persons) in the Bible. This can be seen clearly by anyone who reads the Church Fathers and studies the historic Creeds.* (See

---

*For an in-depth study of the historical development of the doctrine of the Trinity from apostolic times through the final form of the Nicean Creed adopted at the Council of Constantinople in A.D. 381, including a line-by-line comparison of the Creed with New Testament teaching, see Calvin Beisner's *God in Three Persons*. Two other excellent studies are E. Bickersteth's *The Trinity* and Robert Morey's *The Trinity*.[92]

also the Doctrinal Section at the end of this book.)

The Gods Are Evolving

Mormonism teaches that God was not God from all eternity; God was once a man who evolved into Godhood. And to further confuse matters, there are endless numbers of "God."

How do people become Gods? Mormonism believes that all current Gods have attained Godhood through the good works they performed when they were finite. Joseph Smith describes the process by which people become Gods: "When you climb up a ladder, you must begin at the bottom and ascend step by step, until you arrive at the top; and so it is with the principles of the Gospel—you must begin with the first, and go on until you learn all the principles of exaltation ["exaltation" is his term for becoming a God]."[93] An official Mormon publication, *Gospel Principles,* cites this passage and then comments: "This is the way our Heavenly Father became a God."[94] It then quotes Joseph Smith's own evaluation of "The First Principle of the Gospel," which is to realize that God the Father was once a man: "It is the first principle of the gospel to know for a certainty the character of God, and to know that we may converse with him as one man converses with another, and that he was once a man like us; yea that God himself, the father of us all, dwelt on an earth, the same as Jesus Christ himself did; and I will show it from the Bible."[95] This same source states unblushingly that "God is a glorified and perfected man. . . . (See *D&C,* 130:22)."[96]

The Mormon student manual, *Doctrines of the Gospel,* teaches that "God Himself is an exalted man, perfected, enthroned, and supreme."[97] Dr. Stephen Robinson, who is convinced that Mormonism is Christian, confesses, "It is indisputable that Latter-day Saints believe that God was once a human being and that human beings can become gods." The well-known couplet of Lorenzo Snow, fifth president and prophet of the LDS Church, states: "As man now is, God once was; as God now is, man may be."[98]

But Mormonism is divided on how far the process of divine evolution extends. Historically, the church has been uncertain as to whether the Gods continue to evolve forever. Many Mormon presidents and prophets taught that the Gods evolved eternally in power and knowledge, which would never quite make them truly omnipotent and omniscient.[99] Thus it is written: "God himself is increasing and progressing in knowledge, power and dominion, and will do so worlds without end."[100] Others, such as the late Latter-day Saint Bruce McConkie and early Mormon apostle Orson Pratt, believe that God is omnipotent and omniscient, although they at times have been rebuked for it.[101]

So what kind of God does Mormonism teach? Whether we take early or late Mormonism, one fact is clear: Mormonism has no concept of God in the biblical Christian meaning of the term. The Bible asserts in the clearest terms that God is immutable: God never changes in terms of His being, essence or attributes. (The incarnation of Jesus Christ is not an exclusion to this reality; in taking on a sinless human nature, the Second Person of the Godhead did not alter His essential divine nature.) For all eternity God has remained God. God was never originally a man who, incredibly, became God through personal effort.

The following Scriptures testify that God never changes:

I the LORD do not change (Malachi 3:6).

The Father . . . does not change (James 1:17).

God is not a man, that he should lie, nor a son of man, that he should change his mind (Numbers 23:19).

From everlasting to everlasting you art God (Psalm 90:2).

The Mormon God is ultimately a finite one. As Dr. McMurrin concludes in his study: "He is therefore finite rather than absolute."[102] "In its rejection of the classical concept of God as eternal, Mormonism is a most radical digression from traditional theism. This is perhaps its most important departure from familiar Christian orthodoxy, for it would be difficult to overestimate the importance to [Mormon] theology of the doctrine that God is a temporal being."[103]

Jesus Christ

The traditional Christ of whom they [Christians] speak is not the Christ of whom I speak (LDS president Gordon B. Hinkley in Paris; *Deseret News,* June 20, 1998).

From the beginning, the Mormon church has confessed its allegiance to Jesus Christ. Mormon literature emphatically claims to accept and revere the biblical Christ. The publicity booklet *What the Mormons Think of Christ,* published by the Mormon Church, asserts: "Christ is our Redeemer and our Savior. Except for him there would be no salvation and no redemption, and unless men come unto him and accept him as their Savior, they cannot have eternal life in his presence.[104] "He—Jesus Christ—is the Savior of the world and the Divine Son of God."[105]

In his book *Are Mormons Christians?* written in an attempt to prove to the world that Mormons are Christians, Dr. Stephen Robinson emphasizes continually that Mormons believe in the true biblical Jesus Christ. In fact, he claims that the evidence is so persuasive that Mormons believe in Jesus Christ that critics have never even dared to raise the issue![106] Dr. Robinson, apparently, has not read many Christian apologetic works. Christian treatments of Mormonism consistently maintain that Mormons do *not* acknowledge the true Jesus Christ as Lord. For the real issue is which "Jesus Christ" one believes in. The simple truth is that although Mormons proclaim their belief in the biblical Jesus Christ, like other sects and cults theirs is a false, pagan Christ, one who has nothing to do with the biblical Jesus. As the following chart shows, the Mormon Christ and the biblical Christ are so incompatible that not a single resemblance can be found between them.

Mormons deny Jesus Christ's unique deity. Mormonism teaches that Jesus Christ is a created being. That is, Mormonism teaches that every person has two births; first, birth as a spirit child in preexistence and second, much later, birth as a human being. According to Mormon theology, Christ was the first and foremost of subsequent billions of spirit children created through sexual intercourse between the male earth god and his celestial wife. Later, in order to produce the body for this special spirit child, the earth god again had sexual intercourse, this

time with the "virgin" Mary, who then became Jesus' earthly mother.

Jesus Christ is a common God. Mormon teaching implies that Jesus Christ is a "common" God and, in some ways, of minor importance in the larger Mormon cosmology. Mormons do refer to Christ as being "greater" than all other spirit children on earth, but this earth, as discussed previously, is only one of an infinite number of earths, each having their own Gods who have existed and evolved for aeons longer than Christ. Here on earth, Christ is our "senior" only by achievement and position, *not* by nature or essence.

The *essence* of Christ is no different from the essence of any spirit child of Elohim, whether of men or of Satan and his demons. Every person on earth has the same nature and essence as Jesus Christ, and He as they. Although Christ performed better than others in preexistence, He is nevertheless of one nature with all people. Thus, Mormons universally refer to Him as their "elder brother." Jesus Christ is not unique in essence but only in achievement and mission. Thus His divinity is not unique, for every exalted person will attain a similar Godhood. Neither is His incarnation unique, for all persons are incarnated spirit beings—in preexistence, the offspring of the sexual union of the gods, who then take tabernacles of flesh. Indeed, Christ was only unique in His *physical* birth; that is, rather than having a merely human father like the rest of us, His mother had physical sex with the God Elohim.

Christ is also not unique as creator of this earth, because Mormonism teaches that Adam, Joseph Smith and others *helped* Him to create it. Christ "was aided . . . by 'many of the noble and great' spirit children of the Father . . . Adam . . . Noah . . . Joseph Smith. . . ."[107]

Mormonism teaches that Christ is Satan's brother. In Mormon theology, Jesus Christ is the spirit brother of Satan. Since Satan (and his demons) were also preexistent spirit creations of Elohim and his celestial wife, Satan is therefore Christ's brother as well. In fact, the devil and all demons are the spirit brothers of everyone on

Mormon Christ and Christian Christ Incompatibility

THE MORMON JESUS CHRIST	THE BIBLICAL JESUS CHRIST
A created being; the elder brother of Lucifer	Uncreated God
Common (one of many gods) and, in some ways, of minor importance in the *larger* Mormon cosmology	Unique (the Second Person of the one and only Godhead) and of supreme importance throughout time, eternity and all creation
Conceived by a physical sex act between God the Father (Adam or Elohim) and Mary, thus not through a true virgin birth	Conceived by the Holy Spirit, who supernaturally "overshadowed" Mary, thus a true virgin birth
Once sinful and imperfect	Eternally sinless and perfect
Earned his own salvation (exaltation, godhood)	As God, never required salvation
A married polygamist?	An unmarried monogamist

earth. In other words, Christ, the devil and all of us are brothers. Jess L. Christensen, director of the LDS Institute of Religion at Utah State University in Logan, Utah, writes in *A Sure Foundation,* "But both the scriptures and the prophets affirm that Jesus Christ and Lucifer are indeed offspring of our Heaven Father and, therefore, spirit brothers. ... Jesus was Lucifer's older brother."[108] Another Mormon writer concludes, "As for the devil and his fellow spirits, they are brothers to man and also to Jesus and sons and daughters to God in the same sense that we are."[109]

In light of the above, and many more doctrines, we must be careful not to accept Mormon claims concerning belief in Christ's uniqueness or deity. Mormons may claim to exalt Jesus, for, as McConkie says, "He shall reign to all eternity as King of Kings and Lord of Lords, and God of Gods."[110] But what is often not understood is that literally millions of other people will likewise reign, for as Brigham Young emphasized, all men are "the king of kings and lord of lords in embryo."[111]

Mormonism denies the virgin birth. In his controversial Adam-God discourse of April 9, 1852, Brigham Young taught that the body of Jesus Christ was the product of sexual intercourse between God (Adam) and Mary, who then subsequently married Joseph. But since God (Adam) was also the literal, physical Father of Mary (Mary being his literal spirit offspring

through celestial intercourse), this amounts to an incestuous and adulterous relationship, for at the same time she was betrothed in marriage to Joseph. Thus Mary had sexual relations with both her Father in heaven (God Himself) and her spirit brother, Joseph. One apparent effect of this teaching, at least in the minds of some, was to give divine sanction to "spiritual" adultery and even incest, and thus to render the incidents of incestuous polygamy and adultery in Mormon history more acceptable. "After all," they could have reasoned, "God Himself engaged in such practices." (See our *Behind the Mask of Mormonism,* ch. 29.)

This Mormon teaching denies that Jesus Christ was conceived by the Holy Ghost, and it maintains that Jesus was the literal offspring of the Father because, according to Mormon theology, the Holy Ghost does not have a physical body and therefore could not have had sexual intercourse with Mary. Mormon theology teaches that the Father has a physical body, one "of flesh and bones," so He could easily have had physical sex with Mary to conceive the body of Jesus. Thus, the role of the Holy Spirit in the virgin birth of Jesus Christ, so clearly stated in Matthew 1:18 and Luke 1:35, is rejected by Mormons. The following "inspired" statements by Brigham Young make this clear:

Now hear it, O inhabitants of the earth, Jew and Gentile, Saint and Sinner! When our Father

Adam came into the Garden of Eden, he came into it with a *celestial body,* and brought Eve, *one of his wives,* with him. He helped to make and organize this world. He is MICHAEL, *the Archangel,* THE ANCIENT OF DAYS! about whom holy men have written and spoken—he *is our* Father *and our God, and the only God with whom we have to do.* Every man upon the earth, professing Christians or non-professing, must hear it, and will know it sooner or later. . . . When the Virgin Mary conceived the child Jesus, the Father had begotten him in his own likeness. He was not begotten by the Holy Ghost. And who is the Father? He is the first of the human family [Adam]; and when he took a tabernacle [body], it was begotten by *his Father* in heaven, after the same manner as the tabernacles of Cain, Abel, and the rest of the sons and daughters of Adam and Eve.

Now remember from this time forth, and forever that *Jesus Christ was not begotten by the Holy Ghost.* . . . "If the son was begotten by the Holy Ghost, it would be very dangerous to baptize and confirm females and give the Holy Ghost to them, lest he should beget children to be palmed upon the Elders by the people, bringing the Elders into great difficulties."[112]

In his *Doctrines of Salvation,* the tenth Mormon president and prophet, Joseph Fielding Smith, taught, "Christ was begotten of God. He was not born without the aid of Man and *that Man was God!*"[113] The late LDS theologian Bruce McConkie declared, "Christ was begotten by an Immortal Father *in the same way* that mortal men are begotten by mortal fathers."[114] The former president and prophet of the Mormon church, Ezra Taft Benson, also believes that Jesus was not conceived by the Holy Ghost: "The body in which he performed his mission in the flesh was sired by that same Holy Being we worship as God, our Eternal Father. Jesus was not the son of Joseph, nor was he begotten by the Holy Ghost. He is the son of the Eternal Father."[115]

Such teachings are hardly biblical (Matthew 1:18; Luke 1:31–35). They are similar to occult and pagan teachings. Dr. Anthony Hoekema appropriately concludes: "What these men are saying is that, according to Mormon theology, the body of Jesus Christ was a product of the physical union of God the father and the virgin Mary. One shudders to think of the revolting implications of this view, which brings into what is supposed to be 'Christian' theology one of the most unsavory features of ancient pagan mythology!"[116]

Christ was not eternally sinless. While Mormons staunchly affirm that Christ is sinless, what they mean is that Christ was sinless while on this earth. They do not teach that He was sinless for all eternity past.

In Mormon theology, Jesus was only one of innumerable spirit offspring of the earth god and his celestial wife and therefore no different in nature from any other spirit. So He too had to undertake schooling and progression in the spirit world to attain salvation. He had to be tested with good and evil, initially at least, falling into evil like every other spirit son. As we documented in our book *Behind the Mask of Mormonism,* Mormonism teaches that it is only by direct experience of evil that people learn to choose good.

Bruce McConkie confesses that "Christ . . . is a saved being."[117] The official student manual, *Doctrines of the Gospel,* teaches that "the plan of salvation which he [Elohim] designed was to save his children, Christ included; neither Christ nor Lucifer could of themselves save anyone."[118] The same manual also quotes the tenth president and prophet, Joseph Fielding Smith, on the subject:

> The Savior did not have a fullness [of deity] at first, but after he received his body and the resurrection all power was given unto him both in heaven and in earth. Although he was a God, even the Son of God, with power and authority to create this earth and other earths, yet there were some things lacking in which he did not receive until after his resurrection. In other words, he had not received the fullness until he got a resurrected body.[119]

Thus, even though, according to Benson, "Jesus was a God in the pre-mortal existence," He was still imperfect and lacking certain necessary things.[120] McConkie taught: "These laws [of salvation], instituted by the father, constitute the gospel of God, which gospel is the plan by which all of his spirit children, Christ included, may gain eternal life."[121] "Jesus Christ is the Son of God. . . . He came to earth to work out his own salvation."[122] "By obedience and devotion to the truth he attained that pinnacle of intelligence which ranked him as a God."[123] A Mormon publicity booklet, *What the Mormons Think of Christ*, asserts: "Christ, the Word, the First Born, had of course, attained unto the status of Godhood while yet in preexistence."[124]

The above are but several clear statements showing that Mormon theology does not hold a view of God, the Trinity and Jesus Christ that is biblical. The Mormon God is "another Jesus" (2 Corinthians 1:4), who has little if anything to do with the true Christian faith.

Salvation

> We are not saved by grace alone (Boyd K. Packer, acting president of the Quorum of the Twelve Apostles, BYU address, Feb. 1, 1998).

Because Mormonism teaches that "there is no salvation outside the Church of Jesus Christ of Latter-day Saints,"[125] its view of salvation is essential and we need to know what Mormon theology means by it. In the biblical Christian view, salvation is by God's free gift of grace (Ephesians 2:8-9). The Mormon view distorts this in a number of ways, which we will consider here. (A much fuller treatment can be found in our book *Behind the Mask of Mormonism*.)

Mormonism vigorously claims that it believes the biblical teaching of salvation by grace. One Mormon promotional brochure declares: "Salvation by grace is one of the glorious doctrines of Christ."[126] In his apologetic text defending the assertion that Mormons are Christians, Dr. Stephen E. Robinson argues that both the Mormon scriptures and the Mormon church believe that salvation is wholly by grace. Robinson argues: "The charge that Latter-day Saints believe in salvation by works *is simply not true.* That human beings can save themselves by their own efforts is *contrary* to the teachings of the *Book of Mormon*, which eloquently states the doctrine of salvation by grace."[127]

But Dr. Robinson is wrong. The *Book of Mormon* does not state, eloquently or otherwise, the biblical doctrine of salvation by grace. Far from it. In defending his view, the best Dr. Robinson can do is to cite a few weak, if not entirely irrel-evant, scriptures from the *Book of Mormon* (Mosiah 2:21, 24; 5:7, 8; 2 Nephi 2:3-8; 25:23; Alma 5:14, 15; Ether 12:27; Moroni 10:32, 33). Even the strongest of these passages (2 Nephi 2:3-8) is not considered to teach salvation by grace through faith according to Mormon prophets, presidents and doctrinal theologians, at least not in any biblical Christian sense. When Mormonism speaks of "salvation by grace," or when it maintains that salvation does not come by "keeping the law," it means something different from what Christians mean by these things.

It is significant that Robinson cites only the *Book of Mormon*. He never cites *Doctrine and Covenants,* which is the Mormon scripture that most accurately reflects current Mormon beliefs and from which Mormon doctrines were originally derived. Robinson never once mentions that *D&C* adamantly and repeatedly teaches salvation by works. Further, if Mormonism really teaches salvation by grace, why do Mormon presidents, prophets, theologians and lay people staunchly maintain that salvation is by works? Indeed, one of the few Mormon doctrines that has never been altered, suppressed or simultaneously affirmed and denied is the doctrine that salvation is by personal merit, by one's works of righteousness. Mormonism teaches that personal salvation is *never* a free gift secured by grace through faith alone as the Bible teaches. Rather, it is secured by personal merit through zealous good works and impeccable law keeping. One earns salvation by good works and becomes a God in the process. Thus the biblical doctrine of salvation by grace through faith alone is one teaching that the Mormon church never has tolerated.[128]

In his *Articles of Faith*, James Talmage refers to "a most pernicious doctrine—that of justification by belief alone."[129] "The sectarian [Christian] dogma of justification by faith alone has exercised an influence for evil" and leads to "vicious extremes."[130] Mormon theologian McConkie called it a "soul-destroying doctrine."[131] The tenth president and prophet, Joseph Fielding Smith, emphasized that "Mankind [is] damned by [the] 'faith alone' doctrine," and "we must emphatically declare that men must obey these [Gospel] laws if they would be saved."[132] Mormon apostle LeGrand Richards declared: "One erroneous teaching of many Christian churches is: By faith alone we are saved. This false doctrine . . . would teach man that no matter how great the sin, a confession [of faith in Christ as personal savior] would bring him complete forgiveness and salvation."[133] Early Mormon apostle Orson Pratt is just as definite:

> Faith alone will not save men; neither will faith and works save them, unless they are [works] of the right kind. . . . True faith and righteous works are essential to salvation; and without both of these no man ever was or ever can be saved. . . . There are some who believe that faith alone, unaccompanied by works, is sufficient for justification, sanctification, and salvation. . . . [They] . . . are without justification—without hope—without everlasting life, and will be damned, the same as unbelievers.[134]

In order to more fully understand Mormon "salvation by grace," we have to see how some key biblical terms surrounding this Mormon doctrine—grace, justification, the new birth, gift, repentance and sanctification—have been redefined to incorporate works and thus distort the biblical view of salvation as a free gift.

"Grace" incorporates works. When Mormon theologians use the phrase "salvation by grace," they are merely referring to being resurrected from the dead. Beyond that, one's place of residence in eternity is determined wholly by one's good works. Further, according to Mormonism, salvation by grace is merely an infusing of grace based on good works. This is similar to the Roman Catholic doctrine wherein grace itself becomes a "work," so that as people increase in personal righteousness more and more "grace" is granted to them. In other words, "grace" is secured from God on the basis of individual merit and personal righteousness. McConkie explains this clearly:

> Grace is granted to men proportionately as they conform to the standards of personal righteousness that are part of the gospel plan.[135]

> Grace, which is an outpouring of the mercy, love, and condescension of God . . . [is] re-

ceived—not without works, not without righteousness, not without merit—but by obedience and faith![136]

> Many Protestants . . . erroneously conclude that men are saved by grace alone without doing the works of righteousness.[137]

"Justification" incorporates works. Biblically, "justification" is the act of God that declares a sinner righteous entirely apart from works and predicated only upon his or her faith in the atoning death of Christ for their sins. (See Doctrinal Section at end of book.) In Mormon theology the concept of justification is inextricably bound with conditions of personal merit and righteousness. According to the Mormon church, justification does not declare one perfectly righteous before God; it only gives one the opportunity to earn righteousness before God. Notice McConkie's reformulation: "The very atoning sacrifice itself was wrought out by the Son of God so that men might be justified, that is, so they could *do the things* which will give them eternal life in the celestial realm (*D&C*, 20:21–30, emphasis added)."[138] McConkie also stated: "As with all other doctrines of salvation, justification is available because of the atoning sacrifice of Christ, but it becomes operative in the life of an individual only on conditions of personal righteousness."[139]

"New birth" incorporates works. Joseph Fielding Smith taught that "the new birth is also a matter of obedience to law."[140] Smith was echoing the teachings of the *Book of Mormon* (Alma 5:14–30), which declares that to be "born again" a person has to fulfill a number of prerequisites, such as being blameless before God, having an absence of pride and envy. In other words, the new birth is a spiritual *process* secured by good works, not a one-time event secured by faith in Christ. Commenting on this same passage of scripture (about the new birth), McConkie declares that its guidelines enable Mormons "to determine whether and to what extent they have overcome the world, which is the exact extent to which they have in fact been born again."[141]

Biblically, being born again happens in an instant; it is not a process. Scripture repeatedly refers to the fact that every believer has already been (past tense) born again, without works, simply by faith in Jesus (John 5:24; 6:47; Titus 3:5; 1 Peter 1:3, 23).

"Gift" incorporates works. The meaning of the word "gift" is redefined by Mormon theology to mean not something freely given but something that must be earned. The Apostle LeGrand Richards asserts that "to obtain these 'graces,' and the gift of 'eternal salvation,' we must remember that this gift is [given] only to 'all them that obey him.' "[142] McConkie states, "One thing only comes as a free gift to men—the fact of the atoning sacrifice. All other gifts must be earned. That is, God's gifts are bestowed upon those who live the law entitling them to receive whatever is involved."[143]

"Repentance" incorporates works. In Mormonism, the term "repentance" means nothing less than strict obedience to law, rather than the biblical meaning of turning away from one's sins. After a discussion of all the requirements and commandments that must be fulfilled until the end of one's life in order to achieve salvation, Spencer Kimball comments that many people do not understand repentance properly. "They are not 'doing the commandments,' hence they do not repent."[144] In other words, repentance equals obedience. A "transgressor is not fully repentant who neglects his tithing, misses his meetings, breaks the Sabbath, fails in his family prayers, does not sustain the authorities of the Church, breaks the *Word of Wisdom* [church regulations], does not love the Lord nor his fellow man.... God cannot forgive unless a transgressor shows a true repentance which spreads to all areas of his life.... 'Doing the commandments' includes the many activities required of the [Mormon] faithful."[145]

"Sanctification" incorporates works. Similarly, the biblical meaning of sanctification (to be "set apart" to God for His purposes and growth in holiness) is distorted in Mormon theology. *Doctrines of the Gospel: Student Manual* teaches:

Members of the Church of Jesus Christ are commanded to become sanctified.... *To be sanctified is to become holy and without sin....*

Sanctification is attainable because of the atonement of Jesus Christ, but *only if we obey his commandments....* Sanctification is the state of saintliness, a state attained *only by* conformity to the laws and ordinances of the [Mormon] gospel.[146]

Biblically, sanctification involves three aspects. First, we are (past tense) "set apart" to Christ at the moment of regeneration or saving faith. Second, we are (in the present) progressively being sanctified as we grow in the grace, knowledge and obedience of our Lord. Third, we are fully sanctified—fully set apart to God and His purposes—when we become glorified and sinless at the moment of our going to be with Him (the future). The first and third of these aspects are entirely by grace, whereas Mormonism makes everything about sanctification a matter of works.

These are but several Mormon redefinitions of biblical meanings. They should be kept in mind in any discussion with individual Mormons.

Biblical salvation. What the Bible teaches about salvation is completely opposed to Mormon doctrine. The Bible clearly reveals that salvation does not come through one's personal righteousness, or personal merit and good works, but only through the grace of God and the individual's faith in Christ's finished work on the Cross.[147] Consider just several passages from the Bible that indicate salvation by faith, not works:

I tell you the truth, whoever hears my word and believes him who sent me has eternal life and will not be condemned; he has crossed over from the death to life. (John 5:24)

I tell you the truth, he who believes has eternal life. (John 6:47)

Jesus answered and said to them, "This is the work of God, that you believe in Him whom He has sent." (John 6:29 NAS)

All the prophets testify about him that everyone who believes in him receives forgiveness of sins. (Acts 10:43)

For we maintain that a man is justified by faith apart from observing the law. (Romans 3:28)

Just as David also speaks of the blessing upon the man to whom God reckons righteousness apart from works. (Romans 4:6 NAS)

But if it is by grace, it is no longer on the basis of works, otherwise grace is no longer grace. (Romans 11:6 NAS)

For it is by grace you have been saved, through faith—and this not from yourselves, it is the gift of God—not by works, so that no one can boast. (Ephesians 2:8–9)

I do not set aside the grace of God, for if righteousness could be gained through the law, then Christ died for nothing. (Galatians 2:21)

He saved us, not on the basis of deeds which we have done in righteousness, but according to His mercy, by the washing of regeneration and renewing by the Holy Spirit. (Titus 3:5 NAS)

The Atonement

Mormonism claims to hold to the biblical meaning of the atonement of Jesus Christ. One frequently finds statements in Mormon literature to the effect that "Christ died for our sins." When talking with Mormons, they will affirm that they believe Christ died for their sins. Theologian Bruce McConkie claims that "salvation comes because of the atonement." James Talmage argues that Jesus "bore the weight of the sins of the whole world, not only of Adam but of his posterity."[148] The *Doctrines of the Gospel: Student Manual* emphasizes: "No doctrine in the gospel is more important than the atonement of Jesus Christ. . . . The Savior . . . suffer[ed] for the sins of all the children of God. . . . The infinite atonement affects worlds without number and will save all of God's children except sons of perdition."[149] The *Book of Mormon* also claims that Christ died for our sins. It has Jesus saying, "I . . . have been slain for the sins of the world" (3 Nephi 11:14). And it teaches that "the sufferings and death of Christ atone for their [people's] sins, through faith and repentance" (Alma 22:14).

While these statements generally sound Christian, Mormons mean something quite different by them, just as they do the terms surrounding "salvation." Mormons really do not believe that Christ has effectively died for their sins and paid the actual penalty of divine justice necessary for their complete and eternal forgiveness by faith in Christ. Further, Mormons believe that forgiveness of sins is not immediately received upon true faith and repentance. True forgiveness, for them, requires a lengthy probationary period, and serious sins will cause the loss of salvation. Thus Mormon "salvation," and by implication Christ's atonement, does not cover forgiveness of "serious sins."[150]

Consistent with a works-view of salvation, in Mormon theology the atonement includes human obedience, especially to law and commandments. Benson taught that the atonement of Christ's death is effective for "redeeming all of us from physical death, and redeeming those of us from spiritual death *who will obey the laws and ordinances of the gospel*."[151] The *Doctrines of the Gospel: Student Manual* claims that Jesus came to save only those who would obey Him, because mercy is extended only to those who keep God's commandments. "If we do not keep God's commandments, we must suffer for our own sins."[152] The Mormon text *A Sure Foundation* states: "We believe that it is Christ's atonement that saves us but that we must endure to the end in doing good works *if his atonement is to take effect on our behalf*. . . . It is by the atonement of Christ that we are saved, but *it is necessary that we keep the commandments* and obey the ordinances God has given us."[153] In essence, although without Christ's atonement salvation would not be possible, salvation *itself* is the reward for individual merit. Thus point 3 of the *Articles of Faith* of Joseph Smith states: "We believe that through the atonement of Christ, all mankind may be saved, by obedience to the laws and ordinances of the gospel."

Ideas like these explain why Mormon discussions of the atonement are noticeable for their lack of affirming actual forgiveness of sins through Christ's death alone. It also explains, to a large degree, why Mormons do not know the true Gospel, for they have never heard it within Mormonism. A former twenty-year Mormon (who taught doctrine in the church) has said that he never once heard that Christ *actually* died on the Cross for *his* sin. This is not unique within Mormonism; it is characteristic.[154]

Thus, along with Jehovah's Witnesses and other cults, Mormonism teaches that the atonement merely provides the opportunity to earn salvation through personal merit. Just as a college degree does not actually secure a salary, but only makes earning one possible, so Christ's death does not actually secure salvation but only makes earning it possible by good works. In fact, even if all the faith in the world were placed in Christ's death, this still would not forgive a single sin, not apart from law keeping. In Mormonism, then, the substitutionary saving value of the atonement is nonexistent. Their theology denies that Christ's death paid the full penalty for our sins, resulting in complete forgiveness at the moment of faith (1 Corinthians 15:3; Colossians 2:13; Hebrews 9:12). Dr. McMurrin sums up the Mormon distortion on the atonement clearly:

> Mormon theology has with considerable ingenuity constructed its doctrine of salvation around the fall and the atonement, but with radically unorthodox meanings. . . . The meaning of the grace of God given through the atonement of Christ is that man by his freedom can now merit salvation. . . . But that Christ has taken the sins of the world upon himself does not mean, in Mormon theology, that he has by his sinless sacrifice brought the free gift of salvation to mortals steeped in original and actual sin and therefore unworthy of the grace bestowed upon them. In the Mormon doctrine, Christ redeems men from the physical and spiritual death imposed upon them by the transgression of Adam. . . . But he does not in any way absolve them of the consequences of their own actual evil or save them with high glory in the absence of genuine merit.[155]

THE OCCULT

Again we come to one of those points that many Mormons, being uninformed, may find hard to accept about their religion: its occult dimension. But the facts are clear. From Joseph Smith onward, numerous Mormon leaders and prophets have had strong occult interests. For example, the Smith family and Joseph himself were very interested in the occult practice of astrology. (See the authors' text *Astrology: Do the Heavens Rule Our Destiny?* [Harvest House, 1989, pp. 157-257].) This is not the accusation of "enemies" of the Mormon church but of perhaps its most academically qualified, but now excommunicated, historian, Dr. D. Michael Quinn, who holds a Ph.D. in History from Yale:

> Astrology was important to members of the Smith family. . . . Brigham Young stated in 1861 that "an effort was made in the days of Joseph to establish astrology." . . . The Hyrum Smith family preserved a magic dagger inscribed with Mars, the ruling planet of Joseph Smith Sr.'s birth year. The Hyrum Smith family also possessed magic parchments inscribed with the astrological symbols of the planets and the Zodiac . . . and the Emma Smith Badamon family preserved a magic artifact consecrated to Jupiter, the ruling planet of Joseph Smith Jr.'s birth. Based on interviews in 1886 with disaffected Mormons of early Church membership, one anti-Mormon wrote, "The only thing the Prophet believed in was astrology. This is a fact generally known to old 'Nauvoo Mormons.'"[156]

The Smith family also practiced ritual magic. Dr. Quinn observes:

> . . . the Smiths left direct evidence of their practice of ritual magic. In addition to the magic dagger, among Hyrum Smith's possessions at his death were three parchments—lamens, in occult terms—inscribed with signs and names of ceremonial magic. . . . Palmyra neighbors reported that Joseph Smith, Sr., and Joseph Smith, Jr., were drawing magic circles in the mid-1820's. . . . Several sources indicate that Joseph Jr. engaged in folk magic activities during the summers of the 1820s away from Palmyra, often in Pennsylvania.[157]

From the perspective of occult revelation, Smith's dependence upon magic ritual makes the mystical origin of the *Book of Mormon* more credible. Apparently, Smith regularly participated in the occult practice of crystal gazing. He would use "peep stones," or seer stones, in order to receive psychic information. He would place these stones in a hat, bury his face in the hat and then "see" visions of buried treasure, lost property, and suchlike.[158] Of course, this was how the

Book of Mormon was allegedly translated (see previous *"Book of Mormon"* section).

The occult origin of the Mormon religion therefore seems evident. Smith's dependence upon the supernatural for his new religion is clear: 1) the *Book of Mormon* was an occultly derived text; 2) *Doctrine and Covenants* was an occultly derived text containing over one hundred spiritistic revelations; 3) *The Pearl of Great Price* was an occultly derived text, being a second translation done by occult power; and 4) Smith's own revision of the King James Bible, his "inspired translation," may also have been accomplished by occult means.

Occult influence in Mormonism is also seen in Brigham Young, who in some degree held a mediumistic philosophy. This can be seen in his conviction that many of the dead are schooled in the afterlife before being permitted an opportunity to progress spiritually:

> If a person is baptized for the remission of sins, and dies a short time thereafter, he is not prepared at once to enjoy a fullness of the glory promised to the faithful in the Gospel; for he must be schooled while in the spirit, and other departments of the house of God, passing on from truth to truth, from intelligence to intelligence, until he is prepared to again receive his body and to enter into the presence of the Father and the Son. We cannot enter into celestial glory in our present state of ignorance and mental darkness. . . . We have more friends behind the veil than on this side, and they hail us more joyfully than you were welcomed by your parents and friends in this world; and you will rejoice more when you meet them than you ever rejoiced to see a friend in this life.[159]

This mediumistic teaching is endorsed in later Mormonism. A previous president and prophet of the Mormon church, Spencer W. Kimball, taught:

> It is the destiny of the spirits of men to come to this earth and travel a [spiritual] journey of indeterminate length. . . . While we lack recollection of our pre-mortal life, before coming to this earth all of us understood definitely the purpose of our being here. . . . We understood also that after a period varying from seconds to decades of mortal life we would die, our bodies would go

back to Mother Earth from which they had been created, and our spirits would go to the spirit world, where we would further train for our eternal destiny. After a period, there would be a resurrection or a reunion of the body and the spirit, which would render us immortal and make possible our further climb toward perfection and godhood.[160]

Sounding like a typical New Age channeler today, Kimball said: "Men came to earth consciously to obtain their schooling, their training and development, and to perfect themselves."[161]

Mormon theologian Duane S. Crowther has stated various (unbiblical) guidelines in which Mormons can contact spirits and feel safe about it. He also explained that according to Mormon belief there are at least five categories of spirits who can minister to Mormons and others. There are "pre-mortal spirits," "translated beings," "righteous spirits," "evil spirits" and "resurrected beings." The fact that Mormonism offers so many opportunities for contact with the spirits is one reason why Mormonism can be classified as a spiritistic religion. Crowther himself defines one of these categories in characteristically mediumistic terms. Allegedly, "righteous spirits return to earth to: give counsel, give comfort, obtain or give information, serve as guardian angels, prepare us for death, summon mortals into the spirit world, escort the dying through the veil of death."[162]

Joseph F. Smith, the sixth president and prophet of the Mormon church, also supported necromancy, spiritistic and mediumistic contacts with the dead:

> Our fathers and mothers, brothers, sisters and friends who have passed away from this earth, having been faithful . . . may have a mission given them to visit their relatives and friends upon the earth again, bringing from the divine Presence messages of love, of warning, or reproof and instruction, to those whom they had learned to love in the flesh. . . . Joseph Smith, Hyrum Smith, Brigham Young, Heber C. Kimball, Jed M. Grant, David Patten, Joseph Smith, Sen., and all those noble men who took an active part in the establishment of this work, and who died true and faithful to their trust, have the right and privilege, and possess the keys and

power, to minister to the people of God in the flesh who live now. . . . These are correct principles. There is no question about that in my mind. It is according to the scripture; it is according to the revelation of God to the Prophet Joseph Smith; and it is a subject upon which we may dwell with pleasure and perhaps profit to ourselves, provided we have the Spirit of God to direct us.[163]

The fourth Mormon president and prophet, Wilford Woodruff, stated in 1880:

After the death of Joseph Smith I saw and conversed with him many times in my dreams in the night season. . . . I have had many interviews with brother Joseph until the last fifteen or twenty years of my life. . . . I had many interviews with President Young, and with Heber C. Kimball, and Geo. A. Smith, and Jedediah M. Grant, and many others who are dead. *They attended our conference, they attended our meetings.*[164]

This is just the tip of a vast iceberg. The extent of occult practice throughout Mormon history is amazing to contemplate. This can be seen in detail in works like: *Early Mormonism and the Magical Worldview* (Signature Books), by leading Mormon historian D. Michael Quinn; *The Refiner's Fire: The Making of Mormon Cosmology, 1644–1844* (Cambridge University Press), by John L. Brooke; and Lance S. Owen's "Joseph Smith and the Kabbalah: The Occult Connection" (*Dialogue*, Vol. 27, No. 3, 1994), which received the Mormon Historical Association Best Article of the Year award for 1995. So even though the Bible (Deuteronomy 18:9–13) soundly condemns all forms of occultism, including necromancy and spirit contact, everything from automatic writing to out-of-body excursions and other occult practices has been endorsed by Mormons.[165] Mormons who believe that this is acceptable with God have in varying degrees adopted occult philosophy in the guise of divine revelation. One can but wonder how many well-meaning Mormons have been ensnared in occult practices *outside* their church because they were conditioned to accept occult teachings within the church (Compare with our *Behind the Mask of Mormonism*, chapters 19–20).

CRITIQUE

Here we will briefly address three key issues: 1) Mormonism's claim to be a Christian religion; 2) why Mormonism is not a Christian religion; 3) Mormonism's true beliefs about Christianity. (A much more detailed critique—200 pages—in a variety of areas can be found in *Behind the Mask of Mormonism* and in the appendices at the end of this chapter.

The Mormon Claim to Be Christian

"Mormons are Christians precisely because they sincerely say they are. No other criterion is needed . . ." (Daniel C. Petersen and Stephen D. Ricks, "Offenders for a Word"; FARMS, 1998, p. 191).

To be a Christian is to be a devout follower of the biblical Jesus Christ, which logically includes believing in the Bible as God's inerrant Word and in the doctrines of historic Christianity derived from God's Word. This is why the *Oxford American Dictionary* defines "Christian" as "of the doctrines of Christianity, believing in or based on these." "Christianity" is defined as "the religion based on the belief that Christ was the incarnate Son of God and on his teachings."[166]

A true Christian is one who has personally received Jesus Christ as his or her Lord and Savior and who leads a lifestyle in concert with orthodox biblical teaching. It is a loving and committed relationship with the God of the Bible, not merely going to church on Sundays, believing in Jesus in an intellectual sense or attempting to live "a Christian life." It is certainly not claiming to be a Christian while simultaneously rejecting Christian doctrine. Being a true Christian incorporates adherence to accurate doctrine and a godly lifestyle centered around a personal relationship with the living Jesus Christ.

No one can deny that the Mormon church deliberately seeks to be known as a Christian religion. Ezra Taft Benson, answers a resounding "yes" to the question, "Are Mormons Christians?"[167] Jack Weyland, a member of the Rapid City, South Dakota Stake Mission Presidency, mentions that several times he has faced the situation where someone has told him or another Mormon that they are not Christian. "And every time it happens I'm astonished. I usually respond by saying, 'but the name of the church is the Church of Jesus Christ of Latter-day Saints. Every prayer we utter is offered in his name. Every ordinance we perform we do in his name. We believe all the Bible says about him. . . .'"[168] Dr. Harold Goodman, a Brigham Young University professor and Latter-day Saints mission president argues, "Anyone that believes in Christ is a Christian. And we believe that we are Christians."[169]

Perhaps the most comprehensive defense of the idea that the Mormon religion is Christian is found in Dr. Steve Robinson's *Are Mormons Christians?* Robinson, who received a Ph.D. in biblical studies from Duke University,* agrees that the charge that Mormons are not Christians "is often the most commonly heard criticism of the LDS Church and its doctrines."[170] And he allows that "the charge that Mormons are not Christians is a serious charge indeed."[171] However, he argues:

Most of the time the charge that the Latter-day Saints are not Christians has absolutely nothing to do with LDS belief or non-belief in Jesus Christ, or with LDS acceptance or rejection of the New Testament as the word of God. If the term *Christian* is used, as it is in standard English to mean someone who accepts Jesus Christ as the Son of God and the Savior of the world, then the charge that Mormons aren't Christians is false.[172]

But even Robinson, despite his effort, freely concedes that Mormonism: 1) rejects traditional Christian orthodoxy;[173] 2) rejects the historic orthodox view of the Trinity;[174] and 3) rejects the specific orthodox Christian teaching concerning God.[175] Nevertheless, Robinson expresses utter astonishment that Mormonism cannot be considered Christian.

So to many people Mormons appear to be genuine Christians, and Mormons themselves

---

*While his book will undoubtedly convince many that Mormonism is a Christian religion, it will be convincing only to those who are unfamiliar with how to spot logical fallacies and lack knowledge of Mormon history and doctrine and biblical, historic and systematic theology.

are baffled when anyone expresses that they are not Christians. And we have talked with numerous Christians who see nothing at all wrong with Mormonism, believing that it is simply another Christian denomination. Former Mormons Jerald and Sandra Tanner, who for thirty years have diligently sought to help both Mormons and Christians to understand what Mormonism really teaches and why it can not be considered Christian, have told us that the greatest problem the Christian church faces concerning Mormonism is that far too many Christians think Mormonism is a Christian religion.

Why Mormonism Is Not a Christian Religion

In the previous sections of this chapter we have documented many of the Mormon teachings about God, Jesus Christ, salvation, spiritism, the *Book of Mormon* and other unbiblical notions which demonstrate that Mormonism cannot be considered a Christian religion. It is not logically possible that a religion which rejects the biblical Trinity and accepts polytheism, which denies that God always existed and instead maintains that God was once a man who evolved into Godhood, which teaches works-salvation and denies the Virgin Birth and so on can legitimately call itself Christian. Again, this is just the tip of the vast iceberg of nonChristian beliefs and practices within Mormonism (for a fuller treatment see our book *Behind the Mask of Mormonism*).

Mormonism is not true Christianity, and true Mormons cannot be considered Christians. Further, Mormon teaching and practice is not only explicitly antiChristian but also at times pagan, as Dr. Walter Martin has stated.[176] Because there is such widespread uncertainty concerning the religious status of the Mormon church, we will here document for the reader numerous reputable religious scholars and authorities, Christian and nonChristian, who classify Mormonism as a nonChristian religion.

1. As far as we know, even the liberal World Council of Churches refuses to classify Mormonism as a Christian religion.[177]

2. In his book *The Theological Foundations of the Mormon Religion*, Sterling M. McMurrin sets as a purpose: "facilitating understanding of

Mormonism."[178] Noting that Mormon theology has "a radically unorthodox concept of God," he observes that "in its conception of God as in its doctrine of man, Mormonism is a radical departure from the established theology, both Catholic and Protestant."[179] (McMurrin is E. E. Ericksen Distinguished Professor, Professor of History, Professor of Philosophy of Education and Dean of the Graduate School at the University of Utah.)

3. In his book *Is Mormonism Christian?* Gordon Fraser, author of four books on Mormonism, states: "We object to Mormon missionaries posing as Christians, and our objections are based on the differences between what they are taught by their General Authorities and what the Bible teaches."[180]

4. In his work *The Maze of Mormonism,* the late Dr. Walter Martin, acknowledged authority on comparative religion and biblical theology, observes: "In no uncertain terms, the Bible condemns the teachings of the Mormon Church."[181]

5. Former Mormons turned Christians, Jerald and Sandra Tanner, who have done perhaps more in-depth research into Mormonism than anyone else, clearly state: "The Mormon Church is certainly not built upon the teachings of the Bible. . . . Mormonism . . . is not even based on the *Book of Mormon.*"[182]

6. In his book *The Four Major Cults,* theologian Dr. Anthony Hoekema emphasizes, "We must at this point assert, in the strongest possible terms, that Mormonism does not deserve to be called a Christian religion. It is basically anti-Christian and anti-biblical."[183]

7. The *Evangelical Dictionary of Theology* concludes that the Mormon attempt to be Christian "does little justice to either Mormon theology or the Christian tradition."[184]

8. The *Encyclopedia Britannica* classifies Mormonism as a nonChristian religion: "Mormon doctrine diverges from the orthodoxy of established Christianity, particularly in its polytheism, in affirming that God has evolved from man and that men might evolve into gods, that the Persons of the Trinity are distinct beings, and that men's souls have preexisted."[185]

9. *The New Schaff-Herzog Encyclopedia of Religious Knowledge* comments:

So far as the Bible is concerned, Joseph Smith and his successors have taken such liberties with its meaning, and even with its text, that it cannot be said to have any authority for a Mormon. . . . Its doctrine of God, for example, is widely different from that of the Christian Church. The Mormon conception of deity rather resembles that of Buddhism. From it a system of anthropomorphisms has been developed, which far exceeds that of any Christian sect in any age. . . .[186]

10. *The New International Dictionary of the Christian Church* concludes: "An examination of the doctrines taught by the Mormon Church will reveal that they deny most of the cardinal teachings of the Christian faith."[187]

The Real Mormon Beliefs About Christianity

In closing this chapter we thought it might be helpful to cite some of the true views of Christianity that are held by the Mormon church. Because these are in the background of Mormonism, people may find them surprising, being as far different as they are from the neighborly image the church seeks to uphold.

Christians are unbelievers. Brigham Young dogmatically insisted that "Christians profess to believe in Jesus Christ; but, if be told the truth, not one of them really believes in him."[188] In the Introduction to Joseph Smith's *History of the Church,* leading Mormon church historian Brigham Henry Roberts (1857–1933) declares that those who profess belief in the great defining creeds of Christianity (Nicean, Athanasian and so on) "are wandering in the darkness of the mysticisms of the old pagan philosophies."[189] He further claims that these creeds "exhibit the wide departure—the absolute apostasy—that has taken place in respect of this most fundamental of all doctrines of religion—the doctrine of God. Truly, 'Christians' have denied the Lord that bought them, and turned literally to fables."[190]

Christians are satanic false teachers. Joseph Smith, who still remains the most influential man in Mormonism, said that Christian pastors: "Are of their father the devil. . . . We shall see all the priests who adhere to the sectarian [Christian] religions of the day, with all their followers, without one exception, receive their portion with the devil and his angels."[191] In 1 Nephi, chapters 13, 14 and elsewhere, the *Book of Mormon* calls the Christian church "a church which is most abominable above all other churches"; it is "the great and abominable church" founded by the devil; it is "the mother of abominations" and the great "whore of Babylon."[192] In an official compilation of Joseph Smith's writings, *Teachings of the Prophet Joseph Smith*, we find the following assessment: "What is it that inspires professors of Christianity generally with the hope of salvation? It is that smooth, sophisticated influence of the devil, by which he deceives the whole world."[193]

Christians are ignorant of the things of God. Brigham Young, declared:

> With regard to true theology, a more ignorant people never lived than the present so-called Christian world.[194]

> The Christian world, so called, are heathens as to their knowledge of the salvation of God.[195]

> The Christian world, I discovered . . . was groveling in darkness.[196]

> We may very properly say that the sectarian [Christian] world [does] not know anything correctly, so far as pertains to salvation. . . . They are more ignorant than children.[197]

The third president and prophet of the church, John Taylor, held the same view:

> We talk about Christianity, but it is a perfect pack of nonsense. . . . And the Devil could not invent a better engine to spread his work than the Christianity of the 19th century.[198]

> I consider that if I ever lost any time in my life, it was while studying the Christian theology. Sectarian [Christian] theology is the greatest tomfoolery in the world.[199]

> What does the Christian world know about God? Nothing; yet these very men assume the right and power to tell others what they shall and what they shall not believe in. Why, so far

as the things of God are concerned, they are the veriest fools, they know neither God nor the things of God.[200]

> What! Are Christians ignorant? Yes, as ignorant of the things of God as the brute beast.[201]

Mormon apostle Orson Pratt declared that "the whole of Christendom is as destitute of Bible Christianity as the idolatrist Pagans."[202] B. H. Roberts, noted Mormon church historian and member of the "First Council of Seventy," referred to Christians as those, "who are blindly led by the blind."[203]

Christians teach false doctrines. Mormon Apostle Orson Pratt, in a shrill and railing tone, emphasized the evils of Christianity:

> Will Christendom have the unblushing impudence to call themselves the people of God . . . ? How long will the heavens suffer such wickedness to go unpunished![204]

> Another evil of no small magnitude is the vast amount of false doctrines which are taught, and extensively believed, and practiced throughout Christendom. Doctrines which are calculated to ruin the soul. . . . These soul-destroying doctrines . . . are taught in Christendom, and . . . millions have had the wickedness to believe [them]. . . . Now what will become of all these false teachers . . . and what will become of the people who suffer themselves to be led by such hypocrites? They will, every soul of them, unless they repent of these false doctrines, be cast down to hell. . . . Such heaven-daring wickedness is calculated to sink these vile impostors to the lowest hell. And unless the people repent of having received baptism and other ordinances of the Gospel at the hands of such deceivers . . . [and] embrace the fulness of the Gospel which God has revealed anew in the *Book of Mormon* . . . [everyone] of you will, most assuredly, be damned.[205]

In our time the rhetoric is toned down but the view remains. Joseph Fielding Smith has stated that "gospel truth [was] perverted and defiled" by Catholicism until it became a pagan abomination, and even the Reformation "perpetuated these evils and, therefore, the same corrupted doctrines and practices were perpetuated in these Protestant organizations."[206] In his *Mormon Doctrine*, Bruce McConkie universally condemns all non-Mormon churches, asserting that "a perverted Christianity holds sway among the so-called Christians of apostate Christendom."[207] He also observes, commenting on the *Book of Mormon* (1 Nephi, chs. 13–14; 2 Nephi, chs. 28–29): "The *Church of the Devil* and the *Great and Abominable Church* are [terms] used to identify all churches or organizations of whatever name or nature . . . which are designed to take men on a course that leads away from God and his laws and thus from salvation in the kingdom of God [the Mormon Church]. . . . There is no salvation outside this one true Church, the [Mormon] Church of Jesus Christ."[208] In his *Doctrinal New Testament Commentary*, McConkie alleges that Christians are the true enemies of God because the true teachings of God "have been changed and perverted by an apostate Christendom."[209] Further, modern Christians are ignorant of God's true purposes,[210] and Christian doctrines are the "doctrines of devils."[211] Thus, the Christian church is part of "the great and abominable church" of the devil preparing men "to be damned."[212]

One can only conclude that despite the claims of the Mormon church and the sincere conviction of Mormon people, Mormonism is not a Christian religion. From its inception, Mormonism has distanced itself from historic Christian faith, believing that Christianity is an apostate religion that damns the souls of its followers.

TALKING WITH MEMBERS

As is true for most groups in this encyclopedia, talking with Mormons can be difficult because of the semantics barrier. When Christian or biblical words are used, they have a meaning unique to the cult, not one consistent with historic Christian or biblical meaning. Both Mormons and Christians need to understand that when they use terms such as God, Jesus Christ, trinity, grace, virgin birth, salvation, heaven, hell, the scriptures and so on they will be talking past one another unless they understand what each group means by these terms (see Doctrinal Summary). Christians who never discover what Mormons mean by these terms may assume they are talking with another Christian.

In addition, the fact that most Mormons are uninformed on their doctrinal history compounds the problem. A common response to the discussion of specifics of Mormon teaching historically is, "We do not believe that." In this response, they deny the teachings of their own inspired prophets. (See Appendix 4.)

At the very least, Mormons can be informed that their definitions of key theological terms, such as God, Jesus Christ and salvation, do not conform to historic or biblical meanings. The burden of proof remains with LDS to give some evidence for their definitions of words and theological beliefs. So far, none has been provided.

One of the most important issues to discuss with Mormons is the issue of spiritual authority. For example, Joseph Smith's false prophecies clearly prove that he was not a prophet of God. Because he spoke in the name of the Lord and gave false prophecies, the only option available is to consider him a false prophet. Although the contexts are different, the following Scriptures are relevant to Joseph Smith. God tells us the true prophet is "recognized as one truly sent by the LORD *only* if his prediction comes true" (Jeremiah 28:9, emphasis added). This is because "whatever I say *will* be fulfilled, declares the sovereign LORD" (Ezekiel 12:28, emphasis added). God's accuracy will be nothing less than 100 percent, for He is a God "who does not lie" (Titus 1:2); indeed lying is impossible for Him (Hebrews 6:18; cf. 1 John 2:21). Therefore whenever *God* predicts something, it *must* come to pass.

Coupled with visual documentation of Smith's false prophecies cited in this chapter (or others if necessary),* the following verses may be useful in discussion:

> You may say to yourselves, "How can we know when a message has not been spoken by the LORD?" If what a prophet proclaims in the name of the LORD does not take place or come true, that is a message the LORD has not spoken. That

---

*See *Behind the Mask of Mormonism*, ch. 25; or see the material available from Utah Lighthouse Ministry, Box 1884, Salt Lake City, UT 84410.

prophet has spoken presumptuously. Do not be afraid of him. (Deuteronomy 18:21–22)

This verse teaches that Joseph Smith spoke presumptuously when he repeatedly claimed to speak *in the name of the Lord.* (See all the prophecies in *Doctrine & Covenants.*) Therefore, Mormons are not to fear him or heed his words for the simple reason his prophecies did not come to pass.

The following verse teaches that even miracles are not necessarily proof of prophetic claims:

If a prophet, or one who foretells by dreams, appears among you and announces to you a miraculous sign or wonder, and if the sign or wonder of which he has spoken takes place, and he says, "Let us follow other gods" (gods you have not known) "and let us worship them," you must not listen to the words of that prophet or dreamer. The LORD your God is testing you to find out whether you love him with all your heart and with all your soul. It is the LORD your God you must follow, and him you must revere. Keep his commands and obey him; serve him and hold fast to him. That prophet or dreamer must be put to death, because he preached rebellion against the LORD your God.... (Deuteronomy 13:1–5)

Obviously, if a genuine miracle occurs but did not come from God, it had to come from the devil. And it is the devil that is most desirous of robbing God of His glory by having people worship false gods. Thus, the miraculous signs and visions of Joseph Smith are not to be heeded for the simple reason that he counseled people to follow and worship false gods rather than the God of the Bible. Thus, *"you must not listen to the words of that prophet."* In effect, Smith preached rebellion against the Lord.

The next verse illustrates that those who follow their own visions and imaginations may be deceived into thinking that they are receiving revelation from the Lord. In fact, they are so deceived they even expect their predictions to be fulfilled, but they are not fulfilled because God never spoke to such individuals in the first place:

The word of the LORD came to me: "... Say to those who prophesy out of their own imagination: 'Hear the word of the LORD! This is what

the Sovereign LORD says: Woe to the foolish prophets who follow their own spirit and have seen nothing! ... Their visions are false and their divinations a lie. They say, "The LORD declares," when the LORD has not sent them; yet they expect their words to be fulfilled. Have you not seen false visions and uttered lying divinations when you say, "The LORD declares," though I have not spoken?' " (Ezekiel 13:1–7)

As a result of a false prophet's self-deceptions, God will be against them:

"Therefore this is what the Sovereign LORD says: Because of your false words and lying visions, I am against you, declares the Sovereign LORD. My hand will be against the prophets who see false visions and utter lying divinations. They will not belong to the council of my people ..." (Ezekiel 13:8–9)

Because false prophets lead people astray from the one true God, to worship false gods (with all that implies), God declares that He personally opposes those who see false visions and utter lying divinations. Mormons believe that Joseph Smith was a godly prophet and that God had uniquely inspired Smith to reveal the original Christian Gospel that the Christian church had corrupted. But the truth is far more sobering. Joseph Smith never repented of his god or his beliefs. This means that God Himself was opposed to Smith, who died at the hands of an angry mob while in jail. Clearly, false prophets are to have no place among the people of God. Certainly, this speaks volumes to those Christians who believe that Mormons are genuine Christians and who wish to stress commonality and "areas of (alleged) agreement" with them.

Almost everything mentioned in this verse is applicable to Joseph Smith:

Let no one be found among you ... who practices divination or sorcery, interprets omens, engages in witchcraft, or casts spells, or who is a medium or spiritist or who consults the dead. Anyone who does these things is detestable to the LORD.... (Deuteronomy 18:10–12)

Smith practiced divination and sorcery, aspects of witchcraft, interpreted omens, cast spells, was a spiritist and consulted the dead.

According to God, then, Joseph Smith was detestable to the Lord.

Mormons should be challenged to study very carefully the original prophecies of Joseph Smith and determine for themselves whether they are legitimate. Then, at least, should they accept them, they will have no one to blame but themselves for the consequences.

A related issue here involves the dilemma relating to the authority of the LDS church itself. As we documented in *Behind the Mask of Mormonism*, modern Mormon church prophets have denied many of the teachings of the early Mormon prophets, such as Joseph Smith and Brigham Young. On what basis do they do this? Either these men were true prophets or they were not. If they were true prophets, then to change, deny or suppress their revealed teachings is an act of rebellion and blasphemy against God. But if they were not true prophets, no one should have listened to them in the first place. In essence, because modern church authorities have ignored or altered their own prophets teachings (teachings they should never have listened to in the first place), they have no authority to command respect today.

Mormons should, in addition, be encouraged to independently investigate the truth claims of Christianity. If, as Socrates noted, the unexamined life is not worth living, this must also be true for the unexamined belief or religion.

If the most important thing in life is loving God—God himself declares we are to love him with our entire mind (Matthew 22:37)—how are we really going to love God if we won't even examine the evidence to see if our faith is really valid? We are not talking here about examining the 'evidence' for Mormonism through the biased eyes of FARMS or the distorted apologetic research of BYU scholars. The real evidence needs to be examined objectively through the impartial eyes of history, logic, common sense and, most importantly, the basic doctrines of Christianity.

The weight of historical and other evidence against Mormonism is crushing. This may explain why the vast majority of Mormons will not examine it, but it can hardly excuse their irresponsibility at this point. Perhaps the best survey to recommend here is by former Mormons

Jerald and Sandra Tanner, *The Changing World of Mormonism* (Moody Press). Mormons who are unwilling to read this book need to be encouraged to work through the reasons why they will not. (Indeed, the most formidable literature proving that Mormonism cannot be a revelation from God can be found at the Tanners Utah Lighthouse Ministry [PO Box 1884, Salt Lake City, UT, 84110.] They can be reached by phone at 801-485-8894 or at their website: http://utlm.org.) Also, there are many other quality resources available that supply specific techniques for reaching Mormons. These can be found through Alpha and Omega Ministries, Watchman Fellowship and other organizations listed at the front of this volume.

Another point is that if virtually everybody outside of Mormonism recognizes that it is not Christian, and yet Mormons have been told they are Christian, this alone should encourage members to examine the issue for themselves—independently from their church. Any church that can make such an incredible blunder should have the unexamined trust of no one.

Mormons should also be challenged to consider the consequences of failing to prove the truth of their religion. The historic, prophetic and scientific evidence for the truth of Christianity is compelling, as we documented in *Ready with an Answer* (Harvest House, 1997) and in other works. The evidence for Mormonism is nonexistent. For Mormonism to arrive 1800 years after the truths of Christianity are established and claim to all the world that Christianity is a damnable lie is just a bit presumptuous. Certainly, grand claims require grand evidence. For Mormonism to make these claims—without offering a shred of evidence—is pure bluff and disrespect.

If Christianity is true, and the biblical Jesus Christ is the only way to God, then unrepentant faith in the Mormon Jesus will help no one. In fact, it will damn them forever. As Jesus said, "If you do not believe that I am the one I claim to be, you will indeed die in your sins" (John 8:24). "I am the way and the truth and the life. No one comes to the Father except through me" (John 14:6). Based on the evidence for historic Christianity and the lack of evidence for Mormonism, LDS saints sit precipitously on the horns of a dilemma. If this simple fact—that the fate of their eternal soul hangs in the balance—is insufficient to gain their interest in a *truly* independent investigation of the issues surrounding the truth claims of Mormonism and Christianity, then probably nothing will.

APPENDIX 1:
FARMS—THE FOUNDATION
FOR ANCIENT RESEARCH AND
MORMON STUDIES

The Foundation for Ancient Research and Mormon Studies (FARMS) publishes literature in defense of Mormonism, especially the *Book of Mormon*. It describes its work in the following manner:

> The work of the Foundation rests on the premise that the Book of Mormon and other [LDS] scriptures were written by prophets of God. Belief in this premise—in the divinity of scripture—is a matter of faith. Religious truths require divine witness to establish the faith of the believer. While scholarly research cannot replace that witness, such studies may reinforce and encourage individual testimonies by fostering understanding and appreciation of the scriptures.[213]

FARMS has over 100 Brigham Young University scholars working on its projects and a multimillion dollar budget to pursue its goals: "They strongly believe that no other organization on earth can compete with their knowledge of the *Book of Mormon.* They are convinced that as far as human wisdom is concerned they are the ultimate experts on the subject. Consequently, they are very offended if anyone ignores or is ignorant of the research emanating from FARMS." [214]

Although this is clearly the most scholarly venue of Mormon apologetics, unfortunately for FARMS, its first ten years indicate the horse has stumbled at the gate and is close to dying. FARMS cannot defend what does not exist. Its literature may appear persuasive, but so does the literature of evolutionary scientists. Evolution seems persuasive to those with naturalistic spectacles because their assumptions cause them to ignore or misinterpret factual data they might otherwise accept. In a similar fashion,

FARMS materials seem persuasive to those with Mormon spectacles because their assumptions cause them to ignore or misinterpret factual data they might otherwise accept. Here's an analogy from outside Mormonism to help illustrate this point. The "ABC Evening News" of June 2, 1998 reported upon a thorough investigation into the reason why the CIA failed so completely to ascertain that India was going to test nuclear bombs. It was not because the intelligence data was poor. The intelligence data was actually very clear—satellite images unmistakably showed the preparations underway for India's nuclear tests. The real problem was one of preexisting beliefs and, perhaps, naivete. The CIA was so convinced India would not explode a nuclear device, it was actually incapacitated from properly interpreting the evidence. The evidence was there, plainly in front of them. But it was not seen. As a result, the evidence that was there was missed or had to be interpreted otherwise. In a similar manner, Mormons may be so convinced of the truth of their religion that they become incapacitated when it comes to seeing and properly interpreting the evidence that is right before them, in Scripture and history, that discredits their beliefs.

When the basic arguments are examined critically in either case, whether of evolution or Mormonism, they simply do not stand. In fact, in neither case do they even have the possibility of standing. Naturalistic evolution was disproved the day Moses penned Genesis under divine inspiration. It was disproved on the basis of the authority of Scripture and, as we documented in *Darwin's Leap of Faith* (Harvest House, 1998) and elsewhere, has always been disproved by the philosophical, common sense and scientific arguments against it. In a similar fashion, Mormonism was disproved the day Joseph Smith wrote down and published his initial theology. It was disproved on the basis of the authority of scripture that proves it false and on the basis of the historical evidence against it. FARMS thus has an impossible job because it attempts an impossible task: successfully answering critics and "proving" Mormonism true.

Of course, FARMS does not directly claim to prove Mormonism, since the only real "proof" in Mormonism is the subjective "witness" of the

"Holy Spirit" to the alleged divine origin of the *Book of Mormon* (Moroni 10:3–5). FARMS recognizes that it has little hard evidence, which probably explains why it spends so much time attacking critics of Mormonism and "correcting" their endless "errors." Nevertheless, in claiming to reinforce individual Mormon testimonies, etc., through scholarly means, it does suggest its work contributes to the evidential verification of Mormonism. Unfortunately, in making everyone's legitimate criticism and disproof of Mormonism look bad, rather than offering convincing evidence *for* Mormonism, it has established a track record that will be difficult to live down. As Dr. James White wrote in, "Of Cities and Swords: the Impossible Task of Mormon Apologetics": "FARMS regularly promotes an image of scholarship, but serious problems with FARMS scholarship readily appear when they attempt to defend specific and unique elements of the claims of Mormonism. . . . No veneer of scholarly acumen can make a culture appear in history that was not, in fact, there. And no amount of work by FARMS can make Joseph Smith something he was not: a prophet of God."[215] (See Appendix 3 for more on FARMS.)

APPENDIX 2:
EVANGELICAL NEGLECT?

A few evangelical scholars have claimed that Mormon scholars are marshalling truly able defenses of Mormonism, and Mormons have now answered most of the standard evangelical criticisms of their faith. They have also stated that nearly all evangelical responses to Mormonism are inadequate. Other evangelical scholars today have implied or claimed that Mormonism is not as opposed to Christianity as commonly thought.

Evangelicals Carl Mosser and Paul Owen wrote an article entitled "Mormon Scholarship, Apologetic and Evangelical Neglect: Losing the Battle and Not Knowing It?" published in the Fall 1998 *Trinity Journal*.[216] They claim the following: "Currently there are, as far as we are aware, no books from an evangelical perspective that responsibly interact with contemporary LDS scholarly and apologetics writings. . . . At the academic level evangelicals are losing the debate with the Mormons."[217]

They proceed to discuss how they believe current Mormon scholarship is making significant headway in bolstering their faith: "In what intellectually plausible ways are they supporting their unique scriptural canon and doctrinal system? The main body of this paper is devoted to illustrating the answer to this question." They further claim, "Mormons have the training and skills to produce robust defenses of their faith."[218] And, "There are *many* more studies which could be mentioned, but this should suffice to demonstrate that LDS academians are producing serious research which desperately needs to be critically examined from an informed evangelical perspective."[219]

At website www. apologeticsindex.org, Carl Mosser argues that Christian apologists responding to Mormonism have a large degree of responsibility for the dearth of materials responding to recent LDS scholarship and have inadequately informed their readers about its threat: "Frankly, I think that those who have spent years doing apologetics against Mormonism are culpable for this state of affairs. . . . It is wrong that they have not given their readers an accurate portrayal of the level of sophistication to which LDS arguments have risen. It is wrong that they have pridefully insisted that they can handle it all by themselves and . . . have not asked for help from reputable evangelical scholars. If Paul and I have sometimes come across as a little bitter, it's because we are angry that things have been allowed to get so out of hand. There is no reason for things to be the way they are. There "should" be good books out there dealing with this stuff; there are none. Since we became aware of the need we have been doing our darndest to do what we can to remedy this situation. But this is a process and takes time. We began by familiarizing ourselves intimately with the LDS literature and with articulate LDS theology and philosophy. We wrote [this] paper . . . as an attempt to sound the alarm to our own scholars and make them aware that their skills are needed. . . . This is going to require a team effort. The Mormons have a number of scholars with expertise in a variety of disciplines. A full-scale rebuttal will require the help of specialists in Old Testament, New Testament, Ancient Near Eastern Cultures, church history, American history, philosophy, theology, archeology and others."

One can understand Mosser and Owens frustration at this point in discovering a perceived threat and yet finding no Christian responses available as a counterpoint. Fair enough. The LDS have improved their apologetic scholarship and it needs addressing by the evangelical church. We can applaud Mosser and Owen for pointing out the problem and rising to the task apologetically.

Needless Concerns?

What disquiets us about their article is not pointing out that Mormon apologists/scholars have improved their learning in the last generation and are attempting to more forcefully defend their faith academically. As Mosser and Owen noted, "For many years, [Hugh] Nibley may have been conservative Mormonism's only reputable scholar."[220] (Not everyone grants that Nibley was a reputable scholar when forced to defend Mormonism. See Appendix 3.) And it's not that we don't wish to see lay Mormons' apologetic use of FARMS (The Foundation for Ancient Research and Mormon Studies) materials addressed. (Thankfully, Mosser and Owens call to action has worked and recent LDS scholarly apologetics are now being addressed, with several books in various stages of publication.) What we are concerned with is making FARMS/LDS scholarship sound sufficiently important that it distorts both its relevance and the relevance of responsible evangelical work to date. The implication from Mosser and Owen seems to be that almost all evangelical responses to Mormonism are of little or no value, merely because they have not dealt with recent FARMS/LDS scholarship. But interacting with FARMS, pressing as that may be, is not necessary to disproving Mormonism. And we disagree that recent LDS scholarship has adequately answered most evangelical criticisms of Mormonism.

The point we have emphasized is that a Christian response has already, finally and decisively, proved Mormonism a false religion on the basis of biblical doctrine/apologetics, standard Mormon doctrine and extensive historical research. What we are looking at with newer LDS work is a cleaning up after the plane crash. No matter what you do, the plane is not going to fly again. Actually, it never flew to begin with—it was only propped with wires to make it look like it flew. So what can FARMS/LDS scholars do? Granted, like die-hard evolutionists, they can muddy the waters with technical and seemingly scholarly defenses of their faith. This will bolster Mormons and may confuse some Christians, and thus should be addressed. But they can never do more.

Of course we think it is good that the scholarly Christian community should be called upon by those with apologetic ministries to Mormons. We doubt it was a problem of pride as much as one of time and resources dealing with the large amount of poorly reasoned materials. But we are thankful that Mosser and Owen and other scholars are now taking the time to gear up to seriously engage FARMS/LDS scholarship. They deserve our support.

But let's also remember that if Mormonism is *proved* false scripturally—and that a great deal of research by the Tanners and more liberal Mormon scholars proves the same historically—then it seems to be overstating the case to argue that "*important* scholarly arguments" are being ignored against Christianity and in defense of LDS doctrine. Technical, scholarly arguments exist. But it is doubtful there can be *important* scholarly arguments in defense of myths.

Everything we know tells us the *Book of Mormon* is a myth and that Mormonism is a false religion. Arguments exist which deny this, but in light of the facts, one may question their overall importance and impact. To return to the aviation analogy, it's kind of like trying to put that jumbo jet together after it has crashed. It just isn't possible. A Herculean effort with microscopes might put together a small part of the plane, but its fate is sealed. To put it bluntly, Mormonism crashed to smithereens on the mountain of Scripture and history. Great efforts by FARMS, etc., may piece together a wing flap or even erect a part of the tail, but nothing they do will ever make it fly. It's probably not a good idea to suggest otherwise lest some people become confused and believe there's some validity in Mormon claims. We don't think it is good scholarship to try to raise downed airplanes. This is one reason it is easy to view the latest LDS efforts to academically support their faith as more deception common to the history of Mormonism, rather than as true scholarship. After uninterrupted disingenuousness, the ability to trust anything that comes from the mouth of that church has disappeared.

Mosser and Owen point out that gnostic, apocryphal and Kabalistic literature provides some support for Mormonism. And, allegedly, a few church Fathers may have held beliefs similar to Mormonism at certain points. The authors themselves are aware of a problem: "In response to the topics we have been discussing one might assert that they are simply irrelevant to the issue at hand. After all, if Mormons cannot ground their beliefs in the Bible it does not matter whether or not they find support for them among the Dead Sea Scrolls, pseudepigrapha, or church history. Without the Bible it does not matter whether they are using their expertise in Near Eastern history, cultures and languages to defend a possible Near Eastern background for the Book of Mormon. We agree that there is truth in this objection."[221]

Indeed, there is truth in this objection. However, they go on to state, "But the issues are not so simple that they can be dismissed in this way." Mosser and Owen argue that Mormons are now building an effective LDS contextual superstructure "necessary for a *proper* interpretation of the Bible, particularly the New Testament. They are arranging the evidence in a manner that will, if flaws are not demonstrated, *warrant* an interpretation of the New Testament that is *both* historically and culturally based and at odds with evangelicals theology."[222] In other words, they apparently believe Mormons are now laying the groundwork for an interpretation of the Bible that may *effectively* support Mormon beliefs.

We suspect that Mormons are indeed "arranging the evidence"—but not in an objective or credible fashion. Though rarely in a scholarly manner, cultists "arrange the evidence" all the time to make the Bible "support" their beliefs. Liberals like those in the "Jesus Seminar" have also tried to do this and failed, despite their scholarship, as we briefly detailed in *The Facts on False Views of Jesus: The Truth about the Jesus Seminar* (Harvest House, 1997). We would argue that the flaws are already demonstrated in this kind of approach because the facts of history and the accepted historical, grammatical interpretation of the New Testament establishes Christian doctrine, not Mormon doctrine or liberal conclusions about Jesus. Because Christian doctrine is beyond dispute on this very basis, all Mormon attempts to establish their interpretive superstructure, at least for any objective analysis/interpretation of Scripture, are doomed to failure. Again, this does not mean such arguments should not be examined and refuted—they should be. But if LDS faith *is* capable of a robust defense historically, then it is possible to put crashed airplanes back into the air. At that point Christianity itself could be the myth.

At one level it can be argued, as Mosser and Owen do, that "the need is great for trained evangelical biblical scholars, theologians, philosophers and historians to examine and answer the growing body of literature produced by traditional LDS scholars and apologists." But will the new LDS "evidence" be persuasive? It does not seem so, even to Paul Owen. At the same website location, he mentions: "We say that currently evangelicals are 'needlessly' losing this battle. The Mormons have an advantage only because of evangelical neglect, not because their arguments are compelling. It should be obvious that we have read as much of this stuff as anyone, probably more than even most Mormons have, and we remain unconvinced. This ought to be a little troubling to the Latter-day saint who looks to FARMS for inspiration. We have read a good chunk of their best scholarship as charitably as we can and remain unpersuaded." In truth, the evidence will never be persuasive, and the reason is because Christianity is true.

In conclusion, we think that the "threat" of recent LDS scholarship is not quite so alarming as some people indicate. Besides scholarly assessment, what is needed is for Christian scholars to digest this new LDS approach to the data and make it available in chewable form for the layperson who may encounter it in talking with

Mormons. We applaud Mosser and Owen for their contribution toward stirring up Christian scholars to the task at hand. But we still believe that many responsible and current works adequately address LDS doctrine and "older" apologetics that are still popular among LDS. Whatever flaws they have, they should be retained and used because they tell the truth about Mormonism.

REAL CONCERNS

In 1992, we warned that there was an effort underway to reach or use evangelicals to make Mormonism seem Christian, even evangelical, by emphasizing alleged areas of common ground. (We have also seen this with Catholics in the "Evangelical and Catholics Together" statement, and with Unification Church members in their Evangelical/Unification church dialogues, and with others.) A number of books have recently been written by members of both faiths claiming that Mormonism and Christianity are not so opposed as commonly believed. These include *How Wide the Divide? A Mormon and an Evangelical in Conversation* (InterVarsity, 1997), by evangelical Christian scholar Dr. Craig Blomberg and Mormon scholar Dr. Stephen Robinson, Stephen E. Robinson's *Are Mormons Christian?* (1991) and Richard R. Hopkins *Biblical Mormonism* (1994). (The last two have added greatly to the confusion among the uninformed, never mind that they fail to accomplish their goal of showing how Christian Mormonism really is.)

In their book, Craig Blomberg, of Denver seminary, and Stephen Robinson, of Brigham Young University, attempt a dialogue to show areas of agreement and difference. As I, John Weldon, spent the first hour reading this book, I happened to hear in the background not one but two nationally televised ads of the Mormon Church attempting to draw in unsuspecting converts. I thought it ironic. Here I was reading a book by a "progressive" evangelical (one wonders what the term even means anymore), a book that confuses eternal issues, while simultaneously thousands of people were responding to Mormon TV ads making them susceptible to a "gospel" that would damn them forever. Here

is a point no dialogue will ever get beyond. Nevertheless, consider some of the claims and declarations of agreement (all page citations are from the 1997 IVP edition). Dr. Robinson, author of *Are Mormons Christians?* and *Believing Christ,* argues that, "Yes, Latter-day Saints believe things that Evangelicals do not, but the huge amount of doctrinal and scriptural overlap and agreement between us is much greater than the disagreement" (p. 60). Later, he declares, "As the Saints have returned to careful study of the Scriptures, we have been reminded of the importance of what we share with mainline Christians: Christ-centered living, the doctrine of the atonement, grace, justification by faith, and sanctification by the Spirit" (p. 67).

Dr. Blomberg and Dr. Robinson conclude together on the topic of Scripture that there was "more agreement between us than we had expected to find" (p. 75). Their joint conclusion on God is that "both Evangelicals and Latter-day Saints believe in an omniscient, omnipotent, omnipresent, infinite, eternal and unchangeable God" (pp. 109–110). Their joint conclusion on Christ and the Trinity is: "Both sides accept the biblical data about Christ and the Trinity, but interpret them by different extrabiblical standards (the ancient creeds for Evangelicals, the modern revelations of Joseph Smith for Mormons)" (p. 142). Their joint declaration on salvation concludes with the following: "Both Mormons and evangelicals trust that they will be brought into a right relationship with God by Jesus Christ, who is both the Son of God and God the Son. Both believed in the substitutionary atonement of Christ, justification by faith in Christ, and salvation by grace" (pp. 186–87). Later they emphasize, "In fact, adjusted for differences in terminology, the LDS doctrines of justification by faith and salvation by grace are not as different from Evangelical definitions as many on either side believe" (p. 193). Indeed, 12 "foundational propositions of the Christian gospel as we both understand it" are jointly affirmed on p. 195! And their conclusion on the atonement of Christ is that, "We jointly affirm that his death on the cross completed an infinite, vicarious atonement that paid for the sins of the world and reconciled God and humanity" (p. 142).

Unfortunately, Robinson did not accurately portray or represent Mormonism, so Blomberg was taken in by deception. Anyone who reads Phil Roberts review in the *Journal of Christian Apologetics,* Winter, 1997; or Stephen F. Canon's review in The October-December, 1997 *Quarterly Journal;* or the response by Mormon Dave Combe in "Truth-Telling And Shifting Theologies: An Analytical Look At How Wide The Divide?" from *Salt Lake City Sunstone,* Thursday, 7 August 1997 Session 166, 3:30–4:30 P.M.; or Dr. John White's review in the November–December, 1997 *Christian Research Journal;* or many other reviews by evangelicals, will see, once again, why evangelicals should never trust Mormons: the deception never ends. As Cannon points out in the *Quarterly Journal,* and as the Tanners have documented in numerous volumes, "If the LDS/MGS [magisterium] hadn't, through the years, engaged in publicly denying what has been privately believed and then trying to rewrite history to cover it all up, there wouldn't be the need to evaluate closely every word that proceeds from LDS church headquarters" (p. 30).

One can only wonder what the real outcome of this unfortunate dialogue will be. The stated intent was to clarify; regrettably, it will only confuse both Mormons and Christians. Worse, uninformed churches and Christians who take the author's advice at the end of the book may also leave themselves open to deception: "Might we look forward to the day when youth groups or adult Sunday-school classes from Mormon and Evangelical churches in the same neighborhoods would gather periodically to share their beliefs with each other in love and for the sake of understanding, not proselytizing? (This has already happened in some places.)" (p. 191).

If, as the authors concluded, "LDS doctrines of justification by faith and salvation by grace are not as different from Evangelical definitions as many on either side believe" (p. 193), how many young or uninformed Christians might just be open to accepting the Mormon church or even joining it? The Mormons are certainly never going to stop converting everyone they can to their faith. And it's a sure bet that the LDS church will take advantage of every opportunity presented to convert Christians to Mormonism. That's part of their "new" agenda. So, once again, we see the Christian church taken in by deception.

Not surprisingly, L. Ara Norwood, who writes reviews for FARMS, extolled "their landmark book" in his slanted review of Kurt Van Gorden's *Mormonism,* praising the authors for "demonstrat[ing] a mastery of openness and inquiry." To be frank, when someone as biased as Norwood (see the reference to Dr. White's response in Appendix 3) praises a book on Christian-Mormon dialogue, one can be certain that evangelical Christianity has not been the winner.

We think that evangelicals should seriously reconsider this "new" approach to dialogue with Mormons. What is actually indefensible is seeming to, or even partially coming to, the defense of Mormonism. As James White concluded in his *Christian Research Journal* review of *How Wide the Divide?* :

> The most troubling issue raised by this book is not its inaccurate portrayal of Mormonism, nor even the confusion that that portrayal will inevitably cause many who read it. The most troubling issue is this: are we to be seeking this kind of dialogue? . . . Where, biblically, are we encouraged to lay out our areas of "agreement" with false teachers? Did Paul seek to minimize the gulf between himself and the false teachers in Galatia, or the gnostics in Colossae, by focusing on similarities? . . . The result is that the massive gulf that separates orthodox Christians and Mormons is in danger of being seen as a mere interpretational gap, rather than the canyon that yawns between those who worship the one eternal God and those who promote the exalted man-become-God of Joseph Smith" (p. 31).

No doubt the motives are good in this kind of dialogue, but they always are. What is often not considered beforehand in endeavors of this type is the damage done. The average Christian, not infrequently confused as to the true nature of Mormonism by lack of theological study and fraudulent Mormon claims, is now further confirmed in their uncertainty or errors by well-meaning evangelicals who argue that Mormon scholarship is credible or that Mormonism and Christianity are compatible, or not so far apart as thought in key doctrinal points. But as we fully documented in *Behind the Mask of Mormonism* (Harvest House, 1996), Mormonism is one of the most thoroughgoing antiChristian cults in the world. And we do not use the term antiChristian casually. Mormonism is not neutral toward Christianity. It actively opposes it. Because Mormonism is antiChristian, to compromise with it can neither be considered a faithful defense of the gospel nor something conducive to the salvation of souls.

THE CONSEQUENCES OF CONFUSION

To illustrate, some Christians are even calling some Mormons "evangelical Christians" and, apparently, 26% of Mormons now claim to be "born-again" Christians! This figure was reported in the LDS *Sunstone* magazine (August, 1998, p. 21). It further reported LDS' worldwide growth rate from 1978–93 at 156%, U.S growth rate at 82% and Africa's growth rate at an unbelievable 963%—almost 1000%! This is hardly the time, then, to confuse theologies.

If a poll were conducted to determine how many Christians currently believe Mormons are Christian, we would not be surprised if the figure were embarrassingly high. Even former President and Southern Baptist Jimmy Carter illustrates our concerns at this point. According to *The Quarterly Journal* (Vol. 18, no. 2, p. 3):

> [Carter "has] denounced leaders of his denomination for declaring that professing members of The Church of Jesus Christ of Latter-day Saints are non-Christians. . . . [The] former U.S. President also told the Mormon-owned *Deseret News* that his church's leaders were 'narrow in their definition of what is a proper Christian or certainly even a proper Baptist.' The newspaper also declared that Carter had misgivings about 'Christians trying to convert other Christians' [Mormons]."

With confusion like this, Christians obviously need to be better informed on Mormonism.

APPENDIX 3: A BRIEF LOOK AT MORMON SCHOLARSHIP

Scholarship is defined as a "standard of academic work" and "the systematized knowledge of a learned person, exhibiting accuracy, critical ability and thoroughness." Involved in the concepts of accuracy and critical ability, one assumes, is the power of judging rightly and then following the soundest conclusion allowable by an evaluation of the relevant data. Scholarship may not be officially defined as involving ethical considerations, but scholarship without ethics and objectivity is a blight on learning. Unfortunately, Mormon scholars who believe that the LDS scriptures are a divine revelation and that Joseph Smith is a true prophet of God find it difficult to look objectively upon relevant factual data. Indeed, intentionally or not, they often distort it, and thus appear unethical. Why? Because they are forced to interpret the data in light of Mormon scripture and tradition rather than letting the data speak for itself.

When academic skills, however formidable, are pressed into the service of distortion, one finds it difficult to maintain the term "scholarly." When distortion occurs in science and history, this is bad enough, but when it occurs in what is arguably the most important subject of all, theology, it is reprehensible.

While FARMS (see Appendix 1) may have the appearance of scholarship, its agenda forces it to defend Mormonism at the cost of true scholarship. Any who doubt this need only read, for example, Dr. James White's website replies to reviews of his own scholarly material on Mormonism. These include, *"A Study in FARMS Behavior,"* which is a review of L. Ara Norwood's review of White's *Letters to a Mormon Elder* (cf. White's reply to D. L. Barksdale's review of White's *Is the Mormon My Brother?*), and White's analysis of Drs. Peterson and Ricks *Offenders for a Word* in *A Test Case of Scholarship* (Alpha and Omega Ministries at http://www.aomin.org). (Jerald and Sandra Tanner's three volume response to FARMS, *Answering Mormon Scholars* is also relevant.)

Significantly, even some Mormon scholars agree that Mormon scholarship in defense of Mormonism is generally untrustworthy. Karl C. Sandberg (DeWitt Wallace professor of French and Humanities, emeritus, Macalester, College, St. Paul, MN), noted in "Whither (Mormon) Scholarship?" that there are Mormons who do scholarship in lots of areas, but not in Mormonism:

> There are Mormons who do scholarship in all the various disciplines—they play by the same rules as everyone else, they participate in the same dynamics, and they produce the same kind of knowledge. Such is not the case, however, when Mormons do scholarship about Mormonism or directly related subjects. . . . Whenever a claim is raised that differs from the official view (the icon) the first duty, the immediate and only duty, is to defend the icon.[223]

PETERSON AND RICKS

An example of FARMS scholarship can be seen in Drs. Daniel C. Peterson and Stephen D. Ricks, *Offenders for a Word: How Anti-Mormons Play Word Games to Attack the Latter-day Saints* (Aspen 1992; FARMS 1998). Dr. Peterson is executive director and chairman of the Board of Trustees for FARMS, and Dr. Ricks is a Board of Trustees member. Much of their book attempts to document the Mormon claim that the closer one gets to the (alleged) apostasy of the Christian church, the more that evidence for "original" Christianity—Mormonism—will be found. Peterson and Ricks cite the Church Fathers extensively. They allege, for example, that the early Church Fathers taught secret doctrines and rituals and believed in what is called the "deification" of man (theosis). They argue that this supports the Mormon doctrines of, respectively, secret temple ceremonies and exaltation: the doctrine that people can become Gods. In their Introduction they claim that their conclusions concerning early Christian materials "are fully justified by the evidence as well as by reason."[224]

But this is false. In the material that follows we will first supply a few of the comments of Dr. James White concerning Peterson's and Rick's claims about early Christianity, and then we will provide our own analysis in different areas. It is significant that Dr. White set aside the time to check their citations of the Fathers by comparing them in their original context. As we will see, he shows how wrong Peterson and Ricks are and how often these Mormon scholars take quotations out of context merely to support their views.

First, "theosis" was a term used in a relative sense to explain man's creation in the image of God, giving him a spiritual nature, and that he could, by grace, attain union with God. Those who used the term never intended it to mean the Mormon doctrine of exaltation, or anything similar—that people could become Gods and that the God of the Bible was once a man who progressed into Godhood by good works and righteous character. The Church Fathers would have been horrified by such ideas.

As to acceptance of alleged secret rituals in the Fathers, Peterson and Ricks miscite, misinterpret or fail to document their claims with Jeremias, Ignatius of Antioch, Tertullian, Origen and others. For example, "Even a brief reading immediately communicates that Tertullian is, in fact, *arguing directly against the position attributed to him* by the misleading form of citation found in *Offenders*."[225] Dr. White then remarks, "All of us make mistakes. Sometimes we hurry, have deadlines, etc. One major error, such as the above, doesn't prove much. However, if a pattern of such misuse of sources can be discerned and documented, we have cause to wonder. *And just such a pattern can, indeed, be found.*"[226] After citing many additional examples of misquotation, Dr. White reflects:

> Any person desirous of honestly representing the beliefs of the early Fathers could not possibly ignore the context of the passages cited, yet, this is exactly what we find in Peterson and Ricks, and in the earlier work by [Stephen] Robinson [*Are Mormons Christian?* For a good critique of this book, see the *Journal of Christian Apologetics*, Winter, 1997]. Again we have to ask how this kind of a-contextual citation can end up in print, and, in fact, be reprinted by FARMS seven years later, without any correction or emendation, despite it having been

pointed out in *Is the Mormon My Brother?* Scholarship means honestly dealing with historical facts, and quoting items fairly, and in context. How can these scholars present this kind of material? There are, however, many more examples of this kind of lack of concern for accurately handling the words of past Christian writers.[227]

With these preliminary comments aside, we now provide an additional analysis of *Offenders for a Word.* The extent of Drs. Peterson's and Ricks's ignorance of Christianity and lack of sound scholarship can be seen in particular detail in the following citations and discussion. This illustrates that their analysis is flawed throughout with numerous errors, poor reasoning and misrepresentation. (All page numbers are cited from the 1998 FARMS edition):

1) . . . the twenty-ninth chapter of the book of Isaiah . . . is . . . replete with prophecies of . . . the coming forth of the Book of Mormon (p. xiii).

This is incredible, for the context of Isaiah 29 deals with the judgement of God upon Jerusalem (Ariel) for her wickedness. In vivid imagery we see that she is as ignorant of God's purposes as an illiterate man is of writing on a scroll. It does not and cannot, as LDS claims, e.g., refer to Mormon Martin Harris taking the *Book of Mormon* "gold plates" to a Professor Anthon who was unable to read them. We are unaware of a single biblical scholar anywhere in the world, outside the Mormon Church, who accepts Isaiah 29 as a legitimate prophecy of the *Book of Mormon.*

2) . . . examination discloses different views of Christ among the gospel writers, and the apparently older letters of Paul show little interest in the supposed facts about Jesus" (p. 60, quoting C. L. Manschreck). As James D. G. Dunn points out, there was certainly "one Jesus" in history, but there have been "many Christs" in Christian belief—even (or especially) in the period of the New Testament. (ibid.)

Peterson and Ricks apparent confusion over who Christ is biblically cannot be used to blur the distinction between what is Christian and what is nonChristian. They believe that with so many different ideas about Jesus, "the question arises, just where on the opinion spectrum the line will be placed that separates 'Christian' from 'nonChristian.'" (p. 61). In other words, they argue that one can hardly disqualify someone as a Christian (a follower of Christ) when we do not really know who Christ exactly was. Obviously, they missed the point that if we don't know who Christ is biblically, then no one knows what a Christian is, not even Mormons, who can no longer be classified as Christians since no one now knows what a Christian is.

But Peterson and Ricks are wrong. The gospel writers presented a consistent view of who Jesus Christ is. This means we can know with certainty that believing in *this* Jesus Christ makes one a Christian. Even Jesus said, "If you do not believe that I am the one I claim to be, you will indeed die in your sins" (John 8:24). In fact, Jesus was so confident His teachings were clearly known that He appealed to His hearers even at His own trial: "I have spoken openly to the world . . . I said nothing in secret. Why question me? Ask those who heard me. Surely they know what I said" (John 18:20–21). Since Jesus identified who He was so clearly, we are amazed it could be lost on Peterson and Ricks.

In addition, there is no reason to think that the Apostle Paul was suspicious of apostolic teaching about Christ (if this is their argument). For Paul to mention specific biographical details of Christ's life is unnecessary, unless it is relevant to his ministry. Indeed, he must have accepted the teachings of the gospel writers at this point, because he never corrected or contradicted them, an impossible omission if he felt they were wrong, or if he disagreed with them over who Christ was. Paul also taught that the Apostles were the foundation of the Church and that he himself was an Apostle, proving not only his trust in their teachings, but his perceived unity with them (Ephesians 2:20).

3) Trinitarianism hardly seems a valid litmus test for determining who is, and who is not, Christian. Indeed, the metaphysical doctrine of the Trinity is a very late development, and hardly to be found with clarity in the Bible (p. 65).

If biblical accuracy on the nature of God is *not* a determiner of what it means to be Christian, nothing is. Are all nontrinitarians who claim to be Christian truly Christian? Perhaps no doctrine is more important. If we discard God, we may as well be atheists. Peterson and Ricks are wrong again. The doctrine of the Trinity is clearly found in the Bible as we demonstrated in *Knowing the Truth about the Trinity* (Harvest House, 1997).

4) If anyone claims to see in Jesus of Nazareth a personage of unique and preeminent authority, that individual should be considered Christian. Such is the consensus of both scholarly and everyday usage (p. 185).

This would make Jehovah's Witnesses and Mormons Christian, as well as members of other cults and nonChristian faiths.

5) A doctrine known as tritheism was taught by a number of prominent theologians in late antiquity, and can be considered "a definite phase in the history of Christian thought." It is never termed "non-Christian" (p. 67). Obviously, if ancient tritheists were Christians, there is no reason to deny that title to modern tritheists—even if we grant that term is an appropriate one to describe the Mormon understanding of the Godhead, which we do here only for the purposes of argument (p. 68).

This denial of Mormon tri-theism (LDS believes in the Father, Son and Holy Ghost as three separate Gods) is sophistry. If Drs. Peterson and Ricks are unwilling to acknowledge Mormon tri-theism, words lose all meaning. Tri-theism is, of course, a form of polytheism, a belief in more than one god. This has never been Christian teaching because the Bible is clear that there is only one God (Isaiah 44:6, 8). The reason early Christians did not move toward tritheism as they grappled with the doctrine of the Trinity was because of the clear biblical emphasis on monotheism.

6) There are probably few communicant Mormons who would agree to being "polytheists," and none who would claim to worship more than one God. . . . And the late elder Bruce R.

McConkie's consistent instruction to worship the Father only and, in a certain sense, not even the Son, must surely be described as monotheistic" (pp. 71–72).

Although he denied it was polytheism, McConkie wrote in his *Mormon Doctrine* (1977, p. 317): "There are three Gods—the Father, the Son and the Holy Ghost." Belief in more than one God can hardly be called monotheism. Because Mormons believe in three Gods for this earth and endless Gods besides, Mormons are polytheists despite their consistent, if deceptive, denials. Mormons cannot have their cake and eat it too. If we remember correctly, McConkie, finally, actually *rejected* worship of the Son (see note 85). To refuse worship to Jesus hardly makes one a Christian.

7) Mormonism teaches that human beings can become *like* God (p. 75, emphasis added).

In fact, Mormonism teaches that people become God in the fullest sense, not just *like* God.

8) . . . being Arians in the first place did not banish the original followers of Arius from Christendom. . . . Arianism is always termed Christian. . . . As, generally, are the Unitarians" (pp. 63–64).

One hardly knows how to respond. The Church considered Arius and his followers heretics because the denial of cardinal Christian beliefs by those within the Church has always been considered heresy. Heresy involves the denial of vital revealed truth for the acceptance of serious error, and Arius was surely guilty of this in denying the Trinity. To deny such vital truths as the nature of God or the nature of salvation identified one as a deceiver, false teacher and servant of the devil (Matthew 7:15–23; 2 Corinthians 11:2–4, 13–15; Galatians 1:6–9; 2 Peter 2:1). This was grounds for separation or excommunication (Romans 16:17; 2 Corinthians 6:14–18; 2 John 10; cf., 2 Timothy 3:5, 8; 1 John 2:19, 26).

In the words of Robert M. Bowman, heresy in the strict sense is "a teaching or practice which compels true Christians to divide themselves from those who hold it."[228] Thus, the *Evangelical Dictionary of Theology* declares that Arius and all his followers were condemned, whether they were of the "moderate" wing that declared that Christ was of "like" (as opposed to the same) substance as the Father, or of the more radical wing that declared that He was not even of like substance as the Father. All were anathematized by the Council of Nicaea, which was convened on May 20, 325 A.D. Arius and all his followers believed that Christ was only a created being, not God the Son. This denied both Jesus and the Godhead. Thus the "council's anathemas were extended" to every aspect of Arianism—"to all those who claimed 'there was once when he was not'; 'before his generation he was not'; 'he was made out of nothing'; 'the Son of God was of another subsistence or substance'; and 'the Son of God [is] created or alterable or mutable.' "[229] Arianism had "reduced Christ to a demigod and in effect reintroduced polytheism into Christianity."[230]

While it is true many Church leaders were swept into Arianism, this cannot change the fact that Arianism was anathematized or that Christians are specifically commanded to avoid false teachers (Romans 16:17). Harold O. J. Brown points out concerning the gospel in his important work, *Heresies:*

> The early Christians felt a measure of tolerance for the pagans, even though they were persecuted by them, for the pagans were ignorant. "This ignorance," Paul told the Athenians, "God winked at" (Acts 17:30). But Paul did not wink at him who brought "any other Gospel" within the context of the Christian community. "Let him be accursed," he told the Galatian church (Galatians 1:8). Honorable enemies are regarded with less hostility than the traitor from within one's own camp. The Christian life is often presented as spiritual warfare. If the pagans are the enemies, the heretics are the traitors.[231]

And Arians were heretics and traitors, despite the uninformed claims of Dr. Peterson and Dr. Ricks. Indeed, the issue of heresy is precisely the issue of Mormonism, for it denies, among others, the doctrine of salvation by grace, substituting for it salvation by works, and it denies the doctrine of the triune nature of God, substituting for it a theology of polytheism. Joseph Smith deliberately removed himself from the Church when he rejected its teachings for his particular occult revelations (or inventions). The Apostle John wrote: "They went out from us, but they did not really belong to us. For if they had belonged to us, they would have remained with us; but their going showed that none of them belonged to us" (1 John 2:19).

Further, in order for Drs. Peterson and Ricks to make Mormonism Christian, the term Christian has to be redefined or made so mercurial that it can incorporate Mormon beliefs. As a result, the most fundamental misunderstandings of Christianity and biblical and historical theology arise, as can be seen in the following citations by Peterson and Ricks. The embarrassing thing is that Peterson and Ricks condemn themselves by redefining Christianity to incorporate Mormonism even *after* stating the following:

> [There] exists a fairly coherent basic meaning to the term "Christian." . . . Since this meaning is well-established, latecomers have only a very limited ability to alter it. . . . To use the word "Christian" in a new and different sense is to limit communication—or even mislead—until outsiders are able to decode and understand that new and different usage. We . . . shall argue that the historic meaning of the term is clearly broad enough to include The Church of Jesus Christ of Latter-day Saints . . . (p. 17).

Here is the "well-established" and "historic meaning" of "Christian" according to the *Oxford American Dictionary,* cited earlier. "Christian" is defined as "of the doctrines of Christianity, believing in or based on these." "Christianity" is defined as "the religion based on the belief that Christ was the incarnate Son of God and on his teachings." Mormonism clearly fails on both counts. Nevertheless, here are some of Peterson and Ricks arguments:

1) Biblical teaching does not disprove Mormon claims to be Christian:

> Clearly, if it is thought to rest upon standards derived from the New Testament or

from immediately postapostolic Christianity, the anti-Mormon case for expelling Mormons from Christendom is without substance (p. 41).

... the Bible offers no real reason to deny that Mormonism is Christian.... [The] Bible cannot be used to define the Church of Jesus Christ of Latter-day Saints out of Christendom (pp. 43, 54).

To repeat and stress the point: There seems, on the matter of scripture and canon, to be no reason whenever to deny that The Church of Jesus Christ of Latter-day Saints is Christian (p. 128).

The truth is that the Bible everywhere disproves the claim that Mormonism is Christian, as we have already documented.

2) Even a false or heretical view of Jesus would still classify Mormons as Christians:

... if the Mormons were partisans of an individual who ... was in reality a wholly distinct individual from the Jesus of Nazareth whom mainstream Christians worship the world over, Latter-day Saint claims to be Christian could be dismissed *as true* but misleading (p. 55 emphasis added).

How could LDS claims to be Christian possibly still be true when they had denied Jesus Christ? Could Jesus have been clearer on this point? "He who rejects me rejects him who sent me"(Luke 10:16); "Whoever rejects the Son will not see life, for God's wrath remains on him" (John 3:36). Thus, "No one who denies the Son has the Father" (1 John 2:23). Jesus Himself warned against accepting "false Christs" (Matthew 24:23–24), and the Apostle Paul told the Corinthians that they were being deceived by Satan for accepting a false Jesus (2 Corinthians 11:3–4).

3) Points of similarity prove identity. This logical fallacy is seen on page 58, where Peterson and Ricks offer twenty points of similarity between the Mormon Jesus and the Jesus of the Bible to show that they are the same person. "A comparison of twenty elements of personal

identity possessed by 'the Mormon Jesus' and 'the Jesus of the Bible'—and many, many more elements could be compared ... should make it clear to even the most hardened missing persons detective that the two are the same person" (pp. 57–58).

But Peterson and Ricks do not offer even *one* relevant comparison to prove identity of person! The points of similarity include things like birthplace (Bethlehem), Jewish ethnicity, descent from King David, mothers name (Mary), occupation (carpenter), manner of death (crucifixion), time and place of death (under Pontius Pilate, outside Jerusalem), miracles, resurrection, ascension and others. Even atheists, skeptics and Buddhists would accept many of these, and numerous other cults would accept all these items. (Peterson and Ricks neglect to mention that at Alma 7:10, the *Book of Mormon* teaches Jesus was born in *Jerusalem*, not Bethlehem, so it can't be the same Jesus anyway.) Regardless, what is noticeably absent from their list is *all* those biblical teachings that *would* prove identity, vital things like virgin born, eternal Creator, eternally sinless, incarnate, second person of the Trinity and so on. And they understandably fail to mention all the specific teachings of Jesus which deny Mormonism, such as His belief in salvation by faith (John 5:24; 6:47) and in only one God (John 17:3).

3) Mormon words and worldview have priority over biblical Christian words and worldview:

Do the Latter-day Saints somehow deny the Father and the Son? Not according to the first Article of Faith, which specifically affirms belief in both (p. 22).

Do the Latter-day Saints deny that Jesus is the Son of God? No, for the first Article of Faith and literally hundreds of passages in their scriptural books teach his divine Sonship in the most explicit terms (p. 24).

Peterson and Ricks argue that merely mentioning the titles "Father" and "Son," or calling the Son divine, are sufficient to prove that Mormonism does not deny the Father and Son. They neglect to mention that Mormonism has an entirely different "Father" and "Son" than found in Christianity. Which cult *doesn't* mention the Father and Son?

4) The New Testament meaning of the term "Christian" cannot be objectively determined. According to Peterson and Ricks, the applicability of the term Christian should be decided upon an individual's own sincere claim to be Christian. Thus, because the New Testament allegedly gives no clear definition of what a Christian is, "By every New Testament standard, Mormons are Christians" (p. 31). Despite Mormonism having a different Christ, and despite Peterson and Ricks uncertainty over who the biblical Christ was, "What made a person a Christian in the first century, and what makes a person a Christian today, is, simply, a commitment to Jesus Christ. Such commitment is central to the religion of the Latter-day Saints" (p. 27). "In point of fact, the Mormons are Christians precisely because they sincerely say they are" (p. 191). Well, we say, "Mormons aren't Christians precisely because we sincerely say they aren't." "So how are we to determine who is Christian and who is not? It is not altogether clear that we have any responsibility, or any right, to make such a determination" (p. 184).

We can, however, make such a determination by the New Testament standards that Peterson and Ricks ignore. We can only cite the dictionary definition of Christian again: "of the doctrines of Christianity, believing in or based on these." Such doctrines were derived from the New Testament and based in Jesus' teachings, which is why the Apostle Paul emphasized, "You must teach what is accord with sound doctrine" (Titus 2:1). It is why the Apostle John warned, "Anyone who . . . does not continue in the teaching of Christ does not have God . . ." (2 John 9).

Drs. Peterson and Ricks, however, do make a determination about Christians who claim Mormonism isn't Christian. They cite Lloyd Averill's perception of "frustration, outrage, desperation, and latent violence" among Christians who oppose Mormonism (p. 180). They also refer to the "theological bloodlust" of much anti-

Mormonism, which they say has a "super charged, inquisitorial atmosphere" (p. 184).

OTHER MORMON SCHOLARS

To give another illustration of the character of FARMS work, consider the text *New Approaches to the Book of Mormon* (Signature Books, 1993). This is authored by a group of Mormon and other scholars who are critical of the official Mormon story concerning Mormon origins, the *Book of Mormon,* and certain other Mormon beliefs. This book was reviewed by John Wm. Maddox in "A Listing of Points and Counterpoints" in *Review of Books on the Book of Mormon* (RBBM), vol. 8, no.1 (1996). In his review, Maddox attempts to show that the arguments allegedly refuting *New Approaches* published in RBBM's 566-page critique were legitimate criticisms. As he argues:

> Shortly after the *Review of Books on the Book of Mormon,* vol. 6, no. 1, was published, containing over 566 pages of responses to arguments raised in Brent L. Metcalfe's, *New Approaches to the Book of Mormon* (Salt Lake City: Signature Books, 1993), a few people were heard to say that the FARMS publication had failed to address any substantive issues head on. That assessment did not seem to me to describe the contents of the Review that I had read. So I began going through both books to see how many substantive issues had been raised and addressed. . . . I identified about 170 arguments raised in *New Approaches* that find responses in vol. 6, no. 1, or in subsequent issues of the Review. . . . I found the responses of the reviewers to be cogent and sufficiently persuasive."[232]

But it all depends on what one finds convincing. Maddox may be convinced, but this does not change the fact that, clearly, FARMS has not dealt adequately with the material in *New Approaches.* We now offer verbatim illustrations without comment. The term "Critics Claim" summarizes the criticism given in *New Approaches;* the term "FARMS Response" refers to the response by FARMS authors. Although some of the following material may be unfamiliar to those without a prior understanding of Mormon theology and history, the point we wish to make is that in every case, the FARMS response is either wrong or irrelevant. (Abbreviated documentary references have been deleted for ease of reading; also, the responses given often incorporate multiple authors.)

Critics Claim: The *Book of Mormon* reflects Trinitarianism. FARMS Response: The *Book of Mormon* testifies of Jesus' Godhood. It does not fully explain the Godhead. Trinitarianism cannot be found in the *Book of Mormon* or the Bible.

Critics Claim: Sabellianism would explain Nephite belief in Jesus and the Father as two different manifestations of the same being. FARMS Response: Sabellianism is only found by citing a few verses and ignoring the rest of the *Book of Mormon.*

Critics Claim: If the *Book of Mormon* repeats the mistakes of the KJV, we can rule out coincidence. FARMS Response: One cannot prove that the so-called mistakes are actual mistakes.

Critics Claim: Comparing 3 Nephi and Matthew can help determine the historicity of the *Book of Mormon.* FARMS Response: Nobody knows what was and was not in the original Greek.

Critics Claim: Eight mistranslations in the KJV are repeated in the *Book of Mormon.* FARMS Response: The alleged mistranslations involve insubstantial differences. The differences are insignificant, especially in a nineteenth-century context.

Critics Claim: The *Book of Mormon* account of the sermon of Jesus is plagiarized from the KJV. FARMS Response: This argument is neither proved nor disproved. Blind plagiarism cannot explain the complexity of the *Book of Mormon* account.

Critics Claim: Sperry said that if the *Book of Mormon* copied the errors of the KJV, then it should be rejected. FARMS Response: Sperry viewed the *Book of Mormon* as an independent ancient text.

Critics Claim: The New Testament Jesus never claims to be the Father as in the *Book of Mormon.* FARMS Response: The Old Testament and early Christian writers speak of Jesus as the Father.

Critics Claim: The New Testament never claims that Jesus was the god whom the Israelites in the Old Testament worshipped as Jehovah, as in the *Book of Mormon.* FARMS Response: *The Book of Mormon* validates the Bible, not the other way around. Exegesis of Greek and Hebrew Bible texts refutes this hypothesis.

Critics Claim: The *Book of Mormon* must be allowed to speak for itself. FARMS Response: Objectivity is noble but impossible. Narrative theory denies that anyone is free from ideology. The text yields different data depending on the paradigm the reader begins with.

Critics Claim: Speculations about *Book of Mormon* geography are faulty because the geographers accept the *Book of Mormon* as true before they examine the evidence they write about. FARMS Response: This is a straw man argument. What this criticism means is that the geographers' paradigms are different from the claimant's own. Assuming historicity allows one to more easily see historically consistent phenomena.

Critics Claim: The cardinal directions in the *Book of Mormon* must be the same as ours. FARMS Response: Directional concepts are accidents of culture and history.

Critics Claim: The traditional Latter-day Saint view is that all people in the *Book of Mormon* descended from Mulek or Lehi. FARMS Response: The traditional view is not held officially by the Church.

Critics Claim: The traditional view is supported by the *Book of Mormon* text itself. FARMS Response: This is not a careful reading of the text. Some passages from the *Book of Mormon* discredit this claim.

Some FARMS scholars themselves, despite their attempt to bolster Mormonism, have issued warnings about the tentative nature of their research, and all *Book of Mormon* research. This is commendable, but is this ever what Christians must do with standard apologetics? Do typical Christian apologetic works begin with the warning that the "chief source of evidence" for the truth of the Bible and Christianity is subjectively based, or that basic apologetic research is preliminary and conclusions may later be discarded? David Rolph Seely stated the following in his review of *Reexploring the Book of Mormon: The F.A.R.M.S. Updates* (Salt Lake City: Deseret

Book and F.A.R.M.S., 1992) in the FARMS *Review of Books on the Book of Mormon* 5 (1993):

> The editor of this volume, John Welch, clearly delineates in his preface the intended purpose of the authors of the articles in this volume. Quoting from B. H. Roberts, he reminds us of the importance of the Holy Ghost as the "chief source of evidence for the truth of the Book of Mormon." And yet, following Roberts, "Secondary evidences in support of truth, like secondary causes in natural phenomena, may be of first-rate importance, and mighty factors in the achievement of God's purposes" (pp. xiii-xiv). . . . But it should be read with caution. *Book of Mormon* studies are still in their infancy. The editor and authors constantly remind us of the preliminary nature of most of these studies. . . . There is still much to be done, much to be discussed, and many of these preliminary conclusions will be discarded, modified, and enlarged in the years to come.[233]

One might wonder about this, given the lack of academic freedom at BYU. Perhaps the quality of LDS scholarship is thus also hinted at by the June 13, 1998 vote of the delegates of the 84th annual meeting of the American Association of University Professors, which voted to censure Brigham Young University's administration, citing "infringements on academic freedom [that are] distressingly common at the university" and a "climate for academic freedom [that is] distressingly poor."[234] In other words, the Mormon Church tends to run academic matters for its own interests. In fact, the church response to the censure was simply to ignore it. [235]

In conclusion, FARMS may claim scholarship, but the truth lies elsewhere for precisely the reasons given earlier. The "defense" of myths and falsehoods *as genuine history* is difficult to command as a scholarly endeavor. If no historical facts exist, what is there to prove through scholarly analysis?

Dr. Hugh Nibley

No discussion of Mormon scholarship would be complete without considering Dr. Hugh Nibley. He is heralded by Mormons as the premier defender of the Mormon faith. Even evangelicals Mosser and Owen praise him highly:

> Hugh Nibley is without question the pioneer of LDS scholarship and apologetics . . . Since earning his Ph.D. at the University of California at Berkeley in 1939, Nibley has produced a seemingly endless stream of books and articles covering a dauntingly vast array of subject matter. Whether writing on Patristics, the Dead Sea Scrolls, the Apocrypha, the culture of the Ancient Near East or Mormonism, he demonstrates an impressive command of the original languages, primary texts and secondary literature. He has set a standard which younger LDS intellectuals are hard pressed to follow. . . . The few evangelicals who are aware of Hugh Nibley often dismiss him as a fraud or pseudo-scholar. Those wanting to quickly dismiss his writings would do well to heed Madsen's warning: "Ill-wishing critics have suspected over the years that Nibley is wrenching his sources, hiding behind his footnotes, and reading into antique languages what no responsible scholar would ever read out. Unfortunately, few have the tools to do the checking." The bulk of Nibley's work has gone unchallenged by evangelicals despite the fact that he has been publishing relevant material since 1946. . . . No doubt there are flaws in Nibley's work, but most counter-cultists do not have the tools to demonstrate this. Few have tried. . . . [Whatever] flaws may exist in his methodology, Nibley is a scholar of high caliber.[236]

As we mentioned earlier, a religion that has an inherently false theology must necessarily make numerous errors attempting to defend its beliefs doctrinally and historically. Certainly, this would also apply to the writings of Hugh Nibley, despite his "scholar" status. Dr. James White's observation concerning FARMS scholars that "everybody cites Nibley, who, I am hardly alone in asserting, has never once cared about the contextual accuracy of anything he's ever cited" is to the point.[237] We have found serious flaws in Nibley's assertions and documentations. This is not only because he is trying to defend the indefensible, but because when it comes to defending Mormonism, he sacrifices first-rate scholarship to maintaining and propogating the belief that his religion, contrary to the solid research and evidence, is "Christian" and biblically sound.

Here are two brief examples of detailed evangelical responses to Nibley's faulty scholarship.

The Lachish Letters (Lachish ostraca) are late seventh-century B.C. documents that were found at Tell ed-Duweir (ancient Lachish) and written prior to the fall of the Southern kingdom of Judea. One of the reasons they are important is for dating the period, chronicling the fall of the last few cities of Judea. In *Book of Mormon Authorship: New Light on Ancient Origins,* edited by Noel B. Reynolds,[238] Dr. Nibley argues these letters have important parallels to the *Book of Mormon* (he lists 18 parallels), which allegedly illustrate the *Book of Mormon* as an ancient document. But the Lachish Letters cannot be used in this fashion. In "A Review of Hugh Nibley's Comparisons Between the Book of Mormon and the Lachish Letters,"[239] Dr. Thomas J. Finley, professor of Old Testament and Semitics at Talbot School of Theology in La Mirada, California, concluded: "All of the parallels given above are either invalid because of a lack of proper understanding of the Lachish Letters or because they can be explained more easily through parallels with the KJV. No good reason has been given to abandon the rather reasonable assumption that the *Book of Mormon* derives from the time of Joseph Smith and drew heavily on the King James Bible as a literary source."

Another example of Nibley's fundamentally flawed apologetics, again with detailed scholarly analysis, can be seen in Dr. James White's "The Gates of Hell" (www.aomin.org), where he critiques Nibley's biased interpretation of Matthew 16:18.[240] Dr. Nibley believes the gates of hell did overpower the Christian church. He believes the church was entirely apostatized and wasn't restored until Joseph Smith received his "divine" revelations in the nineteenth century. Here, Nibley argues that the "it" in "the gates of Hades will not overcome it" does not refer back to the church. From his perspective, it *cannot refer to the church,* so ways must be devised to reinterpret the obvious meaning of the passage.

It must first be noted that Nibley's interpretation of the passage is not to be found in any stream of scholarly interpretation, whether Protestant or Catholic. We are not aware of a single scholar who attempts to say that the final phrase of Matthew 16:18 is referring to anything other than the Church; that is, that the "it" found in the phrase does not refer back to the term "church" mentioned immediately before. If Nibley is correct, it is amazing that exegetes over the centuries have missed what only he has discovered. Mormons are, by and large, in awe of Hugh Nibley's linguistic abilities. When Dr. Nibley says that the term "it" in Matthew 16:18 is "in the partitive genitive," that must be the case. Yet is it? [No, because, as White points out, there is no specific partitive genetitive form in the Greek.] And what of all those translations of the Bible that do not catch this seemingly basic thing? No wonder Nibley replied to the critique of a Christian minister with, "When ministers start making Greek the argument, it is time to adjourn."

It is also crucial to know that some Mormon scholars also disagree quite strongly with Nibley's methodologies and conclusions. We encourage you to check out their detailed responses and critiques found at the "Honest Intellectual Inquiry" website (www.california.com/~rpcman/ nibley1.htm). An example of Mormon critique of Nibley's work is included in the notes.[241] Is Nibley a scholar of high caliber? True scholars don't wrench sources, hide behind footnotes and read into antique languages what is simply not there.

In very brief fashion, some general comments and simple illustrations are given below as to why we are not impressed with Dr. Nibley (and other LDS scholars). Dr. Nibley, unfortunately, uses his great learning in defense of a false religion. He uses it by every means possible, scholarly and unscholarly. But one could have hoped he would have used his considerable learning to defend the truth instead of leading thousands astray by his writings defending Mormonism. As a Gospel Doctrine teacher in the Mormon Church, he is especially culpable because, in making error and falsehood seem scholarly, he has contributed greatly to the overall deception promoted by the Mormon religion. Here are a few examples of why we do not think Dr. Nibley is a revered scholar when it comes to either adequately defending Mormonism or fairly evaluating Christianity.

In *Tinkling Cymbals,* Nibley cites Eduard Meyer's *Ursprung und Geschichte der Mormonen* as illustrating "at length the 'exact identity' of his [Joseph Smith's] Church both in 'atmosphere' and sundry particulars with that of the early Christians. A 'striking and irrefutable' parallelism supports Mormon claims to revelation; 'with perfect right' they identify themselves with the apostolic church of old."[241a] Since Meyer was "one of the best informed men who ever lived" and had "complete impartiality," according to Dr. Nibley,[242] he couldn't be wrong, could he? The facts are that apostolic Christianity dovetails with Christian doctrine, not Mormon paganism, as eighteen centuries of scholarship have proven time and again.

Dr. Nibley claims solid, genuine evidence for his Churches' most important scripture, the *Book of Mormon*: "Joseph Smith's own story of the book's authorship certainly lies far 'outside the usual and familiar,' and we have *every right* to ask for special proof of it."[243] And, "First and foremost, the Book of Mormon preaches the gospel, but it supports its presentation with *strong evidence*."[244] And, "Upon close examination all the many apparent contradictions in the Book of Mormon *disappear. It passes the sure test of authenticity with flying colors*."[245] And finally, "Since it claims to be translated by divine power, the Book of Mormon also claims *all the authority—and responsibility*—of the original text."[246]

Yet speaking of his *Since Cumorah*, a defense of the *Book of Mormon*, "The whole thing may well impress some as disappointingly inconclusive, for we must insist that we have reached no final conclusions, *even privately*, and that all we can see ahead is more and *ever more problems*."[247] And, "The evidence that will prove or disprove the Book of Mormon *does not exist*."[248] And, "*By far* the most important area in which the Book of Mormon is to be tested is in *the reader's own heart*. The challenge of Moroni 10:4 is by *no means unscientific.* . . ."[249]

Which is it? "Special proof" or "disappointingly inconclusive" evidence? Do we endorse objective or subjective apologetics? Is the definition of science to include the physical or spiritual realm? Since *Book of Mormon* proof is entirely lacking, and disproof is abundant, Dr. Nibley, as a scholar, apparently has to sometimes make it seem like the book has real evidence when he knows better.

When it comes to the Bible and church history, things are not improved according to Dr. Nibley's way of looking at things: "We are now *assured* that the three Synoptic Gospels are not the original *Evangelion* [gospel] at all. . . . the very 'multiplicity of the Gospels' is adequate evidence that someone has been manipulating the records."[250] Dr. Nibley goes on to declare that early Christians "proceeded in the various churches to reinterpret and delete much of the record. . . . [and] after the damage was done the New Testament went forth" throughout the world.[251]

The *Book of Mormon* verses Dr. Nibley discusses here are from 1 Nephi 13, which implies that Christ's gospel suffered great distortion at the hands of the early Christians. The *Book of Mormon* corrects the "devilish and abominable" distortions of the "great and abominable" Christian church by, for example, offering a gospel of works.[252] But the Apostle Paul unmistakably declares the Mormon gospel of salvation by good works is under God's curse, so one has to question which church is actually the abomination. (See Galatians 1:6-9.)

In light of all this, we can only cite Dr. Nibley on the *Book of Mormon* again: "We offer the Book of Mormon to the world in good faith, convinced that it is the truest of books."[253] Also, "Its one and only merit is truth. Without that merit, it is all that non-believers say it is."[254] Given the many errors in the *Book of Mormon* we apparently have little we need to respond to.

Regardless, if what Dr. Nibley says about the corruption of the Christian church is true, no one should ever trust Christianity again: "Wherever we look in the ancient world the past has been controlled, but nowhere more rigorously than in the history of the Christian church. The methods of control, wherever we find them, fall under three general heads, which might be described as (a) the invention, (b) the destruction, and (c) the alteration of documents."[255] Again the facts are to the contrary. It is the history (and doctrine) of the LDS church that has been carefully controlled, as the Tanners and others' research proves repeatedly. Mormons are the ones who have invented, destroyed and altered documents in order to defend their own interests.

These are only a very few illustrations of why we don't trust the scholarship of Dr. Hugh Nibley. In the forward to the 1952 edition of *Lehi in the Desert*, John A. Widtsoe remarked of Nibley's book, "It has been written also under the inspiration of the Spirit of God."

We think not.

APPENDIX 4:
REINVENTING MORMONISM

> "Among Latter-day Saints, his [Mormon president Gordon B. Hinkley's] interviews are also known for his ability to gloss over potentially unpopular church teachings to the point that some Saints have wondered, as President Hinkley admitted in a general conference, whether he in fact understands church doctrine." ("On the Record," *Sunstone: Mormon Experience, Scholarship, Issues and Art*, December 1998 p. 70)

The basic problem for FARMS/LDS is that they insist on their own definition of what Mormonism is. Mormonism is bound by the standard works and what LDS authorities say it is, even though this *denies* official, earlier, divinely revealed church teachings. What is authoritative is only the *Book of Mormon, Doctrine & Covenants, Pearl of Great Price* and the Bible—as interpreted by the General Authorities of the Church and the *current* apostles and prophets. Ezra Taft Benson's widely published, if incredible, 1980 speech at BYU, "Fourteen Fundamentals in Following the Prophets," argued that the living prophet: is the only one to speak for the Lord in everything, more important than the standard works and deceased prophets, will never lead the church astray, has no need for particular earthly training or credentials to speak or act on any subject, does not have to say "thus saith the Lord" to give scripture and is not limited by men's reasoning capacities.

The General Authorities of the past are to be conveniently ignored at points of conflict or controversy, even though these men claimed to be apostles and prophets, were accepted as apostles and prophets or claimed divine revelation and inspiration. For example, President Hinckley, interviewed by Don Lattin of the *San Francisco Chronicle* (4/13/97), declared, "we have a great body of revelation, the vast majority of which came from the prophet Joseph Smith." Brigham Young claimed, "I have never yet preached a sermon and sent it out to the children of men, that they may not call scripture." [235a] But the modern Church authorities, discarding "divine revelation" and vital history in the process, claim that only what *they* say is to be accepted. In essence, the church "guarantee of doctrinal accuracy" is restricted to current teachings only, with the undeclared recognition that its doctrines may change generation by generation. And it's not just that original and modern Mormonism are contradictory, its that the Mormon Scriptures themselves are contradictory. For example, the *Book of Mormon* teaches both Sabellianism and Trinitarianism, neither of which is "official" modern Mormon doctrine. As a divine revelation, this kind of thing makes Mormonism meaningless.

The parallel situation in Christianity would be, first, for the modern Church to have denied numerous cardinal doctrines taught by the Old Testament prophets and New Testament apostles. Second, to have then claimed by divine decree that its modern teachings that contradicted them *alone* were valid. Third, to have claimed that the earlier teachings of the prophets and apostles were *invalid* even though these were also said to be divinely inspired. And fourth, to have covered up anything necessary to maintain the deception. If this had happened, *of course* the Christian church would be worthy of charges of hypocrisy and deception. And, since it had such low regard for its divinely inspired apostles and prophets to begin with, it's hardly surprising if it would have attempted a cover-up to prevent its own embarrassment. If the Christian Church had done all this, Christianity would now be the modern fraud that Mormonism is. And it would deserve the exact same criticism that Mormonism has received.

FARMS is free, of course, to complain about its Christian critics not understanding "true Mormonism," and to falsely condemn them for engaging in shoddy scholarship. But until it deals seriously with its own religion, it can hardly be expected to be granted credibility in the eyes of those who know better. For its part, FARMS claims that it has no bias and is only interested in promoting the truth. The truth would seem to be closer to an interest in distorting or suppressing criticism. Sandra Tanner noted:

There can be no doubt that FARMS is intent on undermining the expanding influence of Signature Books [a publisher whose writers are critical of Mormonism]. In addition, FARMS wishes to destroy the work of Utah Lighthouse Ministry and that of other ministries working with Mormon people. Furthermore, as we will show below, they are willing to spend a great deal of money to accomplish their goals.[257]

At points, it becomes embarrasing. For example, in an alleged defense of Mormonism, FARMS and BYU scholars continue to cite the non-Mormon scholar Lawrence Foster's ill-fated attack on the Tanners. This is despite Foster's own belief concerning Mormonism that "the official line [of the Mormon story] is almost always wrong if you get down the specifics."[258] He also accuses Mormon leadership of "bad religion" and of carrying its zeal to defend Mormonism at all costs to "pathological extremes."[259] He even agreed that in publishing all their works, "the Tanners probably care far more for the Mormon church [than] do the great majority of those Saints who have never rebelled or thought seriously about their faith. . . ."[260] This is a good point. It is not Mormon scholars or authorities—who distort facts and hide the truth—who really care about the Mormon people, it is Christians who have pointed out the truth about Mormonism. They truly care about Mormon people. Indeed, the Tanners research proves beyond doubt that LDS has engaged in suppression of important materials and a protracted cover-up of its deceptions. Mormon people above all else should have the right to this information, if they would only read it.

Some may actually believe that evangelicals are losing the battle with Mormonism by neglect, but the truth is that the battle was won long ago. Mormon scholarship, real or imagined, can never change facts that have existed for over a century, no matter how sophisticated its argumentation. Has LDS scholarship successfully rationalized or corroborated any of the following materials documented in our book *Behind the Mask of Mormonism*?

—The serious confusion and contradiction between official Mormon doctrine historically and today.

—The animosity that Mormonism has shown for God, Jesus and Christianity throughout its history and today.

—The existence of a nonexistent civilization.

—The crude, sexual polytheism and finite godism of Mormon theology.

—The unceasing Mormon defense of salvation by works, a doctrine the Bible declares is cursed by God.

—The *Book of Abraham* and other Mormon scripture that contradict the Bible and given Mormon claims for them, are proven fraudulent.

—That Mormon leaders, writers and apologists should be trusted when they have a history of deception.

—That the fraudulent or occult "first vision" account of Joseph Smith condemning all Christian churches as an abomination to God was a revelation from the God of the Bible.

—That the occult activities of Joseph Smith and Mormonism, historically and in certain cases today, are pleasing to God—that mediumism, astrology, divination, assisting or contacting the dead and other occult practices can be blessed by God.

—That there was a complete apostasy of the Christian Church, despite Jesus' promise that "the gates of hell will not prevail against my church."

—That Mormonism alone is the one true church on earth and Christianity an evil apostate religion.

—That the Mormon priesthood of the unregenerate conveys the spiritual power and blessing of God.

—That Adam was the one true god and that created men and women can become Gods, and that we have a "celestial mother" in heaven.

—That Jesus Christ should be belittled as merely one God among endless billions and the product of a physical sex act between a male Mormon god and Mary.

—That the Christian Church was evil and wrong in declaring justification by faith alone.

—That an eternal hell is not something the majority of humankind, if anyone, must concern himself or herself with.

—That Joseph Smith, despite his hatred of Christianity, his occult practice, false prophecies and all the evil in his personal life was really a true and righteous prophet of God.

—That the errors, contradictions and lies in Mormon scripture and authoritative LDS writings are academically defensible.

From a Christian perspective, what is there for Mormon scholarship to defend here? In William J. Hamblin's review of Paul Toscano's *The Sanctity of Dissent* (1994, Signature books) in *Review of Books on the Book of Mormon*, vol. 7, no. 1, 1995, we see illustrated the basic problem for LDS faith. Hamblin says, referring to the Mormon doctrine of a divine Mother in heaven, "I know of no Latter-day Saint who would deny the existence of our Mother in Heaven. Indeed, there is an article entitled 'Mother in Heaven' in the *Encyclopedia of Mormonism*, in which the existence of our Heavenly Mother is clearly affirmed. Unfortunately, for whatever reason, scripture provides little or no information on this subject."

This is precisely the problem with *all* Mormon doctrine: little or no scriptural (biblical) documentation. So how can it be correct that Mormon scholarship is defensible and Christian scholarship against it is not? Even the most prominent LDS scripture has no support in its behalf. As Dr. White noted, citing a 1973 declaration by Michael Coe:

The bare facts of the matter are that nothing, absolutely nothing, has ever shown up in any New World excavation which would suggest to the dispassionate observer that the *Book of Mormon*, as claimed by Joseph Smith, is a historical document relating to the history of the early migrants to our hemisphere.

These words remain true. Let any person pick up the most popular F.A.R.M.S. materials and

ask themselves a question: would the argumentation presented herein carry weight with me if I was not already committed to the LDS perspective? The current situation in the world of archaeology clearly indicates the answer, for F.A.R.M.S. has yet to convince the scholarly world—including Christian scholars who believe in the supernatural—that the BoM has anything at all to do with the early history of this hemisphere. The same scholars who will readily admit that the Bible has a great deal to do with the history of Palestine find no reason to believe Joseph Smith's story.[261]

William Bennett wrote *The Death of Outrage* to show how Americans have come to accept things that should, and once did, outrage them. Given the previous doctrines of Mormonism, we think that Christians should also be outraged at Mormon teachings. This happened years ago with "The Last Temptation of Christ" movie. But if Christians were outraged then, there is no *less* reason to be outraged here.

Few religions are more blasphemous, anti-Christian and deceitful as Mormonism. This is strong language, to be sure, but that is what has concerned us about Mormon teaching and practice all along. If someone wants to see something "ugly and unchristian" (per Mosser's and Owens' description of our book), don't look in responsible Christian literature. Look at the reprehensible things Mormons have said about Christianity or Christians, or at what Mormons have done historically—opposed the gospel, hindered Christian missions, endorsed blood atonement, practiced deception, endorsed racism, defended the polygamy that infects Utah and other states even to this day, not to mention other evils masquerading as pious religion. If Mormonism were as godly and pristine an institution as its proponents claim, how could Mormonism possibly be responsible for so many evils documented in our book and scores of other books, such as the Tanners works (*Mormon Spies; Hughes and the CIA; The Mormon Purge; Unmasking a Mormon Spy*), Mormon historian Dr. D. Michael Quinn's *Mormon Hierarchy: Extensions of Power*, and sociologist Anson Shupe's *The Darker Side of Virtue: Corruption, Scandal and the Mormon Empire*?

NOTES

1. Pratt, *Seer,* January, 1853, pp. 15-16.
2. *The Salt Lake Tribune,* January 23, 1990.
3. Ankerberg, *Mormonism Revisited,* p. 22.
4. *Time* magazine, July 29, 1991.
5. Ibid., *The Denver Post,* November 21-28, 1982; *Wall Street Journal,* November 9, 1983; *The Arizona Republic,* June 30-July 3, 1991.
6. Walter Martin, *Maze of Mormonism,* pp. 16-21.
7. In Ankerberg, *Mormonism Revisited,* p. 22. See also John Heinerman and Anson Shupe, *The Mormon Corporate Empire.*
8. Ankerberg, *Mormon Officials,* p. 21. See *Living a Christlike Life: Discussion* 5, pp. 14-15.
9. Martin, *Maze of Mormonism,* p. 21.
10. Examine Utah's state politics.
11. Allegedly, up to one-third of the FBI and CIA forces are also Mormon, along with at least 40 key scientists at NASA.
12. *The Utah Evangel* (Salt Lake City, UT), November 1981.
13. Martin, *Maze of Mormonism,* p. 20; Einar Anderson, *Inside Story,* ix; Jerald and Sandra Tanner, *Mormon Spies, Hughes and the CIA* (Salt Lake City, UT: Utah Lighthouse Ministry, 1976), p. 56.
14. Martin, *Maze of Mormonism,* pp. 16-21.
15. *Christianity Today,* October 2, 1981, p. 70.
16. Benson, *Teachings,* p. 240.
17. Ibid., p. 238.
18. Ibid., p. 237.
19. *This People,* (Mormon periodical), Spring 1990, p. 21. The seventy-five percent figure is from Josh McDowell and Don Stewart, *The Deceivers* (Here's Life), 1992, p. 16.
20. Ibid.
21. *The Los Angeles Times,* January 6, 1990.
22. Joseph Smith, *History of the Church,* I 3. (*The Pearl of Great Price* excerpts are originally taken from this text.)
23. Ibid., pp. 4-6.
24. Ibid.
25. Ibid.
26. Ibid.
27. Ibid.
28. Ibid.
29. Ibid.
30. Ibid.
31. Ibid., p. 8.
32. Ibid., p. 9.
33. Ibid., pp. 11-12.
34. Ibid., pp. 12-14.
35. Ibid., p. 15.
36. David Whitmer, "An Address to All Believers in Christ by a Witness to the Divine Authenticity of the Book of Mormon" (Concord, CA: Pacific Publishing Co., 1887, reprint 1972), p. 12.
37. *The Saints Herald,* May 19, 1888, p. 310.
38. See Jerald and Sandra Tanner, *Joseph Smith and Money Digging,* passim.
39. Einar Anderson, *Inside Story,* p. 61.
40. Fawn M. Brodie, *No Man Knows My History,* 2d ed. (New York: Alfred A. Knopf, 1976), pp. 69-70, 72-73.
41. Hal Hougey, *A Parallel,* p. 4; Ropp, *Mormon Papers,* p. 36.

42. Originally cited in *The Rocky Mountain Mason,* Billings, MT, January 1956, pp. 17-31; also in Jerald and Sandra Tanner, *Did Spaulding Write the Book of Mormon?* p. 17.
43. Cf. Martin, *Maze,* p. 68.
44. Taken from the *Book of Mormon* and in part from McConkie, *Mormon Doctrine,* pp. 528-529; Martin, *Maze,* pp. 47-49; McElveen, *Will the Saints?* pp. 59-61; Fraser, *Is Mormonism Christian?* chapter 16; and Arthur Wallace, *Can Mormonism Be Proved Experimentally?* chapter 9.
45. Martin, *Maze,* p. 328.
46. John Ankerberg and John Weldon, *Behind the Mask of Mormonism* (Eugene, OR: Harvest House, 1996), pp. 287–289.
47. Fraser, *Is Mormonism Christian?* p. 135.
48. Hal Hougey, *Archaeology and the Book of Mormon,* rev. ed., pp. 3-4.
49. Fraser, *Is Mormonism Christian?* pp. 143-145.
50. Norman L. Geisler, William E. Nix, *An Introduction to the Bible,* rev. and exp. ed. (Chicago: Moody Press, 1986); F. F. Bruce, *The New Testament Documents: Are They Reliable?* (Downers Grove, IL: InterVarsity Press, 1971).
51. Ibid.
52. Cf. Jerald and Sandra Tanner, *Changing World,* pp. 369-370.
53. Wesley Walters, "Whatever Happened to the Book of Mormon?" *Eternity* magazine, May 1980, p. 32.
54. From Bob Witte, comp., *Where Does It Say That?* p. 4.
55. Jerald and Sandra Tanner, *Changing World,* p. 560, citing *Improvement Era,* 16:344-345.
56. Bernard De Voto, "The Centennial of Mormonism," *American Mercury,* 19 (1930): 5.
57. Church of Jesus Christ of Latter-day Saints, *Sure Foundation,* p. 48.
58. Benson, *Teachings,* p. 116.
59. Hugh Nibley, *No Ma'am, That's Not History,* p. 46, from Jerald and Sandra Tanner, *Mormonism—Shadow or Reality?* p. 5.
60. Ankerberg, *Mormon Officials,* p. 28.
61. Ankerberg, *Mormonism Revisited,* p. 17.
62. Jerald and Sandra Tanner, *The Case Against Mormonism,* 1:86-87.
63. *The Evening and Morning Star,* July 1833, p. 1, emphasis added.
64. Whitmer, *An Address,* pp. 30-31, emphasis added.
65. Ankerberg, *Mormon Officials,* p. 7.
66. Smith, *History,* 1:400.
67. Ibid., pp. 394, 400, 402; Martin, *Maze,* pp. 353-354.
68. Joseph Smith, *History,* 5:336.
69. Cited in Jerald and Sandra Tanner, *Changing World,* p. 419, emphasis added.
70. Ibid., p. 420.
71. This was copied from the microfilm original at the Mormon Church Historian's Library; cf. Jerald and Sandra Tanner, *Changing World,* p. 420.
72. Bob Witte, *Witnessing to Mormons,* p. 17.
73. Church of Jesus Christ of Latter-day Saints, *Doctrines of the Gospel,* p. 6.

74. Joseph Smith, *Teachings*, p. 343.
75. Talmage, *Articles of Faith*, p. 47.
76. Church of Jesus Christ of Latter-day Saints, *Sure Foundation*, p. 93.
77. McConkie, *Mormon Doctrine*, p. 579.
78. Robinson, *Are Mormons Christians?* p. 65.
79. *The Oxford American Dictionary*, s.v. "polytheism."
80. Church of Jesus Christ of Latter-day Saints, *Doctrines of the Gospel*, p. 16.
81. *Pearl of Great Price*, Book of Abraham 4:1; 5-11, 14-17, 25-29; 5:7-8, 11, 14.
82. McConkie, *Mormon Doctrine*, p. 317.
83. Church of Jesus Christ of Latter-day Saints, *Doctrines of the Gospel*, p. 6.
84. Ibid., p. 9.
85. McConkie, *Mormon Doctrine*, pp. 576-577.
86. *Journal of Discourses*, 7:333.
87. Robinson, *Are Mormons Christians?* p. 88, emphasis added.
88. Ibid., p. 79, emphasis added.
89. Ibid., p. 71, emphasis added.
90. Joseph Smith, *Teachings*, p. 372; cf. Joseph Fielding Smith, *Answers to Gospel Questions*, 1:3.
91. Joseph Smith, *Teachings*, p. 370.
92. E. Calvin Beisner, *God in Three Persons* (Wheaton, IL: Tyndale House, 1984); Edward Henry Bickersteth, *The Trinity* (Grand Rapids, MI: Kregel, 1969).
93. Joseph Smith, *Teachings*, pp. 347-348.
94. Church of Jesus Christ of Latter-day Saints, *Gospel Principles*, p. 293.
95. Joseph Smith, *History*, 6:305.
96. Church of Jesus Christ of Latter-day Saints, *Gospel Principles*, p. 6.
97. Church of Jesus Christ of Latter-day Saints, *Doctrines of the Gospel*, p. 17.
98. Robinson, *Are Mormons Christians?* p. 60.
99. E.g., *Journal of Discourses*, 1:93, 123; 6:120.
100. *Journal of Discourses*, 6:120.
101. *Journal of Discourses*, 11:286.
102. McMurrin, *Theological Foundations*, p. 29.
103. Ibid., p. 36.
104. Church of Jesus Christ of Latter-day Saints, *What the Mormons Think of Christ*, 1982 (pamphlet), p. 16.
105. Church of Jesus Christ of Latter-day Saints, *Faith in the Lord Jesus Christ*, p. 4.
106. Robinson, *Are Mormons Christians?* p. 111, emphasis added.
107. McConkie, *Mormon Doctrine*, p. 169; cf. Joseph Fielding Smith, *Doctrines of Salvation*, 1:75.
108. Church of Jesus Christ of Latter-day Saints, *Sure Foundation*, p. 224.
109. H. Evans, *An American Prophet*, 1933, p. 241, cited in Hoekema, *Four Major Cults*, p. 54.
110. McConkie, *Mormon Doctrine*, p. 129.
111. *Journal of Discourses*, 10:223.
112. *Journal of Discourses*, 1:50-51, emphasis added.
113. Joseph Fielding Smith, *Doctrines of Salvation*, 1:18, emphasis added.
114. McConkie, *Mormon Doctrine*, p. 547.
115. Benson, *Teachings*, pp. 6-7.
116. Hoekema, *Four Major Cults*, p. 56.
117. McConkie, *Mormon Doctrine*, p. 257.
118. Church of Jesus Christ of Latter-day Saints, *Doctrines of the Gospel*, p. 15.
119. Ibid., pp. 9-10.
120. Benson, *Teachings*, p. 6.
121. McConkie, *Doctrinal New Testament Commentary*, 2:215.
122. Ibid., 3:238.
123. McConkie, *Mormon Doctrine*, p. 129.
124. Church of Jesus Christ of Latter-day Saints, *What the Mormons Think of Christ*, 1982 (pamphlet), p. 22; cf. McConkie, *Doctrinal New Testament Commentary*, 3:140.
125. McConkie, *Mormon Doctrine*, p. 670.
126. Church of Jesus Christ of Latter-day Saints, *What the Mormons Think*, p. 27.
127. Robinson, *Are Mormons Christians?* p. 109, emphasis added.
128. Cf. Anderson, *Inside Story*, pp. 15, 19.
129. Talmage, *Articles of Faith*, p. 107.
130. Ibid., pp. 479-480.
131. McConkie, *Mormon Doctrine*, p. 671.
132. Joseph Fielding Smith, *Doctrines of Salvation*, 2:139.
133. Richards, *Marvelous Work*, p. 25.
134. Pratt, *Seer*, January 1854, pp. 199-200.
135. McConkie, *Mormon Doctrine*, p. 559.
136. McConkie, *Doctrinal New Testament Commentary*, 2:215; see also LeGrand Richards, *A Marvelous Work*, p. 275.
137. McConkie, Ibid., p. 229.
138. McConkie, *Doctrinal New Testament Commentary*, 2:238.
139. Ibid., p. 230.
140. Joseph Fielding Smith, *The Way to Perfection*, p. 189.
141. McConkie, *Doctrinal New Testament Commentary*, 3:402.
142. Richards, *Marvelous Work*, p. 275.
143. McConkie, *Doctrinal New Testament Commentary*, 2:248.
144. Kimball, *Miracle*, p. 203.
145. Ibid., pp. 203-204.
146. Church of Jesus Christ of Latter-day Saints, *Doctrines of the Gospel*, pp. 49-50, emphasis added.
147. For an excellent popular study, see James I. Packer, *God's Words: Studies of Key Bible Themes* (Downer's Grove, IL: InterVarsity, 1981).
148. Talmage, *Articles of Faith*, p. 76.
149. Church of Jesus Christ of Latter-day Saints, *Doctrines of the Gospel*, p. 22.
150. Talmage, *Articles of Faith*, p. 481; Joseph F. Smith, *Gospel Doctrine*, pp. 214-215.
151. Benson, *Teachings*, p. 14, emphasis added.
152. Ibid., p. 23.
153. Church of Jesus Christ of Latter-day Saints, *Sure Foundation*, p. 156, emphasis added.
154. Ankerberg, *Mormomism Revisited*, p. 25.
155. McMurrin, *Theological Foundations*, p. 83.
156. Quinn, *Early Mormonism*, pp. 58, 60.
157. Ibid., pp. 78, 80.

158. Jerald and Sandra Tanner, *Changing World*, pp. 67-80.
159. *Discourses of Brigham Young*, pp. 378-380, citing *Journal of Discourses*, 7:332; 6:349.
160. Kimball, *Miracle*, pp. 1, 5.
161. Ibid.
162. Crowther, *Life Everlasting*, p. 151.
163. Joseph F. Smith, *Gospel Doctrine*, pp. 436-437.
164. *Journal of Discourses*, 21:317-318, emphasis added.
165. Martin, *Maze*, 226-228, citing *Journal of Discourses*, 3:369.
166. *The Oxford American Dictionary*, s.v. "Christian."
167. Benson, *Teachings*, p. 10.
168. Church of Jesus Christ of Latter-day Saints, *A Sure Foundation*, p. 155.
169. Ankerberg, *Mormonism Revisited*, p. 13.
170. Stephen E. Robinson, *Are Mormons Christians?* p. vii.
171. Ibid., p. 2.
172. Ibid., p. 7.
173. Ibid., p. 34.
174. Ibid., pp. 72, 77.
175. Ibid., pp. 60, 88.
176. Ankerberg, *Mormon Officials*, p. 32.
177. Per John Weldon's conversation with a representation of the WCC, Mar. 26, 1999. Attempts to acquire an official statement were not responded to. Perhaps the WCC would accept LDS membership. Should they even apply?
178. Sterling M. McMurrin, *The Theological Foundations of the Mormon Religion*, p. x.
179. Ibid., pp. ix, 26.
180. Gordon Fraser, *Is Mormonism Christian?* p. 10.
181. Martin, *Maze of Mormonism*, p. 45.
182. Jerald and Sandra Tanner, *Changing World*, p. 559.
183. Hoekema, *Four Major Cults*, p. 30.
184. Irving Hexham, in Walter A. Elwell, ed., *Evangelical Dictionary of Theology* (Grand Rapids, MI: Baker Book House, 1984), p. 736.
185. *Encyclopedia Britannica*, 15th ed., Macropaedia, s.v. "Mormonism."
186. *The New Schaff-Herzog Encyclopedia of Religious Knowledge*, s.v. "Mormonism."
187. Anthony A. Hoekema, in J.D. Douglas, ed., *The New International Dictionary of the Christian Church*, rev. ed. (Grand Rapids, MI: Zondervan, 1979), p. 678.
188. *Journal of Discourses*, 6:198.
189. Brigham Henry Roberts, Introduction to Joseph Smith's *History*, p. lxxxvi.
190. Ibid.
191. *Elders Journal*, 1, 4:59-60. This journal was edited by Joseph Smith. From Jerald and Sandra Tanner, *Mormonism—Shadow or Reality?* p. 3.
192. See *Book of Mormon* index references under "Babylon," "Church of the Devil," "Church, Great and Abominable," and "Churches, False."
193. Joseph Smith, *Teachings*, p. 270.
194. *Journal of Discourses*, 8:199.
195. *Journal of Discourses*, 8:171; cf. 7:333.
196. *Journal of Discourses*, 5:73.
197. *Journal of Discourses*, 5:229.
198. *Journal of Discourses*, 6:167.
199. *Journal of Discourses*, 5:240.
200. *Journal of Discourses*, 13:225.
201. *Journal of Discourses*, 6:25.
202. *Pamphlets by Orson Pratt*, p. 183; cited in Jerald and Sandra Tanner, *Case Against Mormonism*, 1:6.
203. B.H. Roberts, *The Mormon Doctrine of Deity*, p. 233.
204. Pratt, *Seer*, May 1854, pp. 259-260.
205. Pratt, *Seer*, March 1854, pp. 237, 239, 240.
206. Joseph Fielding Smith, *Doctrines of Salvation*, 3:267, p. 287.
207. McConkie, *Mormon Doctrine*, p. 132.
208. Ibid., pp. 137-138.
209. McConkie, *Doctrinal New Testament Commentary*, 2:240, 274; cf. 3:265.
210. Ibid., 2:280.
211. Ibid., 3:85.
212. Ibid., pp. 247, 550-551.
213. "About FARMS" at www.farmsresearch.com.
214. Jerald and Sandra Tanner, "Mormon FARMS: Battling the AntiMormonoids," Utah Lighthouse Ministry website printout, p. 8.
215. *Christian Research Journal* Summer 1996 pp. 33, 35.
216. For our response, we used an earlier, widely circulated internet copy. Pages are listed from that printed out copy, the content of which is essentially the same as the *Journal* article. This copy is online at: www.apologeticsindex.org/cpoint10-2.html. It should be mentioned that *Apologetics Index* hosts articles for research and debate, without necessarily agreeing with the opinions expressed.
217. Ibid., pp. 2-3.
218. Ibid., pp. 4, 7.
219. Ibid., p. 10, emphasis theirs.
220. Ibid., p. 6.
221. Ibid., p. 20.
222. Ibid., p. 21, emphasis added.
223. *Sunstone*, December, 1998, p. 10.
224. Daniel C. Peterson and Stephen D. Ricks, *Offenders for a Word: How Anti-Mormons Play Word Games to Attack the Latter-day Saints* (Aspen 1992; FARMS 1998), p. xiii.
225. James White, "A Test Case of Scholarship," unprinted paginated internet copy, p. 14, emphasis added.
226. Ibid., p. 15, emphasis added.
227. Ibid., p. 17.
228. Rob Bowman, "A Biblical Guide to Orthodoxy and Heresy—Part One: The Case for Doctrinal Discernment: *Christian Research Journal*, Summer, 1990, internet printout, p. 7.
229. V. L. Walter, "Arianism" in Walter A. Elwell, ed. *Evangelical Dictionary of Theology* (Grand Rapids, MI: Baker 1984), pp. 74-75.
230. Ibid., p. 75.
231. Harold O. J. Brown, *Heresies*, p. 3.
232. John Wm. Maddox. "A Listing of Points and Counterpoints," *Review of Books on the Book of Mormon*, vol. 8, no. 1 (1996), internet.
233. Found at www.farmsresearch.com/review/5/Seely3.html.
234. Bryan Watterman, "Policing 'The Lord's University': The AAUP and BYU, 1995-1998," *Sunstone*, December 1998, p. 22.
235a. *Journal of Discourses*, Vol. 13.

235. Ibid., p. 36.
236. Carl Mosser and Paul Owen, "Mormon Scholarship, Apologetic and Evangelical Neglect: Losing the Battle and Not Knowing It?" *Trinity Journal*, Fall 1998, pp. 4-5.
237. James White, "A Study of FARMS Behavior," www.aomin.org.
238. FARMS Reprint Series, Provo, UT: FARMS, 1996, reprint of 1982 ed.; cf. Hugh Nibley, *The Prophetic Book of Mormon*, ch. 18, "The Lachish Letters."
239. Thomas J. Finley, Institute for Religion Research, www.irr.org, a paper originally delivered to the Society for the Study of Alternative Religions (SSAR) at the annual meeting of the Evangelical Theological Society, November 19, 1998, Orlando, Florida.
240. James White, "The Gates of Hell," at www.aomin.org.
241. We found the following on the "Honest Intellectual Inquiry" website: http://www.california.com/~rpcman/NIBLEY1.HTM. It discusses volume 1 of Nibley's collected works and seems to illustrate the quality of his works generally.

"For *BYU Studies* in 1988, Hugh Nibley received an unusual critique from Kent P. Jackson. I have heard others in the church express similar views, but to hear these things from someone like Jackson, published in something like *BYU Studies*, was a bit of a shock. It is refreshing to hear honest opinions like these from orthodox members. Portions of the article have been reproduced below. . . .

[These remarks refer to the Collected Works of Hugh Nibley, Vol. 1, Old Testament and Related Studies. Edited by John W. Welch, Gary P. Gillum, and Don E. Norton (Salt Lake City: Deseret Book and the Foundation for Ancient Research and Mormon Studies, 1986), xiv.]

"Hugh Nibley is the best known and most highly revered of Latter-day Saint scholars. . . . My own serious misgivings about his methodology do not detract from my admiration for his life of scholarship consecrated to the highest cause. . . . Echoing the feelings of Nibley's followers throughout the Church, editor John W. Welch suggests in his Foreword that most of Nibley's lifetime total of nearly two hundred titles are classics (ix). If that is in fact the case, then this volume has been severely shortchanged; nothing in it can be called a classic. It is, in fact, a disappointing collection.

"There are several areas about which I have concerns regarding the material in this book:

"1. In most of the articles Nibley shows a tendency to gather sources from a variety of cultures all over the ancient world, lump them all together, and then pick and choose the bits and pieces he wants. . . . There are serious problems involved in this kind of methodology. . . . Nibley creates an artificial synthesis that never, in reality, existed. The result would be unacceptable and no doubt unrecognizable to any of the original groups. . . .

"This kind of method seems to work from the conclusions to the evidence—instead of the other way around. And too often it necessitates giving the sources an interpretation for which little support can be found elsewhere. I found myself time and time again disagreeing with this book's esoteric interpretations of Qumran passages. In several places Nibley sees things in the sources that simply don't seem to be there (for example, most of the preexistence references in the Dead Sea Scrolls, cited in chapter 7). This is what inevitably happens when scholars let their predetermined conclusions set the agenda for the evidence. . . .

"2. In this book, Nibley often uses his secondary sources the same way he uses his primary sources—taking phrases out of context to establish points with which those whom he quotes would likely not agree. I asked myself frequently what some authors would think if they knew that someone was using their words the way Nibley does (the same question I asked myself concerning his ancient sources as well).

"3. Several of the articles lack sufficient documentation and some lack it altogether. This is to be expected in a collection that includes popular articles and transcripts of speeches. The editors clearly deserve our praise for trying to bring Nibley's footnotes up to professional standards. But given the complexity of the material, it was not always possible. The first article, for example, is riddled with undocumented quotations. Some of Nibley's most puzzling assertions remain undocumented—or unconvincingly documented—even in those articles that are footnoted heavily. The two most extensively referenced articles, "Treasures In the Heavens" and "Qumran and the Companions of the Cave," display the opposite problem. The seemingly endless footnotes in those articles suffer from dreary overkill, and yet too often I was disappointed in searching in vain in them for proof for the claims made in the text.

"4. . . . Nibley frequently misrepresents his opponents' views (through overstatement, oversimplification, or removal from context) to the point that they are ludicrous, after which he has ample cause to criticize them. This may make amusing satire, but it is not scholarship. . . . Among those satirized in this book are 'the learned' (8), archaeologists (chapter 2), 'the clergy' (38-39), 'professional scholars' (39), 'secular scholars' (39), 'the doctors' (217-18), 'the schoolmen' (217), and 'the doctors, ministers, and commentators' (221). . . .

"5. My final area of concern is more properly directed at the editors than at Hugh Nibley. What is the point of publishing some of this material. . . . Several of the chapters in this book, particularly 9 and 10, are so weak that the editors would have been doing Nibley a much greater honor if they had left them out. What is the point of resurrecting such material, which is now completely out-of-date and was not even quality work when first published three decades ago? In doing so they have not done Nibley a service, nor have they served his readers."

[The website piece continues.]

"As noted in *BYU: A House of Faith*, by Bergera and Priddis: 'As a former BYU history professor observed in 1984, "[Nibley] has been a security blanket for Latter-day Saints to whom dissonance is intolerable. . . . His contribution to dissonance management is not so much what he has written, but that he has written. After knowing Hugh Nibley for forty years, I am of the opinion that he has been playing games with his readers all along. . . . Relatively few Latter-day Saints read the Nibley books that they give one another, or the copiously annotated articles that he has contributed to church publications. It is enough for most of us that they are there."³

"[And] reading Nibley reminds me of a quote from a line in Umberto Eco's 'Foucault's Pendulum,' which says, '. . . Wanting connections, we found connections—always, everywhere, and between everything.'"

At the same website, we found this: "I'm putting my own collection of Book of Mormon evidence together, and as I read this, it occurred to me that Nibley is horribly stretching the truth. In fact, I'd say he's lying. . . . Because of everything else he incorrectly stated, I can't bring myself to believe that he's quoting the 1888 Enoch text accurately, or if he's translating it himself, manipulating the words to fit what he believes.

"Sorry, I'm Mormon, and I do respect Nibley's great efforts, but I draw the line at dishonest scholarship, which is what this appears to be."

241a. Hugh Nibley, *Tinkling Cymbols and Sounding Brass* (Salt Lake City: Deseret Book Co. and FARMS, 1991), p. 11.
242. Ibid., p. 10.
243. Hugh Nibley, *The Prophetic Book of Mormon* (Salt Lake City: Deseret Book Co. and FARMS, 1989), p. 59, emphasis added.
244. Ibid., p. 498.
245. Nibley, *Prophetic Book*, p. 67, emphasis added.
246. Ibid., p. 69, emphasis added.
247. Hugh Nibley, *Since Cumorah* (Salt Lake City: Deseret Book Co. and FARMS, 1988), p. xiv, emphasis added.
248. Ibid.
249. Hugh Nibley, *An Approach to the Book of Mormon* (Salt Lake City: Deseret Book Co. and FARMS, 1988), p. 6, emphasis added.
250. Nibley, *Since Cumorah*, pp. 26-27.
251. Ibid., pp. 26-28.
252. We document this thoroughly in our *Behind the Mask of Mormonism*. See also Alma 7:16; Mosiah 5:8,9; 2 Nephi 9:23,24; 3 Nephi 27:14-17,21,22.
253. Nibley, *Approach*, p. 13.
254. Nibley, *Prophetic Book*, p. 86.
255. Hugh Nibley, *Mormonism and Early Christianity* (Salt Lake City: Deseret Book Co. and FARMS, 1987), p. 219.
256. *Journal of Discourses*, Vol. 13, p. 95.
257. Tanners, *Anti-Mormonoids*, p. 5.
258. Ibid., p. 16.
259. Ibid., p. 25.
260. Ibid., p. 29.
261. James White, "A study in F.A.R.M.S. Behavior" printed internet document, p. 12, available at Alpha and Omega ministries website www.aomin.org.

THE MIGHTY I AM

INFO AT A GLANCE

Name: The Mighty I AM.

Purpose: To bring "ascended I AM power" to America, that she might fulfill her cosmic destiny as the world's repository of "Light."

Founder: Guy Ballard (pen name, Godfre Ray King), 1878–1939.

Source of authority: The spiritistic revelations of Guy and Edna Ballard.

Revealed teachings: Yes.

Claim: To be among the vanguard of movements bringing light and truth to the world; to be the only way of attaining the "Ascension"—spiritual resurrection.

Examples of occult potential: Spiritism, voluntary possession, magic, retributive magic.

Key literature: Books by "The Ascended Masters" (such as *Ascended Master Discourses*); "St. Germain" (such as *The "I AM" Discourses*); the "Great Cosmic Beings" (such as *The Magic Presence; Unveiled Mysteries*).

Attitude toward Christianity: Rejecting.

Quotes:

"The Christ [not Jesus] is in reality the MASTER WITHIN!" (*The Voice of the I AM*, December, 1936, p. 37)

"The only ones who know the solution of Life are the Ascended Masters. . . . They have gone every step which you are required to go and know every requirement. Therefore, they are the Ones who can teach you, and the *Only Ones* in the whole world who *can* teach you the Truth of Life. That has been accomplished in the Saint Germain books which are for your use." (Godfre Ray King, *Ascended Master Light*, p. 119)

"[Jesus states:] try always to remember that you are not human beings so-called, but you are Gods and Goddesses in embryo." (Godfre Ray King, *The "I AM" Discourses*, pp. 273–274)

"I want so much to have you feel that you are the Only Authority in this world or any other, so far as your world is concerned. . . . We are going to take this Authority and use it, clear away all discord, and declare with no uncertainty: 'I AM' the Supremacy of man, everywhere I go—'I AM' *God in Action.*" (Ibid., pp. 44–45)

Note: Set historically between Theosophy and the Church Universal and Triumphant, the Mighty I Am is the second of three major religious associations allegedly inspired by the same Ascended Masters. (Before starting the I AM group the Ballards were Theosophists.) While the masters apparently no longer give revelations to the I AM group, the activities of the members are still similar to what they were in its heyday in the late 1930s: giving various Decrees and Demands, reliance upon the "I AM presence," and so on. Literature and books written in its heyday are still reprinted and sold, although with its decline many of the promises and claims of the ascended masters defaulted. The books themselves, like amulets, are reputed to contain occult powers.

DOCTRINAL SUMMARY

God: An impersonal Force, Principle, Energy. There also exists a pantheon of gods and demigods; "St. Germain" is the greatest, but there are many others, including the ascended Guy Ballard and "Jesus."

Jesus: An ascended master.

The Christ: I AM presence within every person.

The Holy Spirit: The I AM presence.

The Trinity: A Christian myth.

Salvation: By a lifetime of good works and occult practice; for example, the "Violet consuming Flame" is called upon to destroy evil thoughts and desires; such as those that do not harmonize with I AM teachings. To be fully enlightened is to attain to the ascension—to be free of all physical limits and to become a God.

Man: Inwardly divine.

Satan: A Christian myth.

The Second Coming: Jesus "returned" when he appeared to the Ballards as an ascended master.

The Fall: Into matter.

The Bible: Subordinate to the ascended masters' new revelations and interpretation.

Death: The individual reincarnates until achieving the status of ascended master.

Heaven and Hell: States of consciousness.

NEW THOUGHT

INFO AT A GLANCE

Name: New Thought.

Purpose: To awaken people to their divine nature.

Founder: The ideas of P. P. Quimby.

Source of authority: Leading New Thought and Mind Science books are important, however ultimately the "higher Self" of the individual is the supreme authority.

Revealed teachings: Yes.

Claim: To offer the means to enable people to live successfully and peacefully.

Occult dynamics: A general openness to the psychic and occult realm reinterpreted through New Thought metaphysics.

Key literature: Scores of books by leading New Thought authors.

Attitude toward Christianity: Rejecting.

Quotes:

"You are the Lord Jesus."[1]

"But even though you are the Christ, you might not be fully aware of the fact."[2]

"The Truth is so shrouded by false dogmas that we have created God and a heaven of our making."[3]

"New Thought emerged because there were, as there still are, those who wished to be liberated from restrictions of outdated religious doctrine. We want to be free from sin and guilt and condemnation, and from the resulting sickness and poverty. We want the truth that would set us free."[4]

Note: Relevant chapters from Vol. 1, *Encyclopedia of New Age Beliefs* (1996), include: A Course in Miracles; Altered States of Consciousness; Enlightenment; New Age Intuition and Inner Work; New Age Meditation; Visualization.

DOCTRINAL SUMMARY

God: Universal Law, "personified" impersonal energy.

Jesus: A great man who attained a high state of awareness and realized his oneness with God.

The Christ: The individualized God-part of mankind.

Holy Spirit: Often, a synonym for God.

Salvation: By proper thought, increased spiritual awareness and inner development leading to knowledge of the truth of who one is.

Man: One essence with God.

Sin: Errors or mistakes resulting from unenlightened consciousness.

The Fall: Into wrong thinking.

The Bible: A spiritually relevant text when interpreted metaphysically in accordance with New Thought principles.

Death: Various interpretations; generally seen as personal advancement.

Hell and Heaven: Mental or physical conditions on earth.

INTRODUCTION AND HISTORY

"I am God. I am not *a* god—I *am* God."[5]

This declaration by Robert Sikking, a minister of the Unity School of Christianity, reflects a typical sentiment within the religion of New Thought. New Thought is an umbrella designation covering hundreds, possibly thousands, of independent churches around the world. Broadly speaking, Religious Science (Science of Mind),* Divine Science, Unity School of Christianity and scores of smaller independent organizations constitute New Thought. Millions of people have been reached with the basic message of New

*Religious Science International and United Religious Science are identical, with the exception that the former refused to join the URS in 1949 and comprises an independent group of 50+ churches.

Thought. In the 1930s and 1940s, New Thought was brought to millions by Frank B. Robinson, head of the Psychiana movement, and today hundreds of leaders have replaced him, all spreading their new "Gospel" of positive thinking with great fervor. In 1980, the former mayor of San Francisco, Dianne Feinstein, issued an official proclamation declaring July 20–25, New Thought Week.[6]

Hundreds of churches and organizations make up the International New Thought Alliance (INTA) headquartered in Mesa, Arizona. Many more exist outside INTA desiring more freedom than its organizational structure and "statement of belief" would restrict them to. Roy Eugene Davis' "Center for Spiritual Awareness," is one example. Often, New Thought groups can be recognized by their allegedly Christian or "New Age" names or emphases. Apart from the above large groups, a sampling of smaller New Thought organizations or groups would include:

Seicho-No-Ie Truth of Life Movement	Unity-Progressive Council	Universal Foundation for Better Living
Affiliated New Thought Alliance Network	Christ Universal Temple	Center for Positive Living
Association of Creative Thought	Golden Key Ministry	Church of Christian Philosophy
Home of Truth	Teaching of the Inner Christ	Association of Progressive Christianity
Metaphysical Bible Institute	Church of Universal Truth	Unity of the Infinite Presence
Christ Haven Center	Church of the Healing Christ	All Faiths Church
Foundation of Living	Esoteric Truth Center	The Science of Awareness
Symphony of Life Association	Christ Circle for Better Living	Sanctuary of Light Church
Center for New Living	Truth Temple	Center for Positive Prayer

Center for Better Living	Church for Today	Church of Truth
Edwene Gaines Prosperity Products	Emerson Institute	New Thought Community
Hillside Chapel and Truth Center	The Inner Voices	A New Thought Gospel Choir
Living Light Ministries	Lifestream Center for Creative Living	Ministry of Truth International
New Thought of Paris	The New Thought Theological Seminary	New Thought Ministries of New Zealand
The Positive Truth: First Interactive Church of the Web	Society of Pragmatic Mysticism	University of Healing
Integral Spirit	Oversoul	Successful Living Foundation

The Annual INTA Congresses have provided glimpses of the message and influence of New Thought. The Sixty-Fifth Congress featured influential persons such as: Dr. C. Norman Shealy, author of *Occult Medicine Can Save Your Life* and, with spiritist Carolyn Myss, *The Creation of Health;* Dr. Gerald Jampolsky, who uses spiritistic literature in his healing practice with children;* Roy Eugene Davis, head of the Center for Spiritual Awareness; Anne Francis, movie-TV actress and head of the Inner Space Foundation and other notables.[7]

The 83rd Annual INTA Congress (1998) held in Scottsdale, Arizona, July 14–19, offered topics such as: "Out of All Chaos We Can Produce Harmony"; "Hidden Bible Secrets"; "Developing Your Healing Hover Touch Skills" (Energy Balancing or Psychic Healing); "Prosperity Step by Step: The Secrets of the Universe in 30 Minutes"; "A Proposal to Establish a New Thought College Worthy of Universally Recognized Accredita-

tion"; "It's All God: The Judaic/Christian Myth in the 21st Century Paradigm."

Some INTA celebrities even have their own TV shows—for example, Dale Balesoles' New Thought-oriented "There is a Way" boasts a half million daily viewers in Southern California.[8] There is also Della Reese, of the hit series "Touched By An Angel," a New Thought minister since 1983 who believes she was guided by God to that vocation. The "Christian" church she founded is called: "Understanding Principles for Better Living" in Los Angeles. (According to its website, Reese was ordained by The Universal Foundation for Better Living in Chicago, an association of 22 independent New Thought churches founded by Reverend Johnnie Coleman in 1974.) Popular speakers such as money man Reverend Ike ("God is money") and V. T. Minto (Alpha Truth Awareness Seminars) are also New Thought oriented. The influential New Age occultist Barbara Marx Hubbard, who receives revelation from "Christ" and has influenced millions of people, has stated, "New Thought is now or will become in the next 30 to 50 years the most important single movement on earth."[9] When someone like Hubbard, the "author" of *The Book of Co-Creation,* and *The Hunger of Eve* and *The Revelation* makes a statement like that, it may be wise to listen.

Two more recent New Thought influences include the Society for the Study of Metaphysical Religion (SSMR), an outgrowth of the American Academy of Religion, and "Process New Thought," which combines the process theology and panentheism of Alfred North Whitehead and Charles Hartshorne and emphasizes practical learning about "offering new opportunities for most wisely engaging in co-creation with God."[10] Concerning the SSMR, its website states:

The SSMR was formed in the mid-1980s largely by people associated with the delivery of certain academic papers at meetings of the American Academy of Religions. These papers related to the New Thought Movement. . . . The "Father of New Thought" was Phineas Parkhurst Quimby, a Maine clockmaker who practiced mesmerism. . . . Among his patients and students were former Methodist minister and Swedenborgian lay leader Warren Felt Evans, who wrote the first books in the field, and Mary Baker Eddy, who

---

*E.g., the second volume, *A Course in Miracles* (see *Encyclopedia of New Age Beliefs*).

later developed Christian Science. A one-time Eddy associate, Emma Curtis Hopkins, founded the first New Thought school and taught founders of the New Thought groups known as Divine Science, Unity, and Religious Science (Science of Mind). . . . New Thought themes are found in teachings of Norman Vincent Peale and Robert Schuller, as well as Alcoholics Anonymous and much success literature. . . . The Society is concerned with metaphysics both in its traditional philosophical meaning (the study of the basic nature of all reality) and in its popular meaning (whatever is beyond the physical). . . . Any group—whether esoteric, theosophical, New Age, or Christian Science—with such emphases would come within the purview of the Society. . . .[11]

INTA recommends the following "basic texts" as representative of New Thought: Dr. Catherine Ponders' *Dynamic Laws of Prosperity* (Dr. Ponders is known as a "prosperity expert" in the movement, having written extensively on all the "millionaires" in the Bible; for example, *The Millionaires of Genesis, The Millionaire Moses, The Millionaire Joshua, The Millionaire from Nazarus*, etc.); Fannie James' *Fundamentals of Divine Science;* H. Emily Cady's *Lessons in Truth;* Dr. Joseph Murphy's *Power of the Subconscious;* Dr. Maxwell Maltz' *Psycho-Cybernetics;* and Dr. Ernest Holmes' *Science of Mind*.[12] Periodicals include *Bright Ideas, Creative Thought, Science of Mind, Daily Word* and *Unity.*

Leading figures within the movement include H. Emile Cady, Dr. Joseph Murphy, Dr. Evarts Loomis, Dr. Marcus Bach, Dr. Gene Emmet Clark, Dr. Vernon A. Shields, Dr. Catherine Ponder, Dr. Joel Goldsmith (head of the "Infinite Way" movement) and lesser notables such as Martha Jean "The Queen" (head of the Order of the Fishermen Ministry).

Almost every leader in the New Thought and Mind Science movement is either a "doctor," reverend or both, but it appears that only a relatively few have legitimate Ph.D.s or the equivalent from accredited institutions. Generally speaking, in New Thought the designation of "minister" or "doctor" does not mean the person is qualified as to the normal Christian or academic meaning of that degree. It is true that some of the New Thought groups do offer more rigor-

ous training courses for ministers at their "colleges," but the course of instruction is often little more than instruction in their particular brand of metaphysics. For example, INTA district president Dr. Anna Maye Dahl offers B.M. degrees (that is, Bachelor of Metaphysics) along with Ph.D.s and D.D.s from her "Academy of Universal Truth," claiming "chartered authority" to issue the degrees.[13]

New Thought can be historically traced to P. P. Quimby (1802–1866), often considered the founder of New Thought. A psychic (then, "magnetic") healer in the Mesmerist movement (our own research has indicated spiritistic influences in his work),[14] Quimby's "healing" of Mary Baker Eddy influenced the beginning of her "Christian Science." In his authoritative work, *Spirits in Rebellion,* C. S. Braden traces other influences on New Thought.[15]

The INTA website indicates the considerable influence of New Thought, both historically and at present. Besides pointing out the influence of New Thought in Christian Science, Divine Science, Unity and Science of Mind, the website also mentions the influence of New Thought on the modern New Age movement, which is now the third largest religious "denomination" in America:* "New Thought is one of the sources of present-day New Age outlooks, as well as much success literature and the positive thinking teachings of Norman Vincent Peale, Robert Schuller, and others. New Thought also contributed significantly to the beliefs of Alcoholics Anonymous (12-step programs), especially through the writings of popular New Thought minister Emmet Fox."[16]

Indeed, the influence of New Thought on Alcoholics Anonymous, which has also had a tradition of occult and Christian interests,[17] is more than incidental:

The most important connection of AA and New Thought was by means of the writings of popular New Thought writer Emmet Fox [described by] Igo I. Sikorsky, Jr., in his *AA's Godparents: Carl Jung, Emmet Fox, Jack Alexander* (Minneapolis: CompCare Publishers, 1990). . . . Si-

---

*See our *Encyclopedia of New Age Beliefs* (Harvest House, 1996), for more detailed information.

korsky says, "Five of the original stories in the Big Book were by early AA members deeply influenced by Emmet Fox (p. 23)." Sikorsky also notes (p. 19) that an early recovering alcoholic who worked with co-founder Bill Wilson was Al Steckman, whose mother was Fox's secretary, and that as a result of this connection early AA groups would often go to listen to Fox. A valuable writing is *New Thought and 12 Step Recovery from Addiction: Practical American Spiritualities* by Kenneth E. Hart. . . .[18]

PRACTICE AND TEACHINGS

New Thought and its derivatives essentially represent a religion of "the Self"; that is people are inwardly divine and it is thus proper that they should receive divine honor, for they are one essence with all God is. Talk of God reigns supreme in New Thought, since it is always pleasant to talk about oneself.

Relevant premises and characteristics of New Thought include:

1. God is One, the only Reality, and everyone is part of that One Reality.

2. Good is omnipresent and life is perfect, we just do not realize it. If we could open our eyes spiritually we would see the divine perfection of all existence. God is "only Good" and God does not "know" or "recognize" things such as evil, lack, illness and poverty; hence, they are "unreal."

3. Thought is creative power. People are God's thought; the creation is the image of God's thought. Thought controls the image of thought. This means that a person's thoughts control his or her life and environment. Since one's consciousness is the cause of one's experience, to alter the consciousness positively or negatively is to alter the experience.

4. Perpetual success is our birthright, such as achieving (recognizing) one's already existing wealth, health, happiness, love and fulfillment.

5. The Bible is a New Thought manual, properly interpreted.

Among the International New Thought Alliance Declaration of Principles, which lists ten key principles, are the following:

1. We affirm the inseparable oneness of God and humankind, the realization of which comes through spiritual intuition, the implications of which are that we can reproduce the Divine perfection in our bodies, emotions, and all our external affairs. . . .

3. We affirm the Good to be supreme, universal and eternal. . . .

6. We affirm our belief in God as the Universal Wisdom, Love, Life, Truth, Power, Peace, Plenty, Beauty and Joy, "in whom we live, and move and have our being". . . .

7. We affirm that our mental states are carried forward into manifestation and become our experience through the Creative Law of Cause and Effect.

8. We affirm that the Divine Nature expressing Itself through us manifests itself as health, supply, wisdom, love, life, truth, power, peace, beauty and joy.

9. We affirm that we are invisible spiritual dwellers within human bodies continuing and unfolding as spiritual beings beyond the change called physical death.

10. We affirm that the universe is the body of God, spiritual in essence, governed by God through laws which are spiritual in reality, even when material in appearance.[19]

There is, however, no "official" New Thought doctrine, so variations of belief may exist among New Thought practitioners. Nevertheless, a core belief is that people can supply for themselves all that could be required of them for time and eternity; potentially, they have no limits. So if a person is divine, the limitations of time and space, for instance, do not necessarily apply. "Time does not exist in Divine Mind. . . . Time is man's creation, not God's creation."[20] Further, people make their own destiny, and their spiritually "enlightened" will is God's will.

Allegedly, through positive thinking people do not affirm *into* existence the good or change the bad, they merely realize that the ALL-GOOD was there all along, waiting to be discovered, and that the bad was "unreal." "Negative" things are simply dark and mysterious shadows upon the world waiting to be diffused by the light of knowledge. Once people turn "on" the light the shadows will disappear, for they cannot exist in the light. Thus:

Man, who is a child of God, is God. . . . so, if man, who is a child of God, is God, then man is Infinite Power. When we awaken to the infinite power which God has given us, all disease will be healed, and poverty will no longer exist.[21]

Nothing is ours except by right of [proper] consciousness. . . . So we work diligently to build our consciousness. All good is ours by right of consciousness.[22]

To know we are the Principle of Being, that I AM consciousness, instead of trying to become It, clears the consciousness of much doubt and confusion. You can never become what you already are.[23]

We know today that we can change our life by changing our thought.[24]

God's will is the recognition of that which is— not of that which will be. Peace is, joy is, love is, harmony is, wholeness is, right action is, wisdom is. God is the Eternal Now. God is timeless and spaceless. So claim your good now! . . . When your wish or desire for harmony, health, peace, joy or abundance becomes a conviction in your subconscious, then it is God's will and is no longer man's wish or choice. . . . In Biblical language, it is no longer "My will" but, "Thy will be done."[25]

New Thought uses "spiritual treatments" or "affirmations" by which it attempts to "integrate" one's fallen consciousness with divine Truth. We have given several examples in our chapters on Religious Science and Unity School of Christianity and do not need to repeat them here. Basically, they affirm the truth of things as seen by New Thought, stressing the mind's ability to "uncover" the world of Reality, the world where there is no sadness, lack or evil, only joy, abundance and goodness.

Positive thinking and positive affirmation are said to be primarily "reminders," not causative agents. However, at the individual level this is merely semantics, for lack of positive thinking

is, practically speaking, the cause of "evil" and disharmony. If one's thoughts are not positive, one will experience the negative. Thus thought is a causative agent, at least from the human perspective.

THEOLOGY

Christianity

Claims to being "fully Christian," or "true Christianity," or "based on the teachings of Jesus" and so on are abundant in New Thought groups. We have also documented this claim in the chapters on the New Thought religions Unity School of Christianity and Religious Science, and readers may turn there for examples. Here we will simply illustrate that, despite its claim to be Christian, New Thought is not Christian. New Thought leaders recognize they have reinterpreted historic Christianity and distorted it to teach their own views. For example, Roy Eugene Davis of the New Thought-oriented Center for Spiritual Awareness (also known as Christian Spiritual Alliance) calls the former Rosicrucian Neville Goddard "one of America's great New Thought teachers" and refers to him as rising "to the peak of professional brilliance," being a "supremely powerful influential teacher in the New Thought field."[26] Goddard reportedly "spent at least eight hours a day reading" the Bible,[27] concluding that God was human imagination. "God is human imagination," he declared, and, "When you hear any priest, any rabbi or any minister speaking of the Lord on the outside [apart from man], bear in mind they do not know the Lord."[28]

William Warch, in his The New Thought Christian, declares that New Thought Christians "seek a new definition of God, Christ and Holy Spirit."[29] Reminiscent of Ernest Holmes, founder of Religious Science, who said, "I did not like the religions I knew of so I made up my own," Warch tells us that we must reject the biblical view of God and make up our own ideas.[30] And the Bible must not be interpreted literally because "certainly literal Biblical descriptions do nothing but terrorize the soul."[31] As a result, he argues that the best "visual aid" for the New Thought journey "is the Holy Bible, metaphysically interpreted."[32] Indeed, Warch reassures his readers that even though the fundamentals of biblical teaching may be tossed aside one can still claim to be a Christian. "If someone asks you, 'Are you a Christian? Do you believe Jesus died for your sins? Are you born again and know that you are a sinner and live with a good deal of guilt and shame?' you can honestly answer, 'Even though I may not believe in those humiliating details, I am a Christian. I am a New Thought Christian because I am developing an awareness of God and my true nature.'"[33]

Veiled and not so veiled sentiments rejecting Christianity are regular features in *New Thought*, the principal journal of INTA.[34] Generally, New Thought members believe that Christians are too rigid, that their "closed theology," their "defining" of God and their "self-defeating experiences of their duality" (human/divine; evil/good, etc.) place them in a spiritually regressive state with little more than "grasshopper consciousness."[35] Christian theology is logically recognized as an "enemy." "Our birthright is wholeness. Our task is to isolate and identify the enemies that keep the potential from being realized."[36] Christianity is "dead dogma," "outrageous theology," "false beliefs" and so on.[37] The Christian religion was not revealed by God but fabricated by man. "And that kind of religion was thought to be God's way, God's religion. How we like to make God into our image and likeness, and to assign Him with laws and regulations that originated from our own developing and struggling consciousness."[38]

New Thought ministers have little problem justifying their particular theology as divine truth, but in its own way their theology is just as "rigid and closed" as the Christian beliefs they condemn. One *must* hold New thought truths to function properly spiritually and to advance metaphysically. As a result, the ministers do not hesitate to infer that those without the proper spiritual mentality are spiritually uncvolved and ignorant of divine truth.

God

I am one with God. ... I am one with all life [God is] one spirit [who] dispenses himself in various bodies, all of us need to adopt the code, 'I am the one with God.' ..."

—Della Reese preaching before standing-room only crowds at her church (Internet; cf. her interview with Anita Belk, *Angel Times* magazine, Vol. 1, No. 4.)

Our future is guided by God. You can't go wrong with that kind of compass point.

—Della Reese, speaking of her and her husband, *ET Spotlight Interview* (Internet)

Perhaps the Christian doctrine most consistently rejected by New Thought is that of creation, of God and people as fundamentally distinct. Obviously, if everyone is not one essence with God, virtually every New Thought doctrine is nullified. "We shall forever be frustrated until we abandon any concept of a 'God-out-there' doing anything to or for us."[39] Biblically, however, God is not our enemy. We can trust in the God "out there," and He will do abundantly well by us. All He asks is that we acknowledge our sin and creaturehood, have faith in His Son, Jesus, and live in dependence, trust and enjoyment of Him rather than attempt to control Him as some "sea of Intelligence which awaits our command."[40] Indeed, the scriptural testimony is that the God of the Bible is far more positive than New Thought practitioners are willing to grant.

That God is good to everyone is indeed the scriptural testimony. Consider just a few scriptures which tells us that God is there, that He is personal, that He is gracious and that He desires we enjoy life. God desires that "none should perish" and that men should "love life and see good days" (1 Peter 3:10). God "gives generously to all without finding fault" (James 1:5). In all past generations, God "did good [to you] and gave you rains from heaven and fruitful seasons, satisfying your hearts with food and gladness" (Acts 14:17 NAS). "I know that there is nothing better for men than to be happy and to do good while they live. That every man may eat and drink, and find satisfaction in all his toil—this is the gift of God" (Ecclesiastes 3:12–13). Truly, "the earth is full of the lovingkindness of the LORD" (Psalm 33:5 NAS). "The LORD is gracious and compassionate, slow to anger and rich in love. The LORD is good to all; he has compassion on all he has made. ... The LORD is faithful to all his promises and loving toward all he has made. The LORD upholds all those who fall and lifts up all who are bowed down. . . . You open your hand and satisfy the desires of every living thing" (Psalm 145:8–9, 13–14, 16).

In New Thought, God is described in many ways. The almost endless variety of descriptions and definitions illustrate the individualist manner of New Thought theology. God is, in the end, whatever one wishes Him to be. The following chart shows numerous New Thought ideas about God.

"Infinite impersonal consciousness"	"Life"	"Truth"
"Divine Consciousness"	"Universal Wisdom and Intelligence"	"Beauty and Joy"
"Presence"	"Father-Mother God"	"the [inner] power to make things right"
"the mood of good"	"the light of life"	"neither person, place or thing"
"the thing called power itself"	"Infinite Spirit"	"the GOOD"
"the eternal NOW"	"Infinite Idea, not a Person"	"Reality"
"Loving Principle"	"It," "I AM"	"Oneness of Spirit"
"the Only Presence, Power, Cause, and Substance"	"Divine Urge, the Divine Impulse, the Absolute Beauty, the Absolute Ongoingness . . . God Itself,"	"all there is, in all, and as all, One presence, One power, One activity"
"Infinite Mellowness"	"Everything,"	"invisible energy-intelligence"
"Good backing us up"	"lavish, opulent"	"One Mind"
"the entire universe"	"Self"	"Perfect and Eternal Being,"
"a Something."[41]	"The Wonder of Life"	"Universal Life Force"

Although New Thought readily berates Christianity for "imprisoning our consciousness in archaic human concepts of the Infinite God,"[42] it fails to realize that its ambiguous theology imprisons Him even more. If God is everything, what is he not? But then, what is he? They like to quote Emerson: "To define God is to defile God." However, this leaves us with little more than a practical agnosticism that allows us to make God whatever we wish, which hardly leaves us with any God at all. One wonders what, essentially, *is* a God that is "Absolute Ongoingness," "a Something," "neither person, place or thing," "Divine Urge," "the Only Presence" and "Infinite Mellowness"? Terms like these are about as vague as it gets. Even the more concrete New Thought descriptions of God still leave one wondering. God is supposedly "All Good" and "Beauty and Joy," but who defines these terms except the individual New Thought practitioner, who can make them mean anything or everything? In the end, God is more like nothing than something divine to love and worship.

It is precisely because the New Thought God remains impersonal and nebulous that He cannot be related to, except perhaps in one's imagination. (Recall Neville Goddard's conclusion earlier.) There is no objective God "out there" to know; there is only oneself. Hence the necessity for borrowing from Christianity becomes evident, and the ineffable thing that is not a Person is called "Good," "Wise," "Presence," "Loving," "Beautiful," "Perfect," "Father" and so on.

In the end, God is impersonal and ultimately reduced to various human feelings and states of consciousness such as emotional love, peace, joy, contentment and psychic consciousness. However, isn't it true that these go only so far in providing meaning to life? If there is no personal God "out there" to worship, no God to obey, no God to love, no God to look forward to eternal fellowship with, what are we really left with? There is no relationship with God at all, and that is the essence of hell. Of course, a "relationship" to "the mood of the good" or to "the Wonder of Life"—to "Something"—can be manufactured by positive thinking, but it comes solely from the human side and cannot be a relationship with the true God, which comes only through Jesus Christ.

One thing we do know is that the New Thought God appreciates money. Reminiscent of Reverend Ike's declaration that "God is money," some New Thought teachers believe "God is financial wealth" and describe God as opulent and opulence. "New Thought calls God opulent. It is the basic idea undergirding all the concepts of a prosperity principle in the Universe. Prosperity and Supply can be demonstrated by Man when he connects himself to Nature and the Universal Life Force."[43] "There is no lack in my life now. There is only rich abundance because I am the child of my rich rich Father-Mother-God."[44] New Thought may tell us that "God appears as the food on your table,"[44a] but would this comfort the hungry? Would the New Thought dictum "all appearance is erroneous," satisfy the poverty stricken or war ravaged?

The God of New Thought is thus unlike the God of the Bible, who in the Person of Jesus experienced poverty, hardship, suffering and shame. The God of New Thought recognizes none of this and sees only one Good, which is one reason why this God is so attractive to the affluent and to those whose goal is personal peace and security.

Jesus Christ

New Thought believes Jesus was only a man who, like some others, became "the Christ" and thus recognized his own divinity. All people are potential Christs. All people are the Son of God in nature, if not yet in consciousness, because anyone can think like Jesus and thus become like Jesus. If Jesus was "unique" in anything, it was His conscious awareness of the truths of New Thought and how He applied them.

What "saved" Jesus Christ was His recognition that He was not the mere limited creature He once thought He was but that He was truly one essence with God. "The Christ is a point of awareness in the mind of God. . . . That is exactly what you are in reality. . . . Many years ago a man named Jesus discovered that all His potential was actually within His own being. . . . He had developed full Christ awareness."[45] According to New Thought, numerous Scriptures describing God (for example, Isaiah 49:26) are interpreted as describing the incarnation of God

in man as man. These verses are "talking about the same thing [proper awareness] that saved Him [Jesus] and worked through Him to save others."[46] By making every person Christ, New Thought undermines the biblical uniqueness of Jesus and His message. "Jesus didn't ask us to follow him as a person."[47] "We revere Jesus the man . . . as one who exemplified . . . the great Principle of perfection and wholeness. Jesus was a Way-Shower—the Savior—in the sense that He drew us out of our limitations."[48] Biblically, however, Jesus is "the way and the truth and the life" (John 14:6) not "a" way-shower. And He teaches us to follow Him. He said, "I am the light of the world; whoever follows me will never walk in darkness, but will have the light of life" (John 8:12). Biblically Jesus is "the Savior of the world" who "bore our sins in His body on the tree" so that "in Him we have redemption through his blood, the forgiveness of sins" (John 4:42; 1 Peter 2:24; Ephesians 1:7). He is God's one and only Son, the incarnation of God (John 3:16). He alone is Christ (or Messiah); He alone was born the Messiah and fulfilled Old Testament prophecies predicting the Messiah (Luke 2:11; 24:25-27, 44-49).

But in New Thought, *every* person's true nature is the "Christ":

You are the [enlightened] Lord Jesus.[49]

Where is the Christ? Wherever you see a man, woman or child.[50]

The Christ is the individual expression of God in and through each one of us.[51]

The word "Christ" is used in many ways. Some think . . . that Jesus had an exclusive association with the word. The New Thought Christian associates the word Christ with that perfect God part of you. . . . It is who you really are.[52]

Perhaps the most bizarre New Thought view of Jesus comes from one of the most influential and celebrated New Thought practitioners, "Neville" (Neville Goddard), cited earlier:

Your own Wonderful Human Imagination is the God of the Universe. That is the one spoken of as the Lord Jesus. . . . I know the truth of what I speak, for I have found him of whom the prophets spoke, Jesus of Nazareth. . . . And that one is man's own wonderful human imagination. That's Jesus, and there is no other. . . . The Lord is your own Wonderful Human Imagination. That's God and there is no other God. That is the Jesus of Scripture. That's the Jehovah of the Old Testament.[53]

Neville teaches that Jesus "incarnated" in human consciousness so that people could become God. "There is no other cross he bears other than the body you wear. He became man that man may become God. I have proved that He is my Imagination."[54] He also believes that no one can come to know God through the Person of Jesus, for the Person of Jesus was only "an acted parable," and Jesus is *not* God's only Son. "When you know God, . . . you aren't going to know him through Jesus. . . ."[55]

Salvation

"I am wonderful, fantastic, beautiful and good. I am the Christ."[56] So declares a typical New Thought "affirmation." If we are Christ, and God, then obviously we need no salvation in the biblical sense. For New Thought, the only "salvation" required is a release from ignorance concerning the oneness that we already have with God. Further, our lack of spiritual knowledge (New Thought) keeps us believing that pain, illness and death are real when everything is actually perfect. Thus, heaven on earth is ours for the asking. Incredibly, New Thought teaches, "You do not have to die, grow old, be ill, suffer lack or experience anything negative."[57]

To "follow Christ" is to follow our higher divine self. Dr. Donald Curtis declares: "Making your decision for Christ today means making your decision to follow the Light of your own being."[58] Regarding New Thought philosophy, Dr. Joseph Murphy declares, "This is the Gospel, the good tidings."[59] Indeed, Dr. Murphy stumbles all over himself in affirming the "good news" of his own deity: "The real Self of man is God. . . . God is my higher self. . . . The Self of me is God. I honor, trust and give all my allegiance to the real Self of me, which is God."[60] William Warch states: "The real you is your personal awareness of yourself as God."[61] "You are the Christ. . . . You are made of the same energy intelligence that holds the planets in orbit and breathes life into infants."[62]

This is the New Thought "gospel," and what it lacks in humility it makes up for in presumption. In its rejection of Christ and its denial of true salvation, it stands condemned by Scripture. "Anyone who rejected the Law of Moses died without mercy on the testimony of two or three witnesses. How much more severely do you think a man deserves to be punished who has trampled the Son of God underfoot, who has treated as an unholy thing the blood of the covenant that sanctified him, and who has insulted the Spirit of grace?" (Hebrews 10:28–29).

New Thought views salvation as the acceptance of what is (Perfection), not as the escape from God's judgment on sin. Hence New Thought salvation is merely a daily experiencing of the positive blessings "resulting" from applying New Thought teachings. "Being 'saved' then, means being *born anew* [in consciousness]. It is the acceptance of an idea or truth principle that will help us to return to the main stream of life and living. . . . Salvation is a here and now experience where and when Truth is consciously known. 'Judgment Day' is every day we take time to review our thoughts and actions, recognize any slippage, and decide to do something about it."[63]

Further, if we do not have "Christ consciousness," we will suffer the unreal appearances. "There is one primary cause of your suffering and that is that you have lost sight of your divinity. . . . If you have forgotten that you are the living expression of God, there is nothing to carry you through negative appearances."[64] Indeed, visiting cancer wards, hospices and caring for the mentally ill, or sending missionaries to the poverty-stricken regions of the world, or working in drug rehabilitation centers or with AIDS patients, would be seen as "negative" environments threatening personal divinity.

An important point in all this is that it is New Thought's frequent use of familiar biblical terms for "salvation" that influence people to think of New Thought as Christian. This also confuses uninformed people as to the biblical meaning of the terms. For example, in *The New Thought Christian*, New Thought redefines the terms "grace" and "born again." "Grace is the upliftment from bondage through greater awareness. If you have made a mistake, you do not have to pay for it. Through Grace (greater awareness) you are free of the limited thinking that caused you to make the mistake in the first place."[65] And being "born again" is a step by step renewal in consciousness that "has nothing to do with Jesus":

> But to the New Thought Christian there is an entirely different meaning to being born again. With each new awakening you are born into a new level of consciousness. In other words, you are constantly being born again as you develop in your awareness of the Christ within. This has nothing to do with Jesus other than the fact that he too entered a constant state of renewal. As you let go of old [e.g., Christian] concepts and beliefs, you release who you were in the past and accept a new understanding of yourself. New ideas about yourself and God are constantly being born in you as your Christ nature reveals itself to you.[66]

Similarly, in his *Immortal Man*, "Neville" gives us the "proper" meaning of salvation, rebirth and forgiveness, because we are assured that *Immortal Man* was "taken from the author's lectures during his spiritually mature years" (front cover). "No one on the outside is going to save you. God and God alone is going to save you. . . . [i.e.,] Your own wonderful I Amness, that is the Lord God Jehovah."[67] "You are told 'Unless you are born again, you cannot enter the kingdom of heaven.' . . . (This means) unless you . . . live in your own wonderful human imagination."[68] "The glory of Christianity is to conquer by forgiveness. . . . Christ is my Imagination. Christ is the Son of Man which is my own Wonderful Human Imagination. This is forgiveness. Scripture is all about forgiveness."[69]

The Afterlife

New Thought rejects the biblical view of death and reward or judgment. Its view of the afterlife is often similar to Eastern and mediumistic perspectives, encompassing post-mortem "schooling" prior to the next incarnation, progression to higher and higher planes and final absorption into "God." Death is not at all negative, but is a glorious Something. Dr. Joseph Murphy declares: "God is life and that is your life now. God cannot die therefore there is no

death. So-called death is an entry into the fourth dimension of life, and our journey is from glory to glory, from wisdom to wisdom, every onward upward and Godward for there is no end to the glory which is man. Death, in Biblical language, is ignorance of the truths of God."[70] Warch declares in his *New Thought Christian*, "There is no such thing as death. . . . You have endless lifetimes."[71]

Satan

The biblical reality of Satan and demons is also discarded. "Since God is the only power, there is no opposite. There is only God."[72] Disregarding a wealth of evidence, New Thought writer Dr. Donald Curtis asserts that "demons" only exist as "negative" human problems. "Of course there aren't any real 'demons.' The so-called demons are merely a focus upon the worries, the despair, the grief, the greed, the selfishness and the negativities stored up in the human race. There aren't any devils. There is no hell. There is no evil. . . . There is no personified God, just as there is no personified devil. These are products of literary invention. God is everywhere."[73] And "Neville" informs us that we should reject reason and the testimony of our senses since these are what constitute hell and the devil. "Turn your back upon the doubters, which are your senses, your reason, for that's hell or the devil or satan in this world."[74]

The Occult

For examples of New Thought acceptance of the occult, see the chapters on Religious Science and Unity School of Christianity. In general, any occult power or practice is potentially acceptable and reinterpreted as divine activity. Although New Thought distances itself from certain forms of the occult, even in these cases it is willing to "accept truth wherever it may be found." The common New Thought teaching that stresses "inner listening" as a means to spiritual guidance is one possible introduction to the psychic realm. Also, some New Thought practitioners have encountered spiritistic inspiration while believing themselves to be a channel for the divine. "The fundamental thing is you must believe that God can positively do anything. Then you must believe in yourself as His channel."[75] As we documented in our *Encyclopedia of New Age Beliefs,* especially the chapters on intuition, inner work and channeling, concepts like the "inner self," "Christ self," higher self, intuition and inner divinity not infrequently become guises for spiritistic inspiration. In their *New Thought: A Practical American Spirituality* (Crossroad), a book highly praised by New Thought leaders, C. Alan Anderson and Deborah G. Whitehouse include chapters on "The Mystical and the Occult or Psychic" and "New Age and the New Thought Movement," in which they observe many parallels between New Thought religion and the New Age movement. They also point out, "New Thought at its best is much inclined toward mysticism. . . ." Not unexpectedly New Thought in general looks favorably on parapsychology, interpreting psychic abilities as "scientific proof" of one's divine potential. (See appendix.)

CRITIQUE

Our chapters on Unity School of Christianity, Christian Science and Religious Science effectively critique New Thought principles from several vantage points and the reader is urged to turn to these pages for a detailed discussion. We now offer some general comments relative to New Thought.

Biblical Distortion

New Thought groups will often quote Jesus, and just as often distort Him. For example, when Jesus said, "Ask and you will receive," they reinterpret this to mean that we are to demand or command God (Cosmic Law) to bring our divine heritage into manifestation. Ask (demand) of the One Mind (which is your real nature, thus a requesting among equals) and you shall receive abundance. Here, New Thought ignores the meaning of biblical words and their context. The asking was to be done "in My (Jesus') name" (John 16:23), which involves a recognition of all Jesus is, including His sovereignty and possible choice not to grant our wishes. "This is the assurance we have in approaching God: that if we ask anything *according to his will,* he hears us" (1 John 5:14).

New Thought also ignores the Greek definition of the word "ask." *Vine's Expository Dictionary of the New Testament* points out that the common word for "to ask" (as in prayer: John 14:13–14; 15:7, 16;16:23–26, etc.) is *aiteo.* It is distinguished from *erotao,* which suggests that "the petitioner is on a footing of equality or familiarity with the person whom he requests"; for example, a king requesting another king in some matter. By contrast, the meaning of *aiteo* "more frequently suggests the attitude of a suppliant, the petition of one who is lesser in position than he to whom the petition is made; e.g., in the case of men asking something from God, Matthew 7:7."[76] Jesus never used *aiteo* when making requests to the Father, which indicate his deity. But when speaking of people requesting things of the Father, He used the word *aiteo,* indicating their creaturehood. In addition, biblically, Satan is the only one who makes demands of God (Job 1:11; Matthew 4:3,6; Luke 22:31).

The biblical distortion by New Thought ministers and practitioners is often extreme (see the Appendix to this chapter). For example, "settle matters quickly with your adversary who is taking you to court. Do it while with him on the way" (Matthew 5:25) means "insisting upon seeing that there is good behind all things."[77] "Jesus called Satan a liar and the father of lies meaning that his existence is based on lies."[78] And John 8:32 is used to prove there is no sin or duality![79] Yet this verse in context refers to being set free by the truth of Jesus' teaching—just two verses later Jesus speaks of being set free from sin—something that New Thought claims that Jesus has just denied as being an illusion. John 1:3, which teaches that Jesus Christ is the Creator, is quoted to show that God is indifferent to evil![80] We are told that "in Hebrew, the word Abraham means 'Father of Height' or a heightened, exalted, prosperous state of consciousness."[81] To the contrary, Abraham means "father of a multitude."[82] Abram, the original name of Abraham, means "Father of Height" or exalted father. But it has nothing to do with personal consciousness.

In theory, there can be as many interpretations of Scripture as there are New Thought believers, since each person is "the greatest authority as to its [the Bible's] true metaphysical meaning."[83] (See this chapter's Appendix for more examples.)

Centering on God?

Centering one's mind upon certain attributes of Deity is a central premise of New Thought. This teaching stresses the awareness of "God" as He or It is "defined" or interpreted in New Thought. Knowledge of God's attributes is said to contribute to a correct perception of the world about us. Without such knowledge, we will misperceive the world, to our own detriment and downfall. For example:

> If God is absolute good and *omniscient* everything is supposedly Good, for God does not "know of" sin and evil so they cannot exist.

> If God is absolute good and *omnipotent*, Good is supposedly all powerful, i.e., any contrary condition of "not good" is infinitely weak by comparison, an illusion without power.

> If God is all power and *omnipresent*, man is supposedly in God as God; creation is God in self-expression. The universe is God's "body." Man can be free from his misperceptions that evil, disease, death, pain, sorrow, etc. (whatever is "not good") has any binding reality.

But apart from accepting a literal interpretation of the Bible, and the Bible as authoritative in an absolute sense, how does any New Thought believer *know* that these are God's attributes? According to New Thought, God has, in truth, *no* distinct attributes (or opinions) apart from those subjectively decided upon by the "enlightened" consciousness. Of what value is this? Each person is God, dictating his or her own theology. We are free to invent God as we wish, just as we are free to label whatever we personally do not like as "unreal," or whatever troubles us as "undivine." But this does not give us a way to determine the divine attributes objectively and authoritatively. So should we determine it on the basis of the pronouncements of New Thought leaders historically? That won't help either because they don't agree. The point is this. If there is no logical basis in New Thought for assurance as to God's attributes, then there can be no logical basis for the New Thought *interpretation* of those attributes. And

without divine authority for this interpretation, New Thought crumbles into the competing subjective opinions of all its members. How can anyone "center on God" when no one knows for sure who or what God is?

Further, if it is human beings who define reality, then people, places, things, events and situations can be divine or not (good or evil) merely depending on how one personally feels. Thus, good or bad emotions, subjective conjecture, prejudices or even evil acts can receive a "divine" blessing, if that's how one feels about it. This has unsavory implications, to say the least.

There are many logical problems to all of this. For example, some New Thought teachers ascribe God as "Matter-Spirit." If matter is God manifesting, as in Process New Thought, how can the "not fully enlightened" (most of us) deny God, who is fully enlightened, His expressions in matter: suffering, decay, lack, evil, disease and death? If these expressions are God (Good), why even try to deny them, let alone try to escape them? Why not *embrace* them, if everything is "God-in-action" or "God becoming"? On the other hand, if New Thought ministers misperceive God—if they misperceive "Good" (God) as "Bad"—how can anyone considered them divinely enlightened? And where and how did this misperception of divine reality ever originate? If they are not fully enlightened, where does their assurance about what God is come from? Further, is the misperception from the mind or from God? If from the mind, then what of the premise that "it is through the mind that we can claim our prosperous heritage of lavish abundance"?[84] If from God, who has any hope at all? If the misperception stems from God—our true nature—where is one's trust possibly to be founded? And why do we need to remind ourselves we are God? If we were God, one would think that no reminder would be necessary. If the mind so forcefully misperceives fundamental earthly reality, how can it possibly be trusted to perceive spiritual heavenly reality accurately?

New Thought Religion, Reality and Rationality

The experience of every man, woman, son and daughter is an experience of life *inconsistent* with the premises of New Thought. Every New

Thought believer realizes his mind is finite, not infinite; that he is limited, not unlimited; that he is morally imperfect, not perfect. This is the testimony of human knowledge, history, common sense and individual experience. As people we are fallen and our minds are subject to all kinds of frailties. If New Thought believers can unleash divine perfection with the mind, why doesn't it work?

There are all kinds of problems with New Thought here. For instance, on the basis of clinical evidence a New Thought father will admit his daughter was raped, but he will also deny rape as an illusion, as an unnecessary misperception. How does this help his daughter? Reality can be denied only until one is forced to accept it. No New Thought believer would deny that someone who fell into a pit of cobras would die a painful death, no matter how illusory they thought the cobra venom to be. Yet until he fell into that pit of cobras, a New Thought believer might deny any necessary reality to pain, illness or death. It is reasonable to ask why the New Thought believer would be the last person in the world to jump into a pit of cobras. Is it because divine perfection would be difficult to find in a pit of angry cobras? But if New Thought is true, why should it matter? It matters because evil *is* real. The folly of New Thought religions is the extent of their denial of reality.

We wonder how the New Thought practitioner really feels during those uncomfortable moments when faced so frequently with what his beliefs say to deny. What about the enthusiastic parishioner who dies of heart disease despite an exemplary mental outlook? What about the friend who was shot and robbed in spite of all the mental affirmations before, during or after the crime; or the financial struggles of divorced Mrs. Jones?

When such failures are encountered they are characteristically interpreted in New Thought as "karmic necessity," lack of faith or false perception. Dr. Joseph Murphy tells us, "The world is not harsh, but it may seem to be because we fail to affirm or claim the presence of God."[85] Again, perhaps the real failure here is in not accepting reality. The simple truth is that when New Thoughts believers are confronted by reality, it is

they who must admit that New Thought, rather than Christianity, is the deceptive philosophy. (See the critique sections of the chapters Unity School of Christianity, Religious Science and Christian Science.) Is it wise to become experts at avoiding reality? Would the consequences of such a life be "all Good"? Isn't even a fool wise in his own eyes?

A further problem is that "accepting" evil sabotages itself because giving *any* power to evil only perpetuates its reality. Thus New Thought places itself in a self-defeating position; like a parasite, it slowly kills the host (the Only Good) upon whose survival it depends. This makes New Thought a terminal illness philosophically. New Thought believers are just as often "corrupted" by duality as those they criticize. The essential dichotomy between God and man, which they so consistently attack in Christianity, is abundantly present in their own religious philosophy and personal lifestyles. New Thought believers must constantly refer to man as *realizing* God, *depending* on God, letting *God* run their lives and so on. Even in New Thought, believers are fallen (in consciousness), need salvation (from error) and are "separate" from God in daily life. If New Thought is true, why does it never work when it really matters?

Incredibly, one New Thought writer declares that "right thought and beneficent motives can change and correct the course of any problem looming in our individual lives or in the national and international scene."[86] This writer suggests that even the Jonestown tragedy could have been prevented had all the participants used "positive" mental energy rather than "negative" energy. She does not seem to consider that, for years, Jonestown members had had a positive mental outlook and good motives; they were simply too naive about false teachings and false prophets. They had all the positive thinking and Utopian hopes one could wish for; that's the very reason they went to Guyana. The problem was that they followed a wolf in sheep's clothing (cf. Matthew 7:15). Anyone who could accept a "Christian" pastor who would throw the Bible on the floor and spit on it, and who "believed he was 'guided' by a supernatural 'spirit,'"[87] could accept anything.

This is the problem with New Thought. How many people who have truly believed that "no harm can come to me because I do not believe in evil"[88] currently reside in prison, the hospital or the morgue? New Thought believers are unable to manifest "the Good" when facing prison, depression, a lawsuit, a divorce, a son or daughter's drug addiction or a thousand other "illusions." Real solutions to problems are not found, because the real problems are not acknowledged sufficiently to begin with; they are glossed over with thoughts of omnipresent goodness.

Our prison population includes thieves, sociopaths, murderers, rapists, the criminally insane and child molesters. Are not some of them, in fact, pretty evil, or, as New Thought teaches, are they merely portions of God who have just forgotten their divine perfection? A New Thought believer tells us in the following words: "Do you approach them as though they were recalcitrants, difficult, troublesome, evil people? Do you think of them as dangerous criminals, attaching their records to them, such as murderer, burglar, or child molester? The answer is a very strong 'no'."[89] In other words, since we are all divine, naturally, "no one is evil."[90] "Anyone who believes that he is bad is supporting a belief in evil."[91] Every prisoner can be told, no matter how vicious and unrepentant he is, "You are Good. You are not evil; no one is evil."[92]

While the author is also pointing out that approaching criminals with kindness can be productive, it hardly helps New Thought ethically. When the fallen self is divinized, the fallen nature can run rampant in full. During the period of the judges in ancient Israel, "Everyone did what was right in his own eyes" (Judges 21:25 NAS) and the terrible consequences were apparent everywhere. Baptizing sin with divinity only compounds it. In ancient Israel, the result of a bad philosophy was sin and anarchy, not righteousness and peace, just as it will be in America. All the kindness in the world will not change an evil, manipulative person who has no desire to change.

To justify their beliefs, New Thought members often interpret pure coincidence as "proof" of New Thought doctrines. One example is a sailor who accidentally locked himself in a submarine compartment with no way out. Turning to New Thought, he repeated that he was "a divine being . . . not confined in any way."[93] After some time a workman passed by and let him out. This incident was hailed as one of many such occasions that proves we are not bound by time, space or form. To the contrary, spending one's time in affirming illusions wastes precious time and prevents logical, rational ways of dealing with a potentially life-threatening event.

Supposedly, "The universe agrees with us. Whatever we agree to, the universe obliges us by its ready agreement . . . but we must be willing to live our assurance night and day."[94] What of the Kansas farmer standing in the path of an oncoming tornado affirming total New Thought protection for his farm and family? What of the New Thought alcoholic, destitute and confined in treatment, affirming, "There is no lack in my life now. There is only rich abundance because I am the child of my rich Father-Mother-God?"[95]

Dr. Joseph Murphy tells of one person's legal difficulties during a five-year lawsuit. When he came to Dr. Murphy, he discovered he had simply not been believing *hard* enough that others had no legal claim over him. Once "he ceased giving his relatives any power to hurt him or deprive him of his good, a power which they never had except in his own thought," the legal suit was soon dropped.[96] Obviously, the dismissal had nothing to do with the length and cost of litigation, only with the mental power that the legal universe submitted to.

New Thought philosophy can filter out all kinds of common sense behavior. For instance, the history of economics has proven the wisdom of saving money. In the world in which we live, it is an unfortunate household that has no savings account. But savings may be *contrary* to New Thought principles, as such action presupposes lack and uncertainty about the future. Therefore, "Never save money! It is vital that the law of circulation, of giving and receiving, is not blocked by the choice to hoard. Your money must be placed into the stream of activity or it will diminish."[97] In other words, if one wants a guaranteed, plentiful supply of money, one should be certain to spend it all! Thrift should be denied; money should be spent as soon as it is received. It should, in particular, be given quickly to New Thought churches, for "not to tithe, not to put God first financially brings the death of your good in many forms."[98]

Morality

New Thought denies the Christian view of morality in many ways. No better example can be found than by quoting "Neville's" view of an amoral Christ, a logical extension of New Thought monistic philosophy. In spite of the clear biblical testimony to the sinless perfection of Jesus, "Neville" blasphemously declares that "Jesus" waits upon him even when he personally wills what is evil. "He creates all things. . . . Yes, good, bad, indifferent. He waits on me just as quickly and just as indifferently when the will in me is evil as when it is good."[99]

Dr. Roy Graves tells us, with emotion, of the travesty of all the Christian ministries "built upon celestial [divine] rewards and punishments" (heaven and hell), and he offers instead the truth "that *nature* rewards and chastises man" in accordance with the principles of New Thought.[100] New Thought cannot tolerate a holy God meting out *just* rewards and punishments; it would apparently rather have an impersonal nature or cosmic law supporting amoral judgments, because "sin and standards of morality are relative."[101]

In a similar manner, Dr. Emma Smiley deplores the kind of gratitude in which we feel thankful for what we have that others do not have. Indeed, because of their superior consciousness New Thought believers *deserve* what others don't have. But New Thought not only makes one feel superior to the less fortunate, it also invalidates their cause altogether. "All is Good and Beauteous. There is no pain, suffering or lack." If, as one New Thought writer declares, "Love and consciousness are one and the same thing," it is easy to conclude that loving actions toward the needy are not so important,[102] because to live in higher consciousness is by definition to be loving toward others, regardless of our actions. We can simply tell them, "There is one primary cause of your suffering and that is that you have lost sight of your divinity."[103] Again, see the chapters on Religious Science and Unity School of Christianity for further discussion of moral concerns relative to New Thought.

TALKING WITH MEMBERS

We have attempted to show that New Thought promises much but delivers little. New Thought tells us that we are separate from God in thought and that consciousness is our redeemer. We are to remind ourselves constantly that we are truly God and perfect, in spite of the fact that our experience constantly denies it. Where is the wisdom here? New Thought promises Godhood but remains stuck with humanity. While we could discuss various approaches one could take toward a New Thought believer, we have already listed some of these in the chapters dealing with the New Thought groups Unity School of Christianity, Religious Science and Christian Science.

In summary, New Thought teachings place one in a fantasy world and for that reason alone they can not be trusted. Its teachings do not work because they deny reality. And they may promote pride, selfishness and hedonism. They cannot provide real life here on earth, nor will they provide real life in eternity, because that life comes only through faith in Jesus Christ. "Now this is eternal life: that they may know you, the only true God, and Jesus Christ, whom you have sent" (John 17:3). Indeed, the very things people so hope for when they turn to New Thought (contentment, meaning, healing), if not denied them in this life, will certainly be denied them in the next. Such concerns need to be openly discussed.

If New Thought teachers are disrespectful of God's Word, they are disrespectful of God (2 Samuel 12:9-10). A spiritual teacher who disrespects God should not be considered an authority on the Bible or spiritual matters. By contrasting biblical teachings and New Thought beliefs, the Christian may help members to see the logical consequences of their ideas and to understand how great the final cost will be. (See Scripture Contrasts chart.) As Jesus said, "What good will it be for a man if he gains the whole world, yet forfeits his soul" (Matthew 16:26)?

Scripture Contrasts

We affirm that the universe is the body of God.[104]	They exchanged the truth of God for a lie, and worshiped and served created things rather than the Creator—who is forever praised. Amen. (Romans 1:25)
Jesus at no time set himself apart from his fellows in *kind*.[105]	But he continued, "You are from below; I am from above. You are of this world; I am not of this world. I told you that you would die in your sins; if you do not believe that I am the one I claim to be, you will indeed die in your sins." (John 8:23-24)
I now decree that God loves me, loves me no matter what I've done or not done, no matter the how I've been behaving.[106]	Do you not know that the wicked will not inherit the kingdom of God? Do not be deceived: Neither sexually immoral nor idolaters nor adulterers nor male prostitutes nor homosexual offenders nor thieves nor the greedy nor drunkards nor slanderers nor swindlers will inherit the kingdom of God. (1 Corinthians 6:9-10)
Rather than praying for health the New Thought Christian prays for his conscious awareness of the perfect health that is already his.[107]	Is any one of you sick? He should call the elders of the church to pray over him and anoint him with oil in the name of the Lord. (James 5:14)
This truth [New Thought] is the savior of the world, for without it we are already lost, with it we can never be lost.[108]	And we have seen and testify that the Father has but sent his Son to be the Savior of the world. (1 John 4:14) This man really is the Savior of the World (John 4:42)

APPENDIX: GEORGE M. LAMSA, ROCCO A. ERRICO AND THE ARAMAIC ARGUMENT

No discussion of New Thought would be complete without an evaluation of the Aramaic interpretation of the late George M. Lamsa (see also The Way, "Aramaic originals") and of Rocco A. Errico's California based "Noohra Foundation." A demonstration of the biblical errors in these writings will prove helpful when talking with people in New Thought (and other) groups who use "the Aramaic argument" to allegedly support New Thought teachings biblically. *(New Thought* magazine regularly carries articles by Errico allegedly substantiating New Thought biblical interpretation.)

Reduced to its simplest form, the Aramaic argument may be summarized as follows. Jesus and the Apostles not only spoke in Aramaic (a Semitic language similar to Hebrew, originally of the Syrian Aramaeans), they also wrote in Aramaic. Therefore, the original inspired writings of the Apostles were written in Aramaic, not in *koine* Greek. Translations from the Aramaic to Greek and then into English have left the Bible with "numerous errors," which must be corrected by someone knowledgeable in the Aramaic language. Lamsa believed the original Aramaic text was the Syriac Peshitta, and thus he argued, "The Peshitta New Testament text varies considerably from the Greek and Latin versions which were made later for the use of new converts to Christianity. There are hundreds of passages where the meaning is different from that of the Greek version."[109] Of course, everything depends on the assumption of the primacy of the Peshitta, an assumption we will show is false.

Before beginning our analysis, we should point out that no one can lightly dismiss the influence of the Aramaic argument. For instance, Lamsa's own translation of the Bible and many of his books are regularly found in evangelical bookstores. Lamsa's translation is published by the A. J. Holman Company, a large publisher of Bibles and Christian books that is now Broadman and Holman. His New Testament has sold hundreds of thousands of copies. Lamsa himself wrote a score of books, among them *Key to the Original Gospels; New Testament Origin; Idioms in the Bible Explained; The Hidden Years of Jesus; Gospel Light; Old Testament Light Commentary;* and *New Testament Commentary.* Classes in "Aramaic and the Bible" are taught nationwide by various "Lamsa groups" and others with related interests.

Despite all this, in considering his life's work, four basic points should be stressed:

1. Scholars reject the basic premise of Lamsa's Aramaic originals.

2. The evidence declares that the Aramaic texts were derived from Greek texts, *not* vice versa, and therefore the Peshitta is the one with translation errors.

3. Lamsa was not the objective scholar he is made out to be; he ended his life in close agreement to many New Thought heresies (for example, he denied the deity of Christ and the atonement).

4. Aramaic is used by more than a dozen cults to *reject* biblical doctrines, rather than to elucidate the meaning of the text.

Nevertheless, Lamsa argued that the original Aramaic text of the Bible was the Syriac Peshitta, hence his *magnum opus* comprises an English translation of this document, titled *The Holy Bible From Ancient Eastern Manuscripts.* We pointed out in our chapter on The Way that there are over a dozen new religious groups (such as Astara, Edgar Cayce study groups and Victor Paul Wierwille's The Way) which make use of this Bible and Lamsa's other writings to change the meaning of the biblical text into their own meanings. Lamsa and his co-workers are particularly adept at using an idiomatic argument to deny Scripture: many things in the Bible are (supposedly) mistranslated or misinterpreted because we do not understand *Aramaic* figures of speech.

For over half a century certain scholars theorized about or attempted to make a case for Aramaic originals.[110] C. F. Burney, in *The Aramaic Origin of the Fourth Gospel* (Oxford, 1922), and C. C. Torrey, in *The Four Gospels: A New Translation* (1933) and Matthew Black in *An Aramaic Approach to the Gospels and Acts* (1946) are representative. Even though all attempts to discover Aramaic originals have failed,[111] George Lamsa was convinced he had succeeded, and his friend and confidant, Rocco A. Errico, broadcasts such information widely as a "fact."

Lamsa's Errors

In the introduction to his Bible, Lamsa claims that "Greek was never the language of Palestine" and that teaching it was forbidden by Jewish Rabbis. Elsewhere he says, "Paul did not write in Greek"; and "not a word of the Scriptures was originally written in Greek." To the contrary, there is abundant evidence that Greek was one of the Palestinian languages, and all doubt has been removed concerning the Greek composition of the original New Testament. Not surprisingly then, historians like Dr. Edwin Yamauchi, a scholar from Miami University, Oxford, Ohio, points out that Lamsa was ignorant of basic facts.[112]

Dr. Yamauchi observes that Lamsa stoops to misquoting Josephus' *Antiquities of the Jews* xx.12.1 to support his beliefs. Lamsa claimed that Josephus argued that "hardly any" Jews succeeded in learning Greek and he quotes Josephus in the previous passage. But what Josephus actually said is that he, personally, did not attain precision in Greek pronunciation. Lamsa also misunderstood Jewish views about learning Greek in the Mishna, Talmud and Tosefta, which ban teaching Greek to children, not adults.[113] The fact that there are about 1,500 Greek loan words in Talmudic literature is evidence of knowledge of Greek among Rabbis. (Half of Rabbian Gamaliel's students—500—studied Greek literature.[114])

In his article, "The Language of the New Testament," J. H. Greenlee of Oxford University provides ample evidence for Greek as a known language in Palestine.[115] For example, when visiting Greeks wished to see Jesus (John 12:20-21), no indication is given that Philip had any problem in communication with them. Neither is there evidence that an interpreter was needed between Pilate and Jesus during His trial. Greenlee argues in detail why the "Aramaic argument" is wrong:

> It is unlikely that the Roman governor was conversant with Aramaic and even less likely that the Jews knew Latin. The logical assumption is that the entire discussion was carried on in Greek. Paul wrote his Epistle to the church at Rome in Greek, not in Latin or Aramaic. Even the Epistle "to the Hebrews" was written in Greek—indeed, in the most literary Greek of any book of the NT. It was in Greek that the Roman tribune and Paul conversed after the apostle had been rescued from the Jewish mob at the temple (Acts 21:37). Peter's communication with the Roman centurion Cornelius and his friends (Acts 10) must have been in Greek, and likewise his sermon on the day of Pentecost. It is noteworthy that Greece is not included in the list of lands in whose (foreign) languages the disciples' praises of God were being heard (Acts 2.5-11). At the same time, local languages were maintained alongside the use of Greek, just as scores of tribal languages are maintained today alongside Spanish, French, and other trade languages. This was clearly the case with the Jews and their use of Aramaic. The fact that certain Aramaic expressions are found in the Gospels ... should not therefore be taken to mean that Jesus normally spoke in another language and interjected this Aramaic phrase for some special effect (though it could be thus interpreted if other evidence supported the hypothesis). It appears, rather, that they were words from expressions the NT writers chose to preserve in their original form because of their special significance or the significance of the events in connection with which they are used.[116]

Nevertheless, Lamsa declared he was the only competent translator (hence interpreter) of the Bible, summarily dismissing all the exegetes of history! In *More Light on the Gospel*, he declared: "The author, through God's grace, is the only one with the knowledge of Aramaic, the Bible customs and idioms, and the knowledge of the English language who has ever translated the Holy Bible from the original Aramaic texts into English and written commentaries on it."[117]

Before we consider specific theological errors from the writings of Lamsa (and Rocco Errico of the Noohra Foundation), we first note the conclusions of Dr. Edwin Yamauchi, a scholar whose academic background eminently qualifies him to assess Lamsa's claims. Dr. Yamauchi is an authority on Mediterranean studies and a specialist in Mandaic, an Eastern Aramaic dialect and author of *Mandaic Incantation Texts*, 1967. The material below is excerpted from his article in *Bibliotheca Sacra*, "Greek, Hebrew, Aramaic or Syriac?: A critique of the claims of G. M. Lamsa for the Syriac Peshitta." He begins by dismissing Lamsa's premises, noting his grave errors in assigning authority to the views of the Assyrian Church of Iraq and the primacy of the Syriac Peshitta:

> It is in fact Lamsa's faith in the dogma of the Assyrian Church of Iraq which he grandiosely calls "the Church of the East" which serves as the basis of his conviction in the superiority of the Syriac Peshitta Version.... The Syriac of the Peshitta is not the language of coastal Syria around Antioch, which was evangelized in the first century A.D., but of the area in the interior around Edessa, one hundred fifty miles from the coast, which was evangelized between A.D. 116 and 216.... No one but an unquestioning adherent of "The Church of the East" would subscribe to the legendary account of the apostolic roots of the Edessene church. In the light of the claims advanced by Lamsa for Syriac, it should be underlined that Syriac is an eastern and not a western dialect of Aramaic, and indeed that it is "a form of Aramaic that emerges toward the beginning of the third century A.D." As such it is one of the least suitable of the Aramaic dialects to use for a reconstruction of the Jewish Palestinian Aramaic used by Jesus. As the basis of his translation Lamsa uses the Peshitta Version of the Old and the New Testaments, which serves as the "authorized version" for the Syrian Orthodox Church. The Peshitta was accepted as the official version before the split of the Syrian Church into the West Jacobite and the East Nestorian

branches in the fifth century. The Peshitta Canon omitted 2 and 3 John, Jude, and Revelation, which Lamsa therefore translates from unidentified "later Aramaic texts."[118]

Dr. Yamauchi also refutes a number of Lamsa's additional teachings, including his claim that the Greek Septuagint was never read by Palestinian Jews who spoke Aramaic and read Hebrew. "Lamsa's contention that the Septuagint 'was never officially read by the Jews in Palestine who spoke Aramaic and read Hebrew,' is flatly contradicted by the discovery of Septuagint fragments at Qumran and the quotations from the Septuagint in the New Testament which are even more numerous than quotations from the Masoretic [Hebrew] type texts."[119] Dr. Yamauchi next dismantles Lamsa's approach to the Old Testament text, noting that his views here are "pure fantasy." About the New Testament, he observes that Lamsa "willfully disregards" the consensus of sound scholarship in order to uphold his own biases:

The suggestion of Lamsa that one can revise the Old Testament text on the basis of the ambiguities in either the consonants or vocalization of the Syriac Peshitta text is pure fantasy. The value of the Peshitta for the text of the New Testament is quite minimal. Lamsa willful disregards the view of scholars that Sinaitic-Curetonian Syriac texts of the New Testament are older than and superior to the Peshitta New Testament.... Since Lamsa quotes from Kenyon's *(Handbook to the) Textual Criticism of the New Testament*, he cannot be ignorant of the evaluation of the Peshitta by scholars but has chosen to deliberately disregard their views. In contrast to Lamsa, all reputable scholars hold the Peshitta New Testament to be based on translations from Greek texts—and from relatively late and inferior Greek texts at that. According to Metzger: "in the Gospels it is closer to the Byzantine type of text than in Acts, where it presents many striking agreements with the Western text."[120]

As Yamauchi continues, he observes that even Lamsa's translation of the Peshitta is of poor quality:

In spite of Lamsa's outrageous and mischievous claims for the Peshitta, he might have done a

service by offering a usable English translation of the Peshitta. Instead, his translation is defective in many respects. In some cases, Lamsa has slavishly copied the King James Version even where the Syriac could be rendered differently. For example, in Philippians 2:6–7.... Where Lamsa does offer an original rendering, it is at times a misleading [one, e.g.] "Caesar's court," in Philippians 1:13 for the Syriac *Pretorin*, which is simply the transliteration of the Latin *praetorium*, the emperor's praetorian guard.[121]

Finally, Dr. Yamauchi observes that one may utilize Aramaic if one does so with caution. He discusses the reasons for this and concludes that the "cautious circumspection" of Aramaic scholars is in marked contrast to the "reckless speculation" of Lamsa. Though it is impossible to lend any credence to the fantastic claims of Lamsa, there:

are sources of Aramaic which can be used with caution. In contrast to Lamsa, who minimizes the dialectical differences between late, eastern Syriac and early, western Aramaic, Fitzmyer warns us: "We should be suspicious of philological arguments about the Aramaic substratum when they depend on texts and dialects of Aramaic that come from a later date (e.g., from the third century A.D. or later), precisely because a new phase of the language begins about that time with clear geographical distinctions".…

How far removed is the cautious circumspection of Aramaic scholars from the reckless speculations of G. M. Lamsa![122]

With this brief background, we now examine the writings of Lamsa and Errico. To start we should observe that Lamsa claimed he was a Christian. "I pray God this translation will benefit Christians everywhere and will help them toward a better understanding of the greatest and most inspiring book of all ages. After all, sincere faith in Jesus Christ has its own reward and devotion to Christ is the principle of all Christianity."[123]

Lamsa and the Bible

Did Lamsa remain faithful to the teachings of Jesus Christ and the Bible in his translation? The plain answer is "no." In his writings, Lamsa denied the deity of Jesus Christ, the biblical teaching on salvation, the judgment, the personality of Satan and demons and numerous other cardinal doctrines of Christianity. Far from being a careful exegete of the Holy Scriptures, Lamsa played so fast and loose with the biblical text that it becomes obvious why so many different cults that deny the Bible turn to him for inspiration.

In his *Idioms in the Bible Explained: A Key to the Holy Scriptures,* we find a typical example of his approach to the Bible: allegorical and nonliteral interpretations abound. The following examples, taken from pages 1–6 and 60–83, in his mind represent the true meaning of the following Scriptures. "Let there be light" in Genesis 1:3 refers to enlightenment or understanding. The Garden of Eden in Genesis 2:8 is a metaphor for a wife or a family. The tree of life in Genesis 2:9 refers to sex or posterity. The angels in Genesis 19:1 indicate God's counsel, or spirits or God thoughts. Wrestling with an angel in Genesis 32:24 refers to being suspicious of a pious man. In Exodus 3:2, the burning bush means that difficulties lie ahead. In Exodus 3:5, "take off your sandals" means to disregard pagan teachings or to cleanse your heart. In Matthew 2:1–10 the wisemen following the star of Bethlehem is interpreted as "walking in the direction of the stars." "The only begotten Son" (KJV), referring to Jesus Christ in John 1:18, signifies "the first one who recognized the fatherhood of God" and "the only God-like man, hence a spiritual son of God." In Matthew 5:22, "fire of hell" means mental suffering or torment.

Lamsa in particular did not like the idea of a real devil or demons, and so in Matthew 8:31, "the demons" refers to insane men. In Matthew 12:43 "evil spirit" means an evil inclination or a demented person. In Mark 1:34, "he would not let the demons speak" is interpreted as Jesus not allowing the insane to speak after he had healed them. In Mark 5:9, "My name is Legion," means that the possessed man had many wrong ideas or that he was a hopeless case. In Luke 4:41, when the demons came out of men, it indicates that many insane men were restored to mental health. In Luke 8:2, "seven demons," refers to seven bad habits or wrong inclinations. In Luke 10:18, "Satan" expresses the idea of to stray, to slide, to mislead and to slip, and "[I saw] Satan fall" indicates that evil is destroyed.

In Lamsa's book, *More Light on the Gospel,* he attempts to explain over 400 New Testament passages. Again, typically, we find non-literal renderings. In Matthew 4:8 the term "high mountain" is figurative and "means he took Him to the summit of his highest human imagination" (p. 2). The word "hated" in Romans 9:13, although perhaps used relatively, still means hate, but for Lamsa it is defined as "to put aside" (p. 187). Lamsa states, "God did not hate Esau. God is love and there is no hatred in Him" (p. 188); never mind that Scripture declares that God does hate (Psalm 5:5; Zechariah 8:17; Malachi 2:16; Revelation 2:6). He denies that God hardened Pharaoh's heart, in spite of Romans 9:17–18 and Exodus 4:21, and he rejects that God judged the Canaanites, in spite of the clear testimony of the book of Joshua (p. 189). He also denies eternal punishment, despite Jesus' clear teaching in Luke 16:19–31, which he calls "wholly allegorical."[124] In relation to 2 Corinthians 5:10, which refers to the judgment seat of Christ Lamsa misinterprets the verse and states, "God and Jesus punish no one. People bring punishment upon themselves through their own evil deeds" (p. 227). This is in direct contrast to 2 Thessalonians 1:6–8 and many other verses. In Revelation 20:13–14, where death and hell are cast into the lake of fire, Lamsa says that "these sayings are used metaphorically," and he again implies there is no eternal punishment (p. 363). Lamsa also has an unorthodox view of the second coming.[125]

Lamsa and Jesus Christ

Even more disturbing are Lamsa's view on Jesus Christ. In *The Hidden Years of Jesus,* Lamsa expresses a characteristic New Thought and Mind Science view of Jesus Christ: "Jesus" was the man; "Christ" was the God-part of him (cf. 1 John 2:22). "Jesus was born a man. He died on the cross a man, but Christ, God dwelling in him—his divinity, was not subject to human suffering nor to birth nor death" (pp. 10–11). The following statements by Lamsa, in *More Light on the Gospels,* also document his false view of Jesus Christ. "Jesus did not believe in the power of death" (p. 37). "Jesus . . . was the first to restore man's divinity . . . he *became* the begotten son of God" (p. 120, emphasis added). "As Jesus advanced in his studies, he *discovered* that he himself was the man [the messiah] who was to take this mantle of the prophets" (emphasis added).[126]

Further, in his 400 page text *Gospel Light,* Lamsa states that Jesus was never worshipped as God (p. 353), and that Jesus was not the Son of God as Christians understand the term (p. 148). "Any claim which Jesus might have made to be greater than God or even to be God himself would certainly have caused misunderstanding even among his own followers. He always declared that he was in accord with God who was greater than he" (p. 369).

Lamsa and Salvation

Lamsa's views on salvation are also heretical. In *More Light on the Gospels* (pp. 117–120), commenting on John 3:16, Lamsa rejects the clear meaning for his own biased interpretation. He actually denies that on the Cross Jesus atoned for the sin of the world:

No verse in the Holy Bible is more quoted than this one and yet none is probably more theologically misunderstood. This is because the Western reader does not understand Eastern customs and mannerisms of speech. . . . It is often said that Jesus Christ died for our sins, and that our sins could never have been forgiven without his death. The Aramaic word *mitol* means "because, or on account of or for" but the preferred meaning is "because." I am inclined to believe that Jesus died because of our sins, because of man's transgression against God's law [i.e., not in an atoning sense but as a victim *because* evil men killed him]. God, being the living father, does not need to be appeased by his children [i.e., Jesus]. No human father would try to appease his wrath by putting one of his sons to death. . . . Assuredly the death of Jesus on the cross was predicted by the prophet Isaiah. . . . The prophet did not at any time say that Jesus' death would reconcile God. . . . The Scripture says "God is love." Indeed, love could not demand human sacrifices because there is nothing in love to be appeased. Jesus died on the cross not to appease God or the evil forces, but to prove that [all human] life is indestruc-

tible and everlasting because God is indestructible and everlasting.

Thus, "Jesus, through his death, became an everlasting example of meekness and loving kindness" (p. 228). "We do not mean that Jesus died to pay a price to the forces of evil for the sins of the people, but that he risked his life to rescue them from sin" (p. 229). "Jesus through his resurrection saved all mankind in that he gave to them an assurance of life here after" (p. 249).

In the quote above, Lamsa claims Jesus' death did not atone for our sins or reconcile us to God. But one only need read Isaiah 53 or the Doctrinal Appendix to see how wrong Lamsa was. Finally, rejecting the biblical meaning of the term regeneration, he says that, "to be born again means to start over, to become like a child, receptive, like the first Adam before the transgression" (p. 310).

From all of this it is clear that Lamsa's theology was not Christian, despite his claims. It is not surprising then, that his chief disciple, Rocco A. Errico, also denies basic Christian teachings.

Rocco A. Errico and the Noohra Foundation

The Noohra Foundation is the brainchild of Rocco A. Errico, whose purpose involves a "special emphasis on the teachings of the Hebrew prophets, Jesus, and related subjects."[127]

Errico and Lamsa were close friends. For seven years Errico studied under Lamsa, whom he believed to be a biblical authority and Aramaic expert. By and large, both Errico and Lamsa have taught doctrines close to New Thought teachings in general. In the quarterly publication *Noohra*, Vol. 4, No. 4, Errico states, "Man is God in disguise" (p. 3) and that false thinking, not sin, is the cause of human misery. "Jesus spoke of true freedom, i.e., freedom from erroneous thinking which is the cause of all human difficulties and enslaving philosophies, politically and religiously."[128]

Errico and Scripture

Looking at Errico's doctrines comprehensively, he denies the biblical nature of God, man, Jesus Christ and salvation as well as the biblical teaching on prayer and many other topics. On page 30 of *The Ancient Aramaic Prayer of Jesus—The Lord's Prayer,* he states, "When we say the words 'our universal Father,' we are automatically recognizing other people's sonship with the Father.... This means that the Chinese, the Russians, the Japanese, the Arabs, and all people everywhere are the sons of God!" Because everyone is already one in essence with God, no one needs repentance from sin or the atoning Savior. People only need to realize that they are fully redeemed children of God; nothing else is necessary.

Like Lamsa, Errico alters the biblical text to conform it to the purported Aramaic original. For example, in Psalm 7:11 we read, "God is a righteous judge, a God who expresses his wrath every day." Errico changes this to "*Alpha* is a just judge and He is *not* angry every day."[129] Errico has changed hundreds of Scriptures like this, and he claims that thousands of others need changing! In effect, Errico and others are rewriting the entire Bible in accordance with their own wishes; they are restructuring biblical teachings into New Thought teachings (or whatever) by appealing to "Aramaic originals." Thus God is defined as "infinite intelligence," "the essence of all things ... the entire cosmic system is alive," "one power," "life forces," "the Source," "inherent spiritual power" and so on.[130] "He [God] is not someone to be feared."[131] God cannot be understood intellectually or doctrinally, He can only be perceived intuitively.[132]

Errico's teachings on Jesus Christ are also quite wrong. To him, Jesus is little more than a New Thought practitioner. To pray in Jesus' name means experiencing the same New Thought awareness that Jesus supposedly felt: that all people are one and God is the universal Father; only the Good exists.[133] In *The Ancient Aramaic Prayer of Jesus,* Errico offers us his new Christ. We are told that Jesus changed the Old Testament concept of God from a God of fear to a God of love.[134] Errico also states, "Jesus knew that man's spirit and God's Spirit are of the same essence.... God and man, then, being of the same spiritual essence, are able to communicate—*the infinite with the Infinite.*"[135] In John 8:24, where Jesus says, "You [will] die in your

sins [if] you do not believe that I am the one I claim to be," Errico argues, "'Ye shall die in your sins' means 'You will die in your mistaken ideas, not knowing the truth.'"[136] John 14:13-14 is translated and given an expanded New Thought meaning from the Aramaic, "And anything you may ask according to my method I will do it for you so that the father may be celebrated through his son. And if you will ask me in my way, I am doing it."[137]

Errico's views on salvation are also unbiblical. What we need is salvation from our ignorance about our oneness with God. Jesus never had to die on the Cross for sin because no one was ever separated from God. "And yet, we have been taught to approach God as if we were totally degraded, no good, unworthy sinners. *Jesus never taught us this! It is a misunderstanding of Scripture! ... At no time can there be separation from God! If we believe that we are cut off or separated from Him, then it is we who bring the sense of division. It is not God who does this; it is our own mental attitude. God is! And He is everywhere! He hasn't changed! We have to change our wrong attitudes!*"[138]

The Occult

Finally, we should note that given their New Thought worldview in general, the teachings of Lamsa and Errico endorse interest in the occult world. Lamsa stated, "Man has unlimited power within himself."[139] Errico has made an approving, if casual reference, to those who "seek aid and assistance from their personal spirit guides."[140]

This openness to the occult is evident in Noohra Foundation publications. Errico teaches psychic development classes titled "Intuitive Development Workshops" where people are taught psychic meditation and how to develop their "intuition"—psychometry, clairvoyance, clairsentience, clairaudience, "auric" and "pranic" healing and so on. Psychic development is also integrated into Errico's Bible studies; for example, titles of his studies include "Moses and the Mystery Schools" and "Seers, Kings and Prophets—The First School of Psychic Development and the Methods Used by Samuel."[141] A Noohra Foundation brochure confuses the supernatural and natural realms when it declares: "Supernatural? Intuitive development will show you just how 'super' the natural in you really is. Learn to develop your healing and intuitive forces. . . . Allow yourself to be receptive; turn within and listen; the voice that speaks to you through you is known as intuition."[142] However, as we documented in our *Encyclopedia of New Age Beliefs* in the chapters on New Age Intuition, Inner Work and Channeling, such attempts at psychic development often lead to occult involvement and have been employed by aspiring mediums and occultists for millennia. The end result here can hardly be different.[143]

In conclusion, we lament that Errico has not taken his own advice: "We have become too bogged down in outward forms and dogmas and have set aside his [Jesus'] original teachings."[144] And, "it is the tendency of so many biblical authorities to complicate the obvious and simple meaning of the Scriptures."[145]

NOTES

1. Taherzadeh, *The Revelation of Baha'u'llah*, p. 146, citing Epistle to the Son of the Wolf (p. 141).
2. William A. Warch, *The New Thought Christian* (Anaheim, CA: Christian Living Publishing, 1977), p. 24.
3. Joseph Murphy, *New Thought*, Winter 1980, p. 33.
4. Herman J. Aaftink, *New Thought a Way of Life* (Clagary, Alberta, Canada: The Centre for Positive Living), p. 7.
5. "Faith for Today," November 1980, p. 14, publication of Christ Church Unity in San Diego.
6. *New Thought*, Summer 1980, p. 43.
7. Ibid., pp. 44-52.
8. Ibid., p. 33.
9. INTA website. See the critique of Hubbard in the *SCP Journal*, Vol. 19, no. 2/3, 1995, pp. 32-49.
10. New Thought Movement home page.
11. Website.
12. *New Thought*, Spring 1978, p. 11.
13. Ibid., Summer 1980, p. 21.
14. See Weldon, Levitt, *Psychic Healing* under "Mesmerism" (Chicago: Moody Press, 1982).
15. C. S. Braden, *Spirits in Rebellion* (Dallas: Southern Methodist University Press), 1977, ch. 2.
16. INTA website.
17. See our *Facts on Self Esteem, Psychology and the Recovery Movement*, pp. 37, 48, note 144.
18. "New Thought Movement" website.
19. INTA website.
20. *New Thought*, Winter 1979, p. 4.
21. Ibid., Summer 1980, p. 20.
22. Ibid., p. 17.
23. Ibid., Winter 1979, p. 13.
24. Ibid., Summer 1979, p. 12.
25. Ibid., pp. 19, 58.
26. "Neville," edited by Marge Broome, *Immortal Man* (Lakemont, GA: CSA Press, 1977), front and back covers.
27. Ibid., p. 9.
28. Ibid., p. 44.
29. Warch, p. 1.
30. Ibid., p. 9.
31. Ibid.
32. Ibid., p. 11.
33. Ibid.
34. For example, Spring 1980, p. 20.
35. *New Thought*, Winter 1980; Summer 1979, p. 60; Winter 1979, p. 13.
36. Ibid., p. 56.
37. Ibid., Autumn 1979, pp. 22-23, 40; Winter 1980, p. 33.
38. Ibid., Spring 1978, p. 18.
39. *New Thought*, Winter 1980, p. 47.
40. Ibid., p. 47.
41. Warch, p. 5; Aaftink, pp. 23-24; *New Thought*, Autumn 1978, p. 36; Spring 1980, pp. 7, 24; Winter 1980, p. 33; Spring 1979, pp. 13, 17, 37; Summer 1979, pp. 3, 9, 19, 26, 58, 60; Winter 1979, p. 9; Summer 1980, pp. 23-27, 73.
42. *New Thought*, Summer 1979, p. 3.
43. Ibid., Summer 1980, p. 80.
44. Ibid., Spring 1978, p. 9.
44a. Ibid., Autumn 1979, pp. 22-23, 40; Winter 1980, p. 33.
45. Warch, p. 15.
46. *New Thought*, Summer 1980, p. 31.
47. Ibid., Autumn 1978, p. 12.
48. Neville, p. 76.
49. Ibid., p. 42, cf. 25.
50. Warch, p. 7.
51. *New Thought*, Autumn 1979, p. 16.
52. Warch, p. 81.
53. Neville, pp. 55, 56, 58.
54. Ibid., p. 76.
55. Ibid., pp. 40, 96.
56. Warch, p. 61.
57. *New Thought*, Spring 1978, p. 49.
58. *New Thought*, Autumn 1978, p. 12.
59. Ibid., Winter 1980, p. 31.
60. *New Thought*, Spring 1978, pp. 4-5.
61. Warch, p. 18.
62. Ibid., p. 28.
63. *New Thought*, Spring 1978, p. 49.
64. Warch, p. 58.
65. Ibid., pp. 90-91.
66. Ibid.
67. Neville, p. 49.
68. Ibid., p. 57.
69. Ibid., p. 76.
70. *New Thought*, Spring 1979, p. 18.
71. Warch, pp. 88-89.
72. *New Thought*, Winter 1979, p. 38.
73. "The Path of Discipleship," *New Thought*, Autumn 1978, p. 12.
74. Neville, p. 20.
75. *New Thought*, Summer 1979, p. 62.
76. W. E. Vine, *An Expository Dictionary of New Testament Words*, p. 79.
77. Warch, p. 59.

78. *New Thought*, Winter 1980, p. 46.
79. Ibid.
80. Neville, p. 15.
81. *New Thought*, Summer 1980, p. 19.
82. *The International Standard Bible Encyclopedia*, Vol. 1, p. 18.
83. Warch, p. 75.
84. *New Thought*, Summer 1980, p. 14.
85. Ibid., Winter 1980, p. 31.
86. Ibid., Spring 1979, p. 14.
87. *Christianity Today*, December 15, 1978, p. 38.
88. Warch, p. 61.
89. *New Thought*, Summer 1980, p. 8.
90. Warch, p. 56.
91. Ibid., p. 57.
92. Ibid.
93. *New Thought*, Summer 1980, p. 15.
94. Ibid., p. 18.
95. Ibid., Spring 1978, p. 9.
96. Ibid., Summer 1980, p. 18.
97. Warch, p. 98.
98. *New Thought*, Autumn 1978, p. 44.
99. Neville, p. 15.
100. *New Thought*, Autumn 1979, pp. 23, 38.
101. Ibid., Spring 1978, pp. 18-19.
102. Ibid., Summer 1979, p. 55.
103. Ibid., p. 58.
104. *New Thought*, Summer, 1979, p. 41.
105. *New Thought*, Winter, 1980, p. 23.
106. *New Thought*, Spring, 1978, p. 10.
107. Werch, p. 40.
108. H. J. Aaftink, *New Thought—A Way of Life*, p. 2.
109. George Lamsa, *The New Testament* (Philadelphia, PA: A. J. Holman, 1968), p. x.
110. Edwin Yamauchi, "Greek, Hebrew, Aramaic or Syriac?" *Bibliotheca Sacra*, October 1974, p. 324.
111. Ibid., pp. 324-325.
112. Ibid., pp. 325-326.
113. Ibid.
114. George Lamsa, *New Testament Origin* (United States: Lamsa Publication, n.d.), p. 38, foreword.
115. J. H. Greenlee in *The Expositor's Bible Commentary*, Vol. 1, pp. 409-416.
116. Ibid., pp. 410-411.
117. George Lamsa, *More Light on the Gospel* (San Antonio, TX: Aramaic Bible Center, 1968), p. xxix.
118. Yamauchi, pp. 327-331.
119. Ibid.
120. Ibid.
121. Ibid.
122. Ibid.
123. Lamsa, *The New Testament*, p. xvi.
124. Lamsa, *Gospel Light*, pp. 284-285.
125. Lamsa, *More Light on the Gospel*, pp. 26, 110.
126. George Lamsa, *The Hidden Years of Jesus* (United States: Lamsa Publication, 1973), pp. 26, 110.
127. Membership pamphlet titled, "Noohra Foundation—A Unique Educational Center of Practical Spiritual Truth," na, nd.
128. *Noohra*, Vol. 6, No. 2, p. 7.
129. *New Thought*, Spring 1980, p. 37.
130. Rocco Errico, *The Ancient Aramaic Prayer of Jesus "The Lord's Prayer"* (Los Angeles, CA: Science of Mind, 1979), pp. 11, 13, 26, 71; *New Thought*, Summer 1979, p. 43; Spring 1978, p. 39.
131. Ibid., p. 26.
132. *New Thought*, Spring 1978, p. 39.
133. Errico, p. 17.
134. Ibid., p. 26.
135. Ibid., pp. 19-20.
136. *Noohra*, Vol. 6, No. 2, p. 6.
137. Ibid., Vol. 4, No. 5, p. 2.
138. Errico, pp. 26-27.
139. *Noohra*, Vol. 6, No. 4, p. 6.
140. *New Thought*, Winter 1979, p. 26.
141. Various brochures describing Noohra Foundation classes: September 15, 22, 29, 1080 at the Church of Daily Living, Santa Ana, CA and September 13, November 0, 1980 at the Noohra Foundation, Santa Ana.
142. Ibid.
143. Cf. John Weldon, *Occult Shock and Psychic Forces*, section on psychic development; Kurt Koch, *Occult Bondage and Deliverance;* M. Unger, *Biblical Demonology, Demons in the World Today*.
144. Errico, pp. 76-77.
145. *New Thought*, Autumn 1978, p. 26.

ONENESS PENTECOSTALISM

INFO AT A GLANCE

Name: Oneness Pentecostalism or "Jesus Only."

Purpose: To defend true (Unitarian) Christianity before the world.

Founder: Possibly R. E. McAlister, during a 1913 Pentecostal camp meeting near Los Angeles, California.

Source of authority: The Bible as interpreted by Oneness founders, theologians and leaders.

Claims: To be the only true Christian church.

Occult dynamics: Some spiritism historically in the formation of the church and its leaders via occult visions or "angel" contacts and guidance.

Attitude toward Christianity: Rejecting.

Examples of key literature: David K. Bernard, Series in Pentecostal theology, *The New Birth*, Vol. 1 and *The Oneness of God*, Vol. 2 (Hazelwood, MI: World Aflame, 1983); Nathaniel A. Urhan, *Consider Him* (St. Louis: United Pentecostal Church, n.d.); Keith G. Morehead, *Fictional Foundations of Trinitarian Thought* (Oneness Ministries, 1988) and *God's Mystery, That Is, Christ Himself* (Oneness Ministries, 1987).

Quotes:

"We do not believe in three separate personalities in the Godhead but we believe in three offices which are filled by one person."[1]

—Nathaniel A. Urshan, "Consider Him" (booklet)

"He himself is the Father; He himself is the Son; He himself is the Holy Spirit"[2]

—Sabellius

"This tract will really open your eyes. It may burst your hide, and if it does, you certainly need it bursted. There is too much smooth, flowery mouthed, preaching, going on, so take heed to this . . . I am obeying my God in writing this tract. I dare you to read it . . . if you will . . . you will be able to tell whether you are in God's truth, or are deceived by Old Satan . . . Old Satan has the vast majority of the church people, sadly deceived, . . .

how smooth and slick that Devil is by coming to us, as an angel of light, and His Preachers, come to us, as the ministers of righteousness. These Preachers and Priests, do not know, they are deceived by Old Satan, and neither do you know you are deceived, until you read this tract . . . let us not believe Old Satan's works. . . . But these Preachers and Priests and you, would rather believe Old Satan's words, before you would God's! . . . So Please don't let Old Satan deceive you any longer with His 3 person 3 god teaching."[3]

—Wilbur King

Note: References to *Encyclopedia of New Age Beliefs* (1996): Angel Contact.

DOCTRINAL SUMMARY

God: One person only (Unitarian).

Jesus: The one true God who exists as the modes of Father, Son and Holy Spirit.

Trinity: A Satanic "doctrine of demons."

Salvation: By faith and works (baptism, speaking in tongues and, often, personal righteousness).

INTRODUCTION

Wilbur King, the writer of the last quotation and a self-styled "One God Jesus Name Preacher," tells Christians that while anyone can see from Scripture that there is a Father, Son and Holy Spirit, it takes a special "revelation from Jesus Himself to find out that the Father, Son and Holy Ghost is all located, in Jesus."[4]

He is typical of hundreds of modern Pentecostal writers who view the historic orthodox Protestant church as an agent of the devil, literally, for its belief in the doctrine of the Trinity. In the past decade or two their numbers have increased dramatically, and thus their beliefs are becoming a genuine concern to the Christian church. Robert M. Bowman, Jr. observes in his critique of the movement: "An astonishing number of professing Christians today reject the doctrine of the Trinity . . . Oneness Pentecostalism began in 1923 [*sic*] and has grown quickly since then to over four million worldwide, making it the second-largest anti-trinitarian movement [behind Mormonism]."[5] (There are now some

estimates that go as high as 17 million adherents, but the dramatic rise of Islam in America now pushes that statement to "third largest.") Oneness Pentecostalism is one of the fastest growing religious movements with 10 to 15 percent increases in international membership for the United Pentecostal Church International (UPCI), alone, according to the UPCI website.

Since its inception, Oneness Pentecostalism (OP) has had a significant impact among Christians. William Branham, a false prophet who was guided by spirits and reached millions of people in the 1930s–50s, was a Oneness preacher. Despite the good (or bad) it does, today's TBN broadcasting, which reaches millions, also supports Oneness Pentecostalism (based on programs we have seen). Thus there exists today yet another sizable and diverse movement which, as we will see, denies both the nature of Christ and the Trinity itself but which also claims to be Christian. While it has emerged under numerous denominations it is most commonly known as the "Jesus Only" or "Oneness Pentecostal" movement, the latter term being preferred by adherents.

It should be noted that the teaching is essentially a Pentecostal phenomena, being born, nurtured and matured within the ranks of Pentecostalism and holiness movements. Modern leaders and apologists in the movement have included John Scheppe, David K. Bernard, R. E. McAlister, Frank Ewart, Glenn A. Cook, Garfield T. Haywood, C. Haskell Yadon, John Peterson, A. McLain and Nathaniel A. Urshan. James D. G. Dunn (author of the excellent and critical treatment, *Baptism in the Holy Spirit*[6] observes, "The largest of these [Jesus Only] churches is the United Pentecostal Church, and in all about twenty-five percent of Pentecostals in the USA are unitarian."[7] In other words, it appears that fully one-fourth of all American Pentecostals are anti-Trinitarian!

According to Bjornstad, Bjorck and Spraker, the modern resurgence of modalism (see below) began in April 1913 during a major Pentecostal camp meeting in Arroyo Seco, near Los Angeles, California. R. E. McAlister preached a sermon on Acts 2:38 where he argued that baptism was to be done in the name of Jesus only and not with a Trinitarian formula. John Scheppe was greatly influenced by the message and in prayer that night encountered a type of "revelation" or mystical experience confirming the power of the name of Jesus. Certain passages of Scripture led Scheppe to adopt a modalistic view of the Godhead that, contrary to Sabellius, made Jesus, not the Father, the one true God. (Some of these passages were Matthew 17:8; John 10:30; Philippians 2:9–11; and Colossians 3:17.)[8] Dr. J. Gordon Melton discusses how the movement grew and attracted prominent Assemblies of God leaders who soon split from the Assemblies of God denomination in 1916:

> The movement spread under the leadership of Ewart and evangelist Glenn A. Cook. They were able to bring in such key leaders as G. T. Haywood of Indianapolis, E. N. Bell, and H. A. Goss, all prominent leaders in the Assemblies of God. . . . The vocalization of oneness ideas, mostly by members of the Assemblies of God, came to a head in 1916 at the Assemblies of God General Council meeting in St. Louis. A strong Trinitarian stance was adopted within the Statement of Beliefs. One hundred and fifty-six ministers were expelled by that act and many Assemblies were lost; the era of formation of "oneness" churches began.[9]

Monarchianism, Modalism and Sabellianism

Historically, the teaching has been known variously as: 1) monarchianism (stressing the *monarchia* (Greek, "single principle"), the absolute unity of the Godhead; 2) modalism, the most popular form of monarchianism (where the Persons of the Godhead are merely transitory and temporal "modes," or expressions, of the one

true God, such as in the "Oneness Pentecostal" movement); and 3) Sabellianism, after Sabellius, a third century proponent of modalism.

In modalism, although the three designated terms of the Godhead (The Father, Son and Spirit) are merely expressions or aspects of the one true God, that one true God is usually designated as either Jesus (modern modalism) or the Father (early modalism). It is important to understand that even though the terms "Jesus" and "Father" are used, they do *not* refer to the manifestations or aspects or offices by that same name. Thus in early modalism, although the one true God is "the Father," that Being also has a manifestation as "the Father" in Scripture. Hence Sabellius believed that it was the Father who was the one true Person of the Godhead and who also expressed himself in the modes of Father, Son and Spirit. Today, the modern Oneness Pentecostal movement believes this one true Person of the Godhead is Jesus. They believe it is Jesus who has expressed himself by the scriptural designations Father, Son and Spirit. In other words, the Father, Son and Spirit as we have them revealed in the Scripture are temporary modes or aspects of the true one Person of the Godhead, who is Jesus. Also, for modern Oneness Pentecostals the term "Father" may refer to the divine nature of Jesus (the one true God) while the term "Son" may refer to the human nature of this unitarian deity.

The broad title encompassing this teaching of the Oneness of God is monarchianism, which has two principle forms historically: dynamic and modalistic. A tabular illustration would look like the chart below.

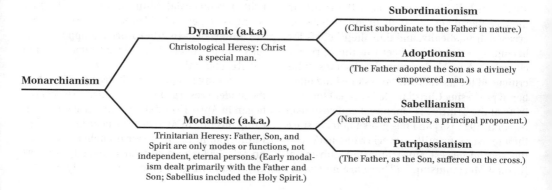

Monarchianism	Dynamic (a.k.a) Christological Heresy: Christ a special man.	Subordinationism (Christ subordinate to the Father in nature.)
		Adoptionism (The Father adopted the Son as a divinely empowered man.)
	Modalistic (a.k.a.) Trinitarian Heresy: Father, Son, and Spirit are only modes or functions, not independent, eternal persons. (Early modalism dealt primarily with the Father and Son; Sabellius included the Holy Spirit.)	Sabellianism (Named after Sabellius, a principal proponent.)
		Patripassianism (The Father, as the Son, suffered on the cross.)

The Specific Christological Heresies of Monarchianism

ADOPTIONISM	MODALISM
• Jesus is a man	• Jesus is the Father
• Preserves the unity of God by sacrificing Christ's deity	• Preserves the unity of God by sacrificing Christ's personality

A number of sub-biblical sects or cults teach modalism today, such as The Local Church of Witness Lee.[10] Some of the largest denominations of the modern "Oneness" movement include: the United Pentecostal Church, the largest denomination with more than 2.3 million members worldwide (3,800 churches in U.S., 16,000 churches in 131 other nations); The Jesus Church; The Bible Way Churches of Our Lord Jesus Christ; The Church of Jesus Christ; Apostolic Overcoming Holy Church of God, Inc.; Assemblies of the Lord Jesus Christ; Pentecostal Assemblies of God; Assemblies of the Lord Jesus Christ; Pentecostal Assemblies of The World; and the Church of the Lord Jesus Christ of the Apostolic Faith. These denominations comprise over 6,000 churches[11] and, if the literature we have perused is representative, many of them are legalistic, authoritarian and exclusivistic. In his definitive refutation of Oneness theology, *Oneness Pentecostals and the Trinity*, Gregory A. Boyd, former Oneness believer and Assistant Professor of Theology at Bethel College, points out that the extreme emphasis on works "gives the UPCI [United Pentecostal Church International] and similar Oneness groups the distinction of being the most legalistic 'Christian' movement in church history."[12]

Oneness apologetic literature in defense of their position, although detailed, frequently cites liberal scholarship (like most cults) and reveals an unfortunate ignorance of church history, Bible doctrine and logical reasoning.[13] For example, it is often held that the doctrine of the Trinity teaches a belief in three Gods, or that it is a doctrine formulated exclusively by the Roman Catholic Church. But the Trinity is not about three Gods, and the teaching of the Trinity was clearly present well prior to the existence of the Catholic Church, which did not begin to take on its present ecclesiastical form until the late 500s. Indeed, belief in the deity of both the Father and the Son as two separate eternal persons concurrently as one God can be seen in the writings of the church fathers from the early second century. (See Doctrinal Appendix.)

SALVATION

Along with the Oneness doctrine of a unitarian, modalistic God, a second major heresy usually exists alongside it: salvation by works, including baptismal regeneration, water baptism in the name of Jesus Only* and the necessity of personal righteousness for gaining entrance into heaven. (Among thousands of Oneness churches, one may expect to find variations of belief here.) Oneness Pentecostals claim to believe in salvation by grace through faith, but their legalism and emphasis on good works obscures or denies their claims.

J. Gordon Melton observes in his *Encyclopedia of American Religions,* "The oneness Pentecostals deny the Trinity and uphold the oneness of God. . . . Salvation is by repentance, and water baptism is considered an essential part of salvation. Baptism is by immersion in the name of Jesus only (Acts 2:38)."[14] Oneness believers reject the term "baptismal regeneration" because they reject infant baptism. However, the basic idea remains: baptism plays an essential part in conferring salvation. The Oneness Pentecostals, then, not only deny the biblical nature of God (see John 4:24) but also reject the biblical nature of salvation, that salvation is solely by grace through faith alone (Ephesians 2:8-9) not by human effort or good works (see Galatians 1:6-8; 2:1-3:25).

This was made evident during a 1985 John Ankerberg Show television debate on this subject, where Dr. Nathaniel Urshan, General Superintendent of the United Pentecostal Church International (UPCI), and Rev. Robert Sabin represented the Oneness views: that in order to have forgiveness of sins and be saved a person

---

*Concerning baptismal regeneration (the teaching that baptism saves, or regenerates), see B. L. Ross, *Acts 2:28 and Baptismal Remission* (Pasadena, TX: Pilgrim Publications, 1976), pp. 1-66 and Cal Beisner, *Is Baptism Necessary for Salvation? A Critical Analysis* (Costa Mesa, CA: CARIS, 1980; Box 2067, Costa Mesa, CA 92628).

"has to obey Acts 2:38," and be baptized in the name of Jesus only.[15] A personal study of this debate illustrates how steadfastly Oneness Pentecostals refuse to accept Trinitarian believers as genuine Christians and how frequently they equivocate, evade key issues, reject evidence, misrepresent Trinitarian theology and use rationalistic cultic argumentation. (In spite of this, their arguments, besides being confusing, can seem at times impressive on the surface, especially to those unfamiliar with their writings and methods of argument.)

Another example is found in a tract of the movement that claims to teach the biblical view of salvation. The tract is titled "New Testament Salvation—Acts 2:38." It states three conditions for salvation, but not one of them is faith. "First, we must repent, turning our back on all sin. Second we must be baptized (immersed) in the Name of Jesus Christ [not of the Father, Son and Holy Spirit] . . . [and] speaking in other tongues . . . is the third step and it takes all three to complete God's plan of Salvation for the church as given in the New Testament, as Jesus told Nicodemus."[16] Examples of OP teachings on legalism and perfectionism, which essentially amount to works-salvation, include: "We are responsible for keeping our salvation until the end," and, "If the sinner has to forsake sin in order to be saved, the Christian must live free from sin in order to stay saved."[17] In sum, 1) repentance, 2) water baptism and 3) Spirit baptism leading to speaking in tongues are the essentials for initiating salvation. And after this, salvation must be maintained by personal holiness. All this is why Dr. Boyd concluded that OP theology denies the finished work of Christ on the Cross when it maintains "that the grace of God through the work of Christ is not alone sufficient for our salvation. Indeed one entire tract of the UPCI is devoted to just this point. It is entitled Grace + 0 = salvation? and in it the UPCI explicitly argues against the view . . . Hence . . . the UPCI and other Oneness groups maintain that it is Grace + Faith + Obedience that equals Salvation."[18] In light of the OP rejection of the biblical doctrine of salvation, Dr. James Bjornstad provides an example to illustrate how the Oneness groups have logically removed themselves from historic orthodox Christian faith (cf., 1 John 2:19, 23):

> The "Jesus Only" or "Oneness" movement is no friend to historic Trinitarian theology. One recent and shocking example of this occurred on July 11, 1981. That was the night when the Rev. Maurice Gordon, pastor of the Lovingway Innercity United Pentecostal Church in Denver, Colorado, nailed his 95 theses to the doors of 1,000 churches and synagogues in Denver, in which he denounced the doctrine of the Trinity as "the most diabolical religious hoax and scandal in history," and concluded with a "Doxology" (revised "Holy, Holy, Holy, / Lord God Almighty, / God is ONE Person: There is / no trinity. / Amen").[19]

Certainly, to this point, we must conclude that to deny the biblical nature of God as Trinitarian is solemn enough, and to further deny the biblical nature of salvation, as being not by grace through faith alone, places groups holding these beliefs outside the pale of orthodox Christianity.

WATER BAPTISM IN JESUS' NAME ONLY?

As noted, water baptism "in the name of Jesus only" is a principal OP tenet based on the belief that since the time of the incarnation the true name of God (the one divine Person) is "Jesus," and on statements in the book of Acts where disciples were said to be baptized "in the name of Jesus." The belief is that since the term "name" is singular in Matthew 28:19, and since baptism was "in the name of Jesus" in Acts, therefore the "name" of the Father, Son and Holy Spirit must be Jesus. Such a conclusion however, fails to take into account the words of Christ Himself as well as historic, literary and other considerations. Thus, concerning the phrasing of Matthew 28:19, the famous Princeton theologian B. B. Warfield observes that a careful reading of the verse disproves the modalistic interpretations:

> The precise form of the formula must be carefully observed. It does not read: "in the names" (plural)—as if there were three beings enumer-

ated, each with its distinguishing name. Nor yet: "In the name of the Father, Son and Holy Spirit," as if there were one person, going by a threefold name. It reads: "In the name (singular) of the Father and of the (article repeated) Son, and of the (article repeated) Holy Spirit," carefully distinguishing three persons, though uniting them all under one name. The name of God was to the Jews Jehovah, and to name the name of Jehovah upon them was to make them His. What Jesus did in this great injunction was to command His followers to name the name of God upon their converts, and to announce the name of God which is to be named on their converts in the threefold enumeration of "the Father" and "the Son" and "the Holy Spirit." As it is unquestionable He here intended Himself by "the Son," He here places Himself by the side of the Father and the Spirit, as together with them constituting the one God. It is, of course, the Trinity which he is describing and that is as much as to say that He announces Himself as one of the persons of the Trinity.[20]

Concerning the use of the phrase "in the name of Jesus" in the book of Acts, we note that there are adequate explanations which do not require the interpretation offered by the Oneness movement. Dr. Henry Heydt comments:

Many people are confused about the difference between Matthew 28:19 and baptism in the book of Acts simply because they do not understand the Jewish background. The Jews had many baptisms or washings. Among these was the baptism of the proselyte, one who turned to Judaism from heathenism. The Talmud says that such baptism had to be in the name of God as assuming the yoke of God's kingdom imposed upon him by the one who leads him to baptism, or else he is not admitted into Judaism. So you have the expressions, "baptized into Moses" (the Greek of 1 Corinthians 10:2), and "into one baptism of John" (the Greek of Acts 19:3). Christian baptism had to be designated as distinct from these. Instead of saying, as we might, "Be baptized in Christian baptism," they followed the mode of expression of the day and used "in the name of Jesus Christ" or "in the name of the Lord Jesus." This expression is not the baptismal formula itself, which is given in Matthew 28:19, but it simply indicates the kind of baptism they needed. In the actual act of bap-

tism loving obedience would certainly have caused the disciples to baptize into the name of the Father, and the Son, and the Holy Spirit."[21]

Bjornstad, Bjorck and Spraker conclude in a similar manner:

A very plausible answer is that when the narrative in Acts indicates a baptism "in the name of Jesus," it is tantamount to saying, "by the authority of Jesus Christ" (see Acts 3:6 and 16:18 where Jesus' authority, "in the name of Jesus," is invoked for healing and exorcism). It is not the formula which accomplishes these things, since in Acts 19:13, the invoking of "in the name of Jesus" by the Jewish exorcists meant nothing because those who invoked it did not have the authority of Jesus Christ.

In other words, baptism was enjoined and carried out under the divine command of the Son. The words employed in the actual rite came from the Matthaean pronouncement. . . . Therefore, it is apparent that we are instructed to use the Triune Formula in baptism by the authority of Jesus Christ's pronouncement in Matthew 28:18-19. Peter, understanding this, commanded baptism on the day of Pentecost by the authority (or in the name) of Jesus (Acts 2:38), precisely as Christ had commanded. The baptismal formula was not in the name of Jesus only. It was by His authority, or literally "in the name of Jesus."[22]

As Dr. Heydt noted, loving obedience to Jesus would have required use of Jesus' baptismal formula. But even *if* we grant that baptism was done verbally with the phrase "in the name of Jesus," there is still no justification for the Oneness interpretation. Judging from the situations where this phrase is used in the Book of Acts, it might have been the means to deal decisively with a brief situation historically where God had implemented a dramatic "new covenant" with stupendous implications. By stressing the vital importance of the Person of Jesus to those already familiar with the God of Abraham, the Apostles underscore the new covenant based on that Person. To stress the importance of Jesus to those related to Judaism, they were baptized in Jesus' name. Pagan converts, however, totally unfamiliar with the triune God, would be baptized in the name of the Father, Son and Holy Spirit. Robert Bowman discusses this possibility:

> In order to reconcile Matthew 28:19 with Acts 2:38 and similar passages it is helpful to see them as pertaining to two different historical contexts. Those who were converted to Christ and baptized in the name of Jesus were either Jews (Acts 2:5, 38; 22:16), Samaritans (Acts 8:5, 12, 16), God-fearing Gentiles (Acts 10:1-2, 22, 48), or disciples of John the Baptist (Acts 19:1-5). Already knowing of the God revealed in the Old Testament, the critical issue for them was a confession of Jesus as Lord and Savior. [Hence, baptism could have been in the name of Jesus.] When pagan Gentiles who knew little or nothing of the God of Israel were led to Christ, however, they would need to confess their faith, not only in Jesus as Lord, but in the one God revealed in Scripture as Father, Son and Holy Spirit. Jesus ordaining that the gospel be taken "to all the nations," made provision for this in His "great commission" (Matthew 28:19).[23]

Whichever conclusion we choose, the fact remains that the Oneness Pentecostal interpretation is unnecessary and erroneous. It is proper to be baptized only in the name of the Father, Son and Holy Spirit. Historically and briefly it may have been permissible to be baptized in the name of Jesus. But in neither case is baptism necessary for salvation. Were baptism needed for salvation, the Apostle Paul would never have made such statements as: "For Christ did not send me to baptize, but to preach the Gospel" (1 Corinthians 1:17).

THE IMPORTANCE OF THE TRINITY

Jesus Christ Himself stressed the vital importance of knowing "the only true God *and* Jesus Christ." "This is eternal life: that they may know you, the only true God, and Jesus Christ, whom you have sent" (John 17:3). It goes without saying that a strictly unitarian or modalistic deity is not "the only true God." If God is unitarian, then Islam, Jehovah's Witnesses, Christadelphians, The Way International and other unitarian groups are right and Christianity is wrong. Biblically, however, the "only true God" is Trinitarian: one God who exists in three Persons and one

substance; one God who is one divine essence but three in centers of consciousness.[24] In their very nature, then, unitarian, monarchian and modalistic theologies are not Trinitarian; they are anti-Trinitarian. Wilbur King, the "One God Jesus Name Preacher," quoted earlier, declares: "Some day our great God who is Jesus is going to utterly destroy that so-called Trinity doctrine. . . ."[25]

The doctrine of the Trinity represents the central hub from which other biblical doctrines radiate. It is the core of the Christian faith; if we abandon it, other crucial doctrines will sooner or later fall by the wayside. Thus, if the Trinity is false and modalism true, many great biblical doctrines are rejected, such as Jesus' preexistence and intercession (Hebrews 7:24-25; 1 John 2:1), the personality and deity of the Holy Spirit, the church as the Body of Christ (union with Christ) and the incarnation and the atonement. Regarding Christ's propitiation of the Father, Harold O. J. Brown points out in his excellent survey, *Heresies,* that historic modalism makes the event of redemption almost a charade, because if the Son of God is not a distinct person, He can hardly represent us before God the Father. If Jesus Christ is not a real, separate person from God the Father—One who can stand before Him, address Him and intercede for us—then what happens to the concept of substitutionary atonement? If Christ does not exist as a separate Person, how did He pay for our sins on the Cross to satisfy the infinite justice of God the Father? In other words, the Jesus who died on the Cross was not the biblical Jesus but the unitarian deity of modalism manifesting a different name and temporarily different form. If there is no Trinity then there is no incarnation and no objective redemption or salvation. There is no one who is acting as a mediator between God and man. Thus Dr. Brown correctly states:

> Logically, modalism makes the events of redemptive history a kind of charade. Not being a distinct person, the Son cannot really represent us to the Father. Modalism must necessarily be docetic and teach that Christ was human in appearance only; the alternative, on the basis of modalistic presuppositions, is that God himself died on the Cross. Since such an idea is considered absurd—except by death-of-God

theologians—the normal consequence is the conclusion that while Christ was fully God, he only appeared to be man. . . . If the Son is not a real Person who can stand before the Father and address him, then the later Christian concept of substitutionary satisfaction, which holds that Christ takes our place and pays our debt to the Father, becomes at best a symbol, not a reality. Where modalism prevails, the concept of substitutionary satisfaction, or vicarious atonement, will necessarily be absent, and so modalism is sometimes adopted by those who object to the doctrine of vicarious atonement. More commonly, however, it simply arises as an attempt to reduce the mystery of the Trinity to a more understandable concept, even at the cost of the true humanity of Jesus and the doctrine of substitutionary satisfaction.[26]

Thus early modalism, which saw the Father as the true divine Person, led to real difficulty with the atonement. If the Son is not a distinct person, how was the Father propitiated? Modern modalism (OP), which see Jesus as the true divine Person, has equal difficulty. If the Father is not a distinct person, who did the Son propitiate?

Instead of the Trinity, the unitarian deity of modalism assumes temporary roles or offices as Father, Son and Spirit. When "the Father" created the universe, it wasn't *really* the Father but the unitarian deity of modalism manifesting for a time as the Father. When the Son died on the Cross, it wasn't *really* the Son who died but the modalistic God manifesting in the temporary form of the Son. When the Holy Spirit guides and sanctifies the Church, it isn't *really* the Holy Spirit but a unitarian deity appearing as the Holy Spirit. Thus, the Persons of the Father, Son and Holy Spirit *do not exist* as eternal Persons but merely as transitory functions. In modalism, therefore, the modes (roles, offices) end up as caricatures of the three divine Persons of the Bible.

The problem for Oneness Pentecostalism is that the biblical doctrines of salvation that are absolutely crucial—regeneration, justification, sanctification and resurrection—are utterly inseparable from Trinitarian theology. When the doctrine of the Trinity is rejected, doctrines related to it are difficult to maintain. Dr. Henry B. Smith observes, "For the Trinity there is a strong, preliminary argument in the fact that in some form it has always been confessed by the Christian Church, and that all that has opposed it has been thrown off. When it has been abandoned, other chief articles, as the atonement, regeneration, etc., have almost always followed it, by logical necessity; as when one draws the wire from a necklace of gems, the gems all fall asunder."[27] As Dr. Loraine Boettner observes in his fine discussion of the Trinity in *Studies in Theology,* "If there were no trinity, there could be no incarnation, no objective redemption and therefore no salvation; for there would then be no one capable of acting as Mediator between God and man. In his fallen condition man has neither the inclination nor the ability to redeem himself."[28]

The drift of the theology away from Trinitarianism also affect the Oneness view of the nature of God:

It is difficult to maintain the independence and self-sufficiency of God on any other than the Trinitarian basis. Those who believe in a unipersonal God almost instinctively posit the eternity of matter or an eternal and necessary creation in order to preserve a subjective objective relationship. . . . It is felt that apart from a creation a unitary God would be a most lonely and solitary Being, limited in companionship, love, mercy, justice, etc., and hence not self-sufficient. The Unitarian conception of God is unstable, and these considerations to quite a large extent account for its distinct tendency toward Pantheism. . . . "A Unitarian, one-personed God," says Dr. Charles Hodge, "might possibly have existed, and if revealed as such, it would have been our duty to have acknowledged His lordship. But, nonetheless, He would have always remained utterly inconceivable to us—one lone, fellowless conscious being; subject without object; conscious person without environment; righteous being without fellowship or moral relation or sphere of right action. Where would there be to Him a sphere of love, truth, trust, or sympathetic feeling? Before creation, eternal darkness; after creation, only an endless game of solitaire, with worlds for pawns.[29]

This is why Boettner concludes as follows:

In the nature of the case Anti-trinitarianism inevitably leads to a radically different system of religion. Historically, the Church has always refused to recognize as Christians those who rejected the doctrine of Trinity. Also, historically, every great revival of Christianity down through the ages has been a revival of adhesion to fullest Trinitarianism. It is not too much to say, therefore, that the Trinity is the point on which all Christian ideas and interests focus, at once the beginning and the end of all true insight into Christianity.[30]

DOES ONENESS DOCTRINE COMPRISE HERESY?

Surprisingly, some evangelicals do not classify Oneness theology as heretical; indeed much of the evangelical community does not appear overly concerned with the issue. After all, it is alleged that Oneness Pentecostals accept Jesus' deity and do not add to Scripture and that they are evangelical in most of their teachings.

This is simply not the case. First, the deity of Christ is not accepted according to the biblical and historic Christian position. There is all the difference in the world between a unitarian God who temporarily manifests as the Son (a unitarian God called Jesus) and the Second Person of the Holy Trinity who incarnated and died on the Cross to appease the wrath of God against sin. The Jesus of OP is *not* the Jesus of the Bible, so it matters little if it accepts Christ's deity. Mormons and many other cults also reject the biblical teaching.

Second, the fact that OP has no additional Scripture is not exactly germane if the Bible it has is so distorted it becomes another Scripture anyway. Further, there are numerous OP claims to divine revelation or illumination of the Scripture which, in principle, amount to an "adding to Scripture." If the Bible can only be interpreted "properly" through the literature of the movement, then such literature is equally important, if not more so, than the Bible, whether or not that literature claims direct divine inspiration.

Third, even though OP may in some areas be more evangelical than traditional cults, it hardly matters. The issue of heresy revolves around key points—the nature of God and the nature of salvation—if it revolves around anything. And Oneness Pentecostalism most certainly denies God's nature and most certainly denies His salvation. The mere fact it is sometimes more sub-

tle in its denials or more biblical in some ways than other cults in no way lessens the severity of rejecting God's self-revelation of His very Being and the way of salvation purchased at so great a cost with the precious blood of Christ. To conclude that such a teaching is not heresy is wrong. As Dr. Harold O. J. Brown points out, heresy by definition involves an abandonment of the faith and has eternal consequences:

In Christian usage, the term "heresy" refers to a false doctrine, i.e., one that is simply not true, and that is, in addition, so important that those who believe it, whom the church calls heretics, must be considered to have abandoned the faith. . . . In the early church, heresy did not refer to simply any doctrinal disagreement, but to something that seemed to undercut the very basis for Christian existence. Practically speaking, heresy involved the doctrine of God and the doctrine of Christ. . . . Paul did not wink at him who brought "any other Gospel" within the context of the Christian community. "Let him be accursed," he told the Galatian church (Galatians 1:8) . . . just as there are doctrines that are true, there are those that are false, so false that they can spell eternal damnation for those who have the misfortune to become entrapped by them.[31]

Robert Bowman concludes that in spite of some of their affirmations OP cannot be classified as Christian; it must be recognized heretical and cultic:

The apostle John warns us, "Whoever denies the Son does not have the Father; the one who confesses the Son has the Father also" (1 John 2:23). Oneness Pentecostals will not admit to denying the Son, of course; but that should come as no surprise. It is doubtful that any heretic, including those about whom John specifically warned, has ever admitted to denying the Son. Instead, heretics of all kinds have simply redefined the meaning of the term "Son" (and along with it the meaning of "Father"). Thus the Jehovah's Witnesses define "Son" as "direct creation," while the Mormons claim that Jesus is the "Son" of God and by virtue of having been begotten through physical union between God and Mary. The Oneness redefinition of "Son" as the human nature of Jesus (and "Father" as His divine nature) may be less offensive than the Mormon version, and less obvious than that of the Jehovah's Witnesses, but it is a redefinition nonetheless. The fact is that the Son and the Father are two persons, co-existing eternally in relationship with one another. To deny this fact is to deny the biblical Son and thus to have a false view of Jesus.

It turns out, then, that one's view of Christ cannot be separated from one's view of the Trinity. Deny the Trinity, and you will lose the biblical Christ; affirm the Christ of Scripture, the Christ who was sent by the Father and who sent the Holy Spirit, and you will find that your God is the Trinity. It is, in fact, the doctrine of the Trinity that is the distinctive feature of the Christian revelation of the nature of the true God. As Calvin expressed it: "For He so proclaims Himself the sole God as to offer Himself to be contemplated clearly in three persons. Unless we grasp these, only the bare and empty name of God flits about in our brains to the exclusion of the true God." Only the Christian God is triune, and consequently, to deny the Trinity is to say that, historically, Judaism and Islam have been right about the being of God, while Christianity has been wrong. Oneness writers have said as much. Therefore, while there may be individual Oneness believers who are saved, the Christian community has no choice but to regard the Oneness movement as a whole as having departed from the Christian faith.

We must conclude, then, that the Oneness teaching is a heresy, that it denies a fundamental, basic belief of biblical Christianity, and that those churches and denominations which teach this heresy are actually pseudo-Christian sects. In popular Evangelical terminology, such a heretical sect is known as a "cult," a term which simply means that the group's beliefs are in some important respect non-Christian. In this sense, we regretfully conclude that the Oneness churches are indeed cults, and we urge Christians to reach out to Oneness believers in love and share with them the triune God revealed in the Scriptures.[32]

SHOULD ONENESS PENTECOSTALISM BE CLASSIFIED AS A CULT?

As we saw, Robert Bowman (and many others) classify OP as a cult, which surprises many people. But they are correct although Oneness Pentecostals would vigorously oppose the label "cult" or "cultic." But again, according to researchers and former members, the label often fits, if not always in every way in every church. Both our biblical and social/psychological definitions of the term cult are relevant for the following reasons (just as our definition of aberrational *Christianity* is not relevant [see Introduction]):

1. Oneness doctrine denies the nature of God.

2. Oneness doctrine denies the nature of Christ.

3. Oneness doctrine denies the nature of the Holy Spirit.

4. Oneness doctrine denies the nature of salvation by grace through faith alone and teaches salvation by works.

5. Oneness practice often harmonizes with cult practice: In "Eight Marks of a Mind Control Cult Applied to the United Pentecostal Church" David Vivas, Jr. lists the following examples:

   a. *Isolation from other churches.* Since only Oneness Pentecostals have the truth, members are warned to avoid other Christians who do not have the truth—virtually all true Christians.

   b. *Social isolation.* Members are encouraged to distance themselves from "outsiders" insuring further isolation and dependence on the particular group.

   c. *Strict obedience to leaders.* Oneness members are not to question their pastor—even if the pastor cannot justify his teaching scripturally.

   d. *Spiritual intimidation.* Members who leave may be told they will be judged by God or turned over to Satan. To leave the church is to forsake God and court damnation.

   e. *Compliance through shame.* Those who violate OP standards of holiness must confess their sins before the entire church.[33]

So far we have shown that Oneness Pentecostalism is not Christian but a heretical teaching. In the following section we wish to examine briefly the reasons behind the historical development of monarchianism to substantiate this conclusion further. While an expanded treatment of the history and forms of monarchianism is not possible here, good discussions are found in Schaff-Herzog,[34] Hastings[35] and Schaff.[36]

The Development of Monarchianism

Monarchianism had two principal forms, dynamic and modalistic. "Dynamic Monarchianism saw in Jesus but a man and in the Holy Spirit a divine influence, while Modalistic Monarchianism regarded the Father, the Son, and the Holy Spirit merely as three modes of manifestation successively assumed by the Godhead."[37] Both had seemingly benevolent motives behind their formation, even if the totality of Scripture was not the authority. As the early Church of the second century developed its theology in a more systematic manner, concern arose in some more rationalistic church circles as to the seeming di-theism (belief in two Gods) implied in asserting Christ's deity.[38] "The doctrine of the Trinity has always bristled with difficulties and therefore it is no wonder that the Church in its attempt to formulate it was repeatedly tempted to rationalize it and to give a construction of it which failed to do justice to the Scriptural data."[39]

The false theology of monarchianism was, then, at least to some degree, motivated by a concern for the unity of God, to preserve monotheism. "Nor is it surprising that these so-called Monarchians should have had a strong following. God is One. For this monotheism the prophets had fought and prevailed."[40] Christians should not forget that they can at this point agree wholeheartedly with monarchianism because Scripture teaches a monotheistic theology. There is only one God and God is one, a unity; there are not two Gods or three Gods in the Godhead. Thus, "there is, of course a legitimate monarchianism, for recognition of the Father, Son, and Holy Spirit does not involve tritheism."[41] But the real issue for monotheism is this: who is the one true God? We must also admit that monarchianism was flawed from the start because it reflected "a desire to evade the inscrutable mystery of three in one."[42] Essentially, monarchians were either embarrassed by the

Trinity or perplexed to the point of abandonment. But to place limited human reasoning above the authority of divine revelation only leads to greater problems. In fact, the serious doctrinal differences between early and modern modalism and their variants only illustrates the greater overall confusion generated from rejecting the Trinity. Thus in adopting a strict unitarianism, monarchianism gave up the biblical teaching of a legitimate diversity within the Godhead:

> It is deceptive, however, to think that Monarchianism was in a better position to hold to the unity of God than was the church. For either it was forced to see in Christ, after his baptism or after his resurrection, a kind of half-God, as was the case with dynamistic Monarchianism; or else, in the attempt to do away with the differences between Father and Son, it became necessary to disregard entirely the Gospel accounts which show the earthly Jesus praying to God the Father. This is what happened in modalistic Monarchianism. Both forms of this movement, therefore, abandoned something which, for the church, was absolutely fundamental.[43]

This abandonment was of course unnecessary, for it was predicated entirely upon rationalistic presuppositions that forced what the Word of God actually taught into its way of reasoning. This is not to say that the doctrine of the Trinity is irrational. But it can be suprarational; that is, not contrary to reason but in places beyond the full grasp of human reason. J. D. Douglas shows how this even flawed the monarchians' concept of the unity of God:

> Their anti-Trinitarianism derives from a presupposition regarding the meaning of unity, rather than from the truth of the Incarnation. ... Traditional presuppositions that unity is simple and undifferentiated have forced many (including Subordinationists and Sabellians) to jettison Trinitarian faith. However, if one sees unity as inclusive rather than exclusive, the problem is at least mitigated. If all approximations to unity are to be measured by a scale of degrees of absence of internal multiplicity, then Trinitarian theology and monotheism are irrevocably incompatible. But if the degree of unity is to be measured by the intensity of the unify-

ing power in the life of the whole, then there is the prospect for at least partially comprehending the unity of the Godhead (cf. John 17:20–23) and other complex unities. That God sent His Son to the cross and that God was in Christ is comprehensible on Trinitarian terms alone.[44]

Having briefly looked at monarchianism, let us consider its two principal forms. (The reader may wish to refer to the earlier chart.) Dynamic monarchianism (also known as adoptionism, after Christ's being "adopted" by the Father) was primarily a Christological heresy. It taught that Christ was a mere man upon whom God's spirit had descended at his baptism, thus filling Him with divine power. In other words, an impersonal divine power was active in the man Jesus and this made Him unique. Thereafter, Christ was adopted by the Father as his Son, becoming the Son of God. "According to one brand of Monarchianism, so-called dynamistic monarchianism, an impersonal divine power was active in the man Jesus. Thereafter Christ was adopted as the Son of God."[45] "In this view Jesus is regarded as a unique man who was divinely energized by the Holy Spirit (usually thought of as occurring at his baptism) and called to be the Son of God."[46] It clearly denied the deity of Christ and never gained a large following. In conceiving "of Jesus as a mere man . . . it was too alien to Christian feeling to make much headway. . . ."[47]

The more popular form, modalistic monarchianism, did gather a sizable number of adherents. "Early in the third century [it] seemed to threaten to become the faith of the church."[48] Modalistic monarchianism also stresses the "monarchy" or unity of the Godhead and ostensibly the deity of Christ, allegedly circumventing the objections to the earlier form. However, it taught that Christ was God *as* the Father, thus denying His eternal, independent existence:

The second class of Monarchians . . . felt the deeper Christian impulse to hold fast to the divinity of Christ; but they sacrificed to it his independent personality, which they merged in the essence of the Father.[49]

The Monarchians fall into two classes. In order to hold fast to the unity of the Godhead the one abandons the Deity of Christ, holding Christ to be a mere man chosen of God, in whom the Holy Spirit dwelt in a (quite) unique sense (Dynamic or Adoptionist Monarchianism). It resembles the Ebionite view. The other, maintaining Christ to be a manifestation of God himself, abandons the personal distinctions and confounds the persons of the Father and the Son (Modalistic Monarchianism). It resembles the Docetic view.[50]

At its simplest, it is the teaching that there is one Godhead which could be designated indifferently as either the Father or the Son. These terms did not indicate any essential distinctions; they were names to be applied to God at different times. God was a monad.[51]

This second form of monarchianism (past and present considered) has a number of subforms depending upon: 1) the emphasis on the One Person (is it the Father or Jesus?) and 2) whether the modes are static (simultaneous) or successive (developmental). Concerning the latter point, some believe the modes (roles, offices) of Father, Son and Spirit are each other simultaneously, while others believe that they represent successive modes where God first becomes the Father, *then* the Son and then *later* the Spirit. (The Local Church of Witness Lee seems to teach both.[52]) Early monarchians taught that God revealed himself "only in one mode at any one time" (successive or development modalism).[53] Thus, "the names Father, Son and Holy Spirit, are simply designations of three different phases under which the one divine essence manifests itself. God reveals Himself as Father in creation and in the giving of the law, as Son in the incarnation, and as Holy Spirit in regeneration and sanctification."[54] Nevertheless, "Its defects were glaring; for if the phases were successive then God ceased to be the Father when He became the Son, and ceased to be the Son when He became the Holy Spirit. The incarnation was reduced to a temporary union of the Divine and the human nature in the man Jesus Christ. This view was so out of harmony with the Scriptures that it was soon rejected."[55] (Of course, it is revived today.)

This western "successive" form of modalistic monarchianism was known as patripassianism, and the Eastern form as Sabellianism, after Sabellius (a principal exponent). In the former title the term was given because the Father *became* the Son, hence the Father was believed to have suffered on the cross (patripassianism, Latin *pater*, "father": and *passus*, "to suffer").[56] In his *Lectures in Systematic Theology*, Dabney describes it this way:

> There is only one substance and person in the Godhead . . . the names, Father, Son, and Holy Ghost, are nothing but names for certain phases of action or roles, which God successively assumes. Christ was the one person, the Godhead or Father, [later] united to a holy man, Jesus, by a proper Hypostatic union. The Holy Ghost is still this same person, the Father, [later] acting His part as revealer and sanctifier. Hence, it is literally true, that the Father suffered . . .[57]

To reiterate, modalistic monarchianism taught that God was one divine essence, a monad expressing itself in three operations or modes. The Father, Son and Spirit were three static or successive phases by which the one divine Person manifested itself.

It must be emphasized that a principal heresy of monarchian theology (irrespective of its forms) is to deny the very persons of the Holy Trinity. "God's different names—Father, Son and Spirit—described the different roles he played at different times."[58] J. G. Davies states:

> In effect this was a form of unitarianism which maintained that the distinction between the Father, and the Son was not real but purely nominal, one single divine person bearing both names at different times . . . God is thus a monad possessing internal powers of expansion, appearing in creation as Father, in redemption as Son and in sanctification as Holy Spirit, not separate realities but aspects of a single reality. This expansion, whereby the three operations are brought into play, is balanced by a process of contraction whereby they are withdrawn again into the one.[59]

Thus in modalism Jesus and the other Persons of the Trinity, remains a "temporary phenomena."[60] After all, if He is merely a temporary expression, or office or function, of the one Person, then He has no permanent or eternal personality,[61] "Athanasius traced the doctrine of

Sabellius to the Stoic philosophy. The common element is the pantheistic leaning view of an expansion and contraction of the divine nature immanent in the world . . . making Father, Son and Holy Ghost only temporary phenomena, which fulfill their mission and return into the abstract monad."[62] Put another way, "The Father is the same as the Son, and the Son the same as the Spirit, three names thus being attached to one and the same Being. This Being is also named Son-Father. And yet God was not Father and Son and Spirit at the same time, but assumed three distinct successive forms of manifestation. . . . As Christ possessed personality only in his historical appearance in the flesh, that personality neither existed previous to his incarnation, nor does it continue to exist now in heaven."[63]

Although the biblical nature of Christ is clearly denied (He does not truly exist),[64] monarchians claim to exalt Jesus.[65] For example, Louis Berkhof discusses the view of Paul of Samosata, a dynamic monarchianist:

> According to him the Logos was indeed *homoousios* or consubstantial with the Father, but was not a distinct Person in the Godhead. He could be identified with God, because He existed in Him just as human reason exists in man. He was merely an impersonal power, present in all men, but particularly operative in the man Jesus. By penetrating the humanity of Jesus progressively, as it did that of no other man, this divine power gradually deified it. And because the man Jesus was thus deified, He is worthy of divine honour, though He cannot be regarded as God in the strict sense of the word.[66]

Modern OP believers may also claim to exalt Jesus. Unfortunately, as should be obvious, it is not the biblical Jesus.

RATIONALISTIC BIAS

Although monarchianism may have begun with proper motives (to safeguard the divine oneness), it nevertheless refused to consider the totality of God's revelation. Something was clearly wrong. Every knowledgeable Christian will defend the unity of God as strongly as he will defend salvation by grace. Yet zeal for the truth of the unity of God does not make him reject the eternality or independent reality of three Persons in the Godhead. The Christian is willing to accept all revelation equally and not sit in judgment on one portion of it. The question must then be raised: why is it that the Monarchianists clearly aligned themselves more to the rationalistic biases of Arianism than to Christianity?

The theological implications of Sabellianism on the orthodox side were serious. A modern form of Sabellianism is Unitarianism.[67]

Nevertheless Paul's school [Paul of Samosata, a dynamic monarchianist] lingered on for a time, giving inspiration to the tenets of Lucian of Samosata (i.v.) and his followers who ultimately developed into the Arians.[68]

[Dynamic monarchianism] was entirely in line with the Ebionite heresy of the early church and with present day Unitarianism.[69]

Essentially, the reason we find such a difference between orthodox Christians and monarchians is because monarchians of all eras have believed in a false God and a false Father and a false Jesus and a false Holy Spirit and therefore never experienced true salvation. Monarchians, generally, have yet to truly come to know Christ personally. Indeed, as an early orthodox opponent of monarchianism declared, "They have impiously slighted the divine Scriptures and repudiated the canon of the ancient faith and have not known Christ. . . ."[70] Only this explains why they do not abide in His word (John 8:31-32) cannot understand Scripture (1 Corinthians 2:14) and willfully separate themselves from other Christians (1 John 2:19). Simply because a person sounds Christian in many areas does not mean salvation is present. Endless cults can sound Christian, e.g., Mormons can sound Christian, yet few groups are as anti-Christian.

According to 1 John 5:12, "He who has the Son, has the life; he who does not have the Son of God does not have the life." In 1 John 5:1a we read, "whoever loves the Father loves the child born of Him." Oneness Pentecostals reject the Father, Son and Holy Spirit and they separate themselves from those born of the Father (Chris-

tians). Do they "love the Father" if they call His children "agents of the devil" and deny the Father Himself? Do they "have" the Son when they deny His very being? This is why the Scripture warns everyone that, at the Second Coming, the Son Himself "will punish those who do not know God and who do not obey the gospel of our Lord Jesus. They will be punished with everlasting destruction and shut out from the presence of the Lord" (2 Thessalonians 2:8-9).

REJECTION BY THE CHURCH

Those who argue that Oneness Pentecostals are "Christian brothers" need to explain why the Church has consistently denied this. While it did take some time for the Church to formulate its theology (indeed, heresy was the common impetus for this), once formulated, all forms of monarchianism were rejected. "The church recognized the errors of both forms of Monarchianism. . . ."[71] "While the great heresy of the second century was gnosticism, the outstanding heresy of the third century was Monarchianism."[72] Further, "The Monarchians were assailed on all sides. . . ."[73] "How grievous were the ravages worked by these Monarchian views can be seen by the frequent condemnation of them. . . ."[74] Cyprian designated the patripassians as "pests and swords, and poisons for the perverting of the truth"[75] (cf., 1 Thessalonians 2:15-16).

As a result, the major proponents of monarchianism were all condemned or excommunicated. "Sabellius and his teaching was condemned at a council at Rome (under Pope Dionysius) in A.D. 263."[76] "Pope Damascus condemned them in the Council held at Rome in 380. . . ."[77] "Paul of Samosata was condemned at a Third Synod in Antioch at A.D. 269 or 268."[78] The Council of Constantinople (381 A.D.) also condemned them, along with the Lateran Council of 649 A.D., and even as late as 1411 A.D. Sabellius was officially condemned.[79] All this was hardly unexpected insofar as Sabellianism was an attack on the God and Savior of all Christians, "to whom every believer felt himself to stand in a personal relation, to whom worship and prayers were addressed [hence], it could not be received by the people of God. Its opposition to Scripture was apparent . . . Sabellianism was, therefore, soon almost universally rejected."[80]

Modern commentators have agreed with their ancient brethren. Schaff, Hastings, Davies, Berkhof and others have labeled such teachings "heresy."[81] And for their part, many OP's have labeled the Trinitarians as "heretics," "apostates" and "emissaries of Satan."* The divide could hardly be greater.

CRITICAL ANALYSIS

The various apologetic tracts of the modalistic community may be confusing or upsetting to a new or untaught Christian, someone who has not systematically studied the scriptural teaching on the nature of God. Oneness pentecostals utilize a number of prooftexts in an alleged substantiation of their position. These include such verses as Isaiah 9:6; John 5:34; 10:30; 14:6–11; 17:6, 11–12; Philippians 2:9–10; Colossians 2:9. Space here does not permit a critique of each verse, but a good in-depth commentary will usually provide adequate refutation of a particular Oneness viewpoint.

To give an idea of how modern Monarchians employ Scripture, consider the following examples. In Luke 23:46 Jesus said, "Father, into your hands I commit my spirit." OP's argue that the humanity of Christ was committing its spirit to the deity of Christ. But is this logical? Does it make sense for the two natures of Christ to relate to one another when Jesus Christ was only *one* person? The Father and Son as two Persons can so relate, but the two natures of one Person cannot so relate by definition. The Bible declares: 1) that the Father loves the Son, 2) that the Son loves the Father and 3) that God loves His children—this requires persons, not natures. If I love my wife and daughter, *I* love them, my person loves them, not my human nature. Like Jehovah's Witnesses, OP's also argue that Christians believe in three Gods. But this has never *once* been the teaching of the Church in its entire 2,000 year history. Arguments like this can

hardly be considered plausible, despite their popularity among cultists.

In the Bible, several scriptures refer to Christ's pre-existence. These are interpreted by OP's as meaning "preexistence" merely in the mind of God, that Christ did not exist in eternity as the Second Person of the Trinity. But Scripture clearly teaches Jesus created all things (John 1:3; Colossians 1:16; Hebrews 1:10). If so, how could something that didn't exist create everything? OP's respond that God made everything with the *thought* of His Son in mind. This not only denies what the Bible plainly teaches, it also seems to make no sense even in Oneness theology. For if the Son is only a different name for a temporary manifestation, or a simultaneous aspect, of the deity, what would be the point of God having such a thought in His mind to begin with?

Regretably, no matter how clearly the Bible refutes OP doctrines, its teachers always seem to discover ways to deny the plain meaning of the text. For example, in Acts 10:43–48, the Gentiles received the Holy Spirit *and* salvation (and spoke in tongues) *before* they were water baptized. This would be impossible according to Oneness doctrine. But rather than correct a false interpretation, they erroneously conclude that in some cases people can receive the Holy Spirit and yet *not* be saved because they have not been baptized. The result is a teaching that sees people without salvation receiving the indwelling ministry of the Holy Spirit.[82]

Refuting Oneness Doctrine

Oneness doctrine generally may be refuted by proving a Trinity as it is historically defined in the church: 1) by documenting a true and definite distinction of actual persons within the Godhead. In other words, by proving a concurrent subject-object relationship between members of the Godhead in which references to interrelationship by foreknowledge, as opposed to actual interrelationships, are shown false; 2) by showing the eternality and deity of three separate Persons. (Cf. Doctrinal Appendix.)

Refuting Oneness theology can probably best be done by first studying the Trinity, such as in E. H. Bickersteth's exceptional work, *The Trinity*.

---

*Some others recognize their "brethren" but declare they will have to suffer through the great Tribulation for their false beliefs.

Once we prove three distinct, eternal persons we have disproven Oneness Pentecostalism. Indeed, proofs of the Trinity are so intricately interwoven throughout Scripture that it is hard to see how they can be missed:

> the whole mass of the New Testament is evidence for the Trinity. For the New Testament is saturated with evidence of the Deity of Christ and the Divine personality of the Holy Spirit . . . the New Testament everywhere insists on the unity of the Godhead; . . . [Yet] it constantly recognizes the Father as God, the Son as God and the Spirit as God; and . . . it cursorily presents these three to us as distinct Persons. . . . That this doctrine underlies the whole New Testament as its constant presupposition and determines everywhere its forms of expression is the primary fact to be noted. . . . The passages in which the three Persons of the Trinity are brought together are much more numerous than, perhaps, is generally supposed . . . the teaching of Jesus is Trinitarianly conditioned throughout . . . all three Persons, God the Father, the Lord Jesus Christ and the Holy Spirit, are brought together, in the most incidental manner, as co-sources of all the saving blessings which come to believers in Christ. . . . To the fact of the Trinity . . . the New Testament testimony is clear, consistent, pervasive and conclusive. There is included in this testimony constant, pervasive and decisive witness to the complete and undiminished Deity of each of these Persons.[85]

In his *Lectures in Systematic Theology* Robert L. Dabney agrees, noting that the distinctions of persons "appear in so many places, [is] asserted in so many forms, [and are] so intertwined with the very woof of the scriptures, that its denial does fatal violence to the integrity of their language." He lists several categories:

> (a) I point to those numerous passages, where one Person is said to act upon, or act through, another. See, e.g., Exodus xxiii:20; Psalms ii:6, cx.; Isaiah xlii; Isaiah liii; 12; John xv:26; xx:21, &c., &c., where God the Father is said to send, to enthrone, to appoint to sacerdotal office, to uphold, to reward the Son, and the Son and Father to send the Holy Ghost. (b) Consider those, in which mutual principles and volitions are said to be exercised by the several persons as such,

towards inferior and external objects. Exodus xxiii:21. (The subject is the Messiah, as will be proved) Ephesians iv:30, Revelation vi:16, &c., &c. Yet, since these principles are all perfectly harmonious, as respects the three persons, there is no dissension of will, breach in unity of council, or difference of perfections. . . . (d) There is still a larger multitude of texts, which assert of the persons as such, actions and agencies toward inferior, external objects. See, for instance, John v:19; 1 Corinthians xii:11, &c., &c. Now, if these personal names of Father, Son, and Holy Ghost, meant no more than three influences or energies, or three phases of action of the same person, or three forms of one substance, is it not incredible that all these properties of personality, choosing loving, hating, sending and being sent, understanding, acting, should be asserted of them? It would be the wildest abuse of language ever dreamed of.[84]

Thus, when Jesus declared that "there is another [*allos* i.e., someone different from the one speaking] who bears witness of Me" (John 5:32 NAS), this must mean that Jesus is not the Father. When the Bible declares that the Father sent the Son and that the Son sent the Holy Spirit, we must be dealing with distinct Persons. For one person to send another person requires two persons, not one person. John 1:6 says God *sent* John the Baptist, but no Oneness writer has ever argued they are one Person. In a similar manner, August H. Strong states in his *Systematic Theology*:

> This tripersonality of the divine nature is not merely economic and temporal, but is immanent and eternal.
>
> 1. Scripture proof that these distinctions of personality are eternal.
>
> We prove this (a) from those passages which speak of the existence of the Word from eternity with the Father; (b) from passages asserting or implying Christ's preexistence; (c) from passages implying intercourse between the Father and the Son before the foundation of the world; (d) from passages asserting the creation of the world by Christ; (e) from passages asserting or implying the eternity of the Holy Spirit.
>
> (a) John 1:1-2—"In the beginning was the Word, and the Word was with God, and the Word was

God"; cf. Genesis 1:1—"In the beginning God created the heavens and the earth"; Philippians 2:6—"existing in the form of God . . . on an equality with God." (b) John 8:58—"before Abraham was born I am"; 1:18—"the only begotten Son who is in the bosom of the Father" (R.V.); Colossians 1:15-17—"firstborn of all creation" or "before every creature . . . he is before all things." In these passages "am" and "is" indicate an eternal fact; the present tense expresses permanent being. Revelation 22:13-14—"I am the Alpha and the Omega, the first and the last, the beginning and the end." (c) John 17:5—"Father glorify thou me with thine own self with the glory which I had with thee before the world was"; 17:24—"Thou lovedst me before the foundation of the world." (d) John 1:3—"All things were made through him"; 1 Corinthians 8:6—"one Lord, Jesus Christ, through whom are all things"; Colossians 1:16—all things have been created through him and unto him"; Hebrews 1:2—"through whom also he made the worlds"; 10—"Thou, Lord, in the beginning didst lay the foundation of the earth, and the heavens are the works of they hands"; Genesis 1:2—"the spirit of God was brooding"—existed therefore before creation; Psalm 33:6—"by the word of Jehovah were the heavens made; and all the host of them by the breath (Spirit) of his mouth"; Hebrews 9:14—"through the eternal Spirit. . . ." Scripture compels us . . . to maintain that there are personal relations between the Father, the Son, and the Holy Spirit independently of creation and of time . . . a social Trinity and an intercourse of love apart from and before the existence of the universe. Love before time implies distinctions of personality before time. There are three eternal consciousness and three eternal wills in the divine nature.[85]

Thus, if Jesus alone is God, and the Spirit, Son and Father His sequential modes, and they cannot co-exist, how is Jesus baptized and *simultaneously* the Spirit descends as a dove and the Father declares, "This is My beloved Son, in whom I am well-pleased" (Matthew 3:17; see 2 Peter 1:17 NAS)? How is Jesus led by the Spirit (Matthew 4:1)? How are the passages in Scripture that refer to the simultaneous (not consecutive) work of each Person to be interpreted? (John 14:23, 31; 15:9, 26; Romans 14:17-18; 15:13, 16-17, 30; 1 Corinthians 6:11, 19; 12:3-6; 2 Corinthians 1:21-22; 2:14-15; 3:3-4; 13:14;

Ephesians 2:18; 3:11, 14, 16; 4:4-6; 5:18, 20; Philippians 1:28 with 2:1, 3:3; 1 Timothy 3:13-16; 2 Timothy 1:13-14; Titus 3:4-6; Hebrews 9:14; 1 John 3:23-4:1.) If the Father, Son and Spirit are present in operation at the same time, then, by definition, they cannot be separate, sequential modes.

When it is understood that each person of the Trinity is simultaneously involved in concurrent, vital operations, sequential modalism must be rejected. Is it not true then that the Father (John 14:23; 2 Corinthians 6:16-18), the Son (John 14:20; Ephesians 3:17; 1 John 4:13) and the Spirit (John 14:17; 1 Corinthians 6:19; 2 Timothy 1:14) all reside "in" the Christian and that the Christian is "in" the Father (1 Thessalonians 1:1; 2 Thessalonians 1:1), Son (John 14:20; Ephesians 1:13; Colossians 2:9-12) and Spirit (Romans 8:9; 9:1; Ephesians 2:18; 4:30; Colossians 1:8)? In other words, the Christian both resides in the Trinity and the Trinity in the Christian. How can this be possible in sequential modalism?

Further, that the Father and Son are distinct and not to be identified or confused as one Person is clear from numerous passages. Neither static nor developmental modalism can be logically defended by the Bible. "My Father is always at his work to this very day, and I, too, am working" (John 5:17). "The Father loves the Son and shows him all he does" (John 5:20). "That all may honor the Son just as they honor the Father" (John 5:23). "The reason my Father loves me is that I lay down my life" (John 10:17). "The miracles I do in my Father's name speak for me" (John 10:25). "Everyone who listens to the Father and learns from him comes to me" (John 6:45). "So whatever I say is just what the Father has told me to say" (John 12:50). "The Holy Spirit, whom the Father will send in my name" (John 14:26). "I am going to the Father, for the Father is greater than I" (John 14:28). "I love the Father and . . . do exactly what the Father has commanded me" (John 14:31). "They have not known the Father or me" (John 16:3).

Also, if the Spirit is a temporary manifestation, how can he "be with you forever" (John 14:16)? How could Jesus pray for the Father to send the Holy Spirit (John 14:16)? In all the above scriptures, is the Father identical with the

Spirit or the Son with the Father? Certainly not. As Bickersteth notes (p. 25) the "will" is the essence of personality. Jesus said that he came down from heaven not to do His own will but the will of Him who sent Him" (John 6:38).

Biblical study will prove that *each* person of the Trinity has a mind, a will, can act and so on. As Bickersteth concludes, after quoting numerous passages documenting the distinct aspects of the personality of the Holy Spirit, "Show me that which has mind, and affection, and will, which can act, and speak, and direct; and that sentient, loving, determining agent, speaker, and ruler, must possess personality, or personality cannot exist."[86] Thus Dr. James Bjornstad observes that one of the most fundamental flaws of the Oneness Pentecostals is, with grave consequences, to ignore the subject-object relationship that exists among the members of the Trinity:

> The most serious weakness in the unipersonal theology of the "Jesus Only" movement is the failure to fully recognize the subject-object relationships among the members of the Godhead. All reality in the realm of personality is based upon this commonly accepted fact. For if there is no object in a given conversation, then there is no meaningful dialogue. One is merely talking to oneself!

> If Jesus alone is God, and the Father and the Holy Spirit are only manifestations of Jesus, many passages of Scripture are meaningless and even deceptive. Did Jesus imitate his Father's voice from heaven (Matthew 3:17)? Who said, "This is *My* (subject) beloved *Son* (object), in whom *I* (subject) am well-pleased?" Where, might we ask, was the Son when the Father (subject) said, ". . . listen to Him" (object)— (Matthew 17:5), and where was the Father when the Son said, "*I* (subject) glorified *Thee* (object) on the earth, having accomplished the work which *Thou* (object) hast given *Me* (subject) to do?"—(John 17:4). The very existence of an "I"-"Thou" relationship denotes personality, and the followers of the "Jesus Only" movement must either ignore or reinterpret (e.g., Jesus as deity is speaking to the human Jesus) these and many other passages to do away with the personal Ego of the members of the Trinity. Our Lord's great plea upon the cross, "*Father,* forgive them . . ." (Luke 23:34), becomes a hollow

sham; his resignation to the Father's will an illusion—". . . not as *I* will, but as *Thou* wilt" (Matthew 26:39); and his final words to his Father on the cross, "Father, into *Thy* hands *I* commit *My* spirit" (Luke 23:46) a pathetic fraud, if there is not a genuine person known as the Father, distinct from the Son.

The same can be said of the Holy Spirit, who manifests every attribute of deity and personality, and of whom Jesus said: "But the Helper, the *Holy Spirit,* whom the *Father* will send in *My* name, *He* will teach you all things, and bring to your remembrance all that I said to you . . . if I do not go away, the *Helper* shall not come to you; but if *I* go, *I* will send *Him* to you . . . *He* will guide you into all the truth; for *He* will not speak on *His* own initiative, but whatever *He* hears, *He* will speak; and *He* will disclose to you what is to come. *He* shall glorify *Me* . . ." (John 14:26; 16:7, 13, 14). The multiple references to the person of the Holy Spirit in a subject-object relationship to Christ and the Father substantiate the Trinitarian claim that the Holy Spirit is a person distinct from the Father and the Son.

It is therefore untenable to maintain the Christology and unipersonal theology of the "Jesus Only" movement when the evidence of Scripture is so clear. There is a person (or Ego) called the Father and designated as God (e.g., 1 Corinthians 8:6); a second co-existent person (Ego) called the Son and designated God (e.g., John 1:1); a third co-existent person (Ego) called the Holy Spirit and designated God (e.g., Acts 5:3, 4); and in the unity of Deity they are collectively termed the "one God" (1 Timothy 2:5).[87]

Finally, who saves us? Who created? Who is eternal yet involved in history? God or each Person? Can an impersonal or temporary "mode" or "function" or "office" accomplish the following? If the modes are successive, how can each mode be involved in such acts when they cannot exist simultaneously? If they are simultaneous why is the distinction of Father, Son and Spirit maintained?

1. *Who saves?*
   a. *Who Regenerates?*
The Father?	(1 Peter 1:3)
The Son?	(John 4:14; 5:21)
The Spirit?	(John 3:6)
Or God?	(1 John 3:9)

b. *Who Sanctifies?*
The Father? (Jeremiah 1:5)
The Son? (Titus 2:14)
The Spirit? (1 Peter 1:2)
Or God? (Exodus 31:13)

c. *Who Justifies?*
The Father? (James 1:17 + Romans 3:24 NAS)
The Son? (Romans 5:9; 10:4; 2 Corinthians 5:19, 21)
The Spirit? (1 Corinthians 6:11; Hebrews 9:14, indirect)
Or God? (Romans 4:6)

d. *Who Propitiates?*
The Father? (John 3:16; 17:5)
The Son? (Matthew 26:28; John 1:29; 1 John 2:2)
The Spirit? (Hebrews 9:14, indirect)
Or God? (Acts. 20:28; 2 Corinthians 5:19)

2. *Who creates?*
The Father? (1 Chronicles 29: 10–12; 1 Corinthians 8:6)
The Son? (Hebrews 1:10; see v. 8)
The Spirit? (Genesis 1:2)
Or God? (Genesis 1:1; Psalm 102:24–26)

3. *Who was involved in Israelite history?*
The Father? (Psalm 103:13–14; Isaiah 63:16; 64:8)
The Son? (1 Corinthians 10:4)
The Spirit? (Nehemiah 9:20)
Or God? (Exodus 17:5–6; 1 Corinthians 10:5)

4. *Who preexisted?*
The Father? (Revelation 1:6)
The Son? (John 17:5; Hebrews 1:8)
The Spirit? (Hebrews 9:14)
Or God? (Deuteronomy 33:27; Habakkuk 1:12)

5. *Who raises the dead?*
The Father? (John 5:21)
The Son? (John 6:44)
The Spirit? (Romans 8:11)
Or God? (2 Corinthians 1:9)

The only conclusion possible is that the Persons of the Trinity are distinct but so united that what is true of one is true of the other:

> Since the three Persons of the Trinity possess the same identical, numerical substance or essence, and since the attributes are inherent in and inseparable from the substance or essence, it follows that all of the Divine attributes must be possessed alike by each of the three Persons and that the three Persons must be consubstantial, co-equal and co-eternal. Each is truly God, exercising the same power, partaking equally of the Divine glory, and entitled to the same worship. When the word "Father" is used in our prayers, as for example in the Lord's prayer, it does not refer exclusively to the first person of the Trinity, but [also to] the three Persons as one God. The Triune God is our Father. The doctrine of the Trinity cannot lead to Tritheism; for while there are three Persons in the Godhead, there is but one substance or essence, and therefore but one God. It is rather a case of the one life substance, Deity, existing consciously as three Persons. The three Persons are related to the divine substance not as three individuals to their species, as Abraham, Isaac and Jacob to human nature; they are only one God,—not a triad, but a Trinity. In the most inmost depths of their being they are inherently and inescapably one. ... Hence it is admitted that our knowledge of the relationships which subsist between the three Persons of the Trinity extends only to the surface. There must be infinite depths in the conscious being of God to which human thought can never penetrate. We are told clearly, however, that God has existed from eternity as three self-conscious persons.[88]

Our examination of OP requires us to conclude that proponents are not biblical in their beliefs but, like cults generally, teaching a serious heresy.

TALKING WITH MEMBERS

As far as talking with a Oneness Pentecostal, comments of former member Gregory Boyd are recommended as useful approaches. Below are brief excerpts from Part One of his article:

> Perhaps the most important thing to remember when dialoguing with Oneness Pentecostals is to demonstrate to them the unconditional love

and acceptance of Jesus Christ. The most problematic aspect of my theology when I was a Oneness Pentecostal was the belief that no one other than us Oneness Pentecostals was going to heaven. Trinitarian Christians simply were not saved! So every time I met Trinitarian Christians who clearly reflected the loving presence of Jesus in their lives by the way they related to me, I confronted more strong evidence that my theology could not be true.

A second vitally important component of witnessing to Oneness Pentecostals is to confront their misunderstandings of what Trinitarians believe. Like most Oneness Pentecostals, I was firmly convinced that Trinitarians worshipped three separate gods and that they didn't "really" believe that Jesus Christ was Himself the Lord God Almighty. This is how Oneness Pentecostals are indoctrinated to perceive Trinitarians. Hence, when dialoguing with Oneness Pentecostals it is vitally important to be utterly empathic about your own belief that there is *only one God*—not three—and that Jesus Christ is *the incarnation of this one God!* . . .

Most importantly, emphasize as strongly as possible that Jesus Christ is the very center of your faith and life. Oneness Pentecostals honestly believe that *they* are the only ones for whom this is true. When I as a Oneness Pentecostal first confronted some informed Trinitarians who successfully conveyed this to me, it effectively loosened the grip which my elitist theology had on me.

The third important ingredient in a witness to Oneness Pentecostals is confronting their theology on its weakest points. . . . Among the erroneous beliefs which Oneness Pentecostals hold, there are four that are especially weak and open to effective refutation: (1) their belief that tongues is the necessary sign of salvation; (2) their denial of the pre-existence of Christ; (3) their belief that Jesus was Himself the Father; and (4) their belief that baptism "in Jesus' name" is necessary for salvation.[89]

Thus Christians should approach Oneness Pentecostals with the following two goals in mind: 1) to display the love *of* Jesus for them and one's love *for* Jesus, and 2) to lead them to a knowledge of the Trinity and personal faith in the true Jesus Christ and salvation by grace alone.

We can best end with the words of Jesus Himself:

> Jesus answered and said to him, "If anyone loves Me, he will keep My word; and My Father will love him, and We will come to him, and make Our abode with him. He who does not love Me does not keep My words; and the word which you hear is not Mine, but the Father's who sent Me." (John 14:23–24)

NOTES

Good "in house" histories of the movement include Fred J. Foster's *Think It Not Strange* (Hazelwood, MO: Pentecostal Publishing House, 1965) and Frank J. Ewart's *The Phenomenon of Pentecost* (1947, rev. 1975; Hazelwood, MO: Word Aflame Press). Robert Bowman, Jr. ("Oneness Pentecostalism and the Trinity," p. 27) refers to a scholarly analysis, David A. Reed, "Origins and Development of the Theology of Oneness Pentecostalism in the United States, " Ph.D. Dissertation (Boston, MA: Boston University Graduate School, 1978).

The doctrinal position of the movement can be found in B. E. Echol, *What Oneness Pentecostals Believe and Teach* (Marshall, TX: BE.E. Echols, 1949); John Paterson, *The Real Truth About Baptism in Jesus Name* (St. Louise: Pentecostal Publishing House, 1953); Kenneth V. Reeves, *The Godhead* (Granite City, IL: Kenneth V. Reeves, 1967); C. Haskell Yodon, *Jehovah-Jesus: The Supreme God* (Twin Falls, ID: C. Haskell Yodon, 1952); and Nathaniel A. Urshan, *Consider Him* (St. Louis: United Pentecostal Church, n.d.). According to Bowman (p. 27), "Probably the best and most complete defense of the Oneness doctrine of God in print" can be found in David K. Bernard, *The Oneness of God* (Hazelwood, MI: Word Aflame Press, 1983).

A definitive refutation can be found in Gregory A. Boyd, *Oneness Pentecostals and the Trinity.* (See note 12.) Good critiques of the movement include The John Ankerberg Show transcript, "The Trinity or Jesus Only—What Do the Scriptures Teach?" series 1 and 2; Robert Bowman, Jr., "Oneness Pentecostalism and the Trinity: A Critique," *Foreword*, Fall 1985, pp. 22-27; Bjorck, Bjornstad, and Spraker, "The 'Jesus Only' or 'Oneness Pentecostal' Movement" (see note 8); and Frank Linquist, *The Truth About the Trinity and Baptism in Jesus' Name Only* (Minneapolis, MN: Northern Gospel Publishing House, 1961).

1. Nathaniel A. Urshan, "Consider Him" booklet (St. Louis: United Pentecostal Church, n.d.).
2. Reinhold Seiberg, *The History of Doctrines, Vol I: History of Doctrines in the Ancient Church* (Grand Rapids, MI: Baker Book House, 1978), p. 168.
3. Wilbur King, "Let Us Make Man in Our Image, After Our Likeness" tract (Salem, OR: n.d.), pp. 1, 2, 3, 10.
4. Ibid., p. 14.
5. Robert Bowman, Jr., "Oneness Pentecostalism and the Trinity: A Biblical Critique," *Foreword*, Fall 1985, p. 23.
6. James G. D. Dunn, *Baptism in the Holy Spirit, Studies in Biblical Theology, Second Series*, Vol. 15 (London: SCM Press, 1973).

7. Tim Dowley, *Eerdman's Handbook to the History of Christianity* (Grand Rapids, MI: Wm. B. Eerdman's, 1977), p. 619.

8. Bjorck, Bjornstad, and Spraker, "The 'Jesus Only' or 'Oneness Pentecostal' Movement" tract, *Christian Research Institute Factsheet* (San Juan Capistrano, CA: Christian Research Institute, 1980), citing David A. Taylor, "Origins and Development of Theology of Oneness Pentecostalism in the United States" (Ann Arbor, MI: University Microfilms International, 1980).

9. J. G. Melton, *The Encyclopedia of American Religion*, vol. 1 (Wilmington, NC: McGrath Publishing House, 1978).

10. Cal Beisner, *The Teachings of Witness Lee and the Local Church* (San Juan Capistrano: Christian Research Institute, 1978), pp. 2-7. For a fuller discussion, see Walter Martin, *The New Cults* (Santa Ana, CA: Vision House, 1980), pp. 379-408.

11. Bjorck, et al., "The 'Jesus Only' or 'Oneness Pentecostal' Movement."

12. Gregory A. Boyd, *Oneness Pentecostals and the Trinity* (Grand Rapids, MI: Baker, 1992), p. 199. Boyd's excellent text has been criticized because of minor problems and his somewhat process, or "open," view of God in *Trinity and Process*. But none of this detracts from its value.

13. For a good illustration see J. F. Solomon, "Questions on the Godhead with Bible Answers," tract no. 125, (Hazelwood, MO: Pentecostal Publishing House, n.d.).

14. J. G. Melton, *The Encyclopedia of American Religion*, vol. 1 (Wilmington, NC: McGrath Publishing House, 1978), p. 288.

15. Transcript, "The Trinity or Jesus Only: What Do the Scriptures Teach?" pp. 75, 80.

16. Hazelwood, MO: Pentecostal Publishing House, Tract No. 111, no author or date.

17. Given in *The Discerner*, Vol. 14, no. 12 (1994), pp. 8-9, citing David Bernard, *The New Birth: Series in Pentecostal Theology*, Vol. 1 (Word Aflame Press, 1983), p. 18 and the UPCI Tract, "Why," p. 15.

18. Boyd, pp. 216-17.

19. James Bjornstad, transcript of an address before the Evangelical Theological Society, December 16, 1983 citing Maurice Gordon, "An Expose and Comprehensive Refutation of the Most Diabolical Religious Hoax and Scandal in History" (Denver, CO: Lovingway Church, n.d.).

20. Lorraine Boettner, *Studies in Theology* (Nutley, NJ: Presbyterian and Reformed, 1980), pp. 144-145 citing B. B. Warfield, *Biblical Doctrines*, p. 204.

21. Henry J. Heydt, *The Chosen* People Question Box II (Englewood Cliffs, NJ: American Board of Missions to the Jews, 1976), pp. 18-19.

22. Bjorck Bjornstad and Spraker.

23. Bowman, p. 25.

24. *The Oxford Dictionary of the Christian Church* (London: Oxford, 1977), p. 1594; Gleason Archer, *Encyclopedia of Bible Difficulties* (Grand Rapids, MI: Zondervan, 1982), p. 361. For treatments see E. W. Bickersteth, *The Trinity* (Grand Rapids, MI: Kregel, rpt., 1969) and Cal Beisner, *God in Three Persons* (Wheaton, IL: Tyndale House, 1984).

25. Wilbur King, "How We Must be Baptized," tract (Salem, OR: n.d.), p. 4.

26. Harold O. J. Brown, *Heresies* (Garden City, NY: Doubleday, 1984), pp. 99-100.

27. Boettner, p. 133.

28. Ibid., p. 135.

29. Ibid., p. 136.

30. Ibid., p. 139.

31. Harold Brown, *Heresies*, pp. 1-3.

32. Bowman, p. 27.

33. Cited in *The Discerner*, Vol. 14, no. 12 (1994), p. 10.

34. S. M. Jackson, *The New Schaff-Herzog Encyclopedia of Religious Knowledge*, Vol. VII, "Monarchianism" (Grand Rapids, MI: Baker Book House, 1977), pp. 453-461.

35. James Hastings, *Encyclopedia of Religions and Ethics*, article on "Monarchianism," Vol. 8, pp. 779-781; cf. "Adoptionism" (New York: Charles Schribner's Sons, n.d.).

36. Philip Schaff, *History of the Christian Church*, Vol. II (Grand Rapids: William B. Eerdman's Publishing Company, 1976), pp. 571-583.

37. Louis Berkhof, *Systematic Theology* (Grand Rapids: William B. Eerdman's Publishing Company, 1974), p. 82.

38. J. N. D. Kelly, *Early Christian Doctrines* (San Francisco: Harper & Row, Publishers, 1978), p. 119, cf., 115-123.

39. Berkhof, *Systematic Theology.*

40. Hastings, *Encyclopedia of Religions and Ethics.*

41. Everett F. Harrison, *Baker's Dictionary of Theology* (Grand Rapids: Baker Book House, 1972), p. 361.

42. Robert L. Dabney, *Lectures in Systematic Theology* (Grand Rapids: Zondervan Publishing House, 1972), p. 175.

43. Bernhard Lohse, *A Short History of Christian Doctrine: From the First Century to the Present* (Philadelphia: Fortress Press, 1978), pp. 42-43.

44. J. D. Douglas, *The New International Dictionary of the Christian Church* (Grand Rapids: Zondervan Publishing House, 1979), p. 986.

45. Lohse, p. 42.

46. Douglas, p. 670.

47. John E. Meeter, *Selected Shorter Writings of Benjamin B. Warfield—Vol. I*, "Antitrinitarianism" (Nutley, NJ: Presbyterian and Reformed Publishing Company, 1970), p. 89.

48. Ibid.

49. Schaff, p. 576.

50. E. H. Klotsche, *The History of Christian Doctrines* (Grand Rapids: Baker Book House, 1979), p. 59.

51. William G. Rusch, *The Trinitarian Controversy* (Philadelphia: Fortress Press, 1980), p. 9.

52. See note 10.

53. Dowley, p. 111.

54. Berkhof, p. 79.

55. Boettner, p. 128.

56. Klotsche, p. 60; Kelly, p. 120.

57. Dabney.

58. Dowley, p. 111.

59. J. G. Davies, *The Early Christian Church: A History of Its First Five Centuries* (Grand Rapids: Baker Book House, 1980), p. 138.

60. Schaff, pp. 582-583.

61. Jackson, p. 457.

62. Schaff.
63. Klotsche, p. 61.
64. I.e., as an eternal Person, in contrast to a temporary mode or expression.
65. Jackson, p. 457.
66. Berkhof, p. 80.
67. Douglas, p. 870.
68. Jackson, p. 457.
69. Berkhof, p. 77.
70. Seiberg, p. 164.
71. Klotsche, p. 61.
72. Berkhof, p. 77.
73. Dowley, p. 111.
74. Hastings, Vol. 8, p. 780.
75. Ibid., p. 169.
76. Harrison, p. 465.
77. Hastings, Vol. 8, p. 780.
78. Schaff, Vol. 2, p. 576.
79. Hastings, Vol. 8, p. 780.
80. Charles Hodge, *Systematic Theology*, Vol. 1 (Grand Rapids: William B. Eerdman's Publishing Co., 1981), p. 452.
81. Schaff, Vol. 2, p. 572; Davies, p. 136; Berkhof, p. 77; Hastings, Vol. 8, p. 773.
82. Steve Lagoon, "What About Oneness Pentecostals—Part 3," *The Discerner*, Vol. 14, no. 12 (1994), pp. 6-7.
83. Benjamin B. Warfield, *Biblical and Theological Studies* (Philadelphia: Presbyterian and Reformed Publishing Company, 1968), pp. 35-37, 47, 51.
84. Dabney, p. 177.
85. A. H. Strong, *Systematic Theology: A Compendium* (Old Tappan, NJ: Fleming H. Revelle Co., 1976), p. 326.
86. E. W. Bickersteth, *The Trinity* (Grand Rapids: Kregel Publications, 1969), p. 124.
87. James Bjornstad, transcript of a lecture delivered to the Evangelical Theological Society, December 16, 1983. Similar content is found in Walter Bjorck and James Bjornstad, "Jesus Only: A New Modalistic Interpretation of the Trinity," *Contemporary Christianity*, Jan-March 1969, pp. 1-4. Cf. Bjornstad, Bjorck, and Spraker.
88. Boettner, pp. 107-108.
89. Gregory A. Boyd, "Sharing Your Faith with a Oneness Pentecostal," Part 1, *Christian Research Journal*, Winter 1991, p. 7.

Rajneesh

INFO AT A GLANCE

Name: Bhagwan Shree Rajneesh

Purpose: Realization of personal divinity through yoga meditation and kundalini yoga; experimentation upon and bringing forth of the "new man." Rajneesh's writings and lectures form the platform for "enlightenment."

Founder: The late Bhagwan Shree Rajneesh.

Source of authority: No absolute authority exists with the possible exception of personal experience.

Revealed teachings: Yes.

Claim: Rajneesh was one of the very few (if not only) fully enlightened masters in the world today.

Theology: Eclectic.

Examples of occult potential: Tantric yoga, spiritism.

Key literature: The writings of Rajneesh, such as *The Rajneesh Bible, Vol. 1; Sannyas* magazine.

Attitude toward Christianity: Rejecting.

Quote:

"To tell you the truth, Jesus is a mental case. . . . He carries the same kind of mind as Adolph Hitler. He is a fascist." (Bhagwan Shree Rajneesh, *The Rajneesh Bible, Vol. 1,* 1985, pp. 9–10.)

"God is the greatest lie ever invented by man." (Rajneesh, personal interview, ABC's "Good Morning America," July 18, 1985.)

"Obedience [to God] is the greatest sin." (Rajneesh, *The Rajneesh Bible, Vol. 1.,* p. 368.)

"My ashram makes no difference between the Devil and the Divine. . . . I use all sorts of energies." (Rajneesh in Swami Anand Yarti, *The Sound of Running Water: A Photo Biography of Bhagwan Shree Rajneesh and His Work 1974–1978* (1980), p. 382.)

DOCTRINAL SUMMARY

God: Impersonal pantheistic essence.

Jesus: A highly evolved man who taught Vedanta Hinduism, among other things.

The Christ: Higher consciousness; for example, Jesus became the Christ (God-realized).

Salvation: By personal effort through use of Rajneesh's psychologized occult techniques.

Man: Inwardly divine.

Sin: Ignorance of personal divinity, mistakes.

Satan: The unenlightened mind, which deceives everyone.

The Fall: Symbolic; man's fallen condition results from his animal ancestry.

The Bible: A document of analogies not to be taken literally.

Death: A spiritual advance.

Heaven and Hell: Temporary states of mind or experiences; God judges no one.

Ram Dass

RELIGIOUS
SCIENCE OF MIND

Info at a Glance

Name: Hanuman Foundation, Ram Dass (Richard Alpert).

Purpose: To further spiritual awakening in society.

Source of authority: Hindu and Buddhist sources, with Ram Dass as the interpreter.

Revealed teachings: Yes.

Examples of occult potential: Eastern meditation; development of psychic powers; spiritism.

Key literature: The books by Ram Dass, such as *Be Here Now; The Only Dance There Is; Grist for the Mill; Journey of Awakening.*

Attitude toward Christianity: Rejecting.

Quote:

"When I said that God came to the United States in the form of LSD, I was quoting my teacher . . . one of the purest and highest beings I have met [who said] . . . 'LSD is like a Christ coming to America'. . . . I honor LSD." (Ram Dass, *The Only Dance There Is*, p. 14.)

"Krishna, Christ, Durga, Kali—all of them [are] the same. The ocean made manifest in different forms. Different strokes for different folks. Each a form you need, if you need form." (Ram Dass, *Grist for the Mill*, p. 153.)

Note: Ram Dass was in the vanguard of the cultural swing to Eastern metaphysics several decades ago; through his writings his influence has been considerable.

Doctrinal Summary

God: Impersonal being and consciousness.

Jesus: An enlightened man.

The Christ: Higher (divine) consciousness.

Man: Inwardly divine.

Sin: Ignorance.

Salvation: By enlightenment.

The Bible: One of many scriptures; interpreted mystically.

Death: A spiritual advance.

Heaven and Hell: States of mind or temporary places.

RELIGIOUS SCIENCE (SCIENCE OF MIND)

INFO AT A GLANCE

Name: United Church of Religious Science (Science of Mind).

Purpose: To help people recognize their essential unity with God, thereby achieving spiritual power and control over their life, bringing abundance and satisfaction.

Founder: Ernest Holmes (1887–1960).

Source of authority: The writings of Ernest Holmes; and the individual "Divine Mind." Most Religious Science ministers and teachers utilize Holmes' *The Science of Mind* as a "Bible." Holmes writings are held to be generally authoritative, although there is a freedom to expand on his ideas in light of one's own "higher consciousness" and the basic principles of Science of Mind.

Claim: To teach the true teachings of Christ.

Occult dynamics: An openness to parapsychological research and certain categories or practices of the psychic/occult world.

Key literature: *The Science of Mind*, by Ernest Holmes; *Science of Mind* (periodical).

Attitude toward Christianity: Rejecting.

Quotes:

"God holds nothing against us, therefore, we need never worry about our relationship with Him."[1]

—Ernest Holmes, *Words That Heal Today*

"Who is Christ? . . . [he is] not the 'only begotten Son of God.'"[2]

—Ernest Holmes, *The Science of Mind*

"Find me one person who is for something and against nothing, who is redeemed enough not to condemn others out of the burden of his soul, and I will find another savior, another Jesus, and an exalted human being. Find me one person who no longer has any fear of the universe, or of God, or of man, or of anything else, and you will have brought to me someone in whose presence we may sit and fear shall vanish as clouds before the sunlight. Find me someone who has redeemed his own soul, and he shall become my redeemer."[3]

—Ernest Holmes, *Sermon by the Sea*

References to Vol. 1, *The Encyclopedia of New Age Beliefs* (1996): Attitudinal Therapy; Altered States of Consciousness; Angel Contact; Dream Work; Enlightenment; Meditation; New Age Inner Work; New Age Intuition; New Age Medicine; Visualization.

Note: Although the terms Religious Science and Science of Mind are technically distinguished, we have employed them interchangeably in accordance with popular usage.

DOCTRINAL SUMMARY

God: Impersonal Mind.

Jesus: A great man who expertly utilized Science of Mind principles and became "Christ conscious," i.e., aware of his own divinity.

The Christ: The divine part of all people.

Holy Spirit: Universal subjectivity.

Trinity: Various triune aspects of reality.

Salvation: By knowledge and positive thinking.

Man: Inwardly divine.

Sin: Error or ignorance.

Satan: A Christian myth.

Second Coming: A Christian myth.

The Fall: Into error.

The Bible: One of many sacred scriptures.

Death: An illusion.

Hell and Heaven: States of mind.

INTRODUCTION AND HISTORY

Religious Science (RS) and its teaching, Science of Mind, are the syncretistic brainchild of Ernest Holmes (1887–1960), who weaved parts of Eastern religions and occult philosophy into a "power of positive thinking" worldview. The late Norman Vincent Peale—himself a promoter of occult and Eastern movements*—said of Holmes: "Only those who knew me as a boy can fully appreciate what Ernest Holmes did for me. Why, he made me a positive thinker!"[4] Holmes' influence has been substantial. For example, today there are about 75 titles published by Science of Mind publications. Most are by Ernest Holmes, but popular modern authors in Religious Science include William Hornaday, Willis Kinnear, David Seabury and others who continue Holmes' tradition. Their combined writings have influenced millions. On the internet one can find hundreds of RS congregations in the United States, plus many others in about 25 countries.

Ernest Holmes

Ernest Holmes' spiritual odyssey[5] began as a young man with the influence of Ralph Waldo Emerson, who was himself influenced by Swedenborgianism, spiritism and Hinduism. (As with Charles Fillmore, founder of Unity School of Christianity, and others, it was partly the influence of Emerson that moved Holmes away from a more biblical worldview.) By the time he was 20, Holmes had rejected Christianity as a viable option for life. He went on to study Christian Science, hypnotism, psychic phenomena, theosophy and spiritism, and was influenced by them all.

Holmes regularly attended séances held by a Mr. Wiggin and was "terrifically impressed by him."[6] At first, uncertain about the idea of spirits speaking through human mediums, he vowed to continue further research. His brother's biography reports, "In later years, he did follow through and attended seances on unnumbered

---

*He has written supporting forewords to a number of nonChristian and psychically oriented books; for example, Helen Keller's *My Religion*, a book about her occult Swedenborgian faith.

occasions."[7] However, he ultimately decided that spiritism was limited in some ways, preferring to trust in himself rather than rely on spirit communications. Despite rejecting spiritism as a personal practice, spiritistic philosophy continued to hold an interest for him. The influence of such famous mediums as Emanuel Swedenborg, Helena Blavatsky, Mary Baker Eddy[8] and others, as well as mystics like Phineas P. Quimby and Meister Eckhart, all had their part in formulating the worldview of Ernest Holmes, Science of Mind and its many modern counterparts. Eventually Holmes coalesced his thoughts in *The Science of Mind* (1926), which became the standard textbook of Religious Science, which became The Church of Religious Science and, later, the United Church of Religious Science, the corporate name undergirding his teachings today.

As is true with most "new" religions, Religious Science practitioners tend to avoid associations to the word "occult." Followers of Holmes tend to deny that Holmes promoted the occult or that his philosophy is occult. However, a study of his life and teachings can lead to no other conclusion. Indeed, Holmes' interest in psychic healing resulted in The Holmes Center for Research in Holistic Healing (founded in 1971 as The Ernest Holmes Research Foundation), which was for many years devoted "solely to research in mental/spiritual/psychic healing." Its directors have included such famous people as Robert Young ("Father Knows Best"); Louis Lundborg, retired board chairman of The Bank of America; Norman Cousins, editor of *Saturday Review*; and Maurice Stans, former United States Secretary of Commerce.[9]

In recent years, Science of Mind has delved more and more into the psychic arena. Its yearly symposiums since 1974 have often dealt with psychic and spiritistic research involving lecturers such as Olga Worrall, William Tiller, Thelma Moss, J. B. Rhine, Gerald Jampolsky, Elmer Green, Hans Engel, Lawrence LeShan, Albert Villoldo and Harold Sherman, all of whom are either parapsychologists, spiritists, psychics or their sympathizers.[10] As the standard Religious Science text, *The Science of Mind* declares, "Spirit communication must be possible."[11]

Spiritist and noted consciousness explorer Jean Houston has written the Foreword to the latest edition of *The Science of Mind* text and, incidentally, has referred to Holmes' Science of Mind as "one of the leading viewpoints in modern metaphysics." The Science of Mind website (www.scienceofmind.com/wwb.html) includes "favorite links" to numerous occultists and occult organizations—Hindu occultist Sai Baba, New Agers and spiritists Caroline Myss and Marianne Williamson, the spiritistic Findhorn Foundation and others.

The United Church of Religious Science was founded in 1927, and is the umbrella organization for about 140 U.S. chartered Religious Science churches. The Holmes Institute is a "graduate center for ministerial education and consciousness studies." A subdivision offers a year long 48 lesson extension study course in RS principles keyed to *The Science of Mind*. It was prepared by Ernest Holmes and has had tens of thousands of graduates. It basically helps one to understand and apply the ideas of Science of Mind, offering assistance through correspondence between the Institute and the individual.

PRACTICE AND TEACHINGS

The Science of Mind website lists the following as its basic principles under the heading, "What We Believe," which is taken from the first issue of *Science of Mind* magazine, October, 1927, written by Ernest Holmes:

- We believe in God, the Living Spirit Almighty. . . .

- We believe in the incarnation of the Spirit in everyone and that all people are incarnations of the One Spirit.

- We believe in the eternality, the immortality, and the continuity of the individual soul, forever and ever expanding.

- We believe that Heaven is within us and that we experience it to the degree that we become conscious of it. . . .

- We believe in the unity of all life, and that the highest God and the innermost God is one God.

- We believe that God is personal to all who feel his Indwelling Presence.

- We believe in the direct revelation of Truth through the intuitive and spiritual nature of the individual, and that any person may become a revealer of Truth who lives in close contact with the indwelling God.

- We believe that the Universal Spirit, which is God, operates through a Universal Mind, which is the Law of God; and that we are surrounded by this Creative Mind which receives the direct impress of our thought and acts upon it.

- We believe in the healing of the sick through the power of this Mind.

- We believe in the control of conditions through the power of this Mind. . . .

Religious Science is a syncretistic system that attempts to harmonize all religions by claiming they contain the same divine truth. As Ernest Holmes put it, "The varying faiths of mankind are unnumbered, but the primal faith of the race is today, as of old, the One Faith; an instructive reliance upon the Unseen, which we have learned to call God. Religion is One. Faith is One. Truth is One. There is One Reality at the heart of all religions, whether their name be Hindu, Mohammedan, Christian or Jewish."[12]

Such an attitude, of course, runs into fatal problems when one examines what various religions actually teach. For example, the Bible declares that Jesus Christ is God (John 1:1–3, 14; Colossians 2:9), but such an idea is blasphemous to a Muslim or a Jew. The impersonal, undefined and amoral Brahman (eternal Spirit) of Hinduism is entirely unlike the personal, revealed and holy Jehovah of the Bible. And both early and late Buddhist beliefs are contrary to Christian, Islamic or Vedantic Hindu beliefs. To claim that all religions are essentially the same is therefore a grave error; the facts of comparative religion do not allow such a conclusion. (See the chapter Baha'i World Faith, critique section.)

Religious Science believes that all people and nature are part of God, the One Spirit or omnipresent Divine Essence. "Every man is an incarnation of God. . . . Our spiritual evolution is a gradual awakening to the realization that the

Spirit is center, source and circumference of all being. It is in everything, around everything and through everything, and It is everything."[13] Unless men and women realize this truth and consciously appropriate their Oneness with God by personal choice, they will not receive any spiritual benefits but will remain in various degrees of spiritual darkness. "The Divine nature must be and is infinite; but we can know only as much of this nature as we permit to flow through us. . . ."[14]

It is through faith (not a biblical faith, but "spiritualization of thought" or positive thinking) that people can claim their oneness with God and receive Its power in their lives. "Religious science not only emphasizes this unity of God and man, it teaches us that in such degree as our thought becomes spiritualized, it actually manifests the Power of God. . . . Religious Science teaches that right thinking can demonstrate [provide] success and abundance . . . and that true salvation comes only through true enlightenment, through a more complete union of our lives with the Invisible."[15] Other basic Religious Science teachings include a belief that people and the universe are fundamentally good and that everyone will be eventually united to the Divine, never having been truly separate from It in essence, only in consciousness.

Positive Affirmations and Negative Confessions

The average Science of Mind practitioner utilizes a type of "positive affirmation" common to nearly all New Thought religions. These "prayers" attempt to change the individual's mind about something, and they can be used to attempt to exert control over other persons, things and events. Because practitioners believe they can unite their minds to the Divine Mind they believe they can, potentially, divinely control their environment and life. They believe that they may function "as God," and that whatever they desire may be realized. There is a relationship here to the premises of occult magic. For example, in *Magic: An Occult Primer*, occultist David Conway speaks in similar terms of the power of the mind, by which practitioners, with the help of spiritual forces, can control the environment and attain whatever they desire.

Craig Carter, in *How to Use the Power of Mind in Everyday Life,* discusses how Religious Science principles work, based on the alleged divine potential of the human mind:

If, for example, your consciousness is one of sickness, you will be sick. Deliberately alter it to one of well-being (prosperity, love, security, happiness, or whatever good thing you desire), and you will soon have that which corresponds to the new state of your belief.

This happens because behind every condition is a belief, and if you can change the belief, you can change the condition . . . the changing of your belief is entirely within your own control.

Because the outer world of your personal experience follows the model of your inner world of mental causation, every time you say, "I am . . ." and add something to it, you set into motion a mental Law of Correspondence, which tends to bring about in actual experience whatever corresponds to your word—your state of consciousness—about yourself. Say, "I feel wonderful!" and that Law will bring you more of something to feel wonderful about. But say to yourself, "I am tired," and you most certainly will be.[16]

If, for whatever reason, practitioners are unable to realize their affirmations, they must begin a process of argument with themselves. "If you cannot achieve such an immediate realization, you must anticipate 'arguing' with yourself. This is a standard technique by which you affirm your belief in peace, denying any contrary appearance, disputing the reality of problems, asserting your belief in answers. Continuing in this fashion, your goal is to attain that state of realization where you can say, *believing,* 'I am at peace.' And at that moment, the great Law of Life will, in truth, have brought you peace!"[17]

Holmes and Kinnear note a point of caution here:

In giving a spiritual mind treatment one should stop when he finds himself tensing and trying to force something to happen. For this "forcing" is an indication that he recognizes the presence of a hostile, opposing power which is arrayed against him, and which he must overcome. This is a belief in duality, the Presence of God and a

supposed opposite; good and evil, health and sickness, prosperity and poverty.

There is nothing but God and good in the universe. Good could only contribute to man's growth and development. *Nothing* is ever trying to oppose him. The secret of accomplishment is in "letting" this good come forth.[18]

Based on this, we can see that the goal in Religious Science is "taking charge of your life by *creating your own destiny.*"[19] The God of Scripture, therefore, does not control our lives; as "God" we do. The following "affirmations" to bring about such control are typical examples of Religious Science methods:[20]

Treatment for Relationships: I now accept God's Love as the law of all my relationships with other people. I see God's Life in them; their life in God. I am in harmony with that Life, for it is my life, too. The God in me salutes the God in all whom I meet today. For this blessing I do give thanks.

Treatment to Remove False Conditions: I know that there is no power opposed to God. There is no false growth or wrong condition in God's Life. That Life is my life now. I let go every contrary belief. I believe only in God, and I give myself utterly to His right action in my life.

Treatment for Healing: Infinite Mind knows only good, and is not confused. I let that Mind be wholly expressed in me. I now see the Father's Perfection in all that I am. It knows how to heal me, and I release my needs to God's action and see myself whole and perfect.

Meditation on "High Vision": The highest God and the innermost God is One God. God, the source of all things, is also that which I am. God's creative activity in me now reaches a point where I can recognize Him for all that He is. As my mind opens up in this new awareness I know that I am the One, and all is complete and perfect.

In the above affirmations, biblical passages are supplied to "support" each affirmation— Psalm 89:1; John 11:41; Psalm 82:6; Colossians 4:2 respectively. These Scriptures, however, in their biblical context, do not in any sense support such affirmations. As anyone with a Bible can see, they either oppose the affirmations or are irrelevant to the ideas in them. Only when these Scriptures are taken out of context and placed into a Science of Mind worldview, and thus had their biblical meanings redefined, can they be interpreted as supporting the affirmations.

There is, of course, an element of truth, biblical and psychological, in the idea of concentrating or meditating on that which is positive. Concentrating on the negative is certainly of little value. Scripture tells us of the benefits of a merry heart; and it says to rejoice always and to meditate on that which is good (Proverbs 17:22; 1 Thessalonians 5:16-18; Philippians 4:4-8). Religious Science, then, has a kernel of truth. But from a Christian perspective there is a major problem. Given biblical revelation, Religious Science has no logical reason upon which to rejoice, since their monistic philosophy actually causes them to meditate upon that which is *not* true. For example, meditation upon oneself as divine, as part of God, is a reflection of self-deception not spiritual enlightenment. The universe is not run by an impersonal divine law that is at our beck and call to answer our every wish. Biblically, the universe is run by an infinite, personal sovereign God, who is working out His own plan, which people cannot alter.

Nevertheless, according to Religious Science, no such God exists and people control their own destiny by consciousness alone. This is why "the gospel of Ernest Holmes" is termed "creative self dominion." The universe and its inviolate, impersonal laws are foolproof. Whatever our thoughts and actions, good or evil, they will bring about a logical corresponding result. Like a magnet, we are always attracting either good or evil to ourselves or repelling one or the other. It is impossible to escape this immutable law of cause and effect that governs all things.[21] However, nature's laws will "obey" people if they first understand and obey them. "*This Law works automatically until it is consciously changed.* To learn how to think is to learn how to live, for our thoughts go into a Medium that is Infinite in Its ability to be and to do."[22]

The reasoning is as follows. People are potentially, one with divine Mind; that is, people are God's thought, although they may not know it. And the creation is the image of God's thought. So thought controls the image of thought, and if a person's consciousness is properly situated, he or she will be able to control the creation and manifest the preexisting divine harmony, rather than succumb to an allegedly false appearance.

If we can control our thoughts and always affirm the good—regardless of contrary appearances—then only the good will be our portion in life. Whatever we desire—happiness, marriage, a new car or home, money, a better business, whatever—"There should be a quiet unstained acceptance of the fact that *it is right for us, is possible for us and already is ours in Mind.*"[23] All we need do is affirm it "into" existence. If we are depressed, in poverty or burdened with a serious illness, all we need to do is to recognize that this is only an *appearance,* not a reality. Through the principles of Religious Science, we can come to understand that the "appearance" is not ultimately real, and let what is real manifest its divine perfection in our lives. Religious Science does not say we never experience ourselves as sick, poor or lonely; it says that such conditions are unnecessary, that the "appearance" can give way to the divine reality. Since the ultimate reality is Divine Mind, and since we are "created" out of it, "we are made of and possess God-like qualities and we have the right and the ability to develop and use them. In fact it is necessary for us to do this if we are to fully express the Life within us."[24] The diagram[25] on the next page illustrates in simple fashion the basic premises of Religious Science.

THEOLOGY

Christianity

Ernest Holmes was rather frank with his opinion of other religions, even his own. "I didn't like any of the religions I was acquainted with and so I made up one that I did like."[26] In one of his last statements before his death, he reflected, "I learned that you must develop faith and confidence in your *own* interpretation of God, man and the universe."[27] Nevertheless, Holmes and Religious Science both claim to be

Christian. Holmes declared that RS "incorporates the precepts of Jesus."[28] "Science of Mind is one of the most significant spiritual experiments since the time of Jesus, I believe. . . . it is Christianity oriented, *fundamentally following the teachings of Jesus*."[29] Despite this, RS claims to have no message "for those who believe that religion is a fixed deposit of revelation, handed down to men in final and complete form."[30]

The Mechanics of Mental Science
God=One Reality=Good=The True Spiritual Universe

Divine Mind / Divine Truth

Blocked

Free-Flowing

PROBLEM

Ignorance
↓
Stifles Power
↓
Lack of
Abundance
(divine life
blocked)
↓
Living in
Unreality
(sin, disease,
crime
poverty,
suffering,
disharmony,
etc.)

SOLUTION

Self-Realization
↓
Spiritualization
of Thought
(faith) by
Positive
Affirmations
(prayer)
↓
Releases
Divine Power
↓
Abundance
(manifesting
divine life)
↓
Living in Reality
(health, joy,
prosperity,
power, divine
perfection and
abundance,
unity)

Man's Mind and Environment

Man = God's thought
Creation = image of God's thought
Thought controls image of thought;
man's divine consciousness
controls creation

Holmes and modern Science of Mind adherents do not believe that biblical Christianity reflects the true teachings of Jesus, even though "it is a historical fact that Jesus Christ lived and taught what the New Testament says He taught."[31] It will become evident in the following that, while they wished to have the benefits of claiming to be followers of Jesus' true teachings, Holmes and his followers deny Jesus' teachings, because their worldview demands it.

Holmes and modern Religious Science writers only rarely assault Christian doctrines openly or directly; they undermine them indirectly. Thus, the "old theology" represents "a superstitious approach to Truth,"[32] or "dogmatism and superstition"[33] or "unreasonable" ideas that tarnish light and truth.[34] In a *Science of Mind* article, H. G. Hill argues in a similar manner. "Now the churches that are shackled and bound by archaic items, offend the modern intellectual and critical minds of up-to-date men. The error is fundamentally one of conceiving of Truth as fixed, static, incapable of change or progress."[35]

Holmes was particularly sensitive about the Christian teaching of eternal punishment and declared that "any religion that casts a shadow across the final deliverance of everyman's soul was born out of chaos."[36] Holmes emphasized, "I do not believe in hell, the devil, damnation, or in any future state of punishment; or any other of the fantastic ideas which have been conceived in the minds of those who are either morbid, or who have felt the need of a future state of damnation to which to consign the immortal souls of those who have not agreed with their absurd doctrines. God does not punish people."[37] It is clear from the Gospels, however, that Jesus taught a belief in a literal, personal Satan and a literal place of future eternal punishment (Matthew 25:46; Luke 4:1-13). Holmes declares that "God does not punish people," but Jesus said of unbelievers, "These will go away into eternal punishment" (Matthew 25:46; cf. Colossians 2:9). God the Father declares, "I will punish the world for its evil and the wicked for their iniquity" (Isaiah 13:11). God also says, "I will punish the men who are stagnant in spirit, who say in their hearts, 'The Lord will not do good or evil'" (Zephaniah 1:12).

If Holmes was the man whose "remarkable mind probed the farthest reaches of the universe and existence,"[38] we might at least expect that mind to have an accurate knowledge of the teachings of Jesus and the Bible. But no. Religious Science opposes conservative Christianity,[39] and its claim to be Christian cannot be substantiated.

The Bible

In RS, the Bible is not held in particularly high regard. Due to its metaphysical premises, Religious Science abandons conventional rules of biblical interpretation, which support its literal interpretation. A person who believed the Bible literally, according to Holmes, had to be healed of his spiritual ignorance.[40] Even though accepted rules of interpretation are universal and well established (see, for example, McQuilkin's *Understanding and Applying the Bible: An Introduction to Hermeneutics* or Berkhof's *Principles of Biblical Interpretation*), RS ignores these rules and transforms the Bible into a Science of Mind text. For example, *Science of Mind* magazine contains "The Daily Guide to Richer Living," which quotes the Scriptures and comments on them. But the comments have little or nothing to do with the accepted meanings of the Bible. Rather, they are figuratively reinterpreted into rejecting what they actually teach. At best the Bible is only a guide for RS. As Holmes states, "Probably God is love—this we believe—but we do not know it just because the Bible says so."[41] (Then how do we know it?) In *The Wonder of Man*, Joseph Krimsky, M.D., states that "the presence of myth, miracle and legend in our Bible"[42] should not concern us because the truth of RS will shine through regardless.

Not unexpectedly, Science of Mind often uses the "Aramaic interpretation" of the Bible as proposed by Rocco A. Errico, a student of George Lamsa. Although they claim scholarship, Errico's or Lamsa's use of biblical data is biased and without justification. RS only employs this Aramaic misuse of the Bible because it supports their own beliefs. (See the chapters on New Thought and The Way International for a critique of Lamsa and Errico and the Aramaic interpretation problem.)

God

Science of Mind teaches monism. In essence, it teaches that All is One and All is God and God is Good. Therefore, All is Good because All is God. Everything is perfect, regardless of our sense perception that tells us otherwise. Contrary evidence in personal experience, history or the testimony of Scripture must be discarded as the illusions or misperceptions of unenlightened consciousness.

Science of Mind also teaches panentheism, that God includes the universe but is not exhausted by the universe. The universe is believed to be God's "Body." *The Science of Mind* glossary defines "Body of God" as "the manifest creation in its entirety."[43] "From our point of view this would mean that mind—God— acting as Energy becomes what we know as the physical world, according to Law. They are one and the same thing, but God, being infinite, could never be depleted by what is created."[44] "An evolved soul is always a worshipper of God. He worships God in everything; for God *is* in everything. God not only is in everything, but He is more than everything He is in!"[45]

But when Holmes said that God was "in everything," he did not mean the Christian sense of God's omnipresence. He meant everything is God in essence. "Everything we see is God—the buttercup, the sunset, the morning dew nestling in the petal of a rose; and love and laughter, they are God."[46]

God is ultimately seen as the infinite essence of and beyond all life, an essence that is believed to manifest attributes of personality. In declaring that God was necessarily personal in some sense, Holmes argued, "To think of God simply as an Infinite Principle would be to resolve the Divine Being into an infinite IT, a cold, impersonal Law, containing no warmth or color, and certainly no responsiveness. Such a concept of God would rob man of his Divine Birthright and throw him, empty-handed, into an abyss of Law and Action, without motive or directions. No worse state of mentality could be imagined than one in which man thought of God simply as Principle."[47]

Strictly, a principle cannot be personal. Yet Holmes frequently used various impersonal synonyms to describe God: "The Thing Itself," "One Law," "It," "Principle." This left Holmes in an uncomfortable position of trying to declare the truth of contradictory beliefs. For example, in the following multiple statements, try and determine if God is impersonal or personal. Holmes seemed confused:

As intelligent beings we must realize that God is a universal Presence, a neutral Force, an impersonal Observer, a divine and impartial Giver, forever pouring *Himself or Itself* upon *His or Its* creation.[48]

We do not think of God as a tremendous Person, but we do think of the Spirit as the Infinite Personalness in and through all Life. Infinite, Self-Knowingness is the Abstract Essence of all personality.[49]

We begin to see that there is an Infinite Personalness in the universe, an Infinite Presence (*not an infinite person*) the abstract and universal cause of all personalities. Then it begins to dawn on us that where our life is personified God is personified . . . hence, it is personal to all who understand its inner presence.[50]

It is *not* personal in the sense of a human personality, but *It* contains within *Itself* the qualities which make up personality.[51]

We have stopped looking for the Spirit, because we have found It. It is what you are and It is what I am; we could not be anything else if we tried. . . . We have found It. In the universe, we call It Universal Subjectivity. . . . In our own experience, we call It the subjective state of our thought, which is our individual use of Universal Law. . . . God is Law. There is a Divine Principle which is God. . . . GOD IS MORE THAN LAW OR PRINCIPLE. God is the Infinite Spirit. . . . The One Infinite Person.[52]

Spirit is the Power that knows Itself, [so that] in each one of us, to each one of us, through each one of us, something is personalized, and that which is personalized is personal to its own personification.[53]

Note that Holmes, who criticized Christianity as chaotic, unreasonable, absurd and irrational, has in these statements declared that God is:

Not a Principle	A Principle
Not an It	An It
Not an Infinite Person	An Infinite Person

Holmes also declared that God:

Is not personal	Contains the qualities of personality
Is a neutral Force	Is Infinite Personalness
Is "Itself"	Is "Himself"

What can we say? Of course, in His ultimate nature, God cannot be both personal and impersonal at the same time. Whatever the RS God ultimately is, to its followers it is whatever they want it to be. As Craig Carter states of God: "It is the *Mother* of the Hindu, the *Father* of the Jew, the *Christ* of the West, and the *Buddha* of the East. Yet, It is always and ever One!"[54]

Science of Mind thus offers a God who reveals Himself or Itself in contradictory forms throughout history—good and evil, moral and amoral, personal and impersonal, infinite and finite, and so on. Many people would find such a God unsatisfactory and hardly God at all. Certainly the RS God is not the Christian God. As to the biblical God Holmes declares, "Now we are more enlightened and we realize that there could be *no such* Divine Being."[55]

The Trinity

Religious Science reinterprets the biblical doctrine of the Trinity to conform to its own ideas. "We have every reason to postulate a three-fold nature of the Universal Being, which we shall call Spirit, Soul, and Body."[56] The Spirit is "the Power that knows Itself"; the Soul is "a blind Force, obeying the Will of Spirit," and Body is "the effect of Spirit, working through Law to produce form."[57] Essentially, Spirit "thinks" (or knows within itself), and by the force or power of the Soul, the Body (the physical universe) is produced. The Trinity is also described as follows: "The Spirit directs and guides, the Law executes, and creation is the result. This is the Trinity: the Thing, the way It works, and what it does."[58] (See Doctrinal Section of this book for the biblical doctrine of the Trinity.)

Jesus Christ

According to Religious Science, Jesus Christ was a highly evolved individual who used Science of Mind principles to an expert degree. Science of Mind, like many Eastern religions, does not deny the deity of Jesus per se, only his unique deity. That is, Jesus is as much a part of God as everyone else. Thus, Jesus only realized "the Christ" (deity) as all people can:

> Christ is God in the soul of man. To practice the Presence of God, is to awaken within us the Christ Consciousness. . . . The birth of Christ is not an historical event, but is an eternal incarnation. Christ is born to each age and reborn in every individual soul.[59]

> Jesus is the name of a man. Christ means the Universal Principle of Divine Sonship. . . . Jesus became increasingly the Christ as his mentality increasingly perceived the relationship of the man Jesus to the Christ principle which is inherent in all people.[60]

> ["Jesus" is merely] the name of a man. Distinguished from the Christ. The man Jesus became the embodiment of the Christ.[61]

Biblically, however, Jesus was uniquely *born* the Christ (Luke 2:11); he did not *become* the Christ later (see 1 John 2:22).

RS philosophy explains why it believes that Jesus is fundamentally no different from anyone else. His consciousness is more evolved, but He had the same nature as anyone. In *Words That Heal Today* (ignoring Scriptures such as Matthew 2:2,11 and John 20:28), Holmes declared: "Jesus never expected us to worship him either as a person or a [unique] God."[62] Elsewhere, "Jesus never thought of himself as different from others."[63] "To think of Jesus as being different from other men is to misunderstand his mission and purpose in life. He was a wayshower and proved his way to be a correct one!"[64] Jesus merely utilized a higher, or transcendent, vision, and it was this alone that enabled him to perform miracles. He understood the laws of the universe better than others, but they were still His equal. Everyone has the potential to do the same miracles that Jesus did, because what He did, anyone can do. Why no one ever has, Religious Science cannot say.

Here we discover one of the Achilles' heels of RS, and of New Thought religion generally. If Christ was *not* unique in nature, why has no one ever been like Him? Who else performed His miracles, lived His powerful life, taught His authoritative teachings and rose from the dead? No one. As we pointed out in *Ready with an Answer* (1997), His entire being, everything having to do with Him and everything He did, was unique. Both friends and enemies recognized this. For example, sin of one type or another can be found in every person, including Ernest Holmes, but not in Jesus. Nevertheless, "Anyone who wishes can be just like Jesus." Sinless. But in 2,000 years no one ever has. Does not this affirm a uniqueness of nature and not simply an expression of higher knowledge?[65]

Holmes' book, *The Philosophy of Jesus*, presents a good overview of Science of Mind teaching about Jesus Christ and what RS thinks He taught. Holmes expressed complete confidence that he knew the real meaning of Jesus' words. He believed that Jesus was fully aware that He was teaching Science of Mind principles. Thus, according to Holmes Jesus "discovered" His divinity, in part, through the truth that "God is incarnated in everything," that each person is "a unique incarnation of God."[66] Further, Jesus did not come to save our souls,[67] and Jesus "did not say there is a heaven which God has provided for us in life after this life; he said that heaven is present with us."[68]

RS practitioners do not seem to understand the implications of making Jesus Christ a Science of Mind practitioner. In rejecting the historical standards of interpretation that powerfully document what exactly Jesus taught, they simultaneously reject the standards that document what Ernest Holmes taught. In other words, if we were to say that Ernest Holmes did not teach Religious Science, his followers would obviously reject the assertion, surprised that we could say such a thing. "Why, all this is historical fact." Of course it is. We cannot logically deny what Holmes taught because it is public record. Well, who Jesus is and what He taught about who He is are also public record. For instance, that He was "the only Son of God" was both His claim and that of His followers

(Matthew 16:16; John 3:16, 18; Romans 1:4; 1 John 4:9). Are we to believe Holmes when he declares, "Jesus understood his own nature"?[69] If so, then Religious Science practitioners must rethink their view of Jesus. Indeed, Jesus proved His nature by His resurrection from the dead, something Ernest Holmes neglected. Why, then, should RS practitioners prefer Holmes' interpretations of Jesus over those of Jesus about Himself?

The only way RS can get around this problem and "accept" Jesus while denying everything He plainly stood for is to employ a double standard. That is, RS interprets Jesus' words metaphysically, but they interpret Holmes' words normally. Indeed, a metaphysical interpretation of the writings of Ernest Holmes and RS principles would distort them just as effectively as their interpretations distort Jesus' teachings.

Some RS ministers use duplicity to get their message across. The Reverend Terry Cole-Whittaker was a national personality and New Age positive thinker as well as former pastor of nine large La Jolla, California, Religious Science churches. Rev. Cole-Whittaker adopts the basic Science of Mind philosophy "of Jesus." "You don't have to try to become Godlike, you are"; and "one of the biggest things in life is money."[70] When she claimed, "Jesus Christ is my personal savior," she sounded biblical and some Christians believed her. But she only meant that the Jesus who was enlightened by RS principles was her savior from false beliefs like those in Christianity. Thus, "Most people who use that term [Jesus as personal savior] and "born again," "saved," all that . . . that Jesus is the only son of God and that you . . . are not divine, only Jesus was . . . [are wrong. My view] is that Jesus said in his teaching that we are all what he is."[71]

But an article in the *Los Angeles Times* noted that Rev. Cole-Whittaker did not always speak publicly what she believes privately. Pressed with the possibility of an extremely disadvantaged and crippled person "becoming all that she wants in life," Cole-Whittaker stepped back from the standard Science of Mind doctrine. She also publicly taught that the Lord's Prayer confirms Science of Mind. It is a positive affirmation of what we already have and contains "not one

line" of beseeching in it. Yet privately she told the reporter there are too many beseeching verbs in it for it to be called an affirmative prayer. There is "something wrong in the translation" (obviously, because) "it does not go with what I think is true." She admitted, "I don't always come out and tell the truth as I see it." So she admits to her own lack of frankness. In a public sermon at her church she noted that "being selfish you are selfless"; that the Bible was written in a universal metaphysical language (for attainment of Christ-consciousness), and (in contrast to the above) that literally nothing was impossible for the one who had faith.[72]

Salvation, Works, the Atonement

According to Religious Science, men and women need no salvation from sin, death or the wrath of God. Everyone is already saved, if they will only realize it. In *Gateway to Life*, Holmes states, "The only salvation necessary is from ignorance"; that is, ignorance of one's innate divinity and the negative effects that flow from this ignorance. "There is no need to *seek* unity with God and the Universe. We already have it. It is something we must become aware of."[73] "Today is the day of salvation. This does not mean a salvation of the soul as though it were lost."[74] Holmes, who claimed to "believe in Jesus' teachings," emphasized, "There is no such thing as a lost soul."[75] "It is *impossible* that any soul can be lost."[76] "DEATH CANNOT ROB HIM [MAN] OF ANYTHING IF HE BE IMMORTAL."[77] "We do not have to save the world; the world is not lost, just confused."[78]

On the other hand, Jesus declared, "What good will it be for a man if he gains the whole world, yet forfeits his soul?" (Matthew 16:26). Jesus also said, "The Son of Man has come to save that which was lost" (Matthew 18:11 NAS); and, "I mention it that you may be saved" (John 5:34). Saved from what? From the "resurrection of damnation" (John 5:29; KJV). In context, He was speaking of a resurrection to judgment for those who refused to believe in Him (John 5:24–34). Indeed, Jesus stated clearly that many people were lost. Judas was, and he "went to his own place" (John 17:12, NAS; Acts 1:25). In fact, Jesus taught that many people are on the broad

road that "leads to destruction," because of the many false teachers in the world (Matthew 7:14–15), teachers who lull people into false security that there is no coming judgment to eternal punishment (Matthew 7:26–27,46).

According to Religious Science, then, Jesus Christ is not man's savior from sin; man is his own savior from ignorance. Holmes stated: "The thing that interests me is that every man shall find his savior within himself. If this is the only place he is going to discover God, you may be sure it is the only avenue through which any way-shower shall lead him to God. There is no other way. Jesus knew this."[79] Did Jesus know this? Was He not the One who said, "*I* am the way.... No one comes to the Father except through *me*" (John 14:6)? Did He not say, "*I* am the door" (John 10:7)? Was He not the One who said that, far from there being an inward Savior, evil came from within?

> And He was saying, "That which proceeds out of the man, that is what defiles the man. For from within, out of the heart of men, proceed the evil thoughts and fornications, thefts, murders, adulteries, deeds of coveting and wickedness, as well as deceit, sensuality, envy, slander, pride and foolishness. All these evil things proceed from within and defile the man." (Mark 7:20-23)

Yet Holmes states in *The Science of Mind*, "There is no way we can know God except by studying man. ... If we study the true nature of man, then we shall have delved into the real nature of God."[80] "Nothing can save us but ourselves."[81]

Biblically, however, Jesus is our "Lord and Savior" (2 Peter 1:11; 3:18), "the Savior of the world" (John 4:42) and our "great God and Savior" (Titus 2:13). He did "not come to judge the world but to save it" (John 12:47). "Salvation is found in no on else, for there is no other name under heaven given to men by which we must be saved" (Acts 4:12), because only Christ died for our sins.

Religious Science also teaches a "gospel" of works-salvation,[82] which the New Testament writers condemned as a false gospel (Galatians 1:6-8, chapters 2–3). Holmes declared in *The Science of Mind:*

By man alone come mistakes. By man alone comes salvation.[83]

No one has the power to hurt us or to save us but ourselves.[84]

No one else can do any of this for me. We alone must do the applying for the Science of Mind to be a practical dynamic factor in everyday living. It's up to us.[85]

Jesus said: "I am the way, the truth, and the life: no man cometh unto the Father but by Me." How true this is! We cannot come unto the Father which art in Heaven except through our own nature. Right here, through our own [divine] nature, is the gateway and the path leads to illumination, to realization, to inspiration, to the intuitive perception of everything.[86]

Note Holmes' rejection of Jesus' words here. Jesus taught that the only way to God was "by Me," by faith in Jesus, in His person. Holmes completely ignores this and interprets "Me" as enlightened human nature. This is the typical pattern in Religious Science biblical usage: to cite a verse, ignore its plain meaning and then distort it to teach RS principles.

Also in Religious Science, when forgiveness is referred to, it is a human act. God cannot "forgive" because there is nothing to forgive. Real man is divine and perfect and requires no forgiveness. Unreal man, within his faulty consciousness, may feel the need for forgiveness, but if so, it is his own act to accomplish. "Forgiveness is our own act."[87]

As there is no sin within people to be forgiven, Christ never died for sin, for sin is an illusion. Further, the divine Essence (God) cannot suffer because there is no suffering in the One reality. "God has forever hung Himself upon the cross of men's indifference; God has forever, but without suffering, given Himself but we have not received the gift."[88]

In *The Voice Celestial* (an "inspired" poem) by Ernest and Fenwick Holmes, we read that "Jesus made no claim that he had paid Man's debt to God, nor must God's wrath be stayed nor be appeased by sacrifice of blood."[89] Further, Jesus never even died on the Cross. "Concealed from sight in sacred mystery. In which the Savior *seems* to die and then the drama ends when he is seen again. The world should witness, it should clearly see there is no death."[90]

But the Scripture and Jesus Himself denied Holmes' teachings when they claim (many times) that He came to die for the world's sins. For instance:

Just as the Son of Man did not come to be served, but to serve, and to give his life as a ransom for many" (Matthew 20:28 NAS).

This is my blood of the covenant, which is to be shed on behalf of many for forgiveness of sins (Matthew 26:28 NAS).

Christ died for our sins according to the Scriptures (1 Corinthians 15:3 NAS).

Without shedding of blood there is no forgiveness (Hebrews 9:22 NAS).

He is the atoning sacrifice for our sins, and not only for ours but also for the sins of the whole world (1 John 2:2).

Religious Science has clearly denied the most plain and fundamental teachings of the Bible, and so it must forfeit the right to be called Christian.

The New Birth

Holmes also redefined the new birth, which to him involved recognizing we are *not* separate from God. "Question—What does the Bible mean by being born again? Answer—Jesus said, 'ye must be born again.' His disciples asked, how can this be? And Jesus answered, 'Ye must be born of Spirit.' We must have a spiritual rebirth. We must be born out of the belief in externalities into the belief of inner realities, out of the belief that we are separated from God, into the belief that we are a part of a Unitary Wholeness [God]."[91] In *The Philosophy of Jesus* Holmes said: "There must come a new impulse to the mind, a new way of looking at things. This is what Jesus called the new birth."[92]

However, the essence of Christian conversion is to recognize oneself as a sinner separate from God and to turn from sin toward God (repentance) by placing faith (trust) in Christ's death for one's sins. If this happens, regeneration, or the new birth, will have occurred (John 3:3–5). One's nature is changed (2 Corinthians 5:17),

eternal life is imparted (John 6:47, 63) and one will discover a desire to live one's life for the one true God. Essential to this whole process is the necessity of recognizing our separation from God due to sin: "But your iniquities have made a separation between you and your God" (Isaiah 59:2). Unless that separation is removed by faith in Christ who died for our sins, we will remain in a state of alienation from God.

Man

Holmes came to believe that everyone was part of God through his study of Eastern and occult philosophy. When Science of Mind followers read the Bible today, they apply to *all* people what it says about believers only. And since they see Jesus simply as a man who evolved to higher consciousness, or "the Christ consciousness," as anyone may, what Jesus (or other biblical writers) said of himself refers to everyone. For example, Bible statements like the following are applied to every one:

I and my Father are one.

We have the mind of Christ.

We know that we dwell in him, and he in us because he has given us his Spirit.

Beloved, now we are the sons of God . . . and because we are sons God has sent forth the Spirit of his Son into your hearts.

He is the image and glory of God.

Do you not know your body is the temple of the Holy Spirit?

Thus, when a person speaks, God speaks:

God is what I am; God may not be what I appear to be, but what I really am must be God or I wouldn't be.[93]

His mind IS the mind of God.[94]

You are the ALL Conquering Son of God.[95]

God *is,* God is what I am; God may not be what I appear to be, but what I really am must be God, or I wouldn't be.[96]

The Scripture, however, takes a dim view of those who exalt themselves in such a manner:

But you said in your heart . . . I will make myself like the Most High. . . . Nevertheless, you will be thrust down to hell. (Isaiah 14:13–15)

Because your heart is lifted up, and you have said "I am a god," I sit in the seat of God. . . . Yet you are a man and not God. . . . You will die the death of those who are slain. (Ezekiel 28:1–2, 10)

Sin and the Fall

Ernest Holmes rejected the moral nature of sin:

Ernest was definitely against it, even as a word . . . [He said] "I have always taught there is no sin but ignorance, following the belief of Emerson."[97]

This enables us to understand the meaning of evil and sin, which are experiences fabricated by misconception or the reverse use of the law.[98]

Ignorance is the only sin there is. It creates hell, devils, limitation and sickness.[99]

There is no sin but a mistake and no punishment but a consequence.[100]

God does not punish sin. As we correct our mistakes, we forgive our own sins.[101]

According to *The Science of Mind*, original sin, or the Fall, was only symbolic. Events and characters in the Fall are interpreted as symbols of some particular Religious Science belief. Thus death and sin never begin with the disobedience of Adam and Eve, even though Romans 5:12 and 19 state that they do.[102] The Fall, as in Mormon theology, merely represents a spiritual advancement. "The story of the Fall in the Old Testament is a symbolic presentation of the evolution of Man, and his spiritual awakening. Taken literally, this story would be ridiculous."[103]

The Afterlife

Religious Science rejects many other key biblical beliefs. For instance, it teaches that angels are merely thoughts and that demons do not exist, or that they exist only as "false beliefs." Further, there is no bodily resurrection, and heaven and hell do not exist. "There is no resurrection life." "There are no evil spirits." "The Angels are your own protective thoughts in the realm of absolute Truth." "Man makes his own heaven or his own hell right here and now."[104] Even in light of Jesus' clear and consistent teaching that not all would be saved (Matthew 7:13; 23:33; 25:46), Holmes declared: "But I am sure that full and complete salvation will come alike to all. Heaven and hell are states of consciousness in which we now live according to our own state of understanding."[105] "Even the lowest and most hopeless savage will sometime attain to Christ consciousness."[106]

In denying hell, Science of Mind uses the writings of Rocco Errico and his "Aramaic" argumentation. In *Science of Mind* magazine Errico claims, "Is it a place of unending separation from the Presence of God? Certainly not, for these fiery concepts of hell and punishment came from certain misunderstood passages of the Bible and from the interpretations of some of the early church fathers such as Tertullian and Augustine. Hell is not a place where God tortures his 'disobedient' children forever and ever, nor was such a meaning ever intended by the original [Aramaic] language of the Bible."[107]

Holmes worked hard to remove people's fear of death and hell. "We need not fear either God or the devil. There is no devil, and God is Love."[108] In the case of a woman who feared God and was concerned about hell he stated, "It took *work* to remove the woman's fear and belief in hell and damnation."[109] In contrast, Jesus said, "And I say unto you my friends, Be not afraid of them that kill the body, and after that have no more that they can do. But I will forewarn you whom ye shall fear: Fear him, which after he hath killed hath power to cast into hell; yea, I say unto you, Fear him" (Luke 12:4-5).

As in other New Thought religions, Holmes denied death. For him, "we must meet the fear of death by an interior awareness that there is no death."[110] Being a part of God, everyone is destined to return to God. "In the long run nothing can harm the soul. In the long run it is bound to . . . return to its source. . . . We can hasten this completion by conscious choice and cooperation with the law."[111] Further, although he eventually denied belief in classical reincarnation theory, he affirmed various "incarnations" on higher planes, and in general chose to believe whatever he wanted:[112]

Ernest believed that as Divine Beings we take our complete identity with us to the next incarnation, for he did believe in *incarnation*. He believed that we move from one plane of experience in living to another, maintaining our individuality, but never with the necessity of having to be reborn as a human.[113]

Our place hereafter will be what we have made it. . . . We confidently expect to meet friends who are on the other side, and to know and be known. . . . But I cannot base my hopes of immortality on the revelation of anyone but myself.[114]

THE OCCULT

We earlier indicated some of the occult involvement of Holmes and modern Religious Science. Like other psychics, Holmes' life was supernaturally "guided." As a result, he was prepared for the proper psychic instruction when his teacher, Emma Curtis Hopkins, appeared and taught him mysticism. (Hopkins also influenced the Fillmores, of Unity, and many others.[115])

The RS periodical *Science of Mind*, also shows its acceptance of the occult by articles it has carried. For example: "Awakening Your Psychic Power" (July, 1982); "Magic and Matter" (Nov., 1978); "Healing at a Distance" (Oct., 1979); "The Experience of Higher Consciousness" (May, 1979); "Awaken Your Intuition" (April, 1979); "What Meditation Does" (Dec., 1978) and "Energy Healing—How It Works" (Feb., 1979). Other RS writers are also generally sympathetic to the occult. J. H. Krimsky, M.D., discussed the importance of particular areas of psychic research,[116] and the noted Marcus Bach discussed his numerous seance experiences.[117]

Religious Science conferences may include mediums and psychics and discussions of various occult topics. For example, the 1978 and 1979 Holmes Center Symposiums included a discussion by Ivan Tors about his spirit guides and lectures by medium Olga Worrall, psychic W. Brugh Joy, parapsychologists Thelma Moss and Robert Miller and spiritist sympathizer Gerald Jampolsky.[118] The late Elisabeth Kubler-Ross also spoke of her spirit guides.[119]

In the end, personal involvement in the occult is simply left up to the dictates of an individual's communion with "divine Mind." The term "occult" may be frowned upon, but occult activity is permitted, and even encouraged, under phrases like: receiving divine illumination, guidance or inspiration.

Reginald Armors' biography observed of Holmes' own spiritual searching what has become a typical approach for many, if not most, of his followers:

His constant search led him to feel very close to the Infinite Presence. He spent many hours and often days in meditation and communion with It. He believed firmly that everyone can commune with this Presence, talk to It, and receive definite guidance in their lives.

His feelings at such times of meditation and communion, he said, could not be described in words. . . . In his later years, in those many hours each day of meditation, some of his experiences bordered on the purely mystical, and I am sure he was aware of flashes of so-called cosmic consciousness. . . . He did not talk about these glimpses of Reality and would not admit to being classified as a mystic, but his inspirational writings are evidence that, in truth, he was.[120]

Spiritistic Revelation as Literary Inspiration

The above reference to Holmes' "inspirational writings" is relevant. In our *Encyclopedia of New Age Beliefs* several chapters discussed how spiritistic revelation was the source for much modern New Age literature.[121] Similarly, it seems that at least two of Holmes' books were spiritistically inspired, and probably more. *The Voice Celestial*, by Ernest and his brother Fenwick, has four principal characters that often mimic modern spirit guides:

1. "The Farer or Wayfarer."

2. "The Presence or The Voice Celestial, becoming audible to all who develop the inner ear" (psychic perception).

3. "The Scribe or observer who reports the conversations between the Farer and the Presence or Voice."

4. "The master of the ages who appears to the Farer while he is in higher states of consciousness."[122]

In another book, *Your Invisible Power*—Part III, the "author" is obviously not Holmes, although the book bears his name. It is a revelation from a spirit being claiming to be God. The spirit speaks to the reader, saying, "Therefore, you may trust what I shall do, for I Am God."[123] Armor points out that even in his lectures, Holmes "was aware often that his mind would open to the creative influx of this Divine Presence, and at such times he was aware of Spirit speaking through him at levels far beyond his intellectual understanding at the moment. He believed in this inspirational type of speaking."[124]

This kind of experience is fairly common among psychics, mediums, gurus and occultists. Edgar Cayce, Sun Myung Moon, H. P. Blavatsky, Ram Dass and hundreds of others have spoken openly in similar terms of their inspiration by spirits. Further, Armor cites that Holmes admitted not always understanding what he was talking about when he was speaking "inspirationally,"[125] which is another common theme in spiritistic communication. In fact, it is possible that the basic Religious Science philosophy, as outlined in *The Science of Mind* and other texts, was first received spiritistically ("inspirationally") and later edited, because it could be argued Holmes was not capable of producing such philosophical works. Holmes "never believed he was an outstanding author, [but] he acknowledged that pure inspiration played a significant role in his literary efforts."[126] Much of what Armor documented about Holmes leaves no doubt about Holmes' heartfelt interest and participation in spiritistic activities. Consider the following:

[Holmes believed] that revelation was a matter of one's desire to receive enlightenment or inspiration on some given idea. When man places himself in a position to listen or accept, he opens his mind to receive from Spirit, that One Source, the desired inspiration or wisdom.[127]

The Originating Power descends into the consciousness which meditates upon It and re-

ceives It. The intellect then abandons itself to the Divine.[128]

Ernest was very interested in spiritualistic mediums and psychic phenomena. . . . After the passing of his beloved wife, Hazel, he tried to establish a definite, conscious contact with her through a medium, but he told me privately after several of these attempts that he was never satisfied. Although 'contact' had been achieved, he was never quite convinced that it actually was Hazel who was speaking to him.[129]

I believe we have to give the spiritualist movement credit for trying to demonstrate objectively what we, as Religious Scientists, believe in—that is, the immortality of the soul and the continuity of life. . . . In so-called communication with departed persons, there is, in my estimation definitely a mingling of consciousness of the individual who has gone on and those who are left behind—I believe this is possible and that it often takes place.[130]

Spiritistic involvement apparently often took place with Holmes. An examination of the glossary of *The Science of Mind* reveals familiarity with numerous spiritistic mediumistic and occult topics: apparition, channel, clairaudience, clairvoyance, cosmic consciousness, discarnate, esoteric, ether, familiar spirits, Father-Mother God, ghost, illumination, levitation, maya, medium, mental medium, mental plane, mysticism, psychic phenomena, planes, psychic, psychometry, psychic world, telekinetic energy, telepathy, theosophy,* trance. The 1926 edition of *The Science of Mind* contained an entire chapter on the law of psychic phenomena; however, it was deleted in 1936 because it was seen as developing into a separate field.[131] Also, in *Letters from Other Dimensions,* by medium Margaret McEathron, it is said that "Ernest Holmes" ostensibly communicated from "the other side" and reportedly gave his brother Fenwick evidence that he could not deny.[133] All this is proof of the occult nature of Religious Science.

---

*Ernest and Fenwick Holmes both declared, "Our message was in [general] harmony with Theosophy."[132] (Theosophy is a heavily spiritistic, occult religion.)

CRITIQUE

In this section we will briefly examine four areas which illustrate why RS claims generally should not be trusted: RS errors of fact; the problem of Ernest Holmes; RS rejection of evil and morality and RS denial of reality.

RS Errors of Fact

Reginald Armor, biographer and lifelong friend of Ernest Holmes, referred to a common view of Holmes, one held by his followers, that Holmes subjected all his beliefs to the test of rationality. "Being very practical, he always submitted his insights, contemplations, and feeling to his reasoning, intellectual mind for verification."[134] We are also told Holmes had a mind that "demonstrated its divinity" and was capable of "probing the farthest reaches of the universe." If so, one might expect unexcelled displays of spiritual power, crisp reasoning abilities, inerrancy in his writing and breathtaking insights from his probes of the universe. Yet in the most important area of all, religion, he was usually in error. For example, in the following quotes we have supplied brief comments or corrections. Holmes argued, "Thus each religion approaches the same God, and must basically believe in the same God."[135] (The Hindu God Brahman, the Muslim God Allah, and the biblical Jehovah, are utterly dissimilar.) "If we study every religion we will find great spiritual consistencies; belief in God [not true of Buddhism, Jainism or Shinto], belief in the Divinity of every individual [not true of Islam, Judaism or Christianity], and of good always triumphant over evil [not true of Hinduism, Zoroastrianism or Religious Science]."[136] Other examples of his numerous errors include the belief that bronchitis and other diseases result from "congested thought";[137] that Jesus' teaching was in "full accord with the Essenes";[138] that polytheism antedated monotheism;[139] and that there are no incurable diseases, only incurable people.[140]

Do the previous examples, and again there are many others, indicate that Ernest Holmes was rational, divine or free from error? A few errors are one thing, for it is human to err, but virtually unremitting error is another matter entirely. So why should anyone place trust in his religion, a religion that even he admitted he simply made up?

The Problem of Ernest Holmes

Holmes was said to have a "reverence for God."[141] He held Jesus to be "a spiritual genius," "the greatest spiritual *realist* who ever lived," and one with solid teaching.[142] This would lead people to assume that he had a reverence for Jesus. But reverence, at the least, includes respect for what a person taught, and Holmes, through his Science of Mind doctrine, denied Jesus' teaching. (See section on "Jesus Christ.") Although Holmes declared, "In this philosophy, no attempt is made to rob Jesus of his greatness or to refute His teachings,"[143] this is precisely what Holmes did. He denied both Jesus' greatness, His Person and His teachings. One wonders, did he really believe he was *not* refuting Jesus and His teachings, or was he unwilling to frankly state that if Jesus was to be understood in a normal sense, he was denying Him?

This brings us to the question of Holmes symbolic interpretation of Scripture. If Holmes was so enlightened, why did he never, anywhere, justify the legitimacy of his figurative, or metaphysical, interpretation of Scripture? The reason is because he could not. He simply demanded that others take his interpretations and invented religion on blind faith. Indeed, he was ill prepared even to *attempt* a defense of his views. As his brother pointed out: "He had no knowledge of either Greek or Hebrew, and traditional exegesis of a text was entirely foreign to him."[144] This may help to account for why he refused to discuss the particulars of Christian beliefs. "Let us not waste time, then, in theological discussions which lead nowhere."[145] What his brother pointed out concerning Holmes' view of the afterlife was relevant generally, "He knew that his philosophy was unclear and probably would not stand the test of theology, but he had no fear of 'authority.' . . ."[146]

Further, Holmes spoke of a perfect religion of the future (his teaching) that would "dehypnotize" people. In a revealing statement, Holmes fairly admitted that Religious Science would purposefully wipe God and biblical teachings out of people's consciousness. "The absence of

God and the devil will clean up the unconscious so that the fear of the unknown will also disappear.... How can this be brought about? That is what our classes and our textbook are designed to show.... The whole problem of sin and salvation is summarized and solved in the realization of the Divine Union.... There is no need for a go-between [Jesus as Savior].... Superstitions like belief in hell, purgatory and a personal devil will have passed away.... There will be justice without judgment."[147]

Clearly, despite Holmes' claim to respect all religions, not to mention his emphasis that he taught true Christianity, the truth is that his personal agenda was to be rid of Christianity once and for all. This is the first problem with Ernest Holmes, by his writings he proved that his respect for Jesus and Jesus' religion was hollow. The second problem with Holmes is that he read the Bible in such a way as to conform it to his personal views, as we've shown. Yet he criticized this approach when he stated, "I have found that Bible interpretation is often the reflection of personal opinion—more a matter of reading something into the Bible rather than getting something out of it."[148] In these words, Holmes has condemned his own approach to the Bible.

A third problem concerns Holmes' hypocrisy in treating the words of Jesus in the very manner that he implored others never to treat his own words. Holmes had one prominent desire when it came to his own words: "HAVING HAD the privilege of starting Religious Science, I would wish, will and desire *above all things else* that the simplicity and purity of our teaching could never be violated."[149] In other words, Ernest Holmes wished above all else that no one would misuse or violate *his words* and his beliefs. Yet his personal reinterpretation of Scripture misused and grossly distorted the Bible and the teachings of Jesus. Is it right for Holmes to do to others what he begged others not to do to himself?

Clearly, his symbolic and figurative interpretation of the Bible had little value apart from its subjectivity, which allowed him to read anything at all into the text. For example, Holmes stated in *Sermon By the Sea*, "There was nothing obscure in the teaching of Jesus.... He said that there is nothing but God."[150] "Holmes said,

"Jesus 'plainly told us' that God was within every man, 'He proclaimed that all men are divine.'"[151] But nowhere in the Gospels did Jesus say anything of the kind; in fact, His words emphatically denied both assertions (for example, John 3:19; 8:44). Can a man who so flagrantly alters another's words expect people to trust or honor his own? (Modern Science of Mind leaders and teachers have not corrected the problem; to the contrary, they have continued it, encouraged it and expanded it.) Holmes also distorted the simplicity and purity of the writings of Moses, the Gospel authors and the Apostle Paul:

—Abraham only *dreamed* God was testing him with Isaac.[152] (This is never stated or even remotely implied in the biblical text.)

—Christ means God-in-us. It means the divine Son at the center of every person's life.[153] ("Christ," from the Greek *Cristos,* means "anointed" and referred solely to Jesus, as the Gospel writers testify.)

—"The original meaning of sin" was to do or allow anything that separates us from the realization of our deity.[154] (The original meaning is from the Greek *hamartia* and meant to "miss the mark" of God's holiness.)

—The Greek word for spirit, *pneuma,* indicates "impersonal creative principle."[155] (By contrast, it means spirit, wind or breath; see Colin Brown, *The Dictionary of New Testament Theology,* Vol. 3, p. 693.)

—Jesus referred to the Holy Spirit as His mother.[156] (This is not stated by any Gospel writer or by Jesus.)

—"I am the way, the truth and the life" means that the infinite I, within the apparently finite you is God.[157] (In the context of John 14:6 Jesus applied this to Himself only, and the Apostle John confirmed it.)

—Resurrection means "rising from a belief in death."[158] (As the Apostle Paul taught, resurrection deals with the raising of the body; cf. Brown, *Dictionary of New Testament Theology,* "resurrection.")

In the following chart, consider examples of Holmes' biblical interpretation, none of which have biblical, historical or logical justification.

Religious Science Distortion of Biblical Terms

BIBLICAL TERM	SCIENCE OF MIND INTERPRETATION
The blood of the Lamb.	The continual flow of spiritual life animating everything.[159]
The lamb slain from the foundation of the world.	A symbol of the outpouring of spirit.[160]
Outer darkness.	Utter darkness; standing in the shade. [161]
Punishment.	Purification.[162]
Demon possession.	Possessed by evil.[163]
The ark of the Covenant; Holy of Holies.	Inner divinity. [164]
The Red Sea; The Flood.	Our Psychic Life.[165]
The Wedding Garment.	Awareness of unity with God.[166]
Elijah and Elisha.	Object lessons, not persons.[167]

RS Rejection of Evil and Morality

Morality involves distinguishing good from evil, discerning what is right or wrong in conduct. But in the perfect universe of RS evil is merely an illusion, and Jesus, the very one who died for sin (evil), was a principal exponent of this idea. "Therefore, following the advice of Jesus, it [Religious Science] refuses to believe that evil has any reality of its own, but that its only claim to existence is that given it *by the belief of man*."[168]

Yet in examining the Gospels, we find that Jesus unequivocally upheld morality and always distinguished good from evil. Clearly, He believed that evil really existed. He spoke of "the evil servant" (Matthew 24:48 KJV), and that from one's heart "come evil thoughts" (Mark 7:21). He urged us to pray, "Deliver us from evil" (Matthew 6:13 NAS). He spoke of "an evil and adulterous generation" (Matthew 12:39), and that God was kind even to evil persons (Luke

6:35). And He said that people loved darkness because their deeds were evil (John 3:19). How can Religious Science deny such statements as: "You brood of vipers, how can you who are evil say anything good? For out of the overflow of the heart the mouth speaks" (Matthew 12:34), and "the world cannot hate you; but it hates me because I testify that what it does is evil" (John 7:7).

Over half a thousand verses in the Bible treat evil as real. Either Jesus, the Bible and the testimony of history and common sense are false, or Religious Science has a terribly deficient worldview. Religious Science loses all credibility when it denies that which is so obvious.

Science of Mind is as much a reaction to evil as a denial of it. As in similar religions (New Thought, Christian Science and others) the popularity of Religious Science is in some ways due to a desire to escape from the real world's evil and suffering. Philosophically, it's a type of emotional buffer against the harsher aspects of reality in order to make life easier in some respects. Holmes wrote:

> How much easier it is to know that I am part of this Light of Lights, that I am supported by it, that I don't have to do everything myself, that behind me is God. Lifting me up is the Energy Force, and smiling at me from ages past and ages to come is the Happy Love of Universal Mind. . . . I don't need to worry any more. . . . I am delighted to know I am on the path of Truth and I am grateful I have this lovingness around me. . . . I look past the body of these people and see the Inner Self. I remember that the spiritual man is always perfect![169]

Thus RS philosophy is severely deficient ethically. Because evil has no reality, and only good exists, what we perceive as evil must really be part of the good. The moral implications of this view are hardly insignificant. This is why the Bible warns, "Woe to those who call evil good and good evil, who put darkness for light and light for darkness. . . . Woe to those who are wise in their own eyes . . ." (Isaiah 5:20–21). Nevertheless, in Religious Science evil is part of the good. Holmes and Kinnear state that "we seek a greater good and we call the lesser good, evil."[170] In *Your Invisible Power,* "God," speaking through Ernest Holmes, says, "I create both saint and sinner, know neither . . . good or bad."[171]

RS denial of morality leads to logical and practical contradictions. For instance, how can we deny that which is intrinsically good? That is, if evil is good, albeit a "lesser good," why not support it rather than deny or oppose it? If All is One and good, including God, what can ever be evil? As we quoted earlier, "There is nothing but God and good in the Universe." Because the "lesser good" is still good, logically it should be affirmed as good. So where are the RS "positive affirmations" for the lesser good? "Right now in Divine Mind I affirm theft, rape, adultery and child abuse as Good, for only Good exists." Can Religious Science live with this? It must, if its first principles are taken seriously. Evil must be affirmed.

But the problem here is compounded. If evil is simply "lesser" good (that is, part of the good), is not this good also the very *evil* we are told we must *not* believe or affirm in order to effectively live the principles of RS? "I let go of every contrary belief. I refuse the appearance of sin sickness and poverty." Even as RS must logically affirm the evil in God, it must simultaneously deny that very affirmation in order to succeed. This means Religious Science can not work in the manner it claims. Consider the following two citations: "It is sometimes difficult for a new student of Science of Mind to see that everything is One. . . . Two things for a person to do and perhaps that individual is you—are to believe all is One and to start consciously thinking of *everything* as one Super Being."[172] "Freedom and bondage, sickness and health, poverty and riches, Heaven and Hell, good and bad, big and little, happiness and misery, peace and confusion, faith and fear, and all conditions which *appear* to be opposites, are not really a result of the operation of *opposing powers,* but ARE THE WAY THE *ONE* POWER IS USED."[173]

Once we admit the One power contains within itself both good and evil and can be used for both good and evil, Religious Science practice is over, for there is no way to win. Thus the illogical resolution is simply to see everything as God. Thus, if the perfect Spirit is always per-

fectly present in one's life, as claimed,[174] then everything one does is by definition a divine act and perfect. The monistic gurus (Sai Baba, Maharishi Mahesh Yogi, Muktananda, Rajneesh and others) say the very same: *whatever* the God-realized person does is, by definition, perfect and divine, even if it is evil. Virtually any crime or immoral act will, in theory, be seen as the perfect working of the Spirit who is perfectly present in one's life. Who are we to judge the motives of the infinite amoral Spirit? After all, some people (even Hitler?) may have seemed evil, but, "We should recognize the divine in them, no matter what the apparent seems to declare. The man who . . . is seeing two powers, good and evil, he has not discovered that the evil is simply the good misdirected."[175] "To think otherwise is to suppose duality, and duality cannot be."[176] "See God in ALL and the trouble will soon be healed."[177]

But can and do RS believers *really* take comfort in the "lesser good," or divinity ("God in ALL"), of the actions of Hitler or groups like Jonestown, or The Branch Davidians (David Koresh), or Aum Shinrikyo, or the pimp and the rapist? Doesn't evil *destroy* millions of lives? It is at precisely this point that RS dismantles itself a second time; no RS practitioner can consistently live or logically justify a philosophy that teaches evil is good.

RS Denial of Reality

Although it is claimed that the principles of Religious Science work, they actually can't work because they deny reality and because RS ideas have serious personal and social consequences. In spite of its claims to be "practical religion," RS is so far removed from reality than any benefits of the applied philosophy can only be superficial at best.

When we sit down and talk with Religious Science followers, we discover they have the same problems most people have—the same concerns over money and circumstances, the same pains and frustrations, the same diseases, the same experience of evil in the world, the same impotence in the face of insurmountable problems that everyone faces as limited creatures. Of course, if our mind "IS the mind of

God" how do we explain such shortcomings?[178] We don't. So RS believers suffer like everyone else. They get sick and die, have car accidents, become emotionally wounded, get robbed and cheated in business and so on. Despite the fact they truly believe they can create and mold inner and outer reality according to their thought life, this is never so. So why continue to accept the philosophy?

Years ago a married couple slowly froze to death in their car, stranded in a Colorado mountain snowstorm. The woman died holding her husband's hand. In the glove compartment was a scribbled note, "I don't want to go this way."[179] Notes found in plane crashes contain sentiments like, "I love you dearly. I never dreamt last night would be our last." As tragic as these stories are, what could such people have done if they were Religious Scientists? Would their philosophy that "ALL is Good" have saved them? Could any Religious Science person anywhere escape death merely by mental power? If not, the theory of Science of Mind cannot be valid because it claims the Mind is divine and *has* all power. Their mind is the mind of God. They speak, and God speaks. All power flows through them. "I am God and there is none else."[180] "He who understands this will take the position of one who wished to work in union with the creative power of God; and to such a one will come all the power that he can conceive of and believe in. His word will become in expression as the very Word of God, and he must realize it to be all powerful."[181]

Why does no one ever experience the realization when it *really* matters? Why are there no manifestations of divine might in impossible circumstances? Does not God's thought (man) control the image of God's thought (the creation)? Infinite power can obviously stop bullets in mid air and raise the dead. But where *is* it in situations like the above? Do RS believers die in these cases merely due to their lack of faith in application of divine law? If Religious Science is true, it must be so. So where is its efficacy? Indeed, really trying to live the philosophy is proof of its error.

Science of Mind "testimonials" (we could more accurately call them "denials") are almost frightening in their implications. We cite four examples from Science of Mind literature. First, is the lady who saw in the rattlesnake which nearly bit her five-year-old daughter the same Spirit of God that "lives in us both, speaks through us both." Earlier she had handled a defanged rattler: "It was God's moment, this moment in time when our lives touched, the snake's life and mine, here in a place so fearful to us both."[182] Would she, however, have continued to love the rattlesnake as God if it had bitten her little girl and caused her painful death? Would the philosophy hold up in the face of a child's death?

Second, there was the woman who, being robbed by a thief and being threatened with death (a knife at her throat) said, smiling, "God is here." With the knife still at her throat she reports: "Looking into his eyes, I saw him in his true identity—God's Life expressing through him." After being hit several times and then robbed, she realized that her thoughts had "erected a protective shield [around her]" and that "any apparent evil [lost] its power to harm. . . ."[183]

Consider a third example, this time of RS parents whose teenagers were engaging in criminal acts, using drugs, abusing alcohol or living promiscuously. Holmes told one distraught mother, almost beside herself with worry over her son's activities, that her son "must work out the evolution of his own soul."[184] The teenager is really "God's life that is seeking expression," and the parents are both to affirm and "salute the God-self in our wonderful teenager, and I know that Divine Love protects and Divine Wisdom instructs and guides him (her) now and always. . . . [Each] young person must learn what Life has to teach. Each one is unique. Each must do his own living; each has a right to express. . . . This is God's perfect child growing up now into perfect adulthood, in a perfect way! Thank you, Father of all!"[185] (The parents of the children killed in the latest school shootings would most certainly disagree!) In typical RS fashion, Proverbs 22:6 ("Train a child in the way he should go, and when he is old he will not turn from it") is quoted as a biblical precedent for the affirmation! One can only wonder how many teenagers given this philosophy today have ruined or even lost their lives to drugs, sexual promiscuity or violence.

In our final example, a woman wrote in desperation that her husband had left her for another woman. She believed in Science of Mind. "I have tried to live one day at a time, holding to the faith that my husband would come back to me." Holmes' cold and unfeeling response was to tell her, "You have no right nor should you seek to coerce your husband. . . . Set him free in your own mind and know that whatever is for his best good and yours will be done."[186] Where is the harmonious thinking here? Where is the power that is supposed to be available in times like this? Where is the Good that is everywhere present? When God has different viewpoints, where is the Unity?

Holmes asserted that in our "prayers" we are to turn from a belief in any evil to a belief in only good, thus accepting "the creativity of the Universe in a constructive way."[187] Thinking of these parents, can we imagine a prayer that says, "God, thank you that my true child really is not taking drugs" or "Thank you that my husband is not really committing adultery"? To the starving can we say, "Thank you that no one dies from starvation, that there are no victims in life"?[188] In the horrors of war, can we say with Religious Science that "Peace is; It is in everything, It is through everything"?[189] After the tornado, flood or hurricane can we accept that "there are disintegrating forces but no destructive forces in nature. The Universe remains only goodness forevermore"?[190] Or can we really accept that "good thoughts always overcome the imperfect ones"?[191] Who can logically believe any of this?

And what about serious or life-threatening illness? Religious Science claims it does not deny the reality of disease in the "outer" man, in the false appearance, ("we do not say a man is not sick").[192] But it also says that a woman with tuberculosis "is a perfect and complete manifestation of Pure Spirit and Pure Spirit cannot be diseased; consequently she is not diseased."[193] In Religious Science "reality," she is both sick and not sick at the same time: the real her is well; the appearance of her is sick. Of course, this is a con. The lady is seriously ill. But how

many Christian Scientists, New Thought, Unity and RS believers have suffered or even died because they chose to deny and ignore the "unreal" appearance?

What comfort does Religious Science offer its devout members, who live it and praise it, when they face major surgery, divorce, the death of a child, terminal illness or some other tragedy? What do they do when they are hit by contradictions and doubts, by a feeling of betrayal? Why is it that even with their sincerest and best efforts to appropriate the All-Good, the Divine Mind, It still lets them down?

RS may make one feel good. Hearing that one is divine and perfect, believing that it is "godly to live as you like," is attractive. But this can never cure people's real problems. Unfortunately, RS practitioners are made up of people who "find their own lives." "It's glorifying yourself, really," admits one practitioner.[194] Yet Jesus said that he who "finds" (or selfishly loves) his own life will lose it, but he who loses his life for Jesus' sake will find it to life eternal (John 12:25; Matthew 10:39).

TALKING WITH MEMBERS

Science of Mind, like religions and cults generally, must agree with Christianity that something is seriously and basically wrong between the divine and the human. The question is who has the more accurate diagnosis of the problem and the best solution? The fact that Science of Mind goes out of its way to deny evil, disease and so on, shows that these conditions really do exist. As in atheism, the constant need to deny affirms the reality of that which is denied. Otherwise, there would be no need for denial. No one feels constrained to build a philosophy against the existence of satyrs, because everyone knows they are a myth. If evil *did not* exist, no one would know it. It is denied because it *does* exist.

Sooner or later RS believers will experience evil in ways they cannot deny. This will lead to doubts about Science of Mind views, and at this point especially they should be challenged to reexamine their spiritual values and commitments. For instance, if sin or evil is merely an appearance that does injustice to the Reality of the divine perfection behind it, why do those in Religious Science *react* to evil like everyone else and fail to manifest perfection? Is not the very reaction to evil and the failure to manifest perfection a betrayal of the principles of Science of Mind? Even Holmes admits, "We only think we believe that God Power is in us."[195] "In discarding the ancient idea of a huge person in the nature of Deity, we are undoubtedly losing something.... Neither can we hope to get very much satisfaction from thinking of God only as an infinite It."[196] The following discussion citing Ernest Holmes underscores fatal problems in RS philosophy. The true betrayer is Religious Science itself:

> I do not believe there is a single fact in human history, or a single manifestation in the universe, which is or could possibly be anything other than a manifestation of the One Divine Mind, the One Universal Presence, the One Infinite Spirit.[197]

> We must realize the Perfect Universe if we wish to embody the greatest good. If the Universe were not perfect it could not exist for a single moment. It is self-evident that we live in a Perfect Universe; and, if so, then everything in it must also be perfect.

> The Truth is Indivisible and Whole. God is Complete and Perfect. A Perfect Cause must produce a Perfect Effect. Disregarding *all evidence to the contrary*, the student of Truth will maintain that he lives in a Perfect Universe and among perfect people; he will regulate his thinking to meet this necessity and will refuse to believe in its opposite. At first he may appear to be weak; but as time goes on, he will prove to himself that his position is a correct one; for that which appears imperfect will begin to slip from his experience.[198]

But as time went on, Ernest Holmes confessed his failure to manifest perfection, just as Charles Filmore, the founder of Unity School of Christianity, also failed in his own confession of divine perfection and died as a result (see chapter on Unity School of Christianity). Contrary to Holmes' own experience, he claimed that it was *not* a matter of choice or conjecture concerning perfection, for "Goodness is already given." But he could never live it. He even understood that his philosophy was a failure:

> We do not appear complete. We act as if we were temporal, limited, unprepared, and afraid. We are not so foolish as to think that people do not suffer; that they do not experience want; that they are not unhappy. But the potential I, the potential you, is just as perfect as the inherent God. *This is why the world will call us stupid: that we do not call this perfection into objective manifestation. It is not a matter of choice that we are potentially perfect. It is not a matter of conjecture....* Goodness is already given.[199]

Holmes was correct. It *is* stupid to remain in imperfection if one can change it. This is a fitting epitaph to Religious Science philosophy: put simply and bluntly, it's just stupid.

Unfortunately, cherished beliefs can die slowly, even when they are shown to be wrong. We reported the following account in *The Coming Darkness*, a book documenting the dangers of occult practice. It discusses a famous although fraudulent medium's shock at learning that people wished to continue to believe in his "divine" powers even after they had been told, *by him*, that they were fraudulent:

> M. Lamar Keene was, at one time, one of the world's highest-paid mediums. He was also considered one of the most proficient and would routinely produce alleged spirit messages, materializations, psychic healings, clairvoyance, trumpet mediumship, apports, etc. But he was a fraud. For over 13 years he practiced his wares before his conscience got the best of him and he decided to confess his unethical methods. In *The Psychic Mafia* he tells his story. "The average person is exceedingly easy to fool," he says.

> In Chapter 5, "Secrets of the Seance," Keene reveals many of the tricks of the trade. Nevertheless, even after he publicly confessed his fraudulent practices, the will to believe persisted. Most of his sitters and even the church board of directors either refused to accept his confession or kept attending the faked seances of Keene's associate!

> Not surprisingly, Keene's reaction was one of shock. After telling them the "spirits" did not exist, that they were fakes, people continued to respond to him on the basis of what they *learned* from the "spirits"! He recalls, "I was crushed. I knew how easy it was to make people believe a lie, but I didn't expect that the same

people, confronted with the lie, would choose it over the truth."

Why did these people continue to believe? Because they wanted to. Belief was more comfortable than unbelief; this is precisely why so many cults and spiritual cons flourish everywhere in America today.[200]

This "will to believe" explains why RS believers may continue to argue the superiority of their beliefs against those of Christianity. A Religious Science church member will often reply to a Christian, "We teach the positive things," as if Christian belief in the reality and effect of sin means that Christianity is entirely negative. To the contrary, nothing is more positive and realistic than Christianity. Man is created in God's image, loved infinitely by Him and capable of an intimately personal eternal relationship with Him. Eternal salvation is an entirely free gift! By contrast, where is the *truly* positive in Religious Science? Is it a *positive* thing to *deny* reality? Is it positive to think you are divine, when you are always confronted with evidence to the contrary? Or, is it positive for a woman or man to attempt to have a personal relationship with an impersonal It? "There *is* a Divine Something, call It what you will."[201] Is it something positive to be absorbed or erased into an impersonal essence at some point in the distant future?

Religious Science practitioner may also respond to a Christian, "But Jesus Himself taught Religious Science when He stressed the power of faith." However, when Jesus said, "Be it done according to your faith," He was clearly and specifically referring to faith in a God beyond the limited resources of the individual. He was referring to a faith that realizes its own creaturely need, rather than one that believes in its own divinity. He was referring to a faith that trusts in God, not in its own arrogance. Had Jesus intended to teach RS, He would simply have said, "Be it done according to your faith in your divine self."

Another Christian response could surround the RS aversion to sin and separation from God. After all, in Religious Science, Christianity represents one of the "greatest handicaps to spiritual progress,"[202] due to its insistence upon man's innate separation from God. A Religious

Scientist may believe that Christians live in "hell," because hell is defined as "a discordant state of being. A belief in duality. A sense of separation from God."[203]

But is this is not *primarily* true of Religious Scientists? (Christians, for their part, are no longer separated from God.) Do Religious Scientists not live in a discordant state of being, wrestling with their perpetual sense of separation from the perfections of "Divine Mind"? Do they not more or less recognize their own constant "separation" from God? Do they not have "sin" constantly in their consciousness? Their own experience cries out "yes!" Man is either one essence with God, or he is not. Religious Science members need to see the logical consequences and expectations of both claims. Do they act like a God according to Religious Science or do they act like a sinner according to Christianity? If they can be helped to answer that question honestly, the battle is half won, and the truth about man's separation from God and Christ's atonement may be introduced.

One good approach may be to center the discussion around Holmes' own teachings that:

> The only reason we have to suppose that Jesus knew (truth) is that he proved his claim. What we should do then is find out exactly what Jesus believed, and why.[204]

> Since the teachings of Jesus contain the key to right living, it is well to consider their meaning. ... We should re-read the words of Jesus as though we had never heard of them before—start all over again, get a completely fresh outlook.[205]

One may then sit down with a Religious Science follower and "start fresh" in the area of biblical study, specifically the teachings of Jesus on sin and salvation and God's love for the person (John 3:16). The RS practitioner will soon see that the Bible teaches something quite different from Science of Mind, and that anyone who interprets the Bible in a normal sense cannot achieve a Religious Science outlook. If Holmes himself was the one who emphasized, "We must have clarity, not confusion; truth, not lies,"[206] where then is "the clarity" (or truth) in Holmes' interpretation of Scripture? Where is "the truth" (or clarity) in his interpretation of experience?

In 1959, Ernest Holmes challenged: "You find me one thousand people in the world who know what Religious Science is and use it, and live it as it is, and I'll myself live to see a new world, a new heaven and a new earth here."[207] But within a year, Holmes had died, having never seen his new millennium. Of course, there have been *millions* of RS practitioners who have known what RS is, who have used it and lived it faithfully, even valiantly. And it changed nothing fundamentally. Holmes was wrong because he refused to accept the world as it is and had forsaken the one true God who created it. This is the God who declared, "It is given for every man to die once, and then comes judgment" (Hebrews 9:27). If RS practitioners do not wish to take the risk Ernest Holmes took, then they must be certain that their philosophy of life is true. Indeed, the difference between being God or being a sinner is the difference between living in heaven or living in hell:

Every word of God is flawless; he is a shield to those who take refuge in him. Do not add to his words or he will rebuke you and prove you a liar. Two things I ask of you, O LORD; do not refuse me before I die: keep falsehood and lies far from me. (Proverbs 30:5–8)

The one who believes in the Son of God has the witness in himself; the one who does not believe God has made Him a liar, because he has not believed in the witness that God has borne concerning His Son. And the witness is this, that God has given us eternal life, and this life is in His Son. He who has the Son has the life; he who does not have the Son of God does not have the life. (1 John 5:10–12 NAS)

In concluding, we can only agree with Science of Mind writer Rev. Margaret R. Stortz in her online article "Science of Mind and the Spirit of Christ," when she writes the following: "In all of Christianity there is no more important single figure than Jesus, the wayshower and inspiration from which the Christian religion began. As an inquirer into Science of Mind, it is very important for you to have a clear understanding about Jesus' relationship to God and to you."

Scripture Contrasts: RS vs. the Bible	
The birth of Christ is not an historical event, but is an eternal incarnation. (*Keys to Wisdom*, p. 39)	But when the time had fully come, God sent his Son, born of a woman, born under the Law. (Galatians 4:4)
It would seem unthinkable and certainly illogical to believe that such states [heaven, hell] could be created by God. (Ibid., p. 18)	Then He will also say to those on His left, "Depart from Me, accursed ones, into the eternal fire which has been prepared for the devil and his angels." (Matthew 25:41 NAS)
This is why the Bible says there is but one mediator between God and man; Christ in us, the *cosmic man*. (*Know Yourself*, p. 94)	For there is one God and one mediator between God and men, the man Jesus Christ, who gave himself a ransom for all men. . . . (1 Timothy 2:5)
Creation is eternally going on. (*Questions and Answers*, p. 11)	And by the seventh day God completed His work which He had done; and He rested on the seventh day from all His work which He had done. (Genesis 2:2)
It is never the will of God or universal harmony to have any person suffer. (Ibid., p. 24)	Therefore, let those also who suffer according to the will of God entrust their souls to a faithful Creator in doing what is right. (1 Peter 4:19 NAS)
Born of the Spirit, your child is changeless, perfect, completely safe and secure in Divine Mind (Ibid., p. 69)	Folly is bound up in the heart of a child, but the rod of discipline will drive it far from him. (Proverbs 22:15) The rod of correction imparts wisdom, but a child left to itself disgraces his mother. (Proverbs 29:15)

(continues)

The devil is an hallucination. (*Gateway to Life*, p. 19)	He replied, "I saw Satan fall like lightning from heaven." (Luke 10:18; see Luke 22:3; Revelation 12:9)
There is no God that heals just because someone crawls up to Him and prays for it. There are no special dispensations of Providence.	And the prayer offered in faith will restore the one who is sick, and the Lord will raise him up, and if he has committed sins, they will be forgiven him. Therefore, (Ibid., p. 70) confess your sins to one another, and pray for one another, so that you may be healed. The effective prayer of a righteous man can accomplish much. (James 5:15–16 NAS)

NOTES

1. Ernest Holmes, *Words That Heal Today* (New York: Dodd, Mead and Company, 10th Printing, 1949), p. 156.
2. Ernest Holmes, *The Science of Mind* (New York: Dodd, Mead and Company, 1939), p. 357.
3. Ernest Holmes, *Sermon by the Sea* (Los Angeles: Science of Mind Publications, 1967), pp. 19-20.
4. Fenwick Holmes, *Ernest Holmes: His Life and Times* (New York: Dodd, Mead and Company, 1970), back cover.
5. Taken in part from Ibid., pp. 73-104, 166-180, 196-204, 281-283.
6. Ibid., p. 93.
7. Ibid.
8. That Mrs. Eddy was for 25 years a medium is documented in Georgine Milmine, *The Life of Mary Baker G. Eddy* (Baker reprint, 1971), pp. 28-31, 66-67, 111-116. See chapter on Christian Science.
9. *Science of Mind*, Nov. 1978, pp. 47-48.
10. See The Science of Mind Publications Order Form; note 3 above.
11. *The Science of Mind*, p. 379.
12. Ernest Holmes, *What Religious Science Teaches* (Los Angeles: Science of Mind Publications, 1978), p. 10.
13. Ibid., p. 57.
14. Ernest Holmes, *What I Believe*, "Science of Mind," Jan. 1965.
15. Holmes, *What Religious Science Teaches*, pp. 24-25.
16. Craig Carter, *How to Use the Power of Mind in Everyday Life* (Los Angeles: Science of Mind Publications, 1978), pp. 4-5.
17. Ibid., p. 6.
18. Ernest Holmes and Willis Kinnear, *Practical Application of Science of Mind* (Los Angeles: Science of Mind Publications, 1977), p. 68.
19. Carter, p. 6. emphasis added.
20. Ibid., pp. 12, 15, 17, 27, 29, 32.
21. Holmes and Kinnear, *Practical Application of Science of Mind*, p. 62.
22. Holmes, *Science of Mind*, p. 133.
23. *Science of Mind*, Nov. 1979, p. 40.
24. Ernest Holmes, *The Basic Ideas of Science of Mind* (Los Angeles: Science of Mind Publications, 1971), p. 13.
25. This chart originally appeared in *The Facts on Mind Sciences* (Harvest House).
26. *Science of Mind*, February 1979, p. 40.
27. Fenwick Holmes, *Ernest Holmes*, p. 95, emphasis added.
28. Holmes, *Sermon by the Sea*, p. 12.
29. Ernest Holmes (compiled and edited by Willis Kinnear), *The Spiritual Universe and You* (Los Angeles: Science of Mind Publications, 1971), p. 9, emphasis added.
30. *Science of Mind*, January 1980, p. 21.
31. Norman Geisler, *A Popular Survey of the Old Testament*, p. 11.
32. Reginald C. Armor, *Ernest Holmes, the Man* (Los Angeles: Science of Mind Publications, 1977), p. 38.
33. Ibid., p. 99.
34. *Science of Mind*, February 1979, p. 41.
35. *Science of Mind*, April 1979, p. 36.
36. Armor, p. 98.
37. Holmes, "What I Believe," *Science of Mind*, January 1965; also published in tract form.
38. *Science of Mind*, January 1970, p. 8.
39. *Science of Mind*, June 1979, p. 38.
40. For example, F. Holmes, *Ernest Holmes*, p. 296.
41. Ibid., p. 293.
42. Joseph Krimsky, *The Wonder of Man—A Doctor's Soliloquy* (Los Angeles: Science of Mind Publications, 1972), p. 110.
43. *The Science of Mind*, p. 578.
44. Holmes, *The Basic Ideas of Science of Mind*, p. 12.
45. *The Science of Mind*, p. 362.
46. Armor, *Ernest Holmes, the Man*, p. 96.
47. *The Science of Mind*, p. 618.
48. Armor, *Ernest Holmes, the Man*, p. 96, emphasis added.
49. *The Science of Mind*, p. 618.
50. Ernest Holmes and Alberta Smith, *Questions and Answers on The Science of Mind* (New York: Dodd, Mead and Company, 1953), pp. 8-9, emphasis added.
51. *Ernest Holmes: His Life and Times*, p. 170, emphasis added.
52. *The Science of Mind*, pp. 364-365.
53. Ibid., pp. 86, 89.
54. Carter, p. 8.
55. *The Science of Mind*, p. 365, emphasis added.
56. Ibid., p. 129.
57. Ibid.
58. Ernest Holmes (compiled and edited by Willis Kinnear), *Know Yourself—You Are More Than You Think* (Los Angeles: Science of Mind Publications, 1974), p. 24.

59. Ernest Holmes, *Keys to Wisdom* (Los Angeles: Sicence of Mind Publications, 1977), pp. 38-39.
60. Holmes and Smith, *Questions and Answers*, p. 10.
61. *The Science of Mind*, p. 603.
62. Holmes, *Words that Heal Today*, p. 90.
63. *The Science of Mind*, p. 361.
64. Ibid. p. 367.
65. *Science of Mind*, January 1979, p. 16.
66. Ernest Holmes (compiled and edited by Willis Kinniar), *The Philosophy of Jesus. . . . For the World Today* (Los Angeles: Science of Mind Publications, n.d.), pp. 48-49.
67. Ibid., p. 59.
68. Ibid., p. 91.
69. *The Science of Mind*, p. 361.
70. *The San Diego Union*, November 4, 1979, p. A-4.
71. Ibid.
72. *Los Angeles Times*, November 16, 1979; verbatim notes taken by Mandy Patterson, November 5, 1978, La Jolla Church of Religious Science.
73. Holmes, *Gateway to Life*, p. 19.
74. Ernest Holmes, *Observations* (Los Angeles: Science of Mind Publications, 1977), p. 63.
75. Ernest Holmes (compiled and edited by Willis Kinnear), *Ideas for Living* (Los Angeles: Science of Mind Publications, 1972), pp. 52-53.
76. *The Science of Mind*, p. 335, emphasis added.
77. Ibid., p. 372.
78. Holmes, *Gateway to Life*, p. 27.
79. Holmes, *Sermon by the Sea*, pp. 15-16.
80. Holmes, *The Science of Mind*, pp. 79-80.
81. Ernest Holmes, *The Larger Life*, p. 72.
82. Ibid.
83. Armor, p. 97.
84. Holmes, *Gateway to Life*, p. 26.
85. Holmes and Kinnear, *Practical Application of Science of Mind*, p. 93.
86. *The Science of Mind*, pp. 358-359.
87. Holmes, *Keys to Wisdom*, p. 72.
88. Holmes, *Sermon by the Sea*, p. 25.
89. Ernest Holmes and Fenwicke Holmes, *The Voice Celestial* (Los Angeles: Science of Mind Publications, 1978), p. 284.
90. Ibid., p. 276.
91. *Questions and Answers on The Science of Mind*, p. 58.
92. Holmes, *The Philosophy Jesus*, p. 16.
93. *Ernest Holmes: His Life and Times*, pp. 286-287.
94. Ibid., p. 23.
95. *Questions and Answers on The Science of Mind*, p. 14.
96. *Ernest Holmes: His Life and Times*, pp. 286-287.
97. Fenwicke Holmes, *Ernest Holmes*, p. 294.
98. Ibid., p. 284.
99. Holmes, *Keys to Wisdom*, p. 10.
100. Armor, p. 98.
101. *The Science of Mind*, p. 633.
102. Holmes and Smith, p. 49.
103. *The Science of Mind*, p. 591.
104. Holmes and Smith, pp. 150, 76, 69, 14 respectively.
105. "What I Believe," *Science of Mind*, January 1965.
106. Holmes and Smith, p. 152.
107. *Science of Mind*, July 1979, p. 51.
108. *The Science of Mind*, p. 383.
109. Fenwick Holmes, *Ernest Holmes*, p. 91.
110. Holmes, *Gateway to Life*, p. 25.
111. Holmes and Smith, p. 52.
112. Fenwick Holmes, p. 179.
113. Armor, p. 42; see Holmes, *The Science of Mind*, pp. 384-388.
114. *The Science of Mind*, pp. 384-388.
115. Fenwick Holmes, *Ernest Holmes*, pp. 196-200.
116. Krimsky, p. 55.
117. Marcus Bach, *The Will to Believe* (Los Angeles: Science of Mind Publications, 1977), pp. 121-130, 172.
118. *Science of Mind*, June-July, 1979, pp. 8-13 and 46-50.
119. *Science of Mind*, April, 1978, pp. 40-46.
120. Armor, pp. 4-6, emphasis added.
121. See chapters on *A Course in Miracles*, Angel Contact, Channeling, New Age Inner Work, New Age Intuition.
122. Holmes and Holmes, *The Voice Celestial*, "list of characters."
123. *Your Invisible Power*—Part III, p. 39.
124. Armor, p. 33.
125. Ibid., p. 32.
126. Ibid., p. 87.
127. Ibid., p. 34.
128. Ibid., p. 94.
129. Ibid., pp. 35-36.
130. Ibid., pp. 34-35.
131. Fenwick Holmes, pp. 201, 253.
132. F. Holmes, p. 167.
133. M. McEathron, *Letters from Other Dimensions*, Forward.
134. Armor, p. 4.
135. Holmes, *The Basic Ideas of Science of Mind*, p. 93.
136. Holmes, *The Spiritual Universe*, p. 27.
137. Ibid.
138. Holmes and Holmes, *The Voice Celestial*, p. 271; cf., for example, F. F. Bruce, *The Teacher of Righteousness in the Qumran Texts* (London: Tyndale Press), 1956, and Wilheim La Sor, *The Dead Sea Scrolls and the New Testament*.
139. Holmes, *The Science of Mind*, p. 131.
140. Armor, p. 32.
141. Ibid., p. 6.
142. Holmes, *The Spiritual Universe*, pp. 16, 33, emphasis added.
143. *The Science of Mind*, p. 631.
144. *Questions and Answers on The Science of Mind*, pp. 166-167.
145. *The Science of Mind*, p. 631.
146. Fenwick Holmes, p. 94.
147. Fenwick Holmes, *Ernest Holmes*, pp. 287-289.
148. Armor, p. 19.
149. *Science of Mind*, pp. 10-11, emphasis added.
150. Holmes, *Sermon by the Sea*, p. 11.
151. *Science of Mind*, December 1978, p. 10; Holmes, *What Religious Science Teaches*, p. 59.
152. *Science of Mind*, February 1979, p. 7.
153. Holmes, *Ideas for Living*, p. 28.
154. Ibid., p. 18.
155. Holmes, *The Voice Celestial*, p. 337.
156. Ibid.

157. Holmes, *Your Invisible Power*, p. 40.
158. Holmes, *The Science of Mind*, p. 630.
159. *Words That Heal Today*, p. 237.
160. Ibid.
161. Ibid., p. 108.
162. Ibid.
163. Ibid., pp. 173-174.
164. Ibid., pp. 61-62.
165. Ibid., pp. 86-88.
166. Ibid., p. 108.
167. *The Philosophy of Jesus*, p. 61.
168. Holmes and Smith, p. 51, emphasis added.
169. *Science of Mind*, May 1979, pp. 62-63.
170. Holmes and Kinnear, *Practical Application of Science of Mind*, p. 75.
171. Holmes, *Your Invisible Power*, p. 36.
172. *Science of Mind*, May 1979, p. 71.
173. *The Science of Mind*, p. 133.
174. Carter, p. 10.
175. Holmes and Smith, p. 71.
176. Ibid., p. 17.
177. Ibid., p. 151.
178. Holmes and Smith, p. 23.
179. *Los Angeles Times*, November 1, 1979.
180. Fenwick Holmes, p. 203.
181. Holmes, *The Spiritual Universe and You*, p. 88.
182. *Science of Mind*, December 1978, pp. 25-28.

183. *Science of Mind*, February 1979, pp. 27-29.
184. Holmes and Smith, p. 157.
185. Carter, p. 49.
186. Holmes and Smith, p. 105.
187. Holmes, *Keys to Wisdom*, p. 93.
188. cf., Ibid., p. 64.
189. cf., Ibid.
190. Holmes, *Gateway to Life*, p. 19.
191. *Science of Mind*, May 1979, p. 71.
192. *Science of Mind*, July 1978, p. 59.
193. Fenwick Holmes, p. 202.
194. *The San Diego Union*, November 4, 1979.
195. Holmes, *Gateway to Life*, p. 51.
196. *Science of Mind*, October 1979, p. 22.
197. Holmes, *Sermon by the Sea*, p. 8.
198. Holmes and Smith, *Questions and Answers on the Science of Mind*, p. 22, emphasis added.
199. *Science of Mind*, March 1979, pp. 24-25, emphasis added.
200. John Ankerberg and John Weldon, *The Coming Darkness* (Eugene, OR: Harvest House Publishers, 1993), p. 242-43.
201. Holmes, *Keys to Wisdom*, pp. 12, 85.
202. Holmes and Smith, pp. 20, 30.
203. *The Science of Mind*, p. 598.
204. *Science of Mind*, December 1978, p. 12.
205. *Ideas for Living*, p. 28.
206. Holmes, *Gateway to Life*, p. 90.
207. Holmes, *Sermon by the Sea*, p. 31.

ROSICRUCIAN FELLOWSHIP

INFO AT A GLANCE

Name: The Rosicrucian Fellowship.

Purpose: To help evolve man's consciousness.

Founder: Max Heindel.

Source of authority: Heindel's writings; for example, *The Rosicrucian Cosmo-Conception.*

Revealed teachings: Yes.

Claim: To reveal the superior "Western Wisdom Teachings" (as opposed to, for example, the Eastern Theosophic teachings).

Occult dynamics: A wide variety of occult practices are accepted, with Rosicrucian choices and interpretations of occult practices constituting the "higher" form of expression over "lower" forms.

Examples of key literature: *The Rosicrucian Cosmo-Conception; the Rosicrucian Philosophy in Questions and Answers; Rays from the Rose Cross* (periodical).

Attitude toward Christianity: Rejecting.

Quotes:

"The Rosicrucian teachings are never in conflict with the Christian religion." (Max Heindel, *The Rosicrucian Philosophy,* p. 99)

"Christ said, 'The Truth shall make you free,' but Truth is not found once and forever. Truth is eternal, and the quest for Truth must also be eternal. Occultism knows of no 'faith once for all delivered.'" (Max Heindel, *The Rosicrucian Cosmo-Conception,* p. 23)

"Jehovistic religions taught and continue to teach a preponderant awareness of sin and error.

To the degree they teach Truth at all, they teach it negatively, from the vantage point of what it is not. They teach the separation of man from the ... Deity. They establish obedience to external authority as the ideal." (Charles Weber, "Religious Authority and the Christian Dispensation," *Rays from the Rose Cross,* June 1978, p. 244.)

Note: In many countries, various Rosicrucian orders, societies or lodges can be found actively promoting variations of occult philosophy and practice. Most United States members are usually found to have former church affiliation in keeping with these occult societies' claim of compatibility with Christianity. In the U.S. there are approximately ten active Rosicrucian sects.

Whatever their differences, all Rosicrucian societies stem from gnostic occult traditions, and they stress the possession of secret wisdom passed down through the ages through a secret brotherhood. They believe that such wisdom can only be received by the initiated, and also that such wisdom leads to the development of "higher" or psychic powers. They stress "inner" enlightenment and usually adopt various tenets of Eastern religious philosophy (such as reincarnation and an impersonal concept of the Deity).

Untangling or ascertaining "genuine" Rosicrucian history is a difficult if not impossible endeavor. Too little reliable historical data exists, and there are too many conflicting claims among the various orders. As is true in Masonry (with which it has common elements) doubtful claims are made by Rosicrucians as to their history. The existence of any order prior to the fifteen century has, to our knowledge, never been demonstrated. Of course, many teachings similar to the Rosicrucians can be found in earlier philosophies—Hermetic, Gnostic, Kabbalistic, spiritistic and the occult in general—but similarity does not prove descent, despite what many Rosicrucian's claim.

AMORC traces its ideological history back to Egyptian mystery schools about 1350 B.C., and in the United States to 1694 A.D. Clymer traces his Rosicrucian Fraternity to 1614 A.D.; Heindel to 1313 A.D. *In The Real history of the Rosicrucians*, A. E. Waite traces Rosicrucianism to a society begun in 1598 A.D., and many authorities cite the first mention of the Rosicrucians to *Fama Fraternitatis* (1614), which tells of the purported Christian Rosenkreuz, a so-called founder of the movement. He allegedly received ancient occult wisdom, including the practice of invocation of spirits, in his travels to Syria, Egypt and Arabia. Some hold Rosenkreuz to be a symbolic representation of the famous alchemist and occultist Paracelsus (1493–1541), in that Rosenkreuz's alleged teachings resemble those of Paracelsus.

A prominent figure during the rise of the Rosicrucians was Jacob Boehme. Although not a Rosicrucian, his teachings influenced what was apparently the first U.S. Rosicrucian society, the Chapter of Perfection, which landed in Germantown, Pennsylvania, in 1694.[1] Boehme (typically known as a Christian mystic) wedded the tradition of the Neoplatonists, the teachings of Paracelsus and other occultists with Protestantism. He influenced both George Fox who founded the Quakers and H. P. Blavatsky who founded Theosophy.[2] Melton notes that Rosicrucianism has had an extensive interaction with Freemasonry and theosophical teachings, and to varying degrees with the tenets of parapsychology and the Western magical tradition.[3]

References to vol. 1, *Encyclopedia of New Age Beliefs* (1996): Altered States of Consciousness, Astrology, Channeling, Divination, Enlightenment, Meditation, New Age Inner Work, New Age Intuition, Visualization.

DOCTRINAL SUMMARY

God: Tripartite: the Absolute, the Supreme Being, God.

Jesus: A highly evolved man.

The Christ: An evolving spirit (a god) who indwelt Jesus and after the crucifixion infused himself into the earth, thus becoming the earth-spirit. Also the Sun spirit.

Holy Spirit: The Race god, Jehovah, who gave mankind its pre-Christian "primitive" religion.

Salvation: Through knowledge of proper occult techniques.

Man: Part of God; a god in the making.

Sin: Ignorance.

Satan: Any adversary in general.

The Fall: Sexual in nature; Adam and Eve are seen as symbolic of men and women in general.

The Bible: A mystical text; only through Rosicrucian "higher consciousness" can it be properly interpreted.

Death: Purgatorial.

Hell and Heaven: No hell exists; however, there are three heavens where human spirits go to prepare for their next incarnation.

NOTES

1. J. Gordon Melton, *Encyclopedia of American Religion*, Vol. 2, p. 179.
2. Robert S. Ellwood, *Religious and Spiritual Groups in Modern America* (Prentice Hall, 1974) p. 62.
3. Melton, Vol. 2, pp. 177-178.
4. Ibid., p. 180.

RUHANI SATSANG

INFO AT A GLANCE

Name: Ruhani Satsang.

Purpose: To experience God as sound and to see Him as light.

Founder: Kirpal Singh (1896–1974).

Source of authority: The revelations of "God-Power" through Singh.

Claim: To represent the teachings of the saints (Sant Mat) and the underlying mystical truth of all religions.

Examples of occult potential: Spiritism, astral travel.

Key literature: *The Path of the Masters,* 2 Volumes (1935) and some 20 other books by Kirpal Singh.

Attitude toward Christianity: Rejecting.

Quote:

"Christians say Christ is the only begotten Son of God—there are no others. This is, excuse me if I use the word, a fallacy." (Kirpal Singh, *Heart to Heart Talks,* Vol. 2, p. 238.)

"Only two scriptures are valid. One is the Koran of the Mohammedans; there has not been a change of even one word. The other is the Sikh scripture, the Adi Granth, which was compiled by Guru Arjan himself. . . . Nothing has been added nor deleted from that. . . . All other scriptures have additions and subtractions. So these two only are valid. (Kirpal Singh, *Heart to Heart Talks,* Vol. 2, p. 173.)

Note: All Sikhs in India take the last name Singh (lion) after Guru Gobind Singh (1666–1708),

the last of their gurus and considered the greatest poet, scholar and warrior. Many Sikhs claim that guruship ended with the tenth guru (Gobind Singh) and that the "Guru" today is their scripture, the Adi Granth. Kirpal Singh, although claiming a Sikh heritage, declares that there are six additional gurus, he and his guru among them. "I tell you, Gurudom continued" (K. Singh, *Heart to Heart Talks,* Vol. 1, p. 72). Obviously, if there have been only six gurus since 1708, Kirpal Singh is a very important figure to disciples (Satsangis). He alleges that the orthodox Sikhs never objected to his idea that Gurudom has continued, and that he was not trying to change the Sikh religion (p. 74). No "orthodox" Sikh, however, would accept this.

The teachings of Ruhani Satsang are very similar to the Radhasoami religion, Kirpal Singh being a disciple of Sawan Singh, leader of the Radhasoami sect at Beas. In many ways the cult of Eckankar comprises a plagarism from Radhasoami teaching.

DOCTRINAL SUMMARY

God: Divine vibration manifesting as Sound and Light.

Jesus: A man who attained God-Realization through the Christ.

The Christ: Divine Power or God Power.

The Holy Spirit: The divine Sound Current.

Salvation: By out-of-the-body experiences and personal merit.

Man: Inwardly divine.

Sin: Violation of the Law of Nature (*Heart to Heart Talks,* Vol. 2, p. 194).

Satan: Kal Niranjan, a lower demi-god.

The Fall: Into matter.

The Bible: Unreliable, not genuine scripture.

Death: A beneficial transition.

Heaven and Hell: Positive or negative experiences or states of consciousness.

THE SAI BABA SOCIETY

INFO AT A GLANCE

Name: The Sai Baba Society, Sri Sathya Sai Publication and Education Foundation.

Purpose: To unite mankind into a New Age of enlightenment; to provide individual enlightenment.

Founder: Sai Baba.

Source of authority: Sai Baba's writings and lectures.

Revealed teachings: Yes.

Claim: To be an avatar of Vishnu, the only incarnation of God on earth today.

Examples of occult potential: Spiritism, psychic abilities.

Examples of key literature: Sai Baba, *Sathya Sai Speaks,* Vols. 1–9.

Attitude toward Christianity: Rejecting.

Quotes:

"Swami can do anything he wishes. He is God" (Murphet, *Sai Baba,* p. 133)

"[You must achieve] elimination of the mind, which is the arch obstacle in the [spiritual] path." (Sai Baba interview in Samuel Sandweiss, *Sai Baba: The Holy Man and the Psychiatrist* (1975), p. 206.)

Note: A good friend of John Weldon, Tal Brooke, was perhaps the highest American disciple of Sai Baba for 18 months before converting to Christ. His valuable insights are contained in *Riders of the Cosmic Circuit* (Lion), a powerful critique of the Eastern gurus, and in

Avatar of Night (Vikas House), a bestselling Indian critique of Sai Baba. Both offer valuable polemics against Indian spirituality in general. Brooke gained insights into Baba that few people ever have access to, in direct contrast to the glowing portraits painted by Baba's biographers and disciples.

DOCTRINAL SUMMARY

God: Brahman (Impersonal Being, Consciousness and Bliss).

Jesus: A Hindu Vedantist who learned wisdom in India.

The Christ: The higher (or "God") consciousness in Jesus, the human way shower.

The Holy Spirit: Psychic energy.

Salvation: Achieving enlightenment or monistic consciousness by placing oneself along Baba's spiritual path.

Man: Inwardly divine.

Sin: Relative; ignorance.

Satan: A figurative term for temptation.

The Second Coming: Sai Baba constitutes the Second Coming of Christ.

The Fall: Into maya (illusion).

The Bible: A holy scripture correctly interpreted by Sai Baba.

Death: Ultimately beneficial.

Heaven and Hell: Positive or negative states of consciousness or temporary places.

SCIENTOLOGY

INFO AT A GLANCE

Description: Scientology is a novel and eclectic religion drawing from Eastern philosophy, modern psychology and occult practice. It seeks to release human potential, free the soul and restore man to his original state as pure, immortal spirit.

Purpose: To "clear" the planet and free Thetans (eternal spirits in bondage to matter).

Founder: L. Ron Hubbard (1911–1986).

Source of authority: L. Ron Hubbard, whose writings have officially been termed "scripture." Claimed to be the only source for solving mankind's problems.

How does it claim to work?: Through its "counseling" procedures (termed "auditing"), Scientology alleges that its methods offer the only final solution to mankind's problems. Auditing "locates" and "resolves" "engrams," or past traumatic experiences, that allegedly inhibit true spiritual enlightenment. Scientology claims that it can eventually free the human spirit from its bondage to the material world.

Scientific evaluation: While the specific religious tenets of Scientology are incapable of scientific evaluation, many or most of its stated beliefs capable of evaluation run contrary to most basic data in the natural and social sciences.

Examples of occult potential: Development of psychic powers, out of body experiences and other occult practice.

Major problem: The specific claims of Scientology in many different fields of study are inconsistent with known data; the extent to which Scientology has or has not reformed its past unconscionable methods of dealing with critics (according to *Time*, 2/10/86, p. 86, the Church had fielded as many as "5,000 'covert agents' to harass opponents"); the rejection of the material world as an "illusion."

Biblical/Christian evaluation: As an occult religion having specific theological beliefs contrary to biblical teaching, membership in the Church of Scientology is logically proscribed for Christians.

Potential dangers: The acceptance of false data carries its own consequences; the physical, psychological and spiritual hazards associated with occult practice; psychological harm from "auditing."

Key literature: The books of L. Ron Hubbard. These include *Dianetics: The Modern Science of Mental Health; Dianetics Today; Dianetics and Scientology Technical Dictionary; Science of Survival; The Church of Scientology* and hundreds of other books, articles and policy letters. Periodicals include: *Advance!; Source; The Auditor; Celebrity; International Scientology News.* Hubbard Communications Office bulletins are abbreviated HCOB.

DOCTRINAL SUMMARY

God: Purposefully undefined; all Theta (life); the Eighth Dynamic/"infinity."

Jesus: A man who was not particularly enlightened whom the church invented as the savior of the world. Some Scientologists may classify Him as an "Operating Thetan" (OT): a person aware of his true nature and abilities.

Salvation: Enlightenment of the thetan as to his true nature and abilities.

Man: In his true nature, an eternal spirit being with divine powers (Thetan).

Sin: Falsehood or ignorance and especially that which opposes Scientology.

Satan: A Christian myth; redefined to include Scientological concepts.

The Second Coming: A misunderstanding of Buddhist teaching.

The Fall: Into matter and ignorance.

The Bible: Accepted as one of the world's religious searchings, but as far as Scientology practices are concerned it is largely irrelevant.

Death: An inconsequential dropping of the body which all Thetans have experienced trillions of times.

Heaven and Hell: Christian myths, or mental implants from previous lives.

PRACTICE AND TEACHINGS

The basic tenets of Scientology result from an eclectic mixture of Eastern philosophy, Hubbard's personal research into a variety of disciplines and the "data" uncovered from "auditing." Auditing is Scientology's "counseling," an extensive examination of the present life and the "past lives" of the initiate, the "preclear." In one of its many definitions, Hubbard has defined Scientology as "the Western anglicized continuance of many earlier forms of wisdom."[1] These include the Vedas, Taoism, Buddhism, Judaism, Gnosticism, early Greek civilization and the teachings of Jesus, Nietzsche and Freud. According to Hubbard, "Scientology has accomplished the goal of religion expressed in all Man's written history, the freeing of the soul by wisdom."[2]

Scientology divides the mind into two components, the analytic and the reactive, roughly parallel to the conscious, or rational, mind and unconscious, or "irrational," mind, respectively. Experiences of extreme shock, pain or unconsciousness cause "engrams," or sensory impressions, to be recorded in the reactive, or unconscious, mind. These mental pictures are the cause of our emotional and physical problems today.[3] They can be dislodged only through Scientology procedures.[4]

While these memory pictures are perfectly recorded, they lay dormant in the brain until restimulated by a similar incident. When restimulated, they cause conditioned, stimulus-response behavior that is counterproductive to the person's well being. Thus, when the brain sees a similar situation to a past negative experience, even if it is not now a personal threat, it responds as if it were, producing inappropriate and self-defeating behavior. For example, a boy falls out of a tree just as a red car passes by and is knocked unconscious. Later, even as a man, red cars (even red things) may restimulate the episode in various ways and cause irrational reactions. This "engram," therefore, may cause the man to refuse to ride in red cars, and he may get ill or dizzy when confronted with the possibility.

In this sense, we are all more or less conditioned "machines" that respond to our "operator" (the reactive mind). Scientology believes that this restimulation is fairly automatic. In other words, we are not free beings; we are slaves of an "aberrated" mind. Scientology maintains that through Dianetic or Scientology therapy we can be exposed to our engrams and "erase" them and become "clear," in control of our behavior ("at cause") rather than at the mercy of a damaged reactive mind ("at effect").

Scientology also teaches that through reincarnation people have been accumulating engrams for trillions of years. In order to resolve hidden engrams, initiates must be mentally whisked back to reexperience the damaging events of their past lives. According to Scientology, each person is really a "thetan," an immortal spirit who has been so damaged by engrams that he has forgotten that he is immortal and a thetan. Thetans have absolute control over bodies but, sadly, they think they are only bodies (a terrible fate) and hence they are bound by the "MEST" (matter, energy, space, time) universe. Each time a body dies, the thetan must enter another body, but he brings with him all his trillions of years' accumulation of engrams. Thetans thus are no longer free but are in bondage to the material universe.[5] Scientology claims it can free the thetan. Many people have spent thousands of dollars to experience "freedom" from engrams.

THEOLOGY

God

The concept of God appears to be panentheistic or perhaps polytheistic depending on one's view of the thetan. Panentheism refers to the belief that all finite entities are within but not identical to God. When Scientology defines God as "all Theta" (life) it indicates a belief similar to panentheism. However, Scientology also seems to grant thetans the status of ontologically independent existence. Thus if thetans, who are eternal, are considered to have divine attributes, or at least "infinite creative potential," and if in some sense each thetan is a "god," then a polytheistic classification seems appropriate.

What the Church refers to as "the Supreme Being" is purposely left undefined and does not become particularly relevant in Scientology theory or practice. It is variously implied to be or referred to as "Nature," "Infinity," "the Eighth Dynamic," "all Theta" (life) and so forth. Usually the individual Scientologist is free to interpret this, God, in whatever manner he wishes.[6]

Man

In their true nature, people are not the limited and pitiful bodies and egos they imagine themselves to be. They are thetans, whose fundamental nature is basically good and divine. They are not morally fallen but simply ignorant of their perfection. Their only "Fall" was into matter, not sin. How did this Fall come about?

Trillions of years ago thetans became bored, so they emanated mental universes to play in. Soon they became so entranced by their own creation and they were so conditioned by the

manifestations of their own thought processes they lost all awareness of their true identity and spiritual nature.[7] In other words, thetans became hypnotized and trapped by MEST. Compounding the problem were the accumulation of countless "engrams" throughout trillions of years of existence. The final result was a materially enslaved entity existing as a mere stimulus–response machine. Today, only slavery to the reactive mind and bondage to the MEST universe (the physical body and environment) are what remain of once glorious spiritual beings who ruled the heavens.

NOTES

1. L. Ron Hubbard, *The Creation of Human Ability* (Los Angeles: The Publications Organization Worldwide, 1968), p. 177.
2. Ibid., p. 180; cf. Church of Scientology Information Service, Department of Archives, *Scientology: A World Religion Emerges in the Space Age* (Los Angeles: U.S. Ministry of Public Relations, 1974), p. 3-17.
3. Impact or injury must be involved for an engram to register, but "the engram is the single and sole source of aberration and psychosomatic illness," L. Ron Hubbard, *Dianetics Today*, pp. 43, 47; cf. pp. 37-106 and especially pp. 38-59.
4. E.g., L. Ron Hubbard, *Dianetics Today*, pp. 947-951; L. Ron Hubbard, *The Volunteer Minister's Handbook* (Los Angeles, Church of Scientology of California, 1976), p. 551; cf. former 14-year member Cyril Vospers' comments in *The Mind Benders* (London: Neville Spearman, 1971), pp. 164-166 and by member Peter Gillham, *Telling It Like It Is: A Course in Scientology Dissemination* (Phoenix, AZ: Institue of Applied Philosophy, 1972), p. 26.
5. See note 3 and L. Ron Hubbard, *Scientology: A History of Man* (Sussex, England: L. Ron Hubbard Communications Office, 1961), pp. 5-76, especially pp. 53-60 for a discussion of alleged evolutionary dynamics and the impact on one's current life; cf. the discussion in Christopher Evans, *Cults of Unreason* (New York: Delta, 1973), pp. 38-47 and Roy Wallis, *The Road to Total Freedom: A Sociological Analysis of Scientology* (New York: Columbia University Press, 1977), pp. 103-104.
6. L. Ron Hubbard, *What Is Scientology?* p. 200. On panentheism see *Scientology: A World Religion Emerges*, p. 21-24 with L. Ron Hubbard; *Dianetics and Scientology Technical Dictionary* (Los Angeles: Church of Scientology of California, 1975), p. 429; cf. L. Ron Hubbard, *Ceremonies of the Founding of the Church of Scientology* (Los Angeles: The American St. Hill Organization, 1971), p. 41; *Reality* magazine, No. 121, p. 3; L. Ron Hubbard, *The Creation of Human Ability*, p. 227; *Advance*, No. 35, pp. 14-15; No. 36, p. 6.
7. See notes 5 and 6.

SELF REALIZATION FELLOWSHIP

TABLE OF CONTENTS

INFO AT A GLANCE

Purpose: To reveal the divine nature of mankind, abolish religious division (such as to reveal the unity of the teachings of Christ and Krishna) and provide direct experience of God through kriya yoga.

Founder: Paramahansa Yogananda (1893–1952).

Source of authority: The writings of Sri Yukteswar, Paramahansa Yogananda, Daya Mata and other qualified leaders, but principally those of Yogananda.

Claim: To possess and disseminate "a knowledge of definite scientific techniques to attaining direct personal experience of God."

Occult dynamics: Incorporates spiritism and psychic meditation; occult yoga practice to activate "psychic centers" (chakras).

Examples of key literature: Yogananda's *Man's Eternal Quest* and *Autobiography of a Yogi*. This latter 600 page book was released in 1946 and is the best known publication of the movement. Issued in some twenty languages, according to the SRF website it is "used as a text and reference work in numerous colleges and universities." It is also considered by many to be a spiritual classic; for example, the website cites Columbia University Press as stating that "there has been nothing before, written in English or any other European language like this presentation of yoga." *Self-Realization* is the principal periodical.

Attitude toward Christianity: Rejecting.

Quote:

"If you want to know Jesus, meditate on the Christ Consciousness in him."
— Paramahansa Yogananda, SRF website

"We worship only Brahman, Spirit,"
— Paramahansa Yogananda, *Man's Eternal Quest*, p. 299.

Note: Two modern offshoots of Self Realization Fellowship (SRF) include sects established by two of Yogananda's disciples, Swami Kriyananda (Melvin Higgins), founder of the Yoga Fellowship, and Roy Eugene Davis, founder of the Center for Spiritual Awareness in Lakemont, GA (a.k.a. Christian Spiritual Alliance). In a letter to John Weldon, SRF declared that these former disciples have not been affiliated with SRF "for many, many years and their activities are not related to those of our Guru's society." They also believe such splinter groups are being disobedient to the divine will. "We are sad because we know, from Guru-Deva's words to us, that this is not the divine will."[1]

References to *Encyclopedia of New Age Beliefs:* Altered States of Consciousness, Astrology, Channeling, Divination, Dream Work, Eastern Gurus, Enlightenment, Mantras and Mandalas, Meditation, Visualization, Yoga.

DOCTRINAL SUMMARY

God: Brahman: impersonal being, consciousness, and bliss (*satchitananda*).

Jesus: A man who realized the Christ.

The Christ: The divine part of man.

The Holy Spirit: Impersonal energy.

The Trinity: Brahman personified; for instance, the Father is Sat (divine Bliss); the Son is tat (universal consciousness); the Spirit is aum (cosmic vibration).

Salvation: By knowledge and works.

Man: Inwardly divine.

Sin: Ignorance.

Satan: Maya (illusion).

The second coming: Cosmic consciousness.

The Fall: Symbolic.

The Bible: One of many scriptures, all of which are believed to teach the same key truths of Yogananda and SRF.

Death: Ultimately one with life.

Heaven and Hell: States of consciousness.

INTRODUCTION AND HISTORY

The Self-Realization Fellowship (SRF) was the second major Hindu movement to come to America after Vedanta. The occasion was the 1920 International Congress of Religious Liberals in Boston, sponsored by the American Unitarian Association (cf. the chapter Unitarian Universalism). This congress had selected Paramahansa Yogananda to come to America to represent India and Hindu spirituality. ("Yogananda" means bliss, *ananda*, through divine union, yoga.)

Yogananda personally initiated over 100,000 students into kriya yoga, the "distinctive" SRF meditative yoga practice. Like all yogas, kriya yoga is designed to awaken and energize the chakras, the purported psychic centers along the spine, which is said to lead to "God-realization," the personal awareness of one's underlying unity with the ultimate divine essence.

Paramahansa Yogananda

Paramahansa Yogananda was born Mukunda Lal Ghosh in Gorakhpur, India, January 5, 1893. He evinced the typical traits of a guru: 1) he displayed various occult powers from childhood, which were interpreted as evidence of divine blessing; 2) though he had been exposed to Christianity early on, he purposefully rejected it by the age of eight and 3) according to his autobiography, he was at times so "drunk with God" from occult practice that he brought numerous problems into his life.

In 1995 the SRF celebrated the seventy-fifth anniversary of their work in the United States. Today SRF has 500 yoga meditation centers on 5 continents in 55 countries, including a network of over 20 schools and colleges in India. In the United States, there are some 30 temples and meditation centers with meditation groups in about 20 states.[2] The most popular lay minister at the Los Angeles headquarters is television star Dennis "McCloud" Weaver, an SRF disciple for some 40 years.

PRACTICE AND TEACHINGS

Among the "Aims and Ideals" of the SRF (as set forth by Yogananda in all SRF literature and as given at their website) are the dissemination of their Hindu spiritual practices throughout the world. They include the following: teaching "that the purpose of life is the evolution, through self effort, of man's limited mortal consciousness into God Consciousness"; "to reveal the complete harmony and basic oneness of original Christianity as taught by Jesus Christ and original Yoga as taught by Bhagavan Krishna"; to promote spiritual and cultural harmony between East and

427

West, to liberate man from spiritual ignorance and to "serve mankind as one's larger Self." Showing the unity between the teachings of Christ and Krishna is held to be central to SRF goals. In other words, SRF maintains that the true, original and principal teachings of Jesus, the Jewish Messiah, were the *same* yoga teachings as those of the mythological god Krishna of the Hindus. We will critically examine this naive idea later.

SRF claims religious tolerance and pluralism, and even to be Christian. However the essentially Hindu outlook of SRF is illustrated in Yogananda's definition of "self realization" as the recognition of our own divinity. It is "The knowing—in body, mind, and soul—that we are one with the omnipresence of God; that we do not have to pray that it comes to us, that we are not merely near it at all times, but that God's omnipresence is our omnipresence. . . ."[3] The essential beliefs of SRF parallel Vedantic Hinduism in the monistic, or non-dualist (*advaita*), tradition. These beliefs however, are modified for Western and Christian consump-

tion. For instance, the highest and *impersonal* God of Vedanta (*Brahman*) is referred to in Christian terms as "The Father."

The third of SRF's 11 "Aims and Ideals" declares that its purpose is not just to reveal the "complete harmony and basic oneness" of Christianity and Yoga but to show that "these principles of truth are the common scientific foundation of all true religions." Three of these "principles of truth" are: (1) the impersonal Brahman alone is real; (2) all else is *maya* (illusion); and (3) that spiritual growth comes by realization of God (Brahman, one's true self) or self-realization through kriya yogic practice.

NOTES

1. *Self-Realization* (Los Angeles, CA: Self Realization Fellowship), Winter 1979, p. 26.
2. *The Illustrated Weekly of India*, Jan. 29, 1978; *Self-Realization*, Summer 1979, pp. 62-63.
3. Paramahansa Yogananda, *Man's Eternal Quest* (Los Angeles, CA: Self Realization Fellowship, 1975), p. 480.

SIKHISM

INFO AT A GLANCE

Name: Sikhism.

Purpose: To foster universal brotherhood.

Founder: Guru Nanak.

Source of authority: The Adi Granth ("the original book"), the Sikh Bible.

Revealed teachings: Guru Nanak was the recipient of visions and claimed divine inspiration, as did many of the principal Sikh Gurus.

Claim: To represent the teachings of the ten historic Sikh Gurus.

Examples of occult potential: General psychic abilities, revelation by the founders.

Key literature: *The Adi Granth*—compiled writings of most of the Sikh Gurus. Gobind Singh compiled the final version and also wrote the *Dasm Granth,* the *Granth* (Book) *Of the Tenth Guru,* which varies in importance among Sikhs.

Attitude toward Christianity: Rejecting.

Quotes:

"To know thyself, is to know God. God is what? God is a totality, and when One knows the total-

ity of one's personality, one is God." (*The Teachings of Yogi Bhajan,* p. 136.)

"But there is only one way and there is only one God and there is only one way to reach Him and there is only one truth to know and there is only one humanity to practice one-pointedness of mind—that is righteousness [righteous consciousness]. Whether you are a Christian, a Jew, a Buddhist, or anything, it doesn't make any difference." (*The Teachings of Yogi Bhajan,* p. 112)

DOCTRINAL SUMMARY

God: Ineffable; One.

Jesus: A human teacher.

Salvation: Achieved by works through the guru's grace.

Man: Inwardly divine.

Sin: Ignorance; one primarily sins against the Nam (holy name of God) or against the gurus.

Satan: A Christian myth.

Scripture: *The Adi Granth.*

Death: Ultimately inconsequential.

Heaven and Hell: Temporal states or places.

SILVA MIND CONTROL

INFO AT A GLANCE

Name: Silva Mind Control (SMC).

Purpose: SMC is a spiritistic, New Age, "self-help" seminar that claims to be able to institute "the next phase of human evolution on this planet."

Founder: Jose Silva (1914–).

Source of authority: Jose Silva; "controlled" esp.

Revealed teachings: Yes.

Claim: SCM claims that it is "the first and only fully guaranteed method known to be effective in developing and controlling Effective Sensory Projection"[1] (i.e., "mind projection" for psychic purposes).

Occult dynamics: Psychic development, spiritism and other forms of occult activity.

Key literature: *The Silva Mind Control Method; I Have a Hunch: The Autobiography of Jose Silva; Reflections; Mysteries to the Keys of the Kingdom;* and other books by Jose Silva.

Attitude toward Christianity: Rejecting

Quote:
"Jesus' purpose on earth was to train everyone to use their 'right brain,' to become clairvoyant."
—Jose Silva, *I Have a Hunch,*
Vol. 1, appendix, p. 8A.

Note: SMC has resulted in a number of "offshoots" that have utilized SMC techniques, including Mind Dynamics and est/The Forum. According to Silva, both Alex Everett, founder of Mind Dynamics, and Werner Erhard, founder of est/The Forum, are SMC graduates.[2] A number of popular books also utilize SMC principles. Jess Stearns' best-selling The Miracle *Power of Alpha Thinking* is basically SMC.[3]

References to *Encyclopedia of New Age Beliefs*: Altered States of Consciousness, Channeling, Hypnosis, Meditation, New Age Inner Work, Visualization.

DOCTRINAL SUMMARY

God: Unipersonal or pantheistic.

Jesus Christ: An enlightened man who used the principles of Silva Mind Control.

Salvation: Employing Silva Mind Control and the right brain hemisphere to achieve spiritual enlightenment and solve the problems of humanity.

Man: Potentially a god.

Sin: Ignorance or failing to think properly.

The Afterlife: Universalist; spiritual progression to higher planes of existence.

INTRODUCTION AND HISTORY

In 1979 a group of people caused worldwide press coverage for their attempt to use "ESP" to affect the orbit of the then faltering Skylab, which later came crashing to earth. After their failure, the project founder logically concluded: "Apparently the height of the orbit was not influenced by the mental projections from earth."[4] This vainglorious effort represented the brainchild of Silva Mind Control International (SMCI), a large occult "human potential" organization, which had earlier attempted to psychically influence astronauts while in space.[5] Since Silva Mind Control claims it is designed to develop psychic powers in anyone within only four days, perhaps the SMC attempt at such stalwart projects is understandable.

Thousands of professionals have been through SMC and utilize some of its principles in their respective professions. Some executives at RCA use it, as do directors in the Mary Kay Corporation. Numerous physicians and psychiatrists use it as well as over nine million others in every American state and in 107 countries and 29 languages around the world.[6] Founder Jose Silva hopes to see literally tens of thousands of ministers, physicians, psychologists, government leaders, law enforcement officials, engineers, archaeologists, meteorologists, astronomers, industrialists, financiers, executives, pilots and others become psychic and change the world into a paradise.[7] Allegedly, "His work signifies and has become one of the first steps taken toward the second phase of human evolution on this planet."[8] It is claimed that Jose Silva is "recognized as a genius in the fields of business, education, athletics, science, art and philosophy," to name a few.[9] Silva himself states unabashedly, "Before we developed this method, there had been no such training since the time of Christ."[10] Jesus, naturally, was an expert in Silva Mind Control.

Today the organization is a large corporate structure. For example, there is the Institute of Psychorientology, which is defined by Jose Silva as "the study of orienting Mind in the subjective world of the [psychic] mind dimension."[11] It is the central organization and manages "research and development," although most of its power has been turned over to Silva Mind Control International, Inc. Another branch, Silva Sensor Systems, coordinates parapsychologically oriented bookstores and provides continuing programs for graduates, tapes and SMC lecturers for the general public. As of 1999, SMC had been taught, often with academic credits available, in scores of colleges and high schools and even numerous elementary schools. SMC offers special lectures and courses for professionals.

PRACTICE AND TEACHINGS

Despite claims to uniqueness, the SMC method is merely a variation on numerous common forms of human potentialism and meditative psychic development, and it often has a "Christian" flavor.

According to SMC, "negative thinking," using terms such as "can't," "won't," "hate" and so on, is forbidden. SMC even believes that employing certain "negative" cultural phrases ("He burns me up") slowly programs people into sickness, pain and death. Hence, a central premise, as in the modern "Christian" "Faith" movement, is the tremendous power of words to impact the psyche (cf. our *The Facts On the Faith Movement*). Silva declares, "Words have special power at deep levels of mind,"[12] and, "Words do not just reflect reality, they create reality."[13]

NOTES

1. Jose Silva, *Silva Mind Control: Alpha Theta Brainwave Function* (Laredo, TX: 1977), brochure, p. 1.
2. Personal conversation with Jose Silva, May 1986.
3. Jose Silva, *I Have a Hunch: The Autobiography of Jose Silva*, Vol. 2 (Laredo, TX: Institute of Psychorientology, 1983), p. 158.
4. *Mind Control Newsletter*, Vol. 10, no. 9, p. 5.
5. Silva, *I Have a Hunch*, Vol. 1, pp. 238ff.
6. Personal conversation with Jose Silva, May 1986.
7. Silva, *I Have a Hunch*, Vol. 1, pp. 11A-24A; Jose Silva, *The Mystery of the Keys to the Kingdom* (Laredo, TX: Institute of Psychorientology, 1984), p. 11.
8. Jose Silva, *Reflections* (Laredo, TX: Institute of Psychorientology, 1982), pp. 5-6.
9. Silva, *I Have a Hunch*, Vol. 2, p. i.
10. Ibid., p. 161.
11. Harry McKnight, *Silva Mind Control: Key to Inner Kingdoms Through Psychorientology* (Laredo, TX: Institute of Psychorientology, rev. 1975, 1976), p. 82.
12. Jose Silva and Philip Miele, *The Silva Mind Control Method* (New York: Simon and Schuster, 1977), p. 60.
13. Ibid., p. 56.

SRI CHINMOY

INFO AT A GLANCE

Name: Sri Chinmoy Centers.

Purpose: Achieving Hindu God-realization through the teachings of *advaita* Vedanta.

Founder: Sri Chinmoy.

Source of authority: The writings of Sri Chinmoy.

Claim: To be the most rapid path to God-realization.

Attitude toward Christianity: Rejecting.

Quotes:

"If you remain calm and quiet, and allow your spiritual [spirit] Guide to enter into you, you will become flooded with Peace. This kind of turning in is not only a valid and correct practice, but is *essential* for one who has placed himself under the guidance of a spiritual Master." (Sri Chinmoy, *Yoga and the Spiritual Life* (1974), p. 113, emphasis added.)

DOCTRINAL SUMMARY

God: The Brahman of *advaita* Vedanta.

Jesus: An advanced being, a Brahman (God-realized) soul.

Salvation: Realization of inner divinity.

Man: Inwardly one essence with Brahman.

Sin: Ignorance.

The Afterlife: Spiritual progression through reincarnation to union with Brahman.

Satan: The embodiment of ignorance.

Prayer: Meditative consciousness.

THE SUFI ORDER

Name: The Sufi Order of Pir Vilayat Inayat Khan, and the Sufi Islamia Ruhaniat Society of Samuel L. Lewis.

Purpose: To help unite East and West and spread the leaders' interpretation of the teachings of Sufism, the original religion of God.

Founder: Hazrat Inayat Khan, Pir Vilayat Inayat Khan, Samuel Lewis.

Source of authority: Hazrat Inayat Khan.

Claim: The Sufi Order constitutes the true essence of all religions.

Examples of occult potential: Development of psychic powers, trance states, spiritism.

Quote:

"The God of the Sufi is the God of every creed, and the God of all. Names make no difference to him. Allah, God, Gott, Dieu, Khuda, Brahma, or Bhagwan." (*The Sufi Message of Hazrat Inayat Khan,* Vol. 1, p. 13.)

"The divinity of Christ means the divinity of man, although divinity itself is the ideal." (Ibid., p. 109.)

Note: Samuel Lewis' Sufi Islamia Ruhaniat Society is a split from the Sufi Order of Pir Vilayat Inayat Khan, and the writings of Hazrat Inayat Khan are foundational to both groups. The individual writings of Samuel Lewis and Pir Vilayat Khan reflect the philosophy of Hazrat Khan, his books being sold and promoted by both groups as their message.

DOCTRINAL SUMMARY

God: God is everything, in everything, transcendent and ultimately indescribable.

Jesus: A saikh or murshid (enlightened spiritual master).

The Christ: The divine part of Jesus, active in all great masters.

Salvation: God-realization through mysticism toward achieving union with God.

Man: Inwardly divine.

Sin: Ignorance of one's true nature.

Satan: Figurative for emotional agitation.

The Bible: One of many scriptures mystically re-interpreted to support Sufi precepts.

Death: In general something good, a normal transition or spiritual advance.

Heaven and Hell: Inner states, e.g., heaven is inner peace.

SUFISM

INFO AT A GLANCE

Name: Sufism.

Purpose: The union of God and man.

Founder: Uncertain.

Source of authority: From one perspective the only authority is individual experience, but Sufi literature (a product of Islam, Hinduism and mysticism) is a reliable guide.

Examples of occult potential: Psychic powers, trance states, possession (although psychic powers are a natural by-product of Sufi practices, some groups do not stress them).

Attitude toward Christianity: Rejecting.

Note: Defining the whole of Sufism in uniform doctrinal terms is impossible. Sufis may make claims for their beliefs or non-beliefs, the accuracy of which may rest upon contradictory traditions, theology, mysticism or mere semantics. Some Islamic traditions within Sufism variously oppose certain Hindu precepts. However, since Sufism is composed of both these religions, others may combine them. Typically, it is Hinduism, not Islam, that gains the upper hand, at least doctrinally if not in practice.

The eclectic and inclusive philosophy of Sufism presents a related difficulty, illustrated by Indries Shah. Possibly the leading exponent of mystical Sufism in the West, he asserts, "Is there a conflict between Sufism and other methods of thought? There cannot be, because Sufism embodies all methods of thought." (Indries Shah, *The Way of Sufi*, pp. 286–287.) According to Shah, the problem of defining Sufism lies not with the internal inconsistencies of Sufism but with the obstinate attitude of the non-Sufis. "So many people profess themselves bewildered by Sufi lore that one is forced to the conclusion that they want to be bewildered." (Ibid., p. 9.) The problem, then, is not due to Sufi secrecy, inscrutability or mysticism but the "ignorance" of the unenlightened. Since Shah maintains that "the knowledge of ordinary people" is not legitimate, one can perhaps understand his position (ibid., p. 238). Thus, one cannot study Sufism "from the single standpoint that it is a mystical system designed to produce ecstasy and based on theological concepts"; and Sufism will not be truly understood "until more scholars avail themselves of Sufi interpretive methods." (Ibid., p. 33; cf. p. 34.) In other words, we cannot know what "true" Sufism is unless we become mystics also. Shah's approach is typically Sufi.

DOCTRNIAL SUMMARY

God: Ineffable.

Jesus: A Sufi master (murshid).

Salvation: The divine aspect of Jesus or (sometimes) the divine part of all great religious teachers.

Man: By psycho-spiritual techniques to achieve mystical union with God. Inwardly man is divine.

The Bible: One of many scriptures; not particularly important.

Death: A spiritual advance.

Heaven and Hell: Mental conditions; temporary experiences or places.

SUFISM REORIENTED/ MEHER BABA

Name: Sufism Reoriented.

Purpose: Achievement of God-realization: awareness that God alone exists and that man in his true being is one with God.

Founder: Meher Baba (1894–1969).

Source of authority: Meher Baba.

Claim: Meher Baba is the avatar, the God-Man of the age.

Examples of occult potential: Eastern meditation, psychic powers, spiritism.

Attitude toward Christianity: Rejecting.

Quotes:

"I am God." (Meher Baba, in Purdom, *The God-Man*, p. 329.)

"If you think Baba is the Devil, say it. Do not be afraid." (Meher Baba, in Purdom, *The God-Man*, p. 218)

Note: Meher Baba gave up verbal communication in 1925 and communicated only by an alphabet board and later by gestures only. Most of his books are by dictation or gesture. All, however, were reputedly confirmed by him as accurate. Meher Baba spent much of his life among the *masts,* pronounced "musts," the insane of India, who achieved this state through devotion to God or Hindu spiritual practice:

"The *masts* are in various stages of involution of consciousness and may be found on any of the 'planes.' They include those who are totally unconscious of physical life, those who are dimly conscious of it, and those who are, at times, more or less fully aware of their surroundings and of what they are doing; among them are various types of *yogis, saliks, sadhus* and others. The God-merged and God-mad are the important *masts,* being the most advanced; they of three main types. (1) Those whose minds become unbalanced through unceasing dwelling upon thoughts about God so that they neglect all normal human requirements. (2) Those whose minds become unbalanced by sudden contact with a highly advanced spiritual being. (3) Those who seek spiritual experience and meet a crisis from which they do not recover. What characterizes all is concentration upon the love of God. (Disciple and biographer C. B. Purdom describing the *Masts,* Meher Baba's beloved, in *The God-Man*, p. 138. Baba declared, "I shall bow down to . . . the masts whom I worship" [p. 199]. The term is apparently derived from the Persian "Masti," "overpowered.")

DOCTRINAL SUMMARY

God: Indescribable unconsciousness.

Jesus: A God-Man or Master.

The Christ: Jesus' spiritual awareness.

Salvation: By works; attaining God-realization.

Man: Inwardly God.

Sin: Error, ignorance, lower consciousness; sanskaras.

Death: Ultimately beneficial.

Heaven and Hell: Temporary states of consciousness after death.

SWAMI KRIYANANDA

Name: Swami Kriyananda, Ananda Cooperative Village.

Purpose: To spread the teachings of Paramahansa Yogananda; to help people find the God Yogananda worshipped (Brahman).

Founder: Swami Kriyananda (James Donald Walters). Kriyananda means: "The bliss of Kriya Yoga.")

Source of authority: The writings of Paramahansa Yogananda and Swami Kriyananda.

Revealed teachings: No direct claim, but Kriyananda's guru was Paramahansa Yogananda, who received spiritistic inspiration.

Claim: To represent the purest, highest and oldest spiritual tradition in the world.

Examples of occult potential: Yoga, astrology, potential spiritism.

Key literature: *The Path* and other books by Kriyananda; Yogananda's *Autobiography of a Yogi.*

Attitude toward Christianity: Rejecting.

Quote:

"What is Christ? St. Simeon the new theologian wrote, 'I move my hand, and Christ moves, who is my hand.' Meister Eckhart wrote, 'Between the only begotten Son and the soul there is no distinction.' . . . My guru explained that the true 'Son' of God is the infinite consciousness at the heart of every atom in creation, as distinct from the infinite Spirit, the Father *beyond* His creation. This 'Son' is present in all of us but it is *manifested* only in those who have overcome the hypnosis of human delusion, of infinitesimal limitation, and realized themselves as one with the Father." (Swami Kriyananda, *Eastern Thoughts Western Thoughts,* pp. 67–68)

DOCTRINAL SUMMARY

God: Brahman (impersonal being, consciousness, bliss).

Jesus: A master.

The Christ: The divine essence.

The Holy Spirit: The cosmic creative vibration, *aum.*

The Trinity: *Sat Tat Aum.*

Salvation: By works (yoga) through higher consciousness.

Man: Inwardly divine.

Sin: Ignorance.

Satan: A universal conscious force, the lila (sport) of Brahman producing maya, the illusion of the creation.

The Second Coming: Inner awakening or Yogananda's vision allegedly carried on in Kriyananda.

The Bible: A lesser scripture that must be interpreted figuratively, or symbolically, to receive its benefit.

Death: An illusion, spiritual advancement.

Heaven and Hell: States of consciousness or temporary planes of existence.

437

SWAMI MUKTANANDA

INFO AT A GLANCE

Name: Swami Muktananda, Siddha Yoga Dham of America (S.Y.D.A.).

Purpose: To help people through kundalini yoga to escape the delusion of duality.

Founder: Muktananda Paramahansa.

Source of authority: The writings of Muktananda.

Revealed teachings: Yes, also several of the texts used by the late Muktananda claim divine inspiration; for example, one of his main texts, the *Shiva Sutras,* are held to be revealed by the God Shiva to a sage, Vasuguptacharya (Muktananda, *Play of Consciousness,* p. 201).

Claim: To be a dispenser of mass *shaktipat* (the transmission of occult power from guru to disciple).

Examples of occult potential: Spiritism, kundalini arousal, ancestor worship.

Attitude toward Christianity: Rejecting.

Quote:

"Muktananda, He is the God of the universe." (Muktananda, *Mukteshiwari,* part 2, p. 158.)

Note: Swami Nityananda, Muktananda's guru has had a direct or indirect influence upon several modern gurus. For example, Swami Rudrananda (1928–1973), the author of S*piritual Cannibalism* (1973), was a disciple of both Nityananda and Muktananda, and Rudrananda went on to heavily influence the spiritual anarchist Da (Bubba) Free John of the Free Primitive Church of Divine Communion (the Dawn Horse Community).

DOCTRINAL SUMMARY

God: Shiva, Nirguna Brahman (impersonal being, consciousness, bliss).

Jesus: A man who attained God-realization.

Salvation: By personal effort and yoga; through kundalini arousal and knowledge of one's innate divinity.

Man: Inwardly divine.

Sin: Ignorance, attachment to maya (illusion).

The Bible: Largely irrelevant.

Death: Non-existent; a benevolent transition.

Heaven and Hell: Inner states or temporary places.

Swami Rama

Swami R

Info at a Glance

Name: The Himalayan International Institute of Yoga Science and Philosophy, Swami Rama.

Purpose: To help unify religions and provide the path to and knowledge of Supreme Reality (Brahman).

Founder: Swami Rama.

Source of authority: Swami Rama.

Revealed teachings: Yes.

Claim: To provide knowledge of the highest of all ways for attaining spiritual reality.

Examples of occult potential: Psychic development, spiritism.

Examples of key literature: Swami Rama, *Lectures on Yoga* and other volumes; Swami Ajaya (ed.), *Living with the Himalayan Masters: Spiritual Experiences of Swami Rama.*

Attitude toward Christianity: Rejecting.

Quote:

"We cannot reach the realm of Divinity in any other way except over the bridge of ego. There-fore he who wants to know God, should know himself." (Swami Rama, *Life Here and Hereafter* (1976), p. 86)

Doctrinal Summary

God: The impersonal Brahman (absolute being, consciousness, bliss).

Jesus: A master or prophet who attained Hindu God-realization.

The Christ: Cosmic ("Christ") consciousness.

Salvation: Enlightenment of one's inner divine nature through yoga meditation.

Man: Inwardly divine.

Sin: Material attachment; ignorance, error; primarily imperfection in consciousness.

Satan: Spiritual ignorance.

The Bible: One of many scriptures properly interpreted in light of Hindu beliefs.

Death: An aspect of life.

Heaven and Hell: States of mind.

Swami Rudrananda

Info at a Glance

Name: Swami Rudrananda (Rudi), Rudrananda Foundation.

Purpose: Spiritual enlightenment through psychic development.

Source of authority: Swami Rudrananda.

Examples of occult potential: Spiritism.

Key literature: *Spiritual Cannibalism.*

Attitude toward Christianity: Rejecting.

Doctrinal Summary

God: Pantheistic.

Jesus: An enlightened man.

Salvation: Through human effort, yoga, meditation.

Man: Inwardly divine.

SWEDENBORG FOUNDATION

TABLE OF CONTENTS

INFO AT A GLANCE

Name: The New Church; The Church of the New Jerusalem; Swedenborg Foundation.

Purpose: To institute the New Church as God's new plan for the world.

Founder: Emanuel Swedenborg (1688–1772).

Source of authority: The writings of Swedenborg; "acceptable" portions of the Bible as interpreted by him (termed "The Word").

Revealed writings: Yes.

Claim: To represent the only true interpretation of "The Word."

Occult dynamics: Swedenborg engaged in regular spiritistic and necromantic contacts; many members today accept this possibility if certain conditions are met.

Key literature: *Arcana Coelestia* (12 vols.); *The True Christian Religion* (2 vols.); *Posthumous Theological Works* (2 vols.); *Apocalypse Explained* (6 vols.); *Spiritual Diary* (5 vols.); *The Word of the Old Testament Explained* (10 vols.); *Logos* newsletter.

Attitude toward Christianity: Rejecting.

Quote:

"The falsities of the dogmas of the faith of the present Church must first be exposed and rejected, before the truths of the dogmas of the New Church are revealed and received."[1]

—Emanuel Swedenborg

DOCTRINAL SUMMARY

God: Unipersonal; modalistic and apparent pantheistic tendencies.

Jesus: Jehovah (The Father) incarnate as man.

Holy Spirit: An "operation" proceeding from God.

Trinity: Defined in terms of a triune nature within the One Divine Person.

Salvation: By faith and works.

Man: The "symbol" of God.

Satan: The personification of evil.

The Second Coming: Swedenborg's writing.

The Fall: Symbolic.

The Bible: Contains the Word of the Lord but is authoritative only when interpreted by Swedenborg.

Death: Continuation of life on earth in the spirit world; its quality being dictated by man's spiritual condition at death.

Heaven and Hell: Temporal "places" or states of mind.

INTRODUCTION AND HISTORY

In 1743 Emanuel Swedenborg claimed he was visited by the Lord God Jehovah Himself and commissioned to reveal to humanity the true interpretation of the Word of God. This event is described by him in a letter written in 1771:

And as the Lord had prepared me for this from my childhood, He manifested Himself in Person before me, His servant, and sent me to do this work. This took place in the year 1743; and afterwards He opened the sight of my spirit, and thus introduced me into the spiritual world, granting me to see the heavens and many of the wonderful things there, and also the hells, and to speak with angels and spirits, and this continually for twenty-seven years.[2]

The life of Emanuel Swedenborg is nothing short of remarkable—even if it was seemingly his spirit guides who were responsible for many of his achievements. He has been called "the Aristotle of the North,"[*] and it seems he was able to master almost any subject he investigated. His breadth of knowledge was encyclopedic and, since his own era, in every generation, he has had an influence on notable persons. To many he was a genius.

Swedenborg excelled as an inventor and scientist. He spoke 9 languages and wrote some 150 works in 18 sciences. These included chemistry, engineering, metallurgy, crystallography, physics, mathematics, mineralogy, paleontology, cosmology, botany, physiology, anatomy, geology, astronomy, and empirical psychology. He invented crudely prefigured airplanes, submarines, hearing aids and other devices. He devised an air-based "machine gun" that discharged a thousand bullets per minute. He created the world's largest drydock as well as the first Swedish texts on algebra and calculus and the first comprehensive texts on metallurgy. He discovered the functions of several areas of the brain and the ductless glands. These are only a few of his accomplishments.

---

[*]D. T. Suzuki, the influential Buddhist who brought Zen to the West and translated Swedenborg into Japanese, referred to him as the "Buddha of the North" in a book by that title: "For you Westerners, it is Swedenborg who is your Buddha, it is he who should be read and followed."

PRACTICE AND TEACHINGS

Swedenborg, despite voluminous writings, presents us with the dilemma of saying too little. "Swedenborg's many writings are characterized by great scholarship and by a fervent search for a synthesis of ancient wisdom and modern experience, empirical science, rationalistic philosophy, and Christian revelation."[3]

Swedenborg detailed a mystical philosophy of the world and a symbolic or allegoric, interpretation of the Bible. Although real, things were not as they seemed. The physical world was actually a symbol, or type, of the spiritual world, corresponding to it in the sense of being a crude reflection of its higher spiritual reality. Swedenborg saw the physical world as a cruder material reflection of corresponding parts in the spiritual world that had in fact given birth to them. In a similar fashion, the words of the Bible represented *corresponding* symbols of higher divine truths. In each case, there are supposedly deeper levels of realization, taking one ultimately back to their source in God.

Every portion of the spiritual world, every part of physical creation including man, and every word of Scripture, allegedly contains degrees of *arcana coelestia*, or heavenly secrets, which only the true mystic or spiritually enlightened can understand. Swedenborg attempted to harmonize this "disparity" between "nature" and "heaven" into one divine unity. He believed that nature (church doctrines, history, ritual and so on) were, in detail, a reflection of heavenly truths. His "system of correspondences" thereby provided a bridge to "join" the worlds of matter and spirit, as it did also the worlds of "outer" biblical teachings with their purported "inner secrets."

NOTES

1. Emanuel Swedenborg, *A Brief Exposition of the Doctrine of the New Church* (London: Swedenborg Society, Inc., 1952), p. 88 (n. 96).
2. Emanuel Swedenborg, *Posthumous Theological Works of Emanuel Swedenborg,* Vol. I (New York: Swedenborg Foundation, Inc., 1969), pp. 590-591.
3. Paul Edwards, *The Encyclopedia of Philosophy,* Vol. 8 (New York: Macmillan Pub. Co. and The Free Press, 1967), pp. 48-50.

THEOSOPHY AND THE THEOSOPHICAL SOCIETY

INFO AT A GLANCE

Name: Theosophy/The Theosophical Society (Wheaton, IL; Pasadena, CA)

Purpose: The three stated objectives of the Society are: 1) to form a nucleus defending the Universal Brotherhood of Humanity; 2) encourage the study of comparative religion, philosophy and science and 3) to investigate and promote the study of "the unexplained laws of nature and the powers latent in man"—that is, to investigate and promote occult philosophy and practice. Originally, a fourth objective was opposition to materialism and theological dogmatism of all types, particularly Christian. Although this fourth point is omitted today in print, it remains in spirit.

Founders: Helena Petrovna Blavatsky (1831–1891), Henry Steel Olcott (1832–1907), William Q. Judge (1851–1896).

Source of authority: The individual; the writings of H. P. Blavatsky, Annie Besant and other prominent Theosophists.

Claim: To be a society of free and open inquiry (nonsectarian, nonpolitical, nondogmatic) into divine wisdom and truth wherever it is found.

Occult dynamics: Spiritism, astrology, psychic development and other occult practices.

Key literature: Blavatsky's *The Secret Doctrine, Isis Unveiled,* and *Collected Writings;* books by Annie Besant and other Theosophical presidents and prominent writers (for example, C. W. Leadbeater, Dora Kunz). Periodicals for the Theosophical Society—Wheaton, Illinois: *The Quest, The American Theosophist* and *The Messenger,* a study paper/newsletter. *Sunrise* is the periodical published by the Theosophical Society headquartered in Pasadena, California.

Attitude toward Christianity: Rejecting.

Quotes:

"O powers of heaven! What I have suffered—there are no words to express it." (H. P. Blavatsky in Ryan, *H. P. Blavatsky and the Theosophical Movement,* p. 129)

"Prayer to God for help is no better than an act of black magic." (H. P. Blavatsky, *The Secret Doctrine,* Vol. 2, p. 133)

"Man tends to become a god and then God, like every other atom in the universe." (*The Secret Doctrine,* 9th fundamental)

"The Theosophical Society is . . . the practical helper, perchance the saviour of Christianity. . . . It is only endeavouring to do the work that Jesus . . . commanded all his followers to undertake." (H. P. Blavatsky, *Collected Writings,* Vol. 8, p. 283)

"Satan, the Serpent of Genesis [is] the real creator and benefactor, the Father of Spiritual Mankind. . . . [Satan] can only be regarded in the light of a Savior. An 'Adversary' to Jehovah . . . he still remains in Esoteric Truth the everloving 'Messenger' . . . who conferred on us Spiritual . . . immortality." "Blessed and sanctified is the name of the Angel of Hades. For the glory of Satan is the shadow of the Lord. . . ." (H. P. Blavatsky, *The Secret Doctrine,* Vol. 3, pp. 238, 246)

"This doctrine of the atonement . . . has proved one of the most pernicious and demoralizing of doctrines. . . . [This] abominable doctrine is the cause of three-fourths of the crimes of so-called Christians." (H. P. Blavatsky, *Isis Unveiled*, Vol. 2, pp. 542, 544)

Note: There are two distinct Theosophical Societies: Pasadena, CA and Wheaton, IL. Both rely upon the writings of Helena P. Blavatsky. These groups trace their founding to the Society begun by Helena P. Blavatsky and Col. Henry S. Olcott in New York, November 17, 1875. The Theosophical Society in Wheaton is the American office of the International Society headquartered in Adyar, Madras, India, and its publishing house is the Theosophical Publishing House. The Theosophical Society in Pasadena is the international headquarters for an entirely separate Theosophical Society headed by Grace F. Knoche. Its publishing facility is Theosophical University Press.

References to *Encyclopedia of New Age Beliefs:* Altered States of Consciousness, Angel Contact, Astrology, Channeling, Divination, Enlightenment, New Age Physics, Meditation, New Age Inner Work/ Intuition, Visualization, Yoga.

DOCTRINAL SUMMARY

God: An indefinable Substance; Principle; Law; One Spirit; Creative Force.

Jesus: A theosophic master.

The Christ: The divine part of every person.

Holy Spirit: Primeval creative power.

Man: A god evolving toward Godhood.

Sin: Ignorance.

Satan: A Christian myth.

The Second Coming: The coming of awareness of the Christ within.

The Fall: From Spirit into matter.

The Bible: Largely a compilation of myths, errors and pagan plagiarism; it does contain some wisdom if interpreted esoterically.

Salvation: Spiritual enlightenment is achieved through the application of theosophic philosophy and practice to eventual union back into the One Principle or the One Life.

Death: A generally beneficial transition to the next "station" prior to reincarnating.

Heaven and Hell: States of consciousness.

TIBETAN BUDDHISM

INFO AT A GLANCE

Name: Tibetan Buddhism. Three prominent Tibetan gurus are the Dalai Lama and the late Lama Govinda, Chogyam Trungpa.

Purpose: To deliver people from *duhkha* (unsatisfactory experience) and enlighten them to the nature of ultimate reality.

Founder: Various schools were founded by various individuals. Perhaps Padmasambhava first began the tradition by translating Tantric texts in Tibet in 810 A.D. and became head of the oldest sect, the Nyingmapa.

Source of authority: Mahayanist Buddhist (especially Tantric) Scripture. Many scholars accept Tantrism as a major Buddhist school, along with Theravadin and Mahayana.

Examples of occult potential: Spiritistic and magical traditions; occult meditation and contact with Hindu deities.

Attitude toward Christianity: Rejecting.

Quote:

"...no one is going to save us." (Chogyam Trungpa, *Cutting Through Spiritual Materialism*, p. 77.)

DOCTRINAL SUMMARY

God: Tibetan Buddhism is ultimately nontheistic, although practically speaking it is polytheistic. Ultimate Reality is One and is usually seen as undifferentiated, impersonal mind.

Salvation: Perception of Ultimate Reality by occult practice.

Man: Inwardly one with Reality.

Sin: Ignorance.

Satan: Some sects use the term symbolically for negative life conditions.

Death: One with life or a state of preparation for rebirth.

Heaven and Hell: Temporary states of consciousness or places.

Transcendental Meditation / The Science of Creative Intelligence

Info at a Glance

Name: Transcendental Meditation, The Science of Creative Intelligence.

Purpose: To usher in a New Age of world enlightenment.

Founder: Maharishi Mahesh Yogi.

Source of authority: The Hindu Scriptures, Maharishi Mahesh Yogi.

Revealed teachings: Yes.

Claim: To be the solution to all mankind's problems, individually and collectively.

Examples of occult potential: Development of psychic powers (siddhas), astrology, spiritism.

Examples of key literature: The books of Maharishi M. Yogi: *Commentary on the Bhagavad Gita,* chapters 1-6; *Transcendental Meditation; Love and God; Meditations of Maharishi Mahesh Yogi, Maharishi's Absolute Theory* (series on Education, Health, Defence, Economy, Management, Rehabilitation, Law and Order); *Modern Science and Vedic Science* is a major periodical.

Attitude toward Christianity: Rejecting.

Quotes:

"I don't think Christ ever suffered or Christ could suffer." *Meditations of Maharishi Mahesh Yogi,* p. 123.

"When America is ready for Hinduism, I will tell them."

> —Maharishi Mahesh Yogi to Anthony D. DeNaro in a private meeting, according to DeNaro's sworn court affidavit. (TranceNet Website, "TM Secret Teachings")

"... there was never a time that TM insiders didn't know TM's secret agenda of making America safe for Hinduism." (Ibid.)

"The Maharishi intended from day one to gradually lead us through small, persistent deceptions to the religion he always knew was best for all of us—an extremely fundamentalist Hinduism." (Ibid.)

Note: www.trancenet.org has a great deal of relevant materials online exposing the deceptions of TM. TranceNet is a consumer protection watchdog agency concentrating on psychological manipulation in cults and the larger society. It has thousands of pages of "insider secrets" from anonymous donors—court records, hospital admissions, internal management reports, tax documents and so on. John M. Knapp is the executive director and a former TMer who wrote or edited TranceNet's TM materials.

TMEX 202–728–7580 is another helpful organization (of former meditators). They publish a quarterly journal and are on the Web through the Meditation Information Network (http://minet.org). They offer a significant number of materials exposing TM as a religion, TM's dangers, testimonies of former members and more.

Since John Weldon published his book on TM in 1975, the interim publications of TM and new books by Maharishi, as well as critiques on the Internet, have only confirmed his initial conclusions reached 25 years ago: Few religions are more defective or deceptive.

DOCTRINAL SUMMARY

God: Impersonal being, consciousness, bliss; that is, the Hindu Brahman described as *satchitananda* or *sat* (being), *chit* (consciousness) *ananda* (bliss).

Jesus: An enlightened teacher of TM.

The Christ: The divine aspect of Jesus. "Christ Consciousness" is seen as vedantic Brahman (God) Realization.

Salvation: By the states of higher consciousness achieved through the practice of Transcendental Meditation.

Man: Inwardly one essence with Brahman.

Sin: Ignorance of one's inner divine nature and the consequences.

The Bible: A relevant Scripture when interpreted through enlightened consciousness.

Death: Reincarnation toward final dissolution into Brahman.

UFOs AND UFO CULTS

One MIT physicist, a fervent proponent in alien abductions and in the process of scientific inquiry, has confirmed that there is not one, single, independently confirmed piece of scientific evidence for an alien abduction. Not one.

—NOVA Online, "Kidnapped by UFO's" (March 1996)

The topic of UFO's seems perennially fascinating, probably because it presents powerful implications globally. In May 1999, an ABC News poll revealed that 70 percent of Americans believe in extraterrestrial life; one percent believed they had personally contacted it.

The influence of the UFO phenomenon in world culture today is nothing short of phenomenal. (See our book, *The Facts On UFOs And Other Supernatural Phenomena.*) From the first modern UFO sighting (alleged) by Kenneth Arnold in 1947, hundreds of millions of people now believe in UFOs, and dramatic public and private efforts to address the phenomena have arisen.

Why is the extraterrestrial "myth" so powerful? Because among all areas of learning, few subjects have the potential to so captivate us. The very idea that there are billions or trillions of extremely advanced civilizations in outer space—alluring races that we might learn from—boggles the mind.

In many ways, ufology and its offshoots have become a new world religion, a universal "church of the stars" so to speak. True believers look yearningly to the heavens in hopes of some kind of alien contact that will bring permanent peace and prosperity to this unceasingly beleaguered planet. Popular culture has been so saturated with extraterrestrial and UFO themes (SETI, NASA, Star Trek, The 'X' Files, Close Encounters), that it would not take much in the way of credible evidence to convert the rest of the world's hopes.

The phenomena of alleged personal contact with aliens (cited in the ABC News poll above) are described in three principal ways in UFO literature: 1) as a "close encounter," where some form of contact with an alien is made, 2) being "abducted" on board a UFO, or 3) as becoming a "contactee," where personal contact continues even for years.

Whatever the public may think they know about UFOs, what the public generally *doesn't* know is that these cases have much in common with the world of the occult.

As far as the UFO phenomena that we are experiencing globally is concerned, the issue of the actual existence or nonexistence of extraterrestrial life is not that germane to the subject of UFO's. Obviously, if life does exist in outer space, then God created it. But due to the occult connection, traveling from that fact to the conclusion that modern UFO's result from such life, involves a leap of faith of Herculean proportions.

Despite the complete lack of legitimate evidence documenting extraterrestrial visitation, despite the profound parallels between UFOs and the occult, despite the many tragedies associated with involvement and investigations in this field, many people are rushing headlong into belief in UFOs, even with the hope of contact. Unfortunately what may "step out" and be contacted is not going to be what is hoped for. If anything is clear in this field, it is that the "aliens" do not have our best interests at heart.

UNIFICATION CHURCH

INFO AT A GLANCE

Name: The Unification Church; The Holy Spirit Association for the Unification of World Christianity; The Unification Movement.

Purpose: To implement "The Divine Principle" and restore the earth to God's original intent.

Founder: Sun Myung Moon (1920–).

Source of authority: Sun Myung Moon and the spirit world.

Revealed teachings: Yes.

Occult dynamics: Spiritism; possible psychic development among members.

Examples of key literature: *The Divine Principle; Master Speaks* (hundreds of transcribed lectures of Sun Myung Moon); the 15 volume *Hoon Dok Hae* set (Gathering for Reading and Learning); *Divine Principle Study Guide for Children;* Dr. Sang Hun Lee's *Report from the Spirit World* and *Life in the Spirit World and on the Earth;* Dr. Mose Durst, *Principled Education.*

Moon's lectures, which claim to be inspired, are so voluminous that hundreds of books could be published. A 200-volume

449

speech set (1956–1995) of Moon's speeches is currently in preparation by Damian Anderson, author of the Unification home page, and a $500, 15 volume set of U.S. speeches is available from HSA Publications (1976 to the present). Samples of books published by Moon to date include *The Tribal Messiah, Blessing and the Ideal Family* and *God's Will and the World*. Heung Jin Moon's *Victory of Love* and *On Internal Guidance* and Rev. Chung Hwan Kwak, editor, *Home Church,* are also relevant titles. Moon's website sells an odd mixture of books by evangelical Christians (C. S. Lewis, James Dobson) as well as books by occultists, psychic researchers, spiritists, mental science practitioners, liberal theologians and noted psychologists.

Attitude toward Christianity: Rejecting.

Quotes:

". . . As soon as a person believes in Jesus, Satan can invade his body." (*Master Speaks,* December 25, 1974, p. 212.)

"I have talked with many Masters, including Jesus. . . . They have subjected themselves to me in terms of wisdom. After winning the victory [his 1945 victory of the spirit world], they surrendered." (*Master Speaks,* March/April, 1965 MS-3, p. 16.)

"I have paid a great amount of indemnity, and because of this I have the right to forgive another's sins." (Ibid.)

"It is only he [Moon] from whom sinless mankind can start. He is the only man in the universe by loving whom my sin is solved, by loving whom I can be born anew, by loving whom I can be given rebirth and new life. Therefore, the fact we can attend him must be the most precious event in our lives. . . ." (Ken Sudo, *The 120 Day Training Manual,* p. 155.)

"One of my most important revelations is that Jesus Christ did not come to die." (Rev. Moon, [interview] in F. Sontag, *Sun Myung Moon and the Unification Church,* p. 134.)

"Do you like to make green bills happy? . . . So many green bills are crying. Have you ever heard them crying? Not yet? You must hear. They are all destined to go to Father. This is our responsibility." (Sudo, *The 120 Day Training Manual,* p. 72.)

Note: The Unification Church (UC) is a multi-billion dollar worldwide enterprise with, allegedly, an incredible 700 to 900 front organizations. (This must be some kind of record.) Critics have charged that with all these front organizations, whatever the UC is involved in, the ultimate purpose was to help Moon achieve his long-term goal of ruling the world as the Lord of the Second Advent. Indeed, our own study of UC history and theology supports this allegation. Further, critics charge that to help achieve this implementation of Moon's lordship, the organization has employed or manipulated the church, business, society, scientific groups, and others, and apparently paid exorbitant sums in the process. The Christian church especially must be on guard here, because its manipulation has occurred in the past, possibly in significant ways.

For someone controlling billions of dollars, what is unusual is that, apparently, despite intense investigation, no one has yet been able to discover exactly how or where Moon and the Unification Movement obtains its money. It would not seem to be from Moon's ventures in America, since the vast majority are said to have carried financial losses. Regardless, in the late 1970's and the early 1980's, the Unification Church claimed its theology was in a state of transition, allegedly towards a more evangelical position. What some did not suspect at the time is that this was a ruse. The UC was attempting to influence Christianity with UC teachings, just as, in a similar manner, Mormonism is currently attempting to do through stressing alleged "areas of agreement" (see chapter on Mormonism). But even prior to 1980, the spurious nature of these claims was evident. Cosmetic, or apparent, changes linked to fundamentally unchanged doctrine have not and never will noticeably alter Unification theology. Thus, the conclusion of the Evangelical Writers—Unification Church dialogue in June 1979 at the Unification Church's World Missions Center in Manhattan was as follows. Evangelical Dr. James Bjornstad, an authority on Unification theology, stated in *Contemporary Christianity,* Jan.–Feb., 1980: "By the end of the dialogue it was clear to all that there were areas which were unchangeable, and that Unification theology was totally distinct from Christian theology. . . . Unification theology may give the appearance of being open, in a state of change and development, and undoubtedly will use more of evangelical terminology, but there have been no changes in the essential areas of doctrine which differentiate them from true Christianity."

The last two decades have changed nothing as far as Moon's goals are concerned. As this chapter makes clear, Moon's real goal is to convert Christians and members of other religions, and to conquer the world, not merely to generate good-will and dialogue.

But as of 1999, Moon's church was in a state of turmoil, if not his corporate empire's "blizzard of organizations." According to a two-part series in the *Washington Post*, November 23/24, 1997, "The founder's advanced age, the lack of clear succession, the failure of recruiting efforts in the United States, a series of scandals and tragedies surrounding Moon's children, and a sense of delusionment among long-term members have left the church reeling, according to former and current members." (Part 2, p. A10.) W. Farley Jones, the president of the Family Federation for World Peace and Unification, a strategic Moon organization, acknowledged, "Things are very much in flux."

Indeed, matters got so bad for Moon he declared that the "period of religion" was passing away and that his beloved Unification Church would actually be dissolved. His disillusionment is understandable. Decades ago, Moon had promised his followers that, through America, God would use him to convert the world. But Moon clearly failed in his "mission" in America. This is why he has recently called Americans stupid, lazy, and evil, even "dirty dung-eating dogs." (Ibid.)

The fact of Moon's advanced age means that he will also never rule the world and that he failed miserably in his personal divine mission. Some observers believe that when Moon dies there will be no powerful successor to replace him, causing even more decline. Time will tell, but no one should be surprised if a dynamic replacement does emerge. Even if the church dissolves and the Family Federation becomes the successor organization as (allegedly) planned, this does not necessarily mean the influence of Moon will be over, far from it. Given its vast wealth, the chances that Moon's corporate empire will disintegrate are slim, not to mention that Moon himself claims that after his death, "I will continue to lead the church from the spirit world." (Ibid.) While Moon will probably be occupied elsewhere, it is clear that the influence of spiritism will continue to guide the church and be a focal point. Clearly, spiritism originated the UC and has sustained it in important ways.

So, whatever form the UC may take, the chances are good that even after Moon is gone he will continue to have significant influence through the corporate empire, front organizations, and Moon's concept of the "home church." The latter involves the idea of Unification Church members returning to their respective faiths in which they grew up to influence churches and synagogues internally rather than from without—essentially another infiltration program.

In addition, the very concept of "world unification" is increasingly powerful and appealing today, and there are many sincere but naive people just waiting to be taken advantage of. It is perhaps significant that the UC web page now begins with, "Welcome to the Unification *Movement*" in large print and then in smaller print it is noted that Moon is the founder of the Unification *Church*.

Whatever the Unification Church is up to, and whether the alleged plans to abandon the church are part of a program of Moon's "heavenly deception" for ulterior motives, one thing is likely: The Unification Church, or whatever replaces it, will be here for some time to come. Even though the current American membership is under 10,000 (the church claims 50,000), South America and Africa are apparently showing significant membership increases. And Moon's limited success in influencing American Christianity cannot negate the fact that his theology and reliance on spiritism are more tailored for success among a variety of nonChristian peoples.

A final point here, is that Moon and his followers have argued that certain embarrassing quotations from the *Master Speaks* (transcripts of Moon's lectures) are often quoted out of context by critics. We have examined dozens of them and not found this to be true, especially given Moon's overall worldview and theology. We suspect that for Moon and Unification

Church members "out of context" means "if you understood how important this mission was you would then understand the validity of such statements in light of UC goals." Even author Frederick Sontag, sympathetic to the Unification Church, admits that the embarrassing quotes substantiate the critics' position. (Thus, we have cited many of them in this chapter.) He would only add that one must cite the positive side of Moon as well. (Sontag, p. 116.) Also, due to its evolution and state of transition, there may be some teachings discussed which are in the process of transition or may no longer be considered official doctrine.

References to *Encyclopedia of New Age Beliefs:* Channeling, Shamanism.

DOCTRINAL SUMMARY

God: Divine energy.

Jesus: A special creation of God.

Holy Spirit: A female aspect of God, a female spirit.

Salvation: By works and personal merit.

Man: One with God (man is God incarnate, although man does not exhaust God).

The Second Coming: Occurred with the advent of Sun Myung Moon.

The Fall: Sexual in nature.

The Bible: One of God's revelations, replaced by Moon's superior revelations. The Bible is largely unreliable and interpreted symbolically.

Heaven and Hell: Various spirit realms and not eternal places.

INTRODUCTION AND HISTORY

Yong Myung Moon was born on January 6, 1920, in a small village in the Pyungan province in Northwestern Korea. Yong eventually changed his first name to "Sun," which meant that his name became "Shining Sun and Moon," a title more reflective of his grandiose cosmo-

logical ambitions. From his earliest childhood Yong was interested in the psychic world, and throughout his life he has drawn sustenance from the spirit world, which became his encouragement and constant companion.

Early Years
In 1936, at the age of 16, Sun Myung Moon claimed that Jesus Christ appeared to him in a vision. Christ purportedly told Moon that he, Moon, had a great mission to accomplish and that He would assist him in this.[1] Apparently more than a mere vision, this experience caused a powerful shamanistic-like transformation and Moon became a medium, afterward communicating regularly with the spirit world.*

Dr. Young Oon Kim, professor of systematic theology at the Unification Theological Seminary in Barrytown, New York, describes the event:

> When Mr. Moon was seventeen years old, Jesus Christ manifested himself to him on Easter morning and told him that he was destined to accomplish a specific mission for which Jesus would work with him.
>
> From this time on, Mr. Moon's spiritual sense was fully opened, and he was able to communicate with the highest level of the spirit world. But, unlike ordinary spiritualists, he did not content himself with merely the demonstration of spiritual phenomena. He began to explore the hidden meanings of the parables and symbols in the Bible and the many unanswered questions of Christianity and other religions.[2]

During the next seven years, Moon received revelations from the spirits concerning "The Divine Principle"; that is, God's will for mankind: the heretofore unknown principles of the creation, the hidden meaning of human history, the secret nature of Satan's crime, the true meaning of the Bible, and how God would restore man and the universe.

Toward the end of World War II, the seeds for the Unification Church (officially founded

---

*See Bryant and Richardson, eds., *A Time for Consideration: A Scholarly Appraisal of the Unification Church* (New York: Edwin Mellen Press, 1978), pp. 278-280.

in 1954) can be traced to events surrounding a number of related spiritistic-pentecostal churches and movements on the East and West coasts of Northern Korea. Moon was directly and indirectly associated with these "churches," which he believed were preparing the way for his "advent." The entire story is reported in the *Master Speaks* (transcribed lectures) of December 27, 1971.[3] One church on the West coast of Northern Korea had been started by a medium named Kim Son Do. Both she and her successor, Ho Ho Bin, also a medium, claimed direct contact with God and Jesus. Jesus told them all about Himself, how His mission had failed and how He was now to guide them to fulfill God's will. The revelations they received included many teachings that were prototypes for the doctrines of the Unification Church of Sun Myung Moon. For example:

—The Lord of the Second Advent (Christ returned) will "return" by physical birth in Korea, the nation that will restore the world.

—A sexual fall of man.

- -The failure of Jesus' mission.

—Marriage is satanic; men and women should not marry; even married couples should abstain from all sex.

—The Lord is coming to establish a new pure blood lineage, erasing the satanic blood of men inherited from the Fall.

If the history of spiritism has taught anything it is that those who give divine authority to "spirits" find the latter are more than willing to use such authority, even in a brutish, tyrannical manner. In his *Master Speaks,* Moon approvingly records this absolute bondage to spirits.

In the following material Moon describes the revelations received from the spirit world by the group on the West coast, which was preparing the way for the "Lord of the Second Advent," who would come as a Korean man, that is, Moon himself. The spirit world had told this group of people that they (and the Lord of the Second Advent) would solve all the problems that Jesus could not solve during His lifetime. They were also told to "indemnify," or repay, to Christ all the things that He was forced to sacrifice while here on earth. In that Jesus was the prince of heaven and yet was rejected by people and forced to live as a pauper on earth, all of this had to be repaid, or restored, to Jesus by those who wished to be His followers on earth. In the following quotations we see an example of the spiritual "enslavement" that is so common in idolatry, animistic societies, ritual magic and anywhere that the spirits are given absolute authority:

So they were told to make clothes the size which Jesus would have worn from his childhood to 33 years old. As many clothes as Jesus could change every three days. So you can imagine how many that would be. And that was not one [style], but in Korean costume and also Western style. One Korean costume and one Western suit every three days. And when they made his clothing they couldn't use sewing machines. They were told not to stitch more than three at a time, and to make this they had to clean out the whole room, and they couldn't stand up until they finished one garment. They didn't allow them to go to the toilet. "Even though you pay such a price, you are not worthy to receive Him," that is what heaven told them. And when they made a mistake in something they were severely chastised from heaven. So they couldn't but follow after heaven's instructions.[4]

Moon discusses how "heaven" (the spirit world) demanded an utterly sadistic amount of work from this group of people. Restoring princely clothes to Jesus was hardly enough. Princely meals had to be prepared three times a day and slavish rituals had to be performed, such as bowing hundreds, even thousands, of times:

At that time the group had more than 1,000 followers. And those 1,000 men worked for 7 years. For the food, they prepared 3 meals a day just like a banquet—meat three times a day. The size of the clothes became larger and larger as he became grown-up. Then, after they finished making clothes for Jesus they were told to make clothes for the Lord to come . . .

When they brought a meal for the Lord, they were told to bow 300 times, sometimes they were told to bow 3,000 times. Heaven told, "Even though you pay your courtesy and respect to the Lord by bowing 3,000 times that is not enough to pay your respect to the Lord." To bow 3,000 times took almost 10 hours; after finishing bowing, they collapsed. Heaven told them all sizes, the length of sleeve, everything.[5] [As we shall see, similar service was rendered to Moon.]

Moon also describes how these persons were "ready at any time to lie down and die if they were told. They were ready to give their lives. They were trained in every way."[6]

Then Moon describes the group on the East coast of Northern Korea and how the failure of the East and West coast groups to merge had forced God to seek a third group to accomplish His purposes. "For Eastern coast spiritual movement, there was another successor. His name was Lee Yong Do.... Centering on Minister Lee, a new Jesus church was started.... The West group went to the Eastern group to be united, but this group did not receive them. By failing to accomplish the unification of these two groups, God had to have a new movement, and pioneer a new field."[7] It was this third group, headed by a Mr. Kim, from which Moon's Unification Church emerged. In the characteristic transmission of spiritual power, Mr. Kim became possessed by the spirit of Mr. Lee as a form of empowerment for the task at hand. "So God wanted to have another man who could receive His direction. That was Mr. Kim.... After that time Mr. Lee died. The spirit of Minister Lee came to Mr. Kim and spiritually Mr. Lee passed on his mission to Mr. Kim. From this Mr. Kim a new group began."[8] Moon refers to these three churches as the formation stage (Mrs. Ho; Mrs. Bin), the growth stage (Mr. Lee Yong Do) and the perfection stage (Mr. Kim) in the preparation and formation of his own ministry.

As it turns out, at the time when Moon was in Southern Korea, the West coast group was waiting for the Lord of the Second Advent (LSA), having prepared everything for him according to the revelations received from the spirits. Moon's own revelations from the spirits told him that he must find the "lady who claims herself to be the wife of Jehovah," otherwise the providence of restoration (God's plan of salvation) could not be continued.[9] Moon thus began a diligent search of all the churches and spiritistic groups in Southern Korea, but was unable to find "Jehovah's wife." In 1945 he met Mr. Kim,

referred to previously, who had a large female following. Eventually Moon inherited Mr. Kim's followers.

The year 1945 was a key year for Moon. It was in this year that he claims he won victory over the spirit world, which then recognized his supreme lordship as "God's true son." In "Sun Myung Moon—From his Message to the World Unification Family in the Year 1964,"[10] we discover that Moon had paid the great price necessary for God to reveal His truth through Moon, truth never before revealed to humanity:

> After nine years of search and struggle, the truth of God was sealed into his hands. At that moment he became the absolute victor of heaven and earth. The whole spirit world bowed down to him on that day of victory.... Satan totally surrendered to him on that day, for he had elevated himself to the position of God's true Son.... The spirit world has already recognized him as the victor of the universe and Lord of creation. The physical world has now only to reflect what he accomplished.[11]

However, Moon still had not found "the wife of Jehovah." Eventually he learned that she was living in Northern Korea. After meeting her, and thus fulfilling yet another divine requisite, Moon sent a messenger to Mrs. Bin's group requesting that she ask God for direction. Moon assumed that Mrs. Bin would be "guided by heaven" to surrender to him. By this time Moon was convinced that he was Jesus Christ returned. He "knew" that a following was being prepared for him, and that these various groups had made the necessary provisions to "receive the Lord." Unfortunately, heaven got its signals crossed. As far as the other groups were concerned, Moon had to come to them. Moon, on the other hand, was told they must come to him as his "bride"; he was not to first seek them out. While he was waiting for his "bride" to come to him, he allegedly had a brutal encounter with the Communists, which subsequently shaped his anticommunist ideology. In 1947, after the Communists had taken power, the leaders of Mrs. Bin's group were arrested.* Moon was also arrested, the authorities

---

*Korea divided politically in 1948 to become North Korea and South Korea.

claiming that he was involved with Mrs. Bin's group. However, Mrs. Bin and the rest of her group had by now rejected Moon as the Lord of the Second Advent (LSA). Moon, of course, claims that they did not really listen to heaven.[12] While in jail, Moon shared the same room with a man who was second in command to Mrs. Bin. Due to a vision, this man gave his allegiance to Moon.

Moon subsequently set out to build his own following. Upon release from jail in 1950, he sought to regain his former followers. Most of them rejected him and he was abandoned once more. After this, he wandered throughout South Korea, gathering any who would believe, one of whom was allegedly Mr. Eu, the former Korean president.[13] By 1954, with sufficient followers, Moon officially began the Holy Spirit Association for the Unification of World Christianity (HSA/UWC), or the Unification Church (UC).

Dr. Young Oon Kim of the Unification Theological Seminary describes the mediumistic practices of the young Church. "He organized a group in Korea in 1954 and began to make the Divine Principles public. In this group not only he but a great number of people communicate with the highest realm of the spirit world through clairvoyance and clairaudience; and some of them converse with Jesus and God under any conditions."[14] Kim describes some of the practices. "Many of them feel spiritual fire and electricity, and some smell spiritual odor. Some go into trances and some hear exquisite heavenly music, and some write automatic writings in languages which they had never learned."[15]

Today's Empire

Today the Unification Church claims representation in over 100 countries, including over 100 churches in the United States. Since its arrival in America, the UC has generated billions of dollars to implement its political goals and other plans. The reason Moon centered his efforts in America was obvious: thousands of devoted recruits soliciting funds day and night could bring in at least several hundred million dollars a year.[16] This money was and is raised by telling donors it is being collected for the poor,

the starving, the handicapped, the underprivileged, the crippled and so on, when in fact most of it goes to Moon and his "church."[17] (Such deceptive fund-raising is practiced by many other cults, such as The Family (Children of God, Love Family) and ISKCON (Hare Krishnas).) However, UC disciples are not to worry about their collection methods because, after all, as their *120 Day Training Manual* declares, little "green bills" are all destined to go to Father:

> Who can dominate the creation and give it the highest joy? Father [i.e., Moon]. Every creation will dash to Father. Father has qualifications to have dominion over everything. Only when the creations are in His hand are creations the happiest.

> Do you like to make green bills happy? When green bills are in the hands of fallen men can they be happy? Why don't you make them happy? So many green bills are crying. Have you ever heard them crying? Not yet? You must hear. They are all destined to go to Father. This is our responsibility.[18]

Green bills dashed to Father with such determination that he had little choice but to live in luxury. "The limousine came by itself, Father never asked for it at all; the limousine came with a speed of 200 miles per hour and said if Father didn't receive it, it would kill him; so, Father received it."[19] Manipulation was and is employed to influence converts to give or raise all the money they can. They could be threatened with losing their eternal life, or promised that $1,000 given now would be the equivalent of one million dollars ten years from now. They are assured that slavish work now will greatly bless their ancestors, parents and their own children after death.[20]

According to a story in the *Washington Post*, there are other reasons to be suspicious of Moon's multi-billion dollar financial empire. Since, apparently, nearly all his business ventures in America have lost money, the source of his revenue must come from other locations. "Executives of Unification-related entities have acknowledged that money from Japan and Korea fuel US operations, but the magnitude and mechanism of those payments, as well as their exact sources, have eluded investigators on three continents over the past three decades."[21] Allegedly, approximately seventy percent of the money comes from Japan, and Moon's South Korea land holdings alone were valued in 1990 at $1,000,000,000. The fact that Moon could subsidize *The Washington Times,* which has never been profitable, to the tune of over $1,000,000,000 is another indicator of his wealth.[22] Further, according to Ron Paquette, president of Moon's Manhattan Center Studio, which was the church's New York recording facility until 1994, "There's always huge amounts of cash involved in doing anything with them. In dealing with them, you have to accept cash."[23]

Moon's network of industries in South Korea, known as the Tong II group, is the 28th largest business conglomerate in South Korea and includes ventures in titanium mining, weapons manufacturing, pharmaceuticals and other interests.[24] Further, because of Moon's aggressive anticommunist stance, he is supported by powerful politically conservative elements in Korea, Japan and the United States, even, allegedly, by some wealthy Christians who are unaware of his theology. Indeed, several major evangelical organizations have worked with Moon on political and social issues,[25] and some evangelical organizations have accepted millions of dollars in loans or gifts from Moon. This is surely a spectacle: Christians taking large amounts of money from an organization headed by a spirit-possessed "Messiah" who claims he has replaced Jesus Christ! One can only wonder, what's next?

When we consider Moon's true goal, to rule the world as the Lord of the Second Advent, one stands back in amazement at his influence. Consider several additional examples of his influence. According to his website, the International Cultural Foundation was begun in 1972 to encourage cultural, scientific and academic exchange among the countries of the world. It has regularly sponsored the International Conference on the Unity of the Sciences, which has been attended by leading scientists worldwide. The International Religious Foundation and the Inter-Religious Federation for World Peace attempts to bring world unity and peace through religious dialogue and harmony. Kenneth

Cracknell with the British Council of Churches claimed, "The Unification Church (which is not an orthodox church) does more for the interfaith movement at an international level than do either the World Council of Churches Dialogue Unit or the Roman Catholic Vatican Secretariat for Non-Christians, or both of them put together."[26] Moon also sponsors the Assembly of the World's Religions that, among other things, attempts to employ Moon's *Divine Principle.* "Many leading Muslims, through study of the *Divine Principle,* have come to see Christianity in a new light."[27] Moon also directed "the compilation of *World Scriptures,* a 900-page volume which brings out the similarities in the Scriptures of all the main religions of the world."[28] Moon owns newspapers in Seoul, Tokyo, Washington, D.C., New York City, Los Angeles, Athens and other places. He also owns the World Media Association, the Women's Federation for World Peace and the Collegiate Association for the Research of the [Divine] Principle (CARP), which is active on campuses in the U.S. and 80 other nations. The Professors World Peace Academy was begun in 1973 and now has chapters in over 100 countries. It attempts to find peaceful solutions to world problems.

But all of these enterprises, directly or indirectly, have the goal of making Moon the world's Messiah. Further, based on Moon's detailed guidance from the spirit world throughout his life, one has to wonder who is actually in control of Moon's enterprises. For example, Moon began the Kirov Academy of Ballet, which despite its bizarre origin, is regarded highly for its quality of dancers and faculty. "Moon created the school in part for Julia Moon, whom Moon considers his daughter-in-law since she married the spirit of his deceased son in a unique church ceremony."[29]

Moon's interest in politics is also more than coincidental. Unification theology sees the "last days" (now) as culminating in a one-world religious-political system under the authority of the Lord of the Second Advent, Moon himself.[30] For God to be happy, Moon must restore all things back to God that were lost at the Fall—essentially the entire world. But Moon can only restore everything back to God when the world is under his control. Thus, everything he does has this goal in mind. His writings, for example *Master Speaks,* indicate that he will rule the world for God. Moon and his workers, however, are the ones responsible for bringing this wonderful New Age to fruition, hence their political interest is required. As noted, the media is another venue of influence. *News World Communications,* a subsidiary of Unification Church International, owns newspapers in Japan, South America, the Middle East and the United States. In the U.S., *Washington Times* and *Noticias del Mundo* (a Spanish language paper) are UC owned newspapers.

Hundreds of alleged front organizations function to support Unification Church goals. Frederick Sontag, author of *Sun Myung Moon and the Unification Church,* admits that "the church does use 1001 organizational names."[31] A brief list includes:

New Yorker Hotel
The Nostalgia Network
World Culture and Sports Festival
University of Bridgeport
American Youth for Just Peace
Committee for Responsible Dialogue
New World Communications
International Cultural Foundation
International Federation for Victory
    Over Communism
Korean Cultural Freedom Foundation
Little Angels of Korea, Little Angels Korean
    Folk Ballet
Ministry of Ecology
New Hope Singers International
One World Crusade
Eden Awareness Training Center
Project Unity
Universal Voice Newspaper
World Freedom Institute

As far back as 1976, the ABC News Closeup documentary of September 1976, "New Religions: Holiness or Heresy" estimated a possible "one hundred religious, educational and business enterprises" under the UC conglomerate. Today, the website of "The Resource Center for Freedom of Mind" declares that there are "religious fronts, political fronts, media fronts, social and cultural fronts, recruiting fronts, educational fronts, and business fronts." A list of some 800–900 past and present organizations associated with Moon can be found at The Resource Center for Freedom of Mind and at http://www.trancent.org/moonism/uclist.shtml. The latter site observes, "Although church members toward the public often vehemently deny ANY affiliation with the UC, inside the church these organizations are probably viewed as 'father's' projects intended to further the establishment of 'God's Kingdom of Heaven on Earth' under Mr. Moon's rule as the Messiah/True Parent of Mankind." (The website also contains quite interesting articles and papers by former members and various exposés on the questionable practices of the Moon organization.) What this means is that many people have financially supported various organizations in the guise of hunger relief, the arts and so on when their finances were, in effect, being used to increase UC influence. As Moon says, "We must manipulate the academic world and the economic world,"[32] and the sports world, church world, political world and so on.

TEACHINGS AND PRACTICE

Moon's worldview involves a combination of complex symbolic historical correspondences, Eastern philosophy, Taoism, occultism and an esoteric-allegoric interpretation of the Bible. Before we go into details, a brief background to Moon's worldview is necessary. Moon believes God poured Himself "out" into the creation, so that the creation itself mirrors certain characteristics of God. God and the creation are really one, although the creation does not exhaust God. After the animal kingdom had evolved, God specially created Adam and Eve. However, they were created as brother and sister, not as husband and wife, and they were not perfect, but still in a stage of spiritual growth. Not until they were perfect could they marry, become husband and wife and have children. As God's highest creation, they would then be able to establish the kingdom of God on earth through their sinless offspring. God would "complete" Himself through their sexual union (Moon teaches God cannot ultimately express His love without sexual union).

However, Satan became jealous of God's love for them and *physically* seduced Eve. This was the *spiritual* Fall of man, and it resulted in Cain. Eve then had intercourse with Adam, which resulted in Abel. This was the *physical* Fall of man. At this point God lost everything—His happiness, His dignity and more.

God's plan had failed. Although He tried desperately to establish "the Providence of Restoration" (restoring man to his original condition), His plans continually failed, thwarted by both man and Satan. Until 2,000 years ago there was no totally obedient man whom God could use to restore people to himself, both physically and spiritually. (Because the Fall was physical and spiritual, "salvation" must encompass both of these.) Not until Jesus Christ was there a man obedient to God, and it was God's hope that Jesus would be able to restore man to Him, and that all religions and cultures would unify under Him. But God's plans were thwarted again. Jesus was crucified—something God never intended.

In Unification theology God is not omniscient. Because God did not know if people would accept Jesus, He put prophecies in the Bible of acceptance and rejection to cover all bases, so to speak. As a result, UC members view Old Testament prophecies about Jesus' crucifixion in light of this "foreseen" failure on the part of people to accept God's will.

God's intent for Jesus was to have Jesus marry the perfect mate and establish "God's family" on earth, eventually achieving the full redemption of mankind. Since the crucifixion killed Him, His mission failed, although in Unification theology God still decided to count it partly toward the spiritual (though not physical) salvation of man. However, all was not lost. God's purpose was that the Lord of the Second Advent would come and restore people completely. This would happen when the Lord of the Second Advent attained perfection, married the proper wife and had sinless offspring. This would bring the full spiritual and physical salvation of man. According to the inner teachings of the church, Moon is this Lord. He has attained perfection, married the proper wife and produced sinless offspring. When Moon married Hak-Ja Han in 1960, the Marriage Supper of the Lamb described in Revelation 19 allegedly oc-

curred. Thus, "the Lord of the Second Advent and His Bride became the True Parents of Mankind."[33] Later, after the birth of children, January 1, 1968 was declared "God's Day" by Moon, because "the sinless family was established on earth."[34] Moon was on the way toward achieving the full redemption of humanity.

With this brief background, we are ready to proceed with a more detailed introduction. What follows becomes complex in places and some readers may wish to skip to our next section. However, the following information is vital to understanding Unification Church theology. According to *Divine Principle* (DP) and other sources, "God is energy itself."[35] God contains or is the source of energy called Universal Prime Energy (UPE). It is the basic energy of God's being and allows all things to maintain their existence. It was poured out *into* the creation. "In the process of creation, God poured out all His Being into the Universe He made."[36] Although in itself the creation does not exhaust God (in this sense, God and the universe are "two" entities), in divine essence they are one. The universe is thus related to God's being in that the entire creation is a *part* of God's energy.

The physical universe itself, then, is divine. Unification theology denies creation in the biblical sense (ex-nihilo), and instead views the creation as a "projection" or emanation of God. As a result, the universe is seen as God's body, and as much God as God is God. This is panentheism. Dr. Young Oon Kim, professor of systematic theology at the Unification Theological Seminary in Barrytown, NY, states that God "makes His presence known in the totality of creation which serves as His body. . . ."[37] In the *Divine Principle* we read that "the universe is the substantial manifestation of the invisible God."[38]

Man, too, as part of the creation, is one essence with God. Indeed, every entity in creation has a nature that mirrors the nature of God. "His nature is displayed in each creation."[39] According to the UC, God's nature consists of pairs of dualities: male and female (perhaps the central UC duality), positivity and negativity, subject and object, internal and external, character and form, horizontal and vertical and so on. Every creation, from sub-atomic particles to giant suns, contains these characteristics.

The Reciprocal Relationships

Every creation also "functions" through a reciprocal relationship, both internal and external. For example, the *internal* duality of sub-atomic particles (positivity, negativity) "reciprocate" to form an atom. Atoms assume either positive or negative characteristics, and reciprocate with other atoms to form molecules. Molecules produce matter, which eventually forms plants and animals who reciprocate with each other based on *external* dual characteristics (for example, male, female), but also containing *internal* duality. In this ontology, every man (and every creation) has a feminine aspect, and vice-versa, and so on down the line. This condition of containing external and internal dualities and reciprocation is true for every creation. "All things are created to exist through a reciprocal relationship between their dual essentialities."[40] Thus, every creation has *external form* (that which is visible) and *internal character* (that which is invisible), a reflection or *projection* of it. They are really "two relative aspects of the same existence," so that external form can be accurately called a "second internal character." Moon calls them dual characteristics or dual essentialities.[41] A diagram with man as the example may help us to understand this.

MAN (consists of)

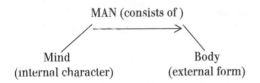

Mind   Body
(internal character)   (external form)

Here the body is really a *projection* of the mind, a "second internal character"; thus Moon calls the body "the 'second mind' or a duplication of the mind."[42] Mind and body together are "the dual characteristics of man."

The internal character (which is invisible) stands in what Moon calls the *subjective position* and is the *cause,* or origin, of the visible external form, which stands in an *objective position.* The reciprocal relationship that exists here comprises the pairs of dualities, such as internal-external, cause-result and subject-object. It logically follows that since the body is the "copy of the mind" it should be completely under the control of the mind. Our chart now looks like this:

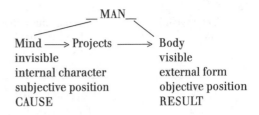

MAN

Mind ———→ Projects ———→ Body
invisible   visible
internal character   external form
subjective position   objective position
CAUSE   RESULT

According to UC theology, the same situation also exists in God, since man (and all creation) is only his "copy."[43] Thus God is comprised of internal character and external form. Internal character is the *subjective position* or "subject." It is invisible and the cause of the *external form* or His *objective position* or "object," the manifested universe. Thus the universe is the *projection* of God's internal character. A diagram of it would look like the one below.

Again, the pairs of dualities within the unmanifested God were manifest in the creation.

The relationship of one creation to another varies, depending upon what it is related to (itself, a person, nature, God). Thus in relation to the universe, God is "the masculine subject representing its internal character."[44]

"B" is in the objective position to God the Subject, but B itself (and each creation in B) contains subject and object, positive and negative and so on in all their constituent parts, which interact with other dualities in all their specific ways. Thus "every creation is [in the position of being] a 'substantial object' of the invisible deity of God."[45] The universe, then, is alive. The universe was created with God at the center, just as man being created in God's image (Genesis 1:27) has been created with his mind at the center.[46]

Universe   Body
←——————————————————————————→
God   Mind

In other words, *Mind* is the center of God's *Body,* which is the universe. The universe is God's body with His Mind (internal character, invisible, subject) at the center. Mind (God) projected the Body (Universe). Thus, "the universe as an organic body has its own internal character and external form, with God as its internal character, while the physical universe is its external form."[47]

A	The Invisible God	Internal Character Subjective Position, Cause	(Male, positive)	
B	The Visible Universe	External Form, Objective Position, Result	(Female, negative)	God = A + B

God as the internal masculine subject created the universe as His external feminine object. God's positivity is masculine; His negativity is feminine. We can begin to see here why God cannot complete Himself without the sex act and why one of Jesus' greatest failures was His failure to marry and have sex. "Unless male and female beings come together and are united, there is no way for God to express His love ultimately."[48] Male and female reflect God and the Universe. In a sense, God is androgynous, currently engaged in "sexual" (emotional) intercourse with the universe, or Himself. (See "God" in the Theology section.)

God as subject gives love as an emotional force to His object; His object (creation) returns beauty as an emotional force to the subject, bringing God perfect joy. When this relationship was ruined in the Fall, God "went to pieces" emotionally. He was extremely upset about this since His chances for perfect joy were thwarted and He lost everything He had hoped for. After all, for eternity God had existed alone—lonely—just as if we humans existed only as a mind in a glass bubble without a body. Projecting a universe gave God the joy our minds get from our having a body.[49] Only now, at the Fall, the Body became "corrupted." God is, in a real sense, a cripple. He must find someone to cure and perfect His Body. He must, or He will be unhappy forever.

"Give and Take Action" is another term Moon uses. It is the process within each created thing that generates the necessary energy for existence and reproduction.[50] It is through the *Universal Prime Force* (UPF) that God's "dual essentialities" form a reciprocal relationship that develops into an external give and take action. And since the creation is God's Body, a created thing does what God does. That is, through the UPF it forms reciprocal relationships that develop into give and take action between its "dual essentialities." For example, animals form reciprocal relationships that develop into give and take action (sex) between their dual essentialities (male and female). There is also give and take action between animals and plants—plants give oxygen, animals return carbon dioxide. Flowers give nectar to bees who pollinate flowers. Solar systems exist through give and take action between the sun and planets, earth and moon and so on. In man there is internal give and take action between male and female (in sex). Give and Take Action (GTA) is thus said to govern all relationships within man and among men.

GTA is also the "cause" of the universe. God's internal unmanifested subject and object entered a relationship through the UPF. The action between the subject and object caused by UPF was the GTA. Through UPF God's GTA resulted in creation. We may diagram this as follows:

Inner GTA
←⎯⎯⎯→
(horizontal)
results in

UPF
Interaction
(vertical)

Causes

Universe which
leads to mutually
sustaining action
(circular)

It is the circular action of this energy that *maintains* creation. God exudes Himself as energy (love) which is returned to Him as energy (love).[51]

Since everything functions "as God" does, Adam and Eve were created in a similar manner. Through UPF, God's dual characteristics entered GTA by forming a reciprocal relationship, causing multiplication; that is, His dual characteristics separated into "two substantial objects centered upon God"[52] (Adam and Eve). These may enter into their *own* GTA by forming a reciprocal relationship through UPF (through intercourse). "By forming one unit they become an object to God."[53] Thus (part of) God is divided into two separate substances that unite to form one body. This process is called Origin-Division Union Action (ODUA). We may diagram ODUA as follows:

```
                    GTA
                   \    /            O
                    \  /             D
                     \ /             U
1st objective         \  |
position to God        \ /
(male and               \            A
female as created)  Adam Eve  (brother, C
                     M   F    sister)  T
                    Sub. Obj.          I
                    When these         O
                    achieve perfection: N

2nd objective
position (male   Husband  GTA   Wife
and female         M  ⟵———⟶   F
perfected)          \            /
                     \          /
                      \        /
                    Union: united in a
                    third objective
                    position to God
3rd objective
position (male
and female in
union)
```

God's dual characteristics (*origin*) multiply by means of GTA into two beings (*division*) who unite (*union*) through GTA. This is ODU Action.

The next discussion in *Divine Principle* concerns the Triple Objective Purpose (TOP) and Four Position Foundation (FPF). These involve a husband, wife and children centered on God. Essentially the FPF is the "proper" relationship of a family to God and each other:

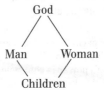

```
            God
           /   \
          /     \
       Man       Woman
          \     /
        Children
```

This relationship involves husbands sometimes submitting to their wives and parents sometimes submitting to their children.

As should be evident by now, the *Divine Principle*, its study guide and the *120 Day Training Manual* are very abstruse. And what we have discussed so far encompasses only a few of the 150-plus diagrammatical charts in the back of the *120 Day Training Manual*, which itself is said to explain Moon's philosophy only in condensed form (diagrams in this chapter are the authors'). Further, Moon and his spirit guides do not always explain key terms. So at the risk of oversimplification we will proceed.

The first group of *four positions* is formed as a result of the division of God into two units which then unite: the position of God, the two unit's positions and the position of union (resulting in children). One takes a subjective position (God); the remaining three stand as objects to God, producing three objective *bases*.[54] This involves the Triple Objective Purpose (TOP), where the three objects unite with the one subject. This leads to the Four Position Foundation (FPF). These three objective positions or bases are Male-Female created as substantial objects (first), Male-Female assuming the role of subject-object (second) and Male-Female in union producing children (third). When these three objective positions are centered on their origin (God), the fourth position is created (the position of centering on God). This is called the Four Position Foundation.

When Moon declares that God's vital purposes with the creation and the salvation of mankind *cannot be achieved* without a God-centered Four Position Foundation resulting from the Triple Objective Purpose through Origin Division Union Action, it involves all that has been discussed to date and a great deal more:

> Until this base is formed on this earth, there cannot be any salvation.[55]

> The four position foundation is the base for the fulfillment of God's goodness and is the ultimate goal of His creation. This is the base through which God's power is channeled to flow into all of His creation in order for the creation to exist. Therefore, the formation of the four position foundation is ultimately God's eternal purpose of creation.[56]

Adam and Eve

The "Four Position Foundation" just discussed is simply Moon's idea of the "proper" relationship of a family to God. It is referred to as establishing a substantial Trinity centered on God, and it relates to Adam and Eve.

The Four Position Foundation was God's purpose of creation and was to be established by God, Adam and Eve and their children in various stages. Adam and Eve were to enter a "Give and Take Action" relationship with God. Had they not fallen, Adam and Eve and all their posterity would have naturally died (death for Moon is normal) and gone into the spirit world. Once there a type of transformation would have taken place in which they would have formed the Body of God with God as the Mind. There would then be one divine entity. Their minds would become spiritual dwellings so God Himself could "become" their mind.[57]

> When Adam and Eve were perfected here on earth and then were elevated to the spirit world, God would have become the mind of Adam and Eve and they would have been the spirit body of God, so that God and men in spirit world would have been inseparable, one body. . . . [Today here] on earth our supreme mission is to prepare ourselves to welcome God as our mind in spirit world. The whole purpose of our physical lives here on earth is to make ourselves dwelling places of God so that when we pass into the spirit world our minds can become spirit bodies in which God can dwell. . . . We are all supposed to be the bodies of God.[58]

Essentially, Moon is proposing that people become redeified. However, the problem was that Adam and Eve failed. They established Give and Take Action with Satan instead of with God, thus establishing a satanic reciprocal base (a Four Position Foundation) that became their "foundation of existence." Thus people no longer stand in relation to God, but to Satan. When Eve fell by having sex with Satan, she took on his sinful characteristics and the literal blood of Satan entered her veins. When she had sex with Adam he was corrupted in the same manner. Then Satan's blood coursed through Adam and Eve and was transmitted to their offspring. Everyone, then, has satanic blood, which must be purified. Further, the mind somehow remained God-centered (more or less), but the body changed "so that Satan has been controlling it." Everyone is physically "possessed" or controlled by Satan, so they must return their bodies to their original position as vehicles of God rather than of Satan.[59]

The goal of history, then, is to establish a perfect race, physically cleansed, in proper familial (FPF), not individual, relationship to God. This is a major goal underlying all the efforts of Moon and his "church." "Our final problem is how to cleanse our blood. All through history God has been working for that."[60] Moon says, "My dispensation is to establish a new lineage of pure blood."[61] (See "Sex Scandals" in Critique section for one of the outcomes.)

Moon divides the 6,000 years of history into three stages, each with many sub-stages. In each stage God attempted to restore the race and failed. It is man's responsibility to meet God's conditions and pay for Adam's sin. Whenever man fails to meet these conditions, he must "pay God back" by punishment and by establishing often more difficult conditions in the future. This is known as "indemnity." (There is also a waiting period between each failure.)

The "providential age for the foundation of restoration" runs from Adam to Abraham, 1,000 years. During this era Noah unsuccessfully attempted to restore the race, since his family failed him. Abraham also failed, but he and his descendants did accomplish enough to begin the "providential age of restoration," 1,930 years, from Israel's Egyptian bondage (indemnity) to

Jesus Christ. The third stage is the "providential age of the prolongation of restoration." This lasts 1,930 years and ends with the "age of preparation for the Lord of the Second Advent." Moon was born in 1920 and we are now preparing for him to be received symbolically as Christ returned. If man fails to receive him, it is back to square one, and everything must begin all over.

The Principle of Restoration Indemnity

Moon describes the vital "principle of restoration indemnity" as follows:

> The "providence of restoration" means God's providence of restoring fallen man to his original state endowed at the creation, thus fulfilling the purpose of creation.... What, then, does "restoration through indemnity" mean? When anything has lost its original position or status, certain conditions must be established in order for the original position or status to be restored. The setting up of such conditions is called "indemnity."[62]

For the UC, "God's" plan of the Providence of Restoration (how to restore the universe to its original position) has been one long and pitiful failure. Moon divides all of history into numerous ages or sections. In each time period God tried and failed to achieve the Four Position Foundation. There are ages of "symbolical" time identity, "image" time identity and "substantial" time identity, each viewed differently. It is quite complex, but if we use only three periods we may have a general idea:

The Age of Law	Old Testament	1st Adam	1st Israel
The Age of Salvation	New Testament	2nd Adam (Jesus)	2nd Israel (Christian Church)
The Age of Restoration	Completed Testament (*Divine Principle*)	3rd Adam (Moon)	3rd Israel (Korea or UC)

Here we see how antiChristian UC theology is. First, according to Unification theology, the age of *salvation* is over because we are now in the age of *restoration*, where God is doing something much more important than saving people. He is restoring man to his original position, ful-

filling the purpose of creation. Second, the Age of the Bible is also over. The Completed Testament is *Divine Principle*, replacing the first (Old) and second (New) testaments. Third, the age of Jesus, the Second Adam, is also over. The Third Adam is Moon, upon whom the salvation (restoration) of the world rests. Finally, the Age of the Christian Church is over. The Second Israel is the Christian Church; the Third Israel is the nation that was to save the world.*

What we discover in Unification theology, then, is the complete replacement of the Bible, Christian salvation, Jesus Christ and the Christian Church with Moon's program for the "providence of restoration."

Restoration Symbolism

Moon's program of restoration indemnity proceeds from the individual level, through the family, tribe and nation levels until finally the whole world is subjugated. Much of this can be "accomplished" by *symbolic* means, although just how much is uncertain.

There are scores of requirements that UC members must fulfill in order to "restore" the world. One of the more outrageous is that a member must find and convert three people who will be willing to die for him. And much of what members are required to do results from the spirits' bizarre system of symbolism, connecting events of history (especially biblical history) to events of today. Thus, UC members must make up for historical failures (indemnify them) by doing them correctly. But there has been 6,000 years of repeated failures to indemnify! For example, "Jesus couldn't restore his tribe. So we have to restore our tribe, and surpass Jesus' mission. By doing that we can restore the nation."[63]

In Moon's writings, hundreds of events in history, religion, politics and his own life are symbolically related and paralleled to hundreds of

---

*Initially, probably Korea; when that did not come to pass, the Third Israel perhaps became the Unification Church members who were to assume power in one nation (America) and use it as a beachhead to subjugate the world for its salvation. Only time will tell how Moon, or whoever replaces him, will deal with his failure in America.

biblical events. Although these events are actually not related to each other, and are often absolutely trivial, in Moon's system they are joined together and made the basis for various teachings. "History both before and after Jesus must be viewed symbolically rather than literally. . . . We say 4, 40, 400, 1600—all have the same meaning. From King Saul to Solomon was 120 years, but in terms of God's providence it only means 40 years, because the three kings only accomplished one thing—the erection of the Temple."[64]

Everything Moon does has some symbolic significance, from his mass weddings to the dates of certain events (numerical symbolism is omnipresent). Due to the additional revelation of the *Divine Principle*, the biblical narrative is even embellished at points to help things "fit." In all of this, UC members will stress that Moon has the "answers" to everything. However, even superficial examination reveals that his analysis and symbolism of history, comparative religion and politics is confused and illogical. Note one example:

> Whenever God's religion comes out then Satan's side can come out also. How do we know this? When Jesus was on the cross, there was a thief on each side of him. Jesus Christ was not supposed to die; so the second coming of Christ was inherited from his crucifixion. Because this happened to Jesus Christ, then two thousand years later this same situation will appear again so that it can be fulfilled. The right thief represents the free democratic nations. We call that the right wing. The left thief represents communism and that's called the left wing sometimes. . . . This was the origin of the left and right political parties at that time. Because of Jesus Christ the thief who was supposed to die got the blessing. That's the Moslem nation.[65]

Man must pay for each historic failure through suffering and set up "proper conditions" to restore the earlier situation. The price may be paid by various means and in various degrees. For example, certain conditions must be met in order to "lay the foundation to receive the Messiah [Moon]."[66] If they are not laid there will be failure, as there was with Jesus, where the proper conditions were not set up beforehand. A wife, for example, was not prepared for

Jesus beforehand, which might have allowed Him to succeed in His mission. After all, how could Jesus form a family centered on God and have sinless children without a wife? So it was inevitable that He should fail. Because of Jesus' failure, man has been paying indemnity for 2,000 years and is now finally ready to set up the "conditions" to receive the Messiah; that is, "conditions" that involve the activities of the UC on Moon's behalf, assuming they are successful.

Unification theology views history in a cyclic or, more accurately, repetitive manner based on the principle of symbolic historic correspondences and the principle of indemnity. Moon is *restoring* history in terms of its past failures, and in the process he is *recreating* it. Wherever redemptive history does not succeed along the intended points (as Moon sees them), future generations must not only pay for the failure (make indemnity) but also achieve the success that earlier generations failed to achieve. For example, "From the Divine Principle we learn that history repeats itself in expanded versions. Because of the failure of the mission of Jesus 2,000 years ago, the pattern of history has to be repeated in our time, and we have to pay the indemnity for the failure at the time of Jesus."[67]

The key is symbolism. Because all history is symbolic Moon can find symbolic correspondences everywhere, and because numbers are symbolic they do not have to be literal; for example, 6 years can represent 600. By this means, Moon arbitrarily molds history to fit his particular theological framework. For example, ancient Israel rejected their Messiah; and Korea today, in the "position" of Israel (the third Israel), must pay indemnity for the first Israel's mistake. So Korea's penalty was to be subjugated by Japan for 36 years, which was "40 years" payment of indemnity: itself the symbolic equivalent of "400" years of Christian tribulation in Rome for their own failure.[68] And since Jesus failed, Moon must succeed where He failed, as well as pay indemnity. His life must not only pass through the stages of Jesus' life but also restore Jesus' failures:

> The time when Jesus was crucified on the cross can be compared to the time of Master's imprisonment. . . . Jesus lost everything on the cross.

So Master had to go through the same situation.[69]

When Jesus was put on the cross He lost His 12 disciples. So Master had to restore those 12 disciples in prison.[70]

For the Lord of the Second Advent to appear on this earth he had to restore all these things lost in the Old Testament Age and in the New Testament Age.[71]

One reason the Communists captured North Korea was so Moon could be tortured to pay the indemnity incurred by Jesus' failure and unexpected crucifixion. Likewise Jesus was rejected by His family, so, correspondingly, Moon could not even witness to his. "He could not witness to or influence his own family. He never once talked about the Divine Principle to his own brother, parents or any relative. Why? He was in the position of Jesus who was driven out by his people."[72] Similarly, since God was willing to sacrifice His own Son for the world, and since He wanted to restore the world at the cost (supposedly) of many martyrs, UC followers, "reliving history," must become martyrs. "Master is in the position of saving the Gentile world at the cost of his own beloved ones."[73]

Moon's theories go on and on, becoming more and more complex. All happenings after Cain and Abel are set by Moon in their respective "positions." With all the evil in the world, Moon argues that the world is in the general position of Cain, who was a *murderer*. The Christian Church is also in the position of Cain. The UC is in the position of Abel, who sacrifices itself for Cain (the world and the Christian Church) even though Cain "murders" or persecutes it.

This entire scheme is carried out with innumerable permutations. "Adam and Eve's fall was on the physical [sexual] level. Therefore, physical abstination [in marriage] is necessary in order to make restitution."[74] There are not only thousands of potentially relevant historical events for the people and events of today to assume their "positions," there are also multiple positions that may be assumed, both horizontally (man to man) and vertically (man to God):

By killing a fallen man, represented by the Egyptian, Moses could liberate God's heart. . . .

God had cherished the feeling of resentment in His heart to kill fallen man, but by Moses' killing of the Egyptian (who represented fallen man), God was liberated from that feeling. So God, instead of hating Moses, loved Moses all the more and set him up as the central figure on that dispensation. Jacob did the same thing on the individual level when he wrestled with the angel and won victory over the angel and could develop the salvation of mankind on the family level. . . . But, they also, the people of the Christian system, have failed to restore and save man. The world of Christianity is now in the position of having failed to do that, because it is relating with Satan. . . . God . . . is now in the position of beating the world of Christianity and finding instead another central figure.[75]

When we encounter Moon, we discover that he is the composite of all history and the one who suffers the sins of other's failures:

I have shed so many tears in discovering the Principle, particularly with such historical figures as Adam, Cain, Abel, Noah, Abraham, Jacob, Moses, Jesus, and so on. . . . It was not Adam's story, but mine. I felt the story of Cain and Abel as my own. Through their mistake, God felt so much sorrow, and I felt the same. So with Noah, Abraham, Jacob, Moses, Jesus. In each event, I put myself in the position of those involved and felt with them, and with God, all through the history. It is not someone else's history, but my own life.[76]

Every period of restoration is my work. My responsibility is to make indemnity for all those from Adam to the Lord of the Second Advent.[77]

Through use of symbolism, Moon can "indemnify" past failures and, through wholly unrelated modern events, such as mass weddings, allegedly change the course of history:

By the blessing of these 36 couples, the period from Adam to Jacob was restored. . . . Then 120 couples were blessed, representing Jesus' 12 disciples, and 120 people who awaited the descent of the Holy Spirit. . . . By the blessing of the 120, the universal blessing could start. . . . I had to pay indemnity for what had been lost by Jacob, Moses and Jesus. . . . By blessing these couples, restoration was completed both physically and spiritually. Therefore, starting from these blessings, heaven and earth, which have been separated, are united. Consequently, international affairs are turning in a new direction. These blessings affected our national affairs in a very conspicuous way.[78]

The Principle of Reversal

As if all this was not difficult enough, Moon's spirit guides demand that things be restored *in reverse order*. For example, in the "Satanic" world the order is first parents, then children. In the restoration age (now) the order must be, at least symbolically, first children then parents. Hence each person must first find three spiritual children (converts) before he or she can be married and be a true parent. Otherwise, even if people are parents, they are not such in God's eyes; they are living in a satanic marriage and union. The principle of reversal also extends at times to roles within the family. Women must sometimes lead men, and children their parents. "In the course of restoration, husband and wife cannot go side by side. One will go ahead of the other, and the other will follow. . . . Men should follow them [women] in this case. After restoration, the order will be reversed. . . . "[79]

Moon himself can learn from and be inspired by anything, even the insane.[80] The Principle of Reversal may also help to explain Moon's view of Satan and the spirit world:

> There is nothing he hates because he likes everything. . . . He is even sympathetic to Satan. In a way, Satan is amicable. Satan has done a great job. He has changed the course of the history of God.[81]

> In teaching the Principle to your children, their spirits will grow faster than yours. Often [spiritistic] messages will come through them to you. . . . The children receive far higher messages for their parents than the parents themselves do. . . . They will tell you what indemnity you have to pay, what punishment you must receive, and so on. Your children can be your guides.[82]

With this introduction to some basics of Moon's theology, we will now turn to a brief examination of several characteristics of the Unification Church or Unification Movement.

Exclusivism

Sun Myung Moon (aka "Father," "Master") alone has the answers to life and all existence. "Throughout history, man has been struggling to solve the fundamental questions of life and the universe. Yet no one [except Moon] has been able to give satisfactory answers, for no one has known the original plan for the creation of man and the universe."[83] Logically, then, the UC is the only path of spiritual restoration. Only the UC is at work in this complex scheme of things to "restore" people to their proper estate. "There is no other way. Prominent religious leaders have no other way to lead the world, or souls, except this method of service and sacrifice, which he (Master) is talking about. This is the position of our Unification Church Family. . . ."[84] Moon says approvingly, "Members of the Unification Church believe that the world cannot be saved except by our group."[85]

Syncretism

God is believed to be the author of all religions; each one, then, is a part of His attempt at restoration.[86] It is also believed that the prophecy of a coming savior is found in each of the world's religions. Since Moon is the personification and fulfillment of all such prophecies, the idea is that all religions will finally accept Moon as their expected savior. Christianity, however, because it is God's best attempt at religion, is where Moon has concentrated his efforts, in the hope that other religions will unify under Christianity—at least his version of it. Thus, with Moon as its monarch, the world will be unified under another, superior worldwide Christianity (however, a "Christianity" more aligned to paganism than to biblical teaching).

Moon also declares that he is in command of the spirit world, and that the spirit world must proclaim him as the truth. As a result, he fully expects that the spirit world (via mediumism and spiritism) will actively help with the process of unifying all religions:

> I stayed in Japan for two weeks before I came here. During that time, five leading members of Buddhism and Shintoism joined our group through the guidance and messages of the spirit

world. In this way, unification of the world will be fulfilled. Otherwise, how could we unify all religions? . . . Buddha comes to them and says that his mission is now over, and that his followers should go to Mr. Moon because he is the one to unify all religions "like rivers run into the ocean." Confucius says the same thing.[87]

Young Oon Kim refers to the fact that in 1954 in Korea, "Some members came to [Moon's] group through direct guidance of the spirit world." Besides Buddhists and Confucists being led by the spirits of their deceased leaders, he also mentions a Catholic woman led to Moon by the Virgin Mary.[88]

Secretive

Moon alleges that "the Unification Church does not have any secrets."[89] Sontag writes: "Does Reverend Moon teach anything different in private to his followers than he admits in his public proclamations? I asked this question of members around the world and got every answer but yes."[90] Of course, in-house replies are hardly evidence that Moon has no secrets, especially if members are instructed not to reveal them.

Not all UC teachings are given up front. Moon himself declares, "If I explain everything plainly about the birth of Jesus, it may stumble many Christians in accepting God's new dispensation. Therefore, I don't want to explain everything too plainly here."[91] This statement could easily have been a reaction to incidents like the following, reported at a UC training camp:

They were talking about how Mary was not a virgin, because she had sex with Zecharias, and that Jesus was the son of Zecharias, and that Joseph had come home and there was Mary in a fallen state in the temple, and this Christian guy just freaked out. He jumped up and went straight through the window glass and took off into the woods. I was shaking, it was so horrible. And apparently, later he didn't remember doing it. They said some people were spiritually weak, and they'd sometimes have to sprinkle salt around them, and exorcise them.[92]

The former member who related this incident claimed, "They're very secretive, and they

were holding back a lot of things."[93] In *The Master Speaks*, Moon admits that he has to be careful to ensure that he does not reveal his real purposes or plans to the wrong people.

Further, there are vital practices that non initiates are not privy to. Moon again admits, "There are many things going on behind the scenes which will be made public much later in history; we cannot do it now."[94] One can only ask, "Why not?", if they are not a secretive organization as they claim?

The fact is, Moon not only guards secret teachings from the general public ("It is all right to say Sun Myung Moon has been here, but don't say who he is"),[95] he has secret teachings that even his own disciples are not ready to hear. Indeed, former President of the UC in America, Neil Salonen, believes that some of Moon's own blood (remember it is pure, not Satanic) was placed into the communion wine at his 1960 wedding and is being preserved by dilution for all future rites.[96] Moon admits, "At the [wedding] ceremony, I use a holy wine that was made through special revelation. Through the use of this holy wine, your body is cleansed. The wine signifies new life. I could not make this wine until I had made enough conditions and received sanction from God. . . . It is made of 12 materials. After it was made, many spirits came and asked for a cup of it."[97] (In some spiritistic traditions, spirits encourage the use and drinking of blood.) As we will see, there is some concern over alleged secret blood purification sex rituals in Moon's early church which, seemingly, were a prerequisite aspect for saving the world.

Superstitious

Spiritistic revelations routinely bring a form of bondage through the superstitious practices demanded. (There is a mansion in California that is an architectural nightmare. Its owner was promised by the spirits that he would never die as long as he kept building additional rooms.)

In his *Youth Brainwashing and Extremist Cults*, sociologist Ronald Enroth records a former member's testimony concerning holy salt, blowing on food and the "exorcism" of unintelligent spirits:

There was also widespread use of "holy salt." Most [members] carry holy salt with them at all times, in order to sanctify their food. Everything has to be sanctified before you eat. If you don't have holy salt to sanctify the food, you must blow on it three times. If you stay in a motel room with a fundraising team, you have to sanctify the room first. You put three handfuls of holy salt in the middle of the room and then sprinkle salt around the room as you repeat a certain prayer. You have to open the windows and doors so the spirits can get out. If they are stupid spirits, they won't realize that they can go through the wall, and so they'll be looking for the door. You have to open the door in case they happen to be stupid spirits.[98]

If you were sick or in a bad mood, you would use holy salt. The spirits supposedly entered through the back of the neck, and you could sanctify yourself by getting them off the back of your neck. If someone freaked out, you would throw holy salt on them. I remember one evening my best girl friend experienced some kind of possession and started talking very strangely. So we threw holy salt on her and immediately felt the atmosphere in the room change. The spirits left, and she became normal. In the movement there was always a lot of talk about spirits and the spirit world. It wasn't anything unusual for me to see a spirit walk into a room and sit down and talk. There was also a tremendous emphasis on visions and personal revelation. It was considered a mark of distinction if you had visions. . . . I heard voices a lot and frequently hallucinated.[99]

SUN MYUNG MOON

In public, Moon denies that he is the new Messiah. "I am not saying 'I am the Messiah.' . . . I am not putting myself in the position of God."[100] "I have never once thought of myself as the authoritative and most powerful one."[101] But when his disciples learn the secret teachings in *The Master Speaks, The 120 Day Training Manual* and elsewhere, they learn the truth. These unveil a virtual god who is prayed to, worshipped and adored. In fact, all the devotion a Christian feels to Jesus Christ is what disciples lavish upon Sun Myung Moon, who, they are told, is far above Jesus Christ in stature. Jesus failed; Moon will succeed. *Moon is now*

the mediator between God and man, not Jesus.[102] From the start Moon claimed that he would succeed where Jesus failed. "But nobody in Korea knew of my vast historical significance. Since I knew the cause of Jesus' failure, I developed my tactic to perfection. I have such a wise tactic that I will not repeat the failure of Jesus."[103]

Even Moon's official title, Lord of the Second Advent, gives credence to the fact that in the UC he is believed to be the Messiah. This is made clear to all disciples even if they deny it publicly. Moon fits every description he has given of the coming Messiah and has fulfilled almost everything the Messiah is to do, including: "birth in the flesh; born in Korea; born around 1920; brings total world salvation; completes the work of Jesus; subjugates Satan; brings the Completed Testament which 'clarifies' the Bible; is the Third Adam; is 'persecuted' by Christians; has the testimony of the spirit world and mediums; is called 'Lord' and 'Father'; will restore the Universe; etc."[104]

In *The 120 Day Training Manual* Moon is viewed as an *atoning Savior.* During his reputed torture by the communists, "Father [Moon] took responsibility for our sins. . . . Therefore, instead of me being tortured, the sinless Messiah was tortured by Satan. . . . The bloody body of the only son on whom Heavenly Father was able to rely was now thrown out into cold, into darkness. . . . Father [Moon] shed blood instead of me, instead of you, instead of us. . . . While I was committing sin, Father was shedding blood to cleanse my sin. Because he shed blood, he was qualified to give life to me."[105] Note that Moon is termed a *"sinless* Messiah." We will later see how patently false this claim is.

Because of Moon's atonement for us, we should "truly feel it is a joy to die for Father."[106] "[Sinless] Father shed blood instead of me. . . . Without Father, there is no life. Father is more precious than myself, than even all mankind. Therefore, even at the price of my life, I can be a joyful offering for Father."[107] Reading through *The 120 Day Training Manual* it is evident not only that Moon has fully replaced Jesus Christ but also that *he exists in the place of God on earth.* This is why he is called Father.[108] "If you want to understand what God is you have only to investigate Father to find what God is," because "Father is visible God."[109] Thus, Moon is the only one to save the world,[110] and he is to be obeyed as God.[111] Six thousand years of human history have been only for him, for God has found him and him alone to be faithful.[112]

The following examples give an idea of the attitude of adoration and worship that a UC member will feel for Moon. "His value is incredible and inestimable and immeasurable. He is greater than the universe. He is more precious than the universe. . . . Therefore through. . . the offering of your mind, your body, your life, and the things you have, you can establish the foundation of faith. . . . Therefore, this attitude toward the Messiah [Moon] is the essential attitude of the Unification Church toward Father [Moon]."[113] The extent of devotion is further indicated by a former UC member, who notes the power and spiritual "presence" of Moon. Reminiscent of many spiritists, gurus and occultists, "Moon had a certain magnificence about him. When he walked into the room, you felt blown against the wall. He had an invisible force around him. . . . He had dominion over creation, and I felt that every leaf, every grain of sand, was truly waiting for his presence."[114] This former member also notes the "service" rendered to Moon by members, reminiscent of the spiritistic groups discussed earlier on the East and West coasts of Korea. Note the spiritual bondage merely in kitchen preparation—incredibly, even banana peels had to be washed with Q-tips:

I was trained for three months to know how to serve him. We spent many hours a day praying in preparation for his visit. It's impossible to pray that long: you have to go into sort of a trance. . . . Preparations for his coming were elaborate. The entire kitchen had to be cleaned out—everything had to be taken out. Everything had to be replaced. If you wanted to use a particular canned good, you had to buy the biggest and most expensive. Even if you had a can which was not opened, you still had to buy a new one. Everything had to be completely new. After all, you were preparing it for "God." If you wanted to use an onion, you would buy a crate of onions and pick out the best one. . . . Every-

thing was washed. If you washed a banana, you had to use Q-Tips. It had to be washed not only physically, but also spiritually.[115]

He also describes the wealth lavished upon Moon and the personal guilt it produced in him:

We bought everything that he could possibly think of needing. I had to call long-distance to New York to find out what kind of underwear he used. I would even have dreams about the doormat not being new. I felt guilty about spending money, because I knew how hard the kids worked to raise it. Yet we were told that it was okay to buy anything. You had to buy things even though you knew he wouldn't need them. Like he doesn't drink coffee, but you had to buy a coffee pot anyway. . . . Every single thing you did had to be done with the correct attitude. While chopping the garlic, if you weren't praying, he [Moon] would know. We were always told that if you weren't prayerful enough, he wouldn't eat the food.[116]

The above devotion is justified because of Moon's divine status. In fact, there are numerous occasions in *Master Speaks,* and other publications, where Moon is equated with God. Although Moon is not all that God is, he is sufficiently close to God to justify the comparisons. "That is why the Leader has appeared to you. . . . If you ask him, 'Who is God?' he will say, 'I am.'"[117] Thus Jesus is really "the Son of Moon." "Jesus will be the first and eldest son, because he was the only one who came to this world as the Son of God. 'Do you mean God's eldest son, or the Master's?' The meaning is the same."[118]

Moon not infrequently compares himself with Jesus, stressing his own superiority. "I am fulfilling what Jesus left undone."[119] "He (our leader) is love and truth itself. Jesus had truth and love, and it was not enough."[120] Even what Jesus endured on the Cross was insufficient to be compared to Moon's sacrifice. "As for Master, during my first 3 years of public ministry, just as Jesus did, I had to go through severe hardships culminating in the torture of prison life, which was more for me than Jesus' cross."[121]

Moon believes that Jesus "could not change the hearts of the people," that Jesus was inferior to him in several respects, that Jesus did not understand truth, was not very wise and had "abstract" love. Moon by contrast, changes the hearts of the people, "is more powerful and wise," and calls himself "the King of Wisdom and the Prince of Love."[122] The following are descriptions of Moon taken from *Master Speaks:* Moon is "the Ultimate Savior"; "the Ultimate One"; "the world Messiah"; "Lord of the entire universe"; "like the ocean"; and as a "man of perfection doesn't need prayer"; thus, "You are connected with God through Master."[123] Further: "Now I have reached the point where I can rule the spirit world using only my physical senses."[124] "I . . . became the Lord in the spirit world first. Then I began struggling on earth, and am now subjugating people and nations with this truth."[125] In light of this, it is not surprising to find that Moon is the one to rule the world, and from there he will proceed to become King and Ruler of the universe. "The Lord of the Second Advent will rule the heaven and the earth with Divine wisdom and power and Fatherly love, and his kingdom will last forever."[126]

We now have some idea of the true position Moon commands among his followers and why they are so devoted to him. Yet guilt, fear and condemnation are also strong motivating factors. God cannot accomplish His purpose without the members' absolute devotion. While Moon lives in palatial estates everything depends on how much they can sacrifice for him. The fate of the world, the spirit world, everyone's salvation, the fate of the universe, even God's happiness—it all depends on the members. If they fail at one level, everything that has been accomplished up to that point will be for nothing. Unless they are supremely committed, they are thieves and parasites unworthy of the Father.

In addition to an inhumane work load (physically and emotionally), UC members carry the burden of believing that they must perfect themselves entirely on their own power. God will not help. "Man's perfection must be accomplished finally by his own effort without God's help."[127] And if they are not very careful, they will lose their salvation.

Political Ambitions

Moon has declared that he has no political interests. "I have no political goals. . . . I do not think in terms of taking over the power or government of a nation."[128] But if anything is clear, it is Moon's desire to rule the world. According to *The 120 Day Training Manual*, Moon first came to America because he was rejected for President of Korea.[129] Moon believes that the amount of territory one conquers on earth determines one's value and position in the spirit world. "In both the physical world and the spirit world, the value of a couple is the same, and the more territory they conquer and embrace with their love here on earth, the more territory they can deal with in spirit world. The scope of that area will determine their depth of understanding in spiritual life and their value in spirit world. Ultimately how much you practice this principle here on earth shall become a measure of how much territory you deserve in heaven."[130] Moon also admits to political interests in the *Master Speaks* publications, and these interests have also been documented elsewhere:

> We will hold a revival movement in established churches and we will organize Christians, and through their strength we will work in a political way. . . . We have to push the Americans to take the right policy.[131]

> He [Moon] is going to work in the U.S. because by doing this he thinks he can have the U.S. influence the Korean government—which will make it easier for us to win the whole nation under our ideology.[132]

> So now we have to make bases in 50 states. We also have to restore Senators. So Master will assign 3 young ladies to each Senator.[133]

> "Tom McDevitt [who attempted an unsuccessful Republican campaign for a Virginia House of Delegates seat in 1993] told me that Father has directed us to get members elected to Congress so we can take over America," said Craig Maxim, a church member who quit in 1995 after spending several years as a regional leader and a singer at Moon's various mansions.[134]

Militaristic and Dictatorial

Moon claims, "I preach [that] our movement is essentially nonviolent and nonmilitaristic."[135] Still, Moon refers to his followers as an "army," and they are asked to affirm their willingness to die, if necessary, on behalf of Moon's divine cause. Total acquiescence is essential. "Utter obedience and belief" in Moon is vital, even if it means disobeying one's parents and one's nation's rulers.[136] Numerous publications make this clear:

> When you join the effort with me, you can do everything in utter obedience to me. Because what I am doing is not done at random but what I am doing is under God's command. There is no complaint, objection against anything being done here until we will have established the Kingdom of God on earth up until the very end! There can never be any complaint! I want to have the members under me who will be willing to obey me even though they may have to disobey their own parents and the Presidents of their own nations.[137]

> You must be ready to be killed a thousand times.[138]

> You must be ready to die . . . you are going to be willing to die in place of him [Moon] or by him.[139]

Although Moon leaves open the possibility of an ideological World War III, he states that there is absolutely no question that World War III will occur, whether it is military or ideological. Members are not given militaristic training, but they are, to a degree, indoctrinated in a militaristic mind set:

> Once we have this rank and this unity and strength here in America, then the ultimate enemy is Soviet Russia. Then the "March to Moscow" is going to be our motto. . . . Our resolution today must be "We fight with our lives to achieve the final victory". . . . So the State Representatives and the Mobile Unit Commanders must realize today that we are very fortunate that God has given us this glorious moment in which we can die for the cause. . . . "YOU MUST BECOME ABSOLUTELY ONE WITH OUR FATHER.". . . We are in the position to die either way. We retreat, then death is waiting for us. We march forward, then death is waiting for us. What shall we do? (March!)[140]

> Through World War I, the Heavenly side established a democratic foundation. . . . Through World War II, the territory of the democratic world was stabilized. . . . Through World War III they must build the democratic foundation of the perfection level. . . . The Third World War must come.[141]

The great world wars are inevitable in order to set up the worldwide condition of indemnity to restore God's three great blessings through the 3 stages. . . . [They] are inevitable in order to have earthly men overcome Satan's three temptations to Jesus on a worldwide basis.[142]

Rabbi Maurice Davis, a long-time opponent of the UC, told a government-citizens panel:

> Senator Dole, ladies and gentlemen, the last time I ever witnessed a movement that had these qualifications: (1) a totally monolithic movement with a single point of view and single authoritarian head; (2) replete with fanatical followers who are prepared and programmed to do anything their Master says; (3) supplied by absolutely unlimited funds; (4) with a hatred of everyone on the outside; (5) with suspicion of parents, against their parents—Senator Dole, the last movement that had those qualifications was the Nazi youth movement, and I tell you, I'm scared.[143]

> This is a movement, sir, in which 35 youngsters have already told me that had they been told to kill, they would have killed, because it was in the name of God, or Moon, take your pick.[144]

Moon and UC members, of course, adamantly oppose the associations. Still, the NBC documentary on the UC for May 17–18, 1975, quoted the following *Master Speaks:*

> We must have an autocratic theocracy to rule the world. The separation between religion and politics is what Satan likes the most.

> Our strategy is to be united into one with ourselves and with that as the bullet, we can smash the whole world.

> The whole world is in my hand and I will conquer and subjugate the world.

Other sentiments in the *Master Speaks* or by former members also indicate the authoritarian nature of the UC:

> We are fighting the democratic world with the Divine Principle.[145]

> Love is the greatest dictator and in this dictatorship we find joy.[146]

> People all over the world . . . must be ready to follow our Master wherever he goes, even

though you may not understand what he is really doing.[147]

The present U.N. must be annihilated by *our* power.... We must make a new U.N.... You may have to *die* or *be killed.* There may be *casualties* by tens of hundreds and thousands. But if you are not ready to *die for the cause*, you cannot live and save the world.... The time will come, without my seeking it, that my words will almost serve as law. If I ask a certain thing, it will be done.[148]

If anyone were to investigate the ideology to any extent, he could see that it is very definitely a very strict, socialist state, centering on a totalitarian dictator.... They said it would take up to seven generations to bring the world under total subjugation.[149]

Democratic citizens are like grasses floating on water.[150]

We do not hesitate to enforce the Will of God.[151]

If all of you are united into one fist like this, I will be the one who will use the fist.[152]

In the New Age ... [free] arrangement of marriage will not be allowed.... Your marriages are not recognized by God because they are satanic, not centered upon God even if you were married in a church. In our church, married couples abstain sexually.[153]

Ancestor Devotion

Moon believes that by strenuous efforts now believers may save not only their ancestors (who, not having had the truth, could not be fully saved or restored) but also their future generations. In fact, the eternal destiny of believers' ancestors and posterity rests squarely upon their ceaseless striving for Moon:

If you are a good worker, a greater number of your ancestors can be liberated by you and through you. You don't understand on earth how greatly they would be saddened if you were to turn away, and how anxious they are for you to succeed.... You can liberate your ancestors and bless your offspring and future generations....[154]

They encourage you to help your ancestors grow through you, so you're aware of the fact that your ancestors are around you. I used to be sitting in a lecture and sometimes I'd sense my grandmother or my mother, and I'd feel, "Oh, they're sitting in with me." There was a spirit there, and they were learning through me; they were seeing through my eyes and hearing through my ears.[155]

THEOLOGY

Christianity

On the one hand, Moon and his followers claim to be a genuinely Christian organization. A biographical note in an official UC publication, *Christianity in Crisis*, informs readers that "only a Christian message that can deal with ultimate questions ... can bring new hope today. Rev. Sun Myung Moon comes bringing such a message."[156] Moon himself declares, "The end of the world is at hand, not only for Christians but for all people throughout the world. The new history of God will begin with the arrival of the Lord [i.e., Moon]. Blessed are those who see him and accept him. It is the hope of Christianity to recognize, receive, and accept the Lord of the Second Advent."[157] UC members collectively view themselves as genuinely Christian; that is, as the true Christians. " 'Christian' means, in this instance, those of the Christian faith who take part actively in God's new dispensation [the Unification Church]."[158] "So what are we? Christians in the real sense."[159]

On the other hand, Moon is clear that the UC and Christianity are mutually exclusive. "The points of difference are complete, not just vague."[160] "When we say we are different, we mean that we are 180 degrees different from the others, not only 90 percent or 90 degrees different."[161] Thus, although Moon and his followers claim to be Christian, no doubt to gain converts from Christianity, an examination of their writings, especially the more private publications, clearly reveals otherwise. As we will now discuss, their beliefs and teachings are not simply neutral toward Christianity, but antagonistic.

Almost 20 years ago Moon's first missionary to the United States, Young Oon Kim (later a professor of systematic theology at Barrytown Seminary) stated that God "is removing His direct guidance from existing churches."[162] Moon himself declared earlier in 1974, "God is now throwing Christianity away and is now establishing a new religion, and this new religion is the Unification Church. . . . We have only one way."[163] The UC is the one and only group on earth fulfilling the mission of Jesus.[164] Moon says that if Christians do not accept the revelations in the Divine Principle as well as the Lord of the Second Advent (Moon), they will be damned.[165]

According to *The 120 Day Training Manual*, Christianity has failed, and Christians are guilty of having betrayed the Lord of the Second Advent. Therefore, God has abandoned them.[166] "Christians all over the world deserve to decline, because they did not accept me."[167] "The mission of the Unification Church is to restore the failure of Christianity. . . . Already the Unification Church has exceeded Christianity. From now on Christianity must obey the Unification Church."[168] "Salvation in Christianity is not enough," because complete salvation comes only from within the Unification Church.[169] Indeed, the contrast could not be clearer: everyone must accept and believe in Moon, but "as soon as a person believes in Jesus, Satan can invade his body."[170] In light of these teachings, it is of great concern to see that in the past so many mainline theologians have supported the Unification Church as a Christian organization. This still remains true today for those who have not examined UC teachings carefully.

At best Moon has had a torturous time with Christianity: he needs it, but he also detests it. Christians must be converted, or his plan of world restoration will be severely hindered. But these very Christians are his greatest enemies.

Major importance in the UC is placed on converting Christians. Since Moon teaches "the unification of world Christianity," his goal is the uniting, under his authority, of Catholics ("even the Papacy will be ours")[171] and Protestants, especially evangelicals:

We are responsible to convey this message to the Christians first. Until our mission with the Christian church is over, we must quote the Bible and use it to explain the Divine Principle. After we receive the inheritance of the Christian church, we will be free to teach without the Bible. Now, however, our primary mission is to witness to the Christian church. When they recognize and accept our movement, the world restoration will be very easy. So go to the Christians. In reality, Christians are quicker to understand the Principle than non-Christians.[172]

In our church we have been preparing on two fronts: one was to work to unify Christianity—i.e., the evangelical movement, the Divine Principle movement.[173]

The numerous dialogues with evangelicals over the last several decades were part of this strategy. Moon attempts to reach Christians in a variety of ways. First, like the Mormons, he places full page advertisements in major newspapers, asserting that his movement is Christian. Second, he has his theologians write liberally-oriented propaganda pieces on theology.[174] Third, he sponsors "dialogues" with both conservatives and the ecumenical-liberal and neo-orthodox ends of the theological spectrum. In the latter groups he has found many theologians willing to support him. One asserted, "I believe that it is clearly a Christian group. . . . More orthodox and more creative in dealing with scripture and the Christian tradition than many other contemporary churches. We should rejoice in their fervor and be glad to learn from them."[175] A student at a liberal Bible college declared: "I learned more about Christianity in a few minutes than I learned in a whole year of Bible college."[176] An editorial in the evangelical magazine *Moody Monthly* made the following observation: "In 1985, some 300,000 pastors and Christian leaders received [UC] materials and videotapes designed to project credibility and build bridges to established churches . . . "[177]

Obviously, if Unification theology were Christian, as many theologians affirm, one wonders how would they explain the following UC statements in which Christianity is referred to as satanic, the enemy and godless?

We know those who hate the Unification Church most are the Christian people. They hate us because Satan is in them.[178]

The satanic power is mobilizing Christian churches to come against us.[179]

The more actively we work, the more swiftly the Christian world will collapse in corruption.[180]

God will get rid of things and people who are against Him, His love or His truth. He will not be tolerant of things and people who are not fully His own.[181]

The three greatest enemies of the Unification Church are Communism, Christianity and members of the opposite sex.[182]

A former member mentioned that the basic attitude towards Christianity and Christians is that they are both satanic:

In Unification theology the cross actually becomes synonymous with Satan. I had been wearing a cross, and no way was I going to continue wearing it. We would comment, as we drove through a city, how ironic that all the churches had crosses on them, because the cross was a symbol of Satan. . . . A Christian is a person that you don't like. [Members] have a horror of Christians. They say their Bibles are like rifles and they come in and shoot Bible verses at you without really understanding the heart of the Bible. They say that Christians are the very ones who will crucify the new messiah. They're the enemy.[183]

Still, "the enemy" is the very one that must be successfully evangelized for UC goals to succeed. As someone once said, the devil is never an easy taskmaster.

God has abandoned Christianity. One reason Christians are to be converted is because they cause such trouble. Since the beginning, God has not been pleased with Christians. After Jesus failed, God had no choice except "to rely on the Christian people . . . [but] God was not pleased with them or pleased to see them."[184] Christianity (and democracy) led to the world's dominion by Satan.[185] "The Christianity which God has been fostering for 6,000 years [sic] is doomed. Up to the present God has been with Christianity. But in Christianity things are stalemated."[186] "The Christian desires only to go to heaven without knowing all these secrets. They can't be admitted! They are lost. They are not doing the right work, and are only greedy."[187] "Have Christians ever . . . attained true liberty from Satan or sin through Jesus? No."[188]

In light of Moon's view of Christianity as an enemy that one needs to convert, it is not sur-

prising that one of the ways he rejects the teachings of Christianity is through his symbolic approach to the Bible.

The Bible

The teachings of Sun Myung Moon are the ultimate source of authority for Unification Church members. Despite UC claims to the contrary, the Bible is not held in especially high regard. It is merely a fallible and primitive human witness.[189] New revelation was needed to update the Bible and to make it relevant and understandable for today. Since "the New Testament was given as a textbook . . . to the people of 2,000 years ago, people whose spiritual and intellectual standard was very low, compared to that of today," it "is thus impossible" that the Bible alone could satisfy man's desire for truth in our modern scientific age, because "today the truth must appear with a higher standard and with a scientific method of expression in order to enable intelligent modern man to understand it."[190] The Bible contains some truth, but the "new, ultimate final truth, however, cannot come from any man's synthetic research in the scriptures. . . . This truth must appear as a revelation from God Himself."[191] Part of this revelation is found in the UC's main text, *Divine Principle*, and in *The 120 Day Training Manual*. This material in the latter is so embarrassing it is hardly surprising that the UC was concerned whenever it fell into the wrong hands. For example, the manual acknowledges that there have been problems with spirit possession among converts, requiring institutionalization and involving the death of at least one person.[192] A former member noted, "I as well as each graduate of that session, was told to guard that manual with my life. Not to show it to even another Unification Church member. We were strongly cautioned that the press and the police would not understand it."[193]

For UC members, then, the Bible is replaced by the *Divine Principle*, which is really "the Word of God,"[194] but still only the beginning of new revelation. The *Divine Principle* forms one-third of a larger revelatory body constituting "The Completed Testament."

As with other new cults who proselytize in Christian churches, means were devised to "accept" the Bible as an "authority" while simultaneously neutralizing any conflicting doctrinal content. Moon knew that he would not convert many Christians by openly teaching his negative views on the Bible. Simply offering "New Revelation" from God is more tactful. "Today's truth is contained in the Divine Principle and in the Completed Testament, which contains the truths which were not revealed in the New Testament."[195] "The Principle is not the word of man, but the Word of God."[196]

Interpreting the Bible in a symbolic sense is another UC method for undermining biblical teaching. "The Divine Principle clearly shows how the Bible is symbolic and how it is parabolic. . . . The Bible is based upon the truth. The Divine Principle gives the true meaning of the secret behind the verse. . . . The story from creation to Abraham . . . is not literal. . . . Unless you truly know the meaning behind it, the Bible can reveal very little."[197] Thus, while UC members can discard the literal words of the Bible, they "cannot miss even one of Father's words." "Unless we know the whole truth, we, like the people of Jesus' time, become victims of the words of the Bible."[198]

God

The God of the Unification Church is an odd, seemingly finite creature who seems to have trouble controlling his emotions and accomplishing his objectives. Far from the holy and sovereign Lord of the Scripture, Moon's God is in many ways similar to the pagan deities, although still conceived of as an infinite energy. Here are several characteristics of the UC God.

God is energy. "God is energy itself."[199] God is "perpetual self-generating energy."[200]

God is dependent on man for His well being. As a solitary being, God is lonely apart from man:

> Even almighty God cannot experience the value of love, life and His ideal when He is alone. That is why God created His object, man.[201]

> Since God did not know how man would respond to His providence for the Messiah, He had no choice but to predict two contradictory results.[202]

In a way God fears man . . . because of man's ability to betray.[203]

If the desire of God and the desire of man differ, God's will cannot be achieved.[204]

We are the loneliest group in the world, because God actually wants to be with us, but He can't. He cannot be with us all the time.[205]

When the Fall occurred "God lost everything. Everything went to pieces."[206] God lost his love, happiness, peace and even the whole creation.[207] God also lost everything at the crucifixion. If man does not "restore" God, He will remain "lost." God has desperately searched for a man for 6,000 years to help Him:

> He is a Being to be pitied. . . . His heart is aching and torn to pieces.[208]

> Do not expect God to comfort you. You must comfort Him! Our Father is most miserable.[209]

> By us and through us it will be possible to . . . liberate even God.[210]

> Through restoration, a man is: "transformed into the holy body of God, your original role. By doing so, you . . . are restoring God's own position and dignity."[211]

God is responsible for evil. Moon teaches that God Himself is largely responsible for the Fall of man, and, in a sense, that God Himself fell. Since the universe is part of God, when it fell, God fell. In part, this explains God's unhappiness. Even the evil within the universe must be considered the "workings" of God's body. "God is taking the major responsibility for the fall of man. God is not making any excuse. The parents of children who commit a crime must be held responsible. So God is not denying it, but is taking first responsibility."[212] (Young Oon Kim, professor at Moon's Unification Theological Seminary, seems to contradict Moon here, saying just the opposite.[213]) "The Lord of the Second Advent must judge this evil and corruption and cleanse the world, making it new. . . . Inwardly speaking, in the realm of heart, families are being destroyed, nations are breaking down. . . . In this way [inwardly] God is destroying and breaking down the satanic world, while outwardly He is preparing and forming the one world He is to establish."[214]

God is not a triune being. In Unification theology, the real Trinity is comprised of man, woman and God in proper orientation.[215] Referring to Genesis 1:26 it is said: "This is not because He was speaking as a trinity."[216]

God can be controlled by people. "What he needs is love. . . . By true love we can enjoy the privilege of controlling Him. If we can do that, we can control our own fate, because we can control God who controls our fate."[217]

Even God worships Sun Myung Moon. Michael Scott, a former member, reported that members were taught of Moon:

> All the spirit world acknowledged that he was the "Lord of Creation," the Messiah. Thereupon every spiritual creature, even God Himself had bowed down and worshipped him![218]

> That is the standard: God, the spirit men and all people should look at the True Parents [i.e., Moon and his wife].[219]

Jesus

Anyone talking with a UC member will probably be impressed with his or her devotion to "Jesus." UC members will say that they believe in Jesus, they love Jesus and they pray to Jesus. They work all day for Jesus. They would even die for Jesus. Unfortunately, they do not refer to the biblical Jesus Christ but rather to Moon, who is the Lord of the Second Advent, the symbolic return of Jesus Christ.

For all practical purposes, the historical Jesus is of little, if any, relevance for today because he has been replaced by Moon. *The 120 Day Training Manual* emphasizes that Moon has completely superseded Jesus, since Jesus failed his mission. In effect, Jesus is not much more important than millions of other spirits now living in the spirit world, although in the spirit world he is conceded to be a messiah of sorts. Nevertheless, Sontag declares that "the interpretation given in the *Divine Principle* of Jesus' role . . . actually is very close to tradition on many major points."[220] Actually, we were unable to find a single point of correspondence. We will now give Moon's view of Jesus, taken from *Divine Principle* and other writings (biblical correctives are provided in parenthesis).

Jesus was not God (see John 1:1; Colossians 2:9; Titus 2:13). According to Moon, when any man has attained the "purpose of creation" he is then "one body" with God and may be called God.[221] At the same time he is not all that God is, since God comprises more than the creation. Jesus, then, could attain what any man could attain, but no more, for Jesus was only a man. Moon and the UC are very careful in making certain that in His nature and essence Jesus is not unique or special; He was not God incarnate in the Christian sense. "He can by no means be God Himself."[222] "It is a great error to think Jesus was God Himself. Jesus is no different from other men."[223] "Jesus was a man even as any other man."[224] "He was a chosen man, but he was a man."[225] "Jesus ranks among us as our elder brother."[226]

Jesus was a failure and under satanic control (see Matthew 4:1–11; 17:5; John 3:35; 4:34; 17:4). In their dialogues with theologians or with potential Christian converts, UC representatives may be evasive, claiming one teaching publicly while denying it privately. Thus, "In the Unification movement, we never ever say Jesus failed. That's put on us from outside. . . . We don't ever talk of Jesus as a failure."[227] But in UC theology, Jesus was a failure. He was unable to attain perfection and unable to accomplish God's will:

> *Well—most of us have come from Christian backgrounds—and a question that has really been bothering me is: exactly how much did Jesus accomplish—because it seems like he accomplished very little. I just wondered how much he really did accomplish.* ANSWER: Nothing. There was but one thing left. He died for God and heaven—that is the only thing he accomplished. He died, "Not my will, but I'll die for God"—that is the only thing he left. Nothing was accomplished, nobody, no disciples at all, nothing, just death. Christianity started after his death anyway.[228]

In addition, incredibly, "God was not happy at all to see the resurrected Jesus."[229] Further, in "Jesus' case . . . His death not only ended his own life, but ended his influence on the whole world."[230] More incredibly, "Jesus could not accomplish the purpose of the providence of physical salvation because his body was invaded by Satan."[231] So, when the UC declares, "We don't ever talk of Jesus as a failure," what is one to think?

Jesus was crucified because He employed occult practices to perform His miracles (see Deuteronomy 18:9-13; Revelation 21:8). "If you indulge in spirit phenomena, you must pay the price; you pay indemnity. Jesus paid much indemnity because he appealed to the people through [spiritistic] phenomena. He paid with a high price for the miracles, in the end, he paid with the crucifixion."[232] Paradoxically, Sun Myung Moon however, who has been a spiritist from an early age, and who boasts of his "divine"—that is spiritistic—powers as proof of his identity as "The Lord," is apparently exempt from paying any such indemnity, due to his superior mission.

Moon and his followers are or can become superior to Jesus (see Matthew 10:24; Philippians 2:9-11):

> History has never seen such a group as ours. . . . We are greater than our predecessors, even greater than Jesus.[233]

> You must be greater and better than Jesus himself. . . . We are in the place of Jesus, but we are going to carry out our mission which is greater than Jesus.[234]

> You can compare yourself with Jesus Christ, and feel you can be greater than Jesus himself.[235]

By implication Jesus was an illegitimate child and not virgin born (see Matthew 1:18-25; Luke 1:26-37). "To be conceived by the Holy Spirit means that Jesus was not born of the lust of his parents. . . . Both were inspired, and in that sense they were almost forced to have the relationship which produced Jesus."[236] "Jesus was born of a father and a mother, just as anyone else is."[237]

Because Jesus was not God incarnate, He had to be born as other men. Young Oon Kim states,

"The virgin birth of Jesus is not securely rooted in the New Testament as a whole" and "Joseph was not the father"—he suggests Zechariah, the husband of Elizabeth, as Jesus' father.[238]

Jesus was spiritually not physically resurrected (see Luke 24:13-39). *"Was Jesus' physical body resurrected?* No. Jesus no longer needed the physical body."[239]

Jesus was ignorant of the truth (see John 1:14; 14:6; Ephesians 4:21). "Many sages couldn't find the truth. Buddha couldn't. . . . Many saints couldn't. Even Jesus wasn't enough to understand the truth. Father [Moon] found it, found the truth."[240] "I have talked with many many masters, including Jesus. . . . They have subjected themselves to me in terms of wisdom."[241]

Jesus needs to be saved (see John 1:4; 2 Corinthians 5:21; 1 John 3:5). "We are in a position to save and liberate Jesus Christ and end his anguish. We can be in a position to liberate even God."[242]

Jesus was not the Messiah (see Matthew 16:15-17; Luke 2:11; John 4:25-26). "Therefore we must understand that while Jesus came as Messiah, he couldn't be Messiah when he was here on earth. . . . Even when Jesus was arisen, he wasn't the Messiah. . . . Therefore, poor Jesus, poor Jesus. He couldn't be Messiah on earth."[243] It was only several weeks after the resurrection that Jesus was somehow approved to become the Messiah, but only in the spirit world. Moon is the Messiah on earth.

Jesus was not the Savior (see John 4:42; Philippians 3:20; 2 Timothy 1:10; Titus 1:4). "We must know today very clearly, that Jesus Christ, the son of God, the Messiah, did not come to die on the cross. That was not the way to save the world."[244]

Jesus is not coming again (see Matthew 24). Jesus Himself will not return literally as Jesus (this is a "very erroneous belief"),[245] but only symbolically in the person of Moon. Moon is Christ returned symbolically, although still greater than Jesus the person. In his 1936 vision he was told, "You will be the completer of man's salvation by being the Second Coming of Christ."[246]

In light of this, it is obvious that the UC entirely rejects the biblical Jesus. When UC members say they believe in Jesus, what they mean is they believe in Sun Myung Moon. The Jesus of the New Testament has little if any relevance for them.

SUN MYUNG MOON	JESUS CHRIST
"Singly pioneered the way of perfect salvation." (Kim, *The Divine Principles,* p. xi)	"Jesus couldn't even save one person in the true meaning." (Sudo, p. 284)
Was perfect	Was sinful
The true Messiah	Not the Messiah
The entire expression of God (because he was married).	Only a partial expression of God (because he was single). (Sudo, p. 120)
Moon's words are more precious than God's. (Sudo, p. 153)	Jesus' words are ignored.
Even God worships Moon.	Jesus is not to be worshiped.

The Holy Spirit

The Holy Spirit is seen variously as a female spirit (a creature) and an impersonal element or essence. "There are many who receive revelations indicating that the Holy Spirit is a female Spirit. . . . The Holy Spirit came as the True Mother."[247] "The Holy Spirit who worked with Jesus was the element of the original Eve. . . . [a] female element of God. . . . When you are speaking of the Holy Spirit, it is all right to say 'it.' You don't need to say 'she.' If it's just wind or power, we can say 'it'."[248]

Salvation, Works and the Principle of Indemnity

UC salvation involves men and women undoing the results of the Fall through the complex symbolism discussed earlier under the leadership of a Savior, Moon, who prepares the way. Moon's concept of salvation centers around the

family, which is ironic because wherever Moon and his teachings predominate, many families are damaged or destroyed.

Since Jesus was crucified before He could marry, He was unable to establish the Four Position Foundation. After two millennia of much travail and agony on the part of God, Moon finally appeared on the scene. He allegedly succeeded where Jesus failed: he married and produced sinless offspring. He has perfected the individual and the family, and, supposedly, his followers will eventually restore the world. By becoming one with Moon and his wife (The True Parents), his followers may continue the process he has implemented. It is hoped by the UC that if Moon gains more power, eventually the world will unite under him and satanic blood will be purged from the race.[249] People will then die natural deaths and, since the physical and spirit worlds will be one, their minds will become their spirit bodies, and God will become their minds. The original purpose of creation will have been fulfilled, and God will then be happy. (Incidentally, the claim to have begotten sinless children was perhaps possible when his children were toddlers. Now that they have grown up it is a different story entirely. For example, one of Moon's sons, according to his former wife, enjoys pornography, uses cocaine and threatened to kill his unborn child (see "Moral Concerns").

As noted, the Principle of Indemnity is a central doctrine in Unification theology, and it has placed extreme physical, emotional and spiritual hardships on UC members. To achieve salvation and restoration they are responsible to pay back to God whatever Moon says they owe Him. God takes care of the remaining deficiency, whatever is lacking. Although the percentages are, supposedly, man 5 percent, God 95 percent, practically speaking it is more 99 percent man, 1 percent God. "There must be a law, The Law of Indemnity. God cannot forgive man who rebelled against Him, unless he [man] sets up the conditions to come back to God, denying Satan."[250]

It is sad indeed to read through the *Master Speaks* publications and reflect upon the extreme bondage that members are placed under. They must work and work, and then work and work even harder. Condition after condition must be met. After all, the fate of the universe rests on their shoulders. Thus, they must sacrifice everything now—not 99 percent, but 100 percent—everything must be sacrificed, even their lives if necessary, or all is lost. In line with the Principle of Reversal, since people fell by exalting themselves rather than God, they must be saved by debasing and sacrificing themselves and thereby exalting God.[251] If members do not attain perfection in this life, or even if they fail at one level, all that God has worked for in the last 6,000 years will be lost. One can imagine the guilt and fear that this brings, and the emotional and spiritual bondage as they work to save everything.

Further, special sins may cause the UC member to bear an even greater load of guilt and fear. For example, fornication (the UC sin of the Fall) is held to be a sin "worse than [physical] murder," because you are not just killing one person (spiritually) but all of your descendants (thus critics charge that detailed accounts of one's sexual history have been submitted to Moon[252]). Moon asserts that fornication is unforgivable, in spite of the fact that many in the Unification Church have committed it. In fact, one is thereby "doomed to Hades." (This is one reason why mixed fellowship and marriages are strictly controlled.) "As I said before, it is worse than murder. If you murder a person, you are killing one person; but by doing this thing, you are killing your descendants and your lineage.... The law to punish this kind of act is going to be the severest.... So, once you commit that kind of mistake, there is no way for me to save you and there is no measurement of how to be saved. You will be doomed to Hades. Then you will have no excuse even in the spirit world when you pass away."[253]

By contrast, Moon himself is exempt from sexual temptation: "I have the iron law in myself and no woman can ever tempt me.... So, in me, there is no temptation possible, and I am not vulnerable to it.... Regarding this problem, I am not a forgiving type of person. I feel rage in me if I find that kind of thing happening here."[254]

The centrality of the Principle of Indemnity lays a basis for the Moon doctrine of requisite sacrifice and suffering. One must pay, and one must pay dearly, just as Moon has. As Moon tells it, "You must exceed even the spirit of Jesus."[255] "We have to be more serious than Jesus."[256] "You must be resolved to bear the cross ten times as much as many [other members] have done."[257] "I will not let you eat or sleep, I will drive you all the time onto the battlefield. . . . The fiercest one history has ever known. . . . There will be no excuse. You all belong to me."[258] Even the spirit world enters the picture at this point. (In light of UC spiritistic involvement historically, the Principle of Indemnity would permit the spirits to afflict whomever they wish behind the scenes, having it interpreted as indemnity.) As Dr. Jack Sparks, author of *The Mind-Benders,* points out, "Moon has set up a complicated system by which such evil spirit people can torment sinful people now living on earth, thereby ultimately gaining salvation for both."[259]

Death for Life

In the following quotations we see self degradation and the glories of martyrdom emphasized as part of the work. Members are told how "satanic" they are and that the only way to serve God is to "kill" themselves in service to him. Devotion must be one hundred percent and then some:

Then, whose blood is it which is running in you? Satan's. Your body, whom does it belong to? You hate to say it, but it belongs to Satan. Your eyes, your mouth, your ears—everything you have belongs to Satan. Can you ever desire to belong to God, if you are going to leave those as they are? ... It is well said that the Word will either kill you or bring you into life again. What I am saying is not from me, it is the Word of Truth from God. If you obey me you have obeyed God. ... Then, are you ready to put your flesh into trial or not? Are you ready for difficulties and hardships? Do you want me to drive you out into the field of death?[260]

Moon emphasizes the importance of dying, if necessary, and of having one's blood shed to advance the cause of the Unification Church:

If God would allow you to be forgiven by cutting one of your arms or one of your legs, would you not be thankful? Furthermore, when you realize that when your human ancestry has been that of murderers, then would you not be willing to kill yourself to save your past ancestry and your future descendants? Would you not be willing to give your life? You cannot but answer affirmatively.

If you are in the position to follow God, follow our Master as God's agent, can you complain on the way? (NO!) Can you say: "I am exhausted, I cannot go any further." (NO!) Never. . . . So, are you going to complain? (NO!). . . . In the world under God, even though you may have to go through untold difficulties and bloodshed, if you live and die for God's cause, you are honored and your future generations will be honored as well.[261]

Moon teaches that those who martyr themselves on earth are guaranteed a "more glorious" position in the spirit world. Whether they are "martyrs" by suffering hardships for Moon's cause, or whether they actually commit suicide to keep themselves from sin (because some future sins cannot be forgiven), they are promised a better life afterwards. This teaching is similar to that in numerous other religions and sects that teach that martyrdom guarantees one salvation, as in Islam, certain Japanese religions (kamakazi pilots) and, in a different form, early Mormon theology. Moon thus counsels a suicide martyrdom for the commission of "dirty sins":

> You must know clearly that those who are near to God's throne in the spirit world are the martyrs. . . . The more they suffered difficulties and hardships on the earth plane, the more glorious their position is in the spirit world. . . . If, after knowing all these facts, after studying the Divine Principle, you commit a dirty sin again, you have no way to be forgiven of that sin. If you may have to be stained in some way or another, it is better for you to kill yourselves than to remain alive. It is a grave matter.[262]

In addition, members must be willing to be geographically separated from their spouses and children, to forgo sexual relations, even when together, and to be paired in reversal, for example, a masculine woman to a feminine man.[263]

How many have actually physically died for Moon is unknown. But given the fear, the exhaustion, the never-ending battle with Satan

and the despair inherent to Moon's theology, not to mention the influence of the spirit world, the numbers could be more than expected. What is known is that life is cheap in comparison to the necessity of world unification:

> So Master's mission is to establish new tradition, new morality, new ways of life, so even if he loses thousands or millions of people, even risking those lives he has to establish new tradition, new culture.[264]

> When you have gained three spiritual children, you must be able to raise them till they become so dedicated to you that they will be willing to die for you—or else your mission will not be a success in the real sense.[265]

> You may have to *die* or *be killed*. There may be *casualties* by tens of hundreds and thousands. But if you are not ready to *die for the cause*, you cannot live and save the world.[266]

> You must keep yourselves pure. If you may have to be stained in some way or another, it is better for you to kill yourself than to remain alive.[267]

Perhaps William Jeffrey Daley had committed the unforgivable sin of fornication or perhaps he was just tired. We do know that he saw no reason to continue living. One day after a UC training session, Bill Daley took off all his clothes, laid his head on a railroad track, and was decapitated. His mother could only wonder, "What did they do to my boy? He was a normal human being. What did they do to my boy?"[268] Unfortunately, there have been similar cases. But Moon promises converts that when they die, they will receive their full reward. He woos them, "I have many secrets to tell you in time. If you could see the place where you will spend eternity."[269] Incidents such as Daley's lay bare the spirit of false religion. Considering the hundreds of similar religions and cults existing today, such consequences can hardly be considered isolated.

Moon's God is impotent in so many areas; it is not surprising he is also impotent in salvation. "Therefore, we must clearly understand that God cannot save me. How ever much He may love me, it is impossible for God to save me by Himself. . . . God by Himself cannot do anything at all. . . . He just hears our cries, but He cannot do anything at all to save us."[270]

The emphasis on works-salvation is so predominant in Unification theology that one is reminded of another spiritistic religion, Mormonism. Thus in the UC:

A man is no more justified by faith alone than he is saved by faith alone.[271]

When you stand at the gate of heaven, you must have met the conditions for entrance. No individual can enter heaven, but [only] as a family. In order to be a family, you must have three [spiritual] sons and daughters. . . . Paying indemnity and helping the restoration is very hard work. Christians believe that they can simply believe in Jesus and go to church in order to go to heaven. . . . No one can take you there, you must do it yourself.[272]

Many people have been following this road: "If I believe in Jesus, I will go to paradise"—but that doesn't work.[273]

Our Leader [Moon] had to pay the indemnity for the entire world, but you are required to pay only the indemnity for your own life. Our Leader worked for the salvation of the world; you are only required to work for your own salvation. He paid the world's debt, but you pay just yours.[274]

In supporting works-salvation, Moon condemns himself as the bearer of a false gospel and thus under God's curse (Galatians 1:8-9; cf. Ephesians 2:8-9 and see Doctrinal Appendix).

The Atonement

The biblical view of the atonement is rejected by Moon when he teaches that God never intended Jesus to die on the Cross.[275] This is repeated endlessly in UC theology:

Do not believe in the Christ on the cross. . . . The cross is the symbol of Satan's victory.[276]

Today's Christianity believes in the crucifixion of Jesus. But that's not the way it should be. Nothing like salvation can come from the cross. . . . By the crucifixion, everything was denied and lost.[277]

This is not biblical teaching. Paul stated, "For I resolved to know nothing while I was with you

except Jesus Christ and him crucified" (1 Corinthians 2:2). "May I never boast except in the cross of our Lord Jesus Christ" (Galatians 6:14). He said this because it was the atonement of Jesus that propitiated God's wrath and provided salvation (Romans 3:21-28). "In him we have redemption through his blood" (Ephesians 1:7, cf., 1 John 2:2). Moon rejects this, as the following statements declare emphatically:

A vast number of Christians throughout the 2,000 years of Christian history have been confident that they have been completely saved by the blood of Jesus' crucifixion. Yet, in reality, not one individual . . . has . . . [been saved].[278]

We must know that the crucifixion of Jesus on the cross was not the original intended will of God. . . . There was no redemption; there was no salvation; and there was no beginning, no beginning of Christianity. So there on the cross, salvation was not given. Today, the Unification Church members must know this truth. . . . We must grimly realize, and rededicate ourselves, knowing first of all, that Jesus did not come to die on the cross. So we must not celebrate a false Christmas in which we believe that Jesus Christ was destined to die on the cross.[279]

A statement like the above, in light of clear biblical teaching, is incredible. Moon claims that his teachings are Christian, yet he ignores the plainest and most central teaching of the entire New Testament: "For what I received I passed on to you as of *first importance:* that Christ died for our sins according to the Scriptures" (1 Corinthians 15:3,* emphasis added).

For Moon, Jesus' death resulted from factors other than propitiating God's anger against sin. Jesus was crucified because He disobeyed God, used occult powers or failed to find a wife! "The reason why Jesus died was because he couldn't have a bride. . . . That was the cause of his

---

*See also Matthew 26:28; Mark 15:21-22; Luke 24: 25-27, 41-46; Acts 2:23-24; 20:28; Romans 3:25; 4:25; 5:10; 2 Corinthians 11:13-14; Galatians 4:4-5; Ephesians 1:7; 2:8, 13; Philippians 3:18; Colossians 1:14, 17-22; 1 Thessalonians 5:9-10; Hebrews 9:1-14, 22; 10:12, 29; 13:12; 1 Peter 1:18-20; 2:24; 1 John 1:7; Revelation 1:5; 5:9; 7:14; 12:11.

death."[280] The *Divine Principle* asserts, "If Jesus had not been crucified, what would have happened? He would have accomplished the providence of salvation both spiritually and physically."[281] It also declares, "From the time of Jesus through the present, all Christians have thought that Jesus came to the world to die. This is because they did not know the fundamental purpose of Jesus' coming as the Messiah."[282] As we have already noted, Moon is viewed as the true atoning Savior of the world: "[Sinless] Father shed blood instead of me. . . . Without Father, there is no life. Father is more precious than myself, than even all mankind. Therefore, even at the price of my life, I can be a joyful offering for Father."[283]

Man

By virtue of his position as the "object" of God, man is considered to be one essence with deity. Moon asserts this quite clearly, as does *Divine Principle:*

> God and man are one. *Man is incarnate God. . . .* So man, the object of God, is as important in value as God Himself.[284]

> He saved not a single ounce of [His] energy when He created them. Thus, man has become the life of God.[285]

> The man whose mind and body have formed a four position foundation of the original God-centered nature becomes God's temple (1 Corinthians 3:16) and forms one body with Him (John 14:20). This means that man attains deity.[286]

> Seen from the principle of creation, the original man of creation should be as perfect as God, having eternal deity because of his oneness with God.[287]

> A man who attains the purpose of creation would become the temple of God's constant abode . . . thus assuming deity. . . . The man who has attained the purpose of creation would assume the divine value of God.[288]

> A perfected man . . . is so valuable as to even possess deity.[289]

Still, because of the physical (sexual) nature of the Fall, man's body is evil. "Your worst enemy is your body."[290] And because Jesus' physical body was given to Satan, man's physical salvation was lost. "Satan's children are born in the satanic body. Our Lord [Moon] is coming to take this physical body away from Satan and return it to God."[291] Moon has allegedly subjugated the spirit world, but apparently not the devil, for the devil is nearly omnipresent in Moon's theology and is seen as the source of many troubles. Also, there is little awareness of demons in their biblical role. As is true in mediumism, evil spirits are seen as the spirits of confused, rebellious or wicked men, rather than in their true identity as the fallen angels (demons).

Death

In UC theology, the existence of death was part of God's original purpose in creation. "God created man to grow old and turn to dust; this would occur even if man had not fallen. Therefore, when Adam died at the Biblical age of 930 and turned to dust, this was not the death which was caused by the fall"[292] (compare Romans 5:12). Moon teaches everyone will be saved in the end, even the devil and his demons. Thus, he also denies the biblical hell, replacing it with temporary, purgatorial concepts:

> The ultimate purpose of God's providence of restoration is to save all mankind. Therefore, it is God's intention to abolish Hell completely, after the lapse of the period necessary for the full payment of all indemnity.[293]

> *The Bible infers that Satan will be case [sic, cast] out forever. Will he be restored completely?* Of course. But it will take almost an eternity for it to happen. He has a great deal of indemnity to pay. Lucifer will not be restored to his original position, but will serve in the lowest position.[294]

> But, as our Principle teaches, God will not desert any person eternally. By some means of restriction they will be restored.[295]

THE OCCULT

"Spiritism is of minor importance."[296] What else could a former president of the UC say to a group of evangelicals familiar with Deuteronomy 18:9–12? The degree of occult involvement in the UC today is difficult to assess, for Moon seems to have his ups and downs with the spirit world, and UC occult interest may vary by country or culture. However, there is no denying that the UC is an occult religion. Thus, if there are ebbtides of interest in the occult, it will only be a matter of time before a period of lull gives way to a period of activity. In this section we will at least document the occult potential of UC beliefs and practices, irrespective of where that church stands on the subject at the time of writing.

The truth is that UC members have developed spiritistic contacts and psychic powers.[297] In the early 1980s Dr. Weldon had been personally informed by an authority on the Unification Church that members were not involved in developing psychic powers. Yet "Instructions from Father," a typed and circulated official directive for the church dated June 2, 1983, and not rescinded to our knowledge, supplied the following instruction to the American UC:

> Cultivate the Spiritually Perceptive Element within Yourself. Report your dreams, visions, intuition to the Korean leaders. Let them train you in spiritual interpretation. Know how to handle spiritual phenomena which occurs. People who act or speak unusually are often influenced spiritually, not crazy. They may even speak in tongues, suddenly changing your topic in an instant. Spirit world uses those people like a microphone. . . .
>
> In each state, you need three spiritually-attuned members, who can function as a barometer of spiritual world. These three represent strong, weak and optimum. You may be instructed from spiritual world to go out at 2 A.M. and speak somewhere. Perceive, gauge, moderate and control spiritual phenomena well.[298]

Members may have opportunities to engage in other occult activities, and as a result of teaching and practices like this, members run the risk of possession. This possibility is admitted, but UC members see it as resulting from causes other than UC spiritism and psychic activity. Because they view themselves as locked in mortal combat with Satan, they naturally see possession as one of the possible hazards. Indeed, even when the *Divine Principle* is being lectured on, or afterwards, people may risk possession simply by their presence:

I know another case in Japan where someone because of spiritual possession died. And it became big trouble. . . . Therefore, this spiritual problem is not so easy. . . . The best method of dealing with possession is prevention. In case someone is possessed . . . [when] he or she is fighting against an evil spirit, if only the person can understand the depths of Divine Principle and can understand how to prevent possession, he or she can do that. Spiritual things can happen when the atmosphere has intense impact. *This is the reason why when a Divine Principle lecture is going on or after a Divine Principle lecture someone may become possessed.*[299]

Given the extensive occult history of their leader and their church, members ought not to be surprised that Moon has been psychic from a young age. "From childhood, I was clairvoyant and clairaudient. I could see through people, see their spirits."[300] His brother was also spiritistic. "His elder brother was . . . taught by spirit world."[301] We don't know for sure, but Moon and his brother may have been predisposed to mediumistic abilities because of the occult activities of their parents. We documented this principle in our book *The Coming Darkness.*[302]

There are other ways in which Unification theology lays the foundation for the potential possession of the UC member. First, one result of Moon's alleged subjugation of the spirit world is that now the spirits must help UC members in their tasks: these spirits will take the initiative. Second, it is taught that spirits must return to the earth in spiritistic or mediumistic communication in order to gain the benefits of each succeeding earth age or epoch.[303] Third, the member's own spirit is seen as his or her "spirit-man," but conceived of as an almost "independent" entity from the body, "which serves as its host."[304] The "spirit-man" is believed to withdraw "vital or life energy" from its host, just as the spirits do in modern channeling and other forms of spiritism. Thus what a UC believer interprets as the spiritual functioning of his own spirit could be a form of demonization. Fourth, it is believed that "spirit-men" (spirits) return to earth and indwell members to help them in their ministries. "Also, the spirit men who left their missions unaccomplished on earth descend to earthly men whose missions are similar to those with which the spirit men were charged while on earth, and cooperate with them for accomplishment of their will. Seen from the standpoint of mission, the physical body of the earthly man serves as the body of the spirit man."[305] Further:

Speaking in tongues is one of the common spiritual experiences. Many people believe that the messages come from the Holy Spirit. The phenomena are accomplished by various spirits who speak through you by using your vocal organs.[306]

When a spirit comes to you, you may not be able to tell the difference at times between your own spirit and the spirit of the one who has come to you. You may behave like someone else.[307]

Before I came to Barrytown I was responsible for Region 8 and we had a Chicago campaign, when one brother got possessed.... He was just learning about Divine Principle, and in the beginning there were many [psychic] phenomena.[308]

While UC members are told to trust entirely in Moon, sooner or later they must also trust in the spirits. As admitted by UC leaders, they may even pray to the spirits.[309] Members may even be told to "ask mediums for verification" of Moon's teachings.[310] As Moon reports concerning his Messiahship, "I have had numerous witnesses from the spirit world through people on earth."[311] He alleges of other mediums, "There are many who are now directly led by me."[312] And, of course, more will be added in the future. "Those mediums or gifted people who witness and testify to him often continue to go their own way. In a little while, they will not be able to do that. They will be stricken by the spirit world if they do not follow what they have received and testified to. Our Leader says he is going to occupy more of these gifted people from now on. They will have to serve him."[313]

Moon also encourages UC members to take their family and friends to mediums, so that people "will be guided by the spirit world to know me.... Teach the Principle first, intellectually, and guide the student to the spiritual experience by having him read books on the spirit world or taking him to a medium."[314]

Although the members we talked with denied it, the truth is that Moon *himself* actually became a medium for the famous Arthur Ford's own spirit guide "Fletcher," as reported in "The Moon Sittings" in Ford's book *Unknown but Known.* Many revelations were given through the possessed Moon, including the common mediumistic teaching that "the coming of the Holy Spirit" was spiritism and, naturally, that Moon's platform was entirely "of God."[315]

The *Divine Principle* itself supports occult practices. "Thus, the spirit men pour out spiritual fire on earthly men, give them the power to heal diseases, and help them do many mighty works. More than that, they enable earthly men to see many facts in the spirit world in a state of trance, give them the gift of prophecy, and inspire them spiritually. Through such activities, substituting for the Holy Spirit, they cooperate with earthly men to fulfill the will of God."[316] Further, members may not only work with occult groups[317] but also expect spiritistic appearances from Moon.[318] Many Eastern gurus and occult leaders have spirit guides who imitate them psychically before disciples. Moon alleges, "I can appear to a thousand people at once."[319] UC members are even encouraged to exercise blind faith in the spirit world:

Sometimes it is good to be blind with faith. The spirit world, then, will add to your power, and you can do much greater work than [in] your own capacity.... If you firmly stand on the Principle, I will appear to you in spirit and teach you everything you need to know.... If you continue to try to develop your mediumship, many spirits will come to you which may lead you into confusion.... But if you stand firmly on the Principle, then the Lord of the entire universe, whom we call in our movement the True Father or True Parent, will appear to you and guide you.[320]

Members may even become like mediums:

They [spirits] are free to associate with you and contact you at any time.[321]

No matter what stage you are in, you can still talk to God directly.... Many mediums talk with God directly through their clairvoyance and clairaudience. It can be done even though you are still in an imperfect stage.[322]

Then for those of us who do have some degree of gift in this area, should we continue to use it? Yes, it is good to have one or two mediumistic people in the group who will help others to grow spiritually.... Through the Principle, did the spirit world not become much more clear to you?[323]

Sometimes you may say something which you never even thought of before. That is a spirit using your mouth to tell you something.[324]

St. Augustine, Luther, John Wesley, St. Paul, and many other great men have come to our members asking us to teach them the Principle.[325]

However, other spirits were not so friendly to Moon's agenda. Moon also encourages one of the goals of magic ritual, the control over spirits. "If you are a clairvoyant and clairaudient, you should know whether your spirit guide is higher than you in spirit. If he is higher, it is all right. If he is not higher than you and you consult him, you lose.... They want to control you.... It is always dangerous, and you don't gain anything, to be controlled by spirit. By understanding the Principle, you are in such a position that you can control and use and guide them."[326]

Despite denials, Moon is clearly a spiritist and has even been a medium. He has urged his followers to engage in spiritistic and mediumistic contacts as part of their "spiritual growth." This is in direct contradiction to biblical warnings that tell us such activity is an abomination to God (Deuteronomy 18:10–12): "Let no one be found among you who sacrifices his son or daughter in the fire, who practices divination or sorcery, interprets omens, engages in witchcraft, or casts spells, or who is a medium or spiritist or who consults the dead. Anyone who does these things is detestable to the Lord, ... "

CRITIQUE

The Unification Church represents a microcosm of many of the characteristics of new religions and cults which, unfortunately, have become such a blight on the Western spiritual landscape: alien and eccentric beliefs, bizarre doctrines, authoritarianism, psychological and spiritual abuse, occultism and dehumanization. In this section we will mention only a few of many areas of concern: UC teachings on the family, morality, the risk of psychological damage and their liberal theological approach.

The Family

Moon claims, "I have never divided families or broken homes."[327] But one would never know it. Sontag observes, "The pattern of family disruption has been universal as the church has expanded in each country, although perhaps it varies in severity."[328] For 50 years Moon has been in the business of disrupting the family, and wherever he goes in the world the disruption appears to be significant. The reason Moon can say he "supports the family" is because his cultic concept of the family is vital to world unification. Without his particular kind of spiritual family, one that is unalterably devoted to him, he cannot succeed.[329]

Even when Moon "supports" the family, he divides it. Moon teaches that when a member is saved, his family will automatically be saved,* although it may be far down the road. As a result, one's family may be sacrificed now (for example, abandoned) since this will assist one's family's salvation after death. But if one "compromises" with one's parents now, it will prevent their salvation and ensure their going to "hell" later.[330] Overall, Moon perceives non-Moon families as satanic. "Your present [marriage and sexual] relationship of love is satanic."[331] "Married life in the satanic world is not recognized by God."[332] "When the 36 couples were blessed, I really took away sons and daughters from satanic families."[333]

Since parents are corrupted by satanic blood, they are "false parents." Moon and his wife, of course, are the "True Parents." "So fallen people came to possess false parents.... God is to love the True Parents, not false parents."[334] *"How do we separate ourselves from Satan when we are in*

---

*Assuming the disciple's continuing sacrifice and dedication. No UC member knows he is "saved" until he has died.

the Satanic world? . . . [Partial answer] You have to cut off the environment of your physical parents, and even the fallen husband and wife relationships."[335] Compared to Moon, one's family is simply irrelevant:

> Friends, relatives or parents are not important. . . . If he [Master] were asked to offer his parents and his children as a sacrifice on the altar he would be willing. . . . He can throw away his parents, throw away his wife and children. . . . It will be the same in the future. There is the course of our Master. If you are a devoted follower you will inherit these thoughts from him.[336]

> Before I was allowed to speak to him, my group leader talked with me for about 10 or 15 minutes, explaining the reason for my mother's sickness. She told me that Satan had invaded her and it was because Satan was working through my family. The general idea is that Satan works through your loved ones to get you away. In fact, anyone who tries to get you to leave the movement is Satanic. . . . I was told again not just that Satan had invaded my mother, my father and the family, but that my family was satanic and evil.[337]

The Unification Church has its own rules for marriage and the family. Moon arranges who marries whom (usually the would-be couples do not know each other). Remarriage is forbidden. Even if the spouse dies, "You must remain single all your life," but the spirit of the dead spouse "will be with you always" as your spiritual "mate."[338] Moon of course is the exception; he has had at least two and allegedly as many as four wives (Sung Kil Choi, "Miss Kim," Mung Hee Kim, Hak Ja Han).

On dozens of occasions, Moon has "married" thousands of couples, sometimes hundreds of thousands or "millions." The consequences and potential for abuse are so great that more than one public proclamation has been issued against such mass marriages. The following is one example:

Joint Declaration Concerning the Moon Organization, September 26, 1997 Endorsed by the following:

Hiroshi Yamaguchi, Secretary General, Network of Lawyers Against the "Spiritual Sales"

National Parents Association of Victims of the Unification Church

The United Church of Christ in Japan Liaison Committee on Unification Association Issues

We oppose the mass communal wedding ceremony. . . . In the planned ceremony, Unification Church leader and self-proclaimed messiah Sun Myung Moon and his third wife Hak Ja Moon are to bless the participating couples. The Unification Church teaches that this ceremony is the sole way to wash away the sins of the human race and of the ancestors of the participants and to enable the participants' children to be born free of original sin. The Unification Church believers are inculcated with the idea that as long as they do not receive the blessing of this ceremony, it will be their fate and the fate of their ancestors to suffer in hell for their sins eternally, even after death. The believers are obliged to participate in the ceremony as the sole way by which they can save themselves (so the participants are made to believe). . . . Persons to be married at the mass wedding ceremony do not know or are not informed of who their marital partner will be until just prior to the ceremony itself. . . .

Although the Unification Church advocates its work in building ideal families, in reality it has led to the destruction of families and homes throughout the world. . . . [Members] are made to think that they are responsible for saving their ancestors who are suffering in hell for sins they have committed. They feel as if they can hear their ancestors in hell calling out and asking them for help. . . . Participants in the mass communal wedding ceremony are requested to pay an exorbitant amount of money as both a fee for participation and as a donation. . . . Each of these people are ordered to pay 300,000 yen as a participation fee and 1,400,000 yen as an obligatory donation paid in order to receive a special blessing. To come up with this excessive amount of money many participants have lied to their family and friends, taken on difficult or hard physical labor jobs or committed illegal acts.

For the upcoming wedding ceremony, already married elderly couples have been persuaded to receive the blessing of Sun Myung Moon again for which they must pay a large sum of money. Also, in Japan, many elderly people who have lost their spouses are being made to pay large sums of money under the pretext that this money is to renew their wedding ceremony with their spouses now living in the spiritual world. In Japan, since 1980, about 10 billion yen was collected each month through "spiritual sales" (of religious objects)—an illegal practice of selling items such as marble vases and ginseng extract at exorbitant prices. . . .

The Unification Church makes the partners of an international marriage register their marriage in both countries so that its believers may work unpaid, live a long time and enter freely into foreign countries, not so that its believers may build their new families. In fact, legally this is a crime of perjury of an official notarized document and/or the crime of being an accomplice to that act. At present, more than 10,000 Japanese women are being dispatched around the world. Due to the absence of these women, their homes, their young children, elderly parents and husbands are suffering. For these women believers, disobeying the instructions of Sun Myung Moon is more frightening than the destruction of their own homes and families. These women are intimidated indirectly with such threats as: "If you do not follow the order of Sun Myung Moon, you will die by the curse of the spiritual world" and "If you get married by any other way than that provided by the Unification Church, then you will not be able to bear children. If you do become pregnant, your child will be born deformed." These women live in foreign countries and solicit people to participate in the mass communal wedding ceremony. In reality, however, they lie to such people and say that they are working as volunteers for the FFWP or the WFWP. This fact has come to light and has been broadcasted to other countries. In November 1996, a Japanese woman who was sent abroad against her will became depressed and committed suicide. . . .

Over the past 10 years since 1987, we lawyers have heard complaints from about 18,000 people who were claiming sums totaling 67,900,000,000 yen. Still these people represent only a fraction of all those who have become victims of the Unification Church.[339]

Further, the UC policy on marriages seems to have shifted. Because marriage was held to be a truly sacred event that would make one's children sinless, members would spend years of sacrifice in the Unification Church for that special blessing of marriage. In fact, you had to be in the church seven years just to be considered for marriage. Now the UC attempts to recruit potential marriage couples almost off the street.

There are other consequences to Moon's doctrine of family. According to Moon's Principle of Reversal, in the "satanic" world the order is first to make parents (that is, for a man and woman to marry) and then make children. Moon's Principle of Reversal turns this backward so that people must first make children (spiritually), and only then can they become "true" parents. In other words, one must gather three converts (who become one's spiritual children) who must be willing to die for you. The result is often that one's spiritual converts become more important than one's own physical family. "In our group, some people have neglected their children and devoted themselves completely to witnessing. This has happened because, if you are not restored, your children will perish automatically. If you don't find three spiritual children, how can your physical children benefit? In that sense, your problem is more urgent. For this reason, some parents have neglected their children."[340] This ends up becoming the bizarre scenario that, in most cases, to ensure the spiritual success of one's own children, one would have to neglect them. Whether or not you are a parent, God does not recognize you as such without three devoted converts, and those converts "must love you so much that they feel they would die for you."[341] Members cannot be "blessed" by God without them.[342] They must also ensure their own spiritual children gather spiritual children and achieve the same "blessing."

One outcome of this is that UC members do not easily surrender to their spiritual "children," and harassment is common for many "backsliders." Further, one can imagine the amount of work it could take to get a convert to be willing, literally, to die for the cause. "One member had a Kendo stick, which is considered a lethal weapon by Rhode Island law, and a canister of Mace. He was specifically looking for an ex-Moon member."[343] Then there is the agony that a member must feel at losing a spiritual child, for such a loss is not only personal failure but also harmful to his ancestors and descendants. After all, another reason Jesus died, they believe, is because he could not get three spiritual children who were willing to die for him. Hence

487

He was murdered and gave His life in vain. Also, "the disciples of Jesus failed and so they were doomed to die."[344] It is hardly surprising members work hard at keeping their converts, and why there is so much furor over deprogramming.

In addition, although officially denied, UC members who have converted to Moon often do divorce their spouses and leave their children in order to marry within the Unification Church. In the end, no other marriage is acceptable to the Lord of the Second Advent. Thus, one woman was told "to divorce [her] husband and leave [her] children if [she] wanted to be a member."[345]

Sexual relations are denied husband and wife because "the spirit world requires you to be completely separated."[346] Consider the consequences when one spouse is converted and another is not. "Married couples must abstain from the marriage relationship at least seven months. There are those in Korea who have been abstaining for over seven years, and live as sister and brother. . . . If the wife only follows the Principle, great conflict arises in the family. The same if only the husband follows. So our church has been accused of destroying families. This is not true. We are uniting them."[347] Clearly, sexual abstention may cause serious strains on the marriage relationship, which is why the Bible counsels, "Do not deprive each other except by mutual consent and for a time, so that you may devote yourselves to prayer. Then come together again so that Satan will not tempt you because of your lack of self-control" (1 Corinthians 7:5). It is not difficult to imagine what it is like to have to stop the marriage union suddenly upon conversion of one partner, or how hard if not impossible it is for married couples to sleep in the same bed as "brother and sister" under a commandment not to have intercourse. Moon admits, "I know there are resentments in your families."[348]

And no wonder. With each family member neglected in so many ways so that "the Father's cause" may advance, with parents occasionally looking to their children for spiritual advice and wives assuming the role of spiritual leadership, with no sex or constant guilt over sexual feelings, and constant pressure to perform spiritu-

ally, one can only imagine the extent of family tragedies that has existed within the Unification Church for the last generation:

> You must let your husband or wife go for the salvation of the whole world, and if necessary, you are separated and work in different corners of the earth, never, never wanting your partner back at the time of trial and difficulty. . . . Your children may cling to you and want you to stay at home. But you must kick them away and with determined and almost cruel mind go out to the battlefield.[349]

The Unification Church has lost the longest and most expensive libel suit in English legal history and was ordered to pay costs estimated at more than $1.5 million. Dennis Orme, leader of Sun Myung Moon's church in Britain, claimed damages against the London Daily Mail for a 1978 article that accused the church of brainwashing converts and breaking up families. The jury, after hearing evidence from more than 100 witnesses over six months, decided unanimously that the Daily Mail was justified in its accusations.[350]

Morality

Sun Myung Moon also claims that he emphasizes the importance of morality both for himself and for his church. "I emphasize honesty, purity, and unselfishness as the principal code of our members. Honesty comes first, particularly between God and man."[351] "Among the people of conscience, the highest people are the members of the Unification Church."[352]

In fact, the morality seen within the Unification Church is less than pure. Honesty is not particularly emphasized. Former members routinely speak of deceiving the public in order to gain funds and for other reasons. This is quaintly termed "heavenly deception." Even Moon himself does not provide the proper moral example, saying "In restoring man from evil sovereignty we must cheat."[353] In an extremely convenient rationalization to excuse the Lord of the Second Advent, we are told, "He is sinless, but in order to pay for the sin that man has committed he must live like a sinner."[354] Perhaps this was why in October, 1981, a federal grand jury in Manhattan "indicted the Korean for tax evasion and conspiracy."[355] He has also served two jail terms in Korea.[356]

One can also see how Moon's teachings could be morally misused by the over-zealous members. A former member notes, "You always had to see things from God's standpoint, and the only representative of God you had was your superior. Whether he's right or wrong, you follow his orders. If he's made mistakes in his command, then he's the one that has to pay for it and not you. So you follow without question."[357] Or consider statements like these by Moon. "I am transcendent of family boundaries, national boundaries and everything else in the Satanic world."[358] "God has his own morality. His own mode of conduct, the heavenly morality."[359] "We are the first ones to restore this earth. So there is no tradition. For us there is no style. We don't have any culture. We have to make a new one. From now, we have to make new customs, new tradition, new culture, new life, a new way of living, new morality, new laws. Are you ready?"[360]

Moon's creation of new laws and a new morality is clearly evident. In the new world "the definition of sin will be different."[361] For example, "Stealing will not exist in the new world. If one has a necessity he can take it from another person. You pray and just take it. It is not stealing."[362] One is tempted to suggest the New World has already arrived. "One former member reported, 'I was told to use my "fallen nature" to get money.... I was exploited. And I did do deceitful things.'"[363] And what of statements like the following? "Love itself is neutral, and is neither good nor evil."[364] "Evil is not something entirely different from love. Evil is the misuse of love.... Good and evil started from one point—love."[365] And what kind of moral indoctrination comes through statements like the following, from a *Master Speaks* publication, which uses the hypothetical example of people being trampled to death on the way into Madison Square Garden to hear Moon? We are asked:

Would you rather have so many people killed and in that way grant that success be yours, or just have fewer people in a calmer atmosphere? Which is your choice? (More!) Then would that mean you would like to have people killed? (Yes! No!) Then you are not good people. In our concept, the definition of good and evil is different from ordinary ones.*[366]

Moon says, "We do not encourage murder,"[367] but one can only wonder about that wonderful New Age with its heavenly dictatorship and its willingness to sacrifice lives for the cause and for Moon's secret teachings. Even now he says of anyone who does not wish to live with his God, "If there is anyone who would answer negatively, he must die."[368] The UC position seems pretty clear:

Would you kill your children for Father [Moon]? one man was asked. "Yes," he replied without hesitation.[369]

Those members who are absolutely truly committed would stop at nothing to do what he said, to do what he asked.... I just came out directly and asked this guy—I said—if, Moon told you to kill your parents, that this was going to forward the kingdom of heaven here on earth, would you do it.... And he looked at me directly in the eye and without flinching said—yes.[370]

Many have said they could easily kill if they were told by the church to kill.[371]

The leader even implied that my life would be threatened if I left.[372]

(This last quotation probably refers to Moon's view that heavenly or "natural" forces will coalesce to destroy his enemies or backsliders.[373] Naturally, it is not safe to be either.)

Other moral failings can be seen in the following:

A Moonie sentenced to 10–18 years for armed robbery he claims was instigated by the church.[374]

Moon reportedly offered the National Council of Churches $50,000 if they would accept him as a member.[375]

One time I disagreed with the leaders. I told them, "You don't even treat people like human

---

*Apparently the "No" answer of some in the audience necessitated the response that they were not good people. They should have no qualms about sacrificing others for the cause.

beings" and I was told that "The Divine Principle" doesn't refer to human beings.[376]

In my opinion, the Moon organization is a pseudo-religious political cult whose existence depends on the deceit and fraud it employs to recruit and raise funds.[377]

Less than 7% of $1 million of Children's Relief Fund went to help children.*[378]

Harvard University refused to rent rooms to CARP on the grounds that CARP had sought permission deceptively (claiming no affiliation with the Unification Church) and had ignored a previous order not to solicit students in dorms.[379]

Perhaps this "morality" is why we find the following in a publisher's blurb of Nansook Hong's *In the Shadow of the Moons: My Life in the Reverend Sun Myung Moon's Family*. Hong became the child bride of Moon's eldest son and heir. Remember, Moon promised that he would produce sinless offspring. But Hong called the estate she lived at, East Garden in New York City, "my personal prison for fourteen years," noting that if she had it to do over again today, "I would escape . . . and leave behind the man who beat me and the false Messiah who let him, men so flawed that now I know that God would never have chosen Sun Myung Moon or his son to be his agents on earth." She alleges that her husband "treated [her] either as a toy for his sexual pleasure or as an outlet for his violent rages," and that Moon is a "fraud."[380] She also claims that Moon had several adulterous affairs and that her husband used cocaine, watched pornography and threatened to kill her unborn child. *The Washington Post*, also commenting upon her, states: "Hyo Jin Moon, 34 is embroiled in a contentious divorce in which his former wife, Nan Sook, has accused him of beating her and 'secreting himself in the master bedroom, sometimes for hours, sometimes for days, drinking alcohol, using cocaine and watching pornographic films,' according to a 1995 affidavit she filed in Massachusetts." The church of course denies all this.

---

*Citizens Freedom Foundation in Southern California.

Sex Scandals

Having the power that it does, sex is routinely exploited in spiritistic religions. In the UC, sex was held to be the cause of the Fall; it is considered "dirty" and is an unforgivable sin outside of marriage, and it is often forbidden within marriage. In his characteristic distortion of Scripture, Moon says, "In the Bible, all men were considered to be as bachelors, and no marriage is recognized in the sight of God."[381] Moon, however, is apparently exempt from sexual restrictions.

Jerry Yamamoto, author of *The Puppet Master*, provides some background information on reputed sex scandals by Moon and his group in the early history of the UC pointing out the theological justification:

What were the "rites" which caused so much controversy concerning the early days of the movement? Moon's critics say that he gleaned ideas from Nam Choo Paik whose Theological Mountain at Wensan he had visited prior to 1945. One of the more important ideas was "pikarume" or blood separation, a secret initiation rite. It is said that the female members of the Unification Church had to have intercourse with Moon in order to be purified. Later, intercourse between husbands and wives would purify the male members. Thereafter their offspring would be pure.[382]

Yamamoto also mentions the UC's denial of such activities but observes that there is reason to suspect the denials:

The Unification Church in the United States now declares that purification is conferred through Moon symbolically at the wedding ceremony. They fervently deny any promiscuous activities on the part of Moon or any other member of the church. There seems to be no reason to suspect Moon of engaging in the rite since his latest marriage. The early days of the movement, however, leave considerable room to doubt the mere symbolism of the rite.[383]

Indeed, the rites do not appear to be symbolic. Although the Unification Church denies any wrongdoing, such early sexual rites were logical in light of Moon's theology. As Moon says, "The point where men and women join together is the very point where God wants to dwell."[384]

In the mid 1970s, reports of Moon's sex with various women (sometimes called "blood cleansing") could be found in *Time* magazine (September 30, 1974); *The Boston Globe* (July 23, 1974); *The Washington Post* (February 15, 1974); *The Christian Crusade Weekly* (April 12, 1974); and *The New York Times* (September 16, 1974). *The International Edition of Newsweek* of June 14, 1976, reported: "The Reverend John E.W. Kim, a Presbyterian pastor whose church was near Moon's church in Pusan at the time, [states], 'Part of Moon's theology was that women converts could only be purified by sleeping with him'—a charge Moon categorically denies."[385] Although it is not directly stated, statements in the *Divine Principle* (pages 110, 141, 216, 218, 367 and 511) do lend support. Does the process of "blood cleansing" through sexual intercourse have a basis in Unification theology? Yes. Eve had sex with Satan and then with Adam, and Adam and his descendants became contaminated with satanic blood. In other words, an imperfect woman (fallen Eve) transmitted unclean blood to a man through the sexual act producing sinful children. The reverse of this (remember "the Principle of Reversal") is for a man who is perfect to transmit clean blood to a woman by the sexual act producing sinless children.

According to *The Washington Post* of November 24, 1997:

At least two of Moon's daughters have expressed public doubts about their father and his faith. ... Moon's own image within the church has been tarnished in recent years by allegations that he has been married at least three times, had affairs and children outside his marriages, and defended sleeping with many women in the 1950s by saying he needed to "purify them." Those accusations, against a man claiming to be the "True Parent" of his theology, are contained in books published in France, Japan and Korea over the past decade.[386]

Dr. Sa Hoon Shin of the Department of Religious Studies, Seoul National University, Seoul, Korea, in a public lecture on April 26, 1975 at the Ho-Sow-Don Girl's High School, Tre-chun, Korea, detailed several cases of Moon's purported sexual episodes. This was on the basis of former female participants who had decided to admit the events. They had not previously done so because at the time they thought that Moon was a God, there were no witnesses to the act, and because of a sense of shame in publicly admitting their adultery.[387]

In a dialogue with Unification Theological Seminary's faculty members, Dr. Jim Bjornstad, author of *The Moon Is Not the Son,* reported: "I brought up his blood impurity scandal of the '40's and they said he was found not guilty and acquitted of all charges. They said they had the proof. I had it checked out also, and found just the opposite."[388] Dr. Bjornstad means that they had no proof. The fact that charges were dropped because witnesses failed to show up does not prove that Moon was innocent. In a personal response to the author, Dr. Bjornstad commented on certain Korean religious sects that are known to engage in religiously justified sexual activity.

Several Korean sects, holding the same interpretation of original sin as Moon does, practice a sexual rite called perikume or "blood-cleansing" to purify individuals of original sin. Accordingly, the taint of Satan's blood which was passed on to the human race by Eve is removed by a woman copulating with the sect's leader or another man who has already been "purified." A man could be "purified" by copulating with a "purified" woman. This was allegedly taught and practiced by Moon and his followers in the early days of his church. The clearest presentation of this was reported in "A Brief Outline of Sun Myung Moon's Doctrine and the Movement of his Group," published in *The Journal of the Royal Asiatic Society.*[389]

Dr. Bjornstad then commented that even though the allegations had never been proven, two facts made one suspect otherwise. First there were the reports of ex-members, and second that such a practice logically fit their overall theology in providing the perfect reversal of their understanding of the Fall.

Finally Moon himself has spoken in the following manner, although he does not clarify what it is that makes him "feel horrible":

You must know that I have gone through a difficult path which you can never imagine. I sometimes even feel fearful of women. In the fallen world, it is easy for fallen women to tempt males. Since I have gone through such difficulties, I wouldn't let you, and I don't want you to go through the same path. Rather, after my having paid the indemnity, I want you to go straight on the road with purity. . . . I hate the idea of my having to go through all those things. So, I did this in order for these kinds of things not to happen. So, even at the idea of those things—when I recall those things—it makes me feel horrible.[390]

How do members react, confronted with these allegations? Reflecting their new morality, some just do not care. "When I asked followers what it would mean to them if the stories of early scandal should prove true, it is interesting to note that some replied it would make no difference. They maintain their loyalty on different grounds."[391]

Mental Hazards

The Unification Church strongly denies that there have been nervous breakdowns, deaths and suicides. Nevertheless Moon's constant diatribe on suffering and sacrifice ("You must not sleep much, rest much, eat much. You must work day and night."[392]) has ruined a number of young lives. *The Christian Century* of September 24, 1975, reported:

In Washington former Moonies, as they call themselves, and a psychiatrist who treats former members testify about life in the cult. "I don't believe any of my patients, except for psychotics who act in response to their hallucinations, have such serious impairment of their free will as that described to me by persons in the Unification Church," says John G. Clark, Jr. of Western Massachusetts. He treated nine members who suffered from sleep deprivation, whose minds had been filled "with ritual, laws, magic and threat . . . group pressure. . . . Many have said they could easily kill if they were told by the church to kill."[393]

A former member who joined the church at 16 alleges, "I had to be taken to a mental institution where a further breakdown took place. And I spent 6 months in the mental institution, paying $75.00 a day. The bill came up to $20,000. The Unification Church takes no responsibility for my condition at all."[394]

The following pieces of information were sent to the author by a pastor who preferred to remain anonymous:[395] "At a CARP table at the University of Massachusetts—Amherst, a woman rushed up and shouted: 'You killed my brother.'[396] He had jumped out of a window." "In the past few years there have been reports of Moonies ending their lives, usually in very violent fashion."[397] "He'd even kill himself if he had the chance 'cause they believe they must die if they fail their missions.'"[398] Dutchess County (New York) Attorney Albert Rosenblat noted an attempted suicide and a "disproportionately high number of hospital admissions" among Unification Church members.[399]

Liberal Theological Approach

In order to support their antiChristian theology, Unification Church theologians largely defer to liberal theology and its higher critical methods.[400] (See Unitarian Universalism for a critique.) For example, "The Epistles of Paul are often opposed to the gospels. . . . The early apostles' knowledge of Jesus [for] Paul is irrelevant . . . the historical Jesus is of no significance to him. . . . [This] reveals a deep gulf between Jesus and Paul, and ends by saying that Christianity was founded not by the Jesus of history but by Paul, who turned it into a religion of redemption."[401] Moon teaches, "But 2,000 years ago Jesus Christ never spoke of himself as a Messiah."[402] (The harmony between the teachings of Jesus and Paul is seen in the chapter on Ba'hai. Jesus did directly call Himself the Messiah in Matthew 26:64 and John 4:26.)

TALKING WITH MEMBERS

If Moon is sinless, perfect, one body with God and deity, then his claim to speak God's words are understandable. But if Moon really speaks God's words why has he also spoken almost nothing but error concerning the Bible and Jesus' teachings?[403] It should be clear by now that it is not God who is inspiring Moon, but the spirit world, and that members need to be warned about the advisability of listening to the spirits.

The *Divine Principle* is "the Word of God." *Master Speaks* lectures are "the Word of God." Nearly everything Moon speaks is "the Word of God." Typical of UC publications are the following statements:

I speak out as God dictates to me.[404]

Rev. Sun Myung Moon seldom uses a text in his speeches. . . . He speaks entirely in the spirit of God.[405]

You must trust my teaching, my words 100 percent because they are not my own. They are God's words.[406]

We must have sympathy for the average Unification Church member who, trapped in a cult, will suffer personal consequences of which he or she is initially unaware. Clearly, much of the information in this chapter can be used to point out the discrepancy between Moon's claims and the reality of how he lives his life and what he teaches. How could such a man possibly be Jesus Christ returned as the Lord of the Second Advent and the most perfect expression of God ever? Is there any way to rationalize the absolute discrepancy between Moon's divine claims and his all too human failures?

Indeed, rejecting biblical teaching and the facts of history, Moon claimed that Jesus had failed in His mission. He declared this entirely on the advice of some unknown spirits who had given him revelations and possessed him. On what logical or historical precedent can those possessed by spirits be trusted? But he also claimed, and promised, he would succeed as the Lord of the Second Advent. Moon, however, was the one who failed miserably to achieve his stated goals: he never converted Korea, he never converted America, he never subjected the spirit world to himself and he never had sinless children. So why should any disciple believe his claim to be the Lord of the Second Advent? How can a UC member logically choose to believe in Moon, who failed at so much, over Jesus Christ,

who failed at nothing? Did Moon resurrect from the dead in proof of his claims, as Jesus did?

Any given UC member may be coming from any given perspective personally—an excited new recruit, a devoted worker, a burned out disillusioned shell of one's former self. Regardless of where a given member is at personally, one should never minimize the importance either of evangelism or pre-evangelism. In addition, just as Jesus warned that, when someone does not understand the Gospel, Satan comes and takes away the seed that was sown in his heart (Matthew 13:19), it is imperative to be certain that the UC member hear and understand the good news. If necessary, one can stress the consequence of Moon's rejection of Jesus and the Bible generally. "If you do not believe that I am the one I claim to be, you will indeed die in your sins" (John 8:24). "There is a judge for the one who rejects me and does not accept my words; that very word which I spoke will condemn him at the last day" (John 12:48). Besides warning members of the dangers of occult involvement, one can certainly warn them of the dangers of eternal judgment. Clearly, if they are wrong and Christianity is true, then they will lose everything, including their soul. So on what objective historical basis do they make their claim for believing in the truth of Moon's revelations?

As is true for cults generally, working with a UC member takes time, understanding and patience. Be prepared to encounter "heavenly deception" and other forms of manipulation. When you do, ask them if lying and moral compromise are the marks of a godly man or woman? Moon says, "You must be able to manipulate those people"[407] because "Father can manipulate the world."[408] So why are Moon followers exempted from being manipulated by Moon? If Moon so freely manipulates others, indeed the whole world, how does the UC disciple gain an assurance that he or she is not part of the program? If lying spirits have been speaking through Moon and influencing him all along, could it be otherwise?

Thus, after having carefully documented Moon's involvement in spiritism from this chapter, one may then point out the biblical prohibitions against spiritism in Deuteronomy 18:9–12.

One could mention that it is impossible for a UC member to be certain that the spirits Moon (or perhaps the member) converses with are themselves telling the truth. How do they know, objectively, that Moon has not been deceived by lying spirits? Indeed, aren't Moon's teachings exactly what one would expect from lying spirits? What else could be the origin for teachings that reject God and Christ, pervert the Bible, ruin the family, deny morality and destroy so many lives?

Or, one might read a quote from *The Way of the World*. The January-February, 1977 issue (pages 45–49) listed 12 "theological affirmations" of official Unification Church beliefs. Of number 10, "The Bible" it declares: "Truth is unique, eternal and unchanging, so any new messages from God will be in conformity with the Bible."*[409] Is *Divine Principle* and the *Master Speaks* "in conformity" with Deuteronomy 18:9-12? Is Moon's theology in general "in conformity" to biblical theology? Not at all.

Another point to mention is that there have been scores of other books allegedly authored by "God" or "Jesus" from the spirit world, and many other people, like Moon, have claimed that Jesus talked with them and gave them vital teachings. However, these books and teachings have contradicted part or all of Moon's teachings. Who, then, is right? Members may say that these are false revelations, and that they came from evil spirits impersonating Jesus. But how can they be certain that Moon is not in the same category? Other people are just as sincere and certain in their claims as Moon is. This point may especially be brought home in light of Ken Sudo's admissions in *The 120 Day Training Manual*:

Even Satan can come in the name of Jesus. So if a spirit may say "I'm Jesus," don't believe so easily. Don't believe until you can check if it is good or not. Sometimes a spirit comes as if he is spirit of Father himself, even through a spiritual

person, spiritual brother or sister, and members who don't know anything are amazed. *We had so many experiences like this and most of them are false.* In the name of Jesus, Moses, Abraham, Mother Mary, and even in the name of Father himself, Satan beguiled us and made us rebel against the providence of God. Spiritual phenomena isn't so easy to understand.[410]

Even the spiritual world is a fallen world. Therefore you cannot rely on [the] spiritual world.[411]

The problem, of course, is that the origin of Moon's teachings is the very fallen spiritual world spoken of! Again, how can the UC members possibly know that Moon's revelations are authentic if UC leaders admit that Satan impersonates Jesus and that even they have been deceived on multiple occasions? Where is the objective standard by which to judge the revelations? Their "answer" to this is certainly self-serving, but hardly a guarantee against deception: "One important direction of evil spirits is to lead people to rebel against Father."[412]

One may also enumerate the potential dangers of UC membership—mental, physical and spiritual. Is joining the Unification Church worth the risk of physical or psychological breakdown or suicide, or perhaps demon possession? For example, Moon relates one story about a psychic healer. A friend requested her to pray for her critically ill son. A [spirit] voice came to the healer and asked her if she would pay any price to heal the boy. She said yes. Three days later the boy was healed. Almost immediately "the healer's only son died. He had been very healthy. The healer was so shocked that she lost her mind. She became insane."[413] Eventually her dead son appeared to her and told her of all his "blessings" in the spirit world because she had healed the boy! Moon uses this as an example of how everything turns out rosy when we obey the voice of a spirit. Biblically, the truth of what happened is far different. Regardless, are spirits who would do such a thing the kind of spirits that members wish to trust?

Further, what are Moon's legitimate credentials for being "Lord" and "Master"? Did he fulfill historic prophecy, or predict his own resurrection from the dead, or perform outstanding miracles, as the "failure" Jesus did?

*. . "and will illuminate it more deeply." This is the "out," but it cannot cover the force of the statement, a deeper illumination is possible with some Scriptures, but it will not contradict something God has said elsewhere. The true interpretation of any Scripture must be in harmony with every Scripture.

How many disciples really know Moon or have spent even more than a few minutes with him? Should one literally entrust one's life and soul to a stranger? How is it possible for the claims of Moon to be so discordant from his actions? And does any UC member really believe he can meet the requirements demanded of him by Moon, without which one loses everything? Isn't freedom from unceasing guilt and effort far better? Jesus said, "Come to me, all you who are weary and burdened and I will give you rest" (Matthew 11:28). Would one not prefer a secure relationship and a truly sovereign God (Romans 8:28–38) as opposed to the insecurities of life with Moon? Would one not desire the complete assurance of all sins forgiven and the joy of knowing one has eternal life (Colossians 2:13; 1 John 5:13)? Indeed, who can deny that the member who leaves now is in good company?

UC leaders themselves have admitted that thousands of disciples have left. Even twenty years ago they confessed:

> In the Unification Church, many have joined and many have left, and few remain. We have lost many, many brothers and sisters. They believed Father was the Messiah; they received the Divine Principle. They made deep determination to sacrifice their entire lives, yet many left because we couldn't raise these members enough. . . . We have killed more than we have saved. It is very true.[414]

Today it is far worse: tens of thousands have now left. Moon himself has failed in his own role as Lord of the Second Advent. Therefore, everything is lost anyway. So why remain a member?

Years ago, however, Moon was right about a few things. He confessed: "Any man who says that he is the source of life and love cannot be trusted, not even Reverend Moon."[415] "Even I cannot be trusted 100 percent because of the innate nature of human weaknesses."[416] Who, then, can one trust 100 percent?

Moon once claimed, "My words will prove to be true. Otherwise there is no God."[417] However time and again his words have not proven true. They consistently contradict God's word, and Moon has failed in his promises. So why should he be trusted at all? Has Moon now concluded that there is no God? Will he realize that listening to the spirit world at the beginning was the source of his troubles?

There is only one God who can be trusted 100 percent—the God of the Bible. He will never fail anyone who trusts in Him: "Never will I leave you; never will I forsake you" (Hebrews 13:5). The only really important thing in life is to come to know Him. As Jesus said, "Now this is eternal life; that they may know you, the only true God, and Jesus Christ, whom you have sent. . . . Sanctify them by the truth; Your word is truth" (John 17:3, 17).

Unification Church	The Bible
I have paid a great amount of indemnity, and because of this I have the right to forgive another's sin. (*Master Speaks* (MS-3) March-April, 1965, p. 16)	Why does this fellow talk like that? He's blaspheming! Who can forgive sins but God alone? (Mark 2:7)
Jesus was a man, not God Himself. (Moon, *Christianity in Crisis*, p. 27)	Looking for the blessed hope and the appearing of the glory of our great God and Savior, Christ Jesus. (Titus 2:13 NAS)
Jesus . . . failed in fulfilling His mission on the earth. (*Master Speaks*, December 26, 1971, p. 2)	I have brought you glory on earth by completing the work you gave me to do. (John 17:4)
We . . . must realize that Jesus did not come to die on the cross. (*Divine Principle*, p. 143)	And He said to them, "O foolish men and slow of heart to believe in all that the prophets have spoken! Was it not necessary for the Christ to suffer these things and to enter into His glory?" (Luke 24:25–26 NAS)
	(continues)

UNIFICATION CHURCH	THE BIBLE
Do not believe in the Christ upon the cross. . . . The cross is the symbol of Satan's victory. (*Master Speaks,* No. 4 (2), p. 6)	It was for this very reason I came to this hour. (John 12:27) For I resolved to know nothing while I was with you except Jesus Christ and him crucified. (1 Corinthians 2:2)

NOTES

Note: Sometimes the *Master Speaks* lectures contain multiple parts. If so, we included the parenthetical numbers to refer to the parts of the lecture (1, 2, 3 etc.). Also Young Oon Kim's texts, *Divine Principle and Its Application* and *The Divine Principles* should be distinguished from the major text of the movement *Divine Principle*, an anonymous book most commentators believe to be authored by Moon, apparently received by him through inspiration.

1. Sun Myung Moon, *For God's Sake* (Washington, D.C.: Holy Spirit Association for the Unification of World Christianity (HSA-UWS)), 1972, p. 23; Young Oon Kim, *The Divine Principles,* (San Francisco: HSA-UWC, 1960), p. ix.
2. Young Oon Kim, *The Divine Principles* (San Francisco: HSA-UWC, 1960), pp. ix-x.
3. Sun Myung Moon, "History of Unification Church," *Master Speaks,* December 27, 1971, pp. 1-10.
4. Ibid., pp. 4-5.
5. Ibid.
6. Ibid.
7. Ibid.
8. Ibid.
9. Ibid., p. 6.
10. Ibid., p. 4.
11. Ibid.
12. Ibid., pp. 6-7.
13. Ibid., p. 8.
14. Kim, *The Divine Principles* (1960), p. xii.
15. Ibid.
16. *Christianity Today,* July 20, 1979, p. 39; Ken Sudo, *The 120 Day Training Manual* (Barrytown, NY: International Unification Church Training Center, n.d.), pp. 56, 111.
17. James Bjornstad, *The Moon Is Not the Son* (Minneapolis, MN: Bethany Fellowship, Inc., 1976), pp. 20-21; J. Isamu Yamamoto, *The Puppet Master* (Downers Grove, IL: Inter-Varsity Press, 1977), p. 23. Ample documentation for this fact has been provided in the popular press.
18. Sudo, *The 120 Day Training Manual,* p. 72.
19. Ibid., pp. 72-73.
20. Sudo, *120 Day Training Manual,* p. 73.
21. Marc Fisher, Jeff Leen, "Unification Church Interests Varied, Part 1," *The Washington Post,* November 23, 1997, internet printout.
22. Ibid.
23. Ibid.
24. Yamamoto, *The Puppet Master,* p. 23; *New York Times,* May 25,1976; *San Francisco Chronicle,* December 11, 1974.
25. E.g., *Christian Research Journal,* Summer 1988 Newswatch; *The Washington Post,* November 23/24, 1997.
26. Unification Church Website, "Global Outreach."
27. Ibid.
28. Ibid.
29. *The Washington Post,* November 23, 1997, Part 1.
30. *Divine Principle* (Washington, D.C.; HSA-UWC), 173; for example, cf. pp. 91, 188, 536.
31. Frederick Sontag, *Sun Myung Moon—and the Unification Church* (Nashville: Abingdon/Parthenon Press, 1977), p. 187.
32. *Master Speaks,* at True Parent's birthday, February 16, 1975.
33. Kim, *Divine Principle and Its Application,* p. 196; cf. *Master Speaks,* December 26, 1971, p. 4.
34. Sudo, *120 Day Training Manual,* p. 236.
35. Kim, *The Divine Principles* (1960), p. 4.
36. Sun Myung Moon, *New Hope* (Washington, D.C.: HSA-UWC, Inc., 1973), p. 78.
37. *Unification Theology & Christian Thought,* p. 6.
38. *Divine Principle,* p. 40.
39. Ibid., p. 20.
40. Ibid., p. 21.
41. Ibid., p. 22.
42. Ibid.
43. Ibid., pp. 20-30.
44. Ibid., p. 25.
45. Ibid., p. 20.
46. Ibid., p. 25.
47. Ibid.
48. Moon, *New Hope,* p. 51.
49. *Divine Principle,* p. 42.
50. Ibid., p. 28.
51. Kim, *The Divine Principle* (1960), p. 4.
52. *Divine Principle,* p. 31.
53. Ibid.
54. Ibid., p. 31.
55. *Master Speaks,* December 23, 1971, p. 3.
56. *Divine Principle,* p. 32.
57. Moon, "The Dignity of God and Man," *The Way of the World,* March-April 1977, p. 5.
58. Ibid.
59. Ibid., pp. 8-11.
60. *Master Speaks,* 319, p. 1.

61. *Master Speaks*, 6, p. 1.
62. *Divine Principle*, pp. 221, 223; cf. p. 226.
63. *Master Speaks*, December 29, 1971, p. 9.
64. *Master Speaks*, 5, p. 4.
65. Ibid.
66. *Divine Principle*, p. 227.
67. *Master Speaks*, July 1, 1973, p. 1.
68. Ibid.
69. *Master Speaks*, 2, p. 3.
70. *Master Speaks*, December 27, 1971, p. 8.
71. *Master Speaks*, December 29, 1971, pp. 1, 6.
72. Ibid., p. 10.
73. *Master Speaks*, 2, p. 6.
74. *Master Speaks*, 2, p. 5.
75. *Master Speaks*, December 12, 1971, pp. 2-3.
76. *Master Speaks*, 3, p. 13.
77. *Master Speaks*, 4, p. 7.
78. *Master Speaks*, 2, p. 3.
79. *Master Speaks*, 2, pp. 6-7.
80. *Master Speaks*, 4 (2), p. 2.
81. Ibid., p. 3.
82. *Master Speaks*, 4, p. 12.
83. *Divine Principle*, p. 19; cf. Moon, *The Way of the World*, March-April 1077, p. 7.
84. *Master Speaks*, 309, January 9, 1972, p. 3.
85. *Master Speaks*, 378, p. 4.
86. Young Oon Kim, *Unification Theology & Christian Thought* (New York: Golden Gate Publishing Co., 1975), p. 286.
87. *Master Speaks*, 1, p. 7.
88. Kim, *The Divine Principles* (1960), p. xiii.
89. Moon, interview in Sontag, p. 138.
90. Sontag, p. 183.
91. *Master Speaks*, 7, p. 4.
92. *Radix Magazine*, September-October 1976, p. 4.
93. Ibid.
94. *The Way of the World*, December 1973, p. 21.
95. *Master Speaks*, 1, p. 5.
96. *Christianity Today*, July 20, 1979, p. 38.
97. *Master Speaks*, 6, pp. 1-2.
98. Ronald Enroth, *Youth Brainwashing and the Extremist Cults* (Grand Rapids, MI: Zondervan, 1977), pp. 118-119.
99. Ibid.
100. *Newsweek* (International edition), June 14, 1976, pp. 48-49.
101. *Master Speaks*, November 9, 1973.
102. Ibid., 381, p. 3.
103. Ibid., 376, p. 3.
104. These are documented throughout the chapter.
105. Sudo, *120 Day Training Manual*, pp. 40-41.
106. Ibid., p. 43.
107. Ibid., p. 61.
108. Ibid., pp. 110, 114.
109. Ibid., pp. 120, 362.
110. Ibid., p. 101.
111. Ibid., pp. 110, 114.
112. Ibid., p. 155; see *The Way of the World*, December, 1973, p. 19.
113. Ibid., p. 155.
114. Enroth, p. 108.
115. Ibid., pp. 106-108.
116. Ibid.
117. *Master Speaks*, 3, p. 10.
118. *Master Speaks*, 4, p. 9.
119. *Master Speaks*, 3, p. 14.
120. *Master Speaks*, 2, p. 12.
121. *Master Speaks*, 372, p. 13.
122. *Master Speaks*, 3, p. 4.
123. *Master Speaks*, 1 (2), pp. 2, 5; *Master Speaks*, 4 (2) pp. 3, 20; *Master Speaks*, 423, p. 4; *Master Speaks*, 3, pp. 5, 10.
124. *Master Speaks*, 3, p. 7.
125. *Master Speaks*, 4, p. 5.
126. Kim, *The Divine Principles*, p. 216.
127. *New Hope News*, October 7, 1974, p. 7, from Yamamoto, *The Puppet Master*, p. 90.
128. *Newsweek* (international edition), June 14, 1976, p. 49, Sontag, p. 141 (interview).
129. Sudo, *The 120 Day Training Manual*, p. 107.
130. Moon, *The Way of the World*, July-August 1977, pp. 25-26.
131. *Master Speaks*, December 27, 1971, p. 10.
132. *Master Speaks*, January 11, 1972, p. 16.
133. *Master Speaks*, December 29, 1971, p. 9.
134. *The Washington Post*, November 23, 1997, internet print-out.
135. Sontag, p. 149 (interview).
136. *Master Speaks*, PD73, p. 3.
137. *Time*, June 14, 1976, p. 49.
138. *Master Speaks*, 346, p. 3.
139. *Master Speaks*, PD73, p. 3.
140. *New Religious Movements Update*, vol. 2, no. 1 (Dialogue Center, April, 1978), pp. 38-39.
141. Ibid., p. 41.
142. Ibid.
143. *Special Report, The Unification Church: Its Activities and Practices*, Unofficial Transcript Government Panel, Citizens Appearing; Dirksen Senate Office Building, Senate Caucus Room, Washington, D.C., February 18, 1976, *Part 1*, p. 40.
144. Ibid., p. 39.
145. *Master Speaks*, December 22, 1971, pp. 6-7.
146. *Master Speaks*, 300, p. 7.
147. Ibid., p. 9.
148. *Special Report, Part I*, pp. 9, 40.
149. Ibid., pp. 10-20.
150. Ibid., pp. 30-31; from *Theory of Education from the Text of Unification Thought*, edited by the Unification Thought Institute in Barrytown, NY.
151. Ibid., p. 11.
152. *Master Speaks*, 430, p. 10.
153. *Master Speaks*, 2, p. 15.
154. *Master Speaks*, 3, p. 27.
155. *Radix Magazine*, p. 3.
156. Sun Myung Moon, *Christianity in Crisis* (Washington, D.C., HSA-UWC), 1973, p. 122.
157. Ibid., p. 114.
158. Kim, *The Divine Principles*, p. 99.
159. *Master Speaks*, February 16, 1975, n.p.
160. *Master Speaks*, 430, p. 3.

161. Ibid., p. 8.
162. Kim, *The Divine Principles*, pp. xiii-xiv.
163. *Time*, September 30, 1974, p. 68.
164. *Master Speaks*, December 26, 1971, p. 3.
165. *Divine Principle*, pp. 533-535.
166. Sudo, *The 120 Day Training Manual*, pp. 96-97.
167. *Master Speaks*, December 25, 1974.
168. Ibid., p. 98.
169. Ibid., p. 212.
170. Ibid.
171. *Master Speaks*, February 16, 1975.
172. *Master Speaks*, 7, p. 1.
173. *Master Speaks*, December 31, 1971, p. 1.
174. Kim, *Unification Theology and Christian Thought*, cf. pp. ix, 86, 93, 97,109-132 (especially 130), 286.
175. *Our Response*, pp. 75-76.
176. Moon, *Christianity in Crisis*, back cover.
177. Editorial, *Moody Monthly*, November 1986, p. 8.
178. NBC documentary, May 17-18, 1975 (citing *Master Speaks*).
179. *Master Speaks*, April 14, 1974, quoted in Sontag, p. 123.
180. *Master Speaks*, 372R, p. 12.
181. *Master Speaks*, 4, p. 1.
182. Dr. Ki-Bum Han, Pastor, Presbyterian Church, Port Chester, NY, quoting Moon. Taken from *A Special Report*, p. 35; also in Janis Feiden's testimony in the *Dallas Morning News*, "Focus," October 19, 1975.
183. Enroth, pp. 119-120.
184. *Master Speaks*, PD73, p. 2.
185. *Master Speaks*, March 23, 1975.
186. *Master Speaks*, 430, p. 3.
187. *Master Speaks*, 2, pp. 13-14.
188. Kim, *The Divine Principles*, p. 44.
189. Kim, *Unification Theology and Christian Thought*, e.g., pp. 97, 113-119; *Divine Principle*, pp. 9-10, 16, 131, 236; Moon, "Christmas in Heart," *The Way of the World*, December 1973, pp. 9-10.
190. *Divine Principle*, p. 131.
191. *Divine Principle*, pp. 15-16.
192. Sudo, *120 Day Training Manual*, pp. 141-148.
193. *Special Report, Part II*, p. 2.
194. *Master Speaks*, 4, p. 11.
195. *Master Speaks*, 3 (2), p. 9.
196. *Master Speaks*, 3, p. 8.
197. *Master Speaks*, 7 (2), p. 1.
198. Moon, *Christianity in Crisis*, p. 106.
199. Kim, *The Divine Principles*, p. 4.
200. Kim, *Divine Principle and Its Application*, p. 5 from Bjornstad Contemporary Christianity, November-December, 1974, p. 3.
201. Moon, *Christianity in Crisis*, p. 4.
202. Ibid., p. 103; cf. *Divine Principle*, pp. 150-152.
203. Ibid.
204. *Master Speaks*, December 14, 1971, p. 1.
205. *Master Speaks*, 309, January 9, 1972, p. 3.
206. *New Hope*, p. 45.
207. Ibid., p. 73.
208. Ibid., p. 39.
209. *Master Speaks*, 3, p. 14.
210. *Master Speaks*, 430, p. 11.
211. Moon, "The Dignity of God and Man," *The Way of the World*, March-April 1977, p. 11.
212. *Master Speaks*, 4 (2), p. 8.
213. Kim, *Unification Theology and Christian Thought*, p. 62.
214. *Master Speaks*, 4, p. 4.
215. *Divine Principle*, pp. 216-218.
216. Ibid., p. 76.
217. Moon, *New Hope*, p. 29.
218. *Contemporary Christianity*, Vol. 5, no. 3, January-February 1976, p. 5.
219. *Master Speaks*, December 23, 1971, p. 3.
220. Sontag, p. 192.
221. *Divine Principle*, pp. 209-210.
222. Ibid., pp. 210-211.
223. Kim, *Divine Principle and Its Application* (1968), p. 75.
224. Kim, *The Divine Principles*, p. 65.
225. *Master Speaks*, 7, p. 4.
226. *Master Speaks*, 1, p. 2.
227. M. Darrol Bryant and Susan Hodges, *Exploring Unification Theology* (New York: Rose of Sharon Press, Inc., 1978), p. 31.
228. *Master Speaks*, 382, p. 3.
229. *Master Speaks*, PD 73, p. 2.
230. *Master Speaks*, 3, p. 15.
231. *Divine Principle*, p. 148.
232. *Master Speaks*, 4 (2), p. 11.
233. *Master Speaks*, 430, p. 9.
234. *Master Speaks*, PD 73, p. 2.
235. *Master Speaks*, 423, p. 4.
236. *Master Speaks*, 7, p. 4.
237. Ibid.
238. Kim, *Unification Theology and Christian Thought*, pp. 113, 116. For good defenses of the virgin birth, see Robert Gromacki, *The Virgin Birth: Doctrine of Deity* and J. Gresham Machen, *The Virgin Birth*.
239. *Master Speaks*, 4 (2), p. 9.
240. Sudo, *120 Day Training Manual*, p. 114.
241. *Master Speaks*, 3, p. 4.
242. *Master Speaks*, 405, p. 6; also in *The Way of The World*, December 1973, p. 19.
243. Sudo, *120 Day Training Manual*, pp. 284, 286.
244. *Master Speaks*, 405, p. 4; also in *The Way of the World*, December 1973, p. 14.
245. *Master Speaks*, 4 (2), p. 9.
246. *The Christian Century*, December 4, 1974, p. 1140.
247. *Divine Principle*, pp. 215-216.
248. *Master Speaks*, 3, p. 20.
249. *Divine Principle*, pp. 179-180.
250. *Master Speaks*, December 14, 1971, p. 3.
251. *Master Speaks*, January 11, 1972, p. 17.
252. Sudo, *The 120 Day Training Manual*, pp. 127-128.
253. *New Religious Movements Update*, Vol. 1, nos. 3-4, pp. 45-47, 57-58, a reproduction of *Master Speaks*, 369, May 20, 1973, second 100-day training session. See Sontag (interview).
254. Ibid., p. 51.
255. *Master Speaks*, 4, p. 7.
256. *Master Speaks*, December 22, 1971, p. 10.
257. *Master Speaks*, December 29, 1971, p. 10.
258. *Master Speaks*, January 11, 1972, p. 11.

259. Jack Sparks, *The Mind Benders* (Nashville: Thomas Nelson, 1977), p. 135.
260. *Master Speaks*, 318, January 18, 1973, pp. 4-5; *Master Speaks*, 319, January 19, 1973, pp. 1-4.
261. Ibid.
262. Ibid.
263. *Master Speaks*, 430, p. 5.
264. *Master Speaks*, December 29, 1971, p. 7.
265. *Update*, Vol. 1, nos. 3-4, p. 56.
266. *Special Report, Part I*, p. 9.
267. *Time*, June 14, 1976, p. 49, from *Master Speaks*.
268. *Special Report, Part I;* also reported in the media.
269. *Master Speaks*, 3 (2), p. 7.
270. Sudo, *120 Day Training Manual*, pp. 39-40.
271. *The Way of the World*, March, 1978, p. 47.
272. *Master Speaks*, 2, pp. 10-12.
273. *Master Speaks*, January 9, 1972, p. 4.
274. *Master Speaks*, 1 (2), p. 6.
275. *Master Speaks*, 2 (2), p. 1.
276. *Master Speaks*, 4 (2), p. 6.
277. *Master Speaks*, 418, May 19, 1974, p. 2.
278. *Divine Principle*, p. 15.
279. Moon, "Christmas in Heart," *The Way of the World*, December 1973, p. 13.
280. *Master Speaks*, December 27, 1971, p. 6.
281. *Divine Principle*, p. 147.
282. Ibid., p. 152.
283. Sudo, *The 120 Day Training Manual*, p. 61.
284. Moon, *Christianity in Crisis*, p. 5.
285. Ibid., p. 15.
286. *Divine Principle*, p. 43.
287. Ibid., p. 104.
288. Ibid., p. 206.
289. Ibid., p. 209.
290. Moon, *The Way of the World*, January-February 1978, p. 5.
291. *Master Speaks*, 4 (2), p. 9.
292. *Divine Principle*, p. 168.
293. Ibid., p. 190.
294. *Master Speaks*, 6, p. 4.
295. *Master Speaks*, 4, p. 1.
296. Neil Salonen, then president, Unification Church, New York World Mission Center, conference between evangelicals and the Unification Church, June, 1979, reported in *Christianity Today*, July 20, 1979, p. 3.
297. *Master Speaks*, 3 (2), p. 8; *Master Speaks*, 3, pp. 4, 15.
298. "Perspective. Instructions from Father: Sun Myung Moon Speaks," *Aeropagus*, Fall, 1987, pp. 29-30.
299. Sudo, *120 Day Training Manual*, p. 144, emphasis added.
300. *Master Speaks*, 1, p. 1.
301. *Master Speaks*, December 29, 1971, p. 11.
302. See John Ankerberg, John Weldon, *The Coming Darkness*, chapter on heredity.
303. *Master Speaks*, 3, p. 22.
304. Kim, *Unification Theology and Christian Thought*, pp. 30-31.
305. *Divine Principle*, p. 187.
306. *Master Speaks*, 3 (2), p. 8.
307. *Master Speaks*, 3, p. 22.

308. Sudo, *120 Day Training Manual*, p. 143.
309. *Christianity Today*, July 20, 1979, p. 39.
310. *Master Speaks*, 1 (2), p. 3.
311. *Master Speaks*, 3, p. 7.
312. *Master Speaks*, 3 (2), p. 7.
313. *Master Speaks*, 3, p. 10.
314. *Master Speaks*, 1, p. 5.
315. Arthur Ford, *Unknown but Known* (New York: Harper and Row, 1968), pp. 121-147.
316. *Divine Principle*, p. 182.
317. *Master Speaks*, 2, pp. 18-19.
318. *Master Speaks*, 3, p. 10.
319. *Master Speaks*, 2, pp. 18-19.
320. *Master Speaks*, 3, pp. 4-5.
321. *Master Speaks*, December 29, 1971, p. 10.
322. *Master Speaks*, 3, p. 3.
323. Ibid., p. 5.
324. Ibid., p. 11.
325. Ibid., p. 17.
326. Ibid., p. 16.
327. Sontag, p. 155.
328. Ibid., p. 177.
329. *Master Speaks*, 2 (2), p. 5.
330. Sudo, *The 120 Day Training Manual*, pp. 160-161.
331. *Master Speaks*, 2, p. 6.
332. Ibid., p. 1.
333. Ibid., p. 12.
334. *Master Speaks*, December 26, 1971, p. 1.
335. *Master Speaks*, December 14, 1971, p. 6.
336. *Master Speaks*, December 22, 1971, p. 10.
337. *Special Report, Part I*, pp. 20-21.
338. *Master Speaks*, 2, p. 8
339. Joint Declaration Concerning the Moon Organization, September 26, 1997, website page http://www.rickross.com/reference/unif15.html.
340. *Master Speaks*, 2, p. 13.
341. *Master Speaks*, 2, p. 2.
342. *Master Speaks*, 2, p. 16.
343. *Special Report, Part I*, p. 33.
344. *Master Speaks*, 2, p. 2.
345. *Des Moines Register* (Iowa), April 4, 1974.
346. *Master Speaks*, 2, p. 6.
347. *Master Speaks*, 2, p. 1.
348. *Master Speaks*, 430, p. 6
349. *Master Speaks*, 430, p. 5.
350. *Christianity Today*, April 24, 1981, p. 48.
351. Official interview in Sontag, p. 150.
352. *Master Speaks*, December 26, 1971, p. 6.
353. From the *Master Speaks* reported in *Time*, June 14, 1976, p. 49.
354. Sudo, *The 120 Day Training Manual*, p. 94.
355. *Time*, October 26, 1981, p. 24.
356. *The Washington Post*, November 23, 1997.
357. Enroth, p. 104.
358. *Master Speaks*, 319, January 19, 1973, p. 7.
359. *Master Speaks*, December 12, 1971, p. 4.
360. *Master Speaks*, December 29, 1971, p. 7.
361. *Master Speaks*, 4 (2), p. 4.
362. *Master Speaks*, 2, p. 14.
363. *Special Report, Part I*, p. 24.

364. *Master Speaks,* 4 (2), p. 5.
365. *Master Speaks,* 5, p. 1.
366. *Master Speaks,* 430, p. 9.
367. *Master Speaks,* 3, p. 13.
368. *Master Speaks,* January 11, 1972, p. 2.
369. *San Francisco Magazine,* July, 1976, p. 41.
370. Transcript of "ABC News Close-Up": "New Religions: Holiness or Heresy?" broadcast September 2, 1976, p. 6.
371. *The Christian Century,* September 24, 1975, p. 813.
372. *Newsweek,* June 14, 1976, p. 47.
373. *Master Speaks,* at True Parent's Birthday, February 16, 1975.
374. KNXFM radio, San Diego, news report, April 14, 1977.
375. *The Catholic News,* February 24, 1977, p. 6.
376. *The Wichita Eagle,* July 14, 1975.
377. Steven Hassan, former CARP director, former assistant director of two U.C. centers, former lecturer, former fundraising team captain, at press conference, Rayburn Bldg., Washington, D.C., November 15, 1979.
378. Steven Hassan, quoted in CFF-IS, June 1, 1980, p. 10.
379. *The Advisor,* December 1979, p. 8, col. 3.
380. Website review at www.littlebrown.com, "About the Book."
381. *Master Speaks,* 2 (2), p. 1.
382. Yamamoto, *The Puppet Master,* pp. 20-21.
383. Ibid.
384. Moon, *The Way of the World,* July-August, 1977 p. 27.
385. *Newsweek,* June 14, 1976, p. 45.
386. *The Washington Post,* November 24, 1997, internet copy.
387. Transcript of April 26, 1975 lecture, on file.
388. Personal letter to John Weldon, June 9, 1976, p. 1.
389. Ibid.
390. *Master Speaks,* 369, cited in *Update,* Vol. 1, Nos. 3-4, pp. 51-52.
391. Sontag, p. 199.
392. *Master Speaks,* January 30, 1973, quoted in Sontag, p. 121.
393. *The Christian Century,* September 24, 1975, pp. 812-813.
394. *Special Report, Part I,* p. 25.
395. Letter sent to John Weldon.
396. *The Advisor,* April, 1980, p. 6, col. 1.
397. Chris Sheridan, "White Plains Rabbi Reunites Families," *Catholic News,* February 24, 1977, p. 14, col. 13.
398. Ted Patrick, quoted in *Crazy for God,* p. 220.
399. *Los Angeles Times,* October 4, 1977, pp. 50-55.
400. E.g., Kim, *Unification Theology and Christian Thought,* pp. 97, 109, 111-127.
401. *The Way of the World,* November-December 1977, pp. 50-55.
402. Excerpts of *Newsweek* interview June 14, 1976, p. 62, international edition.
403. *Master Speaks,* December 26, 1971, p. 2; cf. Moon, *Christianity in Crisis,* p. 107.
404. Sontag, p. 151.
405. Moon, *Christianity in Crisis,* p. vii.
406. *Master Speaks,* January 2, 1977, in Sontag, p. 125.
407. *Master Speaks,* May 20, 1973, p. 6, "Relationship Between Men and Women," second 100-day training session, cited by Sparks, p. 140.
408. Ibid., p. 116.
409. *The Way of the World,* January-February 1977, p. 49.
410. Sudo, *The 120 Day Training Manual,* p. 142, emphasis added.
411. Ibid., p. 141.
412. Ibid.
413. *Master Speaks,* 3, p. 15.
414. Sudo, *The 120 Day Training Manual,* p. 362.
415. *Master Speaks,* August 1, 1976, in Sontag, p. 124.
416. *Master Speaks,* January 2, 1977, Sontag, p. 125.
417. *Master Speaks,* 378R, p. 5.

UNITARIAN UNIVERSALISM

INFO AT A GLANCE

Name: Unitarian Universalism.

Purpose: To provide a humanistic religion of free thought and spiritual growth rather than dogma.

Founder: None per se. Unitarian Universalist ideas are traced to early theological heretics and non-conformists, such as Arius and Pelegius; then to sixteenth and seventeenth-century anti-trinitarians such as Schwenckfeld, Servetus, Catellio, Sigismund, Francis David, Socinus and John Biddle, and later to liberal theologians such as William Ellery Channing. The Unitarian Universalist Association (UUA) is the governing body in Boston, Massachusetts.

Source of authority: The individual: more or less each member believes as he or she wishes.

Occult dynamics: None per se, although many members may be open to occult involvement. On the one hand, the rational, scientific and humanistic emphasis may result in a view of the occult as primitive superstition. On the other hand, the modern New Age emphasis on incorporating alleged scientific backing for occult practice and the parapsychological interpretation of psychic powers, as latent and natural, may result in occult practices being seen as a modern, enlightened and scientific approach to "human potential," or as methods of spiritual advancement.

Examples of key literature: George Chrysside's *The Elements of Unitarianism* (Element, 1998) is probably the best current introduction; *The Epic of Unitarianism; Universalism in America; A History of Unitarianism* (2 Vols.); *The Unitarian Universalist World* (newspaper); and other books published by Beacon Press.

Attitude toward Christianity: Rejecting.

501

Relevant Quotes:

"We indeed grant, that the use of reason in religion is accompanied with danger."

—William Ellery Channing,
May 5, 1819 in Conrad Wright,
Three Prophets of Religious Liberalism, p. 27.

"Perhaps the greatest achievement of the Unitarian Universalist movement has been its liberalizing effect upon the theology and outlook of other churches down through the years."

—John Booth, *Introducing
Unitarian Universalism*, p. 27.

"Unitarianism broke its chains during the nineteenth century. The chain of doctrine, which bound previous generations to the Bible and to Christ, was cast off leaving men free to seek and affirm God within themselves as Reason, Soul and Conscience."

—David Parke, *The Epic of
Unitarianism*, p. 68.

"Christ and the Apostles were the first Unitarians."

—Joseph Priestly, pioneer of English
Unitarianism, 1733–1804, quoted
with approval by G. N. Marshall,
Challenge of a Liberal Faith, p. 208.

"Only 5 to 10 percent of its content [the Gospel of John] can be classified as genuine history."

—Rolland Wolfe, "a noted universalist
biblical scholar," quoted in G. N. Marshall,
Challenge of a Liberal Faith, p. 150.

DOCTRINAL SUMMARY

God: Ultimately undefined, but frequently seen in impersonal or quasi-personal terms, as in pantheism and panentheism, or as evolutionary process.

Jesus: A good man, for some divine in a superhuman, panentheistic sense.

Salvation: Characteristically interpreted in political or social terms, such as liberation theology.

Man: The apex of evolutionary wisdom, for many believers potentially divine.

Sin: Ignorance.

Satan: A Christian myth.

The Second Coming: A Christian myth.

The Fall: A Christian myth.

The Bible: A fallible recording of the evolution of Israelite religion.

Death: Differing beliefs are held; in general the Great Unknown.

Heaven and Hell: Christian myths or states of mind, or personal conditions in this life.

INTRODUCTION AND HISTORY

In the United States and Canada there are over 1,000 Unitarian Universalist (UU) churches within the parent organization, the Unitarian Universalist Association (UUA). The UUA is strongly committed to theological liberalism, religious pluralism, "free-thinking" in all areas and radical social action, the latter primarily sponsored through activism and the printed word. The UUA is a member of the International Association for Liberal Religion, and many of its ministers are trained at three principal universities: Harvard University, Meadville-Lombard (affiliated with the University of Chicago) and the Starr King School for the Ministry in California. A biweekly newspaper, the *Unitarian Universalist World*, was begun in 1970 and is sent 16 times yearly to over 100,000 families. Beacon Press, the publishing arm of the church, has hundreds of titles which sell over a million copies a year. Heavily eclectic, UU organizations and committees are involved with dozens of topics, from abortion rights, environmental concerns and "social justice," to experimental spirituality, feminism, children's education and summer camps, to homosexual activism (for example, The Office for Gay Concerns) and psychic phenomena.

The "Church of the Larger Fellowship" is primarily for those who do not have easy access to local UU fellowships or churches and includes membership from approximately 80 countries. The program provides monthly bulletins, a loan library for sermons and religious-educational programs for the family.

The modern Unitarian Universalist Association represents a merger of two older religious movements. The Universalists, organized in 1793, stressed theological *universalism,* the idea that salvation is universal and therefore everyone will eventually be redeemed to heaven. The Unitarians, organized in 1825, stressed the *unity* of the nature of God as opposed to His trinitarian nature. Historically the two groups were divided by social and theological differences, and it was only after an arduous, painful road towards unity that the two merged in 1961. One historical factor in the growth of Unitarian Universalist thinking was opposition to the theological doctrines of election and imputation, the latter referring to man's inherited depravity and legal condemnation in Adam (Romans 5:12–19).

UU claims an impressive list of followers, which allow one to gauge its influence historically. Their website list of church members, or of those who strongly believed in UU principles, is shown in the chart on the next page.[1]

Reportedly, UU members represent 25 percent of the names in the American Hall of Fame, and they appear more often in *Who's Who,* proportionately, than the members of any other religious group.[2]

PRACTICES AND BELIEFS

If we could list five key beliefs that describe UU best it would be freedom, justice, tolerance, reason and pluralism. These ideals are interpreted from a UU perspective—individualism, rationalism, subjectivism, and liberalism so that Christian and UU interpretations and applications of these concepts would be markedly different in important ways. The UU website succinctly illustrates the UU ideals as follows:

We believe that personal experience, conscience and reason should be the final authorities in religion. In the end religious authority lies not in a book or person or institution, but in ourselves. . . . We will not be bound by a statement of belief. . . . Revelation is continuous. We celebrate unfolding truths known to teachers, prophets and sages through the ages. . . . We believe people should be encouraged to think for themselves. We know people differ in their opinions and lifestyles and believe these differences generally should be honored. We seek to act as a moral force in the world, believing that ethical living is the supreme witness of religion. The here and now and the effects our actions will have on future generations deeply concern us. We know that our relationships with one another, with other peoples, races and nations, should be governed by justice, equity and compassion.[3]

According to their website, in 1997, the largest survey yet conducted had almost 10,000 Unitarian Universalists responding. The average membership was 16 years, and 92.5% of respondents were laypeople. The UU committee "Fulfilling the Promise: A Recovenanting Process for the 21st Century" is "confident [that] the 10,000 responses broadly represent our association." Among its many findings: the largest category, 46.1%, describe themselves as "humanist;" 19% as "earth/Nature centered;" 6.2% as "mystic;" 13% as "theist;" 9.5% as Christian; 3.6% as Buddhist; .04% Hindu; 0.1% Muslim. In addition, a whopping 60% had considered leaving UU. Ninety-five percent of these listed four reasons for this: 1) "lack of spirituality, warmth and joy" (29.2%); 2) "congregational conflict" (24.3%); 3) "too arrogant and cerebral" (19.2%); 4) "too much political correctness" (19.0%). Still, 66% believe their UU congregation should actively seek to spread the UU faith to others. This is done in many ways, such as through the UU Department of Religious Education, which offers specialized programs to reach children and teenagers with their proactive sex education and "anti-bias" propaganda, and through a variety of adult programs and resources.

Clearly no one can argue the UU faith has not been spread far and wide in modern America. Professor Alan Gomes describes their influence when he observes:

[The] philosophy they champion pervades the religious and political left, and is nearly ubiquitous on college campuses. Anyone who has been told that truth is relative; that "tolerance" of "alternative lifestyles" and beliefs—including homosexuality, radical feminism, and abortion on demand—is the highest virtue; that reason, conscience, and experience are the ultimate

FAMOUS UNITARIAN UNIVERSALISTS		
IN ARTS AND LITERATURE	IN SCIENCE AND MEDICINE	IN SOCIAL REFORM
Louisa May Alcott	Alexander Graham Bell	Susan B. Anthony
Horatio Alger	Luther Burbank	Adin Ballou
P. T. Barnum	Charles Darwin	
Ray Bradbury	Samuel F. B. Morse	AS GREAT HUMANITARIANS
Robert Burns	Isaac Newton	
Samuel Taylor Coleridge	Linus C. Pauling	Clara Barton
Norman Cousins	Joseph Priestley	Dorothea Dix
e. e. cummings		Florence Nightingale
Charles Dickens	IN AMERICAN POLITICS	Albert Schweitzer
Ralph Waldo Emerson		John Greenleaf Whittier
Nathaniel Hawthorne	Abigail Adams	
Oliver Wendell Holmes, Jr.	John Adams	IN EDUCATION
Oliver Wendell Holmes, Sr.	John Quincy Adams	
Michael Learned	John C. Calhoun	Mark Hopkins
Henry Wadsworth Longfellow	William S. Cohen	Horace Mann
John Milton	Millard Fillmore	Leland Stanford
Herman Melville	Benjamin Franklin	
Paul Newman	Horace Greeley	BY THEMSELVES
Carl Sandberg	Thomas Jefferson	(NOT AFFILIATED)
Pete Seeger	James Madison	
Rod Serling	Charles P. Steinmetz	Clarence Darrow
Robert Shaw	Adlai Stevenson	Thomas Paine
Mary Wollstonecraft Shelley	Emily Stowe	Paul Revere
Lister Sinclair	William Howard Taft	
Jerry Sohl	Daniel Webster	
Rabindranath Tagore		
Henry David Thoreau		
Frank Lloyd Wright		

guides to truth; and that the Bible is a myth and Jesus Christ but one of many inspirational (but fallible) teachers, has encountered cherished Unitarian Universalist dogmas.

[The] UUA is presently engaged in a militant program of expansion and growth, seeking to increase their ranks by spreading the Unitarian Universalist vision of their politically correct *good news*.[4]

Although UU is clearly a religious movement, and although the history of the two movements compromise an ongoing chronicle of theological concern and speculation, a good number of members today are noncommittal or unconcerned about religion one way or the other. A

brief study of the forerunners of the movements reveals an entirely different worldview from that of the average, modern Unitarian Universalist. Their forefathers utilized both the Bible and human reason in formulating their worldview and theological arguments, although they were never considered Christian by orthodox church leaders. Modern UU members appeal to the Bible only casually, if at all, and they are much more swayed by secular, rationalistic philosophy and thinking and "political correctness."

Over a period of several centuries, we can trace their increasing rejection of the Bible as an authority. Starting with the claim to accept the full authority of Scripture (although often denying this in practice) one biblical doctrine after another was placed under the microscope of human "reason" and then discarded. The Universalists did begin with at least some biblical teachings, such as that Christ died for our sins and the trinitarian nature of God, but they rejected the concept of eternal punishment on what to them were rational grounds. They also allowed the prevailing intellectual climate of the day, during an age of enlightenment and reason, to mold their conscience and interpretation of Scripture. They did not allow divine Scripture to assess the validity of the various theories, cultural fashions and theological trends then in play. Thus, once eternal punishment was deemed "unreasonable," it was only a matter of time before miracles, the Fall, the atonement, the deity of Christ, the Trinity and so on were also found to be deficient according to human "reason." UU theologians and philosophers had, in effect, decided beforehand what was "reasonable" or acceptable, and then they used all the powers at their command to make the Bible conform to their conclusions.

This was a gradual process. For example, in 1847 most Universalists were attempting to refute "the latest form of infidelity," the beginning of the Unitarian denial of the New Testament miracles. Ralph Waldo Emerson had "begun" the Unitarian tirade against miracles in 1838, in his noted Harvard Divinity School lecture at Cambridge. Reflecting his transcendentalist view of the primacy of intuition, he stated: "And thus by his holy thoughts, Jesus serves us, and thus only. To aim to convert a man by [belief in] miracles, is a profanation of the soul. A true conversion, a true Christ, is now, as always, to be made, by the reception of beautiful sentiments."[5] In the end, however, the Christian approach to miracles was labeled "a Monster."[6] For their part, the Universalists reacted by defining the standard for Christian ministry as a belief in "The Bible account of the life, teachings, miracles, death and resurrection of the Lord Jesus Christ."[7] The Unitarians, however, were the more liberal of the two, and were more willing to abandon whichever aspect of Scripture was unreasonable to them; in fact, their impact on Universalist thought eventually influenced the latter away from belief in the Trinity. (New England Transcendentalism, in part, developed out of the theological speculation inherent to Unitarianism. The majority of its early adherents and leaders were Unitarian clergy.[8])

Modern Unitarian Universalists, then, bear little theological resemblance to their forbears, although, practically speaking, they are in full agreement that human "reason" and, paradoxically, sometimes mysticism, are to be the final judge of any purported divine revelation. Mystic George De Benneville (1703–1793), for example, "validated" universalist theology by means of an out of body experience, reported in his *Life and Trance,* and became a pioneer of universalism in America. Today, although only 6 percent classify themselves as mystical according to the most recent poll, a significant minority of UU members, perhaps 15 to 20 percent, could be described as mystical or mystical leaning when we consider the mystical potential in other categories. The tragedy was that in both camps the final result of rejecting one major doctrine of Scripture was the eventual abandonment of them all. Unfortunately, the current trend in many evangelical churches and institutions to abandon belief in inerrancy on the basis of "reason" is equally tragic and could have similar results down the road.

UU members are proud of their liberalizing influence upon Christianity, and indeed it has not been small. As noted earlier, Booth declared that "perhaps the greatest achievement of the Unitarian Universalist movement has been its liberalizing effect upon the theology and outlook of other churches throughout the years."[9] For example, liberal giant Paul Tillich said of UU theologian James Luther Adams that "without him I would not be what I am, biographically as well as theologically."[10]

Obviously the impact of UU has not been upon theology in a vacuum, for in crucial ways as the influence of biblical theology declines, so does the culture. As Rushdoony points out: "In a remarkably brilliant and telling study, Ann Douglas, in *The Feminization of American Culture* (1977), has shown the effects of Unitarianism and religious liberalism on American culture. From a God-centered emphasis . . . a man-centered focus emerged."[11] (By the turn of the millennium, the damage inflicted by feminism and its offshoots alone upon Christianity was difficult to calculate.)

Today the sad results of blendism are everywhere evident. Indeed, if UU is fond of referring to the witness of history as to the alleged "horrors of religious intolerance," we should keep in mind that, put bluntly, from the perspective of salvation in Christ, the witness of eternity will be to the genuine horrors of religious liberalism and Unitarian Universalism. To be damned through the church is a far greater tragedy and mockery of God's love than any supposed religious intolerance.

Early Forerunners

Our next section begins a discussion of contemporary UU theology. Before we turn to that, a brief sampling of the views of a few sixteenth and seventeenth-century forerunners of the

UUA will give us an idea of their beliefs and a basis for comparison. According to *The Epic of Unitarianism,* an edited compilation of basic writings in the liberal tradition, we find the following views.

Michael Servetus (1511–1553). Servetus apparently believed in the virgin birth, but somehow denied the trinity that undergirded it as "blasphemous." Christ in the flesh was man; in the spirit He was God; the Holy Spirit was "the activity of God in the spirit of man," but He did not exist apart from man who was at least in some sense divine.[12] Servetus authored *On the Errors of the Trinity* (1531), in which he stated, "Your Trinity is the product of subtlety and madness. The Gospel knows nothing of it."[13] According to Blunt, in his impressive *Dictionary of Sects, Heresies, Ecclesiastical Parties and Schools of Religious Thought,* Servetus ended up a pantheist.*[14]

---

*Much has been made of the death of Servetus at the hands of the great reformer John Calvin. Indeed, this event has often been cited by enemies of Christianity as a prime example of the evils and "barbaric orthodoxy" of fundamentalist religion.[15] However, this event is hardly proof of "barbaric orthodoxy," nor can all the blame be laid at the feet of John Calvin, who acted in harmony with public law. In his *History of the Church,* Philip Schaff observes that it is easy to misjudge an event in the sixteenth century from the perspective of the modern era:

> Calvin has the misfortune rather than the guilt of preeminence for intolerance among the Reformers. He and Servetus are the best abused men of the sixteenth century; and the depreciation of the good name of the one and the exculpation of the bad name of the other have been carried far beyond the limits of historic truth and justice. Both must be judged from the standpoint of the sixteenth, not the nineteenth, century . . . But the punishment was in accordance with the medieval laws and well nigh universal sentiment of Catholic and Protestant Christendom; it was unconditionally counseled by four Swiss magistrates which had been consulted before the execution (Zurich, Berne, Basel, and Schaffhausen), and was expressly approved by all the surviving reformers: Bullinger, Farel, Beza, Peter Martyr, and (as we have already seen) even by the mild and gentle Melanchthon.[16]

Schaff also discusses the extent of Servetus' blasphemies. There is little doubt as to his guilt or the serious nature of the events at hand:

We may now put a more favorable construction on Servetus' mystic and pantheistic or panchristic Unitarianism than his contemporaries, who seemed to have misunderstood him, friends as well as foes; but he was certainly a furious fanatic and radical heretic, and in the opinion of all the churches of his age a reckless blasphemer, aiming at the destruction of historic Christianity. He was thus judged from his first book (1531), as well as his last (1553). . . . He had abused all trinitarian Christians, as tritheists and atheists; he had denounced the orthodox doctrine of the Holy Trinity, as a dream of St. Augustine, a fiction of popery, an invention of the devil, and a three-headed Cerberus. . . .[17]

Schaff concludes that Calvin was partly justified in his conduct:

He then rushed blindly into the hands of Calvin, whom he denounced, during the trial, as a liar, a hypocrite, and a Simon Magus, with a view, apparently, to overthrow his power, in league with his enemies, the party of the Libertines, which had then the majority in the council of Geneva. Considering all these circumstances Calvin's conduct is not only explained, but even justified in part. He acted in harmony with the public law and orthodox sentiment of his age, and should therefore not be condemned more than his contemporaries, who would have done the same in his position.[18]

Francis David (1510–1579). David was a noted spokesman for Unitarianism in Transylvania. His arguments misconstrued Christian philosophy on the Trinity as "a belief in four or five gods": one substance, God, three separate divine Persons, and one man, Christ. Thus for him the trinitarian view of Christ was "human invention and superstition."[19]

Faustus Socinius. Socinius is frequently termed "the architect of modern Unitarianism." While calling the Old and New Testaments "holy Scripture," he declared that the deity of Christ "is repugnant not only to sound reason, but also to the Holy Scriptures." Like modern Arians (Jehovah's Witnesses, Christadelphians and others), Socinius would quote from the Scriptures teaching the human nature of Christ (his dependence upon the Father and so on), but conveniently reinterpret those that declared Jesus' deity.[20]

Many other examples could be given, illustrating how the increasing acceptance of rationalism produced the increasing rejection of biblical doctrine. As human minds were divinized, God's word was humanized. Mendelsohn observes that the doctrines of the Trinity, Jesus as the God-man, original sin and election were all eventually abandoned. The subsequent consequence was not difficult to predict: "Finally the notion of 'vicarious atonement'—that Jesus provided salvation by paying for the sins of mankind—was examined and discarded."[21]

THEOLOGY

Christianity

It must be remembered that there is no "official doctrine" among modern Unitarian Universalists, since each member believes whatever he or she wishes. Therefore, we cannot properly speak of a UU doctrine of God, Jesus, salvation and so on. However, it does appear there is one nearly universal characteristic of UU members: dislike of biblical orthodoxy. In this sense, there is perhaps at least one "official doctrine" among UU believers. Nevertheless, the following material is representative only—not every member can be categorized according to these beliefs. All quotes, do, however, come from authoritative Unitarian Universalist literature.

While UU believers do proclaim the validity of all religions and spiritual paths, they are peculiarly hostile to the Christian religion. This is ironic in that Christianity is the very religion without which they would not exist, the religion whose Scriptures they may, even today, appeal to in support of their beliefs. Not surprisingly, UU arrives at its view of Christianity from liberal theological scholarship, especially the foolhardy Jesus Seminar:

> The Rev. Katie Lee Crane spoke for many UUs when she delivered her sermon to the congregation at Winchester Unitarian Society, Winchester, Mass., last March: "I was reared a Roman Catholic then abandoned my Christian heritage for a long time. . . . Peeling away all the doctrine and the fluffy stories, I rediscovered a Jesus that I can relate to. . . . No individual has been more important in this re-evaluation of Jesus than Dr. Robert Funk and his controversial Jesus Seminar." Crane had just finished a course on the methods of the Jesus Seminar when she decided to develop what she learned into her worship service of March 9. "There is a real, shared purpose in what the Jesus Seminar does and what Unitarian Universalists have been doing throughout our history," Crane said in a recent interview. . . . The Jesus Seminar on the Road has received warm receptions and universal praise in the UU churches where it has appeared. . . .

However, faith in the Jesus Seminar, rather than in Jesus, exacts its own price. (See "The Problem of Liberal Theology" for a critique of the Jesus Seminar.) As we read on:

> Dr. Davidson Loehr is a Unitarian Universalist minister in Kalamazoo, Michigan, and the only UU in the Jesus Seminar. . . . Loehr remembers something that Funk once told him about learning the truth of Jesus: "Something died in all of us," Funk said of that experience. "It's tormenting us and it's lying there like a lump." Loehr has no remedy for the pain except truth. Jesus, he said, was just a man—a courageous and ethical man, but a man without divine mandate or mission.[22]

A sampling of descriptive phrases which UU writers have applied to the Bible and Christianity leaves little room for acceptance of the UU claim to universal "religious tolerance." It also tends to undermine validity to the stated fundamental UU principle of having "a generous and tolerant understanding of differing views and practices."[23] Although they decry religious bigotry, their attitude toward Christianity is hardly so open and tolerant. They label biblical teachings as: "primitive," "celestial nonsense," "myth," "rubbish," "legends," "impossible history," "excess baggage," "a sham" and "a ghost of superstition in its faded features."[24]

UUs admit that "many of us . . . have . . . strong antipathy to traditional religious language" (that is, Christ as Savior, sin, judgment).[25] The Reverend Ralph N. Helverson of the First Parish in Cambridge, Massachusetts, declares that tolerance means "you tolerate those who differ from you." To illustrate, he mentions a UU's minister friend whose "only theology was Janov's *Primal Scream*" ("scream" therapy), and he can, it seems, accept this. Yet he goes on to declare that "orthodox clergymen speaking about truth voice more nonsense per minute than almost any other group that I hear."[26]

Being tolerant of things like "scream therapy" while being intolerant of basic Bible teaching kind of sums up UU theology. UU is confessedly not Christian. In an official UU report under Section Eleven: Marginalized Groups, "A Non-Christian Religion?", we read "Between 1930 and 1960, the primary theological identity of Unitarianism shifted from Christianity to various understandings of humanism and existentialism." "It is true that *collectively* we are a nonChristian religion . . . [however] one of this century's most controversial theological issues in Unitarian Universalism has been whether one can be genuinely Unitarian Universalist and Christian at the same time."[27] The report implies yes. But as Duke Grey pointed out, in "A Letter to Christians," in the *Unitarian Universalist Christian*, Fall/Winter 1992, p. 42, "The vast majority of congregations now belonging to the UUA consider themselves nonChristians."[28] Indeed, only between 10 to 20 percent consider themselves even "liberal Christians."[29]

Nevertheless, within UU there is an allegedly Christian subset that seeks to stress Christianity. Despite the Christian label, however, their the-

ology is little different from religious liberalism and humanism in general. Richard E. Myers, editor of the *Unitarian Universalist Christian*, the organ of the UU Christian Fellowship (UUCF), declares: "Today, many UU's find traditional Christianity intellectually untenable. It is not just the historical objections to the Trinity and predestination that are the basis of their rejection, but the whole body of theological ideas associated with Christianity, including *even belief in God*. Most of the trappings of traditional religion they view as so much excess baggage."[30] This statement comes from a pamphlet titled, "Can I Be a Unitarian Universalist and Still Be a Christian?" Surprisingly, even in light of this, the author says, "My own answer to that question is: for the present, certainly." But a UU can be considered a Christian only if Unitarian Universalism itself is Christian. If UU rejects the dictionary definition and historic meaning of the term Christian, then even a groundhog could be declared a Christian. The *Oxford American Dictionary* defines "Christian" as "of the doctrines of Christianity, believing in or based on these," and it defines "Christianity" as "the religion based on the belief that Christ was the incarnate Son of God and on his teachings." Any examination of numerous issues of the *Unitarian Universalist Christian* will clearly show repeated denial of central Christian doctrines (see Appendix 1).

The term Christian, like the term UU, is exclusive, not inclusive; it does not, for example, incorporate humanism, atheism or Marxism. A committed Marxist cannot be a Christian, for the entire worldview of one system logically undermines the other. Just so, a committed humanist who rejects all biblical teachings (even though he may uphold Jesus as a good example) would be incorrect in calling his personal worldview "Christian." The Reverend John E. Towbridge argues, "All of us in the liberal church are basically Christians," and he maintains we can "help Christianity be more Christian."[31] But to call UU humanism "Christian" is neither a rational choice of words nor even a credible option. Since UU members pride themselves on reason, credibility and following the dictates of one's moral conscience, a re-evaluation of their use of the term Christian would seem to be in order.

An older poll of 12,151 respondents in 80 UU societies revealed: "Unitarian Universalists no longer regard their faith as distinctly Christian, and an overwhelming majority hope the denomination will move toward a universal or distinctively humanistic religion in contrast to liberal Protestantism or ecumenical Christianity."[32] Clearly, their hopes have been realized. For UU members today to call themselves Christian in any sense is a distortion of language.

There are some UU ministers who are refreshingly more discerning. The Reverend Ralph Bailey argues correctly that UU and Christianity are fundamentally irreconcilable:

Christianity is a religion whose adherents subscribe to an essential core of doctrine which no Unitarian Universalist of my acquaintance would accept. . . . Early Unitarians and Universalists called themselves liberal Christians, though at no time were they ever accepted as any kind of Christians by the great majority of orthodox followers of Christ. In recent years growing numbers of us have felt that, whatever our liberal religious movement might be called, the name of Christianity in no way seemed to fit it. Some of us have tried to explain our variety of religion by defining it in broad Christian terms. This attempt has proved unconvincing to other Unitarian Universalists, unacceptable to orthodox Christians and confusing to anyone attempting to describe or to understand . . . our movement.[33]

One writer, emphasizing this "broad Christian" definition of UU, states, "If Unitarian Universalism is the wave of the future, the demise of Christianity is our greatest threat."[34] But the truth remains evident, for, as Brainard F. Gibbons, the president of the Universalist Church of America in 1951, argued, "Indeed, Universalism has disavowed many essential Christian doctrines. What remains that is uniquely Christian?"[35] Many UU writers almost seem to glory in the destruction of biblical faith. "The old temples of faith are being burned down in the fire of testing. From the ashes a new Phoenix shall rise. Unitarian Universalists are eager to share in the birth."[36]

For many UUs the false prophecy of Theodore Parker, a prominent name in UU history, has actually come true, at least personally. For Parker, Christianity was merely "ephemeral—a transitory fly. It will pass off and be forgotten."[37]

The Bible

The UU view of the Bible is that it is an entirely human product, a result of the thinking of fallible and sometimes ignorant men. UU may thus seek to "correct the corruptions that have obscured the moral emphasis presented by Jesus."[38] While most UUs give the Bible at least a small amount of credit for containing some great teachings, many have also expressed animosity toward it. One such person was radical Universalist Abner Kneeland, a good friend of the prominent early Universalist Hosea Ballou. Reminiscent of the late "People's Temple" cult leader, Jim Jones, he would on occasion quote some "objectionable" passage such as sanitary advice about women's menstruation, "and then hurl the book across the auditorium as unfit for reading."[39]

To a significant degree, it has been the discredited results of liberal higher criticism that has provided the rationale for the modern UU rejection of the divine inspiration of the Bible. Disregarding the data refuting such critical conclusions, UU believers continue to endorse these findings as the "reliable conclusions of modern scholarship." For example, we have already noted their hearty acceptance of the false conclusions of the Jesus Seminar, and they support the "documentary hypothesis" of the Pentateuch, even though it has been discredited for over fifty years.[40] (See "The Problem of Liberal Theology," and Appendix 2.)

The pamphlet, "Unitarian Universalist Views of the Bible" (n.d., Gilbert A. Phillips, editor), comprises a number of UU ministers' views, which provides an overall picture of their attitude toward Scripture. At best the Bible is held to be a guide to truth, but not final truth. Other descriptions are not so flattering, for it is "ignorant," "fetters reason," "hinders progress," has cruel morals and presents primitive views of God. Further, it "ought to be buried," is "very human and therefore very imperfect" and is without "much originality, still less ethical superiority." And, incredibly, we are told that in all the Bible, "no one single unified message or purpose or ethical level is to be found here."

Such an approach does not reflect much concern for reason or careful learning, still less for the true content of Scripture. Yet one of these authors declared, "We must take the Bible for what its authors intended"! As we will show, what the authors intended was neither UU "theology" nor distinct UU ideals and philosophy.

God

As far as belief in God is concerned, UU adherents believe anything or nothing: one is free to be atheist, pantheist, polytheist, agnostic, deist, theist or even Satanist. UUs are free to make God into their own image, or any other image. "God" is ultimately whatever a man might wish God to be. "Unitarian Universalists are free to believe about God whatever seems to them to be truest and most meaningful. . . ."[41]

As noted, theologically, most UUs are noncommittal; however, if there is one object in which UU faith is placed and could be said to be universally "worshipped," it is man and his reason. Mendelsohn points out that "for us a chief resource is human reason. Reason holds the place that is ordinarily accorded to revelation in orthodox religions."[42] In essence, human reason, flawed human reason, becomes the judge of divine revelation. Thus Mendelsohn has the cheek to refer blasphemously to the biblical God as a "brutal deity," "a monstrous being" and "demented."[43]

Indeed, UU adherents are willing to believe in almost *any* concept of God as long as it is not the biblical God. For example, William Ellery Channing gives us an example of the early Unitarian reasoning in his May 5, 1819, address, "Unitarian Christianity":

We . . . protest against the irrational and unscriptural doctrine of the Trinity. . . . We are astonished that any man can read the New Testament, and avoid the conviction that the Father alone is God. . . . We complain of the doctrine of the Trinity, that, not satisfied with making God three beings, it makes Jesus Christ two beings, and thus introduces infinite confusion into our conceptions of his character.[44]

Others are astonished that someone as bright as Channing could fail to miss the doctrine of the Trinity in the New Testament (see Doctrinal Appendix).

Briefly noting a number of Unitarian Universalist ministers' views on God will provide us with a flavor of their "theology." Some are "process" theologians.* For Reverend Donald Harrington: "I see God as the great evolutionary process, the up-thrust of life—whatever it is that has brought life into being in the universe. This evolving life, going into ever-higher forms, it is to me the life of God—and God is a process."[45] Considering the philosopher Spinoza as a prototype of many modern UU believers he states that "God is not a capricious personality, absorbed in the private affairs of his devotees, but the invariable sustaining order of the universe . . . a magnificently credible and impersonal God."[46]

For UU theologian and minister Dr. J. L. Adams, God is human interests—"that which ultimately concerns humanity."[47] For many UU members there is clearly a sense of the reality of God or something divine; however, most UUs refuse to acknowledge a personally transcendent God. A consistent UU theme is to view God in an immanent sense, a natural force rather than a supernatural Person, part of the work of Nature as seen in the evolving creation. We will present five views of God by Unitarian Universalist ministers. The recurring theme is of God as process but not Person:

God is not a person who knows us and loves us. He is the power within us and within all life by virtue of which it is possible for man to love. (Harry Meserve)

The term "God" for me, therefore, does not mean a Supreme Being, a Divine Person; it is rather my affirmation that the universe and life have some principle of coherence and rationality. . . . [A hunger] for truth, the benediction of

---

*Various issues (e.g., Vol. 30, no. 4) of the *UU Christian* have discussed Whitehead's process theology. For brief but excellent critiques, see Gundry and Johnson (eds.) *Tensions in Contemporary Theology*, ch. 6; and Lewis and Demarest (eds.), *Challenges to Inerrancy*, ch. 9; or the longer critique by former process theologian, R. G. Gruenler, *The Inexhaustible God* (Baker, 1983).

love and beauty and the moral imperative within. "God" is the term most generally used to name all this. Its meaning changes and grows. (Arthur Foote)

I cannot accept the personhood of God for in the ultimate nature of things I detect no personal agency. . . . I must reject the idea of God as manager. . . . I reject the idea of God as creator. . . . I prefer to use the term God as a symbol of goodness. . . . I believe in a God which is an impersonal process; which is that part of the total process that has operated and continues to operate so as to result in goodness (including ourselves). . . . My God is not all powerful or all wise, my God is only good. (John MacKinnon)

It is the eternal stillness beneath change and the creative energy of the cosmic process. It is the potentiality within all. (Richard Kellaway)

God, for me, is not some hypothetical being, but rather that which enables us to face faithfully those occasions of every day when and where we ought to be faithful, and to face freely every object less than worthy of our unremitting trust, loyalty, devotion—our faith. (George Beach)[48]

These five views of God may be summarized as follows. Respectively, God is defined as:

- the power within life leading to the capacity for love
- meaning in life
- impersonal process operating for good
- impersonal creative energy
- inner hope and confidence.

These allegedly modern and scientific views have replaced the "inadequate," "primitive" and "superstitious" God of Christianity. According to Reverend Robert Storer, the God of the Bible "has been declared inadequate by the universalist churches. For these liberal churchmen, this God has been dead a long time."[49]

Jesus Christ

Unitarian Universalists have almost as many views of Jesus Christ as are imaginable, but most of them see Him as a good man with good teachings, not so different from the good and wise men in all ages. There is one consensus about Christ, however, which seems to find universal UU agreement: He is not a divine, atoning Savior. UU minister Waldeman Argow declares of UUs: "They do not regard him as a supernatural creature, the literal son of God who was miraculously sent to earth as part of an involved plan for the salvation of human souls."[50] In fact, Argow incorrectly maintains that to accept the biblical portrait (which teaches both Jesus Christ's full humanity and undiminished deity), is to make Him irrelevant, for then, supposedly, He is a God that people cannot relate to. Citing Theodore Parker, "[If] as some early Christians began to do, you take a heathen view, and make him a God, the Son of God in a peculiar and exclusive sense—much of the significance of his character is gone. His virtue has no merit; his love no feeling; his cross no burden; his agony no pain. His death is an illusion; his resurrection but a show."[51] Parker, who originally made the previous statement at his May 19, 1841, Boston lecture, actually began the lecture by quoting Luke 21:33, where Jesus said, "Heaven and earth will pass away, but my words will never pass away"! For most UUs today Jesus' words have passed away and have little if any relevance.

Other UUs of religious persuasion may claim to respect and revere Jesus, but it is principally a Jesus of their own making. They discard any teachings or deeds of Jesus that they personally dislike, particularly His miracles. With liberal theologians generally, UU adherents are "much more impressed by and committed to the historical Jesus than by or to the theological Christ."[52] In other words, UUs prefer the "real" nondivine Jesus of history, whom Christianity allegedly distorted in the process of inventing its own ideas about Jesus as a "theological Christ."

At best, for UU people, Jesus is an example of one who had faith in humanity, but He is never the object of faith for humanity (John 3:16) or a revealer of the one true God (John 17:3). From "the babe in the manger legend" to the "symbolism as poetry" of the resurrection, the life of the *biblical* Jesus is rejected and ridiculed. As far back as 1867 (and before), Jesus Christ was being assaulted by Unitarianism. The "Fifty Affirmations of Free Religion" of the Unitarian Free Religious Association (1867) stated in point

34 their desire that "the completion of the religious protest against authority must be the extinction of faith in the Christian Confession," the belief that Jesus was the Messiah.[53]

By accepting the discredited methods and findings of higher criticism and the Jesus Seminar, most UU ministers and laypeople today believe that they can know little if anything about the "real" Jesus. Therefore, they are free to reinvent Him in any form they wish. The average UU person is not interested in the compelling historic evidence for the biblical portrait of Jesus, but only in whatever he or she wants to believe. "I have my own picture of Jesus, a fictional picture of course, but as valid for me as any of the other fictional pictures. It is based on descriptions and narratives in the Gospels and I admit I have taken only those things that I want for my picture and have ignored those things I do not want."[54]

The most influential English Unitarian, James Martineau (1805–1900), stated what has come to be a common UU belief: "The incarnation is true, not of Christ exclusively, but of Man universally."[55] Further, the Person of Jesus is not unique: "I admire the spiritual force and ethical direction of the Nazarene, but he was neither perfect nor infallible. He is not to be worshipped."[56] This same minister declares, "I accept Jesus as my Christ," and he states that he hopes to be "true to his (Jesus Christ's) discipleship."

Ralph Waldo Emerson, the biblical antagonist and leader of the transcendentalist movement, spent two years in the Unitarian ministry. His famous July 15, 1838 "Harvard Divinity School Address" still reflects the views of a majority of modern UU adherents: "Historic Christianity has fallen into the error that corrupts all attempts to communicate religion. . . . It has dwelt, it dwells, with noxious exaggeration about the *person* of Jesus."[57]

UU minister and professor Jack Mendelsohn repeats the long discredited "Paul invented Jesus" theory, for which there was never a shred of evidence. (See Baha'i chapter for a refutation.) "Most of us believe that on the basis of the evidence available to us, Jesus, at most, thought of himself as the Jewish Messiah. It was

later followers and interpreters, like the Apostle Paul, who transformed Jesus into a Christian Savior atoning to God for the sins of mankind." Incredibly, Mendelsohn claims that the deity of Christ and the doctrine of the Trinity were never accepted by Christians until officially formulated at the Nicean council in A.D. 325. "The deity of Jesus thus became the official orthodoxy of Christian religion."[58] This is proven incorrect by looking at numerous early church Fathers who unequivocally defended Christ's deity. (See Doctrinal Appendix.)

Sin, Salvation, the Atonement

The history of Universalism indicates continued disagreement among its members as to what sin is, whether it exists and whether it could or should be punished by God. Some early UU people insisted that the death of Christ made all punishment of sin unnecessary. Most contemporary religious UU people, if they believe in sin and the afterlife at all, think people are punished for sins only while on earth by the natural consequences of their own mistakes. Others may hold to a purgatorial view. Regardless, in UU, salvation (if we may use the term) is not from sin and God's wrath against it, but from whatever human conditions prevent individual self-fulfillment. This may be referred to in political, sexual, economic, environmental, gender, social or global categories. People need to be saved from the harsh realities of an imperfect world, not from an infinitely righteous God whose holiness demands a judgment upon humans that sin. In one sense (presupposing UU views on ethics and good character), salvation can be achieved by improvement in personal character through sincere effort. In 1803 the Universalists adopted the *Winchester Profession*, which became the expression of Universalist doctrine. It used the phrase "salvation by character," which has continued to this day.

The UU view of "salvation," then, means complete trust in one's own resources and ability to save oneself from whatever one does not like, while God's concerns as to the nature and method of salvation are discarded (Galatians 1:6–9; Romans 3:28). Argow argues: "The concept of original sin and the doctrine that human beings have to be saved from the consequences of that sin are utterly foreign to the thinking of religious liberals. . . . 'Salvation by character' as Unitarian Universalists sometimes call it . . . is at once their faith and their aim."[59] Mendelsohn, referring to good works in general, and faith in man in particular, concludes: "This is what we mean when we say we believe in salvation by character. Perhaps it would be more accurate to say, salvation *is* character, for we do not mean that character saves a man from the flames of an imaginary hell or for the bliss of an equally imaginary heaven. We do not profess to know the precise dimensions of immortality."[60] Parker stated a similar theme: "It is not so much by the Christ who lived so blameless and beautiful eighteen centuries ago, that we are saved directly, but by the Christ we form in our hearts and live out in our daily life, that we save ourselves."[61]

Since UU has no absolute standard for right and wrong, "sin" can only be considered in relative terms. People decide for themselves what sin is or is not, or even if sin is real. What is sin to one person may be joy to another. For those UU who do believe in sin, sin is "atoned" for by character and good works. The good works typically involve social and cultural reconstruction: radical education; liberal ideas of criminal justice; animal, abortion, and homosexual rights; and so on. Unfortunately, they seem oblivious to the social and moral destruction that such ideas have wrought upon society.

Since many UU followers are secular humanists and materialists and believe that this life is all there is, such concern with social action, however misguided by UU philosophical premises, is understandable. However, with no clearly defined sense of God's judgment upon sin in the next life, there is obviously little concern with "saving" someone's soul in this one. Clearly, if one does not believe in Jesus' teachings on eternal punishment for those who reject Him (Matthew 25:46; John 8:24), one can hardly express concern for the lost. Mendelsohn asserts his offense at Jesus Christ, saying that the Jesus of the Gospels "is not the hope of the world": "We were suitably alarmed a few years ago when the World Council of Churches met in Evanston to proclaim impertinently that Christ is 'the hope of the world.' Our sense of the fitness of things was disturbed. We know that a theological Christ is not the hope of the world."[62]

UU minister Tom Owen-Towle declares: "A single savior, be it myself or Jesus Christ will not suffice. . . . We UU's don't promise salvation *from* eternal damnation or anything resembling it. . . . Furthermore, we try, but with no guaranteed success, to save our followers from ignorance, mediocrity and despair. And finally you can rest assured, we will absolutely refuse to save anyone from themselves."[63] This is why Mendelsohn declares, "We are not missionary minded."[64] At least, that is, not for biblical concerns.

Some UUs may claim that UU does not actively seek converts, but this is not the case. Many UU people actively proselytize because those who are wise enough to have become enlightened on the subject of free thinking may naturally attempt to convert others from their "darkness." J. N. Booth refers to the UU necessity to "liberate" others "in body and mind," so they can live properly, in accordance with their own inner divinity.[65] According to Mendelsohn, "a new zeal for 'telling our story' has blossomed among us," and "radio and TV are being increasingly used to present liberal religion."[66]

But UUs have no desire whatever for sharing the truth about Christ's death on the Cross for our sins. The following statement by one UU theologian illustrates UU views on the atonement of Christ: "No scapegoat can carry away the sin and punishment. No Savior can carry away the sin and punishment. No Savior can bear the penalty in our place."[67] Thus, "Salvation is universal. People are capable of infinite improvement, liberalism asserts. When we *raise ourselves* onto a higher moral and spiritual plane, through living the exalted precepts of our religion, we are *achieving our own salvation.* By striving we are capable to build in ourselves, through noble works, an increasingly better character."[68]

A leading Unitarian, William Ellery Channing, "the Colossus of American religious liberalism," declared in his May 5, 1819 address that the idea of Christ's atonement was the most pernicious of errors. "We recollect, however, that, not long ago, it was common to hear of Christ as having died to appease God's wrath and to pay the debt of sinners to his inflexible justice . . . [such views are] a very degrading view of God's character. They give to the multitudes the impression, that the death of Jesus produces a change in the mind of God towards man, and that in this its efficacy chiefly consists. No error seems to us more pernicious."[69] Channing asks in all apparent sincerity, "We ask our adversaries then to point to some plain passage where it [Christ's atonement] is taught."[70] How someone like Channing could miss such obvious passages as the following is explainable only by personal bias, not by lack of scriptural testimony: Matthew 26:28; John 1:29; 6:51; Romans 3:25; 5:8–10; 1 Corinthians 15:3; Galatians 1:4; Ephesians 1:7; Colossians 1:14, 20; Hebrews 9:12; 10:10–12; 1 Peter 2:24; 3:18; 1 John 1:7; 2:2; 4:10; Revelation 1:5. Nevertheless, the atonement and collateral doctrines are for Channing "altogether . . . the fictions of theologians."

> Christianity is in no degree responsible for them. We are astonished at their prevalence. What can be plainer, than that God cannot, in any sense, be a sufferer, or bear a penalty in the room of his creatures? . . . How plain is it also, according to this doctrine, that God, instead of being plenteous in forgiveness, never forgives; for it seems absurd to speak of men as forgiven, when their whole punishment, or an equivalent to it, is borne by a substitute? . . . We believe, too, that this system is unfavorable to the character. It naturally leads men to think, that Christ came to change God's mind rather than their own; that the highest object of his mission was to avert punishment, rather than to communicate holiness. . . . For ourselves, we have not so learned Jesus.[71]

Perhaps this was the problem: UU people never learned of the biblical Jesus.

For UU people generally it is apparently too demeaning personally to believe that they or mankind generally should ever need an atoning Savior. "We are never Christians as he was the Christ, until we worship, as Jesus did, with no mediator, with nothing between us and the Father of all."[72] This kind of spiritual pride betrays a pretentiousness and lack of trust in God.

It illustrates why Jesus emphasized, "I tell you the truth, unless you change and become like little children, you will never enter the kingdom of heaven" (Matthew 18:3). "If you do not believe that I am the one I claim to be, you will indeed die in your sins" (John 8:24). (See Doctrinal Appendix for the biblical view of Christ's atonement.)

Man

Rather than affirm faith in God, UU believers affirm a positive and proactive faith in humanity.[73] A person is the child of God or Nature, full of goodness, with divine or evolutionary qualities latent but always emerging into fuller expression. "We assert the goodness of the individual person; we see the individual as the child of God. . . . We see humans standing high on the evolutionary ladder, with great potential for further growth, and even now possessing evidence of the divine."[74] David Parke, discussing Unitarian history, notes, "Unitarianism broke its chains during the nineteenth century. The chain of doctrine, which bound previous generations to the Bible and to Christ, was cast off leaving men free to seek and affirm God within themselves as Reason, Soul and Conscience."[75]

Emerson stated what is a common belief among many UUs today, concerned as they are with social action and justice. "If a man is at heart just, then in so far is he God; the safety of God, the immortality of God, the majesty of God, do enter into that man with justice. . . . The sublime is excited in me by the great stoical doctrine, 'Obey thyself.' That which shows God in me, fortifies me. That which shows God out of me [Christianity], makes me a wart and a wen."[76]

Indeed, prefiguring New Age teaching, Unitarian Universalists believe that we only obey God when we obey ourselves. God has no meaning apart from Man. "For me, the Eucharist is experiencing what Christ experienced: the willingness to pay any price, even death to maintain integrity and to make the claim, 'I am God.'"[77] UU minister Richard Fewkes asserts: "The divinity of Christ points to the divinity in humankind. . . . A difference in degree, perhaps, but not a difference in kind or nature. . . . Perhaps all of us can also learn to respect the same divinity in all people, including ourselves. Christ's declaration, 'I and my Father are one,' becomes the birthright of all humanity."[78]

The Afterlife

For UU followers, human reason and logic provide the tools for judging what may or may not occur after death. Many UUs have attacked the idea of heaven and hell as immoral. This was the view of William Ellery Channing (1780–1842), the leader of New England Unitarianism. Seeming to deny that one can come to love God because of His love and holiness, Hosea Ballou, a contemporary of Channing and—according to UU historian Cassara—"the greatest thinker produced by the Universalist movement," declared that "the preaching of future rewards and punishments, for the purpose of inducing people to love God and moral virtue, is not only useless, but pernicious."[79] However, the Bible teaches that the very reason we love God is because He loved us first (1 John 4:19). In addition, many biblical passages teach that God is going to reward those who love Him far beyond what they can ever imagine, so the preaching of future rewards is also an inducement to love God. Further, preaching divine judgment is clearly an inducement to moral virtue and has been for 2,000 years. Even Jesus taught it! "I tell you, my friends, do not be afraid of those who kill the body and after that can do no more. But I will show you whom to fear: Fear him who, after the killing of the body, has power to throw you into hell. Yes, I tell you, fear him" (Luke 12:4–5). Further, "Our fathers disciplined us for a little while as they thought best; but God disciplines us for our good, that we may share in his holiness" (Hebrews 12:10).

Many UU adherents do not claim to know about the afterlife; however, UU ideas on the subject run the gamut from non-existence to a basically spiritistic worldview. The one thing all UUs seem certain of is that there is no biblical heaven or hell. Reverend Albert Pery declares that UU believers "are confident that they will not be punished in a 'Hereafter' for errors and sins which they may have made; nor do they expect others, even those who disagree with them,

to so suffer."[80] The reason is because, according to "reason" and human sentiment, it is totally "unthinkable for God, as a loving Father, to damn any of his children everlastingly to hell. The Nicene Creed must then be in error."[81]

Waldeman Argow, minister emeritus of the First Unitarian Church in Toledo, Ohio, after discussing the UU diversity of beliefs on immortality, asserts concerning the biblical views that "it seems safe to say that no Unitarian Universalist believes in a resurrection of the body, a literal heaven or hell, or any kind of eternal punishment."[82] Similarly, John Booth declares: "Merely to accept a particular religious doctrine will not change one's eventual fate, or insure eternal bliss; but to live in the spirit of truth and goodness will have its own reward on earth and, whatever may be true of the afterlife, in the future. Most Unitarian Universalists feel certain there is no physical measurable heaven or hell of future existence. . . . [However] concerning the immortality of influence they hold no doubt."[83]

In a 1966 National Opinion Research Center questionnaire, only 10.5 percent of UU people polled stated a belief in personal existence after death, reflecting their rationalist and humanist presuppositions.[84] Today this figure would probably be much larger, a result of the increasing influence of NDE (Near Death Experience) research, parapsychology, the New Age and Eastern religious and occult ideas on UU.[85]

Regardless, the average UU member seems much more concerned with this life than any possible next life. Reflecting evolutionary presuppositions, he believes death is a normal part of life, not something abnormal. Whatever may be the case after death, man secures immortality in the lifestream of humanity, not necessarily in his own continued personal existence. Reverend Tom Owen-Towle, of the First Unitarian Church in San Diego, stated that "death is not only real and natural, but it seems to me to be eminently desirable." Speaking of the "glory of life" and the "majesty of death," he stated that "both forces are holy." (And in a typical caricature of heaven, he said that it was boring, being characterized by a "terrible constancy with no further growth nor change taking place."[86]

Certainly, for the typical UU, death is not the spiritual enemy of mankind that the Bible declares it is (1 Corinthians 15:26). The Reverend Donald Harrington declares that "death is only an incident in life which brings to an end that one small part of the total evolving-life and makes possible the continuing renewal."[87] (For the biblical view of death and the afterlife, see the Doctrinal Appendix.)

The Occult

Due to its humanism and rationalism, the occult does not have a predominant place in the UU worldview. At least not under that name. Still, anyone who wished to pursue occult interests would not necessarily be frowned upon; it is simply up to them. However, the mysticism of religious humanism and parapsychology, the scientific approach to the occult, claiming to scientifically explore the "hidden or divine powers" of man, would be more consistent with the UU worldview, in which spiritual openness and tolerance for all sorts of religious humanism is only a step away from the world of the occult.[88]

The following statement by one UU minister suggests an openness to the occult through subjectivism and a responsiveness to generalized transcendence. "I used to believe in an anthropomorphic god who governed everything, especially me. I shifted to a being of awesome power and purpose but less personal and divested of human trappings. Then I lost any operative concept of deity. I now am open and responsive to signs of transcendence in my life. Where will my wrangling-with-the-god notion take me next?"[89] Other UU followers are more openly New Age, as indicated by the large percentage (46 percent) classifying themselves as humanist (religious as opposed to secular humanism has a strong New Age connection) and over 20 percent classifying themselves as theist, mystic or Buddhist.

CRITIQUE

The Fallacy of Humanism

UU is primarily a humanist faith. As we saw earlier, 46 percent consider themselves humanists with less than 30 percent considering themselves theists generally, Christian or mystics. "The organized humanist movement in America emerged largely within Unitarianism and Universalism. . . . It is no mere chance that there are proportionately more humanists among Unitarians and Universalists than anywhere else."[90] Secular humanism of course is committed to complete faith in the power of man and his reason and logically denies all power to God. Religious humanism adds a vague concept of God but is often New Age, pantheistic or deistic. While many UU people may claim belief in God, for many of them, practically speaking, God is non-existent.

The adoption of secular humanism means God can bring no meaning into their lives. In pointing out that people cannot have emotional health without purpose and meaning in life, Dr. Rollo May discusses one weakness of the humanist position: "for one cannot live on an island of meaning surrounded by an ocean of meaninglessness. If the universe is crazy, the parts of it must be crazy too."[91] Indeed, the relativism of humanism means there are no answers, nor will there ever be answers: "I have no set creed, no anthropomorphic God, no sure salvation, no ultimate answer, but I have plenty of hunches about the reality of things and am betting my life upon those hunches."[92] This is quite a gamble when one man's hunch is no better than another's. Basing one's view of reality on mere hunches that are inherently void of authority is hardly wise in the face of Jesus' warnings about hell. If "there is a way that seems right to man, but in the end it leads to death" (Proverbs 14:12), we need more than hunches. We need that certainty that only the Bible can logically offer.

The truth is that humanism, the religion of faith in mankind, is a destructive and even dangerous faith. In the midst of a world culture saturated with humanism, some perceptive scholars have attacked it. In *The Arrogance of Humanism*, Rutgers University Professor David Ehrenfeld, points out that it is high time the evils inherent to humanism were recognized, as well as the serious daily damage it does. While he acknowledges that there is a benevolent aspect of humanism (humanitarianism, belief in the value and dignity of man and so on), he maintains that humanism today places far too much faith in man. In the name of humanity, he argues that humanism is destroying "everything upon which human survival and happiness depend"—including the family and small communities, our best agriculture, control over energy, the meaning of language and much more, all because of a misguided faith in the supremacy of human reason and power. In fact, "some of humanism's religious assumptions are among the most destructive ideas in common currency, a main source of peril in this most perilous of epochs."[93]

In what must be considered a naive statement at best, we are told that UU members are "without fear that human error can do any irreparable damage to anyone."[94] But who can logically deny that human error is responsible for tens of millions of deaths every year–from famines in socialist economies, to abortion on demand, to prescription drug and surgical errors, just to name a few. Ravi Zacharias' text, *Can Man Live Without God?* (1994), shows the consequences of humanism and related faiths in its all too gruesome detail.

UU people fail to recognize the accuracy of the biblical portrayal of man as morally and spiritually fallen. For anyone with eyes to see, the events of history—particularly of the last century—clearly endorse the biblical view as far more credible than the humanistic view. Even noted agnostic T. H. Huxley once agreed: "The doctrines of . . . original sin, of the innate depravity of man . . . of the primacy of Satan in the world . . . faulty as they are, appear to me to be vastly nearer the truth than the liberal popular illusions that babies are all born good . . . and other optimistic figments."[95]

For the UU, "Humanism is essentially and above all a religion of hope."[96] By contrast, even J. J. Blackham, a director of the British Humanist Association, once stated that "the most drastic objection to humanism is that it is too bad to be true."[97] One reason for this is that faith in man is unjustified and this has been proven historically. When humanists place the totality of their faith in humanity they are placing complete faith in a race of people who are morally and spiritually fallen; that is, fundamentally self-serving and evil. The teachings of the Bible in general and of Jesus Christ in particular supply ample testimony to the fallenness of humanity. As Jesus Himself said, "If you then, though you are evil, know how to give good gifts to your children, how much more will your Father in heaven give the Holy Spirit to those who ask him!" (Luke 11:13).

Trusting selfish people to do what is good and right, rather than trusting in an infinitely good and wise God, can never be logically defended. Scores of topics could be mentioned, but one will suffice. War is clearly one of the most destructive forces in history, yet humans seem to relish it. As this chapter was being finished, over a dozen wars or conflicts large and small were being waged around the world, including the NATO war against the Serbs, India v. Pakistan, Palestinians v. Israelis, various African conflicts (e.g., Rwanda), and the rebel Kurds in Turkey. An analysis from the *Stockton Herald* (California) tells of a survey utilizing a computer. It found that since 3,600 B.C. the world has known only 292 years of peace. In that period, stretching more than 55 centuries, there have been an incredible 14,531 wars in which over 3.6 billion people have been killed.[98] Indeed, we have read from at least two sources that on any given day in the world there are an estimated 30 to 100 conflicts somewhere.

Again, given mankind's track record, on what basis should faith be placed in people instead of God? Human history and daily experience are all the disproof of humanism needed, and this is consistent with the testimony of Scripture:

It is better to take refuge in the LORD than to trust in man. (Psalm 118:8)

Do not put your trust in princes, in mortal men, who cannot save. (Psalm 146:3)

Stop trusting in man, who has but a breath in his nostrils. Of what account is he? (Isaiah 2:22)

This is what the LORD says: "Cursed is the one who trusts in man, who depends on flesh for his strength and whose heart turns away from the LORD." (Jeremiah 17:5)

Speaking of mortal men, when it comes to deciding spiritual issues, one of the most naive placements for faith is in the vagaries of human reason. Unaided human reason can never ascertain what only divine revelation can supply, because only divine revelation is sufficient for discerning absolute truth concerning the most important issues in life: who we are, where we came from, what the purpose of life is, what God is like and what happens when we die. Only God can meet the needs of people because He is their Creator, who designed them to be in a personal relationship to Him. While we would be the last to deny that reason is a precious God-given gift, daily experience tells us it has its limits, humanist beliefs notwithstanding.

Even among UUs, reason typically becomes perverted from its proper function in support of irrational and false UU ideals. UU followers themselves will sometimes admit this. "Our reason makes many mistakes; it is frequently taken captive by our desires, so that we believe things not because they are true but because we want to believe them."[98a] This is true not only among UUs but also in all people's lives generally. So how can reason deserve the apex of anyone's faith? As we have seen, God's views on humanism are explicit. An absolutely key element in humanism is pride in self. But God hates pride (Proverbs 6:17). "The LORD detests all the proud of heart. Be sure of this: They will not go unpunished. . . . Pride goes before destruction, and a haughty spirit before a fall" (Proverbs 16:5,18). "Do you see a man wise in his own eyes? There is more hope for a fool than for him" (Proverbs 26:12).

No form of humanism, including religious humanism, can ever meet the genuine needs of human beings. This is why so many humanists are unhappy or miserable. Humanism proves useless because it neglects the one true God in whom alone human satisfaction, happiness and contentment can be found. Perhaps this is one reason why the Universalists' membership declined radically from 800,000 in 1840 to 50,000 in 1961, precipitating the 1961 merger with the Unitarians. People weren't satisfied. Besides, everything it offered could be found elsewhere—mostly in political causes, entertainment and social clubs. The merger helped, of course, and the recent push for proselytization will un-

doubtedly bring in new members. But like all false religion, UU can never deliver on its promises in the long run.

False religion will fail people on every level because it denies reality. And to live in denial of reality, as many chapters in this work show, is rarely inconsequential (see Romans 1:18–31). When humanism dethrones God and deifies man, it is a denial of reality. Augustine was right, only the true God can satisfy the God shaped void in every person's life. False gods are formless; their religions empty.

So is it surprising that the uncertainty and indefiniteness of UU beliefs generally fosters a corresponding indifference in attitude to religious concerns, or that this could cause problems in people's lives? As if to confirm their lack of interest in religion, the average UU gives only a few cents a week in support of his or her church.[99] This "is the root of our problem; you have noticed how inarticulate many of us are in a social gathering when asked, 'What do Unitarians believe?' Many of us cannot speak for ourselves, much less invite our thoughtful inquiring friends to share our experience in a UU society."[100]

Indeed, the growth of conservative Christian churches has even been noted by UU members to result from unique elements UUs could not offer or logically justify: biblical salvation, absolute moral guidance and meaning in life.[101] Unfortunately, UUs don't get it because they prefer not to, which leads us to our next section.

Hypocrisy and the Self-Refuting Nature of UU Ideals

UU claims that it upholds the ideals of integrity, tolerance, scholarship, reason and support of truth. UUs are "guided by whatever is noble, true and just"; they "support the free and disciplined search for truth as the foundation of religious fellowship"; and "this church insists that intellectual honesty, moral progress and spiritual growth in religion are dependent upon each person being receptive to all pronouncements of truth."[102]

The problem with these fine ideals is that they are undermined by UU prejudices. When UU people speak of upholding "reason," they mean reason employed in the defense of the false presuppositions of rationalism and humanism. When they speak of "moral freedom," they mean freedom to choose one's own morality autonomously, which often results in moral license. When they speak of "intellectual honesty," they mean freedom to believe whatever one wants to believe, regardless of contrary evidence or the cost to society. When they refer to "perversion of truth," it is a perversion of their total faith in humanity.

If UU believers truly encouraged integrity, tolerance, reason and an independent search for the truth, they would not be subject to critics' charges, which even they confess to. Ed Atkinson writes, "Sometimes our beliefs are logical and consistent. Sometimes they are contradictory."[103] UU minister R. N. Helverson admits that UU adherents are "often prejudiced and irrational."[104] For example, they claim that they are "deeply respectful towards the individuality of other persons,"[105] and they extol "the right of every person to make up his own mind about what he believes,"[106] yet they show no respect at all for the individuality of Christians or their beliefs. Reverend Thomas Owen-Towle, who is "suspicious of tombs of theology," is bold to say, "Let the gaps and inconsistencies of my spiritual pilgrimage shine forth."[107] And shine forth they do.

Writing in the *Journal of Christian Apologetics,* theology professor Alan Gomes, points out that the "corrosive effects" of UU ideology "are manifest and legion" in our society. He also discusses the illogical and self-refuting nature of basic UU philosophy, which stresses an alleged claim to freedom, tolerance and pluralism. "Freedom, tolerance, and pluralism truly are the UUs 'triune God' (if by 'God' we mean whatever is most ultimate). For UUs, this is a Trinity than which no greater can be conceived."[108]

This UU "deity," however, is seriously flawed. Gomes points out that as far as their first principal, religious freedom, is concerned, there is more here than meets the eye. Religious freedom is already embraced by almost everyone in America, so why do UUs preach to the choir and proclaim it so adamantly that an outside observer might suspect that we live in a totalitarian society? The reason is because, for UUs,

"religious freedom" *requires* support for religious diversity based on the premise that all truth is relative. Since truth is relative and not absolute, it must change over time. By definition then, no religion can logically claim absolute truth, and equally valid religious truth can be found in all religions. Christianity is made wrong and demonized merely because it claims absolute truth. The evidence for such a claim is never fairly considered, only the truth of UU premises. Citing well-known UU author Philip Hewett, in *The Unitarian Way* (Toronto: Canadian Unitarian Council 1985, p. 89), "No person, no faith, no one book, no one institution has all the answers, nor ever any patent on the way of finding answers." "Another major Unitarian affirmation is a belief in universality, which excludes all exclusivism."[109]

Thus, hidden in the UU concept of "religious freedom" is the expectation and even the requirement that everyone else accept the "truth" concerning UU views of relativism and pluralism. Gomes points out:

It seems to me that UUs confuse their right to believe with the expectation that others must respect the validity and correctness of UU beliefs, particularly their belief in religious pluralism. Though UUs do have a right to believe whatever they want to . . . it does not follow that they have a "right" to demand that non-UUs embrace their beliefs or even take these beliefs seriously. This is particularly true since Unitarian Universalism is fraught with logical and theological difficulties. . . .[110]

Consider the UU attack against religious exclusivism. The truth is that every religion claims to be the truth, therefore every religion is exclusivistic. Further, for UU pluralism to "exclude all exclusiveness," that is, to exclude all exclusivistic positions, is impossible "since the very act of excluding these positions is in itself an act of exclusivism."[111] Their attack on Christian exclusivism is thus nullified as contradictory, illogical and self-refuting:

Furthermore, the UU attack against "religious exclusivism" based on the notion that "truth is not absolute" is offered as absolutely true. This statement refutes itself. Second, if we should not make exclusivistic claims because "truth changes over time" then what if one of the "truths" that "changes over time" turns out to be the "truth" that "truth changes over time"? Or the "truth" that exclusivism is bad and pluralism is good? Are UUs willing to allow that tomorrow's UU "truth" might be that pluralism is no longer good, and that members of the "religious right," who they regard as hateful, narrow-minded, and exclusivistic, are correct after all? Certainly they are not willing to admit any of these things . . . they have in the same breath undermined the foundation for the very pluralism they espouse.[112]

Further, the UU concept of tolerance is flawed because it is self-serving. UU is not unique; it behaves like every other belief system, excluding some beliefs while affirming others. Thus, "UUs are 'free' to believe anything they want, so long as it does not contradict what UUs are allowed to believe! How this differs from other belief systems—including that of the dreaded 'religious right'—is difficult to see."[113]

In other words, UUs are not quite so tolerant as they would have us believe. Their tolerance is limited to that which doesn't offend them. On the one hand, they proudly assert, "We are tolerant of all beliefs," and that UUs are free to believe whatever they wish. But they simultaneously stress UUs are *not* free to believe anything they wish. For instance, the fact that UU Elizabeth May Strong felt it important to write *Can I Believe Anything I Want?* is to the point. She concludes, "Unitarian Universalism is not the freedom to believe anything or nothing."[114] One's beliefs then, must stay within the confines of, forgive the term, "acceptable dogma."

The truth is that UU followers are especially intolerant of religious exclusivism, in particular Christianity, labeling it hateful, divisive and narrow. In the words of James Luther Adams, "It [Unitarianism] protests against the idolatry of any human claim to absolute truth or authority."[115] But UUs are just as 1) hateful, 2) divisive and 3) narrow for 1) attacking absolute truth claims unmercifully, 2) describing believers in absolute truth with such negative terms and then excluding them from the community of the

tolerant, and 3) proscribing all belief in absolute truth and ruling it void by mere preference. Really on what basis, other than personal subjective preference, are some beliefs excluded and others accepted?

Regardless, if it is arrogant and intolerant to believe one is right and others wrong, UUs are just as arrogant and intolerant as they believe Christians to be, since they believe that they are right and Christianity is wrong. "Arrogance" is not the issue with exclusive truth claims, only whether those claims are true. When Christ claimed that He was the only way to God, this is either true or false. If it is true, when Christians affirm it they are telling the truth. If it is not true, Christians, as Gomes points out, are guilty of having been deceived, but hardly of arrogance. If Jesus' claims are true, then UUs are condemning themselves and being exclusivistic:

for excluding the possibility that what Jesus revealed about himself is true. . . . They do not even consider the possibility that this revelation might be true. So much for being 'open to every revelation,' contrary to the admission of past president Schultz, cited earlier.[116]

Contrary to the UU assertion that conservative Christians are hateful, divisive and narrow because they believe that those who reject Christ—including UUs—will be damned, Christians are actually 'inclusive' in the sense that they want all people to join them as part of God's family. That is, true, biblical Christians are inclusivistic because they desire all people to be saved, even though they are not pluralistic about the way in which one must be saved. If evangelical Christians genuinely were divisive and narrow, as UU writers say, they would ignore UUs and other unbelievers, rejoicing in their sure damnation apart from Christ.[117]

Indeed, the vast majority of John Weldon's 75 books have the gospel and/or sinner's prayer within their pages. Concern for the salvation of all people is a biblical mandate[118] because the evidence for an eternal hell is no less persuasive than that for Christ's resurrection.[119]

UU does not even have a logical basis for its cherished social programs. Christianity, which UU condemns as hateful and divisive, has done far more for the world than UU ever will. Indeed, the social benefits alone that Christianity has given the world are in almost infinite excess to those of UU. (See for example D. James Kennedy, *What If Jesus Had Never Been Born?*) Christian social action is powerful and permanent because it does have a logical, objective basis for condemning many of the same social evils UU does—racism, hatred, violence and so on. However, because UUs teach (as an absolute truth) that all truth is relative, it's moral condemnation is powerless in that it can only be based upon an individual subjective preference. As Gomes points out, there is a great difference between being able to objectively declare something morally wrong and merely personally finding something reprehensible.

Further, UU has to admit that the very ideals it now cherishes as absolutes—even though absolutes do not exist—may one day be rejected by UU on the basis of expediency. Certainly, one could envision a time when its current "tolerance" of Christianity would, given the proper social climate, succumb to hated persecution. Because UU ideals are not based in absolutes, they are permanently subject to the vagaries of social convention or "political correctness." But politically correct views are only infrequently life-affirming; to the contrary, they are often repressive "politically correct death," whether it results from abortion, sexual license or religious persecution, it is in no one's—least of all society's—best interests.

In essence, "one of the best techniques for dealing with the foundational UU errors is to apply their own statements to themselves. Unitarian Universalism is a self-destructive belief system, and this is best shown by advocating it with a thoroughgoing consistency that UUs themselves are unwilling or unable to apply."[120]

Although UU leaders have stated that "happiness is a by-product of having some understanding of the meaning of life,"[121] they reject the only basis for such meaning: knowing the absolute truth that a holy, loving, immutable and infinite-personal God loves us and has revealed Himself to us. The endless speculation in UU only leaves them admitting: "Indeed, sometimes we cannot even agree on what are the most important questions."[122] The reason is evident. Their "faith" is as mercurial as their religion, because "as one's experiences and ideas change, so may one's faith."[123] Faith in God in one era, faith in man in another, perhaps faith in the devil later. Even though William Channing was once "the colossus of American religious liberalism," "many of his views are no longer central" to modern UU concerns.[124] What of "vital" UU beliefs and hopes in the present: are they also to be crushed on the rocks of time? Then of what value were they? Clearly UU has no consistent philosophy, no lasting faith, no answers, no hope to give us. It has no meaning, it offers no eternal life. This is the joy of liberal religion.

In light of the foregoing discussion, one might note some of the conclusions and recommendations of the 1975 General Assembly of the Unitarian Universalist Association's "Commission on Priorities for Unitarian Universalist Advance." We can perhaps understand why their first declaration was the unsurprising conclusion that: "Unitarian Universalists must be doing something wrong, or must not be doing something they should be doing, because after a period of phenomenal growth and extraordinary promise, the movement is declining in both adult and church school membership, financial support and morals in general."[125]

Also, an inter-house poll among UU leaders determined that most believed top priority had to be given to determining just *what* UU does believe! Hence:

Top priority must be given now to the clarification and elaboration of Unitarian Universalist philosophy, goals, and beliefs. Until we know not only how but what we stand for as an identifiable group, we shall not be able to hold our old members or to attract and satisfy new members. Nor shall we know how to educate our children in our schools, develop religious education curriculum and directors, guide our fellowships or develop programs. Nor shall we know how to educate and choose our ministers. Nor shall we have any significant impact upon this frightened age.[126]

But in the subsequent two decades, more UU committees only ran into similar problems.

Until they recognize that the real problem is their most cherished ideal, humanism, little will change. It will always be true that the "urge to save the world [socially] has cost many denominations dearly, and especially the Unitarian-Universalist Association."[127]

The Problem of Liberal Theology, Higher Criticism and the Jesus Seminar

As we have seen, as far as the Bible and Christianity are concerned, Unitarian Universalism holds to liberal assumptions generally, and as far as Jesus is concerned, it holds to Jesus Seminar (JS) conclusions in particular. For reasons that will soon become evident, we can only urge UUs to more carefully consider these things. The following material (to the next section) excerpts slightly revised sections from our book *The Facts on False Views of Jesus: The Truth Behind the Jesus Seminar* to illustrate the problems of unqualified rationalistic approaches to the Bible. The book may be consulted for further information and documentation.

There is little denying the fact that once trust in the Bible as an authoritative revelation is undermined, its teachings will either be doubted or, especially if the teachings are unpopular, considered irrelevant or worse. Yet we don't think that most Christians, and especially the average American, have any idea of the great weight of blame that can be laid at the feet of liberal theology and higher criticism, generally, for destroying America's faith in the Bible, or the terrible consequences, socially, morally and spiritually that have flowed from it.

The liberal approach to the Bible is illustrated by citing the "findings" of the so-called Jesus Seminar, an extensive endeavor of 74 liberal scholars to determine what Jesus "really" said. Many books have been written by liberal theologians in the search for the "historical Jesus," the alleged enigmatic "real" Jesus of history as opposed to the so-called "Christ of faith" that Christians believe in and is found in the Bible. In recent years, this has resulted in dozens of books being written by liberal and non-evangelical theologians rejecting or attacking the very foundation of the Christian faith itself: the biblical Jesus Christ. Among these

books are John Dominic Crossan's *Jesus: A Revolutionary Biography; The Historical Jesus: The Life of a Mediterranean Jewish Peasant* and *Who Killed Jesus?;* Burton Mack's *Who Wrote the New Testament: The Making of the Christian Myth; A Myth of Innocence: Mark and Christian Origins* and *The Lost Gospel: The Book of Q and Christian Origins;* Marcus Borg's *Meeting Jesus Again for the First Time;* Robert Funk's *Honest to Jesus;* and a book published by the "Jesus Seminar," *The Five Gospels: The Search for the Authentic Words of Jesus.*[128]

In recent liberal theology texts, Jesus has been portrayed in diverse and surprising ways—as a Jewish holy man, an occult magician and mystic, a personification of a psychedelic mushroom cult, a homosexual, a twice married divorcee with three kids, a wicked priest, a social cynic, a political revolutionary and more. Unfortunately, these scholars seem more concerned to write about a Jesus whom they are personally comfortable with rather than about the Jesus found in the four Gospels. Luke Timothy Johnson, a Roman Catholic scholar who is critical of the Jesus Seminar, comments quite correctly, "People have no idea how fraudulent people who claim to be scholars can be." Citing another problem, "Americans generally have an abysmal level of knowledge of the Bible. In this world of mass ignorance, to have headlines proclaim that this or that fact about [Jesus] has been declared untrue by supposedly scientific inquiry has the effect of gospel. There is no basis on which most people can counter these authoritative-sounding statements."[129]

We would argue that when it comes to their basic worldview and critical methods, the conclusions of liberal theologians should not be trusted. To illustrate, liberals assume, *apriori*, that the Gospel writers were so overladen with "Christianizing" myths and propaganda that their writings are useless for determining who Jesus really was and, therefore, are essentially valueless as accurate historical documents. If what these scholars say is true, Christianity is not just a false religion, it is a worthless religion and a fraud. One may be tempted to think that such a conclusion is perhaps the aim of the work of many of these scholars. After all, one might wonder why these scholars spend so much of their time and effort attempting to *disprove* what is so obviously a falsehood to begin with. Perhaps they suspect that the Gospels' portrayal of Jesus might really be true after all, but they want to convince themselves otherwise, like the TV narrator who said, "Perhaps the most fearful thing about the Christian hell is that it might be true."[130]

It doesn't take much reading to determine from the New Testament accounts that Jesus claimed to be God and that He said His words would never pass away. Nor does it take a Nobel Prize winner or a Ph.D. from Harvard to ascertain that the New Testament documents are historically accurate and that Jesus rose physically from the dead. What *is* noteworthy is the tremendous amount of legitimate scholarship that some liberal theologians and scholars will disregard in order to maintain their own unestablished biases.

As to knowledge of New Testament reliability, the informed Christian layperson is actually better educated than these scholars, whose skeptical assumptions leave them speaking nonsense or in a hopeless muddle, uncertain what to believe. As one commentator noted, "If a vote were taken on the usefulness of the Jesus Seminar, is there any doubt what the outcome would be?"[131] And because these scholars will not keep their destructive views to themselves, they persuade others not to trust in the biblical picture of Jesus.[132] And they are becoming quite successful. Their "new view of Christ that denies His supremacy is gaining followers all over the world. . . ."[133] This is one reason the Jesus Seminar releases its "findings" just before Easter and Christmas. This is a calculated attempt to target the public at the best possible time to secure maximum exposure for their prejudiced views.

Another problem is that members of the JS fail to recognize that it is the conservative view of Scripture that "passes the rigorous tests of the rules of evidence," not their historical distortions. This has been established by a great weight of evangelical and nonevangelical scholarship. One will find clear and unambiguous refutation of what the liberals are doing, as well

as objective scholarly defenses of New Testament Christianity, in evangelical scholarship such as: the six volume *Gospel Perspectives* (Sheffield, JSOT Press, 1986), a ten year project by an international team of scholars, or N. T. Wright's five volume, *Christian Origins and the Question of God,* or critiques of the JS like Michael Wilkins' and J. P. Moreland's, eds., *Jesus Under Fire,* and Gregory Boyd's *Cynic, Sage or Son of God?*

This is not merely academic debating. Consider the tragic event relayed by William Lane Craig in *The Son Rises.* He recalls the incident of a retired pastor "who in his spare time began to study the thought of certain modern theologians" who denied Jesus' resurrection. This pastor believed that their great learning was superior to his own and concluded that their views must be correct. "He understood clearly what that meant for him: his whole life and ministry had been based on a bundle of lies. He committed suicide." Dr. Craig comments, correctly, "I believe that modern theologians must answer to God for that man's death. One cannot make statements on such matters without accepting part of the responsibility for the consequences."[134] Indeed, in the words of Wilkins and Moreland, "We are not overstating it when we say that these are life and death issues. . . . If Jesus is who he claimed to be and who his followers declare him to be, then we are not dealing simply with academic questions. We are instead dealing with the most important questions of the modern person's daily life and eternal destiny."[135]

What liberal theologians have never dealt with successfully are the philosophical and methodological flaws in their scholarship that are either false or refute their own conclusions. One of the dominant premises of the JS is a philosophical naturalism or scientism that by definition supports its critical agenda. For instance, this scientism can be seen in *The Five Gospels* in its claim, "The Christ creed and dogma . . . can no longer command the assent of those who have seen the heavens through Galileo's telescope. The old deities and demons were swept from the skies. . . . [Science has] dismantled the mythological abodes of the gods and

Satan, and bequeathed us secular heavens."[136] But scientism itself has long been discredited:

> It is well past time to rest content with the politically correct, unjustified assertions of scientism and philosophical naturalism. University libraries are filled with books that show the weaknesses of these views, and the fellows of the Jesus Seminar show virtually no indication that they have so much as interacted with the arguments they contain, much less have they refuted their claims.[137]

Another false assumption of the Jesus Seminar includes the belief that the Christian authors of the Gospels can't be trusted simply *because* they were Christians. This is silly. Does anyone fault the research findings of medical doctors *simply because* they are physicians? Further examples of the JS methodological flaws are seen in the theologians' use of their many "rules and evidence" and "criteria of authenticity" standards, which they employ to allegedly separate out the "real" teachings of Jesus.[138] For example, "The Jesus Seminar formulated and adopted 'rules of evidence' to guide its assessment of gospel traditions. Rules of evidence are standards by which evidence is presented and evaluated in court."[139] But the JS claim to impartiality and use of legal standards of evidence is highly misleading. The truth is that their "rules" are frequently irrelevant or incorporate their own biases against the text so that *applying* the rules only proves the critical conclusions the theologians already held. For example, their "context rule" assumes without justification that the Gospel writers "*invent[ed]* new narrative contexts" for the sayings of Jesus,[140] and their "commentary rule" assumes without justification that the Gospel writers revised Jesus' sayings to conform to their own particularist views.[141] Further, their "false attribution rule" assumes without justification that "the evangelists frequently attribute their own statements to Jesus."[142] And on it goes. In other words, their own "rules of evidence" assume—without justification—that the Gospels as we have them are inventions and myths.

The real issue has nothing to do with the objective and judicial application of rules of evidence, for these *disprove* JS claims and *establish* the Bible, as Dr. John Warwick Montgomery and others have shown.[143] The real issue for the JS is simply to be rid of the biblical Jesus. The JS scholars also violate their own stated safeguard, which they claim "all responsible scholars" practice: "The last temptation is to create Jesus in our own image, to martial the facts to support preconceived convictions. This fatal pitfall has prompted the Jesus Seminar to adopt as its final general rule of evidence: BEWARE OF FINDING A JESUS ENTIRELY CONGENIAL TO YOU."[144] Yet the very next sentence reads: "Eighty-two percent of the words ascribed to Jesus in the gospels were not actually spoken by him . . ."[145]

When liberal theologians condescendingly disparage conservative Christians as "far right fundamentalists," "latter-day inquisitors" and "witch-hunters" and then claim, "Their reading of who Jesus was rests on the shifting sands of their own theological constructions," one can only stand in wonder at the hubris.[146] One reads with further astonishment, "The evidence provided by the written gospels is hearsay evidence. Hearsay evidence is secondhand evidence . . . none of them [the Gospel authors] was an ear or eyewitness of the words and events he records."[147] In the face of this "scholarship," New Testament writers frequently claim to be ear and eyewitnesses: "That which . . . we have heard, which we have seen with our eyes, which we have looked at and our hands have touched—this we proclaim. . . . We proclaim to you what we have seen and heard . . ." (1 John 1:1,3; see Luke 1:2; 24:48; John 3:11; 19:35; 21:24; Acts 2:32; 3:15; 5:32; 10:39; 26:26; 1 Peter 5:1; 1 John 4:14).

The sad fact is that the scholars of the JS care little for objective historical inquiry or truth. If they did, they could never make such a statement as just quoted. The "Dictionary of Terms" concluding *The Five Gospels* defines "critical" [scholarship] as "to exercise careful, considered judgment."[148] This is something JS members have failed to do. After all, why this unwavering bias against the writings of nine men who have, for 2,000 years, been proven to be honest historical reporters? Has even a single argument against their accuracy withstood the test of time? No. In the Gospels we have four accounts, two of which (Matthew and John) were written firsthand by eyewitnesses who spent three years with Jesus and knew Him intimately. The other two, Mark and Luke, received their information from the Apostles (Peter and Paul respectively). They all wrote with great care and an unassailable integrity.

These four accounts have been subjected to the most vigorous criticism for 2,000 years by some of the world's best and most critical scholars who have yet to make a case. As the late noted biblical scholar F. F. Bruce remarks, "There is, I imagine, no body of literature in the world that has been exposed to the stringent analytical study that the four gospels have sustained for the past 200 years. This is not something to be regretted; it is something to be accepted with satisfaction. Scholars today who treat the gospels as credible historical documents do so in the full light of analytical study, not by closing their minds to it."[149] What more could the Christian ask for? What more does the critic want? Dr. Gregory A. Boyd (Yale University Divinity School; Ph.D. Princeton Theological Seminary) correctly points out, "The most compelling argument against any revisionist account of the historical Jesus is not the exposition of its internal weaknesses, as crucial as that is. It is, rather, the *positive* evidence for the reliability of the New Testament's portrait of Christ."[150]

Here is the New Testament portrait of Christ: "I am the light of the world. Whoever follows me will never walk in darkness, but will have the light of life" (John 8:12). "I am the resurrection and the life. He who believes in me will live, even though he dies. . . ." (John 11:25). "I am the way and the truth and the life. No one comes to the Father except through Me" (John 14:6).

Jesus commanded people to love Him in the same way that they love God—with all their heart, soul and mind (Matthew 22:37). Jesus said that God the Holy Spirit would bear witness of Him and glorify Him (John 16:13–14). Jesus said that to know Him was to know God (John 14:7). To receive Him was to receive God (Matthew 10:40). To honor Him was to honor God (John 5:23). To believe in Him was to believe in God (John 12:44–45; 14:1). To see Him was to see God (John 8:19; 14:7). To deny Him was to deny God (1 John 2:23). To hate Him was to hate God (John 15:23).

All these statements, and many more like them, leave us little choice. Either Jesus was who He said He was—God incarnate—or else He was a liar or crazy. But who can believe that?

In time, the research of the Jesus Seminar and all liberal critical biblical "scholarship" will be relegated to the "circular files" of rationalistic, historical skepticism for the simple reason they "evince a prejudice against the New Testament documents that can only be described as historically irresponsible."[151] Crossan himself thinks that in the end, "There could be hopeless disagreement."[152]

What other conclusion might one expect? It is logically impossible to believe the basic assumption of any criticism which, in effect, attributes to a first-century, scattered Christian community the kind of creative power to invent the Jesus Christ of the New Testament. As many have persuasively argued, this is either unbelievable, absurd or both.[153]

Indeed, the more we carefully examine negative criticism generally, the more difficult it is to accept its conclusions. It is nonsense to really believe that most or all of the teachings of Jesus in the New Testament were only myths concocted from the inventive imagination of early Christian believers and that they were then uncritically accepted by other Christian people everywhere—even though these stories were all easily discerned hoaxes. Early Christians could check out the details of the Gospels by talking to those who were eyewitnesses of Jesus' ministry. If what the critics say *were* true, there never would have been a Christianity to begin.

In the end, our only options are to believe in the foolishness of a critical methodology that invents myths or in the soundness of conservative biblical scholarship that has established its methods and conclusions. When Unitarian Universalism looks to the findings of the Jesus Seminar and higher critical methodologies to sustain its views, it is, sadly, only illustrating its own lack of concern with reason, logic and truth.

Moral Concerns

Despite the UU claim to support moral and social progress, their relativism undermines it. Rather than accept a social program based in absolute morality from God, they place absolute authority in the wisdom of their own liberal and radical social programs. Many UUs "deny the immaculate conception of virtue and affirm the necessity of social incarnation."[154] By "placing the measure of right and wrong, of true and false, external to the Bible, in moral conscience and reason,"[155] they have subjected moral verity to personal preference.

It is clearly not true that "that person is likely to behave best who exercises reason most,"[156] for history and contemporary culture are replete with well reasoned support for numerous evils and barbarisms, from adultery, divorce and homosexuality, to abortion, assisted suicide and human sacrifice. If relativism is absolute, reason can only respond, "Do whatever you want." In Unitarian Universalism, and throughout American culture today, reason justifies all sorts of vices and evils, especially hedonism through sex and drugs. Ethical validity in reason all depends on whether reason itself has the support of moral absolutes. If not, reason can justify any vice.

In the sexual area in particular, "reason" has conveniently concluded that no absolutes are necessary.[157] Reason argues especially that the Christian sex ethic is "inadequate," even "perverse." From the Playboy philosophy to Planned Parenthood to pornography to pedophilia, every sexual liberty or perversion has its well-reasoned justification. Fornication, adultery, homosexuality, abortion and pedophilia (see NAMBLA, the North American Man-Boy Love Association) are equally permitted.

Who can logically or compassionately continue to promote such things given the facts of the matter? First, worldwide, literally tens of millions of people (children included!) have been crippled or died from dozens of sexually transmitted diseases.[158] (Worldwide AIDS alone could kill 250,000,000 men, women and children; currently 35 to 45 million are infected.) Second, tens of millions of marriages have been destroyed by "sexual freedom," the consequential radical feminism, liberal divorce laws and

so on. Besides the personal cost to parents, this has also brought moderate to severe dysfunction to millions of children, which society also pays for in numerous ways. Third, the "homosexual lifestyle" is proven beyond doubt to be morally, socially and financially consequential, indeed destructive, to the larger society.[159] Fourth, a trillion dollar pornography industry has destroyed countless marriages and ruined innumerable lives, including children and teenagers. Reasoned support for all this constitutes the height of social irresponsibility and moral degeneracy. (For documentation see our *The Myth of Safe Sex* (Moody, 1993); *The Facts on Homosexuality* (1994); *The Facts on Sex Education* (1993); and *The Facts on Abortion* (1995). UUs however would rather see most such things *defended* from the pulpits. For example, in deference to "freedom of conscience," a UUA president, Eugene Pickett, spoke at the ordination of homosexual minister, Reverend Robert Wheatley, declaring "that it makes no sense to suggest that sexual orientation has any bearing on the condition of one's soul," noting that such ordination was "consistent with, indeed demanded by, my Unitarian Universalist faith." Wheatley was the Director for the UUA Office of Gay Concerns, as well as Associate UUA Director for Social Responsibility.[160]

TALKING WITH MEMBERS

Even though most UU people seem to have an irrational and unjustified bias against Christianity, some might be open to a balanced presentation of Christian truth claims and a reasoned apologetic for faith. For any UU who truly values the ideals of tolerance, openness to all religious convictions, a search for truth and individual freedom, it could hardly be otherwise. Unfortunately, UU ideals are often held in biased fashion. But the very claim to honor such ideals can be pressed to advantage. No UU could easily stomach being properly charged with intolerance, closed-mindedness and bigotry. So how can any UU logically reject a frank evidential discussion of things like religious truth claims, absolute moral values, biblical reliability or the uniqueness and resurrection of Jesus Christ?

Discussion with a UU might begin with the question of the historical reliability and authority of the Bible. As far as sound biblical scholarship is concerned, the integrity and trustworthiness of the biblical text is established.[161] (See Appendix 2.) If the text is uncorrupted, and if what its authors wrote is true, then the Christian view of Christ is the only possible one because no facts anywhere suggest otherwise. Indeed, the truth of Christianity is shown historically by the resurrection of Christ, which proved His claims. UU members may reject Jesus' words, but they cannot logically maintain that He never spoke them or deny His unique deity and universal authority. In all history, who ever made His claims, did His miracles, spoke His teachings? Who else in history ever returned from the dead, let alone was seen alive after death by over 500 people at one time (1 Corinthians 15:6)? It was this same Jesus who stated that the spiritually blessed were "those who hear the word of God and obey it" (Luke 11:28), and that "Man does not live on bread alone, but every word that comes from the mouth of God" (Matthew 4:4).

UUs, however, do not acknowledge the revelation of the biblical God: instead, they "depend on life's unmerited favors," which is their idea of grace.[162] Yet, who gave us these favors? Their view of God is that "this personified God has been declared inadequate by the Unitarian Universalist churches."[163] One can but marvel at the power of a declaration. This rejection of God stands even though UU leaders admit "our constant dependence on forces beyond ourselves."[164] If UUs are really open and tolerant, why such a bias against the God of Scripture? Can they reason this out? As we have seen, the truth is that Unitarian Universalist philosophy is illogical and self-contradictory. It is the Christian philosophy that is established as reasonable. So how can UUs, who pride themselves on rationality and openness, refrain from seriously considering the Person of Jesus?

Biblical teaching is clear that those who reject God's love and mercy in Christ cannot expect to inherit eternal life. Instead, they will separate themselves from God forever. Biblical authority is logically undeniable, and the claims of Christ on everyone's life is unassailable. Can UUs reasonably deny the truth?

For God so loved the world that he gave his one and only Son, that whoever believes in him shall not perish but have eternal life. For God did not send his Son into the world to condemn the world, but to save the world through him. Whoever believes in him is not condemned, but whoever does not believe stands condemned already because he has not believed in the name of God's one and only Son. (John 3:16–18)

As for the person who hears my words but does not keep them, I do not judge him. For I did not come to judge the world, but to save it. There is a judge for the one who rejects me and does not accept my words; that very word which I spoke will condemn him at the last day. (John 12:47–48)

This is how God showed his love among us: He sent his one and only Son into the world that we might live through him. This is love: not that we loved God, but that he loved us and sent his Son as an atoning sacrifice for our sins. (1 John 4:9–10)

We accept man's testimony, but God's testimony is greater because it is the testimony of God, which he has given about his Son. Anyone who believes in the Son of God has this testimony in his heart. Anyone who does not believe God has made him out to be a liar, because he has not believed the testimony God has given about his Son. And this is the testimony: God has given us eternal life, and this life is in his Son. He who has the Son has life; he who does not have the Son of God does not have life. (1 John 5:9–12)

If the Gospels do not contain the Word of Christ, then we have none. UUs who desire to openly consider the words of Jesus may be surprised that their own religion offers some support. In the Constitution of the American Unitarian Association (1825), point 2 states, "The objects of this Association shall be to diffuse the knowledge and promote the interests of pure Christianity throughout the Country."[165] Channing declared, "Jesus is the only master of Christians, and whatever he taught, either during his personal ministry, or by his inspired apostles, we regard as of divine authority, and profess to make the rule of our lives."[166] For Parker, "the

Word of Jesus was real Christianity."[167] Today, UU leaders make the following claims:

It is the religion of Jesus and other notable exemplars of a history, not theological attitudes toward them that will save men and women.[168]

UU's make "Jesus teachings, rather than a conception of his nature, central to their worship."[169]

UU's "join a church as an expression of their faith in religious ideals which Jesus proclaimed and may describe themselves as followers of him."[170]

They "prize the teachings of Jesus rather than the theological ideas about Jesus," and "they appreciate the Biblical text"; "be ye doers of the word, and not hearers only."[171]

The CLF Directed Reading Course states that they "love the person and message of Jesus of Nazareth," and they say, "Christianity should be a religion which seeks to put into practice the ethical principles taught by Jesus, and the Hebrew Prophets, and this we try to do."[172]

For Jesus, the two greatest ethical commandments were to love God with all one's heart, mind, soul and body (which demands love for His word) and to love one's neighbor as oneself (which requires one to express Jesus' own concern for people's salvation). One must ask, "How do the foregoing claims of 'accepting Jesus' teachings square with UU beliefs? And is this hypocrisy?"

UUs may criticize Christians for "dogmatism," and for producing "their" version of truth; however, UU people are just as dogmatic in their view of the "truth," so how can we determine who is right if not on the basis of logic, reason and the historical evidence? If they are really "open to all presentations of the truth," UU followers cannot escape their own *personal* commitment to consider Christian truth. With Pilate, they may ask themselves, "What is Truth?" Hopefully, they will seriously consider the words of Jesus, investigate their credibility and act accordingly. "For this reason I was born, and for this I came into the world, to testify to the truth. Everyone on the side of truth listens to me" (John 18:37).

For a more detailed discussion and suggestions for sharing the true gospel, see our book *Ready with an Answer.*

APPENDIX 1:
THE UNITARIAN UNIVERSALIST CHRISTIAN FELLOWSHIP

The Unitarian Universalist Christian Fellowship (UUCF) was organized in the 1940s to promote liberal Christianity. Members are "United by our belief that one can be both a Unitarian Universalist and a Christian."[173] If our preceding analysis has shown anything, this is impossible. An examination of UUCF literature reveals a constant rejection of Christianity because the UUCF "refuses to endorse as final and sufficient any particular creed of the historical Church."[174] Alan Gomes writes, "Just as, according to UU Philip Hewett, 'It is nonsense for critics to say that one can believe whatever one likes and still be a Unitarian,' even so it is nonsense for [other UUs] to say that a person can disbelieve the core doctrines of Christianity and still call him or herself a Christian."[175]

How then can UUCF be considered Christian by anyone? Former UUCF executive director R. M. Mazur illustrates UUCF beliefs when he declares, "There is a vast difference between taking Jesus literally and taking him seriously. For we do not know him best through the literal words attributed to him in the New Testament."[176] But the literal words attributed to Jesus are the actual words He spoke (see Appendix 2). How then can UUCF members be *followers* of Christ? As the following Appendix proves, we do know Him best (indeed, only) through the literal words of the New Testament. It is just as impossible to take Jesus seriously without taking him literally as it is for UU to reject Christian doctrine and call itself Christian. Further, Mazur states that the beliefs of Jesus "seem irrelevant to modern religious concerns." In fact, they are by far the most relevant to all religious concerns. The teachings of Jesus have so profoundly affected the course of world history for good that without them UUs would probably not even be here to argue the question. (See D. James Kennedy, *What If Jesus Had Never Been Born?*)

We can only ask once more, how does the UUCF believe "seriously" in Jesus? Mazur says UU Christians "must conscientiously decline to become members in any movement which requests assent to dogma." UU dogma aside, in the very same pamphlet, he speaks of "taking Christ seriously" and of worshipping God "in spirit and in truth"! Apart from biblical Christianity, how does he do this with any authoritative standard?

It is not difficult to argue that the intellectual schizophrenia and spiritual vacuum of humanism and liberal Christianity can never satisfy in the long run. "Liberal" chemists do not reinterpret the periodic table. "Liberal" mathematicians do not redefine mathematical theorems. To do so would be folly and lead to confusion. Christianity has a core of undeniable teachings, or "laws," that are as central to its nature and function as the periodic table is to chemistry or theorems are to mathematics. To deny the doctrines of Christianity while retaining the title "Christian" only leads to confusion. This is worse than folly; it is morally unconscionable and even inconsistent with the ideals of Unitarian Universalism.

APPENDIX 2:
THE HISTORIC RELIABILITY OF THE NEW TESTAMENT TEXT*

Christians and skeptical nonChristians have different views concerning the credibility of the Gospels and the rest of the New Testament. For the Christian at least, nothing is more vital than the words of Jesus Himself, who promised, "Heaven and earth will pass away, but my words will never pass away" (Matthew 24:35). This is a promise of no small import. If His words were not accurately recorded in the Gospels, how can anyone know what He really taught? The truth is, we couldn't know. Further, if the remainder of the New Testament cannot be established to be historically reliable, then little if anything can be known about what true Christianity really is, teaches or means.

Who is right in this debate, the Christians who claim that the New Testament is historically accurate or the critics of the New Testament who claim otherwise? The latter group like UUs and the Jesus Seminar authors, usually approach the Bible from a thoroughgoing rationalistic materialistic viewpoint, discounting the Bible's supernatural elements, employing higher critical methods and maintaining that it wasn't even written until the late first or early second century.

The Critical View

The skeptics' argument, usually based on the use of higher critical methods such as source, form and redaction criticism, is often given as follows: by a number of criteria the reliability of the New Testament text may be reasonably doubted. This includes a number of features, such as its dominant "mythological" supernatural) character; the "findings" of the "criteria of dissimilarity" of tradition criticism and of higher criticism in general such as the probability of textual corruption through either the early church (oral tradition, source or form criticism) or a later editor or redactor (redaction criticism); the fabrication of a fictitious view of Jesus on the basis of erroneous Messianic expectation; the hundreds of thousands of variants in extant texts; the dubious theological embellishments of the Apostle Paul, such as in his view of salvation through Jesus Christ; and the invention of most of the teachings of Christ to suit the spiritual or other needs of the early church, or even the removal of the actual teachings of Christ in later church councils for the purpose of political expediency or theological bias. The Jesus Seminar, for example, widely employs the "dissimilarity principle" to supposedly determine what Jesus actually said. Here, a text or saying is reliable only when it *contrasts* with the thinking of the early Christians. Odd or unusual sayings are unlikely to have been invented by the Gospel writers and probably are authentic.

Thomas C. Oden provides a common view of Jesus held by most modern scholars:

> Jesus was an eschatological prophet who proclaimed God's coming kingdom and called his

---

*Excerpted and expanded from our book *Knowing the Truth About the Reliability of the Bible*, Q. 2.

hearers to decide now for or against the kingdom. After he was condemned to death and died, the belief emerged gradually that he had risen. Only after some extended period of time did the remembering community develop the idea that Jesus would return as the Messiah, Son of Man. Eventually this community came to project its eschatological expectation back upon the historical Jesus, inserting in his mouth the eschatological hopes that it had subsequently developed but now deftly had to rearrange so as to make it seem as if Jesus Himself had understood himself as Messiah. Only much later did the Hellenistic idea of the God-man, the virgin birth, and incarnation emerge in the minds of the remembering church, who again misremembered Jesus according to its revised eschatological expectation.

James W. Sire, who cites this view, remarks, "Oden in the following eight pages shows how and why this 'modern view' is seriously at odds with reason." For example, "How such a vacuous implausible interpretation could have come to be widely accepted is itself perplexing enough. Even harder to understand is the thought that the earliest rememberers would actually suffer martyrdom for such a flimsy cause. One wonders how those deluded believers of early centuries gained the courage to risk passage into an unknown world to proclaim this message that came from an imagined revolution of a fantasized Mediator. The 'critical' premise itself requires a high degree of gullibility."[176a]

The conservative view of Scripture takes quite another approach. It maintains that, on the basis of accepted bibliographic, internal, external and other criteria, the New Testament text can be established to be reliable history in spite of the novel and sometimes ingenious speculations of critics who, while often familiar with the facts, refuse to accept them due to a preexisting bias. Textually, there is simply no legitimate basis upon which to doubt the credibility and accuracy of the New Testament writers. Further, the methods used by the critics (higher critical methods) have been weighed in the balance even of secular scholarship and been found wanting. Their use in biblical analysis is therefore unjustified. Even in a positive sense, the fruit they have born is minuscule while, neg-atively, they are responsible for a tremendous weight of destruction relative to people's confusion over biblical authority and their confidence in the Bible.

In this sense, the critics conform to the warnings of Chauncey Sanders, associate professor of military history at The Air University, Maxwell Air Force Base, Montgomery, Alabama. In his book *An Introduction to Research in English Literary History,* Sanders warns the literary critic to be certain that he is also careful to examine the evidence *against* his case:

He must be as careful to collect evidence against his theory as for it. It may go against the grain to be very assiduous in searching for ammunition to destroy one's own case; but it must be remembered that the overlooking of a single detail may be fatal to one's whole argument. Moreover, it is the business of the scholar to seek the truth, and the satisfaction of having found it should be ample recompense for having to give up a cherished but untenable theory.[177]

In order to resolve this issue of New Testament reliability, the following ten facts cannot logically be denied.

Fact one: the bibliographical test (corroboration from textual transmission).
The historical accuracy of the New Testament can be proven by subjecting it to three generally accepted tests for determining historical reliability. Such tests are utilized in literary criticism and the study of historical documents in general. (These are also discussed by Sanders.[178]) They involve 1) bibliographical, 2) internal and 3) external examinations of the text and other evidence.

The bibliographical test seeks to determine whether we can reconstruct the original manuscript from the extant copies at hand. For the New Testament (NT) we have 5,300 Greek manuscripts and manuscript portions, 10,000 Latin Vulgate, 9,300 other versions, plus 36,000 early (100–300 A.D.) patristic quotations of the NT—such that all but a few verses of the entire NT could be reconstructed from these alone.[179] What does this mean?

Few scholars question the general reliability even of ancient classical literature on the basis of the manuscripts we possess. Yet this amount is vastly inferior to that of the NT manuscripts. For example, of sixteen well-known classical authors, such as Plutarch, Tacitus, Sentonius, Polybius, Thucydides and Xenophon, the total number of extant copies is typically *less* than ten and the earliest copies date from 750 to 1600 years *after* the original manuscript was first penned.[180] We need only compare such slim evidence to the mass of biblical documentation, which includes over *24,000* manuscript portions, manuscripts and versions, with the earliest fragments and complete copies dating between 50 and 300 years after originally written.

Given the fact that the early Greek manuscripts (the Papyri and early Uncials) date much closer to the originals than for any other ancient literature and given the overwhelming additional abundance of manuscript attestation, any doubt as to the integrity or authenticity of the New Testament text has been removed—no matter what the "higher" critics claim. Indeed, this kind of evidence supplied by the NT (both amount and quality) is the dream of the historian. No other ancient literature has ever come close to supplying historians and textual critics with such an abundance of data.

Dr. F. F. Bruce, the late Ryland's Professor of Biblical Criticism and Exegesis at the University of Manchester, asserts of the New Testament: "There is no body of ancient literature in the world which enjoys such a wealth of good textual attestation as the New Testament."[181] Professor Bruce further comments, "The evidence for our New Testament writings is ever so much greater than the evidence for many writings of classical writers, the authenticity of which no one dreams of questioning. And if the New Testament were a collection of secular writings, their authenticity would generally be regarded as beyond all doubt."[182]

It is this wealth of material that has enabled scholars such as Westcott and Hort, Ezra Abbott, Philip Schaff, A. T. Robertson, Norman Geisler and William Nix to place the restoration of the original text at 99 percent plus.[183] Thus no other document of the ancient period is as accurately preserved as the New Testament:

> Hort's estimate of "substantial variation" for the New Testament is one-tenth of 1 percent; Abbott's estimate is one-fourth of 1 percent; and even Hort's figure including trivial variation is less than 2 percent. Sir Frederic Kenyon well summarizes the situation: The number of manuscripts of the New Testament . . . is so large that it is practically certain that the true reading of every doubtful passage is preserved in some one or another of these ancient authorities. This can be said of no other ancient book in the world. Scholars are satisfied that they possess substantially the true text of the principal Greek and Roman writers whose works have come down to us, of Sophocles, of Thucydides, of Cicero, of Virgil; yet our knowledge depends on a mere handful of manuscripts, whereas the manuscripts of the New Testament are counted by hundreds and even thousands.[184]

In other words, those who question the reliability of the NT must also question the reliability of virtually every ancient writing the world possesses! So how can the NT logically be rejected by UUs or anyone else when its documentation is 100 times that of other ancient literature? If it is impossible to question the world's ancient classics, it is far more impossible to question the reliability of the New Testament.[185] In addition, none of the established NT canon is lost or missing, not even a verse, as indicated by variant readings. The NT, then, passes the bibliographical test and must, by far, be graded with the highest mark of any ancient literature.

Fact two: the internal evidence test (corroboration from content accuracy). This test asserts that one is to assume the truthful reporting of an ancient document (and not assume either fraud, incompetence or error) unless the author of the document has disqualified himself by their presence. For example, do the NT writers contradict themselves? Is there anything in their writing which causes one to objectively suspect their trustworthiness? The answer is no. There is lack of proven fraud or error on the part of *any* NT writer. But there is evidence of careful eyewitness reporting throughout the NT. The caution exercised by the writers, their personal conviction that what they wrote was true and the lack of demonstrable error or contradiction indicate that the Gospel authors and, indeed, all the NT authors pass the second test as well (Luke 1:1–4; John 19:35; 21:24; Acts 1:1–3; 2:22; 26:24–26; 2 Peter 1:16; 1 John 1:1–3).

The kinds of things the Gospel writers include in their narratives offer strong evidence for their integrity. They record their own sins and failures, even serious ones (Matthew 26:56, 69–75; Mark 10:35–45). They do not hesitate to record even the most difficult and consequential statements of Jesus, such as John 6:41–71. They forthrightly supply the embarrassing and even capital charges of Jesus' own enemies. Thus, even though Jesus was their very Messiah and Lord, they not only record the charges that Jesus broke the Sabbath but also that He was a blasphemer and a liar, insane and demonized (Matthew 26:65; John 7:20, 47; 8:48, 52; 10:20).

To encounter such honesty from those who loved the Person they were reporting about gives one assurance that the Gospel writers placed a very high premium on truthfulness.

Fact three: the external evidence test (corroboration from reliable sources outside the NT).

This test seeks either to corroborate or to falsify the documents on the basis of additional historical literature and data. (In this section, we will look at Christian sources; in the next section, fact four, we will look at non-Christian sources.) Is there corroborating evidence for the claims made in the NT outside the NT? Or are the claims or events of the NT successfully refuted by other competent reports or eyewitnesses? Are there statements or assertions in the NT that are demonstrably false according to known archaeological, historic, scientific or other data?

The New Testament again passes the test. For example, Luke wrote one-fourth of the New Testament. His careful historical writing has been documented from detailed personal archaeological investigation by former critic Sir William Ramsay, who stated after his painstaking research, "Luke's history is unsurpassed in respect of its trustworthiness."[186] A. N. Sherwin-White, the distinguished historian of Rome, stated of Luke: "For [the book of] Acts the confirmation of historicity is overwhelming. Any attempt to reject its basic historicity even in matters of detail must now appear absurd."[187]

Papias, a student of the Apostle John[188] and Bishop of Hierapolis around 130 A.D., observed that the Apostle John himself noted that the Apostle Mark in writing his Gospel "wrote down *accurately* . . . whatsoever he [Peter] remembered of the things said or done by Christ. Mark committed *no* error . . . for he was *careful of one thing*, not to omit *any* of the things he [Peter] had heard, and not to state any of them *falsely*."[189] Further, fragments of Papias' *Exposition of the Oracles of the Lord,* ca. 140 A.D. (III, XIX, XX) assert that the Gospels of Matthew, Mark and John are all based on reliable eyewitness testimony (his portion on Luke is missing).[190]

Even 200 years of scholarly rationalistic biblical criticism (such as form, source and redaction approaches) have proven nothing except that the writers were careful and honest reporters of the events recorded and that these methods attempting to discredit them were flawed from the start.

Fact four (corroboration from nonChristian sources).

The existence of both Jewish and secular accounts, to a significant degree, confirm the picture of Christ that we have in the New Testament. Scholarly research such as that by Dr. Gary R. Habermas in *Ancient Evidence for the Life of Jesus,* and other texts, indicates that "a broad outline of the life of Jesus" and His death by crucifixion can be reasonably and directly inferred from entirely nonChristian sources.[191]

Using only the information gleaned from these ancient extrabiblical sources, what can we conclude concerning the death and resurrection of Jesus? Can these events be historically established based on these sources alone? Of the seventeen documents examined in this chapter, eleven different works speak of the death of Jesus in varying amounts of detail, with five of these specifying crucifixion as the mode. When these sources are examined by normal historical procedures used with other ancient documents, the result is conclusive.

It is this author's view that the death of Jesus by crucifixion can be asserted as a historical fact from this data. . . .[192]

Further, Habermas points out that the empty tomb can reasonably be established as historical from extrabiblical sources and that the resurrection of Christ Himself can be indirectly inferred from nonChristian sources.[193]

Fact five (corroboration from archeology). There exists detailed archaeological confirmation for the New Testament documents.[194] Dr. Clifford Wilson is the former director of the Australian Institute of Archaeology and author of *New Light on the New Testament Letters; New Light on the Gospels; Rock, Relics and Biblical Reliability* and a 17-volume set on the archeological confirmation of the Bible. He writes: "Those who know the facts now recognize that the New Testament must be accepted as a remarkably accurate source book."[195] Many recent scholarly texts confirm this, such as Dr. Randall Price's *The Stones Cry Out: What Archaeology Reveals About the Truth of the Bible* (Harvest House, 1997); A. J. Hoerth, *Archaeology and the Old Testament* (1998); and J. McRay, *Archaeology and the New Testament* (1991).

Fact six (corroboration from enemies' silence). The complete inability of the numerous enemies of Jesus and the early Church to discredit early Christian claims (when they had both the motive and ability to do so) argues strongly for the veracity of the early Christian claims in light of the stupendous nature of those claims (Christ's Messiahship, deity and resurrection) and the relative ease of disproof (Jesus' failure to fulfill prophecy; producing Jesus' body).

Fact seven (corroboration from eyewitnesses). The presence of numerous eyewitnesses to the events recorded in the New Testament[196] would surely have prohibited any alteration or distortion of the facts, just as today false reporting as to the events of the Vietnam War or World War II would be corrected on the basis of living eyewitnesses and historic records.

Some argue that the gospel writers' reporting of miracles can't be trusted because they were only giving their religiously excited "subjective experience" of Jesus, not objectively reporting real miraculous events. They *thought* Jesus did miracles, but were mistaken.

What is ignored by critics is what the text plainly states, and the fact that the gospel writers could not have gotten away with this in their own day *unless* they had been telling the truth. They claimed that these things were done openly, not in a corner (Acts 26:26), that they were literally eyewitnesses of the miraculous nature and deeds of Jesus (Luke 1:2; Acts 2:32; 4:20; 2 Peter 1:16), and that their testimony should be believed *because* it was true (John 20:30-31; 21:24).

Indeed, they wrote that Jesus Himself presented His miracles in support of His claims to be both the prophesied Messiah and God incarnate. In Mark 2:8-11, when He healed the paralytic, He did it so "that you may know that the Son of Man has authority on earth to forgive sins"—a clear claim to being God. In John 10:33, when the Jews accused Jesus of blaspheming because as supposedly only a man He was yet claiming to be God, what was Jesus' response? "Do not believe me unless I do what my Father does. But if I do it, even though you do not believe me, believe the miracles, that you may know and understand that the Father is in me, and I in the Father" (John 10:37-38)—another claim to deity. When John the Baptist was in jail and apparently had doubts as to whether Jesus was the Messiah, what did Jesus do? He told John's disciples to go and report about the miracles that He did, which were in fulfillment of specific messianic prophecy (Matthew 11:2-5). Many other examples could be added.

The truth is that the teachings and miracles of Jesus, as any independent reading of the Gospels will prove, are so inexorably bound together that if one removes the miracles one must discard the teachings and vice versa. It is logically impossible to have any other Jesus than the biblical one. It is precisely the biblical Jesus—His deeds and teachings—who has such abundant eyewitness testimony, as any reading of the Gospels and Acts proves.

Fact eight (corroboration from date of authorship). The fact that both conservatives (F. F. Bruce, John Wenham) and liberals (Bishop John A. T. Robinson) have penned defenses of early dating for the New Testament is a witness to the strength of the data for an early date. For example, in *Redating Matthew, Mark and Luke,* noted conservative British scholar John Wenham presents a convincing argument that the synoptic Gospels are to be dated before 55 A.D. He dates Matthew at 40 A.D. (some tradition says the early 30s); Mark at 45 A.D. and Luke no later than 51–55 A.D.[197]

German papryologist Carsten Peter Thiede has argued that the Magdalen papyrus, containing snippets of three passages from Matthew 26, currently housed at Oxford University, are actually the oldest fragments of the New Testament, dating from about 70 A.D. Thiede's book, *Eyewitness to Jesus* (Doubleday, 1995), points out that the Magdalen papyrus is written in Uncial style, which began to die out in the middle of the first century. In addition, the fragments are from a codex, containing writing on both sides of the papyri, which may have been widely used by Christians in the first century since they were easier to handle than scrolls. Further, at three places on the papyri the name of Jesus is written as KS, which is an abbreviation of the Greek word *kyrios* or Lord. Thiede argues that this shorthand is proof that early Christians considered Jesus a sacred name just as the devout Jews shortened the name of God to Yhwh. This would indicate a very early belief for the deity of Christ. "New papyrus discoveries, Thiede believes will eventually prove that all four gospels, even the problematic one ascribed to John, were written before A.D. 80 rather than during the mid-second century. He argues that a scroll fragment unearthed at the Essene community of Qumran in 1972 almost certainly contains a passage from Mark's gospel and can be accurately dated to A.D. 68. In Thiede's opinion, recent research has established that a papyrus fragment of *Luke* in a Paris library was written between A.D. 63 and A.D. 67."[197a]

Even liberal bishop John A. T. Robinson argued in his *Redating the New Testament* that the entire New Testament was written and in circulation between 40 and 65 A.D.[198] And liberal Peter Stuhlmacher of Tubingen, trained in Bultmann's critical methodology of form criticism, says, "As a Western scripture scholar, I am inclined to doubt these [Gospel] stories, but *as a historian,* I am obligated to take them as reliable." "The biblical texts as they stand are the best hypothesis we have until now to explain what really happened."[199]

Indeed, it is becoming an increasingly persuasive argument that all the New Testament books were written before 70 A.D.—within a single generation of the death of Christ, and probably earlier. Given Jesus' miracles, claims and controversy, which began early in His ministry, it is inconceivable that His disciples would not have recorded Jesus' words as He spoke them or immediately after. Even before He began His public ministry there had to be stories circulating about Him, such as about the unique circumstances surrounding His birth, the visit by the shepherds, His presentation in the temple, the visit by the Magi, His escape to Egypt, the return to Nazareth, the event in the temple as a boy and so on. At His baptism the Holy Spirit descended on Him as a dove and He went to the desert to be tempted by Satan. His first miracle in Cana, the changing of water to wine, His cleansing of the temple, the healing of a nobleman's son and so on were all done in the first six months or so of His public ministry. Even the people of His hometown tried to kill Him at Nazareth (Luke 4:16–30).[199a] It is likely the Gospels would have been constructed from these accounts as soon as necessary, which could have been as early as 40 A.D. or even earlier.

The implications of this are not small. A New Testament written between 40–70 A.D. virtually destroys the edifice on which higher critical premises regarding the New Testament are based. If true, insufficient time elapsed for the early Church to have embellished the records with their own particularist views. What the New Testament reports, it reports accurately.

Fact nine (corroboration from critical methods themselves). Even critical methods indirectly support New Testament reliability. Although higher critical theories in general reject biblical reliability *apriori*, nevertheless, when such theories "are subjected to the same analytical scrutiny as they apply to the New Testament documents, they will be found to make their own contribution to validating the historicity of those records."[200]

Fact ten (confirmation from legal testimony and skeptics).

We must also concede the historicity of the New Testament when we consider the fact that many great minds of legal history have, on the grounds of strict legal evidence, accepted the New Testament as reliable history—not to mention also the fact that many brilliant skeptical intellects, of both history and today, have converted to Christianity on the basis of the historical evidence (Saul of Tarsus, Athanagoras, Augustine, George Lyttleton, Gilbert West, C. S. Lewis, Frank Morrison, Sir William Ramsay, John Warwick Montgomery and others).

Lawyers, of course, are expertly trained in the matter of evaluating evidence, and they are perhaps the most qualified in the task of weighing data critically. Is it coincidence that so many of them throughout history have concluded in favor of the truth of the Christian religion? What of the "father of international law," Hugo Grotius, who wrote *The Truth of the Christian Religion* (1627)? What of the greatest authority in English and American common-law evidence in the nineteenth century, Harvard Law School professor Simon Greenleaf, who wrote *Testimony of the Evangelists* in which he powerfully demonstrated the reliability of the Gospels?[201] What of Edmund H. Bennett (1824–1898), for over 20 years the dean of Boston University Law School, who penned *The Four Gospels From a Lawyer's Standpoint* (1899)?[202] What of Irwin Linton, who in his time had represented cases before the Supreme Court, and who wrote *A Lawyer Examines the Bible* in which he stated:

> So invariable had been my observation that he who does not accept wholeheartedly the evangelical, conservative belief in Christ and the Scriptures has never read, has forgotten, or never been able to weigh—and certainly is utterly unable to refute—the irresistible force of the cumulative evidence upon which such faith rests, that there seems ample ground, for the conclusion

that such ignorance is an invariable element in such unbelief. And this is so even though the unbeliever be a preacher, who is supposed to know this subject if he know no other.[203]

Finally, what of the eminent Lord Chancellor Hailsham, who twice held the highest office possible for a lawyer in England (that of Lord Chancellor), and who wrote *The Door Wherein I Went*, in which he upholds the singular truth of the Christian Religion?[203a] What of hundreds of contemporary lawyers who, on the grounds of strict legal evidence, accept the New Testament as historically reliable?[203b]

Certainly, such men are well-acquainted with legal reasoning and have just as certainly concluded that the evidence for the truthfulness of the Scriptures is beyond reasonable doubt. It is also a fact that on the basis of legal evidence, no competent jury should fail to bring in a positive verdict for either the reliability of the New Testament (see note 203b) or the Resurrection.

Apologist, theologian and lawyer John Warwick Montgomery asks people to consider several things: the "ancient documents" rule (that ancient documents constitute competent evidence if there is no evidence of tampering and they have been accurately transmitted); the "parol evidence" rule (Scripture must interpret itself without foreign intervention); the "hearsay rule" (the demand for primary-source evidence); and the "cross-examination" principle (the inability of the enemies of Christianity to disprove its central claim that Christ resurrected bodily from the dead in spite of the motive and opportunity to do so). All these, writes Montgomery, coalesce directly or indirectly to support the preponderance of evidence for Christianity, while the burden of proof proper (the legal burden) for disproving it rests with the critic, who, in 2,000 years, has yet to prove his case.[203c] We must, then, emphasize that to reject the New Testament accounts as true history is, by definition, to reject the canons of legitimate historical study. If this cannot be done, the NT must be retained as careful historical reporting.

The New Testament has thus proven itself reliable in the crucible of history, while the NT critic has been unable to prove his case. The implications of this are tremendous. Legal scholar

J. N. D. Anderson observes in *Christianity: The Witness of History:*

. . . it seems to me inescapable that anyone who chanced to read the pages of the New Testament for the first time would come away with one overwhelming impression—that here is a faith firmly rooted in certain allegedly historical events, a faith which would be false and misleading if those events had not actually taken place, but which, if they did take place, is unique in its relevance and exclusive in its demands on our allegiance. For these events did not merely set a "process in motion and then themselves sink back into the past. The unique historical origin of Christianity is ascribed permanent, authoritative, absolute significance; what happened once is said to have happened once for all and therefore to have continuous efficacy."[204]

NOTES

1. Website, http://www.uua.org/htm/
2. Waldeman Argow, "Unitarian Universalism: Some Questions Answered," UUA pamphlet, p. 13.
3. Unitarian Universalist Association Online Pamphlet, "We are Unitarian Universalists," Marta Flanagan, http://www.uua.org/bookstore/weare. html, website, p. 1.
4. Alan W. Gomes, "Tolerate This! Answering Unitarian Universalist Pluralism," *Journal of Christian Apologetics*, Vol. 1, no. 2, p. 35.
5. Conrad Wright, *Three Prophets of Religious Liberalism: Channing, Emerson, Park* (Boston, MA: Beacon Press, 1978), pp. 97, 99.
6. Ibid.
7. Ernest Cassar, *Universalism in America* (Boston, MA: Beacon Press, 1971), p. 168.
8. Michael Moran, "New England Transcendentalism," *The Encyclopedia of Philosophy*, Vol. 5, p. 480.
9. John Booth, "Introducing Unitarian Universalism," UUA pamphlet, p. 27.
10. Back cover quote on the 1977 Beacon paper edition of J. L. Adams, *On Being Human Religiously* (Boston, MA: Beacon Press, 1976).
11. R. J. Rushdoony, "The Heresy of Democracy with God," Chalcedon Position Paper No. 6, P.O. Box 158, Vallecito, California 95257.
12. David Parke, *The Epic of Unitarianism Original Writings from the History of Liberal Religion* (Boston, MA: Beacon Press, 1969), p. 6.
13. Jack Mendelsohn, *Why I am a Unitarian Universalist* (Boston, MA: Beacon Press, 1966), pp. 51-52, cf. Parke, pp. 4-6.
14. Parke, pp. 3-6; Blunt, *Dictionary of Sects, Heresies, Ecclesiastical Parties and Schools of Religious Thought*, p. 556.

15. Blunt, op cit., p. 557.
16. Philip Schaff, *History of the Church*, Vol. 7, pp. 66-71.
17. Ibid.
18. Ibid.
19. Ibid., pp. 20-22.
20. Ibid., pp. 24-27.
21. Mendelsohn, op cit., p. 47.
22. Will Moredock, "Who Do Men (People?) Say That I Am? UUs Take a New Look at Jesus," Unitarian Universalist website, http://www.uua.org/WRLD/1197 feature1.html.
23. Mendelsohn, "Meet the Unitarian-Universalist," p. 7, UUA pamphlet.
24. Wright, pp. 144, 117; Mendelsohn, pp. 45, 102; Cassara, 269, 74; Irving Murray (ed.), *Highroad to Advance: Charting the Unitarian Universalist Future* (Pacific Grove, CA: The Boxwood Press, 1976), p. 25; plus from various UUA pamphlets listed in the bibliography.
25. Arthur Foote, "Can I Be a Mystic and Unitarian Universalist?" UUA pamphlet.
26. R. N. Helverson, "A Unitarian Universalist Paradigm," in Irving Murray, op cit., pp. 16, 21, 25.
27. Interdependence: Renewing Congregational Policy: A Report by the Commission on Appraisal, June 1977 (UUA: Boston, MA: 1977).
28. Gomes, p. 41.
29. Ibid.
30. R. E. Myers, "Can I Be a Unitarian Universalist and Still Be a Christian?" UUA pamphlet, p. 1, emphasis added.
31. Richard A. Kellaway (ed.), "Unitarian Universalist Views of Christianity," UUA pamphlet, p. 5.
32. From "The Report of the Committee on Goals," pp. 15-16, published by the UUA in 1967, cf. *Highroad to Advance*, p. 11.
33. Kellaway (ed.), "Unitarian Universalist Views of Christianity," p. 9, UUA pamphlet.
34. W. L. Kitchell in Kellaway (ed.), "Unitarian Universalist Views of Christianity," p. 9, UUA pamphlet.
35. Ibid.
36. Rev. R. F. Boeke in Kellaway (ed.), "Unitarian Universalist Views of Christianity," p. 7, UUA pamphlet.
37. Wright, op cit., p. 144.
38. Marshall, "Unitarian Universalists Believe," p. 4, UUA pamphlet.
39. Cassar, op cit., p. 165.
40. Cf. Cassuto, *The Documentary Hypothesis*; Gleason Archer, *A Survey of Old Testament Introduction;* K. A. Kitchen, *Ancient Orient and the Old Testament.*
41. W. Argow, "Unitarian Universalism—Some Questions Answered," pp. 5-6, UUA pamphlet.
42. J. Mendelsohn, "Meet the Unitarian Universalists," p. 6, UUA pamphlet.
43. Mendelsohn, *Why I Am a Unitarian Universalist*, p. 100.
44. From Wright, op cit., pp. 58, 62-64.
45. Harrington, "I Believe," pp. 6-7, UUA pamphlet.
46. Mendelsohn, *Why I Am a Unitarian Universalist*, p. 112.
47. "Unitarian Universalist Views of God," pamphlet published by the UUA, n.d.
48. Ibid.
49. Ibid., p. 2.

50. W. Argow, op cit., p. 6.
51. Wright, op cit., p. 137.
52. W. Argow, op cit., p. 6.
53. Parke, op cit., p. 123.
54. Gilbert Phillips in Brandock Lovely (ed.), "Unitarian Universalist Views of Jesus," pp. 7-8, UUA pamphlet.
55. Quoted by Richard Fewkes, in Brandock Lovely (ed), op cit., UUA pamphlet, p. 4; cf. Parke, op cit., pp. 72-76.
56. Ronald Mazur, "Viewpoints Within Unitarian Universalist Christianity," p. 5, UUA pamphlet.
57. Wright, Three Prophets of Religious Liberalism, p. 99.
58. Mendelsohn, Why I Am a Unitarian Universalist, p. 43.
59. W. Argow, op cit., p. 9, October 1978, no. 938, UUA pamphlet.
60. Mendelsohn, Why I Am a Unitarian Universalist, p. 31.
61. Wright, op cit., p. 144.
62. Transcribed Sermon, May 6, 1979, "Our Brand of Salvation," First Unitarian Church of San Diego, pp. 5-6.
63. Op cit., pp. 5-6.
64. Mendelsohn, "Meet the Unitarian Universalist," p. 10, UUA pamphlet.
65. "Introducing Unitarian Universalism," pp. 9-10, UUA pamphlet.
66. "Meet the Unitarian Universalist," p. 17, UUA pamphlet.
67. Cassara, op cit., p. 254, quoting Dr. John Van Schaik, Jr., in 1925.
68. J. N. Booth, op cit., p. 16, UUA pamphlet, emphasis added.
69. Wright, op cit., p. 76.
70. From ibid., pp.77-78.
71. Ibid.
72. Ibid., p. 142.
73. G. Marshall, "Unitarian Universalists Believe," p. 2, UUA pamphlet.
74. Ibid.
75. Parke, op cit., p. 68.
76. Ibid. pp. 106, 109.
77. Vern Barnet, "Unitarian Universalist Views of the Sacraments," March, 1978, p. 5, no. 8968-16, UUA pamphlet.
78. Fewkes in Lovely (ed.), p. 65.
79. Cassara, op cit., pp. 152, 17.
80. Robert Storer (ed.), "Unitarian Universalist Views of God," p. 9, UUA pamphlet.
81. J. Mendelsohn, "Meet the Unitarian Universalists," p. 14, March, 1974, UUA pamphlet.
82. W. Argow, op cit., p. 8, October, 1978, no. 938, UUA pamphlet.
83. J. Booth, "Introducing Unitarian Universalism," p. 15, UUA pamphlet.
84. "Unitarian Universalist Views of Death and Immortality," pp. 2, 10-11, UUA pamphlet.
85. Ibid., pp. 10-11; cf. Wilson and Weldon, Occult Shock and Psychic Forces, section III.
86. Thomas Avon Towle, "Both Forces Are Holy, pp. 7-11 (transcript of sermon).
87. D. Harrington, "I Believe," p. 4, April, 1977, no. 4006-02, UUA pamphlet.
88. See Gary North, Unholy Spirits: New Age Humanism and the Occult (Fort Worth, TX: Dominion Press, 1986).
89. Sermon Transcript, "What's Religious About Us?" p. 3, Rev. Thomas Owen-Towle, Feb. 4, 1979, First Unitarian Church of San Diego.
90. E. H. Wilson, in David Miller (Ed.), "Unitarian Universalist Views of Humanism," p. 4.
91. Rollo May, The Art of Counseling, p. 216 (1967 ed.).
92. Thomas Owen-Towle, "What's Religious About Us?" op cit., p. 7.
93. David Ehrenfeld, The Arrogance of Humanism, p. 4.
94. A. Perry, in Brandock Lovely, op cit., p. 9.
95. David Lack, Evolutionary Theory and Christian Belief (London: Methuen, 1957), p. 108.
96. R. E. Green in David Miller (ed.), op cit., p. 7.
97. Clark Pinnock, Set Forth Your Case (Moody, 1971), p. 31.
98. The Stockton Herald, Stockton, California, March 13-18, 1960, or March 3-8, 1963.
98a. J. Mendelsohn, "Meet the Unitarian Universalists," p. 7.
99. The UU World, October 15, 1979, p. 9, reported 11 cents per week.
100. J. R. Clark, "What's Religious in Unitarian Universalism?" in Highroad to Advance—Charting the Unitarian Universalist Future, pp. 4-5 (cf. 1-5).
101. E.g., Ibid., pp. 1-3.
102. Booth, op cit., pp. 29, 12.
103. Ed Atkinson, "Unitarian Universalism," p. 2.
104. Helverson, op cit., p. 16, in Highroad to Advance—Charting the Unitarian Universalist Future.
105. Harry Meserve, op cit., p. 13.
106. J. Mendelsohn, "Meet the Unitarian Universalist," p. 3.
107. Owen-Towle, transcribed sermon, op cit., p. 2.
108. Gomes, p. 36.
109. Gomes, p. 38
110. Ibid., p. 37.
111. Ibid., p 39
112. Ibid., p. 40.
113. Ibid., p 39
114. In ibid., p. 38.
115. Cited in Ibid., p. 38.
116. Ibid., pp. 41-42.
117. Ibid., p. 41.
118. Matthew 28:19-20; Romans 10:13-15; 2 Timothy 2:10.
119. Historical evidence proves that Jesus rose from the dead in proof of His claims to be God incarnate. As God, He is an infallible authority. In that role He spoke more of an eternal hell than of heaven. See our book The Facts on Near-Death Experiences.
120. Gomes, p. 42.
121. Harrington, op cit., p. 6.
122. Atkinson (ed.), "Unitarian Universalism, An Invitation to Growth," p. 2, UUA pamphlet.
123. Marshall, op cit., p. 6.
124. W. E. Channing, "The Free Mind," p. 3, pamphlet.
125. Donald Harrington, "Priorities for Unitarian Universalist Advance," in Murray, Highroad to Advance: Charting the Unitarian Universalist Future, p. 48.
126. Ibid., p. 52.
127. Paul Beathie, "Can the Church Reform Society?" Highroad to Advance, op cit., p. 67.
128. Other books include: Marcus Borg, Meeting Jesus Again for the First Time; Geza Vermes, Jesus the Jew; Barbara

Thiering, *Jesus the Man: A New Interpretation of the Dead Sea Scrolls;* A. N. Wilson's, *Jesus: A Life;* John Shelby Spong, *Born of a Woman: A Bishop Rethinks the Birth of Jesus;* Ian Wilson, *Jesus: the Evidence;* John Allegro, *The Sacred Mushroom and the Cross;* David Spangler, *Reflections on the Christ;* S. G. S. Brandon, *Jesus and the Zealots;* and Morton Smith *The Secret Gospel* and *Jesus the Magician.*

129. David Van Biema, "The Gospel Truth(?)," *Time,* April 8, 1996, p. 57.

130. A & E TV Channel, "Mysteries of the Bible: Heaven and Hell," Oct. 3, 1996.

131. "Who Was Jesus? Reflections on The Jesus Seminar," *Theological Students Fellowship Bulletin,* Feb. 1994, p. 3.

132. Robert W. Funk, Roy W. Hoover and the Jesus Seminar, *The Five Gospels: The Search for the Authentic Words of Jesus* (NY: MacMillan, 1993), p. 34.

133. Adjith Fernando, *The Supremacy of Christ* (Wheaton, IL: Crossway Books, 1995), p. 19.

134. William Lane Craig, *The Son Rises* (Chicago: Moody Press, 1981), p. 135-36.

135. Michael J. Wilkins and J. P. Moreland, "Introduction: The Furor Surrounding Jesus," in Wilkins and Moreland (eds.), *Jesus Under Fire: Modern Scholarship Reinvents the Historical Jesus* (Grand Rapids, MI: Zondervan, 1995), pp. 6, 11.

136. Funk, Hoover and the Jesus Seminar, p. 2.

137. Wilkins and Moreland in Wilkins and Moreland, p. 10.

138. Funk, Hoover and the Jesus Seminar, pp. 16-33.

139. Ibid., p. 16.

140. Ibid., p. 19, emphasis added.

141. Ibid., p. 21.

142. Ibid., p. 23.

143. William Lane Craig, "Did Jesus Rise from the Dead?" in Wilkins and Moreland (eds.) p. 162.

144. Funk, Hoover and the Jesus Seminar, *Five Gospels,* p. 5; the last statement was colored red for emphasis; we capitalized it.

145. Ibid., p. 5.

146. Ibid., pp. 5, 35

147. Ibid., p. 16.

148. Ibid., p. 543.

149. F. F. Bruce, foreword in Craig L. Blomberg, *The Historical Reliability of the Gospels* (Downer's Grove, IL: InterVarsity, 1987), p. ix.

150. Gregory A. Boyd, *Cynic, Sage or Son of God?* (Wheaton, IL: Bridge Point, 1995), p. 163.

151. Craig, "Did Jesus Rise," p. 168.

152. Van Biema, "The Gospel Truth(?)," p. 59.

153. E.g., Walter A. Maier, *Form Criticism Reexamined* (St. Louis: Concordia, 1973), p. 38.

154. J. L. Adams, op cit., p. 9.

155. F. H. Wilson, in Miller (ed.), "Unitarian Universalist Views of Humanism," p. 4.

156. Mendelsohn, "Meet the Unitarian Universalist," p. 6.

157. "Unitarian Universalist Views of Christianity," p. 5; Robert Hill, "Marriage, Remarriage and Divorce," pp. 1, 2, 6.

158. John Ankerberg, John Weldon, *The Myth of Safe Sex* (Chicago: Moody, 1993).

159. See data from *The Family Research Institute,* Washington, D.C.

160. *Unitarian Universalist World,* January 15, 1980, p. 11.

161. See our *Knowing the Truth About the Reliability of the Bible.*

162. Mendelsohn, *Why I Am a Unitarian Universalist,* p. 107.

163. R. A. Storer (ed.), "Unitarian Universalist Views of God," p. 2.

164. Mendelsohn, *Why I Am a Unitarian Universalist,* p. 108.

165. R. E. Myers (ed.), op cit., p. 7.

166. Parke, op cit., p. 89.

167. Wright, op cit., p. 117.

168. Booth, op cit., p. 13.

169. Ibid., p. 18.

170. A. Perry, op cit., p. 9.

171. Argow, op cit., pp. 10-11.

172. George N. Marshall, *Challenge of a Liberal Faith* (Boston, MA: Beacon Press, 1978), pp. 239, 242.

173. Mendelsohn, p. 77.

174. UUCF form letter from Thomas D. Whintle, UUCF President.

175. Gomes, p. 42.

176. UUCF pamphlet, "Unitarian Universalist Christian Affirmations."

176a. James W. Sire, *Why Should Anyone Believe Anything at All?* (Downer's Grove, IL: InterVarsity, 1994), p. 221, citing Thomas C. Oden, *The Word of Life* (New York: Harper and Row, 1989), pp. 223-24.

177. Chauncey Sanders, *An Introduction to Research in English Literary History* (New York: MacMillan, 1952), p. 160. His comments were specifically in reference to the authenticity or authorship of a given text.

178. Ibid.

179. J. McDowell, *Evidence That Demands a Verdict,* rev. 1979, pp. 39-52; and Norman Geisler, William Nix, *A General Introduction to the Bible* (Chicago: Moody Press, 1971), pp. 238, 357-367.

180. McDowell, *Evidence That Demands a Verdict,* p. 42; Newman, "Easter Week Narratives," 281-84.

181. F. F. Bruce, *The Books and the Parchments* (Old Tappan, NJ: Revell, 1963), p. 78.

182. F. F. Bruce, *The New Testament Documents: Are They Reliable?* (Downer's Grove, IL: InterVarsity Press, 1971), p. 15.

183. J. McDowell, *Evidence That Demands a Verdict,* pp. 43-45; Clark Pinnock, *Biblical Revelation: The Foundation of Christian Theology* (Chicago: Moody Press, 1971), pp. 238-39, 365-66.

184. Robert C. Newman, "Miracles and the Historicity of the Easter Week Narratives," in John Warwick Montgomery (ed.), *Evidence for Faith: Deciding the God Question* (Dallas: Probe, 1991), p. 284.

185. See John Warwick Montgomery, *Faith Founded on Fact* (New York: Nelson, 1978); F. F. Bruce, *The New Testament Documents: Are They Reliable?* (Downer's Grove, IL: InterVarsity); John Warwick Montgomery, *History and Christianity* (Downer's Grove, IL: InterVarsity); Norman Geisler, *Christian Apologetics* (Grand Rapids, MI: Baker, 1976), pp. 322-327.

186. William M. Ramsay, *The Bearing of Recent Discovery on the Trustworthiness of the New Testament* (Grand

Rapids, MI: Baker, 1959), p. 81; cf. William F. Ramsay, *Luke the Physician*, 177-179, 222 as given in F. F. Bruce, *The New Testament Documents: Are They Reliable?*, pp. 90-91.

187. A. N. Sherwin-White, *Roman Society and Roman Law in the New Testament* (Oxford: Clarendon Press, 1963) from Norman L. Geisler, *Christian Apologetics*, p. 326.

188. Gary R. Habermas, *Ancient Evidence for the Life of Jesus: Historical Records of His Death and Resurrection* (New York: Nelson, 1984), p. 66.

189. Philip Schaff, Henry Wace, eds., *A Select Library of Nicene and Post-Nicene Fathers of the Christian Church*, 2nd series, vol. 1, Eusebius: Church History, Book 3, Chapter 39, "The Writings of Papias" (Grand Rapids, MI: Eerdmans, 1976), pp. 172-173, emphasis added.

190. Gary R. Habermas, *Ancient Evidence for the Life of Jesus*, pp. 66, 177.

191. Ibid., pp. 112-115.

192. Ibid., p. 112.

193. Ibid., pp. 112-113.

194. See our chapter on archeology in *Ready With An Answer* and F. F. Bruce, "Are the New Testament Documents Still Reliable?", *Christianity Today* (October 28, 1978), pp. 28-33; F. F. Bruce, *The New Testament Documents: Are They Reliable?*, chs. 7-8; Sir William Ramsay, *The Bearing of Recent Discoveries on the Trustworthiness of the New Testament* (Grand Rapids, MI: Baker Books, 1979); C. A. Wilson, *Rocks, Relics and Biblical Reliability* (Grand Rapids, MI: Zondervan, 1977), ch. 2 *New Light on New Testament Letters* and *New Light on the Gospels* (Grand Rapids, MI: Baker, 1975); Edwin Yamauchi, *The Stones and the Scriptures*, Section II (New York: Lippincott, 1972).

195. Wilson, *Rocks, Relics and Biblical Reliability*, p. 120.

196. See any complete concordance listing under "witness," "eyewitness," etc.

197. John Wenham, *Redating Matthew, Mark and Luke*, (Downer's Grove, IL, 1992), pp. 115-19, 136, 183, see pp. xxv, 198, 147, 200, 221, 223, 238-39, 243-45.

197a. John Elson, "Eyewitness to Jesus?" *Time*, April 8, 1996, p. 60.

198. John A. T. Robinson, *Redating the New Testament* (Philadelphia: Westminster, 1976).

199. In Richard S. Ostling, "Who Was Jesus?", *Time*, August 15, 1988, p. 41, emphasis added.

199a. See the chronological "Life of Christ" chart in *The NIV Study Bible*, redletter edition, Zondervan 1985, pp. 1480-1481.

200. F. F. Bruce "Are the New Testament Documents Still Reliable?", p. 33, cf., Craig Blomberg, *The Historical Reliability of the Gospels* (Downer's Grove, IL: InterVarsity, 1987), pp. 247, 253.

201. Reprinted in J. W. Montgomery, *The Law Above the Law* (Minneapolis, MN: Bethany, 1975), appendix, pp. 91-110.

202. Reprinted in *The Simon Greenleaf Law Review*, Vol. 1 (Orange, CA: The Faculty of the Simon Greenleaf School of Law, 1981-1982), pp. 15-74.

203. Irwin Linton, *A Lawyer Examines the Bible* (San Diego: Creation Life Publishers, 1977), p. 45.

203a. *The Simon Greenleaf Law Review*, vol. 4 (Orange, CA: The Faculty of the Simon Greenleaf School of Law, 1984-1985), pp. 28-36.

203b. See our *Ready With An Answer*.

203c. John Warwick Montgomery, *The Law Above the Law* (Minneapolis: Bethany, 1975), pp. 87-88.

204. J. N. D. Anderson, *Christianity: The Witness of History* (Downer's Grove, IL: InterVarsity, 1970), pp. 13-14.

UNITY SCHOOL OF CHRISTIANITY

INFO AT A GLANCE

Name: Unity, Unity School of Christianity.

Purpose: To enable people, through prayer (e.g., mental affirmation), proper knowledge and use of their mental faculties, to become the heir to their true divine nature.

Founder: Charles and Myrtle Fillmore.

Source of authority: The Fillmore's writings; "Divine Mind," individually interpreted.

Claim: To establish the true teachings of Christ and to help men come to knowledge of this truth.

Occult dynamics: Unity believes that innate psychic powers can be developed, and it expresses openness to psychic research generally.

Key literature: *Metaphysical Bible Dictionary;* Charles Fillmore's *Talks on Truth* and other texts; periodicals include *Unity; Daily Word; Wee Wisdom* (for children).

Attitude toward Christianity: Rejecting.

Quotes:

"The Gospel of Jesus Christ is that all men shall become God incarnate."[1]

"We have studied many isms, many cults. People of every religion under the sun claim we either belong to them or have borrowed the best part of our teaching from them. We have borrowed the best from all religions, that is the reason we are called Unity."[2]

"People deal with sacred words in a way that is too superficial to bring results. They juggle with words. They toss them into the air. . . ."[3]

Note: For the most part, Unity remains a religion of the teachings of Charles Fillmore. Although he would undoubtedly change some of his ideas today (as Unity has done since his death), his writings are still authoritative and used by Unity teachers, ministers and laypersons. We have selected both Fillmore's writings and modern Unity authors to present the doctrines and views of Unity.

DOCTRINAL SUMMARY

God: Impersonal Principle and Infinite Mind.

Jesus: A man who attained Christ consciousness (i.e., awareness of the God within).

The Christ: The inner, divine God-self of every person.

Holy Spirit: The "personal"-impersonal function or law of God.

Trinity: Mind, idea, expression or thinker, thought, action.

Salvation: By knowledge, proper thought, mental affirmation.

Man: Inwardly divine.

Sin: Error in thinking.

Satan: False thoughts.

The Second Coming: Building proper mental attitudes in people and their expressions.

The Fall: Into error of thought and personality.

The Bible: The most advanced of mankind's religious Scriptures (when interpreted by Unity).

Death: For the spiritually evolving (eventually everyone), death involves positive transformation leading to higher planes of existence through reincarnation.

Heaven and Hell: States of consciousness.

INTRODUCTION AND HISTORY

The Unity School of Christianity website describes Unity in the following terms: "Unity School of Christianity is a religious, educational organization based on the teachings of Jesus Christ." As the description continues, it claims that Unity is a positive influence in the world and a spiritual "light to all people of the world":

Unity School of Christianity is the world headquarters for the Unity movement, which is founded on Christian principles, spiritual values, and the healing power of prayer . . . [helping others] to apply spiritual principles in pursuit of a happier, healthier, and more prosperous life. Unity embraces all people. Unity transcends religious denominations as a harmonizing, strengthening influence. We believe there is truth in all teachings. Unity leaves all people free to find the truth for themselves . . . Unity School of Christianity is a center of spiritual light for the people of the world . . . [Currently] Unity School serves millions of people in more than 150 countries.[4]

Unity, while not completely like New Thought teaching, can be classed broadly with it (see New Thought chapter). It is one of the few New Thought religions that has become a national organization, and it is the largest of the multitudinous New Thought groups. However, Unity withdrew from the International New Thought Alliance (INTA) in 1922 because Charles Fillmore felt the organization was too broad in its beliefs, some of which he could not support.

Influence

The influence of Unity has been impressive. Even half a century ago Unity boasted more than one million subscribers to its literature, and the Unity Village headquarters of Lee's Summit, Missouri, received over 30,000 letters weekly.[5] Then President James Freeman stated that Unity literature was in print in 12 languages "sent to millions of people in most countries of the earth." Further, through radio "the Jesus Christ message as interpreted by Charles and Myrtle Fillmore goes out to more than three million people."[6] A quarter century ago, *Unity* magazine, *Daily Word* and *Wee Wisdom* (see "Key literature" under "Info at a Glance") had a combined circulation of over a million copies, and 260 TV and 600 radio stations carried Unity programs. Today, Unity remains one of the largest metaphysical groups in the United States, with a large mail order service, publishing house, regular retreats, the Unity School for Religious Studies (ministerial training and continuing education programs), coast-to-coast radio broadcasts and international influence. The *Daily Word*, in continuous publication since 1924, is now printed in ten languages and distributed in 150 countries.

Unity has exercised its influence in other ways. Both the late Norman Vincent Peale (a Mason who often supported nonChristian and occult philosophies*) and student of occult metaphysics, Emmet Fox, were heavily influenced by Charles Fillmore, and in a sense they were his spiritual children. In a 1964 Unity Village 75th anniversary address Peale stated that he had been an orthodox preacher *until* reading Charles Fillmore. He even admitted that the phrase "positive thinking," for which he is so well known, was originally Fillmore's.[7] Peale, of course, has influenced tens of millions of readers with his books, and Fox millions more. In addition, the modern charismatic "positive confession" movement has in part, through E. W. Kenyon, been derived from Unity and related teaching (New Thought, Religious Science, etc.). (See our book *The Facts on the Faith Movement*.)

Today, according to its web site, Unity sends out "more than 33 million pieces of mail annually" and each year "receives more than two million requests for prayer." Over the years tens of millions of prayer requests have been received by Silent Unity, its prayer ministry. With one of the largest publishing houses in the Midwest, Unity now offers over 500 different products to the public, such as books, audio and video cassettes, CDs, magazines and pamphlets. It seems evident that Unity will continue to influence millions of people well into the millennium.[8]

In the minds of these millions of people, Unity teachings appear to be Christian. Unity does, after all, claim to be Christian and to follow Jesus' teachings. This is why it is important to analyze the central beliefs of the Unity School of Christianity to see if these claims are valid.

Charles Fillmore

Charles Fillmore, the founder of Unity, was born on an Indian reservation in 1854 near St.

Cloud, Minnesota, and died 94 years later, in 1948. For a time Fillmore engaged in trading with the Chippewa Indians while he lived among them. He was kidnapped by the Sioux before two years of age and had allegedly been used by them "in some mystical ceremony," which may help to explain some of the occult influences in his life.[9] As a teenager, he had two tutors who immersed him in metaphysics,[10] and he was greatly influenced by Ralph Waldo Emerson and James Russell Lowell, two prominent New England Transcendentalists, who sparked his growing interest in mysticism. In 1881 he married Myrtle Page, a religiously unorthodox Methodist. By 1888 Myrtle was an invalid with TB, having unsuccessfully sought cures in a variety of ways. Finally she turned to New Thought and was unexpectedly healed. His interest in metaphysics now cemented, Charles Fillmore began an intense study of New Thought and related subjects, including Christian Science, Theosophy, Eastern religions, spiritism and other occultism.

In 1889 Charles and Myrtle founded Unity and published the magazine *Modern Thought*, which soon evolved into *Christian Science Thought* (1890). Not unexpectedly, this upset Mary Baker Eddy, the founder of Christian Science. The name of the magazine was then changed to *Thought* (1891), and later that year to *Unity*, the name it retains today. In 1891 The Society of Silent Unity was born. In 1914 this society, which was prayer-oriented, along with "Silent-70" (free literature distribution), the Unity Correspondence School and the Unity Tract Society merged into the Unity School of Christianity.

PRACTICE AND TEACHINGS

Unity attempts to propagate its main ideas through literature, teaching and personal correspondence; for example, Silent Unity's large "prayer ministry," where people can write or phone for help. As their website states: "Prayer is the heart and soul of Unity's work. Unity is one of the oldest prayer ministries in the United States and annually receives more than two million requests for prayer. *Silent Unity,* our

*See for instance his foreword to Helen Keller's *My Religion,* which endorses the occult Swedenborgian faith.

24-hour prayer ministry, prays with anyone in need of spiritual support, whether they contact us by mail or by phone. There is never a charge for this service, and it is always provided in strictest confidence. Silent Unity does not counsel or give advice, but rather helps callers turn to God for counsel."[11] How does Unity claim to help callers "turn to God for counsel"?

Freedom from False Thinking

The main emphasis of Unity is to assist others in achieving freedom from the consequences of "false" thinking. The cause of everyone's problems is their resistance to Truth and their belief in that which is not divine or "not Good." Unity teaches people that if they would be content, happy and have an abundant life, they must learn to reverse their faulty thinking patterns and bring them into harmony with Divine Law. This can be accomplished by understanding the truths that 1) "God is with us" (that is, within us; i.e., that God is potentially present in all circumstances), and 2) that God is All-Good. If we can come to see Reality as it truly is, we can move into a state of harmony with the All-Good, with God, and this will have a life-changing impact. Although we should not expect instant results, we will notice changes as we begin to see the truth that, despite contrary perceptions, everything around us is really all light and divine goodness. Charles Fillmore stated: "Pronounce every experience good, and of God, and by that mental attitude you will call forth only the good. What seemed error will disappear, and only the good will remain."[12]

Belief in evil, an idea that has no necessary reality or power, can also have a great impact on us if we choose to accept it. Unity teaches that there is no reason to accept false beliefs when they have no necessary reality or power. Disease, fear, old age, poverty—anything personally undesirable—is simply unnecessary. Just as faulty consciousness creates all things negative, divine consciousness creates all things good. In effect, ideas make and mold reality because ideas create reality, whether good or bad. Incredibly, Charles Fillmore firmly believed that he would never die because he was in true harmony with universal law. He believed his divine

mind could control the physical condition of his body forever.

In Unity, the term God equals the term Mind, or Spirit, or Universal Principle. "God is the original Mind in which all real ideas exist."[13] Ideas are more real than matter because ideas *create* matter. God created the realm of ideas such that divine thoughts can literally create physical manifestations. Some of God's thoughts created the universe of manifestation (what we see), while others created the spiritual laws by which that universe functions. Thus, Fillmore was convinced that thoughts could create. For instance, he encouraged people to "cease making disease germs" in order to stay healthy.[14] In essence, God, or Spirit or Mind, can be used by the enlightened human mind to create its own perfect reality. If everything that exists is the physical manifestation of ideas, then once the human mind functions in perfect harmony with the Divine Mind, it can control all aspects of the physical and spiritual universes by expressing proper ideas. Thus Unity believes that the basis of true existence has been revealed by Divine intelligence as perfect ideas.

If we accept into our consciousness any ideas other than perfect ones this must lead to negativity and inharmony. Instead of experiencing *only* good, there comes into being good and evil. Unity teaches that sense consciousness—the mental state accrued through believing in the senses (or outer appearances)—is another name for the serpent in the Garden of Eden who deceived man. If we reject divine truth and instead believe in what our senses tell us, this will cause us to "fall" into disharmony: evil will appear to be objectively real, when in fact it was merely the creation of faulty thinking patterns. The world is really perfect, but in our fallen condition we have made it seem imperfect.

In other words, everything that we see about us that is supposedly evil is first picked up by our senses—murder, rape, hate, corruption, cancer, vice, disaster, international discord, and so on. This trust in our senses, or "serpent consciousness," causes us to become *attached* to what we think about and the result is that we then "withdraw" from the awareness of Divine Good. Our link to Spirit, the All Good, is severed and we have gone from an original state of living in Divine consciousness, which is Unity, into *personal* consciousness, which has resulted from our acceptance of limited "selfish" ideas. The end result is that we believe we are separate from God and living in a less than perfect world. Thus, to hold to false (less than perfect) ideas is to follow "the delusive suggestions of the serpent instead of listening to the word of God. Pain, disease, and finally death always result from such ignorant transgression of the divine law."[15] Unity believes that this negative force of consciousness can be countered through its program of "spiritual growth." (For a simple visual diagram of this entire process, see Religious Science.)

Key methods for growing spiritually are meditation and positive affirmation, or "treatments for self-development." When confronted with error or evil, instead of giving them reality and thus power over us, we must choose to mentally affirm their unreality and powerlessness while positively reaffirming the Good. Several examples of "treatments" are found in the back of Fillmore's *Dynamics for Living*. The "Treatment to Realize Freedom" offers a concise view of what Unity teaches at this point. Note the large number of things in life Unity refuses to accept as real:

> God is good and God is all; therefore I refuse to believe in the reality of evil in any of its forms. God is life, and God is all; therefore I refuse to believe in the reality of loss of life, or death. God is power and strength, and God is all; therefore I refuse to believe in inefficiency and weakness. God is wisdom, and God is all; therefore I refuse to believe in ignorance. God is spiritual substance, and God is all; therefore there is no reality in the limitations of matter. God is inexhaustible resource and God is all; therefore I refuse to believe in the reality of lack or poverty. God is love, and God is all; therefore I refuse to believe in hate or revenge.[16]

In the "Treatment to Realize Perfect Manifestation," Fillmore declares his belief in the common spiritistic, New Age and Buddhist idea referred to above: that our consciousness has the power to mold and create reality. "My 'life is hid with Christ in God.' I am the substance of Being made manifest. I am formed in the perfection of the divine-idea man, Christ Jesus. My body is the temple of the living God, and the glory of the Lord fills the temple. My body is not material; it is spiritual and perfect in all its being. By seeing perfection in all things, I help to make it manifest. I see in mind that perfect character which I desire to be."[17]

"Treatment to Develop Prosperity" could have come from either the mouth of New Age spirits or a text of the modern "Christian" positive confession and Word Faith movement. It exclaims: "Infinite wisdom guides me, divine love prospers me, and I am successful in everything I undertake. In quietness and confidence I affirm the drawing power of divine love as my magnet of constantly increasing supply. I have unbounded faith in the omnipresent substance increasing and multiplying at my word of plenty, plenty, plenty."[18] As we will see later, the problem is that it does not work.

We can see here that a basic premise of Unity is the potential omnipotence of the human mind, at least when proper thought patterns harmonize the individual mind with divine mind or universal law. The Fillmores taught that "the Christ" was latent within all people and that this divine aspect (the "I AM power") could be "drawn out" into conscious awareness. One Unity affirmation teaches others to repeat: "I am the resurrection and the life."[19] The end result, according to Unity, is that man "becomes" a perfect child of God, one in essence with God and one's true divine nature.

Because God is "All Good," this higher consciousness brings only good—peace, prosperity, happiness, and so on. The "Kingdom of God," therefore, is the potential *within* man for true unity with God, an infinite potential that is ever present. Once we accept this truth, the Universal Mind (Divine Presence, "God," impersonal law) is deeply and intimately involved in every act, thought, and circumstance in our lives, regardless of our other beliefs: Christian, atheist, Buddhist, Muslim, Satanist, whatever. Since Universal Mind operates all parts of the creation by Universal Law, once we are in harmony with it, this Law is on our side, working smoothly with and for us. Our divine potential can now be used as *power* to bring positive change and even "miracles" into our lives. But, as noted, this Law misused is responsible for people's adversity. By not thinking "properly" (i.e., according to Fillmore's teachings), one is thinking destructively and negative manifestations result.

Essentially, while Law (or God, we could say) may be "All Good" at one level, at another level it is *both* Good and Evil. Informed Unity members know this. Proper thinking, supposedly, allows them to neutralize the "negative" side of the Law, causing "the Good" to manifest. The Law is simply there, like gravity, and we either "obey" it (by believing correctly) or it will work against us to our detriment. There is no middle ground. Only *one way* exists to success and spiritual health: positive thinking.

Would that it were so easy. Even though it is the universal experience of Unity believers that there are many situations in life where all the positive thinking in the world is ineffectual, Unity can respond only by telling members they simply do not have enough "faith." Divine Mind is omnipresent and controls all things, therefore the only possible source of error and imperfect manifestation is one's lack of faith. But even Unity has never explained how the most proficient "positive thinker" ever—Jesus Christ, according to Unity—ended up betrayed by friends, beaten, whipped and crucified, when according to Divine Law only "the Good" could ever have come to Him.[20] But, then, as we will see, Unity has no credible response to a number of serious weaknesses in its worldview.

Basic Creed

The basic "creed" of Unity was issued in 1928, and is reprinted periodically. It includes 11 key beliefs, many of which seem Christian:

We believe in God.
We believe in Christ, the Son of God.
We believe that we live, move, and have our being in God.
We believe that spirit, soul, and body are a unit.
We believe that "God is Spirit," as Jesus taught, and that all of His Spirit is with us at all times, supplying our every need.

We believe that the prayer of faith will heal the sick.
We believe in the supremacy and the eternity of the Good.
We believe that divine intelligence is present in every atom of man and matter.
We believe that the kingdom of heaven or harmony is within man.
We believe in the creative power of thoughts and words.
We believe that the Golden Rule, "Do unto others as you would have them do unto you," should be the paramount rule of life.

As we will see, even the above teachings that seem Christian actually become nonChristian when interpreted in light of Unity's overall worldview.

In many ways, the tenth belief is the most crucial for Unity. Practically speaking, the essence of Unity is manipulating "the creative power of words and thoughts." Indeed, without this, Unity has little to offer. Let's see why this concept is so vital and also summarize our previous discussion to be sure we understand what Unity is saying. In Unity, the universe itself was never actually created (in a Christian sense). It is only an emanation of divine thought. What Unity teaches is that only God exists. God is comprised of Mind (or Divine Principle) and Thought—or how Divine Principle expresses and externalizes itself. What we see about us, including ourselves, is a result of God's thoughts. Put another way, just as our words are an expression of what we are thinking, so the creation is an expression of what God is thinking. Thus, the entire material universe is merely an emanation of God's thought. Apart from God's thinking, the universe has no permanent or independent reality. Again, the universe is not a separate creation of the biblical God, real in itself, but merely an effect of the mental activity of the Divine Principle.

However, because our minds are potentially *one essence* with God's Mind, we can also manipulate the creation just as easily as we manipulate our own thoughts. Why? Because if we are one essence with Divine Mind, then the creation *is* our thought, subject to our complete control.

Here lies the *raison d'etre*, the reason for being, of Unity. We can learn to control the creation absolutely *because* it is *our* creation. We are the Creators, not some biblical God outside of us.

Thus, an essential concept in Unity is that the entire universe is not so much material existence as it is, or results from, divine spiritual ideas. Again, our divine ideas *create* reality: "The good always exists in Divine Mind as ideas. We bring it into manifestation through the prayers of faith, affirmation, praise, and acknowledgment."[21] Our ideas can create reality even to the point of magic. "We are proclaiming that man can use I AM power to restore health and bring increased happiness; in fact, that through righteous, lawful use of the I AM he can have everything he desires."[22] Note the following declaration from the standard Unity *Metaphysical Bible Dictionary:* "There is nothing but Mind and Thought—Principle and its mode of expression. The things made, or externalized, are simply effects, and of themselves would quickly pass away; but Mind and Thought are one and inseparable, self-existent and ever active, the cause of all that appears."[23]

The correspondence here to the premises of ritual magic* becomes more pronounced when Unity teaches that we can, just like the God of the Bible, literally create things from nothing:

It is not an assumption of theoretical metaphysics that we may be able to make our food and clothing from the air, but a logical conclusion that follows the understanding of God as the omnipresent source of all that appears. . . . All people who have studied metaphysics and understand somewhat the action of the mind recognize that there is one underlying law and that through this law all things come into expression; also that there is one universal Mind, the source and sole origin of all real intelligence.[24]

Thus for all practical purposes, we can become God. Here is the basis behind Fillmore's statement, quoted earlier, "The Gospel of Jesus Christ is that all men shall become God incar-

nate." Just so, Unity teaches that "the kingdom of heaven" that Jesus spoke of *is* this perfect state of mind, and that because everything results from mind, mind can literally change everything. Seemingly, the world can itself be harmonized and unified by thought alone. All evil can be removed if we only realize and appropriate the divine power at our disposal.[25] Unfortunately, not too many Unity members seem to have much faith this will actually occur. One wonders why, given their teachings. Regardless, on an individual level at least, proper thinking will at least cease the cycle of reincarnation, and "the weary round of incarnation and reincarnation will cease."[26]

In sum, what Unity teaches is that we are the literal Creators of the universe because our consciousness is God's consciousness. Despite our Fall (into false thinking), our thought processes have divine renewing power. They have the potential to function like magical incantations that will bring us our every desire, provided we engage in the "ritual" of positive affirmation, praise, acknowledgment of the Good and such. Thus, no lack and no evil ever has to happen to us, even death.

THEOLOGY

Christianity

Unity claims to accept the teachings of Jesus Christ and biblical Christianity, and many have believed this to be true. Fillmore himself declared that Unity would revitalize the church: "Unity is the Truth that is taught in all religions, simplified and systemized so that anyone can understand and apply it. Students of Unity do not find it necessary to sever their church affiliations. The church needs the vitalization that this renaissance of primitive Christianity gives it."[27] Hugh D'Andrade, the biographer of Charles Fillmore, called Unity "a movement based on the teachings of Jesus Christ."[28] J. Gordon Melton in his *Encyclopedia of American Religions* asserts that Fillmore, "while heavily leaning on Hinduism at points, was one of the most Christ-oriented teachers in New Thought."[29] Fillmore was even fond of publicly declaring himself to be a personal disciple of Jesus Christ. He felt that he knew Jesus and that Jesus was

---

*Philosophically if not ritually. See for instance the material on the Kabbalistic master ritual in David Conway, *Magic: An Occult Primer.*

his friend. D'Andrade quotes a 50-year friend of Fillmore: "Again and again he would speak of Jesus as a real presence. He felt himself in intimate contact with Jesus. . . . Charles would often say, 'I am a walking disciple of Christ.' Sometimes he would sign a letter with his name and add: 'Representative of Christ at Large.' "[30]

Even though Fillmore had been declaring himself "a representative of Christ at Large" for more than 50 years, he was never a true follower of the biblical Jesus, but rather of a gnostic Christ of his own making. Thus he differentiated between Jesus, a man of history, and the Christ, the divine consciousness dwelling in all men throughout history, and it is not surprising that as he grew older "he spoke more of Christ than of Jesus."[31] He even equated Jesus with the Hindu god Krishna. In his *Christian Healing* he declared: "The Krishna of the Hindu is the same as the Messiah of the Hebrews."[32] But to equate the capricious and amoral Krishna, ultimately an illusion in much Hinduism,* with the infinitely holy Son of God of Christian faith betrays a regrettable lack in Fillmore's understanding of comparative religion, not to mention biblical teaching. The Bible is very clear that Jesus alone is supreme (Colossians 1:15–20). Jesus Himself declared He was the *monogenes* (unique and only) Son of God (John 3:16, 18). The Scripture emphasizes He has a name "above every name" (Philippians 2:9) and that He alone is God incarnate (Isaiah 43:10; 44:6; Philippians 2:6).

Yet in spite of their denials of the biblical Christ and of virtually every major Christian doctrine, Fillmore and Unity, like Mormonism and other cults, have consistently claimed to be Christian and biblical for more than 100 years. Fillmore's *Dynamics for Living* carries a prefatory quote by him about Unity: "Our objective is to discern the truth in Christianity and prove it. . . . Our purpose is to help and teach mankind to use and prove the eternal Truth taught by the Master." Rev. William Cameron declares that in "many ways, Unity is a return to first century Christianity, for it tends not to be a religion *about* Jesus, but it attempts to follow the religion *of* Jesus."[33] In other words, the religion "about" Jesus is the one Christians invented, and the re-

ligion "of" Jesus is what He really believed, which is Unity.

At times, Unity can sound so Christian that an uninformed individual might easily assume that Unity was a Christian denomination. Note the following statements from Charles Fillmore:

> Jesus Christ . . . came to bring a full consciousness of abundant life, complete forgiveness and redemption from all sin, victory over death and the grave.[34]

> The new birth is a change that comes here and now. . . . It is the change from carnal to spiritual consciousness through the begetting and quickening power of the word of Truth. . . . To be born again is to be made a "new creature," having "this mind in you, which was also in Christ Jesus. . . ."[35]

Clear biblical sentiments are expressed here. The right words are used, but unfortunately they have the wrong meanings because they are removed from their biblical worldview. Thus they lose their biblical content and end up expressing ideas contrary to those of the Bible, that is, Unity doctrines. For instance, when Fillmore declares that Jesus came to bring complete forgiveness and redemption from all sin and victory over death, he has Unity beliefs, not biblical beliefs in mind. That is, Jesus' forgiveness of sin is not through His atoning death on the Cross but by His supposed teaching us that we can conquer the illusion of sin through positive affirmation. In a similar manner, having "Christ's mind in you" is not a submission to Jesus' teachings as given in the Bible; it means that we are to realize we are God, just as Jesus realized He was God.

In part, the use of biblical and Christian terms explains why some Christians and many nonChristians think that the Unity School of Christianity is Christian. But there is a larger concern. The modern "Christian" positive confession and Word Faith movement, which boasts thousands of churches worldwide and millions of members, is at places doctrinally similar to Unity. As we noted in our book *The Facts on the Faith Movement:*

> Nevertheless, despite the disclaimers, in many places Faith teachings are either similar or nearly identical to those found in the Mind

---

*In nondual advaita Vedanta Hinduism.

Science religions. The concepts of positive confession, prosperity and success, divine health, manipulation of creation, sensory denial, and the implicit rejection of medical science can all be traced to the cultic Mind Science theologies of the 19th and 20th centuries, such as Unity School of Christianity, New Thought, and Science of Mind. (These three groups, along with the Faith Movement, also teach that "negative confession" can produce disease, tragedy, and even death). . . . Perhaps all this is why charismatic historian D. R. McConnell so readily documents the cultic origin of the Faith Movement through E. W. Kenyon: "[The modern father of the Faith Movement, Kenneth] Hagin plagiarized in word and content the bulk of his theology from E. W. Kenyon. All of the Faith teachers, including Kenneth Hagin and Kenneth Copeland, whether they admit it or not, are the spiritual sons and grandsons of E. W. Kenyon. It was Kenyon, not Hagin, who formulated every major doctrine of the modern faith movement. . . . The roots of Kenyon's theology may be traced to his personal background in the metaphysical cults, specifically New Thought and Christian Science. . . . Kenyon attempted to forge a synthesis of metaphysical and evangelical thought. . . . The result in faith theology is a strange mixture of biblical fundamentalism and New Thought metaphysics."[36]

When both Unity and the Word Faith movement teach the same thing about prosperity and other issues, who should be surprised when some people in the churches become confused about Unity? For example, in the publications of Unity churches there is often a "Practical Christianity" series of articles. These may stress how rich we can become, or how successfully and easily we can solve our problems—if we learn to think properly. Unity may offer members a personal "Prosperity Bank" (made of paper), which will make them rich if they have enough faith. Unity writer Catherine Ponder, author of *The Millionaires of Genesis* series, declares: "The secret of wealth is that it begins *within* your own thoughts and feelings. Through the deliberate action of your mind, you can develop a millionaire consciousness that will lead you to literal wealth as well as to increased abundance in all phases of your life . . . *the millionaire consciousness, developed and enjoyed by the great people of Genesis is still available to you today.*"[37] Al-

though Ponder seems to see every major "positive" character in the Bible as a millionaire, the fact is, that most were decidedly poor, particularly Jesus and the apostles. Jesus' parents were so poor they could not even afford the normal offering at his circumcision rite; they had to bring doves, the offering of the poor (Luke 2:24; Leviticus 12:8). One wonders, would Unity argue that Jesus or His parents were "wrong thinkers"? Unity claims to base its ideas on His words, yet Jesus was much poorer than many whom we today would call poor.

Elissa Lindsey McClain once recalled her former life as a member of Unity. As a new Christian, when she expressed concern over discovering Unity teachings in Christianity, she was rebuffed as being unChristian. Writing with a wry sense of humor, she "wonders if the church should apologize to Unity" for calling it a cult and then teaching its doctrines:

When I complained that the current spirituality of some in the Christian church was like a flashback from my past in the metaphysical Unity cult, I found myself accused of being some nefarious "doom and gloomer." . . . As an adolescent who grew up in the Unity churches I was taught to avoid anything that smacked of fear and negativity. Prosperity, health, and happiness were all divine rights that merely needed to be affirmed repeatedly and visualized until the subconscious mind accepted them as reality.

It would seem that today's brand of "popular Christianity" is catching up to Unity's consciousness level!

As a student of Unity, I was taught to approach God boldly, thanking Him in advance for meeting all my desires, even if the actual results were slow in being manifested. We condescendingly tolerated anyone who actually thought they had to beg or plead to God for anything at all. We merely had to deny the negative condition and receive what God had provided. Unity used these principles long before neo-pentecostal "faith" teachers claimed them as the latest revelation knowledge. . . .

I wonder—should the church apologize to Unity for identifying it as one of the largest and most successful cults of our century? It hardly seems fair to brand it a cult if our own churches are copying it.[38]

Rev. Cameron, a Unity minister, has stated that the Church "has often diverted the original teachings of Jesus into a grim preoccupation with sin, evil, the devil, everlasting punishment and all the negatives of the Dark Ages mentality. (I believe we invented the devil to have something to blame things on.)"[39] Of course, anyone who reads the Gospels can see clearly that Jesus believed in sin, the devil and eternal punishment. There are scores of direct or indirect references to these topics. It is not Christianity that has distorted Jesus' teachings, but Unity and, unfortunately, the Word Faith teachers. Unity may claim to be Christian, but the truth lies elsewhere.

The Bible

In 2,000 years, no critic of Christianity or member of another religion has offered a convincing argument for a nonliteral interpretation of Scripture. Indeed, the only way we can understand the true message of the Bible is to interpret it literally by allowing the words to speak for themselves.

The Bible teaches that the Holy Spirit inspired the words of both the New and Old Testaments. The prophets of old were inspired (1 Peter 1:10-12; 2 Peter 1:19-21) and every word in Scripture is God-breathed (2 Timothy 3:16; 2 Peter 3:2, 15-16). The Holy Spirit and what He inspired, then, literally interpreted, is the authoritative standard for evaluating what is or is not Christian. As we will see, Unity members read the Bible nonliterally rather than literally; in essence, it is interpreted in light of Unity beliefs rather than allowed to speak for itself.

At first Charles Fillmore seems to agree with Christians that the Holy Spirit is the author of Scripture and the authority on the Gospel: "The Holy Spirit is the authority on the gospel of Jesus Christ. He is the only authority ever recognized by Jesus Christ, and whoever attempts to set forth the Christ gospel from any other standpoint is in the letter and not in the Spirit. . . . The Holy Spirit gave His words to the writers of the New Testament."[40] But Unity interprets this statement differently than a Christian would. Unity's view of the Bible is that it represents one of man's many repertoires of spiritual truth, although a higher one generally. According to

Fillmore, it is not divinely inspired in a Christian sense, despite that his previous statement claims such inspiration. Fillmore means that the Holy Spirit or "Divine Mind" of Unity revealed the true Gospel (as Unity teachings) and that Divine Mind generally is the only true interpreter of the Gospel and Scripture. Because the Divine Mind also dwells potentially in everyone, everyone potentially can come to interpret the Bible "properly" and see it as a manual of Unity teachings. Thus Fillmore declares, "We need to divest ourselves of the thought that wise men of the Bible were especially inspired by God, that they were divinely appointed by the Lord to do His work."[41] *All* men are so inspired by God to do His work of "Unity," if they will only choose to do this.

When Fillmore claimed that "the Holy Spirit gave His words to the writers of the New Testament" he did not mean that those words were to be interpreted literally. To interpret the Bible literally "by the letter," or normally, is a serious mistake. Fillmore argued that Jesus' alleged reference to "the letter kills, but the Spirit gives life" is to be interpreted (by Unity) as a scriptural denial to interpret the Bible literally. Besides being wrong on this interpretation, he got the source wrong too. It was the Apostle Paul, commenting upon the law bringing death, not Jesus who said this (2 Corinthians 3:6,7).

In essence, Unity interprets the Bible metaphysically "by the Spirit." What this means is that the divine Spirit in every person will, if people are "open to the Spirit," interpret the Bible "properly" by helping them to see its true meaning (one in conformity with Unity beliefs). What happens is that Unity members slowly become indoctrinated by Unity literature and teachings and interpret this as biblical teaching. Thus they eventually develop a mindset that reads the Bible primarily through the eyes of Unity teachings and not the language, history and culture of the Bible itself. They then understand this as "being led by the Spirit."

However, Fillmore and Unity members encounter something of a double standard here. If the Bible can be interpreted literally, even out of context, they will do so when it supports their position. For example, Fillmore wrote: "I have proved to my own satisfaction that when Jesus said, 'The kingdom of God is within you,' He meant it literally and not figuratively."[42] Fillmore ignores the better interpretation of "among you," which the Greek allows. Jesus spoke these words to God's *enemies* who certainly did *not* have God's Spirit or kingdom within them. But since the words interpreted literally seem to support a Unity belief—the "Kingdom of God" is in all people regardless of their religious beliefs—Fillmore conveniently chooses the literal interpretation. Of course, when the literal interpretation opposes his beliefs, a spiritualizing or allegorizing of Scripture immediately takes precedence.

Further, the "Divine Mind" of the individual supposedly interprets the Word of God properly because Divine Mind *is* the Word of God. In the revised 1979 edition of Fillmore's *Mysteries of Genesis* he says, "So it is not true to say that the Bible is 'the creative Word' of God. The Christ [spiritual principle] in Jesus is the creative Word. Spiritual man is the Word of God. . . . The Word of God is the living, creative force that is man's spiritual mind."[43] Thus, "An understanding of God or universal Mind, is a key to all scriptures and occult writings."[44] But as we will see, Unity ends up with many different interpretations of the same passage and a "Divine Mind" in confusion.

This gnostic approach to Scripture is not unique to Unity. Groups such as the Theosophical Society, the Rosicrucians, the Unification Church, The Way International, Swedenborgianism, Bahai, Self Realization Fellowship, Edgar Cayce, Astara, The Family (Children of God) and many other groups all see the Bible as a hidden book until the proper key (the unbiblical beliefs of the group) is applied to unlock its truths. (This is also true for the more traditional cults such as Jehovah's Witnesses and Mormonism.) The Bible, they would say, can only be interpreted properly by church authorities within the groups. Thus Fillmore declared that the Bible was a sealed book properly interpreted only by Unity: "The New Testament is a sealed book to one who has no knowledge of the laws of mind. It is a secret manual. It reads like an ordinary narrative unless one has the key that unlocks its hidden meaning. Practical Christianity [Unity]

gives that key."[45] (See "Unity Hermeneutics" under "Critical Analysis" section.)

According to Freeman, "the dean of Unity historians," "The Fillmores did not advance any new teachings. All that they taught is based on the Bible, and especially on the teachings of Jesus. . . . They felt that Unity is a return to His original teachings, a return needed for centuries."[46] Again, Unity claims to be truly Christian and to offer Jesus' true teachings but the truth is that it rejects the teachings of Jesus and the Bible.[47] To document this, we will now examine in detail the Unity theology and compare it to biblical teaching.

God

The God of Unity is ultimately described as an *impersonal* Spiritual principle or law that somehow has "personal" attributes. God is already present within everyone, regardless of their religious or non-religious persuasions. What is needed is recognition of and knowledge about this abiding divine presence, and how to use it. Biblically, of course, repentance from sin and faith in Christ brings God's presence, but Freeman tells us that we come to realize God's presence by developing our consciousness along Unity lines:

> God is with you. Yes, God! . . . You have access to God. . . . You may feel, however, that you have no awareness that God is with you. If that is so, you can develop it. How can you develop it? You can develop it through prayer [right thinking]. It may come immediately. It may come slowly. But if you consciously and persistently seek the presence of God, you will find that presence. . . . Many persons have to build a consciousness of the presence of God thought by thought as one builds a house brick by brick.[48]

As to the nature of God, Unity teaches that God is an infinite spiritual Mind that functions as Law. God is an impersonal creative force and law that manifests through ideas as life:

> God is the absolute, incomparable, omnipresent All-Good, the principle of divine benevolence that permeates the universe. . . . God as Principle is the unchangeable life, love, intelligence,

and substance of Being. . . . God as law is Principle in action. . . . God is the one harmonious Principle underlying all being and the Reality out of which all that is eternal comes. . . . God is Spirit, the Principle of creative life, the moving force in the universe. . . . Spirit is not matter. Spirit is not Person. . . . By the term *Mind*, we mean God–the universal Principle. . . . Love, in Divine Mind, is the idea of universal unity. Of all the attributes of God, love is undoubtedly the most beautiful. . . . Divine love is impersonal.[49]

A primary Unity reference work, the *Metaphysical Bible Dictionary (MBD)*, defines "Spirit" as a "name for God. Spirit and Mind are synonymous; therefore we know God-Spirit as Mind, the one Mind, or Intelligence, of the universe."[50] Ultimately, only God (Mind) exists. This is monism and it stands in stark contrast to the theology of biblical Christianity, which teaches that a personal Spirit (God) created a real material universe that is separate from Himself.

Again, in Unity, the expression of Mind, its thought, is the creation around us. Fillmore synthesizes this philosophy into a metaphysical reinterpretation of the Christian Trinity: "First is mind, the mind expresses itself in ideas, then the ideas make themselves manifest [in creation]. This is a metaphysical statement of the divine Trinity, Father, Son and Holy Spirit."[51] Unity ultimately defines God as impersonal in contrast to the God of Scripture who is personal and triune. In *Dynamics for Living* Fillmore argues against belief in a personal God, viewing this as spiritual deception.[52] One Unity member told us that belief in a personal God was actually destructive to humanity.

"All concepts of God as less than universal mind are Baal. Those who believe in a personal God are Baal worshipers."[53] In other words, Unity teaches that Christians are, in effect, worshipers of a false god at best and "devil" worshipers at worst. Because recognition of God as Principle (that is, as Impersonal Law) is so important to realizing the spiritual goals of Unity, one must abandon belief in a personal God. This is because a God who is a Person and Sovereign Lord of all cannot be manipulated the way an impersonal Principle can. He cannot be manipulated at all. Thus, Fillmore declared, "We must

relieve our minds of a personal God ruling over us. . . . God is not person but Principle. . . . The fundamental basis of practical Christianity is that God is Principle."[54]

What are the implications of this, not only for ourselves as individuals but also for our relationship with God? Christians know that a human being, being created in the image of a God who is personal, is also a person. Yet the *Metaphysical Bible Dictionary* declares that "spiritual perception reveals to us *that we are not persons,* but *factors* in the cosmic mind."[55] If we are just "factors" in an impersonal mental Principle, how can we ever have a personal relationship with God as the Bible teaches? Clearly, we cannot. Yet Unity leads people to believe that they can have something they cannot: a personal relationship from an ultimately impersonal Principle. How can a "Principle" have holiness, benevolence, mercy or love? Can a rock love us or a tree answer our prayers? People may have sublime feelings or awe when faced with the grandeur of something impersonal like nature; but nature cannot communicate with them personally, and nature has absolutely no concern for people. Just so, no impersonal Principle can have any concern for people.

What Unity offers people is an alleged Divine Mind that by its very nature can have no concern about them. This is a far cry from the personal God of the Bible who loves, is merciful and desires a personal relationship with us. Anyone who can look at the God of the Bible and at the Jesus of the Gospels and reject them, and choose instead to have a "relationship" with an impersonal Principle, should not be surprised at the outcome. Jesus offers eternal life—personal immortality with a perfect God—as a free gift. What Unity offers is infinitely less.

Jesus Christ

The Jesus Christ of Unity is not the Jesus Christ of the Bible, the Second Person of the Holy Trinity, but the invention of Charles Fillmore to support Unity teachings. The Jesus of Unity is the Unity practitioner and exemplar above all others.

According to Unity, once a person is mentally in harmony with universal law, he or she becomes a "God-man." Jesus, who became the Christ, was such a God-man, and provides the supreme example to help us discover our innate divine nature and power. Our personality, according to Unity, is a barrier to the innate spirituality that allows us to experience our divinity: "We are all, in our personality, wearing the mask that conceals the real, the spiritual I AM [God-self]."[56] If we can remove our personality by becoming absorbed into the divine consciousness, we can become aware of our divine nature and thus experience our divinity. In fact, we "become Christ": "Whoever so loses his personality as to be swallowed up in God becomes Christ Jesus or God-man."[57] Christ is this true hidden self of each individual.

Unity informs us Jesus is not so much unique as he is exemplary, because more than anyone, allegedly, "Jesus Christ knew how the law of divine imagination works."[58] He is the prototype we are destined to become, and the sooner we begin changing our mental habits the quicker this will happen: "There are no miracles in science. Jesus did no miracles. All His marvelous works were done under the laws that we may learn and use as He did."[59] Thus, Jesus is different from the rest of us in degree but not in kind. For Unity, the key difference was in Jesus' thought life; this is what made Him the kind of special man He was. "To say that Jesus Christ was a man as we are men is not correct, because He had dropped that personal consciousness by which we separate ourselves into men and women. He was consciously one with the absolute principle of Being. He had no consciousness separate from that Being, hence He was that Being to all intents and purposes. He attained no more than is expected of each of us."[60] In other words, anyone who wishes can become exactly like Jesus Christ.

As we have seen, in line with its gnostic beliefs, Unity separates "Jesus" and "the Christ." Jesus Christ was not the eternal second Person of the Trinity who became a man to die for man's sins, thus becoming two natures (divine and human) in one Person. Jesus was only a man, a man who attained a higher mental state, "the Christ idea." In other words, the "Christ" is God's idea of man perfected in consciousness. J. Sig Paulson explains in *Unity* magazine:

Because of traditional religious heritage, most of the time we probably think of *Jesus, Jesus Christ,* and *Christ* as synonyms. However, as we come into a greater understanding of these terms, we can see that there are differences. . . . Each individual has within himself the Christ potential, the Christ presence, the Christ reality. . . .

Most of our religious beliefs are based on the idea [erroneous, according to Unity] that Jesus is the only begotten Son of God. When this belief is our foundation, we begin to think of the Kingdom of God as something outside ourself and heaven as a destination toward which we are headed, rather than as a potential that is unfolding within us.[61]

We can become the Christ because the Christ is a "higher" state of consciousness, not a person. Jesus manifested the Christ perfectly and so can we. According to the *Metaphysical Bible Dictionary,* you "reveal yourself to yourself," "by affirming '*I am the Christ, son of the living God*'."[62] Supposedly, this affirmation will inevitably help produce its realization. Another blasphemous affirmation reads: "I am the son of God. . . . I am the only begotten son, dwelling in the bosom of the Father. I am the Christ of God, I am the beloved son in whom the Father is well pleased. He that hath seen me hath seen the Father. I and my Father are one. I am the image and likeness of God. . . . Of a truth I am the son of God."[63]

Again, the ability to live as the absolute Son of God (as Christ was) is a potential that Unity claims resides in every man and woman. It is here that we encounter one of Unity's many practical failures. Unity has never adequately explained the great futility of its program of positive thinking which, it claims, allows people to realize and display their Christ nature. No one in Unity has ever become who Christ is—or even approached His perfection. Yet as we read previously, "He attained no more than is *expected* of each of us." So why has no one ever attained this expectation? Could it be because Unity teachings are false? If Jesus was really so "common," really our true potential, why was He so unique in what He "attained"? If the teachings of Unity have never produced another Christ, not one among millions of people, and yet such potential can be achieved for anyone,

Unity has a serious problem claiming to be "*practical* Christianity." Unity then, is a terrible failure. The obvious conclusion is that people do not have the potential to become Christ.

Take the most celebrated example of the power of positive thinking in Unity history, Charles Fillmore and compare his life with the life of Jesus. Examine both carefully. Did Fillmore, or do his followers, really believe that he was the person Jesus Christ was? How can Jesus be offered as an example of the proof of what Unity can do for us when, normally understood, His teachings deny every fundamental teaching of Unity? How could Jesus have been spiritually *perfect* when He rejected the doctrines of Unity? Because the teachings of Jesus are historically established, even Unity cannot logically deny that they refute Unity beliefs. When Unity claims that Jesus taught Unity ideals, the only evidence provided is Unity's *distortion* of Christ's teachings. Obviously, claims without verification mean little.

Because Unity has a false view of Jesus and a false view of man, it can never attain what it promises. Unity's claim to be a program of spiritual advancement toward Christhood therefore must be rejected. Yet we are asked to believe: "Each of us has within him the Christ, just as Jesus had, and we must look within to recognize and realize our sonship, our divine origin and birth, even as He did. By continually unifying ourselves with the Highest by our thoughts and words, *we too, shall become sons of God, manifest*."[64]

Again, where are the other Christs that have manifested? As we will discuss later, Fillmore himself confessed that the most serious legitimate criticism that others make of Unity is its failure to produce other Christs. If not even Fillmore's advanced positive thinking could achieve the ideal, how can the average Unity member?

Salvation, Works, Atonement

As a gnostic religion, Unity teaches salvation through the application of special knowledge. There is no sin to be forgiven, only something new to understand: believe that you are a Son of God and your belief alone will make it true. To "believe in Jesus" means to believe in your true divine nature; this is Unity's "good news" or gospel. Thus according to Fillmore, salvation in Unity comes by "believing in our divinity."[65]

Fillmore quotes John 17:20–22 (where Jesus prays for all Christians' unity with Him) and teaches this is evidence that every person is potentially the Son of God. Fillmore believes that here Jesus teaches that in our true nature we all are the Son of God. He neglects to quote Jesus' words in context, however, and thus misleads people. Jesus qualified His statement as applying only to believers, who were "not of the [unbelieving] world" according to verse 16. Jesus was even more forceful in verse 9, which qualifies this prayer, "I ask on their behalf; I do *not* ask on behalf of the world, but of those whom Thou hast given me" (NAS). This is only one of many examples of how Fillmore distorts the Bible. Another example is seen in the following citation, where Fillmore rejects the biblical Gospel as an illusion of animal consciousness:

> There can be but one leader for man in his search for God—the Spirit within him. When he unreservedly gives himself to this Spirit. . . . He finds that the church of Jesus Christ is not a church at all. . . . He has looked upon his religion as having to do with the salvation of his soul. . . . That he may be prepared to go to a place called "heaven" after death. When the true church is revealed to his soul, all this illusion of the animal man is dissolved.[66]

In Unity, salvation comes by personal effort, by attaining through mental effort an evolved state of consciousness that "rests" in proper thinking. Thus "the promise of salvation is for everyone. But man must attain it."[67] Fillmore further emphasized salvation by works when he wrote, "Eternal life must be earned," and "No one ever attained spiritual consciousness without striving for it."[68] "Salvation" is achieved by an applied process of "clearer" thinking: "The essential steps that must be taken before man can enter Spirit are: First, there must be an earnest desire to know and feel the presence of God. Second, there must be willingness to eliminate "sense" thoughts from consciousness. This is accomplished through denying error expression, in thought and act, and affirming the substantial ideas of Spirit."[69]

In Unity, man forgives himself (by his own mental processes) when he turns from a (false) *belief* in sin. He does not have to turn from sin itself because there is no sin itself. Forgiveness is defined by Fillmore as the "giving" of truth "for" error because, "All sin is first in the mind; the forgiveness is a change of mind or repentance. We forgive sin in ourself every time we resolve to think and act according to divine law."[70] Thus, "Forgiveness is a process of giving up the false for the true; erasing sin and error from the mind and body. It is closely related to repentance, which is a turning from [a false] belief in sin to belief in God and righteousness.... True forgiveness is only established through renewing of the mind and body with thoughts and words of Truth."[71]

Salvation in Unity is therefore something we achieve for ourselves by mental application; it is not something we receive as a free gift by believing on Jesus Christ. Not surprisingly then, Unity considers it a serious spiritual error to accept the basic biblical doctrine of salvation by faith in Jesus (1 John 5:10–13). It is not the biblical Jesus we must accept, but the Unity Jesus: "The church is not so far wrong in its call to 'follow Jesus.' The error lies in the belief that He was the only begotten Son of God, and that He overcame for us, and that by simply *believing on Him* we are saved."[72] But this is exactly what Jesus and the Bible teach: "Believe in the Lord Jesus, and you will be saved . . ." (Acts 16:31). "For God so loved the world that he gave his one and only Son, that whoever believes in him shall not perish but have eternal life" (John 3:16). "He who believes has eternal life" (John 6:47 NAS).

Unity believes that through a process of spiritual evolution and reincarnation, men can work to inevitably become Jesus Christ. Even if their present state of consciousness is primitive and unevolved, inevitably "they must be equal with Him before they will emerge from the sense of delusion in which they now wander."[73] This "sense of delusion" is how Unity views sin. Because Unity principally defines sin as wrong thinking, rather than as moral violation of God's law, each Unity member learns that by control over his mind he can become "sinless." In their true nature, everyone is already "sinless," and

by realizing and slowly appropriating this "truth" more and more into their thought patterns, they become as they believe: "The whole secret of the demonstration of Christ is that we shall come to realize our original sinlessness. . . . We must be perfect, even as Jesus was perfect. There is no other way."[74]

Salvation, then, is clearly not something received from without by "receiving Christ" as Lord and Savior, but something to be realized from within, the appropriation of a latent innate perfection and deity: "The Kingdom of God is the potentiality within man. . . . The activity of God within us is our salvation. Salvation is not something that is handed to us from an outer source."[75] The *Metaphysical Bible Dictionary* goes so far as to declare that Christians have "devised iniquity and given wicked counsel" in assuring others of salvation by grace through faith alone. In fact, Christians are false prophets:

Many persons today think that by faith in an outer Jesus they will be saved and taken to heaven, to enjoy spirituality and all the blessings of life and good, without really [mentally] overcoming their sinful nature on this earth. They are mistaken, however. Those who teach such a doctrine are false prophets, for Jesus Christ came to save His people from their sins, not in them or in spite of them. Only those who actually put away sin here in the body [i.e., mentally] will be able to enter the heavenly realm and be saved alive and entire.[76]

Only Unity members can truly experience God's grace, "For in order to experience the blessings of the grace of God we must put ourselves in line with them by [mentally] cleansing our mind and heart and life, and by doing the will of the Father, thus keeping the divine law."[77]

It is ironic that Unity speaks of sanctification and of keeping the divine law when it does not accept the biblical teaching on sin. Unity's "sanctification," of course, is far more mental than behavioral. Whereas Christians—who by God's grace and the power of the Holy Spirit—do achieve significant reduction in the commission of sin, Unity claims that people can keep the divine law and attain sinless perfection apart from God's power entirely. Again, where is the evidence? Further, the Bible clearly teaches that salvation is by grace, through faith, and not by works: "For it is by grace you have been saved, through faith—and this not from yourselves, it is the gift of God—not by works, so that no one can boast" (Ephesians 2:8–9). But Fillmore disagrees: "All down the ages, ministers of the gospel have assumed that the requirements are met when men have been persuaded to believe in the Lord Jesus Christ as the Saviour of their souls, and to keep on believing this until they pass out of their bodies; then, the teaching runs, believers are received into the arms of the Lord. But the Holy Spirit does not endorse this assumption, neither does the letter of the Scriptures."[78] But the "letter of the Scriptures" is exactly what proves Fillmore wrong (John 6:29, 40; Acts 7:59; Philippians 1:21, 23; 1 John 3:23; 5:11–12).

Unity has a view of the atonement consistent with its overall philosophy and similar to that of certain occult groups, such as the Holy Order of Mans. Fillmore denied the propitiatory nature of Jesus' death on the Cross and transformed it into a "blood transfusion" for the consciousness of the race. At His ascension, Jesus supposedly translated His body into a spiritual substance and diffused His self-perfected "life essence" into the consciousness of humanity. For Unity this is the "true" meaning of the blood of Jesus giving life to the world. Fillmore wrote in *Dynamics for Living* that there is "life" for all who receive His blood forgiveness (according to Unity's meaning of it). "Jesus Christ broadcast the electrons of His blood into the race thought atmosphere and they may be apprehended by all who believe in Him. These electrons become centers of energy and life in those who appropriate them. Thus, men gradually transform and regenerate their blood and their body. This is the real spiritual meaning of being saved by Jesus Christ."[79]

Here we encounter another serious problem in Unity. If everyone is divine, and if Jesus' ascension actually transferred part of His enlightened essence into the consciousness of humanity, how is it that so few of the human race—much less than .1 percent—ever join Unity? If the human mind is one with God in essence, how could it ever fall into ignorance of who it was? Even Fillmore agrees that "the mind does not always [!] comprehend the I AM in its highest, neither does it discern that the all knowing, omnipotent One is within man."[80] What kind of omniscient, omnipotent mind is this, and why was Unity's Jesus such a failure in His mission?

Regardless, Unity teaches that the biblical atonement of Jesus Christ is fiction. According to Charles Fillmore, the Christian idea of the atonement was invented by the Apostle Paul simply as an extension of his belief in the levitical system of animal sacrifice. As an orthodox Jew, Paul's "consciousness" was so concentrated on the concept of blood atonement that he erroneously extended this idea to the idea of Jesus shedding His blood to forgive the sin of the world:

> By believing that Jesus was more divine than other men, the church has assumed that He had certain privileges that the Father does not extend to all; that in a superhuman way He made good all our shortcomings; that we are saved from suffering for our acts by simply believing on Him and accepting Him, in a perfunctory way, as our Saviour. Paul is responsible for a good share of this throwing of the whole burden upon the blood of Jesus—doubtless the result of an old mental tendency carried over from his Hebrew idea of the blood sacrifice of the priesthood. In order to show the parallel in the life of Jesus, Paul preached to the Jews that He was the great once-for-all blood sacrifice and that no other blood sacrifice would ever become necessary.[81]

Here, Fillmore engages in what religious cults and critics of Christianity do on a routine basis. He ignores history, culture and common sense psychology in dealing with the Christian religion. In fact, the Apostle Paul could never have "invented" the Christian religion for several reasons. One was his intense hatred of Jesus and Christianity. Anyone who reads his words at face value would know that Paul would have been the last person in the world to fabricate Jesus into the atoning Savior of all men (Acts 8:1, 3; 22; 26). Only the appearance of the risen Jesus to Paul can logically explain his conversion to faith in Christ, as Paul himself testified before both Jewish and Roman authorities.

Charles Fillmore, however, claims that he was an advanced reincarnation of Saint Paul.[82] As a result, he could readily "justify" claiming more "enlightened" ideas on the atonement than the relatively "primitive" soul who inhabited Paul's body 2,000 years ago. Thus Fillmore forcefully denied the atonement and argued instead that "the crucifixion of Jesus represents the wiping of personality out of consciousness."[83] Even though Fillmore attributed Paul's teaching (a literal propitiatory atonement) to unenlightened "backward" ideas, Fillmore also declared, "Paul had a better understanding of the relation that we bear to Christ than any other Bible writer"[84] If so, how did Paul emphasize a *literal* propitiatory atonement of Christ *throughout* his writings? And if Paul was so wrong on the atonement, how can we accept anything Charles Fillmore claims about Paul?

The Unity division between "Jesus" the man and "Christ" as spiritual enlightenment is extended into its doctrine of atonement. Thus, the Christ as divine truth cannot possibly suffer or die: "We know that Jesus died on that cross. I say 'Jesus', because Christ did not die, but *Jesus* did in the sense that He was able to give up the body and give up all the outer relationships of the world."[85]

Fillmore is not reading his Bible carefully, for "Jesus Christ [is] the Righteous One . . . the atoning sacrifice for . . . the sins of the whole world," and "Who is the liar? It is the man who denies that Jesus is the Christ" (1 John 2:1-2; 2:22). Jesus never became the Christ (Messiah); He was *born* the Christ: "Today . . . a Savior has been born to you; he *is* Christ, the Lord" (Luke 2:11; cf., 1:35). For Fillmore to argue that the Jewish concept of the Messiah is really a state of "higher" consciousness is nonsense.

Unity not only denies any need for the atonement of Christ or individual repentance from sin but also, like most cults, conceptually insulates a person from these ideas. "Man has unlimited power through thought. . . . If he thinks about the power of sin . . . he forgets his spiritual origin and sees only the human. Thus he thinks of himself as a sinner. . . . If anyone tries to free himself

while holding others in the thought of sin [seeing them as sinners], he will not demonstrate his freedom. . . . The personal man [the individual separate from God] must be eliminated."[86]

"Divine forgiveness" in Unity has no relation at all to the biblical concept because in Unity we forgive ourselves merely by understanding that there is no sin to forgive. As a result of this philosophy, it holds that those who believe in Christ's atonement for sin are deceived and shortsighted. The average "unenlightened" Christian simply does not have the spiritual acumen to understand the true meaning of Christ's death, and the Christian church has only made matters worse. By "materializing" the metaphysical significance of the Cross, the Christian church has permitted a demonic "sense (material) consciousness" to deceive it into teaching falsehoods:

We have been taught by the church that Jesus died for us—as an atonement for our sins. By human sense this belief has been materialized into a flesh-and-blood process, in which the death of the body on the cross played the important part. Herein has the sense consciousness led the church astray. . . .

Jesus of Nazareth played an important part in opening the way for every one of us into the Father's Kingdom. *However, that way was not through His death on the cross,* but through His overcoming [the sense of] death. "I am the resurrection, and the life."

To comprehend the atonement requires a deeper insight into creative processes than the average man and the average woman have attained; not because they lack the ability to understand, but because they have submerged their thinking power in a grosser thought stratum. So only those who study Being from the standpoint of pure mind can ever understand the atonement.[87]

In *The New Birth in Christ* Fillmore criticizes the Christian doctrine of salvation as "shortsighted." For Fillmore, man is the true Savior, not Jesus. Thus, when Christians mistakenly think they are saved "only" by faith in Jesus Christ, such belief betrays a "shortsighted understanding" of the far more complex evolutionary journey of the soul toward divinity throughout many lifetimes:

> Christians who have a "change of heart" and unusual spiritual experiences when they are converted think that they have had the new birth, and that they are saved, and that they will go to heaven and live with Jesus when they die. This is a shortsighted understanding of a process in the evolution of the soul, which progresses in spiritual understanding, incarnation after incarnation, until it reaches its climax in complete overcoming of the sense consciousness and the transformation of the body, as demonstrated by Jesus.[88]

According to Fillmore, the process of the "new birth" (John 3:3–5) occurs *only* when we recognize our divinity, which is when we supposedly begin to reflect the consciousness of Jesus Himself. "When the consciousness of his divinity dawns upon man, he begins the new birth. He is then the infant Jesus, begotten by the Holy Spirit and born of the virgin, pure Truth."[89]

Again, the very idea of the Christian atonement of Jesus Christ is a spiritually destructive teaching, according to Unity. If we trust in a lie about Jesus' atonement, rather than trust in our own potential divinity, we will never progress spiritually. But if we are truly enlightened, we can forgive our own sins and eventually raise our own bodies to eternal life, just like Jesus:

> Everyone who would demonstrate that he is risen with Christ must first lay hold of life by faith and affirm, without wavering, that he is raised out of sin and condemnation and death into life eternal. Then the word of life carries on, day by day, the resurrecting, redemptive work in the mind and in the body. Every day some old limitation or error loses its hold and passes away, and the imperishable incorruptible substance of Truth becomes a little more firmly established in consciousness. In this way the body is transformed and raised up in honor, incorruptible, immortal.[90]

Once again, Unity teaches that positive affirmation has omnipotent power. But once again, no evidence is provided.

Charles Fillmore and modern Unity teachers reject the historic Christian teaching on the atoning death of Jesus Christ.[91] To accept it would undermine their own program of mental and spiritual "salvation." Thus they reject the words of Jesus Himself when He declared that He came to "give his life as a ransom for many" (Matthew 20:28), and that His blood was "poured out for many for the forgiveness of sins" (Matthew 26:28), because "He Himself is the propitiation for our sins; and not for ours only, but also for those of the whole world" (1 John 2:2 NAS).

Man

Earlier we discussed Unity's belief that in essence and true spiritual consciousness, everyone is one with God. The true self is indistinguishable from God because it is God's spiritual idea manifested. Once a person realizes and appropriates his unity with God then he knows "there is no absence or separation in God. His omnipresence is your omnipresence. There can be no absence in Mind."[92] That people can recognize their divinity and "become" God is a doctrine that appears frequently in Unity. "God is man and man is God and there is no separation. . . ."[93] "Every man asks the question at some time, 'What am I?' God answers: 'Spiritually you are My idea of Myself as I see Myself in the ideal; physically you are the law of My mind executing that idea.'"[94] "To 'know thyself' is to know that you are I AM, and not flesh and blood."[95] "Man is by nature an organizer. It is his function in the Godhead to formulate the potentialities of Principle."[96] "Man is spirit, soul, and body. The Spirit is I AM, and I AM is the ego of Deity."[97] Unity author Sue Sikking declares in her book *God Always Says Yes:* "We are God in essence, God to be. Since God is all and in all, what could we ourselves possibly be but God?"[98]

We not only "become" God in essence and nature but also, Unity believes, surpass the dominion and power of Jesus Christ:

> Jesus wants companions in power, dominion, and glory. . . . The gospel of Jesus Christ is that all men shall become God incarnate. It is not alone a gospel of right living. *It shows the way into dominion and power equal to and surpassing that of Jesus of Nazareth.* If we have a sense

of inferiority, if we believe that He has greater wisdom, or power, or love, then we are not fulfilling the requirements. So long as we feel any difference between ourself in the Father and Jesus in the Father, we have fallen short of that "mind . . . which you have in Christ Jesus."[99]

Most Unity members do not seem to realize the serious unbiblical nature of such claims. God has exalted Jesus above everything in creation (Ephesians 1:21; Philippians 2:9–11). To exalt ourselves above Jesus (God) is a true affront to God. In rejecting God's own infinite perfections and glory and by exalting their sinful natures, Unity believers are guilty of pride and blasphemy, which God has sworn to judge and punish:

> You said in your heart, "I will ascend to heaven; . . . I will make myself like the Most High." But you are brought down to the grave, to the depths of the pit. (Isaiah 14:13–15)

> In the pride of your heart you say, "I am a god; I sit on the throne of a god." . . . But you are a man and not a god, though you think you are as wise as a god. . . . Therefore this is what the Sovereign LORD says: ". . . You think you are wise, as wise as a god. . . . Will you then say, 'I am a god,' in the presence of those who kill you? You will be but a man, not a god, in the hands of those who slay you." (Ezekiel 28:2, 6, 9)

> Like the blind we grope along the wall, feeling our way like men without eyes . . . For our offenses are many in your sight, and our sins testify against us. Our offenses are ever with us, and we acknowledge our iniquities: rebellion and treachery against the LORD, turning our backs on our God, fomenting oppression and revolt, uttering lies our hearts have conceived. So justice is driven back, and righteousness stands at a distance; truth has stumbled in the streets, honesty cannot enter. . . . According to what they have done, so will he repay wrath to his enemies and retribution to his foes . . . (Isaiah 59:10, 12–14, 18).

Sin, the Fall

Unity has no divine Savior and no propitiatory atonement because it has no sin. Thus, a common Unity "affirmation" to counteract one's doubts about this is: "There is no evil."[100] Sin

is merely "wrong thinking" according to Fillmore.[101] For Unity writer P. Stovin sin is "our separation from God in consciousness" resulting from belief in any power other than God.[102]

As we have seen, Unity believes that sin, in a biblical sense, is merely an illusion. The real sin is misperception—in this case, to believe sin is real. According to Unity *believing* in sin is what *causes* sin to exist; thinking sin is real is what brings it into being. In other words, the definition of a sinner is simply one who believes in the reality of sin. According to Unity, this belief in sin is unnecessary because sin is unreal and therefore there are no sinners. We *become* sinners if we give sin reality and thus deny our inherent divine perfection. In his *Mysteries of Genesis*, Fillmore defines divine living as recognizing *only* the existence of God or good. Living in such a manner, a person "sees that evil is unreal and unnecessary," and that for anyone who follows God's ways, inevitably "evil will be to him totally unreal."[103]

Obviously then, the Fall of man was through faulty consciousness rather than moral disobedience (to the commandment of God in Genesis). Once the *idea* of evil was entertained in Adam's consciousness, it became a "reality" and man "fell." "Adam, as originally created, was in illumination. Spirit continually breathed into him the inspiration and knowledge that gave him superior understanding. But he began eating (or appropriating) the idea of two powers— God and not-God, good and evil. The result, so the allegory relates, was a falling away from life and all that it involves. This was the first death."[104]

In effect, Adam *created* sin by thinking it was real. Here we can understand one reason why Unity is so opposed to Christianity and why Christianity must be opposed to Unity, just as it was to gnosticism in the early church: Unity makes biblical Christianity a major evil because it causes sin in the world. Because Christianity emphasizes the reality of evil, it is a principal contributor to *producing* evil. Thus Christians, who believe in sin, are actually *originators* of sin. In *The Christ-Based Teachings* Curtis illustrates this idea when he writes: "The only cause for all of the problems in the world is the false belief in duality—in good versus evil."[105] In other words, if everyone just believed there was only good, there would, supposedly, be no evil.

Obviously, the Unity concept of sin has nothing in common with the biblical meaning. Unity's idea involves an ignorance in thinking and so-called "material" contamination. It involves a "falling short" of the Divine Law or Principle in Unity which tells us there is no sin. In Unity, the only real "sin" is not to appropriate the truth of Divine Law and thus remain in "ignorance."

Biblically, of course, sin is real. It is a moral violation of God's infinite holiness and thus separates us from God. "Sin is lawlessness," a transgression of God's law (1 John 3:4). "Your iniquities have separated you from your God" (Isaiah 59:2). The Bible contains more than a thousand references to sin, evil, iniquity, transgression, and such like. Unity, however, declares all this is irrelevant. In Unity it is actually *sinful* to believe we are separate from God. Clearly, to believe what Unity teaches about sin insulates people against the Christian Gospel: no one can trust what Unity teaches and be saved from their sins. Biblically, sin is real. Thus, the Apostle Paul spoke of "the body of this death" and stated that nothing good dwells in our flesh because of the contamination by sin (Romans 7:18-24). Unless sin is forgiven through faith in Christ, sin will send a person to eternal judgment because until a person turns to Christ he is lost and under the wrath of God (John 3:36). Note what a contrast this is to Unity teachings: "We are spiritual beings; there is no sin in us in our spiritual estate, and that estate is the *real*."[106] "Through the Christ Mind, our sins (wrong thinking) are forgiven or pardoned (erased from consciousness). When we have cast all sin (error thought) out of our mind, our body will be so pure that it cannot come under any supposed law of death or corruption."[107] How convenient—the sins of the world can be washed away merely by thinking it so. And also how irreverent—yet another aspersion upon the love of Jesus who was crucified and died a torturous death to freely forgive our sins.

So with stakes so high, upon what biblical or empirical basis can Unity document its view of sin? Did Charles Fillmore ever become sinless? Did he ever physically rise from the dead as proof of his teachings, as Jesus did in confirmation of His? Do Unity members escape the sin common to us all by denying its reality and thinking only of "the omnipotent Good"? What evidence is offered to show that Unity has real power over even its own imagined sin?

Unity will never offer convincing evidence of its views because its views comprise a denial of reality, everything we know about human nature and human history. Here, those who argue that Unity constitutes a platform for self-deception are correct. If any biblical doctrine has empirical proof, it is the doctrine of sin! To deny evil in this day and age, one would have to be less than spiritually enlightened.

The Afterlife

Just as there is no Savior, no atonement and no sin in Unity, there is no death: "There is no need of any state or condition called death. The word 'death' is a denial of God's idea of life."[108]

Death. Death is one more illusion that Unity members think they can avoid. Everyone dies, but Unity teaches that death is unnecessary. If its members will exercise their divine prerogative, they can live forever. In fact, as we will see, Charles Fillmore taught that he would *never* see physical death. Once again Unity is caught in the embarrassment that a denial of a universal human experience brings. Everybody dies, and the Bible teaches that we die because we sin (Romans 6:23). Unity declares that none of this is necessary if we only trust what Charles Fillmore taught. But Charles Fillmore was a sinner like us all and he died like us all, so why should he be trusted when he tells us that death can be avoided?

Charles Fillmore also believed in reincarnation, although not in the traditional Hindu sense. As with other teachings that he borrowed, if there was something he did not like he simply changed it. Fillmore believed the traditional Eastern religious theory was too fatalistic. If people must work out the smallest effect of all their karma from past incarnations through an inviolate universal law, the idea neutralized his concept of spiritual evolution through positive thinking. This would never do for a spiritual optimist like Fillmore. His cosmic law could not possibly constitute an inviolate karma, three millennia of Hindu tradition notwithstanding. His cosmic law had to be subservient to the mind of man.

Fillmore further taught that the progress of each individual was in some way tied to the progress of the race as a whole. The importance of thinking positively is that we not only guarantee "eternal life" for ourselves but help generate it for others. "It is our place to hold ourself in a positive life thought, realizing always the omnipresence and perfection of life in God, thus bringing perfect life more and more into manifestation in ourself and in others. When we realize how much our faithfulness means to the race, we shall rejoice in being true to the great truths that will bring to pass the time when death and the grave will be no more."[109]

Unity teaches that those who have an ignorant primitive thought life are already "dead." This includes Christians who believe God and man are ontologically separate. Such individuals are now experiencing the "first" death, a death in consciousness of their divine nature as a result of spiritual ignorance of divine truth. Biblically, however, the "first death" is *physical* death, separation of the spirit from a dead body, which then decays. Unity defines physical death as the *second* death. According to Unity, Unity thinking leads to life eternal but Christian thinking leads to the second (physical) death:

> [Physical] Death is always the result of a failure to recognize God as the source of wisdom and life. When the soul falls short in this respect, it sins and there is a physical dissolution that is but the outer symbol of mental negation or spiritual inertia.
>
> This death or dissolution of the body is the "second death" over the meaning of which church people have so long contended. The first death is where the consciousness has lost sight of spiritual wisdom and sunk into the belief that God is absent from man and the universe. This belief is the being "dead through your trespasses and sins."
>
> There can be no other explanation of the first and second death.[110]

Unity could not be more wrong here, nor could there be more serious consequences, as our Doctrinal Appendix documents. Biblically, the second death is eternal separation from God, not just physical death or separation from the body (Revelation 20:10–15; 2 Thessalonians 1:9). And this is the condition of all people prior to faith in Jesus Christ, which is why the separation will continue forever at death unless a person turns to Christ for forgiveness of sins (John 3:16–21; 1 John 5:9–13).

Heaven and Hell. In light of our discussion so far, it is not surprising to find that Unity denies heaven and hell as literal places apart from and outside of man. According to Unity, upon death the five principal components of man (spirit, soul, intellect, sense consciousness, body) separate from each other and go to their respective states until a new incarnation occurs: "When the body is destroyed . . . they separate, each going to its own state of consciousness. The spiritual ego reverts to its original essence in the bosom of the Father; soul falls asleep until the next incarnation. Body and sense consciousness are earthbound, and in due season they disintegrate."[111]

Unity distinguishes one's personality (an illusion) from one's individuality, or identity. The "old" personality (who we were) must be forever destroyed, although it is believed that some nebulous undefined sense of individual identity continues. "Identity endures. Personal consciousness does not endure. The personal man is not immortal and he dies. This is clear to anyone who is willing to give up his belief in the reality and importance of the personal consciousness."[112]

Unity argues that neither the personality nor the individual identity experiences heaven or hell in a biblical sense. In one of his more incredible statements, Fillmore declared of heaven: "There is not the shadow of a foundation in either the Old or the New Testament for such doctrine. On the contrary, the teaching is clear that all the heaven which men will ever find will be here."[113] How sad if true. Unfortunately, with its extinction of personality, this is the best Unity can offer men and women. Thus Fillmore believed that heaven was a mental condition:

[Jesus] never did describe it as a place located in some distant realm. In spite of these oft repeated illustrations by Jesus showing the Kingdom of heaven to be a state of consciousness, the great mass of Christians are today teaching that it is a place, to which people who accept Jesus as their Savior will go when they die. *There is no authority in the Bible for such doctrine.* If such a place existed Jesus would certainly have described it plainly instead of giving parable after parable and illustration after illustration showing it to be a state of consciousness to be attained by man.[114]

When Fillmore declares "there is no authority in the Bible" for heaven, he is wrong again, as there are hundreds of references to heaven as a place. For instance, salvation is "reserved in heaven" for believers (1 Peter 1:4 NAS); Stephen "looked up into heaven and saw the glory of God" (Acts 7:55); Jesus said, "I have come down out of heaven" (John 6:42 NAS) and there are "those who dwell in heaven" (Revelation 13:6 NAS). For someone to so thoroughly misread Jesus and the Bible at this point, and in so many other places, can only be described as highly perplexing if Fillmore was who he claimed. But Fillmore was no fool. His genius and his legacy led millions of people to believe that the Bible taught Unity doctrine, and that this was true Christianity. (In the Doctrinal Appendix we have provided biblical documentation describing heaven.)

Unity School of Christianity also denies that hell is a real place of eternal punishment. In spite of Jesus' clear statements that hell is real and that it is a place of eternal punishment, Unity ignores this. In Matthew 25:46 Jesus declared, "Then they will go away to eternal punishment, but the righteous to eternal life." And, "In that *place* there shall be weeping and gnashing of teeth" (Matthew 8:12; 25:30 NAS). But Unity rejects Jesus' words and argues: "There is no warrant for the belief that God sends man to everlasting punishment. . . . Hell is a figure of speech that represents a corrective state of mind."[115] "The fact is everybody has a soul to save, not from the hypothetical hell after death, but from the sins and the delusions of the sense consciousness that make hell here and now."[116]

Unity's *Metaphysical Bible Dictionary,* forever illustrating its level of biblical scholarship, defines hell according to the Saxon root and does not even consider the Greek derivation, usage or meaning: "The booklet, 'The Bible and Eternal Punishment,' by A.P. Barton, gives the following definition of the word 'hell': 'The English word *hell* is from the Saxon verb *helan,* "to cover, or conceal," and intrinsically contains no idea of a place of torment, and never did smell of fire and brimstone in its Saxon home."[117] But the Saxon meaning has nothing to do with the biblical meaning. In the Bible, hell is a place of unending punishment, which is the meaning of the Greek *aionios kolasin* (used in Matthew 25:46). (See an extended discussion in Robert A. Morey, *Death and the Afterlife* [Bethany House].) The meaning of the words used by Jesus that are related to the doctrine of hell (*hades, gehenna, aionios kolasin,* etc.) must come from the language and culture in which the terms are found, not from an outside source to which the biblical usage is unrelated. According to Unity's reasoning here, one could argue that Los Angeles would not be a city because it is derived from the Spanish meaning "angels."

Because it teaches that all people will eventually be "saved" from ignorance of their own deity and merge into the Impersonal Consciousness, Unity may be classed a form of universalism. However, since it also teaches that the individual personality will forever cease to exist, it is also a form of annihilationism.

THE OCCULT

Unity accepts involvement in the psychic and occult world with only minor qualifications. Unity rejects the biblical concepts of Satan and demons and therefore does not believe that the psychic and occult realm is associated with personal evil spirits. Unity maintains that "demons or devils are error states of mind which have to be overcome."[118] In other words, the devil would merely be a personification of lower states of consciousness (like Christian belief). Obviously then, there is no awareness or understanding of the reality of demonic deception.

Although many Unity members are interested in various forms of psychic involvement and the occult, the *Metaphysical Bible Dictionary* seems to warn against this when it teaches: "Astrology, palmistry, the guidance of spirits, mesmerism, hypnotism, are some of the many modern forms of denial of God."[119] In Unity, these practices "deny God," not because they are demonic or anti-biblical but because in various ways they oppose Unity's philosophy and concept of God. Actually, as we will see, this statement is not a denial of the occult generally. The psychic world and spiritism is supported as long as one retains the Unity perspective on it. Following, we will provide several examples. Unity Village offers its "Life-Enhancing Labyrinth," a circular pathway described as "a walking meditation" and "a path of prayer" where people can experience "illumination" and "guidance." Although this is just a normal pathway, when it is used to receive psychic guidance, such guidance may indeed be received and this is part of its purpose.[120] Unity also supports idolatry, one of the oldest forms of pagan demonism there is. This is illustrated by Psalm 106:36–37: "They worshiped their idols, which became a snare to them. They sacrificed their sons and their daughters to demons." But Unity teaches that idolatry isn't idolatry because all idols and gods are part of the one God of Unity: "It is not idolatry to make idols and worship them, if the heart understands their significance. . . . Those who have the love of God quickened in their heart are not disturbed by idols. It makes no difference to them how many representatives there are of God, because their inmost being, the very heart of their existence, is centered in the consciousness of the One. The fact is that every form and shape in existence is representative of God."[121] In theory, Unity would have to accept that even the evil gods of paganism and concepts of the devil himself are "representatives" of the Unity God. Unity members, it seems, rarely consider the implications, and thus the metaphysical outlook of Unity easily predisposes its members to the occult.

Unity stresses the divine power of the mind, so that psychic powers are logically thought to be latent, normal and divine. Charles Fillmore taught that once one comes into proper relationship with "the good," the result is the acquisition of what appear to be supernatural powers which allow one to control "all the so-called forces of nature by word or thought."[122] Unity does not view these occult powers as truly supernatural or demonic but only a reflection of the "natural" outworking of divine mind. Again, Unity rejects the concept of the supernatural because of its view of God. No God exists entirely outside of nature to perform a miracle within nature because all of nature is part of the expression of God. Therefore, no violation of the laws of nature is possible. There is only One Power everywhere and all true laws of nature are laws of the divine. Of course, if Unity's concept of God is wrong, then its denial of the miraculous may also be wrong. And then demons might exist after all. To accept the supernatural in the occult but to call it something else makes little difference as far as the devil is concerned.

Many Unity churches reserve a section in their libraries for occult books and books on ESP.[123] Yoga, meditation and ESP seminars may also be sponsored. Numerous *Unity* magazines contain articles urging the development of "hidden powers," "mystical powers," "subconscious abilities," and so on.[124] Fillmore himself advocated the development of psychic abilities. *Unity* of June 1976, reprinted an earlier article by Fillmore, "How to Handle Psychic Forces," which contains his ideas on the subject: "We should not think of the psychic realm as evil, or be afraid of it. . . . Through our own Christ dominion we develop spiritual powers to handle the psychic realm to great advantage. And that this is a realm in which tremendous forces are present is being discovered by the investigations of physical science."[125]

Here we see how a philosophy of monism can logically reinterpret the demonic as divine activity. If God is the only Power, no demonic power can exist and therefore every manifestation of power, including all occult power, is divine by definition. The result is that Unity members are likely to be open to receive psychic manifestations, including undiscerned psychic or spiritistic inspiration, which according to Unity must be divine. Fillmore teaches that "when a person is established in the Christ power and dominion, he finds that Spirit *often* uses the mental realm to reveal to him some message that is of vital importance to him. Such messages are imparted through dreams and visions."[126] Even overt channeling (its many demonic associations are illustrated in our *Encyclopedia of New Age Beliefs*) should logically be accepted as divine. But this should not be surprising. A brief look at Fillmore's life reveals significant occult involvement and guidance.

Fillmore and the Occult

Freeman's biography of Fillmore points out that both Fillmore and his wife were mystics who believed that their lives were divinely guided. They believed God spoke to them through their dreams.[127] Both were also psychic healers and claimed a high success rate.[128] Modern Unity continues to emphasize "divine" healing, claiming cures for "almost every known physical ailment."[129]

Fillmore's life was directed supernaturally. This was apparently a result of incidents in his youth, his own occult studies and practice and perhaps psychic involvement on the part of his forbearers. Indeed, much of his own teaching and philosophy was directly inspired from the psychic realm. Freeman recalls: "He lived simply and he lived very close to God and he felt very strongly that God was speaking to him, using him to convey divine ideas. Like Joseph and Daniel, he felt that God came to him in dreams and visions of the night *and revealed to him much of the Truth about which he wrote and spoke.*"[130]

One occult dream in particular had a crucial impact on Fillmore's life. He was, of course, a willing recipient to its message because "years of study and meditation . . . had prepared him to obey the promptings of the Spirit in him."[131] In another biography of Fillmore, D'Andrade recorded the dream, which instructed Fillmore that an "invisible power" was to guide him, something consistent with the experience of mediums and psychics generally:

"I had a strange dream," Charles declared, "An unseen voice said, 'Follow me.' I was led up and down the hilly streets of Kansas City and my attention was called to localities I was familiar with. The Presence stopped and said: 'You will remember having had a dream some years ago in which you were shown this city and told you had a work to do here. Now you are being reminded of that dream and also informed that the invisible power that has located you will continue to be with you and aid you in the appointed work.' When I awoke, I remembered that I had such a dream and had forgotten it."[132]

During his life, Fillmore studied a variety of occult and Eastern religious subjects, such as Theosophy, Swedenborgianism, Rosicrucianism and Hinduism. His earliest writings were under the pen name "Leo-Virgo," a reflection of his interest in astrology.[133] The first issue of *Modern Thought* magazine (April 1889) gives one an idea of what attracted his attention. It contained articles on Christian Science, spiritism, Theosophy, psychic powers and general occultism.[134] Like Mary Baker Eddy, Fillmore fell away from overt spiritism and later from occultism in general, divorcing himself from "magnetism, hypnotism, mesmerism, psychometry, palmistry . . . astrology." "Not that we condemn any system, but . . . we wish to confine these pages to that specific doctrine, and Holy Ghost power, taught and demonstrated by Jesus Christ."[135] In other words, without the names or labels, many of the ideas and worldview of the occult continued to be taught, but under the cover of the *teachings of Christ.* For example, Fillmore believed that "the word of Christ as applied to Truth represents an idea that has behind it the occult power necessary" to help harmonize world religious thought.[136]

Reincarnation was another occult philosophy endorsed by Fillmore throughout his life. In 1891, reincarnation was (and is today) regarded by Christians as an antiChristian belief. To teach reincarnation in America back in the nineteenth century was tantamount to declaring oneself a nonChristian. The first issue of *Unity* (June 1891) carried the modern symbol of Unity, a winged globe, of which Fillmore said, "It is a symbol that I feel I knew in a former incarnation in ancient Egypt."[137] The belief in reincarnation remained with him, supported by psychic experiences of alleged "past lives." At age 85, in the booklet *Unity's Fifty Golden Years,* he wrote: "Consulting the light of Spirit, I have been privileged to see states of consciousness formed by my ego thousands of years before its entry into this body."[138] His biographer Freeman reported that Fillmore eventually believed he was the reincarnation of the Apostle Paul.[139] This idea certainly garnered credibility for him as to his alleged biblical expertise. But the reality is that Satan is still an angel of light, still doing his work of deceiving people and seeking to lead others astray (1 Peter 5:8). He is still using false apostles and deceitful workers who transform themselves into apostles of Christ (2 Corinthians 11:13–15; 2 Peter 2:1–3).

Ominously, Fillmore claimed to experience a very real spiritual presence that he believed to be Jesus. "Again and again he would speak of Jesus as a real presence. He felt himself in intimate contact with Jesus."[140] He believed that "no one can know the doctrine of Jesus Christ without going direct to Him for information."[141] Indeed, this is how he developed the religion of Unity. And so, based on his opposition to biblical teaching, we can only conclude that he really encountered spiritistic visions or communications from a spirit entity imitating Jesus. Clearly, the fact that guidance by "Jesus" continually led him to beliefs that were opposed to Christ's must make an unbiased observer suspect that the "presence" was not Christ's. Indeed, in the past century there have been thousands of claimed contacts with spirits claiming to be Jesus who denied His teachings.[142] These spirits' teachings invariably show them to be demons, as in the case of channeled texts such as *God Calling* and *A Course in Miracles* (critiqued in our *Encyclopedia of New Age Beliefs*).

Fillmore also wrote a book on "Christian" Yoga, *The Twelve Powers of Man* (1930), in which he discussed the various "psychic centers" and, incredibly, argued that Jesus was a Hindu yogi. The book was written in response to certain occult experiences in which he psychically examined his own body and consciousness.[143] Again we see guidance by a spirit presence and Fillmore's assumption of its innate benevolence. This assumption was a logical conclusion of his monistic philosophy (all spiritual experiences are divine by definition), but from a biblical, historical and occult perspective such a conclusion was naive at best:

> The most important phase of my experience however was the opening of my spiritual nature. I gradually acquired the ability to go into the silence, and from that source I received unexpected revelations and physical sensations. At first, the revelations were nearly all through dreams. I developed a dream code through which I could get information and answers of marvelous accuracy to my questions. I do not remember that I asked who the author of my guidance was; I took for granted that it was Spirit.
>
> Then the mental and spiritual developed into sensations at the nerve extremities. I was informed by the Presence that I was beginning body regeneration as taught by Jesus Christ.[144]

To be unconcerned as to the identity of a spiritual presence that rejects God, denies Christ and opposes the Bible can hardly be considered an expression of spiritual enlightenment. Unfortunately, what Fillmore permitted here, he also encouraged in others. To be advancing in Truth, "Spirit is constantly infusing us with more of itself. . . . Personality is discarded and spiritual forces begin to renew and rejuvenate."[145] For Fillmore to encourage people to be infused by a spiritual presence or force that stands against the Bible and discards personality is too close to demonism for comfort.

Christ Enthroned in Man, by Cora Fillmore, is presented as a supplement to *The Twelve Powers of Man* and gives psychic "exercises" for "spiritual" development. In certain ways the occult dynamics involved are reminiscent of dangerous *kundalini* yoga exercises (critiqued in our *Encyclopedia of New Age Beliefs*). For example, if one has followed the instructions of *Christ Enthroned,* properly, by the fifth chapter (of 13) one has allowed "the Presence" to have full control over him. Today this book has been somewhat revised by Unity "and harmonized with [their] present understanding of the spiritual principles involved." But "the Presence" has not been expunged. It also retains an emphasis on developing psychic powers: "The exercises in these chapters are an attempt to show step by step how to evolve the natural faculties into highly spiritual faculties, and it is by means of such a development that one comes to learn of salvation through Jesus Christ."[146] "Through our meditation . . . our realization of God as the great Father-Mother is quickened and . . . we begin to discern the soul experiences that have been ours in former lives."[147]

Whatever inspired the Fillmores, it was also interested in influencing the minds of children with occultism. This continues the tradition of spiritism generally. Many spirits and spiritistic religions today give special attention to the "education" of children, for example "Seth," the spirit guide of the late Jane Roberts, and The Church Universal and Triumphant. Unity's *Wee Wisdom* is perhaps the oldest children's magazine in America (1893). Myrtle Fillmore instituted the magazine as a result of a vision given to her about a great crowd of confused children trampling each other. "Who will take care of the children?" she asked in the vision, concerned for their welfare. After being impelled to go to the front of the crowd, a voice told her, "You are to take care of the children. This is your work."[148] For 30 years, as the editor of *Wee Wisdom*, Mrs. Fillmore educated children in Unity teachings and related subjects, and the tradition continues to this day.

In conclusion, although Fillmore did come to warn against certain kinds of occult practice, he always stressed the wisdom and leading of the "God within." But what "the God within" tells one person isn't necessarily what it tells another. Unity teachers and laypersons stress this inner leading today, despite its dangerous subjectivity and lack of any standard by which to check the validity or source of spiritual experience. If the God within leads someone into a form of the occult, who are they to say "No" to the promptings of divine Spirit? In this way, many Unity members are led into demonism under another name.[149] Marcus Bach, who wrote a series titled "Questions on the Quest" for *Unity* magazine, maintains that occultism is a "gift from God," including palmistry, astrology and other kinds of fortunetelling.[150] As it was in the beginning, Unity remains a religion that endorses and participates in the world of the occult.

CRITICAL ANALYSIS

In this section we will undertake a brief critical examination of Unity in terms of its claims to truth, its subjective method of Bible interpretation, its denial of morality and the negative practical implications of its doctrines.

Unity Logic and Science

Charles Fillmore declared that his beliefs were "absolute Truth."[151] Yet he also stated, "What you think today may not be the measure of your thought tomorrow."[152] Over the years, Unity leaders have changed some of his teachings; and so, obviously, Fillmore did *not* teach absolute truth. As his teachings were the philosophy of an occultist, they can hardly be considered divinely authoritative, let alone absolute truth. Nevertheless, Fillmore made many other claims for his beliefs, including claims that he employed rigid logic to arrive at his teachings: "I have a standard of faith which is true and logical, and I must conform to it in my teaching without compromise."[153] "That system of philosophy or religious doctrine which does not admit of the rules of perfect logic in reaching its conclusions from a stated premise must be outside the pale of pure reason and in the realm of manmade dogma."[154] His teachings of "practical Christianity" were "Truth"; they invited "the closest mental scrutiny"; they were a "science of pure reasoning" that used "cold, deductive reasoning" to "arrive at each and every one of the conclusions which are presented." Fillmore continued, Unity students are never "expected to believe anything which they cannot logically demonstrate to be true." And, "We entertain nothing in our statements of Truth that does not stand the most searching analysis, nothing that cannot be practically demonstrated."[155] All this must be so because Fillmore's teachings were divinely inspired from the Infinite Mind:[156] "Practical Christianity and Truth stand upon the same foundation and are interchangeable terms. Practical Christianity is not a theory having origin in the human mind."[157]

Of course, if all of Fillmore's teachings were divinely inspired, Unity would find no need to change them. But perhaps Fillmore's enthusiasm led him to overstate his case. Regardless,

Fillmore's teachings had little to do with logic, science or even common sense. For him, as with many other cults (for example, ISKON, the Hare Krishnas), "true" science investigated the spiritual not the empirical world, thus denying the common meaning of "science." "To know accurately about the reality of things we must disregard all appearances as indicated by the five senses and go into pure reason—the Spirit from which was created everything that has permanent existence."[158] In other words, reason and science can be found only in the subjective realm of Spirit. The material world is impermanent and "opposed" to Spirit, hence it cannot be subjected to "science." Modern Unity writer Ernest Wilson states, "The body of flesh, bones, and blood that the eye of sense beholds is not the true body.... The true body is an ethereal body."[159] So much for modern medicine and physiology!

Fillmore's teachings were not logical or scientific. Yet Fillmore plainly declares that his beliefs express perfect logic and are demonstrable. Further, Fillmore and Unity have made statements that can only be considered embarrassing because they offer evidence that they could not possibly have been divinely inspired, let alone the result of "pure reasoning." For example, Fillmore taught that food and clothing could be created out of thin air: "It is not an assumption of theoretical metaphysics that we may be able to make our food and clothing from the air, but a logical conclusion that follows the understanding of God as the omnipresent source of all that appears."[160] Indeed, if their philosophy is true, Unity members should be able to perform the most astounding miracles. After all, they are one essence with an omnipotent God. They declare that for the enlightened person, "All the powers of God are available to Him."[161] One can only wonder why Unity believers never display such awesome powers?

Fillmore also believed that *mental* thoughts create *physical* germs:

Anger, jealousy, malice, avarice, lust, ambition, selfishness, and in fact all of the detestable patterns that mankind harbors, produce living organisms after their kind. If we had microscopes

strong enough, we should find our body is to be composed of living germs, doing to the best of their ability the tasks which our thoughts have set before them. If you have said, "I hate you," there have been created in your atmosphere hate germs that will do the work for which you have created them.... So the fear, the doubts, the poverty, the sin, the sickness, the thousand erroneous states of consciousness have their germs.[162]

Every thought that flits through the mind of every man, woman, and child in the universe, produces a living organism, a microbe of a character like its producing thought. There is no escape from this conclusion.... [There] is the microbe of fear [also]....This may seem an exaggeration, but we have the authority of Dr. Parker, a physician of New York, who states that he has discovered the microbe of death and experimented with it.[163]

Whoever the good Dr. Parker of New York may have been, it is certain he never found a microbe of death and experimented with it. Believing that "negative" thoughts create viruses and bacteria is sheer fantasy. Are such teachings evidence of spiritual enlightenment or spiritual deception? Fillmore declared his teachings to be absolute truth and divinely inspired. He emphasized that that which is not strictly logical is only "manmade dogma." And he informed his own people they must not believe anything they cannot logically *demonstrate* to be true. We have a few questions. Since Fillmore's teachings deny strict logic, should not Unity members recognize them as merely manmade dogma? If Fillmore's monism and denial of reality cannot be demonstrated and are opposed to logic, how could he have been divinely inspired? If he could not even get basic Christian history and doctrine right, how could he be trusted when he spoke about the errors of Christianity?[164]

If Unity members cannot *demonstrate* these truths of Unity teaching, should they not consider abandoning them based on what Fillmore has stated? Who can demonstrate thought germs? Where are all the miracles they can create from thin air? Why could not even Charles Fillmore demonstrate a genuine healing of his damaged leg from a hip dislocation? Fillmore declares, "Be wise; pronounce nothing evil, and only the good will come,"[165] yet has any Unity member anywhere been able to demonstrate this? Or, "Pain, sickness, poverty, old age and death cannot master me for they are not real,"[166] yet are there no Unity members who are poor, aged or sick? Do Unity members die? Has any Unity member anywhere, any time, ever met the standards of Unity? Then given the evidence for the divine inspiration of the Bible and the logical impossibility of divine inspiration through Fillmore, it seems obvious where the real "man-made dogma" lies.

*Unity Hermeneutics**

Unity rejects both scholarly and common sense understanding when it denies that the proper way to read the Bible is through a normal, literal meaning of its words understood in their immediate and then larger historical and cultural context. Unity believes that the Bible can be understood properly only if one looks for the hidden "spiritual" meaning of words.

The logical basis of Unity's claim to rediscovering "true original Christianity" rests squarely on the credibility of its method of interpreting the Bible. As we will see, that method is entirely subjective and cannot logically claim to teach the truth about anything. Unity relies on its metaphysical and spiritual method of interpretation, not a literal and normal one based on universally accepted rules for interpreting a historical document. In discarding the accepted rules, Unity shares the burden of proof for justifying its method of biblical interpretation, one it has yet to meet. Still, Unity's *Metaphysical Bible Dictionary* (*MBD*) makes the following claims in its Preface, that it "will prove very beneficial to Bible students"; "the aim has been to clarify," and its interpretations "are based on the practical teachings of Jesus."

But none of this is true. The *MBD* frequently defines words on the basis of etymology rather than usage[167] and arbitrarily mixes the literal and metaphysical.[168] It also confuses interpreta-

tion with application,[169] magnifies minor points and gives biblical words almost any meaning but the biblical meaning—hence the name of the dictionary. As in *Alice in Wonderland,* the *MBD* admits that words can mean whatever one wants them to mean: "The interpretations given are suggestions, by no means final . . . If the reader will trust to his own indwelling Spirit of truth for light, he will find in these suggestions a guide to endless inspiration in the understanding of Truth."[170] The phrase "endless inspiration" really means "endless interpretation" because every individual is the final authority in the meaning of words.

One can only wonder how Unity can allege its comprehension of absolute "Truth" with a capital "T" when the "indwelling Spirit of Truth" leads Unity members to contrary meanings for the same words? Worse, on what basis does Unity justify *any* of its metaphysical meanings? On what logical platform, for example, would an Israelite and a Gentile with the same name in Scripture "symbolize different planes of consciousness in the individual," or why would Abraham, being "the father of a multitude" (many nations), refer to a "multitude of manifested thoughts and acts" rather than a multitude of people?[171] How can Unity prove that "Bethlehem" is "the nerve center at the pit of the stomach,"[172] that John the Baptist is "illuminated intellect"[173] or that the kingdom of heaven is "interpenetrating ether"?[174]

The *MBD* speaks of the esoteric interpretation as being "plainly written in the Scriptures."[175] In fact, it is not plain at all, and it is nowhere written in the Scriptures. Once an objective hermeneutic is abandoned, all the Unity member is left with is a purely subjective interpretation. This becomes meaningless in the face of innumerable other claims of "divine illumination" that contradict one another. With various opposing interpretations all laying claim to origination in "divine mind," who can know what is true? So why should anyone logically consider Charles Fillmore's particular interpretation of the Bible, which thinks that it is the true interpretation? Why is it more valid than someone else's partially different view, such as Mary Baker Eddy's?

---

*The authors express their thanks to Dean C. Halverson for some of the ideas in this section.

As an example of this problem, note the following contrary definitions by two leading metaphysicians of the nineteenth century, Mary Baker Eddy, the founder of Christian Science, and Charles Fillmore:

MARY BAKER EDDY (Science and Health Glossary)	CHARLES FILLMORE (Metaphysical Bible Dictionary)
Adam—"Error, a falsity; the belief in 'original sin' sickness and death; evil; the opposite of God . . . nothingness."	Adam—"The first movement of mind in its contact with life and substance . . . harmonious consciousness."
Gad (Jacob's son)—"Science; spiritual being understood."	Gad (Jacob's son)—"The faculty of power . . . but . . . not lifted to truly spiritual expression."
Gihon (a river of Eden; Genesis 2:13)—"The rights of women acknowedged morally, civilly and socially."	Gihon—"Gihon means *formative movement* . . . the deific breath of God inspiring man and purifying his blood in the lungs."
Zion—"Spiritual foundation and superstructure; inspiration; spiritual strength; emptiness, unfaithfulness, desolation."	Zion—"Love's abode in the phase of the subjective consciousness where high, holy thoughts and ideals abide . . . spiritual consciousness."

Which is the true definition of these biblical terms? How is it objectively determined? Who in Unity can prove Fillmore's interpretation is the correct one? No one. The problem here is that if every word people use has numerous subjective metaphysical definitions, then communication is impossible. In the end, Unity's teachings are of little value because they lack authority. Further, if Unity hopes to communicate objective truth about Christianity, and has written hundreds of books attempting to do so, how can it logically claim that one can never go too far in spiritualizing words? "One significance of blasphemy is the tendency in our own mind to fear that we can go too far in spiritualizing our thought and its environment."[176]

The "Preface" to the *MBD* declares: "The Scriptures veil their metaphysical meaning under the names of towns, rivers, seas, and so forth, and the acts of men in connection therewith. The name of each person and of *everything* in the Scriptures has an inner meaning."[177] Note a few of these inner meanings seen given in Fillmore's *Mysteries of John:*

Pontius Pilate = intellect
The Jews = ruling spiritual ideas
Jesus = spiritual man
The seamless garment of Jesus = truth
Golgotha = the front part of the brain[178]

Is this anything other than an exercise in futility? Again, even the *MBD* concurs that there can be more than one "proper" definition and that potential definitions are unlimited.* The *MBD* admits, for example, that Cain, allegedly coming from the root idea of centralized power, could refer either to a benign or to an evil rulership. As a result, the Hebrew language is a potential "source of confusion to many Bible students."[179] So, should Unity members then discard the Hebrew and trust wholly in Fillmore's "Spirit," or should they trust in their own "Spirit" illuminated "intuition"? If the *MBD* accepts "many bypaths of metaphysical deduction" due to differing interpretations of metaphysical authors,[180] who determines what is true? In fact, the Unity student is free to reject any specific interpretation that he does not like, even Fillmore's: "If he does not wish to accept our interpretations, but would rather do his own thinking, entirely apart from our suggestions, we fully recognize his right to do so. . . . As stated before, this book is not final in the field that it covers; at best it is only a stepping-stone to the higher realm of spiritual consciousness, toward attainment of the mind 'which was also in Christ Jesus.'"[181]

Is "the mind of Christ" so confused that it cannot illuminate even Unity teachers consistently? What does this say for Charles Fillmore's lifelong endeavor to explain the truths of the

---

*While it does recognize the literal, historical meanings to biblical terms, practically and spiritually speaking these are of little or no value.

Bible? And even if the leader's definitions and teachings can be discarded, whose can effectively stand?

Unity and the "Mind of Christ"

Perhaps the most serious problem for Unity is its claim to have "the mind of Christ." For Unity, Jesus is the ultimate example of "Christ consciousness." If so, Unity believers should have a genuine interest in how Jesus interpreted Scripture. Unity Rev. Cameron affirmed, "The Christianity of Jesus . . . is what we are supposed to follow. What He thought is the way we are to think."[182] If Unity believers truly have "the mind of Christ" and are "one with Christ" then, logically, they should think on and interpret Scripture just as He did. This ought to be the case especially because Jesus rose from the dead and Fillmore did not. If Unity members choose Fillmore's method of interpretation over Jesus', how can they be expressing the state of perfect spiritual advancement that they claim Jesus had?

Unfortunately for Unity, in the Gospels Jesus never once interpreted Scripture as Unity does. To the contrary, He always interpreted Scripture normally, not metaphysically. Thus Unity cannot logically justify either its claim to have the mind of Christ or its subjective hermeneutic. Jesus' reference to people, cities, and events are always interpreted literally. He mentions Adam, Eve, Abraham, Lot, Noah, Moses, Solomon and David as true persons of history and not once discusses some inner hidden meaning to their names, actions or circumstances. He mentions cities such as Nineveh, Sodom, Gomorrah, Tyre and Sidon and never gives them metaphysical significance. Far from "everything having an inner meaning," for Jesus virtually nothing has an inner meaning. So how did Fillmore ever have, or how does Unity now have, "the mind of Christ" when it comes to properly interpreting the Scriptures?

Further, why is *only* the Bible singled out for this special interpretive treatment? No Unity writer has ever attempted to interpret the writings of Charles Fillmore in the manner that they interpret the Bible, because it would destroy Unity. To interpret Unity according to its own

hermeneutical principles would mean that in Unity one thing could mean ten different things to ten different people. Thus ascertaining the true teachings of Unity would be impossible. (We see the same problem for other groups that attempt the same metaphysical Bible interpretation, such as Swedenborg's New Church.) Indeed, if Unity wanted "credibility" for its teachings, they would have to be understood literally or normally. So why not grant the Bible the same courtesy?

As if such problems were not serious enough, Fillmore even argued that spiritual truth could not be communicated accurately through language: "The revelation [of Spirit] begins the moment we turn from the letter of the gospel and seek for its spirit. To know that every word and sentence of Scripture veils a spiritual truth is the first step in unraveling the gospel. Spiritual truths cannot be expressed in language that will carry correct concepts to the mind."[183] If Fillmore really believed this, one is perplexed that he wrote anything at all! How could he expect to communicate spiritual truth when it was impossible? Either this statement by Fillmore is wrong or his writings convey no spiritual truth. Either way he has a problem. If his writings are bereft of spiritual truth, what value do they have? If he was wrong about interpreting the Bible, then nothing he says about the Bible should be trusted. Yet Fillmore clearly claimed that he *was* communicating spiritual truth through language, which contradicts his previous statement. According to Fillmore's own words, then, he convicts himself as having only "manmade dogma."

Where, too, is the evidence for Fillmore's interpretation of Jesus Christ? If Fillmore really wrote the truth, wouldn't we find Jesus, the highest expression of "the Christ," teaching the same things as Fillmore? To the contrary, the Jesus of Scripture believed in a personal God not in an impersonal principle (John 17). He never says He was "a way shower" among men but rather "*the way* and the truth and the life" (John 14:6). He never declared all men were "the Christ" but that He alone was the Christ (Matthew 16:13ff; 26:63–64; John 10:24ff; 11:25–27). Indeed, the very purpose for writing the book of John was so that "you may believe that Jesus is [not became] the Christ" (John 20:31).

More than any other biblical book, the Gospel of John refutes Unity teachings. How is it then that in the Foreword to *Mysteries of John* (1978) Fillmore claimed that the book of John is "so successful in setting forth metaphysical truths that little interpretation is necessary?" In Matthew 24, Jesus warns against those who would come in His name claiming they were the Christ: "Watch out that no one deceives you. For many will come in my name, claiming, 'I am the Christ,' and will deceive many" (Matthew 24:4–5). Nevertheless, one common Unity affirmation is: "I am the Christ, son of the living God."

If Unity members insist upon a subjective interpretation of the Bible, how do they respond to the following points? The necessity of using the accepted meaning of words for effective communication. Why the Bible gives no indication that it is to be interpreted in any other way. Why Unity's interpretation is directed toward the Bible alone and no other literature, including the writings of Charles Fillmore. How Unity can claim absolute divine truth when its interpretation of Scripture is subjective and therefore meaningless.

Morality

For Unity, only God and Good exist. Fillmore declared: "There is no presence or power of evil, in reality; there is only one Presence and one Power—the good omnipotent."[184] Those who believe in two powers—good and evil—are spiritually dead.[185] Further, one is meant to declare evil as good or as a manifestation of good. Modern Unity writer Sue Sikking states, "Good is not one thing and bad another. There are simply different degrees of good; less good or more good."[186] If so, do Unity members believe that murder and adultery are merely lesser degrees of good than feeding the poor or caring for the sick? Can't this justify all kinds of evil? Also, once Fillmore had declared that evil had no ultimate reality, the outcome was to ignore evil as a genuine power. To even think that there is any power at all to evil gives it power and makes it real. For Unity then, evil must be denied as a power. But if so, any practical response to evil *becomes evil itself.* And thus, if we are to "meet every evil suggestion with a denial of its real-

ity,"[187] how can Unity members resist evil in the world? They cannot. Whether evil is real or not, Unity seems powerless to change it. But if evil is real, then resisting it only in the mind is a travesty and no Unity believer can logically claim to live in reality. "Through the eyes of love, I behold everyone and everything is pure and perfect."[188] Is this reality or self-deception? If there is no evil, why then did the prophets of Israel (Isaiah, Jeremiah, etc.) vigorously oppose and denounce, often at the cost of their own lives, the social and religious evil of Israel? Why did Jesus do the same? The reason is because God had ordered them to this task, a task with which Jesus concurred (Matthew 23:23–39).

Is there no evil in the world? Consider the following "testimony" of a Unity believer recalling her attempted rape:

I had fully embraced the free-love philosophies of my generation. Indeed, I was grateful that my peers were catching up with Unity's stand that "there is no such thing as sin." But one night I foolishly went to a deserted place with a man whose last name I did not even know. I quickly realized I had made a serious mistake. I had no awareness of sin to bother me about involvements of my own choice, but this time it was clear that I was about to be forced into a situation I did not want. We struggled, I fought. I tried to picture this man as a loving child of God and mentally denied that this was actually happening. Inwardly I affirmed "divine order" and pictured myself as calm and in control. Nothing worked. Fear for my own life gripped me just as tightly as my attacker's fists upon my torn blouse.

"Go ahead and scream," he snarled inches from my face. "No one will hear you out here."

I had run out of methods and formulas. Silently I prayed the shortest, most desperate prayer of my life. I pleaded, "Dear God, please help me!"

Though the man could not hear my inaudible prayer, immediately he released his hold and slammed me against the wall. He cursed me disgustedly and growled, "Go on; get out of here."

Before he could change his mind I hurriedly got in my car and sped away, sobbing with gratitude that God mercifully allowed me to escape.[189]

The Unity "God" of positive affirmation was silent and powerless in time of trouble. However, the God of the Bible, who is a God of mercy even to those who have ignored Him, could be found in time of trouble. This person later rejected Unity and discovered the God of Scripture as "the only true God" (John 17:3). The reason is not difficult to comprehend. When confronted with reality, Unity simply did not work.

If there is no evil, there is no violation of righteousness. If there is no violation of righteousness, there is no sin. If there is no sin, then why did Christ die? If there is no sin there are no victims. If there are no victims, why are our jails full? "In Divine Mind there are no evil conditions. . . . Apparent evil is the result of ignorance. . . . Evil appears in the world because man is not in spiritual understanding. He can do away with evil by learning rightly to use the one Power. If there were a power of evil, it could not be changed."[190]

First, this has never been the experience of Unity believers. None have ever vanquished evil in their lives, even though they allegedly have full access to the One Power. Second, the principal message of Christianity is that the power of evil *has* been changed and will one day be vanquished forever because God is righteous and holy and He conquered evil at the cross.

TALKING WITH MEMBERS

Unfortunately, the average Unity believer is unaware of the Bible's true teachings because he or she has allowed the Unity "pastor" to "properly" interpret it for them. They are especially uninformed and have been misinformed concerning church history and formulation of Christian doctrine. Historically, the church councils (Nicea, Chalcedon, etc.) merely organized biblical teachings systematically, often in response to various heresies. These councils neither added to Scripture nor falsely interpreted it, despite Fillmore's claim that Christian doctrine today is the invention of men 300 years after Christ and "not the pure Christianity of Jesus. . . ."[191] Unity members need to be encouraged to examine Scripture and historical theology for themselves. (See the Doctrinal Appendix and Harold O. J. Brown's fine work, *Heresies*.)

Because of Fillmore's teaching, Unity members are characteristically predisposed against a biblical worldview. For example, "Belial refers to the Adversary or . . . to the adverse consciousness in man."[192] Christians who have an "adverse consciousness" are thus "satanic." They cannot understand the truth of Unity: "The unredeemed intellect, because of its limited concepts, cannot grasp absolute truth."[193]

But when Unity's beliefs cause its members to interpret Christian belief as spiritually harmful and destructive (belief in evil, confessing sin, a real devil, hell, etc.), how can it explain that even secular observers of the early church exclaimed of Christians, "See how they love one another"? How can Unity explain the immeasurable good that true Christians have done for the world in the last two millennia? If Unity's Divine Law must bring its necessary retribution to "negative thinkers," why doesn't it work against Christians? The fruit of the Holy Spirit in the lives of Christians (Galatians 5:22–23) invalidates the basic claims of Unity concerning the alleged spiritual evil of Christianity. In essence, Unity believers need to be asked how they can reconcile Unity doctrine with Christian experience.

Even the Apostle Peter once displayed a kind of "positive thinking," a Unity-like attitude to Jesus Christ, and he got rebuked for it, by Christ Himself:

> From that time Jesus Christ began to show His disciples that He must go to Jerusalem, and suffer many things from the elders and chief priests and scribes, and be killed, and be raised up on the third day. And Peter took Him aside and began to rebuke Him, saying, "God forbid it, Lord! This shall never happen to You." But He turned and said to Peter, "Get behind Me, Satan! You are a stumbling block to Me; for you are not setting your mind on God's interests, but man's." (Matthew 16:21–23)

The "evils" of the crucifixion were God's plan to redeem the world (Acts 2:23). Where would the world be today if Christ had been a Unity "positive thinker" in regards to sin, suffering and evil? Indeed Jesus told us that we must deny ourselves, not exalt ourselves, if we would save our souls: "Then Jesus said to His disciples, 'If anyone wishes to come after Me, let him deny himself, and take up his cross, and follow Me. For whoever wishes to save his life shall lose it;

but whoever loses his life for My sake shall find it. For what will a man be profited, if he gains the whole world, and forfeits his soul? Or what will a man give in exchange for his soul?" (Matthew 16:24–26 NAS). What is more important than the salvation of a soul, over which even the angels rejoice (Luke 15:10)?

Another way to address the philosophical barrier erected against the Gospel is to point to the necessity for objective communication. In normal conversation, the Unity member assumes that you understand his words due to a commonly accepted definition of words. On what rational basis then can the Bible be treated differently, especially since God's purpose in giving it was to communicate His concerns effectively? Should we not grant to God what we grant to Charles Fillmore? If no Unity member can explain the objective rules of metaphysical interpretation, how can they ever be certain Fillmore had found "absolute truth"? If they are interpreting the Bible wrongly, how can they claim to be Christian, let alone defend their views before God? In fact, as noted earlier, in the 1978 edition of Fillmore's *Mysteries of John,* he says in the Foreword that "John's Gospel is so successful in setting forth metaphysical truths that little interpretation is necessary." If so, ask the Unity member to sit down with you and read John 3:16 as a starting point. What does he or she think is the normal meaning of those words that need "little interpretation"? At this point the person will at least have heard the Gospel. If one wishes, one could proceed to an in-depth study of John's Gospel. Reading John normally (that is, without metaphysical interpretation) refutes Unity's doctrines entirely.*

One may also cite and discuss the following statement of Charles Fillmore: "Jesus tells us that His words are Spirit, and then tells us to keep them. How can one keep a thing of which he knows nothing? How can one keep the words and sayings of Jesus unless he gets them into his consciousness and grasps them with his mind, his spirit? Surely there is no other way to keep His sayings. Those who are doing so from any

---

*Arthur Pink's *The Gospel of John* is an especially good commentary.

other standpoint are missing the mark."[194] Unity members may not suspect it, but Fillmore here implicated Unity with "missing the mark." Further, he invalidated Unity. The *only* way anyone can know what Jesus meant is to read His words normally. Unity's interpretation of Jesus, then, is the one which "knows nothing."

Another point for discussion involves the denial of reality that must at times wear heavy upon Unity members. The Proverbs declare that "the naive believes everything, but the prudent man considers his steps" (Proverbs 14:15 NAS). We should not accept something as important as claims to spiritual truth without first subjecting them to careful examination, as God directs (Acts 17:11). If we are truly concerned with honoring God, we must be willing to be honest with ourselves before Him, even if it goes against our own beliefs or what we might wish is true. The one who honors God will always be honored by Him in the end: "He who gives attention to the word shall find good, and blessed is he who trusts in the LORD" (Proverbs 16:20). Conversely, the one who dishonors God and leads others astray, or away from Him, will also receive an appropriate recompense. Jesus said, "It is inevitable that stumbling blocks should come, but woe to him through whom they come!" (Luke 17:1 NAS) and "For whoever is ashamed of Me and My words, of him will the Son of Man be ashamed when He comes in His glory" (Luke 9:26 NAS; see Matthew 18:2–6).

It is also important to stress the biblical portrait of fallen humanity. Because people are fallen and corrupt, all are sinners. Sin is part of their very being, their true inner nature even as Jesus said, "For from within, out of the heart of men, proceed the evil thoughts, fornications, thefts, murders, adulteries, deeds of coveting and wickedness, as well as deceit, sensuality, envy, slander, pride and foolishness. All these evil things proceed from within and defile the man" (Mark 7:21–23). Hence Scripture says that "all are under sin"; "there is no one righteous, not even one"; "all fall short of the glory of God" (Romans 3:9-10, 23).

Sin of the flesh cannot be atoned for by a mere mental process, for sin is ingrained too deeply within us. "While we were still helpless, at the right time, Christ died for the ungodly"; "while we were yet sinners Christ died for us" (Romans 5:6–8 NAS). More radical surgery is needed than simply thought reform. If sin were simply ignorance then correct knowledge should in fact remove it, but this is not the experience of Unity members. Complete sinlessness comes only after death for redeemed humanity, because sin resides so deeply within us that only God can completely remove it.

Unity teachings deny the biblical view: "If we say that we have no sin, we are deceiving ourselves and the truth is not in us. . . . If we say that we have not sinned, we make Him a liar, and His word is not in us" (1 John 1:8, 10 NAS). Note a mental affirmation of Unity: "I am able to stand straight before the Lord; I am walking in perfect accord with Him.[195] Who within Unity is sinless, as Christ was? Who has given sight to a man blind from birth? Who has cured the leper, raised the dead and resurrected his own body, appearing to more than 500 people?

> Yet He attained no more than is expected of every one of us. . . . It is all accomplished through the externalization of the Christ consciousness, which is omnipresent and ever ready to manifest itself through us as it did through Jesus. . . . *It must work out surely as a mathematical problem, because it is under immutable law.* The factors are all in our possession and the rule that was demonstrated in one striking instance |Jesus| is before us. By following that rule and doing day by day the work that comes to us, we shall surely put on Christ as fully and completely as did Jesus of Nazareth.[196]

Not even one Unity member in all its history would apply to himself this claim. And perhaps the most poignant example of the ultimate failure and futility of Unity comes from the life of none other than Charles Fillmore. His own death powerfully exhibits the error of Unity's views. The Bible declares the soul that sins will die (Romans 6:23), and that it is appointed for men to die once, and then comes judgment (Hebrews 9:27). At age 46, Fillmore recorded the following thoughts:

> About three years ago, the belief in old age began to take hold of me. I was nearing the half-

century mark. I began to get wrinkled and gray, my knees tottered, and a great weakness came over me. . . . I spent hours and hours silently affirming my unity with the infinite energy of the one true God. . . . Then I went deep down within my body and talked to the inner life centers. I told them with firmness and decision that I would never submit to the old age devil, that I was determined never to give in.[197]

Unity members are fond of stating that Fillmore's mental powers (not his genes) kept him alive for 94 years. Regardless, Fillmore believed that he existed at least since the time of ancient Egypt. This means it took him 5,000 years of "positive thinking" and about a thousand lifetimes just to add maybe 30 years to his life, assuming the life span of the average Egyptian was 60 years. Remember, Fillmore was also the Apostle Paul, whom he claimed was advanced in spirit. If so, then 2,000 years of subsequent positive thinking had only a negligible impact on the decaying process of his body. In other words, if when he was Paul, he was advanced in expressing mental truth (and receiving its benefits), each successive incarnation until Charles Fillmore finally appeared *should* have constituted another improvement. Where, then, is the alleged "Divine Law" in all this, for Charles Fillmore to die at a lowly 94 years? He should have lived on. All his life he had taught: "Through the Christ Mind, our sins (wrong thinking) are forgiven or pardoned (erased from consciousness). When we have cast all sin (error thought) out of our mind, our body will be so pure that it *cannot* come under any supposed law of death or corruption."[198]

Here Fillmore declares that a person with a truly enlightened consciousness has a body that *cannot* die. At age 92, he wrote and emphasized that he would *never* die! (Note again how important the normal use of words is for Fillmore to communicate his argument):

> In my article in the August, 1946 *Unity,* I stated that I had such a vital realization of Jesus' promise "If a man keep my word, he shall never see death" that I should never pass out of this body. Subscribers are now asking if I mean that I shall live forever in the flesh body. *I answered that point in the article as definitely as it can be*

answered in words. I expect to associate with those in the flesh and be known as the same person that I have been for ninety-two years, but my body will be changed in appearance from that of an old man to a young man with a perfectly healthy body.

I do not claim that I have yet attained that perfection, but I am on the way. . . .

Some of my friends think that it is unwise for me to make this public statement of my conviction that I shall overcome death, that if I fail it will be detrimental to the Unity cause. *I am not going to admit to any such possibility.*[199]

He could not possibly admit to such an outcome, for he believed the negative power of that very admission might kill him! If Fillmore agreed that "pain, disease and finally death always result from . . . ignorant transgression of the divine law,"[200] this would confirm that Unity's teachings are false. Even Charles Fillmore could not live up to them, and in the end Unity was of no value to Charles Fillmore. The gospel of Unity is not good news for anyone.

Charles Fillmore tried valiantly, but Charles Fillmore died. Enlightened as he was, he declared he would live. But only one outcome proved true, as the Bible teaches (Romans 6:23).

All the positive thinking in the world did not save Charles Fillmore. His mind (steadfast in harmony with the infinite, inviolate Principle that must irrevocably, inevitably bring us the fruit of our thoughts) resolutely *believed* he would never die. If Unity teachings were valid, Charles Fillmore would not be in the grave. Yet he is dead like other men. If anyone requires proof that Unity is not the truth and that Unity does not work, they need look no further than Charles Fillmore's tombstone.

NOTES

1. Charles Fillmore, *Dynamics for Living* (MO: Unity School of Christianity, 1967), pp. 306-307.
2. Hugh D'Andrade, *Charles Fillmore* (San Francisco: Harper & Row Publishers, 1974), p. 61.
3. Charles Fillmore, *Talks on Truth* (MO: Unity School of Christianity, n.d.), p. 174.
4. See Unity School of Christianity website.
5. James Freeman, *The Story of Unity* (MO: Unity School of Christianity, n.d.), Foreword.
6. Ibid., p. 15.
7. D'Andrade, p. 134.
8. Ibid., p. 142.
9. Freeman, p. 21.
10. D'Andrade, p. 35.
11. website.
12. Fillmore, *Talks on Truth*, p. 107.
13. Fillmore, *Dynamics for Living*, p. 32.
14. Ibid., pp. 147, 183.
15. Ibid., p. 261.
16. Ibid., p. 355.
17. Ibid., p. 353.
18. Ibid., p. 362.
19. Cora Fillmore, *Christ Enthroned in Man* (MO: Unity School of Christianity, n.d.), pp. 24-25, 41.
20. *Unity*, October 1976, p. 64.
21. Fillmore, *Dynamics for Living*, p. 104
22. Ibid., p. 85, emphasis added.
23. Unity School of Christianity, *Metaphysical Bible Dictionary* (MO: Unity School of Christianity, n.d., originally published in 1931), pp. 452-453.
24. Ibid., pp. 82-83.
25. Ibid., pp. 87-88.
26. *Metaphysical Bible Dictionary*, p. 267.
27. D'Andrade, p. 61.
28. Ibid., p. 41.
29. Melton, *Encyclopedia of American Religions*, Vol. 2, p. 59.
30. D'Andrade, pp. 63-64.
31. Ibid., p. 64.
32. Ibid.
33. *Unity*, October 1979, p. 47.
34. Fillmore, *Dynamics for Living*, p. 341.
35. *Metaphysical Bible Dictionary*, p. 481.
36. John Ankerberg and John Weldon, *The Facts on the Faith Movement* (Eugene, OR: Harvest House, 1993), p. 35.
37. *Faith for Today*, May 1977, p. 8 (a publication of San Diego Christ Church Unity).
38. Elissa Lindsay McClain, "Should the Church Apologize to Unity?" *Christian Research Journal*, Winter–Spring 1987, p. 31.
39. *Unity*, October 1979, p. 47.
40. Fillmore, *Talks on Truth*, p. 139.
41. Fillmore, *Dynamics for Living*, p. 10.
42. Fillmore, *Talks on Truth*, p. 34.
43. Charles Fillmore, *Mysteries of Genesis* (MO: Unity School of Christianity, 1979, rev.), p. 43.
44. *Metaphysical Bible Dictionary*, pp. 452-453.
45. Fillmore, *Dynamics for Living*, p. 27.
46. Freeman, *The Story of Unity*, p. 194.
47. Donald Curtis, *The Christ-Based Teachings* (MO: Unity Books, 1976), p. 17.
48. Freeman, "Wherever You Are God Is," pamphlet, pp. 3-5.
49. Fillmore, *Dynamics for Living*, pp. 30-35.
50. Freeman, "Wherever You Are God Is," p. 629.
51. *Metaphysical Bible Dictionary*, pp. 82-83.
52. Fillmore, *Dynamics for Living*, p. 17.
53. *Metaphysical Bible Dictionary*, p. 150.
54. Fillmore, *Dynamics for Living*, p. 30.
55. *Metaphysical Bible Dictionary*, p. 150, emphasis added.
56. Fillmore, *Dynamics for Living*, p. 165.
57. Ibid., p. 321.

58. Cora Fillmore, *Christ Enthroned in Man*, p. 24.
59. Fillmore, *Dynamics for Living*, p. 164.
60. Ibid., p. 322.
61. *Unity*, October 1976, pp. 59-60.
62. *Metaphysical Bible Dictionary*, p. 150.
63. Fillmore, *Dynamics for Living*, pp. 351-353.
64. *Metaphysical Bible Dictionary*, p. 150, emphasis added.
65. Charles Fillmore, *Mysteries of John* (MO: Unity School of Christianity, 1974 edition), p. 38.
66. Fillmore, *Talks on Truth*, p. 110.
67. Fillmore, *Mysteries of Genesis*, p. 139.
68. Fillmore, *Dynamics for Living*, pp. 326, 366.
69. *Metaphysical Bible Dictionary*, p. 233.
70. Fillmore, *Dynamics for Living*, pp. 142-143.
71. Ibid., p. 245.
72. Fillmore, *Talks on Truth*, pp. 166-167.
73. Ibid., p. 143.
74. Ibid., pp. 154-155.
75. *Unity*, October 1976, p. 61.
76. *Metaphysical Bible Dictionary*, pp. 310-311.
77. Ibid., p. 254.
78. Fillmore, *Talks on Truth*, p. 141.
79. Fillmore, *Dynamics for Living*, p. 335.
80. Ibid., p. 84.
81. Fillmore, *Talks on Truth*, pp. 167-168.
82. D'Andrade, p. 41.
83. Fillmore, *Dynamics for Living*, p. 286.
84. Fillmore, "Ye Must Be Born Again," *Unity*, December 1973, pp. 45-46.
85. *Faith for Today*, March 1078, p. 7.
86. Fillmore, *Dynamics for Living*, pp. 142-143.
87. Fillmore, *Talks on Truth*, pp. 164-165; *Dynamics for Living*, p. 318, emphasis added.
88. *Unity*, December 1969, pp. 23-24.
89. Ibid.
90. Fillmore, *Dynamics for Living*, p. 348.
91. Fillmore, *Mysteries of John* (1978), p. 163.
92. Fillmore, *Dynamics for Living*, p. 145.
93. H. E. Caddy, *Lessons in Truth* (Unity, 1967), pp. 95-96.
94. Fillmore, *Dynamics for Living*, p. 45.
95. Fillmore, *Talks on Truth*, p. 77.
96. Ibid., p. 105.
97. Ibid., p. 157.
98. Sue Sikking, *God Always Says Yes* (Santa Monica, CA: Sikking-Davis Publishing, 1974), pp. 35, 62.
99. Fillmore, *Dynamics for Living*, pp. 306-307, emphasis added
100. See Caddy, *Lessons in Truth*, p. 53.
101. Fillmore, *Dynamics for Living*, p. 41.
102. P. Stovin, *Twenty Questions About Unity* (1983), p. 9.
103. Fillmore, *Mysteries of Genesis*, p. 48.
104. Fillmore, *Talks on Truth*, pp. 146-147.
105. Curtis, p. 10.
106. *Metaphysical Bible Dictionary*, p. 129; cf. p. 481.
107. Charles Fillmore, *The Revealing Word* (MO: Unity School of Christianity, n.d.), p. 180.
108. Fillmore, *Talks on Truth*, p. 149.
109. Fillmore, *Dynamics for Living*, p. 348.
110. *Metaphysical Bible Dictionary*, p. 178.
111. Fillmore, *Talks on Truth*, p. 159.
112. Fillmore, *Dynamics for Living*, p. 342.
113. Ibid., p. 292.
114. *Metaphysical Bible Dictionary*, p. 266, emphasis added.
115. Fillmore, *Dynamics for Living*, pp. 278-279.
116. Fillmore, *Talks on Truth*, pp. 139-140.
117. *Metaphysical Bible Dictionary*, p. 271.
118. *Unity*, December 1969, p. 24.
119. *Metaphysical Bible Dictionary*, p. 87.
120. Cf. Lauren Artess, *Walking a Sacred Path*.
121. Ibid., p. 294.
122. Fillmore, *Dynamics for Living*, pp. 18-19.
123. For example, the Christ Church Unity in San Diego; cf. *Faith for Today*, October 1979, p. 21.
124. Cf. June, 1973, p. 36; July, 1973, p. 46; February 1976, p. 20.
125. *Unity*, June 1976, pp. 57-58.
126. Ibid., p. 56, emphasis added.
127. Freeman, *The Story of Unity*, p. 188.
128. D'Andrade, pp. 50, 54.
129. Freeman, *The Story of Unity*, p. 96.
130. Ibid., p. 16, emphasis added.
131. Ibid., p. 42.
132. D'Andrade, p. 21.
133. Ibid., p. 139.
134. Ibid., p. 32; Freeman, *The Story of Unity*, p. 56.
135. Freeman, *The Story of Unity*, pp. 57-58.
136. Ibid., p. 60.
137. Melton, *Encyclopedia for American Religions*, p. 59.
138. Ibid., p. 136.
139. D'Andrade, p. 41.
140. Ibid., p. 63.
141. Fillmore, *Talks on Truth*, p. 133.
142. For examples, see John Ankerberg and John Weldon, *Encyclopedia of New Age Beliefs* (Eugene, OR: Harvest House, 1996), chapters on "A Course in Miracles" and "Channeling," section entitled "Impersonations and Denials of Christianity" pp. 101-103.
143. D'Andrade, pp. 89-90.
144. Freeman, *The Story of Unity*, p. 167.
145. Cora Fillmore, *Christ Enthroned in Man*, p. 38.
146. Ibid., p. 7.
147. Ibid., p. 32.
148. D'Andrade, p. 44.
149. *Unity*, December 1975, p. 53; see also John Ankerberg and John Weldon, *The Coming Darkness*, Appendices A, B, F, G.
150. *Unity*, February 1973, pp. 37-38.
151. D'Andrade, p. 59.
152. Cora Fillmore, *Christ Enthroned in Man*, p. 5, n.d.
153. D'Andrade, p. 59.
154. Fillmore, *Dynamics for Living*, p. 11.
155. Ibid., p. 14.
156. Ibid., pp. 12-13.
157. Ibid., p. 12.
158. Ibid., p. 11.
159. *Unity*, February 1973, p. 34.
160. Fillmore, *Dynamics for Living*, pp. 82-83.
161. Fillmore, *Mysteries of Genesis*, p. 6; *Unity*, October 1979, p. 51.
162. Fillmore, *Dynamics for Living*, p. 177.

163. Fillmore, *Talks on Truth*, p. 19.
164. Fillmore, *Dynamics for Living*, pp. 299-300; Cora Fillmore, *Christ Enthroned in Man*, pp. 24-25, 41.
165. Fillmore, *Dynamics for Living*, p. 131.
166. Caddy, *Lessons in Truth*, p. 53.
167. *Metaphysical Bible Dictionary*, preface, p. 5.
168. Ibid., pp. 17-18.
169. Ibid., p. 6.
170. Ibid., pp. 6-7.
171. Ibid., p. 6.
172. Ibid., p. 119.
173. Ibid., p. 222.
174. Ibid., p. 222.
175. Ibid., p. 129.
176. Ibid., p. 128.
177. Ibid., p. 7.
178. Fillmore, *Mysteries of John*, pp. 162-163.
179. *Metaphysical Bible Dictionary*, p. 5.
180. Ibid., p. 6.
181. Ibid., p. 8.
182. *Unity*, October 1979, p. 52.
183. Fillmore, *Dynamics for Living*, p. 305.
184. *Metaphysical Bible Dictionary*, p. 206.
185. Fillmore, *Talks on Truth*, p. 147.
186. Sikking, *God Always Says Yes*, p. 49.
187. Cora Fillmore, *Christ Enthroned in Man*, p. 38.
188. Ibid., pp. 24-25, 41.
189. McClain, "Should the Church Apologize to Unity?" p. 31.
190. Fillmore, *Dynamics for Living*, p. 72.
191. Ibid., pp. 299-300.
192. *Metaphysical Bible Dictionary*, p. 106.
193. Ibid., p. 297.
194. Fillmore, *Talks on Truth*, p. 175.
195. Cora Fillmore, *Christ Enthroned in Man*, pp. 24-25, 41.
196. Fillmore, *Talks on Truth*, pp. 169-171.
197. Freeman, *The Story of Unity*, p. 197.
198. Fillmore, *Dynamics for Living*, p. 141, emphasis added.
199. Freeman, *The Story of Unity*, pp. 210-211, emphasis added.
200. Fillmore, *Dynamics for Living*, p. 261.

Vedanta, Hinduism and the Ramakrishna Order/Vedanta Society

I. VEDANTA

Info at a Glance

Name: Vedanta

Purpose: To attain knowledge of the ultimate God Brahman in the *Upanishads* (the philosophical portion of the Vedas) and spiritual liberation through yoga and meditation practice.

Founder: Shankara (9th century A.D.); Ramanuja (11th–12th century A.D.); and Madhva (13th century A.D.)

Source of authority: The *Vedas* and *Upanishads;* the *Bhagavad Gita;* the *Brahmasutras of Badarayana*, etc.

Revealed teachings: Yes; the *rishis* (Hindu seers or psychics) experienced the *Vedas* as being divinely revealed (*shruti*) to them.

Claim: To represent the true teachings of the *Vedas.*

Theology: Due to contradictory teachings and textual/hermeneutical difficulties in Vedanta as whole, the overall theology is contradictory, e.g., Vedanta may be monistic, qualified monistic or dualistic; God may ultimately be personal or impersonal, one or many, etc.

Occult dynamics: Development of psychic powers, spiritism, divination, magic and other occult practices.

Key literature: "M" (Mahendranath Grupta), *The Gospel of Sri Ramakrishna,* Swami Nikhilananda; *Vivekananda, The Yogas and Other Works* and large numbers of books from the various Vedantic schools, such as scripture commentaries.

Attitude toward Christianity: Rejecting

Quotes:

"It is blasphemy to think that if Jesus had never been born, humanity would not have been saved. It is horrible. . . . Never forget the glory of human nature. We are the greatest God that ever was or ever will be. . . ."

> — Swami Vivekananda in *Vivekananda, The Yogas and Other Works,* p. 885.

"We are the God of the universe. In worshipping God we have always been worshipping our own hidden Self."[1]

> —Vivekananda

"Let us be God!"[2]

> —Vivekananda

"Among Hindu groups, none has made as great an impact on America as the Vedanta Society."[3]

> —J. Gordon Melton

Note: Vedanta has a variety of subschools. In this introduction we consider only three principal ones. For the principal group cited in illustration of Vedanta (The Vedanta Society/Ramakrishna Order), we provide additional introductory charts.

DOCTRINAL SUMMARY

God: Brahman and lesser deities.

Jesus: A man who realized his divine nature, a yoga adept.

The Christ: The divine part of Jesus.

Trinity: Brahma-Vishnu-Shiva.

Salvation: By human effort.

Man: God (inwardly), part of God, or a creature of God.

Sin: Ignorance or evil.

Satan: Sometimes a synonym for evil.

Fall: E.g., into ignorance of our divine nature.

Bible: One of many world Scriptures; Vedic authority is supreme and provides the proper worldview for biblical interpretation.

Death: A transitory state between incarnations; life and death are one; death is beneficial if one's consciousness has the proper orientation at death. After full enlightenment there is, for example, eventual "absorption" into Brahman.

Heaven and Hell: Largely states of consciousness or temporary experiences here or in between incarnations.

II. THE RAMAKRISHNA ORDER/VEDANTA SOCIETY

INFO AT A GLANCE

Name: The Ramakrishna Order/Vedanta Society.

Purpose: To help people realize their true inner deity.

Founder: Ramakrishna (1836–1886) and Vivekananda (1863–1902).

Source of authority: Official writings plus occult experiences.

Revealed teachings: Yes.

Claim: Ramakrishna is the "one whose teaching is just now, in the present time, most beneficial," (*Teachings of Swami Vivekananda*, p. 227).

Occult dynamics: Spiritism, possession, occult powers.

Examples of key literature: "M" (Mahendranath Guptam), *The Gospel of Sri Ramakrishna*, Swami Nikhilananda, *Vivekananda The Yogas and Other Works*.

Attitude toward Christianity: Outwardly accepting; inwardly hostile; rejected as an incompatible and unenlightened form of religion.

Quotes:

"Who can bind me, the God of the universe?"[4]

—Swami Vivekananda

"Christ, Buddha, and Krishna are but waves in the Ocean of Infinite Consciousness that *I am*."[5]

—Swami Vivekananda

Note: Although relatively small in numbers, the Vedanta Society has had large impact through its influence upon prominent intellectuals such as Gertrude Stein, William James, Aldous Huxley, Christopher Isherwood and Gerald Heard.

DOCTRINAL SUMMARY

God: Brahman (*satchitananda*, or impersonal being: (*sat*), consciousness (*chit*) and bliss (*ananda*).

Jesus: A great son of God like Ramakrishna.

The Christ: The divine part of Jesus.

Holy Spirit: Occult power.

Salvation: By works.

Man: Part of God (inwardly), illusion or maya (outwardly).

Sin: Ignorance.

The Bible: One of many scriptures.

Death: Reincarnation toward eventual union with Brahman.

Heaven and Hell: States of consciousness, not places.

NOTES

1. Swami Nikilananda, *Vivekananda, The Yogas and Other Works* (New York: Ramakrishna-Vivekananda Center, 1953), p. 332.

2. Ibid., p. 517; cf. p. 519.

3. J. Gordon Melton, *The Encyclopedia of American Religions,* Vol. 2 (Wilmington, NC: McGrath Publishing Co., 1978), p. 360.

4. John Yale, ed., *What Religion Is in the Words of Vivekananda* (New York: The Julian Press, 1962), p. 77.

5 Swami Vivekananda in Swami Nikhilananda, *Vivekananda, The Yogas and Other Works* (New York: Ramakrishna-Vivekananda Center, 1953), p. 72.

THE WAY INTERNATIONAL

INFO AT A GLANCE

Purpose: To expand the biblical interpretation of Victor Paul Wierwille.

Founder: Victor Paul Wierwille.

Source of authority: Victor Paul Wierwille's writings.

Revealed teachings: Yes.

Claim: To be the true church of God.

Key literature: L. Craig Martindale's *The Rise and Expansion of the Church; The Way of Abundance and Power* course (this replaces Victor Paul Wierwille's "Power for Abundant Living" course); books by V.P. Wierwille, such as *Receiving the Holy Spirit Today* and *Jesus Christ Is Not God.*

Attitude toward Christianity: Rejecting.

Quotes:

"During my early years of Biblical research, I sometimes did not know enough to be accurate in my teaching."[1]

"One of the predominant concerns in my life has always been 'not handling the Word of God deceitfully.'"[2]

"If my research is a wrong-dividing of God's Word, then I stand before God as an unapproved workman. Either way, I accept full responsibility."[3]

"The first step of all degradation, when the Word of God is wrongly divided, is practical error."[4]

Note: In that the Way has influenced well over 200,000 people, harmed many and often draws recruits from Christian churches, we felt that a more in depth analysis was warranted than the current relatively low numbers of The Way International would seem to require. Only time will tell whether their recent (1998) re-organized structure and new program of church growth will be successful. Still, numerous splinter groups continue to hold to the teachings of Victor Paul Wierwille and so this analysis will have merit for them as well. These splinter groups include: The Christian Educational Service, The Way of Great Britain, The Way of New York, a group in (Gartmore) Scotland and others. As one former member put it, "People who are no longer affiliated with The Way International are still very, very, loyal to the teachings of Victor Paul Wierwille."

DOCTRINAL SUMMARY

God: One Divine Person.

Jesus: The created Son of God, not God the Son.

Holy Spirit: A synonym for God; holy spirit: a synonym for spiritual power.

Trinity: Rejected as a satanic concept.

Salvation: Works/confessional.

Fall: Into the senses world, with a loss of spirit.

Bible: The Word of God as interpreted by Victor Paul Wierwille.

The Afterlife: "Soul sleep" or unconsciousness until the resurrection; according to former members, hell is denied.

INTRODUCTION AND HISTORY

How wrong people can be and still think they are right![5]
—Victor Paul Wierwille

The Way International (TWI) is a multimillion dollar religious enterprise begun by Victor Paul Wierwille (1916–1985), a charismatic leader who stressed "the abundant life" for his many followers. In 1942 Wierwille began a radio ministry on station WLOK (now WIMA) in Lima, Ohio. It was incorporated in 1947 and its name changed to "The Way" in 1955.[6] In 1968 his movement began to experience noticeable growth and within a little over a decade there were possibly 150,000* plus followers and 400 staff. The Way expanded into Europe (especially England), South America and Australia. In light of its missionary activities this was not surprising. The Way once sent out thousands of "Way Over the World (WOW) Ambassadors," or one-year missionaries, as part of its zealous evangelistic endeavors. Ambassadors had to work at a secular job at least 20 hours per week, as well as witness at least 48 hours per week (or 8 hours a day, six days a week).[7] In 1994–95 this program was discontinued, allegedly because about 10 percent of their ambassadors were homosexual; after a "purge" the program was replaced with "Disciples of the Way Outreach Program."

The Way also once funded a nine-member Marketing Department which, following in the steps of the Jehovah's Witnesses, sold literature house to house. In 191 days, this team claimed to introduce nearly 10,000 homes in Wake County, NC, to Wierwille's writings.[8] The Way also once sponsored a slick music outreach that featured the Rock of Ages Music Festivals, a 5000-voice choir (Way Productions), their own radio and TV programs and regular family camps.[9] The Way's publishing arm continues to be American Christian Press and The Way is politically active through its The Word Is Government (TWIG) outreach program. Its purpose is to train its people to use political involvement to help spread Way principles. One noted convert was former Maine Senator Hayes Gahagan, who took the Power for Abundant Living course in September, 1974 during his campaign for the State Senate. He later established the Christian

---

*The Way estimated that 150,000 people had taken the standard "Power for Abundant Living" course. Technically, The Way International has no membership.

Political Alliance in Ohio and was its national executive director.[10] Among the most controversial aspects of The Way, at least non-theologically, is its earlier (and possibly continuing) firearms training of some 800 members and wide circulation of books asserting that the Jewish Holocaust in Nazi Germany was a fabrication (e.g., *The Hoax of the Twentieth Century; The Myth of the Six Million*).[11]

The Way is centrally organized according to the structure of a tree. National Headquarters represents the trunk, State chapters are limbs, county operations are branches, city groups are twigs and individual members are leaves. Shortly after the death of Wierwille in 1985, The Way splintered into several factions (such as Christian Educational Services) and subsequently lost over 70 to 80 percent of its membership. Given the characteristic cultic abuses found in The Way, which critics claim remain today (including spiritual intimidation, authoritarianism, abuse of members, legalistic burdens and immorality), this is hardly surprising.[12] In part, this precipitous decline was largely the consequence of the abuses and ethical violations so common in cults. After his retirement (forced by cancer) and before his death, Wierwille confided in and apparently commissioned Christopher C. Geer (now head of The Way of Great Britain) to issue a stinging indictment against The Way International leadership citing problems that trustees later confessed were true.

"The Fog Years"

Shortly after Wierwille's death, "The Passing of a Patriarch" speech by Geer before Way leaders and clergy hit like a bombshell. It condemned every high level Way leader and led to tremendous infighting, suspicion, paranoia and a struggle for control of power. Its impact was so devastating that this became known as "the fog years." The following is excerpted from a 1997 report on the website of Messiah Lutheran Church: "Great confusion followed the reading of *Passing*. . . . Hundreds of Way leaders were fired and tens of thousands of leaders left TWI to start their own regional groups. While the most intense of 'the fog years' have passed, *Passing . . .* brought about permanent and pervasive effects, including widespread heartbreak, fragmented

groups of followers of V.P. Wierwille, ongoing suspicion, and abrasive condemnations of current Way leaders."[13] For example, splinter groups such as John Lynn's Christian Educational Services and Chris Geer's The Way of Great Britain have accused The Way International of "authoritarianism, misuse of power, adultery, misuse of funds, spiritual corruption, departure from the Word of God and denominationalism."[14]

A former member who had been active in The Way in Germany, New York, Florida, California and Kansas wrote to us about her years in The Way. She said that the priority of The Way is one's "relationship to the organization, but not a personal relationship with Jesus Christ." She also observed the cultic authoritarianism. "Anytime anyone questioned the ministry or the leaders or any of the teachings, it was a major problem. Consequently, I frequently caused problems because I continually researched and found inaccuracies. . . . I was once called by the 'Branch' leader and chewed out because I requested information as to where our collection money (they called it 'abundant sharing') went. He had been calling all the local believers trying to find out 'who was asking devilish questions' and bluntly suggested I was serving Satan himself for having doubts.'"

When L. Craig Martindale became the president of The Way International after Wierwille's death, Martindale soon replaced Wierwille's Power for Abundant Living (PFAL) course with his secret The Way of Abundance and Power (TWAP) course. Martindale also instituted organizational, disciplinary and other changes that observers and former members have declared were also responsible for the decline in TWI membership. For example, the disciplinary practice of "mark and avoid" was applied to all who would not grant supreme allegiance to Martindale and Way leadership. Today many followers of TWI treat Martindale's words as if they were the word of God, just as they did for Wierwille. Nevertheless, the fact that many regional Way groups were started by members who left the Way suggests that overall membership may remain higher than previously thought and that the PFAL and TWAP courses are both in use.

In this chapter, we have primarily cited the books of Victor Paul Wierwille, whose teachings remain authoritative and continue to form the basic theology of The Way and all splinter groups. Not unexpectedly, Martindale's TWAP course offers no fundamental theological change in Way beliefs and for the most part imitates the flawed style, methodology and teachings of VPW.[15]

Reasons for Continued Success

The Way was successful for a number of reasons and could be again after "the fog years" since the following characteristics have remained in The Way and apparently even in its splinter groups. First is their offer of almost Utopian rewards. The Way "guarantees" personal power, success, health and happiness, and this appeals to people. In *The Mind Benders*, Dr. Jack Sparks cites one of their promotional brochures used on college campuses: "How would you like to be set free from all fear, doubt, and bondage; delivered from poverty, sickness, and poor health; overflowing with life, vitality, and zest, rescued from condemnation and self-contempt; cured of drug and sex abuse?"[16]

A second reason for its success is based on the principle that life can be made easier for those who choose to let The Way think for them. In his *Youth Brainwashing and the Extremist Cults*, Dr. Ronald Enroth quotes a former two-year member who confirms Dr. Sparks' observation that The Way is, in part, a "modern behavior modification" cult:[17]

Like most cult groups, Wierwille's Way offers considerable security. "You don't have to worry about the future, because The Way has made all your plans for you. There's always someone in the group to correct you, to take away your doubts, your worries." With security, there is often control. Marie discovered that the group's control extended to everyday necessities: "They explained, 'It's not love to use too much toilet paper.' We were made to feel bad for using too much toilet paper." . . . "Your mind is always geared and directed. You no longer think for yourself. You think what you're told to think. What I experienced when I came out was that it was hard to think, it was hard to put my thoughts together in order to say anything. . . . It's like my mind was asleep for a while. It's a real subtle kind of control over the mind, and no one ever feels it coming over them."[18]

Thus, group indoctrination was and still is employed successfully. This same member admitted:

While I was in it, I never would have come out on my own, because I had found the Truth. Nothing that anyone could say, nothing that I could read, nothing that I could think would have convinced me otherwise. We were told that Satan would stop at nothing to get us away from the truth. They said, "Satan will work through your parents and try to get you away from the Truth." So naturally, when my parents or friends started questioning me about my involvement with The Way, I knew that Satan was using them. Nothing they could say could change my mind.[19]

Several former members told us, in effect, that once their PFAL course was finished, they were not able even to consider that The Way might be wrong. As one said, "I could no longer think thoughts that denied Way teachings." Presumably, this remains true for TWAP courses.

A third reason for its success is the leaders' sincerity, conviction and great enthusiasm. Wierwille was small, but he was a committed and fervent powerhouse as a speaker, and Way leaders were inspired to follow his example. Such an approach obviously carried genuine conviction to an audience eager to learn about the Bible. This seems to continue today, although much of the enthusiasm of years past has been curtailed by current problems.

A fourth, and most important, reason for The Way's success among its converts and even among some Christians can be traced to people's lack of knowledge in biblical doctrine and apologetics. No one can defend themselves against spiritual error if they don't know what the truth is. Hosea's lament concerning knowledge of God is still true, "My people are destroyed for lack of knowledge" (4:6; cf. v. 1).

PRACTICE AND TEACHINGS

The Way has some features that are characteristic of new cults and religious movements. If there are three words that could describe these characteristics of The Way, they would be: undiscerning, unscholarly and extreme. The following material provides examples.

The Supremacy of the Founder

His divine inspiration. On October 5, 1942 at the end of a personal crisis in his own life, Victor Paul Wierwille (typically referred to as "The Doctor") asserted that God spoke to him audibly. Elena S. Whiteside, a writer for The Way and author of *The Way, Living in Love,* records that moment during a personal interview with Wierwille. "God" actually told Wierwille that He would teach him the proper interpretation of the Bible, which had been lost since the first century:

> "I was praying. And I told Father outright that He could have the whole thing, unless there were real genuine answers that I wouldn't ever have to back up on. And that's when He spoke to me audibly, just like I'm talking to you now. He said He would teach me the Word as it had not been known since the first century if I would teach it to others. Well, I nearly flew off my chair. I couldn't believe that God would talk to me." He shakes his head slowly smiling. "It's just too fantastic. People won't believe it. But He spoke to me just as plainly as I'm talking now to you."[20]

But Wierwille still could not believe it so, like Gideon, he asked God for more proof: "You've got to give me a sign so that I really know, so that I can believe."[21] On a crystal clear day he asked God, "Let me see it snow," and just like magic the sky was "white and thick with snow."[22] Whether Wierwille ever heard something audibly, only he knows. However, he had lied about crucial weather conditions on another occasion, so accounts like this may be considered suspect.[23] Regardless, there is little doubt that he claimed divine inspiration in some of his books. In *The New, Dynamic Church* we read: "You too must follow God's truth as told in the Word of God. But if you think this is just Victor Paul Wierwille writing or speaking to you, you will never receive. If you know that what I am saying to you are words which the Holy Ghost has spoken and is speaking to you by me, then you too will manifest the greatness of the power of God."[24]

In *Receiving the Holy Spirit Today,* we find the same doctrine. Since his teachings are unique and divinely revealed, they should be considered "the revealed Word and power of God."[25] Like Mormonism and so many other cults, The Way taught that Christians have been in doctrinal error for the last 2,000 years. In light of this, Wierwille's assertion that "we need the Lord to direct our steps according to the revealed Word of God" seems a clear indication that his particular interpretation is to be viewed as the "revealed Word of God."[26]

Way members have told us that Wierwille was "the greatest teacher since the time of the apostles because he teaches by revelation."[27] In his article "Masters of the Word" he asserted, "Do you think you're reading this by accident? You are being exposed to this knowledge by divine providence."[28] As a result, Way members believe that they alone have the true and proper interpretation of the Bible and that Christianity is in spiritual darkness. As one former member wrote to us in retrospect, "Students and believers are made to feel they are the biblically educated elite.... However, I was actually serving myself and my need to feed my 'far superior' knowledge of the Bible, instead of focusing first on serving the Lord. Being a student with loyalties only to TWI is the number one priority in the TWI teachings. Ultimately of course, this means serving yourself."[29] In our section on Mind Science teachings we will show how this self-serving attitude is generated by Wierwille's philosophy.

His indispensability. Victor Paul Wierwille was a man who needed to be different, to find fulfillment in uniqueness. In his book on The Way, J. L. Williams quotes a schoolmate of Wierwille's: "'If anybody had a $5 bill, he had it.... He has always been an outgoing guy, wanting to be popular.' He was 'always figuring' some way of being the one who knew something special, the man said, adding Wierwille wanted to be the center of attention, 'that's for sure.'"[30]

Although Wierwille claimed, "I have never said that I am a Bible scholar,"[31] one would not assume this from listening to comments by the faithful or even by Wierwille himself. To followers he was and is indeed a Bible scholar—no one else throughout Christian history has interpreted the Bible as accurately as he. Nevertheless, given the dubious nature of his academic background,[32] not to mention his plagiarism (see Critical Analysis), one could think otherwise. For example, why would someone divinely illuminated and inspired need to plagiarize from other people's works? The following comment illustrates that Wierwille was and is believed to be nearly infallible in his interpretation: "The 'Doctor's' oral and written teachings are absolutely authoritative, and they comprise 'the first, pure and correct interpretation of the Word since the first century A.D.' This is the understanding given to members of The Way. Referring to this, one ex-Way member reported of Wierwille that: "He was driving along one day and God told him, 'You are the only person who can interpret the Bible correctly. You are the only one who understands.' That's what we were taught."[33]

As far as The Way's PFAL course was concerned, it was also indispensable, until L. Craig Martindale replaced it with TWAP! Yet when Wierwille was alive, Martindale himself stated a person could not properly understand the Bible without PFAL:

> Any Biblical teaching in a specialized field must have its roots in the foundation class on Power for Abundant Living, or it rests on shaky and fictitious moorings. The foundational class on Power for Abundant Living means to Biblical research and teaching what Michaelangelo's David means to sculpture, the Mona Lisa to painting, Jim Thorpe to athletics and Shakespeare to literature. It is the most comprehensive weaving of life's fundamentals since the seven [sic] church epistles were penned by the Apostle Paul in the first century. Like God's Word, it is timeless in relevancy and potential impact.... The PFAL class is the touchstone of truth from whence every handling of God's Word, however basic or specialized, must germinate and grow. It is the criterion of the study, application and teaching of the Word of God.[34]

Of course, if it were truly "timeless in relevancy" Mr. Martindale would not have needed to revise it. The reason he did was because its errors were exposed by critics—hence his attempt to keep his revision "secret" within the TWAP course.

Extra-Biblical Sources

In light of the previous information about PFAL (and presumably TWAP) being necessary in order for a person to interpret the Bible

properly, as well as Victor Wierwille's claims to unique divine illumination, The Way takes its place with numerous other cults who use alleged new divine revelation as the grid through which the Bible is interpreted—Mormonism, the Unification Church, Jehovah's Witnesses, Christian Science, Armstrong sects and others.

Aramaic Originals and George Lamsa

Another tool by which The Way reinterprets the Bible in an unorthodox manner is the claim that the New Testament was originally inspired in the Aramaic language (a Semitic language similar to Hebrew) and not in Koine Greek. This assumption allows for much greater freedom in New Testament interpretation, since one may claim that the Greek texts in use are merely translations of the Aramaic and incorrect at points of dispute. Supposedly the Aramaic "original" provides the means to the "true" interpretation. In his article "In Search of the God-breathed Original," Walter Cummins, once an assistant of Wierwille claims:

> Even the most objective critics of the New Testament have concluded that a formal Aramaic document lies behind the Greek text of the New Testament.... When Greek translations were made, words were of necessity invented to convey the Aramaic God-breathed meaning which the ordinary Koine Greek (literary Greek dialect used in the New Testament) language could not do.... Other words were totally misunderstood when they were translated.... Because of the practical and doctrinal error that followed the original work of the apostles from the end of the first century on, words were changed, added and omitted in the Aramaic and the Greek texts.[35]

This is entirely false. Unfortunately, The Way's knowledge of Aramaic is based almost entirely on the research of George Lamsa, an anti-Trinitarian member of the Syriac Church, who used Aramaic to justify his particular interpretation of the Bible. Bernita Jess of the Aramaic Department of The Way says that The Way's own research confirms the accuracy of Lamsa. Jess writes: "Also we believe this was the language in which our Bible was first written.... [Way members should understand] the importance of this Estrangelo Aramaic language to our research and teaching of God's Word."[36] Surprisingly then, one wonders why their own Aramaic Interlinear, the *Aramaic-English Interlinear New Testament* (3 vols.), actually refutes their theology at points. The Messiah Lutheran website states:

> The Way's *Aramaic Interlinear* supports the accurate reading of [several] verses, thereby contradicting Wierwille's assertions. Several passages on the deity of Jesus highlight this difference. For instance, Wierwille claimed that John 1:18 must read: "the only begotten Son, which is in the bosom of the Father, he hath declared him" (*Jesus Christ Is Not God*, first edition, pg. 115), and that the words "which is in heaven" should be deleted from John 3:13 (ibid., pg. 140). However, The Way's "Word-by-Word Translation" reads: "The only begotten God that one who is in the bosom of his father has declared (him)" (pg. 594), and, "no man has ascended into heaven but he who descended from heaven, the son of man, who is in heaven" (pg. 608). Moreover, although Wierwille placed the words "my godly Lord" into Thomas' mouth, the Interlinear maintains, "And Thomas answered and said to him, 'My lord and my God.'" (pg. 770).

> The Way's Interlinear also contradicts Wierwille on deletion of the words "of the Father and of the Son and of the Holy Spirit" from Matthew 28:19 (*JCNG*, pg. 19). The Interlinear records the accuracy of the Word, "Go therefore, teach all nations and baptize them in the name of the father and the son and the holy spirit" (pg. 218). The Interlinear also identifies the spirit of truth as "he" in John 16:13 (pg. 734).

> The Way's Aramaic also contradicts Wierwille's wording of Galatians 4:6. While he states it must read that God "sent forth His spirit" (*JCNG*, p. 145), "A Word-by-Word Translation" corrects him, noting that "God sent the spirit of his son." The Interlinear also reads, "which he purchased with his blood" in Acts 20:28, which is a troublesome reading for Wierwille's followers. Wierwille also wanted to delete the word "death" from Philippians 3:10 ("The Knowledge of God," *The Way Magazine*, 1983, p. 6). Yet the *Aramaic Interlinear* clearly reads, "be conformed to his death."

> It is clear that the *Aramaic Interlinear* lists accurate readings of many verses which contradict The Way's preferred teachings. Yet, on other verses the Interlinear goes out of its way to include wording guaranteed to please Way leaders.

Why these differences? Perhaps some of the team members who worked on the book were anxious to please Way leaders, while others intended to reflect the true readings of the Aramaic even when they contradicted The Way's party line.[37]

It should be noted that the books and Bible "translations" of George M. Lamsa are readily found in most Christian bookstores in America. Before his death in 1975 he published over 20 books and many articles. His "translation" of the Bible, plus four of his books, were published by the well-known Bible publisher, A J. Holman, and Spring Arbor, the large Christian distributor, supplies them to Christian outlets around the country. As far as helping Christians to understand their Bible, these companies may as well have been publishing and distributing the literature of the Jehovah's Witnesses or Mormon's.

Lamsa was not an orthodox scholar. He rejected Christ's deity and physical resurrection, and he employed and taught the occult. He denied a personal devil and demons and had unbiblical views on sin and salvation, to name a few problems. He further claimed he alone could accurately translate the Bible, and therefore that only those with access to his insights could accurately teach it. Not surprisingly, his "commentaries" are "inordinately slanted by his metaphysical, political and personal presuppositions" so that the Bible conforms to his personal views rather than its own.[38]

While Lamsa's materials do offer some genuine insights, his overall antiChristian orientation undermines any value his works may otherwise have had for Christians. Indeed, Lamsa's work has frequently been used by numerous cults and occult religions—Unity School of Christianity, Edgar Cayce's Association for Research and Enlightenment, Science of Mind, the Holy Order of Mans, Christadelphians, Jehovah's Witnesses, Astara and others. These groups have consistently cited Lamsa in order to *reject* Christian teachings. Therefore, Lamsa can hardly be considered the "objective" Christian scholar many have claimed him to be. Paradoxically, during his lifetime, Lamsa spoke at hundreds of Christian conferences and churches, and his books continue to enjoy wide circulation, even among Christians.

The idea that an Aramaic text underlies Greek translations is simply not credible. Premier New Testament textual authorities agree on this. For example, Kurt Aland, author of *The Text of the New Testament,* concluded, "There is no longer any doubt that Greek was the language in which all the parts of the New Testament were originally written."[39] Thus, the claims of The Way here are simply wrong. In the chapter on New Thought we have shown in more detail that Lamsa was a biased interpreter whose own biblical translation has numerous crucial errors and that the evidence for Aramaic originals is unconvincing.

Seven of Paul's Epistles

Wierwille taught that the entire Old Testament and 18 books of the New Testament, while useful, were really not necessary for the current church age and hence are of limited value today. What is of prime importance are seven of Paul's 13 epistles. "In these seven epistles we have the perfect 'truth' into which the Spirit was to guide and lead.... The remainder of the epistles in the New Testament are either general or they are specifically addressed to the Hebrews, the twelve tribes, the dispersion, or to individuals."[40] Contradicting the Bible itself, Wierwille forcefully denied that the entire Bible was written for Christians:

> Most people believe that the entire Bible—from Genesis to Revelation—is written to them. This is not true. Believing that the entire Word of God is written to everyone throughout history has caused confusion and contradiction in rightly dividing The Word.... How many groups of people can different segments of The Word be addressed to?... God lists Jew, Gentile, the Church of God—three categories.... The entire Bible is addressed to one or the other of these three groups.... So are the Gospels addressed to us? Not if the Word of God is right.... The Gospels logically belong in the Old Testament.[41]

The seven relevant epistles are, in order (even the correct order is "important to our understanding of life"): Romans, Corinthians (1 and 2 Corinthians are to him one book), Galatians, Ephesians, Philippians, Colossians and Thessalonians.[42] Out of 66 books in the Bible

Wierwille accepted only seven as vital for the believer.* Clearly, such evisceration of the biblical text is equivalent to "subtracting" from the Word of God, something strongly prohibited in Scripture (Revelation 22:19; Proverbs 30:5–6). Perhaps Way members should also carefully reread 2 Timothy 3:16–17: "*All Scripture* is inspired by God and *profitable* for teaching, for reproof, for correction, for training in righteousness; that the man of God may be adequate, equipped for every good work." The words "All Scripture" refer to all 66 books of the Bible, not seven.

Hyper-Dispensationalism

In relation to this concept of seven key books, there are also seven major dispensations or "administrations": the Paradise Administration, the Patriarchal, the Law, the Christ Administration, the Church, the Appearing (also known as the Revelation Administration, the period from the second coming to the Great White Throne Judgment) and the Glory Administration (Revelation 21).[43]

In applying the "proper" section of Scripture to the "proper" age, Wierwille divided up individual books of the Bible.[44] Way writer Dorothy Owens tells us: "The whole Bible is not addressed to us.... So it is MOST IMPORTANT that we see TO WHOM the [given] passage was addressed. What was said TO THE JEW was not said to the Church of God, [for example] the entire book [of Romans] is not addressed to the same group."[45]

Wierwille's approach was similar to that of hyper-dispensationalists like E.W. Bullinger. Bullinger also distorted Scripture; in his case, e.g., it was the result of a numerological approach to the Bible. Wierwille, reflecting on people's lack of appreciation for his work, recalled how appreciative he was of Bullinger's work (we will see just how appreciative later):

> For almost fifteen years, no one thanked me for what I taught . . . when I shared with them what

---

*Technically, Wierwille accepted two "post-Thessalonian" books, James and Hebrews, but these are addressed only to "legally minded" Christians (cf. *Power for Abundant Living,* pp. 212–213).

I had found in God's Word, they would shout "Heresy!" But Dr. E.E. Higgins told me one night . . . that I taught like Bullinger wrote. Then she . . . gave me her copy of *How to Enjoy the Bible.* Back in the early 1900s Bullinger had found and seen many of the things in the Word that I was finding. Reading his book was like getting a drink of cool water from a desert oasis. I still have a great respect and love for the work of E.W. Bullinger.[46]

In effect, Wierwille's hyper-dispensationalism (like his dependence on Aramaic) served a similar function to that of additional revelation. Both were used to reinterpret the Bible in accordance with a preexisting theology that ultimately distorted the plain meaning of the text. Thus Wierwille makes such indefensible distinctions as: the Church of the bride being distinct from the Church of the body,[47] and three separate "gospels": (1) the gospel of the Old Testament, (2) the gospel of the presence of Christ and (3) the gospel of the revealed mystery of the epistles.[48]

Exclusivistic

The Way claims that it is the only group in the world with direct access to the true interpretation of the Bible. Apparently, it alone is most pleasing to God. *The Way Magazine* asks, "When in history has the accuracy of God's Word lived among a group of people? Think about that."[49] Former members recall being told that The Way comprised "the true body of believers." "Marie learned during her PFAL class that Wierwille claims to have rediscovered the long lost 'true' teachings of the original apostles. 'When everyone gets out of this class, they believe that, because he's convinced them. Dr. Wierwille is said to be the greatest teacher since the apostle Paul. It is an unwritten fact that Dr. Wierwille is believed to be an apostle. They believe that they constitute the true body of believers because they have more truth than anyone else.'"[50] Wierwille himself declared that of thousands of Bible teachers only he could teach the word accurately. "The Word is buried today. If there's no one around to teach it, God has to teach it Himself. . . . God knew I would believe His Word. And every day I am more and more deeply convinced of this ministry which teaches people the

accuracy and integrity of God's Word. Without this ministry the world would be in far greater spiritual darkness about His Word. There would be less light in the world. Where else but in this ministry do you find the Word of God so living and real?"[51]

Former Southwestern Regional Director Robert C. Moynihan informed his readers three times that "there is *no other gospel*" than that given by Wierwille:

As in Paul's day, some men and women who once sat under the teaching ministry of The Way International are separating themselves from this fellowship of like-minded believers. But there is *no other gospel.* There is one mystery. What other ministry or individual teaches the mystery of the one Body of Christ? We are men and women who must stand firm on what we know to be the truth. We know there is no other gospel. . . . The International Headquarters and this ministry of the integrity and the accuracy of God's Word shall live as we stand fast in the Lord. There is no other gospel.[52]

To understand the "one mystery" referred to, we must note another particular of the Way.

"The Great Mystery" and the Loss of the Historic Gospel

Here we return to hyper-dispensationalism. We emphasize that The Way claims it alone is pleasing to God, that only they rightly divide the Word, that only they are the one true church and that only they have the true Gospel. As we will see in conjunction with their teaching on the "great mystery" (hinted at previously as the only true Gospel), this must be so. In his book *The New, Dynamic Church* and in his booklet *The Church (The Great Mystery Revealed)*, Wierwille informs us that this "mystery" was lost *before* the death of Paul by deliberate rebellion. "When the first century believers failed to continue to act in the light of the great mystery . . . they lost the . . . center of all true Christian faith. . . . The immediate consequence of the loss of this truth of the great mystery produced glowing errors."[53] Wierwille stresses the extreme importance of this teaching for, as he says, it is "the center of all true Christian faith," for "there is no subject of such significant importance as the *great mystery.*"[54]

What is the "great mystery"? Essentially it involves an arbitrary division of the church into two dispensations: the Church of the bride and the Church of the body. "The Church of the bride" refers to Jewish believers of the Christ dispensation. It is comprised of "two bodies": 1) Christ, and 2) His bride, the Bridegroom or believing Israel. The Church of the bride is related both to the four written Gospels (past) and to the Book of Revelation (future). "The Church of the body" is the "great mystery," that is, the born-again believers of the post-Pentecostal Grace dispensation comprising Jew and Gentile in one Body (not two as before), Christ Himself. "The *ekklesia* of Israel is Biblically called the bride of Christ while the *ekklesia* of Grace is called the Body of Christ. So much error has come about by confusing these two distinct, separate churches."[55] "The Church of the bride, the called out of Israel, temporarily terminated with the death of the Bridegroom. More specifically, the Church of the bride is held in abeyance until the period or administration of the *great mystery* has culminated. Then beginning with the Book of Revelation administration we again have the Church as the bride."[56]

Wierwille taught that Christ is building His bride (Israel) but *not* building His Body which is a clear contradiction of Ephesians 4:11–13. Only believers in the Grace administration can build the Body of Christ. "The Church of the bride is built by the Bridegroom; the Church of the body of Christ is built by the born-again believers."[57] He even declares that without believing his teaching here, one cannot interpret the Bible correctly. And it is also implied one cannot have the truth of the Gospel. Thus, "No believer has a 'sound mind' if he is unsound in his knowledge and understanding of the great mystery."[58] Only this knowledge can bring Church growth: "The growth of the Church is dependent upon rightly dividing the Word of truth as to that which is addressed to us the *body* of Christ."[59]

Wierwille is critical of churches that believe the Bride and Body of Christ are One, or who stress the cross (atonement) of Christ or who neglect his "great mystery."[60] It is hardly surprising that Christians have rejected Wierwille's "great mystery" when they discover that it segments the biblical doctrine of the new birth. On the basis of his "great mystery," Wierwille claims that the new birth was not available until Pentecost. As a result, today we may lead others to the experience of regeneration, "which Christ could not do while on earth."[61] Worse, for Wierwille, this experience of regeneration "is *not* the gospel that Jesus Christ proclaimed to Israel when he walked the earth."[62]

But in John 3:1–6, Jesus himself disproved Wierwille's claim, offering the new birth to Nicodemus prior to Pentecost. Further, the Bible is clear that the blessings of the Gospel were to be known to believers of all "dispensations"—for example, to Abraham, who is listed as an example of believing faith (Romans 4:1–3, 13). Indeed, "The Scripture . . . announced the gospel in advance to Abraham . . ." (Galatians 3:8). The prospect of regeneration, then, was as surely available to Abraham as it was to Nicodemus. But Wierwille, because he presupposes that regeneration or salvation could not be available until after Pentecost, misinterprets the offer to Nicodemus and Abraham. Biblically, the value of the death of Christ on the Cross transcends time, race, culture and also Wierwille's "dispensations."

Extreme Pentecostalism

Although biblically the gift of tongues is not of comparatively great importance to other grace gifts (1 Corinthians 12:30–13:1, 8, 13; 14:5, 19–20), for The Way it is a salvation-truth. Speaking in tongues is a vital practice to The Way, even though, publicly, members may deny this. Without tongues one is not even a Christian, and only with tongues can one truly live for God, as the following five points illustrate.

1. Worship of God is impossible without speaking in tongues. "God is Spirit and can only be worshipped via the spirit and that can only by done by speaking in tongues."[63] Wierwille appeals to John 4:24—"worship [God] in spirit and truth"—to support his teaching. Using one of his many novel techniques for biblical reinterpretation (here it is supposedly a *hendiady*, a certain type of figure of speech), he interprets the clause "spirit and truth" to mean "truly spiritual" or "spiritually true." And "truly spiritual" worship[64] is to worship God "in spirit," which to

Wierwille is tongues worship. Therefore "truly spiritual" worship is speaking in tongues.

2. It is the final proof of salvation. "The only visible and audible proof that a man has been born again and filled with the gift from the Holy Spirit [spiritual power] is always that he speaks in a tongue or tongues."[65]

3. It gives special blessings. "Speaking in tongues gives us special access to God Himself. . . . Speaking in tongues is the one way that we can always speak to God according to His will."[66] "This is the greatest lever of power we've got."[67]

4. It is the proof of the resurrection and Second Coming. "The guarantee that God raised Jesus Christ from the dead and that we have eternal life is that we speak in tongues."[68] "Speaking in tongues is also our proof and assurance of His return to gather together the Church and it is proof of the future resurrections."[69]

5. It is the proof of one's total spiritual commitment (one cannot make Christ Lord without it). "Speaking in tongues is the external manifestation of the internal reality and presence of Christ in you the hope of glory. And that is the proof you've made him lord."[70]

Not unexpectedly, to disagree with Wierwille on his extreme emphasis on tongues proves "we are not spiritual."[71] For Wierwille, nothing was more wonderful. Tongues were "of utmost importance," equal to perfect prayer and so on. Even some of God's other gifts are not available without it. For instance, one cannot do miracles without speaking in tongues.[72]

However, tongues-speaking in The Way is principally a psychological phenomenon. In the PFAL and TWAP courses and in Wierwille's books, members are carefully instructed on how to speak in tongues. They are to do the speaking, but they are told this is God speaking through them. "What you speak is God's business, but that you speak is your business."[73]

Mind Science Teachings

The Way's teachings on success, financial prosperity and healing involve another extreme

and could just as easily be taken from texts of the modern "Word-Faith" movement, Science of Mind, Unity or channeled revelations. Examined in light of historic and worldwide Christian experience and biblical teaching, these Way teachings fall far short of Christian belief and practice. "His will for us is success in everything."[74] "Anyone who follows God's directions will be successful."[75] "Prosperity is dependent upon certain definite laws which everyone may learn and apply."[76] "Christians do not prosper simply because they fail to believe and act on God's Word."[77] Wierwille's "law of believing" is central to all of this:

> The law of believing is dynamically powerful, yet so simple. The law, simply stated, is that what we believe for or expect, we get. This applies in every realm: physical, mental, material, spiritual. Thus it is this law which basically controls the abundant life. . . . The "synchronized life" is simply stated by this formula: confession of belief yields receipt of confession. If you will confess with your mouth at the same time that you confess in your heart what The Word says, you will have power. Your prayers will be answered as you apply these keys in your life by your action. Thus, the abundant resources of heaven are made available to you. But, likewise, if you simultaneously confess with your mouth and heart the negatives of this world, you will manifest these crippling negatives.[78]

According to Victor Wierwille, positive confession or negative confession will bless or curse one's life, respectively. But this is not biblical teaching. Was Jesus financially prosperous? If not, was that because He failed to believe and to act on God's Word by not confessing His material wealth? Did John the Baptist have riches? What about the young martyred Stephen? Why did Paul say he had learned to accept adversity, that he had learned to be *content* while he was hungry, naked, suffering need and in affliction (Philippians 4:11–14)? The Way's misapplication of texts such as Philippians 4:19 and 3 John 2 is characteristic of its many interpretive fallacies. When the Bible says God will "supply all our need in Christ Jesus" the meaning is hardly unending personal prosperity. What God in His wisdom sees as our need and what we might imagine that to be are often two different things.

Simplistic teachings like "the Word of God is the will of God" and "believing equals receiving"[79] frequently lead to disappointment, guilt and defeat in members' lives. Such disillusionment no doubt accounts for some of the recent decline in membership because The Way's response to believer's failures is often cruel. The common rejoinder is to blame the member for "lack of faith," since the laws of prosperity are immutable and never fail. Way members accept this on the authority of Wierwille, who was never wrong.

In his pamphlet "Christians Should Be Prosperous," Wierwille declared that while Christ "fulfilled all the Mosaic Law," "He did not terminate the immutable laws, such as believing and prosperity." In the pamphlet, he also emphasized the importance of "the immutable law of believing."[80] Of course, there is also the law of tithing (to The Way). Tithing "opens the floodgates for prosperity to ourselves," and it is our "financial insurance, health and accident insurance . . . guaranteed by the bank of heaven."[81] Tithing is further linked to the new birth. If one is truly saved, one tithes. If one does not tithe one is presumably not saved. Tithing in a sense, like tongues, is a practical demonstration of the new birth. And if one tithes to The Way, one will be successful financially. "There is a definite new birth spiritually, and there is just as definitely a financially-renewed mind necessary. . . . The Bible clearly indicates that all material manifestation is the result of our spiritual attitude. . . . The belief in lack or need is denied by the tither. . . . All men who have experienced the renewed mind financially and have with systematic accuracy applied the proportionate giving principle have succeeded materially."[82]

These laws are said to work not only for the Christian but also for unbelievers "Immutable laws work for the believer and unbeliever alike. You cannot help but succeed when the principles of the new birth are spiritually applied. Likewise you must succeed when the law of the renewed mind financially is applied."[83] But if these laws work for Muslims, Hindus, atheists, Satanists, Mormons and all others, how do *unbe-* *lievers* "spiritually apply" "the principles of the new birth"?

For The Way, even Christian sanctification proceeds more along the lines of practical mental science than holiness of living. "Believing equals receiving," and believers have a legal right to everything Adam had before the Fall, even everything Christ had, if we will just claim our heritage (see "Salvation" section under "Theology"). "Believe and then receive. The law of believing is the greatest law in the Word of God. As a matter of fact, it is not only the greatest law in The Word, it is the greatest law in the whole world. Believing works for saint and sinner alike."[84] Of course this is simply not true. Faith is not a power to manipulate God to do our bidding. It is trust in His will, Person and wisdom regardless of our personal needs and circumstances.

Regardless, the key to spiritual life in The Way is a renewed mind through proper belief, for "if our minds are renewed, they are perfect, just as our spirit is perfect."[85] Hence, "Christian" sanctification for The Way is not so much godly living as it is prosperous living. "Negative believing" is inspired by Satan and is the root of all sin, illness and evil. "All negatives destroy the mystery" is one slogan.[86] "If I have fear, it has not come from God but through my wrong believing. . . . Above all things; therefore why not believe God's promise of prosperity rather than fear Satan's poverty? The prosperity of your substance and health is dependent upon how much your mind is renewed."[87] As we will see, one logical conclusion is that orthodox Christianity is "inspired by Satan" because it reflects "negative believing."

THEOLOGY

Christianity

There is no doubt that Way members claim to be genuinely Christian. In fact they believe that they are "better" Christians or the "only" Christians. "There have been very few organizations like us in history that want a perfectly biblical view."[88]

In his enthusiasm Wierwille often declared he was willing to debate Christian scholars over his theological beliefs—what was and wasn't Christian. "I'm ready . . . to take on any theologian, any group of scholars, any place in the whole world."[89] Why he turned down the offers is anybody's guess.[90] Despite his claims, Wierwille was no friend of Christianity, which he declared to be "going down the drain, losing, has lost and will continue to lose."[91] The Way opposes Christianity through the following four means.

1. By denying all denominations. Wierwille asserted, "Denominations don't care about teaching God's Word. They perpetuate themselves."[92] "Denominations have dwelt upon methods set up by man rather than actually studying The Word."[93]

2. By attacking all translations and interpretations of the Bible. "The clarity of God's Word has been muddied by passage of time, translations and interpretations. So now we must again study the Word of God and look for clarity on subjects which have been relatively unstudied or on subjects which have been grossly misunderstood and thus inaccurately taught."[94]

3. By denouncing the church. Although The Way claims not to criticize the Christian Church, it does so both in its publications and privately. A former eight year member, Connie M. Heidebrecht recalls, "Belief in the Trinity is a form of 'spiritual whoredom' which can result in demon possession . . . the cross is considered a pagan symbol of death . . . I had been told that the church was an enemy which was keeping us true believers under attack and that I would find only [spiritual] death [in the church]."[95] Wierwille refers to "The so-called 'Christian' Church which purports to teach truth but instead stumbles along in the darkness of its man-made religion."[96] "As a nation we are idolatrous in our beliefs. Our self-exalted religious institutions and leaders are idolatrous, worshipping three-gods-in-one in the name of Christianity and perpetrating the fraud on unsuspecting millions. We must awaken America . . . those who sit in darkness and in the shadow of death."[97]

4. By implying that Christians worship the devil. In light of The Way's overall teachings,

especially on worship (tongue-speaking as the way to worship God) and the Trinity (the doctrine is satanic), the implication is that many Christians are really worshipping the devil. "As human beings, we have two, and only two, alternatives of worship: the true God and the Devil. . . . No good end can come to those who worship anything but the true God."[98]

The chart on the next page shows that The Way is wrong when it claims to be orthodox Christianity.

The Bible

The Way emphasizes its belief in the Bible as God's inspired Word, but its interpretation of the Bible makes the claim meaningless. Wierwille himself even leaned towards bibliolatry. He asserted that "the Word is as much God as God is God."[99] "I believe that The Word takes the place of the absent Christ and that the holy spirit [spiritual abilities] is Christ in us by way of God's Word."[100]

In effect, The Way substitutes the authority of VPW's writings for the authority of Scripture; "the Word of God" becomes VPW's private interpretation. The Bible cannot really be understood without his writings; hence they are as important, if not more important, than the Bible. For example, Wierwille's figures of speech assume great importance, and he believed that a person required knowledge of over 200 of them to interpret Scripture properly. "Figures of speech have a God-designed emphasis which must be grasped and understood in order to fully obtain the impact of The Word. Men are prone to use figures of speech haphazardly, but in the Word of God figures of speech are used with divine design. Each and every one of them may be accurately catalogued and analyzed with precision. There is absolutely no guesswork."[101]

Paradoxically, Wierwille also taught that the Bible cannot edify the spirit because, he believed, the spirit and mind are "two separate and well-defined categories." "Things which are in the senses world cannot feed the spirit. This is a law of God. . . . The Bible is in the senses world . . . and thus can feed only the mind, what then will feed the spirit? The only manifestation God ever gave to edify the spirit is speaking in tongues."[102]

HISTORIC CHRISTIANITY	THE WAY
Jesus is the God-man.	Jesus is a man only.
The Holy Spirit is the Third Person of the Trinity.	The Holy Spirit is a synonym for God (the Holy Spirit is the Father); "holy spirit" refers to spiritual power.
Salvation is solely by grace.	Salvation by grace is claimed but denied in practice.
The Bible normally interpreted is the Word of God and constitutes a completed revelation.	Wierwille's interpretation is the Word of God; additional revelation is accepted.
Propitiatory atonement (completed).	Mediatorial atonement (insufficient).
Repentance from sin.	Repentance as confession.
The human spirit is "dead" or inactive toward God, though not non-existent.	The human spirit is non-existent until the new birth.
Death brings the immediate presence of Christ for the believer or judgment for the unbeliever.	Death brings unconsciousness until the resurrection to eternal life or annihilation.
Hell as an eternal place of divine judgment.	The annihilation of wicked.
Water baptism is commanded.	Water baptism is denied.
Sanctification leads to holiness.	Sanctification leads to successful living.

In The Way, the authority of the Bible is not accepted at face value but is undermined by various means, including: 1. additional sources of revelation from Victor Wierwille or Craig Martindale (PFAL, TWAP, TWI, books, etc.) which, through new illumination and inspiration, interpret the Bible in a biased manner; 2. alleged "new, relevant information" on the biblical languages (e.g., Aramica and mistranslations of the Greek) that illuminate the text; 3. a hyper-dispensationalism that leaves only seven of 66 books relevant for believers; and 4. particular interpretive methods, such as a biased use of nearly endless figures of speech.

God and the Trinity

In his earlier years, Wierwille seems to have believed in the Trinity. In his 1955 book, *Victory through Christ,* he claimed to believe in Christ's deity, and in *Jesus Christ Is Not God* (1975) he claims that at one point in his life he would never have thought about believing that the doctrine of the Trinity was false. It appears that Wierwille came to reject the Trinity through the influence of George M. Lamsa, which began in 1957. Lamsa was a member of a Nestorian church, a heretical branch of Christianity that was condemned in 431 A.D. at the Council of Ephesus.[103] Wierwille's final conclusion was that the doctrine of the Trinity was a satanic deception and a pagan heresy that had undermined the church. The Way is thus adamant about the importance of rejecting the trinitarian doctrine. Indeed, to believe it is to nullify the possibility of salvation. A blazing advertisement for Wierwille's book, *Jesus Christ Is Not God,*[104] reads: "Trinitarian dogma placing Jesus Christ on God's level degrades God and leaves man UNREDEEMED!"

As we will show, Wierwille's denial of the Trinity is based upon his ignorance of church history, comparative religion, systematic theology, biblical studies, the original languages and related subjects. First, he argues that the Trinity is a reflection of false theologies that crept into the Church from pagan converts. Supposedly, the biblical doctrine is related to and derived from the Hindu "trinity" of Brahma, Vishnu and Shiva or other pagan "trinities."[105] But this is nonsense. The so-called trinity of Hinduism, for instance, has nothing to do with the Christian Trinity because the Hindu concepts are comprised of three separate gods and are thus polytheistic, while the biblical Trinity is monotheistic and surrounds the one supreme God. Further, the Hindu trinity is only an illusory manifestation of the ultimate, impersonal, deity Brahman. When we consider the differences between the Christian Trinity and pagan concepts, it is easy to see that Wierwille was mistaken at this point regarding the syncretism.

THE CHRISTIAN TRINITY	PAGAN "TRINITIES" (GREEK, HINDU, ROMAN)
Monotheistic	Polytheistic
Co-equal persons	Unequal deities
Co-eternal persons	Finite deities
One essence in nature	Distinct in nature
Exist in perfect unity	Quarrel and fight with one another
Moral	Immoral

Further, as we document in our Doctrinal Appendix, the Bible does teach the Christian concept of the Trinity; this is how God has revealed Himself to us.

Wierwille also seriously misrepresents the teachings of the church Fathers. During the first three centuries after Christ, we are told that church leaders "*never* referred to them [the Father, Son, Spirit] as co-equal. . . . In fact the opposite was the case. They spoke of the Father as supreme . . . and of the Son as inferior. . . . That there was no formal, established doctrine of the Trinity until the fourth century is a *fully documented* historical fact."[106] In our Doctrinal Appendix we have cited 22 church Fathers who prove Wierwille wrong.

When Wierwille argues that early Christian apologies "were . . . compromises between Christianity and paganism"[107] he displays his ignorance of the writings of early Christian apologists who soundly refuted paganism and other errors, as can be seen from the writings of Athansuis, Ignatius, Polycarp, Ireaeus, Ambrose, Jerome and others. They refuted gnosticism,

various mystery religions and other early heresies, including (Wierwille's dynamic) Monarchianism and Arianism.

Wierwille teaches that Constantine invented the Trinity for political expediency.[108] "Trinitarianism then was confirmed at Nicaea in 325 by Church bishops out of political expediency."[109] As Wierwille's discussion continues, his errors mount. He believes that about 220 bishops were present, but as many as 318 were present, including over a thousand other church leaders. He thinks they were "almost exclusively from the occident," they were predominantly from the East,* although with representatives from all over the world. Incredibly, he argues that the Nicene Creed "was the work of a minority." But the real minority were the two outspoken bishops who refused to sign the creed, and who were summarily excommunicated, and Wierwille's personal hero, Arius, the heretic who had caused so much of the trouble to begin with. That the Trinity was a biblical teaching was the conclusion of almost the entire assembly.** Philip Hughes writes in *The Church in Crisis: A History of the General Councils 325-1870 A.D.,* "The theology of Arius was condemned unanimously."[110]

Further, an "examination of a chain of pre-Arian writers, from every part of Christendom, reveals that 'there was during the second and third centuries a profession and teaching concerning the Holy Trinity, not vague and cloudy, but of a certain determinate character.' "[111] "It is impossible to view [early] historical Christianity apart from the doctrine of the Trinity."[112] Hughes also observes why the specific language of the creed was important. The Bible was not written to refute the technical arguments of heretics, and so it was necessary to declare in technical detail that Scripture meant specifically "this" and specifically "not that" as well.

Wierwille quotes the *Encyclopedia Britannica* to imply that many bishops signed the credal

---

*See Phillip Schaff, *History of the Christian Church*, Vol. 3, pp. 623–624 and Reinhold Seeberg, *The History of Doctrines*, Vol. 1 (Grand Rapids, MI.: Baker Book House, 1978), p. 216.

**See Schaff, *History of the Christian Church*, Vol. 3, pp. 628-632.

statements against their wishes and only because they were overawed by the emperor.[113] However, our edition of the Britannica refutes almost everything he says.[114] Further, as Dr. Jack Sparks points out, the awe was not on the part of the bishops but Constantine himself:

There was indeed some "overawe" there, but it wasn't from the bishops. It was Constantine, the emperor, who was overawed. He'd never seen such a group of men in all his life. There were those there who had gone through some of the most terrifying persecutions imaginable at the hands of the Roman Empire. Some had empty sockets where their eyes had been before they had been gouged out by torturers because they refused to renounce their faith in Jesus Christ. Others had had members of their bodies cut off. Still others had been augured—giant drill bits had been drilled into their arms and legs or other parts of their bodies, because they wouldn't deny Christ. Constantine had never seen such commitment, or devotion, or dedication to anyone. He was so moved that he walked about the assembly and kissed the scars of these heroic confessors. (That's what they called those who had suffered because they preferred to be tortured rather than renounce Christ.)[115]

Dr. Sparks then asks in disbelief: "And we are to assume from Wierwille that the men who met at Nicea were spineless men who were snookered into signing a creed in which they did not believe, because of overawe and political expediency!!??"[116] Thus, about Wierwille, Dr. Sparks correctly points out, "His scholarship in general is irresponsible, slipshod, and false."[117] A good example can be found in his discussion of Martin Luther.

Although Luther's catechism of 1529 declares Jesus as "true God and true man," and although this is only one of many such statements made by Luther, VPW would have people believe: "If Martin Luther would have had more time, and lived in our culture, I'm confident he would have come up with a far better work on *Jesus Christ Is Not God* than I did, because he knew it. But he just didn't have time."[118]

Luther denied Christ's deity and he just didn't have the time to publish a book in confirmation? This is sheer fantasy! Luther penned numerous massive scholarly works, such as his fine commentary on Galatians. If Luther had somehow converted to Arianism, one can be sure he would have written extensively on it. But in his *Epistle to the Hebrews*, Luther stated of chapter 1, verse 12, which refers to God: "We are forced to understand the passage as referring to nobody but the Person of the Son." On chapter 1, verse 1 his commentary reads: "In this way the Apostle established the most powerful argument.... It amounts to this in fact: if the word of the prophets is accepted, how much more ought we to seize the Gospel of Christ, since it is not a prophet speaking to us but the Lord of the prophets, not a servant but a son, not an angel *but God.*"[119]

Wierwille also used sources sympathetic to his position to "document" that there was no doctrine of the Trinity until the fourth century. For example, he quotes from an 1865 text, Alvan Lamson's *The Church of the First Three Centuries.*[120] He does not mention that as a vigorous non-trinitarian Lamson could hardly be expected to provide an objective analysis of historical theology. Wierwille concluded: "Clearly, historians of Church dogma and systematic theologians agree that the idea of a Christian trinity was not a part of the first century Church. The twelve apostles never subscribed to it or received revelation about it."[121] To the contrary, historians and systematic theologians agree that the Trinity was present from the first century Church because it was the teaching of the New Testament.

Wierwille also believed that God is limited by man and limited by His own nature as Spirit: "God's actions are limited by man's believing. And Mary the mother of Jesus was the first woman who believed to the extent that God could create soul-life in her so that she could bring forth God's only begotten Son."[122] "God being Spirit can only speak to what He is. God cannot speak to the natural human mind. . . . But God is Spirit and, therefore, cannot speak to brain cells; God cannot speak to a person's mind. It is a law and God never oversteps His own laws."[123] One wonders, if it is an inviolate "law of God" that God "cannot speak to a person's mind," how did God ever speak to the mind of Wierwille in the first place, on October 5, 1942, and inform him that He would teach him the word "as it had not been known since the first century"?

Clearly, the above examples show that The Way's founder should not be trusted when it comes to pronouncements on Christian doctrine or biblical teaching.

Jesus Christ

A topic so utterly important as God and His Son Jesus Christ certainly deserves both yours and my clearest and best thinking.[124]

—Victor Paul Wierwille

On October 30, 1977, Victor Paul Wierwille stepped from his luxury coach and strutted proudly to the front door of his former United Church of Christ in New Knoxville. There, in an act representing what he saw as "a potentially greater Reformation" than that begun by Martin Luther, he nailed his "version" of Luther's 95 theses to its door. It screamed: JESUS CHRIST IS NOT GOD—Never Was and Never Will Be." Then, "Dr. Wierwille strode back to the custom coach after placing an autographed copy of *Jesus Christ Is Not God* at the foot of the church door for all to see. As the custom coach pulled away, its foghorn blasted three times to signify the ceremony's completion."[125] The Way members present at this important symbolic gesture were thrilled.

According to *Time* magazine, Wierwille arrogantly challenged Christians, "You show me one place in the Bible where it says he [Jesus] is God. . . . I don't want your rapping, your double-talk, your triple-talk; all I want is Scripture."[126] (We list dozens of these Scriptures in the Doctrinal Appendix.) Scripture, however, is exactly what Wierwille did not want, and it is exactly what he would not listen to. For example, as we will see later, to "document" that "Jesus Christ is not God" in John 1:1–14, he had to add over 40 words in brackets in his translation to "clarify" its true meaning. And, although Wierwille claims that it is Christians who "substantiate their beliefs by isolating bits of biblical texts,"[127] the shoe is actually on the other foot, as we will also document.

We may summarize Wierwille's teachings about Jesus under the following seven points.

1. Jesus was first created as a sperm. "Jesus Christ's existence began when God created the sperm with soul-life in Mary."[128]

2. Jesus is the highest creature. "His position is second only to God."[129]

3. Jesus existed with God in the beginning only in God's foreknowledge. "Jesus Christ was not literally with God in the beginning; neither does he have all the assets of God."[130] And, "Where was Jesus Christ before he was born to Mary? Jesus Christ was with God in His foreknowledge. . . . Jesus Christ was with God before the foundation of the world, meaning that God foreknew him. . . . We, as well as Jesus Christ, were with God in His foreknowledge, but not in existence, before the foundation of the world."[131]

4. Jesus is not God. It is crucial that Jesus be only a man. Thus, "When my life is over, I think my greatest contribution may prove to be the knowledge and teaching that Jesus Christ is not God."[132] It is important to observe that Wierwille, like the Jehovah's Witnesses, Christadelphians and other cults, connects salvation to the rejection of Christ's deity. In other words, if Christ is God, the salvation of men and women is impossible. Wierwille's conclusion here is based on a misunderstanding of the Christian view of the nature of Jesus as fully God and fully man—undiminished deity and full humanity in one Person. He argued that if Christ is God, then He could not represent or die for men. "If Jesus Christ is God and not the Son of God, we have not yet been redeemed. The difference is that important, that critical. . . . Our very redemption, the crucial point on which all of Christianity rests, is dependent on Jesus Christ's being a man and not God. Our passover, which was Jesus Christ tortured, crucified, dead and buried, had to be a sheep from the flock. God would hardly qualify as one of our brethren, yet His Son could."[133] Of course, if Jesus was fully human, Wierwille's argument is irrelevant.

5. Jesus is the replacement for Lucifer. "Clearly, Jesus Christ is presently second only to God in power and authority. Lucifer as the morning star was replaced by Jesus Christ who is now the morning star."[134]

6. Jesus was not virgin born. Wierwille apparently teaches that Jesus was born "dead in trespasses and sins, without hope." "Why didn't Jesus come with the spirit upon him when he was born? Because then he could not have redeemed you and me. He had to be born just as we are—a natural man, naturally dead in trespasses and sins, without hope."[135] (See note 152.)

Wierwille believed that Jesus was born of God's sperm but that Mary was a virgin only until the conception of Jesus, but not after. During her pregnancy she had sexual relations with Joseph. Citing Matthew 1:18–20, Wierwille declares: "'Take unto thee' literally means 'to take her as a wife,' not just to take her and watch over her until the baby is born. Mary is already the wife of Joseph so the instruction to 'take unto him' would mean something more; it means intercourse."[136] But Wierwille apparently forgot to read the next few verses. The reason why Christians refer to the virgin *birth*, not the virgin conception, is because the Bible states plainly that Joseph "had no union with her until she gave birth to a son" (Matthew 1:25).

7. Miscellaneous. In addition, Wierwille teaches of Jesus that, after His death, "for three days and three nights he had no consciousness."[137] "The Word of God says that Jesus Christ was dead for 72 hours. How could Jesus Christ be God for God cannot die?"[138] Biblically, however, Jesus was never unconscious for three days, and obviously, the second Person of the Godhead cannot die. But, on the Cross Jesus' human nature expired; it ceased its biological functioning. Since this nature was not eternal, but truly human and began at the incarnation (Philippians 2), it was subject to death.

Wierwille also implies that, at least temporarily, John the Baptist might have been "better than Jesus because he came into the world with more of the power of God than Jesus did."[139] Supposedly, Jesus did not have a spiritual nature until the age of 30, whereas John had "spirit" from the womb. Wierwille teaches that until age 30 Jesus was comprised only of body and soul. Body and soul cannot communicate with God, only spirit can. Wierwille thinks that Jesus had no communion with God until He was 30.

In conclusion, the Jesus of The Way is not the biblical Jesus. While The Way does accept Jesus' physical resurrection, ascension and return, it denies His very nature and mission. For Wierwille, even the term "Son of God" only refers to one who was a special human being.

The Holy Spirit

1. The Holy Spirit is another term for God. Wierwille believes that the Holy Spirit is merely a synonym for God and nothing more. God is holy and God is spirit, therefore Holy Spirit is another name for the one and only God. The Holy Spirit, then, is merely a descriptive term of the Father.

To see how difficult such an idea is, one need only try to translate Scripture according to Wierwille's theory. For example, John 14:16 would read: "I will ask the Father and He will give you the Father . . . that is the Father." How would John 15:26 sound? "When the Father comes, whom I will send to you from the Father, that is the Father, who proceeds from the Father, He will bear witness of me."

Jesus emphasizes the separate personality of the Spirit throughout John 14. He also uses the world *allos* for "another" in 14:16, indicating that the Paracletos, or "Helper," is another one of the same kind. If the word *heteros* had been used, it would have meant one of "a different kind." The Holy Spirit is therefore another of the same kind—another divine Person. One could also ask how Jesus, a mere creature, could *send* the Holy Spirit (God) if indeed Jesus was not God.

2. A crucial distinction between the Holy Spirit and holy spirit. The Way also uses the same term with lower case letters: holy spirit is "power from on high" or spiritual abilities manifested in the outward world of sense as the nine operations or manifestations of God. (Wierwille did not use the term "gifts.") Thus, when the word Holy Spirit is capitalized in his writings (not the Bible's*), Wierwille means God the Father; when the word is not capitalized he means divine power, spiritual power received at the new birth, manifested as the nine "operations" of 1 Corinthians 12:8–10. "The *Giver* is God, the Spirit. His *gift* is spirit. Failure to recognize the

---

*Since the Bible capitalizes Holy Ghost or Holy Spirit, when quoting from the Bible, Wierwille must explain which holy spirit he means.

difference between the *Giver* and His *gift* has caused no end of confusion in the Holy Spirit field of study as well as in the understanding of the new birth."[140]

Wierwille's justification for translating certain usages of the Greek term *pneuma hagion* as "Holy Spirit" (synonymous with God) and others as "holy spirit" (power) is that there is no article "the" before *pneuma hagion* in some 50 passages in the Greek texts, and, he claims, never in the "more accurate" Estrangelo Aramaic texts.[141] "*The* Holy Spirit" for him would imply a distinct person (that is, God the Father); a mere "holy spirit" supposedly does not and is therefore impersonal power. But the presence or lack of the article is irrelevant to the issue of whether the Holy Spirit is a distinct personality within the Godhead, as has been pointed out by Greek authority Thayer, in *Thayer's Greek Lexicon:* "More or less frequently, the article is missing before appellatives (names) of persons or things of which only one of the kind exists, so the article is not needed to distinguish the individual from others of the same kind as sun, earth, Christ, Holy Spirit. . . ." (Cf. Nigel Turner, *Grammatical Insights into the New Testament* [1965], pp. 17–22.)*

3. The apostles received holy spirit by heavy breathing. On the day of Pentecost, believers received "holy spirit" (the power referred to as "it") not the Holy Spirit.[142] Christians are not filled with the Holy Spirit but with "holy spirit." This alleged power has been present since Pentecost but not all Christians receive it. Wierwille's instructions for receiving holy spirit are:

1. Be quiet and at ease (relax).
2. Don't beg God. It is already available.
3. Rest your head back, open your mouth, and breathe in deeply.[143]

---

*Books such as John Walvoord's *The Holy Spirit* (chapter 1), Rene Pache's *The Person and Work of the Holy Spirit* (chapters 1–3), Charles Ryrie's *The Holy Spirit* (chapters 1–3, cf. chapter 19), and the discussion in L. Berkhof's *Systematic Theology* (Part One, VIII) and in A.H. Strong's *Systematic Theology* (Vol. 1, Part IV, chapter II), adequately demonstrate the errors of Wierwille at this point.

Members are also told that "inspiration" means "in-breathing" and that "opening your mouth and breathing in deeply is an act of believing which God honors."[144] Psalm 81:10 is quoted: "Open thy mouth wide, and I will fill it" (KJV) and Psalm 119:131: "I opened my mouth, and panted," (KJV). Also, "the Greek text of Acts 2:2 [referring to the day of Pentecost] . . . should be translated 'as of a heavy breathing'."[145] Thus, the apostles of Jesus Christ apparently congregated around the communion table hyperventilating in hopes of receiving holy spirit.

Salvation

To understand The Way's teaching on salvation, we must begin with the Fall and understand its view of the legal nature of redemption. Wierwille believes man was originally created by God with a body, soul and spirit. But only man's spirit can communicate with Spirit (God); The body (the physical senses) and the soul or mind cannot. Hence God intended man to communicate with Spirit by spirit only. This was the choice in the Garden: either receive natural knowledge by the five senses or spiritual knowledge through the spirit. God intended man to gain spiritual knowledge by his spirit. In other words, God's "image" is solely in the spirit of man. "After God created within man His own image, God had a companion—not in the body and soul parts of man, but in the spirit. . . . This gave them fellowship."[146] The existence of this spirit is what separates man from the animals.

Wierwille distinguishes between the conferred (legal) rights of man and the natural (innate) rights of man, that which man has by virtue of being man. At the creation, God gave Adam certain conferred rights. These included ruling the earth, "the rights to perfect love, to complete joy, to happiness, to perfect health," as well as the right to everlasting life.[147] That is, Adam was not perfectly loving, happy, healthy and immortal innately.

Wierwille also argued that God conferred the earth to Adam to be governed under his authority through a proper relationship to Him (spirit to Spirit). The earth was therefore legally his and under his absolute control. "God limited Himself by giving that legal responsibility to

Adam."[148] But a conferred right, unlike a natural right, can be forfeited by one's own volition. In the Garden, the devil deceived Adam and got him to rely on his senses instead of his spirit. As a result, he lost his spirit and became just like the animals—mere body and soul. Thus, man forfeited his conferred rights to Satan. His spirit was not just dead or unresponsive to God but it was now *nonexistent.* As a result, Adam could no longer communicate with God. Fellowship with God was totally severed because Adam had forfeited his conferred rights. Thus, the Fall gave Satan legal control over all the earth and placed all of Adam's conferred rights under Satan's authority. A complete transfer of power took place. "Adam took those legal rights and transferred by his own willful decision the authority and power of those rights to Satan."[149]

Man no longer controlled the earth. Satan did, and Satan controlled man as well, legally. Man no longer had the right to perfect love, joy, happiness and health. Man was not only without a spirit, and hence unable to communicate with God, but also legally owned by Satan. All that man could do was to live through his five senses, obey his taskmaster and die. Satan now had the power of death over man. "The original sin of man had legal consequences. Adam had the right to transfer the authority and the power and the dominion he had because God had conferred it upon him. . . . Thus when Adam sinned, Satan, who was the supreme enemy of God, obtained absolute control over all that which God had originally given to Adam."[150]

As we shall see, The Way doctrine of salvation involves transferring these legal rights back to man via the death of a special man with pure blood (Jesus). At that point, people will have all the rights that were lost at the Fall legally transferred back to them for use in this life. (This forms the basis of The Way's "prosperity" doctrines.)

With this background, we need to discuss the legal nature of The Way's doctrine of redemption: a legal loss demands a legal redemption. Because God is a just God, He "had to recognize the transferred legal rights." He also had to "redeem man on legal grounds to be just to Himself, to man and to Satan," for a legal forfeiture

of necessity requires a legal re-procurement.[151] Hence, a legal redeemer was necessary. This redeemer could be neither angel nor God, for neither were "legal"—neither had committed the original sin, forfeiting their legal rights; this was only true of man. Thus, the redeemer had to be a man. God thus had to *create* a special man over whom Satan had no authority. Fallen man has impure blood transmitted genetically, so God circumvented this by creating an unpolluted sperm. When Christ was born from God's sperm, Satan had no legal authority over Him because there was no death in His body. "There was no death within His body because the life in His blood was sinless or pure and, subsequently, incorruptible."*[152] The one man over whom Satan had no control had finally arrived. This brings us to The Way's doctrine of the atonement.

The Atonement

The importance of this legal aspect for understanding The Way's view of the atonement is crucial. What forgives people's sin is simply the death of a man with clean blood. This legally transfers all of the rights Satan received at the Fall back to people when they believe. God did not demand any more than a legal transfer, and the requirement was the death of a man with clean blood. This means that even though The Way may use proper terminology when referring to Christ's death (words such as atonement, reconciliation, forgiveness of sins and propitiation), the logical outcome of their doctrine is a blatant *denial* of the biblical nature of the atonement. Nowhere does the Bible teach that the sin of the world is removed by the death of a perfect man with clean blood.

In light of the above we may note the following five points concerning the doctrine of salvation in The Way.

1. Redeemed persons have all the original rights that God conferred on Adam before the Fall. "What man had lost in power, authority, rulership and dominion since Genesis 1:28, he

---

*How this is reconciled with Wierwille's teaching that Jesus was (apparently) born "dead in trespasses and sins" is uncertain.

regains when the holy spirit comes within."[153] Again, this is the basis for The Way's teachings on prosperity and health. Legal rights are something one owns. If a car is legally ours, we own it. Since all of Adam's conferred, or legal, rights (perfect love, joy, moral perfection, happiness, health and immortality) are returned to people at salvation, they own them now by faith. "Jesus Christ legally fulfilled all requirements so that we today can walk without sin and without sickness. Because of his redeeming work . . . we today can walk with our heavenly Father as body, soul and spirit men."[154]

2. These legal rights are available by appropriation. All of our rights are now legally ours if we are redeemed. We only need to appropriate the rights. However, the church has been deceived by Satan into not claiming its legal rights. "The Church has not claimed its rights, power and authority because Satan has talked us out of it."[155] Still, "You have a legal right to victory over all sin and the consequences of sin. . . . You have a legal right to use the authority of the name of Jesus Christ in prayer in order to get results. You have a legal right to the Father's protection, care and guidance."[156] Wierwille also enumerates additional "legal rights" of the believer, including accomplishing more than Jesus did while on earth:

> You have a legal right to be a son of God. . . . You have a legal right to receive the indwelling presence of the holy spirit [God's power that enables man to have spiritual abilities]. You have a legal right to be changed at the second coming. . . . You have a legal right to an immortal body. You have a legal right to an inheritance in the new heaven and the new earth. . . . We have a legal right to everything that Christ had, if we will believe. Everything Jesus did while here upon earth we may do, and more, if we believe.[157]

However, these rights are available only to the believer who appropriates them by choice and action. Remember, legal rights require volition to operate. We may own a car but unless we choose to get inside and drive it, it will sit idle. The same is true for Christians and their "rights":

God has moved in Jesus Christ. Jesus Christ moved to regain legal rights for man. Now it is man's move in the authority and power delegated to him by Jesus Christ for Satan has no legal rights over the converted, born-again man. . . . The unconverted sinner legally belongs in body and soul to the devil. . . . Unless we claim with action and boldness our delegated rights we are tying God's hands. God is limited to the extent of a man's believing and obedience. May I urge you to study God's Word diligently so you will know what are your legal rights in Christ Jesus. This is *the key to power.*[158]

Wierwille teaches that Satan cannot get his legal rights back. He may, however, neutralize Christians by making them think that they do not have these rights; for example, by making them think that health, moral perfection and financial prosperity are beyond their control. Christians may choose not to make use of their legal rights, but they cannot again be transferred to Satan.

3. At salvation, man receives a spirit. The unredeemed have no spirit; they are only body and soul. (This means that until age 30 Jesus had no spirit and was actually unredeemed.) At salvation people receive holy spirit, the spiritual power or essence that enables them to legally produce the nine manifestations of the Holy Spirit (God). Wierwille interprets John 3:6 as "that which is born of the Spirit (the *pneuma*, Spirit, God) is spirit (*pneuma*, gift). . . . In the new birth, man receives spirit from God who is the Spirit."[159] Since the new birth was not available until Pentecost, prior to then no one had a spirit. The holy spirit "is received by the believer at the time of the new birth."[160] The Way emphasizes, "We must constantly remember that Pentecost was the first time in the history of civilization that it was possible for anyone to be born again."[161]

By contrast, scores of Scriptures declare that we have a spirit prior to Pentecost. For example, Pharaoh's spirit was troubled (Genesis 41:8; cf. 1 Chronicles 5:26), and Job said, "There is a spirit in man," and he spoke of "the spirit within me" (32:8, 18 KJV). David said, "Into thy hand I commit my spirit" (Psalm 31:5 NAS) and

Solomon spoke of "the spirit of a man" (Proverbs 18:14 NAS). Isaiah noted, "With my spirit within me I will seek thee" (26:9; KJV). Jesus said, "The spirit is willing" (Mark 14:38). Mary said, "My spirit has rejoiced in God my Savior" (Luke 1:47 NAS). Clearly, Wierwille is wrong again.

4. Before Christ, there was no grace or faith. Until Jesus the perfect man came and legally redeemed people from Satan's control (Jesus legally transferred Satan's rights back to people) there could be no grace, only law. Until the atonement, "God had to recognize the transferred legal rights" at the Fall.[162] As a result, The Way teaches that the Gospels do *not* teach salvation by grace. Salvation in the Old Testament dispensation (which, remember, includes the Gospels) was based on legal means (law-keeping) because Satan's legal rights had not yet been transferred to man. "Before the accomplishments of Jesus Christ, the law had to be kept by man for his salvation."[163] "We must understand that the rules of life change in the various time periods so that we must see each administration within its distinct context.... To whom is Deuteronomy addressed? To the Jews, to Israel. If they kept the law, they would be made righteous. Deuteronomy can be set under law, but it cannot be set under the administration of the Church of Grace. If we observed all the commandments, we would not be righteous because our administration, the Church, operates under changed rules."[164] But Wierwille is wrong again. God is a God of grace for all eternity, even prior to the Law of Moses. Both the Old Testament and the Gospels teach salvation by faith (See John 3:16; 5:24; 6:47; Romans 4).

A related Way belief is that an individual's faith alone does not justify the person, that it cannot be increased and that it was not available until Pentecost. Wierwille teaches that the believer is *not* justified by his or her faith alone but by the faith of Jesus Christ; this is why it can't be increased. "When the man of body and soul hears the Word of God and believes what he hears, Romans 10:9, he receives the 'faith of Jesus Christ' and righteousness."[165] Thus, "All born-again believers have 'the faith of Jesus Christ' which is the measure given to *everyone*

when he believes."[166] "How much faith is the faith of Jesus Christ: All one is ever going to receive. How can a person get more faith?... Whose faith? Not my own, but the faith of Jesus Christ.... A person can never receive or attain more faith than that."[167]

Biblically, none of this is true. Individual faith *does* justify and it was available before Pentecost, as Paul argues so forcefully in Romans and Galatians. Further, we do not have the faith of Christ, otherwise every believer would do the things Christ did. If what Wierwille said was true, why would the disciples tell Jesus, "Increase our faith" (Luke 17:5) if they already had perfect faith? (Wierwille, of course, believes that they didn't have any faith at all, because it wasn't even available until Pentecost.) But then why would Jesus and Paul distinguish degrees of faith (Matthew 8:10; 15:28; Romans 12:6; 14:1)? Why would Paul tell both the post-Pentecostal Corinthians that "your faith grows" (2 Corinthians 10:15 NAS) and the Thessalonians that "your faith is greatly enlarged" (2 Thessalonians 1:3 NAS)?

For Wierwille, all references to faith before the Book of Acts are, conveniently, mistranslations. Thus there are *no* references to faith in the Gospels, and the Old Testament does *not* say that Abraham had faith. "If faith came by Jesus Christ, was there faith in the Old Testament? Was there then faith in the Gospels? There must not have been because Jesus Christ came to make it available.... When we read the word "faith" before the book of Acts, we are simply reading an error in translation.... In the Old Testament, it does not say that Abraham had faith."[168]

This is more nonsense. The Old Testament is full of faith and even New Testament authors agree. In Hebrews 11 we are told again and again that Old Testament saints received the approval of God *by their faith*. The phrase is used 25 times referring to thousands of people. "Faith ... is what the ancients were commended for" (v. 1). "All these people were still living by faith when they died" (v. 13). "These were all commended for their faith" (v. 39). But none of this matters to members of The Way since Wierwille has assured them the entire Old Testament and book of Hebrews were not written for them. Wierwille may try to distinguish between the "faith" that no one had prior to Pentecost and the "belief" that they did have, but the principal Greek words *pistis* and *pisteuo,* are routinely used interchangeably in the Bible for either faith or belief—not a few times, but hundreds of times.

5. The atonement was substitutionary or representational but not propitiatory in a biblical sense. The death of a man with clean blood satisfied God and forgave people's sins because the issue was entirely legal (merely a transfer) and not propitiatory in the biblical understanding. Sins were forgiven because Jesus had pure blood and died, *not* because the sins were laid upon Jesus to satisfy God's wrath. "Jesus Christ was a man like us, only with perfect blood. When he offered himself for our sins, he redeemed us once for all."[169] The legal exchange had been made. Apparently, Jesus' physical death alone, not a propitiatory death, was sufficient. A certain kind of blood was offered within a proper legal environment, rather than making a satisfaction of infinite holiness. Clearly one man alone could never atone for the sins of billions, and according to The Way, Jesus was only a man.

In Wierwille's writings we discover teachings that deny the propitiatory nature of the atonement. As noted earlier, The Way writers will use "figures of speech" to "document" their teachings. Like Wierwille's strangled use of Greek, the figures of speech can awe or mystify the average member. Wierwille uses this ploy to deny that God has anger. "Another example of *condescensio* is Exodus 4:14 which says, 'And the anger of the Lord was kindled.' God is Spirit; He has no anger. When the Bible says the anger of the Lord, what figure is it? *Condescensio.*"[170]

If God has no anger, how can He possibly be angry at sin? How, then, can the atonement possibly be propitiatory? To propitiate, biblically, means to satisfy God's anger against sin by the death of Jesus as our substitute for sins. This is why 1 John 2:2 declares, "He is the atoning sacrifice [propitiation, NAS] for our sins, and not only for ours but also for the sins of the whole world." There are three related Greek words, *hilaskomai, hilasmos* and *hilasterios,* which mean

"propitiation" and are translated as such four times in the NAS (Romans 3:25; Hebrews 2:17; 1 John 2:2; 4:10). The NIV translates them as "atoning sacrifice" for readability, but the meaning of "turning away anger" is central to the Greek terms. But Wierwille teaches God did *not* forsake Jesus because of our sin. Citing Jesus' cry of being forsaken, in Matthew 27:46, he asserts: "This translation is a cry of defeat and as such has misled well meaning people for years. . . . It would appear that God forsook Jesus because Jesus became sin and God could not stand sin. God consequently left Jesus to die alone. This idea contradicts every other pertinent verse in the Word of God."[171]

Christ's death was only a legal transaction, like selling a house. Jesus was simply a better sacrificial animal than the goats and sheep used in Levitical practice. "It took the shed blood of a lamb to save the Israelites from destruction. If the blood of one little lamb could save an entire house from damnation, think of what the shedding of Christ's blood did for you and me."[172]

All this is a terrible blasphemy against Christ. When Way members declare that the sacrifice of Jesus forgave the world's sin, they mean something entirely different than what a Christian would mean. The "atonement" of The Way has nothing to do with the biblical atonement. Biblically, Jesus had to be God to fulfill God's requirements. Only an infinite Being could pay the penalty of infinite wrath against sin. As J. L. Williams states: "Wierwille's Christ is a Christ who cannot save, because He is not fully God and fully man. For Christ to be a bridge between man and God, He *must,* like a physical bridge, be firmly established on both shores. Otherwise the chasm that separates man from God would not be bridged. We would have no mediator. And we would still be lost in our sins."[173]

Works

The Way strongly asserts that it teaches salvation by grace through faith alone. This is said to be official doctrine. However, according to Dr. John Juedes, a Missouri Lutheran Synod pastor in California who has done detailed research into The Way, The Way denies grace in practice and teaches salvation by works:

TWI sometimes refers to grace, but in practice, grace is almost nonexistent in TWI. Instead, TWI constantly emphasizes the law—what people must believe, do, control, or accomplish. . . . On the one hand, leaders will say that righteousness is God-given. But in the same teaching, they will claim that righteousness is only achieved by our own efforts, "Believing brings to pass righteousness, right believing, a true and vital walk with the Father, doing what is correct." . . . In this way, TWI makes righteousness a "right" you claim rather than a gift you receive. . . . The result of this heavy dose of law teaching, is that TWI leaders place an oppressive burden on the backs of its followers. . . . Wayers carry heavy loads, since leaders say that everything is up to their "believing" to attain and prevail.

TWI's word is all law and almost no Gospel. . . . All who have had to submit their lives to the scrutiny of Way leaders and obey them explicitly, who have rushed to sell their homes to get out of debt, who have been forced to give up large parts of their lives to attend every Way meeting, who drove 10 hours every Sunday to New Knoxville, who gave money until it hurt, who have been threatened with "mark and avoid" [discipline] for every little thing, who have been told to "control" [things] and have been condemned for lack of believing and obeying when any negative circumstances arose, and so forth, know that life in TWI is a wearisome burden without any rest.[174]

Victor Wierwille himself taught that believers were to be literally perfect based on the doctrines of the conferral of legal rights and positive confession, or "the Law of Believing." "Somebody may come along and say, 'Well you cannot be perfect?' The Word of God says we are to be."[175] There is not much room for grace here; indeed, as we will see, the hypocrisy was that VPW demanded perfection of his followers while accepting so much imperfection for himself.

There is a secondary problem. In The Way, confessional repentance as a "work" can easily confuse Way members as to their own salvation, i.e., making them believe they have salvation when they do not. Biblical repentance (and faith) must have three components to be genuine: intellectual, emotional and volitional. It is the third element that may be missing in a con-

fessional type of repentance or faith. Here The Way can sound biblical while simultaneously denying the Bible:

> Repentance is to do what God says; and He says in Romans 10:9, "That if thou shalt confess with thy mouth the Lord Jesus, and believe in thine heart that God hath raised him from the dead, thou shalt be saved." Repentance on your part is to confess with your mouth the Lord Jesus as your personal Lord and Savior. It is to believe in your heart, your innermost being, that God has raised Jesus from the dead, that Jesus is resurrected and alive, yes, living *for* you and in you. That is repentance.[176]

> The moment I fulfill these two requirements—believing and confession—I am born again of God's Spirit. . . . When that man by his believing comes to the point of saying, "Jesus is Lord of my life and I believe God raised Him from the dead," he is born again of God's Spirit. That person has instantly changed lords; he is now on the way to heaven and all hell cannot stop him.[177]

The problem with the above statements is not so much the words but in how they are interpreted within the larger context of Way theology and practice. To begin, they are *not* confessing the biblical Jesus Christ as Lord; they are confessing the Wierwille Christ, who is merely a creature. Faith in Jesus as a mere man can no more save a person than faith in Moses or Mohammed. Faith in and confession of the wrong object of faith is powerless to save.

Second, biblical repentance is a change of mind about one's sins and about Christ, and although it leads to verbal acknowledgment of Christ's lordship, verbal confession alone does not save, especially if one is confessing a false Christ. It would not be too difficult to imagine Way members thinking that they are saved simply because they have been told that their audible confession and belief in the Christ of The Way guarantees salvation. To the extent that members of The Way are trusting in what they do in The Way, rather than in what the God-Man has already perfectly accomplished on their behalf, they are trusting in themselves for salvation and not in Jesus as Savior.

Perhaps it is because of Wierwille's ideas on the atonement that he stresses repentance as "confession of Christ" rather than "turning from sin." Again, if God does not get angry at sin, and if the "atonement" was merely a legal transfer, it is reasonable to think that repentance from sin would not be stressed. (This may also explain the immorality in The Way that we discuss later.)

The Way also teaches an unorthodox view of salvation in another manner. Upon verbal confession of "Christ" as "Lord," a person supposedly becomes a child of God legally but not experientially. The latter occurs at the time of manifesting the gift of "holy spirit" (usually at the end of the PFAL and TWAP courses when the person speaks in tongues). In other words, confession puts one on the path to heaven, but the "connection" between the person and God is either not yet received or nonoperative. Thus the believer cannot pray and worship until a later time. Biblically, of course, when one accepts Jesus Christ as Lord and Savior, that person becomes a child of God legally and experientially and can immediately worship and pray (see John 1:12). Further, the stress on audible confession in The Way is carried over to other practical areas of Christian living. For example, "So long as I cannot get my mouth and my heart coordinated on some point that is confirmed by The Word, I have no power with God."[178] In addition, The Way stresses tongues and the manifestations of "holy spirit" so heavily that these can easily become works, things done to attain salvation, or things seen as genuine proof of it.

In summary, salvation according to the Way: 1) is dependent on Christ's creaturehood; 2) has as its proof tongues-speaking; 3) teaches that finding the true Gospel is related to knowing the distinction between the Bride and Body of Christ; 4) involves confession of the Christ of The Way; 5) denies the atonement and salvation by grace; and 6) its sanctification necessitates appropriating one's legal rights through actions or deeds (for example, tithing). This has nothing whatsoever to do with the salvation offered in the Bible.

The Afterlife

The Way teaches that the dead are unconscious, but this teaching is based on a misunderstanding of certain biblical texts. "Except for Christ Jesus, all the rest of the dead are still dead."[179] Psalms 6:5 and 146:4 and Ecclesiastes 9:5, 6 and 10 are often cited as a confirmation.[180] But these verses do not prove that the dead are unconscious or in a state of "soul-sleep." They record the feelings and sentiments of God's people a thousand years prior to New Testament revelation, which make it clear that the dead are not unconscious. But these verses say nothing as to the particular conditions of the afterlife, as commentators such as theologian H. C. Leupold have pointed out.[181] And there are clear Old Testament declarations that the dead are not unconscious, such as Daniel 12:2-3, Isaiah 26:19 and Psalm 16:8-11. (For further exposition of life after death and heaven and hell from a biblical perspective, see the Doctrinal Appendix.)

The Way also teaches the Christian view of death is satanic and that death does not bring the believer immediately into the presence of Christ:

No passage of Scripture teaches that there is conscious existence after death. . . . The teaching that when a person dies he immediately goes to God in heaven is one of the many doctrines of Satan and his fallen angels. Such erroneous thinking can be inspired only by Satan and believed and taught by broken-down clerical institutions and by all other religions which are inaugurated and formed by natural man, and directed by Satan.[182]

If death is the entrance to eternal happiness with the Lord, then death is not an enemy but a welcomed friend. If death brings us into the immediate presence of Christ, then the Scriptures are void and our believing vain.[183]

Wierwille argues that if anyone should have gone to heaven immediately at death, Jesus should have, but instead He was unconscious for three days "as Matthew 12 and Acts 2 state."[184] But Matthew 12:40 and Acts 2 nowhere declared that Jesus was unconscious. (Actually, if we carry the analogy strictly, in Matthew 12:40 Jonah was conscious in the belly of the great fish (see Jonah 1:17 and 2:1, the passage Jesus quoted from), and therefore Jesus must have been conscious after death.)

Wierwille's doctrine of "soul sleep" is based on his illogical views on demonology. He believed that one cannot label the practices of necromancy as satanic *unless* the dead are unconscious. If the dead were conscious, he reasons, seances could then be genuine reappearances of the human dead rather than a satanic counterfeit. Biblically, of course, the saved dead are with Christ and the unsaved are confined to punishment, so the dead do not return to contact the living. But Wierwille is unable to accept the possibility that people can both be conscious after death and also *not* be the source of necromantic contacts. Of course, if demons are behind virtually all contacts with the dead, it hardly matters if the dead are conscious.

But for Wierwille, his "biblical proof " that people are unconscious after death is his real proof that seances are fraudulent. The fact is, they are fraudulent whether or not people have consciousness after death. But for Victor, it seems, the disproof of seances is proven solely by the soul-sleep of men. Thus, according to him, to allow for the possibility of consciousness after death is to allow for a genuine necromancy. "The Bible says that when a man dies, he is dead and he stays dead until the return of Christ and the resurrection. Nobody who has died is living with the exception of the Lord Jesus Christ. . . . If the Church would teach this accurate Word, the spiritualists would be out of business. If the dead are alive and in heaven now having such a glorious time, then the spiritualists are not producing counterfeits."[185]

In his book, *Are the Dead Alive Now?* Wierwille attempts to "refute" some of the major passages supporting the Christian view of what happens at death. Although he claims that Scripture should be interpreted literally whenever possible, he really means literally whenever it is convenient or supports his ideas. Thus the literal meaning of all the following Scriptures is rejected for a symbolic or figurative meaning: 1 Samuel 28, the return of Samuel from the dead; Matthew 17, the transfiguration of Jesus and the appearance of Moses; Matthew 22, the resurrection discussion; Luke 16, Lazarus and the rich man; Luke 23, Jesus' promise to the thief on the cross; Philippians 1, where "to die is gain"; 2 Corinthians 5, where the saved dead are "present with the Lord" (KJV); and Hebrews 11, Enoch's translation.

Finally, although we have never seen it stated formally in Wierwille's writings, former members have said that The Way rejects the biblical doctrine of eternal punishment. We presume that this would be argued on the following grounds: (1) God is not angry over sin; (2) man has no spirit until rebirth; (3) the spirit gives eternal life; therefore, (4) unbelievers are without spirits and without eternal life. Thus their only fate would be annihilation.

The Occult

The question of potential occult involvement in The Way depends upon whether Way members are capable of producing genuinely supernatural manifestations in their exercise of "holy spirit" or "God's" power. Although we cannot deny a prevalence of psychological factors or religious suggestion, truly supernatural manifestations cannot be ruled out for the several reasons, resulting as implications of Way teaching.

1. Receiving "holy spirit" involves the reception of spiritual power. Wierwille himself was concerned over the issue of the source of spiritual power. "I knew that there is such a thing as devil possession and that Satan does supernatural feats. How could I be sure I would not be getting a counterfeit experience when receiving the *pnuema hagion*? This was perhaps my greatest fear."[186] If some members do receive supernatural spiritual power, it is inconceivable that it has come from God because they deny Him (there is no Trinity), His Son (who is a creature), His Spirit (who does not exist) and His Word (as normally understood).

2. Salvation constitutes, in part, receiving a spirit. This is also said to involve acquiring supernatural abilities. Once one receives "holy spirit," the power is held to be inherent. Way members refer to "the awe-inspiring abilities latent within the human mind," and they say, "We have potential power within us," noting, "God has blessed us all alike with the same supernatural equipment, the power of God, to meet the needs of humanity."[187] Thus it is "holy spirit" that is the causative factor for miracles. It is called "this wonderful power."[188] It is not a "he" but an "it," an impersonal power. (One wonders how this teaching is to be distinguished from a medium receiving "power" from a spirit guide?)

3. Wierwille himself claimed to have supernatural powers.[189] In fact, he received his "believing is receiving" theology from "Christian" medium and spiritist Albert E. Cliff, who was once his mentor.[190]

4. The Way stresses operating the "nine manifestations." These are: tongues, interpretation of tongues, prophecy, word of knowledge, wisdom, discerning of spirits, faith, gifts of healing and of working miracles. Seven of these are clearly supernatural.[191] Way members are told they can do the very miracles of Jesus, and more.

Thus if some Way members do operate miraculous gifts, there is reason for concern. Their doctrine tells them to expect to receive "spiritual power" at salvation. But whose spiritual power are they receiving? How could they possibly know its true source? They only have the word of VPW who asserts, "God energizes all manifestations in every believer": one only need to believe to put them into operation.[192] But what are the implications if the source of the spiritual power is not from God?

Wierwille himself teaches that demons can counterfeit every manifestation but tongues. "Speaking in tongues is the only manifestation which basically Satan cannot counterfeit."[193] "Devils *cannot* speak in tongues. Thus, when one speaks in tongues one can never speak devilish or wrong things."[194] No biblical proof is given for these assertions, and indeed there is none. The fact is, Mormons, mediums and many other religious groups claim tongues-speaking by supernatural power. There is no reason why tongues should be exempt from Satan's counterfeits.

5. Wierwille emphasizes the "spirit" world over the "senses" world. "We cannot know anything about the spiritual world by way of the senses. . . . Spiritual things from the spiritual world may be known in this world only by the spirit which dwells in us. Then, and only then, can the Spirit relate impressions and truths to us about the spiritual world and make them logical."[195] He thus encourages people to rely on spirit and to accept communications from the spiritual world. Two "entirely different sets of laws" operate in the spirit and sense worlds. If we understand the laws of the spirit world, we will supposedly no longer have any fear or limit God.[196] But only if we have faith:

The Word declares that the devil both *was* and *is* defeated. It stipulates he has no legal rights over the Christian. If Satan has no power over the Christian, why do you want to confess that he has power over you? Every time you make a negative confession you are contradicting God's Word. If the devil's power is defeated, as it is, then his power cannot touch you when you believe The Word. But, you must *confess* that you know the power of God in your life.[197]

If negative confessions open doors to the devil's influence, which Way member thinks his or her positive confession is perfect? To encourage unbelievers to be open to revelations from the spiritual world is to encourage them to be open to the devil. (For a scriptural view of Satan and the occult, see the Doctrinal Appendix.)

CRITICAL ANALYSIS

Hermeneutics and Changing the Text

Wierwille was a master at the misuse of Scripture, not to mention figures of speech, rules of Greek grammar and word meanings. Nevertheless, he claimed to employ standard rules of biblical interpretation, and he clearly declared that "additions or subtractions" to the Word of God were a sign of poor exegesis. "Now what had Eve done? She had added to the Word of God. When one adds to the Word of God, is it still the Word of God? Again, it becomes private interpretation. The moment a word is deleted or added, one no longer has The Word."[198] "I would estimate that from Genesis to Revelation 85 to 90 per cent of the Word of God interprets itself in the verse."[199] "Whenever one has to remove one passage from the context, we are no longer on the grounds of good biblical exegesis, because the passages in the Bible must interpret themselves and fit together as a perfect pattern without any additions or subtractions since these words make up the Word of God."[200]

Wierwille freely criticized others for misinterpreting the Bible and even for "changing the text,"[201] although he did this very thing routinely. Here and in the Appendix at the end of this chapter, we will illustrate, in order, his: 1) additions to Scripture; 2) logical fallacies; 3) preconceived research; 4) misuse of Greek and Hebrew; 5) plagiarism; and 6) moral lapses. Additional issues will also show that Wierwille was not the "man of God" Way members believe him to be.

Additions to Scripture

Wierwille has added hundreds of words which seriously alter the normal meaning of the Bible and are not found in the original Greek text. The following quotes are verbatim, although we have used ellipses to save space. Bracketed words are Wierwille's insertions to "clarify" the text. As in our chapter on Jehovah's Witnesses, we begin each Scripture by noting his purpose for changing the text.

To deny Christ's deity (John 1:1–14). This is one of the best examples of Scripture twisting to be found in the world of the cults. In these 14 verses, no less than 44 words are added to completely alter the meaning of the text. Observe how the deity of Christ is deleted from this passage through "clarifying" brackets:

> In the beginning was the Word [God], and the [revealed] Word was with [*pros*] God [with Him in His foreknowledge, yet independent of Him], and the Word was God. The same [revealed Word] was in the beginning with [*pros*] God. . . . All things were made by him [God]; and without him [God] was not any thing made that was made. . . . In him [God] was life; and the life was the light of men. . . . And the light [God] shineth in darkness; and the darkness comprehended it not. . . . There was a man sent [*apostello*] from God, whose name *was* John. The same [John] came for a witness, to bear witness of the Light [God], that all *men* through him [John] might believe. He [John] was not that Light [God], but *was sent* to bear witness of that Light [God]. . . . *That* was the true Light [God], which lighteth every man that cometh into the world. . . . He [God] was in the world [by the revealed Word], and the world was made by him [God], and the

world knew him [God] not. . . . He [God] came unto his own [Israel], and his own received him not. . . . But as many [of Israel] as received him [God], to them gave he [God] power [*exousia*, authority, the right] to become the sons of God, *even* to them that believe on [unto] his name [namesake, Jesus Christ]. . . . Which were [who was] born [conceived], not of blood, nor of the will of the flesh, nor of the will of man, but of God. . . . And the Word [revealed Word, Jesus Christ] was made flesh [the conception], and dwelt among us [his birth].[202]

To deny Christ as Creator (Colossians 1:16–17). These verses are supposedly an example of the figure of speech, parembole, a "parenthesis" explaining God as Creator. Again note how Jesus Christ is deleted from consideration, even though two verses earlier the passage has just stated that it refers to Jesus, "the Son in whom we have redemption." But Wierwille makes the pronoun "him" refer to God not to Jesus Christ: "For by him [God] were all things created . . . all things were created by him [God], and for him [God]: And he [God] is before all things, and by him [God] all things consist [cohere, were created]."[203] In Hebrews 1:2, Wierwille's insertion of a new preposition (again to "correct the text") further denies Christ as the Creator: "by [for] whom also he made the worlds."[204]

To deny Jesus His kingdom (Colossians 1:13). Wierwille again changes the preposition to radically alter the meaning: "And hath translated us into the kingdom of [by] his dear Son.[205] Given Wierwille's theology, Christ cannot possibly have a kingdom since He is only a man. Thus, Wierwille comments: "This kingdom cannot be the '. . . kingdom of his dear Son' for the Son has no kingdom of his own; the 'kingdom' is the kingdom of God."[206] One wonders, then, why Scripture many times refers to Christ's kingdom: "the kingdom of the Son" (Colossians 1:15), "the Kingdom of Christ and of God" (Ephesians 5:5), "the kingdom . . . of Christ" (Revelation 1:9), "the eternal kingdom of our Lord and Savior Jesus Christ" (2 Peter 1:11) and so on.

To deny the personality of Holy Spirit (John 16:12–13). Seven times in two verses Wierwille inserts the word "it" after the word "he" to deny the personality of the Holy Spirit as the third Person of the Trinity: "I have yet many things [in concretion] to say [words, of course] unto you, but ye cannot bear them now. Howbeit when he ['it'; Romans 8:16], the Spirit of truth, is come [didn't happen until Pentecost], he [it] will guide you into all [with distinction] truth; for he [it] shall not speak of himself [itself]; but whatsoever he [it] shall hear, that shall he [it] speak; and he [it] will show you things to come."[207] Thus the Person of the Holy Spirit became the impersonal power of God: "And they were all filled with the Holy Ghost [*pneuma hagion*, the gift, power from on high]."[208] "Ye shall receive the gift of (*from*) the Holy Ghost."[209]

To deny the resurrection of Christians (1 Corinthians 15:22–23). Here, all of 1 Corinthians 15:20–28 is said to be "parenthetical" and not to refer to the Church, since grace dispensation believers are "gathered together" not "resurrected."[210] "For as in [the] Adam all die, even so in Christ [also] shall all be made alive [Israel plus the unbelievers].... But every man [each one] in his own order [sequence]: Christ the first fruits; afterward [then] they that are Christ's at [with] his coming [Israel, not the Church of the Body, since the context is that of resurrection]."[211]

Note how Wierwille neglects the plain meaning of the text when he comments on this passage:

"For as in Adam all die," cannot be true of the Church to which you and I belong.... The Church is not going to be resurrected, because to have a resurrection everyone involved must be dead. Since the context of verse 22 deals with the resurrection, we cannot be talking here about the Church.... In other words, "resurrection" in verse 21 refers to all Israel as well as all unbelievers who have died. They are the subject matter of this entire section of scripture. Not rightly dividing verse 22 has caused all the confusion that has resulted in throwing the Church into the first and second resurrections spoken of in the Book of Revelation.... The Bible never speaks of the Church of the Body to which you and I belong as being resurrected, because resurrections apply to Israel and unbelievers. The Church of the Body, on the other hand, at the return of Christ will be gathered together.... After the gathering together of the Church, there is going to be a resurrection. "... They that are Christ's at his coming" should accurately read not *at* his coming, but *with* it. And the "with" is the resurrection *after* the Church of the Body is gathered together. That is the accuracy with which that scripture is written.[212]

To support his charismatic teachings (1 Corinthians 12:30). When the apostle Paul declares that "all do not speak with tongues" (1 Corinthians 12:30 NAS), this rejects Wierwille's theology. So Wierwille adds "in the Church" to the text implying all *should* speak in tongues at home, when they are not in church services. In fact, in 1 Corinthians 12:28 he adds the words "in the Church" seven times.[213] As he explains, "... inserting the words 'in the Church' time and time again, this section of Scripture fit together like a hand in a glove, and it was no longer necessary to explain away one verse or another."[214] How easy it is to conform the Bible to your particular views when you add to or delete from the words of Scripture.

To support his teaching on receiving "holy spirit" by physical inbreathing. In this case, Wierwille twists John 20:22: "And when he had said this, he breathed on [*en*, in; He breathed in] *them* [delete] and saith unto them, Receive [*lambano*] ye the Holy Ghost [*pneuma hagion*]."[215]

In 1 Corinthians 12:8–10 he inserts "for another profit" *seven* times to make each clause read the same. Thus, "gifts of healings are given by the same Spirit for another [*allos*] profit." This "proves" his teaching that each believer has every gift.[216] Wierwille then mistranslates verse 11 so that God's sovereign disposition of His gifts is transferred from His authority to human authority. Wierwille's "true" interpretation is given as follows: "A literal translation of verse 11 is, 'but all these nine manifestations of holy spirit in a believer are produced and energized by the one Spirit, distributing to every man his own, and in the effects produced, as the man wills.'"[217]

In reference to 1 Corinthians 14 he says, "I want you to note and be aware of the exact words that are used throughout,"[218] and then he rewrites the entire chapter! For example, he translates 1 Corinthians 14:1 as: "A literal translation according to usage of I Corinthians 14:1 would be: 'Follow after the love of God in the renewed mind in evidence in the Church, and by doing this you will yearningly desire supernatural manifestations in the Church, and more properly prophecy will be brought forth in the Church.'"[219]

Many other examples could be given, but these are sufficient and serious enough to prove Wierwille dishonestly manipulated the text at will. Wierwille obviously had no respect for the Bible, despite his many claims to the contrary. To be sure, God had already warned him, but he refused to listen: "Every word of God is flawless. . . . Do not add to his words, or he will rebuke you and prove you a liar" (Proverbs 30:5-6).

Logical Fallacies

Victor Wierwille emphasizes that it is other people's use of logic and accuracy in handling the biblical text that is deficient, not his own: "I am trying to show you how confusing and illogical people's thinking basically is because of the lack of concern about rightly dividing God's Word. It is God's Word so we must study it carefully."[220] But Wierwille's use of logic is just as flawed as his use of Scripture. For example, "The Bible is the Word of God; therefore, it is the Will of God,"[221] But would it be true that, "*Paradise Lost* is the word of Milton; therefore it is the will of Milton"? But this generalization does not always apply. Not everything in the Bible can be considered the will of God because the Bible describes things that are clearly not His will. For example, 3 John 2 is the word of God, but Wierwille is wrong to make it teach prosperity doctrine. If prosperity doctrine were the will of God, then poverty, suffering and illness would not also be said to be God's will in the Bible (Mark 14:7; 1 Timothy 5:23; 1 Peter 4:19).

Despite his extreme use of figures of speech, he also frequently appealed to an extreme literalism and routinely engaged in the logical fallacy of equivocation. Thus, he would either ignore the natural flexibility of language (for example, the use of synonyms or Hebrew parallelisms) or use words deceptively to support his beliefs. One example is Luke 23:42-43, referring to the thief on the cross: "Jesus did not say to him, 'Verily, verily I say unto thee, Today thou shalt go to heaven.' No, if Jesus had meant heaven, He would have said heaven. Jesus said 'paradise' because He meant 'paradise' which is referring to a place on earth in the future."[222]

Of course, this "reasoning" can also be used to refute Wierwille's teachings. Had God meant to say "Jesus is a creature," or "the Holy Spirit is a synonym for God," or "tongues are for everyone" or "the Body is not the Bride?" He would have said so. Wierwille can employ this type of argument only when it is advantageous to his theology. When the same argument denies his beliefs, it is rejected. Another example of his use of logical fallacies ("appeal to the majority") is seen in *Jesus Christ Is Not God*, where he applies one of his principles of interpretation: "In applying this principle, we note that Jesus Christ is directly referred to as the 'Son of God' in more than 50 verses in the New Testament; he is called 'God' in four. (Never is he called 'God the Son.') By sheer weight of this evidence alone, 50 to 4, the truth should be evident."[223]

Wierwille is wrong that Jesus is called God only four times (see Doctrinal Appendix), as if a mere four assertions by God are insufficient for us to believe Him. Wierwille, of course, explains them away so they do not become a problem for his followers. Regardless, his logic is flawed. In the New Testament Jesus is called:

the Messiah, *Mesias,* 2 times (John 1:41, 4:25);
the Son of Man 90 times;
the Son of God 50 times;
the Son of David 15 times;
the Christ (*Christos,* the Greek term for the Hebrew word Messiah) 250 times.

Wierwille's ratio was 50:4. Applying his logic, we see a ratio of 90 (the Son of Man) to 15 (the Son of David), proves that Jesus was not the Son of David. The ratio of 250 (the Christ) to 2 (the Messiah) proves Jesus was not the Hebrew Messiah. The ratio of 250 (Christ) to 90 (Son of Man) proves Jesus was not the Son of Man (not a man!), and the ratio of 250 to 50 proves Jesus is not the Son of God either! It seems, applying Weirwille's logic, that Jesus wasn't much of anything.

Wierwille further argues, "According to all laws of logic, one point of dissimilarity *disproves* identity."[224] This is utilized to "prove" Jesus is not God because he is "dissimilar" to Him. Wierwille says God cannot be tempted (true), that Jesus Christ was tempted (true), therefore Jesus cannot be God.[225] However, this says nothing about what conditions would apply if the Second Person of the Trinity took on human nature. His logic is again flawed. A glass of water and a glass of ice are dissimilar in texture but equal in nature.

Preconceived Research

One of his most unfortunate traits was hypocrisy, condemning in others the very things he himself practiced. "Obviously, when a person does unpreconceived research, he does not determine beforehand what he will find. Research doesn't begin with the answers; it looks for the answers."[226] Yet Wierwille *always* wanted the Bible to fit his theology, and he determined beforehand what he would find. As he states, if Jesus really existed before as God then "the problems of Biblical accuracy . . . are going to be overwhelming."[227] "Every truth must fit in the framework of the [holy spirit] manifestations":

> The summer of 1953. . . . I made up my mind that I was going to tie the whole thing together from Genesis to Revelation. So, I did, and in October, I had the very first "Power for Abundant Living" Class. At that time, the Foundational Class and the Advanced Class were together—the whole thing in two weeks. . . . But I knew the greatness of our age—the age of holy spirit and that every truth must fit in the framework of the manifestations. . . . Somewhere in there I wrote the first holy spirit book. . . . I'd been working those 385 scriptures and they began to all fall into place. . . . I spent a week putting that whole thing together. . . . Lots of the stuff I teach is not original. Putting it all together so that it fit—that was the original work.[228]

However, an examination of his use of those 385 Scriptures only proves that Wierwille determined beforehand how they would "fit." Further, is not his research preconceived when he tells us Christ "*had* to be a man and not God"?[229] and that "God *cannot* be born"?[230] If Wierwille's research is not preconceived, why has he had to change so much Scripture?

Misuse of Greek and Hebrew Languages

Wierwille's books regularly appeal to the Greek text, giving them an "air" of authority, impressing and also mystifying the person who has no way of checking his accuracy. Wierwille may use the Greek correctly when convenient, but he consistently misuses it in order to defend his teachings. And when he cannot misuse the Greek he appeals to its mistranslation from the "Aramaic" or to the concept of new revelation. Wierwille always gets what he wants because "believing is receiving."[231] He even resorts to hypothetical "facts" to document his ideas. "Must have" is a favorite phrase of his. When he encounters problems, he invents a solution declaring "it must have been so." Referring to Acts 9:18: "It does not say Paul spoke in tongues, but he must have."[232] Why must he have? Only because Wierwille wants it to confirm his preconceived theology (but see 1 Corinthians 14:18). In *Jesus Christ Is Not God,* we find that the scribes were motivated by private doctrinal concerns to insert the trinitarian formula of Matthew 28:19: "This must have been what happened."[233] In John 1:13 (in order to make the verse refer to Jesus instead of believers), "an earlier text must have had a rendering of 'who' instead of 'which.'"[234] Here, at least, Wierwille is frank enough to admit "there are no manuscripts indicating this."[235] And as we cited earlier, "Was there faith in the Gospels. There must not have been. . . ."

J. L. Williams recorded Wierwille one night during one of his lectures, in which he said, "The other night I was at Johns Hopkins University and there was a professor of Greek and Latin in the audience. He asked to meet me afterwards. When we met, you know what he said? He said, 'Dr. Wierwille, I want to thank you for this service tonight. I've never sat in anything so electrifying! I never saw anybody use Greek as effectively as you did!'"[236] Wierwille certainly did use Greek effectively, but accuracy was another matter. Several examples are given here:

1. 1 Peter 1:20 is quoted to indicate that God knew Christ only in his foreknowledge. He

does not mention that the Greek *ginosko* (cf. *prognisoko*) implies a relationship between the knower and the known, hence the existence of both parties.

2. In his analysis of John 1:1, Wierwille does not mention that the imperfect form of the verb "to be" is used ("was"), which indicates the continuous existence of something in the past. Nonexistence (foreknowledge) is neither stated nor implied.

3. Wierwille tells us that *lambano* (Acts 8:15) means "manifest in the senses world."[237] But this is false. *Lambano* simply means "receive."

4. *"Tartarosas"* in 2 Peter 2:4 is said to be, "a nominative singular masculine participle in the first aorist tense." This is correct, but when he continues with his interpretation he is in error: "Meaning a one time (once and once only) action with continuing results."[238] The aorist tense does not mean that. The aorist relates to the fact of the action; it says nothing about the future—that is, how many times it happened. When Scriptures states, "Jesus went up to Jerusalem," it is in the aorist tense, but He went up six times.

5. In 1 Corinthians 14:22, Wierwille makes the reference to nonChristians—"them that believe not"—refers to Christians—that is, unbelieving Christians. " 'Unbeliever' is the Greek word *apistos*: having been instructed but not sufficiently to fully believe"; . . . "They are 'babes in Christ,' referred to here as 'them that believe not.' "[239] His contention cannot be substantiated. *Apistos* simply means "unbelieving"—that is, nonChristian. Rather than having not believed enough, Paul meant "nonChristian."

6. It is said that a key to proper interpretation is "the mathematical usage of the Greek words." For example, "When a word is used only once it is emphatic and denotes unity," and "each preposition has a precise mathematical meaning."[240] This too is false. (John Weldon illustrated the problems with biblical numerology in chapter three of *Decoding the Bible Code*.)

7. In 2 Timothy 3:17, Wierwille argues, "The word 'furnished' is from the same root word in Greek as the word 'perfect.' The Greek word for 'perfect' is *artios;* the Greek word for

'furnished' in Timothy 3:17 is *exartizo*. *Exartizo* is a verb whereas artios is an adjective. Literally it says, 'That the man of God may be perfect, thoroughly perfect. . . .' Not only is the man to be perfect, but he is to be through and through and thoroughly perfected."[241] Here he picks the variation of the word meaning that he prefers, molding the Greek to fit his doctrine. *Exartizo*, however, does not connote the idea of sinless perfection.

8. *Aiteo* is rendered as "demand." Wierwille's teaching that "the Word of God is the Will of God" causes not only a denial of the humility of biblical prayer but can also ignite a rebellious attitude toward God. For example, denying the clear teaching of 1 John 5:14, Wierwille asserts, "Therefore, if we know the Word of God, we know the will of God. . . . We need no longer pray the pitiful 'If it be Thy will.' Only someone unlearned or ignorant of the Word of God will pray 'If it be Thy will.' "[242] But anyone who reads 1 John 5:14 and James 4:15 can see that Weirwille is wrong: "This is the confidence we have in approaching God: that if we ask anything *according to his will*, he hears us," and, "Instead, you ought to say, *'If it is the Lord's will*, we will live and do this or that.' "

Walter Cummins, in another of The Way approved writings, "Study in Biblical Accuracy," states: "The fourth word [he's been commenting on words for 'ask'] meaning 'to ask' is *aiteo*. . . . The force is strong. A translation which shows a strong asking is 'to demand.' . . . When you ask for something in prayer, believe, and you will absolutely get it. You don't just ask hoping you might get it. You demand it, like demanding a payment on your check, or like demanding your rights as a citizen of the United States.' "[243] Again the Greek word *aiteo* is erroneously said to mean "demand" when used with reference to God in prayer. Is the Lord our puppet? If we pull the correct strings (positive thinking, use of the law of prosperity, tithing and believing, demanding our legal rights) must God act? Note how the author has first added a new meaning (demand) and then used it naturally in translating, as if it were contextually justified and perfectly normal. Thus Philippians 4:6 reads, "Let your requests [*aitema*-demands] be made known unto God."[244] As if by magic "requests" somehow become "demands."

In fact, *aiteo* is never used as "demand" when referring to one's requests of God. It is a forceful word, as in "crave," but still it does not mean "demand." The Way may tell us to "Demand [*aiteo*] what God has already made available,"[245] but no one has a right to make demands upon God, no matter what conditions exist. God is the only One who makes demands. The *International Dictionary of New Testament Theology* states that "in the NT *aiteo, aiteomai* (occurring 70 times) generally means to request, ask (for oneself)." It further observes that when it has the meaning "demand," it is *not* used in the sense that a person makes demands on God, but the opposite, for "when the object of *aiteo* is the subordinate person, it easily assumes the meaning to require, demand." Clearly, God is not subordinate to anyone. Hence, those who trust the interpretation of The Way are in error, for "when man takes this attitude, he is in fact setting himself above God and calling Him to account." The Dictionary does, however, observe that *Satan* makes demands upon God, as in Luke 22:31.[246]

When we turn to the Hebrew the situation is unimproved. In Isaiah 49:16, Wierwille alleges, "The word 'walls' is a very inaccurate presentation."[247] The Hebrew *chomah*, however, does mean "walls," as Hebrew lexicons and various translations show. In another example, in Genesis 1:28 the KJV erroneously translates the Hebrew as "replenish," which means "to fill again." In Genesis 1:22 the same word in the KJV is correctly translated as "fill," referring to a single action. The NAS and the NIV have "fill" in both places. Wierwille uses the mistranslation "replenish" to support his teaching on a repopulated earth using Genesis 1:2.[248] Claiming "great accuracy on God's Word," he also translates the verb "to be" (was) at Genesis 1:2 as "became," to support his teaching of three successive earths.[249] The proper translation is "was."

Plagiarism

Like many other cult leaders, Wierwille engaged in plagiarism. This is documented in John Juedes and Douglas Morton, *The Integrity*

and Accuracy of The Way's Word, and in John Juedes and Jay Valusek, *Will the Real Author Please Stand Up?* (Personal Freedom Outreach, 1980). According to Juedes, Morton and Valusek, Wierwille's *Receiving the Holy Spirit Today* is largely plagiarized from E. W. Bullinger's *The Giver and His Gifts* and from J. E. Stiles, *The Gift of the Holy Spirit. The New Dynamic Church* plagiarizes New Thought writer E. W. Kenyon's (from whom Kenneth Hagin and Copeland received much of their Word-Faith teachings) *The Father and His Family* (chapter 20). *Are the Dead Alive Now?* plagiarizes three of E. W. Bullinger's books, *How to Enjoy the Bible, Selected Writings* and *Figures of Speech Used in the Bible.*[250]

In *Receiving the Holy Spirit Today,* "Wierwille never placed quotation marks around the sections he copied (often virtually word for word), nor did he ever cite a source or even suggest that he had used sources. In fact, he states in the preface that he did not use sources other than the Bible."[251] Further, there was an attempt to cover his plagiarism because the plagiarisms are most noticeable in the first editions "before rewritings obscured them."[252] Thus, "It is clear that Wierwille did use existing sources, including at least six books from at least three authors, all of which were written before Wierwille published his writings. . . . Wierwille clearly practiced plagiarism throughout his 'ministry.' Almost all of Wierwille's theology can be traced to authors such as Bullinger and George Lamsa. . . ."[253]

Morality

In various ways Wierwille's teachings and Way practice have undermined biblical morality. Wierwille leaned toward a gnostic view, seeing the flesh or body as evil and the spirit as holy (holy spirit). "Spirit is holy as opposed to the flesh, which is called by God unholy."[254] But the new spirit received at the new birth is sinless and perfect and cannot sin. "A born-again person cannot sin because he is born of God."[255] Historically, gnosticism has led either to asceticism or license, depending on one's interpretation of the body in relation to the spirit.

Obviously, if the spirit is sinless and the spirit, not the body, is God's primary concern, it matters little what we do with the body. And if a

Way member sins, any sin a Way member commits must be something else. As in all perfectionist systems, the denial of the ability to sin leads to redefining sin and an inability to address one's sin, confess it and repent. Thus several researchers have observed problems with Way morality. Gary Zentmyer states: "What goes on in the body is unimportant. . . . I have interviewed people who are in contact with groups of Wayfarers, including several ex-members. They all agree that moral standards in the Way are consistent with Wierwille's theology."[256]

Michael Harden, writing in *Ohio Magazine*, noted one Way slogan in particular. "Perhaps the most disconcerting of all was, 'Follow the Man of God, right or wrong.' "[257] Further: "More than one Way member reported that there was something of a double standard involving the sex life of Way Corps members. 'There were some weird sexual things going on,' McNulty recalls, 'like talk that said it is okay to sleep with somebody else (other than your spouse) as long as it honors God or builds the ministry or some kind of clowny stuff like that.' "[258] According to *The Quarterly Journal* (Oct.-Dec., 1988, P.4):

> Top former ministry leaders such as John and Pay Lynn, Sue Pierce, Ralph Dubofsky and others have documented that most trustees have approved and practiced adultery and in the process have hurt hundreds of women. Lynn, Steve Sann and others have revealed the authoritarianism of the trustees, their resistance to correction and misuse of finances. It is also clear that Dr. Wierwille himself practiced, taught and defended these to others.

A news report in the *Christian Research Journal* referred to "widespread reports of rampant adultery and promiscuous sex in The Way, including the highest levels of leadership. One ex-member said the Corp's residence training was sometimes like a 'bordello,' with promiscuity, adultery, orgies, wife-swapping, and even gang-rape."[259] Some former members have stated that, as in The Family (formerly Children of God and Love Family), sex has been used as a recruitment tool.

Harden reports on one former short-term member, Cynthia Chiaramonte, who admitted

that "they would, if they felt the end justifies the means, do just about anything this Dr. Wierwille tells them to do."[260] In his travels, Dr. Weldon has also spoken with former members who noted sexual promiscuity and the unquestioning obedience to Wierwille or the current leader.

Wierwille was himself allegedly an adulterer and sexual predator of young women, according to at least two former victims.[261] That many of his followers seem to share his interests, is indicated by a paper on adultery written by Way member John Schoenheit, a 6th Corps graduate, who at the time was employed in TWI's Research Department. Way members were told to report any knowledge of this paper to Way trustees immediately, on pain of severe penalty. The paper was branded as "slipshod research" and "handling the Word deceitfully," and Schoenheit was fired, along with others for their alleged involvement with the paper. Why was TWI leadership so concerned with Schoenheit's paper? Because the paper condemns adultery biblically and refutes Way rationalizations. The paper has 16 pages reviewing numerous passages in Scripture that address and condemn the practice of adultery, including the seventh commandment, "You shall not commit adultery" (Exodus 20:14). In the appendices, twice as many pages list "common" reasons given to justify adultery, followed by a refutation from the Bible. "While the paper never names who practiced and defended adultery, it is obvious that many of them were other leaders in TWI. . . . Way leaders were saying in essence, 'sure, spiritual adultery, that is, unfaithfulness to God, is wrong, but not physical adultery.' "It would be clear to anyone in TWI leadership that these appendices were aimed at then-current Way leaders. One reason leadership condemned the paper so strongly is that they saw themselves being critiqued and biblically condemned in these appendices."

Among the 14 reasons to justify adultery: (1) the Old Testament permitted more than one wife and the Grace period we live in must be less strict than under the law; (2) what made God angry with King David was not his commission of adultery with Bathsheba but his murder of Uriah; (3) Elijah, one of the greatest prophets, lived with a widow many days, so, logically, they must have had a sexual relationship; (4) both Jesus and the apostle Paul traveled with women, so they must have had sexual relations; (5) the marriage relationship is something permitted by God, not commanded by law (1 Corinthians 7), so adultery does not violate the law of God; (6) the use of the term "adultery" in Scripture refers to spiritual adultery not physical adultery; (7) the Word is flexible with the culture; (8) sexual incompatibility permits adultery; (9) flesh is flesh and spirit is spirit; what is done in the flesh can't harm the spirit. "While the leaders may have practiced and defended it the most, many ex-Wayers speak of how promiscuous sex was common even on the twig (local) level."[262]

Physical and Mental Healing

In The Way, the reborn "Christian" has all of Adam's legal "rights," and this includes, as noted, "the right to perfect health." Physical and mental illnesses are therefore entirely unnecessary. Wierwille teaches that all sickness is a result of satanic oppression, which results from lack of faith. "All sickness is some form of oppression of the devil." . . . "Satan causes sickness and disease."[263] Thus mental and physical problems may develop in people who are burdened by (1) lack of faith and (2) oppression by Satan.

A serious problem here is that sound medical practice may be rejected for a positive thinking philosophy of healing, with tragedy as the result. If Wierwille's teachings are accepted then faith alone, not medical practice, is the only proper solution to illness and disease. After all, the medical profession, geared to the sense realm, can hardly fight "the devil;" only "faith" can. "Satan has no legal rights over a believer because all believers have been delivered from Satan's power through Jesus Christ. . . . So the next time you get sick, say, 'Look here, headache [cold, or whatever negative symptom it may be], you have no power over me. You were defeated over nineteen hundred years ago. It says so in The Word, and I believe The Word; therefore, be gone from me.' When we have salvation, we have wholeness, even physical wholeness, if we simply accept it."[264]

Not infrequently, such teachings have lead to tragedy. Many Eastern cults, the Jehovah's Witnesses, traditional Armstrongism, Christian Science and others are responsible for the premature deaths of thousands of people who have believed that illness was an illusion or that it could be cured mentally by "faith" or positive thinking. Family, friends and children have been injured, crippled or died, and the victims have included both cult members and Christians (e.g., the Word-Faith movement). We refuted this teaching in *The Facts on False Teachings in the Church* and *The Facts on the Faith Movement.*[265]

Wierwille teaches that the death of Christ covered our sin and His physical scourging healed our diseases. "There are two parts: sin and disease, one is removed by the blood of the lamb and the other by the flesh of the lamb."[266] When we know the truth "we will no longer tolerate [the existence of] sickness."[267]

Timothy Goodwin* was struck by a truck in 1973 and rendered a quadriplegic. He met The Way in 1975. They promised him "complete healing" within one year if he would just give The Way 15 percent of his $1.4 million insurance settlement ($210,000). (Remember, "believing equals receiving" and tithing is proof of believing.) Wierwille himself wrote out the check and watched Goodwin sign it with a pen held between his teeth. (Wierwille and his brother Harry also received "bonus" checks for a Cadillac and a BMW. The Cadillac no doubt complemented Wierwille's $750,000 jet and two custom motor homes.) Goodwin certainly expected healing. As a musician, he desperately longed for it. "They convinced him that he was gonna walk again and had him talking in tongues and things. He moved a little bit of his right arm, and they attributed it to his new found faith (in The Way)."[268] A year later, Goodwin was still a quadriplegic. He filed a $300,000 lawsuit against Wierwille, charging mental and physical abuse. As a sign of its love for their brother, The Way countersued for $850,000. The problem of course *had* to be Goodwin's "lack of faith" and not Wierwille's theology. The case

---

*Other accounts say James Curtis, perhaps a pseudonym.

was settled out of court, with The Way repaying Goodwin in full.[269]

We have in our files another incident reported by a Pastor in Carlisle, Ohio. "One story has come to me twice of a family whose child had a fatal disease. The family were active in the Church and ready to accept this till Wierwille came and told them the child could be healed. Then the child died and the family had a terrible time. He told them it was because they did not have faith."[270]

Wierwille was being hypocritical when he demanded of others what he failed to do for himself: Victor Paul Wierwille's death certificate lists cancer of the liver and eye as the cause of death. The problem this should present for members of The Way is that it thoroughly undermines Wierwille's teaching on "The Law of Believing." He taught that if a person was fearful of a disease, he or she would manifest that disease, and that the Devil and lack of faith was responsible for disease.[271] His prolonged illness, hidden from Way members, and his subsequent death, proves that he was not the "man of God" he thought he was (since he was so fearful of cancer and therefore lacked in faith) or that his "Law of Believing" was false.[272] In either case, Way members have a problem. But it gets worse. According to Wierwille's own teaching, Way members would have to conclude he was demon-possessed!

According to information given on the Messiah Lutheran Church website (cited earlier), in February 1985, former Way staff member and Way Corps graduate, Rick, was on staff at New Knoxville when Wierwille was ill and died. "He confirmed that TWI never publicly announced any part of Wierwille's illness or cause of death in any publication or announcements in a Sunday night service." He also wrote, ". . . It would be unimaginable to think that the 'man of God' was not able to believe for healing for himself. . . . The other part of the answer is that Wierwille taught that cancer is a devil spirit. Cancer, according to him, is not just caused by a devil spirit, it IS a devil spirit. His logic went something like this: all life is spirit. Cancer has a life of its own. Therefore, cancer is a devil spirit, and anyone with cancer is possessed with a devil spirit. If that teaching was not familiar to the

rank-and-file followers of The Way, it was certainly known to anyone who had taken the Advanced Class on PFAL. It's not hard to imagine the problems that would have been created if Wierwille or anyone else had announced that he had cancer. The idea that 'the greatest man of God since the apostle Paul' was possessed with a devil spirit would have been devastating to say the least!" Devastating, indeed.

TALKING WITH MEMBERS

Although genuine Christians can sometimes be found in The Way, members are generally nonChristians, who need to hear the true Gospel and receive it. Once they are truly regenerated and personally know the true Jesus Christ, they will be unable to remain in a cult that denies God and His Word and betrays their Savior. Thus, Way members need to understand first of all that they reject the true Jesus Christ, and on that basis they cannot be saved. Jesus said, "He who rejects Me rejects the One who sent Me" (Luke 10:16; see John 5:23 NAS). Way members must realize the solemnity of their denial. "Whoever shall deny Me before men, I will also deny him before My Father" (Matthew 10:33 NAS). "If you do not believe I am the One I claim to be, you will indeed die in your sins" (John 8:24).

Our Doctrinal Appendix proves beyond doubt that Christ's deity and the Trinity are biblical teachings. This material can be used to show members that if The Way is wrong about Jesus Christ it can't be trusted on other crucial matters. As one former member recalls, "[I] had such mighty notions about the Way that I was blind to real Christianity, but once I saw The Way exposed just on the Deity [of Christ] the rest of the doctrines also crumbled."[273] Once a Way member sees the truth—that Wierwille, far from being a Bible scholar, was just another cultic manipulator of Scripture—faith in The Way will begin to crumble. "Gradually I began to see that The Way was truly off and that almost everyone in The Way is a follower of Dr. Wierwille more than the Bible."[274]

It is also important for Christians to help former members or new Christian converts with their bitterness at being deceived. As hard as it can be, they need to see their experiences as valuable lessons that may benefit themselves and others. Obviously, patience and understanding here are virtues. Otherwise, members may be tempted to reject everything Christian because of their encounter with The Way. One woman we talked with came close to becoming an atheist. Others have become suicidal:

> There came a time when I could no longer condone the sexual and financial exploitation or ignore the mental manipulation.... [But] how does one walk out on "the greatest man of God since the Apostle Paul"? Where does one go when the only close associations of the past eight years have been with the group which you can no longer endure? How does one admit that eight years of life have been squandered in chasing a lie? Having found no better answer to these questions, I took the bottle of Darvon and lay down to die.[275]

After God graciously spared this young woman's life, she wrote that "the Lord has healed me of the intense bitterness that I had toward The Way. There is a strong delusion prevalent there, Satanic in origin."[276]

Once Way members can understand that The Way has nothing to do with biblical Christianity, they can understand that Christianity cannot be rejected when it was never accepted to begin with. To reject Christianity now would be a far worse error than joining The Way was. Way members also need to be told that God promises to abundantly pardon them and help them through the transition if they turn to Him, the one true God:

> Come, all you who are thirsty, . . . Listen, listen to me, and eat what is good, and your soul will delight in the richest of fare. Give ear and come to me; hear me, that your soul may live. I will make an everlasting covenant with you. . . . Seek the LORD while he may be found; call on him while he is near. Let the wicked forsake his way and the evil man his thoughts. Let him turn to the LORD, and he will have mercy on him, and to our God, for he will freely pardon. . . . You will go out in joy and be led forth in peace; the mountains and hills will burst into song before you, . . . Instead of the thornbush will grow the pine tree, and instead of briers the myrtle will grow. (Isaiah 55:1–3, 6, 12, 13)

If they are relatively new Christian converts, former Way members need to understand that leaving The Way does not mean they must relinquish whatever true happiness or personal confidence they may have found even though they were in The Way. "They are one of the most positive thinking groups that I have ever seen and for me it was just what I wanted in my life. . . . I just cannot emphasize too often the power of the positive approach and thinking of the Way on new people. It feels so good to the person and so any attack on the philosophies of The Way and Dr. Wierwille become an attack on the person's new found happiness and confidence."[277] Nevertheless, happiness and confidence found in The Way would be relatively short lived because doctrines that are not based in the truth can never provide lasting happiness or enduring confidence. Indeed, teachings that are illogical and based on manipulation and distortion of Scripture and a false faith will only lead to destruction in the long run, as happened so frequently in The Way.

Christians should therefore explain to former Way members that by leaving The Way and turning to Christ a new believer receives: 1) the unfailing love of the one true God (Matthew 10:40; John 14:23); 2) full forgiveness of all sins (Ephesians 1:7; Colossians 2:13); and 3) eternal life (John 5:24; 6:47; Hebrews 10:17; 1 John 5:13). What could be better? Or more positive? Or more fruitful? This is what many Way members joined The Way for originally. If they find it now, this is all that matters. Every life has detours, but not every life finds true salvation. Way members must be urged in the clearest way possible to receive the true Jesus and to take advantage of the opportunity while such opportunity remains. "Today, if you hear his voice, do not harden your hearts" for "how shall we escape if we ignore such a great salvation?" (Hebrews 4:7; 2:3).

APPENDIX:
A CRITIQUE OF *JESUS CHRIST IS NOT GOD*

The book *Jesus Christ Is Not God* is "the definitive text" used by Way members to defend their denial of Christ's deity, and it is heralded as "a product of 33 years of Biblical research."[278] In response to it, six points may be discussed.

1. A number of important relevant biblical verses are not even mentioned: Micah 5:2; Zechariah 12:10; John 17:5; Hebrews 1:3, 10; 2 Peter 1:1 and others.

2. Wierwille declares that God had John write his Gospel specifically to *clarify* that Christ was not God. "The true God had the Gospel of John written to clarify Christ's position as the Son of God . . . not 'God the Son' or 'God Himself.' "[279] Why then does Wierwille spend so much time "clarifying" that Gospel? *Jesus Christ Is Not God* runs to 125 pages, and fully one-third is devoted to clarifying merely the first 18 verses of the first chapter of John. Could not God have had John communicate more clearly than that? Put another way, if "words mean what they say," and if 90 percent of the Bible "explains itself word for word," how do a mere 18 verses demand so much clarification when they are supposed to be clearest?

In Appendix B of the book, Wierwille discusses "Common Errors in Understanding"—that is, Scriptures he needs to reinterpret. (His "analysis," however, merely involves simple comments that neither deal with the Scriptures nor the issues.) A numerical breakdown of the Scriptures that he wishes to clarify involves:

John, 26

Old Testament, 7

Colossians, 7

Matthew, 6

Luke, 5

Acts, 5

Titus, 3

Hebrews, 2

Galatians, Jude, 1 John, 1 Timothy and 1 Thessalonians, 1 each.

Again, why does the Gospel of John stand out? Why is it that in comparison to any other New Testament book there are almost four times as many verses in John that need "clarification"? Does this suggest that John succeeded in writing clearly? Is not the real problem found in Wierwille's preconceived theology, which demands revising an already clear text?

3. Way members should prepare a parallel chart of John 1:1-18 in Wierwille's translation with the Bible—any Bible. Many discrepancies will stand out in such an exercise.

4. Chapter Four of *Jesus Christ Is Not God* contains Wierwille's "basis" for his "exegesis" of John 1:1-18. The key to his entire argument is based upon a false assumption that "the Word" of John 1:1 existed only in God's foreknowledge and not in fact. Since only God (unipersonal) existed in the beginning, nothing else could have existed. He defines "the Word" as a) the written word, the Bible; and, b) the revealed word (incarnate), Jesus Christ. These were with God in God's foreknowledge. But this is not what the Bible teaches by stating, "In the beginning *was* the Word." If the oak tree *was* in the park, it existed already. "Was" cannot mean "was in the foreknowledge of the city planners." Jesus Himself referred to "the glory which I had *with* Thee [the Father] before the world was" (John 17:5).

5. To Wierwille "the light" in John 1:5, is God not Jesus, and John the Baptist bore witness of this light (God). Why then does John the Apostle later call *Jesus* the light, and why did John the Baptist "bear witness" to *Jesus* (John 1:26-36)? Why did Jesus say *He* was the light (John 3:19, 8:12, 9:5, 12:46)? If the light had come into the world (Jesus, John 3:19) and if God is the light, what else are we to conclude but that Jesus is God?

6. In verse 13, Wierwille needs a singular, so he changes plurals in the original to singulars in his translation.[280] And he arbitrarily changes the meaning of *logos* seven times in John 1:1-18. "Instead of stumbling over scriptures, we see by careful scrutiny the precision with which God has revealed Himself."[281] Really? Why is it that there is no Greek scholar to support his translation? Can The Way find even one?

If Wierwille's words mean what they say, and say what they mean, we could just as easily cite Wierwille himself to demonstrate Christ's deity. Will Way members listen to "the man of God" here?

Jesus was the fullness of the Godhead.[282]

Christ was filled to capacity with the fullness of the Godhead. . . . Jesus was overflowing with

God's presence, power and Word and thereby declared God.[283]

In all Critical Greek texts and extant manuscripts this verse literally reads, "Looking for that blessed hope and appearing of the glory of the great God even our Saviour Jesus Christ" (citing Titus 2:13).[284]

Do words mean what they say? Will Way members listen further to the greatest teacher since the Apostle Paul when he declares the following?

Every influence which is not based upon the accuracy of God's Word shall come to naught.[285]

I have very little respect for those who stand in the pulpits or stand behind podiums and declare, "This verse is all right, but that one is an interpolation" . . . Which are you going to believe—God's Word or men's opinions?[286]

If we are to rightly divide the Word of God, we must allow the Bible to speak for itself and not read into it the theologies and doctrines of men.[287]

Don't *you* ever compromise on the Word.[288]

"Search the Scriptures. . . ." It does not say search Shakespeare or Kant or Plato or Aristotle or V.P. Wierwille's writings. . . . No, it says, "Search the Scriptures . . ." because all Scripture is God-breathed.[289]

A person must study the Word of God, not what people say around The Word or about The Word. What does *God* say? As I tell many of the people in my classes: Get rid of your other reading material for a while and read the Word of God.[290]

Again, we can only agree. Way members should re-consider the many contradictions between Wierwille's teachings and those of the Bible and ask themselves "What does *God* say?"

SCRIPTURE CONTRASTS	
WIERWILLE	THE BIBLE
Believing equals receiving.	You ask and do not receive, because you ask with wrong motives, so that you may spend it on your pleasures. (James 4:3 NAS)
But Spirit cannot communicate with mind, senses or reason as they are two separate and well-defined categories. Spirit can communicate with spirit only [291]	For to us God revealed them through the Spirit; . . . Now we have received, not the spirit of the world, but the Spirit who is from God, hat we might know the things freely given to us by God. (1 Corinthians 2:10–12 NAS)
Paul pointed out that it was no longer necessary to suffer sickness and disease.[292]	Trophimus I left sick at Miletus. (2 Timothy 4:20) But you know that it was because of a bodily illness that I preached the gospel to you the first time. (Galatians 4:13) Use a little wine because of your stomach and your frequent illnesses. (1 Timothy 5:23)
John made it known that he believed Jesus Christ to be the Son of God, not God.[293]	In the beginning was the Word, and the Word was with God, and the Word was God. (John 1:1, 3)
Paul made it known that he believed Jesus Christ to be the Son of God, not God.[294]	For in Him all the fulness of Deity dwells in bodily form. (Colossians 2:9 NAS)
Simon Peter made it known that he believed Jesus Christ to be the Son of God, not God.[295]	Simon Peter, a bondservant and apostle of Jeses Christ, to those who have received a faith of the same kind as ours, by the righteousness of our God and Savior, Jesus Christ. (2 Peter 1:1 NAS)

NOTES

1. Victor Paul Wierwille, *The Way Magazine*, May-June 1977, p. 22.
2. Ibid.
3. Victor Paul Wierwille, *Jesus Christ Is Not God* (New Knoxville, OH: American Christian Press, 1975), p. 3.
4. Victor Paul Wierwille, *The Church* (New Knoxville, OH: ACP, n.d.), p. 7.
5. Victor Paul Wierwille, *The Word's Way* (New Knoxville, OH: ACP, 1971), p. 63.
6. J. L. Williams, *Victor Paul Wierwille and The Way International*, pp. 22-23.
7. *The Way Magazine*, May-June 1979, p. 21.
8. Ibid., May-June 1976, pp. 11-12.
9. From their four-page catalog.
10. *The Way Magazine*, July-August 1975, p. 6.
11. *Ohio Magazine*, July 1979, pp. 31-33; *Christianity Today*, March 13, 1981, p. 57; N. DiGrovanni, "God's Puppets," *Westchester Illustrated*, June 1979, pp. 55-56; *Dayton, Ohio Journal Herald*, April 4, 1979, cited in Williams, p. 42.
12. Documentation can be found at the website of the Messiah Lutheran Church, Highland, CA, www.empirenet.com/~messiah7.
13. Ibid., Christopher C. Geer, "The Passing of a Patriarch," review by Dr. John Juedes.
14. "News Watch," *Christian Research Journal*, Summer 1996, p. 7.
15. Documentation found at Messiah Lutheran Church website, www.empirenet.com/~messiah7.
16. Jack Sparks, *The Mind Benders*, p.187.
17. Ibid.
18. Ron Enroth, *Youth, Brainwashing, and the Extremist Cults*, p. 131.
19. Ibid., p. 132.
20. Elena Whiteside, *The Way, Living in Love* (New Knoxville, OH: American Christian Press, 1972), p. 178.
21. Ibid., p. 180.
22. Ibid.
23. Messiah Lutheran Church, www.empirenet.com/~messiah7.
24. Victor Paul Wierwille, *The New, Dynamic Church* (New Knoxville, OH: ACP, 1972), p. 116.
25. Victor Paul Wierwille, *Receiving the Holy Spirit Today* (New Knoxville, OH: ACP, 1976), pp. 158, 239, 243.
26. Victor Paul Wierwille, *The Bible Tells Me So*, p. 50.
27. Cf. Williams, p. 90.
28. *The Way Magazine*, May-June 1979, p. 6.
29. Undated letter, 1994.
30. *Dayton, Ohio Journal Herald*, April 3, 1979, cited in Williams, *Victor Paul Wierwille and the Way International*, p. 18.
31. *The Way Magazine*, May-June 1979, p. 22.
32. Whiteside, *The Way, Living in Love*, pp. 174-175, with Walter Martin, *The New Cults* (Ventura, CA: Regal, 1980), pp. 38-39.
33. Jim Bjornstad, "The Pseudo Scholarship of Victor Paul Wierwille," *Contemporary Christianity*, p. 1, cited interview in *Eternity magazine*, November 1977, p. 5.
34. *The Way Magazine*, November-December 1977, p. 8.
35. Ibid., March-April 1976, pp. 10-11.
36. Ibid., January-February 1975, p. 25.
37. John Juedes, "Aramaic Publications by The Way International," Messiah Lutheran Church website: www.empirenet.com/~messiah7.
38. See Dr. John Juedes, "George M. Lamsa: Christian Scholar or Cultic Torchbearer?" *Christian Research International Journal*, Fall 1989, and our discussion under New Thought.
39. Kurt Aland, *The Text of the New Testament* (Grand Rapids, MI: Eerdmans, 1987), p. 52 from James White, *The King James Only Controversy* (Minneapolis: Bethany, 1997), pp. 48-49.
40. Victor Paul Wierwille, "The Church (The Great Mystery Revealed)" pamphlet, p. 5.
41. Victor Paul Wierwille, *Power for Abundant Living*, pp. 207-208, 210.
42. *The Way Magazine*, March-April 1978, p. 9; cf. pp. 8-10.
43. Wierwille, *Power for Abundant Living*, pp. 219, 222; cf. pp. 207-222.
44. Ibid., pp. 216-218.
45. Dorothy Owens, "Keys to Spiritual Light" pamphlet (New Knoxville, OH: ACP, n.d.), p. 7.
46. *The Way Magazine*, May-June 1979, p. 22.
47. Ibid.
48. Victor Paul Wierwille, *God's Magnified Word* (New Knoxville, OH: ACP, 1977), p. 228.
49. *The Way Magazine*, May-June 1977, p. 13.
50. Enroth, *Youth, Brainwashing, and the Extremist Cults*, p. 124.
51. Whiteside, *The Way, Living in Love*, p. 170.
52. *The Way Magazine*, July-August 1977, p. 12.
53. Victor Paul Wierwille, "The Church (The Great Mystery Revealed)," pp. 3-4.
54. Ibid., p. 12.
55. Wierwille, *The New, Dynamic Church*, p. 1.
56. Wierwille, "The Church (The Great Mystery Revealed)," p. 19.
57. Ibid., p. 24.
58. Ibid., pp. 29-30.
59. Ibid., p. 32.
60. Ibid., p. 25.
61. Ibid., p. 26.
62. *The Way Magazine*, November-December 1977, p. 11, emphasis added.
63. Ibid., September-October 1975, p. 19.
64. Victor Paul Wierwille, "What Is True Worship?" *The Way Magazine*, May-June 1978, p 4.
65. Victor Paul Wierwille, *Receiving the Holy Spirit Today*, p. 148; cf. pp. 43, 126, 157, 201, 212, 225, 237, 252.
66. *The Way Magazine*, May-June 1977, p. 6.
67. Ibid., November-December 1975, p. 30.
68. Ibid., July-August 1977, p. 25.
69. Wierwille, *God's Magnified Word*, pp. 235-236.
70. *The Way Magazine*, March-April 1976, p. 4.
71. Ibid., March-April 1978, p. 4.
72. Victor Paul Wierwille, *Receiving the Holy Spirit Today*, pp. 212, 252; P.J. Wade, "Why I Speak in Tongues" pamphlet (New Knoxville, OH: ACP, n.d.), pp. 2, 14.
73. Wierwille, *The New, Dynamic Church*, pp. 117-118.
74. Wierwille, *The Bible Tells Me So*, p. 18.
75. *The Way Magazine*, May-June 1979, p. 9.

76. Victor Paul Wierwille, "Christians Should be Prosperous" pamphlet (New Knoxville, OH: NCP, n.d.), p. 3.
77. *The Way Magazine,* November–December 1978, p. 24.
78. Wierwille, *The Bible Tells Me So,* pp. 29-32.
79. *The Way Magazine,* January–February 1978, p. 21; Wierwille, *The New, Dynamic Church,* p. 236.
80. Wierwille, "Christians Should be Prosperous," p. 5.
81. Ibid., pp. 5, 7, 10, 11.
82. Ibid., pp. 12-13, 16-17; cf. pp. 20-21.
83. Ibid.
84. Wierwille, *Power for Abundant Living,* p. 32.
85. Walter J. Cummins, "The Mind of the Believer" pamphlet (New Knoxville, OH: American Christian Press, n.d.), pp. 11, 6; Dorothy Owens, "Keys to Spiritual Light" pamphlet (New Knoxville, OH: ACP, n.d.), p. 8.
86. See *Westchester (NY) Illustrated,* June 1969, p. 61, and *Ohio Magazine,* July 1979, p. 30.
87. Victor Paul Wierwille, "Studies in Human Suffering" (New Knoxville, OH: ACP, n.d.), pp. 14-18.
88. Williams, p. 46.
89. Ibid., p. 62, transcript of Victor Paul Wierwille interview in his New Knoxville office, February, 1976 with Art Toalston, *The National Courier,* April 1, 1977.
90. Williams, pp. 62-63.
91. Ibid., p. 33, citing Toalston interview, *The National Courier,* April 1, 1977.
92. Whiteside, p. 184.
93. Owens, "Keys to Spiritual Light," p. 10.
94. Victor Paul Wierwille, *The Bible Tells Me So,* p. 103.
95. In James A. Adair, Ted Miller, *Escape from Darkness* (Victor Books, 1982), pp. 26-27.
96. *The Way Magazine,* July–August 1975, p. 30.
97. Ibid., September–October 1975, p. 30.
98. Ibid., May–June 1978, p. 6.
99. *The Way Magazine,* July–August 1977, p. 11.
100. Wierwille, *The Word's Way,* p. 46.
101. Wierwille, *Power for Abundant Living,* pp. 70-71.
102. Wierwille, *Receiving the Holy Spirit Today,* pp. 43-44; *The Word's Way,* p. 27.
103. Douglas V. Morton, "The Lamsa Connection: The Origin of Wierwille's False Christ," *The Quarterly Journal,* Jan.-Mar. 1989, p. 7; cf. "Nestorius" in Walter A Elwell, ed., *Evangelical Dictionary of Theology.*
104. *The Way Magazine,* January–February 1978, p. 6.
105. Wierwille, *Jesus Christ Is Not God,* pp. 11-12, 14-15, 25.
106. *The Way Magazine,* January–February 1975, p. 4; also in *Jesus Christ Is Not God,* p. 12, emphasis added.
107. *The Way Magazine,* January–February 1975, p. 6; also in *Jesus Christ Is Not God,* p. 21.
108. Ibid., January–February 1975; also in *Jesus Christ Is Not God,* pp. 23-27.
109. Ibid., pp. 25-26.
110. P. Hughes, *The Church in Crisis* (1960), p. 32.
111. Ibid., p. 23.
112. Ibid.
113. Wierwille, *Jesus Christ Is Not God,* p. 24, citing 1968 *Britannica.*
114. Cf. article "Arius" in 1958 ed.; or modern eds (*Britannica III*) on related topics. —Nicean Council, Trinity, etc.
115. Sparks, *The Mind Benders,* p. 192.
116. Ibid.
117. Ibid., p. 191.
118. Interview with Art Toalston, *The National Courier,* April 1, 1977, p. 4.
119. James Atkinson, ed., *Luther: Early Theological Works* (1962), pp. 30, 41.
120. Wierwille, *Jesus Christ Is Not God,* p. 13.
121. *The Way Magazine,* January–February 1975, p. 20; also in Wierwille, *Jesus Christ Is Not God,* p. 25.
122. Wierwille, *The Word's Way,* p. 80.
123. Wierwille, *Power for Abundant Living,* p. 78.
124. Wierwille, *Jesus Christ Is Not God,* p. 4.
125. *The Way Magazine,* January–February 1978, p. 22.
126. *Time,* September 6, 1971, p. 54.
127. Wierwille, *The Word's Way,* p. 25.
128. Wierwille, *Jesus Christ Is Not God,* p. 117.
129. Ibid., p. 58., emphasis added.
130. Ibid., p. 5; see bottom note with Wierwille, *The New, Dynamic Church,* p. 60.
131. Ibid., pp. 28-29.
132. Cited in Williams, p. 50; from Mal Miller, "The Way Followers March on New Knoxville Church," St. Mary's (Ohio), *Evening Leader,* October 17, 1977.
133. Wierwille, *Jesus Christ Is Not God,* pp. 6-7.
134. *The Way Magazine,* March–April 1979, p. 4.
135. Ibid., March–April 1976, p. 11; see Wierwille, *The New, Dynamic Church,* p. 60.
136. Wierwille, *The Word's Way,* p. 166.
137. *The Way Magazine,* March–April 1977, p. 6.
138. Wierwille, *Jesus Christ Is Not God,* p. 76 n.
139. Ibid.; *The Way Magazine,* March–April 1976, p. 11.
140. Wierwille, *Receiving the Holy Spirit Today,* p. 4.
141. Ibid., pp. 2-4; cf. pp. 275-277.
142. Edward Bickersteth, *The Holy Spirit* (1967), pp. 7-10, 15, 57.
143. Ibid., p. 60.
144. Ibid., p. 60.
145. Ibid., p. 61.
146. Wierwille, *The Word's Way,* p. 55.
147. Wierwille, *The New, Dynamic Church,* p. 57.
148. Ibid., p. 57.
149. Ibid., p. 58.
150. Ibid., p. 59.
151. Ibid., p. 60.
152. Ibid.
153. Wierwille, *The Word's Way,* p. 23.
154. *The Way Magazine,* September–October 1976, p. 10.
155. Wierwille, *The New, Dynamic Church,* p. 64.
156. Ibid., pp. 63-65.
157. Ibid.
158. Ibid., pp. 66, 69.
159. Wierwille, *Jesus Christ Is Not God,* p. 128.
160. Wierwille, *Receiving the Holy Spirit Today,* p. 175.
161. Ibid., pp. 7-8.
162. Wierwille, *The New, Dynamic Church,* p. 60.
163. Wierwille, *Jesus Christ Is Not God,* p. 105.
164. Wierwille, *Power for Abundant Living,* p. 223.
165. Ibid., p. 274.
166. Wierwille, *The New, Dynamic Church,* p. 29.
167. Wierwille, *Power for Abundant Living,* pp. 274, 276.
168. Ibid., pp. 272-273.
169. *The Way Magazine,* September–October 1976, p. 9.

170. Wierwille, *Power for Abundant Living*, p. 72.
171. *The Word's Way*, pp. 267-268.
172. Wierwille, *Jesus Christ Is Not God*, p. 78.
173. Williams, p. 59.
174. John Juedes, "There's No Grace in The Way International," Messiah Lutheran Church, www.empirenet.com/~messiah7.
175. Wierwille, *Power for Abundant Living*, p. 89.
176. Wierwille, *The Bible Tells Me So*, pp. 18-19.
177. Wierwille, *The Word's Way*, p. 83.
178. Wierwille, *The Bible Tells Me So*, p. 33.
179. Wierwille, *God's Magnified Word*, p. 237.
180. Wierwille, *Are the Dead Alive Now?* p. 23.
181. H. C. Leupold, *Exposition of Psalms* (1974), pp. 86-87, 984.
182. Wierwille, *Are the Dead Alive Now?* p. 97.
183. Ibid., p. 21.
184. Ibid., p. 25.
185. Wierwille, *Power for Abundant Living*, pp. 188-189.
186. Wierwille, *Receiving the Holy Spirit Today*, p. 27.
187. Peter J. Wade, "The Secret of Radiant Living" pamphlet, p. 1; Cummins, "The Mind of the Believer" pamphlet, p. 11; Wade, "I Can Do All Things" pamphlet, p. 4.
188. Wierwille, *Receiving the Holy Spirit Today*, p. 13.
189. Whiteside, *The Way, Living in Love*, p. 193; Wierwille, *Power for Abundant Living*, p. 30.
190. Dr. John Juedes, "The Law of Believing and Prosperity," Messiah Lutheran Church, www.empirenet.com/~messiah7.
191. Wierwille, *Receiving the Holy Spirit Today*, pp. 176-177.
192. Ibid., p. 181.
193. Ibid., p. 253.
194. Ibid., p. 47.
195. Wierwille, *The Bible Tells Me So*, p. 24.
196. Ibid., pp. 24-25.
197. Ibid., p. 32.
198. Wierwille, *Power for Abundant Living*, p. 253.
199. Ibid., p. 147.
200. Wierwille, *Receiving the Holy Spirit Today*, p. 247.
201. Ibid., p. 164.
202. Wierwille, *Jesus Christ Is Not God*, pp. 87, 91, 93-101.
203. *The Way Magazine*, March–April 1979, p. 4; also in *The Word's Way*, p. 41.
204. Ibid., p. 42.
205. *The Way Magazine*, November–December 1978, p. 10.
206. Ibid.
207. Ibid., March-April 1978, p. 8.
208. Wierwille, *Receiving the Holy Spirit Today*, p. 10.
209. Ibid., p. 37.
210. Wierwille, *God's Magnified Word*, pp. 241-246.
211. Ibid., p. 243.
212. Ibid., pp. 241-243.
213. Wierwille, *Receiving the Holy Spirit Today*, p. 196; cf. 189-197.
214. Ibid., p. 247; cf. pp. 242-247.
215. Ibid., p. 62.
216. Ibid., p. 173; cf. pp.180-181.
217. Ibid., p. 184.
218. Ibid., p. 207.
219. Ibid., pp. 210, 212.
220. Wierwille, *God's Magnified Word*, p. 256.
221. Wierwille, *Receiving the Holy Spirit Today*, p. 247.
222. Wierwille, *The Word's Way*, p. 99.
223. Wierwille, *Jesus Christ Is Not God*, p. 30.
224. Ibid., pp. 46, 27.
225. Ibid., p. 46.
226. Wierwille, *Jesus Christ Is Not God*, p. 3.
227. J. P. Wierwille, "In the Beginning" pamphlet, p. 14.
228. Whiteside, *The Way, Living in Love*, pp. 207-209.
229. Wierwille, *Jesus Christ Is Not God*, p. 76, emphasis added.
230. Ibid., p. 73.
231. Williams, p. 94.
232. Wierwille, *Receiving the Holy Spirit Today*, p. 125.
233. Wierwille, *Jesus Christ Is Not God*, p. 19.
234. Ibid., p. 100.
235. Ibid., p. 99.
236. Williams, p. 91.
237. Wierwille, *Receiving the Holy Spirit Today*, pp. 9-10.
238. Wierwille, *Are the Dead Alive Now?* p. 118.
239. Wierwille, *Receiving the Holy Spirit Today*, pp. 228-229.
240. W. J. Cummins, "Fundamentals of Greek Research" pamphlet, pp. 15, 20, 24.
241. Wierwille, *Power for Abundant Living*, pp. 91-92.
242. Wierwille, *The New, Dynamic Church*, p. 236.
243. Walter Cummins, "The Spoken Word" pamphlet, pp. 15-16.
244. Ibid., p. 21.
245. Ibid., p. 22.
246. H. Schonweiss, "Prayer," in Colin Brown, ed., *The New International Dictionary of New Testament Theology*, Vol. 2.
247. Wierwille, *The Bible Tells Me So*, pp. 107-108.
248. Wierwille, *Power for Abundant Living*, p. 242.
249. Wierwille, *The Word's Way*, p. 91. For other examples of misusing the Greek language, see Dr. James Bjornstad, *Contemporary Christianity*, Vol. 8, no. 1; Douglas Morton, "The Way: Ancient Heresy Modernized," *Journal of Pastoral Practice*, Vol. 4, no. 1.
250. John Juedes and Jay Valusek, *Will the Real Author Please Stand Up?* (Personal Freedom Outreach, 1980), pp. 4-6.
251. Jay Valusek and John Juedes, "Eisegesis and Plagiarism: A Further Challenge to the Originality of the Writings of Victor Paul Wierwille," *Personal Freedom Outreach* newsletter, July-Sept. 1987, p. 4.
252. John P. Juedes, "Eisegesis and Plagiarism: A Further Look at the Writings of Victor Paul Wierwille," *Personal Freedom Outreach* newsletter, April–June 1987, p. 6.
253. Valusek and Juedes, p. 6; cf. Whiteside, *The Way, Living in Love*, pp. 207-209.
254. Wierwille, *Receiving the Holy Spirit Today*, p. 4.
255. Wierwille, *Power for Abundant Living*, p. 292.
256. Paper of January 28, 1972 for Professor Howard Happ, Religious Studies 306 (American Sects), California State University, Northridge.
257. Michael Harden in *Ohio Magazine*, July 1979, p. 30.
258. Ibid., pp. 30-31.
259. *News Watch*, *Christian Research Journal*, Summer 1996, p. 7.
260. Harden in *Ohio Magazine*, July 1979, p. 34.
261. Messiah Lutheran Church website, "Letters and Questions Answered" ("Marsha"), www.empirenet.com/~messiah7.

262. Dr. John Juedes, "Review of John Schoenheit's Paper on Adultery," www.empirenet.com/~messiah7; cf. "How Widely Was (Is) Adultery Practiced in TWI?"

263. Wierwille, *Receiving the Holy Spirit Today,* p. 142; Wierwille, *The Bible Tells Me So,* p. 88.

264. Wierwille, *The New, Dynamic Church,* p. 31.

265. For a discussion and refutation see Farah, *From the Pinnacle of the Temple;* Dimagio, *The Wall Street Gospel;* Richard Mahew, *Divine Healing Today* (Chicago: Moody, 1983); Weldon, *Psychic Healing* (Chicago: Moody, 1982, ch. 8).

266. Wierwille, *The Bible Tells Me So,* p. 87.

267. Ibid., p. 90.

268. *Ohio Magazine,* p. 34.

269. Ibid.; Williams, p. 101.

270. Personal letter to Rev. R. K. Wyman, July 27, 1971, p. 6.

271. Wierwille, *Power for Abundant Living* course, pp. 38, 22, 45, 53, 31.

272. Dr. John Juedes, "Why Talk about V. P. Wierwille's Death?" www.empirenet.com/~messiah7.

273. Letter of Patrick Ward, November 22, 1976, to Jim Bjornstad of the Institute for Contemporary Christianity, p. 8.

274. Letter of Patrick Ward, p. 4.

275. In James A. Adair, Ted Miller, *Escape from Darkness* (Wheaton, IL: Victor Books, 1982), p. 27.

276. Ibid., p. 29.

277. Ibid.

278. *The Way Magazine,* January–February 1978, p. 6.

279. Wierwille, *Jesus Christ Is Not God,* p. 16.

280. Ibid., pp. 99-100.

281. Ibid., p. 122.

282. Wierwille, *The Word's Way,* p. 269.

283. Wierwille, *The New, Dynamic Church,* p. 129.

284. Wierwille, *Jesus Christ Is Not God,* p. 148.

285. Wierwille, *The Bible Tells Me So,* p. 5.

286. Wierwille, *Power for Abundant Living,* p. 105.

287. Wierwille, *The Bible Tells Me So,* p. 135.

288. *The Way Magazine,* March–April 1976, p. 5.

289. Wierwille, *Power for Abundant Living,* p. 83.

290. *The Way Magazine,* January–February 1976, p. 5; also in Wierwille, *Power for Abundant Living,* p. 334.

291. *Word's Way,* p. 27.

292. Wierwille, *The Bible Tells Me So,* p. 77.

293. Wierwille, *Jesus Christ Is Not God,* p. 58.

294. Ibid., p. 39.

295. Ibid., p. 41.

YOGI BHAJAN'S "3HO"

INFO AT A GLANCE

Name: Happy-Healthy-Holy Organization ("3HO")

Purpose: Traditional Sikhism is an eclectic faith combining bhakti, or devotional Hinduism, and Sufism, or Islamic mysticism. In this light, "3HO" sees its purpose as helping people realize and live in light of their inherent divine consciousness.

Founder: Yogi Bhajan.

Source of authority: Yogi Bhajan and the ten historic Sikh gurus as interpreted by him.

Revealed teachings: Yes. Besides the divine revelation in their scriptures, a dream revealed to Yogi Bhajan that the teachings of the 10th and final Sikh guru, Gobind Singh (1666–1708), were the truth.

Claim: To accurately represent Sikhism in the Western hemisphere; to be the highest path to God.

Examples of occult potential: Development of psychic powers; kundalini symptomatology, astral travel.

Quotes:

"Who is the savior? It is your own higher consciousness which can save you from your own lower consciousness. (*The Teachings of Yogi Bhajan*, p. 129.)

"I don't care whether you believe in Jesus or not, whether you believe in God nor not, whether you believe in Buddha or not. This is not my problem, it is your problem [that you believe, rather than experience]." (*The Teachings of Yogi Bhajan*, p. 64.)

DOCTRINAL SUMMARY

God: Ineffable, One.

Jesus: A man who attained Christ-consciousness or spiritual enlightenment.

Trinity: Variously defined in 3HO terms.

Salvation: By works (meditation, yoga) toward liberation from ego and wordly attachment.

Man: Inwardly divine.

Sin: Attachment to lower consciousness.

Satan: A Christian myth.

Bible: The Adi (first) Granth and Granth of the Tenth Guru (Dasm Granth) are the only reliable and true scripture.

Death: A normal transition or spiritual advance.

Heaven and Hell: Temporary places or states of consciousness.

ZEN

INFO AT A GLANCE

Name: Zen Buddhism.

Purpose: The attainment of *satori* (enlightenment).

Founder: Unknown; popularly believed to be Bodhidharma.

Source of authority: Zen master's interpretation of Buddhism; the experience of satori.

Claim: Zen is the best or truest path to satori and representative of true Buddhism.

Theology: Monistic, syncretistic.

Occult dynamics: Zen meditation produces *makyo* or psychic phenomena.

Attitude toward Christianity: Rejecting.

Quotes:

"I truly follow God's will if I forget about God."[1]

—The World of Zen

"But after all, Zen teaches nothing. All cosmological and psychological theories of original Buddhism are regarded, according to the phrase of Hui-Hai as arguments which are of the order of nonsense.... As Tao-Yi (Matsu) says, 'We speak of enlightenment in contrast to delusion.' But since there is originally no delusion, enlightenment also cannot stand. This is what is known as 'obtaining which is not an obtaining'; and also 'in the last resort nothing gained.'"[2]

—Lit-sen Chang, former Zen Buddhist

"Smash the Buddha, Patriarchs and Arhats, if you come across them; smash your parents and relations, if you come across them. You will be in real emancipation. . . . Anything that has the resemblance of an external authority is rejected

624

by Zen. Absolute faith is placed in a man's own inner being. Zen wants to live from within, not to be bound by rules, but to be creating one's own rules."[3]

—Dr. D. T. Suzuki

Note: For the interested reader, our chapter on Buddhism has additional relevant material. It should be noted that Zen has many similarities with the religion of Taoism and that Zen influence in the West appears indirectly in numerous places, e.g., Erhard Seminars Training/The Forum is, in many respects, essentially a Zen message. (See our *Encyclopedia of New Age Beliefs*.)

Zen philosophy is inherently contradictory and confusing. We have attempted to spare the reader from as much irrationalism as possible while simultaneously illustrating Zen for what it is.

References to *Encyclopedia of New Age Beliefs:* Altered States of Consciousness, Eastern Gurus, Enlightenment, Hypnosis, Mantras and Mandalas, Martial Arts, Meditation, Visualization, Yoga.

Doctrinal Summary

God: The Absolute, Tao, beyond thought and description.

Jesus: Most Zenists would respect Jesus as a great man but interpret His life and teachings through the philosophical assumptions of Zen.

Salvation: Escaping duality by zazen (meditation) and satori (enlightenment).

Man: In inner essence or reality people are one with the Absolute; ultimately the body and personality are illusions.

Sin: Ignorance of reality.

Heaven and Hell: Mental states or temporary conditions of existence.

Introduction and History

In *The Way of Zen,* the late influential writer Alan Watts described Zen as follows:

But above all it has a way of being able to turn one's mind inside out, and dissolving what seemed to be the most oppressive human problems into questions like "Why is a mouse when it spins?"[4]

This question is a "koan," a nonsense formulation allegedly pointing to absolute truth. The title of one Zen book, *Selling Water by the River,* says a great deal about Zen. As Zen masters admit, Zen is paradoxical at best and nonsense at worst: in effect, the "theatre of the absurd" of religion, and koans are an essential element.

As an undergraduate student, John Weldon once encountered a Zen practitioner and asked the student what Zen was all about. The response was, "Why is the meaning of Zen the legs on a snake?" with the emphasis on "why."

Of course, no one knows and there are no true answers.

Some people view Zen as merely an odd little Eastern sect of little or no import. They could not be more mistaken. Millions of people in the United States have been influenced by Zen directly or indirectly, and there are millions more adherents and sympathizers worldwide. Zen temples currently accept Zen worship in numerous American cities. Over one-half million people to various degrees have had a clandestine experience with Zen through Erhard Seminars Training (est/The Forum) which is predominantly a Zen teaching (see our *Encyclopedia of New Age Beliefs*). Brief research on the Internet indicates that Zen is active in at least 50 countries around the world; there are some 400 Zen centers in the U.S. alone.

Millions of people have been exposed to Zen through its Western popularizers, such as Alan Watts and Christmas Humphreys. Dr. Daisetz Teitaro (D. T.) Suzuki was responsible for bringing Zen to the West in 1906[5] and was often called "the greatest living authority on Zen." He alone has influenced millions through his books and travels.*

---

*Suzuki was also involved with the occult Swedenborg Foundation for some time and colorfully referenced Swedenborg's teachings as "Zen for Westerners" (Robert Ellwood, *Alternative Altars,* pp. 147–148.)

In the last 50 years, hundreds of Zen teachers (*Roshis*) have taken up residence in the United States, leaving a large literary legacy on Zen. For example, Yasutani Roshi alone wrote nearly a hundred volumes before he died.[6] Many popular Zen writers have translated Zen works into English, among them John Blofeld (Chu Ch'an) and Charles Luk (Upasaka Luk'uan Yu). (Zen masters often take several names; there are also Japanese and Chinese equivalencies.)

Zen has influenced many famous individuals. Noted psychoanalyst and occultist Carl Jung was rather sympathetic to Zen.* The book he was reportedly reading on his deathbed was Charles Luk's *Chan and Zen Teachings: First Series;* he asked his secretary to write the author, acknowledging his enthusiasm and personal rapport with Zen ideas.[7] Martin Heidegger, the mentor of Jean Paul Sarte and famous German existentialist philosopher, once stated, "If I understand [Dr. Suzuki] correctly, this is what I have been trying to say in all my writings."[8] The influential neo-orthodox theologian Paul Tillich also admired Zen. Today we find books like James H. Austen's *Zen and the Brain* (MIT: Cambridge Press, 1998), a 900 page "neuroscience" study on Zen states of consciousness and brain physiology. So whatever one thinks of Zen, it is nevertheless a modern force to be reckoned with. Christians especially should take note of its influence on mainline Christianity and the growing movement of so-called "Zen Christians," which we will critique.

Zen and the Major Schools of Buddhism

There are two principal schools of Buddhism: the Hinayana, or Theravada (usually considered the earliest tradition and therefore the most accurate), and the Mahayana, generally thought to be a later tradition which "deified" the Buddha and which represents a more mystical approach,

---

*He wrote the foreword to D. T. Suzuki's *An Introduction to Zen Buddhism* and, with parallels to Swedenborgianism, Jung was also sympathetic to mediumism and attended seances. (See our *The Facts on Psychology,* the Sept. 1995 *ATRI* [Ankerberg Theological Research Institute] *News* magazine; Martin Ebon, "Jung's First Medium," *Psychic,* June 1976, pp. 42–47, and especially Jung's autobiography, *Memories, Dreams, Reflections.*)

hence one closer to Zen. (Many scholars accept Tibetan Buddhism as a third school.) Most scholars regard Zen as Mahayanist, some as Hinayanist, while a few consider it apart from all schools. Zen could also be said to represent a blend of both major schools with additional elements originated during its diverse geographical and historical development.

Zen claims to be the "true" Buddhism, but since no one can prove what true (original) Buddhism is, the claim means little. In Buddhism, generally, four factors have contributed to this uncertainty over the earliest Buddhist teachings: (1) the late nature of the Buddhist manuscripts, (2) their contradictory teachings, (3) Buddhism's long-standing emphasis on subjectivism and (4) Buddha's mixture of legend and history. In the end, Zen is simply one of innumerable conflicting schools of Buddhism, no more no less. Even within its own ranks there are many subschools claiming that they alone constitute the "highest truth" of Zen, and some even claim that conventional Zen cannot offer true enlightenment (such as Zenmar's so-called "Dark Zen").

Because Zenists claim to be the original Buddhism, Zen Roshi Jiyu Kennett attempts to trace the basic doctrines of the earlier Hinayana school to their later development in Zen.[9] And in Blofeld's opinion it is difficult to be dogmatic on the origin of Zen as being strictly Mahayanist, because he argues that the truth of Buddhism is determined subjectively not historically:

Nevertheless, quite apart from the fact that up-to-date research, coupled with closer contacts between Western scholars on the one hand and Chinese, Tibetan and Japanese monks on the other, has demonstrated how impossible it is to be sure that either Mahayana or Hinayana is the more "orthodox" of the two, the folly of such narrow-mindedness is clearly demonstrated by the Blessed One's own words; for, even according to the Theravadins, he seems to have declared soundly that whatsoever is conducive to the welfare of sentient beings is right doctrine and that whatsoever is harmful to their welfare cannot be true Buddha-Dharma. While it is true that some of the schools and sects within the Mahayana are of comparatively later origin than either the Theravadin or the ancient

Mahayanist sects, it is also true that they differ only as to method and never as to the Goal.[10]

This is assuming we know what the Buddha himself said. In fact, Buddhist scholars, such as Edward Conze, Edward J. Thomas and others, have stated that we do not know and cannot know what he said, due to the four points mentioned previously (see also the chapter on Buddhism).

D. T. Suzuki illustrates the problem when he claims: "If the Mahayana is not Buddhism proper, neither is the Hinayana, for the historical reason that neither of them represents the teaching of the Buddha as it was preached by the Master himself."[11] But Suzuki himself is not certain what Buddha said and even admits that Buddhism "refuses to be objectively defined."[12] As a result, he also interprets "true" Buddhism mystically rather than objectively or doctrinally. Suzuki claims to teach a Buddhism "stripped of all its historical and doctrinal garments,"[13] a Buddhism that is "the inner life and spirit of the Buddha" structured around his inmost consciousness.

We do know that the founder of Zen is popularly considered to be Bodhidharma (perhaps a legend), who is said to have brought Zen to China around 520 A.D. Zen's lengthy historical evolution makes its origin difficult to trace. However, the controversial theories of Buddhist monks such as Tao-Sheng (360–434 A.D.) clearly contributed to its development. (Some believe Tao-Sheng was "Zen's actual founder.") Nevertheless, once it arrived in China, the Chinese influence on Zen was crucial, as noted by Dr. Suzuki:

The traditional origin of Zen in India before its introduction into China, which is recorded in Zen literature, is so mixed with legends that no reliable facts can be gathered from it. . . . In fact, Zen Buddhism, as was already discussed, is the product of the Chinese mind, or rather the Chinese elaboration of the [Buddhist] Doctrine of Enlightenment. . . . Some scholars may, however, object to this kind of treatment of the subject, on the ground that if Zen is at all a form of Buddhism, or even the essence of it as is claimed by its followers, it cannot be separated from the general history of Buddhism in India. This is quite true, but as far as facts are con-

cerned, Zen as such did not exist in India—that is, in the form as we have it today; and therefore . . . we must consider Zen the Chinese interpretation of the doctrine of Enlightenment, which is expounded in all Buddhist literature, most intensively in the Mahayana and more or less provisionally in the Hinayana.[14]

In China the two principal schools of Zen, the Rinzai and the Soto, were founded,[15] and from here Zen moved to Japan. In the twelfth century a Japanese Tendai Buddhist monk (Eisai, 1141–1215) went to China to study Zen and returned to found the Rinzai school. Myozen, a disciple of Eisai, initiated Dogen (1200–1253) into Zen, and Dogen became the founder of the Soto school. Today, Zen has a wide influence in Japan. The martial arts of judo, Karate and Kendo (fencing), together with Japanese gardens, architecture, poetry, painting and the tea ceremony all more or less reflect Zen influence.[16] And Dr. Lit-sen Chang observes that Zen "was used by Japanese militarists as an incentive for their aggressive wars."[17]

According to Zen, its "doctrine" and essence were transmitted mystically or psychically from disciple to disciple. Allegedly the Buddha himself transmitted esoteric truth to Mahakasyapa, apparently the only disciple capable of receiving the transmission at the time. As the story goes, the Buddha had picked up a flower after a lecture and held it up for his disciples to see. Only Mahakasyapa understood the meaning and responded with a smile. "Later the Buddha called this disciple to him in private and mystically transmitted to him the wordless doctrine, or 'with Mind transmitted Mind.' Mahakasyapa, in turn, mystically transmitted the Doctrine to Ananda, who thus became second in the line of twenty-eight Indian Patriarchs. The last of these was Bodhidharma, who is said to have travelled to China in the sixth century A.D."[18] Thus, ostensibly, "while all Buddhist sects present the truth in varying degrees, Zen alone preserves the very highest teachings of all—teachings based on a mysterious transmission of Mind which took place between Gautama Buddha and Mahakasyapa."[19]

Again, all of this is unverifiable. Those who believe that Zen can be traced to the Buddha and his "highest" teaching do so on the basis of unsupported Zen claims, not documented history. Even comments by Zenists like John Blofeld are telling. In his translation of one of Hyang Po's writings, *Huan Po Ch'uan Hsin Fa Yao,* he notes the similarity of the Zen experience to that of Plotinus, Meister Eckhart and other famous mystics, and then he illustrates that the story of the Buddha himself originating Zen is based in mysticism, not history:

> Opinions as to the truth of this story naturally vary, but Masters like Huang Po obviously speak from some deep inner experience. He and his followers were concerned solely with a direct perception of truth and cannot have been even faintly interested in arguments about the historical orthodoxy of their beliefs. . . . So however slender the evidence for Zen's claim to have been founded by Gautama Buddha himself, I do not for one moment doubt that Huang Po was expressing in his own way the same experience of Eternal Truth which Gautama Buddha and others, Buddhist and non-Buddhist, have expressed in theirs.[20]

Other Zenists have extended the origin of Zen back far beyond Sakyamuni (the historical Buddha) to earlier "Buddhas," and even far beyond that into eternity past. Zen thus becomes the Eternal Truth that has always existed, and always will.[21] Shunryu Suzuki, a Soto Zen Master, asserts: "There is no Nirvana outside our practice. . . . This practice started from beginningless time, and it will continue into an endless future. Strictly speaking, for a human being there is no other practice than this practice. There is no other way of life than this way of life."[22]

The claims of Zen as to its origin and superiority have not necessarily endeared Zen to other Buddhists, who make similar claims for their own teachings. Zenists accept virtually all Buddhism as representing the genuine teachings of the Buddha, but they distinguish between his "introductory" and "advanced" teachings. From their perspective, they relegate Theravadin teaching, also known as Hinayana, to Buddha's introductory teachings, which were intended for "weaker" souls not up to the rigors of Zen. Roshi Kennett says that "the teachings of Hinayana were for the beginner and the Mahayana

ones were for those who had made greater progress."[23]

This approach harmonizes with the Zen belief that the *experience* of the Buddha was much more important than his *teachings,* which are essentially superficial. Theravadins, for their part, reject Zen as "heretical." They cannot accept what they consider spurious Mahayanist revisions of the Buddha's "true" teachings. If we read the following statement by Dr. Suzuki, we can see why the Theravadins are not content to accept Zen as a legitimate Buddhist school: "Zen claims to be Buddhism, but all the Buddhist teachings as propounded in the sutras and sastras are treated by Zen as mere waste paper whose utility consists in wiping off the dirt of intellect and nothing more."[24]

A recent book title went, *If You Meet the Buddha on the Road, Kill Him.* Those Buddhists who believe that the Buddha is irrelevant and his teachings dangerous can hardly expect sympathy from other Buddhists who reverence him and his words. Dr. Lit-sen Chang observes: "'The Buddha cannot save us,' says Hui-Hai, 'strive diligently, practice the method for yourselves, do not rely on the strength of the Buddha.' It is interesting to note that Buddha is often spoken of as a 'dry stick of dung' and it is also a very popular saying among Zen, 'When you have mentioned Buddha's name, wash your mouth!'"[25] Garma C. C. Chang observes: "If one understands that reality is neither pure nor impure, he finds the Buddha in the dung as well as in Heaven."[26]

PRACTICE AND TEACHINGS

Actually, the issue of Zen origins and orthodoxy is largely irrelevant for most Zen believers. The experience of Zen is what matters to them. As the popular Alan Watts observed, comprehending Zen is like trying to chew one's teeth off; it simply can't be done. Zen only "makes sense" when one enters Zen practice and achieves an altered state of "enlightened" consciousness. Put another way, Zen meditation leading to *satori* (enlightenment) is what makes the irrational in Zen "rational" and its absurdities "meaningful."

Although Zen can be quite profound on one level, as we will see, at another level it is about as profound as "selling water by the river":

The Zen master teaches his student nothing.[27]

There is nothing. Absolutely nothing! I am everything and everything is nothing![28]

To receive trouble is to receive good fortune; to receive agreement is to receive opposition.[29]

Free your mind of notions, beliefs, assumptions. I hit you with my baton (striking student). You cry "Ouch!" That "Ouch!" is the whole universe. What more is there? Is Mu different from that?[30] ["Mu" is a koan.]

Millions of people today are fascinated by Zen, even though Zen teaches them to believe in "nothing" and that they are only illusions. Zen accepts only one reality. This is termed "Not Two," "Only Mind," "Buddha Nature," etc. Separate "things," whether people, places or objects, are illusions "hiding" this one true reality.* Zenists presume that there is no objective world "out there," that it is all in their mind; or, more accurately, since *their* mind does not exist, everything is an illusory manifestation of "Only Mind," or the ultimate reality. The goal of Zen meditation is therefore to recognize the oneness (to experience one's true nature) and then to reconcile, or harmonize, the oneness with the illusory duality. At this point, no observer or reconciler exists, for there is no consciousness of a division between observer and what is observed.

Because Zen is not concerned with the historical Buddha or his alleged teachings, but only with his purported mystical consciousness, the "Buddha" is symbolic of an internal reality, which is found in Zen meditation. "Only Mind" and "the Buddha" are two terms for the monistic (oneness) experience that Zen calls an experience of reality. Although reality is outwardly illusory, everyone is inwardly one essence with

reality, and thus in one sense everyone is the Buddha, or his mystical experience of reality. "People think they are doing various things, but actually it is the Buddha doing them."[31]

Because Zen involves a denial of everything, and is inherently contradictory, readers can expect to encounter significant confusion in studying Zen. However, for the Zenist, it is the *other* six billion people who are deluded: he, at least, has found the "Truth."[52] Suzuki laments, "But in the world, alas, there are so many living corpses wallowing in the mud of ignorance."[53] Another Zen teacher exclaims, "most of the people in the world are heretics."[54]

In the material that follows, we will look at: the definition of Zen; some common beliefs and features of Zen; the two main schools of Zen; the central practice of Zen—meditation or *zazen;* the nonsense riddles (*koans*) given by the *Roshi* or Zen Master and the goal of Zen—enlightenment or *satori.*

Definition of Zen

Like Brahman, who the Hindus define as "not this, not that" ("neti, neti"), Zen is beyond all definition. "Zen masters, in fact, look upon mere definitions and explanations as dry and lifeless, and as ultimately misleading because they are inherently limited."[55] When asked "What is Zen?" by a disciple, Ummon replied, "That's It."[56]

Defining Zen depends on one's perspective. For some, Zen is a philosophy of life. For others it is religion not philosophy. Roshi Kennett declares, "Zen is an intuitive *religion* and not a philosophy or way of life."[57] But D. T. Suzuki argues, "Is Zen a religion? It is not a religion in the sense that the term is popularly understood."[58] Defining Zen is difficult then, since, in an ultimate sense, Zen has no required definition or, allegedly, even beliefs. Suzuki argues, "Zen has nothing to teach us in the way of intellectual analysis; nor has it any set doctrines which are imposed on its followers for acceptance. . . . If I am asked, then, what Zen teaches, I would answer Zen teaches nothing."[59]

Technically speaking, whatever someone may say about Zen can be viewed as wrong, because one can only communicate dualistically

---

*Some Zenists may attempt to restrict "Only Mind" to conscious beings so that plants and rocks do not share the Buddha nature, since they have no mind to perceive it. Others, like D. T. Suzuki, assert that even plants and rocks can become enlightened (Blofeld, *The Zen Teaching of Hui Hai,* p. 139).

(right, wrong; hot, cold), and Zen finds its heart in an experiential realm beyond dualism in oneness. This (Zen) can only be experienced, not communicated. About Zen, one cannot even declare that nothing exists. One cannot declare anything about Zen because to do so one must use concepts and concepts are part of the illusion of duality. Enlightenment means to go *beyond* all concepts, so therefore beyond the ideas of existence and nonexistence, logic and illogic, beyond literally everything.

A good illustration of the problem can be seen at the alt.zen website, "Frequently Asked Questions." Here are the first three questions and partial answers. Question one is, "What is Zen (the simple question)?" We are told that Zen is sometimes called a religion, sometimes a philosophy. "Choose whichever term you prefer, it simply doesn't matter." Question two is, "What is Zen (the real question)?" One reply is that the essence of Zen is, "Have you eaten yet?" Question three is, "Why do people post such nonsense to this group?" The answer is that, according to Zen's intuitive understanding, "words and sentences have no fixed meaning, and logic is often irrelevant." The "Empty Gate Zen Center" is part of the International consortium of Zen centers known as the Kwan Um School of Zen, founded in 1977 by Zen master Seung Sahn. At its website, it describes Zen as follows: "Zen is keeping don't know mind always and everywhere."

So how do we define Zen? Perhaps most simply as an unusual sect of Buddhism that stresses enlightenment attained by mystical technique, contradiction and intuition.

Common Beliefs and Features

In this section, we will briefly note several common beliefs and features of Zen: monism; the centrality of Mind; irrationalism; nihilism; the priority of Self; pantheism; antiauthority; influence by Taoism and Mahayana; exclusivism.

Monism. According to Zen, until one is enlightened one cannot know reality. People may think that there is individual existence, that there is an agreed upon reality, but they are wrong. There is no validity or reality to dualistic

concepts such as Creator and creature, object and subject, right and wrong, life and death, good and evil, heaven and hell and so on. Everything is one. At best, what we perceive around us and in normal patterns of thinking is an illusory manifestation of an underlying unitary reality that is itself indescribable.[40] Soikei-an stated: "Though all day long you are speaking, raising your eyebrows, standing, sitting, walking and lying, nevertheless in reality nothing has happened."[41] Huang Po asserted quaintly: "There has never been a single thing."[42] "The arising and the elimination of illusion are both illusory. Illusion is not something rooted in Reality; it exists because of your dualistic thinking."[43]

Suzuki declared that "with *satori* the whole universe sinks into nothingness."[44] Of course, the universe was nothingness to begin with, so Zenists are really "leaping out of an abyss of absolute nothingness"[45] "into" their version of reality. But paradoxically, one could also describe their reality, at least theoretically, as an experience of absolute nothingness. Reality is Only Mind, the one monistic consciousness that alone "exists." However, Huang Po asserted that even enlightenment and Mind are illusions. "In the teaching of the Three Vehicles it is clearly explained that the ordinary and Enlightened minds are illusions. . . . As thought or sensation arises, you fall into dualism [illusion]. . . . There is no this and no that. . . . Just as those categories [enlightened; ordinary] have no real existence, so Mind is really not 'mind.' 'And, as both Mind and those categories are really illusions wherever can you hope to find anything?'"[46] Zenists, then, find nothing. The "path" of Zen (there is really no path) travels from the perception of "conventional reality as absolute nothingness" to the perception of "Only Mind as absolute nothingness" or what is often termed "the Void." In a sense, Zen begins at absolute nothingness and ends at absolute nothingness.

The Centrality of Mind. Paradoxically, Zen is known as "Hsin-tsung," the discipline of the mind. It emulates the Buddha's supposedly illuminated individual *mind* (an illusion) and produces full realization of Mind or Reality. For

Rinzai and other Zen masters, "Zen is no other than the Mind." "The Buddha is the Mind." The very purpose of the koan is to train the *mind* to experience *satori*. Suzuki states: "According to the philosophy of Zen, we are too much of a slave to the conventional way of thinking, which is dualistic through and through. ... Zen, however, upsets this scheme of thought and substitutes a new one in which there exists no logic, no dualistic arrangement of ideas."[47] Ironically, then, as in *advaita* and other monistic systems stressing enlightenment, Zenists depend entirely upon the mind to subvert the mind and move beyond its normal methods of functioning.

Irrationalism. It is ironic that a system stressing the importance of the mind so radically dismantles the mind by denying its most basic functions, such as rational conceptualization, logic and common sense. How a dualistic entity itself (the mind), which according to Zen has no ultimate existence, can lead to anything, let alone to spiritual enlightenment, is never explained. It is accepted on blind faith. Suzuki himself admitted that "Zen is the most irrational, inconceivable thing in the world."[48] But Suzuki may also contradict himself and claim that Zen "always deals with facts concrete and tangible."[49] The truth, however, is that Zen has no facts; it is irrational in its denial of reason and language, and nihilistic (see following) in its implications.[50]

"Logically considered Zen may be full of contradictions. ... But as it stands above all things, it goes serenely on its own way."[51] Thus, Bodhidharma stressed the necessity of "a special transmission outside the scriptures, no dependence upon the words and letters."[52] Rinzai said, "I tell you this: there is no Buddha, no Dharma, no training and no realization. ... Rather than attaching yourselves to my words, better calm down and seek nothing further."[53] Yashutani Roshi noted, "Buddhism has clearly demonstrated that discriminative thinking lies at the root of delusion. I once heard someone say: 'Thought is the sickness of the human mind.' From the Buddhist point of view this is quite true."[54] "To realize your self-nature you have to break out of the cul-de-sac of logic and analysis."[55]

Now consider Hung Po's (Tuan Chi, Hsi Yun) description of the Zen path:

> That which is fundamentally pure and clean, is beyond word, speech, question and answer. ... Your words and speeches should be disengaged from the worldly way of life thereby [causing] all your utterances to become transcendental [non-dual] in the twinkling of an eye. ... Why do not they, together with me, reduce the mind to the state of empty space, of a withered log, of a stone, of cold ashes and extinct fire? Only then can there be some little degree of responsiveness (to the absolute thatness), otherwise they will have later to be flogged by Yama (the god of the hell) for their sins. You will have only to keep from all that *is* and *is not* so that your mind will be solitary. ...[56]

As Dr. Suzuki said, "Zen is the most irrational, inconceivable thing in the world."

Nihilism. Zen scholars often attempt to deny the charge of nihilism, but Zen is clearly a teaching of meaninglessness and despair. Where can any meaning or purpose be found in Zen?

The experiential state of Zen enlightenment may be described in glowing terms (along with the usual "Nothingness," "Voidness" and "Emptiness"), but that hardly makes it meaningful when "you" do not even really exist to perceive or experience it. If nothing matters, why not become a thief or a hedonist? As one Zen master argued, "In my talks there is nothing absolutely real. If you see it thus, you are a true leaver of home and can spend ten thousand pieces of yellow gold per day (enjoy yourself)."[57] Indeed, why endure the "violent howling, shouting and beating methods" of the Rinzai school in order to break the dualistic mind,[58] when the mind is only an illusion to begin with? Alan Watts described entering the Zen path as "to enter a life which is completely aimless": "To the logician it will of course seem that the point at which we have arrived is pure nonsense—as, in a way, it is. From the Buddhist point of view, reality itself has no meaning. ... To arrive at reality—at "suchness"—is to go beyond karma, beyond consequential action, and to enter a life which is completely aimless."[59]

Zen enlightenment may be described as "full emptiness" rather than "empty emptiness" (implying that "something" remains after enlightenment), but no Zenist has ever been able to say what remains, let alone supply any meaning to Zen enlightenment. Further, one need only examine the lives of people like Alan Watts, who adopted this nihilistic philosophy, to see the personal havoc wrought by this kind of teaching.[60]

Zenists may claim that enlightenment gives one freedom and peace of mind. But "peace of mind" is as meaningless as everything else. What peace? What mind? Can inner peace be experienced by a nonentity? And is it not true that such "freedom" could easily slide into a freedom *from* responsibility? (See Critique section.) Some of this was discussed in our chapter on Eastern Gurus in Vol. 1 of this series, *Encyclopedia of New Age Beliefs*. As the Bible warns, "Do not be misled: 'Bad company corrupts good character'" (1 Corinthians 15:33). "Do not be deceived: God cannot be mocked. A man reaps what he sows" (Galatians 6:7).

What then is the meaning of Zen? The meaning is ostensibly in the simple experience of Zen, but of what value is that within the confines of Zen philosophy? Note a typically characteristic Zen saying: "Who is the teacher of all the Buddhas, past, present, and future? John the cook."[61] Absurd? That's Zen.

The Priority of Self. Zen is a religion that lives and breathes glory to one's true "Self." As the "false" self of individual personality is slowly eradicated, the true Self supposedly emerges in the process of enlightenment. Zen is thus a process "through which self-denial is simultaneously self-election—choice of one's self as infinite and absolute."[62] Akisha Kondo observes: "The answer must come out of oneself, by one's own experience. Single-mindedness is just single-mindedness and leaves no room for interrogation. It is a sheer act of faith in oneself. It implies, therefore, total respect toward the real self."[63] But what is this "real Self"? Zenists cannot say. Even the "real" Self cannot be truly described, since concepts are meaningless. One would assume then that the ineffable Self cannot be described as real when the concept of "real" is meaningless.

Pantheism. Pantheism is both affirmed and denied in Zen. God is and is not the universe. For example, even though Dr. Suzuki asserts that Zen "never subscribes to pantheism,"[64] he also declares "the Creator is the creation and yet the Creator is the Creator."[65] "And the world is God and God is the world, and God exclaims, 'it is good!' . . . God's is-ness is my is-ness and also the cat's is-ness sleeping on her mistress' lap."[66]

Perhaps we could say that Zen is pantheistic in a qualified sense, or that it is panentheistic. In Zen, does it finally matter? Or perhaps Dr. Suzuki was being careless with words: "If I should say 'I am God' it is sacrilegious. No, not that. I am I, God is God, and at the same time I am God, God is I. That is the most important part."[67]

Blofeld argues that if Mind is Only Reality, the illusory, insentient creation itself *cannot* be that Reality.[68] And yet Suzuki admits in an interview, "The banana plant can be saved. Snow, too."[69] Again, what difference should it make?

Antiauthority. On one level, Zen accepts no supreme authority except that of subjective and ineffable experience. After all, what else exists but mystical experience to place authority in? Not Buddha or parents or Scriptures, and certainly not the God of Christianity. Every source of authority must be destroyed: "Followers of the Way, if you wish to see this Dharma clearly, do not let yourselves be deceived. Whether you turn to the outside or to the inside, whatever you encounter, kill it. If you meet the Buddha, kill the Buddha; if you meet the patriarchs, kill the patriarchs; if you meet the Arhats, kill the Arhats; if you meet your parents, kill your parents; if you meet your relatives, kill your relatives; then for the first time you will see clearly."[70]

On the other hand, the Zen master, allegedly enlightened, is the supreme authority, which one must always submit to. What he declares is law. If he tells you that something must be cast aside, you must obey. "Next you must vigorously undertake even what is difficult to do and difficult to endure, without concerning yourself at all with right and wrong and without clinging to your own opinions. You must cast aside anything [even Jesus Christ] that does not accord with the Buddhist truth, even though it be something you most earnestly desire."[71]

Taoism and Mahayana. As noted, Zen claims to be the true Buddhism, its real essence. Dogen argued that Zen is the universal truth, which is also the essence of true Buddhism. "Anybody who would regard Zen as a school or sect of Buddhism . . . is a devil."[72] Zen, however, is simply an odd combination of the occult religion of Taoism and of Mahayana Buddhism. As Alan Watts pointed out, "The origins of Zen are as much Taoist as Buddhist."[73] He notes the first principle of Taoism as: "when everyone recognizes beauty as beautiful, there is already ugliness; when everyone recognizes goodness as good, there is already evil."[74] Dr. Lit-sen Chang describes Zen as a kind of Taoist revolt against Buddhism:

> Zen is not considered classical Buddhism, but a "Chinese anomaly of it." . . . All that we can say with assurance is that in China itself, as early as the Period of Disunity (396–588), the theory of instantaneous enlightenment had been developed. . . . Dr. Hu-Shih describes Zen as a Chinese revolt against Buddhism. He accepts neither the historical reality of Bodhi-Dharma nor the authenticity of the earlier Zen works. . . . Zen grew out of a combination of mahayana Buddhism and Taoism. "From Hui-Neng, Zen lost all its distinctively Indian characteristics, it became thoroughly transformed by the more practical Chinese mentality." It was actually more deeply influenced by Taoism. . . . The central theme of Taoism is "Wu Wei" (non-action). . . . Humphreys asserted more affirmatively, 'The Taoist doctrine of "Wu-Wei" is excellent Zen. "According to him, 'Taoism is "The godmother of Zen".' "[75]

Exclusivism. Religions in general claim tolerance and unity while simultaneously teaching that only their path is valid or is the best path. Zen is no exception: "Few if any achieve 'satori' without Zen training."[76] "There is no Nirvana outside our [Soto Zen] practice."[77]

Two Major Schools of Zen

There are five schools of Zen; however, the two most prominent are the Rinzai and the Soto. The others are the Ummon, the Ikyo and the Hogen schools. The Rinzai stresses very sudden illumination, the use of koans and various "teaching" methods of the Roshi, such as striking a novice. The Soto school of Dogen stresses gradual enlightenment, "no" use of koans and is more gentle. It consists of five stages.[78]

Lin-chi's (Rinzai's) own enlightenment under the tutelage of Huang Po no doubt influenced his own particular screeching and hitting methods:

> When he had been for three years in the Obaku school he approached the Master personally and asked what was the essential truth in Buddha's teaching, all he got was twenty blows with a stick. He went to another Master, Daigu (Tayu), who told him that Obaku had given him the correct treatment for his enlightenment, and further emphasized the matter by roughly manhandling Rinzai's throat and subjecting him to harsh words. This time Rinzai hit back, striking Daigu in the ribs. Nevertheless, he had suddenly become enlightened. Next, Rinzai went back to Obaku to tell him what had happened, but the Master only threatened him with more and gave him a slap in the face, whereupon Obaku gave way to great laughter and roared out the meaningless shout "Katsu."[79]

It is the Rinzai school that has attracted the attention of most Americans. Its most prominent representative is D. T. Suzuki. While the Rinzai and Soto sects are ostensibly distinct, a given Zen master could have various elements of either (or any) school. For example, Yasutani Roshi utilizes both Rinzai and Soto in his own system.[80] "By no means, then, is the koan system confined to the Rinzai sect as many believe. Yasutani Roshi is only one of a number of Soto masters who use koans in their teaching. . . . Even Dogen himself . . . disciplined himself in koan Zen for eight years before going to China and practicing *shikan-taza* [his meditative discipline]."[81]

Zazen (Meditation)

It is sometimes argued that zazen is *not* meditation, although it clearly is. The student sits still in an erect posture, utilizes proper breathing techniques and chants Buddhist sutras while concentrating to induce mental and spiritual transformation. Occult powers are often the eventual result.[82] Zazen does not create Buddhahood; it merely uncovers the eternally existing Buddha nature or Reality (Only Mind):

Thus breathing becomes a vehicle of spiritual experience, the mediator between body and mind. It is the first step towards the transformation of the body from the state of a more or less passively and unconsciously functioning physical organ into a vehicle or tool of a perfectly developed and enlightened mind.... The process of breathing is the connecting link between conscious and subconscious, gross material and fine-material, volitional and non-volitional functions.... The uniqueness of zazen lies in this: that the mind is freed from bondage to *all* thought-forms, visions, objects, and imaginings, however sacred or elevating, and brought to a state of absolute emptiness, from which alone it may one day perceive its own true nature, or the nature of the universe.[83]

Zazen stresses the awakening experience (satori) and its integration into daily life. Because it is about the "state of absolute emptiness" it is accorded absolute value. "Zazen is more than just a means to enlightenment or a technique for sustaining and enlarging it, but it is the *actualization* of our True-nature. Hence it has absolute value."[84]

Zen practice also involves lectures by the Master (*jodo*) and personal interviews with him (*sanzen*). Roshis also supervise meditation periods. While many novices are at first excited to be on the path of enlightenment, few indeed realize what will be required of them. As with nonbiblical forms of religious meditation generally, Zen meditation can be costly. For example, consider what happens to the following tormented soul, bravely doing his best. He is meditating on the famous koan "Mu":

At last the gods are with me! Now I can't miss satori!... Mu, Mu, Mu!... Again roshi leaned over but only to whisper: "You are panting and disturbing the others, try to breathe quietly."... But I can't stop. My heart's pumping wildly, I'm trembling from head to toe, tears are streaming down uncontrollably.... Godo cracks me but I hardly feel it. He whacks my neighbor and I suddenly think: "Why's he so mean, he's hurting him."... More tears.... Godo returns and clouts me again and again, shouting: "Empty your mind of every single thought, become like a baby again. Just Mu, Mu! right from your guts!"—crack, crack, crack!... Abruptly I lose control of my body and, still conscious, crumple

into a heap.... Roshi and Godo pick me up, carry me to my room and put me to bed.... I'm still panting and trembling.... Roshi anxiously peers into my face, asks: "You all right, you want a doctor?"... "No, I'm all right I guess."... "This ever happen to you before?"... "No, never.".... "I congratulate you!"... "Why, have I got satori?"... Roshi brings me a jug of tea, I drink five cups.... No sooner does he leave than all at once I feel my arms and legs and trunk seized by an invisible force and locked in a huge vice which slowly begins closing.... Spasms of torment like bolts of electricity shoot through me and I writhe in agony.... I feel as though I'm being made to atone for my own and all mankind's sins....

Am I dying or becoming enlightened?... Sweat's streaming from every pore and I have to change my underclothing twice.... At last I fall into a deep sleep.[85]

The Koan

Koans are nonsense riddles or stories whose goal involves the restructuring of mental perception to open the mind to "truth" to help it achieve satori. Koans are designed to "attack" the mind, to dismantle its reason, logic, history, ordinary consciousness and duality until it finally "breaks down" and perceives an alternate reality, the monistic perception that Zen considers reality. "Koans are so phrased that they deliberately throw sand into our eyes to force us to open our Mind's eye and see the world and everything in it without distortion.... The import of every koan is the same; that the world is one interdependent Whole and that each separate one of us is that Whole."[86]

Looking at the world logically, morally, reasonably or scientifically *must* be discarded, for only then can one experience true "freedom":

This fundamental overthrowing is necessary in order to build up a new order of things on the basis of Zen experiences.... The *koan*... is only intended to synthesize or transcend... the dualism of the senses. So long as the mind is not free to perceive a sound produced by one hand [clapping] it is limited and is divided against itself. Instead of grasping the key to the secrets of creation, the mind is hopelessly buried in the relativity of things, and, therefore, in their superficiality.[87]

Again, one cannot help but appreciate the irony of Zen enlightenment. Each one of the 1700 or so koans has a "classic" answer, and the poor, unenlightened disciples who "reason" with them—often intermittently beaten with a stick—must try to find it. Koans however are *not* "solved" by reason or intellect, and hence can only be "solved" by recourse to a "deeper" level of mind. Further, to be hit with the stick "does not necessarily mean that the pupil is wrong"; he may be struck "to confirm the disciple's correct interpretation."[88]

Ernest Becker was the author of the seminal, Pulitzer prize-winning *The Denial of Death*. In *Zen: A Rational Critique* he described a number of Zen characteristics: "[Zen is] a technique by which to achieve a mental breakdown of people so that they can be made to accept a new ideology"; *Satori*, its enlightenment: "the final critical collapse under the accumulative pressures of stress" and "a piling up of intellectual frustration that leads to the crumbling of the edifice of logical thought"; and the *koan*, Zen's riddles: "childish dependence upon magical omnipotence" and "a submission to the master's psychological dominance."[89]

The following are some typical koans, the most famous of which is, "What is the sound of one hand clapping?"

> When your mind is not dwelling on the dualism of good and evil what is your original face before you were born?[90]
>
> Q. What is Buddha?
> A. The cat is climbing the post.[91]
>
> Q. Where is emptiness?
> A. It is like a Persian tasting red pepper.[92]
>
> Q. Who is Buddha?
> A. Three measures of flax.[93]
>
> Q. Does a dog have the Buddha-nature?
> A. Wu (nothing).[94]

The Bible, of course, has its own form of "koans," so to speak—pithy sayings intended to lead to spiritual wisdom. With no disrespect intended to Zen masters, we think meditation on the biblical proverbs is more enlightening than the koans. We note a biblical "koan" or two: "Do not answer a fool according to his folly, or you will be like him yourself. Answer a fool according to his folly, or he will be wise in his own eyes" (Proverbs 26:4–5).

Satori

Satori or enlightenment involves the realization of truth that was present all along. "To come to Self-realization you must directly experience yourself and the universe as one. . . . You must let go of logical reasoning and grasp the real thing!"[95] It is the final "psychological" state where everything, paradoxically, "'logically' makes sense." It is a state, one would think, where duality is no longer because one realizes and perceives oneness. But in fact, in satori there is neither duality *nor* oneness; there is only the Void. Suzuki points out that in enlightenment there is no longer even the One:

> Even when Zen indulges in intellection, it never subscribes to a pantheistic interpretation of the world. For one thing, there is no One in Zen. If Zen ever speaks of the One as if it recognized it, this is a kind of condescension to common parlance. To Zen students, the One is the All and the All is the One; and yet the One remains the One and the All the All. "Not two!" may lead the logician to think, "It is One." But the master would go on saying, "Not One either." "What then?" we may ask. We here face a blind alley, as far as verbalism is concerned.[96]

Satori is thus ineffable. Zenists stress satori is an indescribable experience, one that mere words are impotent to explain; hence it can only be experienced. Once achieved, one's previous worldview is radically and often permanently changed into harmony with the Zen worldview. Although Zen meditation is undoubtedly the ultimate cause, satori itself may have a nonspecific causation; for example, any stimuli may "set it off," and for no apparent reason. The mind is apparently "on the brink" at this point, so broken down that even the slightest stimulation can set satori in motion.[97] Satori may also be accompanied by physiological phenomena, trembling, tears, sweating, energy phenomena or possession. And it is mentally hazardous. People have permanently lost their minds through Zen.

Examples of Enlightenment

The satori experience can be radically life-transforming and the "enlightened" individual may rarely be the same person afterwards. For example, the poor soul we quoted earlier is still "mu-ing," but now he has realized the truth:

"Mu'd" silently in temple garden till clock struck one. . . . Rose to exercise stiff, aching legs, staggered into a nearby fence. Suddenly I realized: the fence and I are one formless wood-and-flesh Mu. Of course. . . . Vastly energized by this . . . pushed on till the 4 A.M. gong. . . . Threw myself into Mu for another nine hours with such utter absorption that I completely vanished. . . . I didn't eat breakfast, *mu* did. I didn't sweep and wash the floors after breakfast, *mu* did. I didn't eat lunch, Mu ate. . . . "The universe is One," he [the Roshi] began, each word tearing into my mind like a bullet. "The moon of Truth"—All at once the roshi, the room, every single thing disappeared in a dazzling stream of illumination and I felt myself bathed in a delicious, unspeakable delight. . . . For a fleeting eternity I was alone—I alone was. . . . Then the roshi swam into view. Our eyes met and flowed into each other, and we burst out laughing. . . . "I have it! I know! There is nothing, absolutely nothing. I am everything and everything is nothing!" I exclaimed more to myself than to the roshi, and got up and walked out. . . . I resumed by zazen, laughing, sobbing, and muttering to myself: "It was before me all the time, yet it took me five years to see it."[98]

After all the torment that Zenists submit themselves to, we would be surprised if their minds *did not* break down at some point. (For examples of the torment, see the readings in Kapleau, *The Three Pillars of Zen*, sections III, V.) Note several other accounts of "enlightenment":

Instantaneously, like surging waves, a tremendous delight welled up in me, a veritable hurricane of delight, as I laughed loudly and wildly: "Ha, ha, ha, ha, ha, ha! There's no reasoning here, no reasoning at all! Ha, ha, ha!" The empty sky split in two, then opened its enormous mouth and began to laugh uproariously: "Ha, ha, ha!" Later one of the members of my family told me that my laughter had sounded inhuman. I was now lying on my back. Suddenly I sat up and struck the bed with all my might and beat the floor with my feet, as if trying to smash

it, all the while laughing riotously. My wife and youngest son, sleeping near me, were now awake and frightened. Covering my mouth with her hand, my wife exclaimed: "What's the matter with you? What's the matter with you?" But I wasn't aware of this until told about it afterwards. My son told me later he thought I had gone mad. "I've come to enlightenment! Shakyamuni and the Patriarchs haven't deceived me! They haven't deceived me!"[99]

Now I was in bed, doing zazen again. All night long I alternately breathed Mu and fell into trances. . . . *A strange power propelled me.* I looked at the clock—twenty minutes to four, just in time to make the morning sitting. I arose and calmly dressed. My mind raced as I solved problem after problem. . . . A lifetime has been compressed into one week. A thousand new sensations are bombarding my senses, a thousand new paths are opening before me.[100]

In this state of unconditioned subjectively I, *self-less* I, am supreme. So Shakyamuni Buddha could exclaim: "Above the heavens and below the heavens I am the only honored one."[101] [Yet the attitude of Yun-men (Ummon, the founder of the Ummon school)] was even more radical: "When Sakyamuni was born it is said that he lifted one hand toward the heaven and pointed to the earth with the other, exclaiming, 'Above the heavens and below the heavens, I alone am the Honoured One.' Yun-men comments on this by saying, 'If I had been with him at the moment of his uttering this, I would surely have struck him dead with a blow and thrown the corpse into the maw of a hungry dog.' "[102]

This void is at once the container and the contained, the one and the many. . . . Yet, in truth, we shall have leapt from nowhere to nowhere; hence, we shall not have leapt at all; nor will there be or has there ever been any "we" to make the leap![103]*

In spite of the far-reaching effects of satori, the "enlightened" still have no answers. Dr. Suzuki admits that even *after* enlightenment we still "know not definitely what the ultimate purport of life is."[104] This is in stark contrast to

---

*For other examples of "enlightenment" see our book *The Coming Darkness,* chapter 1, and Vol. 1–*Encyclopedia of New Age Beliefs,* chapters on meditation, enlightenment, yoga, altered states of consciousness and Est/The Forum.

Christian belief. Jesus did tell us the ultimate purpose of life when He said, "This is eternal life: that they may know you, the only true God, and Jesus Christ, whom you have sent" (John 17:3). As we will see, the contrasts between Zen and Christianity are striking wherever we look.

THEOLOGY

Christianity

In this section, we will contrast the teachings of Zen with those of Christianity. At one level, Zenists will admit that the two religions are incompatible, but they will nevertheless argue that a Christian can practice Zen to great benefit. At another level, the Zen doctrine of oneness makes Zen believers religious syncretists: all religions are believed to contain the same *essence* (Zen). Thus a Christian who understands the true *essence* of Christianity will be at home practicing Zen. Consider the following declaration of Zen master Deshimaru (1927–82), who founded some 100 Zen centers throughout Europe and was often called "the Bodhidharma of modern times." At their essence, he saw no difference at all between Christianity and Zen. "In their deepest spirit I find no difference. . . . In essence, it comes down to one and the same religion."[105]

Despite the fundamentally antiChristian nature of Zen, philosophically, theologically and experientially, even some who claim to be Christians endorse Zen. *Zen Meditation for Christians* and *Christian Zen*, written by Roman Catholics, are two of many examples. But the Zen claim and the Zen reality are not one.

The Zen claim: compatibility with Christianity. Zen masters teach that since Zen is supposedly noncommittal religiously, Christians can practice zazen. Soto Master Shunryo Suzuki argues: "Our practice has nothing to do with some particular religious belief. And for you, there is no need to hesitate to practice our way, because it has nothing to do with Christianity or Shintoism or Hinduism. Our practice is for everyone . . . there is no need to worry about the difference between Buddhism and the religion you may believe in."[106] In what must have been a weaker moment, psychoanalyst

Eric Fromm declared: "Zen Buddhism helps man to find an answer to the question of his existence, an answer which is essentially the same as that given in the Judeo-Christian tradition, and yet which does not contradict the rationality, realism, and independence which are modern man's precious achievements."[107] In *Zen Meditation for Christians,* Father H. M. Lassalle firmly declares that "the way of Zen does not conflict theologically with Christian belief" and that Zen can be used by Christians to love God more.[108] He thus asserts that "the Christian need have no misgivings" about practicing Zazen as *Christian* meditation.[109]

However, the parallels Lassalle draws between "Christianity" and Zen are parallels between the practices and beliefs of Christian *mystics*, not the practitioners of biblical Christianity, whose worldview and spiritual practices are based in Scripture, not mysticism. Christian mysticism, to be sure, has felt the influence of Christianity, as opposed to other forms of mysticism that have not. However, our own indepth research into Christian mysticism tells us that we are dealing with aberrational Christianity at best and heresy at worst, not with true biblical Christianity. So in this sense it is not surprising to find parallels between "Christian" mysticism and Zen. John of the Cross, Bonaventure, the Victorines, John Tauler, John Ruysbroeck, Meister Eckhart and others, whatever their orthodoxies may have been, also plant their feet on theological quicksand. Lassalle notes that "their entire way reveals profound similarities with the Zen way."[110] Deshimaru correctly observed, "Father Lassalle never lectures on Christianity; he talks about Zen. Lots of other Christians do the same."[111]

William Johnston, in his equally disturbing *Christian Zen,* "harmonizes" Zen and Christianity, essentially neutralizing the latter by his respect for the former. In 1970 Johnston received the so-called "baptism of the Spirit."[112] "It was through the Pentecostal movement that I came to see the parallel between the Zen *satori* and the Christian conversion or *metanoia* [repentance]. . . . Zen . . . can do a great service to Christians . . . especially to those people who are willing to listen to the voice of the great guru who gave us the Sermon on the Mount."[113]

According to Zen, however, there is no "Great Guru Jesus." Roshi Jiyu Kennett asserts, "The mass-hallucination of the Christian disciples who, after the crucifixion, saw Christ 'risen from the dead,' as they thought, is explained quite easily by the overwrought state of their minds at the time and this type of mass-hallucination is quite well known in Eastern religious circles, being nothing out of the ordinary. The danger comes when we attach importance to such things."[114]

The Zen reality: opposition to Christianity. Zen authorities who are fair with the facts understand full well that Zen and Christianity are entirely incompatible. The chart and quotations below demonstrate this.

As D. T. Suzuki pointed out, in Zen "the story of Creation, the Fall from the Garden of Eden, God's sending Christ to compensate for the ancestral sins, his Crucifixion and Resurrection—they are all symbolic."[116] Western Zenist Alan Watts, who called the idea of God the Father "ridiculous," said that Jesus Christ was a false idol, thus displaying his ignorance of church history and biblical teaching:

> The Zen Buddhists say, "Wash out your mouth every time you say 'Buddha!'" The new life for Christianity begins just as soon as someone can get up in church and say, "Wash out your mouth every time you say 'Jesus!'" . . . Poor Jesus! If he had known how great an authority was to be projected upon him, he would never have said a word. His literary image in the Gospels has, through centuries of homage, become far more of an idol than anything graven in wood or stone, so that today the most genuinely reverent act of worship is to destroy that image. . . . But Christian piety does not let him go away, and continues to seek the living Christ in the dead letter of the historical record. As he said to the Jews, "You search the scriptures, for in them you *think* you have eternal life." The Crucifixion gives eternal life because it is the giving up of God as an object to be possessed, known and held to for one's own safety, "for he that would save his soul shall lose it." To cling to Jesus is therefore to worship a Christ uncrucified, an idol instead of the living God.[117]

ZEN VS. CHRISTIANITY	
CHRISTIANITY	ZEN
God	The void
The Bible is the authoritative Scripture	No authoritative "scripture" but experience
Absolute morality	Relative morality
Jesus as atoning Savior	No savior necessary
Salvation from sin	Enlightenment from ignorance
Repentance involves turning *from* sin	Satori involves a turning to "higher" consciousness that denies sin exists
Self-denial	Self-exaltation
Rational	Irrational
The creation is real	There was no creation
Religious dualism	Monism
Christians "come to sit in fellowship"	Zenists "come to sit in silence"[115]
Eternal life is offered as a free gift (personal immortality)	Personal extinction
Death to self = death to sin; the self is alive to righteousness forever	Death to self = annihilation of self

638

Suzuki is bold enough to write that "Zen followers do not approve of Christians,"[118] and:

> Therefore, in Zen, God is neither denied nor insisted upon; only there is in Zen no such God as has been conceived by Jewish and Christian minds. . . . Make obeisance to the camellia now in full bloom, and worship it if you like, Zen would say. There is as much religion in so doing as in bowing to the various Buddhist gods, or as in sprinkling holy water, or as in participating in the Lord's Supper. All those pious deeds considered to be meritorious or sanctifying by most so-called religiously minded people are artificialities in the eyes of Zen. . . . Zen, therefore, is emphatically against all religious conventionalism.[119]

Thus, "When Buddhists make reference to God, God must not be taken in the Biblical sense."[120] "We see a deep cleavage between Buddhism and Christianity. So long as there is any thought of anybody, whether he be God or Devil, knowing of your doings, Zen would say, 'You are not yet one of us.' . . . In Zen, therefore, there ought not to be left any trace of consciousness after the doing of alms, much less the thought of recompense even by God."[121]

Yasutani Roshi tells us to dissolve our religious delusions "with the fireball of mu!": "The opinions you hold and your worldly knowledge are your delusions. Included also are philosophical and moral concepts, no matter how lofty, as well as religious beliefs and dogmas, not to mention innocent, commonplace thoughts. In short, all conceivable ideas are embraced within the term 'delusions' and as such are a hindrance to the realization of your Essential-nature. So dissolve them with the fireball of Mu!"[122] Sasaki is frank enough to declare that Zen is "diametrically opposed" to basic Christian teaching. "Perhaps for westerners the primary hindrance in understanding Zen, even intellectually, lies in the fact that the great verities that Zen, with Buddhism, takes as basic are diametrically opposed to those the Hebraic-Christian religions have always assumed to be absolute."[123] "Christian" Zenist Lassalle correctly observes that "speaking of God as a person is precisely what annoys the Buddhist."[124] "Whether Zen masters arrive at any explicit belief in God is highly doubtful."[125]

In light of this, Zen and Christianity cannot be reconciled. Entirely apart from the possible dangers of Zen (see the Occult and the Critique sections), for a Christian to accept and practice Zen is a denial of God, Jesus Christ, biblical authority and almost everything distinctively Christian. For example, the Christian who honors the Bible as God's Word could hardly subscribe to a philosophy that teaches, as Hua Hai taught in *The Great Pearl*, "The Scriptures are just words. . . . They are naught but emptiness."[126] But Jesus Himself said, "The *words* I have spoken to you are spirit and they are life" (John 6:63). Can we imagine a Christian acting toward the Bible as Tokusan acted toward his scriptures? "When Tokusan (Te-shan) gained an insight into the truth of Zen he immediately took out all his commentaries on the *Diamond Sutra* once so valued and considered indispensable that he had to carry them wherever he went, and set fire to them, reducing all the manuscripts to ashes."[127]

Despite Zen's dismissal of Christianity, Dr. Lit-sen Chang points out that "modern Zen writers have deliberately borrowed Biblical terminologies to express what they cannot communicate otherwise. In so doing, they are at least unconsciously admitting that the Christian truths are far more adequate than the messages of Zen, even though they so often distort these truths to meet their own ends."[128] For example, Zenists may use the term "God" to describe ultimate reality and "regeneration" to describe satori and "sin" to describe ignorance of Zen truth. At the same time they may argue that it matters not at all whether the resurrection of Christ, the central message of Christianity, was a historical fact. "When Paul insisted that 'if Christ be not raised, your faith is vain; ye are yet in your sins,' he was not appealing to our logical idea of things, but to our spiritual yearnings. It did not matter whether things existed as facts of chronological history or not."[129]

God

Theologically Zen denies relevance to God and practically speaking it is atheistic. Ruth

Fuller Sasaki denies relevance to God while affirming absolute relevance for "THIS":

> Zen does not hold that there is a god apart from the universe who first created this universe and then created man to enjoy, or even master it. . . . Rather, Zen holds that there is no god outside the universe who has created it and created man. God—if I may borrow that word for a moment—the universe, and man are one indissoluble existence, one total whole. Only THIS—capital THIS—is. Anything and everything that appears to us as an individual entity or phenomenon, whether it be a planet or an atom, a mouse or a man, is but a temporary manifestation of THIS in form.[130]

Zen masters may argue they are not atheists since they stress neither belief in God nor disbelief in God. "Is God dead or not? That is the most serious question of all. If you say yes or no, you lose your own Buddha-nature."[131] Lassalle claims: "No understanding Zen master will attack the Christian's faith in God. In most cases, the Zen master himself will not be an atheist. Nevertheless, he will forbid that his disciple think of God, that is think *about* God as one usually does. . . . A Zen master once told his Christian disciple that his idea of God might change after he was enlightened. He did not say that the Christian would or should give up his belief in God."[132]

But Lasalle ignores the fact that this is often exactly what happens. Zen masters do attack the Christian's faith in God because in Zen the very concept of God in Christianity is a delusion preventing enlightenment.

Dr. Lit-Sen Chang was a practitioner of Zen for 50 years before his conversion to Christ. He declares in no mistakable terms that "Zen is a very peculiar and subtle form of atheism."[133] In fact, the practical atheism of Zen is part of its appeal. Westerners or skeptics who have felt themselves "burdened" with a Judeo-Christian concept of God have converted to Zen for just this reason, to "give up belief in God" and live as they wish. Herbert Benoit noted that "Zen demonstrates the nullity of all belief in a personal God, and the deplorable constraint that necessarily flows from this belief."[134] In a telling statement Alan Watts commented:

> Above all, I believe that Zen appeals to many in the post-Christian West because it does not preach, moralize and scold in the st⁻le of Hebrew-Christian prophetism. . . . Absolute morality is profoundly destructive of morality, for the sanctions which it invokes against evil are far, far too heavy. . . . The appeal of Zen, as of other forms of Eastern philosophy, is that it unveils behind the urgent realm of good and evil a vast region of oneself about which there need be no guilt or recrimination, where at last the self is indistinguishable from God. But the Westerner who is attracted by Zen . . . must really have come to terms with the Lord God Jehovah and with his Hebrew-Christian conscience so that he can take it or leave it without fear or rebellion.[135]

In another telling statement, Dr. Lit-Sen Chang describes the beliefs of D. T. Suzuki and Christmas Humphreys (*Zen Comes West*) and then quotes them as declaring that both God and salvation by faith alone must be abandoned by Westerners:

> On the other hand, they not only deny the existence of a living personal God, but rather deify themselves by asserting blasphemously that, 'Before Abraham was I am'; and 'I am the way.' They consider that a greater stumbling block to the acceptance of Zen is the general belief in God. . . . We are told that 'Zen practice has no use for God. Look to no person or Person or God for help.' In the West it is necessary to remove the personal God-concept and all that implies of salvation by faith alone.[136]

The truth is that Zen does attack God, precisely because it understands the implications of belief in the Christian God. Werner Erhard, founder of the Zen driven est/The Forum declares that "the greatest single barrier to God is belief in God." (See *Encyclopedia of New Age Beliefs*, "est, The Forum.") The famous psychoanalyst Eric Fromm observes that in Zen, "I truly follow God's will if I forget about God."[137]

In light of all these denials of God, how is it that Zen is neutral toward God, does not disbelieve in God and should not be considered a form of atheism?

Zen's "theological equivalent" for God is the state of satori or void. The state of "unknowing," the void, is the only truth and the only "God." As noted, while Zen denies the existence of the Christian God, it will use the term God to describe Zen meditation, enlightened Zen practices and the state of satori itself. Consider Deshimaru's response to the following comment: "[Student:] A Zen monk said to me, 'In Zen, when you have satori, you can say, "I am God!"' [Deshimaru:]. . . . Zazen is the same thing as God or Buddha. Gogen, the master of transmission, said, 'Zazen itself is God.' By that he meant that during zazen you are in harmony with the cosmos. . . . The self has dropped away and dissolved. It is the consciousness of God. It is God. . . . We are not separate. There is no duality between God, Buddha, and ourselves."[138] Shunryu Suzuki asserts that *we* are the ones who create the world,[139] while God does not help people at all because "how is it possible for Him to help when He does not realize who He is?"[140] Suzuki tells us that "the *kokoro* . . . is an abyss of absolute nothingness. . . . In Western terminology, the *kokoro* may be regarded as corresponding to God or Godhead,"[141] even as Huang Po asserts that "of the absolute nothing whatever can be postulated."[142]

Zen involves idolatry.

Zen involves idolatry. Everyone worships something in life. Zen rejects worship of the living God but replaces it with prostrations before the Zen master and the worship of Buddhist idols. Indeed, it seems that the lotus position itself indirectly assists in the endeavor. "The fact is that this lotus position somehow impedes discursive reasoning and thinking; it somehow checks the stream of consciousness that flows across the surface of the mind; it detaches one from the very process of thinking."[143] With one's mind sufficiently placed to the side, one suspects that worship of the Zen Master as the personification of the Buddha is thereby made all the easier. Yasutani Roshi tells aspiring Zenists:

> While everyone is free to practice zazen and to listen to the roshi's commentary at sesshin, the essential character of dokusan [the meeting] is the forming of a karmic bond between teacher and disciple, the significance of which is deep in Buddhism. Dokusan therefore is not to be taken lightly. . . . In making your prostrations you should touch the tatami mat with your forehead, with your hands extended in front of your

head, palms upward. Then, bending your arms at the elbows, raise your hands, palms upward, several inches above your head. This gesture of receiving the feet, the lowliest members of the Buddha's body, symbolizes humility and the grateful acceptance into your life of the Way of the Buddha. . . . Bear in mind that the roshi is not simply a deputy of the Buddha but actually stands in his place. In making these prostrations you are in fact paying respect to the Buddha just as though he himself were sitting there, and to the Dharma.[144]

In fact, proper Zen practice provides aspirants with a natural spirit of worship:

> [It is] appreciation of the exalted mind and manifold virtues of the Buddha and the Patriarchs. So there arises within us a desire to express our gratitude and show our respect before their personalized forms through appropriate rituals. These devotions when entered into with a single mind endow the Buddha figure with life; what was formerly a mere image now becomes a living reality with the singular power to obliterate in us awareness of self and Buddha at the moment of prostration.[145]

One Western Zen aspirant recalls his initial recoiling at such idolatry:

> What a weird scene of refined sorcery and idolatry: shaven-headed black-robed monks sitting motionlessly chanting mystic gibberish to the accompaniment of a huge wooden tom-tom emitting other-worldly sounds, while the roshi, like some elegantly gowned witch doctor, is making magic passes and prostrating himself again and again before an altar bristling with idols and images. . . . Is this the Zen of Tanka, who tossed a Buddha statue into the fire? Is this the Zen of Rinzai, who shouted "You must kill the Buddha?". . . . If only he doesn't mar it all by insisting we bow down before those images in the halls. O my prophetic soul! . . . He's brought us into the founder's room and is lighting incense and fervently prostrating himself before a weird statue of Kakuin. . . . "You too may light incense and pay your respects to Kakuin." P__ looks at me and I at him, then he explodes: "the old Chinese Zen masters burned or spit on Buddha statues, why do you bow down before them?" . . . The roshi looks grave but not angry. "If you want to spit you spit, I prefer to bow", . . . We don't spit, but neither do we bow.[146]

But his resistance did not last. Within several weeks this same person records in his diary how he was gladly worshipping a statue of Buddha as God. "Around midnight prostrated myself before statue of Buddha in main hall and desperately prayed: 'O God, O Buddha, please grant me satori and I'll be humble, even bowing willingly before you.'"[147]

Jesus Christ and Christian Zen

Zen avoids the historical Jesus Christ, and for good reason. Zen does not accept differentiated beings as having relevance or reality. *The Gospel of Zen* quotes Christian mystic Meister Eckhart: "Who is Jesus? He has no name"[148]—a fitting epitaph for the Jesus of Zen, who declares, "Split wood: I am there. Lift up the stone, and you will find me there."[149] The *historical* Jesus has no more significance than wastepaper and, as Zenists would say, "wash out your mouth when you say His name." Werner Erhard once blasphemously commented that, Jesus is dog excrement, although he used the four letter equivalent.

The *essence* of Jesus however is everything and nothing, reality, the void. For Zen, Jesus is also the Buddha, as is everything, for All is One. "No matter what the situation, you cannot neglect Buddha, because you yourself are Buddha. Only this Buddha will help you completely."[150] According to Zen, Jesus Christ won't help anyone.

The sight of "Christian" Zenists denying or blaspheming Jesus while worshipping idols of Buddha is a striking one. Sitting in blissful meditation before statues of Buddha they describe the wonders of "Christian mysticism," such as Zen satori. Although they do attempt to comprehend Zen, they cannot seem to comprehend how "the beauty of Christian Zen" only masks an ugly core of rebellion and nihilism.

For Johnston, the author of *Christian Zen*, only a Zen Christ is relevant. This "Christ" is the real Christ and *is* Zen Reality. "Christ is the father of Christian mysticism" and "the great guru who knocked people into enlightenment with remarkable power."[151] "Jesus, I believe, was so filled with God that he no longer had a human personality. . . ."[152] On the other hand, the historical Jesus is depreciated as merely "the finger pointing toward the moon" and not the reality of

the moon itself (enlightenment). Those who want the "real" Christ must not allow the "grubby little merchants" of Christianity to deceive them with their false concepts about Jesus Christ:

> Properly and piously understood, one can say, "if you meet Christ, slay him!" And the meaning is: "What you see is not Christ". . . . It is not necessary to have clear-cut images and concepts of Christ. If you have no such concepts . . . how happy you are! You have left the dirty cave of Plato and are out in the beautiful sunlit air. Don't let these grubby little merchants drag you back to the murky underworld of conceptualization. Stay out. Enjoy your *samadhi*. Christ is with you. . . . The living and risen Christ [is], coextensive with the universe and buried in the hollow recesses of the human heart. . . . So for Paul, Christ is beyond concepts, beyond images, beyond thought, beyond place. . . . He is our original face before we were born.[153]

While "Christian" Zenists are fond of noting the "reverence" that Zen monks display toward Jesus, it is only a Jesus of their own making, one who revels only in Zen. As far as the biblical Christ is concerned, He can only bring spiritual darkness. "The 'Christian' conviction that Jesus is . . . the standard by which everything must be judged, is the depth of darkness to the eyes of Zen."[154]

Just as Zen openly denies the biblical God, Zen openly denies the biblical Jesus Christ. Christian Zen, then, is an oxymoron. It does *not* point anyone to ultimate reality. Put in Zen terms, whenever you say "Christian Zen," wash your mouth out.

Salvation and Works

In order to attain enlightenment, Bodhidharma, the "founder" of Zen, purportedly sat before a wall for nine years without speaking to anyone![155] One can honestly wonder if he felt the effort was worth it? (Following his example, Soto Zenists face a wall or curtain during zazen.) Nevertheless, Zen both denies salvation (or enlightenment) and affirms it.

No one needs salvation. We are perfect just the way we are; we simply do not realize it yet:

If I believe that I *must* achieve my 'salvation' I cannot avoid believing that I *must* lead others to do the same.... The refutation of this error that we are here studying is perfectly expounded in Zen, and as far as we know, nowhere perfectly but there. Zen tells man that he is free now, that no chain exists which he needs to throw off; he has only the illusion of chains. Man will enjoy his freedom as soon as he ceases to believe that he needs to free himself, as soon as he throws from his shoulders the terrible duty of salvation.[156]

In order to realize the truth, all one need *do* is Zen practice, accepting whatever is prescribed by the Zen masters.

Salvation is mystical. "Awakening is to know what reality is not. It is to cease to identify with any object of knowledge whatsoever."[157]

Salvation is by supreme effort. The very essence of Zen is self-salvation, because the way of the Buddhas is the way of unceasing effort. Dogen tells us, "If you practice the Way of the Buddhas and the Patriarchs, you will truly be saved."[158]

Shunryu Suzuki refers to the necessity of "great pure effort," that "the most important point in our practice is to have right or pure effort. Right effort directed in the right direction is necessary."[159] Paradoxically, he also declares: "If it [Buddhism] is unattainable, how can we attain it? But we should! That is Buddhism.... Even though it is impossible we have to do it."[160] Regardless, "it is the effort to improve ourselves that is valuable. There is no end to this practice."[161]

Ruth Fuller Sasaki, the Director of the First Zen Institute of America in Japan, refers to the "hours and hours of meditation upon koan after koan for years and years," noting that "the treasure of Truth lies deep within the mind of each one of us; it is to be awakened or revealed or attained only through our own efforts."[162] D. T. Suzuki informs us that, even though there is no mind: "A thoroughgoing enlightenment, however, is attained only through the most self-sacrificing application of the mind, supported by an inflexible faith in the finality of Zen.... The

necessary requirements are faith and personal effort, without which Zen is mere babble. Those who regard Zen as speculation and abstraction will never obtain the depths of it, which can be sounded only through the highest willpower."[163] According to Shibayama, "there is not a single case where one is enlightened without going through the hard and difficult training process."[164] Regardless, Zen simultaneously undermines its great efforts toward enlightenment. In the words of Deshimaru, "In Zen you must have no goal."

Clearly this is not the biblical teaching of salvation as a free gift of God's grace through faith in Jesus Christ:

"For God so loved the world that he gave his one and only Son, that whoever believes in him shall not perish but have eternal life" (John 3:16).

"For it is by grace you have been saved, through faith—and this not from yourselves, it is the gift of God—not by works, so that no one can boast" (Ephesians 2:8–9).

"He saved us, not because of righteous things we had done, but because of his mercy. He saved us through the washing of rebirth and renewal by the Holy Spirit" (Titus 3:5).

The Atonement

Zen believers reject the atonement of Christ due to Zen philosophy. First, individual spirit, the body and the personality are not real, so no *person* exists to be saved. Second, the true Self in Zen is already perfect, so it cannot require salvation. Third, sin is an illusion, so no atonement for sin is possible. Indeed, Jesus and His atonement are as much an illusion as anything else. Fourth, as human personality is an illusion, it hardly benefits from the atonement of Christ, which bestows personal immortality. Dr. Tucker Callaway observes, "The farther a man walks the Zen Way, the more completely all individuality is erased; the farther a man walks the Jesus Way, the more his individuality is sharpened."[165]

In essence, the Christian concept of the salvation of souls is a myth because there are no souls to save. "Naturally we cannot believe that each individual person has been endowed with a special and individual soul or self. Each one of us is a cell as it were in the body of the Great Self."[166] Alan Watts quotes Sokei-an Sasaki, illustrating how satori obliterates Christian teachings: "One day I wiped out all the notions from my mind. . . . I felt a little queer—as if I were being carried into something, or as if I were touching some power unknown to me . . . and Ztt! I entered. I lost the boundary of my physical body. . . . I had never known this world. I had believed that I was created, but now I must change my opinion: I was never created; I was the cosmos; no individual Mr. Sasaki existed."[167]

Since there really are no parts *of* the whole ("parts" *are* the whole), the Zenist can sincerely proclaim "I *AM* the absolute" or "I *AM* God."[168] "It is incorrect to employ such mystical terminology as 'I dwell in the Absolute,' 'The Absolute dwells in me' or 'I am penetrated by the Absolute,' etc.; for, when space is transcended, the concepts of whole and part are no longer valid; the part is the whole—I AM the Absolute, except that I am no longer 'I.' What I behold then is my real Self, which is the true nature of all things."[169] Thus, "In this state . . . I, selfless, I am supreme."[170] "In the whole universe I am supreme, and it is perfectly natural."[171]

Despite Zen's "death" to the ego, many adherents love to bask in the glory of their new found "Self." After all, if their true nature is supreme; why shouldn't they exalt it? But this easily becomes another trap. In another of Zen's paradoxes, even enlightenment can bring delusion that Zenists may find difficult to avoid. "An ancient Zen saying has it that to become attached to one's own enlightenment is as much a sickness as to exhibit a maddeningly active ego. Indeed, the profounder the enlightenment, the worse the illness. . . . My own sickness lasted almost ten years. Ha!"[172]

In Zen, one need not be humbled by looking to a Savior apart from oneself; one need only look to one's own "real" Self. There one will find true glory because the Zenist himself is the Savior of the world. This is why Zen literature contains references to the Zenist being the "savior" of all. Again, this is not meant in the sense that a Christian would conceive it, since in Zen no individual exists to save. Rather, the individual Zenist is the Savior of the world as soon as he realizes enlightenment, because he knows that all beings are already saved.

This discussion explains why Buddhists generally cringe at the thought of the Cross. Of necessity, the Buddhist must be fundamentally opposed to the Christian concept of redemption. The premise of the atonement, the very means by which God redeems man, involved horrible suffering, but this is something followers of the Buddha cannot accept. At all costs, the Buddhist seeks to escape suffering, not contemplate it or embrace it. Thus, he must not look at the Cross, and he certainly must not accept the platform from which to speak about ignorant concepts such as divine holiness or judgment on sin. Thus the image of the Cross, as well as the sacrament of communion—the perpetual reminders of Jesus' sacrifice—must be forsaken for the vastly "more enlightened" truth of impermanence and nirvana. When D. T. Suzuki contemplates the Cross he comments:

> To the Oriental mind, the sight is almost unbearable. . . . The crucified Christ is a terrible sight and I cannot help associating it with the sadistic impulse of a psychically affected brain. . . . To think that there is a self is the start of all errors and evils. . . . As there is no self, no crucifixion is needed. . . . What a contrast between the crucifixion image of Christ and the picture of Buddha. . . . In these respects, Buddhism proves to be just the opposite of Christianity.[173]

The rotund Buddha smiles serenely from the lotus position; the tormented Jesus screams in agony from a bloody cross. Opposite worldviews are indeed clearly seen. *Of course* biblical Christianity is repulsive to the Zenist or Buddhist. *Of course* it agitates and disturbs. For it has a supreme deity—an infinite, personal, triune God—and this God actually incarnates and suffers to redeem individual people.

Buddhists do their best and go to great lengths to achieve the elimination of suffering. How easy then to not even consider the story of the suffering God and the Cross. Unfortunately, in forsaking everything to end suffering, the Buddhist only guarantees his own suffering. In deliberately rejecting the way of the Cross (faith that God has already endured the suffering for us) for the way enlightenment (faith in one's own ability to end suffering), the result is, biblically, the assurance of eternal suffering. The Buddhist "finds his life"—his concern is with his own Self, his own contentment—he thereby loses it. But Jesus says that the person who loses his life for His sake will find it (Matthew 16:25).

Again, in Zen, the atonement of Christ is as much an illusion as anything else. Only to unenlightened eyes does it appear that Jesus sacrificed Himself on the Cross. As Yasutani Roshi informs us, "There is no real sacrifice."[174]

Death

In Zen, death and judgment are unreal. If there is no soul and if all is one, there can be no death or judgment in biblical terms. "What we see is illusory, without substance, like the antics of puppets in a film. Are you afraid to die? You need not be. For whether you are killed or die naturally, death has no more substantiality than the movements of these puppets."[175] "Our life and death are the same thing. When we realize this fact we have no fear of death anymore, and we have no actual difficulty in our life."[176]

Although no individual soul exists to reincarnate, Zen nevertheless believes in reincarnation. Yasutani-Roshi even notes that Shojo Zen promotes a way of meditation-induced suicide to *escape* rebirth. "With practice this power can be cultivated by anyone. In case there is no wish to die one can enter this trance-like state for a limited period—say an hour or two or one or two days—or one can remain in it indefinitely, in which event death follows naturally and painlessly, without—and this is most important—rebirth. This entire process of death without rebirth is set forth in great detail in a Buddhist philosophical work called the *Kusharon*."[177]

Logically, Zen should not teach belief in personal immortality. Still, some Zenists are agnostic on the issue, perhaps reflecting a desire to escape the despair that Zen leaves one with in its denial of personal immortality. Thus, for Yasutani-Roshi the question of whether there is *personal* survival beyond death "ultimately has no answer."[178]

The Occult

Although for Zen the supernatural, like all else, is illusionary, this does not prevent the supernatural from intruding into the world of Zen. Consider the idolatry that we previously documented in Zen practice. Historically, there is little doubt as to the reality of demons operating behind the mechanism of idolatrous practice. In Zen, as in yoga, chanting and physical postures may become vehicles to open the door to the supernatural world:

> To help awaken us to this world of Buddha-nature, Zen masters employ yet another mode of zazen, namely, the chanting of dharani and sutras. Now, a dharani has been described as "a more or less meaningless chain of words or names that is supposed to have a magical power in helping the one who is repeating it at some time of extremity." Anyone who has recited them for any length of time knows, in their effect on the spirit they are anything but meaningless. When chanted with sincerity and zest they impress upon the heart and mind the names and virtues of Buddhas and Bodhisattvas enumerated in them, removing inner hindrances to zazen and fixing the heart in an attitude of reverence and devotion. . . . Dogen attached great importance to the proper position, gestures, and movements of the body and its members during chanting, as indeed in all other modes of zazen, because of their repercussions on the mind. In Shingon Buddhism particular qualities of Buddhas and Bodhisattvas are evoked by the devotee through certain positions of his hands (called mudra) as well as body postures, and it is probably from the Shingon that this aspect of Dogen's teaching derives. In any event, the prescribed postures do induce related states of mind. . . . Conversely, each state of mind elicits from the body its own specific response. The act of unself-conscious prostration before a Buddha is thus possible only under the impetus of reverence and gratitude.[179]

Zen's emphasis on idolatry, mystical chanting, altered states of consciousness and psychic development can become vehicles to spirit contact. In Zen meditation, and in Eastern meditation generally, the practices adopted sooner or later bring one to the realm of psychic phenomena and spirits.[180] Lassalle observes that the following are to be expected in Zen practice, although they are considered "negative" in one sense, that through fascination with them the practitioner may be distracted from the goal of *satori:*

> Here we shall mention only one of the so-called negative effects: the phenomenon of *makyo* (literally, world of spirits), that is to say, apparitions, fantasies, or illusory sensations. Figures or things not actually present appear to the person meditating. They can be of a pleasant or an unpleasant nature. Sometimes Buddhas appear; at other times the mediator may face the specter of a wild animal or something just as terrifying; or lights may appear to play before the eyes. Less often sounds are heard, but at such times a person may seem to hear his name called out clearly.... Zen masters explain these effects as natural products of the mind.[181]

While such phenomena could at times be entirely mental, they could also at times involve covert or overt consorting with the biblical "principalities and powers." Many people, perhaps most, do not have the stamina to practice Zen for 20 years to achieve satori; some will undoubtedly be sidetracked into the psychic world as a result of Zen meditation. (Gedo Zen has as its main purpose the development and use of psychic abilities.) It seems clear that Zen meditation *itself* develops psychic powers, even if only some schools attempt to cultivate them. Since all Zen practice is the "same" (sitting, breathing, concentration), it is simply a matter of who wishes to *use* these powers, not whether they occur. In part, these powers seem to come by Zen's particular method of concentration (*joriki*):

> The cultivation of certain supranormal powers is also made possible by joriki, as is the state in which the mind becomes like perfectly still water.... The state of blankness in which the conscious functioning of the mind has been stopped. Now, although the power of joriki can be endlessly enlarged through regular practice, it will recede and eventually vanish if we neglect zazen. And while it is true that many extraordinary powers flow from joriki, nevertheless through it alone we cannot cut the roots of our illusory view of the world.[182]

In *The Three Pillars of Zen* we find an in-depth discussion of psychic powers (somewhat reminiscent of mediumism) and how one is to view and approach them:

> *Makyo* are the phenomena—visions, hallucinations, fantasies, revelations, illusory sensations—which one practicing zazen is apt to experience at a particular stage in his sitting. *Ma* means "devil" and *kyo* "the objective world." Hence makyo are the disturbing or "diabolical" phenomena which appear to one during his zazen. These phenomena are not inherently bad.... Broadly speaking, the entire life of the ordinary man is nothing but a makyo.... Besides those which involve the vision there are numerous makyo which relate to the sense of touch, smell, or hearing, or which sometimes cause the body suddenly to move from side to side or forward and backward or to lean to one side or to appear to sink or rise. Not infrequently words burst forth uncontrollably or, more rarely, one imagines he is smelling a particularly fragrant perfume. There are even cases where without conscious awareness one writes down things which turn out to be prophetically true. Very common are visual hallucinations. You are doing zazen with your eyes open.... Without warning everything may go white before your eyes, or black. A knot in the wood of a door may suddenly appear as a beast or demon or angel.... Many makyo involve the hearing. One may hear the sound of a piano or loud noises, such as an explosion (which is heard by no one else), and actually jump....

In the *Zazen Yojinki* we find the following about makyo: "The body may feel hot or cold or glasslike or hard or heavy or light. This happens because the breath is not well harmonized (with the mind) and needs to be carefully regulated." It then goes on to say: "One may experience the sensation of sinking or floating, or may alternately feel hazy and sharply alert. The disciple may develop the faculty of seeing through solid objects as though they were transparent, or he may experience his own body as a translucent substance. He may see Buddhas and Bodhisattvas. Penetrating insights may suddenly come to him, or passages of sutras which were particularly difficult to understand may suddenly become luminously clear to him...." Makyo, accordingly, is a mixture of the real and the unreal, not unlike ordinary dreams....

Never be tempted into thinking that these phenomena are real or that the visions themselves have any meaning. . . . Above all, do not allow yourself to be enticed by visions of the Buddha or of gods blessing you or communicating a divine message, or by makyo involving prophecies which turn out to be true. This is to squander your energies in the foolish pursuit of the inconsequential.[183]

Nevertheless, "as your practice progresses many *makyo* will appear."[184]

Zen's claim that it is "the only teaching which is not to one degree or another tainted with elements of the supernatural" is clearly false.[185] Merely to redefine occult phenomena as "illusions" does not make them so. Zen practice is an occult practice since it produces occult phenomena. Further, discarding these powers is not official doctrine. Nothing is "official doctrine" or "absolute" in Zen, only recommended. Psychic powers may be retained and used by the disciple if his "Zen mind" should desire it.

Zen theory also employs Hindu-Buddhist alleged psychic anatomies, which are themselves theoretically connected to occult powers. The "chakras," for instance, are so-called psychic centers, which when "opened" produce psychic abilities:

In short, by realigning the physical, mental, and psychic energies through proper breathing, concentration, and sitting, zazen establishes a new body-mind equilibrium with its center of gravity in the vita *hara*. . . . *Hara* literally denotes the stomach and abdomen and the functions of digestion, absorption, and elimination connected with them. But it has parallel psychic and spiritual significance. According to Hindu and Buddhist yogic systems, there are a number of psychic centers in the body through which vital cosmic force or energy flows. . . . Hara is thus a wellspring of vital psychic energies. . . . The Zen novice is instructed to focus his mind constantly at the bottom of his hara (specifically, between the navel and the pelvis) and to radiate all mental and bodily activities from that region.

With the body-mind's equilibrium centered in the hara, gradually a seat of consciousness, a focus of vital energy, is established there which influences the entire organism. . . . The "or-

gans," which collect, transform, and distribute the forces flowing through them, are called *cakras*, or centers of force. From them radiate secondary streams of psychic force. . . . In other words, these *cakras* are the points in which psychic forces and bodily functions merge into each other or penetrate each other. They are the focal points in which cosmic and psychic energies crystallize into bodily qualities, and in which bodily qualities are dissolved or transmuted again into psychic forces.[186]

Many books document the frequent hazards that accompany psychic development and occult involvement. We also document this in detail in *The Coming Darkness* and Vol. one in this series. In light of their occult practices, followers of Zen should be far more cautious concerning the so-called "illusions" of their minds.

CRITIQUE

Zen as Self-Disintegration

Sooner or later "zazen leads to a transformation of personality and character."[187] It "effects a fundamental change in oneself, philosophical and intellectual, as well as psychological. It is the total conversion of one's personality."[188]

But Zen constitutes far more than a "conversion" of one's personality; it aims at the destruction of the personality, the "lower" self. The first question that could be raised is whether Zen transformation really benefits the individual. "We have to fix our will on the void, to will the void. . . . This void is fuller than all fullness. . . . This nothingness is not unreal. Compared with it everything in existence is unreal."[189] If Zen's monistic philosophy is in error, then radical personality transformation (destruction) based on it can hardly be considered helpful. If Zen attempts the destruction of the personality, so that the individual is no more, of what value is that—to anyone? What is true for yoga is true for Buddhism; with every step along the Buddhist path the individual is destroyed a little more until there is a complete abolition. In its essence, then, Zen represents a radical denial of life, a denial of what it means to be human. As Professor of Religion Dr. Robert E. Hume remarks in

The World's Living Religions, "An utter extinction of personality and consciousness would seem to be implied by the fundamental principles of Buddhism and also by explicit statements of Buddha...."[190] Buddhist scholar Edward Conze remarks of different Buddhist schools generally, "What is common to all of them is that they aim at the extinction of belief in individuality."[191]

Nevertheless, Zenists have to live in the real world, and it is here we wish to examine an additional consequence of their monistic philosophy: the denial of morality.

Morality

Zen believers claim Zen "also molds our moral character."[192] But this is not true. Or put another way, it is true only from a Zen perspective that denies morality. First, Zen teaches that "only upon full enlightenment" can one distinguish good from evil.[193] As a result, those without Zen enlightenment remain ethically unaware, or blind to Zen's "true morality."

Does Zen really inculcate morality, as it claims? It is interesting that when asked, "What is the primary meaning of the holy reality," the alleged founder of Zen, Bodhidharma, replied first, that there is "nothing that can be called holy" and, second, that reality was "Emptiness, not holiness."[194] When asked if he were a holy man, he replied, "I don't know."[195] If Zen is so moral, why was Huang Po concerned about "harmful" concepts like *virtue,* lest people be led astray into dualism?[196] More than one Buddhist has told us that all actions, even the most virtuous, are to be considered evil if they tie one to duality. Virtually all Christian social work is thus obliterated, not to mention Christian missions.

Buddhists may claim that their moral ideal always consists in the highest good, but it must be remembered that this is said from the perspective of Buddhist philosophy. The highest good in Buddhism is enlightenment, something destructive of morality. Only "enlightened" actions are considered good, because once one is enlightened everything one does is good by definition *even* if it is evil, even if it conflicts with social convention or biblical standards. This approach to ethics is demonstrated by a dialogue between Dom Aelard Graham, author of

Zen Catholicism, and Buddhist Fuji Moto Roshi: "Christians try to conform their conduct to some external law given by God or given by the church. That cannot be, of course, in Buddhism. ... The concept of ethics does not come into Buddhism. ... If one is enlightened, everything he does is good. ... In other words, he lives in the domain where there is no distinction between good and evil. ... As to ethics, we are not concerned with ethics, good and evil, in Buddhism. ... The function of religion is to let us work out or live in accordance with the true nature, with the self-nature."[197] Thus, to adopt a system of Christian ethics, or Christianity itself for that matter, would be to work against one's true nature, and that, naturally, could not be something good in Buddhism. In fact, it would be something evil. Zen does not *exalt* righteousness, it demeans it as an illusion, even as an "evil" concept.

Buddhists argue that practitioners will not abuse the Buddhist denial of ethics. But if Zen's denials of morality will *not* be misused, why does Alan Watts note that "many a rogue has justified himself" by them?[198] Do not people generally live consistently with their presuppositions about life? So will not Zen practitioners be influenced by Zen philosophy, such as its nihilism and amoralism? How could it be otherwise? Buddhist teachings have logical, practical consequences. To think otherwise is foolish. Did not many Zenists of the tenth century use Buddhist philosophy as a means "to antinomianism and even to licentiousness"?[199] Does not Alan Watts himself warn us of our own era: "Therefore Zen might be a very dangerous medicine in a social context where convention is weak, or, at the other extreme, where there is a spirit of open revolt against convention ready to exploit Zen for destructive purposes."[200] In Japan has not Zen been used to justify Japan's aggressive wars against other nations historically? We might ask, what in the name of Buddha did the Zen masters expect? Do they think that when they say that good and evil do not exist, or that evil can be something good, that it will have no impact? Scripture speaks clearly to this: "Woe to those who call evil good and good evil, who put darkness for light and light for darkness, who put bitter for sweet and sweet for bitter. Woe to those who are wise in their own eyes and clever in their own sight." (Isaiah 5:20–21)

We also encounter the ungodliness of Zen morality when we are told that Buddhist love (termed "compassion"), being "all-embracing" and fully non-discriminative, should love even evil. "The greater love is, the less it binds itself to conditions." Thus it is implied we should love heresy, and false gods, and even the Devil![201] In such a philosophy, what then is the *real* evil? "A clinging to the 'one true God,' the 'one true religion.'"[202] Christianity, it seems, is the true malevolent force in this world. Quoting two Western Zenists (Christmas Humphreys and Alan Watts), Lit-sen Chang observes how Zen compromises God's holiness:

> Zen compromises the holiness of God in a very serious manner. In the conception of Zenists, sin against God does not exist. As they boldly declare that the "immaculate Yogins do not enter Nirvana and the precept violating monks do not go to hell; to avoid sin and evil by obedience to any moral law is only an idle attempt. Every being must act according to their Nature." "There is no question and no need of rules of morality." Our Lord says of men "By their fruits ye shall know them." The same rule of judgment applies to doctrines. Even they themselves do not deny that "immature disciples would make the inclusiveness of Zen an excuse for pure libertinism."[203]

And so we find Zen authorities, not to mention mere practitioners, employing Zen philosophy to justify whatever behavior they wish. As the famous novelist Aldous Huxley confessed in his *Ends and Means,* referring to sexual, economic and political liberation, "For myself, as, no doubt, for most of my contemporaries, the philosophy of meaninglessness was essentially an instrument of liberation."[204]

If Zen truly supports moral character, why do we find such appalling statements as the following?

Alan Watts:

> It is indeed the basic intuition of Zen that there is an ultimate standpoint from which "anything goes".... Or as is said in the *Hsin-hsin Ming* [quoting Seng-ts'an]: "If you want to get the plain truth,/Be not concerned with right and

wrong./The conflict between right and wrong/Is the sickness of the mind." Within the conventional limits of a human community, there are clear distinctions between good and evil. But these disappear when human affairs are seen as part and parcel of the whole realm of nature.[205]

The extremes of beat Zen need alarm no one, since, as Blake said, "the fool who persists in his folly will become wise."[206]

Huang Po:

> Then comes the concept "God is good" which, as Christian mystics have pointed out, detracts from His perfection; for to be good implies not being evil—a limitation which inevitably destroys the unity and wholeness inseparable from perfection. This, of course, is not intended to imply that "God is evil," or that "God is both good and evil." To a mystic, He is none of these things, for He transcends them all.[207]

Dogen:

> To offer a diet of beans and water in an effort to save the old and infirm merely caters to the misguided love and deluded passions of this brief life.[208]

> If you renounce this life and enter Buddhism, your aged mother might starve to death.... How can this not accord with the Buddha's will? It is said that if one son leaves his home to become a monk, seven generations of parents will gain the Way. How can you afford to waste an opportunity for eternal peace because of concern for the body in this present fleeting life?[209]

Yet Dogen also says that if we "practice evil" we "violate the will of the Buddha; that we should 'practice good.'"[210] Does he mean to say that moral living is Zen living, because to do good in Zen is as "evil" as to do evil, both being "binding" concepts? Or is he perhaps here speaking of doing good in a Christian sense, as Zenists are sometimes forced to do? If so, we must ask why, if Zen is true, Zenists are forced to live in a Christian world rather than a Zen one?

Yuan-wu:

> If you are a real man, you may by all means drive off with the farmer's ox, or grab the food from a starving man.[211]

Shunryu Suzuki:

When the Buddha comes, you will welcome him; when the devil comes, you will welcome him.[212]

We should find perfection in imperfection.... Good is not different from bad. Bad is good; good is bad.[213]

Christmas Humphreys:

Without any sense of separateness there is no need of benevolence, or of love for one's fellow men.[214]

Alan Watts:

Therefore in Zen there is neither self nor Buddha to which one can cling, no good to gain and no evil to be avoided, no thoughts to be eradicated and no mind to be purified, no body to perish and no soul to be saved.[215]

Hui Hai:

Thinking in terms of good and evil is wrong; not to think so is right thinking.[215a]

Shunryu Suzuki:

Even to have a good thing in your mind is not so good.[215b]

The Apostle Paul, then, from the Zen perspective, is quite mad, "Finally, brothers, whatever is true, whatever is noble, whatever is right, whatever is pure, whatever is lovely, whatever is admirable—if anything is excellent or praiseworthy—think about such things" (Philippians 4:8).

Of course we might ask, given the Zen mindset and philosophy, who is to say good is not evil or that evil should *not* be done? Remember, in Zen, to "do good" is as "evil" as "doing evil." We must thus be mentally "free" from doing good. If "morality . . . must be relinquished"[216] isn't the reason because "doing good" will bind us to illusions and prevent enlightenment?

Scripture supplies a different attitude: "We are God's workmanship, created in Christ Jesus to do good works, which God prepared in advance for us to do" (Ephesians 2:10). The Scripture tells us we are to be "zealous for good

deeds" (Titus 2:14 NAS); and to be "careful to engage in good deeds" (Titus 3:8 NAS); and be "ready for every good deed" (Titus 3:1 NAS). The Apostle Peter illustrates his lack of Zen enlightenment when he writes, "Who is going to harm you if you are eager to do good?" (1 Peter 3:13).

But do not all Zenists live as dualists? Do not Zen monks say to practice *good?* Then why not practice *evil?* If "all is one, what is bad," as Charles Manson once asked? Whatever *is,* is "good"—or simply "IS,"—and this is a tacit *approval* of evil, no matter how uncomfortable practitioners may feel or "logically" attempt to deny it. "In Zen, 'evil' is non-Zen, period."[217]

Dangers, Deceptions and Drug Parallels

Dangers of the Zen path. Individuals attempting to attain "enlightenment" run certain risks, as we documented in-depth in our *Encyclopedia of New Age Beliefs.*[218] The description of "a mosquito trying to bite on a bar of iron"[218a] is an appropo if mild analogy, but obviously a dumb mosquito. The problem is that the human mind was not made to function in the Zen way, and only by serious *abuse* can it be made to do so. As one Zen master urges as part of a ten-point plan to attain "serene-reflection," "try to put your mind into a state as though you had just been shocked."[219] Indeed, it may require two or three years just to "understand" one koan.[220] Satori itself could be years or decades away. And what is our reward? R. F. Sasaki tells aspiring Zenists, "What can they hope to get through all this effort? The classic Zen answer and the Buddhist answer as well is 'Nothing.'"[221]

In the words of Dr. Karl Reichelt, Lit-sen Chang observes that some Zenists "develop very odd qualities. The Chinese have coined a humorous name for them and say that they have become 'mo-wong,' such as 'demon king,' which means they have become mentally deranged."[222] Zen expert Blofeld warns practitioners that "techniques requiring long hours of strenuous meditation and all but the simplest breathing exercises are EXCEEDINGLY DANGEROUS without the guidance of an expert teacher,"[223] although some Zen schools require no teacher. Dr. R. C. Zaehner observes that in

Zen "the risk of madness is always there." He quotes Hui Neng, the sixth Zen patriarch, as warning that some Zenists get "lost" in non-attachment. Because they become attached to *detachment* and stay in a "non-existent" state of mind, "consequently they are so attached to this method as to become insane."[224]

What a contrast to the Christian faith, to the free gift of eternal life in heaven, and to the promise of a God who "is not unjust; he will not forget your work and the love you have shown him as you have helped his people . . ." (Hebrews 6:10). In Christianity, there is no denial or searing of the conscience; there are standards of living that become their own rewards. There are no philosophical hazards for the mind or body, but there is an overall state of well-being generated from God's grace. There is no "disinterestedness toward oneself as a distinct being,"[225] but there is an awareness of oneself as created in God's image and as loved greatly by Him. There is no "let the self perish utterly,"[226] but there is the promise of eternal immortality. There are no evils of idolatry and occultism, no despair over nihilism, there is only the gift of eternal life by grace through faith in Jesus Christ (Ephesians 2:8–9) and the wonderful knowledge that one is loved deeply by God.

Deception. Zen claims uniqueness and finality in mystical experience. But why should Zen mysticism be considered special? For Zen offers only one of many possible mystical states, none of which have absolute authority for determining reality or objectively answering life's fundamental questions. [227] Does Zen have any more convincing claim to absolute reality than any number of other contrary mystical traditions? As Dr. David Clark observes, "the level of agreement among various mystics is so small as to be disappointing to the adherents of one particular world view."[228]

While the Zenist may claim his "nothing" is really "everything," and that he has found Reality, he has no way of knowing that what he thinks is Reality is not simply the deception of his own mind. Given the years of mental and physical abuse the Zenist is subject to, it would surprise us greatly if the mind did not break

down and malfunction perceptually. After all, to sit before a wall for nine years, to listen for an entire year for the sound of one hand clapping,[229] or to mull over the word "Mu" or some other Koan year after year, is bound to have an effect. Like anything else, if regularly abused, the mind will no longer function properly. Far from being a perception of true reality, we think that satori is more the reflection of a serious dysfunction of the mind.

Drug parallels. Significantly, in terms of its mental effects, Zen promoters have noted parallels between Zen use and drug use. R. C. Zaehner comments that "psychedelic drugs can produce every and any kind of mystical experience" from pantheism to Nirvana to intellectual rapture.[230] Zen satori, then, could be partly the consequence of chemical alteration of the brain due to extreme Zen methods:

> To anyone who has neither achieved Zen enlightenment nor a "peak" experience with LSD or similar drugs, however, most descriptions of Zen enlightenment and some of LSD experience would appear to be almost identical. There is the same "oceanic feelings," the same transformation of *self*-consciousness into *cosmic* consciousness, the same "becoming one with Nature and the universe and in this union [the same] experience [of] an immense joy.". . . The resulting experience of seeing all things as One and One as all *does* seem to be the same[231] (brackets in original).

Meditation authority William Johnston observes, "There is, I believe, a second reason why modern people get the hang of Zen rather easily, though I hesitate to mention it lest I be misunderstood. Anyhow, it is this: the widespread use of drugs. . . . All I say here is that they seem to introduce people to a level of psychic life that has something in common with Zen and mysticism."[232]

In conclusion, as a way of life, Zen offers extreme practical difficulties. Its irrationalism and nihilism are destructive to human welfare. Its denial of morality is dangerous. The potential for mental collapse or other pathology is always present. The possibility of spiritual deception likewise. And there are genuine parallels to Zen enlightenment and drug states. Why should all these be accepted to gain literally nothing? What's the point? Is Zen really worth the risk?

TALKING WITH MEMBERS*

Zen vs. Christianity

Based on our discussion of Zen and the documentation supplied, one logical starting point for talking with Zenists would be to point out and then drive home the personal and social consequences of Zen. One could use many of the quotations in this chapter with the following material for this purpose. The basic issue is whether Zen can offer people what they truly need in life, and usually want—purpose, value, peace, meaning and so on. Because no one wishes to end his life and discover he had been deceived, Zen believers can be encouraged to critically examine the implications of their philosophy for themselves, their children and their society. If one were to make a list of what Zen offers through zazen and what Christianity offers through a personal relationship with Jesus Christ, the result would be striking, such as in the chart below.

Nevertheless, Shunryu Suzuki claims that Zen supplies genuine value to life. "When you realize this fact, you will discover how meaningless your old interpretation was, and how much useless effort you had been making. You will find the true meaning of life and . . . you will enjoy your life."[233] We can only disagree. It is logically impossible to find true meaning in life given the acceptance of Zen nihilism. If Zenists find meaning and enjoyment in life it is *not* because of a Zen philosophy that is atheistic, irrational and replete with implications of ultimate despair. In Zen, nothing has value and nothing finally matters. If Zenists find meaning in life, it is because they are living with some Christian assumptions, however unwittingly, not Buddhist ones.

It is also important to discover how open an individual Zen practitioner is to discussion, because some are not willing to talk about such important issues. For many Zenists, "one who knows does not speak and he who speaks does not know."

Clearly, there is little one can say to someone who denies language and reason, and also wishes not to listen. A Zenist may claim, as one did, "I do not care if I go to hell."[234] But some will care. Most of the time, Zenists have to live in the world God created, not the internal Zen world formed by altered states of consciousness. Again, practitioners of Zen must live their lives as if Christian presuppositions were *true* and Zen presuppositions *false*. We have seen this at several points in this chapter. How do Zen practitioners explain this, if their philosophy really is true?

But if their philosophy *is* true, what difference does it make? Nothing matters, *not even Zen*. And if it is false, Zen becomes a terrible waste of time. Indeed, the more one *truly* lives the Zen philosophy, the more open one should be to consider other options. Zen is so contrary

ZEN VS. CHRISTIANITY	
ZEN	CHRISTIANITY
The individual has no value (no self exists)	The individual has eternal value (created in God's image)
Extinction at death	Personal immortality in heaven at death
No God	A loving God who is perfect in every way
The destruction of personal morality with all that this entails	An absolute morality centered in the character of God
No meaning to life (nihilism)	Meaning in life now and forever in eternity

*See also this section in Buddhism chapter.

to the way the world functions and to the manner in which we were created to live that it will sooner or later self-destruct for many practitioners. This is why there are many quite frustrated dabblers, as well as frustrated committed Zenists, who are ready for a change in religious conviction. They are tired of the toil, turmoil, torture and meaninglessness they have experienced under the constraints of Zen.

Dr. Lit-sen Chang's interest in Zen began at a young age. He became an influential Zenist, being elected the first President of Kiang-nan University.[235] He was so committed that he diligently followed the Zen path for some fifty years. Yet upon conversion to Christ, whatever value Zen had for him withered like an unsolved koan. In his exposé, *Zen-Existentialism: The Spiritual Decline of the West,* he warns: "I should say now that what Zen offered me was merely a technique of self-intoxication or a sense of false security.... [satori was] a result of many years of the most strenuous devastation of rational understanding."[236] "Such philosophy of radical freedom and subjectivism which makes man autonomous from all objective forms and divine law and revelation, will surely lead mankind to an horrible chaotic and nihilistic darkness."[237] He concludes:

> In a word, Zen is not only biblically and theologically untenable, but also psychologically and socially detrimental. As we pointed out in another chapter, Zen is a technique by which to achieve "a mental breakdown." It is "a bankruptcy of thought process" or "mental catastrophe".... It is a cult of iconoclasm, a disastrous surrender to Nihilism. Zen has been exaggerated as "the way of liberation," but it is rather a kind of mystical "self-intoxication," "a childish dependence upon magical omnipotence," ... In Japan, it was "condemned by other sects as dangerous to culture because of its iconoclastic teachings." While it had been used by Japanese militarists as an incentive for aggressive war, it is entirely "impotent to do something tangible to aid suffering humanity, judging by the cities and slums and rural misery of Asia." Now many Westerners, weary of their conventional religion and philosophy, find some charm in Zen and have become prey to its plausible teachings. If unchecked, the consequences will be surely disastrous to our culture.[238]

With many millions of people exposed to Zen today, we are already experiencing the consequences. But should not the Zen practitioner bear (and feel) some degree of responsibility for the burdens he has placed upon society by his nihilism? And what of the harm Zen philosophy has wrought to Christian belief in the West? If nothing really matters, why are many Zenists so desirous of converting Christians to Zen and of undermining Christian philosophy? Will they not themselves suffer the consequences culturally and spiritually?

So-called Zen Christians especially should rethink their priorities. As we have seen, in Zen there is no room for Christian morality, or for Jesus Christ (as Savior or anything else), or for a personal God or for personal immortality. In adopting Zen, uninformed Christians seem to have no idea of the consequences or the cost of abandoning Christianity. Is there any idea of what has been exchanged, of what was lost and what was gained? Quite literally, everything was lost and nothing was gained. In any field of life other than mystical religion, such an exchange would not be contemplated for even a moment.

Dr. Tucker Callaway was a Christian personally familiar with Zen and also a missionary to Japan. He spent over twenty years in dialogue with Buddhists in their temples. He also personally took up the practice of zazen so that Zenists would know that he knew Zen as a practitioner and yet still chose to be a Christian. His book, *Zen Way—Jesus Way* contrasts, point by point, the Christian and Zen doctrines, including their presuppositions and views on oneness, Reality, freedom and so on. Dr. Callaway clearly shows that everything is not the same and that the Zen way is *not* the Jesus way. "Those who say all religions are essentially the same either have little substantial information on the matter, or else they are committed to a Zenlike monistic philosophy which demands the denial of all differences as a necessary dogma of their religious faith. These must preach 'tolerance,' with avid intolerance for anyone who disagrees."[239] Further:

> Both Zen and Jesus say, "The truth will make you free." Zen truth is the insight gained in Enlightenment. The freedom it engenders is the liberty to accept everything just as it is with no

hang-ups, no inhibitions; with thankfulness and serenity. No matter how different one set of moral rules may seem from another, Zen knows there is no difference. The Enlightened One is delivered from bondage to all rules. . . . The one limiting factor for Only-Mind is its own nature. . . . Only-Mind is not free to violate its own nature. Only-Mind cannot sin. And since Only-Mind is everything, nothing can sin. The impossibility of sin in Zen is a dramatic evidence of its absolute qualitative difference from the Jesus Way.[240]

Zenists may deny sin, but because sin is real, because all Zenists do sin, and because acknowledgment of sin is necessary to salvation, this is another vital point for discussion with Zen practitioners. Sin constitutes the Zenist's fundamental dilemma before God. "But your iniquities have separated you from your God; your sins have hidden his face from you, so that he will not hear" (Isaiah 59:2). In the end, then, Zen believers must choose between themselves as "no self," or Only Mind, or themselves as personal individuals who need redemption in Jesus Christ: "If anyone would come after me, he must deny himself and take up his cross and follow me. For whoever wants to save his life will lose it, but whoever loses his life for me and for the gospel will save it. What good is it for a man to gain the whole world, yet forfeit his soul? Or what can a man give in exchange for his soul?" (Mark 8:34–37).

Zenists may respond, "The answer, the eternal home, will never, never be found so long as you are seeking it, for the simple reason that it is you yourself."[241] But Jesus says, "Ask and it will be given you; seek and you will find; knock and the door will be opened to you" (Matthew 7:7). And besides, how can the individual be the solution to his own problems when as an individual he does not even exist? Indeed, Zen philosophy has fatal problems at every point one cares to examine it, whether in the field of metaphysics, morality, epistemology or practical living.

Even in all its alleged glory, Zen offers no answers. Indeed, *nothing* exists, so how can there be answers, let alone an eternal home in Zen? There is only a deafening silence. Remember D. T. Suzuki argues that even *after* enlighten-

ment we still "know not definitely what the ultimate purport of life is."[242] But, with Jesus Christ, the Zenist *can* know. "These things I have written to you who believe in the name of the Son of God, in order that you may *know* that you have eternal life" (1 John 5:13 NAS, emphasis added). "Truly, truly, I say to you, he who believes *has* eternal life" (John 6:47 NAS, emphasis added).

Contradictory Teachings

Zen believers may also be challenged to ask themselves how is it possible to know that Zen is true when the philosophy is riddled with contradictions? D. T. Suzuki himself confesses that, "even among the Zen masters themselves there is a great deal of discrepancy, which is quite disconcerting. What one asserts another flatly denies or makes a sarcastic remark about it, so that the uninitiated are at a loss what to make out of all these everlasting and hopeless entanglements."[243] The chart on the next page notes some internal Zen contradictions.

One wonders, was the original face of the Zen practitioner smiling or frowning as he contemplated Zen contradictions?

If they are frank, even committed Zenists must acknowledge the superiority of the Christian view, both philosophically and practically. Tucker Callaway records an interesting discussion that he had with D. T. Suzuki, a discussion which points out the difficulty that even the most devoted Zen teacher has with his own philosophy. "Toward the end of the interview with Daisetz Suzuki, I said that while Buddhism accepts all things, just as they are, as good, [Christians] find things imperfect and therefore strive to change them. To this Suzuki surprisingly replied, 'Yes, that's the good side of Christianity. Buddhists accept everything as it is, perhaps. That is bad. They don't go out of their way to do good.'"[244] Even Suzuki could not live consistently as a Zenist. Callaway points out the implications:

> It is difficult for me not to believe he meant this seriously. It seemed to me that at that moment he departed from his Zen presuppositions and expressed a genuine value judgment. Whether he did, or whether he remained only-mind

"I put samadhi foremost and wisdom afterwards." Master Wanshi (cited in *ZCLA [Zen Center of Los Angeles] Journal*, p. 4)	"I put wisdom foremost and samadhi afterwards." Master Engo (cited in *ZCLA Journal*, p. 4).
"Without it [satori] there is no Zen, for the life of Zen begins with the 'opening of satori'." Dr. Suzuki (Sohl and Carr, *The Gospel According to Zen: Beyond the Death of God*, p. 33)	"It's not that Satori is unimportant, but it's not that part of Zen that needs to be stressed." (Shunryu Suzuki, *Zen Mind, Beginners Mind*, p. 9)
"The achievement of the aim of Zen, as Suzuki has made very clear . . . implies overcoming the narcissistic self-glorification and the illusion of omnipotence." (Ross, *World of Zen: An East–West Anthology*, p. 199)	"I AM the Absolute." The man who has realized Satori . . . being intensely aware of the infinite riches of his nature." (Ross, *World of Zen*, pp. 67, 221)
"Enlightenment, when it comes, will come in a flash. There can be no gradual, no partial Enlightenment. . . . By no means can he be regarded as partially Enlightened." (Huang Po in Ross, *World of Zen* p. 69)	"There are, however, greater and lesser satoris." (R. F. Sasaki in Ross, *World of Zen*, p. 26)
"If your effort is headed in the wrong direction, especially if you are not aware of this, it is deluded effort." (Shunryu Suzuki, *Zen Mind, Beginner's Mind*, p. 59)	"Even if it [your effort] is in the wrong direction, if you are aware of that, you will not be deluded." (Shunryu Suzuki, *Zen Mind, Beginner's Mind*, p. 61)
"So it can be said that a Zen which ignores or denies or belittles satori is not true daijo Buddhist Zen. . . . Today many in the Soto sect hold that since we are all innately Buddhas, satori is not necessary. Such an egregious error reduces Shikantaza, which properly is the highest form of sitting, to nothing more than bompu Zen, the first of the five types."(Yasutani Roshi, *Three Pillars of Zen*, p. 45–46)	"Error has no substance; it is entirely the product of your own thinking." (Huang Po, *The Zen Teaching of Huang Po*, p. 80)
"Zen is most emphatically not to be regarded as a system of self-improvement, or a way of becoming a Buddha. In the words of Lin chi, 'if a man seeks the Buddha, that man loses the Buddha.'" (Alan Watts, *The Way of Zen*, p. 125)	"Because searching one's own mind leads ultimately to enlightenment, this practice is a pre-requisite to becoming a Buddha. No matter whether you have committed either the ten evil deeds or the five deadly sins, still if you turn back your mind and enlighten yourself, you are a Buddha instantly." (Yasutani Roshi, *The Three Pillars of Zen*, p. 161) "It is said in the Diamond Sutra: 'those who relinquish all forms are called Buddhas (Enlightened Ones).'" (*The Zen Teaching of Hui Hai*, p. 53)
"Sages seek from mind, not from the Buddha; fools seek from the Buddha instead of seeking from mind." (Blofield, *The Zen Teaching of Hui Hai*, p. 44)	"The Buddha is none other than Mind." (*The Three Pillars of Zen*, pp. 283–284)
"In point of fact, Zen has no 'mind' to murder; therefore there is no 'mind murdering' in Zen. . . . Nothing really exists throughout the triple world; '*where do you wish to see the mind?*'" (Lit-sen Chang, '*Zen Existentialism*, p. 152, quoting D. T. Suzuki, *Introduction to Zen Buddhism* [New York: Philosophical Library, 1949], pp. 42–43)	"Zen purposes to discipline the *mind* itself, to make it its own master, through an insight into its proper nature. This getting into the real nature of one's *own* mind is the fundamental object of Zen Buddhism." (Chang, *Zen-Existentialism*, quoting D.T. Suzuki, *Introduction to Zen Buddhism*, p. 40)

viewing himself, me, and the entire interview with complete detachment, the value judgment he articulated is crucial.

From the Zen point of view, not going out of one's way to do good is evidence of Enlightenment, as also would be not going out of one's way not to do good. Picking and choosing and the urge to "do good" are evidences of Ignorance. The freedom of the Zen Way is the freedom not to choose. But the freedom of the Jesus Way denies one the freedom not to choose.... If Suzuki seriously meant what he said ... he, at least for that moment, was off the Zen way.[245]

How could Dr. Suzuki possibly admit to Dr. Callaway, as he did, that "Buddhism has a great deal to learn from Christianity,"[246] if Zen is really true? Perhaps Zenists *should* listen to the words of Dr. Suzuki, learn from Christianity and read the words of Jesus Christ in detail. Here they will find true enlightenment, for in Christ "are hidden all the treasures of wisdom and knowledge" (Colossians 2:3).

The difficulty for Zen is that even Zen masters betray Zen by how they live and think. Is a philosophy that one consistently betrays, and that consistently betrays itself, a true philosophy of life? Or is Zen itself the real koan?

Zenists have declared that "ignorance is in reality the Buddha-nature."[247] Read that again, slowly! Based on this statement we might conclude with a "koan" of our own predicated upon Christian presuppositions. "When we say perception is an illusion, are we in our senses or are we not?"

Questions for Practitioners

1. How can koans originate from the Buddha nature?[248]

2. How many Zenists are unnecessarily struggling "no matter what the hardship or anxiety may be?"[249] How many Zenists have committed suicide because of its meaninglessness? "For example, Ch'u Yuan said, 'Everybody in the world is drunk. Only I am sober!' He refused to follow the ways of the world, but he ended his life in the waters of the Ts'ang-lang River."[250]

3. If conflict between right and wrong is the sickness of the mind, why do Zen masters concern themselves with distinguishing right from wrong?[251] If Zen Masters have sick minds should their conclusions be heeded?

4. Some people have practiced Zen for ten years (or longer) without ever attaining enlightenment.[252] Is it wise to spend so much time seeking a condition described even by Zen Masters as encompassing a "half-mad state"?

5. How can Zen monks speak of other Zen "approaches [that] are not authentic, true Zen at all"?[253] If Zen Masters deny each other's basic teachings on zazen,[254] satori and other key elements, how can its disciples be certain that what they learned is true? As Callaway points out:

In fact, Zen cannot even believe that Zen's own doctrine is more true than the doctrine of other religions. The moment one thing is preferred to another, the realization that all things are equally Only Mind has been set aside. This leads to the basic dilemma of Zen and, for that matter, of all other monistic or non-dualistic systems of thought. The only possible conclusion to believing that the insights of Zen are true is to believe that truth cannot be known. But if it is believed that truth cannot be known, it cannot be believed that the premises of Zen are true.[255]

6. After satori is achieved, "When the ecstasy resides, we have acquired nothing extraordinary and certainly nothing peculiar."[256] If it is nothing special, why practice zazen? "If you think you will get something from practicing zazen, already you are involved in impure practice."[257]

7. If the mind does not exist, how can it realize satori and then perceive its own illusion? Is it like discovering one has a mind, after thinking one does not? If the mind does exist, why deny its reasoning abilities? But if so, why teach Zen? As Huang Po said: "If I now state that there are no phenomena and no Original Mind, you will begin to understand something of the intuitive Dharma silently conveyed to Mind with mind.[258]

Scripture Contrasts

ZEN	THE BIBLE
"There is no this and no that." (Huang Po in Ross, *World of Zen*, pp. 70–71)	"In the beginning God created the heavens and the earth." (Genesis 1:1)
"Why seek a doctrine? As soon as you have a doctrine you fall into dualistic thought." (Huang Po, *Zen Teaching of Huang Po*, p. 71)	"You must teach what is in accord with sound doctrine." (Titus 2:1)
"Even to have a good thing in your mind is not so good." (Shunryu Suzuki, *Zen Mind, Beginner's Mind*, p. 127)	"Finally, brethren, whatever is true, whatever is honorable, whatever is right, whatever is pure, whatever is lovely, whatever is of good repute, if there is any excellence and if anything worthy of praise, let your mind dwell on these things." (Philippians 4:8 NAS)
"The master does not 'help' the student in any way, since helping would actually be hindering. On the contrary, he goes out of his way to put obstacles and barriers in the student's path." (Watts, *The Way of Zen*, p. 163)	"In everything I showed you that by working hard in this manner you must help the weak and remember the words of the Lord Jesus, that He Himself said, 'It is more blessed to give than to receive.'" (Acts 20:35 NAS)
"Your own Mind is itself Buddha, the Void-universe. There will then be no anxiety about life or death. . . ." (*The Three Pillars of Zen*, p. 102)	"But I will warn you whom to fear: fear the One who after He has killed has authority to cast into hell; yes, I tell you, fear Him!" (Luke 12:5 NAS)

NOTES

1. Nancy Wilson Ross, *The World of Zen, an East-West Anthology* (New York: Vintage Books), p. 252.
2. Lit-sen Chang, *Zen-Existentialism: The Spiritual Decline of the West* (MA: Presbyterian and Reformed Pub., Co., 1969), p 42.
3. D. T. Suzuki, *Introduction to Zen Buddhism* (New York: Philosophical Library, 1949), pp. 40, 44-45, 64, 131 cited by Lit-sen Chang, *Zen-Existentialism*, pp. 33-34.
4. Alan Watts, *The Way of Zen* (New York: Knopf, Inc. and Random House, Inc., 1957), p. x.
5. Lit-sen Chang, *Zen-Existentialism*, p. 27.
6. *Yasutani Roshi Memorial Issue, ZCLA Journal* (n.d.), p. 26.
7. Philip Kapleau, ed., *The Three Pillars of Zen* (Boston: Beacon Press, 1967), p. xl; cf. Lit-sen Chang, *Zen-Existentialism*, pp. 160-20.
8. Ibid., cf. Lit-sen Chang, *Zen-Existentialism*, pp. 114-125.
9. John Blofeld, *The Zen Teaching of Hui Hai on Sudden Illumination* (New York: Samuel Weiser, Inc., 1972), pp. 24-34; Ernest Wood, *Zen Dictionary* (New York: Philosophical Library, Inc., 1962), pp. 22-24, 78-79; Roshi Jiyu Kennett, *Zen Is Eternal Life* (Emeryvile, CA: Dharma Publishing, 1976), pp. xxiii-xxv, 85-86; Blofeld, *The Zen Teaching of Huang Po, on the Transmission of Mind* (New York: Grove Press, Inc., 1958), pp. 10-12.
10. Blofeld, *The Zen Teaching of Hui Hai*, p. 250.
11. Daisetz Suzuki, *Essays in Zen Buddhism* (New York: Harper and Brothers, 1949), p. 57.
12. Ibid., p. 51.
13. Ibid., p. 52.
14. Daisetz Suzuki, *Essays in Zen Buddhism, First Series*, pp. 161-162.
15. Ibid., p. 226.
16. Ross, section III.
17. Lit-sen Chang, *Zen-Existentialism*, p. 27.
18. Blofeld, *The Zen Teaching of Huang Po*, p. 10.
19. Ibid., p. 8.
20. Ibid., pp. 8-9.
21. Cf. Daisetz Suzuki, *Essays*, p. 168.
22. Shunryu Suzuki, *Zen Mind, Beginner's Mind* (New York: Weatherhill, 1976), pp. 46-47.
23. Kennett, p. 15.
24. Robert Sohl and Audrey Carr, eds., *The Gospel According to Zen, Beyond the Death of God* (New York: The New American Library, 1970), p. 14.
25. Lit-sen Chang, *Zen-Existentialism*, p. 31.
26. Garma Chang, *The Practice of Zen* (New York: Harper and Row Publishers, 1970), p. 175.
27. Ross, p. 25.
28. Tucker N. Callaway, *Zen Way—Jesus Way* (Rutland, VT: Charles E. Tuttle Co., Inc., 1976), p. 26.
29. Watts, citing the Zenrin Kushu.
30. Kapleau, *Three Pillars*.

31. Shunryu Suzuki, p. 126.
32. *ZCLA Journal*, Summer/Fall 1973, p. 26.
33. Daisetz Suzuki, p. 21.
34. *ZCLA Journal*, Summer/Fall 1973.
35. Kapleau, *Three Pillars*, p. 67.
36. Daisetz Suzuki, p. 115.
37. Kennett, p. 13.
38. Sohl and Carr, *Gospel According to Zen*, p. 14.
39. D.T. Suzuki, "What Is Zen," in Ibid., pp. 13-14.
40. Kapleau, *Three Pillars*, pp. 76-79.
41. Ross, p. 64.
42. Blofeld, *The Zen Teaching of Huang Po*, p. 78.
43. Ibid., p. 71.
44. D. T. Suzuki, "The Koan," in Ross, p. 232.
45. Ross, p. 232.
46. Blofeld, trans., "The Zen Teaching of Huang Po on the Transmission of Mind," from the Chun Chow Record of the Zen Master Huang Po (Tuan Chi) in Ross, *World of Zen*.
47. Daisetz Suzuki, Series 1.
48. Daisetz Suzuki, p. 21.
49. Ibid., p. 18; cf. p. 23.
50. Ibid., pp. 70-71.
51. Ibid., p. 18.
52. Ross, p. 5, citing *The Diamond Sutra I Believe*.
53. Irmgard Schloegl, *The Zen Teaching of Rinzai* (The Record of Rinzai) (Berkeley, CA: Shambhala Publications, 1975), pp. 44-45.
54. Kapleau, p. 112.
55. Charles Luk, ed., *The Transmission of the Mind Outside the Teaching* (New York: Grove Press, Inc., 1975), pp. 133-135.
56. Ibid.
57. Schloegl, p. 28.
58. Wood, *Zen Dictionary*, p. 74.
59. Watts, p. 146; cf. p. 125.
60. For a look at the theological consequences, see David Clark, *The Pantheism of Alan Watts*, pp. 41-48. Also see Watt's *Beyond Theology*.
61. Ross, p. 13.
62. Lit-sen Chang, *Zen-Existentialism*, p. 127.
63. Kondo, "Zen in Pyschotherapy: The Virtue of Sitting," in Ross, p. 206.
64. Ross, p. 269.
65. Callaway, pp. 146-147.
66. Ross, pp. 228-229.
67. Callaway, p. 145.
68. Blofeld, *The Zen Teaching of Hui Hai*, p. 139.
69. Callaway, p. 146.
70. Schloegl, pp. 43-44.
71. Beiho Masunaga, *A Primar of Soto Zen* (Honolulu: East-West Center Press, 1971).
72. Z. Shibayama, *A Flower Does not Talk*, p. 81 cited by R. C. Zaehner, *Zen Drugs and Mysticism* (New York: Pantheon Books, 1972), p. 116.
73. Watts, p. 3.
74. Ibid., p. 115.
75. Lit-sen Chang, *Zen—Existentialism*, pp. 30-32.
76. Kapleau, p. 69.
77. Shunryu Suzuki, *Zen Mind, Beginner's Mind*, p. 46.
78. Wood, *Zen Dictionary*, pp. 127-128.
79. Ibid., pp. 109-110.
80. Kapleau, p. xvi.
81. Ibid., p. 8.
82. Yasutani Roshi, "Theory and Practice of Zazen," in Kapleau, p. 43.
83. Kapleau, pp. 11-13.
84. Ibid., p. 20.
85. Ibid., pp. 218-219.
86. Ibid., p. 64.
87. Ross, pp. 50-51.
88. Luk, p. 186n.
89. From Lit-sen Chang, p. 48, citing Ernest Becker, *Zen: A Rational Critique* (New York: Norton, 1961), pp. 14, 76, 57, 81, 140.
90. Ross, p. 49.
91. Wood, p. 82.
92. Ibid., p. 75.
93. Ibid., p. 68.
94. Ibid.
95. Kapleau, p. 106.
96. Ross, p. 260.
97. Suzuki, *Zen Buddhism, Selected Writings*, Barrett, ed. (New York: Doubleday, 1956), pp. 92, 12, cited by Lit-sen Chang, p. 141.
98. Kapleau, pp. 227-228.
99. Ibid., pp. 205-208.
100. Ibid., pp. 244-245, emphasis added.
101. Ibid., p. 16.
102. Lit-sen Chang, p. 31.
103. Blofeld, *The Zen Teaching of Hui Hai*, p. 32.
104. D. Suzuki, "The Sense of Zen" in Ross, pp. 39-40.
105. Deshimaru website: http://www.cwi.nl/~gruau/en/mondo/main/node101.htm1#section 003320000000000 00000)
106. Shunryu Suzuki, *Zen Mind, Beginner's Mind*, p. 76.
107. Sohl and Carr, pp. 11-12.
108. Cover flap; cf. Part Two.
109. H. M. Lassalle, *Zen Meditation for Christians* (LaSalle, IL: Open Court, 1974), pp. 156, 160, emphasis added.
110. Ibid., p. 78.
111. Deshimaru website.
112. Lassalle, p. 100.
113. Ibid., pp. 103-104.
114. Kennett, p. 31.
115. William Johnston, *Christian Zen* (New York: Harper and Row Publishers, 1974), p. 8.
116. Daisetz Suzuki, *Essays*, p. 152.
117. Sohl and Carr, pp. 16-17, 60.
118. Daisetz Suzuki, *Essays*, p. 344.
119. Sohl and Carr, p. 15.
120. Suzuki, "The Awakening of a New Conscience in Zen," in Ross, p. 228.
121. Daisetz Suzuki, *Essays*, p. 343.
122. Kapleau, pp. 79-80.
123. R. F. Sasaki, "Zen: A Method for Religious Awakening," in Ross, p. 17.
124. Lassalle, p. 68.
125. Ibid., pp. 66, 200.
126. Blofeld, *The Zen Teaching of Hui Hai*, p. 92.
127. Sohl and Carr, p. 41.
128. Lit-sen Chang, p. 128.

129. Daisetz Suzuki, *Essays*, p. 43.
130. R. F. Sasaki in Ross, p. 18.
131. Sohl and Carr, p. 5.
132. Lasalle, p. 136.
133. Lit-sen Chang, p. 128.
134. Sohl and Carr, p. 49.
135. "Beat Zen Square Zen and Zen," in Ross, pp. 333-334.
136. Lit-sen Chang, p. 160.
137. Eric Fromm, *Zen Buddhism and Psychoanalysis*, cited by Ross, p. 252.
138. Deshimaru website.
139. Shunryu Suzuki, *Zen Mind, Beginner's Mind*, p. 67.
140. Ibid.
141. Suzuki, "The Awakening of a New Conscience in Zen," in Ross, p. 228.
142. "The Zen Teaching of Huang Po on the Transmission of Mind" in Ross, p. 228.
143. Johnston, p. 5.
144. Ibid., p. 52.
145. Ibid., pp. 18-19.
146. Ibid., pp. 211-212.
147. Ibid., p. 220.
148. Sohl and Carr, p. 92.
149. Ibid., p. 72.
150. Shunryu Suzuki, *Zen Mind, Beginner's Mind*, p. 76.
151. Johnston, pp. 28, 90.
152. Ibid., p. 14.
153. Ibid., pp. 51-53.
154. Callaway, p. 158.
155. Wood, pp. 16-17.
156. Sohl and Carr, pp. 48-49.
157. Watts, p. 171.
158. Masunaga, p. 58.
159. Shunryu Suzuki, *Zen Mind, Beginner's Mind*, p. 59.
160. Ibid., p. 45.
161. Ibid.
162. R. F. Sasaki, "Zen: A Method for Religious Awakening," in Ross, p. 25.
163. Suzuki, "the Koan," in Ross, p. 56.
164. Zaehenr, p. 126, citing *A Flower Does Not Talk*, p. 107.
165. Ross, p. 18.
166. Ibid., p.18
167. Watts, p. 121.
168. Ibid., p. 67.
169. Ross, p. 67 (Huang Po).
170. Kapleau, p. 16.
171. Ibid., pp. 288-289.
172. Kapleau, p. 289.
173. D. T. Suzuki, "Mysticism: Christian and Buddhist," in David W. McKain, ed., *Christianity: Some Non-Christian Appraisals* (Westport, CT: Greenwood Press, 1976), pp. 114, 116-18.
174. *ZCLA Journal*, p. 41.
175. Kapleau, p. 75.
176. Shunryu Suzuki, *Zen Mind, Beginner's Mind*, p. 94.
177. Kapleau, p. 45.
178. Ibid., p. 70.
179. Ibid., pp. 16-18.
180. See our *Encyclopedia of New Age Beliefs* chapters on meditation, yoga, altered states, Eastern gurus, enlightenment, mandalas, visualization.
181. Lassalle, pp. 39-40.
182. Kapleau, p. 47.
183. Ibid., pp. 38-41.
184. Ibid., p. 99.
185. Ibid., p.78.
186. Ibid., pp. 14, 67-68.
187. Ibid., p. 14.
188. Zaehner, p. 126 citing Shibayama, *A Flower Does Not Talk*, p. 117.
189. Ross, p. 288.
190. Robert E. Hume, *The World's Living Religions* (New York: Charles Schribner Sons, 1952), p. 76.
191. Edward Conze, *Buddhism Its Essence and Development*, p. 13.
192. Daisetz Suzuki, *Essays*, p. 25.
193. Kapleau, p. 14.
194. *ZCLA Journal*, p. 19.
195. Kapleau, p. 231n.
196. "The Zen Teaching of Huang Po on the Transmission of the Mind," in Ross, p. 67.
197. Dom Aelard Graham, *Conversations: Christians and Buddhists* (New York: Harcourt Brace Jovanovich, 1968), pp. 100-03.
198. Watts, "Beat Zen Square Zen and Zen," in Ross, pp. 337-338.
199. Wood, p. 159.
200. Watts, p. 143.
201. Garma Chang, *The Practice of Zen*, pp. 196-197.
202. Ibid.
203. Lit-sen Chang, *Zen-Existentialism*, pp. 132-133.
204. Aldous Huxley, *Ends and Means* (London: Chatto and Windus, 1946), pp. 270; cf. 273.
205. Watts, "Beat Zen," in Ross, p. 335.
206. Ibid., p. 339.
207. Blofeld, *The Zen Teaching of Huang Po*, p. 15.
208. Masunaga, p. 88.
209. Ibid., p. 260.
210. Ibid., p. 50.
211. Cited in Watts, p. 147.
212. Shunryu Suzuki, *Zen Mind, Beginner's Mind*, pp. 42-43.
213. Ibid., p. 103.
214. "Christmas Humphreys on Satori," in Ross, p. 47.
215. Watts, pp. 152-153.
215a. Blofeld *The Zen Teaching of Hui Hai*, p. 50.
215b. S. Suzuki *Zen Mind, Beginner's Mind*, p. 127.
216. Blofeld, *The Zen Teaching of Hui Hai*, p. 57.
217. *ZCLA Journal*, pp. 41-42.
218. See *Encyclopedia of New Age Beliefs*, chapters on enlightenment, meditation, yoga, altered states.
218a. Ross, p.13.
219. Chang Chen-Chi, "Practicing Zen Through Observing One's Mind in Tranquility—the Non-Koan Way in Zen," in Ross, p. 219.
220. R. F. Sasaki, "Zen: A Method for Religious Awakening," in Ross, p. 26.
221. Ibid., p. 218.
222. Lit-sen Chang, *Zen—Existentialism*, p. 133, citing *Meditation and Piety in the Far East* (New York Harper, 1954), pp. 14-15.
223. Blofeld, *The Zen Teaching of Hui Hai*, p. 40.

224. Zaehner, p. 132 citing *The Platform Scripture*, p. 14; Wing-Tsit Chan, p. 49.
225. Sohl and Carr, p. 48.
226. Huang Po, in Ross, p. 73.
227. William James, *The Varieties of Religious Experience;* Evelyn Underhill, *Mysticism;* Robert Crookall, *The Interpretation of Cosmic and Mystical Experiences;* R.G. Zaehner, *Mysticism Sacred and Profane;* Walter Pahnke, "Drugs and Mysticism," in *Psychedelics: The Uses and Implications of Hallucinogenic Drugs* and his earlier works; W. T. Stace, *The Teachings of the Mystics.*
228. Clark, *The Pantheism of Alan Watts,* p. 88; cf. chapter 3, pp. 11, 46-47, 86-95.
229. Sohl and Carr, p. 78.
230. Zaehner, p. 83.
231. Ibid., pp. 113-114.
232. Johnston, p. 35.
233. Shunryu Suzuki, *Zen Mind, Beginner's Mind,* p. 95.
234. Suzuki, citing Shinran, a great religious person in Japan, *Essays,* p. 43.
235. Lit-sen Chang, *Zen-Existentialism,* p. 203.
236. Ibid., pp. 206-207.
237. Ibid., p. 159.
238. Ibid., p. 147.
239. Callaway, pp. 231-232.
240. Ibid., pp. 234-235.
241. Sohl and Carr, p. 115.
242. Suzuki, "The Sense of Zen," in Ross, pp. 39-40.
243. Suzuki, "The Koan," in Ross, p. 54.
244. Callaway, pp. 238-239.
245. Ibid.
246. Ibid., p. 148.
247. Watts, p. 146.
248. Wood, p. 66.
249. Masunaga, p. 84.
250. Ibid., p. 44.
251. Ibid., pp.71-72, 106-107; *ZCLA Journal,* pp. 41-42.
252. Kapleau, p. 57.
253. Zaehner, p. 115, citing Shibayama, *A Flower Does Not Talk,* pp. 47-48.
254. Kapleau, p. 56.
255. Ibid., p. 50.
256. Ibid., p. 57.
257. Shunryu Suzuki, *Zen Mind, Beginner's Mind,* p. 60.
258. Blofeld, *The Zen Teaching of Huang Po,* p. 106.

DOCTRINAL APPENDIX

This appendix is designed to provide quick information on major biblical doctrinal themes. It offers quick comparisons and contrasts to any group's teachings on important subjects. For example, if you are reading the Jehovah's Witnesses' view of Jesus Christ as a creation of God and you need a biblical defense of His deity, simply turn to the appropriate section in the Doctrinal Appendix. Virtually all cults and new religions deny almost all key biblical doctrines, so whatever theology section of a chapter you are in, you can know that a biblical corrective is supplied in this appendix.

Each section begins with a brief disclaimer showing that the topic under consideration is not what the cults often claim it is. The goal here is to allow the reader quick access to a few key claims of cults on a given topic and then to present in brief fashion what the Bible itself teaches about that topic. Individually, these sections may also be useful for group Bible study or for talking with members of these groups. Much of the material in the Doctrinal Appendix comes from revised but previously published materials by John Ankerberg and John Weldon and, whether in or out of print, is used with permission.

THE CHRISTIAN FAITH— WHY IT'S TRUE

The Christian faith was not the fabrication of man, for whatever reason. It was not the invention of the disciples, the Apostle Paul or the Council of Nicea in the fourth century. Nor is the Christian faith simply a result of the cultural evolution of the Jewish people, or an ersatz reviving of the ancient mystery religions. By whatever means the cults suggest, Christianity is not the deception they claim it is. Jesus' original teachings were never perverted, only to have them revived by this cult or that cult, whether Mormonism, Jehovah's Witnesses, Christian Science, Unity School of Christianity, Armstrongism, or others.

Historical facts and the canons of logic document that Christianity alone is fully true and the only religion in the world truly based upon divine revelation. To the extent that any Christian body or denomination holds to that divine revelation, it may be considered genuinely Christian, as opposed to being considered aberrational Christianity, heterodoxy, heresy or Christian in name only.

Besides being divine revelation, biblical faith is rational, not blind or based in subjectivism. Christianity is the one religion simultaneously most likely to be true and, given its claims, the easiest to disprove if false. Therefore, an individual searching for truth should begin that search with biblical Christianity. If knowing the truth is in one's best interest, then the claim of Christianity to have the truth and the claim of Jesus Christ to be the truth is worth investigation. Further, because Christianity is a religion based on *divine* revelation (the content of the Bible), it is Christianity which submits to biblical authority. In other words the church does not sit in judgment upon the content or legitimacy of the Bible; the Bible sits in judgment upon the content or legitimacy of religious bodies claiming to be Christian, whether inside the fold of traditional Christianity or outside.

For those who are already searching but who do not share our Christian worldview, especially members of cults and new religions, why might they consider openly evaluating the Christian religion? First, because it is good to do so. All religions can't be true because they all conflict with one another. All might be false, but only one can be true. The honest search for truth is one of the most noble philosophical endeavors of life. As noted earlier, Plato declared, "Truth is the beginning of every good thing, both in Heaven and on earth; and he who would be blessed and happy should be from the first a partaker of the truth." Jesus Christ claims that He is the truth and that people can determine the legitimacy of His claims to their own satisfaction. Any religion that claims and produces solid evidence on behalf of an assertion that it alone is *fully* true is worth serious consideration for that reason alone. Only biblical Christianity does this.

The kind of existence that Christianity offers a seeker is one of deep and abundant satisfaction, regardless of the pain and disappointment one may experience in life. Jesus claimed that He would give us what we really need in life: true meaning and purpose now, and when we die everlasting life in a glorious heavenly existence far beyond our current comprehension. Noted Oxford and Cambridge scholar C. S. Lewis correctly understood one of the most heartfelt yearnings of mankind when he wrote, "There have been times when I think we do not desire heaven but more often I find myself wondering whether, in our heart of hearts, we have ever desired anything else."[1] Jesus declared, "I have come that they may have life, and have it to the full" (John 10:10). He said, "I am the resurrection and the life. He who believes in me will live, even though he dies" (John 11:25). He also said, "I am the truth" (John 14:6). "Everyone on the side of truth listens to me" (John 18:37).

Christianity is unique in both the evidence upon which it rests and the doctrines it teaches. Just as Jesus Christ is unique, so is the religion based upon Him. There is sufficient evidence from virtually every department of human experience and study to objectively demonstrate that Christianity is true. Regardless of the many truth claims in other religions, it is the faith of the nonChristian that is internally and externally lacking. While it may be "politically incorrect" in some minds to say such a thing, the only issue is: "Is it true"? Again, Christian faith is an objective, rational faith. Whatever their merits, nonChristian faiths are typically irrational, subjective and without sufficient grounding as to historical claims, and they lack credible claims to be divine revelation. Despite the widespread misperception that Christianity involves a blind "leap of faith," that description does fit nonChristian religions generally.

Scholars Are Convinced

Christianity is not just intellectually credible, whether considered philosophically, historically, scientifically, ethically or culturally, but from an evidential perspective it is superior to other worldviews, secular or religious. If Christianity were obviously false, as cults and most skeptics charge, how could esteemed scholars and intellectuals logically make their declarations of faith? While testimonies *per se* mean little, if they are undergirded by the weight of scholarly evidence they can hardly be dismissed out of hand. Mortimer Adler is one of the world's leading philosophers. He is chairman of the board of editors for *The Encyclopaedia Britannica*. He is also the architect of *The Great Books of the Western World* series and its amazing *Syntopicon*, and he is director of the prestigious Institute for Philosophical Research in Chicago and author of *Truth in Religion, Ten Philosophical Mistakes, How to Think About God, How to Read a Book*, plus over 20 other challenging books. He simply asserts, "I believe Christianity is the only logical, consistent faith in the world."[2] How could a philosopher of Adler's calibre make such a statement? Because he knows it can't rationally be made of any other religion.

Philosopher, historian, theologian and trial attorney John Warwick Montgomery, holding nine graduate degrees in various fields argues, "The evidence for the truth of Christianity overwhelmingly outweighs competing religious claims and secular world views."[3] His 50-plus books and 100-plus scholarly articles indicate exposure to a wide variety of nonChristian religious and secular philosophies. How could an individual of such intellectual stature use a descriptive phrase as "overwhelmingly outweighs" if it were obviously false?

The individual widely considered to be the greatest Protestant philosopher of God in the world, Alvin Plantinga, recalls, "For nearly my entire life I have been convinced of the *truth* of Christianity."[4] On what basis can one of the world's greatest philosophers make such a declaration if the evidence for Christianity is unconvincing, as cultists and critics charge?

Dr. Drew Trotter is executive director of the Center for Christian Studies at Charlottesville, Virginia. He holds a doctorate from Cambridge University. He argues that "logic and the evidence both point to the reality of absolute truth, and that truth is revealed in Christ."[5]

If we are looking for evident truths, then perhaps we should consider the words of noted economist and sociologist, George F. Gilder, author of *Wealth and Poverty*, who asserts, "Christianity is true and its truth will be discovered anywhere you look very far."[6]

Dr. Alister McGrath is Principal of Wycliffe Hall, Oxford University. He studied at Oxford and Cambridge universities and is research lecturer in theology at Oxford. He is considered one of the most influential Christian writers in the world, and his numerous books include an acclaimed text on apologetics, *Bridge Building*, as well as *Intellectuals Don't Need God and Other Myths*. He declares that the superior nature of the evidence for Christianity is akin to that found in doing good scientific research:

> When I was undertaking my doctoral research in molecular biology at Oxford University, I was frequently confronted with a number of theories offering to explain a given observation. In the end, I had to make a judgment concerning which of them possessed the greatest internal consistency, the greatest degree of correspondence to the data of empirical observation, and the greatest degree of predictive ability. Unless I was to abandon any possibility of advance in understanding, I was obliged to make such a judgment. . . . I would claim the right to speak of the 'superiority' of Christianity in this explicative sense.[7]

The noted Christian scholar, Dr. Carl. F. H. Henry, wrote a 3000-page, 6-volume work titled *God, Revelation and Authority*. After his exhaustive analysis, Henry declared, "Truth is Christianity's most enduring asset. . . ."[8] In his definitive *Baker Encyclopedia of Christian Apologetics* 1999, p. 785, leading Christian scholar Dr. Norman L. Geisler, author of *When Cultists Ask, When Critics Ask* and *When Skeptics Ask*, writes, "The only system of truth is the Christian system." Such accolades could be multiplied repeatedly. Indeed, as Dr. Geisler comments, "In the face of overwhelming apologetic evidence, unbelief becomes perverse. . . ."[9]

There is also Christianity's founder, Jesus Christ, who is utterly original and totally unique when compared to every other religious leader who has ever lived. In the words of an article in *Time* magazine, His life was, simply, "the most influential life that was ever lived."[10] In addition, the Christian Bible itself is clearly the most influential book in human history. If Jesus Christ and the Christian Scriptures continue to exert unparalleled influence in the world, shouldn't they be considered worthy of truly impartial investigation? If objective evidence points to Christianity alone being fully true, then it seems that only personal bias can explain people's unwillingness to consider seriously the claims of Jesus Christ on their life.

A further reason that those of other religious persuasions, secularists too, should be receptive to Christianity is because we live in an increasingly poisonous age experientially. In our pluralistic and pagan culture, almost anyone is a viable target for conversion to any of a wide variety of false beliefs and their consequences—from various cults and New Age occultism to solipsism and nihilism. Philosophies of despair and potent occult experiences can convert even those who think they are the least vulnerable. "There is a great deal of research that shows that all people, but especially highly intelligent people, are easily taken in by all kinds of illusions, hallucinations, self-deceptions, and outright bamboozles—all the more so when they have a high investment in the illusion being true."[11] In other words, even in this life the personal welfare of the nonChristian may be at risk.

When one examines the arguments and attacks made against Christianity for 2,000 years, by some of the greatest minds ever, guess what one finds? Not one is valid. Not one, individually or collectively, disproves Christianity. Even with the most difficult problems, such as the problem of evil, Christianity has the *best* answer of any religion or philosophy; the best solution to the problem.

If the leading minds of the world have been unable to disprove Christianity, this may explain why many of the other leading minds in the world have accepted it. As James Sire correctly points out in *Why Should Anyone Believe Anything At All?* an argument for belief, religious or other, must be secured on the best evidence, validly argued and able to refute the strongest objections that can be mustered against it.[12] The Christian faith fits these criteria.

Obviously, if the God of the universe has revealed Himself and is the only true God, and if Christ is the only true way of salvation, then we would expect convincing evidence to substanti-

ate this. Not just some evidence, or inferior evidence—so that a person has a dozen equally valid options in the choice of their religion—but superior evidence. Dr. John Warwick Montgomery asks:

What if a revelational truth-claim did not turn on questions of theology and religious philosophy—on any kind of esoteric, fideistic method available only to those who are already "true believers"—but on the very reasoning employed in the law to determine questions of fact? . . . Eastern faiths and Islam, to take familiar examples, ask the uncommitted seeker to discover their truth experientially: the faith-experience will be self-validating. . . . Christianity, on the other hand, declares that the truth of its absolute claims rests squarely on certain historical facts, open to ordinary investigation. . . . The advantage of a jurisprudential approach lies in the difficulty of jettisoning it: legal standards of evidence developed as essential means of resolving the most intractable disputes in society. . . . Thus one cannot very well throw out legal reasoning merely because its application to Christianity results in a verdict for the Christian faith.[13]

So, let's assume that a God of truth is dedicated to truth and that He desires that people find Him. Indeed, "From one man he made every nation of men, that they should inhabit the whole earth; and he determined the times set for them and the exact places where they should live. God did this so that men would seek him and perhaps reach out for him and find him, though he is not far from each one of us" (Acts 17:26–27). What is the most logical place to begin our search for divine revelation? Wouldn't it be the one religion that God has made stand out from all the rest? Logically, the best and only practical way to see if one religion is absolutely true is to start with the largest, most unique, influential and evidentiary religion in the world. "In the past God overlooked such ignorance, but now he commands all people everywhere to repent. For he has set a day when he will judge the world with justice by the man he has appointed. He has given *proof of this* to all men by raising him from the dead" (Acts 17:30–31). It seems more reasonable to determine whether or not *this* religion is true than to seek another approach such as examining, one by one, all religions from A to Z, or picking one randomly by personal preference, or by accepting a religion as a result of subjective experience.

The problem is that, not being grounded in objective, historical evidence, all nonChristian religions are experientially based. As such, they prove nothing because of their inherent subjectivism. Thus, having even profound religious experiences, alone, cannot prove one's religion is true. And, obviously, to attempt to examine *all* religions (whether the sequence is random, preferential or alphabetical) would be a daunting, confusing and in the end an impossible task.

If there is only one God, and if only one religion is fully true, then one should not *expect* to discover sustainable evidence in any other religion. And indeed, no other religion, anywhere, large or small, has sustainable evidence in its favor. If no credible evidence exists for any other religion, and if only Christianity has compelling evidence on its behalf, why should time be spent examining religions that have no basis to substantiate their claims, especially when there may be significant negative consequences for trusting in them, not only in this life but the next life as well?

It is much easier, and more logical, to start by examining the probabilities of truth on the highest end of the scale. We examined some of these in our book *Ready with an Answer* (Harvest House, 1997). In "The Value of an Evidential Approach," William J. Cairney (Ph.D., Cornell) discusses some of the possibilities that constitute genuine evidence for the fact God has inspired the Bible and the Christianity based on it:

History Written in Advance. We can all write history in retrospect, but an almighty, omnipotent, Creator would not be bound by our notions of space and time, and would thus be able to write history before it occurs. Suppose that we encountered a sourcebook that contained page after page of history written in advance with such accuracy and in such detail that good guessing would be completely ruled out.

Prescience. Suppose that in this same sourcebook, we were able to find accurate statements written

ages ago demonstrating scientific knowledge and concepts far before mankind had developed the technological base necessary for discovering that knowledge or those concepts. . . .

Historical Evidence. Suppose that in this same sourcebook, we were to find historical assertions that time after time were verified as true as historical scholarship continued. . . .

Archeological Evidence. Suppose that in this same sourcebook, statements that are difficult to verify are made about people and places, but as archeology "uncarths" more knowledge of the past, time after time the sourcebook is seen to be true in its assertions.

Philosophical and Logical Coherence. Suppose that this same sourcebook, even though written piecemeal over thousands of years, contains well-developed common themes and is internally consistent.

And suppose all of these evidences hang together without internal contradiction or literary stress within the same anthology. Collectively, we could not take these evidences lightly.[14]

Indeed, and this is why, overall, the evidence strongly asserts that Christianity *is* true, whether or not anyone agrees. The evidence for Christianity remains powerful whether it is internal (the documents), philosophical, moral, historical, scientific, archeological or when compared with the evidence found in other religions. For example, "The competence of the New Testament documents would be established in any court of law," and, "Modern archeological research has confirmed again and again the reliability of New Testament geography, chronology, and general history."[15] (This is especially true in the biased, liberal biblical studies cited by the cults to reject biblical faith, where we find the paradox of those being closest to the truth often snubbing their noses at it. As the noted classical scholar Professor E. M. Blaiklock points out, "Recent archeology has destroyed much nonsense and will destroy more. And I use the word nonsense deliberately, for theories and speculations find currency in biblical scholarship that would not be tolerated for a moment in any other branch of literary or historical criticism."[16])

In conclusion, no one can successfully argue that Christianity and its origins have not been thoroughly investigated—as if some unrecognized aspect of it might yet prove its downfall. As the fifth edition of *Man's Religions* by John B. Noss points out, "The first Christian century has had more books written about it than any other comparable period of history. The chief sources bearing on its history are the gospels and epistles of the New Testament, and these—again we must make a comparative statement—have been more thoroughly searched by inquiring minds than any other books ever written."[17] In essence, only Christianity meets the burden of proof necessary to say "This religion alone is fully true." When the cults claim otherwise, they are mistaken.

Notes

1. C. S. Lewis, *The Problem of Pain* (New York: Macmillan, 1962), p. 145.
2. As cited in an interview in *Christianity Today*, November 19, 1990, p. 34.
3. John W. Montgomery (ed.), *Evidence for Faith: Deciding the God Question* (Dallas: Word, 1991), p. 9.
4. Alvin Plantinga, "A Christian Life Partly Lived," in Kelly James-Clark (ed.), *Philosophers Who Believe* (Downer's Grove, IL: InterVarsity, 1993), p. 69, emphasis added.
5. As interviewed in the *Chattanooga Free Press*, July 23, 1995, p. A-11.
6. L. Neff, "*Christianity Today* Talks to George Gilder," *Christianity Today*, March 6, 1987, p. 35, cited in David A. Noebel, *Understanding the Times: The Religious Worldviews of Our Day and the Search for Truth* (Eugene, OR: Harvest House, 1994), p. 13.
7. Alister E. McGrath, "Response to John Hick" in Dennis L. Okholm and Timothy R. Phillips (eds.), *More Than One Way? Four Views on Salvation in a Pluralistic World* (Grand Rapids, MI: Zondervan, 1995), p. 68.
8. Ajith Fernando, *The Supremacy of Christ* (Wheaton, IL: Crossway, 1995), p. 109.
9. Norman L. Geisler, "Joannine Apologetics" in Roy B. Zuck (gen. ed.), *Vital Apologetic Issues: Examining Reasons and Revelation in Biblical Perspective* (Grand Rapids, MI: Kregel, 1995), p. 37.
10. Richard N. Ostling, "Who Was Jesus?" *Time*, August 15, 1988, p. 37.
11. Maureen O Hara, "Science, Pseudo-Science, and Myth Mongering," Robert Basil (ed.), *Not Necessarily the New Age: Critical Essays* (New York: Prometheus, 1988), p. 148.
12. James Sire, *Why Should Anyone Believe Anything at All?* (Downer's Grove, IL: InterVarsity Press, 1994), p. 10.
13. John Warwick Montgomery, "The Jury Returns: A Juridical Defense of Christianity," in John Warwick Montgomery (ed.), *Evidence for Faith: Deciding the God Question* (Dallas: Probe Books, 1991), pp. 319-20.
14. William J. Cairney, "The Value of an Evidential Approach," in Montgomery (ed.), *Evidence for Faith*, p. 21.
15. Montgomery, "The Jury Returns: A Juridical Defense of Christianity," in Montgomery (ed.), *Evidence for Faith*, pp. 322, 326.
16. E. M. Blaiklock, *Christianity Today*, Sept. 28, 1973, p.13.
17. John B. Noss, *Man's Religions*, 5th ed. (New York: Macmillan, 1974), p. 417.

Recommended Reading

John Ankerberg, John Weldon, *Ready with an Answer; Knowing the Truth about Salvation;* C. S. Lewis, *Mere Christianity;* Francis Schaeffer, *He Is There and He Is Not Silent;* Norman Geisler, *Baker Encyclopedia of Christian Apologetics.*

THE BIBLE—THE MOST UNIQUE BOOK IN THE WORLD

The Bible is not the product of human invention or ingenuity, nor does it contain a mixture of truth and error. It is not a hidden book requiring "higher" or "enlightened" consciousness in order to interpret it properly. Nor is the Bible, despite the claims of the cults, an incomplete revelation requiring additional scripture to interpret it or to fulfill God's purpose. Biblical claims leave us few options. Either the Bible is what it claims—the literal inerrant Word of God—or it is not possible to know if God has revealed Himself to us truthfully.

The facts of the Bible cannot be explained by recourse to human theories concerning its origin, and the biblical data itself leave inerrancy as the only option concerning its contents. The God of Scripture has revealed Himself as a God of truth, so errors in the autographs (the original writings) would prove that God was not their author. Indeed, since no other religion offers genuine evidence for belief in their God, apart from the Bible we are forced to remain agnostic about God. He might exist, but beyond general revelation we can know nothing about Him. The following seven points are necessary for understanding what the Bible is.

1. Biblical Inspiration

The Bible claims to be the inspired Word of God. "All Scripture is God-breathed [*theopneustos*] and is useful for teaching, rebuking, correcting and training in righteousness, so that the man of God may be thoroughly equipped for every good work" (2 Timothy 3:16). In what sense is the Bible inspired? Biblical inspiration is (a) verbal (extending to the very words, not just the ideas, of Scripture), (b) plenary (extending equally to every part of Scripture) and (c) perspicuous (sufficiently clear for the average person to understand and be spiritually nourished without recourse to scholarly or technical insight). Directly or indirectly, the Bible claims or implies divine inspiration hundreds of times. Here are several examples:

This word came to Jeremiah from the LORD: "Take a scroll and write on it all the words I have spoken to you concerning Israel, Judah and all the other nations from the time I began speaking to you in the reign of Josiah till now." (Jeremiah 36:1–2)

Jesus answered, "It is written: 'Man does not live on bread alone, but on every word that comes from the mouth of God.'" (Matthew 4:4)

For prophecy never had its origin in the will of man, but men spoke from God as they were carried along by the Holy Spirit. (2 Peter 1:21)

For I did not speak of my own accord, but the Father who sent me commanded me what to say and how to say it. . . . Whatever I say is just what the Father has told me to say. (John 12:49–50)

The revelation of Jesus Christ, which God gave him to show his servants what must soon take place. (Revelation 1:1)

In the past God spoke to our forefathers through the prophets at many times and in various ways. . . . (Hebrews 1:1)

The word of the LORD that came to Hosea. . . . (Hosea 1:1)

The word of the LORD came to Ezekiel. . . . (Ezekiel 1:3)

Moses then wrote down everything the LORD had said (Exodus 24:4; see also 31:24).

. . . you should remember the words spoken beforehand by the holy prophets and the commandment of the Lord and Savior spoken by your apostles. . . . [Our] beloved brother Paul, according to the wisdom given him, wrote to you . . . letters, speaking in them of these things,

in which are some things hard to understand, which the untaught and unstable distort, as they do the rest of the Scriptures. (2 Peter 3:2, 15, 16 NAS)

2. The Bible Is Authoritative and Powerful

"'Is not my word like fire,' declares the LORD, 'And like a hammer that breaks a rock in pieces?'" (Jeremiah 23:29). Because the Bible is the Word of God it is the most important literature in all the earth. It is important for what it is and what it does. ". . . My word that goes out from my mouth . . . will not return to me empty, but will accomplish what I desire and achieve the purpose for which I sent it" (Isaiah 55:11). "For the word of God is living and active. Sharper than any double-edged sword, it penetrates even to dividing soul and spirit, joints and marrow; it judges the thoughts and attitudes of the heart" (Hebrews 4:12). Because of its divine nature, ignorance of the Bible is spiritually and otherwise dangerous, a point illustrated throughout this Encyclopedia. As Jesus told the hypocritical religious leaders of His day, "You are in error because you do not know the Scriptures or the power of God" (Matthew 22:29).

3. Scriptural Declarations Concerning the Bible's Own Authority

The Old Testament

Eternal

Isaiah 40:8	The grass withers and the flowers fall, but the word of our God stands forever.
Psalm 119:89	Your word, O LORD, is eternal; it stands firm in the heavens.
Psalm 138:2	I will bow down toward your holy temple and will praise your name for your love and your faithfulness, for you have exalted above all things your name and your word.

Perfect and Trustworthy

Proverbs 30:5–6	Every word of God is flawless; he is a shield to those who take refuge in him. Do not add

to his words, or he will rebuke you and prove you a liar.

Psalm 12:6   And the words of the LORD are flawless, like silver refined in a furnace of clay, purified seven times.

Psalm 18:30   As for God, his way is perfect; the word of the LORD is flaw-less. He is a shield for all who take refuge in him.

Psalm 19:7–9   The law of the LORD is perfect, reviving the soul . . . the judg-ments of the LORD *are* true *and* righteous altogether.

True

Psalm 119:43, 142, 151, 160   The word of truth . . . your law is true . . . all your command-ments are true . . . All your words are true; all your righ-teous laws are eternal.

Holy and Righteous

Psalm 105:42   For he remembered his holy promise given to his servant Abraham.

Psalm 119:123   My eyes fail, looking for your salvation, looking for your righteous promise.

Psalm 119:140   Your promises have been thor-oughly tested, and your ser-vant loves them.

Good

Jeremiah 33:14   I will fulfill the gracious promise I made. . . .

Vital (and verbal)

Isaiah 59:21   "As for me, this is my covenant with them," says the Lord. "My Spirit, who is on you, and my words that I have put in your mouth will not depart from your mouth, or from the mouths of your children, or from the mouths of their de-scendants from this time on and forever," says the LORD.

Jesus Christ and the Gospels

Note Jesus' view of God's Word:

Eternal

Matthew 24:35   Heaven and earth will pass away, but my words will never pass away.

Trustworthy

Matthew 5:18   I tell you the truth, until heaven and earth disappear, not the smallest letter, not the least stroke of a pen, will by any means disappear from the Law until everything is ac-complished.

John 5:47   But since you do not believe what he [Moses] wrote, how are you going to believe what I say?

John 10:35   . . . the Scripture cannot be broken . . .

John 12:49–50   For I did not speak of my own accord, but the Father who sent me commanded me what to say and how to say it. I know that his command leads to eternal life. So whatever I say is just what the Father has told me to say.

John 17:8   I gave them the words you gave me . . .

Luke 16:17   It is easier for heaven and earth to disappear than for the least stroke of a pen to drop out of the Law.

True

John 17:17   Sanctify them by the truth; your word is truth.

Holy

John 7:16   My teaching is not my own. It comes from him who sent me. (compare 12:49–50)

Vital (and Verbal)

Matthew 4:4   Jesus answered, "It is written: 'Man does not live on bread alone, but on every word that comes from the mouth of God.'"

The Rest of the New Testament

Note the Apostles' view of God's Word:

Eternal

1 Peter 1:25 — But the word of the Lord stands forever. And this is the word that was preached to you.

Inspired

2 Timothy 3:16–17 — All Scripture is God-breathed and is useful for teaching, rebuking, correcting and training in righteousness, so that the man of God may be thoroughly equipped for every good work.

2 Peter 1:20–21 — ... no prophecy of Scripture came about by the prophet's own interpretation. For prophecy never had its origin in the will of man, but men spoke from God as they were carried along by the Holy Spirit.

2 Peter 3:2, 15–16 — I want you to recall the words spoken in the past by the holy prophets and the command given by our Lord and Savior through your apostles. . . . Bear in mind that our Lord's patience means salvation, just as our dear brother Paul also wrote you with the wisdom that God gave him. He writes the same way in all his letters, speaking in them of these matters. His letters contain some things that are hard to understand, which ignorant and unstable people distort, as they do the other Scriptures, to their own destruction. (This shows the inspiration of the New Testament.)

Living and Active

Hebrews 4:12 — For the word of God is living and active . . . (compare Acts 7:38)

1 Peter 1:23 — For you have been born again, not of perishable seed, but of imperishable, through the living and enduring word of God.

True

2 Timothy 2:15 — Do your best to present yourself to God as one approved, a workman who does not need to be ashamed and who correctly handles the word of truth.

Not Human

1 Thessalonians 2:13 — And we also thank God continually because, when you received the word of God, which you heard from us, you accepted it not as the word of men, but as it actually is, the word of God, which is at work in you who believe.

1 Thessalonians 4:8 — ... he who rejects this instruction does not reject man but God, who gives you his Holy Spirit.

Holy

2 Timothy 3:15 — ... from infancy you have known the holy Scriptures . . .

Vital (and Verbal)

Revelation 22:18–19 — I warn everyone who hears the words of the prophecy of this book: If anyone adds anything to them, God will add to him the plagues described in this book. And if anyone takes words away from this book of prophecy, God will take away from him his share in the tree of life and in the holy city, which are described in this book.

1 Corinthians
2:12–13   We have not received the spirit of the world but the Spirit who is from God, that we may understand what God has freely given us . . . in words taught by the Spirit. . . . (See v. 14)

Romans 3:2   . . . they have been entrusted with the very words (*logia*) of God.

The Character of God and the Inerrancy and Authority of Scripture

—Sovereign: A sovereign God is able to preserve the process of inspiration from error.

—Righteousness: A righteous God is unable to inspire error.

—Just: A just God could not be untruthful when asserting that His word is inerrant. He would be unjust if He bore witness to errant Scripture as "holy and true."

—Love: A loving God would adequately provide for the spiritual health and safety of His people by inspiring an inerrant word.

—Eternal: An eternal God has had forever to determine the canon and means of inspiration (verbal, plenary, perspicuous) for His word.

—Omniscient: An omniscient God knows every contingency that might arise to inhibit inerrancy.

—Omnipotent: An omnipotent God can effectively respond to every contingency and also preserve the transmission of His Word.

—Omnipresent: An omnipresent God can initially reveal and inspire His word and later illuminate it.

—Immutable: An immutable God could never contradict His word.

—Veracity: A truthful God would not lie when He testifies about the inerrancy of His word.

—Merciful: A merciful God would not be unmerciful in inspiring both truth and error and then have His people vainly attempt to find the parts that are true. He would not leave His people to subjectivism and uncertainty about His vital word.

—Personal: A personal God can inspire verbally, with words, to ensure effective communication.

4. *The Bible Is Proven Reliable Historically* (See Unitarian Universalism chapter.)

5. *The Uniqueness of the Bible*

—The Bible is the only book in the world that offers objective evidence to be the Word of God. Only the Bible gives real proof of its divine inspiration.

—The Bible is the only religious Scripture in the world that logically can be considered inerrant in the autographs.

—The Bible is the only ancient book with documented scientific and medical prevision. No other ancient book is ever carefully analyzed along scientific lines, but many books have been written on the theme of the Bible and modern science.

—The Bible is the only religious Scripture that offers eternal salvation as a free gift entirely by God's grace and mercy.

—The Bible is the only major ancient religious Scripture whose complete textual preservation is established as virtually autographic.

—The Bible contains the greatest moral standards of any book.

—Only the Bible begins with the creation of the universe by divine fiat and contains a continuous, if often brief and interspersed, historical record of mankind from the first man, Adam, to the end of history.

—Only the Bible contains detailed prophecies about the coming Savior of the world and whose prophecies have proven true in history.

—Only the Bible has the most realistic view of human nature, the power to convict people of their sin and the ability to change human nature.

—Only the Bible has unique theological content including theology proper (the Trinity; God's attributes); soteriology (depravity, imputation, grace, propitiation/ atonement, reconciliation, regeneration, union with Christ, justification, adoption, sanctification, eternal security, election and so on); Christology (the incarnation; hypostatic union); pneumatology (the Person and work of the Holy Spirit); eschatology (detailed predictions of the end of history); ecclesiology (the nature of the church as Christ's bride and its organic union with Him); and more.

—Only the Bible offers a realistic and permanent solution to the problem of human sin and evil.

—Only the Bible has its accuracy confirmed in history by archeology and other sciences.

—The internal and historical characteristics of the Bible are unique in its unity and internal consistency despite production over a 1,500 year period by 40-plus authors in three languages on three continents discussing scores of controversial subjects yet having agreement on all issues.

—The Bible is the most translated, purchased, memorized and persecuted book in history.

—Only the Bible is fully one-quarter prophetic, containing a total of some 400 complete pages of predictions.

—Only the Bible has withstood 2,000 years of intense scrutiny by critics, not only surviving the attacks but prospering and having its credibility strengthened by such criticism. (Voltaire, and not a few cult leaders, predicted that the Bible would be extinct within 100 years; within 50 years Voltaire was extinct and his house was a warehouse of the Geneva Bible Society.)

—The Bible has molded the history of Western civilization more than any other book. The Bible has had more influence in the world than any other book.

—Only the Bible has a Person-specific (Christ-centered) nature for each of its 66 books, detailing the Person's life in prophecy, type, anti-type and so on 400–1,500 years before the Person was born.

—Only the Bible proclaims a resurrection of its central figure that is proven in history.

—Only the Bible provides historic proof that the one true God loves mankind.

6. Principles for Interpreting the Bible

The Scripture declares that it is our responsibility to interpret the Bible accurately. "Do your best to present yourself to God as one approved, a workman who does not need to be ashamed and who correctly handles the word of truth" (2 Timothy 2:15). The reason that members of cults and the new religions misinterpret the Bible is because they have never studied or properly applied the rules for correctly interpreting a historical document like the Bible. If this Encyclopedia documents anything, it documents how cults misinterpret the Bible by failing to adhere to accepted rules of textual interpretation. While it is beyond the scope of this section to offer an adequate treatment of hermeneutical principles, these may be secured from any good treatment of biblical hermeneutics, such as McQuilkin's *Interpreting and Applying the Bible.*

In order to approach the Word of God correctly, we must have familiarity with the basic rules of interpretation, such as that the Bible is to be interpreted normally or literally. There is no justification in the text, or anywhere else, for generally interpreting it mystically, or only symbolically or through the alleged insights of so-called "higher consciousness" or alleged new divine revelations that contradict the Bible's earlier revelation. To interpret the Bible normally means attention must be paid to what the authors' intended, what the words they wrote meant to them in their linguistic and historical context. The point is to discover the writer's intent, which is the only true meaning. This meaning is fixed by the author and not subject to alteration by anyone else, cultist or Christian. It should also be noted that while a good English translation is usually reliable, it may not convey all the nuances or force of the original Greek or Hebrew.

Biblical verses must be interpreted with due reference to the original languages of Scripture—Greek, Hebrew and Aramaic—and one must study word meanings and grammar. Comparing corollary or parallel passages relevant to the particular verse or topic is also important. Bible verses must be interpreted both in their immediate and larger context. This may require some understanding of the author, and the general historical context, such as whether the book is pre-exilic or post-exilic. Just as no one interprets a single sentence in a magazine article by itself, but in the context of the entire article, this must be true with the Bible.

Understanding the literary genre of a passage is also important. Thus, one would not interpret the parables of Jesus in the same manner as the historical narrative in, say, the Book of Acts. In addition, because the Bible is a compilation of progressive revelation, the Old Testament text when applicable must be interpreted in light of the greater and final revelation of the New Testament. Also one must interpret unclear passages in light of clear ones, and, because the Bible is inerrant revelation, one must assume that problem passages have a resolution rather than being an error. Time and again history and archaeological discovery have proven the correctness of this approach.

If we respect the Bible as the Word of God, apply proper interpretive principles, and depend upon the Holy Spirit to help us interpret and apply it properly, our reverent study will bring great rewards.

7. Jesus' View of Scripture

All cults must somehow undermine the authority of Scripture. They do this by alleging textual corruption, or a false interpretation by the church or new revelation that corrects or completes the Bible. But what all cults fail to do at this point is to honor the words of Jesus, whom they claim to revere. Jesus said plainly, without any qualification whatsoever, "Your word is truth" (John 17:17). He said that heaven and earth would pass away but that His words would never pass away (Matthew 24:35). In John 14:26 He promised the disciples that the Holy Spirit would teach them all things and bring to remembrance the things Jesus had taught them. He taught that the Holy Spirit, whom He would send, would guide the disciples into all the truth (John 16:13), thus preauthenticating the inspiration and inerrancy of the New Testament. Clearly, Jesus did not believe that the Holy Spirit, whom He called the Spirit of truth (John 14:17), would corrupt His own words or inspire error. As the incarnate son of God, Jesus was an infallible authority. He would hardly teach the infallibility of the Old Testament and not know

that the same condition would apply to the New Testament. As the only man in history to ever resurrect Himself from the dead (John 2:19), His view of Scripture holds precedent over everyone else's.

Recommended Reading

John Wenham, *Christ and the Bible;* Rene Pache, *The Inspiration and Authority of Scripture;* Norman Geisler, *Christ the Theme of the Bible;* Henry Morris, *Modern Science and the Bible;* Gleason Archer, *Encyclopedia of Bible Difficulties;* Norman Geisler, ed., *Inerrancy;* J. Barton Payne, *Encyclopedia of Biblical Prophecy.*

GOD/THE TRINITY

The living God is not what the cults and new religions claim He is, as if only in the last century or so (or even decade!) God had now chosen to reveal Himself "as He truly is" to this or that cult.

God is not some unknowable, impersonal divine essence, such that our own personalities ultimately become an illusion. Nor does "He" or "It" or "She" manifest through our alleged "higher consciousness" so that God and our true self are one. God is not the universe itself, nor is the universe His body (pantheism, panentheism). God is not the originator of all religions (syncretism) or an eternally hidden deity who is perpetually unknowable, unapproachable and indescribable (mysticism). God is not unipersonal or monistic.

The Trinity is not a symbol of various religious, metaphysical or psychological concepts, nor is the Trinity tritheistic (three gods) or exist in three different modes or aspects (modalism). The doctrine of the Trinity was never derived from ancient pagan religions (see our discussion in *Ready With An Answer*). In fact, the only rational explanation of the Trinity is divine revelation.

Among the cults and new religions, we find many different theologies. The chart on the next page lists various concepts of God and which cults and religions subscribe to them.

Among all religions that have ever existed, the Christian concept of God is entirely unique,

DIFFERENT CONCEPTS OF GOD

One God who is personal:

    a. Monotheism—one personal God
    b. Trinitarianism-one personal God, three centers of consciousness
    c. Unitarianism—one God, one person
    d. Modalism—one God, one person, three modes or aspects

Two or more gods who are personal:

    e. ditheism—two gods
    f. tritheism—three gods
    g. polytheism—many gods
    h. henotheism—a variation of polytheism; one principal deity (many gods; only one is worshipped)

One God who is impersonal (and related concepts):

    i. pantheism—the physical universe is God
    j. panentheism—the physical universe is God's "body"
    k. monism—God is one divine unitary essence "behind" or "underneath" the illusory physical universe

No God, or "God" is irrelevant

    l. Atheism

The selected cults and religions below illustrate the diversity of their views about God.

1.	h,g,f	Mormonism
2.	c	Jehovah's Witnesses; The Way International; Judaism
3.	k	Christian Science
4.	d,b	The Local Church
5.	i	Unity School of Christianity
6.	f	Jehovah's Witnesses (caricature of Christianity's God)
7.	j	Process Theology
8.	k,g,h,i	Hinduism
9.	l, g	Buddhism
10.	a	Islam
11.	a,g or a,k	The Masonic Lodge
12.	g	Animism
13.	a	Liberal Christianity
14.	l	Secular Humanism; Materialistic Evolution
15.	k	Transcendental Meditation
16.	a,b	Biblical Christianity

for in the totality of religious history, there is only one concept of an infinite-personal triune God. While every religion fits one of the preceding (or related) descriptions, no other religion has a Trinity. Divine revelation accounts for our knowledge of the Trinity. Indeed, the biblical concept of the Trinity is at once so unexpected and complex, and yet so practical, that it could never have been invented by men in its biblical formula. For example, only the existence of the biblical Trinity logically explains the unity and diversity in creation. Only it explains both the human personality and the many triune manifestations in nature (man as body, soul, spirit; space as height, width, length; time as past, present, future; matter as energy, motion, phenomena; family as man, woman, offspring; and so on). (See also Francis Schaeffer, *He Is There and He Is Not Silent.*)

In the following material and in subsequent sections, we will document that the Bible teaches the doctrine of the Trinity and therefore no other concept of God. It is important to note here that the Bible teaches both monotheism and trinitarianism. It teaches a *monotheistic* view—that there is only one true God—and a *trinitarian* view—that this one true God exists eternally as three Persons. This "triunity" of God was defended from earliest times as Christian theologians and apologists carefully safeguarded both the unity of God against tritheism and maintained the respective deity of the three Persons of the Godhead. As Gregory of Nyssa stated in his letter to Ablabius, "To say that there are three gods is wicked. Not to bear witness to the deity of the Son and the Spirit is ungodly and absurd. Therefore one God must be confessed by us according to the witness of Scripture, 'Hear Israel, the Lord your God is one Lord' (Deuteronomy 6:4), even if the word 'deity' extends through the holy trinity."[1]

There Is Only One True God

The Bible does not teach any form of tritheism or polytheism, as in the Mormon faith, but that there is only one true God from all eternity. As Jesus taught: "Now this is eternal life: that they may know you, the only true God, and Jesus Christ, whom you have sent" (John 17:3).

The following scriptures prove there is only one God:

> . . . the **only** true God . . . (John 17:3)
>
> there is **no God** but one. (1 Corinthians 8:4)
>
> there is **but one** God, . . . (1 Corinthians 8:6)
>
> For there is **one** God . . . (1 Timothy 2:5)
>
> This is what the LORD says . . . "I am the first and I am the last; apart from me **there is no** God." (Isaiah 44:6)
>
> I am the LORD, and **there is no other**; apart from me there is no God. (Isaiah 45:5)
>
> **I am the LORD**, and there is no other. (Isaiah 45:6)
>
> I am God, and there is no other; I am God, and there is **none like me.** (Isaiah 46:9)

God Is a Trinity or Triune

Simultaneously, this one true God has revealed that He is three Persons, or centers of consciousness, within one Godhead. Because the concept cannot be fully comprehended does not mean the doctrine is irrational or cannot be accurately defined. A good definition of the Trinity is provided by noted church historian Philip Schaff:

> God is one in three persons or hypostases [distinct persons of the same nature], each person expressing the whole fullness of the Godhead, with all his attributes. The term *persona* is taken neither in the old sense of a mere personation or form of manifestation *(prosopon,* face, mask), nor in the modern sense of an independent, separate being or individual, but in a sense which lies between these two conceptions, and thus avoids Sabellianism on the one hand, and Tritheism on the other. [Sabellianism taught that God was one person only who existed in three different forms or manifestations; tritheism refers to a belief in three separate gods.] The divine persons are in one another, and form a perpetual intercommunication and motion within the divine essence. Each person has all the divine attributes which are inherent in the divine essence, but each has also a characteristic individuality or property, which is peculiar to the person, and can not be communicated; the Father is unbegotten, the Son begotten, the Holy

Ghost is proceeding. In this Trinity there is no priority or posteriority of time, no superiority or inferiority of rank, but the three persons are co-eternal and coequal.[2]

The biblical doctrine of the Trinity is vital to understand because it concerns *who* God is, which is essential for having a proper realization of the nature of God as Father, Son and Holy Spirit. To understand the Trinity is to understand God as He has revealed Himself to be. To misunderstand the Trinity is to fail to understand who God is.

This is important because if we are to worship God "in spirit and truth" (John 4:24), as Jesus commanded, we must know and worship the one true God as He really is. To fail to do this is to fail to know and worship God, and this cannot bring Him glory. Thus, those who reject the Trinity, by definition, deny the nature of God. Without a biblical theological formulation about God, heretical views arise. This in turn can lead to rejection of the one true God and the worship of a false God. And if the Bible is clear on anything, it is clear that faith in a false God cannot save people from their sins. (See appendix, section on Idolatry.) Jesus Himself emphasized the importance of having an accurate knowledge of God when He said, "This is eternal life: that they may know you, the only true God, and Jesus Christ, whom you have sent" (John 17:3).

In his *Christian Theology,* Christian theologian Millard J. Erickson offers six points that must be included in a proper understanding of the doctrine of the Trinity (the following is the authors' paraphrase of Erickson's points):

1. There is only one God.

2. Each Person in the Godhead is equally deity.

3. The threeness and oneness of God constitute a paradox or an antinomy—merely an apparent contradiction, not a genuine one. This is because God's threeness and oneness do not exist in the same respect; that is, they are not simultaneously affirming and denying the same thing at the same time and in the same manner. God's oneness refers to the divine essence; His threeness to the plurality of persons.

4. The Trinity is eternal—there have always been three Persons, each of whom is eternally divine. One or more of the Persons did not come into being at a point in time or at some point in time became divine. There has never been any change in the essential divine nature of the triune God. God is, and God will be what God has always been forever.

5. The function of one member in the Trinity may for a time be subordinate to one or both of the other members, although this does not mean that that member is in anyway inferior in essence to the others. Each Person of the Trinity has had, for a period of time, a particular function unique to Himself. In other words, the particular function that is sometimes unique to a given Person in the Trinity is only a temporary role exercised for a given purpose. It does not represent a change in His status or essence. When the second Person of the Trinity incarnated and became Jesus Christ, He did not become less than the Father in essence, although He did become subordinate to the Father functionally. In like manner, the Holy Spirit is now subordinated to the ministry of the Son (John 14–16) and to the will of the Father, but He is not less than they are. Certain examples may illustrate this. A wife may have a subordinate role to a husband, but she is also his equal. Equals in some business enterprise may elect one of their number to serve as head or a chairperson for a period, without any change in rank. During World War II, the highest ranking member of an aircraft, the pilot, would nevertheless carefully subordinate his decisions to the bombardier, a lower ranking officer.

6. Finally, the Trinity is incomprehensible. Even when we are in heaven and fully redeemed, we will still not totally comprehend God, because it is impossible that a finite creature could ever comprehend an infinite being. Thus, "Those aspects of God which we never fully comprehend should be regarded as mysteries that go beyond our reason rather than as paradoxes which conflict with reason."[3]

Prior knowledge of the Trinity, especially in its theological formulation, is not necessary for a person to be saved. But once saved, it is vital for Christians to know the true nature of the God who has so graciously pardoned them. This explains why the Church has always recognized the importance of a proper understanding of God and maintained that those who *reject* the scriptural view of God, as long as they do so, cannot be saved. Consider Dr. Schaff's comments about the Athanasian Creed:

[It] begins and ends with the solemn declaration that the catholic [universal] faith in the Trinity and the Incarnation is the indispensable condition of salvation, and that those who reject it will be lost forever. This anathema [divine curse], in its natural historical sense, is not merely a solemn warning against the great danger of heresy, nor, on the other hand, does it demand, as a condition of salvation, a full knowledge, and assent to, the logical statement of the doctrines set forth (this would condemn the great mass even of Christian believers); but it does mean to exclude from heaven all who reject the divine truth therein taught. It requires everyone who would be saved to believe in the only true and living God, Father, Son, and Holy Ghost, one in essence, three in persons, and in one Jesus Christ, very God and very man in one person.[4]

As Vladimir Lossky once put it boldly, "Between the Trinity and Hell there lies no other choice."[5] Only personal bias or ignorance can explain cultic attempts to deny the biblical Trinity. It is significant that even some Unitarians who reject the Trinity still confess it is a biblical teaching based on "its obvious sense, its natural meaning" as found in Scripture. These words of George E. Ellis, a nineteenth-century Unitarian leader (see that chapter), illustrate the biases of anti-trinitarian groups and liberals who refuse to accept the Trinity on personal, not biblical, grounds. Ellis confesses, "Only that kind of ingenious, special, discriminative, and in candor I must add, forced treatment, which it receives from us liberals can make the book teach anything but Orthodoxy."[6] No less an authority than the great Princeton theologian B. B. Warfield pointed out that the doctrine of the Trinity "is rather everywhere presupposed" in Scripture.[7] This is, for example, clearly demonstrated in Edward Bickersteth's fine work, *The Trinity*.

Notes
1. "Gregory of Nyssa Ablabius," in William G. Rusch, trans. and ed., *The Trinitarian Controversy* (Philadelphia: Fortress Press, 1980), pp. 149, 151–52.
2. Philip Schaff, ed., rev. by David S. Schaff, *The Creeds of Christendom: With a History and Critical Notes—Vol. 1: The History of the Creeds* (Grand Rapids, MI: Baker Book House, 1983). The Greek term was transliterated by the authors.
3. Millard J. Erickson, *Christian Theology* (Grand Rapids, MI: Baker, 1986, one vol. edition), pp. 337–338.
4. Schaff, ed., *Creed*, pp. 39-40.
5. Vladimir Lossky, *The Mystical Theology of the Eastern Church* (1957), p. 66.
6. In E. Calvin Beisner, *God in Three Persons* (Wheaton, IL: Tyndale, 1984), p. 25.
7. Ibid., p. 26.

Recommended Reading

Perhaps the best devotional text is Edward Bickersteth's classic, *The Trinity* (Kregel, 1980, rpt.). Notable recent titles include Peter Toon's *Our Triune God* (Bridgepoint, 1996) and Millard J. Erickson's *God in Three Persons* (Baker, 1995). Dr. Robert A. Morey's *The Trinity: Evidence and Issues* (Grandville, MI: World Publ., 1996), is currently the most extensive in-depth analysis of all the biblical, philosophical, and historical issues relating to the doctrine of the Trinity. He deals with epistemology, hermeneutics, heresy, orthodoxy, liberalism, feminism, the Jesus Seminar, Islam, the cults, the occult, early Jewish literature, the Dead Sea Scrolls and the Apostolic Fathers, and he brings to light new information on the history and origins of Arianism and Modalism. The chapter on the deity of Christ, "The Son of God in the New Testament," is over 200 pages with 265-plus footnotes, often with multiple references in each note. And a brief, popular treatment can be found in our booklet *Knowing the Truth About the Trinity*.

JESUS CHRIST:
LORD AND SAVIOR

Jesus Christ is not merely a good man. Nor is He an angel, a preexistent spirit, God's highest creation. He is not one of many special prophets or manifestations of God, or an eastern guru or avatar, or a corruption of the mystery religions or half God–half man. As we documented in *Ready with an Answer,* He is the incarnate second person of the Trinity, the prophesied Messiah predicted hundreds of years in advance through very specific prophecies. He is unique in all creation, virgin born, sinless, deity and the only incarnation of God there is or will be. He is the world's only savior, the only one who died for our sins on the Cross to offer eternal salvation as an entirely free gift. He rose from the dead as proof of His claims, and He is the final judge, the only one who will return personally on the last day to judge every person who has ever lived. Scriptural testimony is clear as to the authority and uniqueness of Jesus Christ:

> All authority in heaven and on earth has been given to me. (Matthew 28:18)

> He is the image of the invisible God, the firstborn over all creation. For by him all things were created: things in heaven and on earth, visible and invisible, whether thrones or powers or rulers or authorities; all things were created by him and for him. He is before all things, and in him all things hold together. And he is the head of the body, the church; he is the beginning and the firstborn from among the dead, so that in everything he might have the supremacy. (Colossians 1:15–18)

> [He is] far above all rule and authority, power and dominion, and every title that can be given, not only in the present age but also in the one to come. (Ephesians 1:21)

> Therefore God exalted him to the highest place and gave him the name that is above every name, that at the name of Jesus every knee should bow, in heaven and on earth and under the earth, and every tongue confess that Jesus Christ is Lord, to the glory of God the Father. (Philippians 2:9–11)

> For God so loved the world that he gave his one and only Son, that whoever believes in him shall not perish but have eternal life. For God did not send his Son into the world to condemn the world, but to save the world through him. Whoever believes in him is not condemned, but whoever does not believe stands condemned already because he has not believed in the name of God's one and only Son. (John 3:16, 18)

Scriptural testimony is clear that Jesus is the Savior of the world:

> And we have seen and testified that the Father has sent his son to be the Savior of the world. (1 John 4:14)

> In the town of David a Savior has been born to you; he is Christ the Lord. (Luke 2:11)

> We no longer believe just because of what you said; now we have heard for ourselves, and we know that this man really is the Savior of the world. (John 4:42)

> Here is a trustworthy saying that deserves full acceptance: Christ Jesus came into the world to save sinners.... (1 Timothy 1:15)

> [But] it has now been revealed through the appearance of our Savior, Christ Jesus, who has destroyed death and brought life and immortality to light through the gospel. (2 Timothy 1:10)

> This is how God showed his love among us: he sent his one and only Son into the world that we might live through him. (1 John 4:9)

> And this is the testimony: God has given us eternal life, and this life is in his Son. He who has the Son has life; he who does not have the Son of God does not have life. (1 John 5:11)

But Christ is not just *a* savior, He is *the* Savior, the only Savior. Because only Christ died for our sin, only faith in Christ has the power to save us from the consequence of our sin. Jesus Himself and the inspired writers of the New Testament teach this so clearly that it is surprising that so many people deny it:

> Jesus answered, "I am the way and the truth and the life. No one comes to the Father except through me. (John 14:6)

> I tell you the truth, I am the gate for the sheep. ... I am the gate; whoever enters through me will be saved.... I have come that they may have life, and have it to the full. I am the good shepherd. The good shepherd lays down his life for the sheep. (John 10:7–11)

> If you do not believe that I am the one I claim to be, you will indeed die in your sins. (John 8:24)

> Salvation is found in no one else, for there is no other name under heaven given to men by which we must be saved. (Acts 4:12)

This is good, and pleases God our Savior, who wants all men to be saved and come to a knowledge of the truth. For there is one God and one mediator between God and man, the man Christ Jesus, who gave Himself as a ransom for all men—the testimony given in its proper time. (1 Timothy 2:3–6)

The Incarnation of Jesus Christ

All cults and religions deny the unique incarnation of the Second Person of the Godhead. The doctrine of the incarnation and its corollary, the virgin birth, are crucial doctrines related both to Christ's deity and our redemption. If Christ was neither incarnate nor virgin born, He could be neither God nor Savior. In other words, if He was not incarnate and virgin born He had to be born like every other man and thus could only be a man, even a sinful man. For reasons relating to God's revelation of Himself in the Old Testament, a finite sinful man, or even a preexistent spirit or an angel, could not redeem the world from the wrath of an infinite God against sin. Jesus had to be both divine and human to satisfy the divine requirements of redemption and to become a satisfactory propitiatory substitute for man. Only an infinite being could satisfy divine wrath, and only a sinless man could become a substitute for others' sins. The Bible clearly teaches that Jesus Christ is incarnate deity:

Therefore the Lord himself will give you a sign: The virgin will be with child and will give birth to a son, and will call him Immanuel [God with us]. (Isaiah 7:14; see Matthew 1:23)

For to us a child is born, to us a son is given.... And he will be called ... Mighty God.... (Isaiah 9:6)

Does not the scriptures say that the Christ will come from David's family and from Bethlehem, the town where David lived? (John 7:42)

As it is written in the second Psalm: "You are my Son; today I have become your Father." (Acts 13:33)

For to which of the angels did God ever say, "You are my Son; today I have become your Father?" (Hebrews 1:5)

The Word became flesh and made his dwelling among us. (John 1:14)

Beyond all question, the mystery of godliness is great: He appeared in a body.... (1 Timothy 3:16)

[The] second man [is] from heaven. (1 Corinthians 15:47)

And being found in appearance as a man, he humbled himself and became obedient to death—even death on a cross! (Philippians 2:8)

Therefore, when Christ came into the world, he said: "Sacrifice and offering you did not desire, but a body you prepared for me." (Hebrews 10:5)

Regarding his Son, who as to his human nature was a descendent of David.... (Romans 1:3)

For the bread of God is he who comes down from heaven and gives life to the world.... I am the bread of life.... For I have come down from heaven.... I am the bread that came down from heaven.... I am the living bread that came down from heaven. (John 6:33, 35, 38, 41, 51)

THE DEITY OF JESUS CHRIST

If there is one biblical doctrine the cults universally deny (generally they deny almost all of them), it is the doctrine of Jesus Christ's deity. Even those who "accept" His deity, do not accept His unique deity, maintaining that Christ is one of many gods, or that the true nature of Christ is divine in the sense that everyone's nature is divine, whether people realize it or not.

However, determining who Christ is is the most important decision to face anyone, anywhere, for one's eternal destiny depends upon the correct answer. Belief in any other God than the true God is idolatry, and as such it will condemn one to judgment. Jesus Himself emphasized, "I told you that you would die in your sins; if you do not believe that I am the one I claim to be, you will indeed die in your sins" (John 8:24). "Moreover, the Father judges no one, but has entrusted all judgment to the Son, that all may honor the Son just as they honor the Father. He who does not honor the Son does not honor the Father, who sent him" (John 5:22-23).

Let's look at five basic questions. If Christ is God, then each point must be true. If He is not, then none can be true.

1. Assuming the Incarnation, Does Christ Make Statements Only God Would Make?

The following Scriptures, given the character of Jesus Christ, are only logically explained on the basis of His deity:

For I have come down from heaven not to do my will but to do the will of him who sent me. (John 6:38)

And now, Father, glorify me in your presence with the glory I had with you before the world began. (John 17:5)

"I tell you the truth," Jesus answered, "before Abraham was born, I am!" (John 8:58)

Then Jesus came to them and said, "All authority in heaven and on earth has been given to me." (Matthew 28:18)

I have told you these things, so that in me you may have peace. In this world you will have trouble. But take heart! I have overcome the world. (John 16:33)

Jesus said . . . "I am the resurrection and the life. He who believes in me will live, even though he dies." (John 11:25)

I tell you the truth, whoever hears my word and believes him who sent me has eternal life and will not be condemned; he has crossed over from death to life. (John 5:24; see John 10:27, 28; 11:25)

I am the vine; you are the branches. If a man remains in me and I in him, he will bear much fruit; apart from me you can do nothing. (John 15:5)

Jesus answered, "I am the way and the truth and the life. No one comes to the Father except through me." (John 14:6)

When he looks at me, he sees the one who sent me. (John 12:45; see John 14:7–11; 17:5)

All that belongs to the Father is mine. That is why I said the Spirit will take from what is mine and make it known to you. (John 16:15)

While I am in the world, I am the light of the world. (John 9:5)

There is a judge for the one who rejects me and does not accept my words; that very word which I spoke will condemn him at the last day. (John 12:48)

Whoever believes in the Son has eternal life, but whoever rejects the Son will not see life, for God's wrath remains on him. (John 3:36)

[The Father has entrusted all judgments to the Son] that all may honor the Son just as they honor the Father. He who does not honor the Son does not honor the Father, who sent him. (John 5:23)

When a man believes in me, he does not believe in me only, but in the one who sent me. (John 12:44)

Can we imagine the president of the United States appearing on national TV and making such claims for himself? Can we imagine even the most exalted angel doing so? The magnitude of these claims are such that if they are not true, Jesus cannot be considered a sane or a good man. He would have to be considered as the founder of the greatest system of idolatry the world has ever seen. Loraine Boettner asserts in his *Studies in Theology* (1980, p. 144):

Certainly on the basis of His own teaching Jesus claimed Deity for Himself. No unprejudiced reader can reach any other conclusion. Such has been the impression of the great mass of those who have read the New Testament. This has led Dr. A. H. Strong to observe that "if He is not God, He is a deceiver or is self-deceived, and in either case, Christ, if not God, is not good." And Dr. E. Y. Mullins has pointed out that if we deny His Deity then "we must conclude that, with all His moral beauty and excellence, Jesus was a pitiable failure as teacher if He did not succeed in guarding His message against corruptions which have led to His own exaltation as God, and to the existence through eighteen centuries of a system of idolatry of which He is the center."

Note again the close relationship between God and Christ in the following Scriptures. No mere creature, however exalted, could rationally make such claims:

I and the Father are One (John 10:30).

He who does not honor the Son does not honor the Father (John 5:23).

If you had known Me, you would have known My Father also (John 8:19).

He who beholds Me, beholds the One who sent Me (John 12:45).

Whatever the Father does, these things the Son also does in like manner (John 5:19).

No one knows the Father except the Son (Matthew 11:27).

You believe in God, believe also in Me (John 14:1).

He who has seen Me, has seen the Father (John 14:9).

He who hates me, hates my Father (John 15:23).

He who receives Me, receives the One who sent Me (Matthew 10:40).

All that belongs to the Father is mine. (John 16:15).

My Father is working until now and I am working (John 5:17).

2. Does Christ Conform to the Attributes of Deity?

In the following condensed descriptions of various Scriptures, we see that Jesus Christ is God because He has the attributes of God.

Eternity

The everlasting Father (Isaiah 9:6).

From everlasting (Micah 5:2).

In the beginning, He always was (John 1:1, 2, 14, 15).

Jesus had glory with God before the world was created (John 17:5).

Omnipresence

Where two or three are gathered in His name, He is there (Matthew 18:20).

He is with us always (Matthew 28:20).

He is in every believer (John 14:20-23).

He fills all (Ephesians 1:23; 4:20).

Omniscience

He knows people's thoughts (Mark 2:8; Luke 6:8; 11:17).

He knew the manner of His death (Matthew 16:21; John 12:33).

He knew the Father (Matthew 11:27; Only God can know Himself, 1 Corinthians 2:11, 16).

He knew who would betray Him (John 6:64, 70-71).

He knew the future (John 2:19-22; John 13:19; 18:4; Matthew 24:35).

He saw Nathaniel under the fig tree (John 1:49).

He knew the history of the Samaritan woman (John 4:29).

The disciples' testimony (John 16:30, 17:30).

He knew all men (John 2:24, 25).

While Christ is God, we must remember that in the incarnation He had surrendered the independent use of His attributes (Philippians 2:6-8; John 5:30). As a true man, He was a servant to the Father as an example to us (John 13:4, 5). Therefore, while on earth, there were some things the Father did not allow Him to know, and in His humanity only He was not omniscient. Thus, He did not know the time of His return (Mark 13:32); He went to see if there was fruit on a fig tree (Mark 11:13); He marveled at both unbelief (Mark 6:6) and belief (Matthew 8:10).

Omnipotence and Sovereignty

He is the Almighty (Revelation 1:8).

He does whatever the Father does (John 5:19).

He upholds all things (Colossians 1:17; Hebrews 1:3).

All authority, including over all mankind, is given to Him (Matthew 28:18; John 17:2, 3).

He is the head over all rule and authority (Colossians 2:10).

He has power to subject all things unto Himself (Philippians 3:21).

He will reign until He has put all enemies under His feet (1 Corinthians 15:25).

He exerts control over His own life and death (John 10:18).

He is the ruler of the kings of the earth (Revelation 1:5).

He has power over nature (Luke 8:25).

He is Lord of all (Revelations 19:16; 1 Peter 3:22; Colossians 1:18; Acts 10:36).

Immutability

He is always and forever the same (Hebrews 13:8; see also 1:12, 8, 10).

His words will never pass away (Matthew 24:35).

Holy

He is holy (Revelation 3:7).

He is the holy offspring that will be called the Son of God (Luke 1:35).

He knew no sin (2 Corinthians 5:21).

He is without sin (Hebrews 4:15).

He is holy, innocent, undefiled and separated from sinners (Hebrews 7:26).

He is unblemished and spotless (1 Peter 1:19).

He committed no sin (John 8:46; 1 John 3:5; 1 Peter 2:22).

Truth

He is full of grace and truth (John 1:14).

The truth is in Jesus (Ephesians 4:21).

He is the truth (John 14:6).

He is faithful and true (Revelation 19:11).

3. Are the Names, Titles and Designations of God Ascribed to Christ?

The chart on pages 682-83 compares descriptions between God in the Old Testament and Christ in the New Testament to prove that Jesus Christ is God. Any created being, however exalted, is unworthy of these statements collectively, and often individually.

4. Are the Prerogatives of Deity Ascribed to Christ?

—Raising the dead while on earth (Matthew 9:25, the Synagogue official's daughter; Luke 7:12-16, the widow's son; John 11:44, Lazarus; John 2:19-22, Himself).

—Doing the works of God (John 10:37-39).

—Giver of eternal life with authority over all mankind (John 17:2, 10:28).

—Worshiped by angels (Psalm 148:2; God, Hebrews 1:6; Jesus, Luke 4:8).

—Addressed in prayer (Acts 7:59).

—Providence and eternal dominion (Luke 10:22; John 3:35; 17:2; Ephesians 1:2; Colossians 1:17; Hebrews 1:3; Revelation 1:5).

—Power to transform the bodies of all believers (Philippians 3:21).

—Raising the dead for judgment (John 5:24–29; Acts 10:42; 17:31).

—Worshiped by people. Only God is worthy of worship (Psalm 95:6). Neither people (Acts 10:25-26) nor angels (Revelation 19:10) are to receive worship, only God (Luke 4:8). But Jesus received worship from: the man born blind (John 9:38); the disciples (Matthew 14:33; 28:17); the wise men (Matthew 2:2, 11); the young ruler (Matthew 9:18); women (Matthew 28:9); the demons (Mark 3:11; 5:6); everyone (Philippians 2:10, 11); the four elders (Revelation 5:14).

—Forgives sin (Matthew 1:21; Mark 2:7).

—Sending the Holy Spirit (a creature cannot send God; John 16:7; compare 14:26).

Even in the baptismal formula, we find Christ clearly asserting His deity. In his *Studies in Theology* (1980, pp. 144–145), Loraine Boettner quotes the great Princeton theologian B. B. Warfield (*Biblical Doctrines*, p. 204):

The precise form of the formula must be carefully observed. It does not read: "In the names" (plural)—as if there were three beings enumerated, each with its distinguishing name. Nor yet: "In the name of the Father, Son and Holy Spirit," as if there were one person, going by a threefold name. It reads: "In the name (singular) of the Father and of the (article repeated) Son, and of the (article repeated) Holy Spirit," carefully distinguishing three persons, though uniting them all under one name. The name of God was to the Jews Jehovah, and to name the name of Jehovah upon them was to make them His. What Jesus did in this great injunction was to command His followers to name the name of God upon their converts, and to announce the name of God which is to be named on their converts in the threefold enumeration of "the Father" and "the Son" and "the Holy Spirit." As it is unquestionable that He here intended Himself by "the Son," He here places Himself by the side of the Father and Spirit, as together with them

PROOF THAT JESUS CHRIST IS GOD		
DESCRIPTION	GOD–OLD TESTAMENT	JESUS–NEW TESTAMENT
1. The first and the last	Isaiah 41:4; 44:6; 48:12	Revelation 2:8; 22:13
2. I AM	Exodus 3:14	John 8:58; John 13:19
3. Author of eternal words	Isaiah 40:8; Psalm 119:89	Matthew 24:35; John 6:68
4. Light	Psalm 27:1	John 1:4–9; 8:12; 1 John 1:5
5. Rock	Deuteronomy 32:31; Psalm 18:2; Isaiah 8:14; Psalm 92:15	1 Peter 2:6–8; 1 Corinthians 10:4
6. Bridegroom	Isaiah 62:5; Hosea 2:16	Mark 2:19; Revelation 21:2
7. Shepherd	Psalm 23:1	John 10:11; Hebrews 13:20
8. Forgiver of sins	Jeremiah 31:34	Acts 5:31
9. Redeemer	Hosea 13:14; Psalm 130:7	Titus 2:13,14; Revelation 5:9
10. Savior	Isaiah 43:3; Hosea 13:4	2 Peter 1:1, 11; Titus 2:10–13; Acts 4:12 (see Titus 1, 3)
11. The Lord of Glory	Isaiah 42:8	John 17:1–5; 1 Corinthians 2:8
12. Judge	Joel 3:12	Matthew 25:31–46
13. The Second Coming God	Zechariah 14:5	Matthew 16:27; 24:29–31
14. The First Coming God	Isaiah 40:3	Matthew 3:3
15. King of Glory	Psalm 24:7, 10	1 Corinthians 2:8; John 17:5
16. Jehovah our righteousness	Jeremiah 23:5–6	1 Corinthians 1:30
17. Jehovah the first and last	Isaiah 44:6; 48:12–16	Revelation 1:8, 17; 22:13
18. Jehovah above all	Psalm 97:9	John 3:31
19. Jehovah's fellow and equal	Zechariah 13:7	Philippians 2:6
20. The Lord Almighty	Isaiah 6:1–3; 8:13–14	John 12:41; 1 Peter 2:8
21. Jehovah	Psalm 110:1	Matthew 22:42–45
22. Jehovah the Shepherd	Isaiah 40:11	Hebrews 13:20
23. Jehovah, for whose glory all things were created	Proverbs 16:4	Colossians 1:16
24. Jehovah the messenger of the Covenant	Malachi 3:1	Luke 7:27
25. Invoked as Jehovah	Joel 2:32; Isaiah 45:22	1 Corinthians 1:2
26. The eternal God and Creator	Psalm 102:24–27	Hebrews 1:8, 10–12
27. The great God and savior	Isaiah 43:11–12	Titus 1:3-4; 2:10, 13; 3:4–6
28. God the Judge	Ecclesiastes 12:14	1 Corinthians 4:5; 2 Corinthians 5:10; 2 Timothy 4:1
29. Emmanuel	Isaiah 7:14	Matthew 1:23
30. The Holy One	1 Samuel 2:2	Acts 3:14
31. Lord of the Sabbath	Genesis 2:3	Matthew 12:8
32. Lord of All	1 Chronicles 29:11–12	Acts 10:36; Romans 10:11–13
33. Creator of all things	Isaiah 40:28; Psalm 148:1–5	John 1:3; Colossians 1:16
34. Supporter, preserver of all things	Nehemiah 9:6	Colossians 1:17

DESCRIPTION	GOD–OLD TESTAMENT	JESUS–NEW TESTAMENT
35. Stumbling rock of offense	Isaiah 8:14	Romans 9:32–33; 1 Peter 2:8; Acts 4:11
36. Confess that He is Lord	Isaiah 45:23 (Jehovah)	Philippians 2:11 (Jesus)
37. The Judge of all men	Psalm 98:9	Acts 17:31
38. Raiser of the dead	1 Samuel 2:6; Psalm 119 (11 times)	John 11:25; 5:21 with Luke 7:12–16;
39. Co-sender of the Holy Spirit	John 14:16 (the Father sends)	John 15:26 (Jesus sends)
40. Led captivity captive	Psalm 68:18	Ephesians 4:7–8
41. Seen by Isaiah	Isaiah 6:1	John 12:41
42. Judge of the nations	Joel 3:12	Matthew 25:31–41
43. Salvation by calling on the name of the Lord	Joel 2:32	Romans 10:13

constituting the one God. It is, of course, the Trinity which he is describing and that is as much as to say that He announces Himself as one of the persons of the Trinity.

5. Does Scripture Declare Unequivocally that Christ Is God?

As if the "Proof that Jesus Christ Is God" chart isn't enough, Scripture plainly declares Christ's deity:

—John 1:1, 14, "The word was God. . . . The Word became flesh and made his dwelling among us."

—John 1:18, "The only begotten God."

—John 20:28, Thomas said to him [Jesus] "My Lord and my God."

—Titus 2:13, "Our Great God and Saviour Jesus Christ."

—Hebrews 1:8, But about the Son he says, "Your throne O God, will last forever and ever."

—2 Peter 1:1, "Our God and Saviour Jesus Christ."

—1 John 5:20, "Jesus Christ. He is the true God and eternal life."

—Colossians 2:9, "In Christ all the fullness of the Deity lives in bodily form."

—Isaiah 9:6, "For to us a child is born . . . and He will be called Mighty God."

—Isaiah 7:14; Matthew 1:23, "Immanuel"— "God with us."

—Hebrews 1:1-3, "The Son is the radiance of God's glory and the exact representation of His being . . ."

—Colossians 1:15–17, "He is the image of the invisible God . . . by him all things were created."

—Acts 20:28, The church was purchased with the blood of God.

—2 Corinthians 4:4, "Christ, who is the image of God."

—Romans 9:5, "Christ, who is God over all, forever praised."

—1 Corinthians 1:24, "Christ the power of God and the wisdom of God."

—2 Thessalonians 1:12, "Our God and Lord Jesus Christ."

—Philippians 2:6, "being in very nature God." (The Greek could be literally translated "continuing to subsist in the form of God.")

Some cult members respond to this previous listing by saying, "Is that all?" Others, even some theologians, have claimed that the actual direct scriptural references to Christ's deity in the New Testament are "exceedingly few."

Only one clear reference of God to Christ's deity should be sufficient; the truth is that we have hundreds of direct and indirect references. The term for "Jehovah God," which is employed some 6,000 times in the Septuagint (LXX, the Greek translation of the Old Testament), is *kurios* (Lord). In other words, *kurios* is the specific term the LXX translators chose to designate the one true God of all the earth. The Apostle Paul and other New Testament writers were well aware of this fact. What is significant is that the very word chosen to designate *God* in the LXX is the word *they* chose to designate Jesus Christ in the New Testament; *kurios*. The implication of this could hardly be lost on either the New Testament writers or its readers. The New Testament writers clearly chose to describe Jesus Christ as God hundreds of times by their use of the term *kurios*.

Other Testimonies

Thomas: "My Lord and my God" (John 20:28).

Peter: "The Son of the living God" (Matthew 16:16; to a Jew, this made Him God's equal, see John 5:18).

John: "Making himself [Jesus] equal with God" (John 5:18).

The Jews: "You a mere man claim[ing] to be God" (John 10:33).

The High Priest: "You have heard the blasphemy" (Mark 14:61–64).

THE DEITY OF CHRIST AND EARLY CHURCH TESTIMONY

Some cults, as well as most liberal theologians, maintain that the doctrine of the Trinity was not part of the teachings of Jesus and the Apostles, but merely invented by the church centuries later. Emanuel Swedenborg, founder of the Church of the New Jerusalem, claimed that the apostolic church knew nothing of the Trinity and that the Trinity was fabricated by the Council of Nicea in the fourth century as a belief in three Gods, not the one true God, which he believed was unipersonal. "A Trinity of Persons was unknown in the Apostolic church, but was hatched by the Nicean Council," and, "No other trinity than a trinity of Gods was understood by the members of the Nicean Council . . . [and] so understood by the whole Christian world as well."[1] Likewise, in a sermon given in August,

1964, at New York City, liberal theologian James A. Pike declared, "The Trinity is not necessary. Our Lord never heard of it. The apostles knew nothing of it." Victor Paul Wierwille, founder of "The Way International," claims in his book, *Jesus Christ Is Not God,* that the early church (to 330 A.D.) never believed in the Trinity or in Christ's deity. He argues, "Certainly, during this time, church leaders spoke of the Father, Son, and Holy Spirit, but they never referred to them as co-equal. . . . In fact, the opposite was the case. They spoke of the Father as supreme, the true and only God . . . and of the son *as inferior* . . . having a beginning, visible, *begotten, immutable.*"[2]

But is this really what we find when we carefully examine the writings of the earliest Christian leaders, or is this merely an invention by those who, for whatever reason, choose not to believe in the Trinity? The following twenty-two chronological examples of key leaders show that the early church clearly believed that Jesus Christ was God.

Ignatius of Antioch (30–107 A.D.). He was born before Christ died and consistently spoke of the deity of Jesus Christ. Consider a few examples. In his writings *To the Ephesians, to the Romans, to the Magnesians* and in other letters, we find references such as the following: "Jesus Christ our God"; "who is God and man"; "received knowledge of God, that is, Jesus Christ"; "for our God, Jesus the Christ"; "for God was manifest as man"; "Christ, who was from eternity with the Father"; "from God, from Jesus Christ"; "from Jesus Christ, our God"; "Our God, Jesus Christ"; "suffer me to follow the example of the passion of my God"; "Jesus Christ the God"; and "Our God Jesus Christ."[3] The fact that Ignatius was not rebuked or branded as teaching heresy by any of the churches or Christian leaders that he sent such letters to proves that the early church, long before 107 A.D., accepted the deity of Christ.

Polycarp (69–155 A.D.). He possibly spoke of "Our Lord and God Jesus Christ."[4]

Justin Martyr (100–165 A.D.). He wrote of Jesus, "who . . . being the first-begotten Word of God, is even God."[5] In his *Dialogue with Trypho,* he stated that "God was born from a virgin," and that Jesus was "worthy of worship" and of being "called Lord and God."[6]

Tatian (110–172 A.D.). This early apologist wrote, "We do not act as fools, O Greeks, nor utter idle tales when we announce that God was born in the form of man."[7]

Theophlius (116–181 A.D.). He was the first to use the term "Trinity" in his *Epistle to Antolycux* II, xv.[8]

Irenaeus of Lyons and Rome (120–202 A.D.). He wrote that Jesus was "perfect God and perfect man"; "not a mere man . . . but was very God"; and that "He is in Himself in His own right . . . God, and Lord, and King Eternal." He also spoke of "Christ Jesus, our Lord, and God, and Saviour and King"[9]

Tertullian of Carthage (145–220 A.D.). He said of Jesus, "Christ is also God" because "that which has come forth from God [in the virgin birth] is at once God and the Son of God, and the two are one. . . . [In] His birth, God and man united." Jesus is "both Man and God, the Son of Man and the Son of God"[10]

Hippolytus (170–255 A.D.). He said, "[It is] the Father who is above all, the Son who is through all, and the Holy Spirit who is in all. And we cannot otherwise think of one God, but by believing in truth in Father and Son and Holy Spirit. . . . For it is through this Trinity that the Father is glorified. . . . The whole Scriptures, then, proclaim this truth." "The *Logos* is God, being *the* substance of God."[11]

Caius (180–217 A.D.). He was a Roman Presbyter who wrote of the universal Christian attestation to the deity of Christ in his refutation of Artemon, who maintained that Christ was only a man. Caius appealed to much earlier writers, all of whom taught Christ's deity. "Justin and Miltiades, and Tatian and Clement, and many others—who is ignorant of the books of Irenaeus and Melito, and the rest, which declare Christ to be God and man? All the psalms, too, and hymns of brethren, *which have been written*

from the beginning by the faithful, celebrate Christ the Word of God, ascribing divinity to Him. . . . [This] doctrine of the Church, then, has been proclaimed so many years ago, . . ."[12]

Gregory Thaumaturgus of Neo-Caesarea (205–270 A.D.) He declared in *On the Trinity* that "all [the persons] are one nature, one essence, one will, and are called the Holy Trinity; and these also are names subsistent, one nature in three persons, and one genus [kind]."[13] He referred to Jesus as "God of God" and "God the Son."[14]

Novatian of Rome (210–280 A.D.). He wrote in his *On the Trinity* of Jesus being truly a man but that "He was also God according to the Scriptures. . . . Scripture has as much described Jesus Christ to be man, as moreover it has also described Christ the Lord to be God. . . . [This] same Jesus is called also God and the Son of God." "Christ Jesus [is] our Lord God."[15] (Note, then, that in the third century we already had widespread discourses on the Trinity.)

Origen of Alexandria (wrote ca 230 A.D.). He stated that Christ was "God and man."[16] In 254 A.D. he wrote, "Jesus Christ . . . while he was God, and though made man, remained God as he was before."[17]

Athanasius (295–373 A.D.). This keen defender of New Testament teaching against the early Arian heresy, which taught that Jesus Christ was not God, declared of Jesus, "He always was and is God and Son," and, "He who is eternally God . . . also became man for our sake."[18]

Lucian of Antioch (300 A.D.). "We believe in . . . one Lord Jesus Christ, his Son, the only-begotten God . . . God of God . . ."[19]

Alexander of Alexandria. Spoke of Jesus' "highest and essential divinity" and that he was "an exact and identical image of the Father."[20]

Eusebius of Caesarea. Stated that "the Son of God bears no resemblance to originated creatures but . . . is alike in every way only to the Father who has begotten [Him] and that he is not from any other hypostasis and substance but from the Father."[21] And (325 A.D.) "We believe in . . . one Lord Jesus Christ, the word of God, God of God . . ."[22]

Cyril of Jerusalem (ca. 350 A.D.). "We believe in . . . One Lord Jesus Christ, the only begotten Son of God . . . very God, by whom all things were made."[23]

Epiphanius of Constantia (374 A.D.). "We believe . . . in one Lord Jesus Christ . . . of the substance of the Father, Light of Light, very God of very God."[24]

Augustine. Declared that Christians "believe that Father, Son, and Holy Spirit are one God, maker and ruler of the whole creation: that Father is not Son, nor Holy Spirit Father or Son; but a Trinity of mutually related Persons, and a unity of equal essence," and that therefore "the Father is God, the Son is God, and the Holy Spirit God; and all together are one God."[25]

Tertullian. Wrote of Jesus that "He is God and man. . . . We have here a dual condition—not fused but united—in one person, Jesus as God and man."[26]

Proclus. "He was born of woman, God but not solely God, and man but not merely man . . . Christ did not by progress become God—heaven forbid!—but in mercy he became man, as we believe. We do not preach a deified man; we confess an incarnate God . . . him alone who was born of a virgin, God and man."[27]

Cyril of Alexandria. Wrote of Jesus, "For he remained what he was; that is, by nature God. But . . . he took it on himself to be man as well," and, "There is nothing to prevent us from thinking of Christ as being the one and only Son at once both God and man, perfect in deity and perfect in humanity. . . . [He] is conceived of as God and is God . . ."[28]

From the very first, the leaders of the Christian church—immediately after the time of the Apostles up to the Council of Nicea in the fourth century and beyond—had consistently believed and taught that Jesus Christ is God. Those who deny this are clearly mistaken when they maintain that the Trinity was "invented" by Christians only in the fourth century or later.

There is only one logical explanation for the abundant early testimony to the deity of Jesus Christ: early church leaders were simply declaring what was already declared by Jesus Christ and the apostles in Holy Scripture: that Christ was indeed God. As Gregory of Nazianzus stated, in his "Third Theological Oration Concerning the Son," "From their [the Apostles] great and exalted discourses we have discovered and preached the deity of the Son."[29] E. Calvin Beisner, author of *God in Three Persons,* states:

> The testimony of the New Testament to the deity of Christ is unanimous. . . . Were there no passages at all which directly call Christ God, we would still have a great weight of evidence that is the New Testament conception of him, for in all senses he is depicted as precisely parallel to God the Father. C. F. D. Moule wrote: "Far more impressive than any single passage are two implicit Christological 'pointers.'" At first is the fact that, in the greetings of the Pauline epistles, God and Christ are brought into a single formula. It requires an effort of imagination to grasp the enormity that this must have seemed to a non-Christian Jew. It must have administered a shock comparable (if the analogy may be allowed without irreverence) to our finding a religious Cuban today inditing a message from God-and-"Che" Guevara. . . .
>
> The other Christological pointer, evidenced early . . . [is the undeniable] fact that Paul seems to experience Christ as any theist reckons to understand God—that is, as personal, but as more than individual: as more than a person. This is evidenced by certain uses (though admittedly not all) of the well known incorporative formulae, "in Christ.". . .[30]

The truth is that for all those groups that deny Christ's deity (see next section)—The Way International, Jehovah's Witnesses, Armstrongism, Christadelphians, modern Modalists and many others—as it was for the early Arians, the Trinity is simply a stumbling block to their rationalism. What they cannot fully comprehend, they will not accept. Thus, the doctrine of the Trinity cannot be rejected on biblical or historical grounds, because the testimony for it is too abundant. It can only be rejected on philosophical and personal grounds which have no merit.

Notes

1. Emanuel Swedenborg, *The True Christian Religion*, Vol. 1, p. 260 (n. 174), 258 (n. 172).
2. Victor Paul Wierwille, *Jesus Christ Is Not God* (New Knoxville, OH: American Christian Press, 1975).
3. Kirsopp Lake, trans., *The Apostolic Fathers*, Vol. 1, *Loeb Classical Library*, Harvard University Press (1965); *To the Ephesians I*, Greeting, I:I, vii.2, xvii.2, xviii.2, xix.3; *To the Magnesians*, xiii.2; *To the Trallians*, vii.1; *To the Romans*, Greeting, iii.3, vi.3; *To the Smyrnaeans* I.I; *To Polycarp*, viii.3; respectively.
4. *The Epistle of Polycarp to the Philippians*, ch. 6, in Alexander Roberts, James Donaldson (eds.), *The Ante-Nicene Fathers Translations of the Writings of the Fathers Down to A.D. 325* (Vol. 1 *The Apostolic Fathers with Justin Martyr and Irenaeus*) (Grand Rapids, MI: Eerdmans, 1977), p. 34.
5. Justin Martyr, "The First Apology," ch. 63, in Roberts and Donaldson, *The Ante-Nicene Fathers*, Vol. 1, p. 184.
6. Justin Martyr, "Dialogue of Justin, Philosopher and Martyr, with Trypho, a Jew," chs. 64, 68, in Roberts and Donaldson, *The Ante-Nicene Fathers*, Vol. 1, pp. 231-233.
7. Tatian the Assyrian, "Address of Tatian to the Greeks," ch. 21, in Roberts and Donaldson, *The Ante-Nicene Fathers*, Vol. 1, p. 74.
8. Roberts and Donaldson, *Ante-Nicene Fathers*, Vol. 2, p. 101.
9. Irenaeus, "Against Heresies" Book III, ch. 16, Title; ch. 19, Title, para. 2; Book I, ch. 10, para. 1, in Roberts and Donaldson (eds.), *The Ante-Nicene Fathers*, Vol. 1, pp. 440, 448-49.
10. Tertullian (Quintus Tertullianus), "A Treatise on the Soul," ch. 41 and "Apology," ch. 21, in Roberts and Donaldson, *The Ante-Nicene Fathers*, Vol. 3, *Latin Christianity: Its Founder, Tertullian* (Grand Rapids, MI: Eerdmans, 1978), 221, 34-35 and *Against Praxaes* in *Ante-Nicene Fathers*, Vol. 3, p. 498, respectively.
11. Hippolytus, *Against the Heresy of Noetus*, p. 14, cited in Harold O. J. Brown, *Heresies* (Garden City, NY: Doubleday & Co., 1984), p. 95; *Refutation of All Heresies*, X, XXIX, *Ante-Nicene Fathers*, Vol. 5, p. 151.
12. Caius, "Against the Heresy of Artemon" in "Fragments of Caius" in Roberts and Donaldson, *The Ante-Nicene Fathers: Fathers of the Third Century*, Vol. 5, p. 601.
13. Gregory Thaumaturgus, "On the Trinity," para. 2, in Roberts and Donaldson, *The Ante-Nicene Fathers*, Vol. 6: *Fathers of the Third Century* (Grand Rapids, MI: Eerdmans, 1975), p. 48.
14. E. Calvin Beisner, *God in Three Persons* (Wheaton, IL: Tyndale, 1984), p. 81.
15. Novatian, a Roman Presbyter, "A Treatise of Novatian Concerning the Trinity," ch. 11, in Roberts and Donaldson, *The Ante-Nicene Fathers: Fathers of the Third Century*, Vol. 5, p. 620.
16. Origen, "Dialogue with Heraclides," 1-4, in Wiles and Santer, *Documents in Early Christian Thought*, p. 23.
17. In Beisner, *God*, p. 80, citing *On the Principles*, Preface, p. 4.
18. Athanasius, "Against the Arians," III, para. 29, 31, in Maurice Wiles and Mark Santer (eds.), *Documents in Early Christian Thought* (Cambridge: Cambridge University Press, 1979), pp. 52, 54.
19. In Beisner, *God*, p. 82.
20. "Alexander of Alexandria's Letter to Alexander of Thessonalica," para. 37, in William G. Rusch (trans./ed.), *The Trinitarian Controversy* (Philadelphia: Fortress Press, 1980), pp. 40, 42.
21. "Eusebius of Caesarea's Letter to His Church Concerning the Synod at Nicaea," para. 13 in Rusch, p. 59.
22. In Beisner, *God*, p. 84.
23. Ibid., p. 86.
24. Ibid., p. 87.
25. Augustine, "On the Trinity," IX, para. 1; XV, para. 28, in Wiles and Santer, *Documents in Early Christian Thought*, 36-37, p. 91.
26. Tertullian, "Against Praxeas," ch. 27, in Wiles and Santer (eds.), *Documents*, p. 46.
27. Proclus, "Sermon I," paras. 2, 4 in Wiles and Santer, *Documents*, pp. 62-64.
28. Cyril of Alexandria, "Second Letter to Successus," 2, 4, in Wiles and Santer, *Documents in Early Christian Thought*, pp. 67, 69-70.
29. Gregory of Nazianzus, "Third Theological Oration Concerning the Son," 17 in Rusch (trans./ed.), *The Trinitarian Controversy*, p. 143.
30. In Beisner, *God*, pp. 33-34.

RELIGIONS, CULTS AND THE DEITY OF JESUS CHRIST

In spite of the importance and centrality of Jesus Christ for human history and welfare, apart from Christianity all the world's religions, ideologies and philosophies reject Him. Biblically, none accept His virgin birth, incarnation, deity, atoning death on the Cross and physical return.

Some four billion people in the world accept at least one of four dominant beliefs: materialism, Marxism, monism or the Muslim faith. In materialism, Jesus Christ is seen as a common product of naturalistic evolution and therefore as having no inherent special status. He was only a man. In Marxism, belief in Jesus Christ is viewed as a falsehood that has deceived millions of people with a religious opiate. Marxist governments have done all they can to oppress or destroy those who believe in Christ, since believers are perceived as enemies of the dialectical advance of history. In monism, such as Hinduism and Buddhism, Jesus, like everyone, is finally an illusion of the deceptive material world of duality. In Islam, Christ is merely one of the prophets of Allah. It is considered an unforgivable sin *(shirk)* to accept His deity. A key tenet of Muslim faith is that Christ is not God and cannot be the Son of God. Since it is unthinkable that Allah would let one of his prophets be crucified, Islam also rejects the biblical teaching that Christ died on the Cross for our sins. Muslims believe that Allah would never condescend to become a man, let alone die on a cross for people's sins. As the Koran declares of Jesus, "They did not slay him, neither crucified him," and, "The Messiah, Jesus son of Mary was only a Messenger of God," and, "They are unbelievers who say, 'God is the Messiah, Mary's son.'"[1]

The following list illustrates sayings of new religions and cults that deny Christ's nature. In the New Testament, Jesus warned that false prophets and false Christs would arrive (Matthew 24:4–5, 24). The Apostle Paul warned that there were false Christs and false gospels (2 Corinthians 11:3–5). The Apostle Peter cautioned against false teachers who would be active within the church and who would "secretly introduce destructive heresies, even denying the Sovereign Lord who bought them" (2 Peter 2:1).

Perhaps the world's denial of Jesus Christ illustrates the difficulty it will face when Christ returns in judgment to the very world He made and lovingly gave His life for:

> He was in the world, and though the world was made through him, the world did not recognize him. He came to that which was his own, but his own did not receive him. Yet to all who received him, to those who believed in his name, he gave the right to become children of God. . . . For God did not send his Son into the world to condemn the world, but to save the world through him. Whoever believes in him is not condemned, but whoever does not believe stands condemned already because he has not believed in the name of God's one and only Son. This is the verdict: Light has come into the world, but men loved darkness instead of light because their deeds were evil. (John 1:10–12, 3:17–19).

The following individuals are the founders or current leaders of the group specified. If a citation is occasionally not by the individual founder or current leader listed, it is excerpted from the group's authoritative literature.

Anthroposophy (Rudolf Steiner). "[Jesus] . . . must be designated in the truest sense of the word as a 'mere man.'"[2]

Association for Research and Enlightenment (Edgar Cayce). "He [Jesus] is an example for man, and only as a man, for He lived only as a man, He died as man."[3]

Astara (Earlyne Chaney). Jesus is "the Master Mystic of all time" who realized the Christ, a state of higher consciousness. Jesus is not the Savior from sin and only incarnation of God.[4]

The Baha'i Faith (The Bab; Baha'u'llah). "Jesus was not the only-begotten Son of God come down from Heaven, crucified and resurrected, nor the unique Saviour."[5]

The Christadelphians (John Thomas). "Jesus Christ did not exist as a person from eternity as one of the triune Godhead. . . . He did not actually come into being until He was begotten of the Holy Spirit and born in Bethlehem."[6]

Christian Science (Mary Baker Eddy). "Jesus Christ is not God, as Jesus Himself declared, but is the Son of God."[7]

The Christian Spiritual Alliance (Roy Eugene Davis). ". . . Jesus was not the only begotten."[8]

Church of the New Jerusalem (Emanuel Swedenborg). "This [belief in the Trinity] is the source and only source from which have sprung monstrous heresies concerning God . . . [and] introduced into the church . . . death as well."[9]

Church Universal and Triumphant (Elizabeth Claire Prophet). "God the Father did not require the sacrifice of His son Christ Jesus or of any other incarnation of the Christ, as atonement for the sins of the world."[10]

The Divine Life Society/Integral Yoga Institute (Sivananda, Satchidananda). "Remember that Christ is not a person. It's an experience—Christhood. Like Nirvana or Buddha. It's an experience."[11]

Divine Science (Nona Brooks). "Someone has said that the greatest discovery of the nineteenth century was Jesus Christ. He was rediscovered and rescued from the superstitious misconceptions regarding him, in which he was thought of as a superman of extraordinary powers which were and ever would be beyond the rank and file of the race."[12]

Eckankar (Paul Twitchell). ". . . do not put Him [Jesus] in a special category, for all saviours and prophets who came to earth to help mankind did their part and passed on to the glory of the heavenly kingdom."[13]

The Foundation of Human Understanding (Roy Masters). "You must not have any concepts of what Christ is like or God is like. It all must be an inward revelation process."[14]

The Free Communion Church (Da Free John). "The conventional cultic and exoteric interpretation of the life and person of Jesus considers him to be an exclusive manifestation of God, representing a history, a way of life, and a destiny that no one else can enjoy or duplicate. . . . Such was absolutely not the point of view of Jesus himself."[15]

The Gurdjieff Foundation (Gurdjieff). "[In a conversation] Gurdjieff said: 'I hate your Jesus, poor Jewish boy'—the emphasis being on 'your.' "[16]

The Hanuman Foundation (Ram Dass). "I have a relative [a brother] who is in a mental hospital. He thinks he is Christ. Well, that's groovy. I am Christ also . . . as far as I'm concerned we are all God."[17]

The Himalayan Institute (Swami Rama). "The Christ is your Soul and you should learn to see Him in all beings."[18]

The Holy Order of Mans (Paul Blighton). "The Master Jesus never made any claims for himself. . . . [He] was a man, and through discipline and striving became receptive enough for the Christ force to enter and change him."[19]

Integral Yoga (Sri Aurobindo). "If Jesus returned today, He would not recognize in Christianity what He Himself taught."[20]

International Society for Krishna Consciousness (A. C. Bhaktivedanta Prabhupada). "Christ's claim to be the only son of God is often misunderstood. . . . When Jesus Christ taught His doctrine in the Middle East, he appeared to be God's only son, or pure devotee. . . . [But] why should God have only one son? . . . God can have billions and trillions of sons and . . . each and every one can be His 'only' son."[21]

Jehovah's Witnesses (Charles Taze Russell). "The incarnation is scripturally erroneous. Indeed, if he (Christ) had been an incarnate being, he could never have redeemed mankind."[22]

The Local Church (Witness Lee). "He has God's nature, and we also have God's nature. He is no longer God's only begotten Son: now by His resurrection He has become God's firstborn Son (Romans 8:29) and we are the many sons of God (Hebrews 2:10)."[23]

Love Family/The Children of God (David Berg). "[There is] no reason why He [Jesus] shouldn't enjoy the sexual fellowship of Mary and Martha! AND HE DID BECAUSE I SAW MARY MAKING LOVE TO HIM in a vision."[24]

Lucis Trust (Alice Bailey). The Incarnation, which is for popular Christianity synonymous with the historical birth and earthly life of Christ, is for the mystic not only this but also a perpetual cosmic and personal process."[25]

The Masonic Lodge. A former Mason reports, "Freemasonry 'carefully excludes' the Lord Jesus Christ from the lodge and chapter, repudiates His mediatorship, rejects His atonement, denies and disowns His Gospel, frowns upon His religion and His church, ignores the Holy Spirit. . . ."[26]

Mighty I AM (Guy Ballard, pen name Godfre Ray King). "I [Jesus] wish it distinctly understood by all who may receive this or ever contact it, that I am not and never was a Special Being created of God different from the rest of humanity!"[27] [Alleged revelation from Jesus.]

Mormonism (Joseph Smith). "Christ is the firstborn spirit Son in the eternal family, and while yet in preexistence he advanced and progressed and became like the Father in power and intelligence; that is, he became a God."[28]

New Thought. "We revere Jesus the man ... as one who exemplified ... the great Principle of perfection and wholeness. Jesus was a Way-Shower—the Savior—in the sense that He drew us out of our limitations."[29]

Nichiren Shoshu Buddhism (Daisaku Ikeda). "The doctrines of the divinity and the resurrection of Christ are outside the province of rational thought. ... Christians are schizophrenic."[30]

Radhasoami/Radhaswami/Radha Soami (Charan Singh; Sawan Singh Ji). "Actually there is no statement in the New Testament, except possibly one or two interpolations, in which Jesus makes any claim to an exclusive divine sonship. This idea was not incorporated into the Christian religion until long after his death."[31]

Rajneesh Foundation International (Bhagwan Shree Rajneesh). "To tell you the truth, Jesus is a mental case. ... He is a fanatic. He carries the same kind of mind as Adolf Hitler. He is a fascist. He thinks that only those who follow *him* will be saved."[32]

Rosicrucianism/AMORC (H. Spencer Lewis). "Nowhere in the teachings and practices of Jesus can we find the least intimation that His great system was intended to bring salvation to the *physical body of man*. Even the salvation of the soul was not taught by Jesus, and all references in the Christian Bible to the salvation of the soul constitute a misinterpretation, a misunderstanding, of the secret [Rosicrucianism] principle that Jesus taught."[33]

Rudrananda Foundation (Swami Rudrananda; Rudi). In *Spiritual Cannibalism* Jesus is described as "a god," a "realized" man, like Buddha and other teachers.[34]

Ruhani Satsang (Kirpal Singh). "Everyone is under the impression that Jesus Christ remains forever. The Christ Power remains forever [not Jesus]; but they [Christians] identify Christ with Jesus, the [solely] human pole, which is not right."[35]

Sai Baba Society (Sathya Sai Baba). "The inner mystery of the Incarnation [is] God incarnating in all. All are One; the One is All."[36]

Science of Mind (Ernest Holmes). "Jesus is the name of a man. Christ means the Universal Principle of Divine Sonship."[37]

Scientology (L. Ron Hubbard). "Neither Lord Buddha nor Jesus Christ were OTs [Operation Thetans, enlightened beings] according to the evidence. They were just a shade above clear [relatively low on the Scientology scale of spiritual advancement]."[38]

Self-Realization Fellowship (Paramahansa Yogananda). "In Christian Scriptures it [Christ] is called the 'only begotten son.' ... It is the universal consciousness, oneness with God, manifested by Jesus, Krishna, and other avatars."[39]

3HO (Happy, Healthy, Holy) Sikhism (Yogi Bhajan). Jesus was a man of God only, who had to become qualified for his spiritual role. He didn't know if Joseph was his father, and his mother created "her son to really be a Christ," but not a savior.[40]

Sri Chinmoy Centers (Sri Chinmoy). "[To] say that Christ is *the* Savior and the only way to salvation is a mistake. ... He laughs when His followers say He is the only Savior. ..."[41]

Tibetan Buddhism (Chogyam Trungpa). "Any kind of savior notion will not function a hundred percent. ..." Worshipping a "deity of any kind" is "the wrong way," and taking refuge in a Father God "is truly self-defeating."[42]

Theosophy (H. P. Blavatsky). "Nowhere throughout the *New Testament* is Jesus found calling himself God, or anything higher than 'a son of God,' the son of a 'Father,' common to all."[43]

Transcendental Meditation (Maharishi Mahesh Yogi). "[When] Christ said, 'Be still and know that I am God,' [He also meant] 'Be still and know that you are God.'" "I don't think Christ ever suffered [on the Cross].... Those who count upon the suffering, it is a wrong interpretation of the life of Christ and the message of Christ. It is wrong."[44]

The Unification Church (Sun Myung Moon). "It is a great error to think Jesus was God Himself. Jesus is no different from other men."[45]

Unitarian/Universalism. Unitarian Universalist minister Waldemar Argow states: "They [Unitarian/Universalists] do not regard him as a supernatural creature, the literal son of God who was miraculously sent to earth as part of an involved plan for the salvation of human souls."[46]

Unity School of Christianity (Charles Fillmore). "Most of our religious beliefs are based on the [erroneous] idea that Jesus is the only begotten Son of God."[47]

Vedanta. Swami Prabhavananda alleges that we "cannot accept Christ as the *only* Son of God. Those who insist on regarding the life and teachings of Jesus as unique are bound to have great difficulty in understanding them."[48]

The Walk (John Robert Stevens and the Church of the Living Word). "The Lord puts you through a process that will bring you into sonship, into deity.... God becoming man means nothing unless we become God, unless we become lost in Him."[49]

The Way International (Victor Paul Wierwille). "Trinitarian dogma placing Jesus Christ on God's level degrades God and leaves man UNREDEEMED!" (advertisement for Wierwille's book, *Jesus Christ Is Not God*). "Our very redemption . . . is dependent on Jesus Christ's being a man and not God."[50]

The Yoga Fellowship (Swami Kriyananda). "What is Christ? St. Simeon the new theologian wrote, 'I move my hand, and Christ moves, who is my hand.'"[51]

Zen Buddhism. *The Gospel According to Zen* quotes Meister Eckhart: "Who is Jesus? He has no name," and "Jesus" declares, "Split wood: I am there. Lift up the stone, and you will find me there."[52]

Almost all of the preceding groups claim that they accept and honor Jesus Christ. But in light of what we have just read, this is impossible. In fact, such groups (there are hundreds more) completely disregard the biblical Jesus and reinvent Christ only to make Him support their own beliefs. Indeed, only *overwhelming* evidence in favor of Christ's deity would have convinced skeptical, staunchly monotheistic and initially frightened Jews to proclaim Christ's deity to a hostile Jerusalem and later to the world.

Notes
1. *The Koran Interpreted*, A. J. Arberry, Trans. (New York. Macmillan, 1976), Sura 4:155, 169; 5:19.
2. Rudolf Steiner, *From Jesus to Christ* (London: Rudolf Steiner Press, 1973), pp. 51-52.
3. Association for Research and Enlightenment, Edgar Cayce, reading #900-10 from *Circulating File: Jesus the Pattern and You* (Virginia Beach: A.R.E. Press, 1971), p. 53 (F).
4. Earlyne Chaney, *Reincarnation* (booklet) (Upland, CA: Astara, 1967), pp. 6-7; Robert Chaney, *Mysticism: The Journey Within* (Upland, CA: Astara, 1979), pp. 117, 163-73.
5. Firuz Kazemzeden (ed.), *World Order* (periodical), Summer, 1978 (The National Spiritual Assembly of the Baha'is of the United States), p. 39.
6. *The Christadelphian Messenger*, No. 46, "The Word Made Flesh," p. 3.
7. Mary Baker Eddy, *Science and Health with Key to the Scriptures* (Boston: The First Church of Christ, Scientist, 1934), p. 361.
8. Roy Eugene Davis, *The Hidden Teachings of Jesus Revealed* (Lakemont, GA: CSA Press, 1968), p. 9, emphasis added.
9. Emanuel Swedenborg, *The True Christian Religion*, Vol. I (New York: Swedenborg Foundation, Inc., 1972), pp. 32-33.

691

10. The Ascended Masters, dictated to Mark and Elizabeth Prophet, *Pearls of Wisdom*, Sept. 16, 1979 (Vol. 22, No. 37), pp. 279-280.

11. Swami Satchidananda, *Satchidananda Speaks* (Annhurst III Integral Yoga Ecumenical Retreat), June 17, 1975, pp. 47-48.

12. Agnes Lawson, *Hints to Bible Study* (Denver: Divine Science Federation International, 1973), pp. 199-200.

13. Paul Twitchell, *The Tiger's Fang* (San Diego: Illuminated Way Press, 1975), pp. 170-71.

14. Roy Masters , "The Mystery of Golgotha," (tape).

15. Da Free John (Franklin Jones), *Scientific Proof of the Existence of God Will Soon Be Announced at the White House* (Clearlake Highlands, CA: The Dawn Horse Press, 1980), p. 218.

16. C. S. Nott, *Teachings of Gurdjieff—A Pupil's Journal* (New York: Samuel Weiser, Inc., 1978), p. 103.

17. Ram Dass, *Be Here Now* (Park Avenue, NY: Crown Publishing, 1971), Section Two, p. 99.

18. Himalayan International Institute, *Meditation in Christianity* (Prospect Heights, IL: Himalayan International Institute, 1973), p. 63.

19. *Discipleship Newsletter* (Cheyenne, WY: Holy Order of Mans Discipleship Movement) p. 7.

20. Sri Aurobindo and The Mother, *A Practical Guide to Integral Yoga* (compiled by Manishai, Pondicherry, India: Sri Aurobindo Ashram, 1973), p. 50.

21. *Back to Godhead* (periodical), Vol. 12, no. 12, pp. 11-12.

22. J. F. Rutherford, *The Harp of God* (1921 edition), p. 101.

23. Witness Lee, *How to Meet* (Anaheim, CA: Stream Publishers, 1970), p. 30.

24. David Berg, *The Mo Letters*, Vol. 4 (Hong Kong: Golden Lion Publishers, 1978), p. 4016, "More on Feedin' the Fish," May, 1976, Disciples Only, No. 549:47-48.

25. Alice Bailey, *From Bethlehem to Calvary* (New York: Lucis, 1976), p. 7.

26. Edmond Ronayne, *The Master's Carpet* (Chicago: Ezra Cook Company, 1879), p. 87.

27. Godfre Ray King, *The "I AM" Discourses* (Santa Fe, NM: Saint Germain Press, 1940), p. 222.

28. Bruce McConkie, *Doctrinal New Testament Commentary*, Vol. 3 (Salt Lake City: Bookcraft, 1973), p. 140.

29. *New Thought* (periodical), Autumn 1978, p. 11.

30. Noah S. Brannen, *Soka Gakkai, Japan's Militant Buddhists* (Richmond, VA: John Knox Press, 1968), pp. 98-99.

31. Joseph Leeming, *Yoga and the Bible* (Punjab, India: Shri S. L. Sondhi, Secretary, Radha Soami Satsang Beas, 1978), p. 3.

32. Bhagwan Shree Rajneesh, *The Rajneesh Bible*, Vol. 1 (Rajneeshpruam: OR: Rajneesh Foundation International, 1985), pp. 9-10.

33. Spencer Lewis, *The Secret Doctrine of Jesus* (San Jose, CA: Supreme Grand Lodge of AMORC), pp. 186-87, 189-91.

34. Rudi (Swami Rudrananda), *Spiritual Cannibalism* (Woodstock, NY: The Overlook Press, 1978), p. 95.

35. Kirpal Singh, *Heart to Heart Talks*, Vol. 2 (India: A.R. Manocha, Secretary, Ruhani Satsang, 1976), p. 54.

36. N. Kasturi, *Sathya Sai Speaks*, Vol. 8, 1st ed. (New Delhi, India, n.p., 1975), p. 144.

37. Ernest Holmes and Alberta Smith, *Questions and Answers on the Science of Mind* (New York: Dodd, Mead and Company, 1953), p. 10.

38. *Ability* magazine, No. 81 [c. 1959], p. 31.

39. Paramahansa Yogananda, *Man's Eternal Quest* (Los Angeles, CA: Self Realization Fellowship, 1975), pp. 470-71; cf. *Self Realization* (Los Angeles: Self Realization Fellowship), Winter 1979, pp. 3-10.

40. *Beads of Truth*, Winter, March 1978, p. 20; Spring 1975, p. 13; Spring 1978, pp. 32, 39; *Beads of Truth*, no. 31, p. 15.

41. Sri Chinmoy, *A Hundred Years from Now* (Jamaica, NY: Agni Press, 1974), pp. 39-43.

42. Chogyam Trungpa, *Garuda III* (Berkeley, CA: Shambhala Publications, Inc., 1973), pp. 25, 39; Chogyam Trungpa, *Cutting Through Spiritual Materialism* (Berkeley, CA: Shambhala Publications, Inc., 1973), pp. 27, 37.

43. Helena Petrovna Blavatsky, *The Secret Doctrine* (India: Theosophical Publishing House, 1971), Vol. 5, p. 369n.

44. Maharishi Mahesh Yogi, *Meditations of Maharishi Mahesh Yogi* (New York: Bantam, 1973), pp. 178, 123-24.

5. Young Oon Kim, *Divine Principle and Its Application* (HSA-UWC, 1968), p. 75.

46. Waldemar Argow, *Unitarian Universalism—Some Questions Answered* (pamphlet) (Boston: Unitarian Universalism Assoc., n.d.), p. 6.

47. *Unity* (periodical), October, 1976, pp. 59-60.

48. Swami Prabhavananda, *The Sermon on the Mount According to Vedanta* (New York: New American Library, 1963), p. 47.

49. *The Living Word This Week*, January 16, 1977, pp. 12-15, 18.

50. *The Way Magazine*, January-February 1978, p. 6; Victor Paul Wierwille, *Jesus Christ Is Not God* (New Knoxville, OH, 1975), p. 7.

51. Swami Kriyananda, *Eastern Thoughts, Western Thoughts* (Nevada City, CA: Ananda Publications, 1975), pp. 67-68.

52. Robert Sohl and Audrey Carr (eds.), *The Gospel According to Zen* (New York: The New American Library, 1970), pp. 92, 72.

THE PERSONALITY AND DEITY OF THE HOLY SPIRIT

Religious groups who deny the Trinity not only characteristically deny the Person and work of Jesus Christ but also the personality and deity of the Holy Spirit. Jehovah's Witnesses teach that "the holy spirit is the active force of God. It is not a person but is a powerful force that God causes to emanate from himself to accomplish his holy will."[1] Victor Paul Wierwille, founder of The Way International, declares, "One of the most misunderstood fields among Christians today is that of the Holy Spirit."[2] Wierwille believes that the Holy

Spirit is merely a synonym for the one Person of the Godhead, the Father, who alone is God. Thus, whenever Wierwille uses the term "Holy Spirit" in his writings (with capital letters), he is merely using a synonym for God. Whenever Wierwille uses small letters, "holy spirit," he means the spiritual gifts given by God the Father. In Wierwille's theology, the biblical Holy Spirit does not exist.[3] Wierwille, Jehovah's Witnesses and many others claim the early church never believed that the Holy Spirit was God.

Although the development of the doctrine of the Holy Spirit was theologically less refined in the early church than that of the doctrine of Jesus Christ, there was still recognition that the Holy Spirit was both personal and God. Here are several sources:

> Athenagoras (his chief work defending the Trinity, *Embassy for the Christians*, is dated 176–180 A.D.) wrote that of the Father, Son and Holy Spirit Christians declared "both their power in union and their distinction in order."[4]

> According to noted theologian, Harold O. J. Brown, "Tertullian [160–230 A.D.] was the first to speak plainly of the Holy Spirit as God and to say that he is of one substance with the Father."[5]

> Tertullian concluded, "Thus the connection of the Father and the Son, and of the Son in the Paraclete [Holy Spirit], produces three coherent Persons, who are yet distinct One from Another. These three are one essence"[6]

> Cyril of Jerusalem wrote that the "Holy Spirit is *honored together* with the Father and the Son *and is fully included* in the holy Trinity. We are not preaching three Gods, so let the Marcionites hold their peace. We do not divide up the holy Trinity, as some do, nor, like Sabellius, do we coalesce it into one. Great indeed is the Holy Spirit, and in his gifts, *omnipotent* and wonderful."[7]

> Athanasius wrote that the "Holy Spirit cannot be a creature, and it is impious to call him so."[8]

> In speaking of the Holy Spirit as a gift to the church, Augustine wrote, "And therefore the Holy Spirit, *God though He is,* is most rightly called also the gift of God."[9]

> Basil of Caesarea wrote, "The Lord has delivered to us as a necessary and saving doctrine that the Holy Spirit is to be ranked *with the Father.*"[10]

Origen argued, "For if [He were not eternally as He is . . .] the Holy Spirit would never be reckoned in the Unity of the Trinity, i.e., along with the unchangeable Father and His Son, unless He had always been the Holy Spirit."[11]

We emphasize again that the early Christians concluded that the Holy Spirit was God for the same reason that they concluded that Jesus was God: because this was the scriptural testimony and the only option they had. Thus, if we examine what the Scripture teaches about the Holy Spirit, we find that the traditional Trinitarian view is clearly seen. For example, the Holy Spirit is distinguished from both the Father and the Son (Isaiah 48:16; Matthew 28:19; Luke 3:21; John 14:16, 17; Hebrews 9:8). Also, the Holy Spirit is clearly not an impersonal force, as Jehovah's Witnesses claim, but a real Person. For instance He loves (Romans 15:30); convicts of sin (John 16:8); has a personal will (1 Corinthians 12:11); commands and forbids (Acts 8:29; 13:2; 16:6); speaks messages (1 Timothy 4:1; Revelation 2:7); intercedes (Romans 8:26); comforts, teaches and guides into truth (John 14:26); and can be grieved, blasphemed and insulted (Ephesians 4:30; Mark 3:29; Hebrews 10:29). Once it is established that the Holy Spirit is a Person, it is easy to see that the impersonal, or even inanimate, terminology in Scripture that is used for Him, such as His "filling us," "being poured out" and so on, is not meant to imply that the Holy Spirit is impersonal, but rather it is illustrating the intimacy of the believer's relationship to Him.

The Holy Spirit is deity because He performs the functions of God and because He is called God in Scripture. He has the attributes of deity, such as omnipresence (Psalm 139:7, 8); omniscience (1 Corinthians 2:10–11); eternality (Hebrews 9:14); omnipotence (Job 33:4). And He gives eternal life (John 3:3–8). He is also the Creator (Job 33:4; Genesis 1:2). It goes without saying that no impersonal force (Jehovah's Witnesses) or finite god (Mormonism) has the personal and divine attributes that Scripture assigns to the Holy Spirit.

It is also clear from Scripture that the Holy Spirit is God by the divine functions that He performs and by the divine associations that He has.

He indwells all believers (John 14:23; 1 Corinthians 6:19 with 2 Corinthians 6:16); strives with all people and convicts the whole world of their guilt and their need of faith in Jesus (Genesis 6:3 with John 16:8; 1 Peter 3:20); divinely inspires (2 Peter 1:21 with Luke 1:68–70 with Acts 1:16, 28:25; Isaiah 6:1–13; Hebrews 10:15–17 with Jeremiah 31:31–34); sanctifies (2 Thessalonians 2:13–14 with 1 Thessalonians 4:7). And in His divine role He sends forth laborers (Matthew 9:38 with Acts 13:2–4; compare Psalm 95:6–9 with Hebrews 3:7–9; Romans 5:5 with 1 Thessalonians 3:12–13 and 2 Thessalonians 3:5). The Holy Spirit is also called God. In Acts 5:3–4, the one lied to is first said to be the Holy Spirit, who is then immediately identified as God. He is called "the Lord" in 2 Corinthians 3:18 and in Hebrews 10:15–16. In Isaiah 6:8–9 and Acts 28:25–26, one passage speaks of "the Lord" (God) speaking to Isaiah, whereas the other passage declares the same message was spoken by the Holy Spirit to Isaiah.

There is only one eternal sin spoken of in all the Bible, the blasphemy against the Holy Spirit (Matthew 12:32). All sins committed against God the Father and God the Son can be forgiven (Matthew 12:32), but blasphemy against the Holy Spirit can never be forgiven. How can this be if the Holy Spirit is merely a creature or an impersonal force? What is the sin spoken of here? Unbelief to the point of death is the only eternal sin: this is the blasphemy against the Holy Spirit and against His testimony concerning Jesus (John 16:8). Thus, persistent resistance of the Holy Spirit's conviction of one's need to believe in Jesus Christ for forgiveness of sins (John 16:8) can never be forgiven. Why? Because one thereby refuses to place faith in Christ, which alone can bring redemption. The Holy Spirit, then, must indeed be God because one can only commit an eternal sin against an eternal God. Indeed, the scriptural testimony to the personality and deity of the Holy Spirit is far more abundant in Scripture than one might think.[12]

The Holy Spirit, whose job it is to glorify Jesus Christ, has been given His rightful place in the Trinity by the historic Christian church. Sadly, He has not been given the honor due Him by the cults.

Notes

1. Watchtower Bible and Tract Society, *Reasoning from the Scriptures* (Brooklyn, NY: Watchtower Bible and Tract Society, 1985), p. 381.
2. Victor Paul Wierwille, *Jesus Christ Is Not God,* (New Knoxville, OH: American Christian Press, 1975), p. 127.
3. Ibid., Appendix A; cf. Victor Paul Wierwille, *Receiving the Holy Spirit Today* (New Knoxville, OH: American Christian Press, 1976), Chapter 1.
4. E. Calvin Beisner, *God in Three Persons* (Wheaton, IL: Tyndale, 1984), p. 53, citing Alexander Roberts and James Donaldson (eds.), *The Ante-Nicene Fathers: Translations of the Writings of the Fathers Down to A.D. 325,* Vol. 2, p. 133, *A Plea for the Christians,* X.
5. Harold O. J. Brown, *Heresies* (Garden City, NY: Doubleday, 1984), pp. 140-141.
6. Tertullian, *Against Praxeas,* p. 25, cited in Brown, *Heresies,* p. 145.
7. Cyril of Jerusalem, "Catechetical Lecture," 16, para. 4, in Maurice Wiles and Mark Santer (eds.), *Documents in Early Christian Thought* (Cambridge: Cambridge University Press, 1979), p. 82.
8. Athanasius, "Third Letter to Serapion," I, in Wiles and Santer, p. 85.
9. Augustine, "On the Trinity," XV, xvii, 32, in Wiles and Santer, p. 94.
10. Basil of Caesarea, "The Book of Saint Basil on the Spirit," Chapter X, para. 25 in Philip Schaff and Henry Wace, *A Select Library of Nicean and Post-Nicean Fathers of the Christian Church, Second Series, Vol. 8* (Grand Rapids, MI: Eerdmans, 1975), p. 17.
11. In Beisner, *God in Three Persons,* p. 64, citing Roberts and Donaldson, *Ante-Nicene Fathers,* Vol. 4, p. 253; *de Principus* I.iii.4.
12. See Edward Henry Beckersteth, *The Holy Spirit: His Person and Work* (Grand Rapids, MI: Kregel, 1967) for an excellent scriptural study on the personality and deity of the Holy Spirit.

SALVATION:
THE GLORY OF THE GOSPEL

Salvation is not achieved by one's personal righteousness, or one's good deeds for God, church or people generally. It is not anything one can earn, no matter how hard a person tries. Salvation is not about removing ignorance of one's alleged divine nature, nor is it about human enlightenment in a general sense or the progress of human evolution. Biblically, salvation is from one thing and one thing only: sin. Salvation occurs only when a person's sin is forgiven by God.

To merit entrance into heaven, humanly speaking, one must be sinless, which means that the Law would have to be kept perfectly, without even a single failure. However, because all men and women have inherited Adam's sin and have a sin nature, they can never keep the Law perfectly in order to merit entrance into heaven:

> All of us have become like one who is unclean, and **all our righteous acts** are like filthy rags; we all shrivel up like a leaf, and like the wind our sins sweep us away. (Isaiah 64:6)

> For I tell you that unless your righteousness **surpasses** that of the Pharisees and the teachers of the law, you will certainly not enter the kingdom of heaven. (Matthew 5:20)

> For whoever keeps the whole law and yet stumbles at **just one point** is guilty of breaking **all of it.** (James 2:10)

> All who rely on observing the law are **under a curse,** for it is written: "Cursed is everyone who does not continue to do **everything** written in the Book of the Law." (Galatians 3:10)

The problem is that no one can keep the Law perfectly because of the inherited tendency to sin and the willful choice to sin. Therefore we all stand guilty before God and are powerless to save ourselves. "You see, at just the right time, **when we were still powerless,** Christ died for the ungodly" (Romans 5:6). "For what the law was **powerless to do** in that it was weakened by the sinful nature, God did by sending his own Son in the likeness of sinful man to be a sin offering. And so he condemned sin in sinful man" (Romans 8:3). Thus, because we are unable to keep the Law, salvation by that means must be considered impossible. The following scriptures prove this beyond dispute and reveal that all religions which teach salvation by law or works are wrong.

The Law, good works and personal righteousness are powerless to save people.

> For if a law **had been given** that could impart life, then righteousness would **certainly** have come by the law. (Galatians 3:21)

> I do not set aside the grace of God, for if righteousness could be gained through the law, **Christ died for nothing!** (Galatians 2:21)

For we maintain a man is justified by faith **apart from observing the law.** (Romans 3:28) To the man **who does not work** but trusts God who justifies the wicked, his faith is credited as righteousness. David says the same thing when he speaks of the blessedness of the man to whom God credits righteousness **apart from works:** Blessed are they whose transgressions are forgiven, whose sins are covered. Blessed is the man whose sin the Lord will never count against him. (Romans 4:5-8)

> We . . . know that a man is **not justified by observing the law,** but by faith in Jesus Christ. So we, too, have put our faith in Jesus Christ that we may be justified by faith in Christ and **not by observing the law,** because by observing the law **no one** will be justified. (Galatians 2:15-16)

> All who rely on observing the law are **under a curse,** for it is written: "Cursed is everyone who does not continue to do everything written in the Book of the Law." Clearly no **one is justified before God by the law,** because, "the righteous will live by faith." The law is not based on faith; on the contrary, "the man who does these things will live by them." Christ redeemed us from the **curse of the law** by becoming a curse for us, for it is written: "Cursed is everyone who is hung on a tree." (Galatians 3:10-13)

> Then they asked him, "What must we do to do the works God requires?" Jesus answered "The **work of God** is this: to believe in the one he has sent." (John 6:28-29)

> Now then, why do you try to test God by putting on the necks of the disciples a yoke that **neither we nor our fathers** have been able to bear? No! We believe it is through the grace of our Lord Jesus that we are saved, just as they are. (Acts 15:10-11)

If salvation does not come by works, salvation must come by faith alone. This is one reason the Scripture declares that our faith is more precious than gold (1 Peter 1:7). Consider the following:

> Yet to all who received him, to those who **believed** in his name, he gave the right to become children of God. (John 1:12)

> For God so loved the world that he gave his one and only Son, that whoever **believes in him** shall not perish but have eternal life. (John 3:16)

695

All the prophets testify about him [Jesus] that everyone who **believes in him** receives forgiveness of sins through his name. (Acts 10:43)

Not having a righteousness of my own that comes from the law, but that which is through faith in Christ—the righteousness that comes from God and is by faith. (Philippians 3:9)

For in the gospel a righteousness from God is revealed, a righteousness that is by faith **from first to last,** just as it is written: "the righteous will live by faith." (Romans 1:17)

Without faith it is impossible to please God. (Hebrews 11:6)

I have come into the world as a light, so that no one who **believes in me** should stay in darkness. (John 12:46)

This righteousness from God comes through faith in Jesus Christ to **all who believe.** (Romans 3:22)

Christ is the end of the law so that there may be righteousness for everyone who believes. (Romans 10:4)

Salvation is therefore a free gift of God's grace.

For it is by grace you have been saved, through faith—and this not from yourselves, it is the **gift** of God—not by works, so that no one can boast. (Ephesians 2:8–9)

For the wages of sin is death, but the **gift** of God is eternal life in Christ Jesus our Lord. (Romans 6:23)

Eternal life cannot possibly be earned by subsequent works and personal righteousness if eternal life is received *at the point of faith.*

Whoever believes in the Son **has** eternal life, (John 3:36)

I tell you the truth, whoever hears my word and believes him who sent me **has** eternal life and will not be condemned; he **has** crossed over from death to life. (John 5:24)

I tell you the truth, he who believes **has** everlasting life. (John 6:47)

I write these things to you who believe in the name of the Son of God so that you may **know** that you **have** eternal life. (1 John 5:13)

FORGIVENESS OF SIN THROUGH GOD'S GRACE AND THE ATONEMENT OF CHRIST

The death of Jesus Christ on the Cross was not merely ethical, a sacrificial example to show us that we need to live good lives no matter what the cost. It was not to illustrate the contamination of materiality (avoiding the "evil" of the material world) or other alleged human problems. The death of Christ did not open an inevitable door to heaven or the next life, or to multiple lives; nor did He infuse His body's "desire over the earth" (Rosicrucian) with divine benevolence toward all people. God's grace is never God's means to enable us to earn our own salvation by effort, as Mormonism teaches, nor is it God's unconditional acceptance of everyone apart from Christ, as Universalism teaches.

As the means to salvation, God's grace is most clearly exemplified in the death of Christ for our sin. Thus, the Bible is clear that salvation is possible *only* because of the atonement of Christ. Salvation is possible because of the divine act of grace where God accepts the offering of Jesus as a substitute for the punishment of sin that was due each of us. Consider the following:

I am the good shepherd. The good shepherd lays down his life for the sheep. (John 10:11)

This is my blood of the covenant, which is poured out for many for the forgiveness of sins. (Matthew 26:28)

This is what is written: the Christ will suffer and rise from the dead on the third day, and repentance and forgiveness of sins will be preached in his name to all nations, beginning at Jerusalem. (Luke 24:46)

The Son of man did not come to be served, but to serve, and to give his life as a ransom for many. (Matthew 20:28)

God . . . [sent] his own Son . . . to be a sin offering. (Romans 8:3)

For all have sinned and fall short of the glory of God, and are justified freely by his grace through the redemption that came by Christ Jesus. God presented him as a sacrifice of atonement, through faith in his blood. He did this to demonstrate his justice . . . so as to be just and the one who justifies those who have faith in Jesus. (Romans 3:23–26)

But we see Jesus, who . . . suffered death, so that by the grace of God he might taste death for everyone. (Hebrews 2:9)

Look, the lamb of God, who takes away the sin of the world! (John 1:29)

For what I received I passed on to you as of first importance; that Christ died for our sins according to the scriptures. (1 Corinthians 15:3)

In him we have redemption through his blood, the forgiveness of sins, in accordance with the riches of God's grace. (Ephesians 1:7)

He himself bore our sins in his body on the tree, so that we might die to sins and live for righteousness. (1 Peter 2:24)

But demonstrates his own love for us in this: while we were still sinners Christ died for us. (Romans 5:8)

But now he has appeared once for all at the end of the ages to do away with sin by the sacrifice of himself. (Hebrews 9:26)

He is the atoning sacrifice for our sins, and not only for ours but also for the sins of the whole world. (1 John 2:2)

But you know that he appeared so that he might take away our sins. And in him is no sin. (1 John 3:5)

This is love: not that we loved God, but that he loved us and sent his Son as an atoning sacrifice for our sins. (1 John 4:10)

Be shepherds of the church of God, which he bought with his own blood. (Acts 20:28)

But when this priest [Jesus] had offered for all time one sacrifice for sins, he sat down at the right hand of God . . . because by one sacrifice he has made perfect forever those who are being made holy. . . . Then he adds, "Their sins and lawless acts I will remember no more." And where these have been forgiven, there is no longer any sacrifice for sin. (Hebrews 10:10–17)

For you know that it was not with perishable things such as silver and gold that you were redeemed . . . but with the precious blood of Christ. (1 Peter 1:18)

THE DOCTRINE OF JUSTIFICATION

"Justification" is the act of God whereby He forgives the sins of believers and declares them righteous by imputing the obedience and righteousness of Christ to them through faith. (Luke 18:9–14)

Justification is one of the most important doctrines in the Bible. It is without question a doctrine that is rejected and opposed by all cults and religions outside of Christianity. In his book *Know Your Christian Life: A Theological Introduction,* theologian Sinclair Ferguson discusses its importance, not only for the church but also for the Christian:

> Martin Luther, whose grasp of the gospel was better than most, once said that the doctrine of Justification was the article by which the Church stands or falls. "This article," he said, "is the head and cornerstone of the Church, which alone begets, nourishes, builds, preserves and protects the Church; without it the Church of God cannot subsist one hour." Luther was right. Although for our understanding of the general shape and direction of the Christian life we have suggested the doctrine of regeneration is important, the doctrine of justification is central. Not only is it the article of the standing or falling Church, but also of the standing or falling Christian. Probably more trouble is caused in the Christian life by an inadequate or mistaken view of this doctrine than any other. When the child of God loses his sense of peace with God, finds his concern for others dried up, or generally finds his sense of the sheer goodness and grace of God diminished, it is from this fountain that he has ceased to drink. Conversely, if we can gain a solid grounding here, we have the foundation for a life of peace and joy.[1]

Ferguson then explains why this doctrine is difficult for some to accept:

> The practical importance of this cannot be exaggerated. The glory of the gospel is that God has declared Christians to be rightly related to him in spite of their sin. But our greatest temptation and mistake is to try to smuggle character into his work of grace. How easily we fall into the trap of assuming that we only remain justified so long as there are grounds in our character for that justification. But Paul's teaching is that nothing we do ever contributes to our justification. So powerful was his emphasis on this that men accused him of teaching that it did not matter how they lived if God justified them.

If God justifies us as we are, what is the point of holiness? There is still a sense in which this is a test of whether we offer the world the grace of God in the Gospel. Does it make me say: "You are offering grace that is so free it doesn't make any difference how you live"? This was precisely the objection the Pharisees had to Jesus' teaching![2]

The biblical doctrine of justification is particularly relevant for the cults who may claim that the doctrine involves only a *partial* justification, which we must maintain by our good works in order to receive final, complete justification or acceptance before God. In essence, these cults argue that the biblical doctrine is a legal fiction because an ultimate self-justification is the only way people can finally earn God's favor. The Bible disagrees because Scripture emphatically teaches that any person who simply and truly believes in Jesus Christ as his or her personal Savior from sin is, *at that moment*, irrevocably and eternally justified. Justification is thus the final verdict of God whereby He not only forgives and pardons the sins of the believer but also declares the believer perfectly righteous by imputing, or crediting, the obedience and righteousness of Christ Himself to the believer—solely through faith. It is therefore on the basis of Christ's life and atonement that God "pronounces believers to have fulfilled all the requirements of the law which pertain to them."[3]

Because justification is an eternal verdict pronounced of God, it is made final the moment a person believes on Christ. This explains why eternal life is granted at the moment of faith (John 6:47; 1 John 5:13). As a result, justification is not a lifelong process and must be distinguished from personal sanctification, which is individual growth in holy living over the period of a lifetime. Both the Old and New Testaments teach the Protestant view of legal (forensic) justification. Consider the following evidence for the Old Testament view of justification:

Concerning the Old Testament word *hitsdiq*, usually rendered "justified," more often than not it is "used in a forensic or legal sense, as meaning, not 'to make just or righteous,' but 'to declare judicially that one is in harmony with the law'. . . . In the Old Testament, the concept of

righteousness frequently appears in a forensic or juridical context. A righteous man is one who has been declared by a judge to be free from guilt."[4]

In his book *Justification*, even Catholic theologian Hans Kung argues for this view when he says, "According to the original biblical usage of the term, 'justification' must be defined as a declaring just by court order."[5] Despite the official Catholic teaching of salvation by works, some other Catholic theologians have agreed with Kung.[6]

The New Testament Scripture agrees with the Old, clearly showing that justification is: (1) a crediting of righteousness on the basis of a person's faith, (2) a completed act of God, and (3) something that occurs wholly apart from personal merit or good works:

1. "[To] the man who . . . trusts God who justifies the wicked, his faith is credited as righteousness. . . . [How blessed is] the man to whom God credits righteousness apart from works." (Romans 4:5–6).

2. "Therefore, since we have been justified through faith, we have peace with God through our Lord Jesus Christ." (Romans 5:1).

3. "For we maintain that a man is justified by faith apart from observing the law." (Romans 3:28).

This explains why the Bible teaches, "There is therefore now no condemnation for those who are in Christ Jesus" (Romans 8:1; also read Luke 18:1–14; Acts 18:38–39; 15:10, 11; Galatians 2:26).

The weight of these Scriptures is formidable; it is indeed logically impossible to deny the biblical teaching of justification by faith alone. For anyone—the Pope or Billy Graham or an angel from heaven—to say that the Bible teaches that sinners "are justified by Christ and by good works"[7] is simply wrong and heretical. As the Apostle Paul emphasized, "I am astonished that you are so quickly deserting the one who called you by the grace of Christ and are turning to a different gospel—which is really no gospel at all. Evidently some people are throwing you into confusion and are trying to pervert the gospel of Christ. But even if we or an angel from heaven should preach a gospel other than the one we preached to you, let him be eternally condemned!" (Galatians 1:6–8).

Scripture clearly rules out all forms of partial justification or salvation by grace and works. And if Scripture is equally clear that salvation comes by grace through faith, then salvation must be by faith alone. Indeed, to make salvation an achievement of "faith plus works" is to destroy Christ's gospel, as Galatians 2:21 and Romans 11:6 teach: "I do not set aside the grace of God, for if righteousness could be gained through the law, Christ died for nothing!" "And, if by grace, then it is no longer by works; if it were, grace would no longer be grace." No one who truly loves God would ever wish to destroy Christ's gospel, especially realizing the infinite price paid by Him so that salvation could be offered as a free gift. Consider the following Scriptures carefully:

> For if those who live by law are heirs, **faith has no value** and the promise is **worthless**.... Therefore, the promise comes **by faith**, so that it may be **by grace** and may be **guaranteed** to all Abraham's offspring—not only to those who are of the law but also to those who are of the faith of Abraham. He is the father of us all. (Romans 4:14, 16)

> Therefore **no one** will be declared righteous in his sight by observing the law; rather, through the law we become conscious of sin. But now a righteousness from God, **apart from law**, has been made known, to which the Law and the Prophets testify. This righteousness from God comes **through faith** in Jesus Christ to all who believe.... [They] are **justified freely** by his grace through the redemption that came by Christ Jesus. (Romans 3:20–24)

> He saved us, **not because of** righteous things we had done, but because of his mercy. (Titus 3:5)

> **Having been justified** [God's legal verdict pronouncing one pardoned forever] by his grace ... (Titus 3:7)

> Since we **have now been justified** by his blood, how much **more** shall we be saved from God's wrath through him! (Romans 5:9)

> Blessed is the man whose sin the Lord will **never** count against him. (Romans 4:8)

These verses indisputably teach that justification is an eternal and final verdict by God, not a lifelong process, and that a person is justified by *faith alone*. There is no hint of any additional requirement or works for salvation that would make justification by "faith plus works" (see Romans 8:30; 10:3–4; 1 Corinthians 6:11; Galatians 3:8–13, 21–25).

What Justification Is Not

1. It is not a *reward* for anything good we have done.

2. It is not something in which we cooperate with God. (It is not sanctification.)

3. It is not infused righteousness that results in good works, which become the basis of justification (the Mormon and Catholic concept of justification).

4. It is not accomplished apart from the satisfaction of God's justice (it is not unjust).

5. It is not subject to degrees. One cannot be more or less justified; one can only be fully justified or fully unjustified.

What Justification Is

1. Justification is an undeserved free gift of God's grace and mercy (Romans 3:24; Titus 3:7).

2. Justification is entirely accomplished by God, *once for all*. (While it is not the process of personal sanctification, knowledge of it helps produce sanctification.)

One of the leading theologians of our time, Dr. James Packer stated:

> This justification, though individually located at the point of time at which a man believes (Romans 4:3; 5:1), is an eschatological once-for-all divine act, the final judgment brought into the present. The justifying sentence, once passed, is irrevocable. "The Wrath" (Romans 5:9) will not touch the justified. Those accepted now are secure forever. Inquisition before Christ's judgment seat (Romans 14:10–12; 2 Corinthians 5:10) may deprive them of certain rewards (1 Corinthians 3:15) but never of their justified status. Christ will not call into question God's justifying verdict, only declare, endorse and implement it.[8]

In other words, if God the Father *justified* believers at the point of faith, would the Son ever repudiate the Father's legal declaration?

3. Justification involves an imputed righteousness entirely apart from works: the righteousness of God Himself has been given to the believer. It has nothing to do with a person's own righteousness (Romans 4:5–6, 17–25).

It is not just that God overlooks our sin and guilt, but that full and entire holiness is credited to our account. Dr. Bruce Milne describes the transaction this way:

> Our justification is not simply a matter of God's overlooking our guilt; our need can be met only if righteousness, full and entire holiness of character, is credited to us. This is the amazing gift of grace. Christ's law-keeping and perfect righteousness are made ours by faith in Him (1 Corinthians 1:30; Philippians 3:9). It is not simply that our abysmal failure in life's moral examination is overlooked; we pass with 100 percent, First Class Honours! Well may Athanasius speak of "the amazing exchange" whereby, as Calvin puts it, "the Son of God though spotlessly pure took upon Himself the ignominy and shame of our sin and in return clothes us with His purity."[9]

Righteousness is imputed by faith because the believer is actually united to Christ. In other words, because the believer is "in Christ," the righteousness of Christ is imputed to him. Justification is the subsequent legal recognition of that fact. We are declared (past tense) righteous, and we *now* (present tense) have perfect righteousness before God, not personally, but legally:

> It is because of him that you are in Christ Jesus, who has become for us wisdom from God—that is, our righteousness, holiness and redemption. (1 Corinthians 1:30).
>
> God made him who had no sin to be sin for us, so that in him we might become the righteousness of God. (2 Corinthians 5:21).

In his book *God's Words: Studies of Key Bible Themes*, J. I. Packer discusses the meaning of justification, contrasting it with the Catholic and Mormon view:

To "justify" in the Bible means to "declare righteous": to declare, that is, of a man on trial, that he is not liable to any penalty, but is entitled to all the privileges due to those who have kept the law. . . . The Church of Rome has always maintained that God's act of justifying is primarily, if not wholly, one of making righteous, by inner spiritual renewal, but there is no biblical or linguistic ground for this view, though it goes back at least as far as Augustine. Paul's synonyms for "justify" are "reckon (impute) righteousness," "forgive (more correctly, remit) sins," "not reckon sin" (see Romans 4:5–8)—all phrases which express the idea, not of inner transformation, but of conferring a legal status and cancelling a legal liability. Justification is a judgment passed on man, not a work wrought within man; God's gift of a status and a relationship to himself, not of a new heart. Certainly, God does regenerate those whom he justifies, but the two things are not the same.[10]

Thus, as *Baker's Dictionary of Theology* points out, every believer in Christ is now treated by God as being righteous (on the basis of their imputed righteousness), not as if they are sinners:

"The righteousness of God" [see Philippians 3:9] is bestowed on them as a free gift (Romans 1:17, 3:21ff.; 5:17, cf. 9:30; 10:3–10): that is to say, they receive the right to be treated and the promise that they shall be treated, no longer as sinners, but as righteous, by the divine Judge. Thus they become "the righteousness of God" in and through Him who "knew no sin" personally but was representatively "made sin" (treated as a sinner, and punished) in their stead (1 Corinthians 5:21). This is the thought expressed in classical Protestant theology by the phrase "the imputation of Christ's righteousness," namely, that believers are righteous (Romans 5:19) and have righteousness (Philippians 3:9) before God for no other reason than that Christ their Head was righteous before God, and they are one with Him, sharers of His status and acceptance. God justifies them by passing on them, for Christ's sake, the verdict which Christ's obedience merited. God declares them to be righteous, because He reckons them to be righteous; and He reckons righteousness to them, not because He accounts them to have kept His law personally (which would be a false judgment), but because He accounts them to be united to the one who kept it representatively (and that is a true judgment). For Paul, union with Christ is not fantasy, but fact—the basic fact indeed in Christianity; and the doctrine of imputed righteousness is simply Paul's exposition of the forensic aspect of it (see Romans 5:12ff.).[11]

4. Justification is accomplished in harmony with God's justice. It displays His holiness; it does not deny it. The only way for the sinner's justification to be truly just in God's eyes is for two requirements to be absolutely satisfied. The first is that every requirement of the law must be satisfied. The second is that the infinitely holy character of God must be satisfied. J. I. Packer comments:

> The only way in which justification can be just is for the law to be satisfied so far as the justified are concerned. But the law makes a double demand on sinners: it requires both their full obedience to its precepts, as God's creatures, and their full endurance of its penalty, as transgressors. How could they conceivably meet this double demand? The answer is that it has been met already by the Lord Jesus Christ, acting in their name. The eternal Son of God was "born under the law" (Galatians 4:4) in order that he might yield double submission to the law in his people's stead. Both aspects of his submission are indicated in Paul's words: "he . . . became obedient—unto death" (Philippians 2:8). His life of righteousness culminated in his dying the death of [the] unrighteous according to the will of God: he bore the penal curse of the law in man's place (Galatians 3:13) to make propitiation for man's sins (Romans 3:25).
>
> And thus, "through one act of righteousness"—the life and death of the sinless Christ—"there resulted justification of life to all men" (Romans 5:18 NAS).[12]

Paul's thesis is that God justifies sinners on a just ground, namely, that the claims of God's law upon them have been fully satisfied. The law has not been altered, or suspended, or flouted for their justification, but fulfilled—by Jesus Christ, acting in their name. By perfectly serving God, Christ perfectly kept the law (cf. Matthew 3:15). His obedience culminated in death (Philippians 2:8); He bore the penalty of the law in men's place (Galatians 3:13), to make propitiation for their sins (Romans 3:25). On the grounds of Christ's obedience, God does not im-

pute sin, but imputes righteousness, to sinners who believe (Romans 4:2–8; 5:19).[13]

This is exactly what Scripture teaches: that God is both just and the justifier of those who place their faith in Jesus:

> For all have sinned and fall short of the glory of God, and are justified freely by his grace through the redemption that came by Christ Jesus. God presented him as a sacrifice of atonement, through faith in his blood. He did this to demonstrate his justice, because in his forbearance he had left the sins committed beforehand unpunished—he did it to demonstrate his justice at the present time, so as to be just and the one who justifies those who have faith in Jesus. (Romans 3:23–26)

Further Scripture Proof

"Abraham **believed** the LORD, and he **credited it to him as righteousness.**" (Genesis 15:6)

"**Blessed is** the man whose sin the LORD **does not count against him.**" (Psalm 32:2)

"'No weapon that is formed against you shall prosper; and every tongue that accuses you in judgment you will condemn. This is the heritage of the servants of the Lord, and **their vindication is from Me,** declares the Lord.'" (Isaiah 54:17 NAS)

"In his days Judah will be saved and Israel will live in safety. This is the name by which he will be called: **the Lord our righteousness.**" (Jeremiah 23:6)

"Behold, as for the proud one, his soul is not right within him; but **the righteous** will live **by his faith.**" (Habakkuk 2:4 NAS)

"For what does the Scripture say? 'AND ABRAHAM BELIEVED GOD, AND IT WAS RECKONED TO HIM AS RIGHTEOUSNESS.' Now to the one who works, his wage is not reckoned as a favor but as what is due. But to the one who does not work, but believes in Him who justifies the ungodly, **his faith is reckoned as righteousness,** just as David also speaks of the blessing upon the man to whom God **reckons righteousness apart from works.**" (Romans 4:3-6 NAS)

"What shall we say then? That Gentiles, who did not pursue righteousness, attained righteousness, even **the righteousness which is by faith;**

but Israel, pursuing a law of righteousness, did not arrive at that law. Why? Because they did not pursue it by faith, but as though it were by works. They stumbled over the stumbling stone, just as it is written, 'Behold, I lay in Zion a stone of stumbling and a rock of offense, and he who believes in Him will not be disappointed.' Brethren, my heart's desire and my prayer to God for them is for their salvation. For I bear them witness that they have a zeal for God, but not in accordance with knowledge. For not knowing about God's righteousness, and seeking to establish their own, they did not subject themselves to the righteousness of God. For **Christ is the end of the law for righteousness to everyone who believes.**" (Romans 9:30–10:4 NAS)

"And such were some of you; but you were washed, but you were sanctified, but **you were justified** in the name of the Lord Jesus Christ, and in the Spirit of our God." (1 Corinthians 6:11 NAS)

"And the Scripture, foreseeing that God would **justify the Gentiles by faith, preached the gospel** beforehand to Abraham, saying, 'All the nations shall be blessed in you.' So then those who are of faith are blessed with Abraham, the believer." (Galatians 3:8–9 NAS)

"Is the Law then contrary to the promises of God? May it never be! For if a law had been given which was able to impart life, then righteousness would indeed have been based on law. . . . Therefore the Law has become our tutor to lead us to Christ, that we may be **justified by faith.**" (Galatians 3:21,24 NAS)

Important Applications of the Doctrine of Justification

1. Justification demands that we trust in Christ's righteousness alone and not our own:

"And through Him everyone who believes is freed **from all things,** from which you could **not be freed** through the Law of Moses." (Acts 13:39 NAS)

"More than that, I count all things to be loss in view of the surpassing value of knowing Christ Jesus my Lord, for whom I have suffered the loss of all things, and count them **but rubbish** in order that I may gain Christ, and may be found **in Him, not having a righteousness of my own derived from the Law,** but that which

is **through faith** in Christ, **the righteousness which comes from God on the basis of faith,** that I may know Him, and the power of His resurrection and the fellowship of His sufferings, being conformed to His death." (Philippians 3:8–10 NAS)

"You have been severed from Christ, you who are seeking to be **justified by law;** you have fallen from grace." (Galatians 5:4 NAS)

2. Justification properly orients Christian morality. The motive for Christian living and service becomes obedience out of love and gratitude to a Savior whose gift of righteousness made law keeping unnecessary:

"So that you may walk in a manner **worthy** of the Lord, to please Him in all respects, bearing fruit in every good work and increasing in the knowledge of God." (Colossians 1:10 NAS)

"I urge you therefore, brethren, by the mercies of God, to present your bodies a living and holy sacrifice, **acceptable to God,** which is your spiritual service of worship. And do not be conformed to this world, but be transformed by the renewing of your mind, that you may prove what the will of God is, that which is good and acceptable and perfect." (Romans 12:1–2 NAS)

The doctrine of justification encourages morality and discourages sin when we consider the One who redeemed us and the cost of our redemption (see Romans 6:10–18):

"What shall we say then? Are we to continue in sin that grace might increase? **May it never be!** How shall we who died to sin still live in it?" (Romans 6:1–2 NAS)

"But thanks be to God that though you were slaves of sin, you became **obedient from the heart** to that form of teaching to which you were committed, and having been freed from sin, you became slaves of righteousness." (Romans 6:17–18 NAS)

"So that you may walk in a manner **worthy of the God** who calls you into His own kingdom and glory." (1 Thessalonians 2:12 NAS)

3. Justification means Christians may be assured that they *now* possess eternal life. A divine

gift is perfect and cannot be taken back. The gifts and calling of God are without repentance (Romans 11:29). Perfect righteousness is a gift (James 1:17; Romans 3:24). If we are declared perfectly righteous by Him, God can only give the gift of perfect righteousness. What condition, then, can exist in the future so that we can lose our righteous standing? If righteousness is a gift to sinners and enemies (if He did the most for us when we hated Him and were His enemies), will God do less for us now that we are His precious children (Romans 5:8–9)?

Also, eternal life could only be a *present* condition on a "just" basis–if from the point of belief we were "eternally righteous," declared eternally righteous. This is why Scripture teaches that the believer now has *eternal* life:

"Truly, truly, I say to you, he who hears My word, and believes Him who sent Me, *has eternal life,* and does not come into judgment, but has passed out of death into life." (John 5:24 NAS)

"He who eats My flesh and drinks My blood *has eternal life,* and I will raise him up on the last day." (John 6:54 NAS)

"The one who believes in the Son of God has the witness in himself; the one who does not believe God has made Him a liar, because he has not believed in the witness that God has borne concerning His Son. And the witness is this, that God *has given us eternal life,* and this life is in His Son. He who has the Son has the life; he who does not have the Son of God does not have the life." (1 John 5:10–13 NAS)

Notes
1. Sinclair Ferguson, *Know Your Christian Life: A Theological Introduction* (Downers Grove, IL: InterVarsity, 1981), p. 71.
2. Ibid., p. 73.
3. As cited in Norman Geisler's manuscript on Roman Catholicism, p. 35.
4. Geisler, p. 34, citing respectively Anthony A. Hoekema, *Saved by Grace* (1989), p. 154 and Millard J. Erickson, *Christian Theology* (1987), 4th printing, p. 955.
5. Hans Kung, *Justification* (Philadelphia: Westminster, 1964), p. 209; Geisler observes, "For an extended treatment of the Old Testament understandings of these terms and the difficulties inherent in translating from the Hebrew into Greek and Latin, see Alister E. McGrath, *Iustitia Dei,* Vol. 1, Cambridge University Press, 1986, pp. 4-16" (from Geisler, Roman Catholicism ms.).

6. E.g., Geisler, Roman Catholicism ms., p. 29
7. Robert C. Broderick, ed., *The Catholic Encyclopedia,* rev. and updated (New York: Thomas Nelson Publishers, 1978), p. 519.
8. James Packer in Everett F. Harrison et al., eds., *Baker Dictionary of Theology* (Grand Rapids, MI: Baker, 1972), p. 305.
9. Bruce Milne, *Know the Truth: A Handbook of Christian Belief* (Downers Grove, IL: InterVarsity, 1982), p. 155.
10. Packer, *God's Words,* pp. 141-42.
11. Packer in *Baker's Dictionary of Theology,* p. 306.
12. Packer, *God's Words,* pp. 141-42.
13. Packer in *Baker's Dictionary of Theology,* p. 306.

DEATH AND THE AFTERLIFE: ETERNITY DECIDED IN TIME

In contrast to the teachings of the cults, death is not merely an illusion, or something good, or eternal extinction, or an inevitable door to heaven or the next life, or multiple lives (reincarnation). Further, heaven is not merely a positive experience in life, such as feeling good, or a higher state of consciousness. Hell is not a negative condition in life, or a temporary purgatory, or the consequences of unenlightened consciousness in this life.

Death per se is a condition of *separation.* According to the Bible, there are only two kinds of death. First, there is physical death, which involves the *temporary* separation of the spirit from the body. In the resurrection, the body is later rejoined with the human spirit. Second, there is eternal spiritual death, or the *eternal* separation of the human spirit from God. This condition has no remedy. Death is not good, it has never been good. Physical death—separation from the body—is not good, since by it man is left "unclothed" in an unnatural state (2 Corinthians 5:4; Philippians 3:21; 1 Corinthians 15:53-54). Spiritual death—separation from God—is not good, since by it one is eternally separated from God.

"Death" and "life" are irreconcilable and opposite *conditions of existence* in both this life and the next. Apart from Christ, death leads to one thing only: eternal judgment. "It is appointed for men to die once and after this comes judgment" (Hebrews 9:27 NAS). But *with* Christ, death leads to life. "I am the resurrection and the life; he who believes in Me shall live even if he dies, and everyone who lives and believes in Me shall never die" (John 11:25–26 NAS). "Truly, truly, I say to you, he who hears My word, and believes Him who sent Me, has eternal life, and does not come into judgment, but has passed out of death into life" (John 5:24 NAS).

The Bible teaches that prior to salvation, even as they are alive, all men and women exist in a state of spiritual death or separation from God. Their human spirits are "dead" to those things that God is truly concerned about (Luke 15:24–32; Ephesians 2:1; 1 Timothy 5:6, Revelation 3:1). Thus, even though they are alive physically, they do not consider the one true God, nor do they honor Him or care about His interests. Whatever God or concept of God they may believe in, they do not concern themselves with the concerns of the one true God (Romans 3:10–18). This is why Jesus Himself referred to "the dead burying their own dead," explicitly teaching that the living human beings around him were, as far as God was concerned, spiritually dead (Luke 9:60).

The Bible teaches that physical and spiritual death exist for one reason: sin. God warned Adam and Eve that if they disobeyed Him, in that day they would die (Genesis 2:17). They died first spiritually and then physically. This is why the Bible teaches, "The wages of sin is death" (Romans 6:23).

Because sin causes death, the problem of sin must be dealt with before death can be dealt with. This is the reason for the Christian teaching on the atonement, that Christ died for the sins of the world. As Jesus taught, "For God so loved the world that he gave his only begotten Son, that whoever believes in him shall not perish but have eternal life" (John 3:16). Whoever receives Christ as personal savior is "born again," regenerated, made alive spiritually. The believer's state of spiritual death is cancelled at the point of receiving Christ. Since Christ paid the full penalty of sin (Colossians 2:13), there is no longer the possibility of the believer suffering God's judgment for his sins, which is the second death. Instead, the believer will join God forever at the point of physical death. This is the essence of the term "saved." And it must be stressed that people must come to belief in the atoning death

of Jesus Christ or they cannot be saved. The only condition is to accept what God has done in the person of Christ. Thus, the biblical view is that the saved are with God; they go to be with Him at the moment of death (Luke 23:43; John 12:26; Acts 7:59; 2 Corinthians 5:8; Philippians 1:23).

The Christian hope, then, is not a cultic or mediumistic view of gradual, spiritual self-progression after death but in physical resurrection and eternal immortality based on Christ's resurrection and life (Romans 4:25; 1 Corinthians 6:14; 2 Corinthians 4:14; 5:1; Ephesians 1:15–21; 2:4–10; Philippians 1:21; 3:21; Colossians 3:4). Those who accept Christ inherit heaven for eternity; those who reject God and His mercy inherit hell for eternity (2 Peter 2:4, 9). There is no possibility of altering one's fate after death (Hebrews 9:27; Luke 16:19–31).

Death, then, is not extinction, as many cults teach. It does not involve a condition of reincarnation, where the soul experiences many lifetimes, as occult religions teach. It does not involve a condition of ultimate union or absorption into some impersonal, divine essence as many Eastern cults teach. (See Ecclesiastes 12:5; Luke 12:46–47; Luke 16:19–31; Acts 1:25; Hebrews 9:27; Psalms 78:39; 2 Corinthians 5:11; Hebrews 10:31; 12:27–29; 2 Peter 2:4, 9; Revelation 20:10, 15).

What Will Heaven Be Like?

The Bible clearly teaches the existence of a place called heaven:

Our Father in heaven.... (Matthew 6:9)

You will have treasure in heaven.... (Matthew 19:21)

He was taken up into heaven.... (Mark 16:19)

No one has ever gone into heaven except the one who came from heaven—the Son of Man. (John 3:13)

You also have a Master in heaven.... (Colossians 4:1)

To wait for his Son from heaven.... (1 Thessalonians 1:10)

He himself will come down from heaven.... (1 Thessalonians 4:16)

Many good books have been written on heaven and we would encourage the reader to read these for greater insights into the eternal existence of the redeemed.[1] Due to space considerations, we can only give a thumbnail sketch.[2]

Heaven is not a perpetual vacation—something that would be terribly boring after only fifty years, let alone for endless time. Heaven is an eternity of purpose and destiny. After the largest conceivable amount of time multiplied by the largest conceivable amount of time, eternity has only just begun. Therefore, heaven must not only be beyond our imagination but also commensurate with the nature and demands of a redeemed eternity itself. Heaven will be an infinitely superb, multi-faceted and glorious paradise because an infinitely superb, multi-faceted, glorious God lives there. Words such as grandeur, exquisite, magnificent, marvelous, resplendent, elegant and superluxurious are, at best, shadows of its descriptions. Heaven is a real and substantial place for real and substantial people. In this place, Jesus told us that we would be glorified and exalted with Him. We will have spiritual bodies (Ephesians 2:6; Romans 8:11–17; Philippians 3:21, 1 John 3:2), and will reign with Him "forever and ever" (Revelation 20:6; 22:5). We will also judge (and perhaps rule) the angels (1 Corinthians 6:3).

In heaven everything that makes life unpleasant or tortuous will be forever vanquished. Those present in heaven will never experience pain, sadness, sorrow, depression, sickness, death, sin, evil, selfishness, fatigue or suffering of any kind, "for the old order of things has passed away" (Revelation 21:4; 22:3). Heaven will be a place of indescribable love, beauty, peace, joy, happiness, rest, adventure, excitement, union and fellowship with God (Revelation 21:3)—multiplied to the degree suggested by what an infinitely loving, omnipotent and omniscient God would do in eternity for those He willingly sacrificed His only Son for. Scripture itself teaches that if God has given us His only Son now, how much more will He give us throughout eternity? (Romans 8:32; 1 Corinthians 2:9; 3:21–23).

Life in heaven will be beyond our wildest imagination. If heaven by definition is devoid of everything old that is negative, it must be saturated with everything new that is positive. "He who was seated on the throne said, 'I am making everything new!' Then he said, 'Write this down, for these words are trustworthy and true'" (Revelation 21:5). Thus heaven will be a place of eternal security and protection where God's creation is redeemed and transformed into an absolutely perfect new earth and heavens (Romans 8:18–23; Revelation chs. 21, 22).

In this never to be equaled universe, which could be inexhaustible, we will be able to explore and never exhaust the ability to explore, just as we will never be able to exhaust our exploration of all there is to know and experience of an infinite God in all His perfections. Obviously, since people are finite beings, there will be never-ending growth in knowledge, truth and wisdom, of God and perhaps of the creation, angels and men and women. We will not only have joyous, intimate, personal fellowship with God, Jesus and the angels but with billions of redeemed people throughout history, and with whatever else God may have created. Yet service and worship to God will be one of our *greatest* joys. As suggested by the parable of the talents (Matthew 25:14–23; Luke 19:11–26), we will also enjoy rewards for service given on earth. These will probably include different positions of honor and authority in heaven. However, all our heavenly blessings and glories will be eternal and indestructible (1 Peter 1:3–4).

But it must also be remembered there is far, far more that we don't know about heaven than we do know; its beauties and glories are indescribable to us now. First Corinthians 2:9 only hints at what awaits those who have made Jesus their Lord and Savior: "No eye has seen, no ear has heard, no mind has conceived what God has prepared for those who love Him." Indeed, "our present sufferings are not worth comparing with the glory that will be revealed in us" (Romans 8:18). In sum, we will inherit all that God *is* and all that God *has* (1 Corinthians 3:21–23) in a true eternal paradise as God originally intended it. As a result, "the righteous will shine like the sun in the kingdom of their Father" forever and ever (Matthew 13:43). We should expect nothing less from a future kingdom prepared by Jesus

Himself, for those He dearly loves and died for personally (Matthew 25:34; John 14:2).

This helps explain why apart from Christ there is no such thing as *real* life, either now or in eternity.

What Will Hell Be Like?

Just as with the doctrine of heaven, the Bible is clear that there is an eternal place termed hell:

> Let him warn them, so that they will not also come to this place of torment. (Luke 16:28)
>
> In danger of the fire of hell. . . . (Matthew 5:22)
>
> God did not spare angels when they sinned, but sent them to hell. (2 Peter 2:4)
>
> Do not be afraid of those who kill the body but cannot kill the soul. Rather, be afraid of the One who can destroy both soul and body in hell. (Matthew 10:28)
>
> They will go away to eternal punishment. (Matthew 25:46)
>
> Who suffer the punishment of eternal fire. . . . (Jude 7)

Hell may be ridiculed and outdated in the minds of many people, and it is universally denied in the cults, but that does not eliminate its reality. Given the infinite holiness of God, one thing is certain: the strongest arguments against hell will be silenced forever on the other side. (Polls since 1944 indicate that although 50 to 60 percent of people believe in hell, only 3 to 4 percent think their chances are good of going there.[3]) Many people think they will never go to hell because they don't "deserve" it. But popular views of Universalism (all will be saved), variations on conditional immortality (the unsaved will be annihilated), and ideas of the opportunity for salvation after death are impossible to defend scripturally.[4] Because of God's infinite righteousness, hell cannot logically be considered immoral. But it could actually be immoral for God to save everyone irrespective of their will, or to annihilate those having intrinsic value, those created in His image.[5]

The most predominant feature of hell will be the eternal absence of an infinitely loving God and the never-ending presence of just punishments for individual sins (2 Thessalonians 1:9; Daniel 12:2; Matthew 10:28). Hell apparently involves degrees of punishment according to the works done in this life (Matthew 11:21-24; 23:23; Luke 12:47-48). In contrast to what most people think, those who are condemned to hell will recognize, and accept, the perfect justice of their presence there. Hell is a subject that all people should contemplate for many reasons, among them[6] are the following.

1) God Himself does not desire that anyone perish, and He has done all He can, this side of death, within the limits of His character and the human condition, to save people (2 Peter 3:9; Acts 17:26-31). It is entirely possible that, given God's infinite knowledge of what every possible created being would do under every possible circumstance, God has so structured human existence so as to save the greatest number. Further, it is equally credible that "of all the possible persons God could have created, the vast majority of those who would have rejected Christ never get created in the first place. The number of people who reject Christ may be an act of mercy on God's part."[7] It is even possible that, given God's holy character and human responsibility, there is *no* world God could have created in which all created persons would have freely accepted Christ. Apparently, "God prefers a world in which some persons freely reject Christ but the number of saved is maximized over a world in which a few trust Christ and none are lost." Thus, "The actual world contains an optimal balance between saved and unsaved, and those who are unsaved would never have received Christ under any circumstances."[8]

2) It is obviously in our own best interest to escape going to hell. Apart from Christ, hell is assured, but this fate can easily be avoided in this life by trust in Jesus for forgiveness of sin (John 1:12; 3:16-18; 5:24; 6:47).

3) Hell is not unjust. The one true God who has revealed Himself as *infinitely* loving and merciful has also spoken of the reality of eternal separation from Him; therefore the doctrine of hell cannot be inconsistent with His love, justice or mercy. Few people balk at the devil going to hell because they assume the devil is bad enough and God just enough to warrant it. Only

when it comes to *us*, do we question its justness. But if it is just for the devil, can we assume it is never just for those of us who are "like" the devil in attitudes and actions, especially as they are directed toward God? (See John 8:44; 1 John 3:8) Indeed, apart from hell, justice itself becomes a myth. All creation will one day understand this (Romans 3:4–6). Even if someone like Adolph Hitler were punished for billions of years and then brought into eternal heaven or annihilated, his time of punishment, compared to eternity, would be essentially meaningless.

4) Hell is not a place where God actively tortures people endlessly as if He were the director of some kind of torture chamber. Hell was made for the devil and his angels (Matthew 25:41), not men and women. But people who continue their rebellion against God must suffer the just judgment of their sins. Since God will not permit unrighteousness or anything unholy to enter heaven (Revelation 21:27; Habakkuk 1:13), there must be some other place for the unrighteous to inhabit eternity. And if the unrighteous are not permanently quarantined from the righteous, all we have is an instant and eternal replay of life on earth, and this is surely not heaven! There will be psychological and physical anguish and torment in hell, but this will result primarily from the conditions of hell and people's own choices and realizations, not from God Himself actively inflicting their torment. A judge and jury who justly send a man to prison do not torment him; his own choices and the conditions of prison do.

5) Sin committed against God is not like sin committed against others. Sinning against an infinite being requires an infinite punishment which, for finite creatures, can only be experienced as eternal punishment. Further, the amount of time it takes to commit a sin has no direct relationship to the punishment it deserves. A bank teller may plan a robbery for months, while his accomplice may murder someone in a moment. The evil of a crime is related more to the *nature* of the crime and the *one* against whom it is committed than the time it takes to commit it. Everyone knows that a man having consensual sex with a prostitute is not the same as a man having sex with an innocent

little boy or girl. No one can accurately gauge how an infinite God, whose holiness is immeasurable, responds to even the smallest human sin. One would think that for a literally infinitely holy Being, even the most minute human sin would be fully heinous and worthy of eternal separation. Also, because the unredeemed *are* unredeemed, they continue to sin *after* death and apparently will continue to sin inwardly *forever* (Matthew 8:12). But the only *just* punishment for eternal sin is eternal punishment. The bottom line is that a good God cannot be unjust in punishing people eternally. What hell means is that there *is* final justice and that hell is no more or less than *perfect* justice (Romans 3:4–6). If, in this life, few things are as satisfying as justice this must also be true in the next life. And hell must also be in full harmony with the love of God. "God loves justice, holiness, and righteousness so much that He created hell. The love of God for His own nature, His law, His universe, and His people, makes hell a product of love as well as justice.[9]

6) Our choice *for* God is important to Him (Luke 13:34). People who refuse Christ in this life would be quite unlikely to accept Him in the next life, in hell, because their basic nature is not altered. If Scripture declares that the unredeemed are God's enemies who want nothing to do with Him (Acts 4:25–27; Romans 1:18–32; 5:6–10), why would anything change just because someone died? Even if they somehow did decide for Christ, it would only be to escape the punishments of hell rather than to love and obey God. They would not be choosing God and Jesus on their own merits, and thus they would not be suited for eternal life with God and Jesus in heaven. No one wants to live forever with someone the person dislikes. The more we understand the nature of heaven as being infused with the nature of God, the more credible is the idea that the unredeemed would not enjoy heaven either.

Of course, the longer we refuse God's gift of mercy now, the harder it becomes to accept it later. Every day, in almost every way, we are either moving closer to God or further from Him. At the end of an unrepentant life, God simply grants our wishes. C. S. Lewis emphasized,

"There are only two kinds of people in the end: those who say to God, 'Thy will be done,' and those to whom God says, in the end, '*Thy* will be done.'"[10] In another book, Lewis writes:

If a game is played it must be possible to lose it. If the happiness of a creature lies in self-surrender, no one can make that surrender but himself (though many can help him to make it) and he may refuse. I would pay any price to be able to say truthfully "all will be saved." But my reason retorts, "without their will, or with it?" If I say, "without their will" I at once perceive a contradiction; how can the supreme voluntary act of self-surrender be involuntary? If I say "with their will," my reason replies "how if they *will not* give in?"[11]

7) The punishment in hell is apparently tempered for some. God can only do what is just in this life and the next. Hebrews 11:6 says that God rewards those who seek Him. Acts 10:35 (NAS) says, "In every nation the man who fears Him and does what is right, is welcome to Him." Abraham asked, "Will not the Judge of all the earth do right?" (Genesis 18:25). The psalmist said, "He will judge the world with justice and the peoples with unfaltering fairness" (Psalm 98:9 BERKELEY). Thus, not everyone experiences the same degree of pain in hell, since there are apparently degrees of punishment. The person who did not know God's will and did not do it will receive "but few" stripes (Luke 12:35–48; Matthew 10:15). It makes sense to believe that those who were less evil in this life are not punished to the same degree as those who were more evil, because God is unable to violate His holy character and give any person *more* punishment than he or she deserves. This means that God, who is infinite in knowledge, knows the perfectly deserved and righteous punishment for every person who has ever lived. In the end, although hell is not what the unrighteous want, it will be seen to be what the unrighteous deserve.

Notes
1. John Gilmore, *Probing Heaven: Key Questions on the Hereafter* (Grand Rapids, MI: Baker, 1989): Joni Eareckson Tada, *Heaven Your Real Home* (Grand Rapids, MI: Zondervan, 1995).
2. Gary R. Habermas and J. P. Moreland, *Immortality the Other Side of Death* (Nashville: Thomas Nelson, 1992).
3. John Ankerberg, John Weldon, *The Facts on UFOs and Other Supernatural Phenomena* and *The Facts on Spirit Guides* (Eugene, OR: Harvest House, 1992).
4. For detailed refutation, see Robert A. Morey, *Death and the Afterlife* (Minneapolis: Bethany, 1984).
5. Habermas and Moreland, *Immortality*, pp. 169-71.
6. Ibid., pp. 157-80.
7. Ibid., p. 178.
8. Ibid., p. 180.
9. Robert A. Morey, *Introduction to Defending the Faith* (Southbridge, MA: Crowne Publications, 1989), p. 38e.
10. C. S. Lewis, *The Great Divorce* (New York: MacMillan, 1946), p. 69.
11. C. S. Lewis, *The Problem of Pain* (New York: MacMillan, 1971), p. 8.

Recommended Reading
For a thorough lexical and exegetical refutation of cultic views, see Robert A. Morey, *Death and the Afterlife* (Bethany).

THE OCCULT: THE MODERN SPIRITUAL COUNTERFEIT

Although all groups discussed in this volume accept occult powers to some degree, but define them as either divine powers or powers of the human mind, most cults and many people generally today also ridicule the idea of a literal devil or demons. To these people, devils and demons are mere primitive superstition. They believe that in our modern scientific age we can finally do away with such medieval nonsense and its corresponding "witchhunts." But is this attitude realistic? Is it "unscientific" to believe in a personal devil, or is there a preponderance of evidence that suggests his existence? The famed evangelist Billy Graham once remarked, "Why do I believe in the devil? *For three reasons.* 1. Because the Bible plainly says he exists. 2. Because I see his work everywhere. 3. Because great scholars have recognized his existence.[1]

It is more logical to assume that Satan does exist than that he does not. As Dr. J. I. Packer, Professor of Historical and Systematic Theology at Regent College in Vancouver, British Columbia, argues:

The natural response to denials of Satan's existence is to ask, who then runs his business?—

for temptations which look and feel like expressions of cunning destructive malice remain facts of daily life. So does hell in the sense defined by the novelist John Updike—"a profound and desolating absence" (of God, and good, and community and communication); and "the realization that life is flawed" (Updike goes on) "admits the possibility of a Fall, of a cause behind the Fall, of Satan." Belief in Satan is not illogical, for it fits the facts. Inept to the point of idiocy, however, is disbelief in Satan, in a world like ours; which makes Satan's success in producing such disbelief all the more impressive, as well as all the sadder.[2]

It is also logical that evil would seek to camouflage itself for strategic purposes, just as the Mafia launders its money through legitimate businesses. Camouflage has been a key ingredient of military tacticians for millennia; it would hardly be unexpected to find employed by the devil. Such camouflage could assume any number of guises, from promoting oneself as myth to the opposite extreme of promoting oneself as God. Indeed, the majority of people in our culture seem to believe either that Satan does not exist or that the realm of the psychic world is something divine. Of course, the only escape from this deception is to unmask the real myth: the lies the devil spreads about himself. Brooks Alexander well argues:

The nature of illusion is the ruse of misdirection. It is the misplacement of our attention through the manipulation of *false images,* both personal and collective. The devil's disappearance provides a clear example of collective misdirection—a form of social deception. Once that image is accepted, *whatever response we make to it* will be as false as the image that provokes it, and therefore play into the devil's hands. Its direction will be amiss by definition. . . . It is less the existence of Satan that should alarm us, than the fact that our social contemporaries are so ill equipped to deal with reality on any level, let alone to recognize the most fundamental danger. De Rougemont's articulation of this point is elegant and concise:

"One of the reasons why confusion is spreading in the world is that we are afraid to face its real causes. We believe in a thousand evils, fear a thousand dangers, but have ceased to believe in

Evil and to fear the true Dangers. To show the reality of the Devil in this world is . . . to cure ourselves. We are never in greater danger than in moments when we deceive ourselves as to the real nature of a threat, and when we summon our energies for defense against the void while the enemy approaches from behind.

It would be irresponsible for us to exclude [the devil] from consideration simply because we dislike the connotations we have given him. Even if we acknowledge the concept without comprehending it, at least it puts us on notice that "spiritual" things may be more subtle and complex than they appear. Healthy caution is an antidote for fear, not its cause."[3]

We may suggest eight lines of reasoning to infer the possibility of a real devil and the reality of spiritual evil:

a. the consensus of history and religion

b. the testimony of active occultists

c. the testimony of former occultists

d. the phenomenon of spirit-possession

e. the authority of the Bible

f. the testimony of Jesus Christ and the New Testament

g. the hostility to historic biblical Christianity displayed in virtually all spiritistically inspired literature

h. destructive power of the occult and the testimony of brilliant thinkers

We examined each of these points in *The Coming Darkness* (Harvest House, 1993) and do not repeat our arguments here except for points e and f.

The Authority of the Bible
Biblical authority is predicated upon its claim to be the Word of God. If the Bible is the Word of God, what it says about the existence of a personal devil must be true; therefore, in light of the overabundance of data supporting its divine inspiration,[4] we may assume that its statements about Satan are authoritative. As Denis De Rougemont observes in his *The Devil's Share: An Essay on the Diabolic in Modern Society,* "If

one believes in the truth of the Bible, it is impossible to doubt the reality of the Devil for a single moment."[5]

The Bible teaches that the spirits who operate in the world of the occult are not what they claim to be—enlightened spirits sent from God—but demonic spirits bent on the deception and destruction of human beings. Thus, God warned ancient Israel not to adopt the occult practices of the pagan nation surrounding it:

When you enter the land the LORD your God is giving you, do not learn to imitate the detestable ways of the nations there. Let no one be found among you who sacrifices his son or daughter in the fire, who practices divination or sorcery, interprets omens, engages in witchcraft, or casts spells, or who is a medium or spiritist or who consults the dead. Anyone who does these things is detestable to the LORD, and because of these detestable practices the LORD your God will drive out those nations before you. (Deuteronomy 18:9–12)

God judged the ancient kings of Israel when they disobeyed Him and practiced occultism. The following reference is to King Manasseh of Judah:

He did evil in the eyes of the LORD, following the detestable practices of the nations the LORD had driven out before the Israelites. He rebuilt the high places his father Hezekiah had demolished; he also erected altars to the Baals [evil gods of human sacrifice] and made Asherah poles. He bowed down to all the starry hosts and worshiped them [astrology]. . . . He sacrificed his sons in the fire in the Valley of Ben Hinnom, practiced sorcery, divination and witchcraft, and consulted mediums and spiritists. He did much evil in the eyes of the LORD, provoking him to anger. (2 Chronicles 33:2–3, 6)

As these verses suggest, in ancient Israel occult practices were associated with idolatry (worship of false gods and spirits) and inevitably led to human sacrifice, as is increasingly occurring in the Western world today. This gruesome practice is discussed in such books as Nigel Davies' *Human Sacrifice in History and Today* (1981). The Bible states:

But they mingled with the nations and adopted their customs. They worshiped their idols, which became a snare to them. They sacrificed their sons and their daughters to demons. They shed innocent blood, the blood of their sons and daughters, whom they sacrificed to the idols of Canaan, and the land was desecrated by their blood. They defiled themselves by what they did; by their deeds they prostituted themselves. Therefore the LORD was angry with his people and abhorred his inheritance. (Psalm 106:35–40)

The Bible further identifies that the spiritistic powers behind idolatry are demonic:

They made him jealous with their foreign gods and angered him with their detestable idols. They sacrificed to demons, which are not God—gods they had not known, gods that recently appeared, gods your fathers did not fear. You deserted the Rock, who fathered you; you forgot the God who gave you birth. (Deuteronomy 32:16–18)

But the sacrifices of pagans are offered to demons, not to God, and I do not want you to be participants with demons. (1 Corinthians 10:20)

At the time of Isaiah, the people had become practitioners of various sorceries, which God condemned:

They [judgments] will come upon you in full measure, in spite of your many sorceries and all your potent spells. You have trusted in your wickedness and have said, "no one sees me." Your wisdom and knowledge mislead you when you say to yourself, "I am, and there is none besides me." Disaster will come upon you, and you will not know how to conjure it away. (Isaiah 47:9b–11a)

In the New Testament, occult practitioners are seen as those who lead people astray from the Christian faith:

There they met a Jewish sorcerer and false prophet named Bar-Jesus, who was an attendant to the pro-counsel, Sergius Paulus. The pro-counsel, an intelligent man, sent for Barnabas and Saul because he wanted to hear the word of God. But Elymas the sorcerer (for that is what his name means) opposed them and tried to turn the pro-counsel from the faith. Then Saul, who was also called Paul, filled with the Holy Spirit, looked straight at Elymas and said, "You are a child of the devil and an enemy of everything that is right! You are full of all kinds of deceit and trickery. Will you never stop perverting the right ways of the Lord?" (Acts 13:6b–11a)

Many also of those who had believed kept coming, confessing and disclosing their practices. Many of those who practiced magic brought their books together and began burning them in the sight of all; and they counted up the price of them and found it 50,000 pieces of silver. So the word of the Lord was growing mightily and prevailing. (Acts 19:18–20)

The New Testament also reveals that when the spirit is cast out from one with occult powers, the powers are lost, revealing that psychic powers are not human (natural and innate) but given by demons. The Apostle Luke reports on one spiritist who was apparently seeking to validate her own practices by linking them with the Apostle Paul's ministry:

Once when we were going to the place of prayer, we were met by a slave girl who had a spirit by which she predicted the future. She earned a great deal of money for her owners by fortune telling. This girl followed Paul and the rest of us, shouting, "These men are servants of the Most High God who are telling you the way [hodon; lit. "a way"] to be saved." She kept this up for many days. Finally, Paul became so troubled that he turned around and said to the spirit, "In the name of Jesus Christ I command you to come out of her!" At that moment the spirit left her. When the owners of the slave girl realized that their hope of making money was gone, they seized Paul and Silas and dragged them into the market place to face the authorities. (Acts 16:16–19)

The following is a selected list of additional Scriptures relating to the existence of the devil, demons and spiritual warfare:

The Spirit clearly says that in later times some will abandon the faith and follow deceiving spirits and things taught by demons. (1 Timothy 4:1)

Finally, be strong in the Lord and in his mighty power. Put on the full armor of God so that you can take your stand against the devil's schemes. For our struggle is not against flesh and blood, but against the rulers, against the authorities, against the powers of this dark world and against the spiritual forces of evil in the heavenly realms. (Ephesians 6:10–12)

I [Jesus] am sending you [Paul] to them [the Gentiles] to open their eyes and turn them from darkness to light, and from the power of Satan to God, so that they may receive forgiveness of sins. (Acts 26:17b–18a)

The god of this age has blinded the minds of unbelievers, so that they cannot see the light of the gospel of the glory of Christ, who is the image of God. (2 Corinthians 4:4)

The coming of the lawless one will be in accordance with the work of Satan displayed in all kinds of counterfeit miracles, signs and wonders, and in every sort of evil that deceives those who are perishing. They perish because they refuse to love the truth and so be saved. (2 Thessalonians 2:9–10)

For such men are false apostles, deceitful workmen, masquerading as apostles of Christ. And no wonder, for Satan himself masquerades as an angel of light. It is not surprising, then, if his servants masquerade as servants of righteousness. Their end will be what their actions deserve. (2 Corinthians 11:13–15)

But the cowardly, the unbelieving, the vile, the murderers, the sexually immoral, those who practice magic arts, the idolaters and all liars—their place will be in the fiery lake of burning sulfur. This is the second death. (Revelation 21:8)

The Testimony of Jesus Christ and the New Testament

No one in human history can speak with more authority than Jesus Christ. No one else both directly claimed to be God (John 5:18; 10:30; 14:9) and proved the truth of His claim by literally rising from the dead (Matthew 20:18, 19; John 20:24–28; Acts 1:3). In *Ready with An Answer* (1997) we detailed the persuasive logical, historical and legal evidence for the fact of Christ rising from the dead. But if He rose from the dead—something unique in all human history—then He is both Lord and God and what He says is true, including His statements about the devil, demons and spiritual warfare.

Satan. The New Testament is replete with references to the reality of a personal devil as an apostate angel who fell from heaven. Most of these references are spoken by Christ Himself (John 8:44; Luke 10:18; Jude 6). The devil is called the tempter (1 Thessalonians 3:5), wicked and evil (Matthew 6:13; 13:19), the prince of devils (Matthew 13:24), the god of this world (2 Corinthians 4:4), the prince of this world (John 12:31; 14:30; 16:11), dragon and serpent (Revelation 12:9; 20:2) and a liar and murderer from the beginning (John 8:44).

Satan has a kingdom (Matthew 12:26), which is hostile to Christ's kingdom (Matthew 16:18; Acts 26:18), and he rules a realm of demons (Matthew 9:34). His key abilities are power and cunning. He is called a "strong man" (Matthew 12:29) and has great power (2 Thessalonians 2:9). His subtlety (Genesis 3:1) is seen in his treacherous snares (2 Timothy 2:26), wiles (Ephesians 6:11), devices (2 Corinthians 2:11) and transforming ability (2 Corinthians 11:14). He is so powerful that he deceives the "whole world," which is said to be "under the control of the evil one" (1 John 5:19; Revelation 12:9; 13:14). He thus works in the children of disobedience (Ephesians 2:2) and occasionally was able to work among the Apostles (Matthew 16:23; Luke 22:31; John 13:2). He opposes the people of God (1 Chronicles 21:1; Zechariah 3:2; Acts 5:3; 1 Thessalonians 2:18; 2 Corinthians 2:11), and He tried to gain the actual worship of God Himself from Christ, an act suggestive of extreme mental imbalance (Mark 1:13; Matthew 4:1-10). Satan unendingly sows seeds of error and doubt in the church (Matthew 13:39), blinds the minds of unbelievers (Mark 4:15; Acts 26:18; 2 Corinthians 4:4), is capable of possessing people (John 13:27), has the power of death (Hebrews 2:14), and prowls about like a roaring lion seeking those he may devour (1 Peter 5:8). Christ appeared to destroy the work of the devil (1 John 3:8), who will soon be defeated (Romans 16:20), to spend eternity in hell (Matthew 25:41; Revelation 20). The biblical testimony concerning the existence of Satan is beyond doubt.

Demons. Demons are not the spirits of dead men, or of some pre-Adamite race, as some cults argue, for the spirits of the human dead are not free to roam but are confined and under punishment (Luke 16:19-31; 2 Peter 2:9). Nor are demons merely personifications of evil, or of natural forces, such as the "gods" of nature, as skeptics assume. Nor are demons the superstitious designation for particular natural diseases, such as epilepsy or mental illness, because Scripture clearly distinguishes these disorders from demon possession, although it is possible that both can be present or that demon possession could induce mental illness.[6] Demons are fallen angels who are now irredeemably corrupted. Demons are set in their ways and have no opportunity for redemption. Thus they will eventually be cast forever into the lake of fire (Revelation 20:2-3, 7-10). This may explain why they responded to Jesus with fear and derision. For example, "What do I have to do with you Jesus, Son of the most high God?" (Mark 5:7; cf., Luke 4:41). And, "Have you come to torment us before our time?" (Matthew 8:29).

These evil angels are morally corrupted spirits who are in rebellion against God (Psalm 106:37; Matthew 12:34; Mark 1:36; John 8:44; 2 Peter 2:4; James 2:19; Jude 1:6). Their rebellion was led by Satan (Jude 6; 1 John 3:8; Matthew 12:24-25, 25:41; Ezekiel 28:12-17) and resulted in their fall and expulsion from heaven (Luke 10:18, Revelation 12:7-9). As a result they became destructive, self-centered creatures who seek to thwart the purposes of God and Christ (Deuteronomy 32:17; Psalm 106:37; Revelation 2:10; 1 Peter 5:8; Ephesians 6:11; Matthew 13:39; Luke 22:31; 1 Thessalonians 2:18; 1 Timothy 4:1; Mark 3:11; 4:15).

One of the demons' principal ploys is to deceive people through false religion or deceptive miracles and thereby blind people to spiritual truth (2 Corinthians 4:4; Acts 26:18; 2 Corinthians 11:14; 2 Thessalonians 2:9, 10; Revelation 16:14; 20:10).

However, it must never be forgotten that Satan and demons are only creatures who are ultimately constrained by the sovereign power and purpose of God. When needed, the Christian has power over them (1 John 4:4; James

4:7) because Christ Himself was victorious over Satan at the Cross (Hebrews 2:14; Colossians 2:15; John 12:31). Jesus proved His complete power over demons (Matthew 12:28; Mark 1:34), often casting demons out of people (Matthew 8:31; 15:22–28), and He commanded His disciples to do the same (Mark 6:13; Matthew 10:1; Luke 10:17).

Using the Bible to catalog the powers and abilities of angels in general would give us a glimpse into their capacities, which would also help us discern the abilities of demons as corrupted angels. The following list indicates the capacities or methods of fallen angels in general. Some listings refer to the good angels to indicate that fallen angels would probably also have these abilities.

1. Power to torment. (Revelation 9:1–11; Luke 8:27–31)

2. Immense power; four angels are released to kill one-third of mankind. (Revelation 9:14–15)

3. Considerable influence; the world is said to be greatly affected by Satan's power. (2 Corinthians 4:4; 1 John 5:19; in Matthew 4 Jesus did not question Satan's right to grant Him the worlds' kingdoms)

4. Purposeful deception. (Genesis 3:1–5, 13)

5. Disguised as good spirits. (2 Corinthians 11:14–15)

6. A particular number of rebellious angels now confined (2 Peter 2:4–5, Jude 6–7), the result of apparent sexual involvement and cohabitation (the exact term "Sons of God," *bene elohim* is only used of angels. C. Fred Dickason, *Angels: Elect and Evil* (Chicago: Moody Press, 1975), pp. 222–25; Ben Adam, *Astrology: The Ancient Conspiracy* (Bethany, 1963), pp. 90–112; Genesis 6:1–4)

7. Producing insanity; great physical strength. (Luke 8:26–35)

8. Inducing sickness for 18 years; producing suffering and deformities. (Luke 13:10–17)

9. Power over nature: Satan produces whirlwinds, fire from heaven and great miracles in the presence of people. (Job 1:16–18; Revelation 13:13; Hebrews 1:7, Psalm 104:4)

10. Power over the human body: Satan produces painful boils or welts. (Job 2:7)

11. Dumbness, blindness, epilepsy, attempted murder. (Genesis 19:11; Matthew 9:32–33; 12:22; 17:15, 18)

12. Multiple possession; apparently seeking "rest" by possessing humans. (Luke 8:30; 11:24–26; Matthew 12:43–45)

13. Convulsions, child possession, mauling. (Luke 9:38–39)

14. Animal possession. (Matthew 8:30–32)

15. A limited prevision of the future; fortune-telling. (Acts 16:16). Despite this apparent ability, demons are not omniscient; any powers they may have are still subject to God's controlling and intervening providence. (Isaiah 44:25–26)

16. Anger, great strength and power. (2 Thessalonians 2:7; 2 Peter 2:11; Acts 19:16)

17. Treacherous natures, scheme wickedly, attack humans. (Ephesians 6:10–16; Judges 9:23)

18. Provide supernatural revelations. (Hebrews 2:2; Acts 7:53; Galatians 3:19)

19. Animals may recognize them. (Numbers 22:23–27)

20. Ability to speak through an animal. (Genesis 3:1–5)

21. Supernatural power to travel. (Job 1:7)

22. Instantaneous projection of a false reality. (Matthew 4:8)

23. Apparent ability to remove thoughts, to implant thoughts and to manipulate the mind. (John 13:2; Matthew 13:19, 38–39)

24. Moral corruption, deception and murder. (John 8:44)

25. Possess humans. (Matthew 8:28; John 13:27)

26. Great wrath. (Revelation 12:12)

27. Ability to incite betrayal. (Luke 22:3–4)

28. Physical ailments. (2 Corinthians 12:7)

29. Deception; blinding minds. (2 Corinthians 4:4)

30. Deceive the nations. (Revelation 12:9; 20:7–8)

31. Invisibility, but an awareness of their presence. (Job 4:15)

32. Ability to terrorize. (1 Samuel 16:14–15)

33. Can assume human form. (Genesis 19:1–10; John 20:12; Acts 12:8–9; Hebrews 13:2)

34. To a degree, they can duplicate God's miracles, changing sticks to snakes, water to blood (control over matter and energy), control over animals. (Exodus 7:10–12, 20–22; 8:6–7; 2 Thessalonians 2:9)

35. Defilement through occult practices and human sacrifice. (Deuteronomy 18:9–13)

36. Transport human beings. (Matthew 24:31; Luke 16:22)

37. Limited ability over events and human actions. (1 Chronicles 21:1; Daniel 10:13; 1 Thessalonians 2:18)

38. Destroying the flesh; power of death. (2 Samuel 24:15–17; 1 Corinthians 5:5; Hebrews 2:14; Acts 12:23)

39. Tempt with evil. (1 Corinthians 7:5)

40. Objects of pagan worship. (Deuteronomy 32:17; 1 Corinthians 10:20; Colossians 2:18)

41. Child sacrifice and murder. (Psalm 106:37)

42. Oppression. (Acts 10:38)

43. Control humans for their own goals. (Revelation 2:10)

44. Pervert the ways of God. (Acts 13:10)

45. Fire and brimstone rained down upon a city. (destruction of Sodom and Gomorrah; Genesis 19:13,24)

46. Influence dream states. (Genesis 31:11)

47. Send pestilence, power to destroy a city. (2 Samuel 24:15–16)

48. Communicate by speech to humans. (1 Kings 13:18; Acts 23:9)

49. Materialize and dematerialize at will. (Luke 2:9, 13, 15)

50. Vast in number. (Hebrews 12:22; Matthew 26:53)

51. Speak to men; control of vocal cords, paralysis and possession. (Luke 1:19–20)

52. Different languages. (1 Corinthians 13:1)

53. Preach a false gospel and deception about God. (1 Kings 22:19–23; Galatians 1:8; 1 Timothy 4:1; 1 John 4:1)

54. False visions and experiences. (Jeremiah 23:16; Colossians 2:18)

55. Miracles. (Revelation 16:14)

This partial listing indicates that demons have more power and influence than most people may realize. And the preceding list is surprisingly relevant for today, when almost everything in this "ancient" list is duplicated somewhere in the world of the cults and the occult. As we documented in detail in volume one in this series, the *Encyclopedia of New Age Beliefs*, evil angels (demons) imitate good angels and express great concern for people's welfare. They give false visions and revelations in dreams or through channeling, automatic writing and so on. They can possess people, perform various miracles, cause insanity or cause murder to be committed. They can produce various physical ailments, sicknesses or mental torments. They can predict the future (albeit in a limited capacity subject to God's sovereignty), encourage occult practices, manipulate the human mind by impressing thoughts, ideas or images, and they can influence nature. They can even assume physical form at will, from human to child, animal to mythological creature. They seek our worship and to pervert God's ways. In the end, however, they destroy people's lives.[7]

Spiritual warfare. Whether or not practitioners accept the categories, the data point unmistakably to the conclusion that the essence of occult practice means trafficking with demons. From this reality flows a number of other concerns: idolatry, spiritual deception, the possibility of possession, psychological and physical harm and the immoral, ethically consequential teachings that inevitably accompany demonic involvement or revelations.

God teaches that spiritual warfare is a reality (Ephesians 6:10–18; 2 Corinthians 2:11; 1 Peter 5:8) and that supernatural manifestations are not to be accepted uncritically but to be tested by the Word of God (1 John 4:1; Revelation 2:2; Acts 17:10–12; Deuteronomy 12:28; 13:5; 18–22; Matthew 24:24). As we have seen, Scripture also speaks of the reality of a personal devil and myriads of demons, who should be regarded as cunning enemies of both the believer in Christ and the non-believer (Isaiah 47:9; John 8:44; 13:27; Matthew 6:13; 9:34; 13:24; Luke 8:12; 13:16; 2 Corinthians 4:4; Colossians 1:13; 2 Thessalonians 2:9; Acts 16:18; 2 Corinthians 2:11; 11:3; 2 Timothy 2:26). Indeed, one of the devil's tactics is to masquerade as an "angel of light" and a servant of righteousness (2 Corinthians 11:13–15).

Scripture warns that false prophets are linked to evil spirits and that there are "doctrines of demons" (1 John 4:11; 1 Timothy 4:1). The Bible also teaches that there is great power in the occult (Isaiah 47:9); that demons work through people by giving them psychic abilities (Acts 16:16–19; Exodus 7:11, 22; 8:7) and that Satan and his hordes are active in the affairs of the planet (Ephesians 2:2; Daniel 10:12, 13, 20). In many instances, Scripture explicitly cites Satan or his demons as the reality behind occult involvement, idolatry and false religion (Deuteronomy 32:16–17; 1 Corinthians 10:10 21; Psalms 106:35–40; 1 Timothy 4:1; 2 Thessalonians 2:9–10; Acts 16:16–19). This is one reason why God considers occult activity in virtually all its forms as an abomination (Deuteronomy 18:9–12), for it links those for whom Christ died to evil spirits who are His enemies. Thus, occult involvement will eventually lead to judgment for those who refuse to forsake it (Revelation 22:15; 2 Chronicles 33:6).

Scripture condemns by name many practices of the cults, such as spiritism, mediumism and necromancy (Deuteronomy 18:9–12; 2 Chronicles 33:2–6; Leviticus 2:6, 27) and various forms of sorcery and divination, such as astrology, (Deuteronomy 18:9–12; Hosea 4:12; Exodus 22:18; Isaiah 44:25; 20:8 9; Ezekiel 21:21; Deuteronomy 17:2–5; 2 Kings 17:15–17; Isaiah 47:9–14). It also condemns magic (Acts 13:8; 19:16–19; Isaiah 47:9, 12). In their numerous forms these basic categories (magic, spiritism, divination, sorcery) cover almost the entire gamut of occult activity. Indeed, all occultism is based to one degree or another in spiritism, which is really demonism. Brooks Alexander notes:

[Spiritism] . . . is one of the oldest known forms of religious expression. It is also one of the deadliest where the certainty of divine judgment is concerned. . . . It is terminal error, since it demonstrates not only an active rejection of God, but an active embrace of his replacement. It is, as the prophets put it, "spiritual adultery," carried to completion. It is faithlessness fulfilled.

The extent to which a society endorses or indulges in widespread spiritism, therefore, is something of a spiritual thermometer. It can give us a rough estimate of our collective state of spiritual health. . . . The Bible levies its judgment against spiritism at two levels. It treats spiritism as a symptom of social decline as well as an act of personal culpability.

All sin provokes God's judgment. Advanced or developed sin provokes it more directly and immediately. As a social symptom, spiritism represents the final stage of a long process of spiritual decay. It is the terminal phase of our flight from God. It is terminal because God's judgment on spiritism is not meant to admonish or correct, but to cleanse and extirpate.

On an individual scale, the practice of spiritism is terminal because it represents an ultimate confusion of values. It trades humanity's privilege of intimacy with God for sheer fascination with a liar who secretly hates all that is human and all that humans hold dear.[8]

In many years of studying spiritistic contacts and literature and the effects on the lives of spiritists, we can confirm this view wholeheartedly. Clearly, Scripture warns against the occult, and just as clearly those who practice it disobey what God's Word commands. In essence, occult activity courts deception and betrayal from the demonic realm, and it evokes judgment from God for engaging in it and thereby promotes spiritual evil under the guise of legitimate religious practice. Therein lies one of the more consequential outcomes of cultic involvement.

Notes

1. In *This Week* magazine, March 2, 1958.
2. J. I. Packer, *God's Words* (Downers Grove, Ill: InterVarsity, 1985), pp. 83-84.
3. Brooks Alexander, "The Disappearance of the Devil," *Spiritual Counterfeits Project Newsletter,* Vol. 10, no. 4, pp. 6-7.
4. Rene Pache, *The Inspiration and Authority of Scripture* (Chicago: Moody Press, 1966); Norman L. Geisler, ed.,

Inerrancy (Grand Rapids, MI: Zondervan, 1979); L. Gaussen, *The Divine Inspiration of the Bible* (Grand Rapids, MI: Kregel, 1971), rpt.
5. Denis De Rougemont, *The Devil's Share: An Essay on the Diabolic in Modern Society* (New York: Meridian, 1956), p. 18.
6. See Matthew 4:24; Mark 1:32, 34; Luke 7:21; 9:1; Kurt Koch, *Occult Bondage and Deliverance* (Grand Rapids, MI: Kregel Publishers, 1970).
7. John Ankerberg, John Weldon, *The Coming Darkness: Confronting Occult Deception* (Eugene, OR: Harvest House, 1993).
8. Brooks Alexander, "What Is Spiritism . . . and Why Are They Saying Those Awful Things About It?" (Berkeley, CA: Spiritual Counterfeits Project, 1986), p. 3.

Recommending Reading

C. S. Lewis, *Screwtape Letters*; John Ankerberg and John Weldon, *The Coming Darkness*.

STUDY SCRIPTURES RELATING TO CULTS AND NEW RELIGIONS

- Introduction
- General Scriptures and Principles
- Approach to Others
- The Importance of Doctrine
- The Devil
- False Apostles
- False Prophets
- False Christs
- False Teachers
- Idolatry
- Spiritual Discernment
- Spiritual Wisdom
- Spiritual Instruction
- Spiritual Deception, Falsehood, Hypocrisy
- God's Concern with Truth
- The Fear of God
- God's Love
- Aberrational Christianity

Introduction

The following verses are selected and coordinated by topic for additional study. They may be utilized in a variety of ways. For example, Bible studies may be developed around them that are coordinated to the general subject of cults or to other modern applications. The sections on doctrine, idolatry, God's love, truth, discernment, wisdom and instruction can be applied to a broad range of topics. Or, after reading a given chapter in this Encyclopedia all the following verses may be read together and particularly relevant verses selected to incorporate in apologetic writing or personal discussion with a member of that particular group. For example, many people believe that Joseph Smith (the founder of Mormonism), or Edgar Cayce (the famous psychic), or Elizabeth Claire Prophet (founder of the Church Universal and Triumphant), were genuine biblical prophets. However, based on the information given in these chapters, did they meet the requirements of a biblical prophet as stated in the following Scriptures? As another example, a number of groups teach that idolatry (actual worship of wooden idols) is a spiritual, godly practice, or at least permissible for those who love God—Vedanta, Zen, Self-Realization Fellowship, Buddhism, Unity. Many of these groups claim to be Christian and biblical in their teachings. But based on the section on idolatry, does the Bible approve of this idea in any form at all? As another example, most groups deny the devil as a real, evil, personal spirit. But since they claim to honor what the Bible teaches, what do they do with the Scriptures cited, not to mention the ones given earlier? Another example of how these Scriptures can be used is to combine relevant topics, such as combining salvation with the Scriptures on heresy or spiritual discernment, or the section on God with the Scriptures on idolatry, or the section on the Bible with the Scriptures on aberrational Christianity or the section on justification with the Scriptures on God's love. Different combinations and other applications may be developed, especially after adding additional relevant Scriptures to these lists.

General Scriptures and Principles

A son honors his father, and a servant his master. "If I am a father, where is the honor due me? If I am a master, where is the respect due me?" says the LORD Almighty. (Malachi 1:6)

God is light; in him there is no darkness at all. If we claim to have fellowship with him yet walk in the darkness, we lie and do not live by the truth. . . . If we claim to be without sin, we deceive ourselves and the truth is not in us. (1 John 1:5–6, 8)

God opposes the proud but gives grace to the humble. Submit yourselves, then, to God. Resist the devil, and he will flee from you. Come near to God and he will come near to you. (James 4:6–8)

Do not merely listen to the word, and so deceive yourselves. Do what it says. (James 1:22)

They claim to know God, but by their actions they deny him. (Titus 1:16)

Not everyone who says to me, "Lord, Lord," will enter the kingdom of heaven, but only he who does the will of my Father who is in heaven. Many will say to me on that day, "Lord, Lord, did we not prophesy in your name, and in your name drive out demons and perform many miracles?" Then I will tell them plainly, "I never knew you. Away from me, you evildoers!" (Matthew 7:21–23)

We know that we have come to know him if we obey his commands. The man who says, "I know him," but does not do what he commands is a liar, and the truth is not in him. (1 John 2:3–4)

He will punish those who do not know God and do not obey the gospel of our Lord Jesus. They will be punished with everlasting destruction and shut out from the presence of the Lord and from the majesty of his power on the day he comes to be glorified in his holy people and to be marveled at among all those who have believed. (2 Thessalonians 1:8–9)

But even if we or an angel from heaven should preach a gospel other than the one we preached to you, let him be eternally condemned! As we have already said, so now I say again: If anybody is preaching to you a gospel other than what you accepted, let him be eternally condemned! (Galatians 1:8–9)

Such is the destiny of all who forget God; so perishes the hope of the godless. What he trusts in is fragile; what he relies on is a spider's web. (Job 8:13–14)

Anyone who does not believe God has made him out to be a liar, because he has not believed the testimony God has given about his Son. And this is the testimony: God has given us eternal life, and this life is in his Son. He who has the

Son has life; he who does not have the Son of God does not have life. (1 John 5:10–12)

Woe to those who call evil good and good evil, who put darkness for light and light for darkness, who put bitter for sweet and sweet for bitter. Woe to those who are wise in their own eyes and clever in their own sight. (Isaiah 5:20–21)

These people honor me with their lips, but their hearts are far from me. They worship me in vain; their teachings are but rules taught by men. . . . Every plant that my heavenly Father has not planted will be pulled up by the roots. Leave them; they are blind guides. If a blind man leads a blind man, both will fall into a pit. (Matthew 15:9, 13–14)

He who listens to you listens to me; he who rejects you rejects me; but he who rejects me rejects him who sent me. (Luke 10:16)

As for the person who hears my words but does not keep them, I do not judge him. For I did not come to judge the world, but to save it. There is a judge for the one who rejects me and does not accept my words; that very word which I spoke will condemn him at the last day. For I did not speak of my own accord, but the Father who sent me commanded me what to say and how to say it. I know that his command leads to eternal life. So whatever I say is just what the Father has told me to say. (John 12:47–50)

Who is the liar? It is the man who denies that Jesus is the Christ. Such a man is the antichrist—he denies the Father and the Son. No one who denies the Son has the Father. (1 John 2:22–23)

The wrath of God is being revealed from heaven against all the godlessness and wickedness of men who suppress the truth by their wickedness, since what may be known about God is plain to them, because God has made it plain to them. (Romans 1:18–19)

For, as I have often told you before and now say again even with tears, many live as enemies of the cross of Christ. Their destiny is destruction, their god is their stomach, and their glory is in their shame. Their mind is on earthly things. (Philippians 3:18–19)

You adulterous people, don't you know that friendship with the world is hatred toward God? Anyone who chooses to be a friend of the world becomes an enemy of God. (James 4:4)

Will you then say, "I am a god," in the presence of those who kill you? (Ezekiel 28:9)

What is your life? You are a mist that appears for a little while and then vanishes. (James 4:14)

Man is destined to die once, and after that to face judgment. (Hebrews 9:27)

But because of your stubbornness and your unrepentant heart, you are storing up wrath against yourself for the day of God's wrath, when his righteous judgment will be revealed. (Romans 2:5)

They went out from us, but they did not really belong to us. For if they had belonged to us, they would have remained with us; but their going showed that none of them belonged to us. (1 John 2:19)

The Spirit clearly says that in later times some will abandon the faith and follow deceiving spirits and things taught by demons. (1 Timothy 4:1)

But whatever was to my profit I now consider loss for the sake of Christ. What is more, I consider everything a loss compared to the surpassing greatness of knowing Christ Jesus my Lord, for whose sake I have lost all things. I consider them rubbish, that I may gain Christ and be found in him, not having a righteousness of my own that comes from the law, but that which is through faith in Christ—the righteousness that comes from God and is by faith. (Philippians 3:7–9)

I want you to know, brothers, that the gospel I preached is not something that man made up. I did not receive it from any man, nor was I taught it; rather, I received it by revelation from Jesus Christ. (Galatians 1:11–12)

For we also have had the gospel preached to us, just as they did; but the message they heard was of no value to them, because those who heard did not combine it with faith. (Hebrews 4:2)

He forgave us all our sins. (Colossians 2:13)

You shut the kingdom of heaven in men's faces. You yourselves do not enter, nor will you let those enter who are trying to. (Matthew 23:13)

They displease God and are hostile to all men in their effort to keep us from speaking to [others] so that they may be saved. (1 Thessalonians 2:15–16)

I give you this charge: Preach the Word; be prepared in season and out of season; correct, rebuke and encourage—with great patience and careful instruction. For the time will come when men will not put up with sound doctrine. Instead, to suit their own desires, they will gather around them a great number of teachers to say what their itching ears want to hear. They will turn their ears away from the truth and turn aside to myths. (2 Timothy 4:1–4)

In the last times there will be scoffers who will follow their own ungodly desires. These are the men who divide you, who follow mere natural instincts and do not have the Spirit. (Jude 18–19)

Anyone who rejected the law of Moses died without mercy on the testimony of two or three witnesses. How much more severely do you think a man deserves to be punished who has trampled the Son of God under foot, who has treated as an unholy thing the blood of the covenant that sanctified him, and who has insulted the Spirit of grace? (Hebrews 10:28–29)

You are of this world; I am not of this world. I told you that you would die in your sins; if you do not believe that I am the one I claim to be, you will indeed die in your sins. "Who are you?" they asked. "Just what I have been claiming all along," Jesus replied. (John 8:23–25)

Whoever believes in the Son has eternal life, but whoever rejects the Son will not see life, for God's wrath remains on him. (John 3:36)

He who belongs to God hears what God says. The reason you do not hear is that you do not belong to God. (John 8:47)

Jesus said, "If you hold to my teaching, you are really my disciples. Then you will know the truth, and the truth will set you free." (John 8:31–32)

Approach to Others

But in your hearts set apart Christ as Lord. Always be prepared to give an answer to everyone who asks you to give the reason for the hope that you have. But do this with gentleness and respect, keeping a clear conscience. (1 Peter 3:15–16)

Be wise in the way you act toward outsiders; make the most of every opportunity. Let your conversation be always full of grace, seasoned with salt, so that you may know how to answer everyone. (Colossians 4:5–6)

Therefore I endure everything for the sake of the elect, that they too may obtain the salvation that is in Christ Jesus, with eternal glory. (2 Timothy 2:10)

Do your best to present yourself to God as one approved, a workman who does not need to be ashamed and who correctly handles the word of truth. (2 Timothy 2:15)

Don't have anything to do with foolish and stupid arguments, because you know they produce quarrels. And the Lord's servant must not quarrel; instead, he must be kind to everyone, able to teach, not resentful. Those who oppose him he must gently instruct, in the hope that God will grant them repentance leading them to a knowledge of the truth, and that they will come to their senses and escape from the trap of the devil, who has taken them captive to do his will. (2 Timothy 2:23–26)

The Importance of Doctrine

You must teach what is in accord with sound doctrine. (Titus 2:1)

Watch your life and doctrine closely. Persevere in them. (1 Timothy 4:16)

Then we will no longer be infants, tossed back and forth by the waves, and blown here and there by every wind of teaching and by the cunning and craftiness of men in their deceitful scheming. (Ephesians 4:14)

If anyone teaches false doctrines and does not agree to the sound instruction of our Lord Jesus Christ and to godly teaching, he is conceited and understands nothing. (1 Timothy 6:3)

Anyone who runs ahead and does not continue in the teaching of Christ does not have God; whoever continues in the teaching has both the Father and the Son. (2 John 9)

The Devil

And even if our gospel is veiled, it is veiled to those who are perishing. The god of this age has blinded the minds of unbelievers, so that they cannot see the light of the gospel of the glory of Christ, who is the image of God. (2 Corinthians 4:4)

We know that . . . the whole world is under the control of the evil one. We know also that the Son of God has come and has given us understanding, so that we may know him who is true. (1 John 5:19–20)

The work of Satan [is/will be] displayed in all kinds of counterfeit miracles, signs and wonders, and in every sort of evil that deceives those who are perishing. They perish because they refused to love the truth and so be saved. (2 Thessalonians 2: 9–10)

You belong to your father, the devil, and you want to carry out your father's desire. He was a murderer from the beginning, not holding to the truth, for there is no truth in him. When he lies, he speaks his native language, for he is a liar and the father of lies. (John 8:44)

No, but the sacrifices of pagans are offered to demons, not to God, and I do not want you to be participants with demons. (1 Corinthians 10:20)

Put on the full armor of God so that you can take your stand against the devil's schemes. For our struggle is not against flesh and blood, but against the rulers, against the authorities, against the powers of this dark world and against the spiritual forces of evil in the heavenly realms. (Ephesians 6:11–13)

Be self-controlled and alert. Your enemy the devil prowls around like a roaring lion looking for someone to devour. Resist him, standing firm in the faith. (1 Peter 5:8–9)

False Apostles

For such men are false apostles, deceitful workmen, masquerading as apostles of Christ. And no wonder, for Satan himself masquerades as an angel of light. It is not surprising, then, if his servants masquerade as servants of righteousness. Their end will be what their actions deserve. (2 Corinthians 11:13–15)

False Prophets

Biblical prophets were unique among the prophets of all religions. Here are some basic characteristics of the biblical prophets that contrast them with the many false prophets in the modern cults and new religions.

1) The biblical prophet is called by the one true God and therefore his message honors the character, nature and purpose of the one true

God. The prophet is inspired by God, not by his own spirit, mind or demons. He speaks in the name of the one true God of Israel and never encourages the worship of false gods.

2) The message of the biblical prophets never contradicts earlier divine revelation but compliments or expands upon it.

3) Their prophecies are 100 percent accurate and therefore, in contrast to false prophets, their prophecy always comes true.

4) Their mission is to keep the people dedicated to the one true God. When the people strayed, they preached God's message of repentance, something which the people did not necessarily want to hear. As a result, the prophets were often rejected and suffered for preaching the message that God had given them to speak. The false prophets do just the opposite. They tell people what they want to hear and do not bring a message of biblical repentance or judgment.

5) The biblical prophet cannot be proven true merely by the fact that he does genuine miracles or by the fact he claims to speak in the name of the one true God. False prophets may also perform miracles or claim to speak in the name of the one true God. However, even though false prophets may claim to speak in the name of the one true God and perform miracles, they never have 100 percent accuracy in their predictions, because the one true God has not spoken to them. Their miracles were accomplished through Satan's power. The following scriptures are some of those relevant to the role of the biblical prophet:

Watch out for false prophets. They come to you in sheep's clothing, but inwardly they are ferocious wolves. (Matthew 7:15)

If a prophet, or one who foretells by dreams, appears among you and announces to you a miraculous sign or wonder, and if the sign or wonder of which he has spoken takes place, and he says, "Let us follow other gods" (gods you have not known) "and let us worship them," you must not listen to the words of that prophet or dreamer. The LORD your God is testing you to find out whether you love him with all your heart and with all your soul. It is the LORD your God you must follow, and him you must revere. Keep his commands and obey him; serve him

and hold fast to him. That prophet or dreamer must be put to death, because he preached rebellion against the LORD your God. (Deuteronomy 13:1–5)

You may say to yourselves, "How can we know when a message has not been spoken by the LORD?" If what a prophet proclaims in the name of the LORD does not take place or come true, that is a message the LORD has not spoken. That prophet has spoken presumptuously. Do not be afraid of him. (Deuteronomy 18: 21–22)

[The prophet] will be recognized as one truly sent by the LORD only if his prediction comes true [because] whatever I say will be fulfilled, declares the Sovereign LORD. (Jeremiah 28:9 with Ezekiel 12:28)

I did not send these prophets, yet they have run with their message; I did not speak to them, yet they have prophesied. (Jeremiah 23:21)

Then the LORD said to me, "The prophets are prophesying lies in my name. I have not sent them or appointed them or spoken to them. They are prophesying to you false visions, divinations, idolatries and the delusions of their own minds." (Jeremiah 14:14) (For a brief treatment on false visions, see our "True v. False Visions and How to Tell Them Apart," *Ankerberg Theological Research Institute News Magazine,* August, 1996.)

Therefore, declares the LORD, I am against the prophets who steal from one another words supposedly from me. Yes, declares the LORD, I am against the prophets who wag their own tongues and yet declare, "The LORD declares." Indeed, I am against those who prophesy false dreams, declares the LORD. They tell them and lead my people astray with their reckless lies, yet I did not send or appoint them. They do not benefit these people in the least, declares the LORD. . . . Every man's own word becomes his oracle and so you distort the words of the living God, the LORD Almighty. (Jeremiah 23:31–36)

Because of your false words and lying visions, I am against you, declares the Sovereign LORD. My hand will be against the prophets who see false visions and utter lying divinations. They will not belong to the council of my people. (Ezekiel 13: 8–9)

They will bear their guilt—the [false] prophet will be as guilty as the one who consults him. (Ezekiel 14:10)

Do not let the prophets and diviners among you deceive you. Do not listen to the dreams you encourage them to have. They are prophesying lies to you in my name. I have not sent them, declares the LORD. (Jeremiah 29:9)

Dear friends, do not believe every spirit, but test the spirits to see whether they are from God, because many false prophets have gone out into the world. (1 John 4:1)

False Christs

Jesus answered: "Watch out that no one deceives you. For many will come in my name, claiming, 'I am the Christ,' and will deceive many.... For false Christs and false prophets will appear and perform great signs and miracles to deceive even the elect—if that were possible." (Matthew 24:4, 24)

You, dear children, are from God and have overcome them [false Christs], because the one who is in you is greater than the one who is in the world. (1 John 4:4)

False Teachers

Keep watch over yourselves and all the flock of which the Holy Spirit has made you overseers. Be shepherds of the church of God, which he bought with his own blood. I know that after I leave, savage wolves will come in among you and will not spare the flock. Even from your own number men will arise and distort the truth in order to draw away disciples after them. So be on your guard! Remember that for three years I never stopped warning each of you night and day with tears. (Acts 20:28-31)

They are ... always learning but never able to acknowledge the truth. Just as Jannes and Jambres opposed Moses, so also these men oppose the truth—men of depraved minds, who, as far as the faith is concerned, are rejected. (2 Timothy 3:6-8)

Evil men and impostors will go from bad to worse, deceiving and being deceived. (2 Timothy 2:13)

But there were also false prophets among the people, just as there will be false teachers among you. They will secretly introduce destructive heresies, even denying the sovereign Lord who bought them—bringing swift destruction on themselves. Many will follow their shameful ways and will bring the way of truth into disrepute. In their greed these teachers will exploit you with stories they have made up. (2 Peter 2:1-3)

They will be paid back with harm for the harm they have done. ... These men are springs without water and mists driven by a storm. Blackest darkness is reserved for them. (2 Peter 2:13, 17)

I felt I had to write and urge you to contend for the faith that was once for all entrusted to the saints. For certain men whose condemnation was written about long ago have secretly slipped in among you. (Jude 3-4)

These men are blemishes ... eating with you without the slightest qualm—shepherds who feed only themselves. (Jude 12)

Because you disheartened the righteous with your lies, when I had brought them no grief, and because you encouraged the wicked not to turn from their evil ways and so save their lives ... (Ezekiel 13:22)

Idolatry

The Bible is clear that the one true God is unique among all the other concepts of God and false gods that people worship. "Who among the gods is like you, O LORD?" (Exodus 15:11). "Among the gods, there is no one like you, O LORD; no deeds can compare with yours" (Psalm 86:8). "How great you are, O Sovereign LORD! There is none like you, and there is no God but you" (2 Samuel 7:22).

Idolatry has been prevalent throughout the past, is so today and, incidentally, will be so at the time of the end, at the return of Christ. "The rest of mankind that were not killed by these plagues still did not repent of the work of their hands; they did not stop worshiping demons, and idols of gold, silver, bronze, stone and wood—idols that cannot see or hear or walk." (Revelation 9:20)

The cults universally promote idolatry, whether by worship of a false concept of God or by worship of an actual idol. Anyone who has studied the effect of idolatry on a people and its culture, whether in the ancient world or in places such as modern Asia and Africa, knows the reasons for the powerfully uncompromising biblical stand against it. "You must not worship the LORD your God in their way, because in worshiping their gods, they do all kinds of detestable things the LORD hates. They even burn their sons and daughters in the fire as sacrifices to their gods" (Deuteronomy 12:31). As Scripture warns, they became like what they worshipped (2 Kings 17:15). "Those who cling to worthless idols forfeit the grace that could be theirs" (Jonah 2:8).

The following excerpt from the *Compton's Interactive Bible–NIV* summarizes succinctly what the Bible thinks of idolatry:

IDOLATRY (Gr. *eidololatria*). Idolatry in ancient times included two forms of departure from the true religion: the worship of false gods (whether by means of images or otherwise); and the worship of the Lord by means of images. All the nations surrounding ancient Israel were idolatrous. . . . The gods had no moral character whatsoever, and worship of them carried with it demoralizing practices, including child sacrifice, prostitution, and snake worship. . . . The word "idolatry" has no exact Hebrew equivalent. There are, however, a number of Hebrew words that are translated "idol." They all give expression to the loathing, contempt, and dread excited in godly men by idolatry. The terms are as follows: (1) *Aven*, "emptiness, nothingness"; that is, a vain, false, wicked thing (Isaiah 66:3). (2) *Emah*, "an object of horror or terror," referring either to the hideousness of the idols or the shameful character of their worship (Jeremiah 50:38). (3) *El*, the name of the supreme god of Canaan; used also as a neutral expression for any divinity (Isaiah 57:5). (4) *Elil*, "a thing of naught, a nonentity," resembling aven in meaning (Leviticus 19:4; 26:1; 1 Chronicles 16:26). (5) *Miphletseth*, "a fright, a horror" (1 Kings 15:12; 2 Chronicles 15:16). (6) *Semel*, "a likeness, semblance" (33:7, 15). (7) *Atsabh*, "a cause of grief" (1 Samuel 31:9; 1 Chronicles 10:9). (8) *Etseb* "a cause of grief" (Jeremiah 22:28 KJV). (9) *Otseb* "a cause of grief" (Isaiah 48:5). (10) *Tsir*, "a form," and hence an idol (45:16). Besides the above words there are a number of others that are not translated "idol" but refer to it, expressing the degradation associated with idolatry: *bosheth*, "shameful thing," applied to Baal and referring to the obscenity of his worship (Jeremiah 11:13; Hosea 9:10); *gillulim*, a term of contempt meaning "shapeless, dungy things" (Zephaniah 1:17); and *shikkuts*, "filth,"

referring especially to the obscene rites associated with idolatry (Ezekiel 37:23; Nahum 3:6). Theologically, idolaters thought of their gods as spiritual beings (or forces) of cosmic significance and, theoretically, to them the idol was as a focal point for worship. The [Old Testament] insists, however, that the heathen worship idols and nothing more (cf. Psalm 115:2-8; Isaiah 44:6-20).

The following Scriptures on idolatry illustrate the preceding condemnation:

Do I mean then that a sacrifice offered to an idol is anything, or that an idol is anything? No, but the sacrifices of pagans are offered to demons, not to God, and I do not want you to be participants with demons. (1 Corinthians 10:19-20)

I am the LORD your God. . . . You shall have no other gods before me. You shall not make for yourself an idol. (Exodus 20:2-3)

Tell us what the future holds, so we may know that you are gods. (Isaiah 41:23)

They exchanged the truth of God for a lie, and worshiped and served created things rather than the Creator—who is forever praised. Amen. (Romans 1:25)

Do you not know that the wicked will not inherit the kingdom of God? Do not be deceived: Neither the sexually immoral nor idolaters nor adulterers nor male prostitutes nor homosexual offenders nor thieves nor the greedy nor drunkards nor slanderers nor swindlers will inherit the kingdom of God. (1 Corinthians 6:9-10)

For all the gods of the nations are idols, but the LORD made the heavens. (Psalm 96:5)

Of what value is an idol, since a man has carved it? Or an image that teaches lies? (Habakkuk 2:18)

But those who trust in idols, who say to images, "You are our gods," will be turned back in utter shame. (Isaiah 42:17)

They followed worthless idols and themselves became worthless. (2 Kings 17:15)

Therefore, my dear friends, flee from idolatry. (1 Corinthians 10:14)

The sorrows of those will increase who run after other gods. (Psalm 16:4)

Do men make their own gods? Yes, but they are not gods! (Jeremiah 16:20)

Some pour out gold from their bags and weigh out silver on the scales; they hire a goldsmith to make it into a god, and they bow down and worship it. They lift it to their shoulders and carry it; they set it up in its place, and there it stands. From that spot it cannot move. Though one cries out to it, it does not answer; it cannot save him from his troubles. (Isaiah 46:6–7)

But their idols are silver and gold, made by the hands of men. They have mouths, but cannot speak, eyes, but they cannot see; they have ears, but cannot hear, noses, but they cannot smell; they have hands, but cannot feel, feet, but they cannot walk; nor can they utter a sound with their throats. Those who make them will be like them, and so will all who trust in them. (Psalm 115:4–8)

But they mingled with the nations and adopted their customs. They worshiped their idols, which became a snare to them. They sacrificed their sons and their daughters to demons. They shed innocent blood, the blood of their sons and daughters, whom they sacrificed to the idols of Canaan, and the land was desecrated by their blood. (Psalm 106:35–38)

All who make idols are nothing, and the things they treasure are worthless. Those who would speak up for them are blind; they are ignorant, to their own shame. . . . Half of the wood he burns in the fire; over it he prepares his meal, he roasts his meat and eats his fill. He also warms himself and says, "Ah! I am warm; I see the fire." From the rest he makes a god, his idol; he bows down to it and worships. He prays to it and says, "Save me; you are my god." They know nothing, they understand nothing. . . . No one stops to think, no one has the knowledge or understanding to say, "Half of it I used for fuel; I even baked bread over its coals, I roasted meat and I ate. Shall I make a detestable thing from what is left? Shall I bow down to a block of wood?" (Isaiah 44:9–19)

Where then are the gods you made for yourselves? Let them come if they can save you when you are in trouble! (Jeremiah 2:28)

Like a scarecrow in a melon patch, their idols cannot speak; they must be carried because they cannot walk. Do not fear them; they can do no harm nor can they do any good. . . . Every goldsmith is shamed by his idols. His images are a fraud; they have no breath in them. They are worthless, the objects of mockery; when their judgment comes, they will perish. (Jeremiah 10:5, 14–15)

Spiritual Discernment

Now the Bereans were of more noble character than the Thessalonians, for they received the message with great eagerness and examined the Scriptures every day to see if what Paul said was true. (Acts 17:11)

See to it that no one takes you captive through hollow and deceptive philosophy, which depends on human tradition and the basic principles of this world rather than on Christ. (Colossians 2:8)

Test everything. Hold on to the good. Avoid every kind of evil. (1 Thessalonians 5:21–22

If anyone acknowledges that Jesus is the Son of God, God lives in him and he in God. . . . Everyone who believes that Jesus is the Christ is born of God, and everyone who loves the father loves his child as well. This is how we know that we love the children of God: by loving God and carrying out his commands. This is love for God: to obey his commands. (1 John 4:15; 5:1–3)

We are from God, and whoever knows God listens to us; but whoever is not from God does not listen to us. This is how we recognize the Spirit of truth and the spirit of falsehood. (1 John 4:6)

Two or three prophets should speak, and the others should weigh carefully what is said. (1 Corinthians 14:29)

Spiritual Wisdom

But the wisdom that comes from heaven is first of all pure; then peace-loving, considerate, submissive, full of mercy and good fruit, impartial and sincere. (James 3:17)

He who gets wisdom loves his own soul; he who cherishes understanding prospers. (Proverbs 19:8)

But where can wisdom be found? Where does understanding dwell? Man does not comprehend its worth; it cannot be found in the land of the living. . . . It cannot be bought with the finest gold, nor can its price be weighed in silver. . . . Neither gold nor crystal can compare with it. . . . God understands the way to it and he alone knows where it dwells. . . . And he said to man, "The fear of the Lord—that is wisdom, and to shun evil is understanding." (Job 28:12–28)

Christ, in whom are hidden all the treasures of wisdom and knowledge. I tell you this so that no one may deceive you by fine-sounding arguments. (Colossians 2:2–4)

The discerning heart seeks knowledge, but the mouth of a fool feeds on folly. . . . The fear of the Lord teaches a man wisdom, and humility comes before honor. (Proverbs 15:14, 33)

Whoever gives heed to instruction prospers, and blessed is he who trusts in the Lord. (Proverbs 16:20)

A rebuke impresses a man of discernment more than a hundred lashes a fool. (Proverbs 17:10)

For the Lord gives wisdom, and from his mouth come knowledge and understanding. (Proverbs 2:6)

The wisdom of the prudent is to give thought to their ways, but the folly of fools is deception. (Proverbs 14:8)

This is what the Lord says: "Let not the wise man boast of his wisdom or the strong man boast of his strength or the rich man boast of his riches, but let him who boasts boast about this: that he understands and knows me, that I am the Lord, who exercises kindness, justice and righteousness on earth, for in these I delight, declares the Lord. (Jeremiah 9:23–24)

Wisdom reposes in the heart of the discerning and even among fools she lets herself be known. (Proverbs 14:33)

The lips of the righteous nourish many, but fools die for lack of judgment. (Proverbs 10:21)

The fear of the Lord is the beginning of knowledge, but fools despise wisdom and discipline. (Proverbs 1:7)

Whoever loves discipline loves knowledge, but he who hates correction is stupid. . . . The way of a fool seems right to him, but a wise man listens to advice. (Proverbs 12:1, 15)

Spiritual Instruction

Let the morning bring me word of your unfailing love, for I have put my trust in you. Show me

the way I should go, for to you I lift up my soul. (Psalm 143:8)

Let him not deceive himself by trusting what is worthless, for he will get nothing in return. Before his time he will be paid in full, and his branches will not flourish. (Job 15:31–32)

The godless in heart harbor resentment; even when he fetters them, they do not cry for help. They die in their youth. (Job 36:13)

Do not be carried away by all kinds of strange teachings. (Hebrews 13:9)

I am writing these things to you about those who are trying to lead you astray. . . . Dear children, do not let anyone lead you astray. (1 John 2:26; 3:7)

This is how we know who the children of God are and who the children of the devil are: Anyone who does not do what is right is not a child of God; nor is anyone who does not love his brother. . . . Do not be surprised, my brothers, if the world hates you. (1 John 3:10, 13)

Do not be deceived: God cannot be mocked. A man reaps what he sows. (Galatians 6:7)

As a prisoner for the Lord, then, I urge you to live a life worthy of the calling you have received. (Galatians 4:1)

Whatever happens, conduct yourselves in a manner worthy of the gospel of Christ. Then . . . I will know that you stand firm in one spirit, contending as one man for the faith of the gospel without being frightened in any way by those who oppose you. This is a sign to them that they will be destroyed, but that you will be saved—and that by God. For it has been granted to you on behalf of Christ not only to believe on him, but also to suffer for him. (Philippians 1:27–29)

Spiritual Deception, Falsehood, Hypocrisy

Many deceivers, who do not acknowledge Jesus Christ as coming in the flesh, have gone out into the world. Any such person is the deceiver and the antichrist. Watch out that you do not lose what you have worked for, but that you may be rewarded fully. (2 John 7–8)

Like a coating of glaze over earthenware are fervent lips with an evil heart. A malicious man disguises himself with his lips, but in his heart he harbors deceit. Though his speech is charming, do not believe him, for seven abominations fill his heart. (Proverbs 26:24–25)

He said to them, "You are the ones who justify yourselves in the eyes of men, but God knows your hearts. What is highly valued among men is detestable in God's sight." (Luke 16:15)

Why do you call me, "Lord, Lord," and do not do what I say? (Luke 6:46)

The Spirit clearly says that in later times some will abandon the faith and follow deceiving spirits and things taught by demons. Such teachings come through hypocritical liars, whose consciences have been seared as with a hot iron. (1 Timothy 4:1–2)

They claim to know God, but by their actions they deny him. (Titus 1:16)

I urge you, brothers, to watch out for those who cause divisions and put obstacles in your way that are contrary to the teaching you have learned. Keep away from them. For such people are not serving our Lord Christ, but their own appetites. By smooth talk and flattery they deceive the minds of naive people. (Romans 16:17–18)

They promise them freedom, while they themselves are slaves of depravity—for a man is a slave to whatever has mastered him. (2 Peter 2:19)

No one who practices deceit will dwell in my house; no one who speaks falsely will stand in my presence. (Psalm 101:7)

You nullify the word of God for the sake of your tradition. You hypocrites! Isaiah was right when he prophesied about you: These people honor me with their lips, but their hearts are far from me. They worship me in vain; their teachings are but rules taught by men. (Matthew 15:6–9)

Rather, we have renounced secret and shameful ways; we do not use deception, nor do we distort the word of God. On the contrary, by setting forth the truth plainly we commend ourselves to every man's conscience in the sight of God (2 Corinthians 4:2)

If we claim to have fellowship with him yet walk in the darkness, we lie and do not live by the truth. . . . If we claim to be without sin, we deceive ourselves and the truth is not in us. . . . If we claim we have not sinned, we make him out to be a liar and his word has no place in our lives. (1 John 1:6, 8, 10)

The man who says, "I know him," but does not do what he commands is a liar, and the truth is not in him. . . . This is how we know we are in him: Whoever claims to live in him must walk as Jesus did. (1 John 2:4–6)

The LORD detests the sacrifice of the wicked, but the prayer of the upright pleases him. . . . The sacrifice of the wicked is detestable—how much more so when brought with evil intent! (Proverbs 15:8; 21:27)

In the same way, on the outside you appear to people as righteous but on the inside you are full of hypocrisy and wickedness. (Matthew 23:28)

Friend deceives friend, and no one speaks the truth. They have taught their tongues to lie; they weary themselves with sinning. You live in the midst of deception; in their deceit they refuse to acknowledge me, declares the LORD. (Jeremiah 9:5)

Hear the word of the LORD, you Israelites, because the LORD has a charge to bring against you who live in the land: There is no faithfulness, no love, no acknowledgment of God in the land. There is only cursing, lying and murder, stealing and adultery; they break all bounds, and bloodshed follows bloodshed. (Hosea 4:1)

God's Concern with Truth

I have no greater joy than to hear that my children are walking in the truth. (3 John 4)

All will be condemned who have not believed the truth but have delighted in wickedness. (2 Thessalonians 2:12)

Jesus answered, "You are right in saying I am a king. In fact, for this reason I was born, and for this I came into the world, to testify to the truth. Everyone on the side of truth listens to me." (John 18:37)

I am . . . the truth. (John 14:6)

The Spirit is the truth. (1 John 5:6)

Have I now become your enemy by telling you the truth? (Galatians 4:16)

The Fear of God

Through love and faithfulness sin is atoned for; through the fear of the LORD a man avoids evil. (Proverbs 16:6)

Although a wicked man commits a hundred crimes and still lives a long time, I know that it will go better with God-fearing men, who are reverent before God. (Ecclesiastes 8:12)

The LORD Almighty is the one you are to regard as holy, he is the one you are to fear, he is the one you are to dread. (Isaiah 8:13)

I tell you, my friends, do not be afraid of those who kill the body and after that can do no more. But I will show you whom you should fear: Fear him who, after the killing of the body, has power to throw you into hell. Yes, I tell you, fear him. (Luke 12:4–5)

The fear of the LORD is the beginning of knowledge, but fools despise wisdom and discipline. (Proverbs 1:6)

Now all has been heard; here is the conclusion of the matter: Fear God and keep his commandments, for this is the whole duty of man. For God will bring every deed into judgment, including every hidden thing. (Ecclesiastes 12:13–14)

God's Love

God is love. This is how God showed his love among us: He sent his one and only Son into the world that we might live through him. This is love: not that we loved God, but that he loved us and sent his Son as an atoning sacrifice for our sins. (1 John 4:8–10)

In love he predestined us to be adopted as his sons through Jesus Christ. (Ephesians 1:7)

To those who have been called, who are loved by God the Father and kept by Jesus Christ. (Jude 1)

But because of his great love for us, God, who is rich in mercy, made us alive with Christ even when we were dead in transgressions—it is by grace you have been saved. (Ephesians 2:4–5)

And I pray that you, being rooted and established in love, may have power, together with all the saints, to grasp how wide and long and high and deep is the love of Christ, and to know this love. (Ephesians 3:17–19)

Be imitators of God, therefore, as dearly loved children. (Ephesians 5:1)

Therefore, as God's chosen people, holy and dearly loved . . . (Colossians 3:12)

For we know, brothers loved by God, that he has chosen you. (1 Thessalonians 1:4)

Brothers loved by the Lord, because from the beginning God chose you to be saved. (2 Thessalonians 2:13)

May the Lord direct your hearts into God's love and Christ's perseverance. (2 Thessalonians 3:5)

Keep yourselves in God's love as you wait for the mercy of our Lord Jesus Christ to bring you to eternal life. (Jude 21)

Aberrational Christianity

The shepherds are senseless and do not inquire of the LORD; so they do not prosper and all their flock is scattered. (Jeremiah 10:21)

But I am afraid that just as Eve was deceived by the serpent's cunning, your minds may somehow be led astray from your sincere and pure devotion to Christ. For if someone comes to you and preaches a Jesus other than the Jesus we preached, or if you receive a different spirit from the one you received, or a different gospel from the one you accepted, you put up with it easily enough. (2 Corinthians 11:3–4)

My people have been lost sheep; their shepherds have led them astray and caused them to roam on the mountains. They wandered over mountain and hill and forgot their own resting place. Whoever found them devoured them. (Jeremiah 50:6–7)

Be shepherds of God's flock that is under your care, serving as overseers—not because you must, but because you are willing, as God wants you to be; not greedy for money, but eager to serve; not lording it over those entrusted to you, but being examples to the flock. (1 Peter 5:2–3)

Turn away from godless chatter and the opposing ideas of what is falsely called knowledge, which some have professed and in so doing have wandered from the faith. (1 Timothy 6:20–21)

Command certain men not to teach false doctrines any longer nor to devote themselves to myths and endless genealogies. These promote controversies rather than God's work—which is by faith. . . . They want to be teachers . . . , but they do not know what they are talking about or what they so confidently affirm. (1 Timothy 1:3–4, 7)

Warn a divisive person once, and then warn him a second time. After that, have nothing to do with him. You may be sure that such a man is warped and sinful; he is self-condemned. (Titus 3:10–11)

Dear children, keep yourselves from idols. (1 John 5:21)

PEOPLE/ORGANIZATION INDEX

Free John, Da (Bubba)–*Da Free John*

Funk, Robert–*Unitarian Universalism*

Geer, Christopher C.–*The Way International*

Goddard, Neville–*New Thought*

Goldsmith, Joel–*Unity School of Christianity*

Govinda, Lama–*Tibetan Buddhism*

Graham, Dom Aelred–*Buddhism/Zen*

Griffiths, Bede–*Vedanta*

Gross, Darwin–*Eckankar*

Gurdjieff, George–*Gurdjieff Foundation*

Hahn, Thich Nhat–*Buddhism*

Hall, Manly P.–*Masonic Lodge*

Hanley, John–*Human Potential Seminars*

Haywood, H.L.–*Masonic Lodge*

Herschel, Milton G.–*Jehovah's Witnesses*

Hinkley, Gordon B.–*Mormonism*

Holmes, Ernest–*Religious Science*

Home Mission Board, Southern Baptist Convention (SBC)–*The Masonic Lodge*

Hong, Nansook–*Unification Church*

Hornaday, William–*Religious Science*

Humphreys, Christmas–*Zen*

Hutchens, Rex R.–*Masonic Lodge*

Ike, Reverend–*New Thought*

Ikeda, Daisaku–*Buddhism*

Institute for the study of American Religion–*How to Use this Encyclopedia*

Internet Cult Watch Group–*How to Use this Encyclopedia*

Isherood, Christopher–*Vedanta*

John Ankerberg Show, The–*How to Use this Encyclopedia*

Khan, Hazrat Inayat–*The Sufi Order*

Kim, Young Oon–*Unification Church*

Kimball, Spencer–*Mormonism*

Kleinknecht, C. Fred–*Masonic Lodge*

Klemp, Harold–*Eckankar*

Knorr, Nathan H. –*Jehovah's Witnesses*

Krishnamurti, Jiddhu–*Krishnamurti Foundation*

Kriyananda, Swami–*Kriyananda, Swami/Self Realization Fellowship*

Kriyananda, Swami–*Self Realization Fellowship*

Lama, Dalai–*Tibetan Buddhism*

Lamsa, George–*New Thought/The Way International*

Lasalle, H.M.–*Zen*

Leazer, Gary–*Masonic Lodge*

Lee, Witness–*The Local Church*

Lewis, Samuel–*The Sufi Order*

Mackey, Albert G.–*Masonic Lodge*

Maharaj Ji, Guru–*Divine Light Mission*

Martindale, Craig L.–*The Way International*

Mashiyach Ministries–*Human Potential Seminars*

Masters, Roy–*Foundation of Human Understanding*

Mata, Daya–*Self Realization Fellowship*

McConkie, Bruce–*Mormonism*

Moon, Sun Myung–*Unification Church*

Muktananda, Swami–*Swami Muktananda*

Murphy, Joseph–*Unity School of Christianity*

Nanak, Guru–*Sikhism*

Newton, Joseph Fort–*Masonic Lodge*

Nikhilananda, Swami–*Vedanta*

OTHER BOOKS BY ANKERBERG/WELDON